The Developing Child

ELEVENTH EDITION

The Developing Child

HELEN BEE

DENISE BOYD

Houston Community College System

PEARSON

Boston   New York   San Francisco
Mexico City   Montreal   Toronto   London   Madrid   Munich   Paris
Hong Kong   Singapore   Tokyo   Cape Town   Sydney

Editor-in-Chief: Susan Hartman
Development Editor: Erin Liedel
Series Editorial Assistant: Debbie Hanlon
Marketing Manager: Kate Conway
Production Editor: Patrick Cash-Peterson
Editorial Production Service: Lifland et al., Bookmakers
Composition Buyer: Linda Cox
Manufacturing Buyer: Andrew Turso
Electronic Composition: Modern Graphics
Interior Design: Ellen Pettengell
Photo Researcher: Annie Pickert
Cover Designer: Linda Knowles

For related titles and support materials, visit our online catalog at www.ablongman.com.

Between the time Web site information is gathered and then published, it is not unusual for some sites to have closed. Also, the transcription of URLs can result in typographical errors. The publisher would appreciate notification where these errors occur so that they may be corrected in subsequent editions.

Library of Congress Cataloging-in-Publication Data

Bee, Helen L., 1939–
    The developing child / Helen Bee, Denise Boyd.—11th ed.
        p. cm.
    Includes bibliographical references and indexes.
    ISBN 0-205-47453-5
        1. Child psychology—Textbooks. 2. Child development—Textbooks. I. Boyd, Denise Roberts. II. Title.

BF721.B336 2006
155.4—dc22
                                                                    2005056463

Printed in the United States of America
10   9   8   7   6   5   4   3   2   1   RRD-OH   10   09   08   07   06

When my two older children, Marianne and Matthew, were 7 and 4 years of age, respectively, I was a graduate student in human development who had developed the questionable habit of trying out everything I was learning in school on my two children. One day, I rather absentmindedly asked Marianne what she wanted to wear to school the next day. She replied, somewhat indignantly, "Do you really want to know, or is this just another one of your studies?" This exchange, and millions of others like it with these two offspring and their younger brother, Christopher, who came along a year or so later, taught me important things about development that no course or textbook or experiment could have. In this spirit, I recommend to all readers of this book that they seek out experiences that will put them in touch with children's everyday thoughts, feelings, and expressions in order to amplify and extend what they learn in their coursework. Further, to express my gratitude to them for teaching me so much about development, I dedicate the eleventh edition of The Developing Child to my children: Marianne Boyd Meece, Matthew Boyd, and Christopher Boyd.

BRIEF CONTENTS

CONTENTS

5 Perceptual Development   125

PART 4   The Thinking Child

6 Cognitive Development 1: Structure and Process   148

LIST OF FEATURES

Integrated Cultural Topics

CHAPTER 1

- Individualism versus collectivism
- Importance of cross-cultural research
- Cross-cultural research methods
- Example of a cross-cultural study
- The role of culture in Bronfenbrenner's and Erikson's theories

CHAPTER 2

- Links between race or ethnicity and genetic disorders

CHAPTER 3

- Cultural variations in the location of birth and the qualifications of birth attendants
- Cultural differences in beliefs about where infants should sleep
- Cross-cultural research on infants' patterns of crying in the early weeks of life
- Cross-cultural consistencies and differences in the techniques parents use to soothe crying babies
- Infant mortality across U.S. racial and ethnic groups

CHAPTER 4

- Cross-cultural consistency in variables associated with early sexual activity among teens
- Culture and childhood obesity

CHAPTER 5

- Cross-cultural variations in object permanence
- Cross-cultural consistencies and differences in children's learning about emotions
- Universals in the interpretation of facial expressions

CHAPTER 6

- The role of socially acquired knowledge in cognitive development
- Cross-cultural research on theory of mind and false belief
- Vygotsky's sociocultural theory
- The link between culture and formal operational thinking
- Cross-cultural research examining changes in information-processing efficiency in middle childhood
- Cultural differences in parents' beliefs about the need to stimulate babies' intellectual development

CHAPTER 7

- Cultural variables associated with historical IQ score gains
- Beliefs about birth order
- The influence of stereotype threat on minority children's IQ scores
- Cultural factors in test score differences across racial and ethnic groups
- Cross-national differences in achievement test scores
- Cultural explanations for sex differences in math achievement

CHAPTER 8

- Motherese across cultures
- Cross-cultural universals and variations in children's first words and in the sequence of stages in language development
- Cross-cultural research examining phonological awareness in early reading
- The developmental advantages and disadvantages of bilingualism
- Second-language learners in U.S. schools
- The use of Black English (Ebonics) in schools

CHAPTER 9

- Cross-cultural research on the Big Five personality traits
- Cross-cultural consistencies and variations in infant temperament
- Cross-cultural differences in parents' interactions with infants
- Minority role models in U.S. culture

CHAPTER 10

- Cross-cultural validity of the identity crisis concept
- Racial and ethnic identity development
- Rites of passage programs for African American children and youth

- The influence of individualism and collectivism on adolescent identity development

- The relevance of culture to sex differences in self-esteem

- Cultural basis of gender roles

- Cross-cultural studies of sex-role stereotypes

- Cultural variables in social-learning explanations of gender role development

CHAPTER 11

- Cross-cultural differences in fathers' interactions with infants

- Cross-cultural studies of stranger and separation anxiety

- Effects on attachment of shared infant caretaking in African cultures

- Cross-cultural research on attachment quality

- Cultural universality of gender segregation in middle childhood

- Peer influence across U.S. racial and ethnic groups

CHAPTER 12

- Racial prejudice in childhood

- Cross-cultural studies of moral reasoning

- The influence of culturally based gender roles on moral reasoning

- Cross-cultural research examining prosocial reasoning

CHAPTER 13

- Bronfenbrenner's ecological theory

- Links between parenting style and race or ethnicity in U.S. culture

- Interactions among race or ethnicity, socioeconomic status, and parenting style

CHAPTER 14

- Variations in child-care arrangements among U.S. racial and ethnic groups

- Associations among race or ethnicity, school achievement, and school engagement

- Racial and ethnic group differences in the effects of employment on adolescent development

- Effects of poverty on development

- Explanation of the difference between race and ethnicity

- Characteristics of African American, Hispanic American, and Asian American families

- Cultural beliefs and child development

CHAPTER 15

- Cross-cultural differences in the incidence of various psychological disorders

- Cultural factors influencing the development of eating disorders

TO THE STUDENT

Hello, and welcome to the study of a fascinating subject—children and their development. Welcome, too, to the adventure of science. From the very first edition of this book, one of Helen Bee's goals has been to convey a sense of excitement about scientific inquiry. We hope that each of you gains some feeling for the way psychologists think, the kinds of questions they ask, and the ways they go about trying to answer those questions. We also want you to gain some sense of the theoretical and intellectual ferment that is part of any science. Think of psychology as a kind of detective story: Psychologists discover clues after hard, often painstaking work; they make guesses or hypotheses; and then they search for new clues to check on those hypotheses.

Of course, we also want you to come away from reading this book with a firm foundation of knowledge in the field. Although there is much that developmental psychologists do not yet know or understand, a great many facts and observations have accumulated. These facts and observations will be of help to you professionally if you are planning (or are already in) a career that involves working with children, such as teaching, nursing, social work, medicine, or psychology; the information will also be useful to you as a parent, now or in the future. We hope you enjoy the reading as much as we have enjoyed the writing.

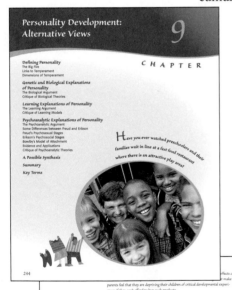

HOW TO WORK WITH THIS TEXTBOOK

To get the most out of any textbook, you should think of yourself as working *with* it so that you can understand and remember the information in it, rather than reading it as you would a magazine, a newspaper article, or a novel. To work with your textbook most effectively, take advantage of its structural and pedagogical features.

Chapter Outlines Before you read each chapter, read over the outline at its beginning. More information will stick in your mind if you have an idea of what to expect.

Vignettes The story at the beginning of each chapter will engage your interest in the major topics and themes.

Headings and Subheadings Think of the headings and their subheadings as a way of dividing the information that follows them into categories. The information in each major section and subsection is linked to the heading and subheading under which it is found. Thinking of the material in this way creates a kind of information network in your mind that will make it easier to recall the material when you are tested. Structuring your notes to correspond to headings will help even more. To have the best chance of creating the information network, stop reading between major sections, reflect back on what you have read, and review your written notes.

Before Going On   To help you review, the text includes "Before Going On" questions near the end of each major section. You should stop reading and try to answer these questions. If you can't answer the questions, go back and review. You will know what parts of the section to review because each question corresponds to a section subheading. Once you've completed this process, take a break before you begin another major section.

Margin Glossary   Key terms are defined in the margins. As you come to each boldfaced term in the text, stop and read its definition in the margin. Then go back and reread the sentence that introduced the key term. Reading over the key terms in the margins just before you take an exam can also be a helpful review strategy if you have thoroughly studied the material in which the terms are introduced.

Critical Thinking Questions   Critical thinking questions and activities encourage you to relate material in the book to your own experiences. They can also help you remember the text because linking new information to things you already know is a highly effective memory strategy.

Chapter Summaries   Looking over the chapter summary can also help you assess how much information you remember. The summaries are organized by major chapter headings.

Key Terms   Key terms are listed alphabetically at the end of each chapter in addition to being defined in the margins. When you finish a chapter, try to recall the definition of each term. A page number is listed for each term, so you can easily look back if you can't remember a definition.

See for Yourself   At the end of each chapter is a feature called "See for Yourself." Some of these provide instructions for testing the findings of research studies in the real world with real children. In Chapter 6, for instance, See for Yourself tells you how to use playing cards to test children's use of organizational memory strategies. Other activities describe ways of finding more information about a topic. For example, in Chapter 7, See for Yourself encourages you to use the Internet to find out more about mandatory standardized testing in your state's public schools. Applying what you learn in this book makes the information more meaningful and memorable.

At this point, the task of understanding and remembering the information in a developmental psychology textbook may seem overwhelming. However, when you finish reading this book, you will have a better understanding of both yourself and other people. So, the benefit you will derive from all your hard work will be well worth it.

Denise Boyd

TO THE INSTRUCTOR

One of the greatest challenges in updating a text is being open to new theories and concepts and willing to rethink and reorganize whole chapters, rather than sticking reflexively (or defensively) to old rubrics. Revising also sometimes includes eliminating favorite examples that are out of date and searching for new metaphors that will speak to current students. Perhaps hardest of all, one must cut as well as add material. Over many editions, the changes accumulate; if you were to compare this edition to the first edition, published in 1975, you would find almost no common sentences, let alone common paragraphs. Still, my goal was to retain most of the threads running from the first through the tenth edition that made Helen Bee's approach to development unique. In particular, four central goals have guided the writing of *The Developing Child*:

- To actively engage the student in as many ways as possible
- To find that difficult but essential balance among theory, research, and practical application
- To present the most current thinking and research
- To maintain a strong emphasis on culture

NEW TO THE ELEVENTH EDITION

The eleventh edition of *The Developing Child* includes updated information about the theories and research presented in the tenth edition, as well as additions to most chapters.

Chapter 1

- The chapter opens with an examination of the modern tendency to look to experts rather than experienced parents for advice on childrearing.
- A new box teaches students how to think critically about media reports of research.
- The section devoted to theories ends with a discussion of eclecticism.

Chapter 2

- The chapter-opening vignette addresses the issue of prosecuting pregnant drug users for child abuse.
- The Research Report discusses assisted reproductive technology.
- Environmental hazards were added to the discussion of teratogens.

Chapter 3

- Research on individual differences in catch-up development exhibited by children who were born prematurely is discussed.
- The discussion of adjustment to parenthood has been expanded.

Chapter 4

- The vignette contrasts media coverage of the "Mozart effect" on brain development to the systematic approach of researchers to such claims.

- There is additional coverage of childhood obesity and how it can be treated.

- Coverage of adolescent drug use, and the factors that predispose teens to addiction, has been expanded.

- A discussion of recent research showing that stress contributes to the relationship between poverty and childhood health has been added.

Chapter 5

- The chapter begins with a discussion of infants' abilities to perceive various aspects of music.

- There is new material in the discussion of object perception.

Chapter 6

- There is greater emphasis than in the previous edition on Baillargeon's and Spelke's work on object perception.

- A discussion of research examining Elkind's adolescent egocentrism now appears in this chapter.

- The role of siblings in theory of mind development is discussed.

- The section on memory now includes a review of information processing theory (first presented in Chapter 1).

Chapter 7

- This chapter opens with a discussion of an award-winning composer, Hiraki Oe, who is mentally retarded.

- The "Flynn effect" and its proposed causes are included in the discussion of intelligence testing.

- The box addressing the use of standardized tests in schools includes a discussion of "No Child Left Behind" legislation.

- A new Research Report box describes research that both supports and challenges the stereotype threat hypothesis.

- The newest version of the WISC, the WISC-IV, is discussed in detail.

- The discussion of birth order effects on IQ scores now includes information about how cultural beliefs may contribute to the relationship.

- The discussion of the possible causes of gender differences in math achievement has been expanded.

Chapter 8

- The chapter opens with a critical look at the notion that hearing babies can benefit from learning sign language.

- The theory section includes a new discussion of the degree to which the various theories can be integrated into a comprehensive explanation of language development.

- Fast-mapping has been added to the discussion of word learning.

- The discussion of ESL and bilingual education has been expanded.

Chapter 9

- The opening vignette addresses notions about personality that are implicit in popular books for parents such as *The Difficult Child* and *The Explosive Child*.

Chapter 10

- The chapter opens with a discussion of the long-term outcomes experienced by individuals who have undergone sex reassignment surgery in infancy.

- Biological theories of gender role development have been added to the chapter.

Chapter 11

- In the opening vignette, the relative influences of parental and peer relationships are discussed in the context of a case in which peer influence led a group of girls from affluent homes to become involved in a spree of armed robberies.

- Discussions of individual differences have been integrated into sections devoted to attachment formation, prosocial behavior, and aggression.

Chapter 12

- The pros and cons of character education are the subject of the opening vignette.

- The Real World box discusses how racial prejudice develops.

Chapter 13

- This chapter's opening vignette analyzes Golding's *Lord of the Flies* from the perspective of systems theory.

- There is a greater emphasis on Bronfenbrenner's theory, now known as the bioecological approach, than in previous editions.

Chapter 14

- The chapter opener recounts the history of *Sesame Street* and its effects on preschoolers' development.

- A new Real World box addresses strategies for choosing a day-care arrangement.

- A discussion of how research on nonparental care should be interpreted has been added to the chapter.

- The discussion of entertainment media now includes the effects of video games on cognitive and social development.

Chapter 15

- In the chapter-opening vignette, the trials associated with parenting a child with disabilities are portrayed in a fictitious case of a boy with profound mental retardation.

- A new section discusses pervasive developmental disorders.

Epilogue

- The epilogue is a comprehensive summary of the book's chapters.

PEDAGOGY

The eleventh edition of *The Developing Child* includes several important pedagogical features.

Chapter Opening Vignettes   Each chapter begins with a compelling vignette, which engages readers' interest in the chapter's topic.

Before Going On   Questions in the margin at the end of each major section prompt students to stop reading and determine whether they can recall information from the section before moving on.

Margin Glossary   All boldfaced terms in the text are defined in the margins as well as in a glossary at the end of the book.

Critical Thinking Questions   The critical thinking questions and activities in the margins encourage students to relate information in the text to their own personal experiences.

Chapter Summaries   Summaries are organized by major chapter heading and include bulleted entries summarizing the information that follows each subheading.

See for Yourself   Each chapter ends with a feature that gives readers instructions for either replicating the findings of a developmental study in an informal way or finding out more about a specific topic.

BOXED FEATURES

The eleventh edition of *The Developing Child* includes two types of boxed discussions: Real World and Research Report.

The Real World   Every chapter includes a boxed discussion of the application of scientific knowledge to a practical question. For example, the Real World feature in Chapter 4 discusses sports for children. The intent of these discussions is to show students not only that it is possible to study such applied questions with scientific methods, but also that all the theory and research they are reading about may have some relevance to their own lives. To facilitate this goal, each Real World box begins with a brief vignette about a parenting issue and ends with questions for reflection, which encourage readers to apply the ideas in the box to that issue.

Research Report   Every chapter includes a boxed discussion of a particularly important study or series of studies. For example, the Research Report in Chapter 15 looks at studies aimed at finding out why boys are more vulnerable to some kinds of disabilities than girls are. Further, each Research Report ends with two questions for critical analysis, which encourage readers to critically evaluate the findings presented in the box.

ACKNOWLEDGMENTS

Thanks to the wonderful people at Allyn & Bacon who participated in the development and completion of this project, including Susan Hartman and Erin Liedel. In addition, I am grateful to all of the reviewers who took time to comment on this and previous editions of *The Developing Child*. The following people provided invaluable feedback through their reviews for the eleventh edition:

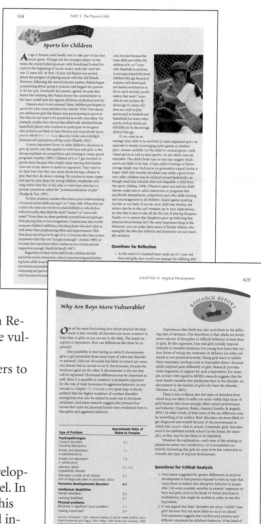

Steven H. Baron
Montgomery County Community College

Elizabeth M. Blunk
Texas State University

Megan E. Bradley
Frostburg State University

Tsu-Ming Chiang
Georgia College and State University

Emily Doolittle
George Washington University

Janet Gebelt
Westfield State College

Celia B. Hilber
Jacksonville State University

Wendy Jordanov
Tennessee State University

Kee Jeong Kim
Virginia Technical University

Brady J. Phelps
South Dakota State University

Jane A. Rysberg
California State University

Delar K. Singh
Eastern Connecticut State University

Gordon Lee Whitman
Tidewater Community College

Thanks also to the following people who provided thoughtful criticism and commentary on earlier editions and drafts:

Janette B. Benson
University of Denver

Marvin W. Berkowitz
Marquette University

Katherine Black
University of Hartford

Peter J. Byrne
Maria College

Saundra K. Ciccarelli
Gulf Coast Community College

Joan Cook
County College of Morris

Rita M. Curl
Minot State University

Wallace E. Dixon, Jr.
Heidelberg College

Jerome Dusek
Syracuse University

Cynthia Erdley
University of Maine

Donna Frick-Horbury
Appalachian State University

Gloria Gartner
Lakeland Community College

Betty K. Hathaway
University of Arkansas at Little Rock

Patricia A. Jarvis
Illinois State University

Janice H. Kennedy
Georgia Southern University

Pamela Ludemann
Framingham State College

Philip J. Mohan
University of Idaho

Terese Morrow
Illinois Central College

Donald Sanzotta
Cayuga Community College

Jane P. Sheldon
University of Michigan–Dearborn

Nancy White
Youngstown State University

Ric Wynn
County College of Morris

Sheri D. Young
John Carroll University

INSTRUCTOR SUPPLEMENTS
FOR QUALIFIED ADOPTERS

The Developing Child Instructor's Classroom Kit and CD-ROM, Volumes I and II Our unparalleled *Classroom Kit* includes every instructional aid a child development professor needs to manage the classroom. We have made our resources even easier to use by placing all of our print supplements in two convenient volumes, and electronic copies of all of our resources on two CD-ROMs which can be found within the print volumes. Organized by chapter, each volume contains an *Instructor's Manual, Test Bank, Grade Aid with Practice Tests*, and slides from *The Developing Child* PowerPoint™ presentation. Electronic versions of the *Instructor's Manual, Test Bank*, and *Grade Aid*, PowerPoint images from the text, and video clips, all searchable by key terms, are made easily accessible to instructors on the accompanying *Classroom Kit* CD-ROMs.

NEW !

Instructor's Manual Prepared by Dara Musher-Eizenman, Bowling Green State University, the *Instructor's Manual* is a wonderful tool for classroom preparation and management. A brand new "easy-to-find" format includes detailed cross-references to features in the *Instructor's Manual* as well as to other print and media supplements and outside teaching resources. The *Instructor's Manual* is both comprehensive and extensive. Each chapter includes the following resources:

- An **At-a-Glance Grid,** with detailed pedagogical information, references to both print and media supplements for each concept, and a chapter overview

- A **detailed chapter outline,** with summaries of key concepts

- **Teaching objectives,** which correlate with the *Grade Aid with Practice Tests* learning objectives

- List of **key terms**

- **Lecture material,** including outlines and suggested discussion topics, with references to pertinent activities in the *Instructor's Manual* and videos from the Allyn & Bacon video library

- **Updated classroom activities and demonstrations**

- An updated **list of video, media, print, and Web resources**

- **Discussion of the CD-ROM** *Development: Journey through Childhood and Adolescence,* including pertinent discussion questions and full table of contents

- **New Web links**

In addition, the appendix includes a compilation of handouts and video offerings.

Test Bank The *Test Bank*, prepared by Carolyn Meyer, Lake-Sumter Community College, helps students prepare for exams with challenging questions that target key concepts. Each chapter includes

- Over 100 questions, including multiple-choice, true/false, short answer, and essay questions—with answers or answer justifications

- Page references, a difficulty rating, a topic heading, and a category designation for each question

In addition, the appendix includes a sample open-book quiz.

The *Test Bank* is also available in TestGen 5.5 computerized format, which makes creating tests for the classroom easy. This version is available from your Allyn & Bacon sales representative.

PowerPoint™ Presentation

Edward Brady, Southwestern Illinois College, prepared a PowerPoint presentation that is an exciting interactive tool for use in the classroom. Each chapter includes

- Key points covered in the textbook
- Images from the textbook, with demonstrations
- A link to the companion Web site for activities

The PowerPoint files are housed on the *Instructor's Classroom Kit* for your convenience.

MyDevelopmentLab

MyDevelopmentLab is a state-of-the-art interactive and instructive solution to the study of human development. This multimedia resource can be used to supplement a traditional lecture course or to administer a course entirely online. It is an all-inclusive tool, a text-specific e-book plus multimedia tutorials, audio, video, simulations, animations, and controlled assessments, to completely engage students and reinforce learning. Fully customizable and easy to use, *MyDevelopmentLab* meets the individual teaching and learning needs of every instructor and every student. Visit the site at **www.mydevelopmentlab.com.**

Transparencies for Human Development

Approximately 125 new, full-color acetates allow instructors to enhance classroom lecture and discussion. Images included are from Bee/Boyd, *Developing Child*, tenth edition; Cook/Cook, *Child Development*; Martin/Fabes, *Discovering Child Development*; and Boyd/Bee, *Lifespan Development*, fourth edition.

Development: Journey through Childhood Video, with Video Guide

A wonderful tool, the video offers two or three clips per chapter, and the *Video Guide* provides critical thinking questions for each clip. Clips cover topics such as a live birth, babies and language development, differences in personality among toddlers, child and parent interaction, and exceptional children. In addition, the *Video Guide* provides Web resources for more information.

Development: Journey through Childhood and Adolescence CD-ROM

This multimedia learning tool is available to be packaged with the text or sold separately. It includes eight units that cover development from the prenatal period through adolescence and introduce all of the biological, cognitive, and psychosocial changes that occur along the way. Clips include footage of live births, interviews with adolescents and the elderly, and toddlers learning to walk. In addition, audio clips, flash animations, and 3-D video animations accompany the footage. Written by Dr. Kelly Welch of Kansas State University, the CD-ROM includes several exercises for students, such as "drag-and-drop" activities, multiple-choice quizzes, flash cards of glossary terms, journal writing, and instant feedback exercises called "Mad Minutes."

Insights into Human Development Video

This new video is available to accompany *The Developing Child*, eleventh edition. The video highlights important high-interest topics in human development, including imagination in early childhood, motivation and school success, and aggression in adolescent romantic relationships. A video user's guide, with critical thinking questions and Web resources, is available to support the use of the video in the classroom.

Allyn & Bacon Digital Media Archive for Human Development, 2006 This comprehensive source includes still images, PowerPoint slides, and video clips from Allyn & Bacon's textbooks on child and lifespan development.

Course Management Use these preloaded, customizable, content and assessment items—available in CourseCompass, Blackboard, and WebCT formats—to teach your online courses.

STUDENT SUPPLEMENTS

MyDevelopmentLab *MyDevelopmentLab* is a state-of-the-art interactive and instructive solution to the study of human development. It is an all-inclusive tool, a text-specific e-book plus multimedia tutorials, audio, video, simulations, animations, and controlled assessments, to completely engage students and reinforce learning. Fully customizable and easy to use, *MyDevelopmentLab* meets the individual learning needs of every student. Visit the site at **www.mydevelopmentlab.com.**

mydevelopmentlab

Grade Aid with Practice Tests Prepared by Kristine Anthis, Southern Connecticut State University, this is a comprehensive and interactive study guide. Each chapter includes

- "Before You Read," providing a brief chapter summary and chapter learning objectives

- "As You Read," a collection of demonstrations, activities, and exercises, including activities that correspond to the CD-ROM *Development: Journey through Adolescence*

- "After You Read," containing three short practice quizzes and one comprehensive practice test

- "When You Have Finished," with Web links to further resources and a crossword puzzle using key terms from the text

An appendix includes answers to all practice tests and the crossword puzzle.

Companion Web Site The book's companion Web site at **www.ablongman.com/bee11e** is a unique resource for connecting the text material to resources on the Internet. Each chapter includes

- Learning objectives

- Updated and annotated Web links for additional sources of information

- Flash cards with glossary terms

- Online practice tests

Development: Journey through Childhood and Adolescence CD-ROM This multimedia learning tool is available to be packaged with the text or sold separately. It includes eight interactive units that cover development from the prenatal period through adolescence and introduce all of the biological, cognitive, and psychosocial changes that occur along the way. Clips include footage of live births, interviews with adolescents and the elderly, and toddlers learning to walk. Flash and 3-D video animations teach students about the inner workings of the human body, including the reproductive organs, conception, and pregnancy. Written by Dr. Kelly Welch of Kansas State University, the CD-ROM includes several exercises for students, such as "drag-and-drop" activities, multiple-choice quizzes, flash cards of glossary terms, journal writing, and instant feedback exercises called "Mad Minutes."

Research Navigator™   Allyn & Bacon's new *Research Navigator*™ is an easy way for students to start a research assignment or research paper. By offering extensive help on the research process and three exclusive databases of credible and reliable source material, including EBSCO's ContentSelect Academic Journal Database, *New York Times* Search by Subject Archive, and "Best of the Web" Link Library, *Research Navigator*™ helps students make the most of their online research time.

Tutor Center   The Tutor Center at www.aw.com/tutorcenter (access code required) provides students with free, one-on-one, interactive tutoring from qualified psychology instructors on all material in the text. The Tutor Center offers students help with understanding major principles as well as methods for study. During Tutor Center hours, students can obtain assistance by phone, fax, Internet, and email. For more details and ordering information, please contact your Allyn & Bacon publisher's representative.

The Developing Child

Basic Issues in the Study of Development

B rowse the shelves of your local bookstore and you will find no shortage of advice and self-help books for parents.

Titles such as *Toilet Training in a Day* and *How to Talk to Your Teenager* abound. Typically, the authors of such books are psychologists, counselors, social workers, educators, or pediatricians. Many are also parents and support their advice with anecdotes from their own parenting experience. In general, though, today's parents regard formal training as a more reliable indicator of expertise on parenting issues than hands-on experience with children (Hulbert, 2003). How did this trend—a fairly recent one, by the way—begin?

According to many observers, parental preoccupation with "expert" child-rearing advice began in the early years of the 20th century, when popular magazines started publishing articles on child-rearing that referred to the theories of Sigmund Freud and other psychologists (Torrey, 1992). Soon, child-rearing books authored by experts became best-sellers. These articles and books recommended "scientific" approaches to child-rearing. No longer were grandparents or other older adults to be viewed as authorities on bringing up children. Instead, young parents were encouraged to turn to pediatricians and psychologists.

One of the first such child-rearing experts was John Watson (1878–1958). He advocated rigid feeding schedules for infants and an orderly approach to child-rearing. Watson believed that American parenting traditions caused children to grow up to be emotionally weak. Accordingly, he advised parents:

> Never hug and kiss them, never let them sit in your lap. If you must, kiss them once on the forehead when they say good night. Shake hands with them in the morning. Give them a pat on the head if they have made an extraordinarily good job of a difficult task. (1928, pp. 81–82)

Watson's popularity ebbed as the radically different ideas of Dr. Benjamin Spock (1903–1990), author of the classic book *Baby and Child Care*, became predominant in the 1950s. Spock urged parents to openly display affection toward children. Influenced by Freud's ideas about the impact of early childhood emotional trauma on later personality, Spock warned parents against engaging in too much conflict with children over weaning or toilet-training. He emphasized the need to wait until children were ready to take on such challenges.

Today, Watson's ideas are viewed as emotionally cold and excessively rigid by pediatricians, psychologists, and parents alike. Similarly, many view Spock's recommendations as overly indulgent. Yet parents continue to look to experts for help with parenting issues, often turning to the rapidly growing number of Internet sites devoted to child-rearing issues. In one survey, 71% of mothers reported that they had searched the Internet for help with a parenting issue (Allen & Rainie, 2002). Child-rearing recommendations representing diverse philosophical orientations abound on the World Wide Web. Consequently, there is no single expert "voice" that predominates. Health-oriented sites, such as kidshealth.org and askdrsears.com, are very popular. Likewise, sites sponsored by child psychologists receive millions of hits each day. But parents also search for advice on their children's spiritual development or for nontraditional treatments for conditions such as attention-deficit hyperactivity disorder (Bussing, Zima, Gary, & Garvan, 2002).

One reason for the diversity and quantity of information available is that, thanks to more than a century of research, we now know a great deal more about the variables that contribute to human development. Identifying variables that influence development and explaining how they work together to shape an individual's life is what developmental science is all about. Developmental scientists develop theories and conduct research aimed at describing, explaining, and predicting age-related changes in behavior, thinking, emotions, and social relationships. Historically, developmental science has been associated with the field of psychology, and most of the developmentalists whose work you will read about in this text were or are psychologists. But developmental science also draws from other fields, including biology, neuroscience, anthropology, sociology, and education.

In addition, most developmental scientists want to find ways to help parents, teachers, therapists, and others who work with children to do so effectively. In pursuit of these goals, developmental researchers often focus on highly specific issues, such as how many items children of different ages can remember. However, a few ideas are central to every theory and research study in developmental psychology. We will begin our discussion with a brief overview of these ideas.

 # Perspectives on Development

Centuries before researchers began to use scientific methods to study age-related changes, philosophers proposed explanations of development based on everyday observations. Many of their questions and assertions about the nature of human development continue to be central to modern-day **developmental science.**

NATURE VERSUS NURTURE

The argument about nature versus nurture, also referred to as heredity versus environment or *nativism* versus *empiricism*, is one of the oldest and most central theoretical issues within both psychology and philosophy. For example, have you ever heard someone say that "baby talk" will interfere with a child's language development? If so, then you have heard an argument for the nurture side of the debate. Such a statement assumes that language development is mostly a matter of imitation. The child must hear language that is properly pronounced and grammatically correct in order to develop linguistic fluency. The nature side would counter that children possess some kind of internal mechanism to ensure that they develop fluent language, no matter how many "goo-goo-ga-gas" they hear from those around them. "Which side is right?" students invariably ask. If there were a simple answer to that question, the debate would have ceased long ago. Instead, the controversy continues today with regard to many developmental processes, including language development.

Philosophically, the nature side of the controversy was represented by the *idealists* and *rationalists*, principally Plato and René Descartes, both of whom believed that at least some knowledge is inborn. On the other side of the argument were a group of British philosophers called *empiricists*, including John Locke, who insisted that at birth the mind is a blank slate—in Latin, a *tabula rasa*. All knowledge, the empiricists argued, is created by experience. From this perspective, developmental change is the result of external, environmental factors acting on a child whose only relevant internal characteristic is the capacity to respond.

In contrast to both rationalists and empiricists, other philosophers believed that development involved an interaction between internal and external forces. For example, the Christian notion of *original sin* teaches that children are born with a

developmental science The study of age-related changes in behavior, thinking, emotions, and social relationships.

3

CRITICAL THINKING ?

See if you can identify one of your own characteristics or behavior patterns that has been strongly affected by "nature" and one that you think is primarily a result of your upbringing.

selfish nature and must be spiritually reborn. After rebirth, children have access to the Holy Spirit, which helps them learn to behave morally through parental and church-based instruction in religious practice.

French philosopher Jean-Jacques Rousseau also believed in the idea of interaction between internal and external forces, but he claimed that all human beings are naturally good and seek out experiences that help them grow. For Rousseau, the goal of human development was to achieve one's inborn potential. "Good" developmental outcomes, such as a willingness to share one's possessions with others who are less fortunate, resulted from growing up in an environment that didn't interfere with the child's expression of his own innate characteristics. In contrast, "bad" outcomes, such as aggressive behavior, were learned from others or arose when a child experienced frustration in his efforts to follow the dictates of the innate goodness with which he was born.

The views of two of psychology's pioneers illustrate the way early psychologists approached the nature-nurture issue. Borrowing an idea from Darwin's theory of evolution, early childhood researcher G. Stanley Hall (1844–1924) believed that the milestones of childhood were dictated by an inborn developmental plan and were similar to those that had taken place in the development of the human species. He thought that developmentalists should identify **norms**, or average ages at which milestones happen. Norms, Hall said, could be used to learn about the evolution of the species as well as to track the development of individual children. So, for Hall, development was mostly about the nature side of the debate.

John Watson, whose views you read about at the beginning of the chapter, explained development in a way that was radically different from that of G. Stanley Hall. In fact, Watson coined a new term, behaviorism, to refer to his point of view (Watson, 1913). **Behaviorism** defines development in terms of behavior changes caused by environmental influences. Watson did not believe in an inborn developmental plan of any sort. Instead, he claimed that, through manipulation of the environment, children could be trained to be or do anything (Jones, 1924; Watson, 1930). As Watson put it,

norms Average ages at which developmental events happen.

behaviorism The theoretical view that defines development in terms of behavior changes caused by environmental influences.

> Give me a dozen healthy infants, well-formed, and my own specified world to bring them up in and I'll guarantee to take any one at random and train him to become any type of specialist I might select—doctor, lawyer, merchant, chief, and yes, even beggar-man and thief, regardless of his talents, penchants, abilities, vocations, and the race of his ancestors. (1930, p. 104)

In a famous study known as the "Little Albert" experiment, Watson conditioned a baby to fear white rats (Watson & Rayner, 1920). As the baby played with the rat, Watson made banging sounds that frightened the child. Over time, the baby came to associate the rat with the noises. He cried and tried to escape from the room whenever the rat was present. Based on the Little Albert study and several others, Watson claimed that all age-related changes are the result of learning (Watson, 1928).

STAGES AND SEQUENCES

The nature-nurture controversy is not the only "big question" in developmental psychology. An equally central dispute concerns the *continuity-discontinuity issue*: Is a child's expanding ability just "more of the same," or does it reflect a new kind of activity? For example, a 2-year-old is likely to have no individual friends among her playmates, while an 8-year-old is likely to have several. We could think of this as a quantitative change (a change in amount) from zero friends to some friends, which suggests that the qualitative aspects of friendship are the same at every age—or, as developmentalists would express it, changes in friendships are *continuous* in nature. Alternatively,

John Watson's pioneering research on emotional learning in infants helped psychologists better understand the role of classical conditioning in child development.

we could think of the difference in friendships from one age to another as a *qualitative* change (a change in kind or type)—from disinterest in peers to interest, or from one sort of peer relationship to another. In other words, in this view, changes in friendships are *discontinuous*, in that each change represents a change in the quality of a child's relationships with peers. Thus, friendships at 2 are quite different from friendships at 8 and differ in ways that cannot be captured by describing them solely in terms of the number of friends a child has.

Of particular significance is the idea that, if development consists only of additions (quantitative change), then the concept of stages is not needed to explain it. However, if development involves reorganization, or the emergence of wholly new strategies, qualities, or skills (qualitative change), then the concept of stages may be useful. Certainly, we hear a lot of "stagelike" language in everyday conversation about children: "He's just in the terrible twos" or "It's only a stage she's going through." Although there is not always agreement on just what would constitute evidence for the existence of discrete stages, the usual description is that a stage shift involves not only a change in skills but some discontinuous change in underlying structure (Lerner, Theokas, & Bobek, 2005). The child in a new stage approaches tasks differently, sees the world differently, is preoccupied with different issues.

INTERNAL AND EXTERNAL INFLUENCES ON DEVELOPMENT

Modern developmental psychologists still debate the nature-nurture and continuity-discontinuity questions. But most agree that essentially every facet of a child's development is a product of some pattern of interaction of nature and nurture (Rutter, 2002). Further, most recognize that some aspects of development are continuous and others are more stagelike. Consequently, the discussions have become a bit more complex.

Maturation Nature shapes development most clearly through genetic programming that may determine whole sequences of later development. Developmentalist

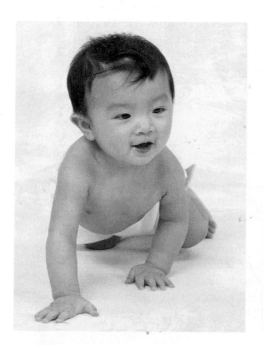

The shift from crawling to walking is a classic example of a maturationally based universal developmental change.

Arnold Gesell (1880–1961) used the term **maturation** to describe genetically programmed sequential patterns of change, and this term is still uniformly used today (Gesell, 1925; Thelen & Adolph, 1992). Any maturational pattern is marked by three qualities: It is universal, appearing in all children, across cultural boundaries; it is sequential, involving some pattern of unfolding skill or characteristics; and it is relatively impervious to environmental influence. In its purest form, a maturationally determined developmental sequence occurs regardless of practice or training. You don't have to practice growing pubic hair; you don't have to be taught how to walk. In fact, only extreme conditions, such as severe malnutrition, prevent such sequences from unfolding. Yet even confirmed maturational theorists agree that experience plays a role.

The Timing of Experience

Modern research tells us that specific experience interacts with maturational patterns in intricate ways. For example, Greenough (1991) notes that one of the proteins required for the development of the visual system is controlled by a gene whose action is triggered only by visual experience. Moreover, experience is required to maintain the neural connections underlying vision (Briones, Klintsova, & Greenough, 2004). So some visual experience is needed for the genetic program to operate. The timing of specific experiences may matter as well. The impact of a particular visual experience may be quite different if it occurs at birth than if it occurs when a baby is older.

Developmentalists' thinking about the importance of timing was stimulated, in part, by research on other species that showed that specific experiences had different or stronger effects at some points in development than at others. The most famous example is that baby ducks will become imprinted on (become attached to and follow) any duck or any other quacking, moving object that happens to be around them 15 hours after they hatch. If nothing is moving or quacking at that critical point, they don't become imprinted at all (Hess, 1972). So the period just around 15 hours after hatching is a **critical period** for the duck's development of a proper following response.

In humans, we more often see sensitive periods than true critical periods. The difference is that a **sensitive period** is a time when a particular experience can be best incorporated into the maturational process, whereas a critical period is a time when an experience *must* happen or a particular developmental milestone will never occur. For example, infancy and early childhood are sensitive periods for language development. A child who is physically isolated from other humans by an abusive parent during these years will not develop normal language, but she will develop some language function once she is reintegrated into a normal social environment.

maturation Sequential patterns of change that are governed by instructions contained in the genetic code and shared by all members of a species.

critical period Any time period during development when an organism is especially responsive to and learns from a specific type of stimulation. The same stimulation at other points in development has little or no effect.

sensitive period A period during which particular experiences can best contribute to proper development. It is similar to a critical period, but the effects of deprivation during a sensitive period are not as severe as during a critical period.

Inborn Biases and Constraints

Another kind of internal influence is described by the concepts of "inborn biases," or "constraints" on development. For instance, researchers such as Elizabeth Spelke (1991) have concluded that babies come into the world with certain "preexisting conceptions," or constraints on their understanding of the behavior of objects. Very young babies already seem to understand that unsupported objects will move downward and that a moving object will continue to move in the same direction unless it encounters an obstacle. Theorists do not propose that these built-in response patterns are the end of the story; rather, they see them as the starting point. Development is a result of experience filtered through these initial biases, but those biases constrain the number of developmental pathways that are possible (Campbell & Bickhard, 1992; Cole, 2005).

The study of identical twins, like these two girls, is one of the classic methods of behavior genetics. Whenever pairs of identical twins are more like each other in some behavior or quality than are pairs of fraternal twins, a genetic influence is likely at work.

How Do Behavior Geneticists Identify Genetic Effects?

Identical twins share exactly the same genetic pattern, because they develop from the same fertilized ovum. Consequently, developmentalists have learned a great deal about behavior genetics from studying identical twins who have been raised by different parents. If identical twins are more like each other on some dimension than other kinds of siblings are, despite having grown up in different environments, this is rather compelling evidence of a genetic contribution for that trait.

In the case of adopted children, the strategy is to compare the degree of similarity between the adopted child and his birth parents (with whom he shares genes but not environment) with the degree of similarity between the adopted child and his adoptive parents (with whom he shares environment but not genes). If the child turns out to be more similar to his birth parents than to his adoptive parents, or if his behavior or skills are better predicted by the characteristics of his birth parents than by characteristics of his adoptive parents, that evidence would again demonstrate the influence of heredity.

Here are two examples, both from studies of intelligence, as measured with standard IQ tests. Bouchard and McGue (1981, p. 1056, Fig. 1) combined the results of dozens of twin studies of the heritability of IQ scores and came up with the results shown in Table 1. The numbers shown in the table are correlations—a statistic explained more fully later in this chapter. For now, you need to know only that a correlation can range from −1.00 to +1.00. The closer a correlation is to 1.00, the stronger the relationship it describes. In this case, the numbers reflect how similar the IQs of twins are. You can see from Table 1 that identical twins reared together have IQs

that are highly similar, much more similar than the IQs of fraternal twins reared together. You can also see, though, that environment plays a role, since the IQs of identical twins reared apart are less similar than are those of identical twins reared together.

The same conclusion comes from two well-known studies of adopted children—the Texas Adoption Project (Loehlin, Horn, & Willerman, 1994) and the Minnesota Transracial Adoption Study (Scarr, Weinberg, & Waldman, 1993). In both studies, the adopted children were given IQ tests at approximately age 18. Their scores on this test were then correlated with the measured IQ scores of their natural mothers and of their adoptive mothers and fathers. These correlations are shown in Table 2. In both cases, the children's IQs were at least somewhat predicted by their natural mothers' IQs, but not by the IQs of their adoptive parents, with whom they had spent their entire childhood. Thus, the adoption studies, like the twin studies of IQ, tell us that there is indeed a substantial genetic component in what is measured by an IQ test.

Questions for Critical Analysis

1. Fraternal twins are no more genetically similar than non-twin siblings, yet the IQs of fraternal twins are more strongly correlated than those of non-twin brothers and sisters. What explanations can you think of to explain this difference?
2. The term *environment* is extremely broad. What are some of the individual variables that comprise an individual's environment?

Table 1

Identical twins reared together	.85
Identical twins reared apart	.67
Fraternal (nonidentical) twins reared together	.58
Siblings (including fraternal twins) reared apart	.24

Table 2

	Texas	Minnesota
Correlation with the biological mother's IQ score	.44	.29
Correlation with the adoptive mother's IQ score	.03	.14
Correlation with the adoptive father's IQ score	.06	.08

Behavior Genetics   The concept of maturation and the idea of inborn biases are both designed to account for patterns and sequences of development that are the same for all children. At the same time, nature contributes to variations from one individual to the next. The study of genetic contributions to individual behavior, called **behavior genetics,** uses two primary research techniques—the study of identical and fraternal twins and the study of adopted children (described more fully in the *Research Report*). Behavior geneticists have shown that heredity affects a remarkably broad range of behaviors (Posthuma, de Geus, & Boomsma, 2003). Included in the list are not only obvious physical differences such as height, body shape, or a tendency to thinness or obesity, but also cognitive abilities such as general intelligence, more specific cognitive skills such as spatial visualization ability, and problems like reading disability (Rose, 1995). Research has also shown that many aspects of pathological behavior are genetically influenced, including alcoholism, schizophrenia, excessive aggressiveness or antisocial behavior, depression or anxiety, even anorexia (Goldsmith, Gottesman, & Lemery, 1997; Gottesman & Goldsmith, 1994; McGue, 1994). Finally, and importantly, behavior geneticists have found a significant genetic influence on children's temperament, including such dimensions as emotionality (the tendency to get distressed or upset easily), activity (the tendency toward vigorous, rapid behavior), and sociability (the tendency to prefer the presence of others to being alone) (Saudino, 1998).

Gene-Environment Interaction   A child's genetic heritage may also affect his environment (Plomin, 1995), a phenomenon that could occur via either or both of two routes. First, the child inherits his genes from his parents, who also create the environment in which he is growing up. So a child's genetic heritage may predict something about his environment. For example, parents who themselves have higher IQ scores are not only likely to pass their "good IQ" genes on to their children, they are also likely to create a richer, more stimulating environment for those children. Similarly, children who inherit a tendency toward aggression or hostility from their parents are likely to live in a family environment that is higher in criticism and negativity—because those are expressions of the parents' own genetic tendencies toward aggressiveness or hostility (Reiss, 1998).

   Second, each child's unique pattern of inherited qualities affects the way she behaves with other people, which in turn affects the way adults and other children respond to her. A cranky or temperamentally difficult baby may receive fewer smiles and more scolding than a placid, even-tempered one; a genetically brighter child may demand more personal attention, ask more questions, or seek out more complex toys than would a less bright child (Saudino & Plomin, 1997). Furthermore, children's interpretations of their experiences are affected by all their inherited tendencies, including not only intelligence but also temperament or pathology (Plomin, Reiss, Hetherington, & Howe, 1994).

Internal Models of Experience   Although we often associate experience exclusively with external forces, it's just as important to consider each individual's view of his or her experiences—in other words, the internal aspect of experience. For instance, suppose a friend says to you, "Your new haircut looks great. I think it's a lot more becoming when it's short like that." Your friend intends it as a compliment, but what determines your reaction is how you hear the comment, not what is intended. If your internal model of your self includes the basic idea "I usually look okay," you will likely hear your friend's comment as a compliment; but if your internal model of self or relationships includes some more negative elements, such as "I usually do things wrong, so other people criticize me," then you may hear an implied criticism in your friend's comment ("Your hair used to look awful").

   Theorists who emphasize the importance of such meaning systems argue that each child creates a set of **internal models of experience**—a set of core ideas or assumptions about the world, about himself, and about relationships with others—through which

behavior genetics The study of the genetic contributions to behavior or traits such as intelligence or personality.

internal models of experience A theoretical concept emphasizing that each child creates a set of core ideas or assumptions about the world, the self, and relationships with others through which all subsequent experience is filtered.

all subsequent experience is filtered (Epstein, 1991; Reiss, 1998). Such assumptions are certainly based in part on actual experiences, but once they are formed into an internal model, they generalize beyond the original experience and affect the way the child interprets future experiences. A child who expects adults to be reliable and affectionate will be more likely to interpret the behavior of new adults in this way and will create friendly and affectionate relationships with others outside of the family. A child's self-concept seems to operate in much the same way, as an internal working model of "who I am" (Bretherton, 1991). This self-model is based on experience, but it also shapes future experience.

Aslin's Model of Environmental Influence

Theoretical models are useful for attempting to organize ideas about how all these internal and environmental factors interact to influence development. One particularly good example of a theoretical approach that attempts to explain environmental influences is a set of models summarized by Richard Aslin (1981), based on earlier work by Gottlieb (1976a, 1976b) and shown schematically in Figure 1.1. In each drawing the dashed line represents the path of development of some skill or behavior that would occur without a particular experience; the solid line represents the path of development if the experience were added.

For comparison purposes, the first of the five models shows a maturational pattern with no environmental effect. The second model, which Aslin calls *maintenance*, describes a pattern in which some environmental input is necessary to sustain a skill or behavior that has already developed maturationally. For example, kittens are born with full binocular vision, but if you cover one of their eyes for a period of time, their binocular skill declines.

The third model shows a *facilitation* effect of the environment, in which a skill or behavior develops earlier than it normally would because of some experience. For example, children whose parents talk to them more often in the first 18 to 24 months of life, using more complex sentences, appear to develop two-word sentences and other early grammatical forms somewhat earlier than do children who are talked to less. Yet less-talked-to children do eventually learn to create complex sentences and use most grammatical forms correctly, so the experience of being talked to more provides no permanent gain.

When a particular experience does lead to a permanent gain, or an enduringly higher level of performance, Aslin calls the model *attunement*. For example, children from poverty-level families who attend special enriched day care in infancy and early childhood have consistently higher IQ scores throughout childhood than do children from the same kinds of families who do not have such enriched experience (Ramey & Ramey, 2004). Aslin's final model, *induction*, describes a pure environmental effect: In the absence of some experience, a particular behavior does not develop at all. Giving a child tennis lessons or exposing him to a second language falls into this category of experience.

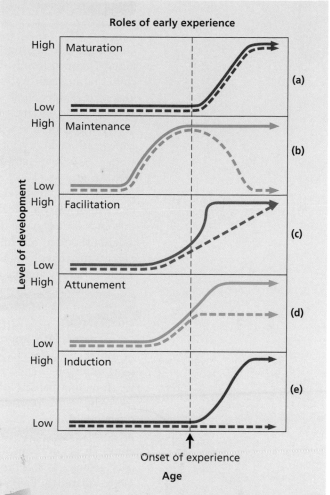

FIGURE 1.1

Aslin's five models of possible relationships between maturation and environment. The top model shows a purely maturational effect; the bottom model (induction) shows a purely environmental effect. The other three show interactive combinations: maintenance, in which experience prevents the deterioration of a maturationally developed skill; facilitation, in which experience speeds up the development of some maturational process; and attunement, in which experience increases the ultimate level of some skill or behavior above the "normal" maturational level.
(*Source*: Aslin, Richard N. "Experiential Influences and Sensitive Periods in Perceptual Development," *Development of perception. Psychobiological perspectives: Vol. 2. The visual system* (1981), p. 50. Reprinted by permission of Elsevier Science and the author.)

THE ECOLOGICAL PERSPECTIVE

Until quite recently, most research on environmental influences focused on a child's family (frequently only the child's mother) and on the stimulation available in the child's home, such as the kinds of toys or books available to the child. If psychologists looked at a larger family context at all, it was usually only in terms of the family's economic status—its level of wealth or poverty. Since the early 1980s, however, there has been a strong push to widen the scope of research, to consider the *ecology*, or *context*, in which each child develops. Urie Bronfenbrenner, one of the key figures in this area of study (1979, 1989), emphasizes that each child grows up in a complex social environment (a social ecology) with a distinct cast of characters: brothers, sisters, one or both parents, grandparents, baby-sitters, pets, teachers, friends. And this cast is itself embedded within a larger social system: The parents have jobs that they may like or dislike; they may or may not have close and supportive friends; they may be living in a safe neighborhood or one full of dangers; the local school may be excellent or poor; and the parents may have good or poor relationships with the school. Bronfenbrenner's argument is that researchers not only must include descriptions of these more extended aspects of the environment but must also consider the ways in which all the components of this complex system interact with one another to affect the development of an individual child.

A particularly impressive example of research that examines such a larger system of influences is Gerald Patterson's work on the origins of antisocial (highly aggressive) behavior in children (1996; Patterson, DeBarsyshe, & Ramsey, 1989). His studies show that parents who use poor discipline techniques and whose monitoring of their children is poor are more likely to have noncompliant or antisocial children. Once established, however, the child's antisocial behavior pattern has repercussions in other areas of his life, leading both to rejection by peers and to academic difficulty. These problems, in turn, are likely to push the young person toward a deviant peer group and still further delinquency (Dishion, Patterson, Stoolmiller, & Skinner, 1991; Vuchinich, Bank, & Patterson, 1992). So a pattern that began in the family is maintained and exacerbated by interactions with peers and with the school system. These relationships are of interest in themselves, but Patterson does not stop there. He adds important ecological elements, arguing that the family's good or poor disciplinary techniques are not random events but are themselves shaped by the larger context in which the family exists. He finds that those parents who were raised with poor disciplinary practices are more likely to use those same poor strategies with their children. He also finds that even parents who possess good child-management skills may fall into poor patterns when the stresses in their own lives are increased. A recent divorce or a period of unemployment increases the likelihood that parents will use poor disciplinary practices and thus increases the likelihood that the child will develop a pattern of antisocial behavior. Figure 1.2 shows Patterson's conception of how the various components of antisocial behavior fit together. Clearly, taking into account the larger social ecological system in which the family is embedded greatly enhances our understanding of the process.

One aspect of such a larger ecology, not emphasized in Patterson's model but clearly part of Bronfenbrenner's thinking, is the still broader concept of *culture*. There is no commonly agreed-on definition for this term, but in essence it describes a system of meanings and customs, including values, attitudes, goals, laws, beliefs, morals, and physical artifacts of various kinds, such as tools and forms of dwellings. The majority U.S. culture, for example, is strongly shaped by the values expressed in the Constitution and the Bill of Rights; it also includes a strong emphasis on "can-do" attitudes and on competition. At a more specific level, U.S. cultural beliefs include, for example, the assumption that the ideal living arrangement is for each family to have a separate house—a belief that contributes to a more spread-out pattern of housing in the United States than what exists in Europe.

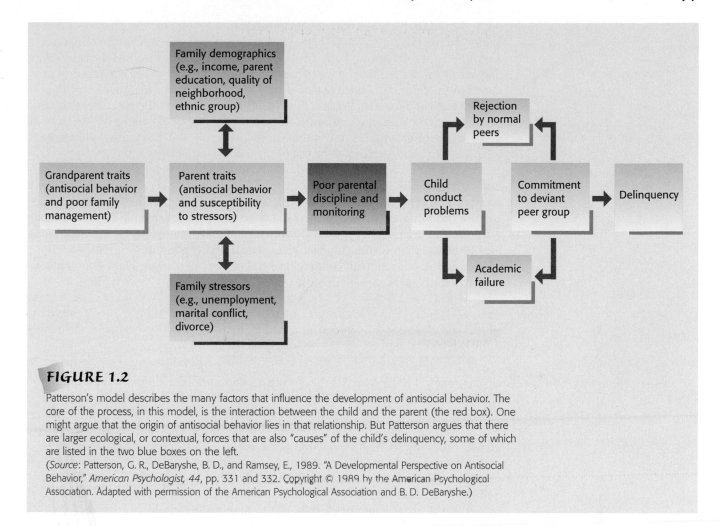

FIGURE 1.2

Patterson's model describes the many factors that influence the development of antisocial behavior. The core of the process, in this model, is the interaction between the child and the parent (the red box). One might argue that the origin of antisocial behavior lies in that relationship. But Patterson argues that there are larger ecological, or contextual, forces that are also "causes" of the child's delinquency, some of which are listed in the two blue boxes on the left.

(*Source*: Patterson, G. R., DeBaryshe, B. D., and Ramsey, E., 1989. "A Developmental Perspective on Antisocial Behavior," *American Psychologist, 44*, pp. 331 and 332. Copyright © 1989 by the American Psychological Association. Adapted with permission of the American Psychological Association and B. D. DeBaryshe.)

For a system of meanings and customs to be called a culture, it must be shared by some identifiable group, whether that group is the entire population of a country or a subsection of such a population; it must then be transmitted from one generation of that group to the next (Cole, 2005). Families and children are clearly embedded in culture, just as they are located within an ecological niche within the culture.

Anthropologists point out that a key dimension on which cultures differ from one another is that of *individualism* versus *collectivism* (e.g., Kashima et al., 2005). People in cultures with an individualistic emphasis assume that the world is made up of independent persons whose achievement and responsibility are individual rather than collective. Most European cultures are based on such individualistic assumptions, as is the dominant U.S. culture, created primarily by whites who came to the United States from Europe. In contrast, most of the remainder of the world's cultures operate with a collectivist belief system in which the emphasis is on collective rather than individual identity, on group solidarity, sharing, duties and obligations, and group decision making (Kashima et al., 2005). A person living in a collectivist system is integrated into a strong, cohesive group that protects and nourishes that individual throughout his life. Collectivism is the dominant theme in most Asian countries, as well as in many African and South American cultures. Strong elements of collectivism are also part of the African American, Hispanic American, Native American, and Asian American subcultures.

Greenfield (1995) gives a wonderful example of how the difference between collectivist and individualist cultures can affect actual child-rearing practices as well as people's judgments of others' child-rearing. She notes that mothers from the Zinacanteco Maya culture maintain almost constant bodily contact with their young babies and do not feel comfortable when they are separated from their infants. They believe that their babies require this contact to be happy. When these mothers saw a visiting American anthropologist put her own baby down, they were shocked and blamed the baby's regular crying on the fact that he was separated from his mother so often. Greenfield argues that the constant bodily contact of the Mayan mothers is a logical outgrowth of their collectivist approach, because their basic goal is interdependence rather than independence. The American anthropologist, in contrast, operates with a basic goal of independence for her child and so emphasizes more separation. Each group judges the other's form of child-rearing to be less optimal or even inadequate.

Such differences notwithstanding, researchers note that it is wrong to think of collectivism and individualism in either-or terms, because there are elements of both in every culture (Green, Deschamps, & Páez, 2005). Consequently, when researchers categorize a given culture as collectivist or individualist, they are referring to which of the two sets of values predominates. It is also true that there is a considerable amount of individual variation within cultures. Thus, people who live in individualistic societies may nevertheless, as individuals, develop a collectivist orientation. The same is true for their counterparts in collectivist societies.

VULNERABILITY AND RESILIENCE

At this point, it should be clear to you that nature and nurture do not act independently in shaping each child's development; they interact in complex and fascinating ways. Consequently, the same environment may have quite different effects on children who are born with different characteristics. One influential research approach exploring such an interaction is the study of vulnerable and resilient children. In their long-term study of a group of children born in 1955 on the island of Kauai, Hawaii, Emmy Werner and Ruth Smith (Werner, 1993, 1995; Werner & Smith, 1992, 2001) found that only about two-thirds of the children who grew up in poverty-level, chaotic families turned out to have serious problems themselves as adults. The other third, described as *resilient*, turned out to be "competent, confident, and caring adults" (Werner, 1995, p. 82). Thus, similar environments were linked to quite different outcomes.

Theorists such as Norman Garmezy, Michael Rutter, Ann Masten, and others (Garmezy, 1993; Garmezy & Rutter, 1983; Masten & Coatsworth, 1995; Rutter, 1987, 2005b) argue that the best way to make sense out of results like Werner and Smith's is to think of each child as born with certain *vulnerabilities*, such as a difficult temperament, a physical abnormality, allergies, or a genetic tendency toward alcoholism. Each child is also born with some *protective factors*, such as high intelligence, good coordination, an easy temperament, or a lovely smile, which tend to make her more resilient in the face of stress. These vulnerabilities and protective factors then interact with the child's environment, and thus the same environment can have quite different effects, depending on the qualities the child brings to the interaction.

A more general model describing the interaction between the qualities of the child and the environment comes from Fran Horowitz (1987, 1990), who proposes that the key ingredients are each child's vulnerability or resilience and the "facilitativeness" of the environment. A highly facilitative environment is one in which the child

Many children who grow up in poverty-stricken neighborhoods are high achievers who are well adjusted. Developmentalists use the term *resilient* to refer to children who demonstrate positive developmental outcomes despite being raised in high-risk environments.

has loving and responsive parents and is provided with a rich array of stimulation. If the relationship between vulnerability and facilitativeness were merely additive, the best outcomes would occur for resilient infants reared in optimal environments, and the worst outcomes for vulnerable infants in poor environments, with the two mixed combinations falling halfway between. But that is not what Horowitz proposes, as you can see represented schematically in Figure 1.3. Instead, she is suggesting that a resilient child in a poor environment may do quite well, since such a child can take advantage of all the stimulation and opportunities available. Similarly, she suggests that a vulnerable child may do quite well in a highly facilitative environment. According to this model, it is only the "double whammy"—the vulnerable child in a poor environment—that leads to really poor outcomes.

In fact, as you will see throughout the book, a growing body of research shows precisely this pattern. For example, very low IQ scores are most common among children who were low-birth-weight babies and were reared in poverty-level families, while low-birth-weight children reared in middle-class families have essentially normal IQs, as do normal-weight infants reared in poverty-level families (Werner, 1986). Further, among low-birth-weight children who are reared in poverty-level families, those whose families offer "protective" factors (such as greater residential stability, less crowded living conditions, and more acceptance, more stimulation, and more learning materials) achieve higher IQ scores than do equivalently low-birth-weight children reared in the least optimal poverty-level conditions (Bradley et al., 1994). The key point here is that the same environment can have quite different effects, depending on the qualities or capacities the child brings to the equation.

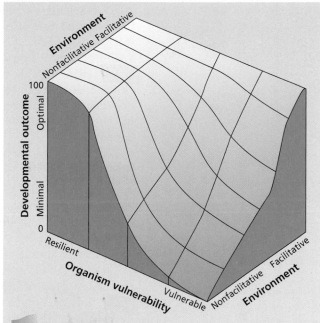

FIGURE 1.3

Horowitz's model describes one possible type of interaction between the vulnerability of the child and the quality of the environment. The height of the surface shows the "goodness" of the developmental outcome (such as IQ or skill in social relationships). In this model, only the combination of a vulnerable infant and a nonfacilitative environment will result in a really poor outcome.
(*Source*: Horowitz, F. D., *Exploring Developmental Theories: Toward a Structural/Behavioral Model of Development*, Fig. 1.1, p. 23. © 1987 by Lawrence Erlbaum Associates, Inc. By permission of the publisher and author.)

Theories of Development

Before going on...

■ How did early philosophers and psychologists explain the roles of nature and nurture in age-related change?
■ What do psychologists mean when they talk about continuity and discontinuity in development?
■ Explain the roles of the various internal and external influences on development.
■ What does Bronfenbrenner's ecological perspective contribute to our understanding of development?
■ Explain the concepts of vulnerability and resilience.

Students often say that they dislike reading about theories; what they want are the facts. However, theories are important, because they help us look at facts from different perspectives. A brief introduction to several important theories will help you understand some of the more detailed information about them presented in later chapters.

PSYCHOANALYTIC THEORIES

The most distinctive and central assumption of the **psychoanalytic theories** is that behavior is governed by unconscious as well as conscious processes. Psychoanalytic theorists also see development as fundamentally stagelike, with each stage centered on a particular form of tension or a particular task. The child moves through these

psychoanalytic theories Developmental theories based on the assumption that age-related change results from maturationally determined conflicts between internal drives and society's demands.

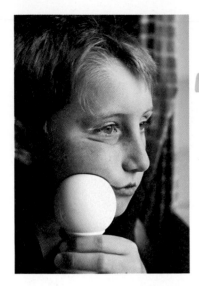

When parents divorce, boys are more likely to show disturbed behavior or poorer school performance than are girls. But why? Theories can help to explain facts like this.

stages, resolving each task or reducing each tension as best he can. This emphasis on the formative role of early experience, particularly early family experience, is a hallmark of psychoanalytic theories. In this view, the first 5 or 6 years of life constitute a kind of sensitive period for the creation of the individual personality. Sigmund Freud (1856–1939) is usually credited with originating the psychoanalytic approach (1905, 1920), and his terminology and many of his concepts have become part of our intellectual culture. Another theorist in this tradition, Erik Erikson (1902–1994), has also had a large impact on the way psychologists think about personality development.

Freud's Theory   Freud proposed the existence of a basic, unconscious, instinctual sexual drive he called the **libido**. He argued that this energy is the motive force behind virtually all human behavior. Freud also proposed that unconscious material is created over time through the functioning of the various *defense mechanisms,* several of which are listed in Table 1.1. We all use defense mechanisms every day, and Freud's ideas about them continue to be influential among psychologists (Cramer, 2000).

A second basic assumption is that personality has a structure, which develops over time. Freud proposed three parts of the personality: the **id**, which is the source of the libido; the **ego**, a much more conscious element, the "executive" of the personality; and the **superego**, which is the center of conscience and morality, since it incorporates the norms and moral strictures of the family and society. In Freud's theory, these three parts are not all present at birth. The infant and toddler is all id—all instinct, all desire, without the restraining influence of the ego or the superego. The ego begins to develop in the years from age 2 to about 4 or 5, as the child learns to adapt her instant-gratification strategies. Finally, the superego begins to develop just before school age, as the child incorporates the parents' values and cultural mores.

Freud thought the stages of personality development were strongly influenced by maturation. In each of Freud's five **psychosexual stages**, the libido is centered in that part of the body that is most sensitive at that age. In a newborn, the mouth is the most

libido The term used by Freud to describe the basic, unconscious, instinctual sexual energy in each individual.

id In Freudian theory, the inborn, primitive portion of the personality, the storehouse of libido, the basic energy that continually pushes for immediate gratification.

ego In Freudian theory, the portion of the personality that organizes, plans, and keeps the person in touch with reality. Language and thought are both ego functions.

superego In Freudian theory, the "conscience" part of personality, which contains parental and societal values and attitudes incorporated during childhood.

psychosexual stages The stages of personality development suggested by Freud: the oral, anal, phallic, latency, and genital stages.

TABLE 1.1	Some Common Defense Mechanisms	
Mechanism	**Definition**	**Example**
Denial	Behaving as if a problem doesn't exist	A pregnant woman fails to get prenatal care because she convinces herself she can't possibly be pregnant even though she has all the symptoms.
Repression	Intentionally forgetting something unpleasant	A child "forgets" about a troublesome bully on the bus as soon as he gets safely home from school every day.
Projection	Seeing one's own behavior or beliefs in others whether they are actually present or not	A woman complains about her boss to a co-worker and comes away from the conversation believing that the co-worker shares her dislike of the boss, even though the co-worker made no comment on what she said.
Regression	Behaving in a way that is inappropriate for one's age	A toilet-trained 2-year-old starts wetting the bed every night after a new baby arrives.
Displacement	Directing emotion to an object or person other than the one that provoked it	An elderly adult suffers a stroke, becomes physically impaired, and expresses her frustration through verbal abuse of the hospital staff.
Rationalization	Creating an explanation to justify an action or to deal with a disappointment	A man stealing money from his employer says to himself, "They won't give me a raise. So what if I took $50?"

sensitive part of the body, so libidinal energy is focused there. The stage is therefore called the *oral stage*. As neurological development progresses, the infant has more sensation in the anus (hence the *anal stage*) and later in the genitalia (the *phallic* and eventually the *genital stages*).

Erikson's Theory The stages Erikson proposed, called **psychosocial stages**, are influenced much less by maturation and much more by common cultural demands for children of a particular age, such as the demand that a child become toilet trained at about age 2 or that the child learn school skills at age 6 or 7. In Erikson's view, each child moves through a fixed sequence of tasks, each centered on the development of a particular facet of identity. For example, the first task, central to the first 12 to 18 months of life, is to develop a sense of *basic trust*. If the child's caregivers are not responsive and loving, however, the child may develop a sense of basic mistrust, which will affect his responses at all the later stages.

In both Freud's and Erikson's theories, however, the critical point is that the degree of success a child experiences in meeting the demands of these various stages will depend very heavily on the interactions he has with the people and objects in his world. This interactive element in Freud's and all subsequent psychoanalytic theories is absolutely central. Basic trust cannot be developed unless the parents or other caregivers respond to the infant in a loving, consistent manner. The oral stage cannot be fully completed unless the infant's desire for oral stimulation is sufficiently gratified. And when a stage is not fully resolved, the old pattern or the unmet need is carried forward, affecting the individual's ability to handle later tasks or stages. So, for example, a young adult who developed a sense of mistrust in the first years of life may have a more difficult time establishing a secure intimate relationship with a partner or with friends.

COGNITIVE-DEVELOPMENTAL AND INFORMATION-PROCESSING THEORIES

In psychoanalytic theories, the quality and character of a child's relationships with a few key people are seen as central to the child's whole development. **Cognitive-developmental theories**, which emphasize primarily cognitive development rather than personality, reverse this order of importance, emphasizing the centrality of the child's actions on the environment and her cognitive processing of experiences.

Piaget's Theory The central figure in cognitive-developmental theory has been Jean Piaget (1896–1980), a Swiss psychologist whose theories (1952, 1970, 1977; Piaget & Inhelder, 1969) shaped the thinking of several generations of developmental psychologists. Piaget was struck by the great regularities in the development of children's thinking. He noticed that all children seem to go through the same kinds of sequential discoveries about their world, making the same sorts of mistakes and arriving at the same solutions. For example, all 3- and 4-year-olds seem to think that if you pour water from a short, fat glass into a tall, thin one, there is more water in the thin glass, since the water level is higher there than in the fat glass. In contrast, most 7-year-olds realize that the amount of water is the same in either glass.

Piaget's detailed observations of such systematic shifts in children's thinking led him to several assumptions, the most central of which is that it is the nature of the human organism to adapt to its environment. This is an active process. In contrast to many theorists, Piaget did not think that the environment shapes the child. Rather, the child (like the adult) actively seeks to understand his environment. In the process, he explores, manipulates, and examines the objects and people in his world.

The process of *adaptation*, in Piaget's view, is made up of several important subprocesses—*assimilation, accommodation*, and *equilibration*—all of which you will learn more about in Chapter 6. What is important to understand at this preliminary point is that Piaget thought that the child develops a series of fairly distinct "understandings,"

psychosocial stages The stages of personality development suggested by Erikson, involving basic trust, autonomy, initiative, industry, identity, intimacy, generativity, and ego integrity.

cognitive-developmental theories Developmental theories that emphasize children's actions on the environment and suggest that age-related changes in reasoning precede and explain changes in other domains.

Piaget based many of his ideas on naturalistic observation of children of different ages on playgrounds and in schools.

or "theories," about the way the world works, based on her active exploration of the environment. Each of these "theories" corresponds to a specific stage. Piaget thought that virtually all infants begin with the same skills and built-in strategies and since the environments children encounter are highly similar in important respects, he believed that the stages through which children's thinking moves are also similar. Piaget proposed a fixed sequence of four major stages, each growing out of the one that preceded it, and each consisting of a more or less complete system or organization of concepts, strategies, and assumptions.

Vygotsky's Theory   Russian psychologist Lev Vygotsky (1896–1934) is normally thought of as belonging to the cognitive-developmental camp because he, too, was primarily concerned with understanding the origins of the child's knowledge (1978/1930). Vygotsky differed from Piaget, however, in one key respect: He was convinced that complex forms of thinking have their origins in social interactions (Duncan, 1995). According to Vygotsky, a child's learning of new cognitive skills is guided by an adult (or a more skilled child, such as an older sibling), who models and structures the child's learning experience, a process Jerome Bruner later called **scaffolding** (Wood, Bruner, & Ross, 1976). Such new learning, Vygotsky suggested, is best achieved in what he called the **zone of proximal development**—that range of tasks which are too hard for the child to do alone but which she can manage with guidance. As the child becomes more skilled, the zone of proximal development steadily widens, including ever harder tasks. Vygotsky thought the key to this interactive process lay in the language the adult used to describe or frame the task. Later, the child could use this same language to guide her independent attempts to do the same kinds of tasks.

Information-Processing Theory   Although it is not truly a cognitive-developmental theory, many of the ideas and research studies associated with **information-processing theory** have increased psychologists' understanding of Piaget's stages and other age-related changes in thinking. The goal of information-processing theory is to explain how the mind manages information (Klahr, 1992). Information-processing theorists use the computer as a model of human thinking. Consequently, they often use computer terms such as *hardware* and *software* to talk about human cognitive processes.

Theorizing about and studying memory processes are central to information-processing theory (Birney, Citron-Pousty, Lutz, & Sternberg, 2005). Theorists usually break memory down into subprocesses of encoding, storage, and retrieval. *Encoding* is organizing information to be stored in memory. For example, you may be encoding the information in this chapter by relating it to your own childhood. *Storage* is keeping information, and *retrieval* is getting information out of memory.

Most memory research assumes that the memory system is made up of multiple components. The idea is that information moves through these components in an organized way (see Figure 1.4). The process of understanding a spoken word serves as a good example. First, you hear the word when the sounds enter your *sensory memory*. Your experiences with language allow you to recognize the pattern of sounds as a word. Next, the word moves into your *short-term memory*, the component of the memory system where all information is processed. Thus, short-term memory is often called *working memory*. Knowledge of the word's meaning is then called up out of *long-term memory*, the component of the system where information is permanently stored, and placed in short-term memory, where it is linked to the word's sounds to enable you to understand what you have just heard.

scaffolding The term used by Bruner to describe the process by which a teacher (or parent, older child, or other person in the role of teacher) structures a learning encounter with a child, so as to lead the child from step to step—a process consistent with Vygotsky's theory of cognitive development.

zone of proximal development In Vygotsky's theory, the range of tasks that are slightly too difficult for a child to do alone but that can be accomplished successfully with guidance from an adult or more experienced child.

information-processing theories A set of theories based on the idea that humans process information in ways that are similar to those used in computers.

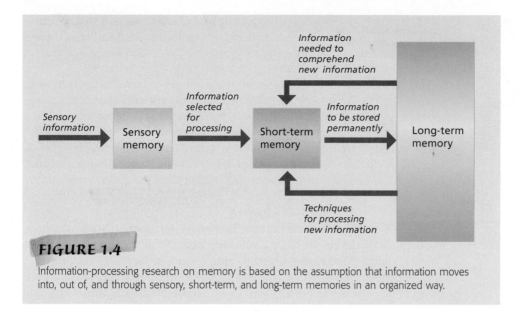

FIGURE 1.4

Information-processing research on memory is based on the assumption that information moves into, out of, and through sensory, short-term, and long-term memories in an organized way.

Each memory component manages information differently. Information flows through sensory memory as if in a stream. Bits of information that are not attended to drop out quickly. Short-term memory is extremely limited in capacity—an adult's short-term memory can hold about seven items at a time. However, information can be retained in short-term memory as long as it is processed in some way—for example, when you repeat your grocery list to yourself on the way to the store.

Long-term memory is unlimited in capacity, and information is often stored in terms of meaningful associations. For example, suppose you read a sentence such as "Bill wrote a letter to his brother." When you think about the sentence later, you might mistakenly recall that it contained the word *pen*. This happens because information about the process of writing and the tools used to do it are stored together in long-term memory.

There are both age-related and individual differences in information processing. As you will learn in Chapter 6, the number of items that can be retained in short-term memory at one time is far more limited in young children than in adults and older children. In addition, among children of the same age, some use more efficient strategies for remembering and solving problems. Looking at differences of both kinds and examining children's thinking from Piaget's and Vygotsky's perspectives provide a more complete picture of how children acquire the ability to reason logically.

LEARNING THEORIES

Learning theories represent a theoretical tradition very different from that of either the psychoanalysts or the cognitive-developmentalists, one in which the emphasis is much more on the way the environment shapes the child than on how the child understands his experiences. Learning theorists do not argue that genetics or built-in biases are unimportant, but they see human behavior as enormously plastic, shaped by predictable processes of learning. Three of the most important learning theories are Pavlov's classical conditioning model, Skinner's operant conditioning model, and Bandura's social cognitive theory.

Classical Conditioning
Classical conditioning, made famous by Ivan Pavlov's (1849–1936) experiments with his salivating dog, involves the acquisition of new signals for existing responses. If you touch a baby on the cheek, she will turn toward the touch and begin to suck. In the technical terminology of classical conditioning, the

learning theories Psychological theories that explain development in terms of accumulated learning experiences.

classical conditioning One of three major types of learning. An automatic, or unconditioned, response such as an emotion or a reflex comes to be triggered by a new cue, called the conditional stimulus, after having been paired several times with that stimulus.

Laboratory research involving animals was important in the development of Skinner's operant conditioning theory.

touch on the cheek is the *unconditional stimulus*; the turning and sucking are *unconditioned responses*. The baby is already programmed to do all that; these are automatic reflexes. Learning occurs when some new stimulus is introduced to the system.

The general model is that other stimuli that are present just before or at the same time as the unconditional stimulus will eventually trigger the same responses. In the typical home situation, for example, a number of stimuli occur at about the same time as the touch on the baby's cheek before feeding: the sound of the mother's footsteps approaching, the kinesthetic cues of being picked up, and the tactile cues of being held in the mother's arms. All these stimuli may eventually become *conditional stimuli* and may trigger the infant's response of turning and sucking, even without any touch on the cheek.

Classical conditioning is of special interest in the study of child development because of the role it plays in the development of emotional responses, as Watson's Little Albert experiment so aptly demonstrated. For example, things or people present when you feel good will become conditional stimuli for that same sense of well-being; things or people previously associated with some uncomfortable feeling may become conditional stimuli for a sense of unease or anxiety. This is especially important in infancy, since a child's mother or father is present so often when nice things happen—when the child feels warm, comfortable, and cuddled. Thus, mother and father usually come to be conditional stimuli for pleasant feelings, a fact that makes it possible for the parents' mere presence to reinforce other behaviors as well. A tormenting older sibling might come to be a conditional stimulus for angry feelings, even after the sibling has long since stopped the tormenting. Such classically conditioned emotional responses are remarkably powerful. They begin to be formed very early in life, continue to be created throughout childhood and adulthood, and profoundly affect each individual's emotional experiences.

Operant Conditioning   The second major type of learning is most often called operant conditioning, although you may also see it referred to as *instrumental conditioning*. **Operant conditioning** is the process through which the frequency of a behavior increases or decreases because of the consequences the behavior produces. When a behavior increases, it is said to have been *reinforced*; when it decreases, the behavior is said to have been *punished*. Psychologist B. F. Skinner (1904–1990) discovered the principles of operant conditioning in a series of animal studies. He believed that these principles strongly influence human development.

Reinforcement occurs when a consequence results in an increase in the frequency of a particular behavior. With **positive reinforcement**, an *added* stimulus or consequence increases a behavior. Certain kinds of pleasant stimuli—such as praise, a smile, food, a hug, or attention—serve as positive reinforcers for most people most of the time. But strictly speaking, a reinforcer is defined by its effect; we don't know that something is reinforcing unless we see that its presence increases the probability of some behavior. For example, if a parent gives a child dessert as a reward for good table manners, and the child's frequency of good table manners increases, then the dessert is a reinforcer. If the frequency does not increase, then the dessert is not a reinforcer.

Negative reinforcement increases a behavior because the reinforcement involves the termination or removal of an unpleasant stimulus. Suppose your little boy is whining and begging you to pick him up. At first you ignore him, but finally you do pick him up. What happens? He stops whining. So your picking-up behavior has been negatively reinforced by the cessation of his whining, and you will be more likely to pick him up the next time he whines. At the same time, his whining has probably been positively reinforced by your attention, so he will be more likely to whine on similar occasions.

operant conditioning The type of learning in which the probability of a person's performing some behavior is increased or decreased because of the consequences it produces.

positive reinforcement The process of strengthening a behavior by the presentation of some pleasurable or positive stimulus.

negative reinforcement The process of strengthening a behavior by the removal or cessation of an unpleasant stimulus.

In laboratory situations, experimenters can be sure to reinforce a behavior every time it occurs or to stop reinforcements completely so as to produce *extinction* of a response. In the real world, however, consistency of reinforcement is the exception rather than the rule. Much more common is a pattern of *partial reinforcement*, in which a behavior is reinforced on some occasions but not others. Studies of partial reinforcement show that children and adults take longer to learn behaviors under partial reinforcement conditions, but once established, such behaviors are much more resistant to extinction. If you smile at your daughter only every fifth or sixth time she brings a picture to show you (and if she finds your smile reinforcing), she'll keep on bringing pictures for a very long stretch, even if you quit smiling altogether.

Both positive and negative reinforcements strengthen behavior. **Punishment**, in contrast, weakens behavior. Sometimes punishments involve eliminating nice things (for example, "grounding" a child, taking away TV privileges, or sending her to her room). Often they involve administering unpleasant things such as a scolding or a spanking. What is confusing about such consequences is that they don't always do what they are intended to do: They do not always suppress the undesired behavior.

Say, for example, a parent suspends a teenager's driving privileges for coming home after curfew in the hope that the penalty will stop the behavior of coming home late. For some teens, this approach will be effective. Others, though, may respond with defiance, by staying out later and later each time their driving privileges are restored. To these teens, the parent's "punishment" is a form of recognition for the defiant attitude they hope to project. For them, the "punishment" is actually a positive reinforcement. Thus, punishment, like reinforcement, must be defined in terms of its effect on behavior; if a consequence doesn't weaken or stop a behavior, it isn't a punishment.

Bandura's Social Cognitive Theory Albert Bandura, whose variation of learning theory is by far the most influential among developmental psychologists today, has built on the base of these traditional learning concepts but has added several other key ideas (1977, 1982, 1989, 2004). First, he argues that learning does not always require direct reinforcement. Learning may also occur merely as a result of watching someone else perform some action. Learning of this type, called *observational learning*, or *modeling*, is involved in a wide range of behaviors. Children learn how to hit from watching other people in real life and on television. They learn how to be generous by watching others donate money or share goods. Bandura also calls attention to another class of reinforcements called *intrinsic reinforcements*. These are internal reinforcements, such as the pride a child feels when she figures out how to draw a star or the sense of satisfaction you may experience after strenuous exercise.

Finally, and perhaps most importantly, Bandura has gone far toward bridging the gap between learning theory and cognitive-developmental theory by emphasizing important cognitive (mental) elements in observational learning. Indeed, he now calls his theory "social cognitive theory" rather than "social learning theory," as it was originally labeled (Bandura, 1986, 1989). For example, Bandura now stresses the fact that modeling can be the vehicle for learning abstract information as well as concrete skills. In abstract modeling, the observer extracts a rule that may be the basis of the model's behavior, then learns the rule as well as the specific behavior. A child who sees his parents volunteering one day a month at a food bank may extract a rule about the importance of "helping others," even if the parents never actually articulate this rule. Thus, through modeling, a child can acquire attitudes, values, ways of solving problems, even standards of self-evaluation.

Being able to use chopsticks is only one example of the myriad skills that are learned through modeling.

CRITICAL THINKING

Think again about your upbringing. What values or attitudes do you think you learned through modeling? How were those values and attitudes displayed (modeled) by your parents or others?

punishment The removal of a desirable stimulus or the administration of an unpleasant consequence after some undesired behavior in order to stop the behavior.

Collectively, Bandura's additions to traditional learning theory make his theory far more flexible and powerful, although it is still not a strongly developmental theory. That is, Bandura has little to say about any changes that may occur with age in what or how a child may learn from modeling. In contrast, both psychoanalytic and cognitive-developmental theories are strongly developmental, emphasizing sequential, often stagelike qualitative change that occurs with age.

COMPARING THEORIES

After learning about theories of development, students usually want to know which one is right. However, developmentalists don't think of theories in terms of right or wrong but, instead, compare them on the basis of their assumptions and how useful they are to understanding human development.

Assumptions about Development   When we say that a theory assumes something to be true, we mean that it begins from a general perspective on development. We can think of a theory's assumptions in terms of its answers to three questions about development.

One question addresses the *active or passive issue*: Is a person active in shaping her own development, or is she a passive recipient of environmental influences? Theories that claim a person's actions on the environment are the most important determinants of her development are on the active side of this question. Cognitive-developmental theories, for example, typically view development this way. In contrast, theories on the passive side of the question, such as classical and operant conditioning, maintain that development results from the action of the environment on the individual.

As you learned earlier in the chapter, the *nature or nurture question* is one of the most important issues in developmental psychology. All developmental theories, while admitting that both nature and nurture are involved in development, make assumptions about their relative importance. Theories claiming that biology contributes more to development than environment are on the nature side of the question. Those that view environmental influences as most important are on the nurture side. Other theories assume that nature and nurture are equally important, and that it is impossible to say which contributes more to development.

Developmental theories also disagree on the *stability versus change issue*. Theories that have no stages assert that development is a stable, continuous process. Stage theories, on the other hand, emphasize change more than stability. They claim that development happens in leaps from lower to higher steps.

Table 1.2 lists the theories you have read about in this chapter and the assumptions each makes regarding these issues. Because each theory is based on different assumptions, each takes a different approach to studying development. Consequently, research derived from each reveals something different about development.

A theory's assumptions also shape the way it is applied in the real world. For example, a teacher who approached instruction from the cognitive-developmental perspective would create a classroom in which children can experiment to some degree on their own. He would also recognize that children differ in abilities, interests, developmental level, and other internal characteristics. He would believe that structuring the educational environment is important, but that what each student ultimately learns will be determined by his or her own actions on the environment. Alternatively, a teacher who adopted the learning theory perspective would guide and reinforce children's learning very carefully. Such a teacher would place little importance on ability differences among children. Instead, he would try to accomplish the same instructional goals for all children through proper manipulation of the environment.

Usefulness   Developmentalists also compare theories with respect to their usefulness. Before reading this section, you should understand that there is a fair amount of dis-

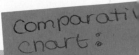

TABLE 1.2	Comparing Theories				
	Theory	**Main Ideas**	**Active or Passive?**	**Nature or Nurture?**	**Stages or No Stages?**
Psychoanalytic Theories	Freud's Psychosexual Theory	Personality develops in five stages from birth to adolescence; in each stage, the need for physical pleasure is focused on a different part of the body.	Passive	Nature	Stages
	Erikson's Psychosocial Theory	Personality develops through eight life crises across the entire lifespan; a person finishes each crisis with either a good or a poor resolution.	Passive	Both	Stages
Cognitive Theories	Piaget's Cognitive-Developmental Theory	Reasoning develops in four universal stages from birth through adolescence; in each stage, the child builds a different kind of scheme.	Active	Both	Stages
	Vygotsky's Socio-cultural Theory	Social interaction is critical to the development of thinking and problem-solving; stages in the development of reasoning reflect internalized language.	Active	Both	Stages
	Information-Processing Theory	The computer is used as a model for human cognitive functioning; encoding, storage, and retrieval processes change with age, causing changes in memory function.	Active	Both	Some theories have stages; others do not
Learning Theories	Classical Conditioning	Learning happens when neutral stimuli become so strongly associated with natural stimuli that they elicit the same responses	Passive	Nurture	No stages
	Operant Conditioning	Development involves behavior changes that are shaped by reinforcement and punishment.	Passive	Nurture	No stages
	Bandura's Social Cognitive Theory	People learn from models; what they learn from a model depends on how they interpret the situation cognitively and emotionally.	Active	Nurture	No stages

agreement among psychologists on exactly how useful each theory is. Nevertheless, there are a few general criteria most psychologists use to evaluate the usefulness of a theory.

One kind of usefulness has to do with a theory's ability to generate predictions that can be tested with scientific methods. For example, one criticism of Freud's theory is that many of his claims are difficult to test. In contrast, when Piaget claimed that most children can solve hypothetical problems by age 12 or so, he made an assertion that is easily tested. Thus, Piaget's theory is viewed by many developmentalists as more useful in this sense than Freud's. Vygotsky, the learning theorists, and the information-processing theorists have also proposed many testable ideas (Thomas, 2000).

Another criterion by which psychologists judge the usefulness of theories is their *heuristic value*, the degree to which they stimulate thinking and research. In terms of heuristic value, we would have to give Freud's and Piaget's theories equally high marks. Both are responsible for an enormous amount of theorizing and research on human development, often by psychologists who strongly disagree with them.

Yet another way of thinking about a theory's usefulness is in terms of practical value. In other words, a theory may be deemed useful if it provides solutions to real-life problems. On this criterion, the learning and information-processing theories seem to stand out because they provide tools that can be used to influence behavior. A person who suffers from anxiety attacks, for example, can learn to use biofeedback, a technique derived from classical conditioning theories, to manage them. Similarly, a student who needs to learn to study more effectively can get help from study-skills courses based on information-processing theories.

Ultimately, of course, no matter how many testable hypotheses or practical techniques a theory produces, it is of little or no value to developmentalists if it doesn't explain the basic facts of development. On this criterion, learning theories, especially those of classical and operant conditioning, are regarded by many developmentalists as somewhat less useful than other perspectives (Thomas, 2000). While they explain how specific behaviors may be learned, the complexity of human development can't be reduced to connections between stimuli and responses or behaviors and reinforcers.

Eclecticism   As you can see, the point of comparing theories is not to conclude which one is true. Instead, we compare them to understand the unique contribution each can make to a comprehensive understanding of human development. Consequently, today's developmental scientists try to avoid the kind of rigid adherence to a single theoretical perspective that was characteristic of theorists such as Freud, Piaget, and Skinner. Instead, most adopt an approach known as **eclecticism**, the use of multiple theoretical perspectives to explain and study human development (Parke, 2004).

To better understand the eclectic approach, think about how ideas drawn from several theories might help us better understand a child's disruptive behavior in school. Observations of the child's behavior and her classmates' reactions may suggest that her behavior is being rewarded by the other children's responses (a behavioral explanation). Deeper probing of the child's family situation may indicate that her acting-out behavior reflects an emotional reaction to a family event such as divorce (a psychoanalytic explanation). The emotional reaction may arise from her inability to understand why her parents are divorcing (a cognitive-developmental explanation). When appropriately applied, each of these perspectives can help us gain insight into developmental issues. Moreover, we can integrate all of them into a more complete explanation than any of the perspectives alone could provide us with.

Before going on · · ·

- What ideas do psychoanalytic theorists propose to explain development?
- What do Piaget's and Vygostky's theories and the information-processing theories suggest about cognitive development?
- How do learning theories explain age-related change?
- What methods do psychologists use to compare theories?

Finding the Answers: Research Designs and Methods

The easiest way to understand research methods is to look at a specific question and the alternative ways in which it can be answered. Suppose we wanted to answer the following question: "What causes children's attention spans to increase as they get older?" How might we go about answering this question?

RELATING GOALS TO METHODS

Developmental psychology uses the scientific method to achieve four goals: to *describe*, to *explain*, to *predict*, and to *influence* human development from conception to death. To describe development is simply to state what happens. "Children's attention spans get longer as they get older" is an example of a statement that represents the description goal of developmental psychology. All we would have to do is measure how long children of various ages pay attention to something to meet this objective.

Explaining development involves telling why a particular event occurs. As you learned earlier in this chapter, developmentalists rely on theories to generate explanations. Useful theories produce predictions researchers can test, or *hypotheses*, such as "If changes in the brain cause children's attention spans to increase, then children whose

eclecticism The use of multiple theoretical perspectives to explain and study human development.

brain development is ahead of that of their peers should also have longer attention spans." To test this biological hypothesis, we would have to measure some aspect of brain structure or function as well as attention span. Then we would have to find a way to relate one to the other.

We could instead test an experiential explanation of attention-span increase by comparing children of the same age who differ in the amount of practice they get in paying attention. For example, we might hypothesize that the experience of learning to play a musical instrument enhances children's ability to attend. If we compare instrument-playing and non–instrument-playing children of the same age and find that those who have musical training do better on tests of attention than their agemates who have not had musical training, the experiential perspective gains support.

If both the biological and the experiential hypotheses are supported by research, they provide far more insight into age-related attention-span change than would either hypothesis alone. In this way, theories add tremendous depth to psychologists' understanding of the facts of human development and provide information that can be used to influence development. Let's say, for example, that a child is diagnosed with a condition that can affect the brain, such as epilepsy. If we know that brain development and attention span are related, we can use tests of attention span to make judgments about how much her medical condition may have already influenced her brain. At the same time, because we know that experience affects memory as well, we may be able to provide her with training that will help her overcome attention-span problems that are likely to arise in the future.

STUDYING AGE-RELATED CHANGES

When researchers set out to study age-related change, they have basically three choices: (1) study different groups of people of different ages, using what is called a **cross-sectional design;** (2) study the *same* people over a period of time, using a **longitudinal design;** or (3) combine cross-sectional and longitudinal designs in some fashion in a **sequential design.**

Cross-Sectional Designs

To study attention cross-sectionally, we might select groups of participants at each of several ages, such as groups of 2-, 5-, 8-, and 11-year-olds. If we find that each group demonstrates a longer average attention span than all the groups that are younger, we may be tempted to conclude that attention span does increase with age, but we cannot say this conclusively with cross-sectional data, because these children differ not only in age, but in *cohort*. (A cohort is a group of individuals who share the same historical experiences at the same period in their lives.) The differences in attention might reflect educational differences and not actually be linked to age or development. Furthermore, cross-sectional studies cannot tell us anything about sequences of change over age or about the consistency of individual behavior over time, because each child is tested only once. Still, cross-sectional research is very useful because it is relatively quick to do and can give indications of possible age differences or age changes.

Longitudinal Designs

Longitudinal designs seem to solve the problems that arise with cross-sectional designs, because they follow the same individuals over a period of time. For example, to examine our attention-span hypothesis, we could test a particular group of children first at age 2, then at age 5, next at age 8, and finally at age 11. Such studies look at sequences of change and at individual consistency or inconsistency over time. And because these studies compare the same people at different ages, they get around the obvious cohort problem. However, longitudinal designs have several major difficulties. One problem is that longitudinal designs typically involve giving each participant the same tests over and over again. Over time, people learn how to

CRITICAL THINKING 9

In contrast to what happened during the Great Depression, the American economy grew at an unprecedented rate during most of the 1980s and 1990s. Do you think these "boom" times influenced the development of individuals in your cohort to the same extent that the Great Depression influenced people who were children and teenagers during the 1920s and 1930s? Do you think your cohort's ideas and expectations about financial success are different from those of earlier cohorts because of the era in which you and your peers grew up?

cross-sectional design A form of research study in which samples of participants from several different age groups are studied at the same time.

longitudinal design A form of research study in which the same participants are observed or assessed repeatedly over a period of months or years.

sequential design A form of research study that combines cross-sectional and longitudinal designs in some way.

Only by studying the same children over time (that is, longitudinally), such as this girl at three ages, can developmentalists identify consistencies (or changes) in behavior across age.

take the tests. Such practice effects may distort the measurement of any underlying developmental changes.

Another significant problem with longitudinal studies is that not everyone sticks with the program. Some participants drop out, others die or move away. As a general rule, the healthiest and best-educated participants are most likely to stick it out, and that fact biases the results, particularly if the study continues into adulthood.

Longitudinal studies also don't really get around the cohort problem. For example, one famous study, the Oakland Growth Study, followed individuals born between 1918 and 1928 into old age. Consequently, the study's participants experienced certain major historical events, such as the Great Depression and World War II, that probably influenced their development. So, we don't know whether the ways in which they changed across these years, when they were children and teenagers, were caused by developmental processes or by the unique historical period in which they were growing up.

Sequential Designs   One way to avoid the shortcomings of both cross-sectional and longitudinal designs is to use a sequential design. To study our attention-span question using a sequential design, we would begin with at least two age groups. One group might include 2- to 5-year-olds, and the other might have 5- to 8-year-olds. We would then test each group over a number of years, as illustrated in Figure 1.5. Each testing point beyond the initial one provides two types of comparisons. Age-group comparisons provide the same kind of information as a cross-sectional study would. Comparisons of the scores or behaviors of participants in each group to their own scores or behaviors at an earlier testing point provide longitudinal evidence at the same time.

Sequential designs also allow for comparisons of cohorts. Notice in Figure 1.5, for example, that those in Group A are 5 to 8 years old at Testing Point 1, and those in Group B are 5 to 8 years old at Testing Point 2. Likewise, Group A members are 8 to 11 at Point 2, and their counterparts in Group B are this age at Point 3. If same-age comparisons of the two groups reveal that their average attention spans are different, the researchers have evidence that, for some reason, the two cohorts differ. Conversely, if the groups perform similarly, the investigators can conclude that their respective performances represent developmental characteristics rather than cohort effects. Moreover, if

		Age at testing point 1	Age at testing point 2	Age at testing point 3
Group	A	5 to 8	8 to 11	11 to 14
	B	2 to 5	5 to 8	8 to 11

FIGURE 1.5

A hypothetical sequential study of attention span across ages 2 to 14.

both groups demonstrate similar age-related patterns of change over time, the researchers can conclude that the developmental pattern is not specific to any particular cohort. Finding the same developmental pattern in two cohorts provides psychologists with stronger evidence than either cross-sectional or longitudinal data alone.

IDENTIFYING RELATIONSHIPS BETWEEN VARIABLES

After deciding how to treat age, a researcher must decide how to go about finding relationships between *variables*. Variables are characteristics that vary from person to person, such as physical size, intelligence, and personality. When two or more variables vary together, we say there is a relationship between them. The hypothesis that attention span increases with age involves two variables—attention span and age—and suggests a relationship between them. There are several ways of identifying such relationships.

Case Studies and Naturalistic Observation

Case studies are in-depth examinations of single individuals. To examine changes in attention span, a researcher could use a case study comparing an individual's scores on tests of attention at various ages in childhood. Such a study might tell a lot about the stability or instability of attention in the individual studied, but the researcher wouldn't know if the findings applied to others.

Still, case studies are extremely useful in making decisions about individuals. For example, to find out if a child is mentally retarded, a psychologist can do an extensive case study involving tests, interviews of the child's parents, behavioral observations, and so on. Case studies are also frequently the basis of important hypotheses about unusual developmental events such as head injuries and strokes.

When psychologists use **naturalistic observation**, they observe people in their normal environments. For instance, to find out more about attention span in children of different ages, a researcher could observe them in their homes or day-care centers. Such studies provide developmentalists with information about psychological processes in everyday contexts.

The weakness of this method, however, is *observer bias*. For example, if a researcher observing 2-year-olds is convinced that most of them have very short attention spans, he is likely to ignore any behavior that goes against this view. Because of observer bias, naturalistic observation studies often use "blind" observers who don't know what the research is about. In most cases, such studies employ two or more observers for the sake of accuracy. This way, the observations of each observer can be checked against those of the other.

Like case studies, the results of naturalistic observation studies have limited generalizability. In addition, naturalistic observation studies are very time-consuming. They must be repeated in a variety of settings before researchers can be sure people's behavior reflects development and not the influences of a specific environment.

Correlations

A **correlation** is a number ranging from −1.00 to +1.00 that describes the strength of a relationship between two variables. A zero correlation indicates that there is no relationship between those variables. A positive correlation means that high scores on one variable are usually accompanied by high scores on the other. The closer a positive correlation is to +1.00, the stronger the relationship between the variables. Two variables that move in opposite directions result in a negative correlation, and the nearer the correlation is to −1.00, the more strongly the two are inversely related.

To understand positive and negative correlations, think about the relationship between temperature and the use of air conditioners and heaters. Temperature and air conditioner use are positively correlated. As the temperature climbs, so does the number of air conditioners in use. Conversely, temperature and heater use are negatively correlated. As the temperature decreases, the number of heaters in use goes up.

case studies In-depth studies of individuals.

naturalistic observation A research method in which participants are observed in their normal environments.

correlation A statistic used to describe the strength of a relationship between two variables. It can range from −1.00 to +1.00. The closer it is to +1.00 or −1.00, the stronger the relationship being described.

If we want to test the hypothesis that greater attention span is related to increases in age, we can use a correlation. All we would need to do would be to administer attention-span tests to children of varying ages and to calculate the correlation between test scores and ages. If there was a positive correlation between the length of children's attention spans and age—if older children attended for longer periods of time—then we could say that our hypothesis had been supported. Conversely, if there was a negative correlation—if older children paid attention for shorter periods of time than younger children—then we would have to conclude that our hypothesis had not been supported.

Useful as they are, though, correlations have a major limitation: They do not reveal *causal* relationships. For example, even a high positive correlation between attention span and age would only tell us that attention span and age are connected in some way. It wouldn't tell us what caused the connection. It might be that older children could understand the test instructions more easily. In order to identify causes, psychologists have to carry out experiments.

Experiments   An **experiment** is a research method that tests a causal hypothesis. Suppose, for example, that we think age differences in attention span are caused by younger children's failure to use attention-maintaining strategies, such as ignoring distractions. We could test this hypothesis by providing attention training to one group of children and no training to another group. If the trained children got higher scores on attention tests than they did before training, and the no-training group showed no change, we could claim that our hypothesis had been supported.

A key feature of an experiment is that participants are assigned *randomly* to participate in one of several groups. In other words, chance determines the group in which the researcher places each participant. When participants are randomly assigned to groups, the groups have equal averages and equal amounts of variation with respect to variables such as intelligence, personality traits, height, weight, health status, and so on. Consequently, none of these variables can affect the outcome of the experiment.

Participants in the **experimental group** receive the treatment the experimenter thinks will produce a particular effect, while those in the **control group** receive either no special treatment or a neutral treatment. The presumed causal element in the experiment is called the **independent variable**, and the behavior on which the independent variable is expected to show its effect is called a **dependent variable** (or the *outcome variable*).

Applying these terms to the attention-training experiment may help you better understand them. The group that receives the attention training is the experimental group, while those who receive no instruction form the control group. Attention training is the variable that we, the experimenters, think will cause differences in attention span, so it is the independent variable. Performance on attention tests is the variable we are using to measure the effect of the attention training. Therefore, performance on attention tests is the dependent variable.

Experiments are essential for understanding many aspects of development. But two special problems in studying child development limit the use of experiments. First, many of the questions developmentalists want to answer have to do with the effects of unpleasant or stressful experiences—for example, abuse or prenatal exposure to alcohol or tobacco. For obvious ethical reasons, researchers cannot manipulate these variables. For example, they cannot ask one set of pregnant women to have two alcoholic drinks a day and others to have none. To study the effects of such experiences, developmentalists must rely on nonexperimental methods, like correlations.

Second, the independent variable developmentalists are often most interested in is age itself, and they cannot assign participants randomly to age groups. Researchers can compare the attention spans of 4-year-olds and 6-year-olds, but the children differ in a host of ways other than their ages. Older children have had more and different experiences. Thus, unlike psychologists studying other aspects of behavior, developmental psychologists *cannot* systematically manipulate many of the variables they are most interested in.

experiment A research method for testing a causal hypothesis, in which participants are assigned randomly to experimental and control groups and the experimental group is then provided with a particular experience that is expected to alter behavior in some fashion.

experimental group A group of participants in an experiment who receive a particular treatment intended to produce some specific effect.

control group A group of participants in an experiment who receive either no special treatment or some neutral treatment.

independent variable A condition or event that an experimenter varies in some systematic way in order to observe the impact of that variation on participants' behavior.

dependent variable The variable in an experiment that is expected to show the impact of manipulations of the independent variable; also called the *outcome variable*.

To get around this problem, developmentalists can use any of a number of strategies, sometimes called *quasi-experiments*, in which they compare groups without assigning the participants randomly. Cross-sectional comparisons are a form of quasi-experiment. So are studies in which researchers select naturally occurring groups that differ in some dimension of interest, such as children whose parents choose to place them in day-care programs compared with children whose parents keep them at home. Such comparisons have built-in problems, because groups that differ in one way are likely to be different in other ways as well. Families who place their children in day care are also likely to be poorer, more likely to have only a single parent, and may have different values or religious backgrounds than those who rear their children at home. If researchers find that the two groups of children differ in some fashion, is it because they have spent their daytime hours in different places or because of these other differences in their families? Such comparisons can be made a bit cleaner if the comparison groups are initially selected so that they are matched on those variables that researchers think might matter, such as income, marital status, or religion. But a quasi-experiment, by its very nature, will always yield more ambiguous results than will a fully controlled experiment. However, as noted in *The Real World* discussion, media reports of research often do not provide consumers with sufficient information about research methods. Such information is vital to determining the validity of a research finding. Likewise, it can help parents and others who work with children determine the relevance of the research to their own lives.

CROSS-CULTURAL (OR CROSS-CONTEXT) RESEARCH

Cross-cultural research, or research comparing cultures or contexts, is becoming increasingly common in developmental psychology. Cross-cultural research is important to developmentalists for two reasons. First, developmentalists want to identify universal changes—that is, predictable events or processes that occur in the lives of individuals in all cultures. Developmentalists don't want to make a general statement about development—such as "Attention span increases with age"—if the phenomenon in question happens only in Western, industrialized cultures. Without cross-cultural research, it is impossible to know whether studies involving North Americans and Europeans apply to people in other parts of the world.

Second, one of the goals of developmental psychology is to produce findings that can be used to improve people's lives. Cross-cultural research is critical to this goal as well. For example, developmentalists know that children in cultures that emphasize the community more than the individual are more cooperative than children in cultures that are more individualistic. However, to use this information to help all children learn to cooperate, developmentalists need to know exactly how adults in collectivist cultures teach their children to be cooperative. Cross-cultural research helps developmentalists identify specific variables that explain cultural differences.

Cross-Cultural Methods   All of the methods you have learned about are used in cross-cultural research. Cross-cultural researchers borrow methods from other disciplines as well. One such strategy, borrowed from the field of anthropology, is to compile an *ethnography*—a detailed description of a single culture or context based on extensive observation. Often the observer lives within the culture for a period of time, perhaps as long as several years. Each ethnography is intended to stand alone, although it is sometimes possible to compare several different studies to see whether similar developmental patterns exist in varying contexts.

Alternatively, investigators may attempt to compare two or more cultures directly, by testing children or adults in each of several cultures with the same or comparable measures. Sometimes this involves comparisons across different countries. Sometimes the comparisons are between subcultures within the same country, as in the increasingly common research that compares children or adults from different ethnic groups

In traditional Kenyan culture, still seen in some rural areas, babies are carried in slings all day and allowed to nurse on demand at night. This cultural pattern, quite different from that in most Western societies, seems to have an effect on the baby's sleep/wake cycle.

cross-cultural research Any study that involves comparisons of different cultures or contexts.

The Real World

Thinking Critically about Research

Two-year-old Jake jumped for joy when his mother, Christina, responded positively to his request to watch his favorite DVD, one that featured the *Sesame Street* character Elmo. For her part, Christina was thankful for the few minutes of peace she would have as Jake sat enthralled in front of the television. "Besides," she told herself, "this DVD will help him learn the alphabet." Nevertheless, a nagging voice in Christina's head reminded her of a news report she had heard the previous day. The report said that researchers had learned that too much television in the early years could cause children to develop some kind of learning problem, though she couldn't recall exactly what that problem was. Like most parents, Christina wanted whatever was best for her child, but she was concerned about the meaning of the research report. "How much television is 'too much'?" she thought. The report had said that some experts recommended that children of Jake's age watch no television at all. "But isn't that a bit extreme?" Christina wondered.

In today's information age, parents are bombarded with this kind of information nearly every day. Thinking about such reports can help you understand why it is important to learn about research methods even if you have no intention of ever doing research yourself. For purposes of illustration, let's take a closer look at a media report like the one that caused Christina to worry about how much time her son spent watching television.

In 2004, the news media carried a number of reports warning parents of young children that watching too much television in the early years might lead to attention deficit hyperactivity disorder (ADHD) later in childhood (e.g., Clayton, 2004). These warnings were based, reporters said, on a scientific study that was published in the prestigious journal *Pediatrics*. How can a person who isn't an expert on the subject in question evaluate claims like these?

The thinking strategies used by psychologists and other scientists can help us sift through such information. *Critical thinking*, the foundation of the scientific method, is the process of objectively evaluating claims, propositions, and conclusions to determine whether they follow logically from the evidence presented. When we engage in critical thinking, we exhibit these characteristics:

- *Independent thinking.* When thinking critically, we do not automatically accept and believe what we read or hear.
- *Suspension of judgment.* Critical thinking requires gathering relevant and up-to-date information on all sides of an issue before taking a position.
- *Willingness to modify or abandon prior judgments.* Critical thinking involves evaluating new evidence, even when it contradicts pre-existing beliefs.

Applying the first of these three characteristics to the television-ADHD study involves recognizing that the validity of any study isn't determined by the authority of its source. In other words, prestigious journals—or psychology

or communities in the United States, such as African Americans, Hispanic Americans, Asian Americans, and European Americans.

An Example of a Cross-Cultural Comparison Study
Cross-cultural researchers Ann Fernald and Hiromi Morikawa took video and audio recordings of 30 Japanese and 30 American mothers with their infants, playing with the infants' own toys in the families' own homes (Fernald & Morikawa, 1993). Ten of the infants in each cultural group were 6 months old, ten were 12 months old, and ten were 19 months old. So, in each culture, Fernald and Morikawa established a cross-sectional study. There were striking similarities in the ways these two groups of mothers spoke to their infants (e.g., Fernald et al., 1989). Both groups simplified their speech, repeated themselves frequently, used sounds to attract the child's attention, and spoke in a higher-pitched voice than usual. Yet the mothers from these two cultural groups differed in the kinds of things they said. One such difference, illustrated in Figure 1.6, was in the American mothers' greater tendency to name toys or parts of toys for their infants. One consequence of this maternal difference appeared to be that the American children knew more words than their Japanese counterparts when they were tested at age 19 months.

textbooks, for that matter—shouldn't be regarded as sources of fixed, immutable truths. In fact, learning to question accepted "truths" is important to the scientific method itself.

The second and third characteristics of critical thinking, suspension of judgment and willingness to change, may require changing some old habits. If you're like most people, you respond to media reports about research on the basis of your own personal experiences, a type of evidence scientists call *anecdotal evidence*. For instance, in response to the media report about television-watching and ADHD, a person might say "I agree with that study because my cousin has such severe ADHD that he had to drop out of high school, and he was always glued to the television when he was little." Another might counter with "I don't agree with that study because I watched a lot of television when I was a kid, and I don't have ADHD."

Suspension of judgment requires that you postpone either accepting or rejecting the study's findings until you have accumulated more evidence. This might involve determining what, if any, findings have been reported by other researchers regarding a possible link between television-watching and ADHD. Finding out about other relevant studies can help to form a comprehensive picture of what the entire body of research says about the issue. Ultimately, when enough evidence has been gathered, a critical thinker must be willing to abandon preconceived notions and prior beliefs that conflict with it.

The quality of the evidence is just as important as the quantity, however. Thus, a critical thinker would evaluate the findings of the television-ADHD study in terms of the methods used to obtain them. Did the researchers randomly assign young children to experimental and control groups who watched different amounts of television and then assess whether experimental and control children differed in ADHD symptoms several years later? If so, then the study was an experiment and media claims that television-watching in early childhood leads to ADHD might be justified. If, however, the researchers simply measured television-watching in early childhood and then correlated this variable with a measure of ADHD later on, then claims of a causal relationship between the two variables wouldn't be justified. Instead, the appropriate response would be to look for underlying variables, such as parental involvement, that might explain the connection. [The research cited in these reports was correlational in nature, so the strong causal claims implied by many media accounts of the study (Christakis, Zimmerman, Giuseppe, & McCarty, 2004) were inappropriate.]

Does a critique of this kind suggest that parents like Christina need not be concerned about how much time their toddlers spend in front of the television? Clearly not. Instead, it confirms a point made at the beginning of the chapter. Development is a complex process involving interactions among many variables. Thus, scientific studies can help parents better understand development, but they must be weighed along with other sources of information, including parents' own priorities and values, in the formulation of parenting decisions.

Questions for Reflection

1. How would you explain the ideas in this discussion to a concerned parent who was not knowledgeable about the principles of critical thinking or about research methods?
2. What variables other than parental involvement might contribute to a relationship between television-watching and ADHD?

RESEARCH ETHICS

Research ethics are the guidelines researchers follow to protect the rights of animals and humans who participate in studies. Ethical guidelines are published by professional organizations such as the American Psychological Association, the American Educational Research Association, and the Society for Research in Child Development. Universities, private foundations, and government agencies have review committees that make sure that all research these organizations sponsor is ethical. Guidelines for animal research include the requirement that animals be protected from unnecessary pain and suffering. Further, researchers must demonstrate that the potential benefits of their studies to either human or animal populations are greater than any potential harm to animal subjects.

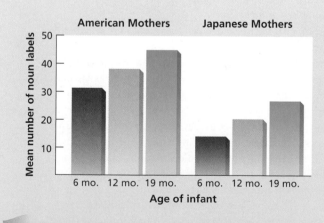

FIGURE 1.6

Cultural differences were evident in Fernald and Morikawa's (1993) study of how mothers speak to their infants.

Ethical standards for research involving human participants are based on the following major themes:

Protection from Harm. It is unethical to do research that may cause permanent physical or psychological harm to participants. Moreover, if there is a possibility of temporary harm, researchers must provide participants with some way of repairing the damage. For example, if the study will remind participants of unpleasant experiences, like rape, researchers must provide them with counseling.

Informed Consent. Researchers must inform participants of any possible harm and require them to sign a consent form stating that they are aware of the risks involved in participating. In order for children to participate in studies, their parents must give permission after the researcher has informed them of possible risks. If children are older than 7, they must also give consent themselves. If the research takes place in a school or day-care center, an administrator representing the institution must also consent. In addition, human participants, whether children or adults, have the right to discontinue participation in a study at any time. Researchers are obligated to explain this right to children in language they can understand.

Confidentiality. Participants have the right to confidentiality. Researchers must keep the identities of participants confidential and must report data in such a way that no particular piece of information can be associated with any specific participant. The exception to confidentiality is when children reveal to researchers that they are being abused or have been abused in any way by an adult. In most states, all citizens are required to report suspected cases of child abuse.

Knowledge of Results. Participants, their parents (if they are children), and administrators of institutions in which research takes place have a right to a written summary of a study's results.

Protection from Deception. If deception has been a necessary part of a study, participants have the right to be informed about the deception as soon as the study is over.

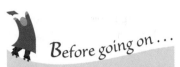

Before going on . . .

- Discuss the pros and cons of cross-sectional, longitudinal, and sequential research designs.
- How do developmentalists use case studies, naturalistic observation, correlations, and experiments to identify relationships between variables?
- Why is cross-cultural research important?
- List the ethical principles researchers follow to protect the rights of participants.
- How does learning about research methods help you be a more critical thinker?

Summary

Perspectives on Development

- The question of the degree to which development is influenced by nature and by nurture has been central to the study of development for thousands of years. Philosophers and early psychologists thought of the nature-nurture issue as an either-or question.
- Psychologists have also debated the question of whether development is continuous or discontinuous. Those who favor continuity emphasize the quantitative aspects of development, while those who view development as discontinuous often propose stage models to explain developmental change.
- One group of influences on development includes internal factors such as maturation, critical and sensitive periods, inborn biases, individual genetic variations, and internal models of experience. Theoretical models try to explain how internal and external factors interact.
- The ecological perspective attempts to explain how external factors such as family and culture influence development.
- Developmental psychologists often discuss development in terms of vulnerability and resilience. The idea is that certain risk factors, such as poverty, predispose children to develop in undesirable ways. However, protective factors, such

as high IQ, prevent some children from being negatively influenced by risk factors.

Theories of Development

- Psychoanalytic theories suggest that internal drives strongly influence development. Both Freud and Erikson proposed stages to explain the process of personality development as people age.
- Cognitive-developmental theories propose that basic cognitive processes influence development in all other areas. Piaget's theory has been especially influential, but interest in Vygotsky's ideas has grown in recent years. Information-processing theory also explains development in terms of cognitive processes.
- Learning theories emphasize the influence of the environment on children's behavior. Classical and operant conditioning principles explain learning in terms of links between stimuli and responses. Bandura's social cognitive theory gives more weight to children's cognitive processing of learning experiences and attempts to explain how modeling influences development.
- Psychologists don't think of theories as "true" or "false." Instead, they compare theories on the bases of assumptions and usefulness.

Finding the Answers: Research Designs and Methods

- The goals of developmental psychology are to describe, to explain, to predict, and to influence age-related change. Developmental psychologists use various methods to meet these goals.
- In cross-sectional studies, separate age groups are each tested once. In longitudinal designs, the same individuals are tested repeatedly over time. Sequential designs combine cross-sectional with longitudinal comparisons.
- Case studies and naturalistic observation provide a lot of important information, but it usually is not generalizable.

- Correlational studies measure relations between variables. They can be done quickly and yield information that is more generalizable than information from case studies or naturalistic observation. To test causal hypotheses, it is necessary to use experimental designs in which participants are assigned randomly to experimental or control groups.
- Cross-cultural (cross-context) research helps developmentalists identify universal patterns and cultural variables that affect development.
- Ethical principles that guide psychological research include protection from harm, informed consent, confidentiality, knowledge of results, and protection from deception.

Key Terms

behavior genetics (p. 8)
behaviorism (p. 4)
case studies (p. 25)
classical conditioning (p. 17)
cognitive-developmental theories (p. 15)
control group (p. 26)
correlation (p. 25)
critical period (p. 6)
cross-cultural research (p. 27)
cross-sectional design (p. 23)
dependent variable (p. 26)
developmental science (p. 3)
eclecticism (p. 22)
ego (p. 14)

experiment (p. 26)
experimental group (p. 26)
id (p. 14)
independent variable (p. 26)
information-processing theories (p. 16)
internal models of experience (p. 8)
learning theories (p. 17)
libido (p. 14)
longitudinal design (p. 23)
maturation (p. 6)
naturalistic observation (p. 25)
negative reinforcement (p. 18)
norms (p. 4)
operant conditioning (p. 18)

positive reinforcement (p. 18)
psychoanalytic theories (p. 13)
psychosexual stages (p. 14)
psychosocial stages (p. 15)
punishment (p. 19)
scaffolding (p. 16)
sensitive period (p. 6)
sequential design (p. 23)
superego (p. 14)
zone of proximal development (p. 16)

See for Yourself

Culture and Informal Theories of Development

Researchers have found that the development of psychological theories is a basic component of human thinking. In other words, we observe human behavior and develop ideas that we think explain our observations. These ideas are often strongly influenced by culture. You can find out about the relationship between culture and informal theories of development by presenting people from different backgrounds with the statement attributed to John Watson at the beginning of the chapter. Next, ask them to explain why they agree or disagree with the statement. Write down or record their responses and analyze them to see how much emphasis each person places on internal (e.g., intelligence) and external (e.g., education) variables. One way of measuring this would be to give each person an "internal" score and an "external" score by assigning 1 point for each internal and each external variable mentioned. Average the scores within each cultural group represented by the people included in your study, and then compare the results across cultures.

Research Design

Almost all the important findings in developmental psychology have resulted from studies employing all of the methods you have learned about in this chapter. For instance, Piaget's theory was built on naturalistic observation, case studies, correlational studies, and experiments. Moreover, many cross-cultural studies have replicated his original results. Think of a question about development that you find intriguing or personally meaningful. How would you look for an answer to that question with each of the methods described in this chapter?

Prenatal Development

C H A P T E R

When Tracy Ward entered an Amarillo, Texas, hospital in November 2003 to give birth to her sixth child, she did not expect to find herself in jail as a result.

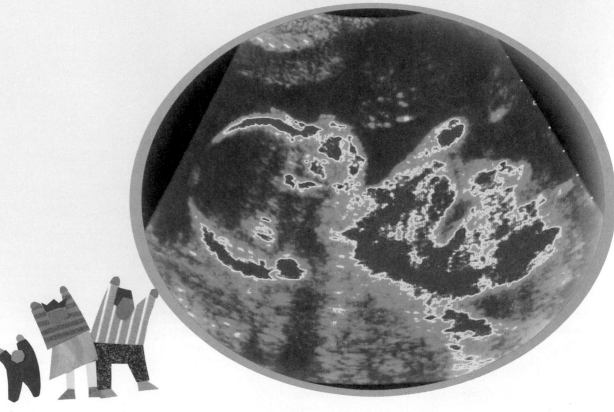

While she was in labor, Ward admitted to caregivers that she was a crack cocaine addict and had frequently used the drug during her pregnancy. As soon as Ward's son was born, he was tested for the drug and was found to have traces of it in his system. As a result, Ward was charged with delivering a controlled substance to a minor, and her children were placed in the custody of relatives. In August 2004, Ward pled guilty and was sentenced to five years' probation. However, her prosecution continues to be controversial and is likely to produce an important appellate court ruling in the near future.

Ward's case and others like it are at the heart of a public policy debate regarding the most effective way to discourage pregnant women from using substances that may endanger the fetuses they carry. In the United States, some have drawn a parallel between drug use during pregnancy and physical abuse of an infant after birth and have suggested that pregnant drug users be criminally prosecuted. Prosecution advocates argue that injecting a newborn with a drug is a crime. Even if no damage is done to the child, "delivering controlled substances to a minor" (the terminology used in most jurisdictions) is itself a crime.

One problem with this approach is that it isn't clear whether a fetus can be considered legally equivalent to a child. U.S. Supreme Court rulings have introduced the issue of fetal viability into abortion law. These rulings allow states to outlaw abortions of viable fetuses and suggest using 24 weeks as the age of viability, based on current research on prenatal development. Thus, it would seem that states could also use existing laws against giving drugs to children and child abuse to prosecute women after the 24th week of prenatal development. In addition, doctors often seek judicial intervention in cases where pregnant women make medical decisions that are potentially damaging to their fetuses (National Abortion and Reproductive Rights Action League [NARAL], 1997). In most such cases, judges make rulings on the basis of the best interest of the fetus.

However, it isn't always easy to find out whether a fetus or newborn has been exposed to drugs. The difficulty is that, while many drugs pass through the placenta, they don't always do so in sufficient amounts to be identifiable in a newborn's blood or urine. In addition, some drugs, like marijuana, remain in the system for a long time, making it possible to test for them several days after birth. But others, like cocaine and alcohol, are excreted from the newborn's body within hours of birth. Thus, drug testing must be carried out almost immediately after birth to determine whether the newborn has been prenatally exposed to potentially harmful drugs (Centers for Disease Control [CDC], 1996b). An additional difficulty is that drug testing at birth usually reveals little or nothing about drug exposure earlier in the pregnancy. Consequently, a pregnant woman could "deliver" a drug to her viable fetus during, for example, the 25th week of pregnancy, but no concrete evidence of this behavior would be available at the time of birth.

Rather than prosecution of pregnant drug users, most public health officials recommend a strategy that combines universal access to early prenatal care, education, and drug treatment (CDC, 1996b). Access to early prenatal care is critical because it provides the context in which education of individual pregnant women can take place. In addition, health care providers can provide pregnant drug users with treatment information. To complete the picture, most public health officials stress the importance of developing treatment programs designed especially for pregnant women (NARAL, 1997).

Near the end of this chapter, you will read about the effects of cocaine and other substances on the developing fetus. The fact that many drug-exposed fetuses are born healthy and develop normally thereafter is testimony to the resilience of the prenatal developmental processes you will learn about in this chapter. The story begins with conception.

 # Conception and Genetics

The first step in the development of a human being is that moment of *conception*, when two single cells—one from a male and the other from a female—join together to form a new cell called a **zygote**. This event sets in motion powerful genetic forces that will influence the individual over the entire lifespan.

THE PROCESS OF CONCEPTION

Ordinarily, a woman produces one **ovum** (egg cell) per month from one of her two ovaries. The ovum is released from an ovary roughly midway between two menstrual periods. If it is not fertilized, the ovum travels from the ovary down the **fallopian tube** toward the **uterus**, where it gradually disintegrates and is expelled as part of the next menstrual flow. If a couple has intercourse during the crucial few days when the ovum is in the fallopian tube, one of the millions of **sperm** ejaculated as part of each male orgasm may travel the full distance through the woman's vagina, cervix, and uterus into the fallopian tube and penetrate the ovum. A child is conceived. The zygote then continues on its journey down the fallopian tube and eventually implants itself in the wall of the uterus. (See the *Research Report.*)

The Basic Genetics of Conception   Except in individuals with particular types of genetic abnormality, the nucleus of each cell in the human body contains a set of 46 **chromosomes**, arranged in 23 pairs. These chromosomes include all the genetic information for that individual, governing not only individual characteristics like hair color, height, body shape, temperament, and aspects of intelligence, but also all those characteristics shared by all members of our species, such as patterns of physical development and inborn biases of various kinds.

The only cells that do not contain 46 chromosomes are the sperm and the ovum, collectively called **gametes**, or *germ cells*. In the early stages of development, gametes divide as all other cells do (a process called *mitosis*), with each set of 23 chromosome pairs duplicating itself. In the final step of gamete division, however, called *meiosis*, each new cell receives only one chromosome from each original pair. Thus, each ga-

zygote The single cell formed from separate sperm and egg cells at conception.

ovum The cell released monthly from a woman's ovaries, which, if fertilized, forms the basis for the developing organism.

fallopian tube The tube between the ovary and the uterus down which the ovum travels to the uterus and in which conception usually occurs.

uterus The female organ in which the embryo/fetus develops (popularly referred to as the *womb*).

sperm The cells produced in a man's testes that may fertilize an ovum following intercourse.

chromosomes The structures, arrayed in 23 pairs, within each cell in the body that contain genetic information. Each chromosome is made up of many segments, called genes.

gametes Sperm and ova. These cells, unlike all other cells of the body, contain only 23 chromosomes rather than 23 pairs.

mete has only 23 chromosomes instead of 23 pairs. When a child is conceived, the 23 chromosomes in the ovum and the 23 in the sperm combine to form the 23 pairs that will be part of each cell in the newly developing body.

The chromosomes are composed of long strings of molecules of a chemical called **deoxyribonucleic acid (DNA)**. In an insight for which they won the Nobel Prize in 1953, James Watson and Francis Crick deduced that DNA is in the shape of a double helix, somewhat like a twisted ladder. The remarkable feature of this ladder is that the rungs are constructed so that the entire helix can "unzip"; then each half can guide the duplication of the missing part, thus allowing multiplication of cells so that each new cell contains the full set of genetic information.

The string of DNA that makes up each chromosome can be subdivided further into segments called **genes**, each of which controls or influences a particular feature of an organism or a portion of some developmental pattern. A gene controlling or influencing some specific characteristic, such as your blood type or your hair color, always appears in the same place (the *locus*; plural is *loci*) on the same chromosome in every individual of the same species. For example, the locus of the gene that determines whether you have type A, B, or O blood is on chromosome 9, and similar genes for blood type are found on chromosome 9 in every other human being. In February, 2001, scientists working on a remarkable group of studies known as the *Human Genome Project (HGP)* announced that they had identified the locus of every human gene (U.S. Department of Energy, 2001) (see Figure 2.1).

There are actually two types of chromosomes. In 22 of the chromosome pairs, called *autosomes*, the members of the pair look alike and contain exactly matching genetic loci. The 23rd pair, however, operates differently. The chromosomes of this pair, which determine the child's sex and are therefore called the *sex chromosomes*, come in two varieties, referred to as the X and the Y chromosomes.

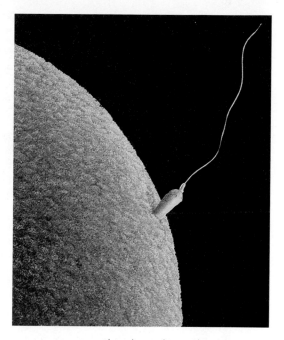

This photo shows the moment of conception, when a single sperm has pierced the coating around the ovum.

deoxyribonucleic acid (DNA) The chemical of which chromosomes are composed.

gene A uniquely coded segment of DNA in a chromosome that affects one or more specific body processes or developments.

Creutzfeldt-Jakob disease	Diabetes insipidus, neurohypophyseal
Gerstmann-Straussler disease	SRY (sex-determining region Y)
Insomnia, fatal familial	McKusick-Kaufman syndrome
Hallervorden-Spatz syndrome	Cerebral amyloid angiopathy
Alagille syndrome	Thrombophilia
Corneal dystrophy	Myocardial infarction, susceptibility to
Inhibitor of DNA binding, dominant negative	Huntington-like neurodegenerative disorder
Facial anomalies syndrome	Anemia, congenital dyserythropoietic
Gigantism	Acromesomelic dysplasia, Hunter-Thompson type
Retinoblastoma	Brachydactyly, type C
Rous sarcoma	Chondrodysplasia, Grebe type
Colon cancer	Myeloid tumor suppressor
Galactosialidosis	Breast cancer
Severe combined immunodeficiency	Maturity onset diabetes of the young, type 1
Hemolytic anemia	Diabetes mellitus, noninsulin-dependent
Obesity/hyperinsulinism	Graves disease, susceptibility to
Pseudohypoparathyroidism, type 1a	Epilepsy, nocturnal frontal lobe and benign neonatal, type 1
McCune-Albright polyostotic fibrous dysplasia	Epiphyseal dysplasia, multiple
Somatotrophinoma	Electro-encephalographic variant pattern
Pituitary ACTH secreting adenoma	Pseudohypoparathyroidism, type 1b
Shah-Waardenburg syndrome	

FIGURE 2.1

This figure represents the genetic "map" of human chromosome #20; the map was produced by scientists associated with the Human Genome Project. Researchers have produced equally specific maps for all 23 human chromosomes. These maps include genes for normal traits (e.g., eye color) as well as for genetic disorders.

Assisted Reproductive Technology

RESEARCH REPORT

In some cases, couples must turn to health professionals for help in conceiving a child. Physicians define *infertility* as the failure to conceive after 12 consecutive months of unprotected intercourse (Mitchell, 2002). To help them conceive and deliver healthy babies, many infertile couples turn to physicians who are specialists in the use of *assisted reproductive techniques (ART)*. The use of *fertility drugs* to stimulate the ovaries to produce eggs is the most common approach to treating infertility. Increasing the number of eggs a woman produces increases the chances of a natural conception. Moreover, fertility drugs play an important role in other assisted reproductive techniques. They are often used along with *artificial insemination*, the process of injecting sperm into a woman's uterus at times when eggs are known to be present.

Fertility drugs are also employed in a more complex assisted reproductive technique known as *in vitro fertilization* (*IVF; in vitro* is Latin for *glass*), popularly known as the "test-tube baby" method. The first step in IVF involves using fertility drugs to stimulate the woman's ovaries to produce

An eight-celled embryo is ideal for an IVF transfer. Pictured here is an embryo on the day of transfer into a woman's uterus.

multiple eggs. The eggs are then extracted from the ovaries and combined with sperm in a laboratory dish. If conception takes place, one or more embryos—ideally at the six-to-eight-cell stage of development—are transferred to the woman's uterus in the hope that a normal pregnancy will develop. The eggs used in IVF can come from the woman who will carry the child or from a donor. Likewise, the sperm can be from the woman's partner or a donor. Extra embryos that result from an IVF cycle but are not used in that particular cycle can be frozen, or *cryopreserved*. These frozen embryos can be transferred at a later date, through a process known as *frozen embryo transfer (FET)*.

However, whether zygotes are cryopreserved or not, IVF is not a highly successful procedure. Less than one-third of such procedures result in a live birth (Wright, Schieve, Reynolds, & Jeng, 2005). The older a woman is, the lower the probability that she will be able to have a successful IVF pregnancy. Roughly 35% of 20- to 29-year-old IVF patients achieve a live birth, but only 13% or so of IVF procedures involving women over age 40 are successful (Schieve et al., 1999). It's important to note here, though, that these are aggregate statistics; each reproductive clinic keeps track of its own success rate, and these can vary considerably from one facility to another (Society for Assisted Reproductive Technology, 2004). Still, in even the most successful clinics, failure rates are high. Considering that most couples resort to IVF after months or years of frustration, it isn't surprising that

A normal human female has two X chromosomes in this 23rd pair (an XX pattern), while a normal human male has one X and one Y chromosome (an XY pattern). The X chromosome is considerably larger than the Y chromosome and contains many genetic loci not found on the Y.

Note that the sex of the child is determined by the sex chromosome it receives from the sperm. Because a woman has only X chromosomes, every ovum carries an X. But because a man has both X and Y chromosomes, when the father's gametes divide, half the sperm will carry an X, and half a Y. If the sperm that fertilizes the ovum carries an X, then the child inherits an XX pattern and is a girl. If the fertilizing sperm carries a Y, then the combination is XY, and the child is a boy.

Geneticists have pushed this understanding a step further, discovering that only one very small section of the Y chromosome actually determines maleness—a segment referred to as TDF, or *testis-determining factor* (Page et al., 1987). In rare instances, TDF is absent from the Y chromosome. In such cases, the resulting embryo is genetically XY but develops female genitalia. Scientists (Arn et al., 1994; Bardoni et al., 1994) have found indications that there may also be a "femaleness" gene, or perhaps a whole collection of genes required to stimulate the appropriate development of female genitalia and internal reproductive organs.

failed IVF can result in depression among some of them (Weaver, Clifford, Hay, & Robinson, 1997). Moreover, IVF is expensive and is typically not covered by health insurance (Jain, Harlow, & Hornstein, 2002).

Successful IVF carries a different set of risks. Babies who are born as a result of IVF conception are more likely to be low-birth-weight and have birth defects than infants who are conceived naturally (Hansen, Kurinczuk, Bower, & Webb, 2002; Schieve et al., 2002). The most important factor explaining these outcomes is the link between IVF and multiple gestation. Multiple births are more frequent among IVF patients, primarily because doctors typically transfer several zygotes at once in order to increase the likelihood of at least one live birth (Society for Assisted Reproductive Technology, 2004). Consequently, 20–25% of IVF patients deliver twins, and another 2–5% give birth to triplets (Schieve et al., 1999). Multiple births are associated with premature birth, low birth weight, and birth defects. Thus, reducing the frequency of multiple births among women undergoing treatment for infertility has become an important goal of reproductive medicine (Jain, Missmer, & Hornstein, 2004). To this end, the Society for Assisted Reproductive Technology (2004) has issued guidelines that strongly discourage physicians from transferring more than two embryos to a woman's uterus.

Nevertheless, researchers have found that, even when only one embryo is transferred, IVF is still associated with a higher rate of multiple births than is natural conception. For reasons that are not yet understood, implanted zygotes conceived through IVF are more likely to spontaneously divide into two embryos than are naturally conceived zygotes (Blickstine, Jones, & Keith, 2003). This finding suggests that multiple births must always be considered as a possible outcome when infertile couples are advised of the risks associated with IVF.

In addition, infants born as a result of IVF conception are twice as likely as naturally conceived infants to be low-birth-weight, even when they are singletons and are born at term. Likewise, birth defects are twice as common among IVF babies of normal birth weight and gestational age as among those who are conceived naturally (Hansen et al., 2002). The causes for these findings are not yet known, but identifying them so as to prevent the occurrence of these problems is one of the major goals of current research on assisted reproductive technology.

Despite the risks associated with IVF, most women who achieve successful pregnancies as a result of this technique deliver babies who are healthy and normal. Further, both comparative (IVF infants and children versus non-IVF ones) and longitudinal studies have shown that children conceived through IVF who are of normal birth weight and who do not have any birth defects develop identically to peers who were conceived naturally (Levy-Shiff et al., 1998; van Balen, 1998). Such findings should give encouragement and hope to those couples who must turn to assisted reproductive technology to fulfill their desire to have children.

Questions for Critical Analysis

1. Look back at the discussion of research ethics in Chapter 1. Would it be ethical to use assisted reproductive technology to experimentally manipulate variables associated with conception, such as the timing of conception in relation to the seasons of the year, in order to determine the effects of such variables on development during infancy and childhood? Why or why not?
2. The use of assisted reproductive technology to help postmenopausal women get pregnant is controversial. What are the arguments for and against this practice?

GENOTYPES, PHENOTYPES, AND PATTERNS OF GENETIC INHERITANCE

When the 23 chromosomes from the father and the 23 from the mother come together at conception, they provide a mix of "instructions," which do not always match. When the two sets of instructions are the same at any given locus (such as genes for type A blood from both parents), geneticists say that the genetic pattern is **homozygous**. When the two sets of instructions differ, the genetic pattern is said to be **heterozygous**, such as a gene pair that includes a gene for type A blood from one parent and a gene for type O blood from the other. How are these differences resolved? Geneticists are still a long way from having a complete answer to this question, but some patterns are very clear. Table 2.1 gives a few examples of physical characteristics that follow the rules you'll be reading about in this section.

Genotypes and Phenotypes First, it's important to know that geneticists (and psychologists) make an important distinction between the **genotype**, which is

homozygous Term describing the genetic pattern when the two genes in the pair at any given genetic locus both carry the same instructions.

heterozygous Term describing the genetic pattern when the two genes in the pair at any given genetic locus carry different instructions, such as a gene for blue eyes from one parent and a gene for brown eyes from the other parent.

genotype The pattern of characteristics and developmental sequences mapped in the genes of any specific individual, which will be modified by individual experience into the phenotype.

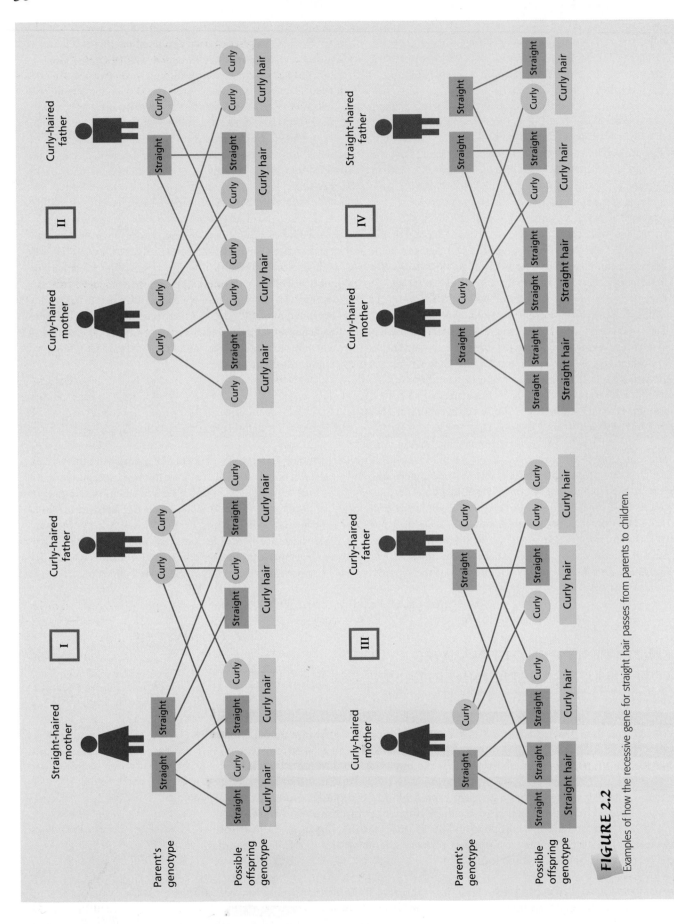

FIGURE 2.2

Examples of how the recessive gene for straight hair passes from parents to children.

TABLE 2.1	Normal Traits	
Dominant	**Recessive**	**Polygenic**
Freckles	Flat feet	Height
Coarse hair	Thin lips	Body type
Dimples	Rh negative blood	Eye color
Curly hair	Fine hair	Skin color
Nearsightedness	Red hair	Personality
Broad lips	Blond hair	
Rh positive blood	Type O blood	
Types A and B blood		
Dark hair		

Source: Tortora and Grabowski, 1993.

phenotype The expression of a particular set of genetic information in a specific environment; the observable result of the joint operation of genetic and environmental influences.

dominant/recessive pattern of inheritance The pattern of genetic transmission in which a single dominant gene influences a person's phenotype, but an individual must have two recessive genes to express a recessive trait.

polygenic pattern of inheritance Any pattern of genetic transmission in which multiple genes contribute to the outcome, such as is presumed to occur for complex traits such as intelligence or temperament.

the specific set of "instructions" contained in a given individual's genes, and the **phenotype**, which is the set of actual observed characteristics of the individual. The phenotype is a product of three things: the genotype, environmental influences from the time of conception onward, and the interaction between the two. A child might have a genotype associated with high IQ, but if his mother drinks too much alcohol during the pregnancy, there may be damage to his nervous system, resulting in mild retardation. Another child might have a genotype including the mix of genes that contribute to a "difficult" temperament, but if his parents are particularly sensitive and thoughtful, he may learn other ways to handle himself.

Dominant and Recessive Genes   Whenever a given trait is governed by a single gene, as is true of some 1,000 individual physical characteristics, inheritance patterns follow well-understood rules. Figure 2.2 offers a schematic look at how the **dominant/recessive pattern of inheritance** works, using the genes for curly and straight hair as an example. Because straight hair is controlled by a recessive gene, an individual must inherit the straight-hair gene from both parents in order for her phenotype to include straight hair. A child who receives only one gene for straight hair will have curly hair, but she may pass the straight-hair gene on to her offspring.

Since curly hair is controlled by a dominant gene, a child who inherits a gene for curly hair from either parent will actually have curly hair. However, her hair may not be as curly as that of the parent from whom she received the gene. Genes vary in *expressivity*, a term that simply means that the same gene may be expressed differently in two individuals who have it.

The dominant/recessive pattern doesn't always work in such a straightforward way. For example, humans carry genes for three kinds of blood type: A (dominant), B (dominant), and O (recessive). Each individual has only two of these genes. If one gene is A and the other is O, then the individual's blood type is A. As you know, an individual must inherit two recessive O genes to have type O blood. But what happens if an individual receives an A and a B gene? Since both are dominant, the individual has type AB blood, and the genes are said to be *co-dominant*. As you can see from Figure 2.3, even the simplest pattern of inheritance can get fairly complicated.

Polygenic and Multifactorial Inheritance   In the **polygenic pattern of inheritance**, many genes influence the phenotype. There are many polygenic traits in which the dominant/recessive pattern is also at work. For example, geneticists think that children get three genes for skin color from each parent (Tortora & Derrickson, 2005). Dark skin is dominant over light skin, but blended skin colors are possible. Thus, when one parent has dark skin and the other has fair skin, their children most likely will have skin that is somewhere between the two. The dark-skinned parent's dominant genes will insure that the children are darker than the fair parent, but the fair-skinned parent's genes will prevent the children from having skin as dark as that of the dark-skinned parent.

Eye color is another polygenic trait with a dominant/recessive pattern (Tortora & Derrickson, 2005). Scientists don't know for sure how many genes influence eye color. They do know, however, that the genes don't cause specific colors. Instead, they cause the colored part of the eye to be dark or light. Dark colors (black, brown, hazel, and green) are dominant over light colors (blue and gray). However, blended colors are also possible. People whose chromosomes carry a combination of genes for green, blue, and gray eyes can have phenotypes that include blue-gray, blue-green,

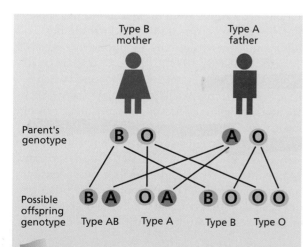

FIGURE 2.3

Possible blood types of offspring of a type B heterozygote and a type A heterozygote.

CRITICAL THINKING

How would you describe your own phenotype? What can you conclude about your genotype by comparing your phenotype to those of your parents?

or gray-green eye color. Likewise, genes that cause different shades of brown can combine their effects to produce variations in children's phenotypes that are different from those of their brown-eyed parents.

Many genes influence height, and there is no dominant/recessive pattern of inheritance among them. Most geneticists think each height gene has a small influence over a child's size (Tanner, 1990) and that a child's height will be the sum of the effects of all of these genes.

Height, like most polygenic traits, is also a result of a **multifactorial pattern of inheritance**—that is, it is affected by both genes and environment. For this reason, doctors use a child's height as a measure of his general health (Sulkes, 1998; Tanner, 1990). If a child is ill, poorly nourished, or emotionally neglected, he will be smaller than others his age. Thus, when a child is shorter than 97% of his agemates, doctors try to determine if he is short because of his genes or because something is causing him to grow poorly (Tanner, 1990).

Genomic Imprinting and Mitochondrial Inheritance   Scientists have discovered some additional principles of genetic inheritance. Through a process called *genomic imprinting*, some genes are biochemically marked at the time ova and sperm develop in the bodies of potential mothers and fathers (Curry, 2002). Apparently, this parental genomic imprint has implications for development. For example, a defective gene on chromosome 15 causes *Prader-Willi syndrome* if it is inherited from the mother. Children with this disorder tend to become obese during the first two years of life and may be mentally retarded. The same gene causes *Angelman syndrome* if a defective copy of it is received from the father. In this disorder, mental retardation is far more severe than in *Prader-Willi syndrome*, and there is no tendency to obesity.

In *mitochondrial inheritance*, children inherit genes located outside the nucleus of the zygote. These genes are carried in structures called *mitochondria* that are found in the fluid that surrounds the nucleus of the ovum before it is fertilized. Consequently, mitochondrial genes are passed only from mother to child. Geneticists have learned that several serious disorders, including some types of blindness, are transmitted in this way. In most such cases, the mother herself is unaffected by the harmful genes (Amato, 1998).

Twins and Siblings   In most cases, babies are conceived and born one at a time. However, 3 out of every 100 births in the United States today are multiple births (U.S. Bureau of the Census, 2001). This number has risen dramatically in recent decades, in large part because widely prescribed new medications given to infertile women frequently stimulate multiple ovulation. The great majority of multiple births in the United States are twins; triplets or higher multiples occur only about once in every 800 births (National Center for Health Statistics [NCHS], 1999).

Roughly two-thirds of twins are **fraternal twins**. Fraternal twins develop when two ova have been produced and both have been fertilized, each by a separate sperm. Such twins, also called **dizygotic twins**, are no more alike genetically than any other pair of siblings and may not even be of the same sex. The remaining one-third of twins are **identical twins** (also called **monozygotic twins**). In such cases, a single fertilized ovum apparently initially divides in the normal way, but then for unknown reasons separates into two parts, with each part developing into a separate individual. Because identical twins develop from precisely the same original fertilized ovum, they have identical genetic heritages. You'll remember from Chapter 1 that comparison of the degree of similarity of these two types of twins is a major research strategy in the important field of behavior genetics.

multifactorial pattern of inheritance The pattern of genetic transmission in which both genes and environment influence the phenotype.

fraternal (dizygotic) twins Children carried in the same pregnancy but who develop from two separately fertilized ova. They are no more alike genetically than other pairs of siblings.

identical (monozygotic) twins Children carried in the same pregnancy who develop from the same fertilized ovum. They are genetic clones of each other.

Before going on . . .

- Describe the process and basic genetics of conception.
- What is the difference between a phenotype and a genotype? Define the dominant/recessive, polygenic, multifactorial, and mitochondrial patterns of inheritance.

Development from Conception to Birth

When we think about prenatal development, our thoughts often focus on the pregnant woman, because the pregnancy is visible. Until very recently, the process of prenatal development was almost completely shrouded in mystery. The only clues scientists had about the process came from examination of embryos and fetuses that were spontaneously aborted or from studies of animal embryology.

Because little was known about prenatal development, there was a lot of confusion about the connection between the experiences of the pregnant woman and the intrauterine development and experiences of the child. For example, pregnancy has traditionally been divided into three *trimesters* of equal length, so doctors as well as expectant couples tended to think of prenatal development as consisting of three analogous stages. One consequence of the confusion was that many people believed that when the mother first *felt* the fetus move, this was the first time the fetus actually had moved.

Of course, technology has changed all this. Thanks to a variety of techniques, scientists have learned that there are indeed three stages of prenatal development, but the developing child has already reached the *third* stage before the mother ends her first trimester. Moreover, we know that spontaneous movement of the fetus begins within a few weeks of conception.

One of the most significant effects of improvements in technology has been to offer fathers greater awareness of the prenatal developmental process. Researchers have found that both the father's and the mother's feelings of attachment to the unborn child intensify when the parents can observe the fetus during an ultrasound examination (Sandelowski, 1994).

THE STAGES OF PRENATAL DEVELOPMENT

The period of gestation of the human infant is 38 weeks (about 265 days). These 38 weeks are divided into three stages of unequal length, identified by specific changes within the developing organism.

The Germinal Stage   The **germinal stage** begins at conception and ends when the zygote is implanted in the wall of the uterus. After conception, the zygote spends roughly a week floating down the fallopian tube to the uterus. Cell division begins 24 to 36 hours after conception; within 2 to 3 days, there are several dozen cells and the whole mass is about the size of the head of a pin. Approximately 4 days after conception, the mass of cells, now called a **blastocyst**, begins to subdivide, forming a sphere with two layers of cells around a hollow center. The outermost layer will form the various structures that will support the developing organism, while the inner layer will form the **embryo** itself. When it touches the wall of the uterus, the outer cell layer of the blastocyst breaks down at the point of contact. Small tendrils develop and attach the cell mass to the uterine wall, a process called *implantation*. When implantation is complete (normally 10 days to 2 weeks after conception), the blastocyst has perhaps 150 cells (Tanner, 1990). The sequence is illustrated schematically in Figure 2.4.

The Embryonic Stage   The **embryonic stage** begins when implantation is complete. The blastocyst's outer layer of cells specializes into two membranes, each of which forms critical support structures. The inner membrane becomes a sac or bag called the **amnion**, filled with liquid (amniotic fluid) in which the embryo floats. The outer membrane, called the **chorion**, develops into two organs, the **placenta** and the **umbilical cord**. The placenta, which is fully developed by about 4 weeks of gestation, is

germinal stage The first stage of prenatal development, beginning at conception and ending at implantation of the zygote in the uterus (approximately the first 2 weeks).

blastocyst Name for the mass of cells from roughly 4 to 10 days after fertilization.

embryo The name given to the developing organism during the period of prenatal development between about 2 weeks and 8 weeks after conception, beginning with implantation of the blastocyst in the uterine wall.

embryonic stage The second stage of prenatal development, from week 2 through week 8, when the embryo's organs form.

amnion The sac, or bag, filled with liquid in which the embryo/fetus floats during prenatal life.

chorion The outer layer of cells of the blastocyst during prenatal development, from which both the placenta and the umbilical cord are formed.

placenta An organ that develops between the fetus and the wall of the uterus during gestation.

umbilical cord The cord connecting the embryo/fetus to the placenta, containing two arteries and one vein.

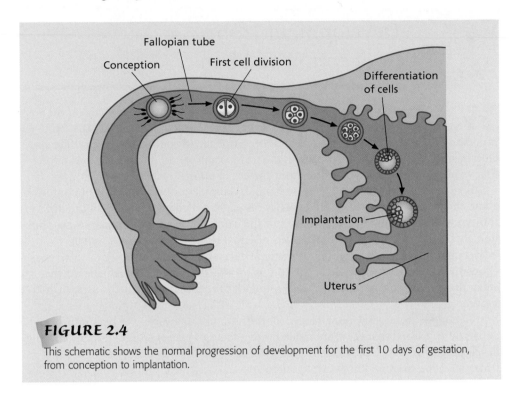

FIGURE 2.4

This schematic shows the normal progression of development for the first 10 days of gestation, from conception to implantation.

a platelike mass of cells that lies against the wall of the uterus. It serves as the liver and kidneys for the embryo until the embryo's own organs begin to function. It also provides the embryo with oxygen and removes carbon dioxide from its blood.

Connected to the embryo's circulatory system via the umbilical cord, the placenta also serves as a critical filter between the mother's circulatory system and the embryo's. Nutrients such as oxygen, proteins, sugars, and vitamins from the maternal blood can pass through to the embryo or fetus; digestive wastes and carbon dioxide from the infant's blood pass back through to the mother, whose own body can eliminate them. At the same time, many (but not all) harmful substances, such as viruses or the mother's hormones, are filtered out because they are too large to pass through the various membranes in the placenta. Most drugs and anesthetics, however, do pass through the placenta, as do some disease organisms.

While the support structures are developing, the mass of cells that will form the embryo itself is differentiating further into several types of cells that form the rudiments of skin, sense receptors, nerve cells, muscles, circulatory system, and internal organs—a process called *organogenesis*.

A heartbeat can be detected roughly 4 weeks after conception; the beginnings of lungs and limbs are also apparent at this time. By the end of the embryonic period, rudimentary fingers and toes, eyes, eyelids, nose, mouth, and external ears are all present, as are the basic parts of the nervous system; these and other developmental milestones are summarized in Table 2.2. The embryonic stage ends when organogenesis is complete and bone cells begin to form, typically about 8 weeks after conception.

The Fetal Stage   Once organogenesis is complete, the developing organism is called a **fetus**. In the 7 months between the beginning of the **fetal stage** and birth, the organ systems are refined. You can get some feeling for the rapidity of the changes by referring to Table 2.2, which lists some of the milestones of fetal development. One vital system that develops mostly during the fetal period is the nervous system, which exists in only the most rudimentary form at the end of the embryonic stage. First to form is a hollow cylinder called the neural tube, out of which both the brain and the spinal cord develop; the neural tube appears during the 4th week following conception (see Figure 2.5).

fetus The name given to the developing organism from about 8 weeks after conception until birth.

fetal stage The third stage of prenatal development, from week 8 to birth, when growth and organ refinement take place.

TABLE 2.2	Milestones in Prenatal Development

Stage/Time Frame	Milestones	
Germinal Stage		
Day 1: Conception	Sperm and ovum unite, forming a zygote containing genetic instructions for the development of a new and unique human being.	
Days 10 to 14: Implantation	The zygote burrows into the lining of the uterus. Specialized cells that will become the placenta, umbilical cord, amnion, and embryonic body are already moving into place.	
Embryonic Stage		
Weeks 3 to 8: Organogenesis	All of the embryo's organ systems form during the 6-week period following implantation.	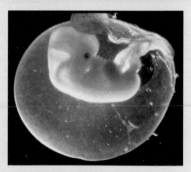
Fetal Stage		
Weeks 9 to 38: Growth and Organ Refinement	The fetus grows from 1 inch long and 1/4 ounce to a length of about 20 inches and a weight of 7 to 9 pounds. By week 12, most fetuses can be identified as male or female. Changes in the brain and lungs make viability possible by week 24; optimum development requires an additional 14 to 16 weeks in the womb. Most neurons form by week 28, and connections among them begin to develop shortly thereafter. In the last 8 weeks, the fetus hears, smells, is sensitive to touch, and responds to light. Learning is also possible.	

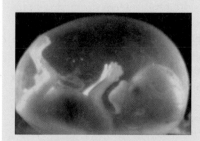 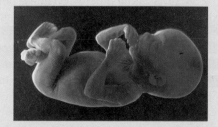 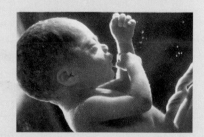

Sources: Kliegman, 1998; Tortora and Grabowski, 1993.

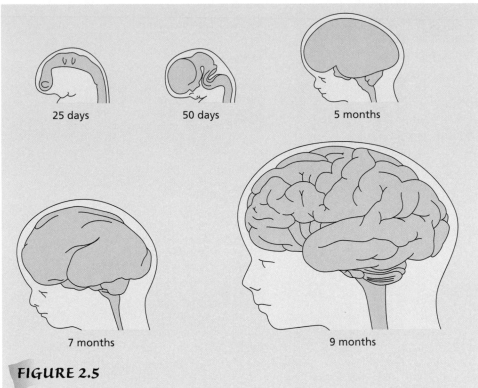

25 days   50 days   5 months

7 months   9 months

FIGURE 2.5

Stages in the prenatal development of the brain, beginning with the neural tube in the embryonic period.
(*Source*: From drawings by Tom Prentiss in "The Development of the Brain" by W. Maxwell Cowan in *Scientific American*, September 1979, pp. 112–114+. Adapted by permission of Nelson H. Prentiss.)

neurons The cells in the nervous system that are responsible for transmission and reception of nerve impulses.

glial cells One of two major classes of cells making up the nervous system; glial cells provide firmness and structure, the "glue" to hold the system together.

dendrites The branchlike part of a neuron that forms one half of a synaptic connection to other nerves. Dendrites develop rapidly in the final 2 prenatal months and the first year after birth.

axon The long tubular extension of a neuron; the terminal fibers of the axon serve as transmitters in the synaptic connection with the dendrites of other neurons.

synapse The point of communication between two neurons, where nerve impulses are passed from one neuron to another by means of chemicals called neurotransmitters.

neurotransmitters Chemicals that accomplish the transmission of signals from one neuron to another at synapses.

The nervous system is made up of two basic types of cells: **neurons** and **glial cells**. The glial cells are the "glue" that holds the whole nervous system together, providing firmness and structure to the brain, helping to remove debris after neuronal death or injury, and segregating neurons from one another. The neurons do the job of receiving and sending messages between parts of the nervous system and between the nervous system and other parts of the body.

Neurons have four main parts, shown schematically in Figure 2.6: (1) a cell body, which is most commonly shaped like a pyramid; (2) branchlike extensions of the cell body (called **dendrites**), which are the major receptors of nerve impulses; (3) a tubular extension of the cell body called the **axon**, which can extend as far as a meter (about 3 feet); and (4) branchlike terminal fibers at the end of the axon, which form the primary transmitting apparatus of the nervous system. Because of the branchlike appearance of the dendrites, physiologists often use botanical phrases when discussing them, speaking of the "dendritic arbor" or of "pruning the arbor."

The point at which two neurons communicate, where the axon's terminal fibers come into close contact with another neuron's dendrites, is called a **synapse**; the communication across the synapse is accomplished with chemicals called **neurotransmitters**, such as serotonin, dopamine, or endorphins. The number of such synapses is vast. A single cell in the part of the brain that controls vision, for instance, may have as many as 10,000 to 30,000 synaptic inputs to its dendrites (Greenough, Black, & Wallace, 1987).

Glial cells begin to develop about 13 weeks after conception and continue to be added until perhaps 2 years after birth. The great majority of neurons are formed between 10 and 18 weeks into gestation (Huttenlocher, 1994; Todd, Swarzenski, Rossi, & Visconti, 1995). Neurons initially form as cell bodies in one part of the brain and then migrate to other sections of the brain (Johnson, 2005). With a few exceptions, these prenatally created neurons are the majority of the neurons an individual will have over his or her entire lifespan; most neurons lost later, either through natural aging or through trauma or disease, are not replaced.

In these early weeks of the fetal period, neurons are very simple. They consist largely of the cell body, with short axons and little dendritic development. It is in the last 2 months before birth and in the first few years after birth that the axons lengthen and the major growth of the "dendritic arbor" occurs. Indeed, the dendrites that first develop in the 8th and 9th months of gestation appear to be sent out as a kind of exploratory system; many of these early dendrites are later reabsorbed, and only the useful extensions remain. In the final fetal months, however, synapse formation is much slower; most synapses are formed after birth. For example, in the part of the brain involved in vision, babies have about 10 times the number of synapses at 6 months as they had at birth (Huttenlocher, 1994).

Similarly, the major growth in fetal size occurs late in the fetal period. The fetus attains about half of birth length by about 20 weeks of gestation, but does not reach half of birth weight until nearly 3 months later, at about 32 weeks.

SEX DIFFERENCES IN PRENATAL DEVELOPMENT

Because nearly all prenatal development is controlled by maturational sequences that are the same for all members of our species—male and female alike—there aren't very many sex differences in prenatal development. Still, there are a few, and they set the stage for some of the physical differences that are evident at later ages.

Sometime between 4 and 8 weeks after conception, the male embryo begins to secrete the male hormone testosterone from the rudimentary testes. If this hormone is not secreted or is secreted in inadequate amounts, the embryo will be "demasculinized," even to the extent of developing female genitalia. Female embryos do not appear to secrete any equivalent hormone prenatally. However, the accidental presence of male hormone at the critical time (such as from some drug the mother may take, or from a genetic disorder called congenital adrenal hyperplasia) acts to "defeminize," or to masculinize, the female fetus, sometimes resulting in malelike genitalia and frequently resulting in masculinization of later behavior, such as more rough-and-tumble play (Collaer & Hines, 1995). Several hormones that affect the prenatal development of genitalia (particularly testosterone in males) also appear to affect the pattern of brain development, resulting in subtle brain differences between males and females and affecting patterns of growth-hormone secretions in adolescence, levels of physical aggression, and the relative dominance of the right and left hemispheres of the brain (Ruble & Martin, 1998; Todd et al., 1995). Although early research has raised some very intriguing questions, the evidence in this area is still fairly sketchy; it is clear that whatever role such prenatal hormones play in brain architecture and functioning is highly complex.

Girls progress a bit faster in some aspects of prenatal development, particularly skeletal development. They are 4 to 6 weeks ahead in bone development at birth (Tanner, 1990). Despite the more rapid development of girls, boys are slightly heavier and longer at birth, with more muscle tissue and fewer fat cells. For example, in the United States, the average birth length and weight for boys is 20 inches and just over 7 pounds, compared with slightly more than 19 inches and 7 pounds for girls (Needlman, 1996).

Boys are considerably more vulnerable to all kinds of prenatal problems. Many more boys than girls are conceived—on the order of about 120 to 150 male embryos for every 100 female ones—but more of the males are spontaneously aborted. At birth, there are about 105 boys for every 100 girls. Boys are also more likely to experience injuries at birth (perhaps because they are larger), and they have more congenital malformations (Zaslow & Hayes, 1986). Male fetuses also appear to be more sensitive to variables such as marijuana and maternal stress, which may negatively affect prenatal development (Bethus, Lemaire, Lhomme, & Goodall, 2005; Wang, Dow-Edwards, Anderson, Minkoff, & Hurd, 2004). The striking sex difference in vulnerability to certain

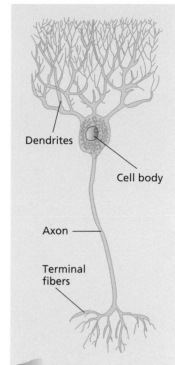

FIGURE 2.6

The structure of a single developed neuron. The cell bodies are the first to be developed, primarily between 10 and 20 weeks of gestation. Axons and dendrites begin to develop in the last 2 months of gestation and continue to increase in size and complexity for several years after birth.

problems seems to persist throughout the lifespan. Males have shorter life expectancy, higher rates of behavior problems, more learning disabilities, and usually more negative responses to stressors such as maternal insensitivity (Warren & Simmens, 2005). One possible explanation for at least some of this sex difference may lie in the basic genetic difference. Because many genes for problems or disorders are recessive and are carried on the X chromosome, the XX combination affords a girl more protection against fragile-X syndrome and against other "bad" recessive genes that may be carried on one X chromosome; the dominant gene on the corresponding X chromosome would be expressed instead. For instance, geneticists have found that a gene affecting susceptibility to infectious disease is carried on the X chromosome (Brooks-Gunn & Matthews, 1979). Because boys have only one X chromosome, such a recessive gene is much more likely to be expressed phenotypically in a boy.

There are also behavioral differences between male and female fetuses. One fairly well documented difference is that male fetuses, on average, are more physically active (DiPietro, Hodgson, Costigan, Hilton, & Johnson, 1996; DiPietro, Hodgson, Costigan, & Johnson, 1996). Further, activity level is fairly stable from the fetal stage through childhood (Accardo et al., 1997; DiPietro, Bornstein, et al., 2002). This means that the sex difference in children's activity level you'll read about in later chapters probably begins in the womb. In addition, female fetuses are more responsive to external stimuli (Groome et al., 1999).

PRENATAL BEHAVIOR

Centuries before scientists began to study prenatal development, pregnant women noticed fetal responses to music and other sounds. However, in recent years, developmentalists have learned a great deal about how such stimuli affect the fetus. For one thing, they know that the fetus responds to sounds with heart rate changes, head turns, and body movements as early as the 25th week of gestation (Joseph, 2000). Researchers have also shown that it is possible to observe fetal brain activity by scanning the mother's abdomen with the same kinds of techniques used to examine brain function postnatally—techniques such as magnetic resonance imaging (MRI). Studies using these techniques have found that late-term fetuses exhibit neurological as well as behavioral responses to sounds (Moore et al., 2001).

Research also suggests that the fetus can distinguish between familiar and novel stimuli by the 32nd or 33rd week (Sandman, Wadhwa, Hetrick, Porto, & Peeke, 1997). In one study, pregnant women recited a short children's rhyme out loud each day between weeks 33 and 37. In week 38, researchers played a recording of either the same rhyme the mother had been reciting or another rhyme and measured the fetal heart rate. Fetal heart rates dropped during the playing of the familiar rhyme, but not during the unfamiliar rhyme, suggesting that the fetuses had learned the sound patterns of the rhyme (DeCasper, Lecanuet, Busnel, Granier-DeFerre, & Maugeais, 1994). The ability to learn in this way seems to emerge along with changes in the nervous system between 24 and 38 weeks that allow the fetal brain to gain greater control of physical movements (Pressman, DiPietro, Costigan, Shupe, & Johnson, 1998).

Evidence for fetal learning also comes from studies in which newborns appear to remember stimuli to which they were exposed prenatally: their mother's heartbeats, the odor of the amniotic fluid, and stories or pieces of music they heard in the womb (Righetti, 1996; Schaal, Marlier, & Soussignan, 1998). Research involving bird embryos is also important to understanding prenatal learning because, unlike the human uterus, egg shells are light-permeable. This allows investigators to expose developing chicks to light as well as to auditory stimuli. They have found that embryonic chicks exposed to multisensory stimulation learn more rapidly than those exposed to a single source of sensory stimulation (Lickliter, Bahrick, & Honeycutt, 2002). Thus, the prenatal learning process appears to directly parallel what happens postnatally. Research with both newborn animals and human infants shows that they learn more rapidly with multisensory stimuli (Sai, 2005).

In a classic study of prenatal learning, pregnant women read a children's story such as Dr. Seuss's *The Cat in the Hat* out loud each day for the final 6 weeks of their pregnancies. After the infants were born, they were allowed to suck on special pacifiers that turned a variety of sounds off and on. Each kind of sound required a special type of sucking. Researchers found that the babies quickly adapted their sucking patterns in order to listen to the familiar story, but did not change their sucking in order to listen to an unfamiliar story (DeCasper & Spence, 1986). In other words, babies preferred the sound of the story they had heard in utero.

Developmentalists are trying to find out if prenatal learning affects later development, and if so, how (Bornstein et al., 2002). In one study, pregnant women wore waistbands equipped with speakers through which they exposed their fetuses to an average of 70 hours of classical music per week between 28 weeks of gestation and birth (Lafuente et al., 1997). By age 6 months, the babies who had heard the music were more advanced than control infants in many motor and cognitive skills. Of course, the exact meaning of this result is difficult to assess, but it does suggest that the prenatal sensory environment may be important in later development.

Researchers have also been able to identify individual differences in fetal behavior. You have already read about the sex difference in activity level. As is true of most sex differences, however, the range of individual differences within each gender is far greater than the difference in *average* activity levels between male and female fetuses. Longitudinal studies have shown that very active fetuses, both males and females, tend to become children who are very active. Moreover, these children are more likely to be labeled "hyperactive" by parents and teachers. In contrast, fetuses who are less active than average are more likely to be mentally retarded (Accardo et al., 1997).

CRITICAL THINKING

Based on the research by Lafuente that you have just read about, if you or your partner were expecting a baby, would you want to expose the fetus to classical music? How could you recreate the conditions used in this experiment in a more natural setting?

Before going on . . .

■ List the milestones of the germinal, embryonic, and fetal stages.
■ What have researchers discovered about prenatal learning and behavior?

Problems in Prenatal Development

One of the most important points about prenatal development is how remarkably regular and predictable it is. However, this sequence of development is not immune to modification or outside influence, as you'll soon see in detail. The potential problems fall into two general classes: genetic and chromosomal problems that begin at conception, and problems caused by damaging substances or events called **teratogens**.

GENETIC DISORDERS

Many disorders appear to be transmitted through the operation of dominant and recessive genes (see Table 2.3). *Autosomal* disorders are caused by genes located on the autosomes. The genes that cause *sex-linked* disorders are found on the X chromosome.

Autosomal Disorders Most recessive autosomal disorders are diagnosed in infancy or early childhood. For example, one recessive gene causes a baby to have problems digesting the amino acid phenylalanine. Toxins build up in the baby's brain and cause mental retardation. This condition, called *phenylketonuria (PKU)*, is found in about 1 in every 10,000 babies (Nicholson, 1998). If a baby consumes no foods containing phenylalanine, however, she will not become mentally retarded. Milk is one of the foods PKU babies can't have, so early diagnosis is critical. For this reason, most states require all babies to be tested for PKU soon after birth.

Like many recessive disorders, PKU is associated with race. Caucasian babies are more likely to have the disorder than infants in other racial groups. Similarly, West African and African American infants are more likely to suffer from *sickle-cell disease*, a recessive disorder that causes red blood cell deformities (Scott, 1998). In sickle-cell disease, the blood can't carry enough oxygen to keep the body's tissues healthy. Few chil-

teratogens Substances such as viruses and drugs or events that can cause birth defects.

TABLE 2.3	Genetic Disorders	
Autosomal Dominant	**Autosomal Recessive**	**Sex-Linked Recessive**
Huntington's disease	Phenylketonuria	Hemophilia
High blood pressure	Sickle-cell disease	Fragile-X syndrome
Extra fingers	Cystic fibrosis	Red-green color blindness
Migraine headaches	Tay-Sachs disease	Missing front teeth
Schizophrenia	Kidney cysts in infants	Night blindness
	Albinism	Some types of muscular dystrophy
		Some types of diabetes

Sources: Amato, 1993; Tortora and Grabowski, 1993.

dren with sickle-cell disease live past the age of 20, and most who survive to adulthood die before they are 40 (Scott, 1998).

Almost one-half of West Africans have either sickle-cell disease or sickle-cell trait (Amato, 1998). Persons with *sickle-cell trait* carry a single recessive gene for sickle-cell disease, which causes a few of their red blood cells to be abnormal. Doctors can identify carriers of the sickle-cell gene by testing their blood for sickle-cell trait. Once potential parents know that they carry the gene, they can make informed decisions about future childbearing. In the United States, about 1 in 650 African Americans has sickle-cell disease, and 1 in 8 African Americans has sickle-cell trait. Sickle-cell disease and sickle-cell trait also occur more frequently in people of Mediterranean, Caribbean, Indian, Arab, and Latin American ancestry than in those of European ancestry (Wong, 1993).

About 1 in every 3,000 babies born to Jewish couples of Eastern European ancestry suffers from another recessive disorder, *Tay-Sachs disease.* By the time he is 1 to 2 years old, a Tay-Sachs baby is likely to be severely mentally retarded and blind. Very few survive past the age of 3 (Painter & Bergman, 1998).

Disorders caused by dominant genes, such as *Huntington's disease*, are usually not diagnosed until adulthood (Amato, 1998). This disorder causes the brain to deteriorate and affects both psychological and motor functions. Until recently, children of Huntington's disease sufferers had to wait until they became ill themselves to know for sure that they carried the gene. Now, doctors can use a blood test to identify the Huntington's gene. Thus, people who have a parent with this disease can make better decisions about their own childbearing and can prepare for living with a serious disorder when they get older.

Sex-Linked Disorders   Most sex-linked disorders are caused by recessive genes. One fairly common sex-linked recessive disorder is *red-green color blindness*. People with this disorder have difficulty distinguishing between the colors red and green when they are next to each other. About 1 in 800 men and 1 in 400 women have this disorder. Most learn ways of compensating for the disorder and thus live perfectly normal lives.

A more serious sex-linked recessive disorder is *hemophilia* (see Figure 2.7). The blood of people with hemophilia lacks the chemical components that cause blood to clot. Thus, when a person with hemophilia bleeds, the bleeding doesn't stop naturally. Approximately 1 in 5,000 baby

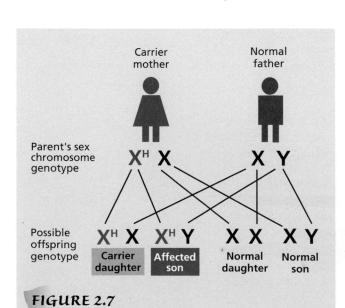

FIGURE 2.7

Compare this pattern of sex-linked transmission of a recessive disease (hemophilia) with the pattern shown in Figure 2.3.

boys is born with this disorder, which is almost unknown in girls (Scott, 1998).

About 1 in every 1,500 males and 1 in every 2,500 females has a sex-linked disorder called *fragile-X syndrome* (Amato, 1998). A person with this disorder has an X chromosome with a "fragile," or damaged, spot. Fragile-X syndrome can cause mental retardation that becomes progressively worse as children get older (Adesman, 1996). In fact, experts estimate that 5–7% of all retarded males have fragile-X syndrome (Zigler & Hodapp, 1991). Fragile-X syndrome is also strongly associated with autism, a disorder that interferes with children's capacity to form emotional bonds with others (Cohen et al., 2005). Fortunately, fragile-X syndrome is one of several disorders that can be diagnosed before birth (see *The Real World*).

CHROMOSOMAL ERRORS

Over 50 different chromosomal anomalies have been identified, and most result in miscarriage. When babies do survive, the effects of chromosomal errors tend to be dramatic.

Note the distinctive facial characteristics of this Down syndrome child.

Trisomies A *trisomy* is a condition in which an individual has three copies of a particular autosome. The most common is **Down syndrome** (also called **trisomy 21**), in which the child has three copies of chromosome 21. Roughly 1 in every 800 to 1,000 infants is born with this abnormality (Rogers, Roizin, & Capone, 1996). These children have distinctive facial features, most notably a flattened face and somewhat slanted eyes with an epicanthic fold on the upper eyelid (an extension of the normal eyelid fold), reduced total brain size, and often other physical abnormalities such as heart defects. Typically, they are retarded.

The risk of bearing a child with trisomy 21 is considerably higher for older mothers. For those age 35, the risk is 1 in 385 births; for a woman of 45, it is 1 in 30 (CDC, 1995a). Research by epidemiologists also suggests a link between exposure to environmental toxins of various kinds and the risk of having a child with Down syndrome. For example, one large study in Canada showed that men employed as mechanics, farm laborers, or sawmill workers, all of whom are regularly exposed to solvents, oils, lead, and pesticides, are at higher risk for fathering Down syndrome children than are men who work in environments lacking these substances (Olshan, Baird, & Teschke, 1989). Findings like these suggest that chromosomal anomalies may not be purely random events but may themselves occur in response to various teratogens. Such results also underline the fact that fathers as well as mothers can contribute to teratogenic effects.

Scientists have identified children with trisomies of the 13th and 18th pairs of chromosomes as well (Amato, 1998). These disorders have more severe effects than trisomy 21. Few trisomy 13 or trisomy 18 children live past the age of 1 year. As with trisomy 21, the chances of having a child with one of these disorders increase with a woman's age.

Sex-Chromosome Anomalies A second class of anomalies, associated with an incomplete or incorrect division of either sex chromosome, occurs in roughly 1 out of every 400 births (Berch & Bender, 1987). The most common is an XXY pattern, called Klinefelter's syndrome, which occurs in approximately 1 out of every 1,000 males. Affected boys most often look quite normal, although they have characteristically long arms and legs and underdeveloped testes. Most are not mentally retarded, but language and learning disabilities are common. Somewhat rarer is an XYY pattern. These children also develop as boys; typically they are unusually tall, with mild retardation.

Down syndrome (trisomy 21) A genetic anomaly in which every cell contains three copies of chromosome 21 rather than two. Children born with this genetic pattern are usually mentally retarded and have characteristic physical features.

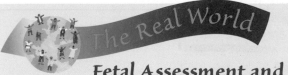

The Real World

Fetal Assessment and Treatment

Shilpa and Rudy Patel are preparing for the birth of their first child. Like many other couples, they are hoping that their child will be healthy. In their case, however, there is real cause for concern because a genetic disorder known as *fragile-X syndrome* runs in Shilpa's family. Prior to her pregnancy, Shilpa was tested and learned that she carries the defect on one of her X chromosomes. Now four months pregnant, she is anxiously awaiting the results of a test that will tell her whether her child is a boy or a girl and, more importantly, whether the genetic defect is present in the fetus's cells.

The procedure used to test Shilpa's fetus is known as *chorionic villus sampling (CVS)*. CVS and another procedure, *amniocentesis*, can be used to identify chromosomal errors and many genetic disorders prior to birth (Curry, 2002). In CVS, cells are extracted from the placenta and subjected to a variety of laboratory tests during the early weeks of prenatal development. In amniocentesis, a needle is used to extract amniotic fluid containing fetal cells between weeks 14 and 16 of gestation. Fetal cells filtered out of the fluid are then tested in a variety of ways to diagnose chromosomal and genetic disorders. In addition, *ultrasonography* has become a routine part of prenatal care in the United States because of its usefulness in monitoring fetal growth in high-risk pregnancies. When an ultrasound test suggests that there may be some kind of brain or spinal cord abnormality, follow-up tests using magnetic resonance imaging are sometimes employed (Levine, 2002). These images are more detailed than those that are produced by ultrasonography.

Many laboratory tests that use maternal blood, urine, and/or samples of amniotic fluid also help health care providers monitor fetal development. For example, the presence of a substance called *alpha-fetoprotein* in a mother's blood is associated with a number of prenatal defects, including abnormalities in the brain and spinal cord. Doctors can also use a laboratory test to assess the maturity of fetal lungs (Kliegman, 1998). This test is critical when doctors have to deliver a baby early because of a pregnant woman's health.

Fetoscopy involves insertion of a tiny camera into the womb to directly observe fetal development. Fetoscopy makes it possible for doctors to surgically correct some kinds of defects (Kliegman, 1998) and has made techniques such as fetal blood transfusions and bone marrow transplants possible. Specialists also use fetoscopy to take samples of blood from the umbilical cord. Fetal blood tests can help doctors identify a bacterial infection that is causing a fetus to grow too slowly (Curry, 2002). Once diagnosed, the infection can be treated by injecting antibiotics into the amniotic fluid to be swallowed by the fetus or by injecting drugs into the umbilical cord (Kliegman, 1998).

Researchers have examined how prenatal diagnosis affects parents-to-be. Compared to parents of 1-year-olds with disabilities who did not know about the problems prior to birth, parents whose infants' difficulties were diagnosed prenatally report greater feelings of stress and depression (Hunfeld et al., 1999). However, specialists in fetal medicine suggest that the negative emotional effects of prenatal diagnosis can be moderated by providing parents-to-be with counseling and specific information about treatment at the time the diagnosis is made rather than waiting until after birth.

Questions for Reflection

1. How do you think you would respond to the news that a child you were expecting was carrying some kind of genetic defect?
2. Suppose Shilpa and Rudy learn that their baby is a girl. Will this news make them more or less concerned about the effect that carrying the fragile-X defect may have on their child's development? Why?

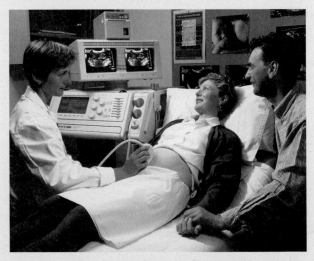

Ultrasound technology allows fathers to experience prenatal development in a more intimate way.

A single-X pattern (XO), called Turner's syndrome, and a triple-X pattern (XXX) may also occur, and in both cases the child develops as a girl. Girls with Turner's syndrome—perhaps 1 in every 3,000 live female births (Tanner, 1990)—show stunted growth and are usually sterile. Without hormone therapy, they do not menstruate or develop breasts at puberty. Neuroimaging studies show that Turner syndrome is associated with abnormal development in both the cerebellum and the cerebrum (Brown et al., 2002). These girls also show an interesting imbalance in their cognitive skills: They often perform particularly poorly on tests that measure spatial ability but usually perform at or above normal levels on tests of verbal skill (Golombok & Fivush, 1994). Girls with an XXX pattern are of normal size but are slow in physical development. In contrast to girls with Turner's syndrome, they have markedly poor verbal abilities and overall low IQ, and they do particularly poorly in school compared with other children with sex-chromosome anomalies (Bender et al., 1995; Rovet & Netley, 1983).

TERATOGENS: MATERNAL DISEASES

Deviant prenatal development can also result from variations in the environment in which the embryo and fetus is nurtured. A particular teratogen, such as a drug or a disease in the mother, will result in a defect in the embryo or fetus only if it occurs during a particular period of days or weeks of prenatal life. The general rule is that each organ system is most vulnerable to disruption at the time when it is developing most rapidly (Moore & Persaud, 1993). Figure 2.8 shows times when different parts of the body are most vulnerable to teratogens. As you can see, the first 8 weeks are the period of greatest vulnerability for all the organ systems.

Rubella The first few weeks of gestation comprise a critical period for a negative effect from rubella (also called German measles). Most infants exposed to rubella in the first 4 to 5 weeks show some abnormality, while only about 10% of those exposed in the final 6 months of pregnancy are affected negatively (Moore & Persaud, 1993). Deafness, cataracts, and heart defects are the most common abnormalities. These effects are observable immediately after birth. But recent research suggests that rubella may also be linked to developmental outcomes, such as the development of schizophrenia, that aren't apparent until adolescence or adulthood (Brown, 2000–2001). Fortunately, rubella is preventable. A vaccine is available, and it should be given to all children as part of a regular immunization program (American College of Obstetrics and Gynecology [ACOG], 2002). Adult women who were not vaccinated as children can be vaccinated later, but the vaccination must be done at least 3 months before a pregnancy to provide complete immunity. Moreover, the vaccine itself can be teratogenic, another good reason to wait several weeks before attempting to conceive.

HIV Worldwide, an estimated 3 million women are infected with HIV, the virus that causes AIDS, and the number of infected women of childbearing age is rising everywhere. In the United States, about 2 out of every 1,000 childbearing women are infected (CDC, 1995b). These grim numbers are counterbalanced by several bits of good news. First, only about a quarter of infants born to HIV-positive mothers actually become infected (Mofenson, 2002). Transmission appears to be much more likely when the mother has developed the symptoms of AIDS than when she is HIV-positive but is not yet experiencing symptoms of the disease (Abrams et al., 1995). Even more encouraging is the finding that infected women who are treated with the drug AZT (short for azidothymidine; also called zidovudine) during their pregnancies have a markedly lower risk of transmitting the disease to their children—as low as 8% (Mofenson, 2002). Because most HIV-positive women are asymptomatic and are unaware they are infected, the Centers for Disease Control recommends routine HIV counseling and vol-

CRITICAL THINKING 9

Do you think all pregnant women should be tested for HIV? Medical ethicists have made strong arguments both for and against testing. How would you explain your opinion to someone who disagreed with you?

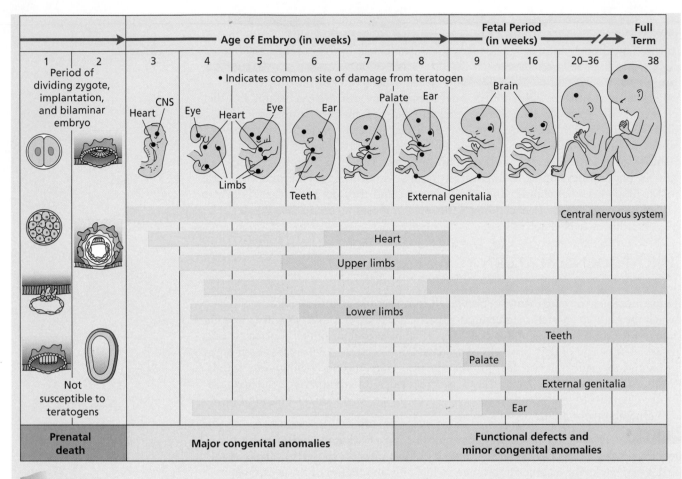

FIGURE 2.8

Critical periods in the prenatal development of various body parts. The light blue portion of each line signifies the period during which any teratogen is likely to produce a major structural deformity in that particular body part. The gold part of each line shows the period in which more minor problems may result. The embryonic period is generally the time of greatest vulnerability.

(*Source*: Moore, K. L. and Persaud T., *The Developing Human: Clinically Oriented Embryology*, 5th ed. © 1993 by W. B. Saunders. By permission.)

untary testing for all pregnant women early in their pregnancies so that they can begin a course of AZT, should that be necessary.

In other parts of the world, HIV is much more prevalent among pregnant women. Unfortunately, many HIV-positive women in nonindustrialized countries know little or nothing about available treatments and possible health consequences of the virus for themselves, their babies, and their partners. For example, one study involving 79 HIV-positive pregnant women aged 18 to 38, in Burkina Faso, West Africa, found that most participants did not intend to inform their partners about their HIV status because they feared being stigmatized (Issiaka et al., 2001). Moreover, none were aware of community organizations from which HIV-positive individuals could obtain information and support. Such findings suggest that the need for basic HIV education in the developing world is critical.

Cytomegalovirus and Other Sexually Transmitted Diseases A much less well known but remarkably widespread and potentially serious sexually transmitted disease (STD) is *cytomegalovirus (CMV)*, a virus in the herpes group. It is now thought to be the single most prevalent infectious cause of both congenital mental retardation and deafness. CMV typically has few, if any, symptoms in an adult. In most cases, an affected person doesn't even know she carries this virus, although in an active phase it sometimes creates symptoms that suggest mononucleosis, including swollen glands and low fever. In infants who are infected prenatally or during birth, however, the virus can sometimes produce crippling disabilities.

Roughly half of all women of childbearing age have antibodies to CMV (Spector, 1996), indicating that they have been infected at some time. Perhaps 2% of babies whose mothers have CMV antibodies become infected prenatally, which means that approximately 1 out of every 100 babies is congenitally infected.

Like CMV, the herpes virus can be transmitted to the fetus during delivery if the mother's disease is in the active phase at that time. Not only will the child then periodically experience the genital sores characteristic of the disease, but he or she may suffer other complications, most notably meningoencephalitis, a potentially serious inflammation of the brain and spinal cord. Because of this increased risk, many physicians now recommend surgical delivery (cesarean section) of infants of mothers with herpes, although vaginal delivery is possible if the disease is inactive.

Two additional STDs, *syphilis* and *gonorrhea*, also cause birth defects. Unlike most teratogens, a syphilis infection is most harmful during the last 26 weeks of prenatal development and causes eye, ear, and brain defects. Gonorrhea, which can cause the infant to be blind, is also usually transmitted during birth. For this reason, doctors usually treat the eyes of newborns with a special ointment that prevents damage from gonorrhea.

Chronic Illnesses   Conditions such as heart disease, diabetes, lupus, hormone imbalances, and epilepsy can also negatively affect prenatal development (Adab, Jacoby, Smith, & Chadwick, 2001; Kliegman, 1998; McAllister et al., 1997; Sandman et al., 1997). And recent research indicates that prenatal exposure to some maternal health conditions, such as the fluctations in metabolism rate characteristic of diabetes, may predispose infants to developmental delays (Levy-Shiff, Lerman, Har-Even, & Hod, 2002). One of the most important goals of the new specialty of *fetal-maternal medicine* is to manage the pregnancies of women who have such conditions so that the health of both mother and fetus will be supported. For example, pregnancy often affects a diabetic woman's blood sugar levels so drastically that it becomes impossible for her to keep them under control. In turn, erratic blood sugar levels may damage the fetus's nervous system or cause it to grow too rapidly (Allen & Kisilevsky, 1999; Kliegman, 1998). To prevent such complications, a fetal-maternal specialist must find a diet, a medication, or a combination of the two that will stabilize the mother's blood sugar but will not harm the fetus.

Environmental Hazards   There are a number of substances found in the environment that may have detrimental effects on prenatal development. For example, women who work with mercury (e.g., dentists, dental technicians, semiconductor manufacturing workers) are advised to limit their exposure to this potentially teratogenic substance (March of Dimes, 2004). Consuming large amounts of fish may also expose pregnant women to high levels of mercury (because of industrial pollution of the oceans and waterways). Fish may also contain elevated levels of another problematic industrial pollutant known as polychlorinated biphenyls, or PCBs. For these reasons, researchers recommend that pregnant women limit their consumption of fish, especially fresh tuna, shark, swordfish, and mackerel (March of Dimes, 2004).

There are several other environmental hazards that pregnant women are advised to avoid (March of Dimes, 2004):

- *Lead*, found in painted surfaces in older homes, pipes carrying drinking water, lead crystal glassware, and some ceramic dishes
- *Arsenic*, found in dust from pressure-treated lumber
- *Cadmium*, found in semiconductor manufacturing facilities
- *Anesthetic gases*, found in dental offices, outpatient surgical facilities, and hospital operating rooms
- *Solvents*, such as alcohol and paint thinners
- *Parasite-bearing substances*, such as animal feces and undercooked meat, poultry, or eggs

TERATOGENS: DRUGS

There is now a huge literature on the effects of prenatal drugs, especially controlled substances such as cocaine and marijuana (Barth, 2001). Sorting out the effects of drugs has proved to be an immensely challenging task because many women use multiple substances: Women who drink alcohol are also more likely than nondrinkers to smoke; those who use cocaine are also likely to take other illegal drugs or to smoke or drink to excess, and so on. In addition, many women who use drugs have other problems, such as depression, that may be responsible for the apparent effects of the drugs they use (Pajulo, Savonlahti, Sourander, Helenius, & Piha, 2001). Furthermore, the effects of drugs may be subtle, visible only many years after birth in the form of minor learning disabilities or increased risk of behavior problems.

Smoking   Recent research suggests that smoking during pregnancy may cause genetic damage in the developing fetus (de la Chica, Ribas, Giraldo, Egozcue, & Fuster, 2005). In addition, the link between smoking and low birth weight is well established. Infants of mothers who smoke are on average about half a pound lighter at birth than infants of nonsmoking mothers (Mohsin, Wong, Baumann, & Bai, 2003) and are nearly twice as likely to be born with a weight below 2,500 grams (5 pounds 8 ounces), the common definition of low birth weight. The more the mother smokes, the greater the negative impact on the infant's weight (Ernst, Moolchan, & Robinson, 2001; Nordentoft et al., 1996), and the older the mother, the more likely it is that her smoking will be linked to low birth weight (U.S. Bureau of the Census, 1997). The primary problem-causing agent in cigarettes is nicotine, which constricts the blood vessels, reducing blood flow and nutrition to the placenta. Whatever the mechanism, the effects of smoking on both height and weight are still evident when the children of smoking and nonsmoking mothers reach school age (Cornelius, Goldschmidt, Day, & Larkby, 2002).

Smokers who quit smoking early in their pregnancy have the same rates of low-birth-weight infants as those who did not smoke at all (Ahlsten, Cnattingius, & Lindmark, 1993). Research also shows a relationship between the "dose" (the amount of nicotine taken in) and the severity of consequences for the child. So a pregnant woman who cannot quit smoking entirely should at least cut back.

Drinking   The effects of alcohol on the developing fetus range from mild to severe. At the extreme end of the continuum are children who exhibit a syndrome called **fetal alcohol syndrome (FAS)**, which affects as many as 3 of every 1,000 infants in the United States (Stratton, Howe, & Battaglia, 1996). Projecting these figures to all children born in the United States means that up to 12,000 children with FAS are born every year. These children, whose mothers were usually heavy drinkers or alcoholics, are generally smaller than normal, with smaller brains and often with distinct physical anomalies or deformities (Swayze et al., 1997). They frequently have heart defects, and their faces have certain distinctive features (visible in the two photos), including a somewhat flattened nose and nose bridge and often an unusually long space between nose and mouth. However, the disorder is often difficult to diagnose. Experts recommend that physicians who suspect that a child may have FAS carry out a multidisciplinary assessment, one that includes a comprehensive medical and behavioral history of both the mother and the child as well as neuropsychological testing (Chudley et al., 2005).

The best single study of the consequences of prenatal alcohol exposure has been done by Ann Streissguth and her colleagues (Olson, Sampson, Barr, Streissguth, & Bookstein, 1992; Streissguth et al., 1980, 1981, 1984, 1989, 1990, 1995, 2004), who followed a group of over 500 women who drank moderate to heavy amounts of alcohol while pregnant and their children. Streissguth tested the children repeatedly, beginning immediately after birth, again later in infancy, at age 4, at school age, and again at ages

fetal alcohol syndrome (FAS) A pattern of abnormalities, including mental retardation and minor physical anomalies, often found in children born to alcoholic mothers.

11 and 14. She found that the mother's alcohol consumption in pregnancy was associated with sluggishness and weaker sucking in infancy; lower scores on measures of intelligence at 8 months, 4 years, and 7 years; and problems with attention and vigilance at 4, 7, 11, and 14. Teachers also rated the 11-year-olds on overall school performance and on various behavior problems, and on both of these measures, children whose mothers had consumed the most alcohol during pregnancy were rated significantly worse. Streissguth also asked mothers about their diet, their education, and their life habits. She found that the links between a mother's alcohol consumption and poor outcomes for the child held up even when all these other variables were controlled statistically. These children are now all young adults, and investigators have found deficiencies in their information-processing skills, demonstrating that the effects of prenatal alcohol exposure persist into adulthood (Connor, Sampson, Bookstein, Barr, & Streissguth, 2001).

Recent evidence also points to milder effects of moderate, or "social," drinking, such as two glasses of wine a day. Children of mothers who drink at this level during pregnancy are more likely to have IQ scores below 85 and to show poorer attention spans. They are also more likely than non-alcohol-exposed peers to have learning problems, both in social situations and in school (Kodituwakku, May, Clericuzio, & Weers, 2001). Thus, we do not yet know whether there is any safe level of alcohol consumption during pregnancy. Research also suggests that alcohol may damage a woman's ova even before they are released (Kaufman, 1997). Given this lack of certainty, the safest course for pregnant women, and for those trying to become pregnant, is not to drink at all.

Cocaine Significant numbers of pregnant women in the United States (and presumably elsewhere in the world) also take various illegal drugs, most notably cocaine. About a third of all cocaine-exposed babies are born prematurely, and among those carried to term, many are lower than normal in birth weight. In addition, cocaine-exposed infants are three times as likely to have a very small head circumference or to show some signs of neurological abnormalities (Needlman, Frank, Augustyn, & Zuckerman, 1995; Singer, Arendt, & Minnes, 1993). Some (but not all) also show significant drug withdrawal symptoms after birth, such as irritability, restlessness, shrill crying, tremors, and lower levels of responsiveness to their mothers (Ukeje, Bendersky, & Lewis, 2001).

What is not yet clear is whether any long-term consequences can be ascribed clearly to prenatal cocaine exposure. Some studies show long-term negative effects (Bender et al., 1995; Mayes, Cicchetti, Acharyya, & Zhang, 2003); others do not (Griffith, Azuma, & Chasnoff, 1994; Richardson & Day, 1994). The most likely possibility is that prenatal cocaine exposure, like prenatal alcohol exposure, does indeed have lasting

These two children, from different countries and different racial backgrounds, have both been diagnosed as having fetal alcohol syndrome (FAS). Both are mentally retarded and have relatively small heads. Note also the short nose and low nasal bridge typical of FAS children.

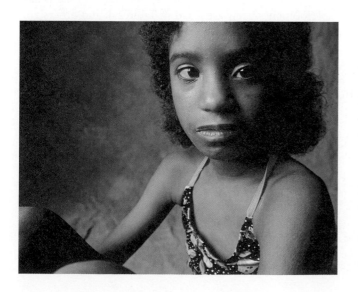
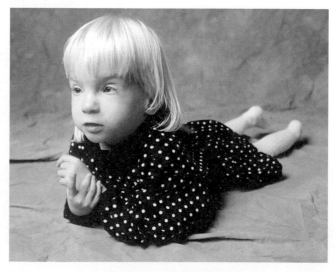

effects on the child, but that the effects are fairly subtle and thus hard to pin down. At the moment, we simply don't know what those long-term effects may be (Lester, Freier, & LaGasse, 1995). However, there are a few studies that suggest that prenatal cocaine exposure is associated with several kinds of deficits in preschool and school-aged children. These include reduced vocabulary at age 6, delayed cognitive and motor development at 3 to 5 years of age, and poor impulse control (Delaney-Black et al., 2000; Hurt, Malmus, Betancourt, Brodsky, & Giannetta, 2001; Savage, Brodsky, Malmud, Giannetta, & Hurt, 2005).

Marijuana and Heroin   Prenatal exposure to marijuana appears to interfere with a child's growth. Even at age 6, children whose mothers used the drug during pregnancy are smaller on average than their non-drug-exposed peers (Cornelius et al., 2002). Researchers also now have evidence suggesting that prenatal exposure to marijuana adversely affects the developing brain (Wang et al., 2004). These findings may help explain why a number of studies have shown that the behavior of infants and children who were prenatally exposed to the drug differs from that of their agemates. For example, the infants of twice-weekly marijuana smokers suffer from tremors and sleep problems. Moreover, they seem to have little interest in their surroundings for up to 2 weeks after birth (Brockington, 1996). How these early differences affect babies' later development is unknown. However, some studies suggest that learning disabilities and attention problems are more common among children whose mothers used marijuana during pregnancy (Fried & Smith, 2001).

Both heroin and methadone, a drug often used in treating heroin addiction, can cause miscarriage, premature labor, and early death (Brockington, 1996). Further, 60–80% of babies born to heroin- or methadone-addicted women are addicted to these drugs as well. Addicted babies have high-pitched cries and suffer from withdrawal symptoms, including irritability, uncontrollable tremors, vomiting, convulsions, and sleep problems. These symptoms may last as long as 4 months.

The degree to which heroin and methadone affect development depends on the quality of the environment in which babies are raised. Babies who are cared for by mothers who continue to be addicted themselves usually don't do as well as those whose mothers stop using drugs or who are raised by relatives or foster families (Brockington, 1996). By age 2, most heroin- or methadone-addicted babies in good homes are developing normally.

OTHER TERATOGENS AND MATERNAL FACTORS

A variety of additional factors, from vitamins to environmental pollutants to maternal emotions, can affect prenatal development. A few are listed in Table 2.4, and others are discussed in more detail in this section.

Vitamins, Drugs, and Other Chemicals   Vitamin A in small doses is essential for the development of the embryo. But when taken in very large doses during the first 2 months of pregnancy—10,000 International Units (IU) or more per day—it may increase the risk of birth defects, particularly malformations of the head, face, heart, and nervous system (Rothman et al., 1995). The recommended daily allowance of vitamin A is 2,700 IU. Most multivitamin pills contain 4,000 to 5,000 units, but some brands contain as much as 10,000; pure vitamin A capsules can contain as much as 25,000 units. Pregnant women should watch their intake of this vitamin.

One of the most widely used drugs, aspirin, is teratogenic in animals when given in high doses. People rarely take high enough doses to produce such effects directly, but research has revealed that aspirin in moderate amounts can have negative effects on the human fetus if it is ingested along with benzoic acid, a chemical widely used as a preservative in such foods as ketchup. This combination, especially in the first trimester, seems to increase the risk of physical malformations in the embryo/fetus.

In most industrialized countries, adults are exposed to fairly high dosages of lead, although the introduction of unleaded gasoline has helped to lower dosages significantly. So did the outlawing of lead-based paint in 1978 in the United States, although any house built before 1978 is quite likely to have at least some lead-based paint. Children may be exposed to lead prenatally, through the mother's blood, or postnatally, through contact with lead paint (from breathing paint dust in the air in an older house or from chewing on a painted windowsill), with car exhaust, or with factory emissions that contain high levels of lead.

Because most children who are exposed to high levels of lead prenatally are also exposed to high levels postnatally, it is extremely difficult to sort out the unique impact of prenatal lead. The best information comes from several excellent longitudinal studies following children from birth through early childhood (e.g., Baghurst et al., 1992, 1995; Dietrich, Berger, Succop, Hammond, & Bornschein, 1993). The researchers found a consistent but small relationship between elevated blood lead levels in newborns and lower IQ scores later in childhood. Exposure to high levels of lead during childhood appears to have a further, even larger, negative effect, not only on IQ scores but also on distractibility and (perhaps) aggressiveness (Needleman, Riess, Tobin, Biesecker, & Greenhouse, 1996). Negative effects are evident even at quite low levels—levels previously classified as "safe" by U.S. guidelines and found in children who live in houses without lead-based paint. For example, a level of 20 micrograms per deciliter was thought to be acceptable, but research showed that children with this level of lead have IQ scores that average 2.6 points lower than do those with only 10 micrograms per deciliter of blood lead (Schwartz, 1994). Because of such evidence, the Centers for Disease Control changed its guidelines, listing 10 micrograms as the desirable upper limit.

By current estimates, 3–6% of U.S. infants and young children have blood lead levels that exceed this amount (CDC, 1997), the greatest percentage of them black or Hispanic children living in inner-city neighborhoods (Berney, 1996). Lead exposure may thus be one of the many small factors contributing to the lower average IQ scores of children living in poverty.

Diet Both the general adequacy of a pregnant woman's diet, measured in terms of calories, and the presence of certain key nutrients are critical to prenatal development. At a minimum, a mother needs sufficient overall calories and protein to prevent malnutrition. When a woman experiences severe malnutrition during pregnancy, particularly during the final 3 months, she faces a greatly increased risk of stillbirth, low infant birth weight, or infant death during the first year of life (Stein, Susser, Saenger, & Morolla, 1975). Autopsies show that infants born to malnourished mothers have smaller brains, with fewer and smaller brain cells than normal (Georgieff, 1994).

The subtle effects of *subnutrition*, or a diet that is barely adequate and lacking in some essential nutrients, is illustrated nicely in the results of a small study by Philip Zeskind and Craig Ramey (1981). They looked at the outcomes for a small group of 10 infants, all born to poverty-level mothers and all extremely thin at birth—usually a sign of prenatal malnutrition. Five of these babies happened to have been assigned randomly to a special enriched day-care program beginning when they were 3 months old. The other five malnourished babies received nutritional supplements but were reared at home in much less stimulating circumstances. Other children in the day-care center had been of normal weight at birth, as were other home-reared children included in the study. The results support Horowitz's vulnerability/resilience model (discussed in Chapter 1). Malnourished infants did well in the stimulating environment of the day-

TABLE 2.4	Some Important Teratogens
Teratogen	**Possible Effects on Fetus**
Maternal Diseases	
Cancer	Fetal or placental tumor
Toxoplasmosis	Brain swelling, spinal abnormalities
Chicken pox	Scars, eye damage
Parvovirus	Anemia
Hepatitis B	Hepatitis
Chlamydia	Conjunctivitis, pneumonia
Tuberculosis	Pneumonia or tuberculosis
Drugs	
Inhalents	FAS-like syndrome, premature labor
Accutane/vitamin A	Facial, ear, heart deformities
Streptomycin	Deafness
Penicillin	Skin disorders
Tetracycline	Tooth deformities
Diet pills	Low birth weight

Source: Amato, 1998; Kliegman, 1998.

care center but extremely poorly in a less supportive environment (average IQ of 96.4 versus 70.6 at 3 years of age). Well-nourished infants also did better in the day-care environment than at home, but the difference was not nearly so large (average IQ of 98.1 versus 87.7 at 3 years of age). Thus, malnutrition appeared to create a "vulnerability" that could be overcome only by an enriched environment.

A vital specific nutrient, whose importance during pregnancy has only recently become clear, is folic acid, a B vitamin found primarily in liver, beans, leafy green vegetables, broccoli, orange juice, fortified breakfast cereals, and grain products, especially wheat germ. Inadequate amounts of this nutrient have been clearly linked to the risk of neural tube defects such as spina bifida, a deformity in which the lower part of the spine does not close (e.g., Butterworth & Bendich, 1996). Many (but not all) such children are retarded; most have some lower-body paralysis. Because the neural tube develops primarily during the very earliest weeks of pregnancy, before a woman may even know she is pregnant, it is important for women who plan a pregnancy to ingest at least the minimum level of folic acid: 400 micrograms daily. Most women, however, do not receive enough folic acid from ordinary food sources or multivitamin pills to reach this minimum level (Daly et al., 1997). To help raise the normal intake above the desired level, new regulations by the Food and Drug Administration in the United States now require that 140 micrograms of folic acid be added to each 100 grams of enriched flour, thus greatly increasing the likelihood that the majority of women will receive sufficient quantities of folic acid.

A woman's caloric needs go up 10–20% during pregnancy in order to support the needed weight gain. As recently as the late 1960s in the United States, physicians routinely advised pregnant women to limit their weight gain to 15 or 20 pounds; greater gains were thought to increase the risk of labor abnormalities and other problems. Beginning in the 1970s, however, new data accumulated showing that weight gains in that low range were associated with increased risk of bearing a low-birth-weight infant and with neurological impairment in the infant (e.g., Carmichael & Abrams, 1997; Hickey, Cliver, McNeal, Hoffman, & Goldenberg, 1996; Zhou & Olsen, 1997). Such information led to significant increases in the recommended weight gain.

Unfortunately, the very women who are otherwise at highest risk for various kinds of problems are also most likely to gain too little weight: those who are lightweight for their height before pregnancy, women older than 35, those with low education, and African American women, for whom higher levels of weight gain during pregnancy seem optimal (Abrams, 1994; CDC, 1992).

There are also risks associated with gaining too much. In particular, women who gain too much weight are more likely to have a cesarean section delivery (Abrams, 1994; Brost et al., 1997); they are also prone to postpartum obesity, which carries a whole set of health risks, including heart disease and diabetes (Johnson & Yancey, 1996). Gains within the recommended ranges appear optimal, although there is wide variability from one woman to the next.

Finally, women who are obese before they become pregnant have some additional risks, regardless of the amount of weight they gain. Such women are about twice as likely to have infants with neural tube defects, regardless of their intake of folic acid (Shaw, Owens, Vondra, Keenan, & Winslow, 1996; Werler, Louik, Shapiro, & Mitchell, 1996)—a finding that argues in favor of weight loss before pregnancy for women who are classed as obese.

The Mother's Age
One of the particularly intriguing trends in modern family life in the United States and many other industrialized countries is the increasing likelihood that women will postpone their first pregnancy into their late 20s or early 30s. In 1970, the average age at which a woman delivered her first child was 21.4 years. By contrast, in 2002, the average age of first-time mothers was 25.1 (National Center for Health Statistics [NCHS], 2003). Of course, women have many reasons for delaying childbearing, chief among them families' increased need for second incomes and the

desire of many young women to complete job training and early career steps before bearing children. Like all important life decisions, such choices have pros and cons. What is relevant to our discussion here is the impact of maternal age on the mother's experience and on the developing fetus.

Current research suggests that the optimal time for childbearing is in a woman's early 20s. Mothers over 30 (particularly those over 35) are at increased risk for several kinds of problems, including miscarriage, stillbirth, complications of pregnancy such as high blood pressure or bleeding, cesarean section delivery, and death during pregnancy or delivery (Berkowitz, Skovron, Lapinski, & Berkowitz, 1990; Hoyert, 1996; McFalls, 1990; Peipert & Bracken, 1993).

Infants born to older mothers also appear to have higher risk of some kinds of problems. In particular, a number of large studies in several industrialized countries show that the risk of fetal death from any of a variety of causes is higher in mothers 35 and older, even when the mothers in every age group have received good prenatal care (Cnattingius, Berendes, & Forman, 1993; Fretts, Schmittdiel, McLean, Usher, & Goldman, 1995). Other than the well-established risk of Down syndrome, children born to older mothers do not seem to be at higher risk for congenital anomalies, but delayed childbearing clearly does continue to carry some added risk for both mother and child, despite improvements in prenatal and neonatal care.

Risks for mother and child are also higher at the other end of the age continuum, among very young mothers. Because teenaged mothers are also more likely to be poor and less likely to receive adequate prenatal care, it has been difficult to sort out the causal factors. An unusually well-designed study, however, makes the link quite clear.

Alison Fraser and her colleagues (1995) studied 135,088 white girls and women, aged 13 to 24, who gave birth in the state of Utah between 1970 and 1990. This is an unusual sample for studies on this subject: Almost two-thirds of the teenaged mothers in this group were married, and most had adequate prenatal care; 95% remained in school. These special conditions enabled Fraser to disentangle the effects of ethnicity, poverty, marital status, and the mother's age—all of which are normally confounded in studies of teenage childbearing. Overall, Fraser found higher rates of adverse pregnancy outcomes among mothers age 17 and younger than among the mothers age 20 and up. The rate of preterm births was twice as high; the incidence of low birth weight was almost twice as high. And these differences were found even among teenaged mothers who were married, in school, and had adequate prenatal care. Outcomes were riskier still among teenaged mothers who lacked adequate prenatal care, but good care alone did not eliminate the heightened risk of problems linked to teen births. Just why such a heightened risk should exist for teen mothers is not entirely clear. The most likely possibility is that there is some negative biological consequence of pregnancy in a girl whose own growth is not complete.

Stress and Emotional State The idea that emotional or physical stresses are linked to poor pregnancy outcomes is firmly established in folklore, but "its foundation in science is much less secure" (DiPietro, 2004; Grimes, 1996). Results from studies in animals are clear: Exposure of the pregnant female to stressors such as heat, light, noise, shock, or crowding significantly increases the risk of low-birth-weight offspring as well as later problems in the offspring (Schneider, 1992). Studies in humans are harder to interpret because they necessarily involve quasi-experimental designs rather than random assignment of participants. Women who experience high levels of stress are quite likely to be different in other ways from those who do not, so it is harder to uncover clear causal connections. Nonetheless, a number of careful studies do show that stressful life events, emotional distress, and physical stress are all linked to slight increases in problems of pregnancy, such as low birth weight, heightened maternal blood pressure, and certain physical problems in the infants, such as cleft palate or respiratory problems (e.g., Hedegaard, Henriksen, Secher, Hatch, & Sabroe, 1996; Henriksen, Hedegaard, Secher, & Wilcox, 1995; Sandman et al., 1997). Moreover, studies involving experimentally induced stressors (e.g., requiring a pregnant woman to take some kind of cognitive test) show that they seem to cause short-term changes in fetal activity, heart rate, and other responses (DiPietro, Costigan, & Gurewitsch, 2003). Whether such changes are sufficient to affect development in any meaningful way is as yet unknown.

Similarly, maternal emotions are associated with measures of fetal response such as activity level. Researcher Janet DiPietro and her colleagues have found that the fetuses of women who have positive emotions toward their condition are less active than those of mothers who feel more negatively about their pregnancies (DiPietro, Hilton, Hawkins, Costigan, & Pressman, 2002). The long-term effects of this association, if there are any, have been difficult to identify. However, researchers have found that severe and prolonged emotional distress during pregnancy can have long-term associations with children's development. Likewise, researchers have found that children of mothers who reported high levels of psychological distress during pregnancy are more emotionally negative at both 6 months and 5 years of age than those of nondistressed mothers (Martin, Noyes, Wisenbaker, & Huttunen, 1999). Other research has shown that prenatal depression predicts children's social skills and behavior problems in the preschool years (Carter, Garrity-Rokous, Chazan-Cohen, Little, & Briggs-Gowan, 2001; Oates, 1998). But critics of such studies claim that the real connection is a matter of maternal genes and/or parenting style; emotionally negative and depressed mothers may use ineffective parenting strategies or simply be more likely, for genetic reasons, to have children who are less emotionally positive than their peers.

One fairly consistent finding, however, is that the fetuses of severely distressed mothers tend to grow more slowly than others (Linnet et al., 2003; Paarlberg, Vingerhoets, Passchier, Dekker, & van Geign, 1995; Weinstock, 1999). Developmentalists hypothesize that this effect may result directly from emotion-related hormones or it may be an indirect effect of the mother's emotional state. A stressed or depressed mother may eat less, or her weakened immune system may limit her ability to fight off viruses and bacteria, either of which may retard fetal growth. Consequently, many psychologists suggest that providing stressed and/or depressed pregnant women with social support and counseling may lead to improvements in both maternal and fetal health (Brockington, 1996). Moreover, many studies suggest that antidepressant drugs do not harm the fetus and may be very helpful for pregnant women who are severely depressed (Rybakowski, 2001).

Poverty   The basic sequence of fetal development is clearly no different for children born to poor mothers than for children born to middle-class mothers, but many of the problems that can negatively affect prenatal development are more common among the poor. For example, in the United States, mothers who have not graduated from high school are about twice as likely as mothers with a college education to have a low-birth-weight infant or a stillborn infant. Poor women are also likely to have their first pregnancy earlier and to have more pregnancies overall, and they are less likely to be immunized against such diseases as rubella. They are also less likely to seek prenatal care, and if they do, they seek it much later in their pregnancies. A significant portion of this difference could be overcome in the United States: Devoting the resources needed to provide good, universal prenatal care could significantly reduce not only the rate of infant death but also the rate of physical abnormalities and perhaps even mental retardation. Equal access to care is not the only answer. In the Scandinavian countries, for example, in which such care is universally available, social class differences in low-birth-weight deliveries and in infant mortality rates remain (Bakketeig, Cnattingius, Knudsen, 1993).

Before going on . . .

■ How do disorders caused by recessive and dominant genes differ?

■ What are the effects of trisomy 21 and the various sex chromosome anomalies?

■ How do maternal diseases affect the developing fetus?

■ What are the potential effects of tobacco, alcohol, and other drugs on prenatal development?

■ Describe the influence of environmental toxins, vitamins, diet, age, and stress on fetal development.

Summary

Conception and Genetics

- At conception, 23 chromosomes from the sperm join with 23 from the ovum to make up the set of 46 that will be reproduced in each cell of the new baby's body. Each chromosome consists of a long string of deoxyribonucleic acid (DNA) made up of segments called genes. The baby's sex is determined by the 23rd pair of chromosomes, a pattern of XX for a girl and XY for a boy.
- Geneticists distinguish between the genotype, which is the pattern of inherited characteristics, and the phenotype, which is the result of the interaction of genotype and environment. Genes are transmitted from parent to child according to complex patterns of inheritance that include dominant/recessive, polygenic, multifactorial, and sex-linked.

Development from Conception to Birth

- During the first days after conception, called the germinal stage of development, the zygote (the initial cell formed by egg and sperm) divides, travels down the fallopian tube, and is implanted in the wall of the uterus. The second stage, the period of the embryo, which lasts until 8 weeks after fertilization, includes the development of the various structures that support fetal development, such as the placenta, as well as primitive forms of all organ systems. The final 30 weeks of gestation, called the fetal period, are devoted primarily to enlargement and refinements in all the organ systems.
- During the embryonic period, the XY embryo secretes the hormone testosterone, which stimulates the growth of male genitalia and shifts the brain into a "male" pattern. Boys are more active, have more slowly developing skeletons, are bigger at birth, and are more vulnerable to most forms of prenatal stress.
- The fetus is responsive to stimuli and appears to learn in the womb. Temperamental differences in the womb (such as activity level) persist into infancy and childhood, and some aspects of the prenatal sensory environment may be important to future development.

Problems in Prenatal Development

- Genes for a variety of disorders can begin to cause problems soon after conception.
- Abnormal numbers of chromosomes or chromosomal damage also cause a number of serious disorders, including Down syndrome.
- Some diseases contracted by the mother, including rubella, AIDS, sexually transmitted diseases, genital herpes, and CMV, may cause abnormalities or disease in the child.
- Drugs such as alcohol and nicotine appear to have harmful effects on the developing fetus; drug effects depend on the timing of exposure and the dosage.
- If a mother suffers from poor nutrition, she faces an increased risk of stillbirth, low birth weight, and infant death during the first year of life. Older mothers and very young mothers also run increased risks, as do their infants. Long-term, severe depression or chronic physical illness in the mother may also increase the risk of complications during pregnancy or difficulties in the infant.

Key Terms

amnion (p. 41)
axon (p. 44)
blastocyst (p. 41)
chorion (p. 41)
chromosomes (p. 34)
dendrites (p. 44)
deoxyribonucleic acid (DNA) (p. 35)
dominant/recessive pattern of inheritance (p. 39)
Down syndrome (trisomy 21) (p. 49)
embryo (p. 41)
embryonic stage (p. 41)
fallopian tube (p. 34)
fetal alcohol syndrome (FAS) (p. 54)

fetal stage (p. 42)
fetus (p. 42)
fraternal (dizygotic) twins (p. 40)
gametes (p. 34)
genes (p. 35)
genotype (p. 37)
germinal stage (p. 41)
glial cells (p. 44)
heterozygous (p. 37)
homozygous (p. 37)
identical (monozygotic) twins (p. 40)
multifactorial pattern of inheritance (p. 40)

neurons (p. 44)
neurotransmitters (p. 44)
ovum (p. 34)
phenotype (p. 39)
placenta (p. 41)
polygenic pattern of inheritance (p. 39)
sperm (p. 34)
synapse (p. 44)
teratogens (p. 47)
umbilical cord (p. 41)
uterus (p. 34)
zygote (p. 34)

See for Yourself

Inheritance Diagram

Look over Table 2.1 and find a dominant or recessive trait that you have. Make a diagram like the one in Figure 2.2 to demonstrate how the trait was passed on to you. Include as many family members as possible in your diagram, and fill in as much of the phenotype and genotype information as you can for your other family members.

Beliefs about Pregnancy

In every culture, there are traditional beliefs about pregnancy, many of which are myths. For example, you may have heard that labor is more likely to begin during a full moon or that boys "carry high" but girls "carry low." Other once-popular ideas include the notion that eating spicy foods or having sex will bring on premature labor. Survey your classmates, friends, and relatives to find out what kinds of things they have heard about pregnancy. If you have access to people from different cultures, analyze the similarities and differences in these beliefs across groups.

Birth and Early Infancy

CHAPTER

3

What do you think concerns women most about giving birth to a child?

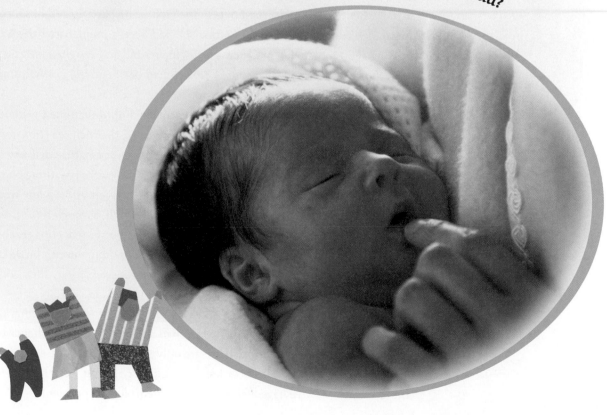

Surveys show that many women worry about the physical pain of labor and delivery, while others are concerned about the financial ramifications of having a baby (Geiss-buehler & Eberhard, 2002). However, anxieties about the health of the newborn outweigh most women's other concerns about pregnancy and birth.

Imagine, then, the response of 23-year-old Mahajabeen Shaik when doctors at Loyola University in Chicago told her that the twin daughters she had been carrying for only 26 weeks would have to be delivered immediately by cesarean section because her blood pressure had become dangerously high (Associated Press, 2005). Ultrasound tests showed that one of the twins was larger than the other. However, Mahajabeen's doctors had only a rough idea about how large that size difference was.

When the twins were born on September 19, 2004, the larger of the two, Hiba, weighed a robust 20 ounces, small but sufficient for her gestational age of 26 weeks. But the other twin, Rumaisa, weighed just 8.6 ounces, a birth weight that gave her the distinction of being the smallest surviving infant ever born. Remarkably, Loyola's experts in neonatal medicine told Mahajabeen and her husband, Mohammed Rahman, that the odds favored a normal infancy and childhood for both girls.

When the couple expressed concerns about Rumaisa's small size, doctors told them the story of one of the "graduates" of Loyola's neonatal intensive care unit (NICU), Madeline Mann, who weighed just 9.9 ounces when she was born in 1989. Madeline's case has been followed carefully by experts in neonatal medicine (Muraskas & Hasson, 2004). The first four months of her life were spent in Loyola's NICU. In the years following her discharge from the hospital, Madeline blossomed into an energetic preschooler. As she progressed through the school years, it became clear that not only was she free from any serious disabilities, but she was quite gifted in a variety of areas. Madeline excelled in school, getting top scores on standardized achievement tests, and learned to play the violin. She participated in sports as well. By her mid-teens, the only indication that she had been a premature baby was her small size. At age 14, Madeline was just 4 feet 7 inches tall and weighed only 60 pounds. Still, throughout her life, her rate of growth had been entirely normal, and she had been free of any major health problems.

Encouraged by Madeline's story, Mahajabeen and Mohammed watched hopefully as their twins grew stronger each day. Tests revealed that neither Hiba nor Rumaisa had suffered any injury to the brain as a result of the premature delivery. At first the girls were on ventilators, but within a few weeks both were breathing on their own and required only small amounts of supplemental oxygen. After a few weeks of intravenous feeding, the girls were able to be fed breast milk through a tube. By the time they reached 3 months of age, both were able to be bottle-fed. Hiba reached the critical weight of 5.5 pounds a couple of weeks before her four-month birthday and was able to go home. Her sister, who had become quite a celebrity by then, joined her family at home a few days before she turned 5 months old.

The case of Rumaisa Rahman, like that of Madeline Mann, is remarkable because most infants who are born weighing less than a pound have little chance of survival. In the entire medical literature, there are only 58 documented cases of surviving newborns who weighed 13 ounces or less (Muraskas & Hasson, 2004). Further, most of those who do survive have lifelong health or neurological problems.

Why do some tiny newborns defy the odds? Clearly, the health of the infant at birth is one critical variable. But even the healthiest preterm babies require care that can be obtained only in high-tech NICUs like the one at Loyola. Technology, though, is only part of the story. As most grateful parents recognize, it is the skilled care, emotional support, and individual attention that their babies receive from the dedicated men and women who work in such facilities that make the difference for infants like Rumaisa and Madeline.

Fortunately, most infants do not require intensive care. In most cases, too, expectant mothers do not deliver under emergency circumstances and can choose the setting in which their babies will be born. We begin our discussion of birth and early infancy with an overview of the array of birth choices available today.

 # Birth

For parents, birth is an experience that combines great physical stress with a wide variety of emotions: the joy of seeing the baby for the first time, curiosity about what kind of individual she will be, worry about possible physical problems, anxiety about the ability to parent effectively, and so on. For the child, of course, birth marks her entrance into the family and community.

BIRTH CHOICES

In the industrialized world, parents must make a number of choices in advance of the delivery. Parents may worry about whether they are making the best choices both for themselves and for the baby.

Drugs during Labor and Delivery   Surveys indicate that about 40% of expectant mothers in the United States fear being in pain during childbirth (Geissbuehler & Eberhard, 2002). Thus, one key decision about the birth process concerns the use of pain-relieving drugs during delivery. Three types of drugs are commonly used: (1) *Analgesics* (such as the common drug Demerol) are given during early labor to reduce pain. All the analgesics in this group are members of the opium family of drugs. (2) *Sedatives* or *tranquilizers* (such as Nembutol, Valium, or Thorazine) may also be given during early labor to reduce anxiety. (3) *Anesthesia* is given during labor and/or delivery to block pain either totally (general anesthesia) or in portions of the body (local anesthesia). Of these three, anesthesia is least often used in the United States, although the use of one form of local anesthesia, the *epidural block*, has been increasing.

Studying the causal links between such drug use and the baby's later behavior or development has proved to be monumentally difficult. Controlled experiments are obviously not possible, since women cannot be randomly assigned to specific drug regimens. In the real world, drugs are also given in myriad different combinations. However, there have been many studies of the immediate effects of obstetric anesthesia on newborns.

One important finding is that nearly all drugs given during labor pass through the placenta and enter the fetal bloodstream. Because the newborn lacks the enzymes necessary to break down such drugs quickly, the effect of any drug lasts longer in the baby than it does in the mother. Not surprisingly, then, drugged infants may show signs of being under the influence of such drugs (Sola, Rogido, & Partridge, 2002). For example, they may have slower or faster than normal heartbeats, depending on which drugs

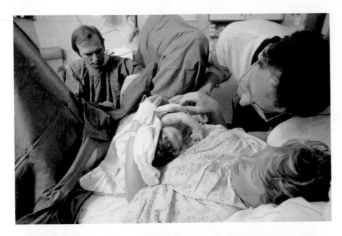

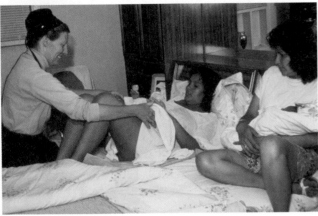

In the United States, the most common delivery setting is in a hospital, assisted by a physician. In other industrialized societies, home deliveries assisted by a midwife are quite common.

their mothers were given. In rare cases, infants of anesthetized mothers experience seizures.

Because of these risks, many women choose to avoid drugs altogether. The general term *natural childbirth* is commonly used to refer to this particular choice. This approach is also often called the *Lamaze method*, after the physician who popularized the notion of natural childbirth and devised a variety of pain management techniques. In natural childbirth, women rely on psychological and behavioral methods of pain management rather than on pain-relieving drugs.

Natural childbirth involves several components. First, a woman selects someone, usually the baby's father, to serve as a labor coach. *Prepared childbirth classes* psychologically prepare the woman and her labor coach for the experience of labor and delivery. For example, they learn to use the term *contraction* instead of *pain*. Further, believing that her baby will benefit from natural childbirth provides the woman with the motivation she needs to endure labor without the aid of pain-relieving medication. Finally, relaxation and breathing techniques provide her with behavioral responses that serve to replace the negative emotions that typically result from the physical discomfort of contractions. Aided by her coach, the woman focuses attention on her breathing rather than on the pain.

The Location of Birth   Another choice parents must make is where the baby is to be born. In the United States, there are typically four alternatives: (1) a traditional hospital maternity unit; (2) a hospital-based birth center or a birthing room located within a hospital, which provides a more homelike setting, with both labor and delivery completed in the same room and family members often present throughout; (3) a freestanding birth center, like a hospital birth center except not located in a hospital, with delivery typically attended by a midwife rather than (or in addition to) a physician; and (4) at home.

At the turn of the century, only about 5% of babies in the United States were born in hospitals; today, the figure is 99% (U.S. Bureau of the Census, 1997). The remaining 1% are born at home or in freestanding birth centers. Limited research in Canada and the United States (e.g., Janssen, Holt, & Myers, 1994; Johnson & Daviss, 2005) indicates that such nonhospital deliveries, if planned and attended by a midwife or equivalent professional, are no riskier than deliveries in hospitals.

The Presence of Fathers at Delivery   The father's presence during labor and delivery has become the norm in the United States, so much so, in fact, that it has become difficult to study this variable. Decades ago, when hospital policies varied greatly with regard to the presence of fathers in the delivery room, it was possible to compare father-present to father-absent deliveries. Such studies found that when fathers were present, laboring women experienced less pain, requested less medication, delivered sooner, and experienced fewer complications than when fathers were absent (Henneborn & Cogan, 1975). However, contrary to the expectations of some, researchers found that being present at the birth of a child had little effect on fathers' emotional bonds with infants (Palkovitz, 1985). These findings suggest that the practice of encouraging fathers to be present in North American labor and delivery rooms is part of a larger cultural trend toward increased father involvement during children's early years rather than the result of research on bonding.

THE PROCESS OF BIRTH

Labor typically progresses through three stages. Occasionally, complications occur, but most of these are managed by health care providers in ways that ensure the health of both mother and baby. Once the child is born, her health is assessed, and the family begins getting to know its newest member.

The Stages of Labor Stage 1 covers the period during which two important processes occur: **dilation** and **effacement**. The cervix (the opening at the bottom of the uterus) must open up like the lens of a camera (dilation) and flatten out (effacement). At the time of actual delivery of the infant, the cervix must normally be dilated to about 10 centimeters (about 4 inches). This part of labor has been likened to what happens when you put on a sweater with a neck that is too tight. You have to pull and stretch the neck of the sweater with your head in order to get it on. Eventually, you stretch the neck wide enough so that the widest part of your head can pass through. A good deal of the effacement may actually occur in the last weeks of the pregnancy, as may some dilation. It is not uncommon for women to be 80% effaced and 1 to 3 centimeters dilated when they begin labor. The contractions of the first stage of labor, which are at first widely spaced and later more frequent and rhythmical, serve to complete both processes.

Customarily, stage 1 is itself divided into phases. In the early (or *latent*) phase, contractions are relatively far apart and are typically not very uncomfortable. In the *active* phase, which begins when the cervix is 3 to 4 centimeters dilated and continues until dilation has reached 8 centimeters, contractions are closer together and more intense. The last 2 centimeters of dilation are achieved during a period usually called the *transition* phase. It is this period, when contractions are closely spaced and strong, that women typically find the most painful.

Fortunately, transition is relatively brief, especially in second or later pregnancies. Stage 1 lasts from 8 to 12 hours for a first birth and about 7 hours for a woman having a second or later child (Moore & Persaud, 1993). Figure 3.1 shows the duration of the several subphases, although neither the figure nor the average numbers convey the wide individual variability that exists. Among women delivering a first child, stage 1 labor may last as little as 3 hours or as long as 20 (Biswas & Craigo, 1994; Kilpatrick & Laros, 1989). The times are generally longer for women receiving anesthesia than for those delivering by natural childbirth.

At the end of the transition phase, the mother will normally have the urge to help the infant come out by "pushing." When the birth attendant (physician or midwife) is sure the cervix is fully dilated, she or he will encourage this pushing, and the second stage of labor—the actual delivery—begins. The baby's head moves past the stretched cervix, into the birth canal, and finally out of the mother's body. Most women find this part of labor markedly less distressing than the transition phase. The average length of

This couple, like so many today, is taking a childbirth class together. Having the father present at the delivery as coach seems to reduce the mother's pain and even shorten the length of labor.

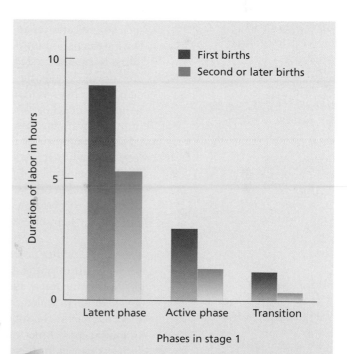

FIGURE 3.1

Typical pattern of timing of the phases of stage 1 of labor for first births and for subsequent births. The relatively long latent phase shown here counts from 0 centimeters dilated, which increases the total hours somewhat. The total length of stage 1 ranges from 8 hours to 12 hours for a first birth and from 6 hours to about 8 hours for later births.
(*Source*: Based on Biswas & Craigo, 1994, from Figures 10–16, p. 216, and 10–17, p. 217.)

stage 2 is about 50 minutes for first infants and 20 minutes for later deliveries (Moore & Persaud, 1993). It rarely takes longer than 2 hours.

Most infants are delivered head first, facing down toward the mother's spine. Three to four percent, however, are oriented differently, either feet first or bottom first (called *breech* presentations) (Brown, Karrison, & Cibils, 1994). Several decades ago, most breech deliveries were accomplished with the aid of medical instruments such as forceps; today, nearly four-fifths of breech presentations are delivered by cesarean section—a procedure discussed more fully in the next section. Stage 3, typically quite brief, is the delivery of the placenta (also called the *afterbirth*) and other material from the uterus. You can see all these steps presented in Figure 3.2.

Complications Many complications are possible during birth. Researchers have found that life-threatening complications during birth (e.g., collapse of the umbilical cord) are associated with poor developmental outcomes, such as excessive aggressiveness, later in childhood and adolescence (Arseneault, Tremblay, Boulerice, & Saucier, 2002). It's important to note, however, that the association between birth complications and later developmental outcomes may not be a causal one. Instead, factors such as poverty and poor maternal health are probably linked to increased risk of both birth complications and poor developmental outcomes.

Still, birth complications that interfere with a child's vital functions can lead to brain damage and, as a result, cause a variety of later developmental problems. One such complication is an insufficiency of oxygen for the infant, a state called **anoxia**. During the period immediately surrounding birth, anoxia may occur because the umbilical circulation system fails to continue supplying blood oxygen until the baby breathes or because the umbilical cord has been squeezed in some way during labor or delivery. Perhaps as many as 20% of newborns experience some degree of anoxia. Long-term effects of anoxia have been hard to pin down. Prolonged anoxia is often (but not invariably) associated with such major consequences as cerebral palsy or mental retardation. Briefer periods of oxygen deprivation appear to have little long-term effect, although that is still a tentative conclusion.

Infants may also dislocate their shoulders or hips during birth. Some experience fractures, and in others, nerves that control facial muscles are compressed, causing temporary paralysis on one side of the face. Such complications are usually not serious and resolve themselves with little or no treatment.

Cesarean Deliveries Sometimes it is necessary to deliver a baby surgically through incisions made in the abdominal and uterine walls. There are several situations that justify the use of this operation, called a **cesarean section** (or **c-section**). A *breech presentation*, in which an infant's feet or bottom is delivered first, represents one of the most compelling reasons for a c-section because it is associated with collapse of the umbilical cord (American College of Obstetrics and Gynecology [ACOG], 2001). Other factors that call for the procedure include fetal distress during labor, labor that fails to progress in a reasonable amount of time, a fetus that is too large to be delivered vaginally, and maternal health conditions that may be aggravated by vaginal delivery (e.g., cardiovascular disease, spinal injury) or may be dangerous to a vaginally delivered fetus (e.g., herpes).

Many observers claim that the current rate of cesarean deliveries in the United States is too high. The National Center for Health Statistics (NCHS, 2003) reports that just over 26% of all deliveries in 2002 in the United States involved a cesarean section. Critics of the frequency with which c-sections occur say that many of these operations are unnecessary. Are their claims justified?

One factor behind current c-section statistics is that, as you learned earlier, more older women are having babies (Joseph et al., 2003). These women are more likely to conceive twins and other multiples. In such cases, surgical delivery almost always increases the odds in favor of the babies' postnatal health. Thus, the benefits of cesarean delivery outweigh its risks.

dilation A key process in the first stage of childbirth, during which the cervix widens sufficiently to allow the infant's head to pass into the birth canal. Full dilation is 10 centimeters.

effacement The flattening of the cervix, which, along with dilation, is a key process of the first stage of childbirth.

anoxia A shortage of oxygen. This is one of the potential risks at birth, and it can result in brain damage if it is prolonged.

cesarean section (c-section) Delivery of the child through an incision in the mother's abdomen.

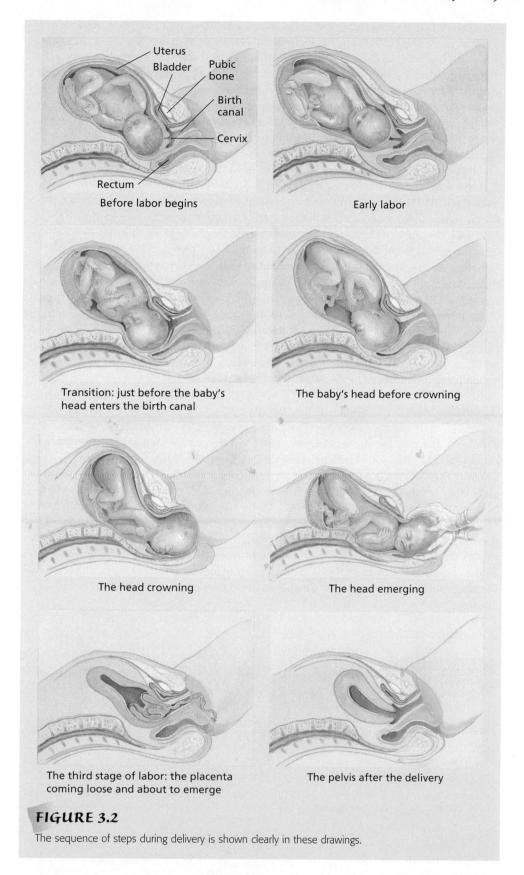

Uterus

Bladder   Pubic
           bone

                Birth
                canal

                Cervix

Rectum

Before labor begins

Early labor

Transition: just before the baby's
head enters the birth canal

The baby's head before crowning

The head crowning

The head emerging

The third stage of labor: the placenta
coming loose and about to emerge

The pelvis after the delivery

FIGURE 3.2

The sequence of steps during delivery is shown clearly in these drawings.

By contrast, a recent survey of hospital records found that nearly one-fourth of c-sections performed in 2002 in the United States were entirely elective (Hall, 2003). In these cases, women who had no medical problems, and who were carrying healthy fetuses, requested a surgical delivery, and their physicians complied. The ethics committee of the American College of Obstetrics and Gynecology (2004) has ruled that elective surgical deliveries are ethical as long as the practitioner is certain that, for the patients who request them, vaginal deliveries carry equal risk. Advocates of elective cesareans say that the surgery spares women from future problems associated with vaginal delivery, such as uterine prolapse and urinary incontinence.

But should cesarean delivery be thought of as just another birth option? Critics say that the possible benefits of elective cesareans do not justify exposing women to their risks (Hall, 2003). They claim that many obstetric patients do not realize that a c-section is major surgery and carries the same risks as other abdominal operations. These risks include allergic reactions to anesthetics, infection, accidental injuries to other organs (as well as to the fetus), and excessive blood loss. Consequently, these critics believe that elective cesarean delivery represents a poorly informed choice on the part of the patient, and an irresponsible practice on the part of the physician. Moreover, some researchers have begun to test the hypothesis that during labor the mother's body produces hormones that cross the placenta prior to the baby's birth and influence immune system functioning in the newborn (Malamitsi-Puchner et al., 2005). If future research provides support for this hypothesis, critics may have yet another reason, a very important one, to argue that cesarean deliveries be avoided except in situations in which vaginal delivery is dangerous to the baby or to the mother.

Assessing the Newborn   It has become customary in most hospitals to evaluate an infant's status immediately after birth, and then again 5 minutes later, to detect any problems that may require special care. The most frequently used assessment system is the *Apgar score*, developed by a physician, Virginia Apgar (1953). The newborn is given a score of 0, 1, or 2 on each of the five criteria listed in Table 3.1. A maximum score of 10 is fairly unusual immediately after birth, because most infants are still somewhat blue in the fingers and toes at that stage. At the 5-minute assessment, however, 85–90% of infants are scored as 9 or 10, meaning that they are getting off to a good start. Any score of 7 or better indicates that the baby is in no danger. A score of 4, 5, or 6 usually means that the baby needs help establishing normal breathing patterns; a score of 3 or below indicates a baby in critical condition, requiring active intervention, although babies with such low Apgar scores can and often do survive (Casey, McIntire, & Leveno, 2001).

TABLE 3.1	Evaluation Method for Apgar Score		
Aspect of Infant Observed	**Score Assigned**		
	0	**1**	**2**
Heart rate	Absent	<100/min.	>100/min.
Respiratory rate	No breathing	Weak cry and shallow breathing	Good strong cry and regular breathing
Muscle tone	Flaccid	Some flexion of extremities	Well flexed
Response to stimulation of feet	None	Some motion	Cry
Color	Blue; pale	Body pink, extremities blue	Completely pink

Source: Francis et al., 1987, pp. 731–732.

Another test used to assess newborns, widely used by researchers, is the Brazelton Neonatal Behavioral Assessment Scale (Brazelton, 1984). In this test, a skilled examiner checks the neonate's responses to a variety of stimuli; his reflexes, muscle tone, alertness, and cuddliness; and his ability to quiet or soothe himself after being upset. Scores on this test can be helpful in identifying children who may have significant neurological problems. More interestingly, several investigators (e.g., Francis, Self, & Horowitz, 1987) have found that teaching parents how to administer this test to their own infants turns out to have beneficial effects on the parent-infant interaction, apparently because it heightens the parent's awareness of all the subtle cues the baby provides.

The First Greeting Many parents experience intense joy as they greet the infant for the first time, accompanied often by laughter, exclamations of delight at the baby's features, and first tentative and tender touching. Here are one mother's reactions to seeing her new daughter:

> She's big, isn't she? What do you reckon? (Doctor makes a comment.) Oh look, she's got hair. It's a girl—you're supposed to be all little. Gosh. Oh, she's lovely. Oh, she's opened her eyes (laughs). Oh lovely (kisses baby). (MacFarlane, 1977, pp. 64–65)

Most parents are intensely interested in having the baby look at them right away. They are delighted if the baby opens her eyes and will try to stimulate her to do so if she doesn't. The parents' initial tentative touches also seem to follow a pattern: The parent first touches the infant rather gingerly with the tip of a finger and then proceeds gradually to stroking with the full hand (MacFarlane, 1977). The tenderness seen in most of these early encounters is striking.

LOW BIRTH WEIGHT

The optimal weight range for infants—the weight that is associated with the lowest risk of later death or disability—is between about 3,000 and 5,000 grams (6.6 to 11 pounds) (Rees, Lederman, & Kiely, 1996). Several different labels are used to describe infants whose weight falls below this optimal range. All babies below 2,500 grams (5.5 pounds) are described with the most general term of **low birth weight (LBW)**. Those below 1,500 grams (3.3 pounds) are usually called **very low birth weight (VLBW)**, and those below 1,000 grams (2.2 pounds) are called **extremely low birth weight (ELBW)**. The incidence of low birth weight has declined in the United States in the past decade but is still high: About 7% of all newborns weigh below 2,500 grams (Guyer, MacDorman, Anderson, & Strobino, 1997; MacDorman & Atkinson, 1999; NCHS, 2003). About 19% of those small babies weighed less than 1,500 grams. Babies who weigh more than 1,500 grams and who receive good neonatal care have close to a 100% chance of survival. However, in the VLBW and ELBW groups, the more the infant weighs, the greater his chances of survival.

Causes of Low Birth Weight Low birth weight occurs for a variety of reasons, of which the most obvious and common is that the infant is born before the full 38 weeks of gestation. Any baby born before 38 weeks of gestation is labeled a **preterm infant**. Multiple births are especially likely to end in preterm delivery. In addition, mothers who suffer from chronic illnesses and those who develop a serious medical condition during pregnancy are more likely to deliver preterm infants (Kliegman, 1998). In most cases of preterm delivery, labor begins spontaneously. However, because of a condition in the fetus or in the mother, physicians sometimes elect to deliver babies prior to 38 weeks of gestation via c-section.

It is also possible for an infant to have completed the full 38-week gestational period but still weigh less than 2,500 grams or to weigh less than would be expected for the number of weeks of gestation completed, however long that may have been. Such

low birth weight (LBW) Term for any baby born with a weight below 2,500 grams (5.5 pounds), including both those born too early (preterm) and those who are small for date.

very low birth weight (VLBW) Term for any baby born with a weight below 1,500 grams (3.3 pounds).

extremely low birth weight (ELBW) Term for any baby born with a weight below 1,000 grams (2.2 pounds).

preterm infant An infant born before 38 weeks gestational age.

an infant is called a **small-for-date infant**. Infants in this group appear to have suffered from prenatal malnutrition, such as might occur with constriction of blood flow caused by the mother's smoking, or from other significant problems prenatally. Such infants generally have poorer prognoses than do equivalent-weight infants who weigh an appropriate amount for their gestational age, especially if the small-for-date infant is also preterm (Korkman, Liikanen, & Fellman, 1996; Ott, 1995).

Health Status of Low-Birth-Weight Infants

All low-birth-weight infants share some characteristics, including markedly lower levels of responsiveness at birth and in the early months of life. Those born more than 6 weeks before term also often suffer from **respiratory distress syndrome**. Their poorly developed lungs lack an important chemical, called a *surfactant*, that enables the air sacs to remain inflated; some of the sacs collapse, resulting in serious breathing difficulties (Sola, Rogido, & Partridge, 2002). Beginning in 1990, neonatologists began treating this problem by administering a synthetic or animal-derived version of surfactant, a therapy that has reduced the rate of death among very low-birth-weight infants by about 30% (Hamvas et al., 1996; Schwartz, Anastasia, Scanlon, & Kellogg, 1994).

Long-Term Consequences of Low Birth Weight

The great majority of infants who weigh more than 1,500 grams and who are not small for date catch up to their normal peers within the first few years of life. However, a small proportion of these infants, especially those with birth weights lower than 1,500 grams, lag behind their peers for many years. As a result, differences in the group averages of normal-weight and LBW infants on many developmental variables persist throughout childhood (Rickards, Kelly, Doyle, & Callanan, 2001; Taylor, Klein, Minich, & Hack, 2000).

You can get a better sense of both the type and the incidence of the problems LBW children experience from the data in Table 3.2, which lists the results of two studies, one from the United States and the other from Australia. Two points are worth making about the findings from follow-up studies like those shown in the table. First, some problems do not appear until school age, when the child is challenged by a new level of cognitive tasks. Many surviving ELBW and LBW children who appear to be developing normally at age 1 or 2 later show significant problems in school. More optimistically, even in the extremely low-birth-weight group, some children seem to be fine. So it is not the case that all LBW children are somewhat affected; rather, some LBW children are significantly affected while others develop normally.

small-for-date infant An infant who weighs less than is normal for the number of weeks of gestation completed.

respiratory distress syndrome A problem frequently found in infants born more than 6 weeks before term, in which the infant's lungs lack a chemical (surfactant) needed to keep air sacs inflated.

TABLE 3.2	Two Examples of Long-Term Outcomes for Extremely and Very Low-Birth-Weight Infants		
	Australian Study[a]	**U.S. Study**[b]	
	500–999 g	**<750 g**	**750–1500 g**
Number of babies followed	89	68	65
Age at testing	8 years	7 years	7 years
Percentage with severe problems of some type (IQ scores below 70, deaf, blind, cerebral-palsied, etc.)	21.3	37.5	17.5
Additional percentage with significant learning problem or IQ scores between 70 and 85	19.1	29.0	20.0

[a]Victorian Infant Collaborative Study Group, 1991. The study included all surviving children of 500–999 grams born in a single state (Victoria) in Australia between 1979 and 1980. A total of 351 infants were born in this weight range, so only a quarter survived. With today's medical techniques, survival rates might be higher.

[b]Heck et al., 1994. The study includes the 68 survivors of a group of 243 children born in an area in Ohio from 1982 to 1986 with birth weights below 750 grams, plus a comparison group born in the same period who weighed between 750 and 1500 grams at birth.

A longitudinal study of LBW infants begun in the mid-1940s suggests that the academic difficulties some of these children experience in the early school years appear to have cumulative effects. That is, because they lag behind peers in elementary school, some children who were LBW infants don't acquire the skills they need for secondary school and college. The researchers found that an increasing number of these children caught up with peers each year between birth and age 8. However, among those who were still behind at age 8, the academic differences between them and normal-birth-weight individuals persisted into middle adulthood (Richards, Hardy, Kuh, & Wadsworth, 2001).

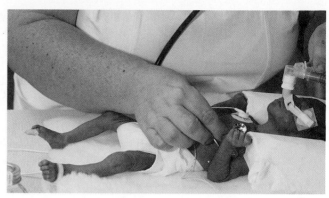

Low-birth-weight infants like this one are not only small; they are also more wrinkled and skinny, because the layer of fat under the skin has not fully developed. They are also more likely to have significant breathing difficulties, because their lungs lack surfactant.

Developmentalists who compare preterm infants to babies born at term often describe premature infants in terms of their "corrected age." For example, a 12-month-old who was born 2 months early would have a corrected age of 10 months. Studies examining preterm babies' neurological functioning, reflexes, and sensory processing have shown that the corrected age concept is valid for assessing the degree to which an individual preterm infant is growing and developing appropriately across the first 2 years of life (Fearon, Hains, Muir, & Kisilevsky, 2002; Sola, Rogido, & Partridge, 2002; Stolarova et al., 2003). Thus, the brain functions, reflexes, and sensory skills of most 12-month-olds who were born 2 months early are very similar to those of full-term 10-month-olds.

But when can parents and health care professionals expect to no longer have to rely on a child's corrected age to assess her development? As you might suspect, the answer to this question is complex. The good news for most parents is that researchers have found that two-thirds to three-fourths of premature infants are no longer distinguishable from peers of the same chronological age by the time they go to school (Bowen, Gibson, & Hand, 2002; Foulder-Hughes & Cooke, 2003a). This means that most parents of first-graders who were born prematurely can reasonably expect their children to display skills that are similar to those of classmates who were born on time. Despite this rosy prognosis, most developmentalists agree that parents and health care professionals should be cautious about basing developmental expectations for an individual child on studies that compare large groups of children to one another. In other words, the development of preterm children is best assessed on a case-by-case basis.

Several factors predict development in preterm infants for many years following birth. Two of these factors are weight and gestational age at birth. Both lower birth weight and earlier gestational age are associated with long-term developmental delays (Foulder-Hughes & Cooke, 2003b; Litt, Taylor, Klein, & Hacks, 2005; McGrath & Sullivan, 2002; Weindrich, Jennen-Steinmetz, Laucht, & Schmidt, 2003). The child's neonatal health is also important. Premature infants who experienced breathing problems, infectious illnesses, or brain injuries during the first few weeks of life are more likely to experience long-term developmental delays than premature infants who did not have such difficulties (McGrath & Sullivan, 2002; Ohgi, Takahashi, Nugent, Arisawa, & Akiyama, 2003). Gender matters as well; premature boys are more likely to display developmental delays than are premature girls (Aylward, 2002). Thus, parents and health care professionals must take these factors into account when assessing an individual child's development.

However, it is also important for parents to know that their responses to the child contribute to how rapidly she develops (White-Traut et al., 2002). For example, a relatively recent innovation in the care of preterm newborns is an intervention called "kangaroo care" in which parents are shown how to increase the amount of skin-to-skin contact infants engage in with them. An important part of the intervention involves allowing parents to hold these tiny newborns for very long periods of time. Researchers have found that babies who receive kangaroo care grow and develop more rapidly than preterm infants given conventional neonatal care (Feldman & Eidelman, 2003; Tessier et al., 2003). Advocates of massage therapy for preterm infants also cite the necessity for skin-to-skin contact. Their research shows that preterm newborns gain weight faster and are more responsive to their environment after a few sessions of massage therapy (Dieter, Field, Hernandez-Reif, Emory, & Redzepi, 2003).

As preterm infants get older, Susan Landry and her colleagues have found, those whose mothers are good at identifying and shaping their attention behaviors develop more rapidly than those whose mothers are less so (Dieterich, Hebert, Landry, Swank, & Smith, 2004; Landry, Smith, Miller-Loncar, & Swank, 1997; Landry, Smith, Swank, Assel, & Vellet, 2001). Of course, responsive parenting is important for full-term babies' development as well. But Landry has found that consistent parental responsiveness over the first several years of life is more critical to preterm than to full-term infants' development (Landry, Smith, Swank, Assel, & Vellet, 2001).

Other researchers have noted that two factors shape parental responses to preterm infants (Bugental & Happaney, 2004). One is the degree to which parents' expectations for a preterm infant's development are realistic. The other is parents' confidence in their ability to manage the challenges associated with caring for an at-risk child. Thankfully, training appears to be of help to parents of preterm infants in both of these areas. Preterm infants whose families participate in parenting skills training programs display better neurobehavioral functioning during the first years of life than preterm infants whose families don't participate in such programs (Heidelise et al., 2004).

Finally, as you can see, the answer to the question of when a preterm child will catch up to his peers is, like so many other questions in the study of human development, "It depends."

Before going on . . .

- What decisions must parents make about the birth process in industrialized societies?
- Describe the physical process of birth and the newborn's first moments with health care providers and parents.
- What is low birth weight, and what are some of its causes and consequences?

Behavior in Early Infancy

Who is this small stranger who brings both joy and strain? What qualities and skills does the newborn bring to the interaction process? He cries, breathes, looks around a bit. But what else can he do in the early hours and days? On what skills does the infant build?

REFLEXES AND BEHAVIORAL STATES

reflexes Automatic body reactions to specific stimulation, such as the knee jerk or the Moro reflex. Adults have many reflexes, but the newborn also has some primitive reflexes that disappear as the cortex develops.

adaptive reflexes Reflexes that are essential to the infant's survival but that disappear in the first year of life.

rooting reflex The reflex that causes an infant to automatically turn toward a touch on the cheek, open the mouth, and make sucking movements.

primitive reflexes Collection of reflexes seen in young infants that gradually disappear during the first year of life, including the Moro and Babinski reflexes.

Moro reflex The reflex that causes infants to extend their legs, arms, and fingers, arch the back, and draw back the head when startled (for example, by a loud sound or a sensation of being dropped).

One important part of the infant's repertoire of behaviors is a large collection of **reflexes**, which are physical responses triggered involuntarily by specific stimuli. In addition, newborns typically display a behavioral cycle that includes periods of alertness, sleepiness, and hunger.

Reflexes Some reflexes persist into adulthood, such as your automatic eyeblink when a puff of air hits your eye or the involuntary narrowing of the pupil of your eye when you're in a bright light. Others, sometimes referred to as **adaptive reflexes**, are essential to the infant's survival but gradually disappear in the first year of life. Sucking and swallowing reflexes are prominent in this category, as is the **rooting reflex**—the automatic turn of the head toward any touch on the cheek, a reflex that helps the baby get the nipple into his mouth during nursing. These reflexes are no longer present in older infants or adults but are clearly highly adaptive for the newborn.

Finally, newborns have a large collection of **primitive reflexes**, controlled by the medulla and the midbrain, both of which are close to being fully developed at birth. For example, if you make a loud noise or startle a baby in some other way, you'll see her throw her arms outward and arch her back, a pattern that is part of the **Moro reflex** (also called the *startle reflex*). Stroke the bottom of her foot, and she will splay out her toes; this reaction is called the **Babinski reflex**.

These various primitive reflexes disappear over the first year of life (see Table 3.3), apparently superseded by the action of the cortex, which by this age is much more fully developed. Yet, even though these reflexes represent neurologically primitive patterns, they are nonetheless linked to important later behavior patterns. The tonic neck reflex (described in Table 3.3), for example, forms the foundation for the baby's later ability to reach for objects, because it focuses the baby's attention on the hand; the grasp reflex, too, is linked to the later ability to hold onto objects.

In a similar way, the walking reflex may be linked to later voluntary walking. In an early study, Zelazo and his colleagues (1972) stimulated the walking reflex repeatedly in some babies every day from the 2nd to the 8th week after birth. By 8 weeks, these stimulated babies took many more steps per minute when they were held in the walking position than did nonstimulated babies. And at the end of the first year, the stimulated babies learned to walk alone about a month sooner than did comparison babies who had not had their walking reflex stimulated. Esther Thelen, an expert on early motor development, points out that to be able to walk, an infant has to have enough muscle strength in his legs to move his legs in a walking movement (1983). Very young infants are light enough to manage such movement, but then they gain weight quickly without an equivalent gain in muscle strength. Only late in the first year do the child's weight and leg muscle strength again come into the appropriate balance. The babies in Zelazo's experiment, however, gained added muscle strength in the early weeks because their legs were exercised—just as you gain muscle strength if you begin a program of regular exercise. According to Thelen, these babies were therefore able to reach the right balance of weight and strength a bit sooner than normal.

Thus, primitive reflexes are not just curiosities. They can be informative, as when a baby fails to show a reflex that ought to be there or displays a reflex past the point at which it normally disappears. For example, infants exposed to narcotics or those suffering from anoxia at birth may show only very weak reflexes; Down

The Moro reflex

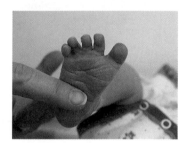

The Babinski reflex

TABLE 3.3	Examples of Primitive and Adaptive Reflexes		
Reflex	**Stimulation**	**Response**	**Developmental Pattern**
Tonic neck	While baby is on his back and awake, turn his head to one side.	Baby assumes a "fencing" posture, with arm extended on the side toward which the head is turned.	Fades by 4 months
Grasping	Stroke the baby's palm with your finger.	Baby will make a strong fist around your finger.	Fades by 3 to 4 months
Moro	Make a loud sound near the baby, or let the baby "drop" slightly and suddenly.	Baby extends legs, arms, and fingers, arches his back, and draws back his head.	Fades by about 6 months
Walking	Hold baby under arms with feet just touching a floor or other flat surface.	Baby will make step-like motions, alternating feet as in walking.	Fades by about 8 weeks in most infants
Babinski	Stroke sole of the baby's foot from toes toward heel.	Baby will fan out his toes.	Fades between 8 and 12 months
Rooting	Stroke baby's cheek with finger or nipple.	Baby turns head toward the touch, opens mouth, and makes sucking movements.	After 3 weeks, transforms into a voluntary head-turning response.

Babinski reflex A reflex found in very young infants that causes them to splay out their toes in response to a stroke on the bottom of the foot.

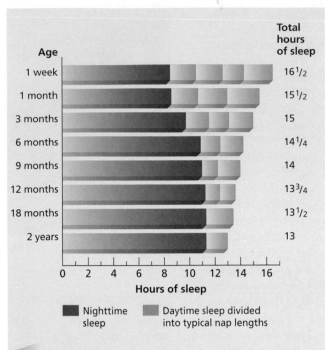

FIGURE 3.3

The total amount of sleep infants need and the number of daytime naps they take typically decline over the first 2 years of life. (*Source*: Reprinted with the permission of Simon & Schuster Adult Publishing Group, from *How to Solve Your Child's Sleep Problems*, by Richard Ferber, M.D. Copyright © 1985 by Richard Ferber, M.D. All rights reserved.)

syndrome infants have only very weak Moro reflexes and sometimes have poor sucking reflexes. When a primitive reflex persists past the normal point, it may suggest some neurological damage or dysfunction (Scerif et al., 2005; Schott & Rossor, 2003). Reflexes are also the starting point for many important physical skills, including reaching, grasping, and walking.

Behavioral States   Researchers have described five different states of sleep and wakefulness in neonates, referred to as **states of consciousness**, summarized in Table 3.4. Most infants move through these states in the same sequence: from deep sleep to lighter sleep to fussing and hunger and then to alert wakefulness. After they are fed, they become drowsy and drop back into deep sleep. The cycle repeats itself about every 2 hours.

Neonates sleep as much as 90% of the time—as much in the daytime as at night, as Figure 3.3 indicates (Sola, Rogido, & Partridge, 2002). By 6 or 8 weeks of age, most infants somewhat decrease their total amount of sleep per day and show signs of day/night sleep rhythms (called *circadian rhythms*). Babies this age begin to string two or three 2-hour cycles together without coming to full wakefulness; at which point, we say that the baby can "sleep through the night." By 6 months, babies are still sleeping a bit over 14 hours per day, but the regularity and predictability of the sleep are even more noticeable. Most 6-month-olds have clear nighttime sleep patterns and nap during the day at more predictable times.

Of course, babies vary a lot around these averages. Of the 6-week-old babies in one study, there was one who slept 22 hours per day and another who slept only 8.8 hours per day (Bamford et al., 1990). (Now there must have been one tired set of parents!) And some babies do not develop a long nighttime sleep period until late in the first year of life.

Moreover, cultural beliefs play an important role in parents' responses to infants' sleep patterns. For example, parents in the United States typically see a newborn's erratic sleep cycle as a behavior problem that requires "fixing" through parental intervention (Harkness, 1998). Put differently, parents in the United States live by the clock themselves and are thus motivated to train their infants to adapt to the cultural context into which they have been born (Cole, 2005). As a result, American parents focus a great deal of attention on trying to force babies to sleep through the night.

states of consciousness The periodic shifts in alertness, sleepiness, crankiness, and so on that characterize an infant's behavior.

TABLE 3.4	The Basic States of Infant Sleep and Wakefulness
State	**Characteristics**
Deep sleep	Eyes closed, regular breathing, no movement except occasional startles
Active sleep	Eyes closed, irregular breathing, small twitches, no gross body movement
Quiet awake	Eyes open, no major body movement, regular breathing
Active awake	Eyes open, with movements of the head, limbs, and trunk; irregular breathing
Crying and fussing	Eyes may be partly or entirely closed; vigorous diffuse movement with crying or fussing sounds

Sources: Based on the work of Hutt, Lenard, and Prechtl, 1969; Parmelee, Wenner, and Schulz, 1964; Prechtl and Beintema, 1964.

By contrast, in the majority of cultures in the world (and in Western cultures until perhaps 200 years ago), babies sleep in the same bed with their parents, typically until they are weaned, a pattern often called *cosleeping*. Such an arrangement is established for any of a number of reasons, including lack of alternative sleeping space for the infant. More often, cosleeping seems to reflect a basic collectivist value, one that emphasizes contact and interdependence rather than separateness (Harkness & Super, 1995). Morelli and her colleagues (1992) reported that the Mayan mothers they interviewed, most of whom had their babies sleep with them, considered the U.S. practice of separate sleeping as tantamount to child neglect. They were shocked and disbelieving when told that U.S. infants often sleep in a separate room, with no one nearby.

Crying is yet another normal part of an infant's cycle of behavioral states. One researcher studying normal newborns found that they cried from 2% to 11% of the time (Korner, Hutchinson, Koperski, Kraemer, & Schneider, 1981). The percentage frequently increases over the first few weeks, peaking at 2–3 hours of crying a day at 6 weeks and then dropping off to less than 1 hour a day by 3 months (Needlman, 1996). Such a peak in crying at 6 weeks has been observed in infants from a number of different cultures, including cultures in which mothers have almost constant body contact with the infant (St. James-Roberts, Bowyer, Varghese, & Sawdon, 1994), which suggests

RESEARCH REPORT

Variations in Infants' Cries

Parents have always known that some babies have cries that are particularly penetrating or grating; other babies seem to have much less irritating crying sounds. Researchers have confirmed this parental observation in a wide range of studies. Many groups of babies with known medical abnormalities have different-sounding cries, including those with Down syndrome, encephalitis, meningitis, and many types of brain damage. This observation has been extended to babies who appear physically normal but who are at risk for later problems because of some perinatal problem, such as preterm or small-for-date babies (Lester, 1987; Lester & Dreher, 1989), or whose mothers were heavy drinkers during pregnancy (Nugent, Lester, Greene, Wieczorek-Deering, & O'Mahony, 1996). Such babies typically make crying sounds that are acoustically distinguishable from those of a normal, low-risk baby. In particular, the cry of such higher-risk babies has a more grating, piercing quality. Interestingly, the cries of babies with colic also have some of these same qualities (Lester, Boukydis, Garcia-Coll, Hole, & Peucker, 1992; Zeskind & Barr, 1997).

On the assumption that the baby's cry may reflect some basic aspect of neurological integrity, Lester also wondered whether one could use the quality of the cry as a diagnostic test. Among a group of high-risk babies, for example, could one predict later intellectual functioning from a measure of the pitch of the baby's cry? The answer seems to be yes. Lester (1987) found that among preterm babies, those with higher-pitched cries in the first days of life had lower scores on an IQ test at age 5 years. The same kind of connection has also been found among both normal babies and those exposed to methadone prenatally. In all these groups, the higher the pitch and more grating the cry, the lower the child's later IQ or motor development (Huntington, Hans, & Zeskind, 1990).

Eventually, it may be possible for physicians to use the presence of such a grating or piercing cry as a signal that the infant may have some underlying physical problem or as a way of making better guesses about the long-term outcomes for babies at high risk for later problems (Barr, Hopkins, & Green, 2000).

Questions for Critical Analysis

1. Suppose you did a study showing that the more irritable the infant's cries are, the more likely parents are to develop hostile attitudes toward their infant. What would be the implications of this finding for neurological explanations of the correlation between the quality of infants' cries and later developmental problems?

2. What kind of research would be necessary to establish norms for infant crying?

that this crying pattern is not unique to the United States or to other Western cultures. Initially, infants cry most in the evening; later, their most intense crying occurs just before feedings.

Moreover, parents across a variety of cultures use very similar techniques to soothe crying infants. Most babies stop crying when they are picked up, held, and talked or sung to. Encouraging them to suck on a pacifier also usually helps. Parents sometimes worry that picking up a crying baby will lead to even more crying. But research suggests that prompt attention to a crying baby in the first 3 months actually leads to less crying later in infancy (Sulkes, 1998).

The basic function of a baby's cry, obviously, is to signal need. Because babies can't move to someone, they have to bring someone to them, and crying is the main way they have to attract attention. In fact, infants have a whole repertoire of cry sounds, with different cries for pain, anger, or hunger. The anger cry, for example, is typically louder and more intense, and the pain cry normally has a very abrupt onset—unlike the more basic kinds of hunger or distress cries, which usually begin with whimpering or moaning.

However, not all infants cry in precisely the same way. Some, as you can see in the *Research Report*, have particularly piercing or grating cries, a pattern that may be diagnostic of an underlying problem of some sort. In the end, each parent learns the sounds of her or his own baby. Alen Wiesenfeld and his colleagues (1981) found that mothers (but not fathers) of 5-month-olds could discriminate between taped cries of anger and pain from their own babies, while neither parent could reliably make the same discrimination with the taped cries of another baby.

For the 15–20% of infants who develop **colic**, a pattern involving intense bouts of crying totaling 3 or more hours a day, nothing seems to help (Coury, 2002). Typically, colic appears at about 2 weeks of age and then disappears spontaneously at 3 or 4 months of age. The crying is generally worst in late afternoon or early evening. Neither psychologists nor physicians know why colic begins, or why it stops without any intervention. It is a difficult pattern to live with, but the good news is that it does go away.

Finally, the infant behavioral state most enjoyed by many caregivers is the one in which babies are awake and alert. However, neonates are in this state only 2 to 3 hours each day, on average, and the total amount of waking time is unevenly distributed over a 24-hour period. In other words, 15 minutes of waking time may happen at 6:00 a.m., then 30 minutes at 1:00 p.m, another 20 minutes at 4:00 p.m., and so on. Over the first 6 months, advances in neurological development enable infants to remain awake and alert for longer periods of time as their patterns of sleeping, crying, and eating become more regular.

PHYSICAL AND COGNITIVE ABILITIES

Newborns come into the world equipped with an array of motor skills that allow them to act on their environments. Through such actions, they acquire new behaviors through learning.

Motor Skills   The infant's motor skills emerge only gradually in the early weeks. By 1 month, a baby can hold her chin up off the floor or mattress. By 2 months, she can hold her head steady while she's being held and is beginning to reach for objects near her. These improving motor skills follow two broad patterns originally identified by Gesell: Development proceeds from the head downward, in a pattern called **cephalocaudal**, and from the trunk outward, in another pattern called **proximodistal**. Thus, the baby can hold up her head before she can sit or roll over and can sit before she can crawl.

Another interesting feature of young babies' motor skills is how repetitively they perform their limited range of movements (Adolph & Berger, 2005). They kick, rock, wave, bounce, bang, rub, scratch, or sway repeatedly and rhythmically. These repeated

---

colic A pattern of persistent and often inconsolable crying, totaling more than 3 hours a day, found in some infants in the first 3 to 4 months of life.

cephalocaudal One of two basic patterns of physical development in infancy (the other is proximodistal), in which development proceeds from the head downward.

proximodistal One of two basic patterns of physical development in infancy (the other is cephalocaudal), in which development proceeds from the center outward, that is, from the trunk to the limbs.

patterns become particularly prominent at about 6 or 7 months of age, although you can see instances of such behavior even in the first weeks, particularly in finger movements and leg kicking. These movements do not seem to be totally voluntary or coordinated, but they also do not appear to be random. For instance, Thelen (1995) has observed that kicking movements peak just before the baby begins to crawl, as if the rhythmic kicking were a part of the preparation for crawling. Thelen's work has revealed certain patterns and order in the seemingly random movements of the young infant, but even this understanding does not alter the fact that, by contrast with perceptual abilities, the baby's initial motor abilities are quite limited.

Sensory and Perceptual Abilities Babies come equipped with a surprisingly mature set of perceptual skills. The newborn can do several things:

- Focus both eyes on the same spot, with 8–10 inches being the best focal distance; discriminate his mother's face from other faces almost immediately; and, within a few weeks, follow a moving object with his eyes—although not very efficiently.
- Easily hear sounds within the pitch and loudness range of the human voice; roughly locate objects by their sounds; discriminate some individual voices, particularly his mother's voice.
- Taste the four basic tastes (sweet, sour, bitter, and salty) and identify familiar body odors, including discriminating his mother's smell from the smell of a strange woman.

Brief as this summary is, several points stand out. First of all, newborns' perceptual skills are a great deal better than most parents believe—better than most psychologists or physicians believed until a few years ago. The better research techniques have become, the more we have understood just how skillful the newborn baby really is—important evidence for the significance of nature in the nature-nurture interaction.

Even more striking is how well adapted the baby's perceptual skills are for the interactions he will have with the people in his world. He hears best in the range of the human voice, and he can discriminate his mother (or other regular caregiver) from others on the basis of smell, sight, or sound almost immediately. The distance at which he can focus his eyes best, about 8–10 inches, is approximately the distance between his eyes and his mother's face during nursing.

As you'll see in Chapter 5, a newborn has a long way to go in the development of sophisticated perceptual abilities, but the infant begins life able to make key discriminations and to locate objects through various perceptual cues.

Classical Conditioning The bulk of the research on learning in newborns suggests that they can be classically conditioned, although it is difficult (Herbert, Eckerman, Goldstein, & Stanton, 2004). Conditioning that relates to feeding in some way is most likely to be successful, perhaps because this activity is so critical for the infant's survival. As one example, Elliott Blass and his colleagues (1984) gave 1- and 2-day-old infants sugar water in a bottle (the unconditional stimulus), which prompted sucking (the unconditioned response). Then, just before they were given the sugar water, the babies' foreheads were stroked (the conditional stimulus). After several such repetitions, the experimenters stroked the infants' foreheads without giving the sugar water to see if the infants would begin sucking—which they did, thus showing classical conditioning.

By the time infants are 3 or 4 weeks old, classical conditioning is no longer difficult to establish; it occurs easily with many different responses. In particular, this means that the conditioned emotional responses you read about in Chapter 1 may begin to develop as early as the first week of life. Thus, the mere presence of mom or dad or another favored person may trigger the sense of "feeling good," a response that may contribute to the child's later attachment to the parent.

Operant Conditioning Newborns also clearly learn by operant conditioning. Both the sucking response and head turning have been successfully increased by the

Young Lucy was 5 months old when this photo was taken, showing her "airplaning." You can see that by this age, she is able to hold up not only her head but also part of her chest—a big advance over the motor skills seen in newborns.

use of reinforcements, such as sweet-tasting liquids or the sound of the mother's voice or heartbeat (Moon & Fifer, 1990). At the least, the fact that conditioning of this kind can take place means that the neurological basis for learning to occur is present at birth. Results like this also tell us something about the sorts of reinforcements that are effective with very young children. It is surely highly significant for the whole process of mother-infant interaction that the mother's voice is an effective reinforcer for virtually all babies.

Schematic Learning   The fact that babies can recognize voices and heartbeats in the first days of life is also important, because it suggests that another kind of learning is going on as well. This third type of learning, sometimes referred to as **schematic learning**, draws both its name and many of its conceptual roots from Piaget's theory. The basic idea is that from the beginning the baby organizes her experiences into expectancies, or known combinations. These expectancies, often called *schemas*, are built up over many exposures to particular experiences but thereafter help the baby to distinguish between the familiar and the unfamiliar. Carolyn Rovee-Collier (1986) has suggested that we might think of classical conditioning in infants as being a variety of schematic learning. When a baby begins to move her head as if to search for the nipple as soon as she hears her mother's footsteps coming into the room, this is not just some kind of automatic classical conditioning, but the beginning of the development of expectancies. From the earliest weeks, the baby seems to make connections between events in her world, such as between the sound of her mother's footsteps and the feeling of being picked up or between the touch of the breast and the feeling of a full stomach. Thus, early classical conditioning may be the beginnings of the process of cognitive development.

Habituation   A concept related to schematic learning is habituation. **Habituation** is the automatic reduction in the strength or vigor of a response to a repeated stimulus. For example, suppose you live on a fairly noisy street, where the sound of cars going by is repeated over and over during each day. After a while, you not only don't react to the sound, you quite literally do not perceive it as being loud. The ability to do this—to dampen down the intensity of a physical response to some repeated stimulus—is obviously vital in our everyday lives. If we reacted constantly to every sight and sound and smell that came along, we'd spend all our time responding to these repeated events, and we wouldn't have energy or attention left over for things that are new and deserve attention. The ability to dishabituate is equally important. When a habituated stimulus changes in some way, such as a sudden extra-loud screech of tires on the busy street by your house, you again respond fully. The reemergence of the original response strength is a sign that the perceiver—infant, child, or adult—has noticed some significant change.

A rudimentary capacity to habituate and to dishabituate is built in at birth in human babies, just as it is in other species. In 10-week-old babies, this ability is well developed. An infant will stop looking at something you keep putting in front of her face; she will stop showing a startle reaction (Moro reflex) to loud sounds after the first few presentations but will again startle if the sound is changed; she will stop turning her head toward a repeating sound (Swain, Zelazo, & Clifton, 1993). Such habituation itself is not a voluntary process; it is entirely automatic. Yet in order for it to work, the newborn must be equipped with the capacity to recognize familiar experiences. That is, she must have, or must develop, schemas of some kind.

The existence of these processes in the newborn has an added benefit for researchers: It has enabled them to figure out what an infant responds to as "the same" or "different." If a baby is habituated to some stimulus, such as a sound or a specific picture, the experimenter can then present slight variations on the original stimulus to see

schematic learning The development of expectancies concerning what actions lead to what results or what events tend to go together.

habituation An automatic decrease in the intensity of a response to a repeated stimulus, enabling a child or adult to ignore the familiar and focus attention on the novel.

the point at which dishabituation occurs. In this way, researchers have begun to get an idea of how the newborn baby or young infant experiences the world around him—a point you'll read more about in Chapter 5.

TEMPERAMENT AND SOCIAL SKILLS

Clearly, many aspects of early development are universal, such as reflexes and the capacity to respond to conditioning. However, there are also important individual differences among infants. All babies cry, but some cry more than others; some are easily irritated by a wet diaper, while others seem to be more tolerant of physical discomforts. Moreover, human newborns, unlike those in many other species, are a very long way from being independent. If they are to survive, someone must provide consistent care over an extended period. So the infant's capacity to entice others into the caregiving role is critical. It is here that the "social" skills of infants, along with the ability of parents to adapt to the caregiving role, come into play.

Temperament   Babies vary in the way they react to new things, in their typical moods, in their rate of activity, in their preference for social interactions or solitude, in the regularity of their daily rhythms, and in many other ways. Developmentalists collectively call these differences **temperament**. You'll be reading a great deal more about temperament in Chapter 9, but because the concept will come up often as we go along, it is important at this early stage to introduce some of the basic terms and ideas.

In classic research, developmentalists Alexander Thomas and Stella Chess (1977) described three categories of infant temperament, the **easy child**, the **difficult child**, and the **slow-to-warm-up child**. Easy children, who comprised approximately 40% of Thomas and Chess's original study group, approach new events positively. They try new foods without much fuss, for example. They also exhibit predictable sleeping and eating cycles, are usually happy, and adjust easily to change.

By contrast, the difficult child is less predictable with regard to sleep and hunger cycles and is slow to develop regular cycles. These children react vigorously and negatively to new things, are more irritable, and cry more. Their cries are also more likely to have the higher-pitched, grating quality you read about in the *Research Report* on page 77 (Huffman et al., 1994). Thomas and Chess point out, however, that once the difficult baby has adapted to something new, he is often quite happy about it, even though the adaptation process itself is trying. In Thomas and Chess's original sample, about 10% of children were clearly classifiable in this group.

Children in the slow-to-warm-up group are not as negative in responding to new things or new people as are the difficult children. They show instead a kind of passive resistance. Instead of spitting out new food violently and crying, the slow-to-warm-up child may let the food drool out and may resist mildly any attempt to feed her more of the same. These infants show few intense reactions, either positive or negative, although once they have adapted to something new, their reaction is usually fairly positive. Approximately 15% of Thomas and Chess's sample followed this pattern.

While these differences in style or pattern of response tend to persist through infancy into later childhood, no psychologist studying temperament suggests that such individual differences are absolutely fixed at birth. Inborn temperamental differences are shaped, strengthened, bent, or counteracted by the child's relationships and experiences. Infants enter the world with somewhat different repertoires or patterns of behavior, and those differences not only affect the experiences an infant may choose, but also help to shape the emerging pattern of interaction that develops between infant and parents. For example, toddlers and preschoolers with difficult temperaments are more often criticized or physically punished by their parents than are easy children, presumably because their behavior is more troublesome (Bates, 1989). Yet once it is established, such a pattern of criticism and punishment itself is likely to have additional consequences for a child. Nonetheless, not all parents of difficult children respond in

A baby's smile and laughter are an utter delight for parents. Laughing is one of the important social/emotional responses that contribute to the emerging parent-child bond, part of the "glue" that cements the relationship together.

CRITICAL THINKING ?

In what ways do you think the temperament types discussed in the text are exhibited by adults?

temperament Inborn predispositions that form the foundations of personality.

easy child An infant who adapts easily to change and who exhibits regular patterns of eating, sleeping, and alertness.

difficult child An infant who is irritable and irregular in behavior.

slow-to-warm-up child An infant who may seem unresponsive but who simply takes more time to respond than other infants do.

Of course, you can't evaluate a baby's temperament on the basis of one picture, but you might guess that young Benjamin, smiling delightedly, has an easier temperament than Eleanor, who is pushing away her food and who may have a slow-to-warm-up temperament.

this way. A skilled parent, especially one who correctly perceives that the child's "difficultness" is a temperamental quality and not a result of the child's willfulness or the parent's ineptness, can avoid some of the pitfalls and can handle the difficult child more adeptly.

The Emergence of Emotional Expression

There is really no way to know just what emotion a baby actually feels. The best we can do is to try to judge what emotion a baby appears to express through body and face. Researchers have done this by confronting babies with various kinds of events likely to prompt emotions, photographing or videotaping those encounters, and then asking adult judges to say which emotion the baby's face expresses (Izard et al., 1995; Izard & Harris, 1995; Izard & Malatesta, 1987).

Table 3.5 summarizes the current thinking about the ages at which various important emotional expressions first appear. As you can see, some rudimentary emotional expressions are visible at birth, including a sort of half-smile that delights parents even though they cannot figure out how to elicit it consistently. Within a few weeks, though, babies begin to show a full social smile. Happily, one of the earliest triggers for this wonderful baby smile is the kind of high-pitched voice that all adults seem to use naturally with infants. So adults seem to be preprogrammed to behave in just the ways that babies will respond to positively. Within a few weeks, babies will also smile in response to a smiling face, especially a familiar face.

Within a few months, babies' emotional expressions differentiate even further, so that they express sadness, anger, and surprise. Four-month-olds also begin to laugh—and there are few things in life more delightful than the sound of a giggling or laughing baby! Fear appears as a discrete emotional expression at about 7 months.

Taking Turns

Yet another social skill the baby brings to interactions is the ability to take turns. As adults, we take turns all the time, most clearly in conversations and

TABLE 3.5	The Emergence of Emotional Expressions in Infancy and Toddlerhood	
Age	**Emotion Expressed**	**Examples of Stimuli That Trigger That Expression**
At birth	Interest	Novelty or movement
	Distress	Pain
	Disgust	Offensive substances
	Neonatal smile (a "half smile")	Appears spontaneously for no known reason
3 to 6 weeks	Pleasure/social smile (precursor to joy)	High-pitched human voice; clapping the baby's hands together; a familiar voice; a nodding face
2 to 3 months	Sadness	Painful medical procedure
	Wariness (precursor to fear)	A stranger's face
	Frustration (precursor to anger)	Being restrained; being prevented from performing some established action
	Surprise	Jack-in-the-box
7 months	Fear	Extreme novelty; heights (such as in the visual cliff experiment)
	Anger	Failure or interruption of some attempted action, such as reaching for a ball that has rolled under a couch
	Joy	Immediate delighted response to an experience with positive meaning, such as the caregiver's arrival or a game of peekaboo

Sources: Izard and Malateste, 1987; Mascolo and Fischer, 1995; Sroufe, 1996.

eye contacts. In fact, it's very difficult to have any kind of social encounter with someone who does not take turns. Kenneth Kaye (1982) argues that the beginnings of this turn-taking can be seen in very young infants in their eating patterns. As early as the first days of life, a baby sucks in a "burst-pause" pattern. He sucks for a while, pauses, sucks for a while, pauses, and so on. Mothers enter into this process, such as by jiggling the baby during the pauses, thus creating an alternating pattern: suck, pause, jiggle, pause, suck, pause, jiggle, pause. The rhythm of the interaction is really very much like a conversation. It is not clear whether this conversational quality of very early interaction occurs because the adult figures out the baby's natural rhythm and adapts her own responses to the baby's timing or whether some mutual adaptation is going on. Nonetheless, it is extremely intriguing that this apparent turn-taking is seen in infants only days old.

The advent of a new baby—especially a first child—is one of those richly ambivalent times for many adults: They are delighted and proud, and yet they also typically feel increased strain.

Adapting to the Newborn Learning their baby's subtle temperamental and social cues is one of the several adaptational tasks facing parents of infants. For most adults, the role of parent brings profound satisfaction, a greater sense of purpose and self-worth, and a feeling of being grown up. It may also bring a sense of shared joy between husband and wife (Umberson & Gove, 1989). At the same time, the birth of the first child signals a whole series of changes in parents' lives, not all of which are absorbed without strain. Mark Bornstein offers a particularly clear description of the process:

> By their very coming into existence, infants forever alter the sleeping, eating, and working habits of their parents; they change who parents are and how parents define themselves. Infants keep parents up late into the night or cause them to abandon late nights to accommodate early waking; they require parents to give up a rewarding career to care for them or take a second job to support them; they lead parents to make new circles of friends with others in similar situations and sometimes cause parents to lose or abandon old friends who are not parents. . . . Parenting an infant is a 168-hour-a-week job, whether by the parents themselves or by a surrogate who is on call, because the human infant is totally dependent on parents for survival. (1995, pp. 3–4)

One common consequence of all these changes and new demands is that marital satisfaction typically goes down in the first months and years after the first child is born (Glenn, 1990). Individuals and couples report a sense of strain made up partly of fatigue and partly of a feeling that there is too much to cope with, anxiety about not knowing how best to care for the child, and a strong sense of loss of time spent together and intimacy in the marriage relationship (Feldman, 1987). In longitudinal studies in which couples have been observed or interviewed during pregnancy and then again in the months after the first child's birth, spouses typically report fewer expressions of love, fewer positive actions designed to maintain or support the relationship, and more expressions of ambivalence after the child's birth than before (Belsky, Lang, & Rovine, 1985). Such strains and reduced satisfaction are less prevalent when the child was planned rather than unplanned and for those couples whose marriage was strong and stable before the birth of the child. But virtually all couples experience some strain.

It's important to keep in mind, though, that new parents who are married or cohabiting experience a much smaller decline in overall life satisfaction than new single parents, whose lives are far more complicated and stressful (Lee, Law, & Tam, 1999). Likewise, single parents are more likely to suffer from health problems and are less likely to advance to management positions at work (Khlat, Sermet, & Le Pape, 2000; Tharenou, 1999). Instead of focusing on declines in relationship satisfaction, some developmentalists suggest that more attention be paid to the consistent finding that having a parenting partner—especially one to whom one is married—is a significant protective factor in managing the stressful transition to parenthood.

Before going on . . .

- Describe the newborn's reflexes and states of consciousness.
- What are the physical and cognitive abilities of newborns?
- How do newborns differ in temperament, and what skills do they bring to social interactions?

Health and Wellness in Early Infancy

You may have heard references to the increasing life expectancy in the United States. At the beginning of the 20th century, Americans' average life expectancy was only about 49 years, but by the century's end, it was 76 years. One of the most significant factors behind this statistic is the reduction in infant mortality that occurred in industrialized societies during the 20th century. Improved medical technology and better understanding of newborns' nutritional and health care needs are responsible for this trend. Sadly, though, many infants die in the first year of life. In fact, infancy continues to be associated with a higher death rate than any other period of life except old age. Many such deaths are due to genetic disorders, but others result from causes that are more easily preventable.

NUTRITION, HEALTH CARE, AND IMMUNIZATIONS

Newborns, of course, are completely physically dependent on their caretakers. To develop normally, they need adequate nutrition, regular medical care, and protection against diseases.

Nutrition   Eating is not among the states listed in Table 3.4, but it is certainly something that newborn babies do frequently! Given that a newborn's natural cycle seems to be about 2 hours long, she may eat as many as ten times a day. Gradually, the baby takes more and more milk at each feeding and doesn't have to eat so often. By 2 months, the average number is down to five or six feedings each day, dropping to about three feedings by age 8 to 12 months (Overby, 2002). Breast-fed and bottle-fed babies eat with the same frequency, but these two forms of feeding do differ in other important ways (see the *The Real World*).

Up until 4 to 6 months, babies need only breast milk or formula accompanied by appropriate supplements. For example, pediatricians usually recommend vitamin B_{12} supplements for infants whose nursing mothers are vegetarians (Tershakovec & Stallings, 1998). Doctors may recommend supplemental formula feeding for infants who are growing poorly, but breast milk meets the nutritional needs of most infants.

There is no evidence to support the belief that solid foods encourage babies to sleep through the night. In fact, early introduction of solid food can actually interfere with nutrition. Pediatricians usually recommend withholding solid foods until 4 to 6 months of age (Overby, 2002). The first solids should be single-grain cereals, such as rice, with added iron. Parents should introduce their baby to no more than one new food each week. If parents follow a systematic plan, food allergies can be easily identified (Tershakovec & Stallings, 1998).

Health Care and Immunizations   Infants need frequent medical check-ups. While much of *well baby care* may seem routine, it is extremely important to babies' development. For example, babies' motor skills are usually assessed during routine visits to a doctor's office or a health clinic. An infant whose motor development is less advanced than expected for his age may require additional screening for developmental problems such as mental retardation (Sulkes, 1998).

One of the most important elements of well baby care is vaccination of the infant against a variety of diseases. Although immunizations later in childhood provide good protection against these diseases, the evidence suggests that immunization is most effective when it begins in the first month of life and continues across childhood and adolescence (Umetsu, 1998). Even adults need occasional "booster" shots to maintain immunity.

As recently as 1992, only 55% of children in the United States had received the full set of recommended immunizations—a schedule that includes three hepatitis, four

The Real World

Breast or Bottle?

Expectant mother Suzanne found it easy to decide where she wanted to give birth and whom she wanted to serve as her labor coach. Now, her greatest worries centered around how she would feed her baby. She had heard that breast-feeding was best, but she expected to return to work within a few weeks after the birth. Consequently, she was leaning toward bottle-feeding but was seeking information that would reassure her that her baby would develop properly on formula.

All parents, like Suzanne, want to do what's best for their babies, and developmentalists today generally agree that breast-feeding is superior to bottle-feeding for meeting infants' nutritional needs (Overby, 2002). However, not all mothers *can* breast-feed. Some have an insufficient milk supply. Others suffer from medical conditions that require them to take drugs that may filter into breast milk and harm the baby. Furthermore, viruses, including HIV, can be transmitted from mother to child through breast milk. And what about adoptive mothers?

Developmentalists are quick to reassure mothers who can't nurse that their babies will most likely develop as well as breast-fed infants. However, it is important to understand that several decades of extensive research in many countries comparing large groups of breast- and bottle-fed infants make it clear that breast-feeding is nutritionally superior to bottle-feeding. On average, breast-fed infants are less likely to suffer from such problems as diarrhea, gastroenteritis, bron-

chitis, ear infections, and colic, and they are less likely to die in infancy (Barness & Curran, 1996; Beaudry, Dufour, & Marcoux, 1995; Golding, Emmett, & Rogers, 1997a, 1997b; López-Alarcón, Villapando, & Fajardo, 1997). Breast milk also appears to promote the growth of nerves and the intestinal tract, to contribute to more rapid weight and size gain (Prentice, 1994), and to stimulate better immune system function (Pickering et al., 1998). Research also suggests that breast-feeding may protect infants from becoming overweight in later years (Dietz, 2001). For these reasons, physicians strongly recommend breast-feeding if it is at all possible, even if the mother can nurse for only a few weeks after birth or if her breast milk must be supplemented with formula feedings (Tershakovec & Stallings, 1998).

For those who cannot breast-feed at all, nutrition experts point out that infants who are fed high-quality, properly sterilized formula typically thrive on it (Furman et al., 2004; Tershakovec & Stallings, 1998). Moreover, there are a wide variety of formulas available today to fulfill the requirements of infants who have special needs, such as those who are lactose-intolerant. It is also reassuring to know that the social interactions between mother and child seem to be unaffected by the type of feeding. Bottle-fed babies are held and cuddled in the same ways as breast-fed babies, and their mothers appear to be just as sensitive and responsive to their babies and just as bonded to them as are mothers of breast-fed infants (Field, 1977).

Questions for Reflection

1. If Suzanne were your friend and asked you for advice regarding this important decision, what would you tell her?
2. The research linking breast-feeding to obesity protection was correlational. What other variables might explain this relationship?

diphtheria/tetanus/pertussis, three influenza, three polio, one measles/rubella, and one varicella zoster virus vaccine (American Academy of Pediatrics Committee on Infectious Diseases, 2000). Vaccination against hepatitis A is also recommended in some cities (Centers for Disease Control [CDC] National Immunization Program, 2000). By 1999, after intensive efforts, the vaccination rate was raised to more than 90% (CDC National Immunization Program, 1999).

However, recent history suggests that the public can easily become complacent about immunizations (CDC National Immunization Program, 1999). For example, declines in measles immunizations during the late 1980s and early 1990s led to epidemics of this potentially fatal disease in many urban areas (Umetsu, 1998). Thus, it is important to remember that infectious diseases like measles will remain rare only as long as parents are diligent in obtaining immunizations for their children.

ILLNESSES

Virtually all babies get sick, most of them repeatedly. Among infants around the world, three types of illnesses are most common: diarrhea, upper respiratory infections, and ear infections.

Diarrhea   Worldwide, one of the most common and deadly illnesses of infancy and early childhood is diarrhea, accounting for the deaths of an estimated 3.5 million infants and children each year. In developing countries, 1 out of 4 deaths of children under age 5 is due to diarrhea; in some countries, the rate is even higher (Gorter et al., 1995). In the United States, diarrhea rarely leads to death in infants, but virtually every infant or young child has at least one episode of diarrhea each year; about 1 in 10 cases is severe enough for the child to be taken to a doctor (Kilgore, Holman, Clarke, & Glass, 1995). In most such cases, the cause of the illness is a viral or bacterial infection, the most common of which is *rotavirus*, a microorganism that is spread by physical contact with others who are infected with the disease (Laney, 2002).

Virtually all the deaths from diarrhea could be prevented by giving fluids to rehydrate the child (Laney, 2002). In serious cases, this rehydration should involve a special solution of salts (oral rehydration salts, or ORS). The World Health Organization has for some years been involved in a program of training health professionals around the world in the use of ORS, with some success (Muhuri, Anker, & Bryce, 1996). Still, diarrhea remains a very serious illness for infants and children in many parts of the world.

Upper Respiratory Infections   A second common illness during infancy is some kind of upper respiratory infection. In the United States, the average baby has seven colds in the first year of life. (That's a lot of nose-wipes!) Interestingly, research in a number of countries shows that babies in day-care centers have about twice as many such infections as do those reared entirely at home, presumably because babies in group-care settings are exposed to a wider range of germs and viruses (e.g., Collet et al., 1994; Hurwitz, Gunn, Pinsky, & Schonberger, 1991; Lau, Uba, & Lehman, 2002; Louhiala, Jaakkola, Ruotsalainen, & Jaakkola, 1995). In general, the more different people a baby is exposed to, the more colds she is likely to get. This is not as bad as it may seem at first. The heightened risk of infection among infants in day care drops after the first few months, while those reared entirely at home have very high rates of illness when they first attend preschool or kindergarten. Attendance at day care thus simply means that the baby is exposed earlier to the various microorganisms typically carried by children.

Ear Infections   One of the most common infections in infants is an ear infection (more properly called *otitis media*), the early childhood illness that in the United States most often leads to a visit to a doctor (Lau, Uba, & Lehman, 2002). Such an infection very often follows a cold or an allergic reaction, either of which may lead to congestion in the eustachian tube—the tube through which middle ear fluid drains. The fluid thus accumulates in the middle ear, creating pressure and pain, most often accompanied by fever, headache, and other signs of illness.

In the United States, as many as 90% of children have at least one serious ear infection before age 2, with the incidence peaking between ages 6 and 18 months (Daly, 1997; Paradise et al., 1997). The earlier a child's first episode, the more likely she is to have repeated infections. The risk of otitis media is unusually high among many Native American groups as well as among Alaskan and Canadian Inuits and is higher among Caucasian American than among black or Hispanic American infants. It is more common in boys than in girls, more common in children in day care than those reared at home, more common among children whose parents smoke, and less common among infants who are breast-fed (Alho, Laära, & Oja, 1996; Golding, Emmett, & Rogers, 1997b; Kemper, 1996; Klein, 1994). It is a serious condition, requiring consistent medical treatment, which is not equally available to all children. When not treated appropriately, repeated episodes can sometimes lead to some permanent hearing loss, which in turn may be linked to language or learning problems at later ages (Gravel & Nozza, 1997; Roberts & Wallace, 1997; Vernon-Feagans, Manlove, & Volling, 1996).

INFANT MORTALITY

A small minority of babies face not just a few sniffles but the possibility of death. In the United States, about 7 babies out of every 1,000 die before age 1 (MacDorman & Atkinson, 1999; Matthews, 2005). The rate has been declining steadily for the past few decades (down from 20 per 1,000 in 1970), but the United States continues to have a higher infant mortality rate than other industrialized nations. Almost two-thirds of these infant deaths occur in the first month of life and are directly linked to either congenital anomalies or low birth weight (MacDorman & Atkinson, 1999). Fewer than 3 deaths per 1,000 births occur in the remainder of the first year.

Sudden Infant Death Syndrome   A sizeable fraction of deaths in the first year are attributable to **sudden infant death syndrome (SIDS)**, in which an apparently healthy infant dies suddenly and unexpectedly. In the United States, SIDS is the leading cause of death in infants more than 1 month of age (Fein, Durbin, & Selbst, 2002). SIDS occurs worldwide; for unexplained reasons, however, the rate varies quite a lot from country to country. For example, SIDS rates are particularly high in Australia and New Zealand and particularly low in Japan and Sweden (Hoffman & Hillman, 1992).

Physicians have not yet uncovered the basic cause of SIDS, although they have learned a fair amount about the groups that are at higher risk: babies with low birth weight, male babies, African American babies, babies with young mothers, and those whose mothers smoked during pregnancy or after birth. SIDS is also more common in the winter and among babies who sleep on their stomachs (Fein, Durbin, & Selbst, 2002; Hoffman & Hillman, 1992; Mitchell et al., 1997; Ponsonby, Dwyer, Gibbons, Cochrane, & Wang, 1993; Taylor et al., 1996), especially on a soft or fluffy mattress, pillow, or comforter. The growing evidence on the role of sleeping position persuaded pediatricians in many countries to change their standard advice to hospitals and families about the best sleeping position for babies. The American Academy of Pediatrics, for example, has been recommending since 1992 that healthy infants should be positioned on their sides or backs when they are put down to sleep. Physicians in many other countries have made similar recommendations, a change in advice that has been followed by a significant drop in SIDS cases in every country involved (Fein, Durbin, & Selbst, 2002; Willinger, Hoffman, & Hartford, 1994). In the United States, for example, the number of SIDS cases has dropped by nearly 30% since 1992. Still, sleeping position cannot be the full explanation, because, of course, most babies who sleep on their stomachs do not die of SIDS.

Ethnic Differences in Infant Mortality   Large variations in infant mortality rates exist across ethnic groups in the United States, as shown in Figure 3.4 (MacDorman & Atkinson, 1999; Matthews, 2005). Rates are lowest among Asian American infants; about 5 of every 1,000 die each year. Among white American babies, the rate is approximately 6 deaths per 1,000. The three groups with the highest rates of infant death are Native Americans (9.1 deaths per 1,000), Native Hawaiians (9 deaths per 1,000), and African Americans (13.9 deaths per 1,000). One reason for these differences is that Native American and African American infants are two to three times more likely to suffer from congenital abnormalities and low birth weight—the two leading causes of infant death—than babies in other groups. Furthermore, SIDS is two to three times as common among them.

sudden infant death syndrome (SIDS) The unexpected death of an infant who otherwise appears healthy; also called crib death. The cause of SIDS is unknown.

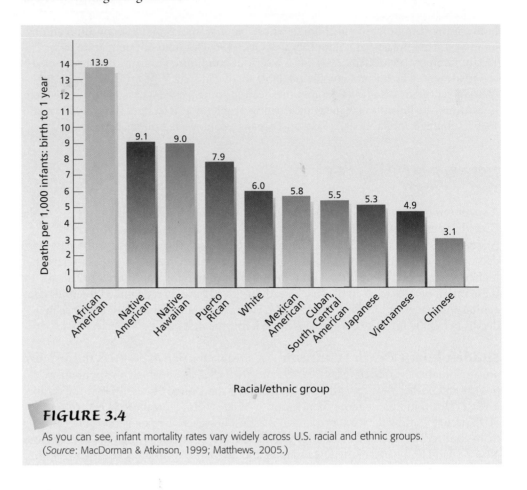

FIGURE 3.4

As you can see, infant mortality rates vary widely across U.S. racial and ethnic groups. (*Source*: MacDorman & Atkinson, 1999; Matthews, 2005.)

Because babies born into poor families, regardless of race or ethnicity, are more likely to die than those whose families are better off economically, some observers have suggested that poverty explains the higher rates of infant death among Native Americans and African Americans, the two groups with the highest rates of poverty. However, infant mortality rates among Hispanic American groups suggest that the link between poverty and infant mortality is not so straightforward. The infant mortality rate among Mexican American babies is 5.8 per 1,000, and the mortality rate for infants of Cuban, South, and Central American ancestry is only 5.5 per 1,000 (MacDorman & Atkinson, 1999). These groups are almost as likely to be poor as African Americans and Native Americans. In contrast, Puerto Rican families are not likely to be poorer than other Hispanic American families, but the mortality rate is 7.9 per 1,000 among their infants. Similarly, rates of early prenatal care—defined as consulting a doctor or midwife during the first trimester of pregnancy—are nearly identical for African American women and Hispanic American women (U.S. Bureau of the Census, 2001). Consequently, access to prenatal care cannot explain differences in infant mortality across these groups.

Interestingly, mortality rates among the babies of immigrants of all racial and ethnic groups are lower than those among babies of U.S.-born mothers. This finding also challenges the poverty explanation for racial and ethnic group differences in infant mortality, because immigrant women are more likely to be poor and less likely to receive prenatal care than women born in the United States (MacDorman & Atkinson, 1999). Many researchers suggest that lower rates of tobacco and alcohol use among women born outside the United States may be an important factor.

Another indication that complex factors influence infant mortality is the finding that, even when researchers compare only infants born to college-educated mothers, those born to African American women are more likely to die (Schoendorf, Hogue,

Kleinman, & Rowley, 1992). Moreover, when only full-term, normal-weight babies are compared, infant mortality is still higher among African American infants. Consequently, researchers believe that understanding racial and ethnic differences in infant mortality is critical to gaining insight into the basic causes of infant death. Thus, explaining group differences has become an important goal of research examining the causes of death in the first year of life.

Before going on...

- What are the infant's nutritional, health care, and immunization needs?
- What kinds of illnesses typically occur in infancy?
- Define SIDS, and describe racial and ethnic differences in infant mortality in the United States.

Summary

Birth

- Most drugs given to a woman during delivery pass through to the infant's bloodstream and have short-term effects on infant responsiveness. In uncomplicated, low-risk pregnancies, delivery at home or in a birth center may be as safe as hospital delivery. The presence of the father during delivery has a variety of positive consequences, including reducing the mother's experience of pain, but being present for the birth does not appear to affect the father's attachment to the infant.
- The normal birth process has three stages: dilation and effacement, delivery, and placental delivery. Several types of problems may occur at birth, including reduced oxygen supply to the infant (anoxia). Slightly more than one-quarter of all deliveries in the United States today are by cesarean section. Newborns are typically assessed using the Apgar score, which is a rating on five dimensions. Most parents show intense interest in the new baby's features, especially the eyes.
- Infants born weighing less than 2,500 grams are designated as low birth weight (LBW); those below 1,500 grams are very low birth weight (VLBW); those below 1,000 grams are extremely low birth weight (ELBW). The lower the weight, the greater the risk of neonatal death or of significant lasting problems, such as low IQ score or learning disabilities.

Behavior in Early Infancy

- Infants have a wide range of reflexes. Some, such as the sucking reflex, are essential for life. Other primitive reflexes are present in the newborn but disappear in the first year. Cycles of sleeping, waking, and crying are present from the beginning.
- Motor skills are only rudimentary at birth. Perceptual skills include the ability to focus both eyes; visually track slowly moving objects; discriminate the mother by sight, smell, and sound; and respond to smells, tastes, and touch. Babies cry for several hours per day, on average, with the amount of crying peaking at about 6 weeks. Newborns can learn from the first days of life and can habituate to repeated stimulation.
- Babies differ from one another on several dimensions, including vigor of response, general activity rate, restlessness, irritability, and cuddliness. Infants develop the ability to express a range of emotions, such as pleasure and distress, over the first year. Most parents experience delight and pleasure at their new role, but it also places strains on their relationship.

Health and Wellness in Early Infancy

- Breast milk or formula supply all of an infant's nutritional needs until 4 to 6 months of age. Babies require periodic check-ups to track their growth and development. They also need to be immunized against a variety of diseases.
- Common illnesses of childhood include diarrhea, upper respiratory infections, and ear infections. Of these, ear infections (otitis media) are often the most serious. All forms of upper respiratory illness are more common among children in day care than among those reared at home.
- In the United States and other industrialized countries, most infant deaths in the first weeks are due to congenital anomalies or low birth weight; after the first weeks, sudden infant death syndrome (SIDS) is the most common cause of death in the first year. African American, Hawaiian American, and Native American infants display higher rates of infant mortality than whites and other racial groups in the United States. Poverty may be a factor, but other groups with similar rates of poverty, such as Hispanic Americans, have lower infant mortality rates than whites.

Key Terms

adaptive reflexes (p. 74)

anoxia (p. 68)

Babinski reflex (p. 75)

cephalocaudal (p. 78)

cesarean section (c-section) (p. 68)

colic (p. 78)

difficult child (p. 81)

dilation (p. 67)

easy child (p. 81)

effacement (p. 67)

extremely low birth weight (ELBW) (p. 71)

habituation (p. 80)

low birth weight (LBW) (p. 71)

Moro reflex (p. 74)

preterm infant (p. 71)

primitive reflexes (p. 74)

proximodistal (p. 78)

reflexes (p. 74)

respiratory distress syndrome (p. 72)

rooting reflex (p. 74)

schematic learning (p. 80)

slow-to-warm-up child (p. 81)

small-for-date infant (p. 72)

states of consciousness (p. 76)

sudden infant death syndrome (SIDS) (p. 87)

temperament (p. 81)

very low birth weight (VLBW) (p. 71)

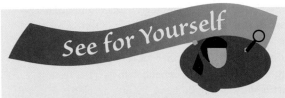

Concerns about Childbearing

You can find out more about women's childbearing-related worries by carrying out what researchers call a *free response* study. Simply ask several women to express their concerns in their own words. Write down what they say or, better yet, make audio or video recordings. When you have collected a number of responses, analyze them for common themes. It is likely that the women's concerns will fall into categories such as physical pain, financial concerns, health of the child, and so on. Once you have determined the categories, calculate the percentage of women who expressed concerns in each. Another way of measuring categories in free responses is to note the order in which categories are mentioned. In other words, you might determine the percentage of women who mentioned physical pain first. Another possible approach to analysis would be to take into account women's experiences with childbearing. The responses of women who have had children may be different from those of women who have not.

Physical Development

4

C H A P T E R

Have you ever shopped for a child's birthday gift? If so, you may have noticed that the labels on toys and other products for children often include claims regarding an item's effect on children's development.

For instance, many videos and music CDs are promoted as having beneficial effects on children's brain development. Sometimes these claims are framed in ways that make parents feel that they are depriving their children of critical developmental experiences if they can't afford to buy such products.

Are such claims justified? Certainly, as you will learn in this chapter, it is true that experience plays a critical role in brain development. However, many observers have noted that the concerns of today's parents about the necessity of providing children with stimuli specifically geared to enhancing brain development have little support in scientific research. Still, "brain-stimulating" toys and media continue to be popular, and many people believe that they are necessary to children's development. Stanford University researchers Adrian Bangerter and Chip Heath have written about how such ideas take root, using the history of a phenomenon known as the Mozart effect as an illustration (Bangerter & Heath, 2004).

In 1993, the news media touted a study published in the scientific journal *Nature* (Rauscher, Shaw, & Ky, 1993) in which researchers reported that listening to a Mozart sonata appeared to raise college students' IQ scores. Almost immediately, the results of this study were dubbed the Mozart effect (ME) and were generalized to infants and children by the popular press. However, neither this study nor any other at the time had addressed the question of whether music could raise children's IQs. Bangerter and Heath also noted that media reports failed to include the information that the IQ increases reported in the study were temporary. In hundreds of newspaper articles and other media reports that appeared between 1993 and 2001, Bangerter and Heath found that, over time, discussions of the ME lost all connection to the original study, and the idea that Mozart sonatas can increase children's IQs came to be assumed to be true. Over the same period, say Bangerter and Heath, the news media ignored numerous carefully designed research studies debunking the Mozart effect that were published in scientific journals (e.g., Chabris, 1999; Steele, Bass, & Crook, 1999). In response to the news media's one-sided representation of the ME, policy makers in some jurisdictions went so far as to provide parents of newborns with free CDs and to require publicly funded preschool programs to include music by Mozart in their curricula. As a result, the ME was perceived by the public as being endorsed by the government, lending further weight to the assumption that it must be real.

This child is still unsteady on her bike, but once she masters this new physical skill, her life will change as she becomes more independent.

Today it is widely known among developmental scientists that there is no empirical support for the ME (Jones & Zigler, 2002; McKelvie & Low, 2002). Nevertheless, many popular books and Internet sites devoted to parenting and teaching continue to promote the idea that listening to music by Mozart raises children's IQ scores (Krakovsky, 2005). Bangerter and Heath say that believing in the ME helps parents and teachers control the emotions associated with their concerns about fostering children's intellectual development. Consequently, anxious parents and teachers are open to discussions that validate their beliefs and turn a deaf ear to scientists' attempts to invalidate them.

As noted earlier, experience is important to brain development and to other aspects of physical development. However, the evidence suggests that physical changes, including those in the brain, rely on an inborn maturational plan as well. Thus, as is true of every domain of development, physical changes appear to arise from the interaction of this maturational plan with environmental factors.

The Brain and Nervous System

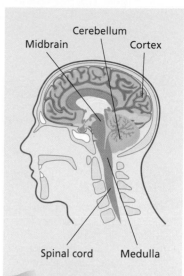

FIGURE 4.1

The medulla and the midbrain are largely developed at birth. In the first 2 years after birth, it is primarily the cortex that develops, although increases in the dendritic arbor and in synapses also occur throughout the nervous system.

Figure 4.1 shows the main structures of the brain. At birth, the **midbrain** and the **medulla** are the most fully developed. These two parts, both in the lower part of the skull and connected to the spinal cord, regulate vital functions such as heartbeat and respiration as well as attention, sleeping, waking, elimination, and movement of the head and neck—all tasks a newborn can perform at least moderately well. The least developed part of the brain at birth is the **cortex**, the convoluted gray matter that wraps around the midbrain and is involved in perception, body movement, thinking, and language. Changes in the brain and nervous system continue throughout childhood and adolescence. There are several critical processes that contribute to these changes.

GROWTH SPURTS

One of the most important principles of neurological development is that the brain grows in spurts rather than in a smooth, continuous fashion (Fischer & Rose, 1994). Each of these spurts involves all of the major developmental processes you'll read about in the sections that follow, and each is followed by a period of stability. In infancy, the intervals of growth and stability are very short. There are short growth spurts at approximately 1-month intervals until the baby is about 5 months old. As the infant gets older, the periods of both growth and stability become longer, with spurts occurring at about 8, 12, and 20 months of age. Between ages 2 and 4, growth proceeds very slowly, and then there is another major spurt at age 4.

Interestingly, many growth spurts are *localized*; that is, they are restricted to one or a few parts of the brain rather than applying to the whole brain (Thompson et al., 2000). Neuropsychologists have correlated some of these localized brain growth spurts with milestones of cognitive development (Fischer & Rose, 1994). For example, the spurt at 20 months of age happens at the same time as most infants show evidence of goal-directed planning in their behavior. A toddler may move a chair from one location to another so that he can climb high enough to reach a forbidden object. Similarly, the spurt around age 4 is accompanied by attainment of an impressive level of fluency in both speaking and understanding language.

Two major growth spurts happen in the brain during middle childhood (Spreen, Risser, & Edgell, 1995). The first is linked to the striking improvements in fine motor skills and eye-hand coordination that usually emerge between 6 and 8 years of age. During the spurt experienced by 10- to 12-year-olds, the frontal lobes of the cerebral cortex become the focus of developmental processes (van der Molen & Molenaar, 1994). Predictably, logic and planning, two cognitive functions that improve dramatically during this period, are carried out primarily by the frontal lobes. In addition, this spurt is associated with improvements in memory function (Hepworth, Rovet, & Taylor, 2001).

There are also two major brain growth spurts in the teenage years. The first occurs between ages 13 and 15 (Spreen, Risser, & Edgell, 1995). For the most part, this growth spurt takes place in parts of the brain that control spatial perception and

midbrain A section of the brain lying above the medulla and below the cortex that regulates attention, sleeping, waking, and other automatic functions; it is largely developed at birth.

medulla A portion of the brain that lies immediately above the spinal cord; it is largely developed at birth.

cortex The convoluted gray portion of the brain, which governs most complex thought, language, and memory.

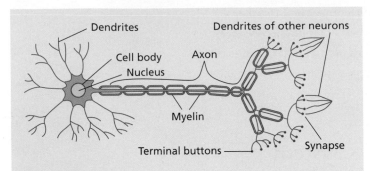

FIGURE 4.2

A typical neuron has three major parts: (1) a cell body, which carries out the metabolic functions of the neuron; (2) branched fibers called dendrites, which are the primary receivers of impulses from other neurons; and (3) a slender, tail-like extension called an axon, the transmitting end of the neuron, which ends in many branches, each with an axon terminal. The axon is covered with myelin, a fatty substance that makes the transmission of neural impulses more efficient.

motor functions. Consequently, by the mid-teens, adolescents' abilities in these areas far exceed those of school-aged children.

Neuropsychologists Kurt Fischer and Samuel Rose believe that a qualitatively different neural network also emerges during this brain growth spurt, a network that enables teens to think abstractly and to reflect on their cognitive processes (Fischer & Rose, 1994). As evidence, they cite neurological and psychological research, from study after study, revealing that major changes in brain organization show up between ages 13 and 15 and qualitative shifts in cognitive functioning appear after age 15. They claim that the consistency of these research findings is too compelling to ignore.

The second brain growth spurt begins around age 17 and continues into early adulthood (van der Molen & Molenaar, 1994). This time, the frontal lobes of the cerebral cortex are the focus of development (Davies & Rose, 1999). You may recall that this area of the brain controls logic and planning. Thus, it is not surprising that older teens perform differently from younger teens when dealing with problems that require these cognitive functions.

SYNAPTIC DEVELOPMENT

One of the processes that contribute to brain growth is called **synaptogenesis**, or the process of creating connections (*synapses*) between neurons (Johnson, 2005). Recall from Chapter 2 that the brain is composed of two basic types of cells: neurons and glial cells. Virtually all of both types of cells are already present at birth. The developmental process after birth primarily involves the creation of synapses, or connections between neurons. Synapse development results from growth of both dendrites and axons (see Figure 4.2). Synaptogenesis occurs at a rapid rate in the cortex during the first 2 years after birth, resulting in a tripling of the overall weight of the brain during those years (Nowakowski, 1987). This burst in synaptogenesis, as well as others that occur later in development, is followed by a period of "pruning," when unnecessary connections are eliminated, making the whole system operate more efficiently.

For example, early in development, each muscle cell seems to develop synaptic connections with several motor neurons in the spinal cord. But after the pruning process has occurred, each muscle fiber is connected to only one neuron. Some neurophysiologists have suggested that the initial surge of synapse formation follows a built-in pattern (Greenough, Black, & Wallace, 1987). The organism seems to be programmed to create certain kinds of neural connections and does so in abundance, creating redundant pathways. According to this argument, the pruning that takes place beginning at around 18 months is a response to experience, resulting in selective retention of the most efficient pathways. Putting it briefly, "experience does not create tracings on a blank tablet; rather, experience erases some of them" (Bertenthal & Campos, 1987). However, neurophysiologists point out that some synapses are formed entirely as a result of experience, and that synaptogenesis continues throughout our lives as we learn new skills.

Consistent with the overall "start-and-stop" pattern of brain development, pruning does not occur at the same time in all parts of the brain. For example, the maximum density of synapses in the portions of the brain that have to do with language comprehension and production occurs at about age 3 years. In contrast, the part of the cortex devoted to vision is maximally dense at 4 months of age, with rapid pruning thereafter (Huttenlocher, 1994).

synaptogenesis The process of synapse formation.

One of the most intriguing points about this process of synaptogenesis is that the combination of the early surge of synaptic growth and then pruning means that the 1-year-old actually has a greater density of dendrites and synapses than an adult does—a piece of information that has surprised many psychologists. Even at age 4, when the early burst of pruning has occurred in all areas of the brain, synaptic density is about twice that in an adult's brain. Pruning continues in spurts throughout childhood and adolescence.

The crucial new understanding that has emerged from research examining the process of synaptic growth and pruning is that the whole process is heavily dependent on the child's specific experience. Each time some experience stimulates a neural pathway, it leaves behind a kind of chemical signal, which is strengthened with each repeated use of that same pathway. When the signal strength reaches some threshold level, that particular neural connection appears to become immune to the pruning process and becomes a permanent part of brain architecture. Conversely, pathways that are not used at all or not used often enough do not reach this threshold strength and are later pruned out.

This new information has several critical implications. First, it becomes clear that brain development follows the old dictum "Use it or lose it." A child growing up in a rich or intellectually challenging environment will retain a more complex network of synapses than a child growing up with fewer forms of stimulation—a variation of the nature-nurture interaction that Aslin calls *attunement.* The evidence to support this proposal comes from several kinds of research, including work with animals. For example, rats that are reared in highly stimulating environments as infants will have a denser network of neurons, dendrites, and synaptic connections as adults than rats that do not receive as much stimulation (Escorihuela, Tobena, & Fernández-Teruel, 1994). Also, in both nonhuman primates and humans, infants who experience significant sensory deprivation, such as from being blind in one eye, develop (or retain) less dense synaptic networks in the part of the brain linked to that particular function (Gordon, 1995). Finally, there is growing evidence showing the importance for human babies of being talked to—not by an inanimate source like a television, but by an attentive, conversational adult. Such conversation appears to help stimulate and organize the infant's brain (Fifer & Moon, 1994; Kuhl, 1993); babies exposed to more of such verbal stimulation retain denser and more complex networks of synapses. This denser network, in turn, provides an enduring base for later complex thinking. Thus, these early months appear to be a sensitive period for the retention of synapses; neural complexity that is not retained in these early years does not redevelop later. Love and affection, while critical to an infant for other reasons, are not enough to optimize brain organization; the baby needs patterned visual and auditory stimulation, particularly language.

A second implication of researchers' emerging understanding of synaptic growth is that the very flexibility of the early brain means that babies and children can adapt to whatever environmental demands they may face; those adaptations are then built into their brains throughout their lives. A child growing up in a physically dangerous environment may retain and strengthen an acute sensitivity to certain signals of danger; a child who lives in a hunting culture will retain an especially acute ability to notice some categories of environmental detail; a child growing up in a noisy urban environment learns how to filter out unnecessary noise (Shore, 1997).

A third basic point is that the "programmed plasticity" of the brain appears to be at its height in infancy. Perhaps paradoxically, this period of maximum plasticity is also the period in which the child may be most vulnerable to major restrictions on intellectual stimulation—such as physical or emotional neglect—making these early years a kind of critical period for brain development. Just as the time of most rapid growth of any body system prenatally is the time when the fetus is most vulnerable to teratogens, so the young infant needs sufficient stimulation and predictability in her environment to maximize the early period of rapid growth and plasticity (de Haan, Luciana, Maslone, Matheny, & Richards, 1994).

Finally, we must raise one additional point about plasticity. Nearly everything scientists know about the role of experience in brain development is derived from studies of children whose environments are characterized by deficiencies (Bruer, 1999). For instance, we know that inadequate nutrition can slow brain development and, consequently, interfere with both cognitive and social development (Liu, Raine, Venables, & Mednick, 2004). However, these findings do not imply that *supernutrition*, or a diet that provides nutrition beyond what is required for normal growth, accelerates brain growth and cognitive development. Indeed, this kind of fallacious conclusion, often inferred from studies emphasizing the importance of experience to brain development, leads to inappropriate beliefs, such as those associated with the Mozart effect you read about at the beginning of the chapter.

Similarly, in recent years many educators have suggested that teachers should employ instructional strategies that are geared toward the developmental processes going on in the brains of their students (e.g., Berninger & Richards, 2002). It is probably beneficial for teachers to understand brain development. However, research aimed at establishing milestones for normal brain development, such as those that have long been known for motor skills (crawling precedes standing, standing precedes walking, and so on), has only just begun (Giedd et al., 1999). Thus, most neuroscientists agree that it is far too soon to form conclusions about how knowledge of brain development might inform "brain-based" teaching strategies for students of different ages.

MYELINATION

A second crucial process in neuronal development is the creation of sheaths, or coverings, around individual axons, which insulate them from one another electrically and improve the conductivity of the nerves. These sheaths are made of a substance called *myelin* (see Figure 4.2 on page 94); the process of developing the sheaths is called **myelination.**

The sequence of myelination follows both cephalocaudal and proximodistal patterns. Thus, nerves serving muscle cells in the hands are myelinated earlier than those serving the feet. Myelination is most rapid during the first 2 years after birth, but it continues at a slower pace throughout childhood and adolescence. For example, the parts of the brain that govern motor movements are not fully myelinated until about age 6 (Todd, Swarzenski, Rossi, & Visconti, 1995).

Myelination leads to improvement in brain functions. For example, the **reticular formation** is the part of the brain responsible for keeping your attention on what you're doing and for helping you sort out important and unimportant information. Myelination of the reticular formation begins in infancy but continues in spurts across childhood and adolescence. In fact, the process isn't complete until the mid-20s (Spreen et al., 1995). So, teenagers have longer attention spans than children, who, in turn, have longer attention spans than infants.

Also of importance is the myelination of the neurons that link the reticular formation to the frontal lobes. It is well documented that **selective attention**, the ability to focus cognitive activity on the important elements of a problem or situation, increases significantly during middle childhood (Lin, Hsiao, & Chen, 1999). It seems likely that myelination of linkages between the frontal lobes and the reticular formation work together to enable school-aged children to develop this important kind of concentration (Sowell et al., 2003).

To understand the importance of selective attention, imagine that your psychology instructor, who usually hands out tests printed on white paper, gives you a test printed on blue paper. You won't spend a lot of time thinking about why the test is blue instead of white; this is an irrelevant detail. Instead, your selective attention ability will prompt you to ignore the color of the paper and focus on the test questions. In contrast, some younger elementary school children might be so distracted by the unusual color of the paper that their test performance would be affected. As the nerves connecting the retic-

CRITICAL THINKING ❓

How does this chapter's information about development of the reticular formation influence your beliefs about children's ability to attend to stimuli for long periods of time?

myelination The process by which an insulating layer of a substance called myelin is added to neurons.

reticular formation The part of the brain that regulates attention.

selective attention The ability to focus cognitive activity on the important elements of a problem or situation.

ular formation and frontal lobes become more fully myelinated during the school years, children begin to function more like adults in the presence of such distractions.

The neurons of the **association areas**—parts of the brain where sensory, motor, and intellectual functions are linked—are myelinated to some degree by the time children enter school. However, from age 6 to age 12, the nerve cells in these areas become almost completely myelinated. Neuroscientists believe that this progression of the myelination process contributes to increases in information-processing speed. For example, suppose you were to ask a 6-year-old and a 12-year-old to identify pictures of common items—a bicycle, an apple, a desk, a dog—as rapidly as possible. Both would have equal knowledge of the items' names, but the 12-year-old would be able to produce the names of the items much more rapidly than the 6-year-old. Such increases in processing speed probably contribute to improvements in memory function you'll read about later in Chapter 6 (Kail 1991; Johnson, 2005).

Neurons in other parts of the brain, such as the **hippocampus**, are also myelinated in childhood (Tanner, 1990). The hippocampus is involved in the transfer of information to long-term memory. Maturation of this brain structure probably accounts for improvements in memory function across childhood (Rolls, 2000).

LATERALIZATION

Equal in importance to synapse formation and myelination is the specialization in function that occurs in the two hemispheres of the brain. The **corpus callosum**, the brain structure through which the left and right sides of the cerebral cortex communicate, grows and matures more during the early childhood years than in any other period of life. The growth of this structure accompanies the functional specialization of the left and right hemispheres of the cerebral cortex. This process is called **lateralization**.

Left- and Right-Brain Dominance   Figure 4.3 illustrates how brain functions are lateralized in 95% of humans, a pattern known as *left-brain dominance*. In a small proportion of the remaining 5 percent, the functions are reversed, a pattern called *right-brain dominance*. However, most people who are not left-brain dominant have a pattern of *mixed dominance*, with some functions following the typical pattern and others reversed. (By the way, the terms *left-brain* and *right-brain* are sometimes used to describe personality or learning style. Such usage has nothing to do with the physical lateralization of functions in the two hemispheres of the brain.)

Neuroscientists suspect that our genes dictate which functions will be lateralized and which will not, because some degree of lateralization is already present in the human fetus (de Lacoste, Horvath, & Woodward, 1991). For example, both fetuses and adults turn their heads in order to be able to listen to language with the right ear. Because sounds entering the right ear are routed to the left side of the brain for interpretation, such findings suggest that language begins to be lateralized in most fetuses. Full lateralization of language function, though, doesn't happen until near the end of the early childhood period (Spreen et al., 1995).

It appears that the experience of learning and using language, not simply genetically programmed maturation of the brain, is the impetus behind hemispheric specialization. Young children whose language skills are the most advanced also show the strongest degree of lateralization (Mills, Coffey-Corina, & Neville, 1994). Neuroscientists have not determined whether some children advance rapidly in language acquisition because their brains are lateralizing at a faster pace. It could also be that some children's brains are lateralizing language function more rapidly because they are learning it faster.

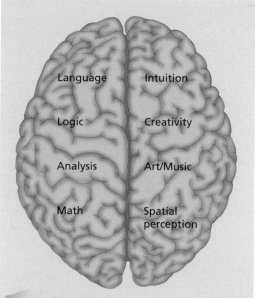

FIGURE 4.3

Brain functions are lateralized, as shown in the figure. Neurologists think that the basic outline of lateralization is genetically determined, whereas the specific timing of the lateralization of each function is determined by an interaction of genes and experiences.

association areas Parts of the brain where sensory, motor, and intellectual functions are linked.

hippocampus A brain structure that is involved in the transfer of information to long-term memory.

corpus callosum The structure that connects the right and left hemispheres of the cerebral cortex.

lateralization The process through which brain functions are divided between the two hemispheres of the cerebral cortex.

Studies of deaf children who are learning sign language also suggest that experience contributes to brain development (Johnson, 2005; Mills et al., 1994). These children use the same area of the brain to process sign meanings as hearing children use for spoken word meanings. Likewise, deaf children's sign vocabularies grow at about the same rate as the vocabularies of children learning spoken language. However, deaf children's processing of sign language grammar happens in an entirely different area of the brain from that used by hearing children to understand the structure of spoken language. In addition, deaf children acquire grammatical knowledge at a slower pace. These observations indicate that some aspects of brain development are linked more to the kinds of linguistic stimuli to which the brain is exposed—in other words, to experience—than to a rigid genetic plan.

Spatial Perception   Lateralization is also linked to the development of **spatial perception**, the ability to identify and act on relationships of objects in space. For example, when you use a map to get from one place to another, you are using spatial perception to read the map and to relate it to the real world. Across early and middle childhood, spatial perception is lateralized to the right hemisphere of the brain in most people. Perception of objects such as faces lateralizes in the preschool years. However, complex spatial perception, such as map-reading, isn't strongly lateralized until after age 8 (Roberts & Bell, 2000). At the same time, the areas of the corpus callosum that are involved in interhemispheric communication related to spatial perceptual tasks grow rapidly (Thompson et al., 2000). As a result of both lateralization and corpus callosum growth, children beyond age 8 exhibit spatial perceptual skills that are superior to those of younger children.

A behavioral test of spatial perception lateralization that neuroscientists often use involves **relative right-left orientation**, the ability to identify right and left from multiple perspectives. Such tests usually show that most children younger than 8 know the difference between their own right and left. Typically, though, only those older than 8 understand the difference between statements like "it's on *your* right" and "it's on *my* right." Lateralization of spatial perception may also be related to the increased efficiency with which older children learn math concepts and problem-solving strategies. In addition, it is somewhat correlated to performance on Piaget's conservation tasks (van der Molen & Molenaar, 1994).

However, the development of spatial perception is more than just a physiological process. Developmentalists know this because this function lateralizes much more slowly in blind children than in those who have sight. Thus, it appears that visual experience plays an important role in this aspect of brain development.

Furthermore, differences in visual experiences have been postulated to explain sex differences in spatial perception and in a related function called **spatial cognition**, the ability to infer rules from and make predictions about the movement of objects in space. For example, when you are driving on a two-lane road and you make a judgment about whether you have enough room to pass the car ahead of you, you are using spatial cognition. From an early age, boys score much higher than girls, on average, when asked to perform spatial cognition tasks (Halpern, 1986; Voyer, Voyer, & Bryden, 1995). Some developmentalists suggest that boys' play preferences, such as their greater interest in video games, help them develop more acute spatial perception and cognition. Indeed, several studies suggest that playing video games fosters good spatial cognition skills (Greenfield, Brannon, & Lohr, 1994). These studies indicate that video-game playing has a particularly marked effect on mental rotation ability—precisely the dimension on which boys and girls differ the most. However, it should also be noted that, throughout childhood and adolescence, the parts of the brain that serve spatial perception possess more volume in boys than in girls (Durston et al., 2001). Similarly, these areas mature at faster rates among males (Giedd et al., 1999). Of course, the faster maturation rates may be at least partly attributable to boys' play preferences. Still, the cross-cultural consistency of male-female differences in spatial per-

spatial perception The ability to identify and act on relationships of objects in space; in most people, this skill is lateralized to the right cerebral hemisphere.

relative right-left orientation The ability to identify right and left from multiple perspectives.

spatial cognition The ability to infer rules from and make predictions about the movement of objects in space.

ception supports the hypothesis that the difference probably stems from some kind of biological factor (Lippa, 2005).

Handedness Handedness, the tendency to rely primarily on the right or the left hand, is another important aspect of neurological lateralization (Tanner, 1990). Studies relating brain lateralization to handedness suggest that a common neurological process may be involved in both. About 96% of right-handers possess the typical pattern of language-on-the-left (Pujol, Deus, Losilla, & Capdevila, 1999). However, only 75% of left-handers are left-brain dominant. About 1% of left-handers have complete right-brain language specialization, and the rest have a mixed pattern of dominance (Pujol et al., 1999).

It used to be thought that right-handedness increased among humans as societies became more literate. The idea was that, when teaching children how to write, parents and teachers encouraged them to use their right hands. In this way, right-handedness became sort of a custom that was passed on from one generation to the next through instruction. By examining skeletons that predate the invention of writing, archaeologists have determined that the proportions of right- and left-handedness were about the same in illiterate ancient populations as they are among modern humans: 83% right-handed, 14% left-handed, and 3% ambidexterous (Steele & Mayes, 1995). These findings suggest that the prevalence of right-handedness is likely to be the result of genetic inheritance. Moreover, geneticists at the National Cancer Institute (NCI) have identified a dominant gene for right-handedness that they believe to be so common in the human population that most humans receive a copy of it from both parents (Talan, 1998, October 28).

Further evidence for the genetic hypothesis can be found in studies demonstrating that handedness appears very early in life—often before the first birthday—although it doesn't become well established until the preschool years (Stroganova, Posikera, Pushina, & Orekhova, 2003). Research comparing children's right-hand and left-hand performance on manual tasks, such as moving pegs from one place to another on a pegboard, also supports the genetic hypothesis. Most of these studies show that older children are better at accomplishing fine-motor tasks with the nondominant hand than younger children are (Dellatolas et al., 2003; Roy, Bryden, & Cavill, 2003). Findings from studies comparing nondominant hand use in children and adults follow the same pattern (Annett, 2003; Cavill & Bryden, 2003). Thus, experience in using the hands appears to moderate, rather than strengthen, the advantage of the dominant over the nondominant hand.

Before going on . . .

- Describe the pattern of growth spurts in brain development.
- What are synapses, and how do they change?
- How does the process of myelination contribute to brain development?
- What kinds of cognitive and motor skills are linked to lateralization?

Bones, Muscles, and Motor Skills

As you've seen, changes in children's nervous system have powerful influences on their development. But changes in other systems are influential as well.

PATTERNS OF CHANGE IN SIZE AND SHAPE

By age 2, a toddler is about half as tall as he will be as an adult (hard to believe, isn't it?). You may also find it surprising that growth from birth to maturity is neither continuous nor smooth. Figure 4.4 shows the different phases in height gain for boys and girls.

During the first phase, which lasts for about the first 2 years, the baby gains height very rapidly, adding 10 to 12 inches in length in the first year and tripling his body weight in the same span. At about age 2, the child settles down to a slower but steady addition of 2 to 3 inches and about 6 pounds a year until adolescence.

handedness A strong preference for using primarily one hand or the other; it develops between 3 and 5 years of age.

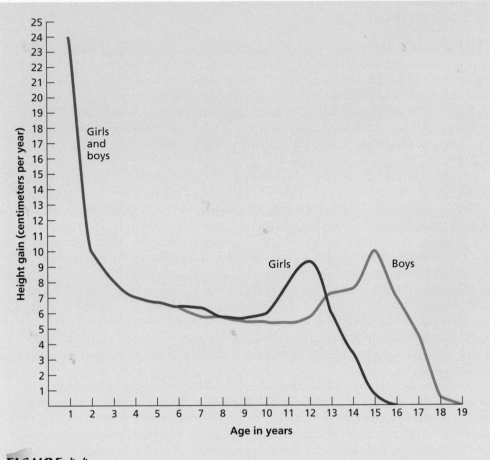

FIGURE 4.4

These curves show the gain in height for each year from birth through adolescence, based on recent data from many hundreds of thousands of American children. You can see the several clear phases: very rapid growth in infancy, slower growth in the preschool and elementary school years, a growth spurt at adolescence, and the cessation of growth at adulthood.
(*Sources*: Malina, 1990; Tanner, 1990, p. 14.)

The third phase is the dramatic adolescent "growth spurt," when the child may add 3 to 6 inches a year for several years, after which the rate of growth again slows until final adult size is reached. Figure 4.4 makes it clear that this growth spurt is, on average, larger for boys than for girls, but virtually all children show a period of more rapid growth sometime between the ages of about 9 and 15.

The shape and proportions of the child's body also change. In an adult, the head is about an eighth to a tenth of the total height. In a toddler, the head is proportionately far larger in order to accommodate the nearly adult-sized brain of the infant. And a child's hands and feet normally reach full adult size sometime in late elementary school or early adolescence, causing his appearance to be somewhat awkward. However, researchers have found no point in the adolescent growth process at which teenagers become consistently less coordinated or less skillful in physical tasks (Butterfield, Lehnhard, Lee, & Coladarci, 2004).

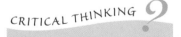

CRITICAL THINKING

How do you think boys' slower pace of motor development affects their experiences in school?

BONES

The hand, wrist, ankle, and foot all have fewer bones at birth than they will have at full maturity. An adult has nine separate bones in his wrist, while a 1-year-old has only three; the remaining six bones develop over the period of childhood. Like many aspects of physical development, this process occurs earlier in girls than in boys. For example, the nine adult wrist bones are normally visible on x-rays, though not yet fully hardened or completely "articulated" (meaning they don't yet work as well together as they will in adulthood), by 51 months in girls but not until 66 months in boys (Needlman, 1996). Consequently, in the early years of school, girls display more advanced coordination in skills such as handwriting than boys do.

In one part of the body, though, the bones fuse rather than differentiate. The skull of a newborn is made up of several bones separated by spaces called **fontanels**. Fontanels allow the head to be compressed without injury during the birth process, and they give the brain room to grow. In most children, the fontanels are filled in by bone by 12 to 18 months, creating a single connected skull bone.

Bones also change in quality as well as in number over the course of development. An infant's bones are softer, with a higher water content, than an adult's bones. The process of bone hardening, called **ossification**, occurs steadily from birth through puberty, following such a regular and predictable pattern that physicians use **bone age** as the best single measure of a child's physical maturation; x-rays of the hand and wrist show the stage of development of wrist and finger bones. In infancy and toddlerhood, the sequence of development generally follows the cephalocaudal and proximodistal patterns. For example, bones of the hand and wrist harden before those in the ankles or feet.

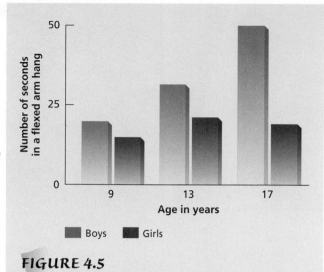

FIGURE 4.5

Both boys and girls get stronger between childhood and adolescence, but boys gain much more strength.
(*Source:* Smoll & Schutz, 1990, from Table 1, p. 363.)

MUSCLES AND FAT

Although virtually all muscle fibers are present at birth, muscles—like bones—change in quality from infancy through adolescence, becoming longer and thicker and developing a higher ratio of muscle to water at a fairly steady rate throughout childhood. At adolescence, muscles go through a growth spurt, just as height does, so that adolescents become quite a lot stronger in just a few years. Both boys and girls show this increase in strength, but the increase is much greater in boys. For example, in a classic cross-sectional study in Canada involving 2,673 children and teenagers, Smoll and Schutz (1990) measured strength by having each child hang as long as possible from a bar, keeping his or her eyes level with the bar. As you can see in Figure 4.5, 9-year-old boys could maintain this flexed arm hang for about 40% longer than could girls of the same age; by age 17, boys could sustain it almost three times as long as girls. Similar results have been found for other measures of strength (Butterfield et al., 2004). This substantial difference in strength is one reflection of the sex difference in muscle mass. In adult men, about 40% of total body mass is muscle, compared to only about 24% in adult women.

Such a sex difference in muscle mass (and accompanying strength) seems to be largely a result of hormone differences, although sex differences in exercise patterns or fitness may also play some role. For example, the sex difference in leg strength is much less than the difference in arm strength, a pattern that makes sense if we assume that all teenagers walk and use their legs a similar amount but that boys use their arm muscles in various sports more than girls do, especially in the teenage years, when girls increasingly drop out of sports programs (Kann et al., 1995). Still, there does seem to be a basic hormonal difference as well, because very fit girls and women are still not as strong as very fit boys and men.

Another major component of the body is fat, most of which is stored immediately under the skin. This subcutaneous fat first develops beginning at about 34 weeks prenatally and has an early peak at about 9 months after birth (the so-called baby fat); the thickness of this layer of fat then declines until about age 6 or 7, after which it rises until adolescence.

fontanel One of several "soft spots" in the skull that are present at birth but disappear when the bones of the skull grow together.

ossification The process of hardening by which soft tissue becomes bone.

bone age A measure of physical maturation based on x-ray examination of bones, typically the wrist and hand bones. Two children of the same chronological age may have different bone age because their rates of physical maturation differ.

By age 1, Nellie not only can walk; she can navigate stairs. By age 5 or 6, most children have developed very good gross motor skills, needed to run and kick. Yet a 5- or 6-year-old will approach a task requiring fine motor skills, such as using scissors, with tense concentration and slow, still imprecise body movements.

| Category | Drawing Model | |
	Cube	Cylinder
1 Scribbles (up to 30 mos.)		
2 Single Units (30 mos. to 46 mos.)		
3 Differentiated Figures (46 mos. to 7 years)		
4 Integrated Whole (7 years +)		

FIGURE 4.6

Examples of drawings in each category of two object forms. (*Source*: Toomela, A. (1999). Drawing Development: Stages in the Representation of a Cube and a Cylinder. *Child Development, 70*, 1141–1150. Reprinted with permission from the Society for Research in Child Development.)

Once again, there is a sex difference in these patterns. From birth, girls have slightly more fat tissue than boys do, and this difference becomes gradually more marked during childhood. At adolescence, the difference grows still further. The size of the change is illustrated in results of the Canadian study cited earlier (Smoll & Schutz, 1990). Between ages 13 and 17, the percentage of body weight made up of fat rose from 21.8% to 24.0% among the girls in this study but dropped from 16.1% to 14.0% among the boys. So during and after puberty, proportions of fat rise among girls and decline among boys, while the proportion of weight that is muscle rises in boys and declines in girls.

USING THE BODY

The ability to use the body to carry out physical activities involves interactions of several separate systems.

Stamina   *Stamina* is the capacity to sustain motor activity. For example, if you observe children on playgrounds, you will notice that preschoolers display short bursts of physical activity followed by periods of rest. School-aged children show a similar pattern, but their periods of activity are longer and their periods of rest are shorter than those of younger children because they possess more stamina.

Changes in stamina are linked to growth of the heart and lungs, which is especially evident during puberty. As the heart and lungs increase in size, the heart rate drops. Both of these changes are more marked for boys than for girls—another of the factors that increases boys' capacity for sustained effort relative to that of girls. Before puberty, boys and girls are fairly similar in physical strength, speed, and stamina, although even at these earlier ages, when a difference exists, it favors the boys. After puberty, boys have a clear advantage in all three areas (Smoll & Schutz, 1990).

motor development Growth and change in ability to perform both gross motor skills (such as walking or throwing) and fine motor skills (such as drawing or writing).

Motor Development   **Motor development** includes both movement skills, often called *gross motor skills*, such as crawling, walking, running, and bike riding, and manipulative skills, often called *fine motor skills*, such as grasping or picking up objects, holding a crayon or a pencil, or threading a needle. Both gross motor and

TABLE 4.1	Sequences of Development of Various Motor Skills	
Age	**Locomotor (Gross Motor) Skills**	**Manipulative (Fine Motor) Skills**
1–3 mos.	Stepping reflex; lifts head; sits with support	Holds object if placed in hand; begins to swipe at objects
4–6 mos.	Rolls over; sits with self-support by 6 months; creeps	Reaches for and grasps objects, using one hand to grasp
7–9 mos.	Sits without support	Transfers objects from one hand to the other; can grasp with thumb and finger ("pincer grasp") by 9 months
10–12 mos.	Pulls self up to standing; walks grasping furniture, then walks without help; squats and stoops	Grasps a spoon across palm, but has poor aim of food at mouth
13–18 mos.	Walks backward and sideways; runs (14–20 months)	Stacks two blocks; puts objects into small containers and dumps them out
2–4 yrs.	Runs easily; walks up stairs using one foot per step; skips on both feet; pedals and steers a tricycle	Picks up small objects (e.g., Cheerios); holds crayon with fingers (age 2–3), then between thumb and first two fingers (age 3–4); cuts paper with scissors
4–7 yrs.	Walks up and down stairs using one foot per step; walks on tiptoe; walks a thin line; jumps, throws, and catches fairly well	Threads beads but not needle (age 4–5); threads needle (age 5–6); grasps pencil maturely but writes or draws with stiffness and concentration

Sources: Capute et al., 1984; Connolly and Dalgleish, 1989; Den Ouden, Rijken, Brand, Verloove-Vanhorick, and Ruys, 1991; Fagard and Jacquet, 1989, Gallahue and Ozmun, 1995; Hagerman, 1996; Needlman, 1996; Overby, 2002; Thomas, 1990.

fine motor skills are present in some form at every age, as you can see in Table 4.1. As a general rule, however, gross motor skills develop earlier, with fine motor skills lagging behind. Thus, 6-year-olds can run, hop, skip, jump, and climb well; many can ride a two-wheeled bike. But children this age are not yet skilled at using a pencil or crayon or cutting accurately with scissors (see Figure 4.6). When they use such tools, their whole body gets involved—the tongue moving and the whole arm and back involved in the writing or cutting motion—a pattern plainly evident in the photograph of the boy cutting. In the elementary school years, fine motor skills improve rapidly, making it possible for most children not only to write more clearly and easily, but also to play a musical instrument, draw, and develop sports skills that require fine motor coordination. Indeed, the emergence of fine motor skills also has an impact on the appropriate timing of children's sports activities—a topic explored in *The Real World*.

Before going on . . .

- How do children change in shape and size?
- How do the bones of an adult differ from those of an infant?
- In what ways do muscle and fat tissue change with age?
- Describe age-related changes in stamina and motor skills.

The Endocrine and Reproductive Systems

*O*ne of the most obvious sets of physical changes involves the development of sexual maturity. The whole process is controlled by special chemical signals and is somewhat different in girls and boys.

HORMONES

Hormones, which are secretions of the various **endocrine glands** in the body, govern pubertal growth and physical changes in several ways, which are summarized in Table

endocrine glands Glands (including the adrenals, the thyroid, the pituitary, the testes, and the ovaries) that secrete hormones governing overall physical growth and sexual maturing.

Sports for Children

At age 6, Katara could hardly wait to take part in her first soccer game. Though not the strongest player on the team, she enjoyed playing soccer with friends and looked forward to the beginning of soccer season each year until she was 12 years old. At first, 12-year-old Katara was excited about the prospect of playing soccer with her old friends. However, following the second practice session, Katara began complaining about going to practice and begged her parents to let her quit. Eventually her parents agreed, because they feared that insisting that Katara honor her commitment to the team would turn her against all forms of physical activity.

Katara's story is not unusual. Many children participate in sports for a few years and then lose interest. Why? One reason pre-adolescent girls like Katara stop participating in sports is that they do not want to be perceived as overly masculine. For example, studies have shown that athletically talented female basketball players who continue to participate in the game after puberty are likely to have found a way to positively incorporate athleticism into their identities while maintaining a feminine self-perception off the court (Shakib, 2003).

A more important factor in older children's decisions to give up sports, one that applies to both boys and girls, is the strong emphasis on competition and winning in many sports programs (Anshel, 1990). Children of 6 or 7 get involved in sports more because they simply enjoy moving their bodies than out of any desire to defeat an opponent. They want to do their best, but they care more about having a chance to play than they do about winning. Yet coaches in many organized sports, even those for young children, emphasize winning rather than fun or fair play or even basic exercise—a process sometimes called the "professionalization of play" (Hodge & Tod, 1993).

Further, amateur coaches often have a poor understanding of normal motor skills among 6- or 7-year-olds. When they see a child who does not yet throw a ball skillfully or who kicks a ball awkwardly, they label the child "clumsy" or "uncoordinated." From then on, these perfectly normal boys and girls get little playing time or encouragement. Coaches may also overtly compare children's abilities, criticizing those who don't play as well rather than emphasizing effort and improvement. Children drop out of sports by age 10 or 11 because they have a clear impression that they are "not good enough" (Anshel, 1990) or because they experience their coaches as too critical and not supportive enough (Smith & Smoll, 1997).

Regardless of their initial skill levels, children should spend the earlier elementary school years learning and perfecting basic skills in activities that are fun and that involve as much movement as possible. Among sports activities, soccer and swimming are particularly likely to meet these conditions, not only because everyone is likely to get at least some aerobic exer-

cise, but also because the basic skills are within the abilities of 6- or 7-year-olds. Baseball, in contrast, is not a good sport for most children this age because it requires well-developed eye-hand coordination to hit or catch the ball, coordination that most 7-year-olds do not yet have. By about age 10, many children are ready to play sports such as baseball and basketball, but many other sports, such as tennis, are still difficult for the average child of this age.

If you want to encourage your child to be involved in some organized sport (as opposed to simply encouraging active games or outdoor play), choose carefully. Let the child try several sports—individual sports as well as team sports—to see which ones are enjoyable. The child's body type or size may suggest which sports are likely to be best. A lean child of average or below-average height may find soccer or gymnastics a good choice; a larger child with broader shoulders may make a good swimmer; taller children may be inclined toward basketball—although small size certainly does not disqualify a child from this sport (Malina, 1994). Whatever sport you and the child choose, make sure to select instructors or programs that specifically deemphasize competition and offer skills training and encouragement to all children. Guard against pushing too fast or too hard. If you do, your child may develop the notion that he or she can't measure up to your expectations, an idea that is sure to take all the fun out of playing the game. Finally, try to ensure that daughters grow up believing that physical attractiveness isn't the most important thing in life. Moreover, you can make them aware of female athletes who exemplify the idea that athletics and femininity are not mutually exclusive.

Questions for Reflection

1. As the coach of a baseball team made up of 7-year-old boys and girls, how would you manage the differing ability levels and expectations of the children?
2. How might the parents of an athletically talented 13-year-old girl who wants to quit participating in sports deal with the situation?

4.2. The **pituitary gland** provides the trigger for release of hormones from other glands; thus, it is sometimes called the *master gland*. For example, the thyroid gland secretes thyroxine only when it receives a signal from the pituitary in the form of a secretion of a specific thyroid-stimulating hormone.

The rate of growth of children is governed largely by thyroid hormone and pituitary growth hormone. Thyroid hormone is secreted in greater quantities for the first 2 years of life and then falls to a lower level and remains steady until adolescence (Tanner, 1990). Secretions from the testes and ovaries, as well as adrenal androgen, are also at very low levels in the early years of childhood. As Figure 4.7 shows, this changes at age 7 or 8, when adrenal androgen begins to be secreted in greater amounts—the first signal of the changes of puberty (Rosenthal & Gitelman, 2002).

Although **puberty** is often thought of as a single event, it is actually a series of milestones that culminate in the ability to reproduce. After the initial hormonal changes that happen around age 7 or 8, there is a complex sequence of additional hormonal changes. The pituitary gland begins secreting increased levels of **gonadotrophic hormones** (two hormones in males, three in females). These in turn stimulate the development of glands in the testes and the ovaries that then secrete more of the so-called *sex hormones*—testosterone in boys and a form of estrogen called *estradiol* in girls.

Along with the gonadotrophic hormones, the pituitary gland secretes three other hormones that interact with the sex hormones and affect growth: *adrenal androgen, thyroid-stimulating hormone*, and *general growth hormone*. Adrenal androgen, which is chemically very similar to testosterone, plays a particularly important role for girls, triggering the growth spurt and affecting pubic hair development. For boys, adrenal androgen is less significant, presumably because they already have so much male hormone in the form of testosterone in their bloodstreams. The increased levels of sex and growth hormones trigger two sets of body changes: development of the sex organs, and a much broader set of changes in the brain, bones, muscles, and other body organs.

The most obvious changes of puberty are those associated with sexual maturity. Changes in *primary sex characteristics* include growth of the testes and penis in the male and of the ovaries, uterus, and vagina in the female. *Secondary sex characteristic* changes include breast development in girls, changing voice pitch and beard growth in boys, and the growth of body hair in both sexes. These physical developments occur in

Gains in coordination, strength, and stamina enable these adolescent girls to perform far better on the basketball court than was possible just a couple of years earlier.

TABLE 4.2	Major Hormones Involved in Physical Growth and Development	
Gland	**Key Hormone(s) Secreted**	**Aspects of Growth Influenced**
Thyroid	Thyroxine	Normal brain development and overall rate of growth
Adrenal	Adrenal androgen (chemically very similar to testosterone)	Some changes at puberty, particularly the development of skeletal maturity and mature muscles, especially in boys
Leydig cells in the testes (in boys)	Testosterone	Crucial in the formation of male genitals prenatally; triggers the sequence of primary and secondary sex characteristic changes at puberty; stimulates increased output of growth hormone and affects bones and muscles
Ovaries (in girls)	Several estrogens, the most critical of which is estradiol	Development of the menstrual cycle, breasts, and pubic hair
Pituitary	Growth hormone (GH), thyroid-stimulating hormone (TSH), and the gonadotrophic hormones: follicle-stimulating hormone (FSH) and luteinizing hormone (LH)	Growth hormone governs the rate of physical maturation; other pituitary hormones signal the respective sex glands to secrete; follicle-stimulating hormone and luteinizing hormone help control the menstrual cycle

Source: Tanner, 1990.

pituitary gland Gland that provides the trigger for release of hormones from other glands.

puberty The series of hormonal and physical changes at adolescence that bring about sexual maturity.

gonadotrophic hormones Two hormones secreted by the pituitary gland at the beginning of puberty that stimulate the development of glands in the testes and ovaries, which then begin to secrete testosterone or estrogen.

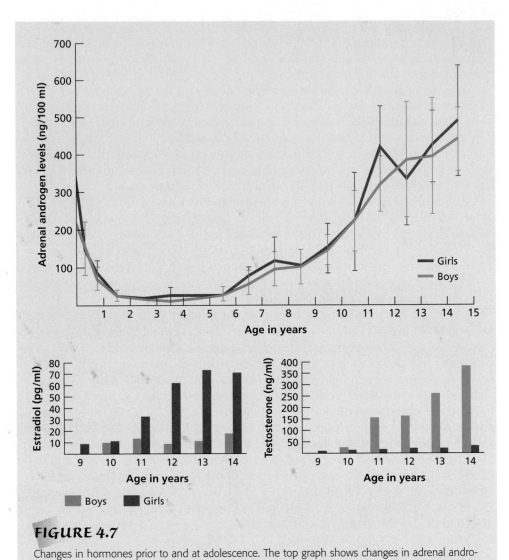

FIGURE 4.7

Changes in hormones prior to and at adolescence. The top graph shows changes in adrenal androgen, which are equivalent in boys and girls; the bottom graphs show increases in estradiol for girls in picograms per milliliter, and testosterone for boys in nanograms per milliliter.
(*Sources*: Androgen data from M. K. McClintock and G. Herdt, from "Rethinking Puberty: The Development of Sexual Attraction," *Current Directions in Psychological Science*, Vol. 5, No. 6 (December 1996), p. 181, Fig. 2. © 1996 American Psychological Association. By permission of Cambridge University Press. Estradiol and testosterone data from Elizabeth Susman, Fig. 2 from "Modeling Developmental Complexity in Adolescence: Hormones and Behavior in Context," p. 291, *Journal of Research on Adolescence*, 7, 1997. © 1997 by Lawrence Erlbaum Associates, Inc. By permission of the publisher and author.)

a defined sequence, customarily divided into five stages following a system originally suggested by J. M. Tanner (1990) (see Table 4.3). Stage 1 describes the preadolescent stage, stage 2 the first signs of a pubertal change, stages 3 and 4 the intermediate steps, and stage 5 the final adult characteristic.

SEQUENCE OF CHANGES IN GIRLS AND BOYS

Studies of preteens and teens in both Europe and North America show that in girls, the various sequential changes are interlocked in a particular pattern, shown schematically in Figure 4.8 (Malina, 1990). The first steps are the early changes in breasts and pubic hair, followed by the peak of the growth spurt and by the beginnings of stages 4 and 5, which involve further breast and pubic hair development. Usually, only after the growth spurt does first menstruation occur, an event called **menarche** (pronounced

menarche Onset of menstruation.

TABLE 4.3	Examples of Tanner's Stages of Pubertal Development	
Stage	**Female Breast Development**	**Male Genital Development**
1	No change except for some elevation of the nipple.	Testes, scrotum, and penis are all about the same size and shape as in early childhood.
2	Breast bud stage: elevation of breast and the nipple as a small mound. Areolar diameter increases compared to stage 1.	Scrotum and testes are slightly enlarged. Skin of the scrotum reddens and changes texture, but little or no enlargement of the penis.
3	Breast and areola both enlarged and elevated more than in stage 2, but no separation of their contours.	Penis slightly enlarged, at first mainly in length. Testes and scrotum are further enlarged.
4	Areola and nipple form a secondary mound projecting above the contour of the breast.	Penis further enlarged, with growth in breadth and development of glans. Testes and scrotum further enlarged, and scrotum skin still darker.
5	Mature stage. Only the nipple projects, with the areola recessed to the general contour of the breast.	Genitalia achieve adult size and shape.

Source: Petersen and Taylor, 1980, p.127.

men-ARE-kee). Menarche typically occurs 2 years after the beginning of other visible changes and is succeeded only by the final stages of breast and pubic hair development. Among girls in industrialized countries today, menarche occurs, on average, between ages $12^{1}/_{2}$ and $13^{1}/_{2}$; 95% of all girls experience this event between the ages of 11 and 15 (Adelman & Ellen, 2002).

Interestingly, the timing of menarche changed rather dramatically from the mid-19th to the mid-20th century. In 1840, the average age of menarche in Western industrialized countries was roughly 17; the average dropped steadily from that time until the 1950s at a rate of about 4 months per decade among European populations, an example of what psychologists call a **secular trend** (Roche, 1979). The change was most likely caused by significant changes in lifestyle and diet, particularly increases in protein and fat intake along with reductions in physical exercise, that resulted in an increase in the proportion of body fat in females. In developing countries, where diets are leaner or even inadequate and children engage in physical labor, menarche still tends to happen in the middle rather than the early teen years.

It is possible to conceive shortly after menarche, but irregularity is the norm for some time. For about two years after menarche, ovulation occurs in only 30% of girls' menstrual cycles (Adelman & Ellen, 2002). Over the next two years, that ovulation percentage rises to the adult rate of 80%. Such irregularity no doubt contributes to the widespread (but false) assumption among girls in their early teens that they cannot get pregnant because they are too young.

In boys, as in girls, the peak of the growth spurt typically comes fairly late in the sequence, as you can see in Figure 4.9. These data suggest that, on average, a boy completes stages 2 and 3 of genital development and stages 2 and 3 of pubic hair development before he reaches his growth peak. The development of a beard and the lowering of the voice occur near the end of the sequence. Precisely when in this sequence the boy begins to produce viable sperm is very difficult to determine. It appears that a boy

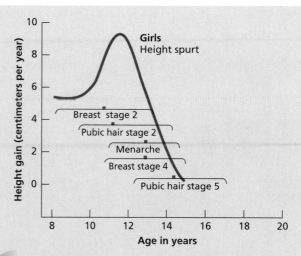

FIGURE 4.8

The figure shows the normal sequence and timing of pubertal changes for girls. The red box on each black line represents the average age when the change occurs; the line indicates the range of normal times. Note the wide range of normality for all of these changes. Also note how relatively late in the sequence the growth spurt and menarche occur.
(*Sources*: Malina, 1990; Tanner, 1990.)

secular trend A pattern of change in some characteristic over several cohorts, such as systematic changes in the average timing of menarche or in average height or weight.

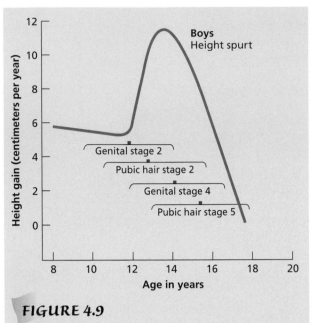

FIGURE 4.9

The sequence of pubertal changes begins about 2 years later for boys than for girls, but as with girls, the height spurt occurs relatively late in the sequence.
(*Sources*: Malina, 1990; Tanner, 1990.)

can attain fertility as early as age 12 or as late as age 16 and still be within the normal range (Adelman & Ellen, 2002). Sequentially, fertility usually occurs just before a boy reaches his full adult height.

While the order of pubertal development seems to be highly consistent, there is quite a lot of individual variability. Figures 4.8 and 4.9 depict the normative, or average, pattern, but individual teenagers often deviate from the norm. For instance, a girl might move through several stages of pubic hair development before the first clear changes in the breasts become evident or might experience menarche much earlier in the sequence than normal. It is important to keep this variation in mind if you are trying to make a prediction about an individual teenager.

THE TIMING OF PUBERTY

In any random sample of 12- and 13-year-olds, you will find some who are already at stage 5, and others still at stage 1 in the steps of sexual maturation. In U.S. culture today, most young people seem to share the expectation that pubertal changes will happen sometime between ages 12 and 14. Coincidentally, most girls acquire a culturally undesirable *endomorphic*, or somewhat flabby, body type, as a result of puberty. Thus, early-developing girls should have more adjustment problems than average- or late-developing girls. Similarly, puberty provides most boys with a culturally admired *mesomorphic*, or lean and muscular, body type. Thus, early-developing boys should display better psychological and social adjustment than average- or late-developing boys.

Research in the United States confirms some of these predictions. Girls who are early developers (before age 11 or 12 for major body changes) show consistently more negative body images, such as thinking they are too fat (Sweeting & West, 2002). Such early-developing girls are also more likely than girls who are average or late developers to get into trouble in school and at home, to get involved with misbehaving peer groups, to engage in delinquent behavior, to be depressed, to begin smoking in adolescence, and to develop eating disorders (Alsaker, 1995; Caspi, Lynam, Moffitt, & Silva, 1993; Dick, Rose, Viken, & Kaprio, 2000; Kaltiala-Heino, Rimpela, Rissanen, & Rantanen, 2001; Rierdan & Koff, 1993; Silbereisen & Kracke, 1993).

In early studies, researchers found, as expected, that the earlier a boy's development, the more positive his body image, the better he does in school, the less trouble he gets into, and the more friends he has (Duke et al., 1982). However, in more recent longitudinal research, early-developing boys have been found to be more hostile and aggressive than their on-time peers (Ge, Conger, & Elder, 2001). Moreover, early development appears to render boys more likely to suffer ill effects from stressful life experiences (e.g., parental divorce). And in poor neighborhoods, early puberty is associated with affiliation with deviant peers (Ge, Brody, Conger, Simons, et al., 2002). Consequently, developmentalists are reexamining the notion that early puberty is entirely beneficial to boys.

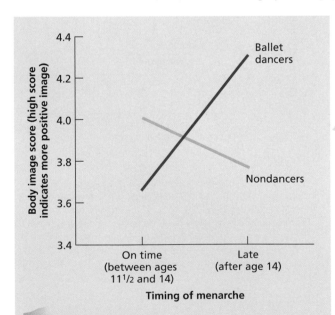

FIGURE 4.10

Serious ballet dancers clearly prefer to have a very late puberty. In this study, dancers whose menarche was "on time" by ordinary standards actually had poorer body images than those who were objectively quite late, while the reverse was true for nondancers. Thus, it is perception of timing and not actual timing that is critical.
(*Source*: Brooks-Gunn & Warren, 1985, from Table 1, p. 291.)

In nearly all studies examining pubertal timing, though, earliness or lateness has been defined in terms of the actual physical changes. The results have been somewhat clearer when researchers have instead asked teenagers about their internal models of earliness or lateness. The link between the internal model and the outcome is especially vivid in a classic study of ballet dancers by Jeanne Brooks-Gunn (Brooks-Gunn, 1987; Brooks-Gunn & Warren, 1985). She studied 14- to 18-year-old girls, some of whom were serious ballet dancers studying at a national ballet company school. A very lean, almost prepubescent body is highly desirable among such dancers. Brooks-Gunn therefore expected that dancers who were very late in pubertal development would actually have a better image of themselves than those who were on time. And that is exactly what she found (see Figure 4.10). Among the nondancers, menarche at the biologically average time was associated with a better body image than was late menarche, but exactly the reverse was true for the dancers. Thus, as predicted, it is the discrepancy between a teenaged girl's internal model of puberty and her experiential reality that predicts the effects of pubertal timing. Research has yet to examine the relationship between boys' internal models of puberty and their actual experiences.

Before going on ...

- How do hormones affect physical growth and puberty?
- What are the normative sequences of pubertal development in girls and boys?
- How does the timing of puberty influence an individual's development?

Sexual Behavior in Adolescence

In the United States, most people become sexually active sometime before age 20, about half before they leave high school (see Figure 4.11). For some teens, being "sexually active" constitutes a single act of intercourse sometime during the high school years. However, many others have multiple partners and frequently engage in unprotected sex acts. Consequently, a fairly large proportion of teenagers in the United States suffer from **sexually transmitted diseases (STDs),** diseases acquired through sexual activity (also called *venereal diseases*). In addition, many experience unplanned pregnancies.

PREVALENCE OF SEXUAL BEHAVIOR

Figure 4.11 shows findings from a large-scale national survey of high school students in the United States (Centers for Disease Control [CDC], 2004a). As you can see from the figure, high school boys were found to be more sexually active than girls.

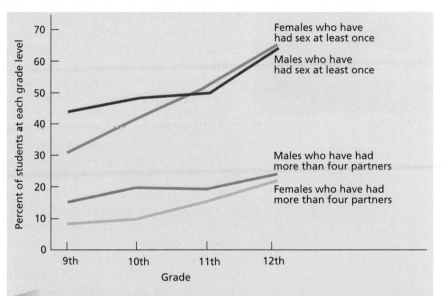

FIGURE 4.11

The graph illustrates the data from a representative sample of more than 15,000 high school students interviewed in 1999. As you can see, the number of students who have had sex at least once increases substantially from 9th to 12th grade, and an alarming percentage of teens have had four or more partners by the end of the high school years. (*Source*: CDC, 2004a.)

Furthermore, the proportion of sexually experienced teens increased across grades 9 to 12. One statistic illustrated by the figure that is particularly worrisome to public health officials is the proportion of teens who have had multiple partners before leaving high school. Research has shown that the more partners a teenager (or an adult, for that matter) has, the more likely he or she is to contract a sexually transmitted disease.

Sexual experience varies across ethnic groups (CDC, 2004a). About 67% of African American high school students report having had sexual intercourse at least once in their lives. The rates among Hispanic American and white students are 51% and 42%, respectively. African American students are also more likely than Hispanic Americans

sexually transmitted diseases (STDs) Category of disease spread by sexual contact, including chlamydia, genital warts, syphilis, gonorrhea, and HIV; also called venereal diseases.

CRITICAL THINKING ?

Think about your own experience of puberty. Was it early, late, or on time? How did the timing of the various milestones of puberty affect your self-image? How did it affect your status with peers?

Early dating is associated with early sexual activity.

and white teens to have had their first sexual encounter before age 13 (19% versus 8.5 and 4.2%, respectively).

There are also age and ethnic differences among students who are sexually active—defined as having had sex at least once within 3 months of responding to the survey. For example, roughly 43% of 11th-grade females report recent sexual activity, while 18% of 9th-grade females do so. With respect to ethnic differences, 49% of African American students, as compared to 37% of Hispanic Americans and 31% of whites, report being currently sexually active.

Among students who are sexually active, 63% say that they use condoms (CDC, 2004a). African Americans are more likely than students in other groups to report using condoms (73% versus 57% for Hispanic Americans and 63% for whites). Birth control pills are used even less frequently. Only 21% of sexually active females report being on the pill. In addition, pill usage is far more common among white high school girls (27%) than among their African American and Hispanic American peers (12% in both groups).

EXPLAINING ADOLESCENT SEXUAL BEHAVIOR

Although sexual activity of boys is somewhat correlated with the amount of testosterone in their blood, social factors are much better predictors of teenagers' sexual activity than hormones (Halpern, Udry, Campbell, & Suchindran, 1993; Udry & Campbell, 1994). In fact, cross-cultural evidence suggests that the same factors are related to sexual behavior even in societies with very low rates of teenage sexual activity, such as Taiwan (Wang & Chou, 1999). Those who begin sexual activity early are more likely to live in poor neighborhoods in which young people are not closely monitored by adults. They come from poorer families or from families in which sexual activity is condoned and dating rules are lax. They are more likely to use alcohol. Many were abused and/or neglected in early childhood (Herrenkohl, Herrenkohl, Egolf, & Russo, 1998).

Among girls, those who are sexually active are also more likely to have had early menarche, to have low interest in school, to have had their first date at a relatively early age, and to have a history of sexual abuse (Billy, Brewster, & Grady, 1994; Buzi, Roberts, Ross, Addy, & Markham, 2003; Hovell et al., 1994; Miller et al., 1998; Schvaneveldt, Miller, Berry, & Lee, 2001; Small & Luster, 1994). In general, these same factors predict sexual activity among whites, blacks, and Hispanics. And in every group, the greater the number of these risk factors present for an individual teenager, the greater the likelihood that he or she will be sexually active.

Adolescents' moral beliefs and the activities in which they participate also predict to some extent whether they will become sexually active. For example, teens who believe premarital sex is morally wrong and who attend religious services frequently are less likely than their peers to become sexually active before reaching adulthood (Miller et al., 1998). Rates of sexual activity are also lower among teens who are involved in sports or other after-school pursuits than among their peers who do not participate in such activities (Savage & Holcomb, 1999). Moreover, alcohol use is associated with 25–30% of adolescent sexual encounters; thus, teens who do not use alcohol are less likely to be sexually active than those who drink (CDC, 2000). Finally, gay and lesbian youth report having more sexual partners, engaging in a higher proportion of unprotected sex acts, and using alcohol or drugs prior to engaging in sexual activity more frequently than do their heterosexual peers (Blake et al., 2001).

SEXUALLY TRANSMITTED DISEASES AND SEX EDUCATION

Despite their high levels of sexual activity, many teens are woefully ignorant of sexually transmitted diseases and their potential consequences, although about 90% of high school students report having learned about sexually transmitted diseases in school

(CDC, 2000; Rosenthal, Lewis, Succop, & Burklow, 1997; Sharma & Sharma, 1997). Even when they are knowledgeable about STDs, many teens lack the assertiveness necessary to resist sexual pressure from a romantic partner or to discuss condom use.

Although infection rates have declined in recent years, *chlamydia*, a disease that is preventable through condom use, continues to be the most commonly reported STD in the United States (CDC, 2004b). Officials estimate that 5% of 15- to 24-year-old females in the United States are infected with chlamydia. Higher rates are found in several subgroups. For instance, in some states, rates as high as 33% have been found among women who are incarcerated (CDC, 2004b). Public health experts estimate that 75% of females and 50% of males who suffer from chlamydia are symptomless (CDC, 2000). Thus, they suggest that routine chlamydia screening of asymptomatic, sexually active teens and young adults is critical to reducing the prevalence of this disease. Left untreated, chlamydia can lead to infertility in females and a number of genital and urinary tract disorders in males.

To combat the spread of STDs among teens, many developmentalists and public health advocates say that more effective sex education programs are needed. Most suggest that programs that include social and decision-making skills training, along with information about STDs and pregnancy, are more likely to reduce the prevalence of sexual activity and increase the number of teens who protect themselves against disease and pregnancy when they do have sex than are information-only approaches. However, no clear consensus about the effectiveness of various approaches to sex education has emerged (Hovell et al., 1998). Moreover, researchers have found that students prefer to get information about sex from their parents (Measor, 2004; Somers & Surmann, 2004). Information provided by peers and young adults who have had personal experiences with unplanned pregnancy and sexually transmitted diseases may also influence teens' sexual decision-making to a greater degree than formal educational programs (Kidger, 2004).

TEENAGE PREGNANCY

The rate of teenage pregnancy is higher in the United States than in any other Western industrialized country (Ambuel, 1995; Singh & Darroch, 2000). For example, the overall annual rate is about 50 pregnancies per 1,000 teens in the United States; it is only 17 pregnancies per 1,000 in Israel and 4 per 1,000 in Japan (Merrick & Morad, 2002). Ethnic differences exist within the United States as well (U.S. Bureau of the Census, 1998). Births to teenagers represent about a quarter of all births to African American women. Among whites, only 11% of births involve teenaged mothers; among Hispanic women, about 17% of all births are to teenagers.

However, teen pregnancy statistics can be confusing, because they usually refer to all pregnancies among women under age 20. To clarify the extent of the teen pregnancy problem, it is useful to break down the statistics by adolescent subgroups. For example, in the United States, the annual pregnancy rate is 1–2 pregnancies per 1,000 for girls younger than 15; 72 per 1,000 among girls aged 15 to 17; and 213 per 1,000 among 18- to 19-year-olds (Ventura, Mosher, Curtin, Abma, & Henshaw, 2000). Looking at the numbers this way shows that teen pregnancy is far more frequent among older adolescents and, in fact, is most likely to happen after a girl leaves high school.

The age at which an adolescent becomes a parent is only one aspect of the teen pregnancy issue. Birth rates among teenagers have actually dropped in the entire U.S. population since the 1960s, including among 15- to 19-year-olds. What has increased is the rate of births to unmarried teens. During the 1960s, more than 80% of teens who gave birth were married. By contrast, in 2003, about 20% of teenaged mothers were married (CDC, 2004a).

The proportion of teenaged mothers who eventually marry the baby's father has also declined in recent years, and, again, there are ethnic differences. Less than 5% of African American teen mothers marry the baby's father, compared to 26% of Hispanics and 41% of whites (Population Resource Center, 2004). Moreover, across ethnic

CRITICAL THINKING 9

Why do you think teens continue to display little knowledge of the basic facts of sexuality when so many are exposed to sex education in schools? In your opinion, how could such programs be designed to be more effective?

groups, 17% of teen mothers maintain romantic relationships with their babies' fathers beyond the first few months after birth (Gee & Rhodes, 1999, 2003).

Whether a girl becomes pregnant during her teenage years depends on many of the same factors that predict sexual activity in general (Miller, Benson, & Galbraith, 2001). The younger a girl is when she becomes sexually active, the more likely she is to become pregnant. Among teenaged girls from poor families, from single-parent families, or from families with relatively uneducated parents, pregnancy rates are higher (Vikat, Rimpela, Kosunen, & Rimpela, 2002). Likewise, girls whose mothers became sexually active at an early age and bore their first child early are likely to follow a similar path. Peer rejection also increases the likelihood that a girl will become pregnant, especially among girls who are high in aggressiveness (Underwood, Kupersmidt, & Coie, 1996).

In contrast, the likelihood of pregnancy is lower among teenaged girls who do well in school and have strong educational aspirations. Such girls are both less likely to be sexually active at an early age and more likely to use contraception if they are sexually active. Girls who have good communication about sex and contraception with their mothers are also less likely to get pregnant.

When teenaged girls become pregnant, in most cases, they face the most momentous set of decisions they have encountered in their young lives. About one-third of teen pregnancies across all ethnic groups end in abortion, and about 14% result in miscarriages (Alan Guttmacher Institute, 2004). Among whites, 7% of teens carry the baby to term and place it for adoption, while 1% of African American teens relinquish their babies to adoptive families.

The children of teenaged mothers are more likely than children born to older mothers to grow up in poverty, with all the accompanying negative consequences for the child's optimum development (Burgess, 2005; Osofsky, Hann, & Peebles, 1993). For instance, they tend to achieve developmental milestones more slowly than infants of older mothers (Pomerleau, Scuccimarri, & Malcuit, 2003). However, the children of teenaged mothers whose own parents help with child care, finances, and parenting skills are less likely to suffer such negative effects (Birch, 1998; Uno, Florsheim, & Uchino, 1998). Moreover, social programs that provide teenaged mothers with child care and the support they need to remain in school positively affect both these mothers and their babies. Such programs also improve outcomes for teenaged fathers (Kost, 1997).

HOMOSEXUALITY

Estimating the proportion of adolescents who identify with a homosexual orientation is exceedingly difficult because many teens, like adults, find sexual orientation to be too private a matter to discuss with researchers. In addition, most individuals do not commit to a gay or lesbian orientation until early adulthood. Thus, many teens experience same-sex attraction but do not identify themselves as homosexual; further, many such teens eventually commit to a heterosexual orientation (Moshman, 2005). Nevertheless, when asked to estimate how many teens in the United States are homosexual, experts often rely on the results of a study of nearly 35,000 youths in Minnesota public schools in which researchers found that about 1% of the adolescent boys and approximately 0.4% of the adolescent girls defined themselves as homosexual. A much larger number said they were unsure of their sexual orientation (Remafedi, Resnick, Blum, & Harris, 1998). These figures are generally consistent with the data on adults in the United States (Laumann, Gagnon, Michael, & Michaels, 1994).

Several twin studies have suggested a genetic basis for homosexuality (Lippa, 2005). Most of these studies indicate that when one identical twin is homosexual, the probability that the other twin will also be homosexual is 50–60%, whereas the concordance rate is only about 20% for fraternal twins and only about 11% for pairs of biologically unrelated boys adopted into the same family (Bailey & Pillard, 1991; Bailey, Pillard, Neale, & Agyei, 1993; Whitam, Diamond, & Martin, 1993). Family studies also suggest that male homosexuality runs in families—that is, the families of most gay men have a higher proportion of homosexual males than do the families of heterosexual men (Bailey et al., 1999; Kirk, Bailey, & Martin, 2000). Such findings strengthen the hypothesis that homosexuality has a biological basis (Gladue, 1994; Pillard & Bailey, 1995).

Additional studies suggest that prenatal hormone patterns may also be a causal factor in homosexuality (Lippa, 2005). For example, women whose mothers took the drug diethylstilbestrol (DES, a synthetic estrogen) during pregnancy are more likely to be homosexual as adults than are women who were not exposed to DES in the womb (Meyer-Bahlburg et al., 1995). Moreover, there is evidence that many boys who demonstrate strong cross-sex play preferences in early childhood show homosexual preferences when they reach adolescence (Bailey & Zucker, 1995). Interestingly, too, studies show that the long bones in the legs and arms of school-aged children who grow up to be homosexual do not grow as rapidly as those of children who eventually become heterosexual (Martin & Nguyen, 2004). These findings indicate that maturational differences between homosexuals and heterosexuals are evident before puberty and involve body systems other than the sexual organs themselves. Taken together, prenatal hormone exposure studies, research examining early childhood activity preferences, and studies comparing the processes of physical maturation in heterosexuals and homosexuals are consistent with the hypothesis that homosexuality is programmed in at birth.

Such evidence does not mean that environment plays no role in homosexuality. For example, when one of a pair of identical twins is homosexual, the other twin does *not* share that sexual orientation 40–50% of the time. Something beyond biology must be at work, although developmentalists do not yet know what environmental factors may be involved.

Whatever the cause of variations in sexual orientation, the process through which an individual comes to realize that he or she is homosexual appears to be a gradual one. Some researchers think that the process begins in middle childhood as a feeling of doubt about one's heterosexuality (Carver, Egan, & Perry, 2004). Retrospective studies have found that many gay men and lesbians recall having had homosexual fantasies during their teen years, but few fully accepted their homosexuality while still in adolescence (Wong & Tang, 2004). Instead, the final steps toward full self-awareness and acceptance of one's homosexuality appear to take place in early adulthood.

As homosexual teens grapple with questions about their sexual orientation, many report feeling isolated from and unaccepted by their peers (Galliher, Rostosky, & Hughes 2004; Martin & D'Augelli, 2003). This may help explain why a higher proportion of homosexual than heterosexual teens suffer from depression and attempt suicide (Cato & Canetto, 2003; Remafedi, French, Story, Resnick, & Blum, 1998; Safren & Heimberg, 1999; Savin-Williams & Ream, 2003). Many mental health professionals suggest that, to respond to these adolescents' needs, school officials provide emotional and social support for homosexual teens (Rostosky, Owens, Zimmerman, & Riggle, 2003; van Wormer & McKinney, 2003).

While homosexual adolescents clearly face unique challenges, they share many of the same concerns as their heterosexual peers. For example, both homosexual and heterosexual girls are more likely than boys to be dissatisfied with their physical appearance (Saewyc, Bearinger, Heinz, Blum, & Resnick, 1998). Consequently, dieting is more common among both homosexual and heterosexual girls than among boys of either sexual orientation. Like their heterosexual counterparts, homosexual male adolescents drink alcohol more often and engage in more risky behavior than do female teenagers.

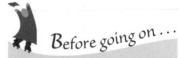

Before going on · · ·

- How prevalent is adolescent sexual activity in the United States?
- What are the factors that influence a teenager's decision to become sexually active?
- List some of the issues related to the incidence of sexually transmitted diseases among teens.
- Which teenaged girls are most likely to become pregnant?
- What does research suggest about the origins of homosexuality?

 Health and Wellness

You read about infants' physical health in Chapter 3, and children have many of the same needs. However, their needs, and the focus of concerns about their health, change significantly after puberty, so it's important to separate our discussion of health issues and look first at childhood and then at adolescence.

HEALTH IN CHILDHOOD

Typically, childhood is a fairly healthy period of life. However, children have many accidents, and the health habits formed during these years can persist for a lifetime, influencing individual health for good or for ill.

Health Care Needs   Just as infants do, young children continue to require periodic medical check-ups and a variety of immunizations (Overby, 2002). At yearly check-ups, doctors monitor preschoolers' growth and motor development. At the same time, doctors and nurses often serve as parents' first source of help with children who have sensory or developmental disabilities that were not diagnosed in infancy (Sulkes, 1998).

School-aged children benefit from regular medical care as well. For one thing, there are a few important immunizations that are usually administered during this period (Umetsu, 1998). In addition, many school-aged children have undiagnosed health problems. For example, 10–20% have difficulty sleeping (Owens, Spirito, McGuinn, & Nobile, 2000; Sadeh, Gruber, & Raviv, 2002). In most cases, parents of school children are unaware of such problems until a physician or nurse specifically asks a child about sleep patterns as part of a routine check-up. Sleep difficulties are associated with attention, concentration, and behavioral problems, so picking up on an undetected sleep problem, and correcting it, may improve a child's life considerably (Sadeh et al., 2002).

Illnesses and Accidents   In the United States, the average child has four to six brief bouts of sickness each year, most often colds or the flu (Sulkes, 1998). Children who are experiencing high levels of stress or family upheaval are more likely to become ill (Guttman & Dick, 2004). For example, an early nationwide study in the United States showed that children living with their mothers only have more asthma, more headaches, and a generally higher vulnerability to illnesses of many types than do those living with both biological parents (Dawson, 1991). Figure 4.12 shows one comparison from this study, which used a "health vulnerability score" that was the sum of nine questions answered by parents about their child's health. You can see in the figure that the average score was only about 1.0 out of a possible 9.0, which implies that most children are quite healthy. But it is clear that children living in more stressful family structures had higher health vulnerability scores—and this was true even when such other differences between the families as race, income, and mother's level of education were factored out.

Another danger for children is accidents. In any given year, about a quarter of all children under 5 in the United States have at least one accident that requires some kind of medical attention, and accidents are the major cause of death in preschool and school-aged children (Fein, Durbin, & Selbst, 2002). At every age, accidents are more common among boys than among girls, presumably because of their more active and daring styles of play. The majority of accidents among children occur at home—falls, cuts, accidental poisonings, and the like. Automobile accidents are the second leading source of injuries to school-aged children in the United States, followed by bicycle-related mishaps (National Center for Injury Prevention and Control [NCIPC], 2000). In fact, 80% of bicycle-related head injuries involve children. Research suggests that wearing a helmet while riding a bike reduces the chances of head injury by more than 85%. Consequently, many cities and states have enacted laws requiring both children and adult bicyclists to wear helmets. Finally, some "accidents" are actually the result of parental abuse (see the *Research Report*).

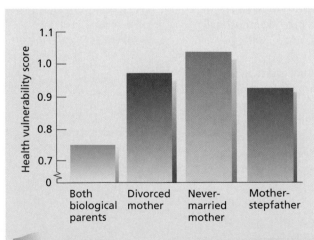

FIGURE 4.12

Assuming that single-parent and stepparent families contribute to higher stress for children (an assumption supported by research), the results shown here are yet another illustration of the link between higher stress and increased rates of illness. (*Source*: Dawson, 1991, from Table 3, p. 577.)

Nutrition Because children grow more slowly during the early childhood years than in infancy, they may seem to eat less than when they were babies. Moreover, food aversions often develop during the preschool years. For example, a child who loved carrots as an infant may refuse to eat them at age 2 or 3. Consequently, conflicts between young children and their parents often focus on the child's eating behavior (Overby, 2002).

Nutritionists point out that it is important that parents keep in mind that young children eat only half as much food as adults. Thus, parents should not become so concerned about the quantity of food a child consumes that they cater to her preferences for sweets and other high-calorie, high-fat foods (Wong, 1993). Although young children are rarely overweight, many children acquire eating habits during these years that lead to later weight problems. Nutritionists recommend keeping a variety of nutritious foods on hand and allowing a child's appetite to be a good guide to how much food she should eat. Of course, this approach only works if young children's access to sweets and other attractive, but nonnutritious, foods is limited.

During the school years, children become more open to new foods, but different kinds of nutritional problems arise. Many school-aged children make food choices without adult supervision for the first time in their lives. They use their allowances to purchase items from vending machines at school, or they stop at a corner store on the way to or from school. Not surprisingly, school-aged children's food choices in such circumstances are not always wise, and many consume a great deal of "junk" food—sodas, candy bars, and the like of which their parents may not be aware.

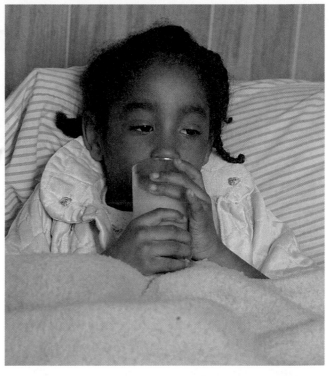

Most kids this age are sick in bed about 5 days a year, most often with a cold or the flu.

Obesity One of the most significant health risks of childhood is obesity, which usually develops in the school years. Estimates of the prevalence of obesity vary. Approximately 16% of children and adolescents are obese (National Center for Health Statistics [NCHS], 2005). Several studies indicate that the incidence of obesity is increasing; see Figure 4.13 (NCHS, 2005). Moreover, obesity is a significant health problem throughout the industrialized world. For example, researchers in Italy found that 23.4% of a sample of 10-year-old boys and 12.7% of girls were obese (Maffeis, Schutz, Piccoli, Gonfianttini, & Pinelli, 1993).

Obesity is most often defined as a body weight 20% or more above the normal weight for height, but recently health care providers have begun using a measure called the *body mass index (BMI)* that estimates a child's proportion of body fat (NCHS, 2000). The BMI is a ratio of weight to height that allows care providers to more easily distinguish between children who seem to be overweight because they are very muscular and those who are actually obese. (Try calculating the BMI yourself in the *See for Yourself* activity at the end of the chapter.)

The older overweight children get, the more likely they are to remain obese into their adult years (NCHS, 2000). Few overweight babies are still overweight as adults, but half of those who are obese in elementary school continue to be overweight in adulthood (Overby, 2002). In addition, more than half of obese children possess one or more risk factors, such as elevated levels of cholesterol or high blood pressure, that predispose them to heart disease later in life (National Center for Chronic Disease Prevention and Health Promotion [NCCDPHP], 2000). Obese children are also often rejected by their peers and unhappy with their physical appearance (Crystal, Watanabe, & Chen, 2000; Vander Wal & Thelen, 2000; Williams, Wake, Hesketh, Maher, & Waters, 2005).

This overweight child not only has different kinds of encounters with his peers—he is also more likely to be fat as an adult, with all the increased health risks that accompany being overweight.

obesity Most often defined as a body weight 20% or more above the normal weight for height, or a Body Mass Index at the 85th percentile or above.

Child Abuse and Neglect

Figuring out what qualifies as abuse is not always simple; most psychologists today tend to follow definitions proposed by Douglas Barnett and his colleagues (1993) as well as other researchers (Rogosch, Cicchetti, Shields, & Toth, 1995): *Physical abuse* involves the nonaccidental infliction of bodily injury on the child—anything from a bruise to injuries so extreme that the child requires hospitalization or dies; *sexual abuse* involves any kind of sexual contact between a child and a responsible adult that is for the purpose of the adult's gratification or gain; *physical neglect* includes either failure to provide adequately for the child's nurturance and basic care or failure to provide supervision adequate for the child's age, or both.

There is no standardized reporting system for abuse and neglect, and it is often difficult for health care professionals to determine whether an injury is due to abuse or an accident. Consequently, estimating the prevalence of abuse is difficult. The best estimate is that about 1 million cases of abuse in the United States each year come to the attention of law enforcement officials and/or health care professionals (Fein, Durbin, & Selbst, 2002; Lamb & Lewis, 2005). Interviews with emergency room physicians and nurses suggest that an additional 1 million children visit hospitals and clinics with injuries that are suspected to have been caused by abuse or neglect but these suspicions cannot be confirmed (Sulkes, 1998). Of course, an unknown number of children are abused or neglected without anyone ever knowing about it. Analyses of

medical and police records aimed at classifying abuse/neglect cases suggest that two-thirds involve physical injuries, another quarter involve sexual abuse, and 5% are the result of neglect, such as underfeeding an infant (Sulkes, 1998). Sadly, estimates of the number of deaths that result from abuse and neglect range from 1,000 to 5,000 per year.

Certain risk factors predispose parents to abuse and/or neglect their children, but abuse does not normally occur unless several of these risk factors occur in the same family at the same time (Rogosch, Cicchetti, & Aber, 1995; Rogosch et al., 1995; Spieker, Bensley, McMahon, Fung, & Ossiander, 1996). First, the risk of abuse is higher in any family experiencing significant stress, whether that stress arises from unemployment, poverty, neighborhood violence, a lack of social support, or an especially difficult or demanding infant. Second, some parents, particularly those who were themselves abused, simply know no other way to deal with frustration and stress or with disobedience in their child, other than striking the child in some way. Other parents are depressed or unable to form the kind of emotional bond to the child that would help to prevent abuse (Wiehe, 2003). Parental alcohol and drug dependence, too, play a significant role in a great many cases (Emery & Laumann-Billings, 1998). A third key element is a lack of social support or some degree of social isolation.

Overeating or eating too much of the wrong foods causes obesity in children just as it does in adults (NCCDPHP, 2000). Predictably, research shows that weight-management programs for obese children must involve parents in order to be effective (Berry et al., 2004). There are several barriers to parental involvement, however. For one, researchers have found that parents of obese children often have no idea what or how much their children eat (Steinberg et al., 2004; Tanofsky-Kraff, Yanovski, & Yanovski, 2005). Clearly, getting a child's weight under control requires that this lack of information, whether attributable to the child's "sneakiness" or to parental indifference, be addressed. In addition, some parents have little knowledge of children's nutritional needs, so they must learn the basics of good nutrition before they can implement a weight-management plan for their children. What's more, parents of obese children must confront their own weight issues and be willing to change their eating and exercise habits to serve as good role models for their children.

Parents who are willing to help children get control of their weight gain need to realize that weight-management diets must be tailored to children's growth needs (Overby, 2002). Pediatricians point out that the goal of a dietary intervention for an obese child is to slow down his or her weight gain to a rate that is appropriate for the child's overall rate of growth. Put differently, the idea is to stabilize an obese child's weight so that he or she can grow into it. As you might suspect, both parents and chil-

A fourth factor often cited by sociologists and anthropologists involves cultural traditions that view children as property and include no moral prohibitions against abusing them (Mooney, Knox, & Schacht, 2000).

Some children who are frequently or severely abused develop *post-traumatic stress disorder (PTSD)* (Kendall-Tackett, Williams, & Finkelhor, 1993; Margolin & Gordis, 2000; Morrissette, 1999; Pynoos, Steinberg, & Wraith, 1995). This disorder involves extreme levels of anxiety, flashback memories of episodes of abuse, nightmares, and other sleep disturbances. Abused children are also more likely than nonabused peers to exhibit delays in all domains of development (Cicchetti, Rogosch, Maughan, Toth, & Bruce, 2003; Glaser, 2000; Malinosky-Rummell & Hansen, 1993; Rogosch, Cicchetti, & Aber, 1995).

On the positive side, children who are physically neglected typically recover rapidly once the abuse stops. In studies involving abused and/or neglected children who were placed in foster care, developmentalists have found that differences between abused and nonabused children in physical, cognitive, and social development disappear within 1 year (Olivan, 2003). As you might suspect, though, these studies suggest that the critical factor in the catching-up process is the quality of the post-abuse environment.

Preventing abuse begins with education. Informing parents about the potential consequences of some physical acts, such as the link between shaking an infant and brain damage, may help. In addition, parents need to know that injuring children is a crime, even if the intention is to discipline them. Parenting classes, perhaps as a required part of high school curricula, can help inform parents or future parents about principles of child development and appropriate methods of discipline (Mooney, Knox, & Schacht, 2000).

Another approach to prevention of abuse involves identification of families at risk. Physicians, nurses, and other professionals who routinely interact with parents of infants and young children have a particularly important role to play in this kind of prevention. Parents who seem to have problems attaching to their children can sometimes be identified during medical office visits. These parents can be referred to parenting classes or to social workers for help. Similarly, parents may ask doctors or nurses how to discipline their children. Such questions provide professionals with opportunities to discuss which practices are appropriate and which are not.

Finally, children who are abused must be protected from further injury. This can be accomplished through vigorous enforcement of existing child abuse laws. As noted, health professionals must report suspected abuse. However, in most states, ordinary citizens are also legally required to report suspected abuse. And reporting is only part of the picture. Once abuse is reported, steps must be taken to protect injured children from suspected abusers.

Questions for Critical Analysis

1. As a researcher, how might you set up a study to determine the qualities that distinguish abuse victims who experience long-term negative consequences from those who appear to experience no lasting effects?
2. What underlying factor or factors might explain the correlation between family stressors such as parental unemployment and child abuse?

dren can find this long-term approach to weight control frustrating, and consequently many abandon the special diets designed for them by physicians.

Because children and parents often fail to adhere to dietary interventions and because lack of activity is just as important to obesity as overeating, physicians stress the need to include exercise in weight-management programs for children (Overby, 2002). Researchers have found that obese children begin to establish a sedentary lifestyle as early as age 3 (Reilly et al., 2004). The primary characteristic of this lifestyle is a preference for passive activities such as television-watching over those that require physical activity, such as bicycling and organized sports. Thus, parents can play a critical role in preventing obesity by recognizing this lifestyle pattern when it appears and regulating children's activities. If children are already obese, parents must commit themselves to encouraging their children to be more physically active and, if necessary, prohibiting them from spending too much time in sedentary activities.

Clearly, environmental factors play a role in childhood obesity. However, researchers have also found evidence suggesting that genes may be important as well. Both twin and adoption studies suggest that obesity probably results from an interaction between a genetic predisposition and environmental factors that promote overeating or low levels of activity (Stunkard, Harris, Pedersen, & McClearn, 1990). Whatever the experiential and genetic contributions might be, public health officials contend that

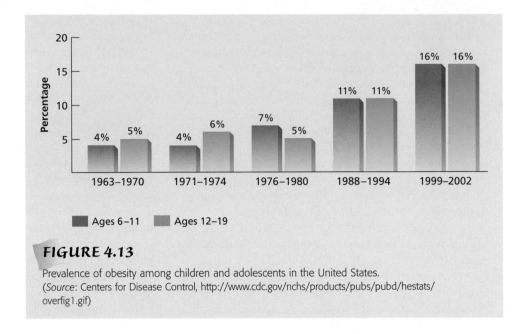

FIGURE 4.13

Prevalence of obesity among children and adolescents in the United States. (*Source*: Centers for Disease Control, http://www.cdc.gov/nchs/products/pubs/pubd/hestats/overfig1.gif)

CRITICAL THINKING

What would you say to the parent of an overweight child who said she believed that her son was just carrying extra "baby fat" that he was sure to outgrow later in life?

a cultural pattern involving decreased levels of physical activity and increases in the consumption of high-calorie convenience foods have led to the current epidemic of obesity among both children and adults in the United States (NCCDPHP, 2000).

Dieting   Many nonobese children are fearful of developing an unattractive body. Serious eating disorders—which you'll read about in detail in Chapter 15—don't become common until well into adolescence. However, most school-aged children are quite knowledgeable about weight-loss diets and products (Kostanski & Gullone, 1999). Moreover, research suggests that children as young as 7 years of age sometimes express dissatisfaction with their weight or physical appearance, and some begin dieting as early as age 9 (Kostanski & Gullone, 1999; NCHS, 1996a; Nutter, 1997). Moreover, weight concerns increase among both boys and girls across the elementary school years (Gardner, Friedman, & Jackson, 1999). These concerns sometimes lead to binge eating, a pattern that increases the risk that a child will develop an eating disorder during adolescence (Tanofsky-Kraff et al., 2005).

ADOLESCENT HEALTH

For most individuals, adolescence is one of the healthiest periods of life. However, as adolescents gain independence, they encounter numerous health risks.

Health Care Issues   Even though they get sick less often than children and infants, teenagers are frequent visitors to health care facilities. Many adolescents believe themselves to be less healthy than they actually are and may develop physical symptoms in response to perceived parental or peer rejection (Wickrama, Conger, Lorenz, & Elder, 1998). In contrast, teens who perceive their parents to be emotionally supportive tend to think of themselves as healthier and experience fewer physical symptoms than peers whose parents seem to be less supportive (Wickrama, Lorenz, & Conger, 1997). Further, like younger children, teens are most likely to need medical care because of an accident, often as a result of their own behavioral choices.

Sensation-Seeking   Many teenagers appear to have what developmentalists describe as a heightened level of **sensation-seeking**, or a desire to experience high levels of arousal such as those that accompany high-speed driving or the highs that are associated with drugs. Sensation-seeking leads to recklessness (what most developmental

sensation-seeking A strong desire to experience the emotional and physical arousal associated with risky behaviors such as fast driving and unprotected sex.

researchers call "risky" or "high-risk" behavior), which, in turn, leads to markedly increased rates of accidents and injuries in this age range. For example, adolescents drive faster and use seat belts less often than adults do (CDC, 2000). To reduce the number of accidents among teenaged drivers, many states in the United States have enacted laws that allow only "graduated" driver's licenses (Cobb, 2000). Sixteen-year-olds can drive in most such states, but they must remain accident- and ticket-free for a certain period of time before they can have privileges such as driving at night.

Risky behaviors may be more common in adolescence than in other periods because such behaviors help teenagers gain peer acceptance and establish autonomy from parents and from other authority figures (Jessor, 1992). In fact, researchers have found that teens who show high rates of reckless behaviors are likely to have had poor school records or to have suffered early rejection by peers, neglect at home, or some combination of these problems (Robins & McEvoy, 1990). In addition, adolescents to whom popularity is important are more likely to engage in risky behaviors than peers who value popularity less (Stein, Roeser, & Markus, 1998). Portrayals of risky behavior in entertainment media may also be a factor, as you'll learn in Chapter 14.

Alcohol and Drug Use

Alcohol and Drug Use   Teenagers who express the most interest in sensation-seeking are those who are most likely to use drugs and consume alcohol (Donohew et al., 1999). Indeed, researchers have found that individual levels of sensation-seeking predict peer associations—that is, teens who are high sensation-seekers choose friends who are similar. Once such groups are formed, sensation-seeking becomes a central feature of their activities. So, for example, if one member tries marijuana or alcohol, others do so as well. However, teens who spend a lot of time alone may also be vulnerable to substance abuse. Researchers have found that shy adolescents, particularly those who are high in neuroticism, are more likely to use alcohol and drugs than are peers who are more outgoing (Kirkcaldy, Siefen, Surall, & Bischoff, 2004).

Sensation-seeking also interacts with parenting style to affect the likelihood of drug use. Authoritative parenting seems to provide high sensation-seeking teenagers with protection against their reckless tendencies (Pilgrim, Luo, Urberg, & Fang, 1999). In fact, for African American adolescents, authoritative parenting may entirely negate the potential influence of drug-using peers. Moreover, parents who have realistic perceptions of the prevalence of teenaged drinking are also less likely to have teenaged children who are drinkers. These parents, who are aware of the prevalence of alcohol use among adolescents, try to prevent their children from getting into situations, such as unsupervised social events, where drinking is likely to happen (Bogenschneider, Wu, Raffaelli, & Tsay, 1998). Surveys suggest that parents do indeed need to take a proactive approach to preventing alcohol and drug use among teens.

Many types of teenaged drug use are on the rise in the United States. For example, in 1974, about 23% of adolescents reported that they had used marijuana. By 1992, the percentage had fallen to 11.7 (U.S. Bureau of the Census, 1995). A federal government survey conducted in 2003 found that 22% of high school students had used marijuana within 3 months of responding to the survey (CDC, 2004c). Longitudinal studies have shown that marijuana use during the teen years is associated with lower income and poorer health in adulthood (Ellickson, Martino, & Collins, 2004). This association may be the result of an underlying factor that predicts both marijuana use in adolescence and poor outcomes in adulthood. However, it seems likely that marijuana use itself is at least partly responsible for these effects.

Alcohol use is also fairly common among teens, at least in the United States. For example, in 2003, 37% of twelfth-graders, 32% of tenth-graders, and 27% of eighth-graders reported that they had engaged in binge drinking (defined as consuming five or more drinks on a single occasion) at least once in the last month (CDC, 2004c). Alcohol use is highest among teens in situations where "racial or ethnic minorities live in circumscribed, impoverished areas such as ghettos, barrios, and Indian reservations" (Mitchell et al., 1996, p. 152).

Smoking   Surveys suggest that 22% of U.S. adolescents are regular smokers, and 58% have tried smoking. Ethnic groups differ in tobacco use. Less than 6% of African American and Hispanic American high school students smoke daily, compared to about 12% of whites (CDC, 2004c).

Some developmentalists speculate that teenagers begin smoking because they really don't understand its health consequences. Consequently, many anti-smoking campaigns emphasize health risks. However, teenagers seem to be well aware of these risks, including the link between smoking and lung cancer (Taylor et al., 1999). Further, many teens cite moral and ethical reasons for not smoking when asked about it by researchers. Thus, it seems that adolescents are very familiar with all the reasons they shouldn't smoke. So, why do they start smoking if they know they shouldn't?

One finding that may help to answer this question is that teenagers who believe they are already in poor health are more likely to smoke than those who think of themselves as healthy (Kirkaldy, Siefen, Surall, & Bischoff, 2004; Leff et al., 2003). Note, however, that *perceptions* of one's health can be very different from one's actual health status. So, the key here is that teens who begin smoking *believe* their health is poor, regardless of how healthy they may actually be. They also seem to think they have little or no power to affect their future health. In other words, adolescent smokers of this kind have a fatalistic "What have I got to lose?" attitude about smoking because they view themselves as doomed to a future of poor health no matter what they do. To some degree, these negative self-perceptions are driven by personality traits. Adolescents who are introverted and who tend to have a negative outlook on life are more likely to take up smoking than their more optimistic peers (Kirkaldy et al., 2004). Similarly, teens who have a long history of minor physical complaints, such as headaches and stomach upset, appear to be more likely to smoke (Leff et al., 2003). Thus, vulnerability to smoking is at least partly a function of factors that are within the individual.

Peer influences appear to outweigh perceptions of future health risks for many teenagers (Chopak, Vicary, & Crockett, 1998; West, Sweeting, & Ecob, 1999). In fact, some developmentalists advise parents that if their teenaged child's friends smoke, especially close friends with whom the child spends a lot of time, parents should probably assume that their child smokes as well (Urberg, Degirmencioglu, & Pilgrim, 1997). Moreover, the period between ages 15 and 17 seems to be the time during which a teenager is most susceptible to peer influences with regard to smoking (West et al., 1999). Clearly, then, by monitoring the friends of their 15- to 17-year-olds and discouraging them from associating with smokers, parents may help prevent their teens from smoking (Mott, Crowe, Richardson, & Flay, 1999).

Parental influence is important, too—a pattern that is especially clear for mothers and daughters (Kandel & Wu, 1995). When an adult stops smoking, the likelihood that her children will smoke decreases. Thus, another way to prevent teenaged smoking is to encourage parents to give up the habit. In addition, having a family rule against substance use—including drugs, alcohol, and tobacco—has a lot more influence on teenagers' decisions about using such substances than most parents think (Abdelrahman, Rodriguez, Ryan, French, & Weinbaum, 1998; Mott et al., 1999). Similarly, teens who view smoking as morally wrong are less likely to smoke than peers who do not think of smoking as a moral issue (Taylor et al., 1999). Thus, parents who think tobacco use is morally wrong should discuss their beliefs with their children.

POVERTY AND HEALTH

In the United States, just under 17% of children younger than 6 live in poverty (defined as a yearly income of less than $12,400 for a one-child family; Proctor & Dalaker, 2003). Children growing up in poverty have significantly more health problems than do those living in more affluent circumstances, as you can see from Table 4.4. This pattern is not unique to the United States. Equivalent risk differentials exist in virtually all countries.

TABLE 4.4	Comparison of Health Problems of Poor and Nonpoor Children	
Problem		**Rate for Poor Children Compared to Nonpoor Children**
Low birth weight		1.5 to 2 times higher
Delayed immunization		3 times higher
Asthma		Somewhat higher
Lead poisoning		3 times higher
Neonatal mortality		1.5 times higher
Deaths from accidents		2 to 3 times higher
Deaths from disease		3 to 4 times higher
Number reported to be in fair or poor health (rather than good health)		2 times higher
Percentage with conditions limiting school activity		2 to 3 times higher
Physical stunting (being in the 5th percentile or lower for height)		2 times higher
Days sick in bed or lost school days		40 percent higher
Severely impaired vision		2 to 3 times higher
Severe iron-deficiency anemia		2 times higher

Sources: Brooks-Gunn, J., and Duncan, G. J., "The Effect of Poverty on Children," *The Future of Children, 7*(2), 1997, pp. 55–71; Starfield, B., "Childhood Morbidity: Comparisons, Clusters, and Trends," *Pediatrics*, 88, 1991, pp. 519–526.

Psychologist Edith Chen has found that the relationship between stress and immune system functioning underlies the link between poverty and children's health (Chen, 2004). Chen hypothesizes that poverty exposes children to physical stressors such as pollution along with psychological stressors like anxiety and social stressors such as neighborhood instability. Her research suggests that the combined effects of all these stressors impair immune system functioning in children from low-income homes, leaving them vulnerable to a whole host of health problems.

The effects of poverty on children's health are not limited to their physical well-being. For instance, as Table 4.4 indicates, children from low-income families miss more days of school because of illness than children who come from higher-income homes. Fewer days in school can lead to deficits in learning which, in turn, decrease children's chances of graduating from high school. As adults, these children cannot qualify for jobs that would enable them to provide better living conditions for their own children. Consequently, the cycle of poverty–poor health–low achievement–poverty repeats itself in the next generation. Thus, poverty has a direct and cumulative effect not only on children's development but also on society as a whole.

MORTALITY

Those of us who live in countries with relatively low rates of infant and childhood mortality are accustomed to thinking of childhood as a basically healthy time. Yet worldwide, over 10% of children die before age 5; in many countries, the rate is higher than 20%, as you can see in Figure 4.14 (Public Health Policy Advisory Board, 2001). In less developed countries, the most common cause of death is diarrhea, confounded by malnutrition (Dillingham & Guerrant, 2004). In contrast, the leading cause of children's deaths in the United States is accidents, particularly motor vehicle accidents (Hoyert, Kung, & Smith, 2005).

Happily, the rate of childhood deaths in the United States has been declining an average of about 2% every year for the past five decades (Hoyert et al., 2005; Singh & Yu, 1996), suggesting that, as a society, we have begun to control at least some of the

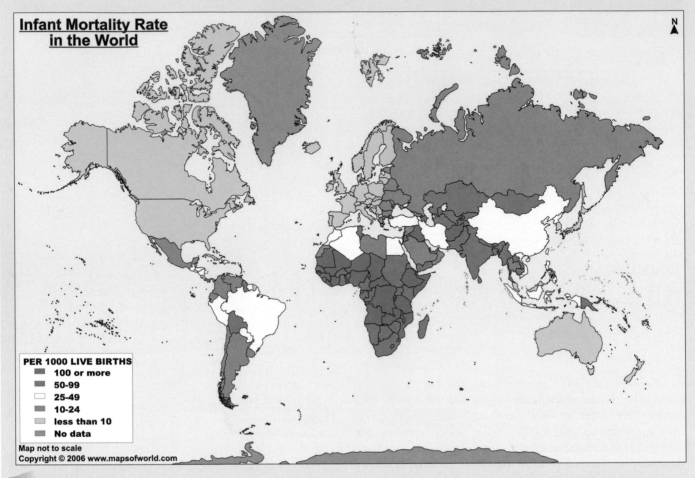

FIGURE 4.14

Infant mortality rate.

(Source: From Maps of the World (mapsoftheworld.com/infant-mortality-rate-map.htm). Reprinted with permission.)

Before going on . . .

- List the major health concerns of early and middle childhood.
- What kinds of risky behavior threaten teenagers' health?
- Describe the relationship between poverty and health.
- What are the leading causes of death among children and adolescents?

causes of mortality, particularly through the use of car seats, seat belts, and bicycle helmets. However, the United States continues to have wide ethnic variation in mortality rates among children. African American children—especially African American boys—have the highest death rates, primarily because of much higher rates of accidents and homicides; Asian American children have the lowest rates, with Caucasian American children falling in between (Hoyert et al., 2005; Singh & Yu, 1996).

During the teen years, accidents continue to be the most frequent cause of death in most groups in the United States. However, among African Americans, homicide surpasses accidents as the leading cause of death after age 15 (Hoyert et al., 2005; U.S. Bureau of the Census, 2001). In fact, African American teenaged boys are nearly ten times as likely as their white peers to die as a result of homicide. The ratio of African American to white teenaged girls who die as a result of homicide is almost as high, although homicide rates are a great deal lower among females than among males across all ethnic groups. Suicide and accident rates are lower among African American teens than in other ethnic groups. And deaths due to disease occur about as often among African Americans as among other teens. However, the very high incidence of homicide deaths raises the overall mortality rates for African American adolescents higher than that of teens in other groups.

Summary

The Brain and Nervous System

- The brain develops in spurts. Several short spurts occur in the first years, followed by longer periods of growth at about ages 4, 6, 10, 13, and 17.
- In most parts of the brain, dendritic and synaptic development reaches its first peak between 12 and 24 months, after which there is a "pruning" of synapses. Periods of synaptic growth followed by pruning of redundant pathways continue to occur throughout childhood and adolescence.
- Myelination of nerve fibers also occurs rapidly in the early years but continues throughout childhood and adolescence. Brain structures that are critical to memory and other forms of complex information processing become myelinated later in childhood.
- Significant changes in brain lateralization happen in early childhood. Handedness is weakly related to brain lateralization, but the association between the two is poorly understood at the present time.

Bones, Muscles, and Motor Skills

- Changes in height and weight are rapid during the first year and then level off to a steady pace until adolescence, when a sharp growth spurt occurs.
- Bones increase in number in some joints (e.g., the wrist) but decrease in quantity in others (e.g., the skull). Bone hardening, or ossification, contributes to development of motor skills.
- Muscle tissue increases primarily in density and length of fibers, with a much larger increase at adolescence for boys than for girls. Fat cells are added in the early years and then again rapidly at adolescence, in this case more for girls than for boys.
- Children of 6 or 7 have confident use of most gross motor skills, although there are refinements still to come; fine motor skills needed for many school tasks are not fully developed until sometime in the elementary school years.

The Endocrine and Reproductive Systems

- The physical changes of adolescence are triggered by a complex set of hormonal changes, beginning at about age 8. Very large increases in gonadotrophic hormones, which in turn trigger increased production of estrogen and testosterone, are central to the process.
- In girls, sexual maturity is achieved in a set of changes beginning as early as age 8 or 9. Menarche occurs relatively late in the sequence. Boys achieve sexual maturity later, with the growth spurt occurring a year or more after the start of genital changes.
- Variations in the rate of pubertal development have some psychological effects. In general, children whose physical development is markedly earlier or later than they expect or desire show more negative effects than do those whose development is "on time."

Sexual Behavior in Adolescence

- Sexual activity among teens has increased in recent decades in the United States, where roughly half of all high school students are sexually active and 1 in 10 teenaged girls becomes pregnant each year.
- Compared to teens who delay sexual activity until leaving high school, teens who begin sexual activity earlier are more likely to come from poorer families or from families in which sexual activity is condoned, to use alcohol, and to have been abused.
- Adolescents in the United States suffer from a variety of sexually transmitted diseases. Most adults support sex education programs to combat the spread of STDs, but there is no consensus regarding the effectiveness of various approaches.
- Long-term consequences for girls who bear children during adolescence are negative on average, although a significant minority of such girls are able to overcome their early disadvantages.
- About 1% of adolescent boys and approximately 0.4% of girls define themselves as homosexual. Research suggests that both heredity and environment contribute to the development of sexual orientation.

Health and Wellness

- Like infants, older children benefit from regular medical check-ups. Many immunizations are required for initial and continued school enrollment. In addition, parents' conversations with health care professionals may lead to discovery of previously unknown problems.
- Acute illnesses are a normal part of children's early lives, and accidents are fairly common. Children of all ages need regular check-ups and immunizations. Obesity is a serious health risk in middle childhood.
- Adolescents sometimes believe themselves to be less healthy than they actually are. Also, sensation-seeking behaviors (e.g., driving too fast) are a significant health risk for this age group. Tobacco, alcohol, and drug use are additional risks for some teens.
- Virtually all forms of physical disability, chronic illness, acute illness, and accidents are more frequent among children living in poverty. Explanations focus on limited access to health care and on more dangerous home and neighborhood situations among the poor, as well as on the effects of stress on the immune system.
- After early infancy, mortality rates are low among children, with most deaths being due to accidents. Among teens, homicide is a significant cause of death, especially for African American males.

Key Terms

association areas (p. 97)
bone age (p. 101)
corpus callosum (p. 97)
cortex (p. 93)
endocrine glands (p. 103)
fontanel (p. 101)
gonadotrophic hormones (p. 105)
handedness (p. 99)
hippocampus (p. 97)
lateralization (p. 97)

medulla (p. 93)
menarche (p. 106)
midbrain (p. 93)
motor development (p. 102)
myelination (p. 96)
obesity (p. 115)
ossification (p. 101)
pituitary gland (p. 105)
puberty (p. 105)
relative right-left orientation (p. 98)

reticular formation (p. 96)
secular trend (p. 107)
selective attention (p. 96)
sensation-seeking (p. 118)
sexually transmitted diseases (STDs)
    (p. 109)
spatial cognition (p. 98)
spatial perception (p. 98)
synaptogenesis (p. 94)

Calculating Your BMI

You can see for yourself whether the BMI is a more accurate measure of obesity than weight-for-height comparisons by trying it out on a few of your fellow students (and yourself!). First, find out a few of your classmates' heights and weights. (It may be best to collect these data anonymously.)

The formula for calculating the BMI is

$$\text{Weight in kilograms}/(\text{Height in meters})^2$$

First, convert pounds to kilograms (1 lb = .4536 kg) and feet to meters (1 ft = .3048 m). Then enter your data on your classmates into the formula and calculate each person's BMI. BMI scores below 18 are classified as underweight, while those between 19 and 25 are considered normal. Scores between 26 and 29 fall into the overweight category. Individuals with BMI scores over 30 are classified as obese, and those with scores that exceed 35 are considered severely obese. Provide each of your classmates with his or her BMI and its classification. Do the scores fit with your subjective impression of whether each individual is obese? You may want to do the BMI and weight-for-height comparisons for a few children as well. Be sure to explain your study to both the children and their parents and obtain their permission before collecting any data.

Gender Differences in Dieting

Studies of dieting behavior have shown that elementary school girls are five or six times as likely as boys to have dieted at least 10 times in the past year. Do you think a survey of your classmates would produce similar results? Try asking about 20 male and 20 female students how many times they have deliberately tried to lose weight in the past year. Develop a theory to explain why dieting rates change or remain stable from early adolescence to young adulthood—whichever result your study shows.

Perceptual Development

CHAPTER

5

Think about how often you hear music each day. Sometimes it happens intentionally, as when you listen to a favorite CD or tune your car radio to your favorite station.

At other times, you hear it inadvertently as an element of an advertisement, in the background at a store, or in an elevator. The point is that music is pervasive, and it's hard to imagine life without it.

As a student of developmental science, you might wonder when children acquire the ability to appreciate music as a distinct element of the sensory environment. If you observe parents of infants, you will see that they appear to believe that babies are born with this ability. In fact, singing to babies, even those who are only a few minutes or hours old, is just as universal as music itself (Custodero, Britto, & Brooks-Gunn, 2003; Custodero & Johnson-Green, 2003). Moreover, parents the world over sing to infants in a distinctive manner, one that includes a high-pitched tone and exaggerated rhythms (Bergeson & Trehub, 1999; Trainor, Clark, Huntley, & Adams, 1997; Trehub, Hill, & Kamenetsky, 1997). But what does the baby get out of it?

One answer to this question is clear. Babies know when they are being sung to, as indicated by the different behaviors they display when being sung to and talked to by their mothers (Nakata & Trehub, 2004). When mothers sing, babies move less and stare more intently at them than when mothers speak. Moreover, babies as young as 2 days old can tell when a videotaped adult is singing to an infant rather than to an older child or adult (Masataka, 1999). Thus, the capacity to recognize that, to put it simply, "This song is for me" appears to be inborn.

Infants appear to be born with much more than just the ability to recognize that a song is being directed to them (Trehub, 2003). They respond to dissonant notes (i.e., tones that don't sound pleasant when played together) just as adults do (Trainor, Tsang, & Cheung, 2002). Likewise, they recognize familiar melodies, no matter what key they are played in. They also notice when a familiar melody is played on an instrument that differs from the one with which they were familiarized with the song (Trainor, Anonymous, & Tsang, 2004). Likewise, they can discriminate between songs that have different meters, such as waltzes and marches.

Interestingly, too, infants are able to recognize another universal in infant-directed singing—the distinction between play songs (e.g., "The Itsy-Bitsy Spider") and lullabies (e.g., "Rock-a-Bye Baby"). Babies respond to lullabies by turning their attention toward themselves and playing with their hands or sucking their thumbs (Rock, Trainor, & Addison, 1999). In contrast, they display externally directed responses to play songs and behave in ways that seem to encourage adults to continue singing (Rock et al., 1999). This ability to discriminate song type may arise out of the capacity to recognize the emotional characteristics of a piece of music, another aspect of musical perception that appears to be inborn (Adachi, Trehub, & Abe, 2004; Schmidt, Trainor, & Santesso, 2003).

Thinking about how infants respond to music can help you understand the critical distinction between *sensation* and *perception*. The process of sensation involves the acquisition of information through the sensory organs—the eyes, ears, skin, nose, and mouth—and the transmission of that information to the brain. Perception is the attribution of meaning to sensations. Another way of saying this is that sensation furnishes the raw material of sensory experience, while perception provides the finished product. With regard to music, the sensory process of hearing is involved when babies recognize that one pitch differs from another. Every other aspect of infants' responses to music involves perception: Knowing that a song is being sung to them rather than to someone who is older, preferring some combinations of pitches to others, distinguishing between marches and waltzes, and recognizing the difference between a play song and a lullaby all involve perception. Because these aspects of music perception appear so early in life, it seems likely that they are inborn.

By contrast, no one would expect a baby to visualize a spider crawling up a waterspout, no matter how much she appears to enjoy listening to "The Itsy-Bitsy Spider." Preschoolers would be more likely to respond to the song with a visual image because they would know what the song's words meant. On the other hand, infants appear to be more able than adults to recognize music that is structurally different from that which is common in their own culture (Hannon & Trehub, 2005). Thus, some aspects of perception are obviously learned. Moreover, some of the learned aspects of perception broaden our perceptual abilities, while others narrow them. That is, learning language enhances our ability to attribute meaning to a song's lyrics, while long-term exposure to our own culture's music limits our ability to perceive the structural characteristics of music from other cultures.

As the example of music perception illustrates, research examining perceptual development provides fertile ground for developmentalists on both sides of the nature-nurture debate. We will begin our discussion with an examination of the theories and evidence on both sides.

Success! The spoon is in the mouth! At 1 year, Genevieve isn't very skillful yet, but she is already able to coordinate the perceptual and motor skills involved in this complex task at least a bit.

Thinking about Perceptual Development

The study of perceptual development has been significant because it has been a key battleground in the dispute about nature versus nurture—though theorists who study perceptual development refer instead to the contrast between *nativism* and *empiricism*. **Nativism** is the view that most perceptual abilities are inborn. **Empiricism** argues that these skills are learned. This issue has been so central in studies of perception that researchers have focused almost all their attention on young infants; only by observing infants can they observe the organism when it is relatively uninfluenced by specific experience (Bornstein, Arterberry, & Nash, 2005).

WAYS OF STUDYING EARLY PERCEPTUAL SKILLS

It took a while for psychologists to figure out how to study infants' perceptual skills. Babies can't talk and can't respond to ordinary questions, so how were researchers to decipher just what they could see, hear, or discriminate? Eventually, clever researchers figured out three basic methods for "asking" a baby about what he experiences. With the preference technique, devised by Robert Fantz (1956), the baby is simply shown two pictures or two objects, and the researcher keeps track of how long the baby looks at each one. If many infants shown the same pair of pictures consistently look longer at one picture than the other, this result not only indicates that babies see some difference between the two but also may reveal something about the kinds of objects or pictures that capture babies' attention.

nativism The view that perceptual abilities are inborn.

empiricism The view that perceptual abilities are learned.

Another strategy takes advantage of the processes of habituation and dishabituation you learned about in Chapter 3. Researchers first present a baby with a particular sight or sound over and over until he habituates—that is, until he stops looking at it or showing interest in it. Then experimenters present another sight or sound or object that is slightly different from the original one and watch to see if the baby shows renewed interest (dishabituation). If the baby does show renewed interest, they know he perceives the slightly changed sight or sound as "different" in some way from the original.

The third option is to use the principles of operant conditioning described in Chapter 1. For example, an infant might be trained to turn her head when she hears a particular sound, using the sight of an interesting moving toy as a reinforcement. After the learned response is well established, the experimenter can vary the sound in some systematic way to see whether the baby still turns her head.

EXPLANATIONS OF PERCEPTUAL DEVELOPMENT

We noted earlier that the study of perception, more than any other topic in developmental psychology except perhaps intelligence, has been dominated by questions of nature versus nurture, or nativism versus empiricism. Certainly there are other theoretical issues worthy of study, but given the importance of the historical argument between the nativists and the empiricists, it's worthwhile to take a closer look at current understanding of this question about perceptual development.

Arguments for Nativism　It is not hard to find strong arguments for a nativist position on perceptual development. As researchers have become more and more clever in devising ways to test infants' perceptual skills, they have found more and more skills already present in newborns or very young infants: Newborns have good auditory acuity, poor but adequate visual acuity, and excellent tactual and taste perception. They have at least some color vision and at least a rudimentary ability to locate the source of sounds around them. More impressive still, they are capable of making quite sophisticated discriminations from the earliest days of life, including being able to identify their mothers by sight, smell, or sound.

Newborn or very young babies also do not have to be taught what to look at. There are "rules" for looking, listening, and touching that can be detected at birth. As Kagan puts it: "Nature has apparently equipped the newborn with an initial bias in the processing of experience. He does not, as the 19th-century empiricists believed, have to learn what he should examine" (1971, p. 60). Furthermore, studies on babies' object understanding point to the strong possibility that other "assumptions," or biases about the way the world is organized, may also be built-in.

The fact that the "rules" seem to change with age can also be explained in nativist terms, since the nervous system is undergoing rapid maturation during the early months of life, much of it apparently in an automatic way, as preprogrammed synapses are formed rapidly. Furthermore, these rule changes seem to occur in bursts. One such set of changes seems to occur at about 2 to 3 months, when infants appear to shift away from focusing their eyes on contours or edges and toward more detailed visual analysis of objects or figures. At about the same age, a baby becomes able to track objects smoothly. Another shift seems to occur at about 4 months, when a whole host of discrimination skills, including depth perception based on kinetic cues and cross-modal transfer, especially coordination of auditory and visual information, first become evident.

Of course, it is possible that this apparent pileup of changes at 4 months reflects the accidental fact that many researchers have chosen to study babies of this age rather than younger babies. Perhaps, though, one major reason why researchers choose to study babies this age is that they are significantly easier to test—because there has been some underlying maturational shift that makes them more attentive, more able to focus, more stable in state.

Finally, we can find support for a nativist position in comparisons of the perceptual development of babies born after the normal gestational period versus those born preterm or at the normal term. In one such study, Yonas (1981) compared the response of two groups of 6-week-old babies: a group of normal-term babies and a group of babies born 3 to 4 weeks late (postterm). Both sets of infants were tested for depth perception using the method of looming objects. Yonas found that the postterm infants showed more consistent reactions to the looming objects, even though both groups had had precisely the same number of weeks of experience with objects since birth. Thus, it looks as if it is maturational age, and not experience, that matters in this case, which strengthens a nativist, or biological, position.

Arguments for Empiricism   On the other side of the ledger, however, we can find a great deal of evidence from research with other species that some minimum level of experience is necessary to support the development of the perceptual systems—the pattern of environmental effect Aslin calls *maintenance*. For example, animals deprived of light show deterioration of the whole visual system and a consequent decrease in perceptual abilities (Hubel & Weisel, 1963). Likewise, animals deprived of auditory stimuli display delayed or no development of auditory perceptual skills (Dammeijer, Schlundt, Chenault, Manni, & Anteunis, 2002).

It is also possible to find support for the negative version of Aslin's facilitation effect: Infants lacking sufficient perceptual stimulation may develop more slowly. Wayne Dennis's study of orphanage babies in Iran (1960) illustrates this possibility. The infants who didn't have a chance to look at things, to explore objects with hands and eyes and mouth, and who were deprived of the opportunity to move around freely were retarded in the development of both perceptual and motor skills.

Attunement may also occur. Evidence from studies of other species suggests that animals that are completely deprived of visual experiences in the early months of life never develop the same degree of depth perception as do those with full visual experience (Gottlieb, 1976b).

Integrating the Nativist and Empiricist Positions   We can best understand the development of perceptual skills by thinking of it as the result of an interaction between inborn and experiential factors. The relationship between the built-in process and the role of the environment is a little like the difference between a computer's hardware and its software. The perceptual hardware (specific neural pathways, rules for examining the world, a bias toward searching for patterns, and the like) may be preprogrammed, while the software (the program that governs the child's response to a particular real environment) depends on specific experience. A child is able to make visual discriminations between people or among objects within the first few days or weeks of life. That's built into the hardware. The specific discriminations she learns and the number of separate objects she learns to recognize, however, will depend on her experience. She is initially able to discriminate all the sound contrasts that exist in any spoken language, but the specific sound contrasts she eventually focuses on and the actual language she learns depend on the language she hears. The basic system is thus adapted to the specific environment in which the child finds herself. A perfect example of this, of course, is the newborn's ability to discriminate her mother's face from a very similar woman's face. Such a discrimination must be the result of experience, yet the capacity to make the distinction must be built in. Thus, as is true of virtually all dichotomous theoretical disputes, both sides are correct. Both nature and nurture are involved.

CRITICAL THINKING ?

Think of some other kinds of skills that could be explained from the nativist perspective—skills that appear very early in life and that improve regardless of experience.

Before going on . . .

■ Describe the three approaches to studying infants' perceptual skills.
■ List the arguments for nativist and empiricist views of perceptual development.

Sensory Skills

When developmentalists study sensory skills, they are asking just what information the sensory organs receive. Does the structure of the eye permit infants to see color? Are the structure of the ear and the cortex such that a very young infant can discriminate among different pitches? The common theme running through all of what you will read about sensory skills in this section is that newborns and young infants have far more sensory capacity than physicians or psychologists thought even as recently as a few decades ago. Perhaps because babies' motor skills are so obviously poor, we assumed that their sensory skills were equally poor. But we were wrong.

SEEING

Until 25 or 30 years ago, many medical texts stated that newborn infants were blind. Now we know that the newborn has poorer visual skills than older children but is quite definitely not blind.

Visual Acuity In adults, the usual standard for **visual acuity**—how well one can see—is 20/20 vision. If you have 20/20 vision, you can see and identify something that is 20 feet away that the average person can also see at 20 feet. A person with 20/100 vision, in contrast, has to be as close as 20 feet to see something that the average person can see from 100 feet. In other words, the higher the second number, the poorer the person's visual acuity. At birth, an infant's visual acuity is in the range from 20/200 to 20/400, but it improves rapidly during the first year as a result of all the swift changes occurring in the brain described in Chapter 4, including myelination, dendritic development, and pruning. Most infants reach the level of 20/20 vision by about 2 years of age (Keech, 2002).

The fact that the newborn sees so poorly is not so negative a thing as it might seem at first. Of course, it does mean that a baby doesn't see faraway things very clearly; he probably can't see well enough to distinguish two people standing nearby. But he sees quite well close up, which is all that is necessary for most encounters with the people who care for him or with objects immediately at hand, such as breast, bottle, or mobiles hanging above his crib.

Tracking Objects in the Visual Field When an infant tries to get a spoon in her mouth, one of the things she needs to do is keep her eyes on her hand or the spoon as she moves it toward herself. This process of following a moving object with your eyes is called **tracking**, and you do it every day in a variety of situations. You track the movement of other cars when you are driving; you track as you watch a friend walk toward you across the room; a baseball outfielder tracks the flight of the ball so that he can catch it. Because a newborn infant can't yet move independently, a lot of her experiences with objects are with things that move toward her or away from her. If she is to have any success in recognizing objects, she has to be able to keep her eyes on them as they move; she must be able to track.

Studies by Richard Aslin (1987) and others show that tracking is initially fairly inefficient but improves quite rapidly. Infants younger than 2 months show some tracking for brief periods if the target is moving very slowly, but a shift occurs somewhere around 6 to 10 weeks, and babies' tracking becomes skillful rather quickly. You can see the change graphically in Figure 5.1, taken from a study by Aslin.

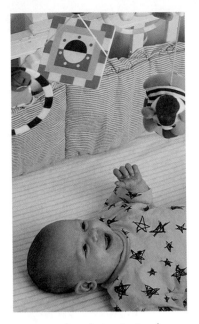

At 2 months, Eleanor's visual acuity is good enough that she can clearly see the colorful mobile hanging above her crib.

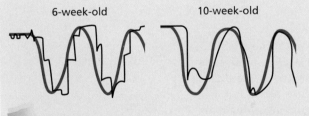

6-week-old   10-week-old

FIGURE 5.1

The red line in each figure shows the trajectory of the moving line that babies tried to follow with their eyes in Aslin's experiment. The black line represents one baby's eye movements at 6 weeks and again at 10 weeks. At 6 weeks, the baby more or less followed the line, but not smoothly. By 10 weeks, the same baby's tracking skill was remarkably smooth and accurate. (*Source*: Aslin, Richard N., "Motor Aspects of Visual Development in Infancy," *Handbook of Infant Perception: Vol. 1, From Sensation to Perception*, P. Salapatek and L. Cohen, eds. © 1987 by Academic Press. Adapted by permission.)

visual acuity How well one can see.

tracking Following a moving object with the eyes.

Color Vision Researchers have established that the types of cells in the eye necessary for perceiving red and green (the cones) are clearly present by 1 month, perhaps at birth; the cones required for perceiving blue are probably present by then as well (Bornstein et al., 1992). Thus, infants can and do see and discriminate among various colors (Pereverzeva, Hui-Lin Chien, Palmer, & Teller, 2002).

Taken together, research findings on tracking and color vision certainly do not support the notion that an infant is blind at birth. While it is true that the infant's visual acuity is initially poor, it improves rapidly, and other visual capacities are remarkably well developed early on. There are also some interesting hints that some kind of "shifting of gears" may take place at approximately 2 months; a number of skills, including the scanning of objects and tracking, improve incrementally at about that age (Bronson, 1994). But we don't yet know whether such changes are the result of such neurological changes as the rapid proliferation of synapses and the growth of dendrites, of changes in the eye itself, or perhaps of the child's experience.

HEARING AND OTHER SENSES

As you learned in Chapter 2, babies can hear long before they are born. However, like vision, hearing improves considerably in the early months of life. The other senses follow a similar course.

Auditory Acuity Although children's hearing improves up to adolescence, newborns' **auditory acuity**—how well they hear—is actually better than their visual acuity. Research evidence suggests that within the general range of pitch and loudness of the human voice, newborns hear nearly as well as adults do. Only with high-pitched sounds is their auditory acuity less than that of an adult; high-pitched sounds must be louder for a newborn to hear them than for older children or adults (Werner & Gillenwater, 1990).

Detecting Locations Another basic auditory skill that exists at birth and improves with age is the ability to determine the location of a sound. Because your two ears are separated from one another, sounds arrive at one ear slightly before the other, which allows you to judge location. Only if a sound comes from a source equidistant from the two ears (along the midline) does this system fail. In this case, the sound arrives at the two ears at the same time and you know only that the sound is somewhere on your midline. Newborns can judge at least the general direction from which a sound has come because they turn their heads in roughly the right direction toward some sound. More specific location of sounds, however, is not well developed at birth. For example, Barbara Morrongiello has observed babies' reactions to sounds played at the midline and then sounds coming from varying degrees away from the midline. Among infants 2 months old, it takes a shift of about 27 degrees off midline before the baby shows a changed response; among 6-month-olds, only a 12-degree shift is needed, while by 18 months, discrimination of a 4-degree shift is possible—nearly the skill level seen in adults (Morrongiello, 1988; Morrongiello, Fenwick, & Chance, 1990).

Smelling and Tasting Babies' senses of smell and taste have been studied much less than other senses, but we do have some basic knowledge about them. As in adults, the two senses are intricately related—that is, if you cannot smell for some reason (for example, when you have a cold), your taste sensitivity is also significantly reduced. Taste is detected by the taste buds on the tongue, which register at least four basic tastes: sweet, sour, bitter, and salty. (Some scientists believe there is a fifth basic taste: *umami*, the taste elicited by glutamate, an amino acid in meat, fish, and legumes.) Smell is registered in the mucous membranes of the nose, which can discriminate nearly unlimited variations.

auditory acuity How well one can hear.

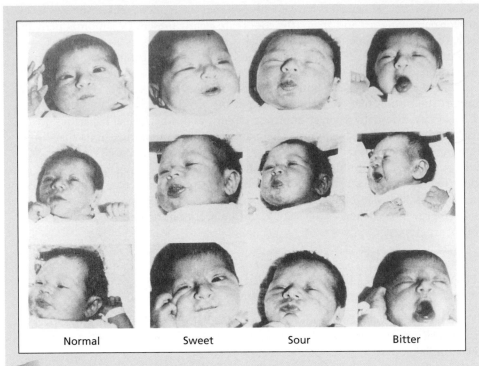

| Normal | Sweet | Sour | Bitter |

FIGURE 5.2

These are three of the newborns Steiner observed in his experiments on taste response. The left-hand column shows each baby's normal expression; the remaining columns show the change in expression when they were given sweet, sour, and bitter tastes. What is striking is how similar the expressions are for each taste.

(*Source*: Steiner, J. E., "Human Facial Expressions in Response to Taste and Smell Stimulation," in *Advances in Child Development and Behavior*, Vol. 13, H. W. Reese and L. P. Lipsitt, eds. © 1979 by Academic Press. By permission.)

CRITICAL THINKING ❓

In your opinion, what is the significance of information on babies' sensory skills for infant caregivers?

Before going on . . .

■ Describe the visual abilities of infants. How do these skills change across the first months?
■ How do infants' senses of hearing, smell, taste, touch, and motion compare to those of older children and adults?

Newborns appear to respond differentially to four of the basic tastes (Crook, 1987). Some of the clearest demonstrations of this fact come from an elegantly simple set of early studies by Jacob Steiner (Ganchrow, Steiner, & Daher, 1983; Steiner, 1979). Newborn infants who had never been fed were photographed before and after flavored water was put into their mouths. By varying the flavor, Steiner could determine whether the babies reacted differently to different tastes. As you can see in Figure 5.2, babies responded quite differently to sweet, sour, and bitter flavors. Babies as young as 1 week old can also tell the difference between such complex smells as personal body odors. Specifically, they can discriminate between their mother's and other women's smells (Rattaz, Goubet, & Bullinger, 2005).

Senses of Touch and Motion   The infant's senses of touch and motion may well be the best developed of all. The research you read about in Chapter 3 on the effects of massage on preterm infants illustrates that even the youngest infants are sensitive to touch (Dieter, Field, Hernandez-Reif, Emory, & Redzepi, 2003). Motion perception is clearly present even in the youngest infants, although a considerable degree of fine-tuning takes place over the first year of life (Bosworth & Birch, 2005).

Everything you have read about these sensory abilities is fairly dry and technical. The important point for you to remember is that, as Reisman puts it, "We think of infants as helpless but they are born with some exquisitely tuned sensory abilities" (1987, p. 265).

Perceptual Skills

In studies of perceptual skills, developmentalists are asking what the individual does with the sensory information—how it is interpreted or combined. Researchers have found that very young infants are able to make remarkably fine discriminations among sounds, sights, and physical sensations, and they pay attention to and respond to patterns, not just to individual events.

LOOKING

One important question to ask about visual perception is whether the infant perceives his environment in the same way as older children and adults. Can he judge how far away an object is by looking at it? Does he visually scan an object in an orderly way? Developmentalists believe that infants' patterns of looking at objects tell a great deal about what they are trying to gain from visual information.

Depth Perception   One of the perceptual skills that has been most studied is depth perception. You need this ability any time you reach for something or decide whether you have room to make a left turn before an oncoming car gets to you. Similarly, an infant needs to be able to judge depth in order to perform all kinds of simple tasks, including judging how far away an object is so that he can reach for it, or how far it is to the floor if he has ideas about crawling off the edge of the couch, or how to aim a spoon toward a bowl of chocolate pudding.

It is possible to judge depth using any (or all) of three rather different kinds of information: First, *binocular cues* involve both eyes, each of which receives a slightly different visual image of an object; the closer the object is, the more different these two views are. In addition, information from the muscles of the eyes also tells you something about how far away an object may be. Second, pictorial information, sometimes called *monocular cues*, requires input from only one eye. For example, when one object is partially in front of another one, you know that the partially hidden object is farther away—a cue called *interposition*. The relative size of two similar objects, such as telephone poles or two people you see in the distance, may also indicate that the smaller-appearing one is farther away. Linear perspective (the visual effect that makes railroad tracks seem to get closer together at a distance) is another monocular cue. Third, *kinetic cues* come from either your own motion or the motion of some object: If you move your head, objects near you seem to move more than objects farther away (a phenomenon called *motion parallax*). Similarly, if you see some object moving, such as a person walking across a street or a train moving along a track, the closer it is, the more distance it appears to cover in a given time.

How early can an infant judge depth, and which of these cues does he use? This is still an active area of research, so scientists do not have any final answers. The best conclusion at the moment seems to be that kinetic information is used first, perhaps by about 3 months of age; binocular cues are used beginning at about 4 months; and pictorial (monocular) cues are used last, perhaps at 5 to 7 months (Bornstein et al., 1992).

In a remarkably clever early study, Eleanor Gibson and Richard Walk (1960) devised an apparatus called a visual cliff. You can see from the photo that it consists of a large glass table with a checkerboard pattern immediately below the glass; on the other side—the "cliff" side—the checkerboard is several feet below the glass. A baby placed on the apparatus could judge depth by several means, but it is primarily kinetic information that would be useful, since the baby in motion would see the nearer surface move more than the farther surface. If a baby has no depth perception, she should be equally willing to crawl on either side of the table, but if she can judge depth, she should be reluctant to crawl out on the "cliff" side.

In an experiment using a "visual cliff" apparatus, like the one used by Gibson and Walk, mom tries to entice her baby out onto the "cliff" side. But because the infant can perceive depth, he fears that he will fall if he comes toward her, so he stays put, looking concerned.

One of the many skills 5-month-old Peter has to have in order to reach for and grasp his toy is the ability to judge depth. He must determine how far away the toy is and whether it is near enough for him to reach with his hand.

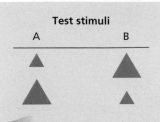

FIGURE 5.3

In the Carons' study, the researchers first habituated each baby to a set of training stimuli (all "small over large" in this case). Then they showed each baby two test stimuli: one that had the same pattern as the training stimuli (A), and one that had a different pattern (B). Babies aged 3 and 4 months showed renewed interest in the B stimulus but not the A stimulus, indicating that they were paying attention to the pattern, and not just to specific stimuli. (*Source*: Caron, A. J., and Caron, R. F., "Processing of Relational Information as an Index of Infant Risk," *Pre-term Birth and Psychological Development*, S. Friedman and M. Sigman, eds. © 1981 Academic Press. By permission.)

Since an infant had to be able to crawl in order to be tested in Gibson and Walk's procedure, the babies they studied were all 6 months old or older. Most of these infants did not crawl out on the cliff side but were quite willing to crawl out on the shallow side. In other words, 6-month-old babies have depth perception.

What about younger infants? The traditional visual cliff procedure can't give an answer to this question, since a baby must be able to crawl in order to show this evidence of depth perception. Researchers have studied younger babies' use of kinetic cues by watching them react to apparently looming objects. Most often, the baby observes a film of an object moving toward him, apparently on a collision course. If the infant has some depth perception, he should flinch, move to one side, or blink as the object appears to come very close. Such flinching has been consistently observed in 3-month-olds (Yonas & Owsley, 1987). Most experts now agree that this is about the lower age limit of depth perception.

What Babies Look At   Even though a baby cannot judge depth right away, her behavior is governed by visual information from the very first minutes of life. From the beginning, babies look at the world around them in a nonrandom way. In Marshall Haith's phrase (1980), there are "rules babies look by." Furthermore, those rules seem to change with age.

In the first 2 months, a baby's visual attention is focused on where objects are in her world (Bronson, 1991). Babies scan the world around them—not very smoothly or skillfully, to be sure, but nonetheless regularly, even in the dark. This general scanning continues until they come to a sharp light/dark contrast, which typically signals the edge of some object. Once she finds such an edge, a baby stops searching and moves her eyes back and forth across and around the edge. Thus, the initial rule seems to be: Scan till you find an edge and then examine the edge. Motion also captures a baby's attention at this age, so she will look at things that move as well as things with a noticeable light/dark contrast.

These rules seem to change between 2 and 3 months of age, perhaps because by then the cortex has developed more fully. At about this time, the baby's attention seems to shift from where an object is to what an object is. To put this another way, the baby seems to move from a strategy designed primarily for finding things to a strategy designed primarily for identifying things. Babies this age begin to scan rapidly across an entire figure rather than concentrating on edges. As a result, they spend more time looking at the internal features of some object or array of objects and are thus better able to identify the objects.

What is amazing about this shift at about 3 months is the degree of detail infants seem to be able to take in and respond to. They notice whether two pictures are placed horizontally or vertically, they can tell the difference between pictures with two things in them and pictures with three things in them, and they clearly notice patterns, even such apparently abstract patterns as "big thing over small thing."

One early study that illustrates this point particularly well was done by Albert and Rose Caron (1981), who used "training stimuli" in a habituation procedure. The babies were first shown a series of pictures that shared some particular relationship, such as "small over big." After the baby stopped being interested in the training stimuli (that is, after he habituated), the Carons showed him another figure (the "test stimulus") that either followed the same pattern or followed some other pattern, such as those in Figure 5.3. If the baby had really habituated to the pattern of the original pictures (small over big), he should show little interest in a picture like test stimulus A ("Ho hum, same old boring small over big thing"), but he should show renewed interest in test stimulus B ("Hey, here's something new!"). Caron and Caron found that 3- and 4-month-old children did precisely that. So even at this early age, babies find and pay attention to patterns, not just to specific stimuli.

Faces: An Example of Responding to a Complex Pattern   From the beginning of the era of research on infant perception, researchers have been especially

RESEARCH REPORT

Langlois's Studies of Babies' Preferences for Attractive Faces

Many studies on infant perception seem to point toward the conclusion that more perceptual rules are built-in than had been supposed. One such built-in rule appears to be a preference for attractive faces. In the first study in an important series of experiments, Langlois and her colleagues (1987) tested 2- to 3-month-olds and 6- to 8-month-olds. Each baby was shown color slides of adult Caucasian women, half rated by adult judges as attractive, half rated as unattractive. On each trial, the baby saw two slides simultaneously, with each face approximately life-size, while the experimenter peeked through a hole in the screen to count the number of seconds the baby looked at each picture. Each baby saw some attractive/attractive pairs, some unattractive/unattractive pairs, and some mixed pairs. With mixed pairs, even the 2- and 3-month-old babies consistently looked longer at the attractive faces. Several later studies, including some in which pictures of individuals of different races were used, produced similar findings (Langlois, Roggman, & Rieser-Danner, 1990; Langlois, Ritter, Roggman, & Vaughn, 1991).

It is hard to imagine what sort of learning experiences could account for such a preference in a 2-month-old. Instead, these findings raise the possibility that there is some inborn template for the "correct" or "most desired" shape and configuration for members of our species, and that we simply prefer those who match this template better.

Questions for Critical Analysis

1. If there is an inborn template that is used as a standard against which faces are compared, how might such a template affect our interactions with others?
2. How would researchers determine the degree to which attractiveness affects adults' perceptions of infants' faces? Why would such research be unable to tell us whether the concept of attractiveness is inborn?

interested in babies' perception of faces, not only because of the obvious relevance for parent-infant relationships, but because of the possibility that there might be a built-in preference for faces or facelike arrangements—a variant of the nativism/empiricism issue. But 30 years of research has not supplied all the answers. In fact, research brings new surprises all the time. Here is a sample of what developmentalists think they know at this point.

First, there is little indication that faces are uniquely interesting to infants, which fails to support one of the early assumptions of many nativists. That is, babies do not systematically choose to look at faces rather than at other complex pictures. On the other hand, researchers have some evidence from brain-imaging studies suggesting that there is an area of the brain dedicated to face processing in both adults and infants as young as 3 months of age (Johnson, 2005). Moreover, among faces, babies clearly prefer some to others. They prefer attractive faces (an intriguing result discussed in the *Research Report*), and it now seems apparent that they prefer the mother's face from the earliest hours of life, a finding that has greatly surprised psychologists, although it may not surprise you.

For years, psychologists have been telling parents that there was clear research showing that babies can't recognize their mothers' faces until at least 1 or 2 months of age but that they can recognize the mother by sound or smell immediately. In response, parents often said, "I don't care what the research says; I know my baby could recognize my face right away." It looks like they were right, and the older research was wrong.

Several studies have supported newborns' face recognition ability (e.g., Pascalis, de Schonen, Morton, Derulle, & Fabre-Grenet, 1995). A study that offered some of the clearest evidence was conducted by Gail Walton and her colleagues (1992). Walton videotaped the faces of 12 mothers of newborns and then matched each of these faces

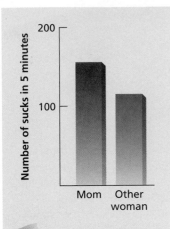

FIGURE 5.4

The babies in this study were 12 to 36 hours old at the time they were tested. They sucked more to see a picture of mom than a picture of another woman who looked very like her, thus showing that they could discriminate between the two faces. (*Source:* Walton et al., 1992, p. 267.)

CRITICAL THINKING 🤔

Does psychologists' history of being wrong about infants' perceptual abilities mean that they ought to believe mothers and fathers more often when they describe their infants and what the babies can do? How should scientists weigh anecdotal evidence against research evidence?

with the face of another woman whose hair color, eye color, complexion, and hair style were the same as the mother's. Each baby was then tested with one picture at a time in a modification of the preference technique. The babies could keep the picture turned on by sucking on a pacifier. The experimenters could count how often the babies sucked in order to keep mom's picture available, compared to their sucking rate for the photo of the woman who was not mom. These babies, who were only a day or two old at the time of the testing, clearly preferred to look at their moms, as you can see in Figure 5.4.

Recent research indicates that recognition of the mother's voice directs the newborn's attention to her face (Sai, 2005). Recall from Chapter 3 that maternal voice recognition happens prenatally. After birth, once the association between the mother's voice and her face has happened, the newborn spends more time looking at her face than at other visual stimuli, setting the stage for the formation of a memory for the face.

Beyond the issue of preference, there is also the question of just what it is that babies are looking at when they scan a face. Before about 2 months of age, babies seem to look mostly at the edges of the faces (the hairline and the chin), a conclusion buttressed by the finding by Pascalis and his colleagues (1995) that newborns could not discriminate mom's face from a stranger's if the hairline was covered. After 4 months, however, covering the hairline did not affect the baby's ability to recognize mom. In general, babies appear to begin to focus on the internal features of a face, particularly the eyes, at about 2 to 3 months.

LISTENING

When we turn from looking to listening, we find similarly intriguing indications that very young infants not only make remarkably fine discriminations among individual sounds but also pay attention to patterns. For starters, researchers have established that babies as young as 1 month old can discriminate between speech sounds such as *pa* and *ba* (Trehub & Rabinovitch, 1972). Studies using conditioned head-turning responses have shown that by perhaps 6 months of age, babies can discriminate between two-syllable "words" such as *bada* and *baga* and can even respond to a syllable that is hidden inside a string of syllables, as in *tibati* or *kobako* (Fernald & Kuhl, 1987; Goodsitt, Morse, Ver Hoeve, & Cowan, 1984; Morse & Cowan, 1982). Even more remarkable, it doesn't seem to matter what voice quality is used in saying the sound. By 2 or 3 months of age, babies respond to individual sounds as the same whether they are spoken by male or female voices or by a child's voice (Marean, Werner, & Kuhl, 1992). Research also indicates that infants can rapidly learn to discriminate between words and nonwords in articifial languages that researchers invent strictly for the purpose of such experiments (Aslin, Saffran, & Newport, 1998).

That's pretty impressive evidence that infants perceive quite fine variations in speech sounds, not just at the beginnings of words but in other vocal positions as well. Even more striking is the finding that babies are actually better at discriminating some kinds of speech sounds than adults are. Each language uses only a subset of all possible speech sounds. Japanese, for example, does not use the *l* sound that appears in English; Spanish makes a different distinction between *d* and *t* than occurs in English. It turns out that up to about 6 months of age, babies can accurately discriminate all sound contrasts that appear in any language, including sounds they do not hear in the language spoken to them. At about 6 months of age, they begin to lose the ability to distinguish pairs of vowels that do not occur in the language they are hearing; by age 1, the ability to discriminate nonheard consonant contrasts begins to fade (Polka & Werker, 1994).

Some of the best evidence on this point comes from the work of Janet Werker and her colleagues (Werker & Desjardins, 1995; Werker & Tees, 1984). They have tested 6- and 10-month-old infants on various consonant pairs, including one pair that is meaningful in English (*ba* versus *da*); a pair that occurs in a North American Indian language, Salish (*ki* versus *qi*); and one from Hindi, a language from the Indian subcontinent (*ta* versus *ta*). Other infants were tested with both English and German vowel contrasts. Figure 5.5 shows the results on contrasts that do not occur in English for babies growing up in English-speaking families. You can see that at 6 months, these babies could still readily hear the differences between pairs of foreign consonants but were already losing the ability to discriminate foreign vowels. Infants aged 10 and 12 months could not readily hear either type of contrast. Similarly, Werker has found that 12-month-old Hindi infants can easily discriminate a Hindi contrast but not an English contrast. So each group of infants loses only the ability to distinguish pairs that do not appear in the language they are hearing.

These findings are entirely consistent with the pattern of rapid, apparently preprogrammed, growth of synapses in the early months of life, followed by synaptic pruning. Many connections are created initially, permitting discriminations along all possible sound continua, but only those pathways that are actually used in the language the child hears are strengthened or retained.

Pattern perception is evident in other aspects of auditory perception. For example, as you learned at the beginning of the chapter, infants can recognize various kinds of patterns in music. Evidence supporting the pattern-seeking aspect of infants' responses to auditory stimuli also comes from research showing that, by 5 months of age, they can recognize their own names (Newman, 2005). Thus, just as with patterns of looking, infants appear to pay attention to and respond to patterns of sound and not just specific sounds.

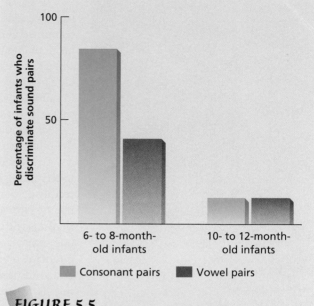

FIGURE 5.5

These data from Werker's studies are for babies growing up in English-speaking families, but she has similar results from infants in families that speak Hindi and families that speak Salish. In every case, 6-month-olds can still "hear" the distinctions between consonant pairs that do not occur in their family's language, but by 12 months that ability has largely disappeared. Discrimination of nonheard vowel pairs disappears even earlier. (*Source*: "Listening to Speech in the First Year of Life: Experimental Influences on Phoneme Perception" by Werker and Desjardins, *Current Directions in Psychological Science*, Vol. 4, No. 3 (June 1995), p. 00, Fig. 2. By permission of Blackwell Publishers.)

COMBINING INFORMATION FROM SEVERAL SENSES

If you think about the way you receive and use perceptual information, you'll realize that you rarely have information from only one sense at a time. Ordinarily, you have both sound and sight, touch and sight, or still more complex combinations of smell, sight, touch, and sound. Psychologists have been interested in knowing how early an infant can combine such information. For example, how early can an infant integrate information from several senses, such as knowing which mouth movements go with which sounds? Even more complex, how early can a baby learn something via one sense and transfer that information to another sense (for example, at what age can a child recognize solely by feel a toy he has seen but never felt before)? The first of these two skills is usually called **intersensory integration**, while the latter is called **cross-modal transfer** (or *intermodal transfer*).

Piaget believed that both these skills were simply not present until quite late in the first year of life, after the infant had accumulated many experiences with specific objects and how they simultaneously looked, sounded, and felt. Other theorists, including the eminent perceptual psychologists James J. Gibson (1904–1979) and Eleanor J. Gibson, have argued that some intersensory integration or even transfer is built in at birth (Gibson, 2002). The baby then augments that inborn set of skills with specific experience with objects. Research favors the Gibsonian view: Empirical findings show that cross-modal transfer is possible as early as 1 month and becomes common by 6 months (Rose & Ruff, 1987; Schweinle & Wilcox, 2004). Moreover, research comparing these skills in children born prematurely and those born at term suggests that basic maturational processes play an important role in their development (Espy et al., 2002).

intersensory integration The combining of information from two or more senses to form a unified perceptual whole (such as combining the sight of mouth movements with the sound of particular words).

cross-modal transfer The ability to transfer information gained through one sense to another sense at a later time (for example, identifying visually something you had previously explored only tactually).

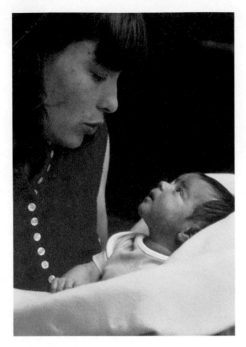

At 3 weeks, this infant can already discriminate her mother's face from the face of another woman; she can also identify mom by voice and smell.

Even though 7-month-old Leslie is not looking at this toy while she chews on it, she is nonetheless learning something about how it ought to look based on how it feels in her mouth and in her hands—an example of cross-modal transfer.

Research also suggests that intersensory integration is important in infant learning. One group of researchers found that babies who habituated to a combined auditory-visual stimulus were better able to recognize a new stimulus than infants who habituated to either the auditory or the visual stimulus alone (Bahrick & Lickliter, 2000). For example, suppose you played a videotape of someone singing for one baby, played the videotape without the sound for another, and played an audio recording of the song for a third. Research suggests that the first baby would recognize a change in either the singer (visual stimulus) or the song (auditory stimulus) more quickly than either of the other two infants.

In older children, intersensory integration and transfer, not only between touch and sight but between other modalities such as sound and sight, can be readily demonstrated. For instance, in several delightfully clever early experiments, Elizabeth Spelke showed that 4-month-old infants can connect sound rhythms with movement (1979). She showed babies two films simultaneously, one showing a toy kangaroo bouncing up and down, the other a donkey bouncing up and down, with one of the animals bouncing at a faster rate. Out of a loudspeaker located between the two films, the infant heard a tape recording of a rhythmic bouncing sound that matched the bounce pattern of one of the two animals. In this situation, babies showed a preference for looking at the film showing the bounce rate that matched the sound.

An even more striking illustration of the same basic process comes from the work of Jeffery Pickens (1994). He showed 5-month-old babies two films side by side; each film showed a train moving along a track. Then out of a loudspeaker he played various sequences of engine sounds, such as getting gradually louder (thus appearing to come closer) or getting gradually fainter (thus appearing to be moving away). The babies in this experiment looked longer at the film of the train whose movement matched the pattern of engine sounds. That is, they appeared to have some understanding of the link between the pattern of sound and the pattern of movement—knowledge that demonstrates not only intersensory integration but also surprisingly sophisticated understanding of the accompaniments of motion.

In the same vein, researchers have shown that 4- to 5-month-old babies will look longer at a face of a person mouthing a vowel that the baby hears spoken over a loudspeaker than at the face of a person mouthing another vowel (Kuhl & Meltzoff, 1984; Walton & Bower, 1993). Similarly, somewhat older infants shown a photo of a male and one of a female will look longer at the face that matches the gender of a voice heard over a loudspeaker—although only when the photo/voice match is female (Poulin-Dubois, Serbin, Kenyon, & Derbyshire, 1994).

Neither intersensory integration nor cross-modal transfer is a completely automatic process in young infants. In some 4- and 5-month-olds, these processes occur only under special circumstances (Lewkowicz, 1994). What is clear is that young infants have at least some ability to link simultaneous information from several senses, a conclusion that raises several interesting theoretical issues. For one thing, it is now perfectly clear that a baby or child does not need language to transfer information from one mode to another. And the fact that at least some transfer is possible within the first few weeks of life points rather strongly to the possibility that some connections may be built-in, although experience with specific objects and combinations clearly makes a difference as well. So this body of information enriches but does not settle the nativism-empiricism debate.

IGNORING PERCEPTUAL INFORMATION

Although babies are remarkably skillful at making perceptual discriminations of various kinds, they must acquire another, very different, kind of perceptual skill: the ability to ignore some kinds of perceptual data. Specifically, the child must acquire a set of rules called **perceptual constancies**.

When you see someone walking away from you, the image of the person on your retina actually becomes smaller. Yet you don't see the person getting smaller, but rather as the same size and moving farther away. When you do this, you are demonstrating **size constancy**; you are able to see the size as constant even though the retinal image has changed. Other constancies include the ability to recognize that shapes of objects are the same even though you are looking at them from different angles, called (logically enough) **shape constancy**, and the ability to recognize that colors are constant even though the amount of light or shadow on them changes, called **color constancy**.

Taken together, the several specific constancies add up to the larger concept of **object constancy**, which is the recognition that objects remain the same even when the sensory information you have about them has changed in some way. Babies begin to show signs of these constancies at 3 or 4 months of age and become more skilled over the first several years (Kavšek, 2002). Think about shape constancy as an illustration.

Shape constancy has perhaps the most obvious day-to-day relevance for a baby. She has to realize that her bottle is still her bottle even though it is turned slightly and thus presents a different shape to her eyes; she has to figure out that her toys are the same when they are in different positions. The beginnings of this understanding seem to be present by about 2 or 3 months of age. The classic study was done by Thomas Bower (1966), who first trained 2-month-old babies to turn their heads when they saw a particular rectangle. He then showed them tilted or slightly turned images of the same rectangle to see if the babies would respond to these as "the same," even though the retinal image cast by these tilted rectangles was actually a trapezoid and not a rectangle at all. Two-month-olds did indeed continue to turn their heads to these tilted and turned rectangles, showing that they had some shape constancy.

One of the ironies about perceptual development is that at a later age, when learning to read, a child has to unlearn some of these shape constancies. Pairs of letters such as *b* and *d*, *p* and *q*, and *p* and *b* are the same shape except with the direction reversed— flopped or upside down. So to learn to read (at least the Latin alphabet) the child must learn to pay attention to something she has learned to ignore—namely, the rotation of the letter in space. Of course, learning to read involves a good deal more than simply ignoring shape constancy, but 5-year-olds who have difficulty discriminating between mirror images of shapes also have more difficulty learning to read (Casey, 1986).

INDIVIDUAL DIFFERENCES IN PERCEPTUAL SKILLS

In Chapter 4, you learned that very similar patterns of physical development are seen in all children. The same is clearly true for many of the patterns of perceptual development. Nonetheless, like physical development, perceptual development shows significant individual variations, of which the most interesting are the indications that babies may differ in the efficiency with which they are able to deal with perceptual information.

The most extensive body of research has dealt with variations in infants' *recognition memory,* or the ability to recognize that one has seen or experienced some object or person before. One way to measure this is with a standard habituation test, that is, by counting how many repeated exposures it takes before a baby stops responding with interest to some stimulus. The speed with which such habituation takes place may indicate something about the efficiency of the perceptual/cognitive system and its neurological underpinnings. And if such efficiency lies behind some of the characteristics we normally call "intelligence," then it is possible that individual differences in rate of habituation in the early months of life may predict later intelligence test scores.

perceptual constancies A collection of mental rules that allow humans to perceive shape, size, and color as constant even when perceptual conditions (such as amount of light, angle of view, and the like) change.

size constancy The ability to see an object's size as remaining the same despite changes in size of the retinal image; a key element in size constancy is the ability to judge depth.

shape constancy The ability to see an object's shape as remaining the same despite changes in the shape of the retinal image; a basic perceptual constancy.

color constancy The ability to see the color of an object as remaining the same despite changes in illumination or shadow.

object constancy The general phrase describing the ability to see objects as remaining the same despite changes in sensory information about them.

This is exactly what researchers have found in studies over the past 15 years. The rate of habituation shown by 4- to 5-month-old babies is correlated positively with IQ and language development at 3 or 4 years of age or older. That is, faster habituation is associated with higher IQ and better language, and slower habituation is associated with lower IQ and poorer language. The average correlation in studies in both the United States and England is in the range of .45 to .50 (Rose & Feldman, 1995; Rose, Feldman, & Jankowski, 2004; Slater, 1995). This correlation is certainly not perfect, but it is remarkably high, given the difficulties involved in measuring habituation rate in babies.

Certainly these correlations do not prove that intelligence, as measured by an IQ test, is only a reflection of some kind of "speed of basic processing." Results like these nonetheless underline the potential importance of individual differences in perceptual efficiency in early infancy.

Before going on . . .

■ Describe the development of depth perception, and explain what babies look at and how they respond to faces.
■ How do infants perceive human speech, recognize voices, and recognize sound patterns other than speech?
■ What are perceptual constancies, and why are they important to perception?
■ What is the significance of individual differences in habituation rate?

The Object Concept

Acquiring the various perceptual constancies is only part of a larger task facing the child; he must also figure out the nature of objects themselves. First of all, an infant must somehow learn to treat some combinations of stimuli as "objects" but not others, a process usually referred to as *object perception*. A still more sophisticated aspect of the infant's emerging concept of objects is the understanding that objects continue to exist even when they are out of view, an understanding usually referred to as **object permanence**.

OBJECT PERCEPTION

The most thorough and clever work on object perception in infants has been done by Elizabeth Spelke and her colleagues (Spelke, 1982, 1985; Spelke, von Hofsten, & Kestenbaum, 1989). Spelke believes that babies are born with certain built-in assumptions about the nature of objects. One of these is the assumption that when two surfaces are connected to each other, they belong to the same object; Spelke calls this the *connected surface principle*. To study this (Spelke, 1982), she first habituated some 3-month-old babies to a series of displays of two objects; other babies were habituated to the sight of one-object displays. Then the babies were shown two objects touching each other, such as two square blocks placed next to each other so that they created a rectangle. Under these conditions, the babies who had been habituated to two-object displays showed renewed interest, clearly indicating that they "saw" this as different, presumably as a single object. Babies who had seen the one-object displays during habituation showed no renewed interest. Spelke has also shown that babies as young as 2 and 3 months old are remarkably aware of the kinds of movements objects are capable of, even when the objects are out of sight. They expect an object to continue to move on its initial trajectory, and they show surprise if the object's movement violates this expectancy. They also seem to have some awareness that solid objects cannot pass through other solid objects.

In one experiment, Spelke (1991) used the procedure shown schematically in the upper part of Figure 5.6. Two-month-old babies were repeatedly shown a series of events like that in the "familiarization" section of the figure: A ball was rolled from the left-hand side to the right and disappeared behind a screen (the dashed line in Figure 5.6). The screen was then taken away and the baby could see that the ball was stopped against the wall on the right. After the baby got bored looking at this sequence (habituated), he or she was tested with two variations, one "consistent" and one "inconsistent." In the consistent variation, a second wall was placed behind the screen and the sequence was conducted as before, except now when the screen was removed, the ball

object permanence The understanding that objects continue to exist even when they cannot be directly perceived.

could be seen resting up against the nearer wall. In the inconsistent variation, the ball was surreptitiously placed on the far side of the new wall. When the screen was removed, the ball was visible in this presumably impossible place. Babies in this experiment were quite uninterested in the consistent condition but showed sharply renewed interest in the inconsistent condition, as you can see in the lower part of Figure 5.6, which shows the actual results of the experiment.

Spelke is not suggesting that all of a child's knowledge of objects is built-in; she is suggesting that some rules are built-in and that others are learned through experience. Other researchers, such as Renée Baillargeon (1994), argue that basic knowledge is not built-in, but that strategies for learning are innate. According to this view, infants initially develop basic hypotheses about the way objects function—how they move, how they connect to one another. These early basic hypotheses are quite rapidly modified, based on the baby's experience with objects. For example, Baillargeon finds 2- to 3-month-old infants are already operating with a basic hypothesis that an object will fall if it isn't supported by something, but they have no notion of how much support is required. By about 5 months of age, this basic hypothesis has been refined, and they understand that the smiling-face block in the upper arrangement of Figure 5.7 (condition a) will stay supported, but the block in the bottom arrangement (condition b) will not (Baillargeon, 1994). However, other psychologists question Baillargeon's conclusions. For example, developmental psychologist Leslie Cohen and his associates have conducted similar experiments with 8-month-olds, and they argue that infants respond to the stimuli used in such studies on the basis of novelty rather than because of an understanding of stable and unstable block arrangements (Cashon & Cohen, 2000). Such varying interpretations demonstrate just how difficult it is to make inferences about infants' thinking from their interactions with physical objects.

Recent research has also examined the degree to which infants can make practical use of their understanding of objects and object movements. For example, several studies have shown that 2-year-olds experience difficulty when they are required to use this understanding to search for a hidden object (Keen, 2003). In one study, 2-, 2.5-, and 3-year-olds were shown a display similar to that in the top portion of Figure 5.6 and responded in exactly the same way as younger infants to the consistent and inconsistent displays (Berthier, DeBlois, Poirier, Novak, & Clifton, 2000). Next, a board in which there were several doors took the place of the screen; however, the barrier protruded several inches above this board (see Figure 5.8). Across several trials, children were shown the ball rolling behind the board and were asked to open the door behind which they thought the ball would be found. Even though the children could clearly see behind which door the barrier was placed in every trial, none of the 2-year-olds and only a few of the 2.5-year-olds were able to succeed on this task, in contrast to the large majority of 3-year-olds. Developmentalists interpret such results to mean that young infants' understanding of objects is the foundation upon which the object concept is

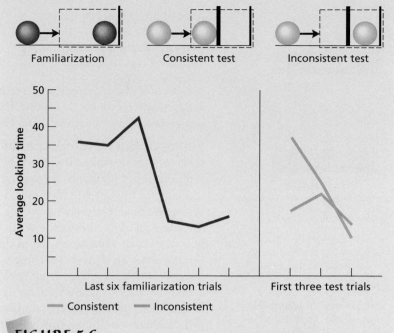

FIGURE 5.6

The top part of the figure shows a schematic version of the three conditions Spelke used. The graph below the conditions shows the actual results. You can see that the babies stopped looking at the ball and screen after a number of familiarization trials, but they showed renewed interest in the inconsistent version—a sign that the babies saw this as somehow different or surprising. The very fact that the babies found the inconsistent trial surprising is itself evidence that infants as young as 2 months have far more knowledge about objects and their behavior than most developmentalists had thought

(*Source*: E. S. Spelke, from Figures 5.3 and 5.4, "Physical Knowledge in Infancy: Reflections on Piaget's Theory" in *The Epigenesis of Mind: Essays on Biology and Cognition*, S. Carey and R. Gelman (eds.). © 1991 by Lawrence Erlbaum Associates, Inc. By permission of the publisher and author.)

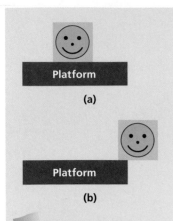

FIGURE 5.7

Renée Baillargeon's research suggests that 2- and 3-month-old babies think that the smiling-face block will not fall under either of these conditions, but by 5 months, they realized that only the condition shown in (a) is stable. In condition (b), the block will fall. (*Source*: "How Do Infants Learn About the Physical World?" by Baillargeon, R., *Current Directions in Psychological Science*, Vol. 3, No. 5 (October 1994), p. 134, Fig. 1. By permission of Blackwell Publishers.)

gradually constructed and applied to real-world interaction with objects over the first 3 years of life (Keen, 2003).

OBJECT PERMANENCE

The study of object perception is a rather new area of research. In contrast, object permanence has been extensively studied. This has happened in large part because this particular understanding was strongly emphasized in Piaget's theory of infant development.

Stages in the Development of Object Permanence   According to Piaget's observations, replicated frequently by later researchers, the first sign that a baby is developing object permanence comes at about 2 months of age. Suppose you show a toy to a child of this age and then put a screen in front of the toy and remove the toy. When you then take away the screen, the baby shows some indication of surprise, as if she knew that something should still be there. The child thus seems to have a rudimentary schema, or expectation, about the permanence of an object. However, infants of this age show no signs of searching for a toy they may have dropped over the edge of the crib or that has disappeared beneath a blanket or behind a screen—a pattern of reaction that parents take advantage of when an infant is fussing for some toy or object he can't reach or when they want him to stop fooling with some object. So, with young infants, there is a fleeting concept of the permanence of objects, but it isn't yet well developed enough to motivate them to search for a hidden object.

At about 6 or 8 months of age, this begins to change. Babies of this age look over the edge of the crib for the dropped toy or over the edge of the high chair for food that was spilled. (In fact, babies of this age may drive their parents nuts playing "dropsy" in the high chair.) Infants this age will also search for partially hidden objects. If you put a favorite toy under a cloth but leave part of it sticking out, the infant will reach for the toy, which suggests that in some sense the infant recognizes that the whole object is there even though she can see only part of it. Yet if you cover the toy completely with the cloth or put it behind a screen, the infant will stop looking at it and will not reach for it, even if she has seen you put the cloth over it.

This changes again somewhere between 8 and 12 months. At this age, the "out of sight, out of mind" parental strategy no longer works at all. Infants this age will reach for or search for a toy that has been covered completely by a cloth or hidden by a screen. Thus, by 12 months, most infants appear to grasp the basic fact that objects continue to exist even when they are no longer visible.

Object constancy has intrigued researchers and theorists in part because it forms one kind of bridge between studies of perception and studies of early cognitive development. Many developmentalists have also been struck by a possible link between the emergence of object constancy and the infant's earliest attachment. It seems reasonable to assume that some kind of object permanence is required before a baby can become attached to an individual person, such as his mother or father. Since clear single attachments don't appear much before 5 months, right about the time that the baby is showing signs of object permanence, the connection seems very reasonable.

Interestingly, and surprisingly to a lot of developmentalists, most direct tests of this hypothesis have not shown much sign of such a causal link. Still, the problem may be with the research techniques rather than the hypothesis. As John Flavell (1985, p. 135) wonders, "However could a child persistently yearn and search for a specific other person if the child were still cognitively incapable of mentally representing that person in the person's absence?" Flavell's logic is persuasive, but as usual we will have to wait for further research evidence to be sure.

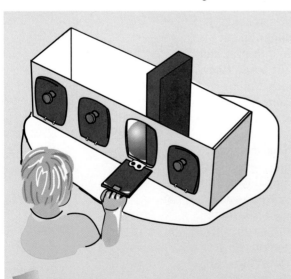

FIGURE 5.8

Researchers use devices such as this one to find out whether toddlers can predict that a moving object will be stopped by the barrier that protrudes above the wall of doors. Children younger than 3 typically fail to identify the door behind which the object will be found.

Object Permanence and Cultural Practices   It might seem that experiences manipulating objects contribute to the development of object permanence. However, Susan Goldberg's classic longitudinal study of 38 Zambian infants (1972) indicated that this is not the case. From shortly after birth, Zambian babies are carried about in slings on their mothers' backs. They spend very little time on the floor or in any position in which they have much chance of independent movement until they are able to sit up at about 6 months. At that point they are usually placed on a mat in the yard of the house. From this vantage the baby can watch all the activity around the house and in the neighborhood, but he has few objects to play with.

Yet despite this very limited experience manipulating objects, tests of object permanence showed that, on average, the Zambian babies were ahead of U.S. babies on a measure of the object concept at 6 months of age. At 9 and 12 months of age, the Zambian babies were slightly behind U.S. babies, but Goldberg believes that this difference is due not to any cognitive failure but to the fact that at these ages the Zambian babies were quite unresponsive and passive toward objects and thus were very difficult to test. She observed that Zambian adults actively discourage older infants from touching and manipulating objects, and so, she hypothesized, the infants may have interpreted the objects in the experiment to be things that they weren't supposed to respond to. Nevertheless, Goldberg's research revealed a clear progression toward object permanence across the first 18 months of life that was quite similar to that observed in Western infants.

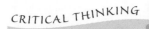

CRITICAL THINKING 9

Research on object permanence suggests that, if you take an object away from a 6-month-old, she will forget about it as soon as it is out of sight. How might this characteristic of younger infants be useful for caregivers?

Before going on...

- What kinds of rules do infants appear to use in perceiving objects?
- What is object permanence, and how does it develop?

Perception of Social Signals

The description of the infant's ability to discriminate faces presented earlier in this chapter treats faces as if they were purely physical objects, with fixed properties such as eye characteristics, hairlines, and so forth. But, of course, other people's faces also provide social signals in the form of varying emotional expressions. Variations in vocal intonations and body language similarly provide social cues. These are important bits of information for a baby to detect and decipher. Parents, teachers, and other adults convey a great deal of information through their emotional expression. In peer interactions, too, the ability to read another's emotion is essential for any kind of sustained cooperative play or for the subtle adaptations required for the formation of enduring friendships.

EARLY DISCRIMINATION OF EMOTIONAL EXPRESSIONS

Research evidence suggests that infants begin to pay attention to social/emotional cues in faces at about 2 or 3 months of age. For example, at that age, infants begin to smile more to human faces than to a doll's face or another inanimate object, suggesting that at this early stage, the baby is already responding to the added social signals available in the human face (Ellsworth, Muir, & Hains, 1993; Legerstee, Pomerleau, Malcuit, & Feider, 1987). The orientation of the face seems to be one critical ingredient in this early preferential smiling. Albert Caron and his colleagues (1997) find that babies smile more only when the face is turned toward them; if the face is turned aside, the baby does not smile more.

Infants this age are also beginning to notice and respond differently to variations in others' emotional expressions. Initially, they discriminate emotions best when they receive information on many channels simultaneously—such as when they see a particular facial expression and hear the corresponding emotion expressed in the adult's voice (Walker-Andrews, 1997). For example, Haviland and Lelwica (1987) found that when mothers expressed happiness with both face and voice, 10-week-old babies looked happy

CRITICAL THINKING ?

You judge others' emotions quite automatically, using all the subtle cues you have learned. Analyze the process for a moment, though: What are the specific cues you use to decide that someone is expressing pride, or shame, or ambivalence? How are these complex emotions expressed in the face or body movement? Is tone of voice part of the picture?

FIGURE 5.9

What emotion is being expressed in each of these photos? If you said fear and happiness, you agree with virtually all observers, in many countries, who have looked at these pictures. (Copyright Paul Ekman.)

social referencing Using another person's emotional reaction to some situation as a basis for deciding one's own reaction. A baby does this when she checks her parent's facial expression or body language before responding positively or negatively to something new.

and interested and gazed at the mother; when the mothers expressed sadness, babies showed increased mouth movements or looked away; when the mothers expressed anger, some babies cried vigorously, while others showed a kind of still or "frozen" look.

By 5 to 7 months, babies can begin to "read" one channel at a time, responding to facial expression alone or vocal expression alone, even when the emotions are displayed by a stranger rather than mom or dad (Balaban, 1995). Specifically, they can tell the difference between happy and sad voices (Walker-Andrews & Lennon, 1991) and between happy, surprised, and fearful faces (Nelson, 1987). They also seem to have some preliminary understanding that vocal and facial emotional expressions typically go together.

For example, Nelson Soken and Anne Pick (1992) showed 7-month-olds pairs of faces displaying happy and angry expressions while the babies listened to words spoken in either a happy or an angry voice. The infants looked longer at the face that matched the emotion in the speaking voice. Recent research suggests that younger infants (12 to 14 weeks of age) display an understanding of facial/vocal matches and mismatches only when these are demonstrated by the babies' own mothers (Kahana-Kalman & Walker-Andrews, 2001).

Late in the first year of life, infants take another important step and link the information about a person's emotional expression with the environmental context. For example, a 12-month-old, faced with some new and potentially fearful event such as a new toy or a strange adult, may first look at mom's or dad's face to check for the adult's emotional expression. If mom looks pleased or happy, the baby is likely to explore the new toy with more ease or to accept the stranger with less fuss. If mom looks concerned or frightened, the baby responds to those cues and reacts to the novel situation with equivalent concern or fear. Researchers have described this as a process of **social referencing** (Thompson & Goodvin, 2005; Walker-Andrews, 1997). Not only do babies use the emotions of others to guide their own responses, but recent research suggests that, by 12 months of age, they can use nonverbal cues to identify the cause of another person's emotional response (Moses, Baldwin, Rosicky, & Tidball, 2001). Moreover, 1-year-olds can calm themselves when their caregivers behave in expected ways (Cole, Martin, & Dennis, 2004). For example, a baby who is frustrated by hunger will calm down when she sees her caregiver preparing to nurse her or to provide her with some other kind of nourishment. However, infants' basic ability to perceive emotions carries potential risks for those whose mothers are depressed (see *The Real World*).

CROSS-CULTURAL COMMONALITIES AND VARIATIONS

It is reasonable to ask whether children in every culture learn about emotions in this same way. The Utka, an Inuit band in northern Canada, have two words for fear, distinguishing between fear of physical disaster and fear of being treated badly. Some African languages have no separate words for fear and sorrow. Samoans use the same word for love, sympathy, and liking, and Tahitians have no word at all that conveys the notion of guilt. These examples, drawn by James Russell (1989) from the anthropological literature, remind us that we need to be very careful when we talk about the "normal" process of a child learning about emotional expression and emotional meaning. From an English-speaking, Western perspective, emotions such as fear and anger seem like "basic" emotions that all infants understand early and easily. But what would be the developmental sequence for a child growing up in a culture in which fear and sorrow are not distinguished?

The work of Paul Ekman (1972, 1973, 1989) has provided evidence of a strong cross-cultural similarity in people's facial expressions when conveying certain of these same "basic" emotions, such as fear, happiness, sadness, anger, and disgust. (Figure 5.9 shows two such common expressions.) In all cultures studied so far, adults understand these facial expressions as having the same core meaning. Cultural

Infant Responses to Maternal Depression

Marsha, a new mother, had just been diagnosed with postpartum depression. Her doctor assured her that there was a good chance that the antidepressants she had begun taking, along with the psychotherapist he had recommended, would enable her to pull out of the depression in a few weeks. Still, Marsha told her psychotherapist that she worried about how her depression might affect her 1-month-old's development. In response, the therapist encouraged Marsha to participate in a training program designed to help depressed mothers recognize how their illness was affecting their parenting behaviors. Further, the program would help Marsha learn how to exhibit more effective parenting behaviors in their place.

Marsha was right to be concerned about the effects of her own depression on her baby's development. For one thing, one of the characteristics of people who suffer from depression is the exhibition of sad facial expressions even in situations in which they feel happy. And, as you've learned, babies use parents' facial expressions to guide them in the expression of their own emotions. So, what are the effects on babies of day-to-day interactions with a depressed mother?

Developmentalists have found that babies who interact regularly with depressed mothers express more negative and fewer positive emotions. They smile less, show more sad and angry facial expressions, and are more disorganized and distressed (Dawson, Panagiotides, Klinger, & Spieker, 1997; Field, Healy, Goldstein, & Guthertz, 1990; Pickens & Field, 1993). Such children are also at higher risk for later behavior problems, including either heightened aggression or withdrawal (Cummings & Davies, 1994).

Recent findings, though, suggest that more may be involved than just infants' perceptions of their depressed mothers' facial expressions. Specifically, brain-imaging studies show that similar patterns of activity exist in the brains of mothers who were depressed while they were pregnant and in the brains of their newborn infants (Field et al., 2004). These studies suggest that the relationship between maternal and infant depression may derive from babies' prenatal exposure to the biochemical features of their mothers' emotional state. Further, studies have shown that stress- and depression-related hormones are passed from mother to infant via breast-feeding (Hart et al., 2004).

Whether the link between maternal and infant depression arises from babies' ability to perceive facial expression or is biochemical in nature, it seems clear that maternal behaviors are important as well. There appear to be three problematic behavior patterns in depressed mothers. In one pattern, moth-

ers are withdrawn and detached; they look at, touch, or talk to their babies less often and are less affectionate toward them than are nondepressed mothers (Field, 1995; Hart, Jones, Field, & Lundy, 1999). Children of these depressed mothers are less likely to form a secure attachment with the mother. They are also at higher risk for later behavior problems, including either heightened aggression or withdrawal (Cummings & Davies, 1994; Murray et al., 1999; Teti, Gelfand, Messinger, & Isabella, 1995). In the second pattern, mothers are overly involved with their infants, often interrupting and overstimulating them. Babies seem to respond to this kind of treatment by withdrawing both from their mothers and from others in their environments (Hart et al., 1999). The third group of depressed mothers overreact and respond angrily to babies' undesirable behaviors. Infants of these depressed mothers are more likely than others to display aggressive behavior in early childhood (O'Leary, Smith Slep, & Reid, 1999).

By contrast, infants whose depressed mothers exhibit sensitive parenting behaviors are less likely to display long-term negative effects than babies of other depressed mothers (NICHD Early Child Care Research Network, 1999). In other words, when depressed mothers exhibit the same kinds of parenting behaviors as most nondepressed mothers, their emotional status doesn't appear to have negative effects on their babies' development. Thus, because the link between maternal depression and its effects on infants is a behavioral one, parent training may provide an avenue through which the potential negative effects of maternal depression can be moderated. Indeed, several studies have shown that training can increase the frequency of sensitive behaviors in depressed mothers and, as a result, lead to changes in infants' attachment status (van den Boom, 1994, 1995). Moreover, antidepressant medications positively affect many aspects of depressed mothers' behavior, including making the tone of their verbal interactions with infants more like that of nondepressed mothers (Kaplan, Bachorowski, Smoski, & Zinser, 2001).

Questions for Reflection

1. How might researchers study whether genetics plays a role in the correlation between maternal and infant depression?
2. Based on this discussion, what items might be included in a brief observational checklist that health care professionals could use to identify problem behaviors in depressed mothers?

variations are laid on top of these basic expressive patterns, and cultures have different rules about which emotions may be expressed and which must be masked. One could hypothesize that infants and toddlers are quite good at discriminating and understanding the core, shared patterns; even 2-year-olds can recognize and categorize happy and sad expressions. Beyond that basic understanding, the child must then slowly learn all the cultural overlays—the links between emotion and situation that hold for each culture, the specific meanings of emotional language, and the scripts that govern the appropriate expression of emotion in a given culture. This is no small task. What is remarkable is just how much of this information the preschooler already comprehends and reflects in his own behavior.

Before going on...

- Describe changes in infants' perceptions of emotions across the first year of life.
- What cross-cultural differences in emotional perception have been noted?

Summary

Thinking about Perceptual Development

- Studies of perceptual development have been greatly aided by methodological advances, such as Fantz's preference technique and the use of habituation or operant conditioning techniques with very young infants.
- A central issue in the study of perceptual development continues to be the nativism-empiricism debate. Many basic perceptual abilities, including strategies for examining objects, appear to be built into the system at birth or to develop as the brain develops over the early years. But specific experience is required both to maintain the underlying system and to learn fundamental discriminations and patterns.

Sensory Skills

- Color vision is present at birth, but visual acuity and tracking ability are relatively poor at birth. These skills develop rapidly during the first few months.
- Basic auditory skills are more fully developed at birth; auditory acuity is good for the range of the human voice, and the newborn can locate at least the approximate direction of a sound. The sensory capacities for smelling and tasting and the senses of touch and motion are also well developed at birth.

Perceptual Skills

- Depth perception is present in at least rudimentary form by 3 months of age. The baby initially uses kinetic cues, then binocular cues, and finally pictorial cues by about 5 to 7 months. Visual attention appears to follow definite rules, even in the first hours of life. Babies can discriminate the mother's face from other faces, and the mother's voice from other voices, almost immediately after birth.
- From the beginning, babies appear to attend to and discriminate among all possible speech sound contrasts; by the age of 1 year, the infant makes fine discriminations only

among speech sounds that occur in the language she is actually hearing.
- By 4 months, babies also attend to and discriminate among different patterns of sounds, such as melodies or speech inflections.
- Touch/sight and sound/sight cross-modal transfers have been demonstrated in infants as young as 1 month old and are found reliably in 4-month-olds.
- Perceptual constancies such as size constancy, shape constancy, and color constancy are all present in at least rudimentary form by 4 months of age.
- Babies differ in the apparent speed or efficiency of perceptual processes, such as habituation to a repeated stimulus. Such variations in habituation rate are correlated with later measures of IQ and language skill.

The Object Concept

- Young babies have quite complex understanding of objects, their properties, and their possible movements.
- The understanding of object permanence (the realization that objects exist even when they are out of sight) begins at 2 or 3 months of age and is quite well developed by 10 months.

Perception of Social Signals

- Babies' ability to discriminate among emotional expressions appears early in the first year. By 6 months of age, most infants can discriminate between emotional information contained in facial expressions and that represented by vocal tone.
- Cross-cultural research has shown that facial expressions are given the same meaning in every culture studied so far. What varies across cultures to some degree is the situations associated with various emotions as well as social rules for expressing them.

Key Terms

auditory acuity (p. 131)
color constancy (p. 139)
cross-modal transfer (p. 137)
empiricism (p. 127)
intersensory integration (p. 137)

nativism (p. 127)
object constancy (p. 139)
object permanence (p. 140)
perceptual constancies (p. 139)
shape constancy (p. 139)

size constancy (p. 139)
social referencing (p. 144)
tracking (p. 130)
visual acuity (p. 130)

See for Yourself

Object Permanence

You can learn more about object permanence by carrying out your own experiment with an infant between 6 and 12 months old. Obtain permission from the baby's parents and ask the mother and/or father to be present during the study. Obtain from the parents one of the baby's favorite toys. Place the baby in a sitting position or on his stomach in such a way that he can reach for the toy easily. Then perform the following steps:

Step 1: While the baby is watching, place the toy in full view and within easy reach. See if the infant reaches for the toy.
Step 2: In full view of the infant, cover part of the toy with a handkerchief, so that only part is visible. Does the baby reach for the toy?
Step 3: While the infant is reaching for the toy (you'll have to pick your moment), cover the toy completely with the handkerchief. Does the baby continue reaching?
Step 4: In full view of the child, while the child is still interested in the toy, cover the whole toy with the cloth. Does the baby try to pull the cloth away or search for the toy in some way?

You may need to use more than one toy to keep the baby's interest and/or spread the tests over a period of time. Jackson, Campos, and Fischer (1978) report that Step 2 (in which the baby reaches for the partly covered toy) is typically "passed" at about 26 weeks, Step 3 at about 28 or 29 weeks, and Step 4 (reaching for the toy that was fully covered before the child began to reach) at about 30 or 31 weeks. Did the baby's performance conform to those expectations? If not, why do you think your experiment was different? Do you think it mattered that a familiar toy was used? Did it matter that the mother or father was present?

Infants' Responses to Lullabies and Play Songs

If you have access to a 3- to 6-month-old infant, you can replicate the research findings showing that infants respond differently to play songs and lullabies. Ask the baby's mother or father to sing the two types of songs and note whether the infant displays the kinds of behavior described in the text. Recall that researchers have found that lullabies elicit inwardly directed behaviors, such as thumb-sucking, and play songs elicit externally directed behaviors, such as babbling and smiling.

Cognitive Development I: Structure and Process

C H A P T E R

6

It was a beautiful sunny day, so the 2-year-old boy's conscientious caregiver, she securely strapped him nanny decided to take him out for a walk. Ever the into his stroller before heading for a nearby park.

As the pair made their way through the park, a man suddenly accosted the nanny, separating her from the stroller and knocking her to the ground. His goal, it appeared, was to kidnap the child, but the strap that had been so carefully secured by the nanny foiled his attempt at a quick getaway. The nanny collected herself, got up off the ground, and attacked the man with all her might. As she pummeled him with her fists, he grabbed her arms to stop the attack, leaving several deep scratches in her forearms. Just then, a police officer came to the rescue, captured the would-be kidnapper, and carried him off to jail. The nanny comforted the boy, who was crying, and then hurried home. That evening, she recounted the story to the boy's parents, who were so grateful that they gave her an expensive wristwatch as a reward.

Over the years, the story became standard family fare, the kind of story that was retold whenever relatives got together or when a new person entered the family and needed to be advised of critical events in the family's history. Each time the story was retold, the boy assured the listeners that, despite his tender age at the time, he had a vivid memory of the event. The kidnapper's face, he said, was emblazoned in his memory, as was his nanny's valiant struggle to save him.

Several years later, the nanny, who had moved on to another position, had a religious experience that would change both her life and that of the family whose child she had saved. Consumed by the urge to relieve herself of the guilt she felt over her past wrongdoings, the nanny set out to correct each of them one by one. Eventually, she made her way to the family of the almost-kidnapped boy. By then, the boy was 15 years old, and the kidnapping episode was firmly rooted in his sense of personal history. Thus, he was shocked when he learned from the morally burdened former nanny that the entire story had been a fabrication. Moreover, she had given herself the scratches in order to make her story more convincing. The ex-nanny begged the family's forgiveness, which they graciously gave her, and returned the watch.

Along with the moral relief the former nanny no doubt felt, an event that would have far-reaching consequences occurred that day. The young man, still troubled by the fear associated with the "memory" of his near-kidnapping, found himself fascinated with the workings of the human mind. How, he wondered, was it possible that the mind could construct such a vivid memory of an event that had never actually occurred? His search for an answer to that question, as well as many others about cognitive functioning, would ultimately lead to a career in psychological research. And by the time the young man reached the age of 30, he would be credited with having made some of the most important discoveries in the history of psychology. That young man was Jean Piaget (Piaget, 1962).

In this chapter, you will learn about the developmental patterns Piaget discovered and how he explained them. You will also read about the ideas and findings of many *other psychologists who have attempted to explain age-related changes in cognitive functioning, including a few who have found possible explanations for the vividness and durability of Piaget's false memory.*

Piaget's Basic Ideas

The metaphor of the child as a "little scientist," constructing his understanding of the world, comes directly from Piaget's theory.

Piaget set out to answer a fundamental question: How does a child's knowledge of the world change with age? In answering this question, Piaget's most central assumption was that the child is an active participant in the development of knowledge, constructing his own understanding. This idea, perhaps more than any other, has influenced the thinking of all developmentalists who have followed Piaget. In addition, after three decades of research devoted to challenging his assertion that cognitive functioning develops in stages, the whole concept of cognitive stages is enjoying a resurgence of interest among developmental psychologists (Feldman, 2004). Of course, the hundreds of studies that have been done since Piaget first proposed the stages have revealed a number of shortcomings in his original account of cognitive development. Still, the basic outline he first sketched more than 70 years ago of cognitive changes from infancy to adolescence appears to be fairly accurate.

SCHEMES

A pivotal Piagetian concept—and one of the hardest to grasp—is that of a **scheme** (sometimes called a *schema*). This term is often used as a rough synonym for the word *concept* or the phrases *mental category* or *complex of ideas*, but Piaget used it even more broadly than that. He saw knowledge not as merely passive mental categories but as actions, either mental or physical; each of these actions is what he meant by a scheme. So a scheme is not really a category, but the *action* of categorizing in some particular fashion. Some purely physical or sensory actions are also schemes. If you pick up and look at a ball, you are using your "looking scheme," your "picking-up scheme," and your "holding scheme."

Piaget proposed that each baby begins life with a small repertoire of simple sensory or motor schemes, such as looking, tasting, touching, hearing, and grasping. For the baby, an object is a thing that tastes a certain way, feels a certain way when touched, or has a particular color. Later, the toddler develops mental schemes as well, such as categorizing or comparing one object to another. Over the course of development, the child gradually adds extremely complex mental schemes, such as deductive analysis or systematic reasoning. In fact, humans continue to add new schemes, both physical and mental, throughout the lifespan. So where, you might be wondering, do these new schemes come from?

According to Piaget, as people act on their environments, an inborn mental process called *organization* causes them to derive generalizable schemes from specific experiences. For example, when an infant handles a spherical object, such as a ball, the scheme she constructs will be applied to all similar objects. So, when she observes a decorative glass ball, she will attempt to handle it in the same way she would a rubber ball. Schemes organize our thinking according to categories that help us determine what kinds of actions to take in response to variations in environmental characteristics. Obviously, each

scheme Piaget's word for the basic actions of knowing, including both physical actions (sensorimotor schemes, such as looking or reaching) and mental actions (such as classifying, comparing, and reversing). An experience is assimilated into a scheme, and the scheme is created or modified through accommodation.

ball is a little bit different from those we have encountered in the past. As a result, our schemes don't always work the way we expect them to. So, according to Piaget, the mental process he called *adaptation* complements organization by working to change schemes that don't quite fit the challenges offered by our environments. Three subprocesses are involved in adaptation: *assimilation*, *accommodation*, and *equilibration*.

ASSIMILATION AND ACCOMMODATION

Assimilation is the process of taking in, of absorbing some event or experience and making it part of a scheme. Piaget would say that when a baby handles a decorative glass ball in the same way she learned to manipulate a rubber ball, she has assimilated the ball to her ball-handling scheme. The key here is that assimilation is an active process. For one thing, we assimilate information selectively. We don't behave like a blotter, absorbing everything we experience; instead, we pay attention only to those aspects of any experience for which we already have schemes. For example, when you listen to an instructor give a lecture, you may try to write everything down in your notebook or store it in your brain, but in fact you assimilate only the thoughts you can connect to some concept or model you already have.

The process complementary to assimilation is **accommodation**, which involves changing a scheme as a result of new information taken in by assimilation. The baby who grasps a glass ball for the first time will respond to the slipperiness of the surface, compared to what she expected based on her experience with rubber balls, and will accommodate her ball-handling scheme. In this way, she will develop a ball-handling scheme that can take into account different surface characteristics of different kinds of balls. Thus, in Piaget's theory, the process of accommodation is the key to developmental change. Through accommodation, we reorganize our thoughts, improve our skills, and change our strategies.

EQUILIBRATION

The third aspect of adaptation is **equilibration**, the process of bringing assimilation and accommodation into balance. This is not unlike what a scientist does when she develops a theory about some body of information. The scientist wants to have a theory that will make sense out of every observation—that is, one that has internal coherence. When new research findings come along, she assimilates them into her existing theory; if they don't fit perfectly, she makes modifications (accommodations) in the theory so that it will assimilate information that previously did not fit. However, if enough nonconfirming evidence accumulates, the scientist may have to throw out her theory altogether or change some basic theoretical assumptions; either response is a form of equilibration.

A road map analogy may be helpful. Suppose you have just moved to a new city, and instead of buying a local map, you try to learn your way around with only a hand-drawn map given to you by a friend. As you make your way through the new city, you make corrections on your map—redrawing it and writing notes to yourself. The redrawn and revised map is certainly an improvement over the original version, but eventually you will find that it is both impossible to read and still seriously flawed. So you start over and draw a new map, based on all your information. You carry this around with you, revising it and writing on it until it, too, is so full of annotations that you need to start over. The corrections and annotations you make to your map are analogous to accommodations in Piaget's theory; the process of starting over and drawing a new map is analogous to equilibration. Each modification of an existing map or drawing of a new map allows you to more easily assimilate your driving or walking experiences. Put more simply, with each modification, your map works better than before.

assimilation That part of the adaptation process proposed by Piaget that involves absorbing new experiences or information into existing schemes. Experience is not taken in "as is," however, but is modified (or interpreted) somewhat so as to fit the preexisting schemes.

accommodation That part of the adaptation process proposed by Piaget by which a person modifies existing schemes as a result of new experiences or creates new schemes when old ones no longer handle the data.

equilibration The third part of the adaptation process proposed by Piaget, involving a periodic restructuring of schemes to create a balance between assimilation and accommodation.

Piaget thought that a child operated in a similar way, creating coherent, more or less internally consistent schemes. However, since the infant starts with a very limited repertoire of schemes (a very primitive initial map), the early structures the child creates are simply not going to be adequate. Such inadequacies, Piaget thought, force the child to make periodic major changes in the internal schemes.

Piaget saw three particularly significant reorganization, or equilibration, points in childhood, each ushering in a new stage of development. The first occurs at about 18 months, when the toddler shifts from the dominance of simple sensory and motor schemes to the use of the first symbols. The second equilibration point normally falls between ages 5 and 7, when the child adds a whole new set of powerful schemes Piaget calls **operations**. These are far more abstract and general mental actions, such as mental addition or subtraction. The third major equilibration point is in adolescence, when the child figures out how to "operate on" ideas as well as on events or objects.

The three major equilibration points yield four stages during which children use different ways of acting on the world around them. During the **sensorimotor stage**, from birth to 18 months, infants use their sensory and motor schemes to act on the world around them. In the **preoperational stage**, from 18 months to about 6 years, youngsters acquire symbolic schemes, such as language and fantasy, that they use in thinking and communicating. Next comes the **concrete operations stage**, during which 6- to 12-year-olds begin to think logically. The last phase is the **formal operations stage**, in which adolescents learn to think logically about abstract ideas and hypothetical situations.

CAUSES OF COGNITIVE DEVELOPMENT

Since Piaget's stages represent a fixed sequence, you might think that they are controlled by an inborn genetic plan, much like the sequence of motor skill development you read about in Chapter 4. Piaget suggested that just such an inborn plan for cognitive development exists, but that it depends on environmental factors for its full expression. He proposed four main causes of cognitive development: two that are internal, and two that are found in a child's environment (Piaget & Inhelder, 1969).

As you learned in the preceding section, Piaget believed that equilibration was the chief process through which new stages of cognitive development are reached. He hypothesized that the process of equilibration is an inborn, automatic response to conflicts between a child's current schemes and the challenges of her environment. Likewise, he assumed that the basic pattern of brain maturation common to all human beings that you learned about in Chapter 4 contributed to cognitive development. So, he claimed, individual differences in the pace at which children proceed through the four stages of cognitive development may be partly explained by different rates of brain maturation, which may be the result of either inborn differences or environmental factors such as nutrition.

The two environmental factors Piaget posited to explain progression through the stages were social transmission and experience. *Social transmission* is simply information the child gets from other people. According to Piaget, parents, teachers, and others provide children with information, such as the names and characteristics of objects, as well as with models of more mature cognitive development. Say, for example, a preschooler believes that her dresser turns into a monster every night when the light is turned off. To reassure her, her parent turns the light on and off repeatedly to demonstrate that the dresser remains a piece of furniture whether the light is on or off. In so doing, the parent is demonstrating use of a logical scheme that has many applications to the physical world: "If this object was a dresser with the light on, it must still be a dresser when the light is off. Darkness cannot change the 'dresserness' of the dresser; it can't change one object into another." The parent's logical scheme conflicts with the magical scheme on which the child bases her belief that pieces of furniture can change into monsters in the dark. As a result, the experience stimulates the process of equili-

operation Term used by Piaget for a complex, internal, abstract scheme, first seen at about age 6.

sensorimotor stage Piaget's term for the first major stage of cognitive development, from birth to about 18 months, when the child uses sensory and motor skills to act on the environment.

preoperational stage Piaget's term for the second major stage of cognitive development, from about 18 months to about age 6, marked by the ability to use symbols.

concrete operations stage Piaget's term for the stage of development between ages 6 and 12, during which children become able to think logically.

formal operations stage Piaget's name for the fourth and final major stage of cognitive development, occurring during adolescence, when the child becomes able to manipulate and organize ideas or hypothetical situations as well as objects.

bration for the child. Piaget suggested that adults contribute a great deal to children's progression from one stage to the next through these kinds of informal demonstrations.

By *experience*, Piaget meant the child's own opportunities to act on the world and to observe the results of those actions. If you watch preschoolers playing on the beach or in a sandbox, you will notice that one of their favorite activities is to fill containers with sand, empty them out, and fill them up again. You might see a group of children making a "mountain" out of sand in this way. In so doing, they notice that the mountain doesn't hold together very well unless a little water is mixed with the sand, but then they see that too much water also prevents the mountain from holding together. Through this kind of experimentation and modification of actions, Piaget believed, children often stimulate their own cognitive development.

One place where children are exposed to many opportunities for both social transmission and experience is in school. In fact, studies all over the world have shown that children who attend school progress through Piaget's stages more rapidly than those who do not (Mishra, 1997). These studies lend weight to Piaget's claim that movement from one cognitive stage to another is not simply a matter of maturation but is the result of a complex interaction between internal and environmental variables. Each of these variables, Piaget suggested, is *necessary but not sufficient* to produce movement from one cognitive stage to the next. In other words, a certain degree of brain maturation is required for each stage, but brain development by itself cannot cause a child to progress to the next stage. All of the causal factors—equilibration, maturation, social transmission, and experience—must interact and support one another in order for cognitive development to proceed.

Before going on . . .

- What is the role of schemes in cognitive development?
- How do assimilation and accommodation change schemes?
- What is equilibration, and how does it contribute to cognitive development?
- Explain the four causes of cognitive development proposed by Piaget.

Infancy

Piaget's theory assumes that the baby assimilates incoming information into the limited array of sensory and motor schemes she is born with—such as looking, listening, sucking, and grasping—and accommodates those schemes based on her experiences. This is the starting point for the entire process of cognitive development.

PIAGET'S VIEW OF THE SENSORIMOTOR PERIOD

In the beginning, in Piaget's view, the baby is entirely tied to the immediate present, responding to whatever stimuli are available. She does not remember events or things from one encounter to the next and does not appear to plan or intend. John Flavell summarizes all of this very nicely:

> [The infant] exhibits a wholly practical, perceiving-and-doing, action-bound kind of intellectual functioning; she does not exhibit the more contemplative, reflective, symbol-manipulating kind we usually think of in connection with cognition. The infant "knows" in the sense of recognizing or anticipating familiar, recurring objects and happenings, and "thinks" in the sense of behaving toward them with mouth, hand, eye, and other sensory-motor instruments in predictable, organized, and often adaptive ways. (1985, p. 13)

This pattern gradually changes during the first 18 months as the baby comes to understand that objects continue to exist even when they are out of sight (see

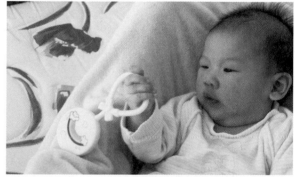

Three-month-old Andrea may be showing a secondary circular reaction here, shaking her hand repeatedly to hear the sound of the rattle. A learning theorist would say that the pleasure she experiences from hearing the sound is reinforcing her hand-shaking behavior.

CRITICAL THINKING

Think of some common infant behaviors (such as a baby's throwing a toy on the floor every time a parent or sibling hands it to her). How do they seem to fit with Piaget's ideas about primary, secondary, and tertiary circular reactions?

Chapter 5) and as she becomes able to remember objects, actions, and individuals over periods of time. Yet Piaget insisted that in the sensorimotor period, the infant is not yet able to manipulate these early mental images or memories. Nor does she use symbols to stand for objects or events. It is the new ability to manipulate internal symbols, such as words or images, that marks the beginning of the next stage, the stage of preoperational thought, which starts at 18 to 24 months of age.

The change from the limited repertoire of schemes available to the newborn to the ability to use symbols at about 18 months is gradual, although Piaget identified six substages, summarized in Table 6.1. Each substage represents some specific advance. Substage 2 is marked by the beginning of those important coordinations between looking and listening, reaching and looking, and reaching and sucking that are such central features of the 2-month-old's means of exploring the world. The term **primary circular reactions** refers to the many simple repetitive actions seen at substage 2, each organized around the infant's own body. The baby accidentally sucks his thumb one day, finds it pleasurable, and repeats the action. **Secondary circular reactions**, in substage 3, differ only in that the baby is now repeating some action in order to trigger a reaction outside his own body. The baby coos and mom smiles, so the baby coos again, apparently in order to get mom to smile again; the baby accidentally hits the mobile hanging above his crib, it moves, and he then repeats his arm wave, apparently with some intent to make the mobile move again. These initial connections between bodily actions and external consequences

primary circular reactions
Piaget's phrase to describe a baby's simple repetitive actions in substage 2 of the sensorimotor stage, organized around the baby's own body; the baby repeats some action in order to have some desired outcome occur again, such as putting his thumb in his mouth to repeat the good feeling of sucking.

secondary circular reactions
Repetitive actions in substage 3 of the sensorimotor period, oriented around external objects; the infant repeats some action in order to have some outside event recur, such as hitting a mobile repeatedly so that it moves.

TABLE 6.1	Substages of Piaget's Sensorimotor Stage		
Substage	**Age**	**Piaget's Label**	**Characteristics**
1	Birth–1 month	Reflexes	Use of built-in schemes or reflexes such as sucking or looking; no imitation; no ability to integrate information from several senses
2	1–4 months	Primary circular reactions	Accommodation of basic schemes (grasping, looking, sucking), as baby practices them endlessly. Beginning coordination of schemes from different senses, such as looking toward a sound; baby does not yet link bodily actions to some result outside the body.
3	4–8 months	Secondary circular reactions	Baby becomes much more aware of events outside his own body and makes them happen again, in a kind of trial-and-error learning. Imitation may occur, but only of schemes already in the baby's repertoire. Beginning understanding of the "object concept."
4	8–12 months	Coordination of secondary schemes	Clear intentional means-ends behavior. The baby not only goes after what she wants, she may combine two schemes to do so, such as knocking a pillow away to reach a toy. Imitation of novel behaviors occurs, as does transfer of information from one sense to the other (cross-modal transfer).
5	12–18 months	Tertiary circular reactions	"Experimentation" begins, in which the infant tries out new ways of playing with or manipulating objects. Very active, very purposeful trial-and-error exploration.
6	18–24 months	Beginning of representational thought	Development of use of symbols to represent object or events. Child understands that the symbol is separate from the object. Deferred imitation first occurs at this stage.

are fairly automatic, very like a kind of operant conditioning. During this substage, infants build the important schemes that underlie the *object concept*, a set of milestones discussed extensively in Chapter 5. Recall that **object permanence**, or the understanding that objects continue to exist even when they are out of sight, is one of the most important of these milestones.

Substage 4 brings with it the beginnings of a real understanding of causal connections. At this point, the infant moves into exploratory high gear. In substage 5, this exploratory behavior becomes even more marked with the emergence of what Piaget called **tertiary circular reactions**. In this substage, the baby is not content merely to repeat the original triggering action but tries out variations. He might try out many other sounds or facial expressions to see if they will trigger mom's smile or try moving his hand differently or in new directions in order to make the mobile move in new ways. At this stage, the baby's behavior has a purposeful, experimental quality. Nonetheless, Piaget thought that even in substage 5 the baby does not have internal symbols to stand for objects. The development of such symbols is the mark of substage 6.

Piaget's descriptions of this sequence of development, largely based on remarkably detailed observations of his own three children, provoked a very rich array of research, some that confirms the general outlines of his proposals and some that does not. Research results described in Chapter 5, along with other research on infant memory and imitation, point to the conclusion that in a number of important respects, Piaget underestimated the ability of infants to store, remember, and organize sensory and motor information.

CHALLENGES TO PIAGET'S VIEW OF INFANCY

Although research has generally supported the sequence of cognitive development discovered by Piaget, there are many findings that challenge his view. As you learned in Chapter 5, research by Elizabeth Spelke and Renée Baillargeon, among others, has given us a more detailed account of infants' understanding of objects than Piaget's studies did. Their work suggests that infants have a much more sophisticated understanding of objects than Piaget concluded. Likewise, research examining infants' memory functioning and their capacity for imitation also suggests that Piaget may have underestimated their capabilities.

Memory   One hint that infants are capable of greater feats of memory than Piaget proposed is research showing that habituation and dishabituation are already present at birth—research you read about in Chapter 3. Habituation, you'll recall, involves a lessening of response to a repeated stimulus. For instance, a newborn stops exhibiting a startle response to a sound after she has been exposed to it several times. For habituation to be possible, the baby must have at least some ability to store (remember) information about the previous occurrences. Similarly, for dishabituation to occur, the baby must recognize that a new event is somehow different, which suggests that the baby's memory contains a fairly detailed image or template of the original event (Schneider & Bjorklund, 1998).

A second source of evidence that quite young babies can remember specific events over periods of time comes from a series of clever studies by Carolyn Rovee-Collier and her colleagues (Bhatt & Rovee-Collier, 1996; Gerhardstein, Adler, & Rovee-Collier, 2000; Hartshorn & Rovee-Collier, 1997; Hayne & Rovee-Collier, 1995; Rovee-Collier, 1993). In her most widely used procedure, Rovee-Collier uses an ingenious variation of an operant conditioning strategy. She first hangs an attractive mobile over a baby's crib and watches to see how the baby responds. In particular, she is interested in how often the baby normally kicks her legs while looking at the mobile. After 3 minutes of this "baseline" observation, she attaches a string from the mobile to the baby's leg, as you can see in Figure 6.1, so that each time the baby

FIGURE 6.1

This 3-month-old baby in one of Rovee-Collier's memory experiments will quickly learn to kick her foot in order to make the mobile move. And several days later, she will remember this connection between kicking and the mobile.
(*Source*: Rovee-Collier, 1993, p. 131.)

object permanence The understanding that objects continue to exist even when they cannot be directly perceived.

tertiary circular reactions The deliberate experimentation with variations of previous actions, characteristic of substage 5 of the sensorimotor period, according to Piaget.

kicks her leg, the mobile moves. Babies quickly learn to kick repeatedly in order to make this interesting new thing happen (what Piaget would call a secondary circular reaction). Within 3 to 6 minutes, 3-month-olds double or triple their kick rates, showing that learning has clearly occurred. Rovee-Collier then tests the baby's memory of this learning by coming back some days later and hanging the same mobile over the crib, but not attaching the string to the baby's foot. If the baby remembers the previous occasion, she should kick at a higher rate than she did when she first saw the mobile, which is precisely what 3-month-old babies do, even after a delay of as long as a week.

Such studies show that the young infant is cognitively a whole lot more sophisticated than developmentalists (and Piaget) had once supposed. At the same time, Rovee-Collier's work also offers some support for Piaget's views, since she observes systematic gains over the months of infancy in the baby's ability to remember. A 2-month-old can remember the kicking action for only 1 day; a 3-month-old can remember for over a week; and by 6 months, a baby can remember for more than 2 weeks. Rovee-Collier has also found that all these early infant memories are strongly tied to the specific context in which the original experience occurred. Even 6-month-olds do not recognize or remember the mobile if the investigator makes even a very small change, such as hanging a different cloth around the crib in which the child was originally tested. Thus, babies do remember far more than Piaget believed—but their memories are highly specific. With age, their memories become less and less tied to specific cues or contexts (Learmonth, Lamberth, & Rovee-Collier, 2004).

Imitation   Another active area of study has been the ability of the infant to imitate. If you look again at Table 6.1, you'll see that Piaget thought that the ability to imitate emerged quite gradually over the early months. In broad terms, Piaget's proposed sequence has been supported. For example, imitation of someone else's hand movements or their actions with objects seems to improve steadily during the months of infancy, starting at 1 or 2 months of age; imitation of two-part actions develops only in toddlerhood, perhaps at 15 to 18 months (Poulson, Nunes, & Warren, 1989). In two areas, however, Piaget may have been wrong about infants' imitative abilities.

First, although Piaget thought babies could not imitate other people's facial gestures until about substage 4 (8–12 months), quite a lot of research now shows that newborns are able to imitate at least some facial gestures, particularly tongue protrusion (Anisfeld, 1991; Field, Woodson, Greenberg, & Cohen, 1982; Meltzoff & Moore, 1977; Nagy & Molnar, 2004), as shown in the photo in Figure 6.2. Nevertheless, newborns' capacity for imitation appears to be quite limited. Researchers have found that neonates imitate tongue-protrusion but not mouth-opening (Anisfeld et al., 2001). Taken together, studies of imitative behavior in newborns indicate that Piaget was probably wrong in his assertion that very young infants are incapable of imitation. However, it seems likely that he was accurate in his view that imitation is not a general strategy infants use for developing their understanding of the world until they are a bit older.

Piaget also argued that *deferred imitation*, in which a child sees some action and then imitates it at a later time when the model is no longer visible, became possible only in substage 6 (at about 18 months of age), since deferred imitation requires some kind of internal representation. Once again, more recent research points to earlier development of this ability (Learmonth et al., 2004). At least one study (Meltzoff, 1988)

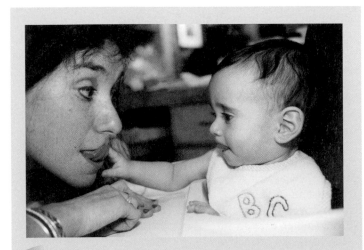

FIGURE 6.2

Although researchers still disagree on just how much newborns will imitate, everyone agrees that they will imitate the gesture of tongue protrusion.

shows that babies as young as 9 months can defer their imitation for as long as 24 hours. By 14 months, toddlers can recall and later imitate someone's actions over a period of 2 days (Hanna & Meltzoff, 1993). This finding makes it clear that children of this age can and do learn specific behaviors through modeling, even when they have no chance to imitate the behavior immediately.

The Preschool Years

Piaget's theory and research findings suggest that preschoolers' ability to use symbols such as words significantly enhances their ability to understand and act on the world around them. But their ability to reason about the world is still fairly poor.

PIAGET'S VIEW OF THE PREOPERATIONAL STAGE

Piaget saw evidence of symbol use in many aspects of the behavior of children aged 2 to 6. For example, children this age begin to pretend in their play. Such symbol use is also evident in the emergence of language and in the preschooler's primitive ability to understand scale models or simple maps (DeLoache, 1995).

Other than symbol use, Piaget's description of the preoperational stage focused on all the other things the preschool-aged child still cannot do, giving an oddly negative tone to his description of this period. Piaget saw the preschooler's thinking as rigid, captured by appearances, insensitive to inconsistencies, and tied to her own perspective—a quality Piaget (1954) called **egocentrism**. The child is not being selfish; rather, she simply thinks (assumes) that everyone sees the world as she does.

Figure 6.3 illustrates a classic technique used to measure this egocentrism. The child is shown a three-dimensional scene with mountains of different sizes and colors. From a set of drawings, she picks out the one that shows the scene the way she sees it. Most preschoolers can do this without much difficulty. Then the examiner asks the child to pick out the drawing that shows how someone else sees the scene, such as a doll or the examiner. At this point, preschoolers have difficulty. Most often, they again pick the drawing that shows their own view of the mountains (Gzesh & Surber, 1985). In Piaget's view, for a child to be able to succeed at this task, she must *decenter*—must shift from using herself as the only frame of reference to seeing things from another perspective. Piaget thought that preschool children could not yet do this.

The preschool child's focus on the appearance of objects is an equally important part of Piaget's description of this period, evident in some of the most famous of his studies, those on conservation (see Figure 6.4). **Conservation** is the understanding that the quantity of a substance remains the same even when its appearance changes. Piaget's measurement technique involved first showing the child two equal objects or sets of objects, getting the child to agree that they were equal in some key respect, such as weight, quantity, length, or number, and then shifting, changing, or deforming one of the objects or sets and asking the child if they were still equal. Next, Piaget asked how the child knew the answer was correct. Children who were using preoperational schemes would

Before going on...

- How do primary, secondary, and tertiary circular reactions differ?
- Describe infants' ability to remember.
- How does the process of imitation change over the first 2 years of life?

CRITICAL THINKING ?

Think of examples of egocentrism in your own behavior. For example, how does egocentrism affect the way you communicate with others?

egocentrism A cognitive state in which the individual (typically a child) sees the world only from his own perspective, without awareness that there are other perspectives.

conservation The understanding that the quantity or amount of a substance remains the same even when there are external changes in its shape or arrangement. Typically, children do not have this understanding until after age 5.

FIGURE 6.3

The experimental situation shown here is similar to one Piaget used to study egocentrism in children. The child is asked to pick out a picture that shows how the mountains look to her, and then to pick out a picture that shows how the mountains look to the doll.

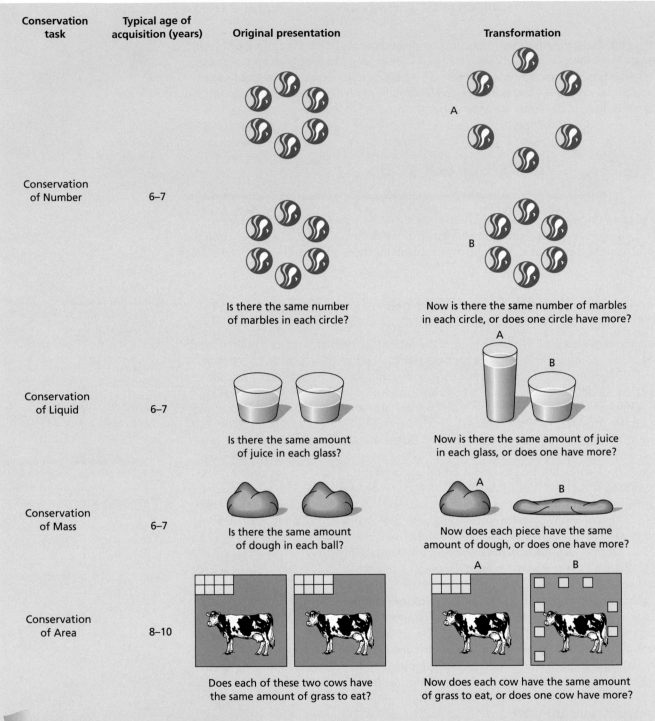

Conservation task	Typical age of acquisition (years)	Original presentation	Transformation
Conservation of Number	6–7	Is there the same number of marbles in each circle?	Now is there the same number of marbles in each circle, or does one circle have more?
Conservation of Liquid	6–7	Is there the same amount of juice in each glass?	Now is there the same amount of juice in each glass, or does one have more?
Conservation of Mass	6–7	Is there the same amount of dough in each ball?	Now does each piece have the same amount of dough, or does one have more?
Conservation of Area	8–10	Does each of these two cows have the same amount of grass to eat?	Now does each cow have the same amount of grass to eat, or does one cow have more?

FIGURE 6.4

Piaget's research involved several kinds of conservation tasks. He classified children's thinking as concrete operational with respect to a particular task if they could correctly solve the problem and provide a concrete operational reason for their answer. For example, if a child said, "The two circles of marbles are the same because you didn't add any or take any away when you moved them," the response was judged to be concrete operational. Conversely, if a child said, "The two circles are the same, but I don't know why," the response was not classified as concrete operational.

give justifications, such as "the sausage has more clay because it is longer now." By contrast, concrete operational thinkers would respond with an answer such as "the sausage looks like more because its longer now, but you didn't add any clay or take any away so it must still be the same." Piaget insisted, based on his evaluations of both children's solutions and their reasoning, that children rarely exhibit a true understanding of conservation before age 5 or 6.

CHALLENGES TO PIAGET'S VIEW OF EARLY CHILDHOOD

Studies of conservation have generally confirmed Piaget's predictions. Although younger children can demonstrate some understanding of conservation if the task is made very simple, most children cannot consistently solve conservation problems until age 5 or 6 or later (e.g., Andreucci, 2003; Ciancio et al., 1999; Gelman, 1972; Sophian, 1995; Wellman, 1982). Nevertheless, evidence suggests that preschoolers are somewhat more cognitively sophisticated than Piaget thought.

Egocentrism and Perspective Taking   Children as young as 2 and 3 appear to have at least some ability to understand that another person sees things or experiences things differently than they do. For example, children of this age will adapt their play or their speech to the demands of their companions. They play differently with older and younger playmates and talk differently to a younger or a handicapped child (Brownell, 1990; Guralnick & Paul-Brown, 1984).

However, such understanding is clearly not perfect at this young age. Developmental psychologist John Flavell has proposed two levels of perspective-taking ability. At level 1, the child knows that another person experiences something differently. At level 2, the child develops a whole series of complex rules for figuring out precisely what the other person sees or experiences (Flavell, Green, & Flavell, 1990). Two- and 3-year-olds have level 1 knowledge but not level 2 knowledge; the latter only begins to emerge in 4- and 5-year-olds. For example, a child of 4 or 5 understands that another person will feel sad if she fails or happy if she succeeds. The preschool child also begins to figure out that unpleasant emotions arise in situations in which the relationship between desire and reality is unequal. Sadness, for example, normally occurs when someone loses something or fails to acquire some desired object (Harris, 1989).

Appearance and Reality   The child's movement away from egocentrism seems to be part of a much broader change in her understanding of appearance and reality. Flavell has studied this understanding in a variety of ways (Flavell, 2004; Flavell, Green, & Flavell, 1989; Flavell, Green, Wahl, & Flavell, 1987). In the most famous Flavell procedure, the experimenter shows the child a sponge that has been painted to look like a rock. Three-year-olds will say either that the object looks like a sponge and is a sponge or that it looks like a rock and is a rock. But 4- and 5-year-olds can distinguish the two; they realize that it looks like a rock but is really a sponge (Flavell, 1986). Thus, the older child understands that an object may not be what it seems.

Using similar materials, investigators have also asked whether a child can grasp the **false belief principle** (Lamb & Lewis, 2005). Individuals who understand the false belief principle can look at a problem or situation from another person's point of view in order to discern what kind of information can cause that person to believe something that isn't true. For example, after a child has felt the sponge/rock and has answered questions about what it looks like and what it "really" is, a researcher might ask something like this: "John [one of the child's playmates] hasn't touched this; he hasn't squeezed it. If John just sees it over here like this, what will he think it is? Will he think it's a rock or will he think that it's a sponge?" (Gopnik & Astington, 1988, p. 35). Most 3-year-olds think that the playmate will believe the object is a sponge because they themselves know that it *is* a sponge. By contrast, 4- and 5-year-olds realize that, because the playmate hasn't felt the sponge, he will have a false belief that it is a rock. Some studies show that 3-year-olds can perform more accurately if they are given a hint or clue. For example, if experimenters tell them that a "naughty" person is trying to fool their playmate, more of them will say that he will falsely think the sponge is rock (Bowler, Briskman, & Grice, 1999). But the child of 4 or 5 more consistently understands that someone else can believe something that isn't true and act on that belief.

THEORIES OF MIND

Evidence like that just described has led researchers to examine children's understanding of others' thoughts and feelings in a new way. In the past 15 years, a number of develop-

false belief principle The understanding that another person might have a false belief and the ability to determine what information might cause the false belief. A child's understanding of the false belief principle is one key sign of the emergence of a representational theory of mind.

mentalists have examined a theoretical notion known as **theory of mind**, or a set of ideas that explain other people's ideas, beliefs, desires, and behavior (Flavell, 1999, 2000, 2004). As you might suspect, research indicates that adolescents and adults have a much more fully developed theory of mind than children do (Flavell & Green, 1999; Flavell, Green, & Flavell, 1998, 2000; Flavell, Green, Flavell, & Lin, 1999). However, research also suggests that the degree of sophistication in young children's theory of mind is probably greater than either Piaget or casual observers of children would expect.

Understanding Thoughts, Desires, and Beliefs
As early as 18 months, toddlers begin to have some understanding of the fact that people (but not inanimate objects) operate with goals and intentions (Meltzoff, 1995). By age 3, they understand some aspects of the links between people's thinking or feeling and their behavior. For example, they know that a person who wants something will try to get it. They also know that a person may still want something even if she can't have it (Lillard & Flavell, 1992). But 3-year-olds do not yet understand the basic principle that each person's actions are based on his or her own representation of reality and that a person's representation may differ from what is "really" there. For example, a person's *belief* about how popular she is has more influence on her behavior than her actual popularity. It is this new aspect of the theory of mind that clearly emerges at about age 4 or 5.

Furthermore, not until about age 6 do most children realize that knowledge can be derived through inference. For example, researchers in one study showed 4- and 6-year-olds two toys of different colors (Pillow, 1999). Next, they placed the toys in opaque containers. They then opened one of the containers and showed the toy to a puppet. When asked whether the puppet now knew which color toy was in each container, only the 6-year-olds said yes.

Understanding of the reciprocal nature of thought seems to develop between age 5 and age 7 for most children. This is a particularly important development, because it is probably necessary for the creation of genuinely reciprocal friendships, which begin to become evident in the elementary school years (Sullivan, Zaitchik, & Tager-Flusberg, 1994). In fact, an individual preschooler's rate of development of theory of mind is a good predictor of her social skills both later in early childhood and during the school years (Moore, Barresi, & Thompson, 1998; Watson, Nixon, Wilson, & Capage, 1999).

Influences on Theory of Mind Development
Developmentalists have found that a child's theory of mind is correlated with his performance on conservation tasks as well as egocentrism and understanding of appearance and reality (Melot & Houde, 1998; Yirmiya & Shulman, 1996). In addition, pretend play seems to contribute to development of theory of mind. Shared pretense with other children, in particular, is strongly related to theory of mind (Dockett & Smith, 1995; Schwebel, Rosen, & Singer, 1999). However, recent longitudinal research indicates that the link between theory of mind and pretend play may be in the opposite direction from what some psychologists have assumed. That is, development of a theory of mind may precede and, to some extent, cause the emergence of sophisticated forms of pretend play, such as the kind of role-play observed when children play house (Jenkins & Astington, 2000).

Recent findings suggest that interactions with siblings may be more important than those with peers (Hughes et al., 2005). In one study, researchers compared children with either older or younger siblings to those who had only co-twins or no siblings (Wright, Fineberg, Brown, & Perkins, 2005). They found that only children and twin-only children performed more poorly on theory of mind tasks than those who had either older or younger siblings. Various explanations have been proposed for what is called the *sibling advantage* in theory of mind development. To date, the best such theory focuses on the mentor-apprentice roles that often characterize siblings of different ages. You will learn more about these roles in Chapter 11.

Language skills, such as knowledge of words for feelings, desires, and thoughts—for example, *want, need, think,* and *remember*—are also related to theory of mind (Astington & Jenkins, 1995; Green, Pring, & Swettenham, 2004; Hughes et al., 2005). Furthermore,

theory of mind Ideas that collectively explain other people's ideas, beliefs, desires, and behavior.

children whose parents discuss emotion-provoking past events with them develop a theory of mind more rapidly than their peers do (Welch-Ross, 1997). Indeed, some level of language facility may be a necessary condition for the development of theory of mind. Developmentalists have found that preschool children simply do not succeed at tests of false-belief skills until they have reached a certain threshold of general language skill (Astington & Jenkins, 1999; Jenkins & Astington, 1996; Watson et al., 1999). Differences in rate of language development may also explain why preschool-aged girls, whose language skills are, on average, more advanced than those of boys, demonstrate higher levels of success on tests of false-belief skills (Charman, Ruffman, & Clements, 2002).

Further support for this point comes from the finding that children with disabilities that affect language development, such as congenital deafness, mental retardation, or autism, develop a theory of mind more slowly than others (Lundy, 2002; Peterson & Siegal, 1995; Peterson, Wellman, & Liu, 2005; Pilowsky, Yirmiya, Arbelle, & Mozes, 2000; Sicotte & Sternberger, 1999). Research has also demonstrated that, among mentally retarded and autistic children, development of theory of mind is better predicted by language skills than by disability category (Bauminger & Kasari, 1999; Peterson & Siegal, 1999; Yirmiya, Eriel, Shaked, & Solomonica-Levi, 1998; Yirmiya, Solomonica-Levi, Shulman, & Pilowsky, 1996).

FALSE BELIEF AND THEORY OF MIND ACROSS CULTURES

Research suggests that the false belief principle develops between ages 3 and 5 across a variety of cultures. For example in one classic study Jeremy Avis and Paul Harris (1991) adapted the traditional false belief testing procedure for use with children in a pygmy tribe, the Baka, in Cameroon. The Baka are hunters and gatherers who live together in camps. Each child was tested in his or her own hut, using materials with which he or she was completely familiar. The child watched one adult named Mopfana (a member of the tribe) put some mango seeds into a bowl. Mopfana then left the hut, and a second adult (also a tribe member) told the child that they were going to play a game with Mopfana: They were going to hide the seeds in a cooking pot. Then the second adult asked the child what Mopfana was going to do when he came back. Would he look for the seeds in the bowl or in the pot? The second adult also asked the child whether Mopfana's heart would feel good or bad before he lifted the lid of the bowl. Younger children—2- and 3-year-olds and those who had recently turned 4—were much more likely to say that Mopfana would look for the seeds in the pot or to say that he would be sad before he looked in the bowl; older 4-year-olds and 5-year-olds were nearly always right on both questions.

Research indicates that the sequence of development of theory of mind is highly similar across cultures.

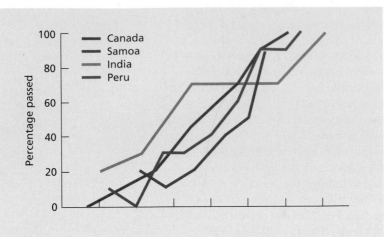

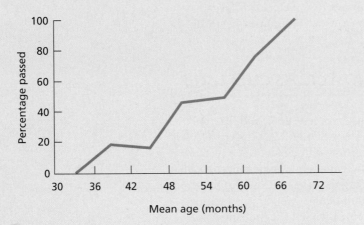

FIGURE 6.5

Percentage of children passing the false-belief test as a function of age. In the top panel, data are plotted separately for Canada, Samoa, India, and Peru. In the bottom panel, results for these four cultures are combined. Data from 13 Samoan and all Thai children were excluded from this analysis because their birth dates were not available.

(*Source*: Callaghan et al. (2005). "Synchrony in the Onset of Mental State." *Psychological Science, 16*(5), 378–384, Fig. 1 on page 382. Reprinted with permission of Blackwell Publishing.)

In another classic study, when Flavell used his sponge/rock task with children in mainland China, he found that Chinese 3-year-olds are just as confused about this task as are American or British 3-year-olds, whereas 5-year-old Chinese children had no difficulty with it (Flavell, Zhang, Zou, Dong, & Qi, 1983). In these very different cultures, then, something similar seems to be occurring between ages 3 and 5. In these years, all children seem to understand something general about the difference between appearance and reality.

Research also suggests that certain aspects of theory of mind development may be universal. For example, similar sequences of such development have been found in the United States, China, Europe, and India (Cole, 2005; Flavell et al., 1983; Joshi & MacLean, 1994; Tardif & Wellman, 2000). Figure 6.5 shows the results of one study comparing the performance of children from five cultures on a false-belief task (Callaghan et al., 2005). Moreover, participation in shared pretending has also been shown to be related to theory of mind development cross-culturally (Tan-Niam, Wood, & O'Malley, 1998).

ALTERNATIVE THEORIES OF EARLY CHILDHOOD THINKING

In recent years, a number of interesting theoretical approaches have attempted to explain both Piaget's original results and more recent findings that appear to contradict them.

Neo-Piagetian Theories   One set of alternative proposals is based on the information-processing model (explained in Chapter 1). These are called **neo-Piagetian theories** because they expand on, rather than contradict, Piaget's views (Birney, Citron-Pousty, Lutz, & Sternberg, 2005). For example, the late neo-Piagetian Robbie Case explained age differences in cognitive development as a function of changes in children's use of their short-term memories (Case, 1985, 1992). Case used the term **short-term storage space (STSS)** to refer to working memory capacity. According to Case, there is a limit on how many schemes can be attended to in STSS. He referred to the maximum number of schemes that may be put into STSS at one time as **operational efficiency**. Improvements in operational efficiency occur through both practice (through tasks that require memory use, such as learning the alphabet) and brain maturation as the child gets older. Thus, a 7-year-old is better able to handle the processing demands of conservation tasks than a 4-year-old because of improvements in the operational efficiency of the STSS.

A good example of the function of STSS may be found by examining *matrix classification*, a task Piaget often used with both preschool and school-aged children (see Figure 6.6). Matrix classification requires the child to place a given stimulus in two categories at the same time. Young children fail at such tasks because, according to neo-Piagetian theory, they begin by processing the stimulus according to one dimension

neo-Piagetian theory A theory of cognitive development that assumes that Piaget's basic ideas are correct but that uses concepts from information-processing theory to explain children's movement from one stage to the next.

short-term storage space (STSS) A neo-Piagetian term for working memory capacity.

operational efficiency A neo-Piagetian term for the number of schemes an individual can place into working memory at one time.

(either shape or color) and then either fail to realize that it is necessary to reprocess the stimulus along the second dimension or forget to do so.

However, researchers have trained young children to perform correctly on such tasks by using a two-step strategy. They are taught to think of a red triangle, for example, in terms of shape first and color second. Typically, instruction involves a number of training tasks in which researchers remind children repeatedly that it is necessary to remember to reclassify stimuli with respect to the second variable. According to Case, both children's failure prior to instruction and the type of strategy training to which they respond illustrate the constraints imposed on problem-solving by the limited operational efficiency of the younger child's STSS. There is only room for one scheme at a time in the child's STSS, either shape or color. The training studies show that younger children can learn to perform correctly but do so in a way that is qualitatively different from the approach of older children. The older child's more efficient STSS allows her to think about shape and color at the same time and therefore to perform matrix classification successfully without any training.

However, it appears that children must be exposed to multiple training sessions that take place over a fairly extended period of time, as long as an entire year, in order to effect permanent changes in their matrix completion behaviors (Siegler & Svetina, 2002). Comparative research has shown that children who develop these skills on their own do so over an equivalent period of time and demonstrate transitional behaviors that are quite similar to those of children who are trained by experimenters. Thus, some developmentalists have suggested that there is no advantage to be gained by training children to exhibit skills that they are known to acquire in the natural course of cognitive development. Moreover, with regard to research methodology, when children must be trained over long periods of time, it becomes impossible to distinguish between the effects of training and those of the natural developmental processes that are occurring contemporaneously with such training.

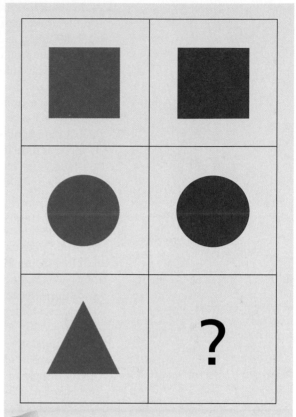

FIGURE 6.6

Neo-Piagetians have used Piaget's matrix classification task in strategy training studies with young children. Before training, most preschoolers say that a blue triangle or a red circle belongs in the box with the question mark. After learning a two-step strategy in which they are taught to classify each object first by shape and then by color, children understand that a red triangle is the figure that is needed to complete the matrix.

Vygotsky's Socio-Cultural Theory In Chapter 1, you learned that psychologists' interest in Russian psychologist Lev Vygotsky's views on development has grown recently. Vygotsky's theory differs from both Piagetian and neo-Piagetian theory in its emphasis on the role of social factors in cognitive development. For example, two preschoolers working on a puzzle together discuss where the pieces belong. After a number of such dialogues, the participants internalize the discussion. It then becomes a model for an internal conversation the child uses to guide himself through the puzzle-solution process. In this way, Vygotsky suggested, solutions to problems are socially generated and learned. Vygotsky did not deny that individual learning takes place. Rather, he suggested that group learning processes are central to cognitive development. Consequently, from Vygotsky's perspective, social interaction is required for cognitive development (Thomas, 2000).

You'll recall that two important general principles of Vygotsky's theory are the *zone of proximal development* and *scaffolding*. Vygotsky also proposed specific stages of cognitive development from birth to age 7. Each stage represents a step toward the child's internalization of the ways of thinking used by adults in his society.

In the first period, called the *primitive stage*, the infant possesses mental processes that are similar to those of lower animals. He learns primarily through conditioning until language begins to develop in the second year. At that point, he enters the *naive psychology stage*, in which he learns to use language to communicate but still does not understand its symbolic character. For example, he doesn't realize that any collection of sounds could stand for the object "chair" as long as everyone agrees on the sounds; that is, if all English speakers agreed to substitute the word *blek* for *chair*, they could do so because they would all understand what *blek* meant.

Once the child begins to appreciate the symbolic function of language, near the end of the third year of life, he enters the *egocentric speech stage*. In this stage, he uses language as a guide to solving problems. In effect, he tells himself how to do things. For example, a 3-year-old walking down a flight of stairs might say to himself "Be careful." Such a statement would be the result of his internalization of statements made to him by more mature individuals in his environment.

Piaget also recognized the existence and importance of egocentric speech. However, he believed that egocentric speech disappeared as the child approached the end of the preoperational stage. In contrast, Vygotsky claimed that egocentric speech becomes completely internalized at age 6 or 7, when children enter the final period of cognitive development, the *ingrowth stage*. Thus, he suggested that the logical thinking Piaget ascribed to older children resulted from their internalization of speech routines they had acquired from older children and adults in the social world rather than from schemes they had constructed for themselves through interaction with the physical world.

At present, there is insufficient evidence to support or contradict most of Vygotsky's ideas (Miller, 2002). However, some intriguing research on children's construction of theory of mind ideas during social interactions lends weight to Vygotsky's major propositions. It seems that children in pairs and groups do produce more sophisticated theory of mind ideas than individual children who work on problems alone. However, the sophistication of a group's ideas appears to depend on the presence of at least one fairly advanced individual child in the group (Tan-Niam, Wood, & O'Malley, 1998). Thus, Vygotsky's theory may ignore the important contributions of individual thought to group interaction.

Before going on · · ·

- List the characteristics of children's thought during what Piaget called the preoperational stage.
- How has recent research challenged Piaget's view of this period?
- What is a theory of mind, and how does it develop?
- What does research indicate about the universality of children's understanding of false beliefs and their theory of mind?
- How do Vygotsky's theory and the neo-Piagetian theories explain the changes in children's thinking that happen between the ages of 2 and 6?

The School-Aged Child

The new skills that emerge at age 6 or 7 build on all the small changes that have already taken place in the preschooler, but from Piaget's perspective, a great leap forward occurs when the child discovers or develops a set of immensely powerful, abstract, general rules or strategies for examining and interacting with the world. Piaget called these new rules *concrete operations*.

PIAGET'S VIEW OF CONCRETE OPERATIONS

Piaget defined concrete operations as a set of powerful, abstract schemes that are critical building blocks of logical thinking, providing internal rules about objects and their relationships.

Reversibility   Piaget thought that the most critical of all the concrete operations was **reversibility**—the understanding that both physical actions and mental operations can be reversed. The clay sausage in a conservation experiment can be made back into a ball; the water can be poured back into the shorter, fatter glass. This understanding of the basic reversibility of actions lies behind many of the gains made during this period.

For example, if you understand reversibility, then knowing that A is larger than B also tells you that B is smaller than A. The ability to understand hierarchies of classes, such as "Fido," "spaniel," "dog," and "animal," also rests on this ability to go backward as well as forward in thinking about relationships. Both Piaget's original observations and more recent research have demonstrated that at about age 7 or 8 the child first grasps the principle of **class inclusion**, the idea that subordinate classes are included in larger,

reversibility   One of the most critical of the operations Piaget identified as part of the concrete operations period: the understanding that actions and mental operations can be reversed.

class inclusion   The principle that subordinate classes of objects are included in superordinate classes.

superordinate classes. Bananas are included in the class "fruit," fruits are included in the class "food," and so forth. Preschool children understand that bananas are also fruit, but they do not yet fully understand the relationship between the classes—that the class "fruit" is superordinate, including all bananas as well as all other types of fruit, such as oranges and apples.

Piaget also proposed that reversibility underlies the school-aged child's ability to use **inductive logic**: She can reason from her own experience to a general principle. For example, she can move from the observation that when you add another toy to a set and then count the set, it has one more toy than it did before, to a general principle that adding always makes more.

Because elementary school students are good at observational science and inductive reasoning, field trips like this fossil-hunting expedition are a particularly effective way of teaching.

Elementary school children are pretty good observational scientists and enjoy cataloging, counting species of trees or birds, or figuring out the nesting habits of guinea pigs. What they are not yet good at is **deductive logic**, which requires starting with a general principle and then predicting some outcome or observation, like going from a theory to a hypothesis. For example, suppose someone asked you to think of all the ways human relationships and societies would be different if women were physically as strong as men. Answering this question requires deductive, not inductive, logic; the problem is hard because you must imagine things that you have not experienced. The concrete operational child is good at dealing with things he knows or can see and physically manipulate—that is, he is good with concrete, or actual things; he does not do well with mentally manipulating ideas or possibilities. Piaget thought that deductive reasoning did not develop until the stage of formal operations in adolescence.

Horizontal Decalage   Note that Piaget did *not* argue that all concrete operational skills popped out at the same moment, as if a light bulb had gone on in the child's head. He used the term **horizontal decalage** to refer to children's tendency to be able to solve some kinds of concrete operational problems earlier than others. The French word *decalage* means "shift." The shift into concrete operational thinking is "horizontal" because it involves applying the same kind of thinking—concrete operational logic—to new kinds of problems. A "vertical" decalage would be a shift from one kind of thinking to another, as happens when children move from the preoperational to the concrete operational stage.

An early longitudinal study of concrete operations tasks by Carol Tomlinson-Keasey and her colleagues (1979) demonstrated just how long the period of horizontal decalage may actually be. They followed a group of 38 children from kindergarten through third grade, testing them with five tasks each year: conservation of mass, weight, and volume; class inclusion; and hierarchical classification. You can see from Figure 6.7 that the children got better at all five tasks over the 3-year period, with a spurt between the end of kindergarten and the beginning of first grade (at about the age Piaget thought that concrete operations really developed) and another spurt during second grade. However, even at the end of third grade, not every child had mastered all of the concrete operations tasks.

Understanding the concept of horizontal decalage is especially important for teachers, parents, and others who interact with children every day. For example, a 9-year-old may grasp the logic of some mathematical relationships (e.g., If $6 + 2 = 8$ and $4 + 4 = 8$, then $6 + 2 = 4 + 4$). Her understanding of such relationships demonstrates concrete operational thought. However, the same child, when asked by a parent to recall where she left her backpack, has difficulty applying concrete operational logic to the problem. As adults, we might use our concrete operations schemes to think of the problem this way: "If I had my backpack when I came in the door after school, and I didn't have it when I sat down in the living room, then it must be somewhere between the door and the living room." However, a 9-year-old who can grasp the concrete

CRITICAL THINKING   ？

How does reversibility come into play when you watch a magician perform? Do you think an understanding of reversibility makes the performance more or less interesting for you than for a young child who has yet to develop reversibility?

inductive logic Reasoning from the particular to the general, from experience to broad rules, characteristic of concrete operational thinking.

deductive logic Reasoning from the general to the particular, from a rule to an expected instance or from a theory to a hypothesis, characteristic of formal operational thinking.

horizontal decalage Piaget's term for school-aged children's inconsistent performance on concrete operations tasks.

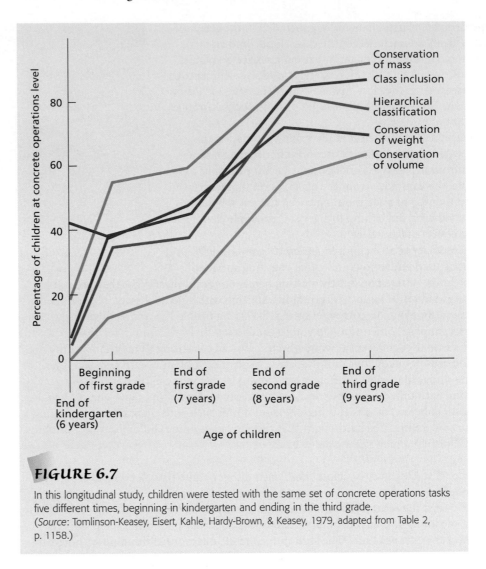

FIGURE 6.7

In this longitudinal study, children were tested with the same set of concrete operations tasks five different times, beginning in kindergarten and ending in the third grade.
(*Source*: Tomlinson-Keasey, Eisert, Kahle, Hardy-Brown, & Keasey, 1979, adapted from Table 2, p. 1158.)

operational logic of mathematical relationships may demonstrate horizontal decalage by responding to the lost backpack problem with preoperational thinking: "I don't know where my backpack is; someone must have stolen it." In such situations, teachers or parents may think a child is being difficult or lazy; in reality, she simply may not yet be capable of using concrete operational thinking to solve everyday problems that seem simple to adults but are actually quite complex.

A DIFFERENT APPROACH TO CONCRETE OPERATIONAL THOUGHT

Some psychologists have suggested that the problem of horizontal decalage calls into question Piaget's assertion that concrete operational thinking is a stage of cognitive development. The work of Robert Siegler (1996; Siegler & Chen, 2002) has shown that individual children may use a wide variety of types of rules—from very simple to quite sophisticated—on the same type of problem in different attempts on the same day. For example, if you give first- or second-graders simple addition problems (3 + 6, 9 + 4, etc.), they may solve each problem in any of a variety of ways. If they have committed a particular sum to memory, they may retrieve the answer directly from memory without calculation—the strategy most adults use for simple addition problems. On other problems, children may simply count, starting at 1, until they reach the sum. So 6 + 3 becomes "One, two, three, four, five, six, . . . seven, eight, nine." Alternatively, they may use what some researchers call the *min strategy*, a somewhat more sophisti- cated rule in which the child starts with the larger number and then adds the smaller one by counting. In this method, the child arrives at the sum 3 + 6 by saying to herself, "Seven, eight, nine." The child mentally counts each number as it is added. So, when she begins at 6 and counts to 7, she knows that one number has been added. Similarly, she knows that two numbers have been added when she gets to 8, and three have been added when she arrives at 9. Finally, a child might use a still more sophisticated *decomposition strategy*, which involves dividing a problem into several simpler ones. For ex- ample, a child might add 9 + 4 by thinking, "10 + 4 = 14, 9 is one less than 10, 14 − 1 = 13, so 9 + 4 = 13" (Siegler, 1996, p. 94). (You may use this method for more complicated prob- lems, such as multiplying 16 × 9. You might think, "9 × 10 = 90; 9 × 6 = 54; 54 + 90 = 144.")

With increasing age, elementary school children use counting less and less while increasing their use of retrieval, the min strategy, and decomposition—a finding that is en- tirely consistent with the notion of a gradual increase in use of more complex strategies. What Siegler has added to this information is the finding that the same child may use all these different strategies on different addition problems on the same day. So, it isn't that each child systematically shifts from one level of strategy to another, but rather that any given child may have a whole variety of strategies and may use some or all of them on different problems. Over time, the child's repertoire of likely strategies does indeed shift toward more and more complex or sophisticated ones, just as Piaget and others have described. But the process is not steplike; instead, it is more like a series of waves, as shown in Figure 6.8. When children add a new strategy, they do not immediately give up old ones; instead, they continue to use the old and the new for a while. Gradually, as the new strategies be- come more firmly established and better rehearsed, the less efficient or less effective strategies are dropped.

Despite research findings that challenge some of Piaget's hypotheses, his core concept of *constructivism*—that children are active thinkers, constantly trying to con- struct new strategies and more advanced understandings—is strongly supported by considerable research. Siegler points out that children will continue to construct new strategies for solving some kinds of problem, such as addition problems, "even when they already know perfectly adequate ones for solving them" (Siegler & Ellis, 1996, p. 211). Piaget also seems to have been on the mark in arguing for genuine qualitative change in the form of the child's thinking. An 8-year-old approaches new tasks dif- ferently than a 4-year-old does. He is more likely to attempt a complex strategy; if that strategy fails, he is more likely to try another one. Yet the appearance of these new cognitive skills is apparently much more gradual, and far less stagelike, than Pi- aget originally thought.

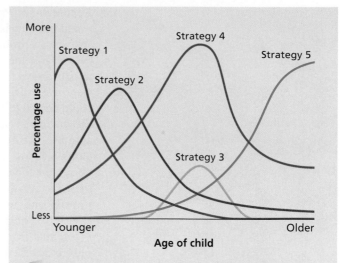

FIGURE 6.8

Siegler's "overlapping wave" model of cognitive development is probably a better description of the way children move toward more complex forms of thinking than the steplike stage model Piaget originally proposed.
(*Source*: "Figure 4.4: Overlapping waves depiction of cognitive development," from *Emerging Minds: The Process of Change in Children's Thinking* by Robert S. Siegler, copyright © 1996 by Oxford University Press, Inc. Used by permission of Oxford University Press, Inc.)

Before going on . . .

- What are concrete operations, and how do they represent an advance over earlier forms of thought?
- What does Siegler's research suggest about Piaget's view that concrete operational thinking develops in a single, coherent stage?

Adolescence

PIAGET'S VIEW OF FORMAL OPERATIONS

The formal operations stage, which Piaget believed emerged fairly rapidly between about ages 12 and 16, has a number of key elements.

One aspect of formal operations is the use of deductive logic, which is normally required first in high school, especially in math and science classes like this chemistry class.

hypothetico-deductive reasoning Piaget's term for the form of reasoning that is part of formal operational thought and involves not just deductive logic but also the ability to consider hypotheses and hypothetical possibilities.

Systematic Problem Solving One important feature of formal operational thinking is the ability to search systematically and methodically for the answer to a problem. To study this ability, Piaget and his colleague Barbel Inhelder (Inhelder & Piaget, 1958) presented adolescents with complex tasks, mostly drawn from the physical sciences. In one of these tasks, participants were given various lengths of string and a set of objects of various weights that could be tied to one of the strings to make a swinging pendulum. They were shown how to start the pendulum by pushing the weight with differing amounts of force and by holding the weight at different heights. The participants' task was to figure out whether the length of the string, the weight of the object, the force of the push, or the height of the push (or a combination of these factors) determines the period of the pendulum, that is, the amount of time for one swing. (In case you've forgotten your high school physics, the answer is that only the length of the string affects the period of the pendulum.)

If you give this task to a concrete operational child, she will usually try out many different combinations of length, weight, force, and height in an inefficient way. She might try a heavy weight on a long string and then a light weight on a short string. Because she has changed both string length and weight in these two trials, however, there is no way she can draw a clear conclusion about either factor. In contrast, an adolescent using formal operational thinking is likely to be more organized, attempting to vary just one of the four factors at a time. She may try a heavy object with a short string, then with a medium string, then with a long one. After that, she might try a light object with the three lengths of string. Of course, not all adolescents (or all adults, for that matter) are quite this methodical in their approach. Still, there is a very dramatic difference between the overall strategy used by 10-year-olds and that used by 15-year-olds, which marks the shift from concrete to formal operations.

Logic Another facet of the shift from concrete to formal operations is the appearance of what Piaget called hypothetico-deductive reasoning in the child's repertoire of skills. Piaget suggested that the concrete operational child can use inductive reasoning, which involves arriving at a conclusion or a rule based on a lot of individual experiences. **Hypothetico-deductive reasoning**, a more sophisticated kind of reasoning, involves using deductive logic, considering hypotheses or hypothetical premises, and then deriving logical outcomes. For example, the statement "If all people are equal, then you and I must be equal" involves logic of this type. Although children as young as 4 or 5 can understand some deductive relationships if the premises given are factually true, both cross-sectional and longitudinal studies support Piaget's assertion that only at adolescence are young people able to understand and use the basic principles of logic (Mueller, Overton, & Reene, 2001; Ward & Overton, 1990).

A great deal of the logic of science is hypothetico-deductive logic. Scientists begin with a theory and propose, "If this theory is correct, then we should observe such and such." In doing this, they are going well beyond their observations; they are conceiving of things they have never seen that ought to be true or observable. We can think of the change to this type of thinking at adolescence as part of a general decentering process that began much earlier. The preoperational child gradually moves away from his egocentrism and comes to be able to view things from the physical or emotional perspective of others. During the formal operations stage, the child takes another step by freeing himself even from his reliance on specific experiences.

Piaget also suggested that in many adolescents, hypothetico-deductive thinking leads to an outlook he called *naive idealism* (Piaget & Inhelder, 1969). Adolescents can use this powerful intellectual tool to think of an ideal world and to compare the real world to it. Not surprisingly, the real world often falls short of the ideal. As a result, some adolescents become so dissatisfied with the world that they resolve to change it. For many, the changes they propose are personal. For example, a teen whose parents

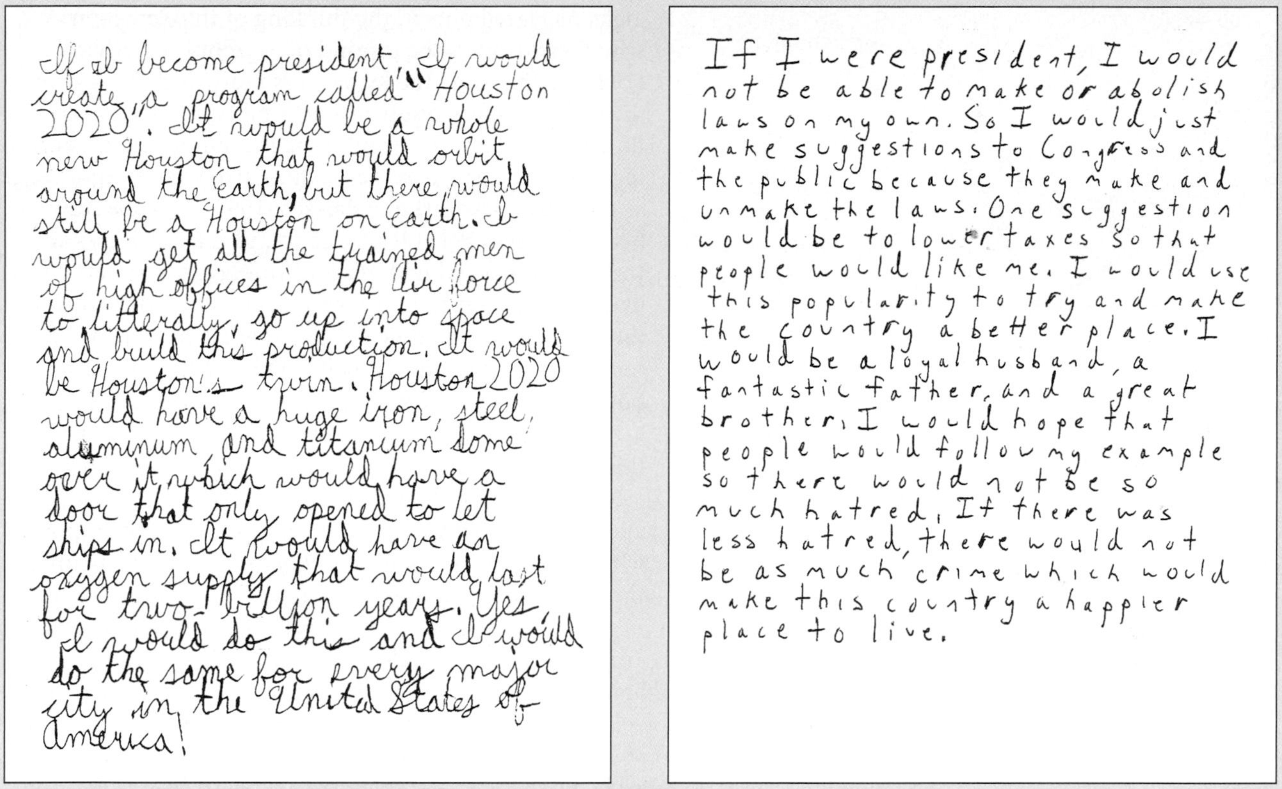

If I become president, I would create a program called "Houston 2020". It would be a whole new Houston that would orbit around the Earth, but there would still be a Houston on Earth. I would get all the trained men of high offices in the Air Force to litterally, go up into space and build this production. It would be Houston's twin. Houston 2020 would have a huge iron, steel, aluminum and titanium dome over it which would have a door that only opened to let ships in. It would have an oxygen supply that would last for two billion years. Yes I would do this and I would do the same for every major city in the United States of America!

If I were president, I would not be able to make or abolish laws on my own. So I would just make suggestions to Congress and the public because they make and unmake the laws. One suggestion would be to lower taxes so that people would like me. I would use this popularity to try and make the country a better place. I would be a loyal husband, a fantastic father, and a great brother. I would hope that people would follow my example so there would not be so much hatred. If there was less hatred, there would not be as much crime which would make this country a happier place to live.

FIGURE 6.9

The same boy wrote both of these compositions. The one on the left was written when the boy was 10, and the other when he was 13. The compositions illustrate the difference between concrete operational and formal operational thinking in response to the hypothetical question "What would you do if you became president of the United States?"
(*Source*: Author.)

have been divorced for years may suddenly decide she wants to live with the noncustodial parent because she expects that her life will be better. Another may express naive idealism by becoming involved in a political or religious organization.

The two compositions in Figure 6.9 illustrate how concrete operational and formal operational thinking lead to very different results when children are asked to reason deductively from an untrue premise. Both essays were written by the same boy, one at age 10 and the other at age 13, in response to the question "What would you do if you became president of the United States?" The 10-year-old boy's response is full of ideas about the president's ability to manipulate the concrete world. Significantly, it proposes building replicas of American cities in space, nicely illustrating the concrete operational thinker's tendency to replicate concrete reality when asked to think hypothetically. By contrast, the composition written at age 13 reflects both better deductive thinking and Piaget's notion of naive idealism. Moreover, it contains abstract ideas, such as the hypothesized relationship between hatred and crime, that are completely absent from the composition written at age 10. Thus, as Piaget's theory suggests, at 13, this boy not only knew more about the office of the president (e.g., that the president doesn't make laws singlehandedly), but he also thought quite differently about the world than he did at age 10.

POST-PIAGETIAN WORK ON ADOLESCENT THOUGHT

A good deal of post-Piagetian research confirms Piaget's basic observations. Adolescents, much more than elementary school children, operate with possibilities in addi-

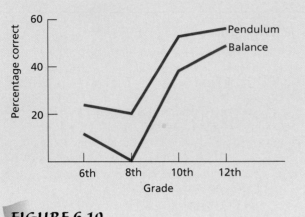

FIGURE 6.10

These are the results from 2 of the 10 different formal oper-
ations tasks used in Martorano's cross-sectional study.
(*Source*: Martorano, 1977, p. 670. Copyright by the American
Psychological Association.)

tion to reality, and they are more likely to use deductive
logic. As Flavell puts it, the thinking of the elementary
school child "hugs the ground of . . . empirical reality"
(1985, p. 98), while the teenager is more likely to soar into
the realm of speculation and possibility. An 8-year-old
thinks that "knowing" something is a simple matter of finding out the facts; a teenager is more likely to see knowledge
as relative, as less certain (Bartsch, 1993). Deanna Kuhn and
her colleagues (1995) have also found that teenagers and
young adults, faced with disconfirming evidence, are more
likely than younger children are to change their theories or
their initial guesses; they are also more systematic in seeking
out new information that will help hone their hypotheses—
both hallmarks of formal operational reasoning.

A research illustration clearly illustrates the change in
thinking. In an early cross-sectional study, Susan Martorano
(1977) tested 20 girls at each of four grades (6th, 8th, 10th,
and 12th) on 10 different tasks that required one or more of
what Piaget called *formal operations skills*. Indeed, many of
the tasks Martorano used were those Piaget himself had de-
vised. Results from two of these tasks are shown in Figure 6.10. The pendulum problem
is the same one described earlier; the balance problem requires a youngster to predict
whether two different weights, hung at varying distances on either side of a scale, will
balance. To solve this problem using formal operations, the teenager must consider both
weight and distance simultaneously. You can see from the graph that a significant improvement in scores occurred between 8th and 10th grades (between ages 13 and 15).

Formal Operations and Adolescent Decision Making   In a more practical vein, Catherine Lewis (1981) has shown that teenagers' new cognitive abilities alter
the ways in which they go about making decisions. Older teenagers are more focused
on the future, on possibilities, and on options when they consider decisions. Lewis
asked 8th-, 10th-, and 12th-grade students to respond to a set of dilemmas, each of
which involved a person facing a difficult decision, such as whether to have an operation to remove a facial disfigurement or how to decide which doctor to trust when different doctors give differing advice. Forty-two percent of the 12th graders, but only
11% of the 8th graders, mentioned future possibilities in their answers to these dilemmas. In answer to the cosmetic surgery dilemma, for example, a 12th grader said, "Well,
you have to look into the different things . . . that might be more important later on in
your life. You should think about, will it have any effect on your future and with,
maybe, the people you meet . . . " (Lewis, 1981, p. 541). An 8th grader, in response to
the same dilemma, said, "The different things I would think about in getting the operation is like if the girls turn you down on a date, or the money, or the kids teasing you at
school" (Lewis, 1981, p. 542). The 8th grader, as is characteristic of the preadolescent or
early adolescent, is focused on the here and now, on concrete things. The teenager is
considering things that might happen in the future.

Note, though, that even among the 12th graders in Lewis's study, nearly three-fifths
did not show this type of future orientation. And take another look at Figure 6.10; only
about 50–60% of 12th graders solved the two formal operations problems. In fact, only
2 of the 20 12th graders in Martorano's study used formal operational logic on all 10
problems. These findings reflect a common pattern in research on adolescent thinking:
By no means do all teenagers (or adults) use these more abstract forms of logic and
thought. Keating (1980) estimates that only about 50–60% of 18- to 20-year-olds in industrialized countries use formal operations at all, let alone consistently. In nonindustrialized countries, the rates are even lower.

There are several possible explanations for such low levels of formal operational
thought. One is that the parts of the brain needed to connect hypothetico-deductive

thought to everyday problems may not be sufficiently developed to make these connections until the late teens. Neuroimaging studies comparing the brain activity of children, teens, and adults while they were engaged in a gambling task provide support for this hypothesis (Crone & van der Molen, 2004).

Expertise may also be a crucial factor. That is, most of us have some formal operational ability, but we can apply it only to topics or tasks with which we are highly familiar. Willis Overton and his colleagues (1987) have found considerable support for this possibility in their research. They have found that as many as 90% of adolescents can solve quite complex logic problems if the problems are stated using familiar content, while only half can solve identical logic problems when they are stated in abstract language.

Another possibility is that most everyday experiences and tasks do not require formal operations. Inductive reasoning or other simpler forms of logic are quite sufficient most of the time. We can elevate our thinking a notch under some circumstances, especially if someone reminds us that it would be useful to do so, but we simply don't rehearse formal operations very much.

Finally, psychologist David Elkind (1967) has proposed that, paradoxically, it is formal operational thinking itself that impairs adolescents' ability to make sound decisions about everyday matters. Elkind has proposed that the hypothetico-deductive capabilities associated with formal operational thought enable teenagers to construct unrealistic ideas about both the present and the future. In effect, these ideas lead teens to view their lives with either excessive optimism or excessive pessimism. Elkind's ideas have had a great deal of influence on the approaches taken by researchers to understanding teens' decisions with regard to risky behaviors such as drug use (see the *Research Report*).

Culture and Formal Operational Thinking   The fact that formal operational thinking is found more often among young people or adults in Western or other industrialized cultures can be interpreted as being due to the fact that such cultures include high levels of technology and complex life-styles that demand more formal operational thought. By this argument, all nonretarded teenagers and adults are thought to have the capacity for formal logic, but only those of us whose lives demand its development will actually acquire it.

Notice that all these explanations undermine the very notion of a universal "stage" of thinking in adolescence. Yes, more abstract forms of thinking may develop in adolescence, but they are neither universal nor broadly used by individual teenagers or adults. Whether one develops or uses these forms of logic depends heavily on experience, expertise, and environmental demand.

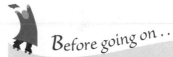

Before going on . . .

- What are the key elements of formal operational thinking?
- What does post-Piagetian research suggest about this stage?

Development of Information-Processing Skills

As the story of Piaget's "kidnapping" at the beginning of the chapter illustrates, our memories do not function as mental tape recorders. Instead, memory is a constructive process, one that sometimes leads to errors and can even result in the invention of pseudomemories depicting events that never actually happened (Loftus, 1993). Piaget's case illustrates, too, that the constructive aspect of memory can begin quite early in life, as discussed in *The Real World* on page 174. Further, constructive memories can be made more vivid, and our confidence in their veracity increased, by repetition (Thomas, Bulevich, & Loftus, 2003). Thus, the frequent retelling of Piaget's kidnapping story probably contributed to his belief that he remembered the event. Moreover, false memories that carry deep personal significance, like Piaget's, are more likely to become

Elkind's Adolescent Egocentrism

Psychologist David Elkind hypothesized that another common manifestation of hypothetico-deductive reasoning is a type of thought he called adolescent egocentrism, that belief that one's thoughts, beliefs, and feelings are unique. One component of adolescent egocentrism, Elkind said, is the personal fable, the belief that the events of one's life are controlled by a mentally constructed autobiography (Elkind, 1967). For example, a sexually active teenage girl might be drawing upon such a personal fable when she says "I just don't see myself getting pregnant" in response to suggestions that she use contraception. In contrast to this inappropriately rosy view of the future, a teen who is involved in a violent street gang may say "I'll probably get shot before I make 18" when advised to leave the gang and focus on graduating from high school.

Elkind also proposed that adolescent egocentrism drives teenagers to try out various attitudes, behaviors, and even clothing choices in front of an *imaginary audience*, an internalized set of behavioral standards usually derived from a teenager's peer group. Think about the example of a teenaged girl who is habitually late for school because she changes clothes two or three times every day before leaving home. Each time the girl puts on a different outfit, she imagines how her peers at school will respond to it. If the imaginary audience criticizes the outfit, the girl feels she must change clothes in order to elicit a more favorable response. Similarly, a boy may spend hours in front of the mirror trimming his sideburns in an effort to achieve a look he thinks his peers will approve of.

Many developmentalists have found Elkind's personal fable and imaginary audience to be helpful in explaining a variety of adolescents' everyday behaviors. However, research has produced mixed results (Bell & Bromnick, 2003; Vartanian, 2000). For one thing, while it is true that adolescents use idealized mental models to make all kinds of decisions about their own and others' behavior, researchers have found that school-aged children exhibit similar forms of thought (Vartanian, 2001). Thus, the idea that the personal fable and the imaginary audience are not evident until adolescence is not supported by research. Further, if school-aged children display this kind of thinking, then it is not as strongly correlated to formal operational thinking as Elkind claimed. Not surprisingly, this is exactly what has been found by researchers who have looked for relationships among measures of formal operational thinking, personal fable thought, and judgments based on the reactions of an imaginary audience (Vartanian, 2000).

Despite the shortcomings of Elkind's proposed construct of adolescent egocentrism, developmentalists agree that the tendency to exaggerate others' reactions to one's own behavior and to base decisions on unrealistic ideas about the future are two characteristics that distinguish adolescents from younger children. However, social-cognitive theorists have argued that both kinds of thinking result from the teenager's growing ability to take the perspective of another person, or her role-taking skills (Lapsley & Murphy, 1985). Research examining teens' role-taking skills and their tendency to think in terms of an imaginary audience and a personal fable has shown that role-taking is linked to the personal fable but not to the imaginary audience (Jahnke & Blanchard-Fields, 1993; Vartanian & Powlishta, 1996; Vartanian, 1997). Thus, the social-cognitive perspective doesn't provide us with a complete explanation.

A theory that shows more promise than either Elkind's original view or the social-cognitive approach is a model known as the *new look theory* (Vartanian, 2000). The new look theory claims that both the imaginary audience and the personal fable are rooted in social-emotional development, not in Piaget's formal operational stage (Lapsley, 1993; O'-Connor, 1995). Specifically, new look theorists say that both forms of ideation result from teenagers' attempts to establish identities that are separate from those of their parents. In the process, the stress associated with separating from parents causes teenagers to use a defense mechanism you may recall from Chapter 1, called *projection*—the attribution of one's own thoughts to others. Consequently, say new look theorists, teens who are concerned about their physical appearance believe that others are concerned about it as well. There is some evidence supporting their point of view. Several studies have shown correlations between identity development and personal fable/imaginary audience ideation. In one such study, teens whose parents were unsupportive turned to these forms of thought as a source of ideas for forming an identity (Vartanian, 2000). Research further suggests that teens who use this kind of thinking as a coping mechanism when faced with a lack of support from parents are less likely to be depressed than peers who do not cope in this way (Goossens, Beyers, Emmen, & van Aken, 2002). Thus, in contrast to Elkind's negative characterization of the personal fable and imaginary audience, both may actually be facilitators of, rather than hindrances to, a teenager's identity development. Moreover, what Elkind called adolescent egocentrism may actually turn out to be one of many manifestations of the identity development process you will learn about in Chapter 10.

Questions for Critical Analysis

1. In what ways might the personal fable and imaginary audience positively influence a teenager's decisions about risky behaviors such as smoking and unsafe sex? How might they negatively influence such decisions?
2. What are the roles of the imaginary audience and the personal fable in adults' perceptions of themselves?

embedded in our minds than those that concern less important matters (Kronlund & Whittlesea, 2005).

You may recall from Chapter 1 that the information-processing perspective is the view that has most often been used to study human memory. The information-processing model of memory postulates that information is processed, stored, and retrieved in different ways by the various components of the memory system, each of which has unique characteristics (see Figure 1.4). Although information-processing theory is not truly a developmental theory, research derived from this perspective has shed considerable light on age-related changes in memory and other aspects of cognitive development (Lamb & Lewis, 2005).

CHANGES IN PROCESSING CAPACITY AND EFFICIENCY

One obvious place to look for an explanation of developmental changes in memory skills is in the "hardware" itself. With any computer, there are physical limits on the number of different operations that can be performed simultaneously or in a given space of time. In the human memory system, the limiting factor is the short-term memory, as you'll recall from Chapter 1. It seems likely that as the brain and nervous system develop in the early years of life, the capacity of short-term memory increases (Johnson, 2005).

This has turned out to be a very difficult hypothesis to test. The most commonly cited evidence in support of an increase in short-term memory capacity is the finding that over the years of childhood, children are able to remember longer and longer lists of numbers, letters, or words, a pattern clear in the data shown in Figure 6.11. The difficulty with these results, however, is that they could also be simply another reflection of age differences in experience, because older children naturally have more experience with numbers, letters, and words. Thus, the memory-span data don't give a clear-cut answer to the question of whether basic processing capacity increases with age. Nevertheless, most developmental psychologists today agree that it is plausible to assume that short-term memory capacity increases across childhood, although most also admit that measuring such capacity is difficult (Cowan, Nugent, Elliott, Ponomarev, & Saults, 1999).

Researchers have also produced persuasive evidence that processing efficiency increases steadily with age. Indeed, most developmentalists now see such a change in efficiency as the basis on which cognitive development rests (Case, 1985; Halford, Mayberry, O'Hare, & Grant, 1994; Kuhn, 1992; Li et al., 2004). The best evidence on this point is that cognitive processing gets steadily faster with age. Robert Kail (1991, 2004; Kail & Hall, 1994) has found an exponential increase with age in processing speed on a wide variety of tasks, including such perceptual-motor tasks as tapping out a given rhythm or responding to a stimulus (for example, by pressing a button when you hear a buzzer) and cognitive tasks such as mental addition. He has found virtually identical patterns of speed increases in studies in Korea and the United States, adding a bit of cross-cultural validity to his results.

One plausible explanation for this common pattern is that over time, the brain and nervous system change physically in some fundamental way that allows increases in both response speed and mental processing. The most likely sources for such a basic change are the "pruning" of synapses and the myelination of the nerves, both of which you learned about in Chapter 4 (Hale, Fry, & Jessie, 1993). For example, assuming that pruning begins at about 12 to 18 months of age and then continues steadily

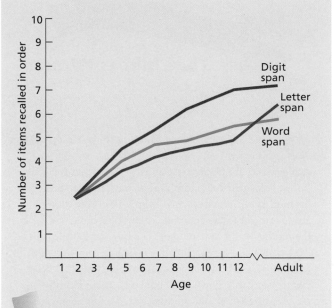

FIGURE 6.11

Psychologists have tried to measure basic memory capacity by asking research participants to listen to a list of numbers, letters, or words and then repeat the list items in order. This figure shows the number of such items that children of various ages are able to remember and recall accurately.
(*Source*: Dempster, 1981, from Figures 1–3, pp. 66–68.)

The Child as Witness

On April 30, 2004, Gerald Amirault walked out of a Massachusetts prison after serving 18 years of a 30- to 40-year sentence for child sexual abuse ("Convicted Day-Care Rapist Released," 2004). Amirault's conviction, and those of his mother and sister, resulted from a 1986 allegation of abuse brought to the attention of law enforcement officials by the mother of a 4-year-old boy. The boy was enrolled at the Amiraults' child-care facility, the Fells Acre Day School in Malden, Massachusetts. In response to the report, officials immediately shut down the school and began interviewing other 3- and 4-year-old children. Based on these interviews, the Amiraults found themselves accused not only of abuse but also of trafficking in child pornography. They were also accused of exposing children to bizarre acts such as ritualistic animal sacrifices. Ultimately, the convictions of Amirault's mother and sister were overturned because of research showing that the techniques used by the interviewers were likely to have implanted false memories in the children's minds (Rabinowitz, 2003). However, Gerald Amirault's conviction still stands, although he has been paroled. Law enforcement officials in Massachusetts continue to claim that the conviction was just. Further, Amirault's accusers maintain that their reports were accurate and actively worked to prevent his release from prison.

The Amiraults were among a handful of people who were prosecuted for abuse during the 1980s based solely on eyewitness testimony provided by witnesses who were preschoolers at the time the alleged abuse took place (Rabinowitz, 2003). Such cases led a number of psychologists to study the accuracy of children's eyewitness memories. The results of these studies have helped mental health professionals and those in the criminal justice system better understand the extent to which children's memories can be influenced by leading questions and other behaviors exhibited by interviewers (Crossman, Scullin, & Melnyk, 2004; Melinder, Goodman, Eilertsen, & Magnussen, 2004). These studies focused on two issues: (1) Can young children accurately remember faces or events and report on their experiences, even after a period of time has passed? (2) Are children more suggestible than adults about what they might have seen or experienced? (Will they report what they have been told to say or what may have been suggested to them, as opposed to what they actually saw or felt?) The answer to both questions seems to be "yes," which leaves developmentalists in a real dilemma regarding the overall accuracy of children's testimony (Ceci & Bruck, 1995, 1998).

First, recall of specific events or of the faces of people seen in the past does improve with age, but even preschoolers can recall events with considerable accuracy. Children often report less detail than adults do, but they rarely report something that didn't actually occur (Baker-Ward, 1995; Baker-Ward, Gordon, Ornstein, Larus, & Clubb, 1993;

throughout childhood, one effect is to make the "wiring diagram"—the connections within the nervous system—ever more efficient and thus able to operate faster.

However, experience using the memory system also contributes to increases in processing efficiency. For example, one of the most important ways in which processing becomes more efficient is through the acquisition of **automaticity**, or the ability to recall information from long-term memory without using short-term memory capacity. For example, when children can respond to the question "How much is 7 times 7?" by saying "49" without thinking about it, they have achieved automaticity with respect to that particular piece of information.

Automaticity is achieved primarily through practice and is critical to efficient information-processing because it frees up short-term memory space for more complex processing. Thus, the child or teenager who knows automatically what 7×7 is can use that fact in a complex multiplication or division problem without giving up any of the short-term memory space he is using to solve the problem. As a result, he is better able to concentrate on the "big picture" instead of expending effort trying to recall a simple multiplication fact. Not surprisingly, researchers have found that elementary school children who have automatized basic math facts in this way learn complex computational skills more rapidly (Kail & Hall, 1999). Similarly, kindergarteners who display automaticity with regard to naming letters and objects are more likely to be fluent

automaticity The ability to recall information from long-term memory without effort.

Ceci & Bruck, 1993; Davies, 1993). Even when they were under stress at the time of some event, such as being injured in an accident and treated at a hospital, young children remember the event quite accurately (Peterson & Bell, 1996).

At the same time, younger children, particularly preschoolers, are more suggestible than older children or adults (Ceci & Bruck, 1995; Hardy & Van Leeuwen, 2004). One common way to study this is to show a film or tell a story to children and adults. Then, while asking questions about what the participant saw, the investigator injects some misleading question into the set—a question that assumes something that didn't really happen (e.g., "He was carrying a pipe wrench when he came into the room, wasn't he?"). Young children are more affected than are older children or adults by such misleading suggestions (Leichtman & Ceci, 1995).

Research by Maggie Bruck and Stephen Ceci (1997) also makes it clear that repeated questioning influences children's testimony. Even when an event did not happen, many preschoolers and some school-aged children will say that it did after they have been asked about it many times (Ceci & Bruck, 1998; Muir-Broaddus, 1997). Thus, when an interviewer believes that some event has occurred, that belief may affect the way the interview is conducted and can influence the content of the child's recall, especially with preschool children (Ceci & Bruck, 1995). When misinformation comes from parents, children are even more likely to incorporate the parents' version into their own free recall (Ricci, Beal, & Dekle, 1995). Furthermore, these incorporated false reports persist over time; when children are reinterviewed later, many of them repeat the false reports.

To further complicate the issue, recent research suggests that children's personalities influence the accuracy of their eyewitness testimony. Shy children appear to be less likely to give truthful answers to questions than children who are more outgoing (Roebers & Schneider, 2001).

From the legal point of view, neither the findings on the cognitive aspects of children's testimony nor those suggesting that personality influences their answers to questions mean that children should not testify; they suggest only that adults should carefully evaluate how much weight to give their recollections. The research also points to the vital importance of extensive training for interviewers, so that they can use appropriate care in framing questions, beginning with the very first interview with the child (Bruck, Ceci, & Hembrooke, 1998).

Questions for Reflection

1. Suppose you are the parent of a preschooler. When you pick your child up from day care after a long day at work, the teacher tells you that your child hit one of his classmates and asks you to talk to him about it. Your first instinct is to try to find out from your child what the circumstances surrounding the incident were, so you begin by asking him to tell you what happened. Based on the research regarding young children's memories, how should you proceed if you want to get the most accurate report?

2. Think about possible conflicts between the rights of individuals who are accused of crimes and those of children who must be protected from people who would exploit them. How might research-based interviewing techniques help to protect both?

readers by the end of second grade than peers who require more time and effort to produce such names (Schatschneider, Fletcher, Francis, Carlson, & Foorman, 2004).

METAMEMORY AND METACOGNITION

One way in which a child's information-processing "software" changes is in her increasing awareness of her own mental processes. If a memory researcher had you learn a list of everyday words (*chair, spaghetti, lettuce*, and so on) and asked you afterward what techniques you used to remember them, you could describe your mental processes. You could also relate other things about the way your mind works, such as good ways to study particular subjects or which kinds of tasks are hardest for you, and why. These are examples of **metamemory** and **metacognition**—knowing about remembering and knowing about knowing. Such skills are a part of a larger category that information-processing theorists refer to as *executive processes*: planning what to do and considering alternative strategies.

Research suggests that such skills emerge in early childhood. For example, John Flavell's appearance/reality research has demonstrated that children between ages 3 and 5 know that in order to tell if a rock painted like a sponge is really a sponge or a rock, a

metamemory Knowledge about one's own memory processes.

metacognition General and rather loosely used term describing knowledge of one's own thinking processes: knowing what one knows, and how one learns.

person needs to touch or hold the object. Just looking at it doesn't give enough information (Flavell, 1993; O'Neill, Astington, & Flavell, 1992). In a similar vein, 4-year-olds (but not 3-year-olds) understand that to remember or forget something, one must have known it at a previous time (Lyon & Flavell, 1994). Flavell's research also suggests that by age 4, a child understands that there is a process called *thinking* that people do and that is distinct from knowing or talking (Flavell, Green, & Flavell, 1995). They also understand in some preliminary way that people can think about imaginary objects or events as well as real ones. Despite these major advances, however, 4- and 5-year-olds do not yet understand that thinking occurs continuously (Wellman & Hickling, 1994). In particular, they don't realize that other people are thinking all the time, and when asked, they are bad at guessing what another person might be thinking about, even when the clues are quite clear—such as when the other person is reading or listening to something. All of these skills are much more highly developed in 7- and 8-year-olds, who seem to have figured out that their own and other people's thinking goes on constantly and follows certain rules.

These skills are of particular interest because performance on a whole range of everyday tasks is better if the child can monitor her own performance or can recognize when a particular strategy is called for and when it is not. Four- and 5-year-olds do show some such monitoring, but it is rarely seen earlier than that, and it clearly improves fairly rapidly across the elementary school years. For example, 10-year-olds are more likely than 8-year-olds to know that understanding a story requires that the reader or listener exert mental effort to prevent his or her mind from wandering (Parault & Schwanenflugel, 2000).

Among other things, some metacognitive ability is critical for learning to read skillfully. A child learning to read needs to recognize which words he knows and which he does not, or which sentences he understands and which he does not, and needs to have some idea of how to get the information he needs. He needs to be able to recognize the difference between easy sentences and hard ones so that he can concentrate more and put more effort into the harder ones. A variety of research reveals that younger and poorer readers are less adept at all these metacognitive tasks, while better or older readers can do them more readily and skillfully (Flavell, Miller, & Miller, 1993).

By age 14 or 15, the metacognitive and metamemory skills of an adolescent far exceed those of a younger child. These gains result from improvements in working memory efficiency and increases in knowledge (Kail, 1990, 1997). As a result, teenagers outperform school-aged children on even simple memory tasks, such as remembering faces, and are far better than younger children at using complex strategies that aid memory (Gathercole, Pickering, Ambridge, & Wearing, 2004; Itier & Taylor, 2004). For example, one classic study of metamemory involved offering fifth-graders, eighth-graders, and college students the opportunity to earn money by remembering words (Cuvo, 1974). Researchers designated to-be-recalled words as being worth either 1 cent or 10 cents. Fifth-graders rehearsed 1-cent and 10-cent words equally. In contrast, eighth-graders and college students put more effort into rehearsing 10-cent words than 1-cent words. At the end of the rehearsal period, fifth-graders recalled equal numbers of 1- and 10-cent words, while older participants remembered more 10-cent items. Further, college students outperformed eighth-graders in both rehearsal and recall. These findings suggest that the capacity to apply memory skills selectively based on the characteristics of a memory task appears early in the teen years and continues to improve throughout adolescence.

MEMORY STRATEGIES

The notion that older children and adolescents intentionally use strategies for solving problems or for remembering things has been the basis for a whole new view of cognitive development (Schneider & Bjorklund, 1998).

CRITICAL THINKING ?

Write down three good ways to study. In choosing one of these methods, does it matter what subject you are studying? How do you know all this? Do you think about it consciously when you are starting to study?

Rehearsal Strategies Suppose you need to run the following errands: stop at the dry cleaner; buy some stamps; copy your IRS forms; and buy milk, bread, orange juice, carrots, lettuce, spaghetti, and spaghetti sauce at the grocery store. To remember such a list, you might use any one of several possible strategies, some of which are listed in Table 6.2. In this particular case, one option would be to rehearse the list over and over in your mind. Do children do this when they try to remember? One classic early study (Keeney, Cannizzo, & Flavell, 1967) indicated that school-aged children do but younger children do not. Keeney showed children a row of seven cards with pictures on them and told the children to try to remember all the pictures in the same order they were laid out. A helmet was then placed over the child's head to prevent the child from seeing the cards but allow the experimenter to see if the child seemed to be rehearsing the list by muttering under his or her breath. Children under 5 almost never showed any rehearsal, but 8- to 10-year-old children usually did. Interestingly, when 5-year-olds were taught to rehearse, they were able to do so and their memory scores improved. Yet when these same 5-year-olds were given a new problem without being reminded to rehearse, they stopped rehearsing. That is, they could use the strategy if they were reminded to, but they did not produce it spontaneously—a pattern described as a **production deficiency**.

More recent work suggests that preschool-aged children show some kinds of strategies in their remembering if the task is quite simple, such as the game of hide-and-seek that Judy DeLoache (DeLoache, 1989; DeLoache, Simcock, & Marzolf, 2004) has used in her studies. In one of DeLoache's studies, the child watches the experimenter hide an attractive toy in some obvious place (e.g., behind a couch) and is then told that when a buzzer goes off she can go and find the toy. While playing with other toys during the 4-minute delay interval before the buzzer sounded, 2-year-olds often talked about, pointed to, or looked at the toy's hiding place—all of which seem clearly to be early forms of memory strategies.

These results and others like them indicate that there is no magic shift from non-strategic to strategic behavior at age 5 or 6 or 7. Children as young as 2 use primitive strategies, but school-aged children seem to have larger repertoires of strategies and to

TABLE 6.2	Some Common Strategies for Remembering
Strategy	**Description**
Rehearsal	Perhaps the most common strategy, which involves either mental or vocal repetition or repetition of movement (as in learning to dance). May be used by children as young as 2 years under some conditions.
Clustering	Grouping ideas, objects, or words into clusters to help in remembering them, such as "all animals," or "all the ingredients in the lasagna recipe," or "the chess pieces involved in the move called castling." This is one strategy that clearly benefits from experience with a particular subject or activity, since possible categories are learned or are discovered in the process of exploring or manipulating a set of materials. Primitive clustering is used by 2-year-olds.
Elaboration	Finding shared meaning or a common referent for two or more things to be remembered. The helpful mnemonic for recalling the names of the lines on the musical staff ("Every Good Boy Does Fine") is a form of elaboration, as is associating the name of a person you have just met with some object or other word. This form of memory aid is not used spontaneously by all individuals and is not used skillfully until fairly late in development, if then.
Systematic Searching	Scanning the memory for the whole domain in which something might be found. Children aged 3 and 4 can begin to do this to search for actual objects in the real world but are not good at doing this in memory. Search strategies may be first learned in the external world and then applied to inner searches.

Source: Flavell, 1985.

production deficiency A pattern whereby an individual can use some mental strategy if reminded to do so but fails to use the strategy spontaneously.

use them more flexibly and efficiently, a quality of thinking that becomes increasingly evident in older schoolchildren (Bjorklund & Coyle, 1995). For example, when learning a list of words, 8-year-olds are likely to practice the words one at a time ("cat, cat, cat"), while older children practice them in groups ("desk, lawn, sky, shirt, cat"). The 8-year-olds, tested again a year later, show signs of a shift toward the more efficient strategy (Guttentag, Ornstein, & Siemens, 1987).

Clustering   Another strategy that helps improve memory involves putting the items to be learned or remembered into some meaningful organization. For example, in trying to remember a list of items you need to buy at the grocery store, you could aid your memory by thinking of the items as ingredients in a recipe (e.g., "what I need to make spaghetti and meatballs"). Another common strategy is to mentally group the items into categories such as "fruits and vegetables" and "canned goods," a strategy called clustering, or chunking.

Studies of clustering often involve having children or adults learn lists of words that have potential categories built into them. For example, in a study of categorical clustering, a researcher would ask you to remember this list of words: *chair, spaghetti, lettuce, cat, desk, chocolate, duck, lion, table.* You would be given 2 minutes to try to memorize the list, using whatever method(s) you wished. Then the researcher would ask you to list the words you could recall. If you used some kind of clustering technique, you would be likely to list the same-category words together (*cat, duck, lion; chair, desk, table*; and *spaghetti, chocolate, lettuce*).

School-aged children show this kind of internal organization strategy when they recall things, while preschoolers generally do not. And among school-aged children, older children use this strategy more efficiently, using a few large categories rather than many smaller ones (Bjorklund & Muir, 1988; Schlagmüller & Schneider, 2002). Interestingly, research shows that children often spontaneously use such a strategy but derive no apparent memory benefit from it, a pattern called a **utilization deficiency** (Bjorklund, Miller, Coyle, & Slawinski, 1997; Schneider & Bjorklund, 1998)—in a sense the opposite pattern from a production deficiency, in which a child will use and benefit from a strategy if reminded to do so but will not use it spontaneously. Utilization deficiencies are intriguing to theorists because they suggest that the child assumes that using some kind of strategy is a good thing to do but does not fully understand how to go about it. This form of deficiency is more common in children younger than 6 or 7, but it occurs among older children and teenagers as well (Bjorklund et al., 1997).

Strategy Training   Training studies, in which children and adolescents are taught to use a particular memory strategy, suggest that teens benefit more from training than younger children do. For example, in one of the early strategy training studies, researchers taught elementary school and high school students a strategy for memorizing the manufacturing products associated with different cities, for example, "Detroit—automobiles" (Pressley & Dennis-Rounds, 1980). Once participants had learned the strategy and were convinced of its effectiveness, researchers presented them with a similar task: memorizing Latin words and their English translations. Experimenters found that only the high school students made an effort to use the strategy they had just learned to accomplish the new memory task. The elementary school children used the new strategy only when researchers told them to and demonstrated to them how it could be applied to the new task. The high school students' success seemed to be due to their superior ability to recognize the similarity between the two tasks—an aspect of metamemory.

The differences between elementary school children's and adolescents' ability to learn strategies for processing meaningful text, such as newspaper articles or material in textbooks, are even more dramatic. In a classic study of text processing, experimenters asked 10-, 13-, 15-, and 18-year-olds to read and summarize a 500-word passage (about 1 page in a typical college textbook). The researchers (Brown & Day, 1983) hypothesized that participants would use four rules in writing summaries. First, they would delete trivial information. Second, their summaries would show categorical organization; that is, they would use terms such as *animals* rather than specific names of animals mentioned in the text. Researchers also speculated that participants would use

utilization deficiency Using some specific mental strategy without deriving benefit from it.

topic sentences from the text in their summaries and would invent topic sentences for paragraphs that didn't have them.

The results of the research suggested that participants of all ages used the first rule, because all of their summaries included general rather than detailed or trivial information about the passage. However, the 10- and 13-year-olds used the other rules far less frequently than did the 15- and 18-year-olds. There were also interesting differences between the two older groups. Fifteen-year-olds used categories about as frequently as 18-year-olds did, but the oldest group used topic sentences far more effectively. This pattern of age differences in strategy use suggests that complex information-processing skills such as text summarizing improve gradually during the second half of adolescence.

Studies of text outlining reveal a similar pattern (Drum, 1985). Both elementary school and high school students know that an outline should include the main ideas of a passage along with supporting details. However, research suggests that 17-year-olds generate much more complete outlines than do 14-year-olds. Moreover, 11-year-olds' outlines usually include only a few of the main ideas of a passage and provide little or no supporting details for the main ideas they do include.

These school-aged chess players, unless they are rank novices, would remember a series of chess moves or the arrangement of pieces on a chessboard far better than would nonplayers, regardless of their ages.

EXPERTISE

All of the apparent developmental changes that we have discussed may well turn out to be as much a function of expertise as they are of age. Piaget thought that children apply broad forms of logic to all their experiences in any given stage. If that's true, then the amount of specific experience a child has had with some set of materials shouldn't make a lot of difference. A child who understands hierarchical classification but who has never seen pictures of different types of dinosaurs still ought to be able to create classifications of dinosaurs about as well as a child who has played a lot with dinosaur models. A child who understands the principle of transitivity (if A is greater than B and B is greater than C, then A is greater than C) ought to be able to demonstrate this ability with sets of strange figures as well as she could with a set of toys familiar to her. But, in fact, that seems not to be the case.

Developmentalists now have a great deal of research showing that specific knowledge makes a huge difference (Kail, 2004). Children and adults who know a lot about some subject or some set of objects (dinosaurs, baseball cards, mathematics, or whatever) not only categorize information in that topic area in more complex and hierarchical ways, they are also better at remembering new information on that topic and better at applying more advanced forms of logic to material in that area. Furthermore, such expertise seems to generalize very little to other tasks (Ericsson & Crutcher, 1990). A child who is a devout soccer fan will be better than a nonfan at recalling lists of soccer words or the content of a story about soccer, but the two children are likely to be equally good at remembering random lists of words (Schneider & Bjorklund, 1992; Schneider, Reimers, Roth, & Visé, 1995).

Research on expertise also shows that even the typical age differences in strategy use or memory ability disappear when the younger group has more expertise than the older. For example, Michelene Chi, in her now-classic early study (1978), showed that expert chess players can remember the placement of chess pieces on a board much more quickly and accurately than can novice chess players, even when the expert chess players are children and the novices are adults—a finding since replicated several times (e.g., Schneider, Gruber, Gold, & Opwis, 1993). To paraphrase Flavell (1985), expertise makes any of us look very smart, very cognitively advanced; lack of expertise makes us look very dumb.

Before going on . . .

- How do cognitive processing capacity and efficiency change with age?
- What are metamemory and metacognition, and what is their importance to cognitive functioning?
- What kinds of improvements in strategy use happen across childhood and adolescence?
- How does expertise influence memory function?

Summary

Piaget's Basic Ideas

- Piaget assumed that the child was an active agent in his own development, constructing his own understandings and adapting to the environment through his actions on the world. Cognitive structures called schemes underlie the stages of cognitive development.
- Schemes change through the processes of assimilation, accommodation, and equilibration.
- Conflict between a child's existing schemes and his observations of the world leads to actions that eventually result in resolution of such conflicts, or equilibration, as Piaget called the process. Each stage of development represents a more adaptive equilibration.
- Equilibration interacts with maturation, social transmission, and experience to produce changes in children's thinking.

Infancy

- Piaget's first stage is the sensorimotor period, from birth to 18 months; the infant begins with a small repertoire of basic schemes, from which she moves toward symbolic representation in a series of six substages.
- Post-Piagetian studies of infant cognition show infants' memory skills to be far more advanced than Piaget thought. Infants can imitate in the earliest weeks but do not show deferred imitation for several months.

The Preschool Years

- In Piaget's preoperational period, from 2 to 6 years, the child is able to use mental symbols to represent objects to himself internally. Despite this advance, the preschool-aged child still lacks many sophisticated cognitive characteristics. In Piaget's view, such children are still egocentric, rigid in their thinking, and generally captured by appearances.
- Research on the cognitive functioning of preschoolers makes it clear that they are much less egocentric than Piaget thought. By age 4, children can distinguish between appearance and reality in a variety of tasks.
- Preschoolers develop a surprisingly sophisticated theory of mind—that is, ideas of how other people's minds work. They understand that the actions of others are often based on thoughts and beliefs.
- Recent theorizing about the preschool period has been influenced by neo-Piagetian theories that explain Piaget's stages in information-processing terms.

- Vygotsky's socio-cultural theory emphasizes the role of social interactions in children's cognitive development. Moreover, Vygotsky suggested that language provides the framework necessary to support many of the general concepts children acquire in the preschool years.

The School-Aged Child

- In Piaget's third stage—concrete operations—occurring from age 6 to age 12, the child acquires powerful new mental tools called operations, such as reversibility.
- Recent research on this period confirms many of Piaget's descriptions of sequences of development but calls into question his basic concept of stages. Siegler's work shows that cognitive development is less steplike than Piaget proposed; children may use a variety of different strategies, varying in complexity, on the same kind of problem. Still, the repertoire of strategies does become more complex with age.

Adolescence

- Piaget's fourth stage—formal operations—is said to develop from age 12 onward and is characterized by the ability to apply basic operations to ideas and possibilities as well as to actual objects and by the emergence of systematic problem solving and hypothetico-deductive logic.
- Researchers have found clear evidence of such advanced forms of thinking in at least some adolescents.

Development of Information-Processing Skills

- Most theorists agree that there are age-related changes in the capacity of the mental "hardware" as well as improvements in speed and efficiency.
- Children's capacity to think about their own mental processes also contributes to improvements in memory functioning.
- Processing efficiency improves because of increasing use of various types of processing strategies with age, including strategies for remembering. Preschoolers use some strategies, but school-aged children use them more often and more flexibly.
- Studies of expertise show that prior knowledge contributes to both individual and age-related differences in memory functioning and strategy use.

Key Terms

accommodation (p. 151)

assimilation (p. 151)

automaticity (p. 174)

class inclusion (p. 164)

concrete operations stage (p. 152)

conservation (p. 157)

deductive logic (p. 165)

egocentrism (p. 157)

equilibration (p. 151)

false belief principle (p. 159)

formal operations stage (p. 152)

horizontal decalage (p. 165)

hypothetico-deductive reasoning (p. 168)

inductive logic (p. 165)

metacognition (p. 175)

metamemory (p. 175)

neo-Piagetian theory (p. 162)

object permanence (p. 155)

operation (p. 152)

operational efficiency (p. 162)

preoperational stage (p. 152)

primary circular reactions (p. 154)

production deficiency (p. 177)

reversibility (p. 164)

scheme (p. 150)

secondary circular reactions (p. 154)

sensorimotor stage (p. 152)

short-term storage space (STSS) (p. 162)

tertiary circular reactions (p. 155)

theory of mind (p. 160)

utilization deficiency (p. 178)

Children's Use of Clustering Strategies

You can use a deck of playing cards to examine memory improvement. Do your research with a 7-year-old and a 10-year-old. Make sure that the children know the names of the suits and the conventional way of referring to cards (7 of hearts, 2 of spades, etc.). For the first trial, select 12 cards, 3 from each suit, making sure that the cards are all of different values. Arrange the cards in front of the child in such a way that no card is next to another of the same suit. Test each child separately, allowing 1 minute for the child to memorize the cards. When the minute has passed, take up the cards and ask each child to recall them. For the second trial, repeat the experiment with a different set of 12 cards, but tell the children that they may rearrange the cards if they think it will help their memory. The 7-year-old probably won't rearrange the cards by suit, but the 10-year-old will. This shows that the older child is attempting to use categories as a memory aid, a clustering strategy. The 10-year-old should exhibit better recall than the 7-year-old across both trials, but the difference between the two should be greater when the older child is allowed to use the clustering strategy.

Using Play Behavior to Assess Stage of Cognitive Development

Across the ages of 1 to 3, children's play behaviors are correlated with the transition from the sensorimotor to the preoperational stage. Careful observation of these behaviors can provide you with useful information about an individual child's stage of cognitive development. Use the chart below to record observations of individual 1- to 3-year-olds' play behaviors in a natural setting, such as a park or a preschool classroom. Based on these observations, determine whether each child is best described as being in the sensorimotor stage, in the preoperational stage, or in transition between the two. Note differences in age-stage correlations across children. (Be sure to obtain permission from children's parents and teachers before carrying out your study.)

Stage/Typical Age	Typical Object Play Behaviors	Typical Pretend Play Behaviors	Observed Object Play Behaviors	Observed Pretend Play Behaviors
Sensorimotor 12–18 months	Uses motor skills (e.g., grasping, banging) and senses (e.g., vision, taste) to explore objects	Simple pretending (e.g., goes to the door and pretends to go "bye-bye")		
Transition 18–24 months	Limited constructive play; structures are often unstable	Combines objects (e.g., doll and toy bottle) in pretend play		
Preoperational 24–36 months	More complex constructive play; structures have greater stability	Uses substitute objects in pretend play (e.g., pretends a block is a car); role play (e.g., playing "house")		

Cognitive Development II: Individual Differences in Cognitive Abilities

7

C H A P T E R

Kenzaburo Oe was just 23 years old in 1958, when a novel he authored was awarded a prestigious literary prize in his native Japan.

By the time Oe married in 1960, he was one of Japan's most successful novelists. But as the delivery date for his first child approached in 1963, he was having doubts about his ability to live up to the expectations that had been created for him by his early successes. The news that his wife had given birth to a son who had a serious birth defect seemed like the final blow to his fragile sense of self-worth (Cameron, 1998).

The doctors told Oe and his wife that their newborn son's brain was herniated outside of his skull, and only a dangerous operation, one that would leave the boy mentally retarded and vulnerable to other neurological difficulties, could save his life. The doctors' recommendation that the couple allow the child to die peacefully did little to lift Oe's spirits. Instead of taking their advice, Oe turned to doctors who had spent their lives treating survivors of the atomic bomb that was dropped on the Japanese city of Hiroshima at the end of World War II. These doctors agreed that the child would likely be severely disabled by the surgery, but they encouraged Oe and his wife to adopt the view that human life is precious and that hope and joy can be found even in the most dire of circumstances. With that philosophical outlook, Oe named the boy Hikari, the Japanese word for "light," and told surgeons to operate on his son.

As the doctors had predicted, it was quite clear by the time Hikari was just a few years old that he was mentally retarded. He also suffered from epileptic seizures and had extremely poor vision. In addition, Hikari appeared to be incapable of forming social relationships. Still, Oe gained inspiration from his own and his wife's efforts to reach the boy. His writing became embued with a sense of hope that can be developed only in the midst of a human tragedy. As a result, his career prospered, and his work achieved worldwide acclaim. Soon, two more children, both healthy and normal, were born into the Oe family.

When Hikari was about 6 years old, his parents noticed that he had an unusual ability to memorize and sing songs, though his ability to speak and to understand language was quite limited. They decided to give him piano lessons and found a teacher who was willing to take on the challenging student. As the teacher worked with Hikari, it became apparent that the child had remarkable musical gifts. Within months, he was playing difficult classical pieces with ease. Moreover, he began to improvise on classical forms to create his own pieces. Though she doubted the effort would be successful, Hikari's piano teacher decided to try to teach him musical notation so that he could write down his compositions. To her surprise, he mastered the difficult skill of writing classical music in a relatively short time. Today, as a middle-aged man, Hikari Oe is an accomplished and celebrated composer of classical music. Yet his scores on standardized tests of intelligence are far below average, and he is unable to live independently.

Hikari Oe is just one of the thousands of individuals with mental retardation and other severe mental disabilities who display savant syndrome, the exhibition of remarkable talents in the context of a severe disability. Psychologists have studied savants such as Hikari for more than a hundred years, yet do not yet know why some abilities in these individuals become accentuated while others are destroyed. But studying savants has led to the development of new theories of normal intellectual functioning, theories that have led psychologists to look beyond conventional intelligence tests in the quest for an accurate definition of human intelligence.

In this chapter, you will learn about the history of intelligence testing and the study of human intelligence. You will also learn about the range of individual differences in intelligence and some of the controversies surrounding group differences. At the end of the chapter, you will read about a theory of intelligence that is based on studies of savants such as Hikari Oe.

Measuring Intellectual Power

Psychologists have argued for decades about whether test performance is an adequate definition of intelligence. At a conceptual level, though, most psychologists agree that **intelligence** includes the ability to reason abstractly, the ability to profit from experience, and the ability to adapt to varying environmental contexts. Consequently, most tests of intelligence include tasks that require examinees to use these abilities.

Still, most of us have a greatly inflated notion of the permanence or importance of an IQ score. To acquire a more realistic view, it helps to know something about what such tests were designed to do and something about the beliefs and values of those who devised them.

THE FIRST IQ TESTS

The first modern intelligence test was published in 1905 by two Frenchmen, Alfred Binet and Theodore Simon (1905). From the beginning, the test had a practical purpose—to identify children who might have difficulty in school. For this reason, the tasks that made up the test Binet and Simon devised were very much like some school tasks, including measures of vocabulary, comprehension of facts and relationships, and mathematical and verbal reasoning. For example, could a child describe the difference between wood and glass? Could a young child touch his nose, his ear, his head? Could he tell which of two weights was heavier?

Lewis Terman and his associates at Stanford University modified and extended many of Binet and Simon's original tasks when they translated and revised the test for use in the United States (Terman, 1916; Terman & Merrill, 1937). The several Terman revisions, called the **Stanford-Binet**, consist of six sets of tests, one set for children of each of six consecutive ages. A child taking the test begins with the set of tests for the age below his actual age, then takes the set for his age, then those for each successively older age until he has either completed all the tests for older ages or has reached a point where the remaining tests are too difficult for him.

Terman initially described a child's performance in terms of a score called an **intelligence quotient**, later shortened to **IQ**. This score was computed by comparing the child's chronological age (in years and months) with his **mental age**, defined as the level of questions he could answer correctly. For example, a child who could solve the

intelligence A set of abilities defined in various ways by different psychologists but generally agreed to include the ability to reason abstractly, the ability to profit from experience, and the ability to adapt to varying environmental contexts.

Stanford-Binet The best-known U.S. intelligence test. It was written by Lewis Terman and his associates at Stanford University and based on the first tests by Binet and Simon.

intelligence quotient (IQ) Originally defined in terms of a child's mental age and chronological age, IQ is now computed by comparing a child's performance with that of other children of the same chronological age.

mental age Term used by Binet and Simon and Terman in the early calculation of IQ scores to refer to the age level of IQ test items a child could successfully answer. Used in combination with the child's chronological age to calculate an IQ score.

problems for a 6-year-old but not those for a 7-year-old would have a mental age of 6. Terman devised a formula to calculate the IQ score:

$$\frac{\text{Mental Age}}{\text{Chronological Age}} \times 100$$

This formula results in an IQ score above 100 for children whose mental age is higher than their chronological age and an IQ score below 100 for children whose mental age is below their chronological age.

This old system for calculating IQ scores is not used any longer, even in the modern revisions of the Stanford-Binet. IQ score calculations are now based on a direct comparison of a child's performance with the average performance of a large group of other children of the same age, with a score of 100 still typically defined as average.

The majority of children achieve Stanford-Binet scores that are right around the average of 100, with a smaller number scoring very high or very low. Figure 7.1 shows the distribution of IQ scores that will result when the test is given to thousands of children. You can see that 67% (about two-thirds) of all children achieve scores between 85 and 115, while 96% achieve scores between 70 and 130. The groups that developmentalists refer to as "gifted" or "retarded," both of which you'll read about in some detail in Chapter 15, clearly represent only very small fractions of the distribution.

One advantage of the modern method of calculating IQ scores is that it allows the test makers to restandardize the test periodically, so that the average remains at 100. Such readjustments are needed because IQ test scores have been rising steadily over the past 50 or 60 years. If the same standards were used today as were applied in 1932, when tests such as the Stanford-Binet were first devised, the average score would be 115 and not 100—an increase that has been found among children and adults all over the world (Dickens & Flynn, 2001; Flynn, 1994, 1999). That is, the average child today can solve problems that only an above-average child could solve 60 years ago. This historical shift upward in scores on cognitive ability tests is known as the *secular trend* in IQ scores. You may recall this term from Chapter 4, where you read about its use in relation to historical changes in the timing of menarche. The secular trend in IQ scores is also sometimes called the *Flynn effect*, because it was discovered by psychologist Raymond Flynn (1994).

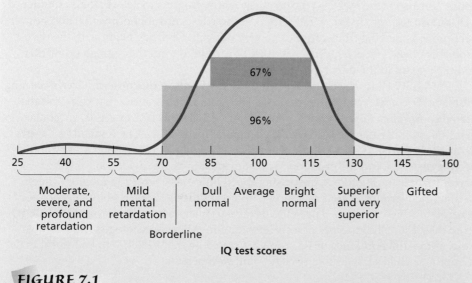

FIGURE 7.1

The approximate distribution of scores on most modern IQ tests, along with the labels typically used for scores at various levels. The tests are designed and the scoring is standardized so that the average score is 100 and two-thirds of the scores fall between 85 and 115. Because of brain damage and genetic anomalies, there are slightly more low-IQ children than there are very high-IQ children.

When thinking about the ways in which children's IQ scores have changed over the past 70 years, it's important to keep in mind that both maturational and experiential variables influence IQ scores. Further, historical changes in these two sets of factors have followed different patterns. Most observers attribute changes in the maturational components of IQ test performance to improvements in health and nutrition (Williams, 1998), most of which took place during the first half of the 20th century. In support of this hypothesis, comparisons of average scores exhibited by children in the mid-1980s to those of children in the early years of the 21st century show that the maturational components underlying cognitive ability test scores have not changed at all over this period (Nettelbeck & Wilson, 2004). Studies of test score changes in nations that have experienced significant improvements in the physical environment over the same period (e.g., Singapore, Estonia, and rural Kenya) lend further weight to this hypothesis. These studies reveal that children's performance on maturationally loaded tasks has risen dramatically along with improvements in diet and health (Cocodia et al., 2003; Daley, Whaley, Sigman, Espinosa, & Neumann, 2003; Must, Must, & Raudik, 2003).

By contrast, scores on tests that reflect the experiential elements of the Flynn effect are continuing to increase in industrialized societies (Nettelbeck, 2004). This increase is usually attributed to environmental factors that have changed more in recent years than in the early decades of the past century. Two likely factors are the explosion in information media and children's increased preschool attendance. In addition, test scores attained by today's children may reflect their tendency to be a bit more "testwise" than earlier cohorts simply because they take more tests and do more test-like activities in the early years of school (Cocodia et al., 2003).

MODERN IQ TESTS

The three tests most frequently used by psychologists today are the Stanford-Binet V (the fifth revision of the original Stanford-Binet), the third edition of the Wechsler Preschool and Primary Scale of Intelligence (the **WPPSI-III**), and the fourth edition of the Wechsler Intelligence Scales for Children, (the **WISC-IV**). The two Wechsler tests are derived from an intelligence test for children originally developed by psychologist David Wechsler (1974). The WPPSI-III is designed for children between the ages of $2\frac{1}{2}$ and 7. Norms for the WISC-IV begin at age 6 and progress to age 16. (Several other well-known tests are listed in Table 7.1.) All three tests feature both verbal and nonverbal problems ranging from very easy to very difficult. Children begin with the easiest problems of each type, continue with that type of item until they can go no further, and then go on to the next type of problem.

The WISC-IV is the test most often used in schools to diagnose children's learning problems. It consists of 15 different tests. Five of these tests, those that comprise the **verbal comprehension index**, rely strongly on verbal skills (for example, vocabulary, describing similarities between objects, general information). The remaining 10 tests demand nonverbal types of thinking, such as arranging pictures to tell a story and repeating digits back to the examiner. The nonverbal tests are divided among the **perceptual reasoning index**, **processing speed index**, and **working memory index**. Each of these groups of tests measures a different kind of nonverbal intelligence and generates its own IQ score. The WISC-IV also provides a comprehensive **full scale IQ** score that takes all four types of tests into account. Many psychologists find comparisons of the different kinds of IQ scores generated by the WISC-IV to be helpful in determining a child's intellectual strengths and weaknesses.

Infant Tests   Neither the Stanford-Binet nor either of the Wechsler tests can be used with children much younger than about 3. Infants and toddlers don't talk well, if at all, and most childhood tests rely heavily on language. (Even the Peabody Picture Vocabulary Test, described in Table 7.1, requires that the child understand individual words.) So how do developmentalists measure "intelligence" in an infant? This becomes

WPPSI-III The third revision of the Wechsler Preschool and Primary Scale of Intelligence.

WISC-IV The most recent revision of the Wechsler Intelligence Scales for Children, a well-known IQ test developed in the United States that includes both verbal and performance (nonverbal) subtests.

verbal comprehension index Tests on the WISC-IV that tap verbal skills such as knowledge of vocabulary and general information.

perceptual reasoning index Tests on the WISC-IV, such as block design and picture completion, that tap nonverbal visual-processing abilities.

processing speed index Timed tests on the WISC-IV, such as symbol search, that measure how rapidly an examinee processes information.

working memory index Tests on the WISC-IV, such as digit span, that measure working memory efficiency.

full scale IQ The WISC-IV score that takes into account verbal and nonverbal scale scores.

TABLE 7.1	Intelligence Tests That May Be Used in Place of the Stanford-Binet and the WISC
Test	**Description**
Peabody Picture Vocabulary Test (PPVT)	Not originally designed as an IQ test, but widely used as a quick measure of intelligence because the scores correlate so highly with Binet or Wechsler scores. Includes 150 pages, each page with four pictures, the pages arranged in order of increasing difficulty. The examiner says a word and asks the child to point to the appropriate picture, as in the example to the right. Widely used with preschool children. 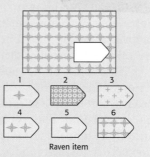 PPVT item (word is *emerge*)
Raven's Progressive Matrices	Each of the 36 items shows a pattern on a rectangular space, such as a set of dots covering the space. One section of the rectangle is blanked out, and the child must choose which of six alternative fill-in options will match the original matrix, as in the example to the right. Designed as a nonverbal measure of intelligence.
Kaufman Assessment Battery for Children (KABC)	Kaufman himself does not call this an intelligence test, although it is often used in this way. Suitable for children aged 2½ to 12, it includes three tests of *sequential processing* (such as number recall) and seven tests of *simultaneous processing* (including face recognition), combined to provide an overall score based primarily on nonverbal measures. Six achievement subtests can also be given, including vocabulary, riddles, and reading. The test also allows flexible testing procedures, including the use of other languages, alternative wording, and gestures, all of which make the test one of the fairest for ethnic minorities and children from poverty-level families.

At 22 months, Katherine would clearly pass the 17-month item on the Bayley Scales of Infant Development that calls for the child to build a tower of three blocks.

an important question if they want to be able to identify, during infancy, those children who are not developing normally or to predict later intelligence or school performance.

Most "infant IQ tests," such as the widely used **Bayley Scales of Infant Development** (Bayley, 1969, 1993), have been constructed rather like IQ tests for older children in that they include sets of items of increasing difficulty. However, instead of testing school-like skills—skills an infant does not yet have—the items measure primarily sensory and motor skills, such as reaching for a dangling ring (an item for a typical baby at 3 months), putting cubes in a cup on request (9 months), or building a tower of three cubes (17 months). Some more clearly cognitive items are also included, such as uncovering a toy hidden by a cloth, an item used with 8-month-old infants to measure an aspect of object permanence.

Bayley's test and others like it, such as the Denver Developmental Screening Test, have proved helpful in identifying infants and toddlers with serious developmental delays (Lewis & Sullivan, 1985). As a more general predictive tool to forecast later IQ scores or school performance, however, such tests have not been nearly as useful as many had hoped. On the whole, it looks as if what is being measured on typical infant tests is not the same as what is tapped by the commonly used intelligence tests for children and adults (Birney, Citron-Pousty, Lutz, & Sternberg, 2005; Colombo, 1993).

Bayley Scales of Infant Development The best-known and most widely used test of infant "intelligence."

In the United States, virtually all fourth graders—like these in Austin, Texas—are given achievement tests so that schools can compare their students' performance against national norms.

Achievement Tests   Another kind of test of intellectual skill with which you are probably familiar is the achievement test, which nearly all of you have taken in elementary and high school. **Achievement tests** are designed to test specific information learned in school, using items like those in Table 7.2. The child taking an achievement test doesn't end up with an IQ score, but his performance is compared to that of other children in the same grade across the country.

How is an achievement test different from an IQ test? An IQ test is intended to reveal something about how well a child can think and learn, while an achievement test tells something about what a child has already learned. Or to put it another way: Designers of IQ tests thought they were measuring a child's basic capacity (underlying **competence**), while an achievement test is intended to measure what the child has actually learned (**performance**). This is an important distinction. Each of us presumably has some upper limit of ability—what we could do under ideal conditions if we were maximally motivated, healthy, and rested. Yet, since everyday conditions are rarely ideal, people typically perform below their hypothetical ability.

The creators of the widely used IQ tests believed that by standardizing the procedures for administering and scoring the tests, they could come close to measuring competence. But because scientists can never be sure that they are assessing any ability under the best of all possible circumstances, they have to settle for measuring performance at the time the test is taken. What this means in practical terms is that the distinction between IQ tests and achievement tests is one of degree rather than of kind. IQ tests include items that are designed to tap fairly fundamental intellectual processes such as comparison and analysis; achievement tests call for specific information the

achievement test Test designed to assess a child's learning of specific material taught in school, such as spelling or arithmetic computation; in the United States, achievement tests are typically given to all children in designated grades.

competence A person's basic, underlying level of skill, displayed under ideal circumstances. It is not possible to measure competence directly.

performance The behavior shown by a person under real-life rather than ideal circumstances. Even when researchers are interested in competence, all they can ever measure is performance.

TABLE 7.2	Some Sample Items from a Fourth-Grade Achievement Test

Vocabulary

jolly old man

1. angry
2. fat
3. merry
4. sorry

Language Expression

Who wants _____ books?
1. that
2. these
3. them
4. this

Mathematics

What does the "3" in 13 stand for?
1. 3 ones
2. 13 ones
3. 3 tens
4. 13 tens

Reference Skills

Which of these words would be first in ABC order?
1. pair
2. point
3. paint
4. polish

Spelling

Jason took the *cleanest* glass.

right _____ wrong _____

Mathematics Computation

79	149	62
+14	−87	×3

Source: From Comprehensive Tests of Basic Skills, Form S, Reprinted by permission of the publisher, CTB/McGraw-Hill, Del Monte Research Park, Monterey, CA 93940. Copyright © 1973 by McGraw-Hill, Inc. All rights reserved. Printed in the USA.

child has learned in school or elsewhere. Thus, the strong link between IQ and performance on achievement tests calls into question the notion that such tests are good measures of what has been taught and learned in a particular school (see *The Real World*). High scores in one school may simply mean that the students are brighter rather than indicating anything about the quality of the school's curriculum or the methods used by its teachers.

College entrance tests, such as the SAT, fall somewhere in between IQ and achievement tests. They are designed to measure basic "developed abilities," such as the ability to reason with words, rather than specific knowledge. But all three types of tests measure aspects of a child or young person's performance and not his or her competence.

STABILITY OF TEST SCORES

One of the bits of folklore about IQ tests is that a particular IQ score is something you "have," like blue eyes or red hair—that a child who achieves a score of, say, 115 at age 3 will continue to score in about the same range at age 6 or 12 or 20. Psychologists use the term *reliability* to refer to the stability of a test score. By definition, a reliable test yields scores that are stable over time. That is, if a child takes a reliable test several times, her scores will be very similar at each testing. In this sense, IQ scores are, in fact, very stable, although there are also some exceptions to this general rule. One such exception is the weak link between scores on infant IQ tests such as the Bayley Scales and later IQ scores. The typical correlation between a Bayley score at 12 months and a Stanford-Binet IQ score at 4 years is only about .20 to .30 (Bee et al., 1982)—significant but not robust. Newer tests of infant intelligence, such as those based on habituation rates or other basic processes, may ultimately prove to be more helpful predictors of later IQ scores (Colombo, 1993); currently, however, there is no widely used method that allows developmentalists to predict with any reliability which 1-year-olds will later have high or low IQ scores.

However, beginning at about age 3, consistency in performance on IQ tests such as the Stanford-Binet or the WISC-IV increases markedly (Birney et al., 2005). If such a test is taken twice, a few months or a few years apart, the scores are likely to be very similar. The correlations between adjacent-year IQ scores in middle childhood, for example, are typically in the range of .65 to .80 (Bartels, Rietveld, Van Baal, & Boomsma, 2002; Honzik, 1986). Moreover, correlations among IQ scores measured in late childhood, early adolescence, and adulthood are also quite high, typically ranging from .70 to .85, including adult IQs that are measured when people are in their 70s and 80s (Deary, Whiteman, Starr, Whalley, & Fox, 2004; Mortensen, Andresen, Kruuse, Sanders, & Reinisch, 2003). However, many children show quite wide fluctuations in their scores. When children are given IQ tests repeatedly over a period of years, the common finding is that about half show little or no significant fluctuation in their scores while the remaining half show at least small changes from one testing to another, with perhaps 15% showing rather substantial change (Caspi, Harkness, Moffitt, & Silva, 1996; McCall, 1993).

One example comes from a New Zealand longitudinal study in which all 1,037 children born in the town of Dunedin over a 1-year period in the 1970s were followed through childhood and adolescence. Among many other measures, the researchers measured the children's IQs with the WISC every 2 years starting at age 7. They found that over any 2-year period, 10% of the children's IQ scores changed as much as 15 points—a very large change (Caspi et al., 1996). Another 13% showed major changes over longer periods; 15 of the children showed cumulative shifts of more than 50 points over 6 years. In most cases, however, these large shifts represented "bounce" or "rebound" rather than permanent shifts upward or downward. That is, some children seemed to respond to specific life experiences—stresses or special advantages—with a decline or a rise in IQ score. A few years later, their IQ score returned to something closer to the original score.

Using Standardized Tests to Improve Schools

Like many 17-year-olds at the beginning of their senior year of high school, Krystal is looking forward to graduation with eager anticipation. So far, she has passed all of the required courses she has taken, and after graduation she plans to attend a local community college to become a physical therapist. There is just one problem with Krystal's plan. Students in her state are required to pass a standardized test in order to qualify for a high school diploma. Krystal failed the exam the first time she took it during her junior year, so she took the required remedial coursework in summer school and retook the exam. Now she is awaiting the results and hoping that she scored high enough to earn the right to participate in her school's graduation ceremony.

Tests such as the one Krystal had to take represent one of the most recent manifestations of the *test-based school reform movement*, a series of changes in educational policy that have taken place over the past four decades in the United States. These changes have emphasized the use of standardized tests to improve schools (Bond, Braskamp, & Roeber, 1996).

The test-based reform movement, say historians of education, began with the development of the National Assessment of Educational Progress (NAEP). The NAEP, nicknamed "the nation's report card," was designed to compare what American school children know to what experts think they should know. Students are described as performing at the advanced, proficient, or basic level, as indicated in the table.

In 1990, the federal government asked states to voluntarily participate in state-by-state NAEP score reporting. Thirty-seven states agreed, and results were reported in local papers and on TV news programs. The public became accustomed to hearing reports such as "The Nation's Report Card shows that fourth-graders in California are scoring lower than children in most other states on math achievement tests." Such reports raised public concerns about education and increased the demand for instructional reforms. By the late 1990s, these concerns had coalesced into a national "school accountability" movement that continues to be a major political issue. As a result, governments at all levels began moving toward an increased emphasis on standardized testing.

On the national level, the most prominent outgrowth of the test-based reform movement is a comprehensive set of educational reforms known collectively as *No Child Left Behind (NCLB)*, signed into law by President George W. Bush in 2001. These reforms address many aspects of public education, but one overriding theme of the legislation is that standardized testing should play an important role in school improvement (U.S. Department of Education, 2004). NCLB requires that comparative testing programs be developed within local school districts (U.S. Department of Education, 2004). The idea behind this requirement is that parents should be able to use test score information to compare results obtained by students in their own child's school to those achieved by children in other district schools. Moreover, NCLB requires that local school districts allow parents to move their children out of low-scoring schools if they choose to.

However, designing tests that can be used to compare one school to another isn't as simple as it might seem. Before

Such fluctuations, while intriguing, occur against a background of increasing IQ test score stability with age. The general rule of thumb is that the older the child, the more stable the IQ score becomes. Older children may show some fluctuation in scores in response to major stresses such as parental divorce, a change in schools, or the birth of a sibling, but by age 10 or 12, IQ scores are normally quite stable.

Despite the evidence for stability, it is worth pointing out that IQ scores are not etched on a child's forehead at birth. Although these scores do become quite stable in late childhood, individual children can and do shift in response to especially rich or especially impoverished environments or to any stress in their lives (McCall, 1993; Pianta & Egeland, 1994a).

WHAT IQ SCORES PREDICT

The information on long-term stability of IQ test scores reveals something about the reliability of the tests. What about their validity? *Validity* has to do with whether a test is measuring what it is intended to measure. One way to assess a test's validity is to see the test development process can even begin, educators must develop *measurable standards*. An example of a measurable standard is "Fourth-graders will be able to multiply single-digit numbers with 80% proficiency." Many proponents of test-based reform suggest that the creation of such standards is just as important in improving schools as the tests themselves. Analyses show that such standards typically include greater emphasis on fundamental reading, writing, and mathematical skills than existed in a state's schools prior to the implementation of a standards-based testing program (Council on Basic Education, 1998).

Advocates of test-based reform also point out that experimental evidence indicates that students try harder and get higher scores on tests when passing tests is tied to high-stakes outcomes such as high school graduation (DeMars, 2000). And in some states, these tests seem to have had a positive impact on student achievement. For example, the NAEP math scores of Texas school children, especially African American students, increased a great deal in the 1990s as a result of an extensive testing program implemented at all grade levels (Carnoy, Loeb, & Smith, 2001).

However, critics claim that state-mandated tests encourage teachers to restrict what they teach to the content of the tests (Neill, 2000). This problem is made worse, they say, when penalties are attached to low scores. A school in danger of losing money or being closed may force students to memorize things they really don't understand just to improve their test scores.

Other critics point to research demonstrating that average and above-average students learn a great deal when preparing for high-stakes tests, but low-achieving students seem to benefit far less from such approaches (Fuchs et al., 2000). Lack of funding for the mandates associated with legislation such as NCLB is another area of concern often cited (Fair Test, 2004). Furthermore, say critics, despite decades of test-based reform, American public schools continue to turn out thousands of graduates who lack the skills to do college work (Schmidt, 2000). So, the test-based reform movement may have yielded some improvements, but it is hardly a cure-all for the problems of education in the United States.

Level	Description
Advanced	This level signifies superior performance.
Proficient	This level represents solid academic performance for each grade assessed. Students reaching this level have demonstrated competency over challenging subject matter, including subject-matter knowledge, application of such knowledge to real world situations, and analytical skills appropriate to the subject matter.
Basic	This level denotes partial mastery of prerequisite knowledge and skills that are fundamental for proficient work at each grade.

Source: National Center for Education Statistics, 1999.

Questions for Reflection

1. Given that Krystal's grades are satisfactory, do you think that it is fair to require her to pass a standardized test in order to get a high school diploma?
2. If you were the parent of a child whose school received low scores on a standardized test of the type required by NCLB, would you remove your child from the school? Why or why not?

whether scores on that test predict real behavior in a way that makes sense. In the case of IQ tests, the most central question is whether IQ scores predict school performance. That was what Binet originally intended his test to do; that is what all subsequent tests were designed to do. The research findings on this point are quite consistent: The correlation between a child's IQ test score and her grades in school or performance on other school tests typically falls between .45 and .60 (Brody, 1992, 1997; Carver, 1990; Neisser et al., 1996; Peterson, Pihl, Higgins, Seguin, & Tremblay, 2003). A correlation in this range suggests a strong but by no means perfect relationship. It indicates that, on the whole, children with high IQ scores are more likely than their peers with average and low scores to be among the high achievers in school, and those who score low are likely to be among the low achievers. Still, some children with high IQ scores don't shine in school while some children with lower scores do.

IQ scores predict future grades as well as current grades. Preschool children with high IQ scores tend to do better when they enter school than those with lower scores; elementary school children with higher IQ scores do better later in high school. Further, IQ scores predict the total number of years of education a child is likely to complete. Higher-IQ elementary school children are more likely to complete high school and are more likely to decide to go on to college (Brody, 1997).

CRITICAL THINKING ❓

Given the variability in individual IQ scores, does it make sense to select children for special classes, such as classes for the gifted, on the basis of a single test score? How else could you go about choosing students?

Among these high school students, those with higher IQ are not only likely to get better grades, they are more likely to go on to college. Intelligence also adds to a child's resiliency—his ability to survive stress, including poverty.

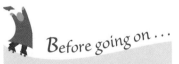

Before going on . . .

- Describe early efforts to measure intelligence.
- What intelligence tests are used today, and how do they differ from the first such tests?
- How stable are IQ scores throughout childhood and adolescence?
- Explain what IQ scores predict.

It is important to point out that these predictive relationships hold within each social class and ethnic group in the United States. Among the poor, among African Americans and Hispanic Americans, and among middle-class white Americans, children with higher IQ are most likely to get good grades, complete high school, and go on to college (Birney et al., 2005; Brody, 1992; Rushton & Jensen, 2005). Such findings have led a number of theorists to argue that intelligence adds to the child's *resilience*—a concept you learned about in Chapter 1. Numerous studies show that poor children—whether they are white American, Hispanic American, African American, or from another minority group—are far more likely to develop the kind of self-confidence and personal competence it takes to move out of poverty if they have higher IQ scores (Luthar & Zigler, 1992; Teachman, Paasch, Day, & Carver, 1997; Werner & Smith, 1992).

At the other end of the scale, low intelligence is associated with a number of negative long-term outcomes, including adult illiteracy, delinquency in adolescence, and criminal behavior in adulthood (Birney et al., 2005; Stattin & Klackenberg-Larsson, 1993). For example, in a 20-year longitudinal study of a group of children born to African American teenage mothers in Baltimore, Nazli Baydar found that the best single predictor of adult literacy or illiteracy was each participant's childhood IQ score (Baydar, Brooks-Gunn, & Furstenberg, 1993). This is not to say that all lower-IQ individuals are illiterate or criminals—obviously that is not the case. But low IQ makes a child more vulnerable, just as high IQ increases a child's resilience.

Clearly, then, IQ tests can be said to be valid. They measure what they purport to measure, which is school performance. However, they do not measure everything. Later in the chapter, you will read about two models, those of Robert Sternberg and Howard Gardner, that place the kind of intelligence measured by IQ tests into a much broader framework that encompasses many other aspects of cognition. And in Chapter 12, you will learn about *emotional intelligence*, a theoretical approach that represents a new way of thinking about children's understanding of their own and others' emotions.

Most importantly, intelligence tests cannot tell you (or a teacher or anyone else) that a child has some specific, fixed, underlying intellectual capacity. Traditional IQ tests also do not measure a whole host of skills that are likely to be highly significant for getting along in the world. IQ tests were originally designed to measure only the specific range of skills that are needed for success in school. They do this reasonably well, so, for this limited purpose, they are valid. But these tests do not predict how well a particular person may perform other cognitive tasks requiring skills such as creativity, insight, "street smarts," or ability to read social cues.

Explaining Individual Differences in IQ Scores

You will not be surprised to discover that the arguments about the origins of differences in IQ test scores nearly always boil down to a dispute about nature versus nurture. When Binet and Simon wrote the first IQ test, they did not assume that intelligence as measured on an IQ test was fixed or inborn. However, many of the American psychologists who revised and promoted the use of IQ tests did believe that intellectual capacity is inherited and largely fixed at birth. Those who hold this view and those who believe that the environment is crucial in shaping a child's intellectual performance have been arguing—often vehemently—for at least 60 years. Both groups can muster research to support their views.

EVIDENCE FOR THE IMPORTANCE OF HEREDITY

Both twin studies and studies of adopted children show strong hereditary influences on IQ scores, as you already know from the *Research Report* in Chapter 1. Identical twins are more like one another in IQ scores than are fraternal twins, and the IQs of adopted children are better predicted from the IQs of their natural parents than from those of their adoptive parents (Brody, 1992; Loehlin, Horn, & Willerman, 1994; Rushton & Jensen, 2005; Scarr, Weinberg, & Waldman, 1993). This is precisely the pattern of correlations we would expect if there were a strong genetic element at work.

EVIDENCE FOR THE IMPORTANCE OF ENVIRONMENT

Adoption studies also provide some strong support for an environmental influence on IQ scores, because the IQ scores of adopted children are clearly affected by the environment in which they have grown up (van IJzendoorn, Juffer, & Poelhuis, 2005). Early studies of adopted children involved mostly children born to poverty-level parents who were adopted into middle-class families. Such children typically have IQ scores 10 to 15 points higher than those of their birth mothers (Scarr et al., 1993), suggesting that the effect of being brought up by a middle-class adoptive family is to raise the child's IQ score. What this finding doesn't indicate is whether a less stimulating adoptive family would lower the test score of a child whose birth parents had average or above-average IQs. Information on that question comes from a French study by Christiane Capron and Michel Duyme (1989), who studied a group of 38 French children, all adopted in infancy. Approximately half of the children had been born to better-educated parents of higher social class, while the other half had been born to working-class or poverty-level parents. Some of the children in each group had then been adopted by higher-social-class parents, and the others by poorer families. Table 7.3 shows the children's IQ scores in adolescence. If you compare the two columns in the table, you can see the effect of rearing conditions: The children reared in upper-class homes had IQ scores that were about 11 points higher than those of children reared in lower-class families, regardless of the social class or education of the birth parents. At the same time, you can see a genetic effect if you compare the two rows in the table: The children born to upper-class parents had higher IQ scores than children from lower-class families, no matter what kind of environment they were reared in.

Social Class Differences This relationship between social class and IQ score, so clear in the Capron and Duyme study, is echoed in a great deal of other research. But just what is meant by *social class*? Every society is divided into social strata of some kind. In Western societies, an individual's social status or social class is typically defined or measured in terms of three dimensions: education, income, and occupation. Thus, a person with more education, a higher income, and a more prestigious occupation has higher status. In other societies, the dimensions of status might be different, but some

TABLE 7.3	IQ Scores at Adolescence for Capron and Duyme's Adopted Children		
		Social Class of Adoptive Parents	
		High	**Low**
Social Class of Biological Parents	**High**	119.60	107.50
	Low	103.60	92.40

Source: From Capron, C., and Duyme, M., "Assessment of Effects of Socio-Economic Status on IQ in a Full Cross-fostering Study," *Nature*, 340, 1969, p. 553. By permission of the publisher, Macmillan Magazines, Ltd. and the authors.

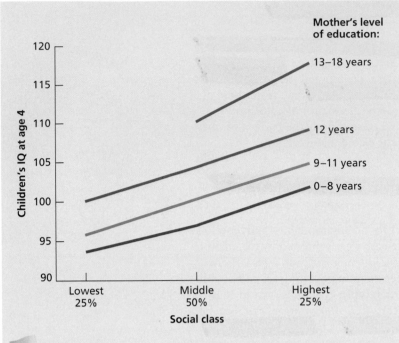

FIGURE 7.2

Each line represents the IQ scores of 4-year-old white children whose mothers had a particular level of education, and whose families fit in one of three broad social class levels. Both elements are obviously related to the child's IQ. (*Source*: Broman et al., 1975, p. 47.)

status differences exist in every society. Distinctions between "blue collar" and "white collar" and between "middle class" and "working class" are fundamentally status distinctions.

Dozens of research studies reveal that children from poor or working-class families, or from families in which the parents are relatively uneducated, have lower average IQ scores than do children from middle-class families (e.g., Gale, O'Callaghan, Godfrey, Law, & Martyn, 2004). You can see this effect particularly vividly in Figure 7.2, which is based on data from a huge national study of more than 50,000 children born in 12 different hospitals around the United States between 1959 and 1966 (Broman, Nichols, & Kennedy, 1975). In order to make sure that the effects are due to social class and not racial differences, the figure shows only the results for white children who were tested with the Stanford-Binet at age 4, a total sample of more than 11,800 children. As you can see, the average IQ score of the children rises as the family's social class rises and as the mother's education rises.

Such differences are not found in the results of standardized tests of infant intelligence such as the Bayley Scales (Golden & Birns, 1983). Later in childhood, test score differences associated with social class appear in most studies (Cox, 1983; Misra, 1983), producing what is sometimes called a **cumulative deficit**. That is, the longer a child lives in poverty, the more negative the effect on IQ test scores and other measures of cognitive functioning (Duncan, 1993; Smith, Brooks-Gunn, & Klebanov, 1997). These cumulative effects are especially large for verbal tests (Jordan, Huttenlocher, & Levine, 1992).

Genetic differences are obviously contributing to the pattern in Figure 7.2, since brighter parents typically acquire more education and better jobs and also pass on their "bright" genes to their children. Clearly, though, environment plays a significant role in accentuating the genetic differences, particularly for those parents who live in poverty. Poverty exerts a significant negative effect on children's IQ scores, over and above what may be contributed by the parents' own genes or the level of enrichment they may provide to their children. As you'll recall from Chapter 4, children born into or living in poverty are at higher risk for prenatal problems and poorer general health. For example, poor children are likely to be exposed to higher levels of lead, and lead exposure is known to be causally linked to lower test scores (Baghurst et al., 1992, 1995; Dietrich, Berger, Succop, Hammond, & Born-Schein, 1993; Tesman & Hills, 1994). Children living in poverty are also more likely to suffer from periodic or chronic nutritional deficits. Developmentalists know that nutrition contributes to lower IQ scores because experimental studies in developing countries show that when children living in poverty are given nutritional supplements in infancy and early childhood, they later have higher IQ scores or vocabularies compared to children who do not receive the supplements (Grigorenko, 2003; Pollitt & Gorman, 1994).

In addition to all these physical factors, real differences in the ways infants and children are treated in poor versus middle-class families are important in cognitive development. It is these differences in early experiences that have been the focus of most of the research on environmental effects on IQ.

cumulative deficit Any difference between groups in IQ or achievement test scores that becomes larger over time.

Specific Family Characteristics and IQ Scores When you read about correlations between poverty and IQ scores, it's easy to get the idea that children in low-income homes are doomed to have below-average intellectual abilities. However, there are several factors that help protect children against the risks associated with poverty. In fact, researchers have found that the quality of parent-child interactions may be a more important factor than income in determining a child's IQ (Robinson, Lanzi, Weinberg, Ramey, & Ramey, 2002). Research has shown that, no matter what the economic status of a child's family is, there are at least five dimensions of family interaction or stimulation that influence her IQ. Parents of children who have higher IQ scores or scores that increase with age tend to do several things:

This kind of rich, complex, stimulating environment is consistently linked to higher IQ scores in children.

■ They provide an interesting and complex physical environment for their children, one that includes play materials that are appropriate for each child's age and developmental level (Bradley et al., 1989; Englund, Luckner, Whaley, & Egeland, 2004; Luster, Lekskul & Oh, 2004; Molfese, DiLalla, & Bunce, 1997; Pianta & Egeland, 1994a). Research on brain development in infancy and childhood, discussed in Chapter 4, makes it clear that such a complex environment in the early months and years is a critical factor in stimulating the retention of greater synaptic density.

■ They are emotionally responsive to and involved with their children. They respond warmly and appropriately to a child's behavior, smiling when the child smiles, reacting when the child speaks, answering the child's questions, and responding to the child's cues in myriad other ways (Barnard et al., 1989; La Paro, Justice, Skibbe, & Pianta, 2004; Lewis, 1993; Murray & Hornbaker, 1997).

■ They talk to their children often, using language that is diverse, descriptive, and accurate (Fewell & Deutscher, 2003; Hart & Risley, 1995; Sigman et al., 1988).

■ When they play with or interact with their children, they operate in what Vygotsky referred to as the zone of proximal development (described in Chapter 1), aiming their conversation, their questions, and their assistance at a level that is just above the level the children could manage on their own, thus helping the children to master new skills (e.g., Landry, Garner, Swank, & Baldwin, 1996; Tamis-LeMonda, Shannon, Cabrera, & Lamb, 2004).

■ They avoid excessive restrictiveness, punitiveness, or control, instead giving their children room to explore, even opportunities to make mistakes (Bradley et al., 1989; Murray & Hornbaker, 1997; Olson, Bates, & Kaskie, 1992). In a similar vein, they ask questions rather than giving commands (Hart & Risley, 1995).

■ They expect their children to do well and to develop rapidly. They emphasize and encourage school achievement (Englund et al., 2004; Entwisle & Alexander, 1990).

You may have figured out the methodological problem in research on parent-child interactions: the same problem that surfaces in comparisons of the IQs of children in families that differ in social class. Because parents provide both the genes and the environment, it isn't clear that these environmental factors are really causally important. Perhaps these are simply the environmental features provided by brighter parents, and it is their genes and not the environment that cause the higher IQ scores in their children. The way around this problem is to look at the link between environmental factors and IQ in adopted children. In fact, the few studies of this type do point to the same critical environmental features. That is, adoptive parents who behave in the ways listed above have adopted children who score higher on IQ tests (Plomin, Leohlin, & DeFries, 1985; van IJzendoorn et al., 2005).

Differences in Environments within Families Within families, the experiences of individual children also differ in ways that affect IQ test scores. Being the oldest of a large family, for example, is a very different experience from being the youngest or being in the middle; being the only girl in a family of boys is different from being a girl with only sisters. Psychologists are just beginning to study these within-family

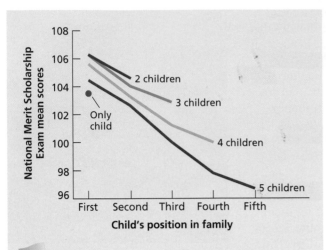

FIGURE 7.3

These data from the 1965 National Merit Scholarship Examination show the commonly found relationship between test scores and family size and birth order. Within each family size, the average score is highest for the first-born and declines with each position in the birth-order sequence.

(*Sources*: Data from Breland, 1974, recalculated by Storter, 1990, Table 7, p. 32.)

variables. Thus far, they have been looking mostly at obvious differences, such as the number of children in a family or the child's position within the family, both of which seem to be at least slightly related to a child's IQ score. (You will read more about the impact of family size and birth order on children's development in Chapter 13.) On average, the more children in a family, the lower the IQ scores of the children. And, on average, first-born children have the highest IQ scores, with average scores declining steadily down the birth order (Zajonc, 1983; Zajonc & Marcus, 1975; Zajonc & Mullally, 1997). Children who are born very close together also have slightly lower IQ scores on average than do those born further apart (Storter, 1990). One fairly typical set of data is illustrated in Figure 7.3, which is based on scores of nearly 800,000 students who took the National Merit Scholarship Examination in 1965, with the scores converted to the equivalent of IQ scores.

It is important to note two points about results like those in Figure 7.3. First, these differences are found consistently when IQ scores are averaged over many children or adults. However, when you look at individual families, the pattern is much weaker or not obvious at all. (Similarly, researchers know that if they compare large groups of smokers and nonsmokers, the smokers have a much higher probability of developing lung cancer than the nonsmokers, but this doesn't mean that every smoker will develop cancer [Zajonc & Mullally, 1997].) So you should be careful about extrapolating the aggregated data illustrated in Figure 7.3 to your own family or to other individual families. Some significant effect of birth order is detectable with large samples, but that particular effect may or may not be present in an individual family.

A second point about birth-order comparisons is that the absolute differences in IQ scores are not huge, even in the aggregated data. Still, this pattern has been observed repeatedly, in Europe as well as in the United States, leaving developmentalists with a puzzle. Why would such a pattern occur? Robert Zajonc's hypothesis is that, on average, the birth of each succeeding child "dilutes" the intellectual climate of the home. The oldest child initially interacts only with adults (parents) and thus has the most complex and enriching environment possible in that family at that time. Second or later children, in contrast, experience a lower average intellectual level simply because they interact with both other children and adults.

Some developmentalists have suggested that cultural beliefs about the significance of birth order may be just as important as any "dilution" that may occur as family size increases (Herrera, Zajonc, Wieczorkowska, & Cichomski, 2003). For example, many first-born sons in Europe and North America are named after their fathers. This practice, known as *namesaking*, may influence the expectations that adults have for the child. These expectations may, in turn, cause adults to do a better job of supporting the namesaked child's intellectual development than that of a later-born child (McAndrew, King, & Honoroff, 2002). Likewise, among the Balinese, standard syllables signifying children's birth rank are added to their names. The rationale for this practice is that the higher a child's birth rank, the greater the status he or she must be afforded by members of the culture. As a result, every person a child meets instantly knows his or her status and the cultural prescriptions regarding how he or she is to be treated. Similarly, cultural beliefs about only children may influence the way parents and teachers treat them, thereby indirectly affecting their intellectual development. For instance, only children are widely believed to be spoiled, self-centered, and disliked by their peers. Expectations for only children based on these beliefs may help explain why, in most studies, they do not display the advantages of other first-borns.

SCHOOL EXPERIENCE AND SPECIAL INTERVENTIONS

Home environments and family interactions are not the only sources of environmental influence. Many young children also spend a very large amount of time in day care, special programs like Head Start, or preschool. How much effect do these environments have on a child's intellectual performance?

Answers to this question are of theoretical interest because they may reveal something about the general effects of early experience and about the resiliency of children. Are the effects of an initially impoverished environment permanent, or can they be offset by an enriched experience, such as a special preschool? In Aslin's terms (refer back to Figure 1.1, p. 9), the question is whether special programs can produce *attunement*—a permanent gain over the level of performance the child would have shown without the added enrichment. On a practical level, programs like Head Start are based on the assumption that it is possible to modify the trajectory of a child's intellectual development, especially with early intervention.

Children who have attended Head Start programs like this one don't show permanent increases in IQ, but they are less likely to repeat a grade or to be assigned to special education classes.

Attempts to test this assumption have led to a messy body of research. In particular, children are rarely assigned randomly to Head Start or non–Head Start groups, so interpretation is difficult (Ripple & Zigler, 2003). Still, researchers agree generally on the effects. Children enrolled in Head Start or other enriched preschool programs show a gain of about 10 IQ points during the year of the Head Start experience compared to similar children without such experience. This IQ gain typically fades and then disappears within the first few years of elementary school (Ripple & Zigler, 2003; Zigler & Styfco, 1993). However, recent research suggests that the contributions made by Head Start teachers to children's beliefs about their ability to attain educational goals continue to be evident in adolescence (Slaughter-Defoe & Rubin, 2001).

On other measures, a clear residual effect can be seen as well. Children with Head Start or other quality preschool experience are less likely to be placed in special education classes, somewhat less likely to repeat a grade, and somewhat more likely to graduate from high school (Darlington, 1991; Haskins, 1989). They also are healthier, have better immunization rates, and show better school adjustment than their peers (Ripple & Zigler, 2003; Zigler & Styfco, 1993). In addition, Head Start programs provide a useful context for identifying and helping children who exhibit behavior patterns, such as aggression, that put them at risk for adjustment difficulties in elementary school (Kamps, Tankersley, & Ellis, 2000). So although poor children with preschool experience typically do not test much higher on standardized achievement tests (and, in most studies, do not have higher IQ scores) than their peers who did not attend preschool, they function better in school. When some kind of supportive intervention continues into the early years of elementary school or when the elementary school is of good quality, the beneficial effects of preschool or Head Start on school performance are even clearer (Currie & Thomas, 1997; Reynolds, 1994; Zigler & Styfco, 1993).

Furthermore, the one study that has looked at adult outcomes of such preschool attendance suggests lasting effects. Young adults who had attended a particularly good experimental preschool program, the Perry Preschool Project in Milwaukee, had higher rates of high school graduation, lower rates of criminal behavior, lower rates of unemployment, and a lower probability of being on welfare than did their peers who did not have the advantage of the preschool experience (Barnett, 1993). Thus, the potential effects of such early education programs may be broad—even though the programs appear to have no lasting effect on standardized IQ test scores (Ripple & Zigler, 2003).

Note that the Perry Preschool Project was not a Head Start program, so developmentalists have no equivalent information about children who have attended Head Start. Thus, they can't be sure that the long-term effects of Head Start would be as great as in the Perry Project, although it is reasonable to expect that well-run, comprehensive Head Start programs would have similar effects (Zigler & Styfco, 1996).

Overall, despite the bits of encouraging information, sweeping assertions about the benefits of Head Start should not be made. Edward Zigler—the nation's leading expert on Head Start—says, "Early childhood intervention alone cannot transform lives. Its positive effects can be overpowered by the longer and larger experience of growing up in poverty" (Zigler & Styfco, 1996, p. 152). Programs like Head Start are well worth public support, but no one should expect them to solve all problems. Indeed, research suggests that schooling can affect IQ scores at any age, so even if Head Start appears to provide only a small "push" toward improvement when its effects are measured at early ages, it is still likely that the benefits gained in early childhood will form a foundation for continuing improvement during the elementary years and beyond.

More promising still—although far more expensive and complex—are enrichment programs that begin in infancy rather than at age 3 or 4. IQ scores of poverty-level children who have attended such very early programs do show an attunement effect: The scores remain elevated even after the intervention has ended—a result that might be expected, given what psychologists now know about the importance of early stimulation for the growth of neural connections in the brain. The best-designed and most meticulously reported of such infancy interventions has been carried out by Craig Ramey and his colleagues at the University of North Carolina (Burchinal, Campbell, Bryant, Wasik, & Ramey, 1997; Campbell, Pungello, Miler-Johnson, Burchinal, & Ramey, 2001; Campbell & Ramey, 1994; Ramey, 1993; Ramey & Campbell, 1987; Ramey & Ramey, 2004). Infants from poverty-level families whose mothers had low IQ scores were randomly assigned either to a special day-care program, 8 hours a day, 5 days a week, or to a control group that received nutritional supplements and medical care but no special enriched day care. The special day-care program, which began when the infants were 6 to 12 weeks of age and lasted until they began kindergarten, involved the kinds of optimal stimulation described earlier. When they reached kindergarten age, half the children in each group were enrolled in a special supplemental program that focused on family support and increasing educational activities at home. The remaining children had only the normal school experience.

The average IQ scores of the children at various ages are shown in Figure 7.4. You can see that the IQ scores of the children who had been enrolled in the special day-care program were higher at every age, whether they were in the school-age supplementary program or not, although the scores for both groups declined in the elementary school years. What is not shown in the figure but is perhaps more practically significant is the fact that 44.0% of the control group children had IQ scores classified as borderline or retarded (scores below 85), compared to only 12.8% of the children who had been in the special day-care program. In addition, the enriched infant-care group had significantly higher scores on both reading and mathematics achievement tests at age 12 and were only half as likely to have repeated a grade (Campbell & Ramey, 1994). And a follow-up study of the participants at age 21 revealed that the early advantage associated with participation in the program persisted into young adulthood (Campbell et al., 2001).

Ramey also gained insight from the varying experiences of the children in the control group. Some of them had been reared primarily at home; others had spent periods of time in other types of day-care or preschool programs. When he compared the IQ scores of these two groups with those who had been in the special day-care program, he found a consistent rank order: Children in the special program had the highest scores, followed by those who had had some kind of day-care experience, with those reared entirely at home having the lowest. The IQ scores at age 4 for these three groups were 101.1, 94.0, and 84.2, respectively (Burchinal, Lee, & Ramey, 1989). So the length and quality of the intervention appeared to be directly related to the size of the effect. Other researchers have confirmed the basic conclusion that the most effective programs are those that begin early and provide consistent, frequent stimulation (Ramey & Ramey, 1998, 2004).

CRITICAL THINKING ❓

Considering the results of Ramey's study, would you be in favor of providing enriched day care to all infants from high-risk or poverty-level families? What are the arguments, pro and con?

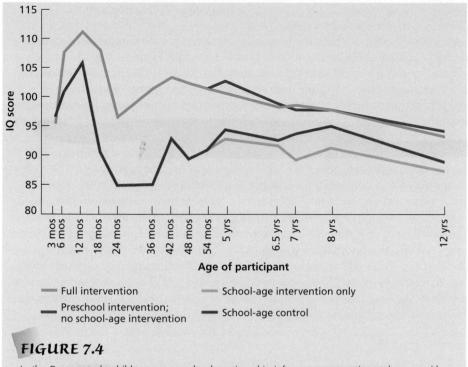

FIGURE 7.4

In the Ramey study, children were randomly assigned in infancy to an experimental group with special day care (the "full intervention" group) or to a control group. From kindergarten through third grade, half of each group received supplementary family support, while the other half received none. Thus, the "preschool intervention" group had the intervention for 5 years, but nothing beyond that; the "school-age intervention" group had no intervention before school age but did have assistance in early elementary school. The difference in IQ between the intervention and control groups remained statistically significant even at age 12.

(*Source*: Campbell, F. A., and Ramey, C. T., "Effects of achievement: A follow-up study of children from low-income families," Fig. 1, p. 690, *Child Development*, 65 (1994), 684–698. By permission of the Society for Research in Child Development.)

INTERACTIONS OF HEREDITY AND ENVIRONMENT

Putting together all the information about the influence of heredity and environment on IQ scores makes it clear that both factors are highly significant. Studies around the world consistently yield estimates that about half the variation in IQ scores within any population is due to heredity (Neisser et al., 1996; Plomin & Rende, 1991; Rogers, Rowe, & May, 1994; Rushton & Jensen, 2005). The remaining half is clearly due to environment or to interactions between environment and heredity.

One useful way to think about this interaction is with the idea of a **reaction range**—a range within upper and lower boundaries of possible functioning established by one's genes. Where a child's IQ score falls within those boundaries is determined by environment. Richard Weinberg (1989) estimates that the reaction range for IQ scores is about 20 to 25 points. That is, given a specific genetic heritage (a genotype), a child's actual IQ test performance (the phenotype) may vary by as much as 20 or 25 points, depending on the richness or poverty of the environment in which the child grows up. When a child's environment is improved, the child moves closer to the upper end of his reaction range. When the environment becomes worse, the child's effective intellectual performance falls toward the lower end of his reaction range. Thus, even though a reaction range of intelligence (as measured with an IQ test) is highly heritable, the IQ score within that range is determined by environment. Research showing that the IQ scores of identical twins are more weakly correlated in poor families than in those with

reaction range Term used by some psychologists for the range of possible outcomes (phenotypes) for some variable, given basic genetic patterning (the genotype). In the case of IQ scores, the reaction range is estimated at 20 to 25 points.

more economic resources amply demonstrates this idea (Turkheimer, Haley, Waldron, D'Onofrio, & Gottesman, 2003).

We could also think about the interaction between heredity and environment in terms rather like those Horowitz used in his model (recall Figure 1.3, p. 13), or we could use Aslin's concept of maintenance. Some theorists (Turkheimer & Gottesman, 1991) have argued that within the normal range of environments, IQ scores may be largely a function of heredity, not because environment is unimportant but simply because most environments are sufficiently rich to support or maintain normal intellectual development. It is only when environmental quality falls below some crucial threshold that it has a major effect on the level of measured IQ, as might be true for children reared in an orphanage or in a severely impoverished environment. This view does not necessarily contradict the concept of a reaction range. Rather, the argument is that the lower end of any given child's reaction range is likely to be manifested only if the child is reared in an environment that falls below the critical threshold. If we think about the effect of environment in this way, it makes sense that special programs like Ramey's are effective for children from poverty-level environments, since such a program improves the child's environment to the point that it adequately supports normal intellectual development. The same program provided to a child from a more enriched family environment, however, should have little or no effect on IQ scores—which is essentially what researchers have found.

Before going on . . .

- What do twin studies suggest about the heritability of IQ scores?
- How do social class and family environment affect IQ scores?
- In what ways do school experience and early interventions affect IQ scores and school performance?
- Describe some possible models for examining interactions between heredity and environment.

Explaining Group Differences in IQ or Achievement Test Scores

So far, we have sidestepped a difficult issue: group differences in IQ or achievement test scores. Because group differences have powerful personal and political ramifications and can easily be blown out of proportion, it's important not to place too much emphasis on them and to point out that individual variation in IQ and achievement is far greater than variation across groups. But you should be aware of what psychologists know, what they don't know, and how they explain these group differences.

RACIAL DIFFERENCES

Evidence points to several racial differences in intellectual performance (Rushton & Jensen, 2005). First, Asian and Asian American students typically test 3 to 6 points higher on IQ tests and do consistently better on achievement tests (especially math and science tests) than do Caucasian children (Geary, 1996; Geary, Bow-Thomas, Liu, & Siegler, 1996; Stevenson et al., 1990; Sue & Okazaki, 1990; Williams & Ceci, 1997). More troubling for researchers and theorists is the finding that in the United States, African American children consistently score lower than Caucasian children on standard measures of intelligence. This difference, which is on the order of 12 IQ points, is not found on infant tests of intelligence or on measures of infant habituation rate (Fagan & Singer, 1983), but it becomes apparent by the time children are 2 or 3 years old (Brody, 1992; Peoples, Fagan, & Drotar, 1995; Rushton & Jensen, 2005). There is some indication that the size of the IQ difference between African American and Caucasian children declined during the 1970s and 1980s and may now be less than 10 points (Neisser et al., 1996; Williams & Ceci, 1997). A noticeable difference persists.

Some scientists, while acknowledging that the environments of the two groups are, on average, substantially different, nonetheless argue that the IQ score difference must reflect some genetic differences between the races (Jensen, 1980; Rushton & Jensen, 2005). Other scientists, even granting that IQ is highly heritable, point out that a

10- or 12-point difference falls well within the presumed reaction range of IQ. They emphasize that there are sufficiently large differences in the environments in which African American and white American children are typically reared to account for the average difference in score (Brody, 1992). African American children are more likely to be born with low birth weight, more likely to suffer from inadequate nutrition, more likely to have high blood levels of lead, and less likely to be read to or provided with a wide range of intellectual stimulation. Each of these environmental variations is known to be linked to lower IQ scores.

Further evidence for the environmental hypothesis comes from studies of Asian American families, who tend to emphasize academic achievement more than either African American or white families. As teens, Asian Americans prioritize their time differently than do adolescents in other groups: Family and school take precedence over social activities with peers (Fuligni, Yip, & Tseng, 2002). Such differences have been cited in explanations of Asian American children's higher IQ scores.

Cultural differences also clearly contribute to observed differences between African American and Caucasian children's test scores, as African American psychologists have long pointed out (e.g., Ogbu, 1994, 2004). One such cultural effect is discussed in the *Research Report*. We can see such differences at work in the way children from different subcultures respond to the testing situation itself. For example, in a classic study of adopted African American children, Moore (1986) found that those who had been reared in white families (and thus imbued with the values of the majority culture) not only had a higher average IQ score than those adopted into African American families (117 versus 103) but also approached the IQ-testing situation quite differently. They stayed more focused on the tasks and were more likely to try some task even if they didn't think they could do it. African American children adopted into middle-class African American families did not show this pattern of persistence and effort. They asked for help more often and gave up more easily when faced with a difficult task. When Moore then observed each adoptive mother teaching her child several tasks, he could see parallel differences. The white mothers were more encouraging and less likely to give the child the answer than were the African American mothers.

Findings like these suggest that the observed IQ differences among racial or ethnic groups are primarily a reflection of the fact that IQ tests and schools are designed by the majority culture to promote a particular form of intellectual activity and that many African American or other minority families rear their children in ways that do not promote or emphasize this particular set of skills. Consequently, some developmentalists have argued for banning intelligence testing altogether. However, most psychologists agree that there are still some good reasons for using IQ tests, as long as their limitations are understood. Likewise, studies examining a new approach to individualized assessment suggest that it may be possible for psychologists who are testing children from disadvantaged backgrounds to duplicate the test-familiarity advantage of middle-class children in the testing situation itself. In *dynamic assessment*, children are informed about the purpose of an intelligence test and are given a chance to practice with each kind of problem-solving task on the test prior to actually being tested. Studies show that dynamic assessment significantly increases the proportion of minority children who attain above-average scores (Lidz & Macrine, 2001). Further, whenever possible, intelligence testing of ethnic minority children should be carried out by testing professionals with ethnic backgrounds similar to those of the children being tested. Research has shown that children from minority groups get better scores under such conditions (Kim, Baydar, & Greek, 2003).

CROSS-CULTURAL DIFFERENCES

Awareness of different emphases is also helpful in understanding variations in intelligence test scores across cultures. Many cross-cultural psychologists have argued that comparisons of IQ scores across cultures are meaningless, because each culture

Stereotype Threat

Suppose that on the first day of class, your professor says that women usually get higher grades than men in child development courses. Do you think such a statement will cause male students to slack off? If so, you are in agreement with the central hypothesis of a perspective known as *stereotype threat theory.*

Stereotype threat theory was first proposed by psychologists Claude Steele and Joshua Aronson (Steele & Aronson, 1995). Stereotype threat is a subtle sense of pressure that members of a particular group feel when they are attempting to perform well in an area in which their group is characterized by a negative stereotype. According to Steele and Aronson, African American students experience stereotype threat whenever they are faced with an important cognitive test, such as a college entrance exam or an IQ test, because of the general cultural stereotype that African Americans are less intellectually able than members of other groups. In order to avoid confirming the stereotype, says the theory, African Americans avoid putting forth their best effort because to fail after having put forth one's best effort would mean that the stereotype was true.

In their seminal study of stereotype threat, Steele and Aronson (1995) randomly assigned African American and white college students to groups that were given different descriptions of a test they were about to take. In the "threat" condition, students were told that the test measured general intellectual ability. In the "non-threat" condition, participants were led to believe that the test was designed to tap problem-solving skills and were assured that the test was unrelated to general intellectual ability. As you can see in the graph on the facing page, African American and white students' scores differed in the threat condition but not in the non-threat condition.

Over the past ten years, numerous studies have confirmed the existence of stereotype threat (Steele & Aronson, 2004; Suzuki & Aronson, 2005). As a result, stereotype threat has become an integral part of most cultural explanations of racial group differences in scores on cognitive tests. However, the notion that stereotype threat can account for such group differences is not without its critics. Perhaps the most important criticisms have been offered by a team of researchers at the University of Minnesota led by psychologist Paul Sackett (Sackett, Hardison, & Cullen, 2004a, 2005). These researchers point out that statistical techniques used in Steele and Aronson's original study equated the experimental and control groups with regard to intellectual ability. Thus, their study demonstrated that a stereotype threat manipulation can induce differences among people who are actually equal in intellectual ability; their findings did not show that removing stereotype threat would cause groups who were unequal to perform equally. For their part, Steele and Aronson (2004) agree that stereotype threat cannot possibly provide a full explanation for group differences on cognitive tests, but they do believe that the variable will ultimately be found to be an important component of a complete explanation.

In addition, Philippe Rushton and Arthur Jensen (2005), two of the most ardent advocates of the genetic explanation of racial differences, claim that group differences in IQ scores show up in early childhood, long before children's social-cognitive development would allow them to be vulnerable to stereotype threat. They cite Steele's own outline of stereotype threat theory in support of their position. Steele says that individuals

emphasizes different aspects of intelligence in child-rearing practices (Mishra, 1997). Further, each develops its own methods of assessing individual differences in these aspects of intelligence, which are tied to the society's beliefs about the relative importance of different kinds of skills. Consequently, in the industrialized world, tests of intelligence look very much like achievement tests (as you learned earlier), because school performance is the primary arena in which children are expected to apply their intellectual abilities. Thus, using such tests to measure intelligence in a culture where children are expected to use their cognitive gifts differently is invalid.

Because of the difficulty inherent in developing tests that provide comparable scores across very different cultures, research attempting to directly compare the intelligence of individuals in one culture to that of those in another has generally been restricted to comparisons of industrialized societies. For example, several studies have found that Chinese, Japanese, and Korean children tend to score slightly higher on traditional intelligence tests than do their American and European counterparts (Lynn, 1991; Lynn & Song, 1992; Rushton & Jensen, 2005).

would have to be aware of negative stereotypes and be sensitive to the relevance of a test to their own self-esteem before their performance could be affected by stereotype threat. Thus, two questions must be answered before developmentalists can determine whether stereotype threat theory might explain group differences in test scores among children. First, researchers must find out whether children are aware of negative stereotypes. Second, researchers need to know whether children believe that negative stereotypes might be applied to them on the basis of their test performance.

Researchers Clark McKown and Rhona Weinstein (2003), of the University of California, Berkeley, have taken the first steps toward answering these two questions. In their initial study, McKown and Weinstein found that some children as young as 6 years of age were aware of negative stereotypes. Their research also revealed that children in groups that are often the target of such stereotypes, such as African Americans, were more aware of them than children in non-stigmatized groups. Still, not until age 8 or so were a majority of the children in the study aware of negative stereotypes. Further, when McKown and Weinstein replicated the Steele and Aronson study with groups of 6- to 11-year-olds, they found that group differences in the threat condition were much smaller than those Steele and Aronson had found among college students. Consequently, while the power of stereotype threat to influence adults' performance on cognitive tests has been well established by researchers, the jury is still out with regard to its importance in explaining group differences among children.

Finally, Sackett and his colleagues have raised concerns about the degree to which the importance of stereotype threat has been misinterpreted in the popular press and in introductory psychology textbooks (Sackett, Hardinson, & Cullen, 2004b). Often, they say, Steele and Aronson's findings are presented in ways that cause naive individuals to believe that racial differences would disappear if somehow stereotype threat could be eliminated. In some cases, the inference has been drawn that scientists should refrain from publishing or even discussing racial group differences so as not to engender feelings of stereotype threat among members of minority groups.

By contrast, continued discussion of these differences serves to accentuate the need for more research on the topic and to affirm the practical utility of research aimed at identifying environmental, and presumably malleable, factors that may explain racial group differences.

Questions for Critical Analysis

1. If discussion of group differences in intelligence test scores contributes to racial prejudice, do you think society would be better off if researchers stopped trying to discover the causes for them? Why or why not?
2. How might parents and teachers moderate the effects of stereotype threat on children's test performance?

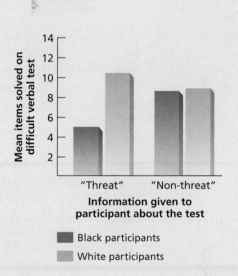

Source: From "A threat in the air: How stereotypes shape intellectual identity and performance" by Claude M. Steele, *American Psychologist*, 52 (June 1997), p. 621, Fig. 2. © 1992 American Psychological Association. Reprinted within guidelines of the American Psychological Association and by permission of the author.

However, cross-national comparisons of intellectual skills have focused more on the domains of math and science achievement than on IQ scores. The reason for this focus is that cross-national studies have often found that children in the United States demonstrate substantially lower levels of performance in these areas than children in other industrialized nations (Caslyn, Gonzales, & Frase, 1999; National Center for Education Statistics [NCES], 2000). These comparisons have focused on Asian children because their scores have been found to be significantly higher than those of children in other nations.

Harold Stevenson and others have argued that the differences between Asian and American children in performance on mathematics achievement tests result not from genetic differences in capacity, but from differences in cultural emphasis on the importance of academic achievement, in the number of hours spent on homework, and in the quality of math instruction in the schools (Chang & Murray, 1995; Geary, 1996; Schneider, Hieshima, Lee, & Plank, 1994; Stevenson & Lee, 1990; Stigler, Lee, & Stevenson, 1987). For example, Singaporean parents start teaching their children about numbers and mathematical reasoning long before the children begin school (Sharpe, 2002).

Moreover, teachers in Asian nations take a different approach to mathematics instruction than do teachers in the United States. For example, James Stigler and Harold Stevenson (1991) observed teaching practices in 120 classrooms in Japan, Taiwan, and the United States. Asian teachers typically devoted an entire class period to a single type of problem. In U.S. classrooms, in contrast, teachers rarely spent 30 or 60 minutes on a single coherent math or science lesson involving the whole class of children and a single topic. Instead, they shifted often from one topic to another during a single math or science lesson. They might do a brief bit on addition, then talk about measurement, then about telling time, and then shift back to addition. Stigler and Stevenson also found striking differences in the amount of time teachers spent leading instruction for the whole class. In the U.S. classrooms they observed, group instruction occurred only 49% of the time; it occurred 74% of the time in Japan and 91% of the time in Taiwan. More recent studies have produced similar findings (NCES, 2003c).

Asian and American math instruction also differs with respect to emphasis on *computational fluency*, the degree to which an individual can automatically produce solutions to simple calculation problems. A number of mathematicians and professors of mathematics have claimed that American math instruction has been influenced more by fads than by a sound understanding of the role of computational fluency in mathematical problem-solving (Murray, 1998). They point out that research has demonstrated that computational fluency is related both to calculation skills and to facility in solving word problems (Geary et al., 1999; Kail & Hall, 1999).

Asian and American cultures differ with respect to beliefs about achievement as well. For example, developmentalists have found that North American parents and teachers emphasize innate ability, which they assume to be unchangeable, more than they emphasize effort. For Asians, the emphasis is just the opposite: They believe that people can become more capable by working harder (Serpell & Hatano, 1997). Because of these differences in beliefs, some developmentalists claim, Asian parents and teachers have higher expectations for children and are better at finding ways to motivate them to do schoolwork.

Another difference between Asian and American schools, especially at the elementary level, involves the use of rewards. Because of the influence of Skinner's operant conditioning theory on education in the United States, teachers commonly use material rewards, such as stickers, to motivate children. Such rewards may be effective when they are unexpected and tied to high standards (Deci, Koestner, & Ryan, 1999; Eisenberger, Pierce, & Cameron, 1999). Giving a surprise sticker to the only child in a class who gets a grade of 100 on a spelling test is an example of this approach to using rewards. However, when teachers use such rewards routinely to try to motivate children to do everyday tasks, such as turning in homework, they clearly undermine both intrinsic motivation and interest in the tasks to which the stickers are linked (Deci et al., 1999). So, Asian students may be more intrinsically motivated to achieve because they are provided with fewer material rewards; achievement itself is their reward.

In elementary school, girls get better grades and higher scores on achievement tests than do boys. What explanations can you think of for such a difference?

SEX DIFFERENCES

Comparisons of overall IQ test scores for boys and girls do not reveal consistent differences. It is only when researchers break down the overall score into several subscores that reflect separate skills that some patterns of sex differences emerge (Lippa, 2005). On average, girls are slightly better at verbal tasks. Boys, on the other hand, are somewhat better at numerical reasoning, a difference that becomes clearer on tests in high school, when reasoning problems make up a larger portion of math exams.

Sex differences in spatial abilities are also found regularly and are evident in the early preschool years (Levine, Huttenlocher, Taylor, & Langrock, 1999). Boys have somewhat higher average scores on tests of spatial visualization, such as those illustrated in Figure 7.5. On measures of mental rotation, like that illustrated in part (c) of the figure, the sex difference is substantial and becomes larger with age (Eagly, 1995; Karadi, Szabo, Szepesi, Kallai, & Kovacs, 1999; Lippa, 2005; Voyer, Voyer, & Bryden, 1995). Differences in such abilities are manifested in everyday tasks such as route learning. In learning to follow a new way to get from one place to another, both preschool and elementary school boys make fewer errors than girls (Beilstein & Wilson, 2000).

Of course, even on tests of mental rotation, the two distributions overlap. That is, some girls and women are good at this type of task, while some boys and men are not. Still, the average difference is quite large. The fact that girls score lower on such tests does not mean that no women are qualified for occupations that demand such skill, such as being an architect or engineer. Indeed, there are many girls who display exceptional levels of spatial ability, and the link between spatial ability and skills such as model building is just as strong for girls as for boys (Brosnan, 1998). However, the difference in boys' and girls' averages on tests of spatial ability does mean that fewer girls or young women will be able to meet the training requirements for such jobs.

Where might such differences come from? The explanatory options should be familiar by now. Biological influences have been most often suggested as the cause of sex differences in spatial abilities (Newcombe & Baenninger, 1989). Specifically, boys show greater coherence in brain function in areas of the brain devoted to spatial tasks, while girls display more organized functioning in parts of the brain where language and social information are processed (Hanlon, Thatcher, & Cline, 1999). Advocates of this position also point out that research with adults has demonstrated that hormonal differences between men and women, as well as hormonal variations among women, are linked to performance on spatial tasks (Halpern & Tan, 2001; Josephs, Newman, Brown, & Beer, 2003). As a result, some argue that hormonal differences between boys and girls or hormonal variations in the prenatal environment may affect spatial abilities.

More purely environmental explanations have also been prominent in discussions of the sex differences in mathematical or verbal reasoning. For instance, longitudinal studies have shown that parents' beliefs about their children's talents at age 6 predict those children's beliefs about their own abilities at age 17 (Fredricks & Eccles, 2002). Thus, findings regarding parental attitudes towards sons' and daughters' performance on mathematics tests may help explain sex differences in this area. For one, parents are more likely to describe sons as competent in mathematics (Furnham 2000; Tiedemann, 2000). Parents are also more likely to characterize a daughter who performs well in math classes as a "hard worker," while a son who does well in mathematics is often described as "talented" (Räty, Vänskä, Kasanen, & Kärk Käinen, 2002). Not surprisingly, when children reach high school age, their self-descriptions mirror the beliefs expressed by parents of young children. That is, boys say that natural ability enables them

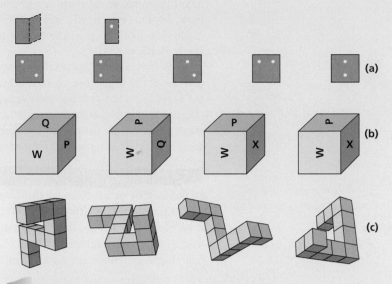

FIGURE 7.5

Three examples of spatial ability tasks. (a) *Spatial visualization*. The figure at the top represents a square piece of paper being folded. A hole is punched through all the thicknesses of the folded paper. Which figure shows what the paper looks like when it is unfolded? (b) *Spatial orientation*. Compare the three cubes on the right with the one on the left. No letter appears on more than one face of a given cube. Which of the three cubes on the right could be a different view of the cube on the left? (c) *Mental rotation*. In each pair, can the three-dimensional objects be made congruent by rotation?

(*Source*: D. Halpern, *Sex Differences in Cognitive Abilities*, Figures 3.1 and 3.2, pp. 50 and 52. © 1986 by Lawrence Erlbaum Associates, Inc. By permission of the publisher and author.)

CRITICAL THINKING

A lot of effort has been spent trying to explain possible sex differences in mathematical ability. What are the practical implications of viewing such differences as genetic versus viewing them as caused by environmental factors?

to get good scores on math tests, while girls say that they "work hard" to do so (Reis & Park, 2001). Thus, it isn't surprising that even the most mathematically talented girls are far less likely to aspire to careers in math and science than are boys (Webb, Lubinski, & Benbow, 2002).

Environmental explanations notwithstanding, it is clear that males far outnumber females at the highest levels of mathematical giftedness, often quantified as scores in the top 1% on tests of quantitative reasoning, such as the math portion of the SAT (Lippa, 2005). Researchers have yet to find an adequate explanation for this sex difference. However, recent findings suggest that the disproportionate male to female ratio among the mathematically gifted may be but one manifestation of a larger phenomenon, that of greater variability among males than females. In other words, there are more males than females at the highest levels of mathematical ability, but the same is probably true of lowest levels (Deary, Thorpe, Wilson, Starr, & Whalley, 2003). Such findings do not constitute an explanation for sex differences in mathematical giftedness. However, they do help us conceptualize these differences more dispassionately— that is, as "differences" rather than some form of "superiority" or "advantage" that has been unjustly conferred upon males.

Before going on . . .

- Describe differences in IQ scores across U.S. racial and ethnic groups and the hypotheses posited by psychologists to explain them.
- What kinds of factors appear to contribute to cross-cultural differences in IQ and achievement test scores?
- How do males and females differ with respect to IQ and achievement test performance?

Alternative Views of Intelligence

Using IQ tests to define and explain individual and group differences in intelligence is called the *psychometric approach* (Birney et al., 2005). Recently, developmentalists of diverse theoretical orientations have argued that this approach is too narrow. That is, many are beginning to believe that psychologists have placed too much emphasis on defining intelligence in terms of correlations between IQ tests and school achievement. Moreover, a number of developmentalists have suggested that we still do not really know what it is that intelligence tests measure. Thus, several alternative approaches to defining and measuring intelligence have been proposed in recent years.

INFORMATION-PROCESSING THEORY

In Chapter 6, you read about developmental changes in information-processing strategies. Several developmentalists have argued that some of the same concepts can be used to explain what specific processes are measured on IQ tests.

Speed of Information Processing   As you learned in Chapter 6, it is becoming increasingly clear that increases in speed or efficiency of processing underlie age-related changes in cognitive skills. Thus, it makes sense to hypothesize that differences in processing speed may also underlie individual differences in IQ scores (Thomas & Karmiloff-Smith, 2003). A number of investigators have found just such a link: Participants with faster reaction times or speed of performance on a variety of simple tasks also have higher average IQ scores on standard tests (Fry & Hale, 1996; McRorie & Cooper, 2004; Rindermann & Neubauer, 2004; Vernon, 1987). A few studies have even linked speed of processing directly to central nervous system functioning and to IQ. For example, it is now possible to measure the speed of conduction of impulses along individual nerves, such as nerves in the arm. Philip Vernon (1993; Vernon & Mori, 1992) has found a correlation of about .45 between such a measure and IQ test score.

Most of this research has been done with adults, but a link between speed of reaction time and IQ scores has also been found in a few studies with children (Keating, List, & Merriman, 1985; Rindermann & Neubauer, 2004; Saccuzzo, Johnson, & Guertin, 1994). Furthermore, there are some pretty clear indications that such speed-of-processing differences may be built in at birth. Indeed, the link be-tween infant habituation (or recognition memory) and later IQ score seems to be primarily a result of basic variations in speed of processing (Rose & Feldman, 1997).

Other Links between IQ and Information Processing

Other researchers have explored the connec-tions between IQ and information processing by comparing the information-processing strategies used by children of nor-mal intelligence with those used by retarded children. In one classic study, Judy DeLoache compared the searching strate-gies of groups of 2-year-olds who were either developing nor-mally or showed delayed development (DeLoache & Brown, 1987). When the search task was very simple, such as looking for a toy hidden in an obvious location in a room, the two groups did not differ in search strategies or skill. But when the experimenter surreptitiously moved the toy before the child was allowed to search, normal children were able to search in alternative plausible places, such as in nearby loca-tions; delayed children simply persisted in looking in the place where they had seen the toy hidden. They either could not change strategies once they had settled on a particular approach or did not have alternative, more complex strategies in their repertoires.

Other research underlines this difference in the flexibility of strategy use. In several early studies, Joseph Campione and Ann Brown (1984; Campione, Brown, Ferrara, Jones, & Stein-berg, 1985) found that both retarded and normal-IQ children could learn to solve problems such as those in parts (a), (b), and (c) of Figure 7.6, but the retarded children could not transfer this learning to a more complex problem of the same general type, such as part (d), whereas normal-IQ children could. Both sets of stud-ies suggest that flexibility of use of any given strategy may be another key dimension of individual differences in intelligence.

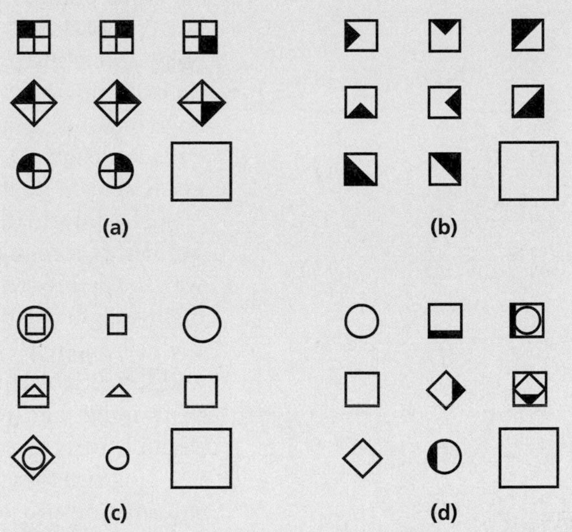

(a)   **(b)**

(c)   **(d)**

FIGURE 7.6

For parts (a) through (d), the child must figure out the "sys-tem" in each set and then describe what pattern should go in the empty box in the bottom right-hand corner. Part (a) shows rotation; part (b) shows addition of two elements; part (c) shows subtraction. The figure in part (d) is harder because the child must apply *two* principles at once, in this case both addition and rotation. Retarded children and chil-dren of normal IQ could do problems like those in parts (a), (b), and (c), but retarded children did much more poorly on problems like the one in part (d).
(*Source*: Campione et al., 1985, Figure 1, p. 302, and Figure 4, p. 306.)

Evaluating the Information-Processing Approach

The information-processing approach offers some important bridges between testing approaches to intel-ligence and stage theories such as Piaget's. It now looks as if children are born with some basic, inborn cognitive strategies (such as noting differences or similarities). It is also clear that these strategies or rules change during the early years of life, with more com-plex ones emerging and old ones being used more flexibly. Plain old experience is a key part of the process of change. The more a child plays with blocks, the better she will be at organizing and classifying blocks; the more a person plays chess, the better he will be at seeing and remembering relationships among pieces on the board. So some of the changes that Piaget thought of as changes in the underlying structure of intelligence are instead specific task learning. But there does seem to be some structural change as well, such as the emergence of new strategies, particularly metacognitive strategies.

Individual differences in what is normally thought of as intelligence can then be conceived of as resulting both from inborn differences in the speed or efficiency of the basic processes (differences in the hardware, perhaps) and from differences in expertise or experience. The child with a slower or less efficient processing system will move through all the various steps and stages more slowly; he will use the experience he has less efficiently or effectively and may never develop as complete a range of strategies as the child who is initially quicker. But when this less innately gifted child has sufficient expertise in some area, that specialized knowledge can compensate for the lower IQ.

This point is nicely illustrated in a study of expertise done in Germany (Schneider & Bjorklund, 1992). School-aged children who were experts (very knowledgeable) about soccer had better recall of soccer-related lists than did nonexperts. But high-IQ novices did as well as low-IQ experts on these same tasks. So rich knowledge in some area can compensate somewhat for lower IQ, but it does not result in equality. High-IQ experts will still be better than medium- or low-IQ experts in any given area.

The information-processing approach may also have some practical applications. Studies of recognition memory in infancy, for example, may give developmentalists a way to identify retarded children very early in life or to sort out from among low-birth-weight infants those who seem at particular risk for later problems. Identifying the key differences between retarded and nonretarded children (or between brighter and less bright children) may also allow developmentalists to identify specific kinds of training that would be useful for a retarded child or for a child with a learning disability.

It is well to remember, though, that developmentalists do not yet have any tests of information-processing ability that could realistically replace the careful use of IQ tests in schools and clinics, although a few psychologists believe that a clinically useful biological measure of intelligence will be available within several decades (Matarazzo, 1992). Nor are the sequential theories of information-processing development yet able to explain all the observed differences among infants, preschoolers, and older children in performance on various Piagetian tasks. In short, information-processing theory is an important addition to psychologists' understanding of cognitive development, but it does not replace all the other approaches.

STERNBERG'S TRIARCHIC THEORY OF INTELLIGENCE

triarchic theory of intelligence A theory advanced by Robert Sternberg, proposing the existence of three types of intelligence: analytical, creative, and practical.

analytical intelligence One of three types of intelligence in Sternberg's triarchic theory of intelligence; the type of intelligence typically measured on IQ tests, including the ability to plan, remember facts, and organize information.

creative intelligence One of three types of intelligence described by Sternberg in his triarchic theory of intelligence; includes insightfulness and the ability to see new relationships among events or experiences.

practical intelligence One of three types of intelligence in Sternberg's triarchic theory of intelligence; often called "street smarts," this type of intelligence includes skill in applying information to the real world or solving practical problems.

Some developmentalists say that the problem with relying on IQ tests as the primary means of understanding and studying intelligence is that these tests fail to provide a complete picture of mental abilities. Psychologist Robert Sternberg, while conceding that conventional tests are good predictors of academic performance and other important outcomes (Sternberg, Grigorenko, & Bundy, 2001), argues that there are components of intellectual functioning that these tests measure poorly. He suggests that there are actually three aspects, or types, of intelligence (1985, 2003; Sternberg & Wagner, 1993). Consequently, Sternberg's theory is known as the **triarchic theory of intelligence**.

Sternberg has developed a test, the Sternberg Triarchic Abilities Test, to measure the three aspects of intelligence he hypothesizes (Sternberg, Castejon, Prieto, Hautamaeki, & Grigorenko, 2001). The first of the three, which Sternberg calls **analytical intelligence** (originally called *componential intelligence*), includes what is normally measured by IQ and achievement tests. Planning, organizing, and remembering facts and applying them to new situations are all part of analytical intelligence.

The second aspect Sternberg calls **creative intelligence** (originally labeled *experiential intelligence*). A person with well-developed creative intelligence can see new connections between things, is insightful about experiences, and questions what is sometimes called the "conventional wisdom" about various kinds of problems (Sternberg, 2001). A graduate student who comes up with good ideas for experiments, who can see how a theory could be applied to a totally different situation, who can synthesize many facts into a new organization, or who critically examines ideas that most professionals in the field accept as true is high in creative intelligence.

The third aspect Sternberg calls **practical intelligence** (originally labeled *contextual intelligence*), sometimes called "street smarts." People who have a high degree of practical intelligence are good at seeing how some bit of information may be applied to the real world or at finding some practical solution to a real-life problem—such as coming up with shortcuts for repetitive tasks or figuring out which of several different-sized boxes of cereal is the best buy. Practical intelligence may also involve being skilled at reading social cues or social situations, such as knowing not to give your boss bad news when she is clearly angry about something else or knowing how to persuade your supervisor to invest a large amount of money in your proposed sales plan (Sternberg, Wagner, Williams, & Horvath, 1995).

Sternberg's most basic point about these several types of intelligence is not just that standard IQ tests do not measure all three, but that in the world beyond the school walls, creative or practical intelligence may be required as much as or more than the type of skill measured on an IQ test (Sternberg & Wagner, 1993). These are important points to keep in mind when considering the origins of individual differences in IQ scores. What developmentalists know about "intelligence" is almost entirely restricted to information about analytical intelligence—the kind of intelligence most often demanded (and tested) in school. They know almost nothing about the origins or long-term consequences of variations in creative or practical intelligence.

GARDNER'S MULTIPLE INTELLIGENCES

Developmental psychologist Howard Gardner has also argued that a multidimensional view of intelligence provides both a better understanding of individual differences and, at least potentially, strategies for measuring these differences in more meaningful ways. Accordingly, he has proposed a theory of **multiple intelligences** (Gardner, 1983). This theory claims there are eight types of intelligence, as shown in Figure 7.7:

- *Linguistic*: People who are good writers or speakers, learn languages easily, or possess a lot of knowledge about language possess greater than average linguistic intelligence.
- *Logical/mathematical*: Logical/mathematical intelligence enables individuals to learn math and to generate logical solutions to various kinds of problems.
- *Spatial*: Spatial intelligence is used in the production and appreciation of works of art such as paintings and sculpture.
- *Bodily kinesthetic*: Professional athletes possess high levels of this kind of intelligence.
- *Musical*: Musicians, singers, composers, and conductors possess musical intelligence.
- *Interpersonal*: Those in the "helping professions"—counselors, social workers, ministers, and the like—have high levels of interpersonal intelligence.
- *Intrapersonal*: People who are good at identifying their own strengths and choosing goals accordingly have high levels of intrapersonal intelligence.
- *Naturalistic*: Scientists are high in this type of intelligence involving the ability to recognize patterns in nature.

Gardner's theory is based on observations of people with brain damage, mental retardation, and other conditions, such as the savant syndrome displayed by Hikari Oe. Gardner points out that brain damage usually causes disruption of functioning in very specific mental abilities rather than a general decline in intelligence. He also notes that many individuals with mental deficits have remarkable talents: some are gifted in music; others can perform complex mathematical computations in their heads. Critics claim that Gardner's view, while intuitively appealing, has little empirical support (Aiken, 1997).

CRITICAL THINKING ?

It's fairly easy to come up with a list of occupations for which analytical intelligence is especially useful, but in what jobs might a high level of practical intelligence be especially useful?

multiple intelligences Eight types of intelligence (linguistic, logical/mathematical, spatial, bodily kinesthetic, musical, interpersonal, intrapersonal, and naturalistic) proposed by Howard Gardner.

Before going on . . .

- How do information-processing theorists explain individual differences in IQ scores?
- What is the triarchic theory of intelligence?
- Describe the eight types of intelligence proposed by Howard Gardner.

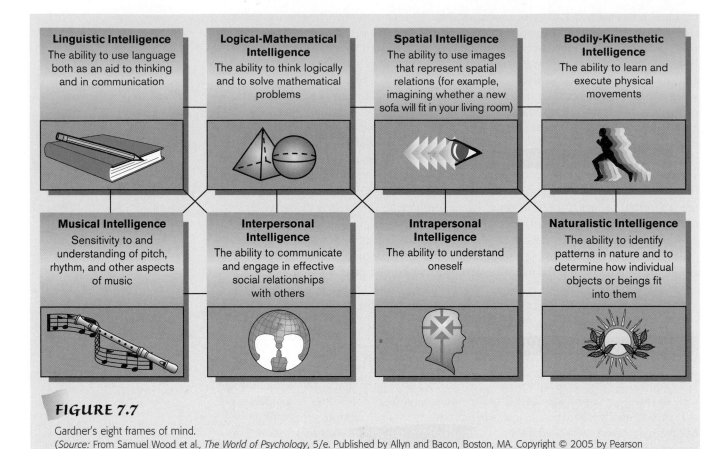

FIGURE 7.7

Gardner's eight frames of mind.

(*Source:* From Samuel Wood et al., *The World of Psychology*, 5/e. Published by Allyn and Bacon, Boston, MA. Copyright © 2005 by Pearson Education. Reprinted by permission of the publisher.)

Summary

Measuring Intellectual Power

- Early tests of intelligence, such as that devised by Binet, were designed to identify children who might have difficulty in school. Scores were based on a child's mental age.
- Modern intelligence tests compare a child's performance to that of others of the same age. Scores above 100 represent better than average performance; scores below 100 represent poorer than average performance. The most commonly used individually administered tests for children are the current revisions of the Stanford-Binet and the Wechsler Intelligence Scales for Children (WISC).
- IQ scores are quite stable from one testing to the next, especially as a child gets older. But individual children's scores may still fluctuate or shift by 20–30 points or more over the course of childhood.
- IQ test scores are quite good predictors of school performance and years of education, a correlation that gives one piece of evidence for the validity of the tests.

- An important limitation of IQ tests is that they do not measure many other facets of intellectual functioning that might be of interest.

Explaining Individual Differences in IQ Scores

- Studies of identical twins and of adopted children clearly show a substantial genetic influence on measured IQ scores. Most psychologists agree that approximately half of the variation in individual IQ scores can be attributed to heredity.
- The remaining half of the variation in IQ scores is attributed to environmental variation. Poor children consistently score lower on IQ tests than do children from middle-class families; children whose families provide appropriate play materials and encourage intellectual development score higher on IQ tests.

- Environmental influence is also shown by increases in test performance or school success among children who have been in enriched preschool or infant day-care programs and by children who attend school longer.
- One way to explain the interaction of heredity and environment is with the concept of reaction range: Heredity determines some range of potential; environment determines the level of performance within that range.

Explaining Group Differences in IQ and Achievement Test Scores

- A consistent difference in IQ scores of about 10 to 12 points is found between African American and Caucasian children in the United States. It seems most likely that this difference is due to environmental and cultural differences between the two groups, such as differences in health and prenatal care and in the type of intellectual skills taught and emphasized at home. Stereotype threat may also play some role in lowering test scores for African Americans.
- Some researchers have argued that the differences between Asian and American children in performance on mathematics achievement tests result not from genetic differences in capacity but from differences in cultural emphasis on the importance of academic achievement, the number of hours spent on homework, and the quality of math instruction in the schools.
- Males and females do not differ on overall IQ test scores, but they do differ in some subskills. The largest differences are on measures of spatial reasoning, on which males are consistently better.

Alternative Views of Intelligence

- Information-processing theory provides developmentalists with an alternative approach to explaining individual differences in intelligence. Higher-IQ individuals, for example, appear to process information more quickly and to apply strategies or knowledge more broadly.
- Sternberg's triarchic theory of intelligence suggests that IQ tests measure only analytical intelligence, one of three aspects of intellectual ability. According to his theory, these tests measure neither creative nor practical intelligence.
- Gardner has proposed eight distinct types of intelligence: linguistic, logical/mathematical, spatial, bodily kinesthetic, musical, interpersonal, intrapersonal, and naturalistic.

Key Terms

achievement test (p. 188)
analytical intelligence (p. 208)
Bayley Scales of Infant Development (p. 187)
competence (p. 188)
creative intelligence (p. 208)
cumulative deficit (p. 194)
full scale IQ (p. 186)

intelligence (p. 184)
intelligence quotient (IQ) (p. 184)
mental age (p. 184)
multiple intelligences (p. 209)
perceptual reasoning index (p. 186)
performance (p. 188)
practical intelligence (p. 208)
processing speed index (p. 186)

reaction range (p. 199)
Stanford-Binet (p. 184)
triarchic theory of intelligence (p. 208)
verbal comprehension index (p. 186)
WISC-IV (p. 186)
working memory index (p. 186)
WPPSI-III (p. 186)

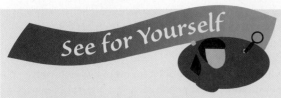

Standardized Testing Programs

How much do you know about your own state's standardized testing program? You can learn more about testing policies and issues in your state by doing the following:

- Talk to public school teachers and administrators about your state's testing program. Do they think standardized tests have improved education?
- Check your state education agency's Web site for information on standards and testing.
- Locate newspaper articles that report on what your governor and state legislators think about test-based school reform. Do these officials support a national test?
- Visit the *fairtest.org* and *edexcellence.net* Web sites to find out how experts on opposite sides of the testing issue rate your state's standards and testing program.

Stereotype Threat in Women

You can use the figure on page 207 (Figure 7.6) to find out more about stereotype threat. Randomly assign an equal number of your male and female classmates or friends to threat and non-threat conditions. Tell those in the threat condition that the tasks in the figure measure sex differences in cognitive ability. Point out that men often outperform women on such tasks. Tell participants in the non-threat condition that you have to collect data on the tasks for your psychology class. Score participants' responses to sets (a) through (d) as correct or incorrect according to the explanations provided in the figure caption. You should find that women in the threat condition make more errors than those in the non-threat condition. Men should score about the same in both. You may also want to note the time each participant requires to complete the tasks. Some studies suggest that individuals who are working under stereotype threat conditions take longer to solve problems because they are trying to prevent themselves from making errors (Seibt & Förster, 2004).

The Development of Language

CHAPTER

In recent years, countless programs geared toward teaching sign language to infants who can hear have been developed.

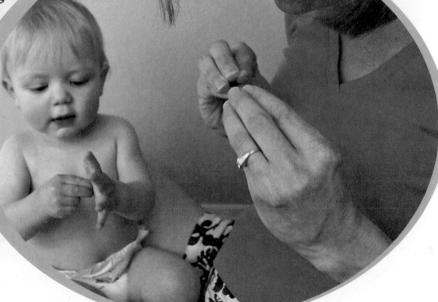

The authors and publishers of these programs claim that acquiring sign language will speed up the language development process, enabling children to acquire larger vocabularies and more complex grammatical structures than others their age. As a result, in the future they will be better readers and better academic learners. Anecdotal reports about the benefits of teaching babies to sign are found on the dozens of Internet sites that market sign-language training products to eager parents (e.g., babysigns.com, sign2me.com). You learned in Chapter 1 that developmental scientists approach such claims by asking whether evidence supports them. There are several kinds of studies that are relevant to this question.

To start with, it is quite clear that infants can learn sign language. Researchers have been studying sign-language acquisition in deaf children for decades. These studies have shown that, given an equal amount of input, deaf babies learn sign language just as easily as hearing children acquire spoken language. Further, acquisition of sign and spoken language appears to follow the same timetable. For example, deaf children use their first symbolic signs at the same age as hearing children utter their first meaningful words, around the first birthday (Petitto, 1988).

Studies of hearing children of deaf parents provide a somewhat different slant on the issue. Again, given equal input, these infants have no difficulty acquiring sign language and spoken language at the same time. In fact, the developmental timetable exhibited by these children is quite similar to that of hearing children learning only spoken language, although a few studies show that they learn the signs for some objects before they learn the verbal equivalents (Capirci, Iverson, Montanari, & Volterra, 2002; Folven & Bonvillian, 1991; Johnston, Durieux-Smith, & Bloom, 2005; Petitto et al., 2001). So, it would appear that it is entirely feasible to teach a hearing child to use sign language without interfering with his or her development of spoken language.

Keep in mind that, in all of the studies discussed so far, researchers were observing babies learning language naturally. The infants in these studies were learning either sign or spoken language to communicate with their parents. Language learning was built in to their normal daily activities; there were no "lessons" in either how to sign or how to speak. Thus, the results of these studies can't be generalized to learning contexts in which parents are intentionally teaching babies to sign for the purpose of enhancing their language development.

Nevertheless, research indicates that it is possible to teach infants to use signs in a lesson-type format, one that does not involve communicative necessity. In one experiment, researchers were able to teach a sign vocabulary to infants as young as 6 months of age within a remarkably short time: 4 hours, to be exact (Thompson, McKerchar, & Dancho, 2004). Moreover, after the training period was over, the researchers observed the babies using the signs independently. However, there was no follow-up to determine how long the babies retained these signing skills after the experiment ended. Thus, it is impossible to determine what long-term effects there might have been from the sign-language training. Suppose, though, that research had clearly demonstrated that it is possible to teach infants to use sign language in brief training sessions, that they form long-term memories of the signs, and that they use them in their everyday lives after receiving the training. We would still be left with the question of whether signing enhances language development.

To address this issue, researcher Cyne Johnston and her colleagues at the Universities of Ottawa and Waterloo carried out an extensive review of sign-language training programs for hearing infants (Johnston, Durieux-Smith, & Bloom, 2005). They began by compiling detailed descriptions of all the programs that are commercially available. They identified dozens of such programs and found that most included training aids such as videotapes and flash cards. Moreover, all of the programs claimed to enhance language development and cited research in support of their claims.

Next, Johnston's team examined the methods and findings of the cited studies to determine whether the authors' claims of support were justified. Johnston and her colleagues concluded that almost all of the studies had been carried out in ways that made it impossible to determine whether any of the training programs actually influenced language development. For the most part, the studies lacked experimental methods, such as random assignment, that would support claims of causality. Further, many failed to control variables, such as parental enthusiasm, that might account for program effects. Some involved very small numbers of participants and purely descriptive research methods such as naturalistic observation and case studies.

Based on their analysis, Johnston and her colleagues concluded that there is no evidence that teaching hearing babies to use sign language enhances their language development. Thus, they noted, developmental scientists should not encourage parents to teach their babies sign language as a means of enhancing language development. The researchers did note, however, that teaching sign language to infants does not appear to be harmful to the process of spoken language development. Consequently, if parents find it useful or enjoyable to do so, there doesn't appear to be any reason why they shouldn't.

Do such conclusions mean that parents have no influence on infants' language development? Clearly not, because, at a minimum, a child must have linguistic input and be able to engage in linguistic interactions with other people in order to acquire language. Thus, as you'll see throughout this chapter, both maturation and experience are critical to language development.

Chimpanzees can fairly easily learn signs for individual objects or actions and can understand and follow quite complex instructions. Here Nim Chimpsky, one of the first chimps trained to use signs to communicate, signs "I see." But is it advisable to teach human infants to use sign language?

Before the First Word: The Prelinguistic Phase

Before delving into the topic of language development, we need to be clear about just what it is we're studying. Language has several dimensions. The sound patterns that a particular language uses and the rules that govern those patterns are its **phonology**. **Semantics** refers to how language represents meaning. The rules a language uses for combining words into sentences is known as **syntax**. You will see each of these terms again as we trace the development of language from its early, preverbal beginnings to the emergence of true linguistic fluency many years later.

phonology The sound patterns of a particular language and the rules for combining them.

semantics A particular language's system of meaning and the rules for conveying meaning.

syntax The rules for forming sentences in a particular language.

Chimpanzees can learn to communicate by using sign language or by pointing to sequences of symbols. However, in most cases, it takes a good deal of effort to teach them to use **expressive language**—sounds, signs, or symbols that communicate meaning (Savage-Rumbaugh et al., 1993). In contrast, as Flavell puts it, "Draconian measures would be needed to prevent most children from learning to talk" (1985, p. 248). And as any parent can tell you, once children do learn, it is virtually impossible to shut them up! The process of language development actually begins in the months before the baby speaks his first word, a period called the **prelinguistic phase**.

EARLY PERCEPTION OF LANGUAGE

A baby cannot learn language until he can hear the individual sounds as distinct. Just how early can he do that? Recall from Chapter 5 that babies are born with, or very soon develop, remarkably good ability to discriminate speech sounds. By 1 or 2 months of age, they pay attention to and can tell the difference between many individual letter sounds; within a few more months, they clearly can discriminate among syllables or words. They have also figured out that these speech sounds are matched by the speaker's mouth movements.

Researchers have also found that babies in these early months are sensitive to the intonational and stress patterns of the speech they are listening to. For example, Anne Fernald (1993) has found that 5-month-olds will smile more when they hear tapes of adults saying something in a positive or approving tone than when they hear someone speaking in a negative tone, whether the words are in Italian, German, or English. By 8 months, babies demonstrate clear preferences for the language most often spoken by their mothers (MacWhinney, 2005). Even more impressive is a study showing that by 9 months of age, babies listening to English prefer to listen to words that use the typical English pattern of stress on the first syllable (such as *fal*ter, *com*et, or *gen*tle) rather than those that stress the second syllable (e.g., com*ply* or as*sign*) (Jusczyk & Hohne, 1997). Presumably, babies listening to another language would prefer listening to whatever stress pattern was typical of that language. All this research shows that very early on—from birth and perhaps even before birth—the baby is paying attention to crucial features of the language she hears, such as stress and intonation.

EARLY SOUNDS AND GESTURES

A baby's early perceptual skill is not matched right away by much skill in producing sounds. From birth to about 1 month of age, the most common sound an infant makes is a cry, although infants also make other fussing, gurgling, and satisfied sounds. This sound repertoire expands at about 1 or 2 months with the addition of some laughing and **cooing**—making repetitive vowel sounds, like *uuuuuu*. Sounds like this are usually signals of pleasure in babies and may show quite a lot of variation, including increases and decreases in volume or pitch.

Consonant sounds appear only at about 6 or 7 months of age, when for the first time the baby has the muscle control needed to combine a consonant sound with a vowel sound. From 6 months on, there is a rapid increase in the amount of vowel-consonant combinations. This type of vocalization, called **babbling**, makes up about half of babies' noncrying sounds from about 6 to 12 months of age (Mitchell & Kent, 1990).

Much early babbling involves repetitive strings of the same syllables, such as *dadadada* or *nananana* or *yayayaya*. Adults find babbling delightful to listen to; Lois Bloom (1998), one of the foremost theorists and observers of children's language, points out that these new sound combinations are also much easier for adults to imitate than are the earlier baby sounds, because babbling has more of the rhythm and sound of adult speech. The imitative game that may then develop between parent and child is not only a pleasure for both but may help the baby to learn language.

CRITICAL THINKING ?

Next time you're engaged in a conversation, notice how you and the person you're speaking with use combinations of words and gestures. For example, some people point to their teeth when talking about a visit to the dentist. You may lift your hand when you describe how fast your young nephew is growing. Do you think such gestures help you communicate, or are they distracting to your conversation partner?

expressive language Sounds, signs, or symbols used to communicate meaning.

prelinguistic phase The period before a child speaks his or her first words.

cooing Making repetitive vowel sounds, particularly the *uuu* sound; the behavior develops early in the prelinguistic period, when babies are between about 1 and 4 months of age.

babbling The repetitive vocalizing of consonant-vowel combinations by an infant, typically beginning at about 6 months of age.

Babbling is an important part of the preparation for spoken language in other ways as well. For one thing, developmentalists have observed that infants' babbling gradually acquires some of the intonational pattern of the language they are hearing—a process Elizabeth Bates refers to as "learning the tune before the words" (Bates, O'Connell, & Shore, 1987). At the very least, infants do seem to develop at least two such "tunes" in their babbling. Babbling with a rising intonation at the end of a string of sounds seems to signal a desire for a response; a falling intonation requires no response.

A second important thing about babbling is that when babies first start babbling, they typically babble all kinds of sounds, including some that are not part of the language they are hearing. Then, beginning at about 9 or 10 months of age, the sound repertoire of infants gradually begins to shift toward the set of sounds they are listening to, with the nonheard sounds dropping out (Oller, 1981)—a pattern that clearly parallels the findings of Werker's research, illustrated in Figure 5.5 (page 137) and that reflects what psychologists know about early synaptic development and pruning. Findings like these do not prove that babbling is necessary for language development, but they certainly make it look as if babbling is part of a connected developmental process that begins at birth.

Another part of that connected developmental process appears to be a kind of gestural language that develops near the end of the first year (MacWhinney, 2005; Rodrigo, González, de Vega, Muñetón-Ayala, & Rodríguez, 2004). Pointing is the most common gesture infants use. However, it is not unusual to see a baby of this age ask for things by using a combination of gestures and sounds. A 10-month-old baby who apparently wants you to hand her a favorite toy may stretch and reach for it, opening and closing her hand, making whining sounds or other heartrending noises. There is no mistaking the meaning. At about the same age, babies enter into those gestural games much loved by parents, like "patty-cake," "soooo-big," or "wave bye-bye" (Bates et al., 1987).

Researchers have also found that deaf children of deaf parents show a kind of "sign babbling" between about 7 and 11 months of age, much as hearing children of this age babble sounds. Then, at 8 or 9 months of age, deaf children begin using simple gestures, such as pointing, and such gestures emerge in hearing babies of hearing parents at just about the same age. At about 12 months of age, deaf babies seem to display their first referential signs—that is, gestures that appear to stand for some object or event, such as signaling that they want a drink by making a motion of bringing a cup to the mouth (Petitto, 1988).

What do you think this young girl is "saying" with her pointing gesture? Before they speak their first words, babies successfully use gestures and body language in consistent ways to communicate meaning.

RECEPTIVE LANGUAGE

Interestingly, the first signs that an infant understands the meaning of individual words spoken to her (which linguists call **receptive language**) also become evident at about 9 or 10 months (MacWhinney, 2005). Larry Fenson and his colleagues (1994) asked hundreds of mothers about their babies' understanding of various words. The mothers of 10-month-olds identified an average of about 30 words their infants understood; for 13-month-olds, that number was up to nearly 100 words. Since infants of 9 to 13 months of age typically speak few, if any, individual words, findings like these make it clear that receptive language comes before expressive language. Children understand before they can speak. Babies as young as 9 or 10 months old are already actively learning the language they are listening to. Not only can they understand some simple instructions, but they can benefit from being exposed to a rich array of language.

receptive language
Comprehension of spoken language.

Before going on . . .

■ Describe infants' speech perception abilities.
■ What are the characteristics of cooing and babbling?
■ What have researchers learned about infants' receptive language skills?

These bits of information point to a whole series of changes that seem to come together at 9 or 10 months: the beginning of meaningful gestures, the drift of babbling toward the heard language sounds, the first participation in imitative gestural games, and the first comprehension of individual words. It is as if the child now understands something about the process of communication and is intending to communicate to the rest of the world.

Learning Words and Word Meanings

Somewhere in the midst of all the babbling, the first words appear, typically at about 12 or 13 months (Fenson et al., 1994). Once she has learned the first few words, the infant begins the work of identifying specific links between words and the objects or actions for which they stand.

CHARACTERISTICS OF THE FIRST WORDS

A *word*, as linguists usually define it, is any sound or set of sounds that is used consistently to refer to some thing, action, or quality. But for a child, a word can be any sound; it doesn't have to be a sound that matches words adults are using. Brenda, a little girl studied by Ronald Scollon (1976), used the sound *nene* as one of her first words. It seemed to mean primarily liquid food, since she used it for "milk," "juice," and "bottle," but she also used it to refer to "mother" and "sleep." (Some of Brenda's other early words are listed in the left-hand column of Table 8.1.)

Often, a child's earliest words are used only in one or two specific situations and in the presence of many cues. The child may say "doggie" or "bow-wow" only in response to such promptings as "What's that?" or "How does the doggie go?" Typically, this early word learning is very slow, requiring many repetitions for each word. In the first 6 months of word usage (roughly between 12 and 18 months of age), children may learn

TABLE 8.1	Brenda's Vocabulary at 14 Months and 19 Months		
14 Months		**19 Months***	
aw u (I want, I don't want)	baby	nice	boat
nau (no)	bear	orange	bone
d di (daddy, baby)	bed	pencil	dimb
d yu (down, doll)	big	write	checkers
nene (liquid food)	blue	paper	cut
e (yes)	Brenda	pen	I do
ada (another, other)	cookie	see	jump
	daddy	shoe	met
	eat	sick	Pogo
	at	swim	Ralph
	(hor)sie	tape	you too
	mama	walk	
	mommy	wowow	

*Brenda did not actually pronounce all these words the way an adult would. The columns show the adult version, since that is easier to read.

Source: R. Scollon, *Conversations with a one-year-old*. Honolulu: University of Hawaii Press, 1976, pp. 47, 57–58.

to say as few as 30 words. Most linguists (e.g., Nelson, 1985) have concluded that in this earliest word-use phase, the child learns each word as something connected to a set of specific contexts. The toddler has apparently not yet grasped that words are symbolic—that they refer to objects or events regardless of context.

THE NAMING EXPLOSION

Somewhere between 16 and 24 months, after the early period of very slow word learning, most children begin to add new words rapidly, as if they have figured out that things have names. According to Fenson's very large cross-sectional study, based on mothers' reports, the average 16-month-old has a speaking vocabulary of about 50 words (a shift you can see illustrated by young Brenda's 19-month vocabulary in Table 8.1); by 24 months of age, this speaking vocabulary has multiplied more than sixfold to about 320 words (Fenson et al., 1994). A parallel study in Italy by Elizabeth Bates and her colleagues (Caselli, Casadio, & Bates, 1997) showed that this rapid rate of vocabulary growth is not unique to children learning English. In this new phase, children seem to learn new words after very few repetitions and to generalize these new words to many more situations.

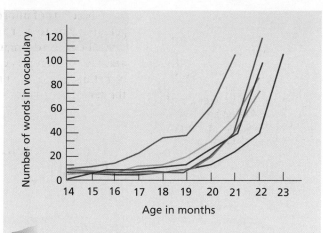

FIGURE 8.1

Each line in this figure represents the vocabulary growth of one of the children followed by Goldfield and Reznick in their longitudinal study.
(*Source*: B. A. Goldfield and J. S. Reznick, Figure 3, p. 177, "Early lexical acquisition: Rate, content, and the vocabulary spurt," *Journal of Child Language*, 17 (1990), 171–183. By permission of Cambridge University Press.)

For the majority of children, the naming explosion is not a steady, gradual process; instead, a vocabulary spurt begins once the child has acquired about 50 words. You can see this pattern in Figure 8.1, which shows the vocabulary growth curves of six children studied longitudinally by Goldfield and Reznick (1990); the same pattern has been found by other researchers as well (e.g., Bloom, 1993). Not all children show precisely this pattern. In Goldfield and Reznick's study, for example, 13 children showed a vocabulary spurt; 11 other children in the study followed varying growth patterns, including several who showed no spurt at all but only gradual acquisition of vocabulary. Still, a rapid increase over a period of a few months is the most common pattern.

During this early period of rapid vocabulary growth, the majority of new words are names for things or people. Verblike words tend to develop later, perhaps because they label relationships between objects rather than just individual objects (Bates et al., 1994; Gleitman & Gleitman, 1992). For example, in Fenson's large cross-sectional study (1994), 63.0% of the words mothers said their children knew by age 2 were nouns, while only 8.5% were verbs. Studies of children learning other languages show very similar patterns, as you can see in Table 8.2.

Some studies suggest that noun learning may precede verb learning because infants lack the ability to consistently associate words with actions until about 18 months of age (Casasola & Cohen, 2000). However, recent cross-linguistic research also suggests that English-speaking parents, compared to Korean-speaking parents, for example, emphasize nouns more than verbs in speaking and reading to infants (Choi, 2000). Thus, the noun-before-verb learning pattern may be influenced by the characteristics of the language being learned as well as by the behavior of mature speakers toward the infant.

The naming explosion may also rest on new cognitive understandings. In several studies, Alison Gopnik and Andrew Meltzoff (1987, 1992) have found that the naming explosion typically occurs at the same time as or just after children first categorize mixed sets of objects, such as putting balls into one group and blocks into another. Having discovered categories, the child may rapidly learn the names for already existing categories. However, such a linkage is still uncertain: In a more recent set of studies, Lisa Gershkoff-Stowe and her colleagues (1997) repeatedly failed to replicate the results obtained by Gopnik and Meltzoff. Gershkoff-Stowe proposes that while some basic

CRITICAL THINKING

For those of you who have seriously studied another language: Do you think that the process of learning vocabulary in a second language is similar to the process infants go through—a first stage in which each word is learned laboriously with many repetitions, followed by a vocabulary spurt?

TABLE 8.2	Early Words Acquired by Children in Four Cultures			
	German Boy	**English Girl**	**Turkish Girl**	**Chinese Girl**
Words for people or things	Mommy	Mommy	Mama	Momma
	Papa	Daddy	Daddy	Papa
	Gaga	babar	Aba	grandmother
	baby	baby	baby	horse
	dog	dog	food	chicken
	bird	dolly	apple	uncooked rice
	cat	kitty	banana	cooked rice
	milk	juice	bread	noodles
	ball	book	ball	flower
	nose	eye	pencil	wall clock
	moon	moon	towel	lamp
Nonnaming words	cry	run	cry	go
	come	all gone	come	come
	eat	more	put on	pick up
	sleep	bye-bye	went pooh	not want
	want	want	want	afraid
	no	no	hello	thank you
Total percentage of naming words	67%	69%	57%	59%

Source: Gentner, 1992.

understanding of the existence of kinds of things, or categories, may well be required for a child to experience the naming explosion, such an understanding is not sufficient. Many other factors can influence the precise timing of the naming explosion and of the ability to classify objects into different types.

At the same time, causality also runs the other way, from language to thought: Once the child understands in some primitive way that names refer to categories, learning a new name suggests the existence of a new category (Waxman & Hall, 1993); thus, the name affects the child's thinking as much as new mental skills affect word learning.

LATER WORD LEARNING

During the preschool years, children continue to add words at remarkable speed. At age $2\frac{1}{2}$, the average vocabulary is about 600 words, about a quarter of which are verbs (Bates et al., 1994); by age 5 or 6, total vocabulary has risen to perhaps 15,000 words—an astonishing increase of 10 words a day (Pinker, 1994). What accounts for this amazing rate of word learning? Researchers have found that a momentous shift in the way children approach new words happens around age 3. As a result of this shift, children begin to pay attention to words in whole groups, such as words that name objects in a single class (e.g., types of dinosaurs or kinds of fruit) or words with similar meanings. In a sense, understanding of the categorical nature of words helps children develop what we might think of as mental "slots" for new words. Once the slots are in place, children seem to automatically organize the linguistic input they receive from parents, teachers, peers, books, television programs, advertisements, and every other source of language to extract new words and fill the slots as quickly as possible.

Psychologists use the term **fast-mapping** to refer to this ability to categorically link new words to real-world referents (Carey & Bartlett, 1978). (*Referents* are the real objects and events to which words refer.) At the core of fast-mapping, say researchers, is a

fast-mapping The ability to categorically link new words to real-world referents.

rapidly formed hypothesis about a new word's meaning (Behrend, Scofield, & Kleinknecht, 2001). The hypothesis is based on information derived from the child's prior knowledge of words and word categories and from the context in which the word is used. Once formed, the hypothesis is tested through use of the word in the child's own speech, often immediately after learning it. The feedback the child receives in response to use of the word helps him judge the accuracy of the hypothesis and the appropriateness of the category to which he has assumed that the word belongs. Perhaps this helps explain why preschoolers do so much talking and why they are so persistent at getting their listeners to actively respond to them.

In middle childhood, children continue to add vocabulary at the rate of 5,000 to 10,000 words a year. This figure comes from several careful studies by Jeremy Anglin (1993, 1995), who estimates children's total vocabularies by testing them on a sample of words drawn at random from a large dictionary. Figure 8.2 shows Anglin's estimates for first-, third-, and fifth-grade children. Anglin finds that the largest gain from third to fifth grade occurs in knowledge of the type of words he calls "derived words"—words such as *happily* or *unwanted*, which have a basic root to which some prefix or suffix is added. Anglin argues that at about age 8 or 9, the child shifts to a new level of understanding of the structure of language, figuring out relationships between whole categories of words, such as between adjectives and adverbs (*happy* and *happily, sad* and *sadly*) and between adjectives and nouns (*happy* and *happiness*). Once he understands such relationships, the child can understand and create whole sets of new words, and his vocabulary thereafter increases rapidly.

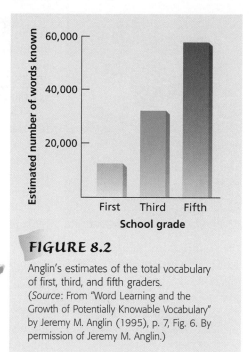

FIGURE 8.2

Anglin's estimates of the total vocabulary of first, third, and fifth graders. (*Source*: From "Word Learning and the Growth of Potentially Knowable Vocabulary" by Jeremy M. Anglin (1995), p. 7, Fig. 6. By permission of Jeremy M. Anglin.)

EXTENDING THE CLASS

Just what kind of categories does the child initially create? Suppose your 2-year-old, on catching sight of the family cat, says, "See kitty." No doubt you will be pleased that the child has applied the right word to the animal. But this sentence alone doesn't tell you much about the word meaning the child has developed. What does the word *kitty* mean to the child? Does she think it is a name only for that particular furry beast? Or does she think it applies to all furry creatures, all things with four legs, things with pointed ears, or what?

One way to figure out the kind of class or category the child has created is to see what other creatures or things a child also labels with the word *kitty*. That is, how is the class extended in the child's language? If the child has created a "kitty" category that is based on furriness, then many dogs and perhaps sheep would also be called "kitty." If having a tail is a crucial feature for the child, then some breeds of cat that have no tails might not be labeled "kitty." Or perhaps the child uses the word *kitty* only for the family cat, or only when petting the cat. This would imply a very narrow category indeed. The general question for researchers has been whether young children tend to use words narrowly or broadly, overextending or underextending them.

Research indicates that **underextension**—use of a word for only one specific object or in a single context—is most common at the earliest stages of vocabulary development, particularly before the naming explosion (MacWhinney, 2005), which suggests that most children initially think of words as belonging to only one thing, rather than as names for categories.

Once the naming explosion starts, however, the child appears to grasp the idea that words go with categories, and **overextension**—the use of a single word for an entire category of objects or in multiple contexts—becomes more common. At that stage, we're more likely to hear the word *kitty* applied to dogs or guinea pigs than we are to

Does this toddler know the word doll because she first had a concept of doll and later learned the word, or did she learn the word first and then create a category or concept to go with the word?

underextension The use of words to apply only to specific objects, such as a child's use of the word *cup* to refer only to one particular cup.

overextension The inappropriate use of a word to designate an entire category of objects, such as when a child uses the word *kitty* to refer to all animate objects.

For most toddlers, the word ball stands for a variety of round objects: balls of various kinds, round fruits such as oranges and peaches, and decorative objects such as globes and paperweights.

hear it used for just one animal or for a very small set of animals or objects (Clark, 1983). All children seem to show overextension, but the particular classes a child creates are unique to that child. One child Eve Clark observed used the word *ball* to refer not only to toy balls but also to radishes and stone spheres at park entrances. Another child used the word *ball* to refer to apples, grapes, eggs, squash, and a bell clapper (Clark, 1975).

These overextensions may reveal something about the way young children think, for example, that they have broad classes. However, linguists such as Clark point out that these children don't know very many words. A child who wants to call attention to a horse may not know the word *horse* and so may say *dog* instead. Overextension may thus arise from the child's desire to communicate and may not be evidence that the child fails to make the particular discriminations. As the child learns the separate labels that are applied to the different subtypes of furry four-legged creatures, overextension disappears.

CONSTRAINTS ON WORD LEARNING

Another fundamental question about word meanings, the subject of hot debate among linguists in recent years, is just how a child figures out which part of some scene a word may refer to. The classic example: A child sees a brown dog running across the grass with a bone in its mouth. An adult points and says "doggie." From such an experience, the toddler is somehow supposed to figure out that *doggie* refers to the animal and not to "running," "bone," "dog with bone," "brownness," "grass," or any other combination of elements in the whole scene.

Many linguists have proposed that a child could cope with this monumentally complex task only if he operated with some built-in biases, or **constraints** (e.g., Golinkoff, Mervis, & Hirsh-Pasek, 1994; Waxman & Kosowski, 1990; Woodward & Markman, 1998). For example, the child may have a built-in assumption that words refer to whole objects and not to their parts or attributes—this is referred to as the *whole object constraint*. The *mutual exclusivity constraint* leads children to assume that objects have only one name.

Suppose this little girl already knows the word flower. If her mother points to the flower and says "petal," is the girl likely to think that flower and petal mean the same thing? According to the principle of contrast, she will not be confused, because children approach word learning with the assumption that each word has a different meaning. Thus, she will assume that "petal" refers to some aspect of the flower whose name she doesn't yet know.

Another built-in constraint is the **principle of contrast**, which is the assumption that every word has a different meaning. Thus, if a new word is used, it must refer to some different object or a different aspect of an object (Clark, 1990). For example, in a widely quoted early study, Carey and Bartlett (1978) interrupted a play session with 2- and 3-year-old children by pointing to two trays and saying, "Bring me the chromium tray, not the red one, the chromium one." These children already knew the word *red* but did not know the word *chromium*. Nonetheless, most of the children were able to follow the instruction by bringing the tray that was not red. Furthermore, a week later, about half of the children remembered that the word *chromium* referred to some color and that the color was "not red." Thus, they learned some meaning by contrast.

Early proponents of constraints argued that such biases are innate—built into the brain in some fashion. Another alternative is that the child learns the various constraints over time (e.g., Merriman, 1991; Merriman & Bowman, 1989). For example, Carolyn Mervis and Jacquelyn Bertrand (1994) have found that not all children between the ages of 16 and 20 months use the principle of contrast to learn the name of a new, unknown object. Children in their sample who did use this principle had larger vocabularies and were more likely to be good at sorting objects into categories. Results like these suggest that constraints may be a highly useful way for children to learn words quickly but that they may be a product of cognitive/linguistic development rather than the basis for it.

A more sweeping argument against the notion of built-in constraints comes from Katherine Nelson (1988), who points out that a child rarely encounters a situation in which an adult points vaguely and gives some word. It is far more common for the adult to follow the child's lead, labeling things the child is already playing with or pointing at (Harris, 1992). In fact, children whose parents do more of such responsive, specific labeling seem to learn language somewhat faster (Dunham, Dunham, & Curwin, 1993; Harris, 1992). Other theorists also emphasize that the situations in which children hear new words are rich with cues to help the children figure out what the words may refer to—including the parents' facial expressions, the emphasis in their words, and the entire context in which the new word is given (Akhtar, Carpenter, & Tomasello, 1996; MacWhinney, 2005; Samuelson & Smith, 1998). To the extent that this is true, then, the child doesn't need a collection of constraints in order to figure out new words.

Before going on . . .

- Describe infants' first words.
- What is the naming explosion, and how long does this phase of development last?
- How does word learning proceed in the later preschool and elementary school years?
- What kinds of errors do young children make in their attempts to apply words to new objects and actions?
- What are some proposed constraints on word learning?

Learning the Rules: The Development of Grammar and Pragmatics

After learning the first words, the next big step the child takes is to begin to string words into sentences, initially putting only two words together, then three, four, and more. The first two-word sentences are usually formed between the ages of 18 and 24 months. This is not a random or independent event. Research such as Fenson's (Fenson et al., 1994) suggests that sentences appear only when a child has reached some threshold level of vocabulary size—somewhere around 100 to 200 words.

HOLOPHRASES

Just as the first spoken words are preceded by apparently meaningful gestures, the first two-word sentences have gestural precursors as well. Toddlers often combine a single word with a gesture to create a "two-word meaning" before they actually use two words together in their speech. Bates suggests an example: A child may point to daddy's shoe and say "daddy," as if to convey "daddy's shoe." Or she may say "cookie!" while simultaneously reaching out her hand and opening and closing her fingers, as if to say "Give cookie!" (Bates et al., 1987). In both cases, the meaning conveyed by the use of a gesture and body language combined with a word is more than that of the word alone. Linguists call these word-and-gesture combinations **holophrases**; they are common between the ages of 12 and 18 months.

Once children actually begin speaking two-word sentences, they move rapidly through a series of steps or stages. Thus, within a year or two, most children are able to create remarkably complex sentences.

FIRST SENTENCES

The first sentences—which Roger Brown, a famous observer of child language, called *stage 1 grammar*—have several distinguishing features: They are short (generally two or three words), and they are simple. Nouns, verbs, and adjectives are usually

constraint As used in discussions of language development, an assumption that is presumed to be built-in or learned early (a "default" option") by which a child figures out what words refer to. Examples include the principle of contrast and the whole object constraint.

principle of contrast The assumption that every word has a different meaning, which leads a child to assume that two or more different words refer to different objects.

holophrase A combination of a gesture and a single word that conveys more meaning than just the word alone; often seen and heard in children between 12 and 18 months old.

TABLE 8.3	Some Meanings Children Express in Their Earliest Simple Sentences

Meaning	Examples
Agent-action	Sarah eat; Daddy jump
Action-object	Eat cookie; read book
Possessor-possessed object	Mommy sock; Timmy lunch
Action-location	Come here; play outside
Object-location	Sweater chair; juice table
Attribute-object	Big book; red house
Nomination	That cookie; it dog
Recurrence	More juice; other book

Source: Maratsos, 1983.

included, but virtually all purely grammatical markers (which linguists call *inflections*) are missing. At the beginning, for example, children learning English do not normally add -*s* to the ends of nouns to make them plural, put the -*ed* ending on verbs to make the past tense, or use -*'s* for the possessive or auxiliary verbs such as *am* or *do*. For example, they might say "I tired" or "Me tired" rather than "I am tired," or "I not want it" rather than "I don't want it." Because only the really critical words are present in these early sentences, Brown (1973; Brown & Bellugi, 1964) described them as **telegraphic speech**. The child's language sounds rather like old-fashioned telegrams, in which people included all the essential words—usually nouns, verbs, and modifiers—but left out all the prepositions, auxiliary verbs, and the like (because they had to pay for each word in a telegram).

Interestingly, linguists are no longer sure that precisely this form of telegraphic speech occurs in children learning all languages. Some research seems to show that what determines the words children use in their early sentences is the amount of stress normally placed on such words when that particular language is spoken. In English (and in many other languages), nouns, verbs, and adjectives are stressed in speech, whereas inflections are not. In some languages, however, such as Turkish, inflections are stressed, and children growing up hearing Turkish seem to use inflections much earlier (Gleitman & Wanner, 1988). Findings like these certainly raise some interesting questions about the universality of some of the patterns Brown and others have described.

In contrast, there is no dispute about the assertion that even at this earliest stage, children create sentences following rules—not adult rules, to be sure, but rules nonetheless. Children focus on certain types of words and put them together in particular orders. They also manage to convey a variety of different meanings with their simple sentences.

For example, young children frequently use a sentence made up of two nouns, such as "mommy sock" or "sweater chair" (Bloom, 1973). We might conclude from this that a two-noun form is a basic grammatical characteristic of early language, but such a conclusion misses the complexity. For instance, the child in Bloom's classic study who said "mommy sock" said it on two different occasions. The first time was when she picked up her mother's sock, and the second was when the mother put the child's own sock on the child's foot. In the first case, "mommy sock" seemed to mean "mommy's sock," which is a possessive relationship. In the second instance, the child was conveying that "mommy is putting a sock on me," which is an agent-object relationship.

Table 8.3 lists some other meanings that children convey with their earliest sentences. Not all children express all these relationships or meanings in their early word combinations, and there does not seem to be a fixed order in which these meanings or constructions are acquired, but all children appear to express at least a few of these patterns in their earliest, simplest sentences (Maratsos, 1983).

telegraphic speech Term used by Roger Brown to describe the earliest sentences created by most children, which sound a bit like telegrams because they include key nouns and verbs but generally omit all other words and grammatical inflections.

THE GRAMMAR EXPLOSION

Just as a vocabulary explosion follows an early, slow beginning, so a grammar explosion follows several months of short, simple sentences. One sign of this change is that children's sentences get longer, as you can see in Figure 8.3, which shows the maximum sentence length reported by parents of toddlers of various ages, drawn from Fenson's study. Most 18- to 20-month-olds are still using one- and two-word sentences. By 24 months, children include four and five words in their longest sentences; by 30 months, their maximum sentence length has almost doubled again.

Vocabulary and the Grammar Explosion

The grammar explosion is strongly linked to vocabulary development. Fenson finds a correlation of .84 between the complexity of a child's sentences and the size of her speaking vocabulary—an astonishingly high correlation for behavioral research (Fenson et al., 1994). That is, children whose grammar is more complex and advanced also have larger vocabularies. Just what such a link may indicate about how children learn language is still a matter of debate. Is a large vocabulary necessary for grammar development? Alternatively, perhaps having begun to understand how to construct sentences, a child can also understand new words better and hence learn them more readily. Whatever the eventual explanation, Fenson's research gives developmentalists important data to work with.

During the grammar explosion, children's speech ceases to be telegraphic, as they rather quickly add many of the inflections and function words. Within a few months, they use plurals, past tenses, auxiliary verbs such as *be* and *do*, prepositions, and the like. You can get a feeling for the sound of the change from Table 8.4, which lists some of the sentences spoken by a boy named Daniel, recorded by David Ingram (1981). The left-hand column lists some of Daniel's sentences at about 21 months of age, when he was still using the simplest forms; the right-hand column lists some of his sentences only 2½ months later (age 23 months), when he had shifted into a higher gear. As you can see, stage 2 grammar includes longer sentences and a few inflections, such as "doggies."

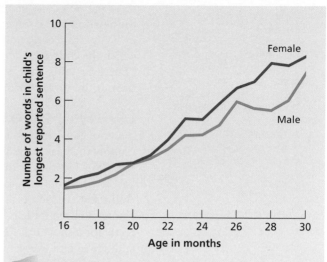

FIGURE 8.3

In their cross-sectional study, Fenson and his colleagues asked 1,130 parents of toddlers (aged 16 to 30 months) to describe the longest sentence used by their child.

(*Source*: From "Variability in Early Communicative Development" by Fenson, Dale, Reznick, Bates, Thal, and Pethick, *Monographs of the Society for Research in Child Development*, 59, No. 242 (1994), p. 82, Fig. 27. By permission of the Society for Research in Child Development.)

Adding Inflections

Daniel obviously did not add all the inflections to his sentences at once. As you can see in Table 8.4, he uses only a few, such as *-s* for plural, although the beginning of a negative construction is apparent in "No book," and the beginning of a question form shows in "Where going?" even though he has not yet added the auxiliary verb to the question.

Within each language community, children seem to add inflections and more complex word orders in fairly predictable sequences. In a classic early study, Roger Brown (1973) found that the earliest inflection used by children learning English is most often *-ing* added onto a verb, as in "I playing" or "doggie running." Then come (in order) prepositions such as *on* and *in*; the plural *-s* on nouns; irregular past tenses such as *broke* or *ran*; possessives; articles (*a* and *the*); the *-s* on third-person verb forms, as in *he wants*; regular past tenses such as *played* and *wanted*; and the various forms of auxiliary verbs, as in *I am going*.

Questions and Negatives

There are also predictable sequences in the child's developing use of questions and negatives. In each case, the child seems to go through periods when he creates types of sentences that he has not heard adults use but that are consistent with the particular set of rules he is using. For example, in the development of questions in English,

TABLE 8.4	Examples of Daniel's Stage 1 and Stage 2 Sentences
Stage 1 (Simple) Sentences, Age 21 Months	**Stage 2 (More Complex) Sentences Age 23 Months**
A bottle	A little boat
Here bottle	Doggies here
Hi Daddy	Give you the book
Horse doggie	It's a boy
Broke it	It's a robot
Kitty cat	Little box there
Poor Daddy	No book
That monkey	Oh cars
Want bottle	That flowers
	Where going?

Source: Reprinted by permission of the publisher. D. Ingram, Early patterns of grammatical development, in R. E. Stark (Ed.), *Language behavior in infancy and early childhood*. Tables 6 and 7, pp. 344–345. Copyright © 1981 by Elsevier Science Publishing Co., Inc.

there is a point at which the child puts a *wh* word (*who, what, when, where,* or *why*) at the beginning of a sentence but doesn't yet put the auxiliary verb in the right place, as in "Why it is resting now?" Similarly, in the development of negatives, there is a stage in which the child uses *not* or *-n't* or *no* but omits the auxiliary verb, as in "I not crying," "There no squirrels," or "This not fits" (Bloom, 1991). Then children rather quickly figure out the correct forms and stop making these mistakes.

Overregularization   Another intriguing phenomenon of this second phase of sentence construction is *overregularization*. What English-speaking 3- to 4-year-olds do is apply the basic rules to irregular words, thus making the language more regular than it really is (Maratsos, 2000). You can hear this phenomenon in children's creation of past tense forms such as "wented," "blowed," or "sitted," and plurals such as "teeths" or "blockses" (Fenson et al., 1994; Kuczaj, 1977, 1978). Stan Kuczaj has pointed out that young children initially learn a small number of irregular past tenses and use them correctly for a short time. Next, children rather suddenly seem to discover the rule of adding *-ed* and overgeneralize this rule to all verbs. Then, they relearn the exceptions one at a time. Even among preschoolers, this type of error is not hugely common, comprising only about 2–3% of all past tenses in English, according to one study (Marcus et al., 1992). These overregularizations nonetheless stand out because they are so distinctive and because they illustrate yet again that children create forms that they have not heard but that are logical within their current understanding of grammar.

LATER GRAMMAR LEARNING

Even though most children are reasonably fluent in their first language (or languages) by age 3 or 4, there are still many refinements to be made. These refinements gradually appear in children's language over the course of the later preschool, elementary, and even early teen years.

Complex Sentences   Soon after young children have figured out inflections and basic sentence forms such as negation and questions, they begin to create remarkably complex sentences, using conjunctions such as *and* and *but* to combine two ideas or using embedded clauses. Here are some examples, taken from the speech of 3- and 4-year-olds, from de Villiers and de Villiers (1992):

> I didn't catch it but Teddy did!
> I'm gonna sit on the one you're sitting on.
> Where did you say you put my doll?
> Those are punk rockers, aren't they?

Children add still more complex and difficult sentence forms to their repertoires throughout elementary school, and recurrent overregularization errors are eliminated (Bowerman, 1985). (However, children have trouble understanding and using passive forms, such as "The food is eaten by the cat" and do not use them much in spontaneous speech until they are 8 or 9.) But these are refinements. The really giant strides occur between ages 1 and about 4, as the child moves from single words to complex questions, negatives, and commands.

Further Refinements   During middle childhood, children become skilled at managing the finer points of grammar (Prat-Sala, Shillcock, & Sorace, 2000; Ragnarsdottir, Simonsen, & Plunkett, 1999). For example, by the end of middle childhood, most children understand various ways of saying something about the past such as *I went, I was going, I have gone, I had gone, I had been going,* and so on. Moreover, they use such tenses correctly in their own speech. During the middle childhood years, children also learn how to maintain a topic of conversation, how to create unambiguous sentences, and how to speak politely or persuasively (Anglin, 1993).

PRAGMATICS

For about a decade, linguists have also been interested in a third aspect of children's language—the way children learn to use speech, either to communicate with others (an aspect of language called **pragmatics**) or to regulate their own behavior. How early do children know what kind of language to use in specific situations? How early do they learn the "rules" of conversation, for example, that people conversing take turns?

Children seem to learn the pragmatics of language at a remarkably early age. For example, children as young as 18 months show adult patterns of gazing when they are talking with a parent: They look at the person who is talking, look away at the beginning of their own speaking turn, and then look at the listener again when they are signaling that they are about to stop talking (Rutter & Durkin, 1987).

Furthermore, a child as young as 2 years old adapts the form of his language to the situation he is in or the person he is talking to—a point made in Chapter 6 in the discussion of children's egocentrism. A child might say "Gimme" to another toddler as he grabs the other child's cup but say "More milk" to an adult. Among older children, language is even more clearly adapted to the listener: 4-year-olds use simpler language when they talk to 2-year-olds than when they talk to adults (Tomasello & Mannle, 1985); first-graders explain things more fully to a stranger than to a friend (Sonnenschein, 1986) and are more polite to adults and strangers than to peers. Both of these trends are even clearer among fourth-graders. Thus, very early on—probably from the beginning—the child recognizes that language is meant to communicate, and he adapts the form of his language in order to achieve better communication.

These children already know many of the social rules about how language is used, including rules about who is supposed to look at whom during a conversation.

LANGUAGE AND SELF-CONTROL

Children also use language to help control or monitor their own behavior. Such *private speech*, which may consist of fragmentary sentences, muttering, or instructions to the self, is detectable from the earliest use of words and sentences. For example, when 2- or 3-year-olds play by themselves, they give themselves instructions, stop themselves with words, or describe what they are doing: "No, not there," "I put that there," or "Put it" (Furrow, 1984).

Piaget thought that this was egocentric speech, but Vygotsky believed that Piaget was quite wrong in this case. Vygotsky insisted instead that the child uses private speech to communicate with herself for the explicit purpose of guiding her own behavior. He believed that such self-directing use of language is central to all cognitive development.

In young children, such self-directing speech is audible. In older children, it is audible only when the child is facing a challenging task; in other situations, it goes "underground." For example, you may recall from Chapter 6 that Flavell found that young elementary school children muttered to themselves while they were trying to remember lists; among 9- or 10-year-olds, this behavior is much less common (Bivens & Berk, 1990). Thinking of this set of findings in terms of the work on information processing described in Chapter 6 leads to the view that the child uses language audibly to remind himself of some new or complex processing strategy; as the child rehearses the strategy and learns it more flexibly, audible language is no longer needed. Such an

pragmatics The rules for the use of language in communicative interaction, such as the rules for taking turns and the style of speech that is appropriate for different listeners.

Before going on...

- What is a holophrase?
- Describe children's first sentences.
- What is the significance of the grammar explosion?
- List the refinements children make in their language skills in the preschool, elementary, and teen years.
- Describe children's acquisition of pragmatic rules.
- What is private speech, and what is its significance for cognitive development, according to Vygotsky and Piaget?

interpretation is bolstered by the observation that even adults use audible language in problem solving when they are faced with especially difficult tasks.

Even this brief foray into the research on children's use of language points out that a full understanding of language development requires knowledge of both cognitive development and children's social skills and understanding. Lois Bloom argues that "children learn language in the first place because they strive to . . . share what they and other persons are feeling and thinking" (1993, p. 245). From birth, the child is able to communicate feelings and thoughts through facial expressions, and somewhat later through gestures. But these are imperfect vehicles for communication; language is much more efficient. Such an argument reminds us once again that child development is not divided into tidy packages labeled "physical development," "social development," and "language development" but is instead a coherent, integrated process.

 # Explaining Language Development

If merely describing language development is difficult, explaining it is still harder. Indeed, explaining how a child learns language has proved to be one of the most compelling challenges in developmental psychology.

IMITATION AND REINFORCEMENT

The earliest theories of language were based either on learning theory or on the commonsense idea that children learn language by imitation. Imitation obviously has to play some part, because a child learns the language she hears. Furthermore, those toddlers who most readily imitate an adult when the adult speaks a new word are also the ones who show the most rapid vocabulary growth in the first year or two of the language explosion; this fact indicates that imitation is an important ingredient in the process (Masur, 1995). Still, imitation alone can't explain all language acquisition, because it cannot account for children's tendency to create words and expressions they have never heard, such as "footses" and "I goed."

Reinforcement theories such as Skinner's (1957) fare no better. Skinner argued that in addition to the role they play in imitation, parents shape language through systematic reinforcements, gradually rewarding better and better approximations of adult speech (the process of *shaping*). Yet when researchers have listened to parents talking to children, they find that parents don't seem to do anything like what Skinner proposed. Instead, parents are remarkably forgiving of all sorts of peculiar constructions and meaning (Brown & Hanlon, 1970; Hirsh-Pasek, Trieman, & Schneiderman, 1984); they reinforce children's sentences on the basis of whether the sentence is true rather than whether it is grammatically correct. In addition, children learn many forms of language, such as plurals, with relatively few errors. In sum, it is plain that some process other than shaping must be involved.

NEWER ENVIRONMENTAL THEORIES

Still, it seems obvious that what is said to a child has to play some role in the process of language formation. Developmentalists know that children whose parents talk to them often, read to them regularly, and use a wide range of words in their speech begin to talk sooner, develop larger vocabularies, use more complex sentences, and learn to read more readily when they reach school age (Hart & Risley, 1995; Huttenlocher, 1995; Snow, 1997). Thus, the sheer quantity of language a child hears is a significant factor.

Environment and Language Development   Children who are exposed to less (and less varied) language in their earliest years don't seem to catch up later in vocabulary, a point illustrated with the data in Table 8.5. These numbers come from the National Longitudinal Survey of Labor Market Experience of Youth (NLSY), a 12-year longitudinal study of a large sample of young women in the United States, begun when they were still teenagers. Table 8.5 shows one piece of information about the preschool-aged children of these young women: the percentage who had vocabulary scores below the 30th percentile on the most commonly used measure of vocabulary—the Peabody Picture Vocabulary Test (PPVT). Developmentalists know that the amount and quality of language a child hears varies with the mother's income level: Poor mothers talk to their children less, use less complex sentences, and read to their children less. The data in Table 8.5 reveal that one consequence of poverty for children is a considerably higher risk of poor language skills.

By age 4, the difference in vocabulary between poor and better-off children is already substantial, and the gap only widens over the school years. Similarly, Catherine Snow (1997) has found that 4-year-old children reared in poverty use shorter and less complex sentences than do their better-off peers. Many factors no doubt contribute to these differences, but the richness and variety of the language a child hears are obviously highly significant. Of all these factors, being read to may be one of the most critical.

Motherese   Beyond the mere quantity of language directed at the child, the quality of the parents' language may also be important in helping the child learn language. In particular, developmentalists know that adults talk to children in a special kind of very simple language, originally called **motherese** by many linguists and now more scientifically described as **infant-directed speech**. This simple language is spoken in a higher-pitched voice and at a slower pace than is speech to older children or other adults. The sentences are short and grammatically simple, with concrete vocabulary. When speaking to children, parents also repeat a lot, introducing minor variations ("Where is the ball? Can you see the ball? Where is the ball? There's the ball!"). They may also repeat the child's own sentences but in slightly longer, more grammatically correct forms—a pattern referred to as an *expansion* or a *recasting*. For example, if a child said "mommy sock," the mother might recast it as "Yes, this is mommy's sock," or if a child said "Doggie not eat," the parent might say "The doggie is not eating."

Developmentalists also know that babies as young as a few days old can discriminate between motherese and speech directed to other adults and that they prefer to listen to motherese, whether it is spoken by a female or a male voice (Cooper & Aslin,

CRITICAL THINKING

Imagine yourself talking to an infant you are holding in your arms. Can you hear yourself using motherese?

TABLE 8.5	Percentage of Children Aged 4 to 7 Who Score below the 30th Percentile on the Peabody Picture Vocabulary Test, as a Function of Poverty		
Type of Family	**Number of Cases**	**Observed Percentage**	**Adjusted Percentage***
Recipients of Federal Aid to Families with Dependent Children, or AFDC ("welfare" families)	196	60%	52%
Poor but not receiving AFDC	116	47%	42%
Not poor	659	27%	30%

*These percentages have been adjusted statistically to subtract out the effects of differences in parents' education, family structure, family size, and age, sex, and ethnicity of the child.

Source: From "The life circumstances and development of children in welfare families: A profile based on national survey data" by Zill, Moore, Smith, Stief, and Coiro, *Escape from poverty: What makes a difference for children*, P. L. Chase-Lansdale and J. Brooks-Gunn, eds., p. 45, Table 2.3. © 1995 by Cambridge University Press. By permission of Cambridge University Press.

motherese (infant-directed speech) The simplified, higher-pitched speech that adults use with infants and young children.

1994; Pegg, Werker, & McLeod, 1992). This preference exists even when the motherese is being spoken in a language other than the one normally spoken to the child. Janet Werker and her colleagues (1994), for example, have found that both English and Chinese infants prefer to listen to infant-directed speech, whether it is spoken in English or in Cantonese (one of the major languages of China).

The quality of motherese that seems to be particularly attractive to babies is its higher pitch. Once the child's attention is drawn by this special tone, the very simplicity and repetitiveness of the adult's speech may help the child to pick out repeating grammatical forms. Children's attention also seems to be drawn to recast sentences. For example, Farrar (1992) found that a 2-year-old was two or three times more likely to imitate a correct grammatical form after he had heard his mother recast his own sentences than he was when the mother used that same correct grammatical form in her normal conversation. Experimental studies confirm this effect of recastings. Children who are deliberately exposed to higher rates of specific types of recast sentences seem to learn the modeled grammatical forms more quickly than do those who hear no recastings (Nelson, 1977).

The theory makes sense, doesn't it? The language the child hears is important, perhaps even formative. Still, this theory of language acquisition has some holes in it. For one thing, while children who hear more expansions or recastings may learn grammar sooner, in normal parent-toddler conversations, recastings are actually relatively rare, and in some cases almost nonexistent. Yet children nevertheless acquire complex grammar, which suggests that the kind of feedback provided by recastings is unlikely to be a major source of grammatical information for most children (Morgan, Bonamo, & Travis, 1995). And although motherese does seem to occur in the vast majority of cultures and contexts, it does not occur in all. For example, Pye (1986) could find no sign of use of motherese in one Mayan culture, and studies in the United States show that it is greatly reduced among depressed mothers (Bettes, 1988). Children of these mothers nonetheless learn language. Thus, while infant-directed speech may be helpful, it is probably not necessary for language acquisition.

NATIVIST THEORIES

On the other side of the theoretical spectrum are the nativist theorists, who argue that much of what the child needs for learning language is built into the organism. Early nativist theorists such as Noam Chomsky (1965, 1975, 1986, 1988) were especially struck by two phenomena: the extreme complexity of the task the child must accomplish, and the apparent similarities in the steps and stages of children's early language development across languages and among all children. Newer cross-language comparisons make it clear that there is more variability than at first appeared, as will be described in the next section of this chapter. Nonetheless, nativist theories are alive and well and are becoming increasingly accepted.

One particularly influential nativist is Dan Slobin (1985a, 1985b), who assumes that every child is born with a basic language-making capacity, made up of a set of fundamental operating principles. Slobin argues that just as the newborn infant seems to come programmed with "rules to look by," infants and children are programmed with "rules to listen by." You've already encountered a good deal of evidence consistent with this proposal in earlier sections. Researchers have established that very young infants focus on individual sounds and syllables in the stream of sounds they hear, that they pay attention to sound rhythm, and that they prefer speech of a particular pattern (motherese). Slobin also proposes that babies are preprogrammed to pay attention to the beginnings and endings of strings of sounds and to stressed sounds—a hypothesis supported by research (e.g., Morgan, 1994). Together, these operating principles help to explain some of the features of children's early grammar. In English, for example, the stressed words in a sentence are normally the verb and the noun—precisely the words that English-speaking children use in their earliest sentences. In Turkish, on the other hand, prefixes and suffixes are stressed, and Turkish-speaking children learn both very early. Both of these patterns make sense if we assume that the preprogrammed rule is not "pay attention to verbness" or "nounness" or "prefixness" but "pay attention to stressed sounds."

CONSTRUCTIVIST THEORIES

The fact that the nativist model is consistent with growing knowledge of apparently built-in perceptual skills and processing biases is certainly a strong argument in its favor. Even so, this is not the only compelling theoretical option. In particular, some theorists argue persuasively that what is important is not the built-in biases or operating principles but the child's construction of language as part of the broader process of cognitive development.

One prominent proponent of this view, Melissa Bowerman, puts the proposition this way: "When language starts to come in, it does not introduce new meanings to the child. Rather, it is used to express only those meanings the child has already formulated independently of language" (1985, p. 372). Even more broadly, as noted earlier, Lois Bloom argues that from the beginning use of language, the child's intent is to communicate, to share the ideas and concepts that are in his head. He does this as best he can with the gestures or words he knows, and he learns new words when they help him communicate his thoughts and feelings (1993, 1997).

One type of evidence in support of this argument comes from the observation that it is children, not mothers, who initiate the majority of verbal exchanges (Bloom, 1997). Further evidence comes from studies showing links between achievements in language development and the child's broader cognitive development. For example, symbolic play (such as pretending to drink from an empty cup) and imitation of sounds and gestures both appear at about the same time as the child's first words, suggesting some broad "symbolic understanding" that is reflected in a number of behaviors. In children whose language is significantly delayed, both symbolic play and imitation are usually delayed as well (Bates et al., 1987; Ungerer & Sigman, 1984).

Another example reinforces this argument: At about the point at which two-word sentences appear, children begin to combine several gestures into a sequence in their pretend play, such as pouring imaginary liquid, drinking, and then wiping the mouth. Children who are the first to show such sequencing in their play are also the first to show two- or three-word sentences in their speech (e.g., McCune, 1995; Shore, 1986).

We need not choose between Slobin's and Bowerman's approaches. Both may be true. The child may begin with built-in operating principles that aim her attention at crucial features of the language input. The child then processes that information according to her initial (perhaps built-in) strategies or schemes. Then she modifies those strategies or schemes as she receives new information, such as by arriving at some of the constraints about word meanings. The result is a series of rules for understanding and creating language. The strong similarities observed among children in their early language constructions come about both because all children share the same initial processing rules and because most children are exposed to very similar input from the people around them. But because the input is not identical, because languages differ, language development follows less and less similar pathways as the child progresses.

AN ECLECTIC APPROACH

Many developmentalists believe that a theory of language development that draws from all of the views discussed above provides the best understanding of language development. One important point is that we now have a much greater understanding of how the environment influences language development than when Skinner and Chomsky began their historic debate in the 1950s. Also, it seems clear that a complete understanding of language development must incorporate the nativist and cognitivist theories. Before adding these two perspectives to a contemporary understanding of how the environment influences language development, we have to find a way to reconcile them to each other.

First, it seems clear that, as the nativists claim, some kind of capacity for processing linguistic information is "hard-wired" into the infant brain. However, many developmentalists have argued that this phenomenon is best understood when it is integrated into a constructivist view of language development. This integrated view proposes that the child begins with built-in operating principles that aim the child's attention at crucial features of the language input. The child then processes that information according to her initial (perhaps built-in) strategies or schemes. Then she modifies those strategies or rules as she receives new information—for example, arriving at some of the constraints on word meanings. The result is a series of rules for understanding and creating language. The strong similarities we see among children in their early language constructions come about both because all children share the same initial processing rules and because most children are exposed to very similar input from the people around them. But because the input is not identical, because languages differ, language development follows less and less common pathways as the child progresses.

Before going on . . .

- How do learning theorists explain language development?
- What do environmental theories of language development suggest about the importance of talking to a child?
- What kinds of evidence supports the nativist theories?
- How do constructivist theories differ from other approaches?
- How can the behaviorist, nativist, and constructivist approaches be integrated into a comprehensive explanation of language development?

Individual and Group Differences in Language Development

The description you've read of the sequence of language development is accurate on the average, but the speed with which children acquire language skill varies widely. There also seem to be important style differences.

DIFFERENCES IN RATE

There is a great deal of individual variation in language development. Some children begin to use words at 8 months, while others do not do so until 18 months. Similarly, the normal range of variation in vocabulary size among 2-year-olds is from a low of 10 words to a high of several hundred (MacWhinney, 2005).

You can see the range of normal variation in sentence construction very clearly in Figure 8.4, which shows the average number of meaningful units per sentence [referred to by linguists as the **mean length of utterance (MLU)**] of 10 children, from longitudinal studies by Roger Brown (1973), Ira Blake (1994), and Lois Bloom (1991). The figure includes a line at the MLU level that normally accompanies a switch from simple, uninflected two-word sentences to more complex forms.

You can see that Eve was the earliest to make this transition, at about 20 months, while Adam and Sarah passed over this point nearly a year later. These variations are confirmed in Fenson's much larger cross-sectional study of more than 1,000 toddlers whose language was described by their parents. In this group, the earliest age at which parents reported more complex sentences than simple sentences was about 22 months, with an average of about 27 months. However, as many as a quarter of children had not reached this point by 30 months (Fenson et al., 1994).

At present, MLU is frequently used by physicians, teachers, and others to identify children who need additional screening to determine whether they have some kind of language disability (Hewitt, Hammer, Yount, & Tomblin, 2005). More than half of children who are behind schedule during the early months of language development even-

mean length of utterance (MLU) The average number of meaningful units in a sentence. Each basic word is one meaningful unit, as is each inflection.

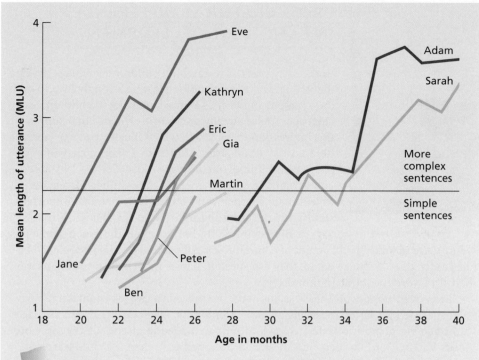

FIGURE 8.4

The 10 children whose language is charted here, studied by three different linguists, moved at markedly different times from simple one- and two-word sentences to more complex sentences. (*Sources*: Reprinted and adapted by permission of the publisher from *A First Language: The Early Stages*, by Roger Brown, p. 55, Cambridge, MA: Harvard University Press, Copyright © 1973 by the President and Fellows of Harvard College. Lois Bloom, *Language Development from Two to Three*, p. 92, Table 3.1; Cambridge, England: Cambridge University Press, 1991. I. K. Blake, "Language Development and Socialization in Young African-American Children," *Cross-Cultural Roots of Minority Children*, Greenfield and Cocking, eds., p. 169, Table 9.1 and p. 171, Fig. 9.1; Hillsdale, NJ: Lawrence Erlbaum Associates, Inc., 1994.)

tually catch up to their agemates. The subset who do not catch up is primarily made up of children who also have poor receptive language (Bates, 1993; Thal, Tobias, & Morrison, 1991). Research suggests that some kind of defect in the fast-mapping process may be responsible for the leveling off in vocabulary growth that many of these children exhibit around the age of 3 (Alt, Plante, & Creusere, 2004). Such children appear to remain behind in language development and perhaps in cognitive development more generally. In practical terms, this means that parents of a child who is significantly delayed in understanding as well as speaking language should seek professional help to try to diagnose the problem and begin appropriate intervention.

How can these variations in speed of early language development be explained? The alternative possibilities should be familiar by now. One possibility is that the rate of language development may be something one inherits—in the same way that intelligence or the rate of physical development may be affected by heredity. Twin studies designed to test this possibility show that vocabulary size (but not grammatical complexity) is more similar in identical twins than in fraternal twins (Mather & Black, 1984). However, adoption studies show that 2-year-olds' language skill can be predicted about equally well from the IQ scores or the language skills of either their biological or their adoptive parents (Plomin & DeFries, 1985). So it seems that parents who talk more, who read to their children more and elicit more language from them, and who respond appropriately to their children's language may have children who develop language more rapidly, regardless of genetic inheritance. Overall, as with IQ, it seems obvious that both the particular genes the child inherits and the environment in which the child grows up contribute to her rate of language development.

CROSS-CULTURAL DIFFERENCES IN LANGUAGE DEVELOPMENT

Parents who talk a lot to their babies and ask them questions, as this man appears to be doing, have children who learn to talk sooner.

In the early years of research on children's language development, linguists and psychologists were strongly impressed by the apparent similarities across languages in children's early language. You've already seen some evidence that supports this impression in Table 8.2, which illustrated large similarities in early vocabularies. Studies in a wide variety of language communities, including Turkish, Serbo-Croatian, Hungarian, Hebrew, Japanese, a New Guinean language called Kaluli, German, and Italian have revealed important similarities in young children's language (Maitel, Dromi, Sagi, & Bornstein, 2000). For example, the prelinguistic phase seems to be identical in all language communities. All babies coo, then babble; all babies understand language before they can speak it; babies in all cultures begin to use their first words at about 12 months.

Moreover, a one-word phase seems always to precede a two-word phase in every language, with the latter appearing at about 18 months. Likewise, across all languages studied so far, prepositions describing locations are added in essentially the same order. Words for "in," "on," "under," and "beside" are learned first; then the child learns the words for "front" and "back" (Slobin, 1985a). Finally, children everywhere seem to pay more attention to the ends of words than to the beginnings, so they learn suffixes before they learn prefixes.

Interestingly, the universal tendency of children to attend to the ends of statements produces cross-cultural differences in language learning. Such differences happen because different languages use different kinds of words at the ends of sentences. In English, the last word in a statement is most likely to be a noun. However, in Mandarin Chinese and Korean, the last word is often a verb. Consequently, while children who are learning English tend to use more nouns than verbs in their first attempts at speaking, children learning Mandarin Chinese and Korean produce just as many verbs as nouns (MacWhinney, 2005). Further, this linguistic difference is associated with cross-cultural variations in the way mothers speak to their babies. Those who speak languages that often use verbs at the ends of statements talk about verbs more to their babies. By contrast, mothers who speak English and other noun-focused languages more often explain nouns to infants.

Another interesting cross-linguistic difference is that the specific word order a child uses in early sentences is not the same for all children in all languages. In some languages, a noun/verb sequence is fairly common; in others, a verb/noun sequence may be heard. In addition, particular inflections are learned in highly varying orders from one language to another. Japanese children, for example, begin very early to use a special kind of marker, called a *pragmatic marker*, which tells something about the feeling or the context of what is being said. For instance, the word *yo* is used at the end of a sentence when the speaker is experiencing some resistance from the listener; the word *ne* is used when the speaker expects approval or agreement. Japanese children begin to use these markers very early, much earlier than children whose languages contain inflections.

Most strikingly, children learning certain languages do not appear to go through a stage of using simple two-word sentences with no inflections. Children learning Turkish, for example, use essentially the full set of noun and verb inflections by age 2 and never go through a stage of using uninflected words. Their language is simple, but it is rarely ungrammatical from the adult's point of view (Aksu-Koc & Slobin, 1985; Maratsos, 1998).

Finally, cross-cultural studies of language development provide us with several good examples of how such research informs our understanding of universals in human development. For example, researchers at one time thought that individual differences in the types of words babies use might be universal (e.g., Shore, 1995). This difference was termed a *style* of language acquisition. Early studies suggested that some toddlers exhibited a *referential* style that focused on labeling objects, while others showed an *expressive* style that concentrated more on social and emotional words. Further research, however, demonstrated that these differences, while somewhat useful for describing the development of English-speaking children, were not manifested in the development of children who were learning other languages (Camaioni & Longobardi, 1995). As a result, researchers took a closer look at English-speaking toddlers, and they found that the apparent style difference disappears with age and has no impact on later language development (Bates et al., 1994).

Before going on . . .

■ Are differences in rate of language development related to later linguistic proficiency?
■ What are the expressive and referential styles, and how do they affect language development?
■ In what ways does language development vary across language groups?

Learning to Read and Write

Finally, throughout the industrialized world, and increasingly in developing nations, using language to read and write is just as critical to a child's development as using spoken language. Certainly, spoken language forms the foundation on which children build literacy skills. However, learning to read and write taps into children's cognitive and motor skills as well.

CRITICAL THINKING

As an adult reader, when do you use your phonological awareness skills?

THE EARLY FOUNDATION: PHONOLOGICAL AWARENESS

Certain aspects of early childhood language development, such as rate of vocabulary growth, predict how easily a child will learn to read and write when she enters school (Wood & Terrell, 1998). However, one specific component of early childhood language development—phonological awareness—seems to be especially important (Anthony & Lonigan, 2004; Schatschneider, Fletcher, Francis, Carlson, & Foorman, 2004). **Phonological awareness** is a child's awareness of the rules governing sound patterns that are specific to his or her own language. It also includes the child's knowledge of that particular language's system for representing sounds with letters. Researchers measure English-speaking children's phonological awareness with questions like these: "What would *bat* be if you took away the [b]? What would *bat* be if you took away the [b] and put [r] there instead?" (see the *Research Report*).

Young children can learn phonological awareness skills either through formal means, as these preschoolers are doing, or informally through word games and rhymes.

Developmentalists now have abundant evidence that children who are more phonologically aware at age 3, 4, or 5 later learn to read much more easily (Adams, Trieman, & Pressley, 1998; Bryant, MacLean, Bradley, & Crossland, 1990; Hansen & Bowey, 1994; Wagner et al., 1997; Whitehurst, 1995). Furthermore, if you train preschoolers or kindergartners in phonological awareness, their reading skills in first grade improve—a result that has been found in studies in Scandinavia and Germany as well as the United States (Nelson, Benner, & Gonzalez, 2005; Schneider, Reimers, Roth, & Visé, 1995).

Of course, a child doesn't have to acquire phonological awareness in early childhood. Phonological skills can be learned in elementary school through formal instruction (Ball, 1997; Bus & van IJzendoorn, 1999; Segers & Verhoeven, 2004). However, numerous studies have shown that the greater a child's phonological awareness *before* he enters school, the faster he learns to read (Christensen, 1997; Gilbertson & Bramlett, 1998; Schatschneider, Francis, Foorman, Fletcher, & Mehta, 1999; Wood & Terrell, 1998). In addition, phonological awareness in the early childhood years is related to rate of literacy learning for languages as varied as English, Punjabi, and Chinese

phonological awareness
Understanding of the rules governing the sounds of a language as well as knowledge of the connection between sounds and the way they are represented in written language.

African American Vernacular English

The term *Standard American English (SAE)* refers to written English and to dialects that are very similar to written English. *African American Vernacular English (AAVE)*, also known as *Black English* and *Ebonics*, is a dialect spoken by many African Americans. In recent years, this particular dialect has been the subject of much discussion, most of which has centered around the relationship between AAVE and reading achievement. Research indicates that African American children who are less proficient in SAE than they are in AAVE get lower scores on reading achievement tests than peers who are more familiar with SAE (Charity, Scarborough, & Griffin, 2004). Psycholinguists believe that differences such as these arise out of phonological variations across AAVE and SAE (Treiman, 2004). For example, AAVE tends to drop consonants at the ends of words. As a result, children who acquire AAVE as their first language possess good phonological awareness skills for AAVE but lack them for SAE (Sligh & Connors, 2003). Predictably, experimental studies show that African American children who speak AAVE benefit from specific training in the sound patterns of SAE (Laing, 2003).

Many educators have also argued that children who speak AAVE need support in improving other SAE-related skills. Some have suggested that schools use teaching strategies that build on children's knowledge of AAVE to help them become more skilled in the use of SAE. For example, some teachers put up posters in their classrooms that remind students of AAVE-SAE translations, such as "I had went = I had gone" (Delpit, 1990). In some schools, African American children study the history of the dialect and its relationship to the West African cultures from which many slaves were taken centuries ago. In others, children learn about other dialects, like Australian English, along with AAVE and SAE (Wolfram, Schilling-Estes, & Hazen, 1996).

The use of AAVE in schools, even as a means of teaching SAE, is controversial, however. Some Americans still regard AAVE as an inferior form of English that has no place in formal education (Wolfram, 1990). In addition, some African Americans believe that reinforcing children's use of the dialect will make it more difficult for them to succeed in a culture dominated by SAE (Fillmore, 1997). They point out that not all African American children speak AAVE, and those who don't shouldn't be forced to learn it strictly on the basis of their race. Some critics have been persuaded to support teaching strategies that involve AAVE, however, on learning that children's reading and writing skills have improved in schools where such strategies have been tried (Council of the Great City Schools, 1997).

Questions for Critical Analysis

1. In what ways are the challenges faced by AAVE-speaking children similar to those of children whose home language is not English, and in what ways do they differ?
2. As implied in this discussion, African American children vary in the degree to which they are proficient in both AAVE and SAE. What are some of the variables that might account for these variations?

(Chiappe & Siegel, 1999; Ho & Bryant, 1997; Huang & Hanley, 1997; McBride-Chang & Ho, 2000). Large gains in phonological awareness appear to take place between children's fourth and fifth birthdays, just before most children enter kindergarten (Justice et al., 2005).

Researchers have also found that many of the everyday activities preschoolers engage in foster the development of phonological awareness. For example, among English-speaking children, learning and reciting nursery rhymes contributes to phonological awareness (Bryant, MacLean, & Bradley, 1990; Bryant, MacLean, Bradley, & Crossland, 1990; Layton, Deeny, Tall, & Upton, 1996; MacLean, Bryant, & Bradley, 1987). For Japanese children, a game called *shiritori*, in which one person says a word and another comes up with a word that begins with its ending sound, helps children develop these skills (Norboru, 1997; Serpell & Hatano, 1997). Educators have also found that using such games to teach phonological awareness skills to preschoolers is just as effective as using more formal tools such as flash cards and worksheets (Brennan & Ireson, 1997). *Shared reading*, or *dialogic reading*, has also been found to contribute to growth in phonological awareness (Burgess, 1997).

Young children with good phonological awareness skills often use a strategy called **invented spelling** when they attempt to write (see Figure 8.5). In spite of the many errors they make, children who use invented spelling before receiving formal instruction in reading and writing are more likely to become good spellers and readers later in childhood (McBride-Chang, 1998). Thus, the evidence suggests that one of the best ways parents and preschool teachers can help young children prepare for formal instruction in reading is to engage them in activities that encourage word play and invented spelling.

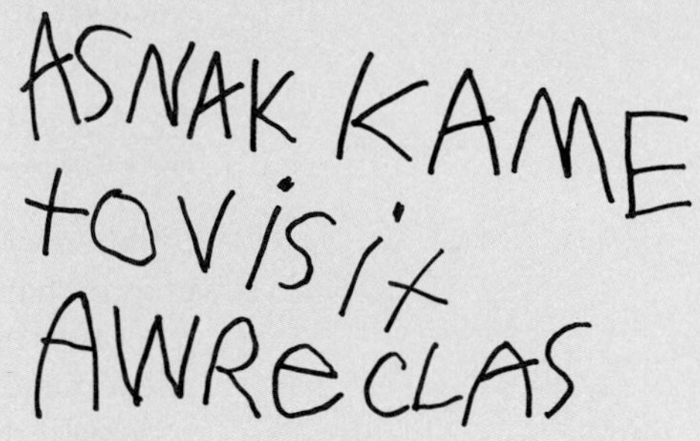

BECOMING LITERATE IN SCHOOL

Across the early elementary years, phonological awareness skills continue to increase (Shu, Anderson, & Wu, 2000). Children who are behind their peers in phonological awareness skills at the start of school are likely to fall further behind unless some systematic effort is made to provide them with a base of phonological knowledge (Torgesen et al., 1999). Indeed, all beginning readers, both those who have high levels of phonological awareness and those who know less about sounds and symbols, seem to benefit from specific instruction in sound-letter correspondences (Adams & Henry, 1997).

It also appears that beginning readers gain a significant advantage when they achieve automaticity with respect to identifying sound-symbol connections (Samuels & Flor, 1997). Thus, they need plenty of opportunities to practice translating written language into spoken words. For this reason, reading experts suggest that oral reading is critical to success in the early years (Adams, 1990).

Once children have learned the basic reading process, learning about meaningful word parts, such as prefixes and suffixes, helps them become more efficient readers and to better understand what they read (Adams & Henry, 1997; McBride-Chang, Shu, Zhou, & Wagner, 2004; Nagy, Berninger, Abbott, Vaughan, & Vermeulen, 2004). Instruction in comprehension strategies, such as identifying the purpose of a particular text, also helps improve reading skill and understanding (Pressley & Wharton-McDonald, 1997; Van den Broek, Lynch, Naslund, Ievers-Landis, & Verduin, 2004). Of course, all along the way, children need to be exposed to good literature, both by reading on their own and by having teachers and parents read to them.

Some of the strategies used to teach reading also help children learn writing—the other component of literacy. For example, instruction in sound-symbol connections helps children learn to spell as well as to read. Of course, good writing is far more than just spelling; it requires instruction and practice, just as reading does. Specifically, children need to learn about writing techniques such as outlining and paragraph development in order to become good writers. They also need to learn about language mechanics, such as grammar and appropriate uses of words, as well as how to edit their own and others' written work (Graham & Harris, 1997).

Despite educators' best efforts, many children fall behind their classmates in literacy during the early school years. In general, reading researchers have found that poor readers have problems with sound-letter combinations (Agnew, Dorn, & Eden, 2004; Gonzalez & Valle, 2000; Mayringer & Wimmer, 2000). Thus, many children who have reading difficulties benefit from highly specific phonics approaches that provide a great deal of practice in translating letters into sounds and vice versa (Berninger et al., 1999).

However, curriculum flexibility is also important in programs for poor readers. Some do not improve when phonics approaches are used. In fact, programs such as the *Reading Recovery* program, which combine sound-letter practice and comprehension training, have proven to be highly successful in helping poor readers catch up, especially when the programs are implemented in the early elementary years (Klein &

FIGURE 8.5

Translation: *A snake came to visit our class.*

A 5-year-old used a strategy called "invented spelling" to write this sentence about a snake's visit (hopefully accompanied by an animal handler!) to her kindergarten class. Invented spelling requires a high level of phonological awareness. Research suggests that children who have well-developed phonological awareness skills by the time they reach kindergarten learn to read more quickly. (*Source:* Author.)

invented spelling A strategy young children with good phonological awareness skills use when they write.

Swartz, 1996). Consequently, teachers need to be able to assess the effectiveness of whatever approach they are using and change it to fit the needs of individual students.

LEARNING A SECOND LANGUAGE

Children whose home language is different from the language spoken at school face unique challenges in acquiring literacy in school (see *The Real World*). Although schools in other countries serve populations who do not speak the local language, this phenomenon seems to be far more pervasive in the English-speaking nations. World-wide patterns of population growth and movement have led to tremendous increases in the number of non–English-speaking children who attend school in the United States, Canada, Great Britain, and Australia. About two-thirds of these children speak English well enough to function in school, but the rest essentially speak no English. Educators in English-speaking countries use the term *limited English proficient (LEP)* to refer to both immigrant children and native-born children who don't speak English.

About 8% of school-aged children in North America are classified as LEP (Statistics Canada, 2000; National Center for Education Statistics [NCES], 2003a). However, as you probably realize, these children are not equally distributed across schools. Some systems have relatively few, while others, as Table 8.6 shows, must cope with a large number of such pupils. Furthermore, in many urban areas in North America, LEP children come from widely varying linguistic backgrounds. In Toronto, for example, school children

One Language or Two?

Chan, a Chinese American, and Luisa, a Mexican American, are the proud parents of a 3-month-old girl. Chan is fluent in Chinese and English, and Luisa is a Spanish-English bilingual. However, neither speaks the other's native language; the only language they have in common is English. Both were raised in monolingual homes and learned to speak English when they went to school. Their own experiences have convinced them that being bilingual is a great asset. They hope to provide their daughter with an even greater asset—that of being fluent in three languages. However, they are somewhat worried about the advisability of raising a child with more than one language in the home. When they were children, they clearly distinguished between their home language and the language they spoke at school. Further, they began learning their second language at an age when they could ask questions of their peers or teachers whenever they were confused about a word or grammatical device. For this reason, Chan and Luisa are concerned about the possibility that their daughter will become confused about which language is which. What would a developmental scientist advise them to do?

Knowing two or more languages clearly provides social and economic benefits to an adult. However, research suggests that there are cognitive advantages *and* disadvantages to

growing up bilingual. On the positive side, being bilingual seems to have no impact on early language milestones such as babbling (Oller, Eilers, Urbano, & Cobo-Lewis, 1997). Also, infants in bilingual homes readily discriminate between the two languages both phonologically and grammatically from the earliest days of life (Bosch & Sebastian-Galles, 1997; Holowka, Brosseau-Lapré, & Petitto, 2002; Koeppe, 1996). Further, learning a grammatical device, such as using *-s* to signify plurals, in one language seems to facilitate learning parallel devices in the other language (Schlyter, 1996).

In preschool and elementary school children, being bilingual is associated with a clear advantage in *metalinguistic ability*, the capacity to think about language (Bialystok, Shenfield, & Codd, 2000; Mohanty & Perregaux, 1997). In addition, most bilingual children display greater ability to focus attention on language tasks than do monolingual children (Bialystok & Majumder, 1998). These two advantages enable bilingual children to more easily grasp the connection between sounds and symbols in the beginning stages of learning to read (Bialystok, 1997; Oller, Cobo-Lewis, & Eilers, 1998).

On the negative side, infants in bilingual homes reach some milestones later than those learning a single language. For example, bilingual infants' receptive and expressive speak more than 80 different languages (Toronto District School Board, 2001). In the U.S. cities of Los Angeles, New York, Chicago, and Washington, DC, more than 100 languages are spoken in the homes of children (NCES, 1997).

The home languages of children in London schools, where LEP students represent about 20% of school enrollment, number more than 300 (National Literacy Trust, 2003). In Australia, issues surrounding LEP students include an added dimension. Schools in urban areas, such as Melbourne and Sydney, face the same challenges as their counterparts in other English-speaking countries. However, most of Australia's LEP children live in remote rural areas and speak one of 10 aboriginal languages (Australian Clearinghouse for Youth Studies, 2005). Their language issues are compounded by poverty, social isolation, and limited availability of teachers (Nicholls, 2005).

Because the issues involved in educating LEP children are so diverse across nations and even across regions within nations, there is no one-size-fits-all solution for school systems that must deal with growing numbers of such students. Frequently, policymakers must adopt an eclectic approach that takes into consideration all of the various approaches to second-language education that have been tried over the past few decades. As you will see, there are important variations among them.

In many North American cities, a substantial proportion of school children come from homes in which a language other than English is spoken. With support, these children can become fluent in English and can excel in school.

vocabularies are as large as those of monolingual infants, but the words they know are divided between two languages (Patterson, 1998). Consequently, they are behind monolingual infants in word knowledge no matter which language is considered, a difference that persists into the school years. In addition, children growing up in bilingual homes in which the two languages vary greatly in how they are written (e.g., English and Chinese) may acquire reading skills in both languages more slowly than peers in monolingual homes (Bialystok, Majumder, & Martin, 2003). Even in adulthood, bilingualism is sometimes associated with decreased efficiency in memory tasks involving words (Gollan & Silverberg, 2001; McElree, Jia, & Litvak, 2000). However, bilingual people appear to develop compensatory strategies that allow them to make up for these inefficiencies. Consequently, those who are bilingual often perform such memory tasks with equal accuracy, even though they may respond to the tasks more slowly than those who are monolingual.

Research indicates that bilingual children who are equally fluent in both languages encounter few, if any, learning problems in school (Vuorenkoski, Kuure, Moilanen, & Peninkilampi, 2000). Similarly, teens and adults who are equally fluent in two languages demonstrate few if any differences in verbal memory efficiency (McElree et al., 2000). However, most children do not attain equal fluency in both languages (Hakansson, Salameh, & Nettelbladt, 2003). As a result, they tend to think more slowly in the language in which they are less fluent (Bernardo & Calleja, 2005; Chincotta & Underwood, 1997). When the language in which they are less fluent is the language

in which their schooling is conducted, they are at risk for learning problems (Anderson, 1998; Thorn & Gathercole, 1999). Further, in adulthood, these "unbalanced bilinguals" are more likely to display reduced speed and accuracy on verbal memory tasks than either monolingual people or bilingual people with equivalent fluency in two languages (McElree et al., 2000). Therefore, parents who choose to speak two languages with their children should probably take into account their ability to fully support the children's acquisition of fluency in both languages.

Clearly, the advantages in adulthood of being bilingual are substantial, and these advantages may outweigh any disadvantages experienced in childhood. Bilingual parents need to balance the various advantages and disadvantages, as well as their long-term parenting goals, to reach an informed decision about the kind of linguistic environment to provide for their infants and children.

Questions for Reflection

1. What kind of linguistic environment would you provide for your child if you were in the same position as Chan and Luisa?

2. In your opinion, how likely is it that the little girl will achieve her parents' goal of fluency in three languages? What factors will influence her eventual level of fluency in each of the three languages?

TABLE 8.6	Percentage of LEP Students in Some of North America's Largest School Systems
Los Angeles	42%
Toronto	41%
Dallas	33%
Houston	28%
San Diego	27%
Denver	25%
Miami	19%
Albuquerque	18%
Chicago	14%
New York City	14%
District of Columbia	12%
Vancouver	12%

Sources: British Columbia Ministry of Education, 2001; NCES, 2003b; Toronto District School Board, 2001.

bilingual education As practiced in the United States, a school program for students who are not proficient in English in which instruction in basic subject matter is given in the children's native language during the first 2 or 3 years of schooling, with a gradual transition to full English instruction over several years.

structured immersion An alternative to traditional bilingual education used in classrooms in which all children speak the same non-English native language. All basic instruction is in English, paced so that the children can comprehend, with the teacher translating only when absolutely necessary.

English-as-a-second-language (ESL) An alternative to bilingual education; children who are not proficient in English attend academic classes taught entirely in English but then spend several hours in a separate class to receive English-language instruction.

submersion An approach to education of non–English-speaking students in which they are assigned to a classroom where instruction is given in English and are given no supplemental language assistance; also known as the "sink or swim" approach.

Some LEP children, mostly those whose first language is Spanish, participate in a bilingual education program (NCES, 1997). In **bilingual education**, instruction is presented in the children's native language during the first 2 or 3 years of schooling, and teachers make a gradual transition to instructing totally in English over the next few years. Such programs have been developed for Spanish-speaking children because they constitute by far the largest group of LEP students in U.S. schools. In other English-speaking countries, bilingual education is available to children from large non–English-speaking groups as well. For example, schools in Canada have provided both English- and French-speaking students in Quebec, a primarily French-speaking province, with bilingual education for decades.

An alternative to bilingual education is **structured immersion**, used in classrooms in which all the children speak the same non-English native language and the teacher speaks both English and the children's native language. In such classrooms, the basic instruction is in English, paced so that the children can comprehend, with the teacher translating only when absolutely necessary. French language programs of this kind for English-speaking children have been very successful in Quebec (Allen, 2004; Holobow, Genesee, & Lambert, 1991). In these programs, students are taught exclusively in French for two years of elementary school. During the remaining elementary years, they receive bilingual instruction. Research shows that, in the early grades, these pupils are somewhat behind monolingual English-speakers in literacy skills. However, when these children reach high school age, they get higher scores on reading achievement tests than their monolingual peers.

However, it is often logistically impossible to provide bilingual education or structured immersion for most LEP children. For one thing, if a school system has only a handful of students who speak a particular language, it is not financially feasible to establish a separate curriculum for them. In addition, it may be impossible to find bilingual teachers for children whose language is spoken by very few people outside their country of origin. For these reasons, most LEP school children in the United States, about 76%, are enrolled in **English-as-a-second-language (ESL)** programs (NCES, 1997). In ESL programs, children attend academic classes that are conducted entirely in English and spend part of each day in English-language classes.

In addition to bilingual education, structured immersion, and ESL approaches, there is **submersion**, sometimes called the "sink or swim" approach, in which a non–English-speaking child is simply assigned to a regular classroom where instruction is given in English and is given no added support or supplemental instruction. While submersion programs implemented in the early school grades are typically associated with positive outcomes for children, the same cannot be said for this approach in secondary school. One study of more than 12,000 Chinese-speaking students who enrolled in English-speaking high schools in Hong Kong found that negative achievement effects were especially evident in mathematics, history, geography, and science classes (Marsh, Hau, & Kong, 2000). However, submersion led to improved achievement test scores in both English and Chinese language classes.

There is some indication that programs of any of these four types that also include a home-based component, such as those that encourage parents to learn the new language along with their children, may be especially effective (Koskinen et al., 2000). However, the only way to find out which alternative is best is to conduct studies in which children are assigned randomly to several of these types of programs and then followed over time. Christine Rossell and Keith Baker (1996), in their comprehensive review of all such controlled, comparative studies, found that bilingual education is not consistently better than submersion, ESL, or structured immersion. Indeed, on measures of English reading proficiency, students in structured immersion programs performed consistently better than those in traditional bilingual education or ESL programs. Rossell and Baker conclude that some version of structured immersion is best. However, the research findings are inconclusive, and the issue remains fraught with controversy (e.g., Crawford, 1991; Goldenberg, 1996; Rossell & Baker, 1996). Different observers draw various conclusions from the existing research evidence, while the great majority of bilingual educators remain committed to some version of traditional bilingual education.

Note that even the very best program will not be effective for children who come to school without good spoken language skills in their native language. And studies involving college students learning a new language suggest that, for older LEP students, facility with written language in their first language is probably also important for success in English-speaking schools (Meschyan & Hernandez, 2002).

With respect to overall achievement, LEP students' performance in school is very similar to that of English-speaking children (NCES, 1997). In fact, in U.S. schools, native-born English-speaking children are more likely to fail one or more grades than children whose home language is either Asian or European. Native-born Spanish-speaking children fail at about the same rate as English speakers. And in U.S. schools, adolescents who are recent immigrants are more likely to complete high school than peers who entered the United States at younger ages or who are native-born (White & Glick, 2000). In fact, studies suggest that, with the help of special programs designed to ease their transition into a new language, ESL children can outperform their monolingual peers on standardized tests of reading achievement as early as second grade, even if they enter school with no knowledge whatever of English (Lesaux & Siegel, 2003). Thus, there is no evidence that a child who enters school with limited English skills has any greater risk of failure than a child whose first language is English.

One cautionary note is important, however: An LEP student does not have an increased risk of failure as long as the school provides some kind of transition to English-only instruction *and* school officials take care to administer all standardized tests in the language with which the child is most familiar (Bernardo & Calleja, 2005; Cushner, McClelland, & Safford, 1992). The first is necessary to optimize the LEP child's potential for achievement. The second ensures that non–English-speaking children are not misclassified as mentally retarded or learning disabled because of their limited English skills. Beyond these requirements, LEP students represent no particular burden to schools. Moreover, in all likelihood, their presence enriches the educational experience of U.S.-born children.

Before going on...

- What is the relationship between phonological awareness and success in learning to read?
- What specific kinds of skills help children become better readers in school?
- How do educators try to help children who have difficulty learning to read?
- Describe the various kinds of programs that schools in English-speaking countries provide for students whose first language is not English.

Summary

Before the First Word: The Prelinguistic Phase

- Many of the developments during the prelinguistic phase (before the first word)—for example, the ability to discriminate different kinds of language sounds—are significant precursors to language.
- An infant coos and produces babbling sounds that gradually more closely approximate the sounds he hears, and he uses gestures in communicative ways.
- By 10 months of age, infants understand 30 or more words, though their speaking vocabulary is still extremely limited.

Learning Words and Word Meanings

- The earliest words appear at about 1 year of age. The first words are simple and are typically used only for specific objects or situations.

- Vocabulary grows slowly at first and then usually spurts in a naming explosion. By 16 to 20 months of age, most children have a vocabulary of 50 or more words; by 30 months, the average vocabulary is 600 words.
- Children continue to learn new words throughout the preschool years and add approximately 10 words a day by the time they are ready to begin elementary school.
- The earliest words are typically highly specific and context-bound in meaning; later, children typically overextend word usage.
- Many (but not all) linguists have concluded that in determining word meanings, a child has built-in constraints or biases, such as the assumption that words refer to objects or actions but not both and the principle of contrast. Others linguists believe that such constraints exist but are acquired rather than built-in.

Learning the Rules: The Development of Grammar and Pragmatics

- Linguists use the term *holophrase* to refer to infants' use of single words, or single words combined with gestures, as sentences. For example, the utterance "cookie" may mean "This is a cookie" or "May I have a cookie?" depending on the context.
- The first two-word sentences normally appear between the ages of 18 and 24 months and are short and grammatically simple, lacking the various inflections. The child can nonetheless convey many different meanings, such as location, possession, or agent-object relationships.
- During the grammar explosion, the child quickly adds many grammatical inflections and learns to create questions and negative sentences.
- By age 3 or 4, most children can construct remarkably complex sentences. Later skills are primarily refinements of established skills, such as learning to understand and use passive sentences.
- As early as age 2, children adapt their language to the needs of the listener and begin to follow culturally specific customs of language usage.
- Children also use language to regulate their own behavior.

Explaining Language Development

- Several theories have been offered to explain language development. Two early environmental explanations, one based on imitation and one on reinforcement, have been largely set aside.
- More recently, emphasis has been placed both on the helpful quality of the simpler form of parent-to-child language called *motherese*, or infant-directed language, and on the role of expansions and recastings of children's sentences.
- Nativist theories are also prominent. They assume that the child is born with a set of operating principles that focus him on relevant aspects of language input.
- Constructivist theories hold that a child constructs language at the same time and in the same way as he constructs all cognitive understandings.

- The eclectic approach to explaining language development recognizes the contribution of the environment while at the same time acknowledging that some inborn mechanism is involved in language development. This approach also notes that information-processing skills interact with both environmental and inborn factors to shape language development.

Individual and Group Differences in Language Development

- Children show differences in the rate of development of both vocabulary and grammar, differences explained by both heredity and environmental influences. Despite these variations in rate of early development, however, most children learn to speak skillfully by about age 5 or 6.
- In the early years of language development, two styles of language can be distinguished: referential (focusing on objects and their description) and expressive (focusing on words and forms that describe or further social relationships).
- The sequence of language development is remarkably consistent across all languages. There are a few exceptions, however. For example, children learning Turkish do not exhibit a two-word stage in grammar acquisition.

Learning to Read and Write

- Development of an awareness of the sound patterns of a particular language during early childhood is important in learning to read and write. Children seem to acquire this skill through word play.
- In school, children need specific instruction in sound-letter correspondences, word parts, and comprehension strategies to become good readers. They also need to be exposed to good literature and to have lots of appropriate practice in using literacy skills.
- Children with limited English perform as well as English-speaking peers when they receive specific kinds of support in school.

Key Terms

babbling (p. 216)
bilingual education (p. 240)
constraint (p. 222)
cooing (p. 216)
English-as-a-second-language (ESL) (p. 240)
expressive language (p. 216)
fast-mapping (p. 220)
holophrase (p. 223)

invented spelling (p. 237)
mean length of utterance (MLU) (p. 232)
motherese (infant-directed speech) (p. 229)
overextension (p. 221)
phonological awareness (p. 235)
phonology (p. 215)
pragmatics (p. 227)
prelinguistic phase (p. 216)

principle of contrast (p. 222)
receptive language (p. 217)
semantics (p. 215)
structured immersion (p. 240)
submersion (p. 240)
syntax (p. 215)
telegraphic speech (p. 224)
underextension (p. 221)

Private Speech

As noted in this chapter, Vygotsky and Piaget differed about the function of private speech. You can observe children using private speech in a preschool, kindergarten, or first-grade classroom. (Remember to get permission from school officials and from the children's parents.) Focus on one child at a time, keeping a record of the child's self-directed statements. Determine the proportion of such statements that appear to be for the purpose of guiding behavior, as Vygotsky suggested. An example of such a statement might be a preschooler's utterance of "this goes here" while putting a puzzle together. After you have collected data on several children, decide whether you agree with Vygotsky.

Mean Length of Utterance

You can gain more insight into Roger Brown's research by doing some observations of your own. Locate a child who is still in the earliest stages of sentence formation or who is just beginning to add a few inflections. This is most likely to be a child 20 to 24 months old, but a child between 24 and 30 months may be fine. The one essential ingredient is that the child be speaking at least some two-word sentences. Arrange to spend enough time with the child at his or her home or in any other convenient setting that you can collect a list of 50 different spontaneous utterances, including both one-word utterances and two-word (or longer) sentences. Try to avoid actively eliciting language from the child, although it is fine to collect samples while the child is playing with an adult or doing some activity with a parent or older sibling. Write down the child's sentences in the order in which they occur and stop when you have 50. Whenever you can, make notes

about the context in which each sentence occurred so that you can judge the meaning more fully. When you have your list of 50 utterances, calculate the mean length of utterance by counting the number of meaningful units in each sentence. (Each word is a meaningful unit, but so is each grammatical inflection, such as the -s for a plural and the -ed ending for a past tense.)

Following are some specific rules to follow in calculating the MLU:

1. Do not count such sounds as *uh* or *oh*, but do count "no," "yeah," and "hi."
2. Compound words, such as *birthday, choo-choo, night-night,* or *pocketbook*, should be counted as single units.
3. Count all irregular past tenses, such as *got, did, want,* or *saw*, as single units. But count as two units any regular past tense, such as *play-ed*, or any erroneous extension of the past tense, such as *went-ed*.
4. Count all diminutives, such as *doggie* or *mommy*, as single units.
5. Count all combinations, such as *gonna, wanna,* or *hafta*, as single units.
6. Count each auxiliary, such as *is, have, will, can,* or *must*, as a single unit, as well as each inflection, such as the -s for a plural or a possessive, the -s for the third-person singular verb form, and the -ing on a verb.

Compare the MLU you obtain with those shown in Figure 8.4, and discuss any special conditions of your observation that you think might have affected the results.

Personality Development: Alternative Views

9

C H A P T E R

Have you ever watched preschoolers and their families wait in line at a fast food restaurant where there is an attractive play area?

When their children ask to go to the play area, most parents follow a script that goes something like this: "As soon as we get our food, we'll go over there, but you have to finish eating before you can play." In response, some children look longingly at the play area but remain steadfastly at their parents' side. Others whine a bit but soon distract themselves from their unfulfilled desire to play by focusing on their anticipation of the toy they will get with their food. Still others behave as if they had just been told the world as they know it was coming to an end. They cry loudly and may even scream in frustration. Many of these children fall onto the floor and injure themselves, adding more drama to the display. Some even hit or kick the refusing parent. Others defiantly run to the play area, seemingly oblivious to their parents' instructions to stay in line. Remarkably, these variations often occur among children from the same family.

Thinking about the differences that appear when children are in frustrating situations captures the essence of what psychologists mean when they use the term **personality**. Formally, this term is defined as the individual's enduring patterns of responses to and interactions with others and the environment. Practically, it pervades all of children's relationships, thereby exerting just as powerful an influence on developmental outcomes as their cognitive abilities. What causes such differences? When we look for answers to this question, whether in the countless books on child-rearing that are available today or in the professional literature, we inevitably encounter the debate that pervades every discussion of human development: the nature-nurture controversy. Before turning to psychologists' views on the subject, let's look at the issue from a parenting perspective.

In 1985, the notion that some children are born with characteristics that make it nearly impossible to parent them effectively found its way into public discourse through the publication of a book called *The Difficult Child*, authored by psychiatrist Stanley Turecki. The book was revised in 2000 and continues to be a best-seller. In it, Turecki describes the challenges he faced in raising his own difficult child, Jillian, the youngest of his three daughters. Even in infancy, Jillian appeared to be in a permanent state of discontent. Adaptation to any kind of routine seemed to be out of the question for both the girl and her unfortunate family. Even at 6 months of age, Jillian was still waking up at unpredictable times every night, sometimes several times in the same night. She displayed fits of temper in response to every transition, even those as commonplace as transitioning from indoor to outdoor play and back again. In public, Jillian's tantrums were so loud and embarrassing that, by the time the child was 2 years old, Turecki and his wife were forced to carefully plan each outing so as to avoid any situation that might trigger an outburst. They were also concerned about the effect that living in a family ruled by the whims of a 2-year-old might have on their older daughters.

In search of an explanation for Jillian's behavior, Turecki examined the research literature. After rereading the classic research of Stella Chess and Alexander Thomas (1984), he concluded that his daughter's behavior was not pathological but was within the normal range of variation in infant temperament. Jillian possessed, Turecki decided, a constellation of inborn traits that made her what Turecki termed a "difficult" child. These traits included a high level of physical activity, poor concentration, emotional intensity, stubbornness, hypersensitivity to physical and sensory stimuli, a tendency to cling to parents in social situations, difficulty adapting to change, and negative mood. After successfully implementing a number of changes in his approach to parenting Jillian, Turecki began recommending them to the parents of difficult children he saw in his private practice. Ultimately, he turned his own experiences and those of his clients into a popular book.

When *The Difficult Child* was published, many parents of children like Jillian regarded it as a godsend. At best, these parents were frustrated; at worst, they felt helpless in the face of what seemed to be an impossible task. Many felt guilty because they had been told by well-meaning relatives, friends, and even mental health professionals that their child's behavior was caused by their own inept attempts at parenting. Some had given up altogether. By adopting parenting techniques that Turecki claimed were appropriate for such children, many of these parents regained hope and learned to appreciate their children's unique characteristics. As a result, many of their children, like Turecki's own daughter, blossomed into manageable, and even enjoyable, children and teenagers.

The concept of the difficult child is not without its critics, however. Noted pediatrician Dr. Lawrence Diller (2001), for instance, has argued that Turecki's book served as the impetus for the development of a dangerous trend in American parenting practices. While applauding Turecki's original book, Diller points out that it led to a succession of similar best-selling books, including those describing the "spirited" child (Kurcinka, 1992) and the "explosive" child (Greene, 1998). Such books, says Diller, encourage parents to regard every troublesome behavior their child exhibits as a manifestation of an inborn, unchangeable trait. As a result, he says, many parents have abdicated responsibility for disciplining their children. When children become too out-of-control to live with, such parents often turn to physicians, who have become all too willing to prescribe medications that make children's behavior more manageable, argues Diller. Instead of turning to pharmacological solutions, says Diller, parents need to better understand how their parenting strategies and the environments they create influence their children's personalities.

Diller and others who have expressed similar ideas—including Stanley Turecki, by the way—say that it is the interaction between a child's inborn traits and the characteristics of his or her environment, not one or the other, that determines personality. In other words, parenting practices should be based on an understanding of all the factors that influence children's personalities. For instance, as you'll learn in this chapter, modeling of various behaviors by both parents and peers can influence children's personalities. However, parenting that relies solely on either the notion that behavior is determined by inborn traits or the idea that modeling influences personality is likely to be ineffective. Instead, parents need to have a better idea of how and when inborn traits and modeling, as well as a number of other factors, come into play.

In this chapter, we will review how various theorists have approached the explanation of personality development. When you finish reading this chapter, you will have a better appreciation for the complexities of human personality. You will see that, like most developmental variables, it isn't simply a matter of either inborn traits or environmental influences.

 # Defining Personality

Like the concept of intelligence, the concept of personality has been hard to define clearly. Most theorists and researchers have thought of **personality** in terms of variations on a set of basic traits or dimensions, such as shyness versus gregariousness or activity versus passivity. If researchers could identify the basic dimensions of personality, they could then describe any individual's personality as a profile of those key traits. That sounds straightforward, but coming to agreement on the nature of the key dimensions has been no simple task. Over the years, researchers and theorists have disagreed vehemently about how many such dimensions there might be, how they should be measured, or even whether there are any stable personality traits at all. However, in the past decade, somewhat to the surprise of many psychologists, a consensus has emerged.

THE BIG FIVE

Researchers now agree that adult personality can be adequately described as a set of variations along five major dimensions, often referred to as the **Big Five**, and described in Table 9.1: **extraversion**, **agreeableness**, **conscientiousness**, **neuroticism**, and **openness/intellect** (Caspi, Roberts, & Shiner, 2005; Digman, 1990; John, Caspi, Robins, Moffitt, & Stouthamer-Loeber, 1994; McCrae & John, 1992). The Big Five have been

personality The collection of relatively enduring patterns of reacting to and interacting with others and the environment that distinguishes each child or adult.

Big Five The five primary dimensions of adult personality identified by researchers: extraversion, agreeableness, conscientiousness, neuroticism, and openness/intellect.

extraversion One of the Big Five personality traits; a person who scores high on this trait is characterized by assertiveness, energy, enthusiasm, and outgoingness.

agreeableness One of the Big Five personality traits; a person who scores high on this trait is characterized by trust, generosity, kindness, and sympathy.

conscientiousness One of the Big Five personality traits; a person who scores high on this trait is characterized by efficiency, organization, planfulness, and reliability.

neuroticism One of the Big Five personality traits; a person who scores high on this trait is characterized by anxiety, self-pity, tenseness, and emotional instability.

openness/intellect One of the Big Five personality traits; a person who scores high on this trait is characterized by curiosity, imagination, insight, originality, and wide interests.

TABLE 9.1	*The Big Five Personality Traits*	
Trait	**Basic Feature(s)**	**Qualities of Individuals High in the Trait**
Extraversion	The extent to which a person actively engages the world versus avoiding social experiences	Active, assertive, enthusiastic, outgoing, talkative
Agreeableness	The extent to which a person's interpersonal interactions are characterized by warmth and compassion versus antagonism	Affectionate, forgiving, generous, kind, sympathetic, trusting
Conscientiousness	The extent and strength of a person's impulse control	Efficient, organized, planful, reliable, responsive, thorough, able to delay gratification in the service of more distant goals
Neuroticism; also called emotional (in)stability	The extent to which a person experiences the world as distressing or threatening	Anxious, self-pitying, tense, touchy, unstable, worrying
Openness/Intellect	Reflects the depth, complexity, and quality of a person's mental and experiential life	Artistic, curious, imaginative, insightful, original, having wide interests

Sources: Caspi, 1998, p. 316; John et al., 1994, Table 1, p. 161; McCrae and Costa, 1994.

Even in the early years of life, differences in personality are evident.

identified in studies of adults in a variety of countries, including some non-Western cultures, which lends some cross-cultural validity to this list. At the very least, researchers know that this set of dimensions is not unique to American adults (Bond, Nakazato, & Shiraishi, 1975; Borkenau & Ostendorf, 1990; Lüdtke, Trautwein, & Köller, 2004; McCrae & Terracciano, 2005).

There is also good evidence that the Big Five are stable traits: Among adults, personality test scores on these five dimensions have been shown to be stable over periods as long as a decade or more (Caspi et al., 2003; Costa & McCrae, 1994). In addition, the usefulness of the Big Five as a description of personality has been validated by a variety of studies linking scores on these dimensions to behavior in a wide variety of real-life situations (Caspi et al., 2005; Furnham, Petrides, Tsaousis, Pappas, & Garrod, 2005). For example, college students who score high on the dimensions of conscientiousness and openness to experience tend to have higher GPAs than their peers who score lower on these traits. Those high in neuroticism have poorer health habits (they more often smoke, for example) and complain more about their health than do those low in neuroticism (Costa & McCrae, 1984). Thus, the Big Five, as measured either through self-reports or through reports by observers, appear to be both reliable and valid descriptions of personality.

Researchers who wish to apply this model to children's personality have to ask two questions. The first is, do these same five dimensions accurately describe children's personality? The second question is much trickier: What connection, if any, do these five dimensions have to infant and early childhood temperament—that is, to inborn predispositions, reactions, moods, and the like? The great bulk of research on individual differences in infants' and children's styles and manners of interaction with the world has been couched in terms of temperament, not personality. How can these two bodies of research be linked? Let's take the easier question first.

A small but growing body of research suggests that the Big Five provide a decent description of personality structure in late childhood and adolescence as well as adulthood (e.g., Baker, Victor, Chambers, & Halverson, 2004; Caspi, 1998; Hartup & van Lieshout, 1995; Huey & Weisz, 1997). For example, Cornelis van Lieshout and Gerbert Haselager (1994), in a large study of children and adolescents in the Netherlands, found that the five clearest dimensions on which they could characterize their young participants matched the Big Five very well, and this was true for both boys and girls and for preschoolers as well as adolescents. In this sample, agreeableness and emotional (in)stability (the equivalent of the neuroticism dimension) were the most evident dimensions of personality, followed by conscientiousness, extraversion, and openness.

Similar results have come from longitudinal studies in the United States, in which researchers have found that measures of the Big Five in childhood predict academic achievement and a variety of social variables in adolescence (Shiner, 2000). In one particularly influential study, Oliver John and his colleagues (1994) studied a random sample of nearly 500 boys initially selected from among all fourth graders in the Pittsburgh public school system and followed until age 13. Like the Dutch researchers, John found strong evidence that the five-factor model captured the personality variations among these preteen boys.

John's study was also helpful as a test of the validity of the five-factor model because he gathered information on other aspects of the boys' behavior, such as their school success or their delinquent behavior. By comparing the personality profiles of boys who differed in some other way, he could check to see if their personality patterns differed in ways that made theoretical and conceptual sense. For example, Figure 9.1 contrasts the personality profiles of boys who reported delinquent activity versus boys who reported none. As John predicted, delinquent boys were markedly lower than non-

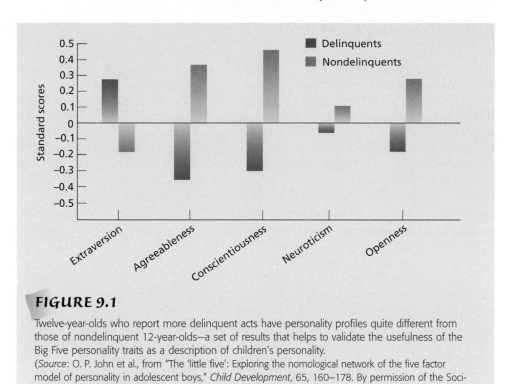

FIGURE 9.1

Twelve-year-olds who report more delinquent acts have personality profiles quite different from those of nondelinquent 12-year-olds—a set of results that helps to validate the usefulness of the Big Five personality traits as a description of children's personality.

(*Source*: O. P. John et al., from "The 'little five': Exploring the nomological network of the five factor model of personality in adolescent boys," *Child Development*, 65, 160–178. By permission of the Society for Research in Child Development.)

delinquent boys in both agreeableness and conscientiousness. John also found that boys higher in conscientiousness did slightly better in school, just as would be expected. Subsequent studies supported John's findings. However, some of these studies also found a positive correlation between neuroticism and delinquency (e.g., Retz et al., 2004). Likewise, research examining relationships among the Big Five and delinquency in adolescent girls shows that neuroticism predicts criminal behavior among them as well (ter Laak et al., 2003). In addition, the link between a low level of conscientiousness and delinquency holds for girls. However, researchers have not found a correlation between a low level of agreeableness and delinquency among females.

A nice cross-cultural validation of the five-factor model comes from a study by Geldolph Kohnstamm and his colleagues (Havill, Allen, Halverson, & Kohnstamm, 1994; Kohnstamm, Halverson, Havill, & Mervielde, 1994). Researchers asked parents in the United States, the Netherlands, Belgium, and Surinam to describe their children, using whatever wording they wished. The researchers found that 70–80% of the qualities mentioned by parents in each of these four cultures could be classified as one of the Big Five personality traits. A similar study comparing American, Dutch, Greek, and Chinese parents' descriptions of their children's personalities, carried out by Kohnstamm's colleague Charles Halverson, produced similar findings (Halverson et al., 2003).

These results are impressive and point to the usefulness of the five-factor model, but it is still too soon to tell whether the Big Five will turn out to be the optimal way of describing children's personality. In particular, researchers may need more than five dimensions to describe children. For example, both John and his colleagues in their U.S. study and van Lieshout and Haselager in their Dutch study found two additional dimensions that describe children's personality: irritability and activity level. Since both these dimensions typically appear in descriptions of temperament, this brings us to the more difficult question: What is the connection between research on the Big Five traits and studies of infant and child temperament?

CRITICAL THINKING

Look over the list of qualities for each of the Big Five, given in Table 9.1. How would you rate yourself on each of these dimensions? Has your personality changed since you were a child?

LINKS TO TEMPERAMENT

You read about temperament in Chapters 1 and 3, so the concept is not completely new. What is confusing (even to most psychologists) is the question of whether *temperament* is just another word for *personality* or whether the two concepts are really different. Mary Rothbart and John Bates, two of the leading researchers in this area, define temperament as "individual differences in emotional, motor, and attentional reactivity and self-regulation" that children consistently display in all kinds of settings and situations (1998, p. 109). These authors, and most others who study temperament, conceive of these qualities as the emotional substrate of personality—the set of core qualities or response patterns that are visible in infancy and reflected in such things as typical activity level, irritability or emotionality, "soothability," fearfulness, and sociability (Hartup & van Lieshout, 1995, p. 658; Rothbart, Ahadi, & Evans, 2000). In this way of thinking, temperament is the foundation on which adult personality is built (Ahadi & Rothbart, 1994; McCrae, Costa, Ostendorf, & Angleitner, 2000).

This distinction between temperament and personality is a little like the difference between a genotype and a phenotype. The genotype sets the basic pattern, but the eventual outcome depends on the way the basic pattern is affected by specific experience. Thus, temperament may represent the basic pattern; what is measured as personality later in childhood or adulthood reflects how the basic pattern has been affected by myriad life experiences. For example, recent longitudinal research suggests that mothers' responses to toddlers' temperaments can serve to either strengthen or weaken inborn temperamental variables such as shyness (Rubin, Burgess, & Hastings, 2002; Rubin & Coplan, 2004). Toddlers of mothers who are critical of their shy behavior display more shyness as preschoolers than children of mothers who are accepting of this trait in their children. If this interactive model is correct, then variations in temperament ought to bear some (perhaps even considerable) resemblance to the five basic personality dimensions seen in adulthood, although the matchup will probably not be perfect.

DIMENSIONS OF TEMPERAMENT

Discovering whether data support the notion of temperament as a substrate of personality has been made difficult by the fact that temperament researchers, unlike adult-personality researchers, have not yet agreed on the best way to characterize variations in early temperament. Instead, they have proposed several rather different category systems, each influencing a body of research.

Three Views of Temperament   One of the most influential temperament category systems has been Stella Chess and Alexander Thomas's (1984) description of *difficult, easy,* and *slow-to-warm-up* temperaments, reflecting profiles on nine different dimensions—a system described in Chapter 3. In contrast, Arnold Buss and Robert Plomin originally proposed only three key dimensions: activity level, emotionality (primarily negative emotionality), and sociability (Buss, 1989; Buss & Plomin, 1984, 1986). The questionnaire they devised to measure these three qualities has been widely used by researchers studying infants, children, and adults. Yet another key figure has been Jerome Kagan, who has focused on only a single dimension, which he calls *behavioral inhibition*—an aspect of what most people mean by "shyness" (Kagan, Reznick, & Snidman, 1990; Kagan, Snidman, & Arcus, 1993). None of these conceptualizations has been universally accepted.

An Emerging Consensus   Temperament researchers are still struggling to define the key dimensions and have not reached a clear agreement (Thompson & Goodvin, 2005). However, over the past decade, a consensus has emerged, one that is reflected in the writings of the leading researchers in the field (Ahadi & Rothbart, 1994; Belsky, Friedman, & Hsieh, 2001; Belsky, Hsieh, & Crnic, 1996; Kagan, 1997; Martin, Wisenbaker, & Huttunen, 1994; Rothbart, 2004; Rothbart & Bates, 1998). Many theorists are now emphasizing the following five key dimensions of temperament and are actively exploring the possible links between these and the Big Five personality dimensions (e.g., Caspi, 1998, 2000):

■ *Activity level.* A tendency to move often and vigorously, rather than to remain passive or immobile. High activity is most often hypothesized to be a precursor of extraversion (Martin et al., 1994), a link found in one longitudinal study in Sweden (Hagekull & Bohlin, 1998).

■ *Approach/positive emotionality.* A tendency to move toward rather than away from new people, situations, or objects, usually accompanied by positive emotion. This dimension is similar to what Buss and Plomin call *sociability* and seems to be another obvious precursor of extraversion at later ages. It may also be a precursor of what is later measured as agreeableness (Caspi, 1998; Rothbart & Bates, 1998).

■ *Inhibition and anxiety.* The flip side of approach is a tendency to respond with fear or to withdraw from new people, situations, or objects. This dimension has been intensely studied by Kagan and his colleagues (e.g., Kagan, 1994, 1997; Kagan et al., 1990), who see it as the precursor of what is called *shyness* in everyday language. In the five-factor model, inhibition and anxiety would be reflected in very low scores on extraversion and low scores on openness and might also contribute to high scores on neuroticism at later ages.

■ *Negative emotionality/irritability/anger.* A tendency to respond with anger, fussiness, loudness, or irritability; a low threshold of frustration. This dimension appears to be what Thomas and Chess are tapping with their concept of the "difficult" child and what Buss and Plomin call *emotionality*. It is an obvious precursor of what is later called *neuroticism* (e.g., Hagekull & Bohlin, 1998).

■ *Effortful control/task persistence.* An ability to stay focused, to manage attention and effort, which psychologist Jay Belsky has suggested contributes to infants' ability to adapt to the demands of schooling later in childhood (Belsky et al., 2001). Caspi (1998) suggests that this temperamental quality may contribute to several later personality dimensions, including conscientiousness, agreeableness, and openness to experience.

This is obviously not a final list; temperament researchers are still working their way toward common ground. But this set of traits or qualities is probably fairly close to the list they will eventually agree on. At the very least, developmentalists know that babies and young children do differ on these dimensions, and they have some reasonable hypotheses about how these early variations may link with later stable personality characteristics.

Four-year-old Sayde appears to have a high degree of "effortful control," one of the dimensions of temperament identified by researchers.

Temperament across Cultures   Despite knowing something about temperament, researchers are still left with several huge questions to answer. One such question concerns the universality of these dimensions of temperament. Early research by Daniel Freedman (1979) suggested that Chinese and Native American infants were less active than Caucasian American or Japanese babies. Kagan and his colleagues (1994) replicated part of these results in their comparison of Chinese, Irish, and Caucasian American 4-month-olds. They found that the Chinese infants were significantly less active, less irritable, and less vocal than were babies in the other two groups. The Caucasian American infants showed the strongest reactions to new sights, sounds, or smells. Similarly, Chisholm (1989) has replicated Freedman's research on Native American babies, finding them to be significantly less irritable, less excitable, and more able to quiet themselves than Caucasian American babies.

Since such differences are evident in newborns, they cannot be the result of systematic shaping by the parents. But the parents bring their temperaments as well as

Before going on . . .

- List and define the Big Five.
- Outline the similarities between the Big Five and dimensions of infant temperament.
- What are the dimensions of temperament that most psychologists agree on?

their cultural training to interactions with their newborns, which may tend to strengthen or perpetuate the babies' temperamental differences. For instance, Freedman and other researchers have observed that both Japanese and Chinese mothers talk to their infants much less than Caucasian mothers do. These differences in mothers' behavior were present from the mothers' first encounters with their infants after delivery, so the pattern is not a response to the babies' quieter behavior. Nonetheless, a correspondence between a mother's culturally defined behaviors and a baby's temperamental pattern is likely to strengthen the pattern in the child, which would tend to make the cultural differences larger over time.

Genetic and Biological Explanations of Personality

Many researchers, such as Robert Plomin, maintain that the evidence that heredity plays a strong role in the determination of personality is powerful and must be taken into account in any theoretical explanation of individual differences (Plomin, 2001, 2004). The genetic approach includes a number of persuasive propositions. However, there are many critics of this perspective.

THE BIOLOGICAL ARGUMENT

Broadly expressed, the argument that the origins of personality are biological is based on four major propositions.

Proposition 1: Each individual is born with genetically determined characteristic patterns of responding to the environment and to other people. Virtually every researcher who studies temperament shares the assumption that temperamental qualities are inborn, carried in the genes. This idea is not so very different from the notion of "inborn biases," or "constraints," you have read about in earlier chapters, except that in this case the focus is on individual rather than shared behavioral dispositions.

There is clear, strong evidence to support this assertion (Rose, 1995; Saudino, 1998), both in studies of adult personality and in studies of childhood temperament. Studies of twins in many countries show that identical twins are much more alike in their temperament or personality than are fraternal twins (Rose, 1995). Hill Goldsmith and his colleagues (1997) have recently combined the results from many studies in which twins have been rated by their parents on some version of the Buss and Plomin temperament categories. Their research shows that the correlations on each dimension are a great deal higher for pairs of identical twins than for pairs of fraternal twins, indicating a strong genetic effect. Further support for the genetic hypothesis comes from researchers who have found that non-twin siblings are far more similar in personality than many parents believe them to be. Developmentalist Kimberly Saudino (Saudino, Wertz, Gagne, & Chawla, 2004) compared parents' ratings of siblings' activity levels to computerized assessments of videotapes of the children's behavior. She found that the parental ratings differed significantly across siblings but the computerized assessments did not. She found a similar pattern when she compared parents' ratings of siblings' shyness to those of objective observers. Such findings mean that parents tend to exaggerate temperamental differences among their children. Thus, studies that rely on parental ratings may fail to capture similarities across siblings that may have a genetic basis.

Proposition 2: Genetic differences operate via variations in fundamental physiological processes. Many (but not all) temperament theorists take Proposition 1 a step further and trace the basic differences in behavior to variations in underlying physiological patterns, particularly to variations in the reactivity of under-lying neural systems (Derryberry & Rothbart, 1998; Gunnar, 1994; Gunnar et al., 2003; Nelson, 1994; Plomin, 2004; Rothbart & Bates, 1998).

As an example, Kagan has suggested that differences in behavioral inhibition are based on differing thresholds for arousal in those parts of the brain—the amygdala and the hypothalamus—that control responses to uncertainty (1994; Kagan et al., 1990, 1993; Schwartz, Wright, Shin, Kagan, & Rauch, 2003). Arousal of these parts of the brain leads to increases in muscle tension and heart rate. Shy or inhibited children are thought to have a low threshold for such a reaction. That is, they more readily become tense and alert in the presence of uncertainty, perhaps even interpreting a wider range of situations as uncertain. What we inherit, according to this view, is not "shyness" or some equivalent behavioral pattern but a tendency for the brain to react in particular ways.

This 1-year-old may just be having a bad day. But if this is typical behavior, one sign of a "difficult" temperament, she will be at higher risk for a variety of problems at later ages.

In support of this argument, Kagan reports correlations in the range of .60 between a measure of behavioral inhibition in children aged 2 to 5 and a series of physiological measures, such as muscle tension, heart rate, dilation of the pupil of the eye, and chemical composition of both urine and saliva, which strongly suggests that temperament is based on physiological responses and is not simply a set of learned habits (1994; Kagan et al., 1990). Moreover, Kagan and his associates have found that behavioral measures of inhibition taken in infancy are correlated with measures of brain reactivity to stimuli at ages 10 to 12; the correlation held for adults as well (Schwartz et al., 2003; Woodward et al., 2001). Other researchers have demonstrated that temperamental differences are associated with different levels of activity in the left and right hemispheres of the brain (Fox, Henderson, Rubin, Calkins, & Schmidt, 2001; McManis, Kagan, Snidman, & Woodward, 2002).

Proposition 3: Temperamental dispositions persist through childhood and into adulthood. No theorist in the biological camp proposes that initial temperamental dispositions remain unchanged by experience. Still, if temperamental patterns create a bias toward particular behaviors, temperament ought to exhibit at least some stability over time. Such stability ought to show itself in the form of at least modest correlations between measures of a given temperamental dimension at different ages.

Although the research evidence is somewhat mixed, there is growing evidence of consistency in temperamental ratings over rather long periods of infancy and childhood (Rothbart, Ahadi, Hersey, & Fisher, 2001). In one study involving a group of 450 Australian children, researchers found that mothers' reports of children's irritability, cooperation/manageability, inflexibility, rhythmicity, persistency, and tendency to approach (rather than to avoid) contact were all quite consistent from infancy through age 8 (Pedlow, Sanson, Prior, & Oberklaid, 1993). Similarly, in a longitudinal study of American children from age 1 to age 12, Diana Guerin and Allen Gottfried (1994a, 1994b) found strong consistency in parents' reports of their children's overall "difficultness" as well as approach versus withdrawal, positive versus negative mood, and activity level. In fact, research suggests that temperament differences are stable from the preschool years into adulthood (Caspi, 1998, 2000).

Kagan has also found considerable consistency over the childhood years in his measure of inhibition, which is based on direct observation of the child's behavior rather than on the mother's or father's ratings of the child's temperament. He reports that half of the babies in his longitudinal study who had shown high levels of crying and motor activity in response to a novel situation when they were 4 months old were still classified as highly inhibited at age 8, while three-fourths of those rated as uninhibited at 4 months remained in that category 8 years later (Kagan et al., 1993). Furthermore, the inhibited toddlers in Kagan's sample were less likely than their more uninhibited peers to be rated as highly aggressive or delinquent at age 11 (Schwartz, Snidman, & Kagan, 1996).

Thus, babies who readily and positively approach the world around them continue to be more positive as young teenagers; cranky, temperamentally difficult babies continue to show many of the same temperamental qualities 10 years later; and strongly behaviorally inhibited babies are quite likely to continue to show such "shyness" at later ages. Such consistency is probably stronger among children whose temperamental patterns are initially fairly extreme, such as highly inhibited youngsters or those with particularly clear patterns of negative emotionality (e.g., Rubin, Hastings, Stewart, Henderson, & Chen, 1997), but even among children with less extreme patterns, researchers find some degree of consistency.

Proposition 4: Temperamental characteristics interact with the child's environment in ways that may either strengthen or modify the basic temperamental pattern. Despite all the clear evidence for genetic/biological influences on temperament, genetics is clearly not destiny; there is still a good deal of room for environmental influences. For example, the extent to which parents direct the behavior of their children and express warmth toward them seems to be a significant factor in shaping the children's tendency toward positive affect and approach rather than withdrawal (Rothbart & Bates, 1998; Rubin, Cheah, & Fox, 2001; Rubin & Coplan, 2004). In most cases, the resultant personality develops through some interaction between the child's temperamental tendencies and the environment the child encounters or creates. One factor that tends to strengthen a child's built-in qualities is the fact that we all—including young children—choose our experiences. Highly sociable children seek out contact with others; children low on the activity dimension are more likely to choose sedentary activities like working puzzles or playing board games rather than baseball. Similarly, temperament may affect the way a child interprets a given experience—a factor that helps to account for the fact that two children in the same family may experience the family pattern of interaction quite differently.

Imagine, for example, a family that moves often, such as a military family. If one child in this family has a strong built-in pattern of behavioral inhibition, the myriad changes and new experiences will likely trigger repeated fear responses. This child comes to anticipate each new move with dread and is likely to interpret his family life as highly stressful. A second child in the same family, with a more strongly approach-oriented temperament, finds the many moves stimulating and energizing and is likely to think of his childhood in a much more positive light.

A third environmental factor that often reinforces built-in temperamental patterns is the tendency of parents (and others in the child's world) to respond differently to children with different temperaments. The sociable child, who may smile often, is likely to elicit more smiles and more positive interactions with adults, simply because she has reinforced their behavior by her positive temperament. Buss and Plomin (1984) have proposed the general argument that children in the middle range on temperament dimensions typically adapt to their environment, while those whose temperament is extreme—for example, extremely difficult children—force their environment to adapt to them. Parents of difficult children, for example, adapt to the children's negativity by punishing them more, although often less consistently, than do parents of more adaptable children (Lengua & Kovacs, 2005). This pattern may well contribute to the higher rates of significant emotional problems in such children.

Buss and Plomin's proposal, while it may be accurate, doesn't convey the additional complexities of the process. First, sensitive and responsive parents can moderate the more extreme forms of infant or child temperament; a particularly nice example comes from the work of Megan Gunnar (1994) and her colleagues, who studied a group of highly inhibited toddlers who differed in the security of their attachment to their mothers. In a series of studies (Colton et al., 1992; Nachmias, 1993), researchers found that insecurely attached inhibited toddlers showed the usual physiological responses to challenging or novel situations. Securely attached temperamentally inhibited toddlers, on the other hand, showed no such indications of physiological arousal in the face of novelty or challenge. Thus, secure attachment appears to have modified a basic

CRITICAL THINKING ?

The finding that difficult children are punished more often could be interpreted in several ways. How many alternative explanations can you think of?

physiological/temperamental response. Another example, also involving inhibited/fearful children, comes from the work of Kenneth Rubin and his colleagues (1997), who found that highly inhibited children with oversolicitous mothers showed more persistent inhibition across situations than did those whose mothers were more relaxed and less intrusive or intense.

Thus, while many forces within the environment tend to reinforce a child's basic temperament and thus create stability and consistency of temperament/personality over time, environmental forces can also push a child toward new patterns or aid a child in controlling extreme forms of basic physiological reactions.

CRITIQUE OF BIOLOGICAL THEORIES

The biological approach to the origins of personality has two great strengths. First, it is strongly supported by a large body of empirical research. There is simply no refuting the fact that built-in genetic and physiological patterns underlie what we think of as temperament or personality. This approach thus provides a powerful counterweight to the longtime dominance of psychoanalytic and learning theories of personality development, both of which strongly emphasized environmental influences.

Paradoxically, the second strength of this approach is that it is not purely biological; it is an interactionist approach, very much in keeping with much of the current theorizing about development. The child is born with certain behavioral tendencies, but his eventual personality depends on the transactions between his initial characteristics and the responses of his environment.

On the other side of the ledger, though, there appear to be a number of problems, not the least of which is the continuing lack of agreement on the basic dimensions of temperament. Researchers have used such varying definitions and measures that it is often difficult to compare the results of different investigations.

A second problem has been that many biologically oriented temperament theories have not been fundamentally developmental theories. They allow for change through the mechanism of interaction with the environment, but they do not address the question of whether there are systematic age differences in children's responses to new situations or to people; they do not focus on whether the child's emerging cognitive skills have anything to do with changes in the child's temperamental patterns. They do not, in a word, address how the shared developmental patterns may interact with inborn individual differences. A few theorists have begun to talk about such developmental patterns (e.g., Rothbart & Bates, 1998), but this remains a set of questions in need of exploration.

Neither of these concerns constitutes a refutation of any of the basic tenets of this theoretical approach. Clearly, genetic differences and basic biology are important in shaping individual differences in temperament or personality.

This child, clinging to her mom's leg, might be rated as relatively high in "behavioral inhibition." She may also be being reinforced for her clinging or shy behavior by her mother's approval of the behavior.

Before going on . . .

- Summarize the four basic propositions of the biological approach to explaining personality.
- What are some important criticisms of this perspective?

Learning Explanations of Personality

Instead of focusing on what the child brings to the equation, learning theorists have looked at the reinforcement patterns in the environment as the primary cause of differences in children's personality patterns. Of course, theorists in this tradition do not reject biology. Albert Bandura, arguably the most influential theorist in this group, agrees that biological factors (such as hormones) or inherited propensities (such as temperament, presumably) also affect behavior. But he and others of this persuasion look to the environment as the major source of influence.

THE LEARNING ARGUMENT

The learning camp includes several distinct schools of thought. Some investigators, often called *radical behaviorists*, argue that only the basic principles of classical and operant conditioning are needed to account for variations in behavior, including personality. Others, among them Bandura, emphasize not only observational learning but also important cognitive elements. However, like the biological explanations, all of the learning approaches are organized around a set of basic propositions. Both groups of learning theorists agree with the first two propositions listed below; the remaining propositions emerge primarily from Bandura's work.

Proposition 1: Behavior is strengthened by reinforcement. If this rule applies to all behavior, then it should apply to attachment patterns, shyness, sharing behavior, and competitiveness. Children who are reinforced for clinging to their parents, for example, should show more clinging than children who are not reinforced for it. Similarly, a nursery school teacher who pays attention to children only when they get rowdy or aggressive should find that the children in her care get steadily more rowdy and aggressive over the course of weeks or months.

Proposition 2: Behavior that is reinforced on a partial schedule should be even stronger and more resistant to extinction than behavior that is consistently reinforced. You read about partial reinforcement in Chapter 1, so you have some idea of what is involved. Most parents are inconsistent in their reinforcement of their children, so most children are on partial schedules of some kind, whether the parents intend that or not. That is, they are sometimes reinforced for a particular behavior, but not every time. Because behavior that is rewarded in this way is highly persistent—highly resistant to extinction, in the language of learning theory—partial reinforcement is a major factor in the establishment of those distinctive and stable patterns of behavior defined as personality.

An immense collection of studies supports these first two propositions. For example, in several studies, experimenters systematically rewarded some children for hitting an inflated rubber clown on the nose. When the researchers later watched the children in free play with peers, they found that the children who had been rewarded showed more hitting, scratching, and kicking than did children who hadn't been rewarded for punching the clown (Walters & Brown, 1963). Partial reinforcement in the form of inconsistent behavior from parents also has the expected effect. For example, one study (Sears, Maccoby, & Levin, 1977) found that parents who permit fairly high levels of aggression in their children, but who occasionally react by punishing it quite severely, have children who are more aggressive than do parents who neither permit nor punish aggression.

Gerald Patterson's research on families with aggressive or noncompliant children, described in Chapter 1, also illustrates the significance of these basic principles. If you look again at Figure 1.2 (p. 11), you'll see that the heart of Patterson's model is a link between "poor parental discipline" and resultant conduct problems in the child. Patterson argues that both normal personality patterns and deviant forms of social behavior have their roots in daily social exchanges with family members. For example, imagine a child playing in his very messy room. The mother tells the child to clean up his room. The child whines or yells at her that he doesn't want to do it or won't do it. The mother gives in and leaves the room, and the child stops whining or shouting. Patterson analyzes this exchange as a pair of negatively reinforced events. When the mother gives in to the child's defiance, her own behavior (giving in) is negatively reinforced by the cessation of the child's whining or yelling. This makes it more likely that she will give in the next time. She has learned to back down in order to get the child to shut up. At the same time, the child has been negatively reinforced for whining or yelling, since the unpleasant event for him (being told to clean his room) stopped as soon as he whined. So he has learned to whine or yell. Imagine such exchanges occurring over and over, and you begin to understand how a family can create a system in which an imperious, demanding, noncompliant child rules the roost (Snyder, Edwards, McGraw, Kilgore, & Holton, 1994).

As you learned in Chapter 1, Patterson's thinking has moved beyond the simple propositions outlined here. Like current temperament theorists, he emphasizes that what happens in a given family, for a particular child, is a product of the child's own temperament or response tendencies, the parents' discipline skills, the parents' personalities, and the social context of the parents' lives. Patterson is nonetheless still assuming that basic learning principles can both describe and explain the ways in which the child's behavior pattern (his "personality") is formed or changed. And he and others have shown that it is possible to change the child's typical behavior by helping families learn new and more effective reinforcement and management strategies, and in this way reduce the likelihood of later delinquency (Tremblay, Kurtz, Mâsse, Vitaro, & Pihl, 1995; Wierson & Forehand, 1994).

By observing and working next to his dad, this 3-year-old is not only learning how to wash a car; he's also learning his father's attitudes about work and perhaps the beginnings of self-efficacy.

Proposition 3: Children learn new behaviors largely through modeling. Bandura has argued that the full range of social behaviors, from competitiveness to nurturance, is learned not just by direct reinforcement but also by watching others behave in those ways. Thus, the child who sees her parents taking a casserole next door to the woman who has just been widowed will learn generosity and thoughtful behavior. The child who sees her parents hitting each other when they are angry will most likely learn violent ways of solving problems.

Children learn from television, too, and from their peers, their teachers, and their brothers and sisters. A boy growing up in an environment where he observes playmates and older boys hanging around street corners, shoplifting, or selling drugs is going to learn those behaviors. His continuous exposure to such antisocial models makes it that much harder for his parents to reinforce more constructive behavior.

These many effects of observational learning have been demonstrated experimentally in literally hundreds of studies (Bandura, 1973, 1977). One interesting—and very practical—sidelight to the process of modeling has been the repeated finding that modeling works better than preaching. So, parents' displaying of desired behavior—such as generosity, fairness, or diligent work—is more effective than simply telling children that it is good to be generous, fair, or hardworking. For example, in one early study, Joan Grusec and her colleagues (1978) had elementary school children play a miniature bowling game, ostensibly to test the game. The children first observed an adult "test" the game and saw the adult win 20 marbles. Near the bowling game was a poster that said "Help poor children. Marbles buy gifts." Under the poster was a bowl with some marbles in it. Half of the participants saw the adult model donate half his newly won marbles to this bowl; the other half of the children did not see the model donating marbles. In addition, the model either "preached" about donating marbles or said nothing. To some of the children, the adult preached in specific terms, saying that the child should donate half his marbles when he played the game, since it would be good to make poor children happy by doing that. To the other children, the adult preached in more general terms, saying that the child should donate half his marbles because it is a good thing to make other people happy by helping them any way one can. After demonstrating the game, the adult model then left the room, and the child had an opportunity to play the bowling game and to decide whether to donate any marbles. You can see in Figure 9.2 how many children in each group (out of a maximum of 16) donated marbles. Clearly, modeling increased the

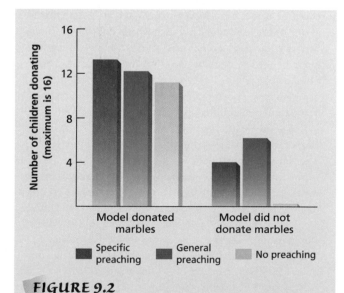

FIGURE 9.2

These results from Grusec's modeling study illustrate the general finding that modeling is more powerful than preaching in changing children's behavior.

(*Source:* Grusec, Saas-Kortsaak & Simutis, 1978, from Table 1, p. 922.)

CRITICAL THINKING ?

Suppose you were trying to learn a new sport, such as tennis or soccer, by observing an expert. How might Bandura's four conditions affect what you could learn from the model?

effectiveness of preaching. The results also illustrate the point that when a conflict exists between what a model says and what the model does—such as when parents smoke but tell their children not to—children generally follow the behavior and not the verbal message. So the old adage "Do what I say and not what I do" doesn't seem to work.

However, learning from modeling is not an entirely automatic process (see *The Real World*). Bandura points out that what a child (or adult) learns from watching someone else will depend on four things: what she pays attention to and what she is able to remember (both cognitive processes), what she is physically able to copy, and what she is motivated to imitate. Because attentional abilities, memory, and other cognitive processes change with age through infancy and childhood, what a baby or child can or will learn from any given modeled event also changes through development (Grusec, 1992).

Proposition 4: From reinforcement and modeling, children learn not only overt behavior but also ideas, expectations, internal standards, and self-concepts. The child learns standards for his own behavior and expectancies about what he can and cannot do— which Bandura (1997) calls **self-efficacy**—from specific reinforcements and from modeling. In this way, the child internalizes what he has learned. Once those standards and those expectancies or beliefs are established, they affect the child's behavior in con-

self-efficacy Bandura's term for an individual's belief in his or her ability to accomplish tasks.

Role Models in Life and in the Media

Like many youngsters, Chérie idolizes professional athletes. Her current heroine is professional tennis star Serena Williams. Like her idol, Chérie is African American, and she is inspired not only by Williams's dynamic style of play, but also by the fact that Williams has become a star in what was once an all-white sport. Interestingly, Chérie's uncle is a professor of English literature at an ethnically diverse private college. He, too, has achieved success in a profession that was at one time closed to minorities. So, why does Chérie idolize Serena Williams and other professional athletes rather than her own uncle and others like him? This question has been examined by researchers who are concerned about the ways in which media portrayals of African Americans in various occupational roles influence children's career aspirations.

A good illustration of the complex nature of the influence of models comes from research examining African American children's ideas about which adults they consider to be their role models. Researchers conducted a survey in which 4,500 African American boys aged 10 to 18 were asked to name an important role model outside their own families (Assibey-Mensah, 1997). Investigators thought that these boys would name teachers as important role models because of their frequent interactions with them. However, a large majority of the boys named a professional athlete, and not a single boy named a teacher as an important personal role model (which is astounding when you think of the number of boys who participated in the study). These findings suggest that entertainment media are a more important source of role models for these youths than their real-life experiences with adults. Clearly, neither frequency of interaction with a model nor similarity between the observer and the model explain these findings. However, comparisons of portrayals of teachers to those of athletes in media may help explain why these boys responded as they did.

News reports about public education often characterize schools with large proportions of minority students as failures. The implication is that teachers in such schools are ineffective. Fictional teachers are often portrayed as inept, and many popular TV programs geared to young audiences (for example, "South Park" and "The Simpsons") depict teachers and other school officials as buffoons who are not respected by their students. In contrast, stories about both real and fictional athletes are dominated by themes of fame, wealth, popularity, and achievements such as league championships and record-breaking statistics. Considering the contrast between the two, it isn't surprising that African American boys prefer athletes as role models rather than teachers, even though they know many teachers and most likely have themselves no personal interactions with professional athletes.

Questions for Reflection

1. How might frequent interaction make it less likely that someone would be viewed by a child as a role model?
2. In your opinion, to what extent are the concerns highlighted by these researchers equally true for children of other ethnicities?

sistent and enduring ways and form the core of what can be called personality (Bandura, Caprara, Barbaranelli, Gerbino, & Pastorelli, 2003).

CRITIQUE OF LEARNING MODELS

Several implications of the learning approach to personality are worth emphasizing. First of all, learning theories can explain either consistency or inconsistency in children's behavior. The behavior of a child who is friendly and smiling both at home and at school, for example, could be explained by saying that the child is being reinforced for that behavior in both settings rather than by assuming that the child has strong "approach tendencies" or a "gregarious temperament." Similarly, if the child is helpful at school but defiant at home, learning theorists invoke the principle that different reinforcement contingencies are at work in the two settings. To be sure, because individuals tend to choose settings that support or reward their accustomed behavior and because a person's behavior tends to elicit similar responses (reinforcements) from others in many settings, there is a bias toward consistency. But learning theorists have less trouble accounting for normal "situational variability" in behavior than do other theorists.

This girl may be excited about learning how to throw a pot (yet another example of modeling), but there is no guarantee that she will be equally interested in learning to cook or to throw a football—a kind of inconsistency that learning theorists can explain more easily than biological temperament theorists can.

A related implication is that learning theorists are supremely optimistic about the possibility of change. Children's behavior can change if the reinforcement system (or their beliefs about themselves) changes, so problem behavior can be modified. In contrast, biologically oriented temperament theorists, while agreeing that environmental variations can alter or shift the child's built-in temperamental tendencies, are more pessimistic about the likelihood of change, particularly for children whose temperamental pattern is extreme. Extremely inhibited children, for example, tend to remain that way, even in supportive environments; extremely irritable, angry, inattentive children ("difficult" children in Chess and Thomas's conceptualization) are highly likely to become aggressive, difficult schoolchildren with a higher-than-normal likelihood of developing antisocial or delinquent patterns later, unless they learn extremely good strategies for self-control (e.g., Eisenberg et al., 2005; Moffitt & Harrington, 1996).

The great strength of the learning view of personality and social behavior is that it gives an accurate picture of the way in which many specific behaviors are learned. It is perfectly clear that children *do* learn through modeling; it is equally clear that children (and adults) will continue to perform behaviors that "pay off" for them.

The cognitive elements in Bandura's theory add further strength, offering a beginning integration of learning models and cognitive-developmental approaches. If we were to apply Piaget's language to Bandura's theory, we might refer to the acquisition of a "self-scheme"—a concept of one's own capacities, qualities, standards, and experiences. New experiences are then assimilated to that scheme. You will recall from Chapter 6 that one of the characteristics of the process of assimilation as Piaget proposed it is that new information or experiences are modified as they are taken in. Similarly, Bandura is saying that once the child's self-concept is established, it affects what behaviors he chooses to perform, how he reacts to new experiences, whether he persists or gives up on some new task, and the like. If a child believes he is unpopular, for example, then he will not be surprised if others do not choose to sit by him in the lunchroom; if someone does sit next to him, he's likely to explain it in such a way that he retains his central belief, such as by saying to himself, "There must have been no place else to sit." In this way, the underlying scheme isn't modified (accommodated) very much.

Just as biological temperament theorists argue that inborn temperament serves as a central mediating force, shaping the child's choices and behavior, so in social learning theory the self-concept (or self-scheme) acts as a central mediator, leading to stable differences in behavior of the kind we typically call personality. The self-concept can be modified (accommodated) if the child accumulates enough experience or evidence that doesn't fit with the existing scheme (that is, in learning theory language, if the reinforcement contingencies change in some dramatic way). If an "unpopular" child noticed that classmates regularly chose to sit next to him at lunch even when there were other seats available, he might eventually change his self-scheme, coming to think of himself as "somewhat popular." However, since the child (like an adult) will choose activities or situations that fit his self-concept, such as sitting in the corner where no one is likely to see him, he will be partially protected from such nonconfirming experiences.

To be sure, Bandura and Piaget would not agree on how this self-concept develops. Piaget emphasizes internal processes, while Bandura emphasizes reinforcement and modeling as causal factors. What they agree on is the impact that such a scheme will have once it has developed.

The learning theories, particularly the more radical versions, also have significant weaknesses. First, from the perspective of many psychologists, these theories still place too much emphasis on what happens to the child and not enough on what the child is doing with the information she has. Bandura's theory is much less vulnerable to this charge, but most learning theories of personality are highly mechanistic and focused on external events. Second, like biological temperament theories, learning theories are not really developmental. They can say how a child might acquire a particular behavior pattern or belief, but they do not take into account the underlying developmental changes that are occurring. Do 3-year-olds and 10-year-olds develop a sense of self-efficacy in the same way? Do they learn the same amount or in the same way from modeling? Given Bandura's emphasis on the cognitive aspects of the modeling process, a genuinely developmental social learning theory could emerge in the coming years. Still, despite these limitations, all the theories in this group offer useful descriptions of one source of influence on the child's developing pattern of behavior.

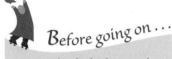

Before going on . . .

- Summarize the basic propositions of learning explanations of personality.
- What are some criticisms of this perspective?

Psychoanalytic Explanations of Personality

Like many temperament theorists and those social learning theorists like Bandura, psychoanalytic theorists believe that the interaction between the child's inborn characteristics and the environment plays a central role in shaping differences in personality. However, unlike most temperament or learning approaches, psychoanalytic theories are clearly developmental as well, describing systematic changes in children's sense of self, in their needs or drives, and in their relationships with others.

THE PSYCHOANALYTIC ARGUMENT

You read about psychoanalytic theories in Chapter 1, so the major propositions of this approach should be familiar.

Proposition 1: Behavior is governed by unconscious as well as conscious motives and processes. Freud emphasized three sets of instinctual drives: the sexual drive (libido); life-preserving drives, including avoidance of hunger and pain; and aggressive drives. Erikson emphasizes a more cognitive process, the drive for identity.

Proposition 2: Personality structure develops over time, as a result of the interaction between the child's inborn drives and needs and the responses of the key people in the child's world. Because the child is often prevented from achieving instant gratification of his various drives, he is forced to develop new skills—planning, talking, delaying, and other cognitive techniques that allow gratification of the basic needs in more indirect ways. Thus, the ego is created, and it remains the planning, organizing, thinking part of the personality. The superego, in turn, develops because parents and other adults try to restrain certain kinds of gratification; the child eventually incorporates these adult standards into his own personality.

Proposition 3: Development of personality is fundamentally stagelike, with each stage centered on a particular task or a particular basic need. You'll read about both Freud's and Erikson's stages in some detail below. The key point is simply that there are stages in these theories.

Proposition 4: The specific personality a child develops depends on the degree of success the child has in moving through the various stages. In each stage, the child requires a particular kind of supportive environment in order to successfully resolve that particular dilemma or meet that need. A child lacking the needed environment will have a very different personality from one whose environment is partially or wholly adequate. However, while each stage is important, all the psychoanalytic theorists strongly emphasize the crucial significance of the very earliest stages and focus especially on the adequacy of the relationship between the baby and the central caregiver, usually the mother. This is not quite like saying that infancy is a sensitive period for personality development; rather, Freud and later psychoanalytic theorists argue that the earliest relationship establishes a pattern and sets the child on a particular pathway through the remainder of the stages.

SOME DIFFERENCES BETWEEN FREUD AND ERIKSON

All four of these general propositions are contained in both Freud's and Erikson's theories, but both the details and the emphases differ in important respects. In Freud's theory, for example, cognitive skills develop only because the child needs them to obtain gratification; they have no independent life. In Erikson's theory (and in many other variations of psychoanalytic theory), cognitive skills are part of a set of ego functions that are presumed to develop independently, rather than arising entirely in the service of basic gratification.

Basic physical maturation is also more central to Freud's theory than to Erikson's. In Freud's theory, the stages shift from one to the next in part because of maturation of the nervous system. In each stage, the child is attempting to gratify basic physical ("sexual") needs through stimulation of a particular part of the body—that part of the body that is most sensitive at that time. As neurological development proceeds, maximum body sensitivity shifts from the mouth to the anus to the genitals, and this maturational change is part of what drives the stage changes. Erikson acknowledges such physical changes but places greater emphasis on shifts in the demands of the social environment. For Erikson, each stage centers on a specific social conflict, resulting in a psychosocial crisis. For example, stage 4 ("industry versus inferiority") begins at about age 6, because that is when the child goes off to school; in a culture in which schooling is delayed, the timing of the developmental task might be delayed as well.

Because of such theoretical differences, Erikson and Freud have described the stages of development differently. Because both sets of stages have become part of the vocabulary of developmental psychology, you need to be conversant with both.

FREUD'S PSYCHOSEXUAL STAGES

psychosexual stages The stages of personality development suggested by Freud, consisting of the oral, anal, phallic, latency, and genital stages.

Freud proposed five **psychosexual stages**, which are summarized in Table 9.2.

The Oral Stage: Birth to 1 Year

The mouth, lips, and tongue are the first centers of pleasure for the baby, and his earliest attachment is to the one who provides pleasure in the mouth, usually his mother. For normal development, the infant requires some optimal amount of oral stimulation—not too much and not too little. If the optimal amount of stimulation is unavailable, then some libidinal energy may remain attached to ("fixated on," in Freud's terms) the oral mode of gratification. Such an individual, Freud thought, will continue to have a strong preference for oral pleasures in later life, as you can see in the right-hand column in Table 9.2.

The Anal Stage: 1 to 3 Years

As the body matures, the baby becomes more and more sensitive in the anal region. And as she matures physically, her parents begin to place great emphasis on toilet training and express approval when she manages to perform in the right place at the right time. These two forces together help to shift the major center of physical and sexual sensitivity from the oral to the anal region.

The key to the child's successful completion of this stage (according to Freud) is how parents manage toilet training. If toilet training becomes a major battleground, then some fixation of energy at this stage may occur—with the possible adult consequences of excessive orderliness and stinginess or the opposite of these.

The Phallic Stage: 3 to 5 Years

At about 3 or 4 years of age, the genitals become increasingly sensitive, ushering in a new stage. One sign of this new sensitivity is that children of both sexes normally begin to masturbate at about this age. In Freud's view, the most important event that occurs during the phallic stage is the so-called **Oedipus conflict**. He described the sequence of events more fully (and slightly more believably!) for boys.

According to Freud, during the phallic stage, the boy, having discovered his penis, rather naively wishes to use this newfound source of pleasure to please his oldest source of pleasure, his mother. He becomes envious of his father, who has access to the mother's body in a way that the boy does not. The boy also sees his father as a powerful and threatening figure who has ultimate power—the power to castrate. The boy is caught between desire for his mother and fear of his father's power.

Oedipus conflict The pattern of events that Freud believed occur between ages 3 and 5, when the child experiences a sexual desire for the parent of the opposite sex; the resulting fear of possible reprisal from the parent of the same sex is resolved when the child identifies with that parent.

TABLE 9.2		Freud's Stages of Psychosexual Development		
Stage	**Age (years)**	**Sensitive Zones**	**Major Developmental Task (potential source of conflict)**	**Personality Traits of Adults "Fixated" at This Stage**
Oral	0–1	Mouth, lips, tongue	Weaning	Oral behavior, such as smoking and overeating; passivity and gullibility
Anal	1–3	Anus	Toilet training	Orderliness, stinginess, obstinacy, or the opposites
Phallic	3–5	Genitals	Oedipus conflict; identification with same-sex parent	Vanity, recklessness, or the opposites
Latency	5–12	No specific area; sexual energy is quiescent	Development of ego defense mechanisms	None; fixation does not normally occur
Genital	12–18 and adulthood	Genitals	Mature sexual intimacy	None; adults who have successfully integrated earlier stages should emerge with a sincere interest in others and mature sexuality.

Most of these feelings and the resultant conflict are unconscious. The boy does not have overt sexual feelings or behave sexually toward his mother. But unconscious or not, the result of this conflict is anxiety. How can the little boy handle this anxiety? In Freud's view, the boy responds with a defensive process called **identification**: The boy "incorporates" his image of his father and attempts to match his own behavior to that image. By trying to make himself as much like his father as possible, the boy not only reduces the chance of an attack from the father; he takes on some of the father's power as well. Furthermore, it is the "inner father," with his values and moral judgments, that serves as the core of the child's superego.

In elementary school, boys play with boys, girls play with girls. How would Freud explain this?

According to Freud, a parallel process occurs in girls. The girl sees her mother as a rival for her father's sexual attentions and has some fear of her mother (though less than the boy has of his father, since the girl may assume she has already been castrated). In this case, too, identification with the mother is thought to be the "solution" to the girl's anxiety.

The Latency Stage: 5 to 12 Years   Freud thought that after the phallic stage came a sort of resting period before the next major change in the child's sexual development. The child has presumably arrived at some preliminary resolution of the Oedipus conflict and now experiences a kind of calm after the storm. One of the obvious characteristics of this stage is that the identification with the same-sex parent that defined the end of the phallic stage is now extended to others of the same sex. So it is during these years that children's peer interactions are almost exclusively with members of the same sex and that children often have "crushes" on same-sex teachers or other adults.

The Genital Stage: 12 to 18 and Older   The further changes in hormones and the genital organs that take place during puberty reawaken the sexual energy of the child. During this period, a more mature form of sexual attachment occurs. From the beginning of this period, the child's sexual objects are people of the opposite sex. Freud placed some emphasis on the fact that not everyone works through this period to a point of mature heterosexual love. Some people have not had a satisfactory oral period and thus do not have a foundation of basic love relationships. Some have not resolved the Oedipus conflict and arrived at a complete or satisfactory identification with the same-sex parent, a failure that may affect their ability to cope with rearoused sexual energies in adolescence.

Optimal development at each stage, according to Freud, requires an environment that satisfies the unique needs of each period. The baby needs sufficient oral and anal stimulation; the 4-year-old boy needs a father present with whom to identify and a mother who is not too seductive. An inadequate early environment will leave a residue of unresolved problems and unmet needs, which are then carried forward to subsequent stages. This emphasis on the formative role of early experience, particularly early family experience, is a hallmark of psychoanalytic theories. In this view, the first 5 or 6 years of life are critical for the development of the individual personality.

ERIKSON'S PSYCHOSOCIAL STAGES

Erikson shared most of Freud's basic assumptions, but there are some crucial differences between the two theories. First, Erikson placed less emphasis on the centrality of sexual drive and instead focused on a stepwise emergence of a sense of identity. Second, although he agreed with Freud that the early years are highly important, Erikson argued that identity is not fully formed at the end of adolescence but continues to

identification The process of taking into oneself (incorporating) the qualities and ideas of another person, which Freud thought was the result of the Oedipus conflict between ages 3 and 5. The child attempts to become like the parent of the same sex.

CRITICAL THINKING ?

Does the idea that one carries unresolved issues forward into adulthood make sense to you? Think of some examples from your own experiences.

move through further developmental stages in adult life. You can see in Table 9.3 the eight **psychosocial stages** that Erikson proposed, three of which are reached only in adulthood.

In Erikson's view, maturation plays a relatively small role in the sequence of stages. Far more important are common cultural demands on children of a particular age, such as the demand that the child become toilet trained at about age 2, that the child learn school skills at age 6 or 7, or that the young adult form an intimate partnership. Each stage, then, centers on a particular *dilemma*, or social task. Thus, Erikson called his stages psychosocial stages rather than psychosexual stages.

Basic Trust versus Basic Mistrust: Birth to 1 Year　The first task (or dilemma) occurs during the first year of life, when the child must develop a sense of basic trust in the predictability of the world and in his ability to affect the events around him. Erikson believed that the behavior of the major caregiver (usually the mother) is critical to the child's successful or unsuccessful resolution of this task. Children who reach the end of the first year with a firm sense of trust are those whose parents are loving and respond predictably and reliably to the child. A child who has developed a sense of trust will go on to other relationships, carrying this sense with him. Those infants whose early care has been erratic or harsh may develop mistrust, and they too carry this sense with them into later relationships.

Erikson never said, by the way, that the ideal or "correct" resolution to any of the dilemmas was to arrive at the ego quality at one end of the continuum. In the first stage, for example, there is some risk in being too trusting. The child also needs to develop some healthy mistrust, such as learning to discriminate between dangerous and safe situations.

Autonomy versus Shame and Doubt: 2 to 3 Years　Erikson saw the child's greater mobility during the toddler years as forming the basis for the sense of independence or autonomy. But if the child's efforts at independence are not carefully guided by the parents and she experiences repeated failures or ridicule, then the results of all the new opportunities for exploration may be shame and doubt instead of a basic sense of self-control and self-worth. Once again, the ideal is not for the child to have *no* shame or doubt; some doubt is needed for the child to understand which behaviors are acceptable and which are not, which are safe and which are dangerous. But the ideal does lie toward the autonomy end of the continuum.

Initiative versus Guilt: 4 to 5 Years　This phase, roughly equivalent to Freud's phallic stage, is also ushered in by new skills or abilities in the child. The 4-year-old is able to plan a bit, to take the initiative in reaching particular goals. The child tries out these new cognitive skills and attempts to conquer the world around him. He may try to go out into the street on his own; he may take a toy apart, and then find he can't put it back together and throw the parts at his mother. It is a time of vigorous action and of behaviors that parents may see as aggressive. The risk is that the child may go too far in his forcefulness or that the parents may restrict and punish too much—either of which can produce guilt. Some guilt is needed, since without it the child would develop no conscience and no self-control. The ideal interaction between parent and child is certainly not total indulgence, but too much guilt can inhibit the child's creativity and interactions with others.

Industry (Competence) versus Inferiority: 6 to 12 Years　The beginning of schooling is a major force in ushering in this stage. The child is now faced with the need to win approval by developing specific competences—learning to read, to do math, and to succeed at other school skills. The task of this period is thus simply to develop the repertoire of abilities society demands of the child. If the child is unable to develop the expected skills, she will develop instead a basic sense of inferiority. Yet some failure is necessary so that the child can develop some humility; as always, bal-

psychosocial stages The stages of personality development suggested by Erikson, involving tasks centered on trust, autonomy, initiative, industry, identity, intimacy, generativity, and ego integrity.

TABLE 9.3	*Erikson's Eight Psychosocial Stages of Development*

Approximate Age (years)	Ego Quality to Be Developed	Some Tasks and Activities of the Stage
0–1	Basic trust versus basic mistrust	Develop trust in mother or central caregiver and in one's own ability to make things happen, a key element in an early secure attachment
2–3	Autonomy versus shame, doubt	Develop walking, grasping, and other physical skills that lead to free choice; complete toilet training; child learns control but may develop shame if not handled properly
4–5	Initiative versus guilt	Learn to organize activities around some goal; become more assertive and aggressive
6–12	Industry versus inferiority	Absorb all the basic cultural skills and norms; including school skills and tool use
13–18	Identity versus role confusion	Adapt sense of self to physical changes of puberty, make occupational choice, achieve adultlike sexual identity, and search for new values
19–25	Intimacy versus isolation	Form one or more intimate relationships that go beyond adolescent love; marry and form family groups
26–40	Generativity versus stagnation	Bear and rear children, focus on occupational achievement or creativity, and train the next generation
41+	Ego integrity versus despair	Integrate earlier stages and come to terms with basic identity; accept self

ance is an issue. Ideally, the child must have sufficient success to encourage a sense of competence but should not place so much emphasis on competence that failure is unacceptable or that she becomes a "workaholic."

Identity versus Role Confusion: 13 to 18 Years   The task that faces the child during puberty is a major one in which the adolescent reexamines his identity and the roles he must occupy. Erikson suggested that two "identities" are involved—a sexual identity and an occupational identity. What should emerge for the adolescent from this period is a reintegrated sense of self, of what one wants to do and be, and of one's appropriate sexual role. The risk is that the child may suffer confusion, arising from the profusion of roles opening up at this age.

BOWLBY'S MODEL OF ATTACHMENT

Erikson was not the only influential modern theorist whose thinking was strongly affected by Freud or psychoanalysis. Among those interested specifically in very early child development, John Bowlby (1907–1990) had a particularly large impact with his theory of the development of attachment (1969, 1973, 1980). Bowlby offered an interesting blend of psychoanalytic and biological approaches. Like Freud, he assumed that the root of human personality lies in the earliest childhood relationships. Significant failure or trauma in those

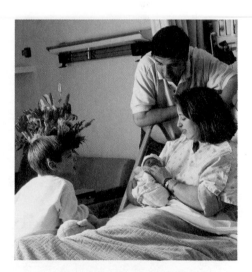

This preschooler, who is in the stage Erikson calls initiative versus guilt, may develop resentful or aggressive thoughts about his new baby brother. If so, the guilt he feels may help him inhibit any actions that may arise from these feelings.

relationships will permanently shape the child's development (see the *Research Report*). Bowlby focused his attention on the child's first attachment to the mother because it is usually the earliest and arguably the most central. To describe how that attachment comes about, Bowlby introduced several concepts from ethological theory, which brings evolutionary concepts to bear on the study of behavior.

Human evolution, Bowlby suggested, has resulted in each child's being born with a repertoire of built-in, instinctive behaviors that elicit caregiving from others—behaviors such as crying, smiling, and making eye contact. Similarly, the mother (or other adult) responds with various instinctive behaviors toward the infant, such as picking up the baby when he cries or speaking to the baby in a high-pitched voice. These instinctive patterns bring mother and infant together in an intricate chain of stimulus and response that causes the child to form a specific attachment to that one adult—a process you'll be reading about in some detail in Chapter 11.

Although Bowlby's model is not a full-fledged stage theory of development like Freud's or Erikson's, it is nonetheless based on many underlying psychoanalytic assumptions. It has also stimulated and profoundly influenced the large body of current research on attachment.

EVIDENCE AND APPLICATIONS

Empirical explorations of Freud's or Erikson's theories are relatively rare, largely because both theories are so general that specific tests are very difficult to perform. For example, to test Freud's notion of fixation, researchers would need much more information about how to determine whether a given child is fixated at some stage. What is a sign that a child is fixated at the oral or the anal stage? Is there some automatic connection between how early a child is weaned and such ostensibly oral adult behavior as smoking or overeating? When researchers have searched for such direct linkages, they have not found them.

Despite these difficulties, researchers have managed to observe instances of some of Freud's psychosexual stages. For instance, one 4-year-old boy, after his mother told him that she loved him, said, "And I love you too, and that's why I can't ever marry someone else" (Watson & Getz, 1990a, p. 29). In their studies of Oedipal behavior, Malcolm Watson and Kenneth Getz (1990a, 1990b) have indeed found that children of about 4 or 5 are likely to make comments like this. More generally, they have found that 4-year-olds, more than any other age group, show more affectionate behavior toward the opposite-sex parent and more aggressive or antagonistic behavior toward the same-sex parent. You can see the results of a study of aggressive and antagonistic behavior in Figure 9.3. Whether Freud's explanation of this phenomenon is the correct one remains to be seen, but these observations are certainly consistent with his theory.

A second research area that has its roots in psychoanalytic theory is the current work on the security or insecurity of children's early attachments. Both Erikson and Freud argued that the quality of the child's first relationship with the central caregiver will shape her relationships with other children and other adults at later ages. And of course Bowlby's theory is designed specifically to examine that earliest relationship. You'll be reading a great deal more about early attachments in Chapter 11, but here it is sufficient to note that research in this area provides a good deal of support for the basic psychoanalytic hypothesis that the quality of the child's earliest relationship affects the whole course of her later development. Dozens of longitudinal studies have assessed

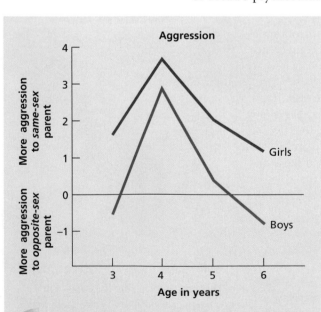

FIGURE 9.3

This figure graphs data from the detailed reports of parents on their children's affectionate and aggressive behavior toward them. Scores above 0 mean that the child was more aggressive toward the same-sex parent than toward the opposite-sex parent; scores below 0 mean the reverse.
(*Source:* Watson & Getz, 1990b, from Table 3, p. 199.)

Adoption and Development

Most people who adopt a child assume that if they provide enough love and support, the child will develop both cognitively and emotionally along the same pathway as their biological children. Indeed, Bowlby's theory would predict that adopted children should have no particular difficulty forming attachments to their adoptive parents as long as the parents provide the infant with a warm, secure environment. However, like most relationships in development, the links between adoption and developmental outcomes are not that simple.

For one thing, as you learned earlier in the chapter, many aspects of temperament and personality are inherited. Therefore, an adopted child is likely to have different personality traits than adoptive parents. Developmentalists speculate that a lack of "fit" between the adopted child's temperament and the parents' personalities can give rise to difficulties in the parent-child relationship. For example, if two extremely shy parents adopt a child who is very outgoing, the parents may find themselves at a loss as to how to handle the child's behavior; in an extreme case, they might come to view the child's personality as "disturbed" in some way rather than just different from theirs.

Of course, infant temperament isn't the only relevant variable. The child's circumstances prior to the adoption also matter. Generally, children adopted before the age of 6 months, who have no history of institutionalization or abuse, are generally indistinguishable from nonadopted children in security of attachment, cognitive development, and social adjustment. This is true both when adoptive parents and children are of the same race and/or nationality and when their races and/or nationalities are different (Juffer & Rosenboom, 1997). For example, in one study involving 211 teenagers adopted into Swedish families at an early age, 90% thought of themselves as Swedish even though many were of non-European birth (Cederblad, Hook, Irhammar, & Mercke, 1999). Similarly, Korean children adopted into American families at very young ages tend to grow up thinking of themselves as sharing the ethnicities of their adoptive parents unless these parents explicitly teach them about their Korean heritage (Lee & Quintana, 2005). Such findings suggest that raising a low-risk adopted child differs little from raising a biological child.

However, children who are adopted later, who have histories of abuse and/or neglect, or who have lived in institutions for long periods tend to have more problems, both cognitive and emotional, than nonadopted children (Castle et al., 1999; O'Connor, Bredenkamp, & Rutter, 1999; Marcovitch, Goldberg, Gold, & Washington, 1997; Rebollo, Molina, & Muñoz, 2004; Roy, Rutter, & Pickles, 2000; Verhulst & Versluis-Den Bieman, 1995). One study found that 91% of children who had been adopted after being abused, neglected, and institutionalized suffered from emotional problems even after having been in their adoptive families for an average of 9 years (Smith, Howard, & Monroe, 1998). Not surprisingly, parents of such children report experiencing more parenting-related stress than parents of either adoptees from favorable backgrounds or biological children (Mainemer, Gilman, & Ames, 1998). Consequently, people who adopt such children should expect that parenting them will not be easy.

However, there are a few important facts parents who adopt high-risk children should keep in mind. First, despite increased risks, the large majority of adopted children are indistinguishable from nonadopted children in social behavior and emotional functioning by the time they reach adolescence (Brand & Brinich, 1999; Cederblad et al., 1999).

Second, the task of raising high-risk children can be made more manageable through parent training (Juffer, Bakermans-Kranenburg, & van IJzendoorn, 2005). Thus, adoptive parents should take advantage of any training offered by the institutions through which their adoptions are arranged or elsewhere, perhaps at a local community college.

Third, at the first sign of difficulty, adoptive parents should seek help from a social worker or psychologist who specializes in treating children. In fact, many developmentalists recommend that agencies who place high-risk children in adoptive or long-term foster families should routinely provide them with post-adoption therapeutic services (Mainemer, Gilman, & Ames, 1998; Minty, 1999; Smith, Howard, & Monroe, 2000). Therapists can help with routine challenges such as toilet-training and teach parents strategies for dealing with behavior that reflects severe emotional disturbance, such as self-injury.

Finally, despite the ups and downs that come with adopting a high-risk child, parents can take heart in the frequent finding that these children are better off developmentally than their peers who remain institutionalized or who are returned to the biological parents who abused and/or neglected them (Bohman & Sigvardsson, 1990).

Questions for Critical Analysis

1. What might the various theoretical models of attachment (e.g., those of Bowlby and Erikson) predict about the risks associated with adopting a child older than 6 months of age?
2. What kind of study might you design to examine the degree to which temperamental mismatch between adoptive parents and children results in adjustment problems for adopted children?

children's attachment security at age 1 or 2 and then followed them over a period of years—in some cases throughout childhood and adolescence. The consistent finding is that children who had a more secure attachment in infancy have more positive relationships with others and are more socially skillful later on (Thompson, 1998). Thus, the relationship formed during the earliest stage of psychosocial development seems to create a prototype for later relationships, as Bowlby and Erikson proposed. Recall, too, the result from the study by Gunnar (1994) described earlier: Temperamentally inhibited toddlers who have formed a secure attachment to their mothers show little or no physiological sign of fearfulness in a novel setting. Thus, the quality of the child's early attachment can at least partially override basic temperamental tendencies as the personality is formed.

CRITIQUE OF PSYCHOANALYTIC THEORIES

Freud's and Erikson's psychoanalytic theories are attractive for several reasons. Perhaps their greatest strength is that they provide us with a better account of the complexities of personality development than other perspectives, especially the learning theories (Seligman, 2005). In psychoanalytic theory, a particular characteristic of the environment, such as inconsistent parenting, is not hypothesized to have a specific effect on development. Instead, psychoanalysts predict that the effects of such factors depend on how individual children perceive them, the stage of development in which children experience them, and, in Erikson's case, the cultural context in which they occur.

Moreover, psychoanalytic theories focus on the importance of the emotional quality of the child's relationship with caregivers. These theories suggest that the child's needs or tasks change with age, so that the parents must constantly adapt to the changing child. One of the implications of this observation is that "good parenting" should not be thought of as if it were a global quality. Some parents may be very good at meeting the needs of an infant but terrible at dealing with a teenager's identity struggles; others may have the opposite pattern. The child's eventual personality and her overall emotional health thus depend on the interaction, or *transaction*, that develops in a particular family. This is an attractive element of psychoanalytic theories, because research within developmental psychology is increasingly supporting a transactional conception of the process of development.

Psychoanalytic theory has also given psychologists a number of helpful concepts, such as defense mechanisms and identification, that have been so widely adopted that they have become a part of everyday language as well as theory. These strengths have led to a resurgence of influence of both Erikson's theory and several related psychoanalytic approaches such as Bowlby's.

The great weakness of all the psychoanalytic approaches is the fuzziness of many of the concepts. Identification may be an intriguing theoretical notion, but how can it be measured? How do researchers detect the presence of specific defense mechanisms? Without more precise operational definitions, it is impossible to test the theories. The general concepts of psychoanalytic theories have furthered an understanding of development only when other theorists or researchers have offered more precise definitions or clearer methods for measuring some psychoanalytic construct, such as Bowlby's concept of security of attachment. Psychoanalytic theory may thus sometimes offer a provocative way of thinking about personality, but it is not a precise theory of development.

Before going on . . .

- What are the major points of the psychoanalytic view of personality development?
- List some of the differences between Freud's and Erikson's theories.
- How does Freud's theory explain personality development?
- How does Erikson's theory explain personality development?
- Explain Bowlby's model of attachment.
- What evidence is there to support the psychoanalytic perspective on personality development?
- What are some criticisms of psychoanalytic theories?

A Possible Synthesis

You have read about three different views of the origins of those unique, individual patterns of behavior we call personality. Each view can be at least partially sup-

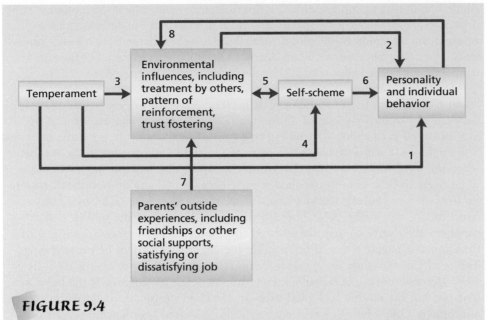

FIGURE 9.4

Here is one version of a complex interactive model describing the formation of individual personality. The effects of inborn temperament and environmental influences do not merely add. Each affects the other, helping to create the child's unique self-scheme, which in turn affects the child's experiences. All this occurs within the context of the family, which is itself influenced by the parents' own life experiences. What developmentalists think of as personality is a complex product of all these forces.

ported with research evidence; each has clear strengths. Do developmentalists need to choose just one of them, or can the views be combined in a way that makes sense? Some argue that theories as different as these cannot ever be combined, because they make such different assumptions about the child's role in the process of personality development (Lerner, Theokas, & Bobek, 2005; Overton & Reese, 1973). Nonetheless, combinations of these varying perspectives, like the one shown in Figure 9.4, may still be fruitful. This model suggests that the child's inborn temperament is a beginning point—an initial, highly significant bias in the system. Arrow 1 suggests a direct relationship between that inborn temperament and the eventual personality seen in the child and later in the adult.

Arrow 2 suggests a second direct effect, between the pattern of the child's environment and his eventual personality and social behavior. Whether the parents respond reliably and appropriately to the infant will affect his trust, or the security of his attachment, which will show up in a range of behaviors later; whether the parents reinforce aggressive or friendly behavior will influence the child's future as well.

These direct effects are straightforward, even obvious, but most of what happens is much more complicated than that. The way the child is treated is influenced by her temperament (arrow 3), and both that basic temperament and the family environment affect the child's self-scheme, or self-concept—her expectations for others and herself, her beliefs about her own abilities (arrows 4 and 5). This self-scheme (including the child's sense of self-efficacy), in turn, helps to shape the child's overt behavior, which reflects her "personality" (arrow 6).

This system does not exist in a vacuum. In keeping with the ecological approach of Bronfenbrenner and others, arrow 7 suggests that the parents' ability to maintain a loving and supportive relationship with their child is influenced by the parents' own outside experiences, such as whether they like their jobs or whether they have enough emotional support to help them weather their own crises.

For example, Mavis Hetherington (1989) reports that children with difficult temperaments show more problem behavior in response to their parents' divorce than do children with easier temperaments, but this difference exists only if the mother is also depressed and has inadequate social support. In this study, those difficult children whose divorcing mothers were not depressed did not show heightened levels of problems. Thus, the child's temperament clearly seems to have an impact, but the effect of temperament can be and is modified by the parents' pattern of response.

Another illustration of the intricacy of the system comes from the work of Susan Crockenberg (e.g., Crockenberg & Leerkes, 2004). In one early study (1981), Crockenberg studied a group of 48 mothers and infants over the first year of life. She measured each child's irritability (an aspect of temperament) when the baby was 5 to 10 days old and assessed the security of the child's attachment to the mother when the child was 12 months old. We might expect that irritable babies would be more likely to be insecurely attached, merely because they are more difficult to care for. In fact, Crockenberg found a small effect of this kind (see Table 9.4). But Crockenberg didn't stop there. She also measured the level of the mother's social support—the degree of help she received from family and friends in dealing with the strains of having a new child or other life changes she might be experiencing. The results of the study show that insecure attachment in the child was most likely when the mother had an irritable infant and low levels of support. If the baby was irritable, but the mother had good support, the child nearly always developed secure attachment. Only when two difficult conditions occurred together did a poor outcome result for the child.

In a later study, Crockenberg (1987) found that a higher level of anger and noncompliant behavior (perhaps reflections of what is called *neuroticism* in the Big Five) was common in toddlers who had been irritable as infants and whose mothers were angry and punitive toward them. Furthermore, such angry and punitive behavior by the mother was more likely if the mother had experienced rejection in her own childhood and if she experienced little support from her partner. Clearly, Crockenberg's work reveals a system of effects.

Returning to Figure 9.4, you'll see that arrow 8 emphasizes the transactional elements of the system. Once the child's unique pattern of behaviors and attitudes (personality) is formed, this pattern affects the environment she will encounter, the experiences she will choose, and the responses of the people around her, which in turn affect her behavior (Bandura, 1997; Scarr & McCartney, 1983; Sroufe, Carlson, & Schulman, 1993).

No doubt even this fairly complex system underestimates the intricacy of the process of personality development in the child. Most research does not yet encompass all the pieces of the puzzle. But the very fact that developmental psychologists are turning toward such complex models is a very good thing. Development *is* complex, and developmentalists will not be able to describe it or explain it until they begin to examine and try to measure all these separate forces.

TABLE 9.4	Influence of Child's Temperament and Mother's Social Support on the Child's Secure or Insecure Attachment		
Child Irritability	**Mother's Social Support**	**Securely Attached Children**	**Insecurely Attached Children**
High	Low	2	9
High	High	12	1
Low	Low	7	2
Low	High	13	2

Source: From S. B. Crockenberg, Table 5, 862, "Infant Irritability, Mother Responsiveness, and Social Support Influences on the Security of Infant-Mother Attachment," *Child Development*, 52, 1981, p. 857–865. By permission of the Society for Research in Child Development.

Summary

Defining Personality

- Researchers studying adult personality have agreed on a set of five dimensions (the Big Five) that capture most of the variation among individuals: extraversion, agreeableness, conscientiousness, neuroticism, and openness/intellect. Recent research suggests that the same five dimensions may give an accurate picture of variations in children's and adolescents' personalities as well.
- Researchers studying infants and young children have studied temperament rather than personality. Temperament is now widely seen as a set of built-in, behavior tendencies that form the emotional substrate of personality.
- There are sizeable differences among temperament theorists regarding how best to characterize the basic dimensions of temperament, but there is general agreement on five key dimensions: activity level, approach/positive emotionality, inhibition and anxiety, negative emotionality/irritability/anger, and effortful control/task persistence.

Genetic and Biological Explanations of Personality

- Biological explanations of temperament and personality, focusing on genetic differences in patterns or styles of reacting to people and the environment, are well supported by research. Evidence is also accumulating that specific differences in neurological and chemical responses underlie many observed variations in behavior.
- However, temperament is clearly not totally determined by heredity or ongoing physiological processes, although the child's built-in temperament does shape her interactions with the world and affect others' responses to her.

Learning Explanations of Personality

- Traditional learning theorists emphasize the role of basic learning processes, such as reinforcement, in shaping individual behaviors, including patterns of interaction with others. Social/cognitive learning theorists such as Bandura also emphasize the role of observational learning as well as the role of the child's learned expectancies, standards, and self-efficacy beliefs in creating more enduring patterns of response.
- Critics argue that learning theories place too much importance on what is happening to the child and pay too little attention to how the child acts on his environment. They also suggest that learning theories explain only how children acquire specific behaviors, not the underlying processes that drive personality development.

Psychoanalytic Explanations of Personality

- Psychoanalytic theorists emphasize the importance of unconscious motives and processes as well as the stagelike emergence of personality. This approach views the relationship of the child with significant adults, particularly in early infancy, as critical.
- While Freud's and Erikson's theories share a common set of assumptions, they differ with respect to the importance of the libido. In addition, Freud proposed that personality development was completed in childhood, while Erikson claimed that change continued throughout the lifespan.
- Freud's psychosexual stages are strongly affected by maturation. Particularly significant is the phallic stage, beginning at about age 3 or 4, when the Oedipus conflict arises and is resolved through the process of identification.
- Erikson's psychosocial stages are influenced both by social demands and by the child's physical and intellectual skills. Each of the major stages has a central task, or dilemma, relating to some aspect of the development of identity.
- Bowlby's theory of attachment, with roots in psychoanalytic thought, is particularly influential today.
- Psychoanalytic theories have been broadly confirmed in some aspects, such as the impact of early attachment on later functioning.
- Critics point out that psychoanalytic theories are difficult to test because of their imprecision.

A Possible Synthesis

- Elements of all three views can be combined into a transactional, or interactionist, view of personality development. Temperament may serve as the base from which personality grows, both by affecting behavior directly and by affecting the way others respond to the child. Both the child's temperament and the specific pattern of response from the people in the child's environment affect the child's self-concept, or self-scheme, which then helps to create stability in the child's unique pattern of behavior.

Key Terms

agreeableness (p. 247)

Big Five (p. 247)

conscientiousness (p. 247)

extraversion (p. 247)

identification (p. 263)

neuroticism (p. 247)

Oedipus conflict (p. 262)

openness/intellect (p. 247)

personality (p. 247)

psychosexual stages (p. 261)

psychosocial stages (p. 264)

self-efficacy (p. 258)

See for Yourself

Validity of Parental Ratings of Temperament

Much of the research on temperament in young children re-lies on parental ratings of children's behavior. The validity of this approach to measurement of temperament is often tested by comparing parents' ratings to those of objective observers. You can carry out a validity study of this kind by using the temperament scale found at http://www.adopting.org/ weidmanTemperament.html. This scale is intended for adop-tive families, but you can adapt it for use in your validity study. First, identify a few families with children who would be willing to participate. Second, observe the children in a natural setting, such as in a preschool classroom or at home. You may want to enlist the help of a classmate to serve as an additional objective observer. (Be sure to observe all the chil-dren in the same setting.) Next, ask parents to complete the checklist. Finally, compare your ratings—and those of your classmate, if applicable—to those of parents. If you find dif-ferences, note on which dimensions of temperament they occur. Develop a theory as to why parents might rate children either higher or lower on those dimensions than objective raters. Think about the degree to which the setting in which you observed the children might have influenced your own ratings.

Gender Segregation on the School Playground

As Freud's description of the latency stage would predict, re-searchers have found that the tendency for school-aged chil-dren to segregate themselves by gender is universal. There also appear to be universal rules defining socially acceptable contact between boys and girls (Sroufe, Bennett, England, Urban, & Schulman, 1993). Some examples of acceptable girl-boy interactions are (1) accidental contact; (2) contact com-pelled by an adult, as when a teacher forces a boy to work with a girl in class; (3) and contact accompanied by verbal taunts, insults, or mild physical aggression such as pushing. You can observe both gender-segregated play and rule-governed cross-gender contact on any school playground. As you watch children at play, note the following: (1) the num-ber of contacts between boys and girls; (2) the type of contact (accidental, compelled, or aggressive); (3) children's com-ments to or about a boy or girl who violates gender segrega-tion rules; and (4) the kinds of activities exhibited by boys' groups and girls' groups. Use your data to hypothesize some additional rules governing children's relations with peers of the same sex and of the opposite sex.

Concepts of Self, Gender, and Sex Roles

The terms sex and gender are common in everyday speech, but have you ever thought about the difference between the two?

Usually, *sex* is reserved for the biological aspects of maleness and femaleness. Thus, as you learned in Chapter 2, the X and Y chromosomes are referred to as the *sex chromosomes*. You probably recall, too, that males follow the XY pattern, while females are XX. By contrast, *gender* refers to the psychological and social aspects of maleness and femaleness. Typically, male children grow up to have a sense of male gender that helps them to be comfortable with most of the behaviors that their cultures regard as acceptable for males. Likewise, most female children develop a sense of female gender that is consistent with the cultures in which they are raised. But what happens when sex and gender are in conflict?

Consider the tragic case of John/Joan, who, along with an identical twin brother, was born in the mid-1960s. In those days, many researchers believed that hormones played no role in the development of gender. They thought that a child could be successfully brought up as either male or female, regardless of his or her chromosomal makeup. As a result, when an accident during a routine circumcision left John with a severely damaged penis, doctors recommended that his parents allow him to undergo sex reassignment surgery and that they raise him as a girl. Their thinking was that the child would be better able to develop a healthy sense of self with surgically sculpted female genitalia than with mutilated male genitalia. The parents agreed, and John became Joan.

Joan's parents exposed her to all the typical female experiences and never hinted that she might have ever been anything other than a girl. The famous sex researcher John Money reported that the "experiment" had been a success and had provided strong support for the notion that gender roles are acquired through learning (Money, 1975). Still, Joan was emotionally troubled and was sometimes teased by her schoolmates for being too "masculine" to be a girl. By the time she reached adolescence, Joan was convinced that she was different from others in some fundamental way. When her parents revealed the truth, Joan became John once again and began to live as a male. She, now he, underwent sex reassignment surgery and eventually married. Though John and his wife adopted children and, to outsiders, appeared to be a normal couple, he was never really happy. Unfortunately, in May 2004 John committed suicide.

The Joan/John case provides compelling evidence for the view that gender is strongly influenced by the physiological aspects of biological sex. In fact, longitudinal studies indicate that when individuals are born as males but, because of birth defects or circumcision mishaps, undergo sex reassignment surgery, most choose to live as males once they become aware of their early experiences (Reiner & Gearhardt, 2004). Researchers generally attribute this phenomenon to exposure to prenatal testosterone. But how can we explain cases in which individuals appear to be physically normal and are brought up in ways that are consistent with their biological sex, but their gender is the opposite of their biological sex?

Despite having normal genitalia and a typical, gender-typed upbringing, individuals who are *transgendered* develop a sense of gender that is the opposite of their biological sex. Many wear clothing that is more typical of the opposite sex; others pose as the opposite sex. Transgendered individuals who do so on a full-time basis are known as *transsexuals*. Some transsexuals are so anguished by their sex-gender conflict that they undergo sex reassignment surgery in order to achieve a match between the two. Research shows that, following the surgery, transsexuals are generally satisfied with the results and rarely experience regret about their decision (Lawrence, 2003). Studies suggest that some transgendered individuals may have been exposed to atypical amounts of sex hormones while in the womb, but most of them do not have such histories (Lippa, 2005). Thus, the cause of transgenderism remains a mystery.

From these widely varying examples of a mismatch between sex and gender we can form some conclusions about the role of sex and gender in a person's overall sense of self. First, it seems clear that neither nature nor nurture alone determines gender. If nature determined gender, then transgenderism wouldn't exist. Likewise, if nurture alone were responsible for gender development, infant boys raised to believe they were girls would not develop a male gender identity. Second, the health of one's sense of self seems to depend on achieving some degree of integration of sex and gender. This is why most of the little boys who were raised as girls felt relieved when they learned the truth and adopted a male life-style. Further, this assertion provides an explanation for why some transgendered individuals report higher levels of life satisfaction after undergoing sex reassignment surgery.

Finally, there is an important distinction between sex and gender. Biological sex is categorical. That is, aside from rare instances of chromosomal errors or other kinds of birth defects, individuals are either male or female. By contrast, gender is noncategorical. In other words, psychologically speaking, none of us is either male or female. Instead, gender varies by degrees. We all have some characteristics that we share with others of our sex and some that are more common among those of the opposite sex. What seems not to vary across individuals is that both sex and gender are important elements in one's global sense of self.

How children develop a coherent sense of self is the topic of this chapter. First, we will explore how children come to understand "self" as a concept. Next, we will turn to the topic of self-esteem. Finally, we will return to the critical issue of how individuals integrate biological sex and psychological gender and incorporate them into a sense of self.

 ## The Concept of Self

Developmentalists' thinking about the child's emerging sense of self has been strongly influenced by both Freud and Piaget. Each of these theorists assumed that a baby begins life with no sense of separateness. Freud emphasized what he called the symbiotic relationship between the mother and young infant, in which the two are joined together as if they were one. Predictably, Piaget's theory has provided the basis for explanations of the sense of self that emphasize the child's knowledge of and thinking about himself. Even more influential than either Freud or Piaget, however, has been the thinking of the early American psychologist William James (1890, 1892), who compartmentalized the global **self-concept** into one component he called the "I" and another he termed the "me." The "I" self is often called the **subjective self**; it is that inner sense that "I am," "I exist." The "me" aspect is sometimes called the **objective self**; it is the individual's set of properties or qualities that are objectively known or knowable, including physical characteristics, temperament, and social skills.

self-concept One's knowledge of and thoughts about the set of qualities attributed to the self.

subjective self The component of the self-concept that involves awareness of the "I," the self that is separate from others.

objective self The component of the self-concept that involves awareness of the self as an object with properties.

THE SUBJECTIVE SELF

Most modern students of self-development dispute Freud's claim about the initial symbiotic link between infant and parent in which the infant has no sense of separateness (Harter, 1998). Most now argue that the baby has some primitive sense of separateness from the beginning. In the early months, the baby's task is to begin to coordinate the various sources of information he has about his own actions and their impact. In particular, over the first year, the infant develops a sense of himself as an agent in the world—as able to make things happen. The delight the baby shows when he is able to make a mobile move or create a noise by squeezing a squeaky toy is evidence of the baby's emerging sense of himself as an agent—the first step in the formation of a self-concept. Albert Bandura argues that the roots of the sense of self-efficacy are found during this first year, when the infant realizes he can control certain events in the world.

This sense of efficacy or control occurs not just with inanimate objects but perhaps even more centrally in interactions with adults, who respond appropriately to the child's behavior—smiling back when the baby smiles, making funny faces when the baby does particular things, playing repetitive games like peek-a-boo while changing diapers or feeding the baby. Of course the baby is not "causing" these things to happen in most cases; it is the parents who are initiating the games or patterns. But within these games and patterns are myriad repetitions of sequences in which the baby does something and the parent responds with some predictable behavior. From the baby's perspective, he has "made it happen," and his sense of self, of efficacy or agency, is established.

Piaget also argued that a critical element in the development of the subjective self is the understanding of object permanence that develops at about 9 to 12 months. Just as the infant is figuring out that mom and dad continue to exist when they are out of sight, he is figuring out—at least in some preliminary way—that he exists separately and has some permanence.

THE OBJECTIVE SELF

At 4 months, Lucy's pleasure at looking at herself in a mirror comes from the fact that this is an interesting moving object to inspect—not from any understanding that this is herself in the mirror.

The second major step in the development of a self-concept is for the toddler to come to understand that she is also an object in the world. Just as a ball has properties—roundness, the ability to roll, a certain feel in the hand—so the self also has properties, such as gender, size, a name, and qualities like shyness or boldness, coordination or clumsiness. It is this self-awareness that is the hallmark of the "me" self.

Studying Self-Awareness   Babies as young as 4 months old respond differently to live video or still photographic images of themselves and others (Rochat & Striano, 2002). For example, they look longer at images of others than they do at images of themselves. They also smile more in response to pictures of other babies. However, developmentalists believe that this type of discrimination is only a precursor to true self-awareness.

The most common procedure psychologists use to measure self-awareness involves a mirror. First the baby is placed in front of a mirror, just to see how she behaves. Most infants of about 9 to 12 months will look at their own images, make faces, or try to interact with the baby in the mirror in some way. After allowing this free exploration for a time, the experimenter, while pretending to wipe the baby's face with a cloth, puts a spot of rouge on the baby's nose and then again lets the baby look in the mirror. The crucial test of self-recognition, and thus of awareness of the self, is whether the baby reaches for the spot of rouge on her own nose rather than for the spot on the nose in the mirror.

The results from one of Michael Lewis's studies using this procedure are shown in Figure 10.1. As you can see, none of the 9- to 12-month-old children in this study touched their noses, but by 21 months, three-quarters of the children showed that level of self-recognition. The figure also shows the rate at which children refer to themselves by name when they are shown a picture of themselves, which is another commonly used measure of self-awareness. You can see that this development occurs at almost exactly the same time as self-recognition in a mirror. Both are present by about the middle of the second year of life (Lewis & Ramsay, 2004).

Once the toddler achieves such self-awareness, his behavior is affected in a wide range of ways. Self-aware toddlers begin to insist on doing things for themselves and show a newly proprietary attitude toward toys or other treasured objects ("Mine!"). Looked at this way, much of the legendary behavior in the "terrible twos" can be understood as an outgrowth of self-awareness. In a quite literal sense, toddlers are self-willed for the first time.

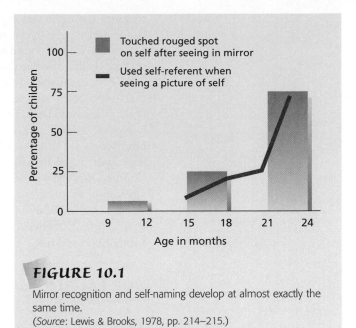

FIGURE 10.1

Mirror recognition and self-naming develop at almost exactly the same time.
(*Source*: Lewis & Brooks, 1978, pp. 214–215.)

Another behavioral change ushered in by the toddler's newly emerging self-awareness is the expression of such self-conscious emotions as embarrassment, pride, or shame. These emotions are not normally expressed until late in the second year of life, presumably because they all involve some aspect of self-evaluation, not present until the toddler has achieved at least minimal self-awareness (Lewis, Allesandri, & Sullivan, 1992; Lewis, Sullivan, Stanger, & Weiss, 1989; Thompson & Goodvin, 2005). According to Lewis, emotions such as shame or pride require the child to be aware of some standards of conduct and to compare himself to those standards— a development that also occurs late in the second year of life. It is only at this age, for example, that children begin to use words like *dirty* to describe themselves or an object, suggesting that they are judging themselves or others against some standard. The child then expresses shame when he feels he has not met the standard, or pride when he is able to meet the standard—to build the block tower as high as the teacher wants, say, or to wash his hands so that they are clean, or the like. One aspect of this phase of development is that after age 2, children become increasingly eager for adult approval, using the adult's response to gauge whether they have met some standard or lived up to some expectation. By school age, children have largely internalized those standards and expectations and thus become more autonomous in their self-judgments (Schaffer, 1996). Likewise, they internalize their parents' rules and regulations, thereby becoming better able to regulate their emotional expression and behavior.

Early Self-Definitions Having achieved an initial self-awareness, the preschool child begins to define "who I am" by learning about her own qualities and her social roles. The 2-year-old not only knows her own name; she can probably also tell you if she is a girl or a boy and whether she is big or little. By about age 5 to 7, a child can give you quite a full description of herself on a whole range of dimensions. For example, Susan Harter (1987, 1990, 1999; Harter & Pike, 1984) has found that children of this age have clear notions of their own competence on a variety of specific tasks, such as solving puzzles, counting, knowing a lot in school, climbing or skipping or jumping rope, or being able to make friends.

Beginning in the second year, children also seem to become aware of themselves as players in the social game. By age 2, the toddler has already learned a variety of social "scripts"—routines of play or interaction with others. Case (1991) points out that the toddler next begins to develop an implicit understanding of her own roles in these scripts. So she begins to think of herself as a "helper" in some situations or as "the boss" when she is telling another child what to do. You can see this clearly in

CRITICAL THINKING **9**

Can you think of some social scripts that a 2- or 3-year-old is likely to learn? Bedtime rituals? Others?

sociodramatic play among preschoolers, who begin to take explicit roles: "I'll be the daddy and you be the mommy" or "I'm the teacher." As part of the same process, the preschool child also gradually understands her place in the network of family roles—she knows that she has sisters, brothers, father, mother, and so on.

These are major advances in the child's understanding. Yet the self-definition is still tied to concrete characteristics. For one thing, each facet of a preschool child's self-concept seems to be quite separate, rather like a list: "I'm good at running"; "I don't like to play with dolls"; "I live in a big house"; "I have blue eyes" (Harter, 1998). These separate aspects of the self-scheme, or internal working model of the self, have not yet coalesced into a global sense of self-worth (Harter, 1987, 1990, 1999; Harter & Pike, 1984). Children this age do not say "I am a terrible person" or "I really like myself." Their perceptions of themselves are more tied to specific settings and specific tasks. Moreover, a preschooler's self-concept tends to focus on his own visible characteristics—whether he's a boy or girl, what he looks like, what or who he plays with, where he lives, what he is good or bad at doing—rather than on more enduring, inner qualities.

THE EMOTIONAL SELF

Another facet of self that emerges during the early years is the child's ability to understand and regulate her own expressions of emotion (Dunn, 1994; Hoeksma, Oosterlaan, & Schipper, 2004). Part of this process is the development of *impulse control*, sometimes called *inhibitory control*—the growing ability to inhibit a response, for example, to wait rather than to weep, to yell rather than to hit, to go slowly rather than to run (Kochanska, Murray, & Coy, 1997). When an infant is upset, it is the parents who help to regulate that emotion by cuddling, soothing, or removing the child from the upsetting situation. Over the preschool years, this regulation process is gradually taken over more and more by the child as the various prohibitions and instructions are internalized. A 2-year-old is only minimally able to modulate feelings or behavior in this way; by age 5 or 6, however, most children have made great strides in controlling the intensity of their expressions of strong feelings, so they don't automatically hit someone or something when they are angry, cry inconsolably when they are frustrated, or sulk when they are denied (Sroufe, 1996).

A second aspect of the child's regulation of emotion—one that is clearly linked to the cognitive processes discussed in Chapter 6—is the need to learn the social rules of specific emotional expressions. For example, as early as age 3, children begin to learn that there are times when they ought to smile—even when they do not feel completely happy (Liew, Eisenberg, & Reiser, 2004). Thus, they begin to use the "social smile," a facial expression that is quite distinct from the natural, delighted smile. Similarly, children gradually learn to use abbreviated or constricted forms of other emotions, such as anger or disgust (Izard & Abe, 2004; Izard & Malatesta, 1987), and they learn to conceal their feelings in a variety of situations. An ability to conceal feelings appears to rest on the child's emerging theory of mind. For example, for a child to conceal some emotion in order not to hurt someone else's feelings requires that she have some sense of what will cause the other person's feelings to be hurt. Equally, the preschool child learns to use her own emotional expressions to get things she wants, crying or smiling as needed. This control of emotions, in turn, rests at least partially on her grasp of the links between her behavior and others' perception of her behavior, an understanding that develops rapidly between ages 3 and 4 as a consequence of the child's growing theory of mind (see Chapter 6).

Developmentalist Nancy Eisenberg argues that emotion regulation is the foundation on which a child's entire repertoire of social skills is built (Eisenberg, 2001). Research lends some support for this notion, as the ability to regulate emotions during the preschool years is strongly predictive of a wide variety of social skills later in life (Rubin, Burgess, Dwyer, & Hastings, 2003). For instance, self-control in early childhood is related to children's ability to obey moral rules and to think about right and wrong during the school years (Kochanska et al., 1997). Further, young children who are skilled in controlling negative emotions, such as anger, are less likely to display behavior problems during the school years (Eisenberg et al., 1999; Eisenberg et al., 2005). Emotional regulation skills appear to be particularly important for children whose temperaments include high levels of anger proneness (Diener & Kim, 2004). Research also suggests that children who poorly control their negative emotions are less popular with peers (Denham et al., 2003; Eisenberg, Liew, & Pidada, 2001; Fantuzzo, Sekino, & Cohen, 2004).

The process of acquiring emotional control is one in which control shifts slowly from the parents to the child (Houck & Lecuyer-Marcus, 2004). Here again, the child's temperament is a factor. For example, preschoolers who have consistently exhibited "difficult" behavior since infancy are more likely to have self-control problems in early childhood (Schmitz et al., 1999). Similarly, preschoolers who were born prematurely or who were delayed in language development in the second year of life experience more difficulties with self-control during early childhood (Carson, Klee, & Perry, 1998; Schothorst & van Engeland, 1996).

However, parents' age-based expectations and parenting behaviors are also important. For instance, most parents know that it is unreasonable to expect toddlers to wait for long periods of time, so they provide external control mechanisms such as reminding them of prohibitions and repeating requests. Over the years from 3 to 6, children gradually internalize such parental standards and expectations and take on more of the control task for themselves. For example, if you were to observe parents and children in a doctor's waiting room, you would see that parents of bored toddlers often physically direct and redirect their behavior. A parent of a 2-year-old might take the child onto his lap and read to her. In contrast, you would notice that older preschoolers look for things to do on their own. In response to such evidence of emotional maturity, parents expect more control from older preschoolers and use verbal instructions, rather than physical control, to help them manage their behavior.

In addition to parenting behavior, the way parents express emotions themselves is related to their children's ability to regulate emotions. Generally, parents who are very expressive of their negative emotions tend to have children who poorly control their negative feelings (Eisenberg, Gershoff et al., 2001; Eisenberg, Liew, & Pidada, 2001). Interesting, too, is the finding that positive emotional expressivity in parents does not predict children's emotional self-regulation as consistently as negative emotional expressivity.

SELF-CONCEPT AT SCHOOL AGE

Over the elementary school years, the child's concrete self-concept gradually shifts toward a more abstract, more comparative, more generalized self-definition. A 6-year-old might describe herself as "smart" or "dumb"; a 10-year-old is more likely to say he is "smarter than most other kids" or "not as good at baseball as my friends" (Rosenberg, 1986; Ruble, 1987). The school-aged child also begins to see her own (and other people's) characteristics as relatively stable and, for the first time, develops a global sense of her own self-worth.

A number of these themes are illustrated nicely in a classic study by Montemayor and Eisen (1977) of self-concepts in 9- to 18-year-olds. Using the question "Who am I?" these researchers found that the younger children they studied were still using mostly surface qualities to describe themselves, as in the description by this 9-year-old:

My name is Bruce C. I have brown eyes. I have brown hair. I have brown eyebrows. I am nine years old. I LOVE! Sports. I have seven people in my family. I have great! eye site. I have lots! of friends. I live on 1923 Pinecrest Dr. I am going on 10 in September. I'm a boy. I have an uncle that is almost 7 feet tall. My school is Pinecrest. My teacher is Mrs. V. I play Hockey! I'm almost the smartest boy in the class. I LOVE! food. I love fresh air. I LOVE school. (pp. 317–318)

These fourth graders are already developing fairly clear ideas about their academic abilities, comparing their own successes and failures to those of other children in their class. These ideas then become incorporated in the children's self-schemes, affecting their choices and sense of self-efficacy.

In contrast, look at the self-description of this 11-year-old girl in the sixth grade:

My name is A. I'm a human being. I'm a girl. I'm a truthful person. I'm not very pretty. I do so-so in my studies. I'm a very good cellist. I'm a very good pianist. I'm a little bit tall for my age. I like several boys. I like several girls. I'm old-fashioned. I play tennis. I am a very good swimmer. I try to be helpful. I'm always ready to be friends with anybody. Mostly I'm good, but I lose my temper. I'm not well-liked by some girls and boys. I don't know if I'm liked by boys or not. (pp. 317–318)

This girl, like other youngsters of her age in Montemayor and Eisen's study, not only describes her external qualities but also emphasizes her beliefs, the quality of her relationships, and her general personality traits. Thus, as the child moves through the elementary school years (Piaget's concrete operations period), her self-definition becomes more complex, more comparative, less tied to external features, and more focused on feelings and ideas.

The increasingly comparative self-assessments seen in middle childhood are particularly visible in the school context. Kindergarten and first-grade children pay relatively little attention to how well others do at a particular task; in fact, the great majority will confidently tell you that they are the smartest kid in their class—an aspect of a general tendency at this age to identify self-qualities as positive (Harter, 1998). By third grade, however, children begin to notice whether their classmates finish a test sooner than they do or whether someone else gets a better grade or more corrections on his spelling paper (Stipek, 1992). Their self-judgments begin to include both positive and negative elements.

Teachers' behavior shows a related progression: In the first few grades, teachers emphasize effort and work habits. Gradually, they begin to use more comparative judgments. By junior high, teachers compare children not only to each other but to fixed standards, students at other schools, or national norms (Stipek, 1992). These comparisons are sometimes subtle, but they can be powerful. Robert Rosenthal (1994), in a famous series of studies, has shown that a teacher's belief about a given student's ability and potential has a small but significant effect on his or her behavior toward that student and on the student's eventual achievement. This set of results has now been replicated many times. Rosenthal's standard procedure is to tell teachers at the beginning of a school year that some of the children in the class are underachievers and just ready to "bloom" intellectually, although in fact the children labeled in this way are chosen randomly. At the end of the year, those students labeled as having more potential have typically shown more academic gains than those who have not been labeled in this way.

Similarly, parents' judgments and expectations also play a role. For example, you may recall from Chapter 7 that parents in the United States are more likely to attribute a daughter's good performance in math to hard work but a son's good math grades to ability. Children absorb these explanations and adjust their behavior accordingly (Fredricks & Eccles, 2005).

The beliefs about their own abilities that students develop through this process of self-assessment are usually quite accurate. Students who consistently do well in comparison to others come to believe that they are academically competent. Further, and perhaps more important, they come to believe that they are in control of academic outcomes—in Bandura's terms, they have a strong sense of their own academic self-efficacy.

SELF-CONCEPT AND IDENTITY IN ADOLESCENCE

The trend toward greater abstraction in self-definition continues during adolescence, and the self-concept blossoms into a mature sense of identity.

Self-Descriptions Compare the answers of this 17-year-old to the "Who am I?" question with the ones you read earlier:

> I am a human being. I am a girl, I am an individual. I don't know who I am. I am a Pisces. I am a moody person. I am an indecisive person. I am an ambitious person. I am a very curious person. I am not an individual. I am a loner. I am an American (God help me). I am a Democrat. I am a liberal person. I am a radical. I am a conservative. I am a pseudoliberal. I am an atheist. I am not a classifiable person (i.e., I don't want to be). (Montemayor & Eisen, 1977, p. 318)

Obviously, this girl's self-concept is even less tied to her physical characteristics or even her abilities than is that of the 11-year-old. She is describing abstract traits or ideology. Figure 10.2 shows this shift from concrete to abstract self-definitions, based on the answers of all 262 participants in Montemayor and Eisen's study. Participants' answers to the "Who am I?" question were placed in one or more specific categories, such as references to physical properties ("I am tall," "I have blue eyes") or references to ideology ("I am a Democrat," "I believe in God"). Figure 10.2 makes it clear that physical appearance was still a highly significant dimension of self-concept in the preteen and early teen years but became less dominant in late adolescence.

The adolescent's self-concept also becomes more differentiated as the teenager comes to see herself somewhat differently in each of several roles: as a student, with friends, with parents, and in romantic relationships (Harter & Monsour, 1992; Thompson & Goodwin, 2005). Once these ideas are formed, they begin to influence adolescents' behavior. For example, teens whose academic self-concepts are strong take more difficult courses in high school than those who believe themselves to be less academically able. Further, they tend to select courses in disciplines in which they believe they have the greatest ability and to avoid courses in perceived areas of weakness (Marsh & Yeung, 1997). Further, as you might suspect, teens with weak academic self-concepts are more likely to get into trouble in school than those who have more confidence in their ability to succeed academically (Pisecco, Wristers, Swank, Silva, & Baker, 2001).

Adolescents' academic self-concepts seem to come both from internal comparisons of their performance to a self-generated ideal and from external comparisons to peer performance (Bong, 1998). It also appears that perceived competency in one domain affects how a teenager feels about his ability in other areas. For example, if a high school student fails a math course, it is likely to affect his self-concept in other disciplines besides math. This suggests that teens' self-concepts are hierarchical in nature. Perceived competencies in various domains serve as building blocks for creating a global academic self-concept (Yeung, Chui, & Lau, 1999).

Erikson's Identity Crisis
A somewhat different way to look at adolescent self-concept is through the lens of Erikson's theory. In this model, the central task (or dilemma) of adolescence is that of **identity versus role confusion**. Erikson argued that the child's early sense of identity comes partly "unglued" at puberty because of the combination of rapid body growth and the sexual changes of puberty. He described this period as a time when the adolescent mind is in a kind of moratorium between childhood and adulthood.

During this stage, the adolescent's old identity will no longer suffice; a new identity must be forged, one that allows a place for the young person in each of the myriad

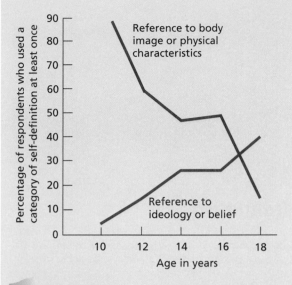

FIGURE 10.2

As they get older, children and adolescents define themselves less by what they look like and more by what they believe or feel.
(*Source*: Montemayor & Eisen, 1977, from Table 1, p. 316.)

If you asked them to define themselves, these teenagers would surely give much more abstract and comparative answers than you would hear from a 6-year-old.

identity versus role confusion As hypothesized by Erikson, the psychosocial stage in which a teenager must develop a sense of personal identity or else enter adulthood with a sense of confusion about his or her place in the world.

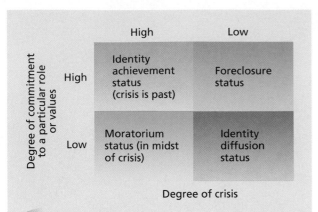

FIGURE 10.3

Marcia's four proposed identity statuses, based on Erikson's theory. To come to a fully achieved identity, according to this model, the young person must examine his or her values or goals and reach a firm commitment.
(*Source*: Marcia, 1980.)

identity achievement One of four identity statuses proposed by Marcia, involving the successful resolution of an identity "crisis" and resulting in a new commitment.

moratorium One of four identity statuses proposed by Marcia, involving an ongoing reexamination of identity but no new commitment.

foreclosure One of four identity statuses proposed by Marcia, involving an ideological or occupational commitment without a previous reevaluation.

identity diffusion One of four identity statuses proposed by Marcia, involving neither a current reevaluation of identity nor a firm personal commitment.

roles of adult life—occupational roles, sexual roles, religious roles. Confusion about all these role choices is inevitable. The teenage clique, or crowd, thus forms a base of security from which the young person can move toward a unique solution of the identity process. Ultimately, each teenager must achieve an integrated view of himself, including his own pattern of beliefs, occupational goals, and relationships.

Marcia's Identity Statuses   Nearly all the current work on the formation of adolescent identity has been based on James Marcia's descriptions of *identity statuses* (Marcia, 1966, 1980), which are rooted in but go beyond Erikson's general conception of the adolescent identity crisis. Following one of Erikson's ideas, Marcia argues that the formation of an adolescent identity has two key parts: a crisis and a commitment. By a "crisis," Marcia means a period of decision making when old values and old choices are reexamined. This may occur in a sort of upheaval (the classic notion of a crisis), or it may occur gradually. The outcome of the reevaluation is a commitment to some specific role, some particular ideology.

If you chart the two elements of crisis and commitment together, as in Figure 10.3, you can see that four different "identity statuses" are possible:

- **Identity achievement**: The young person has been through a crisis and has reached a commitment to ideological or occupational goals.
- **Moratorium**: A crisis is in progress, but no commitment has yet been made.
- **Foreclosure**: A commitment has been made without the person's having gone through a crisis. No reassessment of old positions has been made. Instead, the young person has simply accepted a parentally or culturally defined commitment.
- **Identity diffusion**: The young person is not in the midst of a crisis (although there may have been one in the past), and no commitment has been made. Diffusion may represent either an early stage in the process (before a crisis) or a failure to reach a commitment after a crisis.

Evidence for Erikson's and Marcia's Theories   Erikson's and Marcia's theories assume that some kind of identity crisis is both normal and healthy. These assumptions have not been entirely supported by the evidence. For one thing, the whole process of identity formation may occur later than Erikson thought, if it occurs at all. In one combined analysis of eight separate cross-sectional studies, Alan Waterman (1985) found that most young people attained the identity achievement status in college, not during high school. Waterman also found that the moratorium status was relatively uncommon, except in the early years of college. So if most young people are going through an identity crisis, the crisis is occurring fairly late in adolescence and is not lasting terribly long. What's more, about a third of the young people at every age were in the foreclosure status, which may indicate that many young people simply do not go through a crisis at all, but follow well-defined grooves.

As a further caveat, all the participants in the studies Waterman analyzed were either in college or in college-preparatory high school programs. This may give a false impression of the process of identity formation for young people who do not go to college, who do not have the luxury of a long period of questioning but must work out some kind of personal identity while still in their teens (Munro & Adams, 1977).

In addition, cognitive development may be more strongly related to identity formation than either Erikson or Marcia believed. Research suggests that teens who are most advanced in the development of logical thinking and other information-processing skills are also the most likely to have attained Marcia's identity achievement status (Klaczynski, Fauth, & Swanger, 1998). This may help to explain why the process takes place at somewhat later ages than Erikson's and Marcia's theories predict. There is also evidence that the quest for personal identity continues throughout the lifespan, with alternating periods of instability and stability (Marcia, 2002). For example, a person's sense of being "young" or "old" along with her integration of that idea into a sense of belonging to a particular generation appears to change several times over the course of the adolescent and adult years (Sato, Shimonska, Nakazato, & Kawaai, 1997). Consequently, adolescence may be only one such period among several.

Other research suggests that males and females experience the adolescent or early adulthood identity crisis differently (Lytle, Bakken, & Romig, 1997; Moretti & Wiebe, 1999). For example, girls seem to fit Erikson's and Marcia's hypotheses about adolescent identity formation better than boys. They consolidate their identities at a younger age, and they do so by integrating internal beliefs about themselves with information gained through social relationships. Conversely, boys are more likely to delay identity achievement until adulthood and to focus more on internal than on social sources of information in the identity construction process.

Further, teens facing extreme stressors, such as life-threatening illnesses, seem to be most optimally adjusted when they adopt the foreclosed status (Madan-Swain et al., 2000). Accepting others' goals for them, at least temporarily, seems to protect these teens against some of the negative emotional effects of whatever difficulties they are enduring. Thus, the idea that progression to the identity achievement status is the most psychologically healthy resolution of the identity crisis clearly doesn't apply to some adolescents.

Finally, the conception of an adolescent identity crisis is also strongly influenced by cultural assumptions in industrialized Western societies, in which full adult status is postponed for almost a decade after puberty. In such cultures, young people do not normally or necessarily adopt the same roles or occupations as their parents. Indeed, they are encouraged to choose for themselves. In such a cultural system, adolescents are faced with what may be a bewildering array of options, a pattern that might well foster the sort of identity crisis Erikson described. In less industrialized cultures, especially those with clear initiation rites, there may well be a shift in identity from that of child to that of adult, but without a crisis of any kind. Some anthropologists, in fact, refer to such cultures as "foreclosed," in the sense that adolescent identity alternatives are distinctly limited (Coté, 1996).

For all these reasons, both Marcia and Waterman now agree that the various identity statuses do not form a clear developmental progression that all or most teenagers and young adults follow, even in Western cultures. Instead, the four identity statuses may more reasonably be thought of as different approaches young people may take to the task of identity formation, depending on culture as well as on the young person's individual situation (Marcia, 1993; Waterman, 1988). In this view, it is not correct to say that a young person who is in the foreclosure status has not achieved any identity. She has an identity, which she has adopted from parental or other societal rules without significant questioning.

Thus, the developmental aspect of the Erikson or Marcia model is very likely not correct. In contrast, the other implication of the model—the notion that experiencing an identity crisis and its resolution is a psychologically healthy process—is confirmed by a variety of research. In Western cultures, at least, young people who have made a commitment to some identity (that is, those who are classed in either identity achievement or foreclosure status) have higher self-esteem and lower levels of depression and are more goal-directed. Those in a foreclosure status tend to be more stereotyped in their approach to relationships, while those in identity diffusion status have the most difficulties with intimacy (Waterman, 1992). All this evidence suggests that while a variety of roads may lead to some kind of personal identity, not all roads are psychologically equivalent.

ETHNIC AND RACIAL IDENTITY IN ADOLESCENCE

Minority teenagers, especially those of color in a predominantly white culture, face another task in creating an identity in adolescence: They must also develop an ethnic or

In addition to establishing a sense of personal identity, minority teens must also develop an ethnic identity. Some resolve this developmental task by creating a bicultural identity for themselves, one that allows them to interact comfortably with members of the majority group, individuals who belong to other minority groups, and members of their own group.

racial identity, including self-identification as a member of some specific group, commitment to that group and its values and attitudes, and some evaluative attitudes (positive or negative) about the group to which they belong. Some of this self-identification occurs in middle childhood (Aboud & Doyle, 1995): 7- and 8-year-old minority children already understand the differences between themselves and majority children, and most often prefer their own subgroup.

Further steps in the ethnic identity process occur in adolescence. Jean Phinney (1990; Phinney, Ferguson, & Tate, 1997; Phinney & Rosenthal, 1992) proposes that the development of a complete ethnic identity moves through three rough stages during adolescence. The first stage is an *unexamined ethnic identity*, equivalent to what Marcia calls a foreclosed status. For some subgroups in U.S. society, such as African Americans and Native Americans, this unexamined identity typically includes the negative images and stereotypes common in the wider culture. Indeed, it may be during adolescence, with the advent of the cognitive ability to reflect and interpret, that the young person becomes keenly aware of the way in which his own group is perceived by the majority.

The second stage in Phinney's model is the *ethnic identity search*, parallel to the crisis in Marcia's analysis of adolescent identity. This search is typically triggered by some experience that makes ethnicity relevant—perhaps an example of blatant prejudice or merely the wider realm of experience offered by high school. At this point, the minority teenager begins to arrive at her own judgments.

This exploration stage is eventually followed by a *resolution of the conflicts and contradictions*—analogous to Marcia's status of identity achievement. This is often a difficult process, as teenagers become aware of what Prentice and Miller (2002) call *homegrown stereotypes*. These stereotypes involve instructions for how a group member is supposed to present herself to other members of the same group. They often include the notion that one's own beliefs are at variance with those of the group, but that certain behaviors are required when presenting oneself to the group in order to maintain their acceptance. For example, an African American teen might learn that she is supposed to behave in certain ways toward white peers in order to continue to be accepted by African American peers. Hispanic teens often report similar experiences. Some resolve this pressure by keeping their own racial or ethnic group at arm's length. Some search for a middle ground, adopting aspects of both the majority and minority cultures, a pattern Phinney calls a "blended bicultural identity" (Phinney & Devich-Navarro, 1997). Others deal with it by creating essentially two identities (a pattern Phinney calls an "alternating bicultural identity"), as expressed by one young Hispanic teen interviewed by Phinney:

> Being invited to someone's house, I have to change my ways of how I act at home, because of culture differences. I would have to follow what they do. . . . I am used to it now, switching off between the two. It is not difficult. (Phinney & Rosenthal, 1992, p. 160)

Still others resolve the dilemma by wholeheartedly choosing their own racial or ethnic group's patterns and values, even when that choice may limit their access to the larger culture.

In both cross-sectional and longitudinal studies, Phinney has found that African American teens and young adults do indeed move through these steps or stages toward a clear racial or ethnic identity. Furthermore, there is evidence that African American, Asian American, and Mexican American teens and college students who have reached the second or third stage in this process—those who are searching for or who have reached a clear identity—have higher self-esteem and better psychological adjustment than do those who are still in the "unexamined" stage (Phinney, 1990). In contrast, among Caucasian American students, racial identity has essentially no relationship to self-esteem or adjustment.

Further, Phinney has found that racial identity seems to provide African American teens with an important protective factor. For one thing, those who possess a strong sense of racial identity get better grades than peers who do not (Oyserman, Harrison, & Bybee, 2001). The "bicultural" pattern of Phinney's last stage has been found to be a consistent characteristic of adolescents and adults who have high self-esteem and enjoy good relations with members of both the dominant culture and their own racial or ethnic group (Farver, Bhadha, & Narang, 2002; Phinney, Horenczyk, Liebkind, & Vedder, 2001; Yamada & Singelis, 1999). Further, African American teens are more likely than Asian American and Caucasian American youths to choose friends whose racial identity statuses are the same as their own (Hamm, 2000). As the discussion in *The Real World* indicates, such research has led some developmentalists to propose programs aimed at helping African American teens acquire a strong sense of cultural identity (Phinney, Kim-Jo, Osorio, & Vilhjalmsdottir, 2005).

Of course, the search for identity is affected by cultural norms. It is likely that parent-teen conflict is common and even socially acceptable in North American and European families because these individualistic cultures associate separation from parents with psychological and social maturity. As a result, parents in North America and Europe expect to experience these conflicts and endorse adolescents' efforts to demonstrate independence. For example, many American parents think that part-time jobs help teens mature. Thus, if an American parent prohibits a teenager from getting a job, but the adolescent presents a good argument as to why he should be allowed to work, the conflict is seen as a sign of maturity. In contrast, cultures that emphasize the community rather than the individual view teens' acceptance of family responsibilities as a sign of maturity. An issue such as whether a teen should get a job is decided in terms of family needs. If the family needs money, the adolescent might be encouraged to work. However, if the family needs the teenager to care for younger siblings while the parents work, then a part-time job will be forbidden. If the teenager argues about the parents' decision, the conflict is seen as representing immaturity rather than maturity.

Research involving Asian American teenagers helps to illustrate this point. Psychologists have found that first-generation Asian American teens often feel guilty about responding to the individualistic pressures of North American culture. Their feelings of guilt appear to be based on their parents' cultural norms, which suggest that the most mature adolescents are those who take a greater role in the family rather than try to separate from it (Chen, 1999). Thus, for many Asian American adolescents, achievement of personal and ethnic identity involves balancing the individualistic demands of North American culture against the familial obligations of their parents' cultures.

Phinney's stage model is a useful general description of the process of ethnic identity formation, but as research involving Asian American teens demonstrates, the details and content of racial and ethnic identity differ markedly from one subgroup to another. Further, those groups that encounter more overt prejudice will have a different set of experiences and challenges than will those who may be more easily assimilated; those whose own ethnic culture espouses values that are close to those of the dominant culture will have less difficulty resolving the contradictions than will those whose subculture is at greater variance with the majority. Whatever the specifics, young people of color and those from clearly defined racial or ethnic groups have an important additional identity task in their adolescent years.

Cultures determine the kinds of behaviors that signify the transition from childhood to adulthood. For example, European American families might consider teenagers' quest for independence to be a sign of normal, healthy development. By contrast, to Asian American parents, increased willingness to fulfill family obligations would be considered a more appropriate way for teenagers to express their growing understanding of the adult roles they will shortly assume.

Before going on . . .

- What is the subjective self, and how does it develop?
- In what way is the acquisition of an objective self an improvement in self-understanding?
- In what way is the ability to regulate emotions in preschool related to social functioning later in childhood?
- How do school-aged children describe themselves?
- How do Erikson's and Marcia's theories explain identity development in adolescence?
- What are the stages of ethnic identity development, according to Phinney?

Adolescent Rites of Passage

An expression of intense concentration appeared on 13-year-old Aisha's face as she stood before a mirror, wrapping a brightly colored cloth around her head. She had learned the art of Gele headwrapping just a few hours earlier and wanted to demonstrate it for her mother and younger sister. Headwrapping is just one of many traditional African skills Aisha has learned in the rites of passage program she is attending at a local community college. The purpose of the program, one of hundreds across the United States, is to help Aisha and other African American teens develop a sense of ethnic identity and to provide them with critical social support as they enter the teen years.

Programs such as the one Aisha attends have arisen out of concern about the lack of formal rites of passage in Western society. As a result, passage into adult status is much fuzzier for American youth, perhaps contributing to a greater sense of "identity crisis." And many developmentalists argue that the fuzziness of the adolescent-to-adult transition in U.S. culture is even more problematic for African American teens than for other American teens. They point out that other minority groups practice rites of passage that connect their young people with a centuries-long cultural heritage—such as the Jewish *bar mitzvah* and *bat mitzvah* and the *quinceañera* for young Hispanic girls. By contrast, the institution of slavery separated African Americans from the traditions of their ancestors.

Consequently, many African American churches and other institutions have devised formal initiation rites preceded by a period of instruction in traditional African cultural values and practices, typically called *rites of passage programs*. The goal of such programs is to enhance African American teens' sense of racial identity and self-esteem, thereby making them

less vulnerable to drug abuse, pregnancy, and other risks associated with adolescence (Harvey & Rauch, 1997; Warfield-Coppock, 1997). Most such programs are implemented over a fairly long period of time, usually a year or more, and include formal instruction for both the teens and their families (Gavazzi & Law, 1997). Many programs target teens in situations that carry especially high risks, such as those who are incarcerated or in foster care (Gavazzi, Alford, & McKenry, 1996; Harvey & Coleman, 1997).

Research indicates that rites of passage programs can make a difference (Harvey & Hill, 2004). In one program, six underachieving sixth-grade African American boys with histories of school behavior problems participated in a rites of passage program for an entire school year (Bass & Coleman, 1997). In-depth case studies of all the boys revealed that by the end of the year, their classroom behavior had improved considerably, they exhibited less antisocial behavior, and they had acquired a great deal of knowledge about African cultures, symbols, and ideas. A larger group participated in a rites of passage program involving both boys and girls in the fifth and sixth grades, over a 2-year period (Cherry et al., 1998). At the end of this program, participants exhibited higher self-esteem, a stronger sense of racial identity, a lower incidence of school behavior problems, and greater knowledge of African culture.

The experiences of many African American youth in rites of passage programs suggest that there may be some real advantage to providing teens with formal instruction and initiation into adult roles. What many see as a vestige of a bygone era may actually serve a very important function in adolescent identity development.

Questions for Reflection

1. Rites of passage programs include three separate components that may explain their positive effects on teenagers: contact with adults, contact with peers, and information about ethnicity. Which factor do you think is most important and why?
2. When you were a teenager, did you participate in any formal rites of passage, such as a confirmation, *bar mitzvah,* or *quinceañera?* If so, what effect did it have on you? If not, in what way do you think such a program might have been helpful to you?

Self-Esteem

Our discussion thus far has treated self-concept as if there were no values attached to the categories by which we define ourselves. Yet clearly one's self-concept contains an evaluative aspect, usually called *self-esteem*. Note, for example, the differences in tone in the answers to the "Who am I?" question quoted earlier in the chapter. The 9-year-old makes a lot of positive statements about himself, whereas the two older respondents offer more mixed evaluations.

THE DEVELOPMENT OF SELF-ESTEEM

Over the years of elementary school and high school, children's evaluations of their own abilities become increasingly differentiated, with quite separate judgments about skills in academics or athletics, physical appearance, peer social acceptance, friendships, romantic appeal, and relationships with parents (Harter, 1990, 1998; Jacobs, Lanza, Osgood, Eccles, & Wigfield, 2002). A consistent feature of self-competence judgments across domains is that they become less positive as children get older. The declines may be based on children's experiences. For example, social self-esteem, the assessment of one's own social skills, is higher in popular children than in those who are rejected by their peers (Jackson & Bracken, 1998).

Another striking feature of self-competence judgments is that they differ for boys and girls. Developmentalists believe that these differences are influenced both by cultural expectations and by children's own experiences. To fully understand this sex difference, it's important to understand that each component of self-esteem is valued differently by different children. Initially, the standards and beliefs of the larger culture influence these values, so almost all young boys rate themselves as competent in sports, because they know that the culture values sports achievement in males. However, over time, children come to value domains in which they experience real achievements. So, as children get older, both boys and girls who view themselves as highly competent in sports, because of their own actual successes, also value sports achievement very highly (Jacobs et al., 2002). And lack of demonstrated skill in sports leads to a decline in the value placed on sports achievement among children of both genders.

As children develop domain-specific self-competence judgments, they also create for themselves a global self-evaluation that stands alongside these self-judgments. It is this global evaluation of one's own worth that is usually referred to as **self-esteem**. Self-esteem is not merely the sum of all the separate assessments the child makes about his skills in different areas.

Instead, as Susan Harter's extremely interesting research on self-esteem reveals, each child's level of self-esteem is a product of two internal assessments (Harter, 1987, 1990, 1999). First, each child experiences some degree of discrepancy between what he would like to be and what he thinks he is—a gap between his ideal self and what he perceives to be his real self (Harter, 1998). When that discrepancy is small, the child's self-esteem is generally high. When the discrepancy is large—when the child sees himself as failing to live up to his own goals or values—self-esteem is much lower. The standards are not the same for every child. Some value academic skills highly; others value sports skills or having good friends. The key to self-esteem, Harter proposes, is the amount of discrepancy between what the child desires and what the child thinks he has achieved. Thus, being good at something—singing, playing chess, or being able to talk to one's parents—won't raise a child's self-esteem unless the child values that particular skill.

Another major influence on a child's self-esteem, according to Harter, is the overall sense of support the child feels from the important people around her, particularly

self-esteem A global evaluation of one's own worth; an aspect of self-concept.

Playing catch with dad is a classic father-son activity in American culture. One of the side effects is likely to be that the son comes to believe that his father values skill in sports.

CRITICAL THINKING ?

Think about the following somewhat paradoxical proposition: If Harter's model is correct, then one's self-esteem is most vulnerable in the area in which one appears (and feels) the most competent. Does this fit with your experience?

parents and peers (Franco & Levitt, 1998). Both these factors are clear in the results of Harter's own research. She asked third, fourth, fifth, and sixth graders how important it was to them to do well in each of five domains and how well they thought they actually did in each. The total discrepancy between these sets of judgments made up the discrepancy score. (A high discrepancy score indicates that the child reported that she was not doing well in areas that mattered to her.) The social support score was based on children's replies to a set of questions about whether they thought others (parents and peers) liked them as they were, treated them as a person, or felt that they were important. The findings for the fifth and sixth graders were virtually identical, and both sets of results strongly supported Harter's hypothesis, as does other research, including studies of African American youth (DuBois, Felner, Brand, Phillips, & Lease, 1996; Luster & McAdoo, 1995): A low discrepancy score alone does not protect the child completely from low self-esteem if she lacks sufficient social support. And a loving and accepting family and peer group do not guarantee high self-esteem if the youngster does not feel she is living up to her own standards.

A particularly risky combination occurs when the child perceives that parental support is contingent on good performance in some area—getting good grades, making the first-string football team, being chosen to play the solo with the school orchestra, being popular with classmates. If the child does not measure up to the standard, he experiences both an increased discrepancy between ideal and achievement and a loss of support from the parents.

If we accept Harter's model and assume that self-esteem is a product of a person's comparison of her desired or valued qualities with her actual qualities, we still have to ask where each child's values and self-judgments come from. First, of course, a child's own direct experience with success or failure in various arenas plays an obvious role. Second, the value a child attaches to some skill or quality is obviously affected fairly directly by peers' and parents' attitudes and values. Peer standards (and general cultural standards) for appearance establish benchmarks for all children and teens. A child who is "too tall" or "too fat" or who deviates in some other way from the accepted norms is likely to feel a sense of inadequacy. Similarly, the degree of emphasis parents place on the child's performing well in some domain—whether schoolwork, athletics, or playing chess—is an important element in forming the child's aspirations in each area.

CONSISTENCY OF SELF-ESTEEM OVER TIME

A number of longitudinal studies of elementary school children and teenagers show that self-esteem is moderately stable in the short term but somewhat less so over periods of several years. The correlation between two self-esteem scores obtained a few months apart is generally about .60. Over several years, this correlation drops to something more like .40 (Alsaker & Olweus, 1992), a level that has been found over periods as long as a decade, from early adolescence into early adulthood (Block & Robins, 1993). So while it is true that a child with high self-esteem at age 8 or 9 is likely to have high self-esteem at age 10 or 11, it is also true that there is a good deal of variation around that stability.

Self-esteem seems to be particularly unstable in the years of early adolescence, especially at the time of the shift from elementary school to junior high school. In one study, Edward Seidman and his colleagues (1994) followed a group of nearly 600 Hispanic, black, and white youngsters over the 2 years from sixth grade through junior high. Seidman found a significant drop in average self-esteem between the last year of elementary school and the first year in junior high, a decline that occurred in each of the three ethnic groups. Similarly, David DuBois and his colleagues (1996), in a cross-sectional study of 1,800 children in grades 5 through 8, found that eighth graders had significantly lower self-esteem than did fifth graders.

On average, self-esteem tends to rise in the later teen years (Diehl, Vicary, & Deike, 1997; Harter, 1990; Wigfield, Eccles, MacIver, Reuman, & Midgley, 1991). However, both the decline in average self-esteem in the early teen years and the average increase that follows can obscure important individual differences (Harter & Whitesell, 2003). Underlying the averages, researchers often find four patterns of self-esteem change among adolescents (Diehl et al., 1997; Zimmerman, Copeland, Shope, & Dielman, 1997). The largest group of teens, about half in most studies, display consistently high self-esteem throughout adolescence. The second group exhibit low self-esteem early in adolescence, but it rises steadily as they get older. The self-esteem ratings of the third group are low in both early and late adolescence. Teens in the fourth group enjoy moderate to high self-esteem at the beginning of the period but exhibit steady declines as adolescence progresses. As you might suspect, differences in self-esteem are related to some important developmental outcomes.

Harter and others have found that a child who has low self-esteem is more likely than are her high self-esteem peers to suffer from depression in both middle childhood and adolescence, especially when she also exhibits high levels of neuroticism (see the *Research Report*) (Harter, 1987; Renouf & Harter, 1990). Bear in mind, though, that this is correlational evidence. These findings don't prove that there is a causal connection between low self-esteem and depression. They only indicate that the two tend to go together.

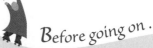

Before going on · · ·

- Describe the development of self-esteem.
- How consistent is self-esteem across childhood and adolescence, and what are the consequences of variations in self-esteem?

The Development of the Concepts of Gender and Sex Roles

As noted at the beginning of this chapter, biological sex and psychological gender are integral components of each individual's sense of self. Thus, in this final section, we turn our attention to the process through which sex and gender become woven into each child's self-concept. We begin by examining how children come to understand several important concepts that are associated with sex and gender.

DEVELOPMENTAL PATTERNS

Those of us who want to understand ourselves—and developmentalists who may wish to advise parents about child-rearing—need to know more about the ways in which children learn about gender and sex roles.

What Must Be Learned   Acquiring an understanding of sex roles involves several related tasks. On the cognitive side, a child must learn the nature of the sex/gender category itself—that *boyness* or *girlness* is permanent, unchanged by such things as modifications in clothing or hair length. This understanding is usually called the **gender concept**. On the social side, the child has to learn what behaviors go with being a boy or a girl. That is, the child must learn the **sex role** (sometimes called the *gender role*) defined as appropriate for his or her gender in the particular culture.

All roles involve sets of expected behaviors, attitudes, rights, duties, and obligations. Teachers are supposed to behave in certain ways, as are employees, mothers, or

gender concept The full understanding that gender is constant and permanent, unchanged by appearance.

sex role The set of behaviors, attitudes, rights, duties, and obligations that are seen as appropriate for being male or female in any given culture.

A Troublesome Cluster of Traits

Some teenagers exhibit a pattern of behavior that includes academic failure, social rejection, and depression. Developmentalists have found that such teens often possess a cluster of personality traits that include the introversion and neuroticism dimensions of the Big Five along with low self-esteem (Beautrais, Joyce, & Mulder, 1999). As you'll recall, introversion is the preference for solitary over social activities; individuals who score high on tests of neuroticism are pessimistic and irritable, and they worry a lot. Most adolescents who show such personality traits resist efforts by parents and friends to help them and are at greater risk than their peers for all kinds of adjustment problems.

An additional factor for most such adolescents is a trait known as *locus of control*, a set of beliefs about the causes of events (Rotter, 1990). There are important correlations between locus of control and behavior (Janssen & Carton, 1999). An *external* locus of control attributes the causes of experiences (for example, school failure) to factors outside the individual, and it is associated with procrastination and poor academic performance. An adolescent with an external locus of control might claim that he failed a class because the teacher didn't like him or because the class was too difficult.

An *internal* locus of control views variables inside a person, such as ability and effort, as responsible for outcomes. A teen who believes that he failed a class either because he lacked ability or because he didn't try hard enough has an internal locus of control. Both teens and adults with an internal locus of control are more likely to complete tasks and to succeed in school.

Developmentalists have found that teens across a variety of cultures who are high in introversion and neuroticism, who are low in self-esteem, and who possess an external locus of control have a very negative outlook on life and seem to have little ability or interest in changing their circumstances. For instance, these adolescents are more likely to use *avoidant coping* when they face problems (Gomez, Bounds, Homberg, Fullarton, & Gomez, 1999;

Gomez, Homberg, Bounds, Fullarton, & Gomez, 1999; Medvedova, 1998). This means that they ignore problems or put off dealing with them. For example, a high school student with these traits who finds out he is failing a class may wait until it is too late to try to do anything about it. However, because he tends to blame others for his problems, he is unlikely to be able to learn from the experience. Such teens get into these situations over and over again and appear to be unable to prevent this or to pull themselves out of trouble in any effective way. The consequence of their negative outlook combined with repeated experiences of disappointment and failure is that these adolescents are prone to depression (del Barrio, Moreno-Rosset, Lopez-Martinez, & Olmedo, 1997; Ge & Conger, 1999). Once depressed, such teens are likely to attempt suicide (Beautrais, Joyce, & Mulder, 1999). Their emotional difficulties are compounded by the fact that most are rejected by peers (Young & Bradley, 1998).

The outlook for teens with this set of characteristics is not good. Their beliefs about themselves and the social world are resistant to change and persist into adulthood (Gomez, Gomez, & Cooper, 2002; Offer, Kaiz, Howard, & Bennett, 1998). In addition, as adults, they continue to be subject to bouts of depression and a variety of academic, occupational, and relationship difficulties. Consequently, developmentalists are searching for assessment tools and intervention strategies that can be used to identify and help such individuals in middle childhood or early adolescence (Young & Bradley, 1998).

Questions for Critical Analysis

1. What kind of research would be required to test the effectiveness of an intervention program for the type of adolescent described in this discussion?
2. How would theorists on either side of the nature-nurture debate explain the development of this troublesome cluster of traits?

baseball managers—all roles in our culture. Gender roles are somewhat broader than most other roles, but they are nonetheless roles—sets of expected behaviors, attitudes, rights, duties, and obligations involved in filling the role of "girl," "woman," "boy," or "man." Put another way, a gender role is a "job description" for being a male or a female in a given culture.

Sex-typed behavior is behavior exhibited by a child or an adult that matches culturally defined gender-role expectations for that person's gender. A girl may know quite well that she is a girl and be able to describe the cultural sex roles for girls accurately but may still behave in a tomboyish way. Such a girl's sex-role behavior is less sex-typed than the behavior of a girl who adopts more traditional behavior patterns.

The Gender Concept

Research suggests that gender is a highly significant variable for children from the earliest days of life. For example, infants as young as 3 months of age distinguish between photos of male and female infants (Shirley & Campbell, 2000). Curiously, these young infants pay more attention to male babies and to male infant activities than to females. As you'll read later, by as early as 18 months of age, children prefer playmates of the same sex. By 4, children can readily identify the gender of a speaker of their own age on the basis of vowel sounds in speech patterns (Perry, Ohde, & Ashmead, 2001).

How soon does a child apply gender categorization to herself or himself? Research suggests that the process of self-categorization is linked to cognitive development (Trautner, Gervai, & Nemeth, 2003). In other words, a child's understanding of gender progresses along with his or her general understanding of the world. Moreover, like general cognitive development, understanding of gender appears to involve a universal sequence of stages (Munroe, Shimmin, & Munroe, 1984).

The first stage is **gender identity**, which is simply a child's ability to label his own sex correctly and to identify other people as men or women, boys or girls. By 9 to 12 months, babies already treat male and female faces as if they were different categories, apparently using hair length as the primary differentiating clue (Fagot & Leinbach, 1993; Ruble & Martin, 1998). Within the next year, they begin to learn the verbal labels that go with these different categories. By age 2, if you show children a set of pictures of a same-sex child and several opposite-sex children and ask "Which one is you?" most children can correctly pick out the same-sex picture (Thompson, 1975). Between ages 2 and 3, children learn to identify and label others correctly by sex, such as by pointing out "which one is a girl" or "which one is a boy" in a set of pictures (Ruble & Martin, 1998). Hair length and clothing seem to be especially important cues in these early discriminations.

Next comes **gender stability**, the understanding that people stay the same gender throughout life. Researchers have measured this understanding by asking children such questions as "When you were a little baby, were you a little girl or a little boy?" or "When you grow up, will you be a mommy or a daddy?" Slaby and Frey, in their classic study (1975), found that most children understand this aspect of gender by about age 4, as Figure 10.4 suggests.

The final stage in development of a gender concept, usually referred to as **gender constancy**, is the understanding that someone's biological sex stays the same even though he may appear to change by wearing different clothes or changing his hair length. For example, boys don't change into girls by wearing dresses. This is an appearance/reality problem very much like Flavell's sponge/rock test described in Chapter 6. The child must figure out that although a boy wearing a dress may look like a girl, he is really still a boy, just as the sponge painted to look like a rock may look like a rock but is really still a sponge. When children are asked the gender constancy question in this way, many 4-year-olds and most 5-year-olds can answer correctly, just as 4- and 5-year-olds understand other appearance/reality distinctions (Martin & Halverson, 1983). Sandra Bem has found that to reach this level of understanding, a child must have at least some grasp of the basic genital differences between boys and girls and some understanding that genital characteristics are what make a child "really" a boy or a girl. In

This mother is not only teaching her daughter how to cook; she is also transmitting information about sex roles and reinforcing traditional sex typing.

sex-typed behavior Behavior that matches a culturally defined sex role.

gender identity The first stage in the development of gender concept, in which a child labels self and others correctly as male or female.

gender stability The second stage in the development of gender concept, in which the child understands that a person's gender stays the same throughout life.

gender constancy The final stage in development of gender concept, in which the child understands that gender doesn't change even though there may be external changes (in clothing or hair length, for example).

FIGURE 10.4

In describing this self-portrait, the 5-year-old artist said, "This is how I will look when I get married to a boy. I am under a rainbow, so beautiful with a bride hat, a belt, and a purse." The girl knows she will always be female and associates gender with externals such as clothing (gender stability). She is also already quite knowledgeable about gender role expectations.
(*Source:* Author.)

Four-year-olds and 9-year-olds think it is okay for a boy to play with dolls, but many 6-year-olds think it is simply wrong for boys to do girl things or for girls to do boy things.

her study, 4-year-olds who did not yet understand genital differences also did not show gender constancy (Bem, 1989). In sum, children as young as 2 or 3 know their own sex and that of people around them, but children do not have a fully developed concept of gender until they are 4 or 5.

SEX-ROLE CONCEPTS AND STEREOTYPES

Obviously, figuring out your gender and understanding that it stays constant is only part of the story. Learning what goes with, or ought to go with, being a boy or a girl is also a vital part of the child's task.

Sex-Role Stereotypes Studies of children show that stereotyped ideas about sex roles develop early, even in families that espouse gender equality (Lippa, 2005). Even 2-year-olds already associate certain tasks and possessions with men and women, such as vacuum cleaners and food with women and cars and tools with men. By age 3 or 4, children can assign stereotypic occupations, toys, and activities to each gender (Ruble & Martin, 1998; Signorella, Bigler, & Liben, 1993). By age 5, children begin to associate certain personality traits with males or females, and such knowledge is well developed by age 8 or 9 (Martin, 1993; Serbin, Powlishta, & Gulko, 1993).

Studies of children's ideas about how men and women (or boys and girls) ought to behave add an interesting further refinement to what developmentalists know about sex-role stereotypes, and an early study by William Damon (1977) illustrates this element particularly nicely.

Damon told children aged 4 through 9 a story about a little boy named George who likes to play with dolls. George's parents tell him that only little girls play with dolls; little boys shouldn't. The children were then asked a batch of questions about the story, such as "Why do people tell George not to play with dolls?" or "Is there a rule that boys shouldn't play with dolls?" Four-year-olds in this study thought it was okay for George to play with dolls. There was no rule against it, and he should do it if he wanted to. Six-year-olds, in contrast, thought it was wrong for George to play with dolls. By about age 9, children had differentiated between what boys and girls usually do and what is "wrong." One boy said, for example, that breaking windows was wrong and bad, but that playing with dolls was not bad in the same way: "Breaking windows you're not supposed to do. And if you play with dolls, well you can, but boys usually don't."

What seems to happen is that the 5- or 6-year-old, having figured out that she is permanently a girl or he is a boy, is searching for a rule about how boys and girls behave (Martin & Halverson, 1981; Martin & Ruble, 2004). The child picks up information from watching adults, from watching television, from hearing evaluations of different activities (e.g., "Boys don't cry"). Initially they treat these as absolute, moral rules. Later they understand that these are social conventions, at which point sex-role concepts become more flexible (Katz & Ksansnak, 1994).

In a similar way, many kinds of fixed, biased ideas about other people—such as biases against obese children, against those who speak another language, or against those of other races—are at their peak in the early school years and then decline throughout the remaining years of childhood and into adolescence (Doyle & Aboud, 1995; Powlishta, Serbin, Doyle, & White, 1994). Another way to put it is that children of 5 to 7 years of age have a strong sense of "us" versus "them," of in-group versus out-group.

They classify other children as "like me" or "not like me" on some dimension, and they develop strong preferences for those who are like themselves and highly stereotyped (often negative) ideas about those who are not like themselves.

This entire stereotyping process seems to be totally normal, part of the child's attempt to create rules and order, to find patterns that can guide his understanding and his behavior. In fact, children's beliefs about the degree to which they "fit in" with peers of the same sex may be an important component of healthy psychological adjustment during the elementary school years (Egan & Perry, 2001). Thus, just as an English-speaking 2- or 3-year-old discovers the rule about adding *-ed* to a verb to make the past tense and then overgeneralizes that rule, so the 6- or 7-year-old discovers the "rules" about boys and girls, men and women, "us" and "them," and overgeneralizes. In fact, most 6- and 7-year-olds believe that gender-role differences are built-in along with biological gender differences. By age 9, they understand that at least some differences in behavior between boys and girls are the result of training or experience (Taylor, 1996).

Sex-Role Stereotypes across Cultures

The content of sex-role stereotypes is remarkably similar in cultures around the world. John Williams and Deborah Best (1990), who have studied adults' gender stereotypes in 28 different countries and children's gender stereotypes in 24 countries, find that the most strongly stereotyped traits are weakness, gentleness, appreciativeness, and softheartedness for women and aggression, adventurousness, cruelty, and coarseness for men. There are a few differences, naturally. German children, for instance, choose "adventurous," "confident," and "steady" as female items, although these are more normally male items in other cultures. Pakistani children identify "emotional" with men; Japanese children associate independence and severity with neither sex. But these are variations on a common theme. Researchers have presented children with a story in which the sex of the main character was not explicitly stated. When asked to tell whether the character was better represented by a male or a female doll, in all 24 countries, 8-year-olds chose the male figure for stories about aggression, strength, cruelty, coarseness, and loudness, and they chose the female figure for stories about weakness. In 23 of 24 countries, 8-year-olds also chose the female character for gentleness, appreciativeness, and softheartedness. Thus, not only does every culture appear to have clear sex-role stereotypes, but the content of those stereotypes is remarkably similar across cultures.

Another of the interesting revelations of cross-cultural research is that the male stereotype and sex-role concept seem to develop a bit earlier and to be stronger than the female stereotype and sex-role concept—and this is true in virtually all countries studied. Whatever the reason for this phenomenon, it is clear that in Western societies, the qualities attributed to males are more highly valued than are female traits (Broverman, Broverman, Clarkson, Rosenkrantz, & Vogel, 1970; Lippa, 2005). Research has demonstrated that children assign higher status to a job with which they are unfamiliar when it is portrayed as being done by a man than when researchers tell them the job is usually performed by a woman (Liben, Bigler, & Krogh, 2001).

It's also important to note that children's stereotypical beliefs about men and women are probably different from their beliefs about boys and girls (Sani & Bennett, 2001). Consequently, children do not attribute higher status to boys in the same way as they do to men. For example, psychologist Gail Heyman showed second and third graders pictures of unfamiliar children and told them about behaviors the children had exhibited—behaviors that could be interpreted in several different ways (Heyman, 2001). Heyman found that both boys and girls were likely to classify the behavior as "bad" or "naughty" if the pictured child was a boy. Still, despite their beliefs about the gender-based status of adult occupations and apparent stereotypical negative bias toward boys, children as young as 4 years old recognize that excluding someone from an activity strictly on the basis of gender is morally wrong (Killen, Pisacane, Lee-Kim, & Ardila-Rey, 2001).

CRITICAL THINKING ❓

How many rules for boys' and girls' behavior (e.g., "Boys don't cry") can you think of?

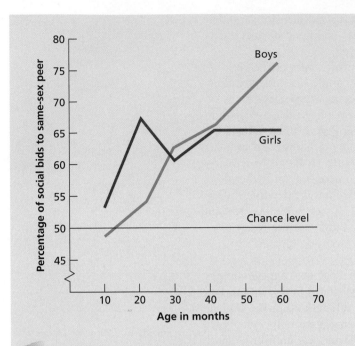

FIGURE 10.5

Same-sex playmate preference among preschoolers.
(*Source*: La Freniere et al., from Fig. 1, p. 1961, "The emergence of same-sex affiliative preference among pre-school peers: A developmental/ethological perspective," *Child Development*, 55 (1984), 1958–1965. By permission of the Society for Research in Child Development.)

Sex-Role Behavior The final element in the development of a sex-role concept is the actual behavior children show with those of their own sex and of the opposite sex. The unexpected finding here is that children's behavior is sex-typed earlier than are their ideas about sex roles or stereotypes. For example, by 18 to 24 months, children begin to show some preference for sex-stereotyped toys, such as dolls for girls or trucks or building blocks for boys, which is some months before they can normally identify their own gender (O'Brien, 1992).

A similar pattern exists for playmate preference. Long before age 3, girls and boys begin to show a preference for same-sex playmates and are much more sociable with playmates of the same sex—at a time when they do not yet have a concept of gender stability (Lippa, 2005; Maccoby, 1988, 1990; Maccoby & Jacklin, 1987). By school age, peer relationships are almost exclusively same-sex. You can see the early development of this preference in Figure 10.5, which shows the results of a seminal study of preschool play groups. The researchers counted how often children played with same-sex or opposite-sex playmates (La Freniere, Strayer, & Gauthier, 1984). You can see that by age 3, over 60% of play groups were same-sex groupings, and the rate rose for older children.

Not only are preschoolers' friendships and peer interactions increasingly sex-segregated, it is also becoming clear that boy-boy interactions and girl-girl interactions differ in quality, even in these early years. One important part of same-sex interactions seems to involve instruction and modeling of sex-appropriate behavior. In other words, older boys teach younger boys how to be "masculine," and older girls teach younger girls how to be "feminine" (Danby & Baker, 1998).

Sex Roles and Adolescent Identity Development

In adolescence, teens' understanding of and attitudes toward sex roles become central to the search for identity that you read about earlier in the chapter. Certainly, the physical changes of puberty contribute to the significance of gender issues for teens. Indeed, as you learned in Chapter 4, the timing of puberty can have a profound impact on individual teenagers' perceptions of themselves. Unlike younger children, adolescents understand that sex roles are social conventions, so their attitudes toward them are more flexible (Katz & Ksansnak, 1994). And, by the mid-teens, most adolescents have largely abandoned the automatic assumption that whatever their own gender does is better or preferable (Powlishta et al., 1994).

However, increased flexibility may mean that teens experience more anxiety about how they should or should not behave, since cultural stereotypes are no longer seen as rigid dictates that must be followed. Because teens are actively searching for ways to incorporate gender into their own identities, parental attitudes as well as behavior become increasingly important in shaping teens' ideas about gender and sex roles (Castellino, Lerner, Lerner, & von Eye, 1998; Cunningham 2001; Ex & Janssens, 1998; Jackson & Tein, 1998; Raffaelli & Ontai, 2004).

EXPLAINING SEX-ROLE DEVELOPMENT

Theorists from most of the major traditions have tried their hand at explaining these patterns of sex-role development. Freud relied on the concept of identification to explain the child's adoption of appropriate sex-role behavior, but his theory founders on the fact that children begin to show clearly sex-typed behavior long before age 4 or 5, when Freud thought identification occurred.

Social Learning Theory Social learning theorists, such as Albert Bandura (1977) and Walter Mischel (1966, 1970; Bandura & Bussey, 2004), have naturally emphasized the role of both direct reinforcement and modeling in shaping children's sex-role behavior and attitudes, as well as the availability of stereotypical sex-role models in the various media to which children are exposed. This approach has been far better supported by research than have Freud's ideas.

Social learning theorists point out that children are constantly exposed to sex-role stereotypes in entertainment media. The most current estimates suggest that in virtually every kind of TV programming in the United States, males outnumber females by 2 or 3 to 1; in programming aimed specifically at children, the ratio is more like 5 to 1 (Huston & Wright, 1998). The frequency of males and females is more equal in commercials, but the "voice-over" on commercials is nearly always male. In both commercials and regular programming, women are more often shown at home or in romantic situations; men more often appear in work settings, with cars, or playing sports. Men are shown solving problems and being more active, aggressive, powerful, and independent. Women are most often portrayed as submissive, passive, attractive, sensual, nurturing, emotional, and less able to deal with difficult situations (Golombok & Fivush, 1994; Huston & Wright, 1998).

Advocates of the social learning perspective also point out that parents reinforce sex-typed activities in children as young as 18 months old, not only by buying different kinds of toys for boys and girls, but by responding more positively when their sons play with blocks or trucks or when their daughters play with dolls (Bussey & Bandura, 2004; Fagot & Hagan, 1991; Lytton & Romney, 1991). Some evidence also suggests that toddlers whose parents are more consistent in rewarding sex-typed toy choice or play behavior, and whose mothers favor traditional family sex roles, learn accurate gender labels earlier than do toddlers whose parents are less focused on the gender-appropriateness of the child's play (Fagot & Leinbach, 1989; Fagot, Leinbach, & O'Boyle, 1992)—findings clearly consistent with the predictions of social learning theory.

Similarly, parents of school-aged children are often guided by gender stereotypes when they select leisure-time activities for their children. For instance, parents more strongly encourage boys to participate in sports and in computer-based activities than they do girls (Fredricks & Eccles, 2005; Simpkins, Davis-Kean, & Eccles, 2005). They do so because of their beliefs about gender differences in various abilities. Research shows that, over time, children's own views about gender differences in athletic talent come into line with those of their parents and influence their activity preferences.

Cross-cultural evidence also supports a social learning view. Anthropologist Beatrice Whiting, after examining patterns of gender socialization in 11 different cultures, concluded that "we are the company we keep" (Whiting & Edwards, 1988). In most cultures, girls and boys keep different company, beginning quite early, with girls spending more time with women as well as having more child-care responsibilities. To the extent that this is true, it would provide both girls and boys with more same-sex than opposite-sex models and more opportunity for reinforcement of sex-appropriate behavior.

Still, helpful as it is, a social learning explanation is probably not sufficient. In particular, parents differentially reinforce "boy" versus "girl" behavior less than you'd expect, and probably not enough to account for the very early and robust discrimination children seem to make on the basis of gender (Fagot, 1995; Gauvain, Fagot, Leve, & Kavanagh, 2002). Moreover, parents' reinforcement of gender-typed behavior is far from consistent (Power, 2000). Experimental studies have shown that parents neither encourage girls to engage in stereotypically female play behaviors nor discourage them from engaging in stereotypically male activities. By contrast, fathers, but not mothers, take more interest in the gender-appropriateness of boys' play behaviors. For the most part, though, parents treat boys and girls similarly.

Social learning theorists argue that little boys prefer to play with trucks because parents buy them more trucks and reinforce them directly for such play.

Social attitudes toward "tomboys," as this young female soccer player might be labeled, have changed a great deal in recent decades. As a result, girls are often encouraged to take up traditionally male activities. By contrast, boys who express interest in traditionally female activities, such as ballet, are still discouraged from participating in them.

Even children whose parents seem to treat their young sons and daughters in highly similar ways nonetheless learn gender labels and show same-sex playmate choices. Moreover, once they reach adulthood, the gender-related behavior of the large majority of girls who exhibited male-stereotypical behavior in childhood is indistinguishable from that of other women (Burn, O'Neil, & Nederend, 1996), despite the relative lack of discouragement girls experience when they exhibit tomboyish behavior. So, there seems to be something more to sex-role development than modeling and reinforcement.

Cognitive-Developmental Theories

A second alternative, based strongly on Piagetian theory, is Lawrence Kohlberg's suggestion that the crucial aspect of the process of sex-role development is the child's understanding of the gender concept (1966; Kohlberg & Ullian, 1974). Once the child realizes that he is a boy or she is a girl forever, he or she becomes highly motivated to learn to behave in the way that is expected or appropriate for that gender. Specifically, Kohlberg predicted that systematic same-sex imitation should become evident only after the child has shown a full understanding of gender constancy. Most studies designed to test this hypothesis have supported Kohlberg: Children do seem to become much more sensitive to same-sex models after they understand gender constancy (Frey & Ruble, 1992). What Kohlberg's theory cannot easily explain, however, is the obvious fact that children show clearly differentiated sex-role behavior, such as toy preferences, long before they have achieved full understanding of the gender concept.

Gender Schema Theory

The most fruitful current explanation of sex-role development is usually called **gender schema theory** (Bem, 1981; Martin, 1991; Martin & Halverson, 1981; Martin & Ruble, 2004), a model that has its roots in information-processing theories of cognitive development as well as in Kohlberg's theory. Just as the self-concept can be thought of as a "self-scheme" or "self-theory," so the child's understanding of gender can be seen in the same way. The gender schema begins to develop at about 18 months, once the child notices the differences between male and female, knows his own gender, and can label the two groups with some consistency; the gender schema is generally fully developed by age 2 or 3.

Why would children notice gender so early? Why is it such a significant characteristic? One possibility, suggested by Maccoby (1988), is that because gender is clearly an either/or category, children seem to understand very early that this is a key distinction. Thus, the category serves as a kind of magnet for new information. Another alternative is that young children pay a lot of attention to gender differences because their environment provides so many gender references. Adults and other children emphasize gender distinctions in innumerable small ways. The first question we ask about a new baby is "Is it a boy or a girl?" We buy blue baby clothes for boys and pink for girls; we ask toddlers whether their playmates are boys or girls. A preschool teacher emphasizes gender if she says "Good morning, boys and girls" or divides her charges into a boys' team and a girls' team (Bigler, 1995). In all these ways, adults signal to children that this is an important category and thus further the very early development of a gender scheme that matches cultural norms and beliefs. Whatever the origin of this early scheme, once it is established, a great many experiences are assimilated to it, and children may begin to show preferences for same-sex playmates or for gender-stereotyped activities (Martin & Little, 1990).

The key difference between gender-schema theory and Kohlberg's cognitive-developmental theory is that for the initial gender schema to be formed, children need not understand that gender is permanent. When they come to understand gender constancy at about 5 or 6, children develop a more elaborated rule, or schema, about "what people who are like me do" and they treat this "rule" the same way they treat other rules—as absolute. By early adolescence, teenagers understand that sex-role concepts are social conventions, and not rigid rules (Katz & Ksansnak, 1994). Indeed, a significant minority of teenagers and youths begin to define themselves as having both masculine and feminine traits—a point we'll return to in a moment.

gender schema theory A theory of the development of gender concept and sex-role behavior that proposes that, between about 18 months and age 2 or 3, a child creates a fundamental schema by which to categorize people, objects, activities, and qualities by gender.

Many of us, committed to the philosophical goal of equality for women, have taken the rigidity of children's early sex stereotypes ("Mommy, you can't be a psychology doctor, you have to be a psychology nurse") as evidence that there has been little progress toward gender equality. Gender schema theorists emphasize that such rule learning is absolutely normal, and so is the rigid stereotyping seen in children's ideas about sex roles between ages 5 and 8 or 9. Children are searching for order, for rules that help to make sense of their experiences. And a rule about "what men do" and "what women do" is a helpful schema for them.

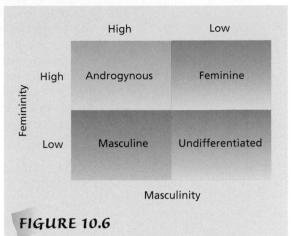

FIGURE 10.6

Thinking of masculinity and femininity as separate dimensions rather than as two ends of the same dimension leads to the creation of four sex-role types.

Individual Gender Schemas   A different approach to the study of sex-role development can be found in research on individual gender schemas, or orientations. Researchers can ask, about any given child, adolescent, or adult, not only how closely the individual's behavior matches the sex-role stereotype, but also how the person thinks of herself or himself and gender-related qualities. In the early years of this research, the issue was usually phrased as masculinity versus femininity, and these were thought of as being on opposite ends of a single continuum. A person could be masculine or feminine but couldn't be both. Following the lead of Sandra Bem (1974) and Janet Spence and Robert Helmreich (1978), psychologists today most often conceive of masculinity and femininity as two separate dimensions, with masculinity centered around agentic/instrumental qualities and femininity centered around expressive/communal qualities. A person can be high or low on either or both. Indeed, categorizing people as high or low on each of these two dimensions, based on each individual's self-description, yields four basic sex-role types, called masculine, feminine, androgynous, and undifferentiated—as you can see in Figure 10.6. The masculine and feminine types are the traditional combinations in which a person sees himself or herself as high in one quality and low in the other. A **masculine** person, according to this conceptualization, is one who perceives himself or herself as having many traditional masculine qualities and few traditional feminine qualities. A **feminine** person shows the reverse pattern. In contrast, **androgynous** individuals see themselves as having both masculine and feminine traits; **undifferentiated** individuals describe themselves as lacking both kinds of traits—a group that sounds a lot like those with a "diffuse" identity in Marcia's system.

This categorization system says nothing about the accuracy of the child's or the adult's general sex-role schema. A teenaged girl, for example, could have a clear notion of the norms for male or female behavior and still perceive herself as having some stereotypically masculine qualities. In some sense, then, when developmentalists study masculinity, femininity, and androgyny, they are studying the intersection between the self-scheme and the gender scheme.

Perhaps because young children's ideas about sex roles are still quite rigid, researchers find few signs of androgyny among children younger than 9 or 10. Among older elementary school students and adolescents, however, there are clearly variations in androgyny, masculinity, and femininity. In the United States, 25–35% of high school students define themselves as androgynous (e.g., Lamke, 1982; Rose & Montemayor, 1994). More girls than boys seem to show this pattern, and more girls fall into the masculine category than boys into the feminine group.

More striking is the finding that either an androgynous or a masculine sex-role self-concept is associated with higher self-esteem among both boys and girls (Boldizar, 1991; Burnett, Anderson, & Heppner, 1995; Gurnáková & Kusá, 2004; Rose & Montemayor, 1994). This finding makes sense if we assume that there is a "masculine bias" in the United States and other Western societies, in that traditionally masculine qualities such as independence and competitiveness are more valued by both men and women than are many traditionally female qualities. If such a bias exists—and there is plenty of evidence that it does—then the teenaged boy's task is simpler than the teenaged girl's. He can achieve high self-esteem and success with his peers by adopting

masculine One of four sex-role types suggested by the work of Bem and others; a type characterized by high scores on masculinity measures and low scores on femininity measures.

feminine One of four sex-role types suggested by the work of Bem and others; a type characterized by high scores on femininity measures and low scores on masculinity measures.

androgynous One of four sex-role types suggested by the work of Bem and others; a type characterized by high levels of both masculine and feminine qualities.

undifferentiated One of four sex-role types suggested by the work of Bem and others; a type characterized by low scores on both masculinity and femininity measures.

a traditional masculine sex role, whereas a girl who adopts a traditional feminine sex role is adopting a less valued role, with attendant risks of lower self-esteem and a reduced sense of competence (Massad, 1981; Rose & Montemayor, 1994).

Findings like these suggest the possibility that while the creation of rigid rules (or schemas) for sex roles is a normal and even essential process in young children, a blurring of those rules may be an important process in adolescence, particularly for girls, for whom a more masculine or androgynous self-concept is associated with more positive outcomes.

BIOLOGICAL APPROACHES

The theories we have discussed so far flourished in an era when most developmentalists had turned away from the idea that hormonal differences between males and females contributed to sex-role development. Today, developmentalists are taking another look at decades-old experimental studies with animals showing that prenatal exposure to testosterone powerfully influences behavior after birth (Lippa, 2005). Female animals exposed to testosterone behave more like male animals; for instance, they are more aggressive than females who do not experience prenatal exposure to testosterone. Similarly, when experimenters block the release of testosterone during prenatal development of male animal embryos, the animals exhibit behavior that is more typical of the females of their species.

Nature has provided some important evidence regarding the behavioral effects of prenatal exposure to testosterone in humans. Normally developing female embryos produce miniscule amounts of testosterone. Occasionally, however, genetic defects cause unusually large amounts of testosterone to be produced (Rosenthal & Gitelman, 2002). These defects can cause physical defects in the genitalia. In addition, girls with these conditions are more likely to exhibit stereotypically male behavior than are girls who do not have them (Lippa, 2005).

Hormonal influences have been proposed to explain the outcomes of cases involving sex reassignment of infants (like those you read about at the beginning of the chapter). Many such boys carry a genetic defect that causes them to develop deformed genitalia. This defect, however, interferes only with testosterone's effects on the sex organs (Rosenthal & Gitelman, 2002). The brains of these fetuses are exposed to normal amounts of testosterone throughout prenatal development. The hormonal hypothesis asserts that boys with this kind of genetic defect develop a masculine gender identity, despite being raised as girls, because their brains have been exposed prenatally to amounts of testosterone that are typical for male fetuses. As a result, like other boys, they come into the world with the tendency to look for "boy" things and to subtly incorporate such things into their developing self-concepts. According to this view, one could not reasonably expect to inculcate a sense of "femaleness" into these boys' self-concepts by raising them to believe they were girls. Moreover, research indicates that even when these individuals elect to retain the feminine identity with which they have been raised, they possess many attributes and exhibit a number of behaviors that are more typical of males than of females (Reiner & Gearhardt, 2004).

Finally, note that our discussion of biological approaches has focused largely on research aimed at explaining the role played by biological factors in atypical development. It is always legitimate to question the degree to which findings based on such cases can be generalized to the more common course of development experienced by the majority of children. Although we must keep this caution in mind, research examining how variations in prenatal hormones caused by genetic defects influence behavior after birth suggests that hormones may be far more important in normal sex-role development than theorists once believed.

Before going on . . .

■ Describe the development of ideas about gender and sex roles across childhood and adolescence.

■ In what ways does children's behavior reflect cultural sex-role stereotypes, and how does sex-typed behavior change across childhood and adolescence?

■ How do various theories explain gender concept and sex-role development?

Summary

The Concept of Self

- The child's emerging self-concept has several elements, including the awareness of the self as separate from others and the understanding of self-permanence (which may collectively be called the subjective self) and awareness of the self as an object in the world (the objective self). The subjective self develops in the first year of life.
- Real self-awareness and the objective self emerge in the second year. In early childhood, the child begins to categorize herself in basic ways such as by age, size, and gender.
- Children gain an understanding of their emotions during early childhood. The ability to regulate emotion during early childhood predicts how well children function in social settings during the school years.
- The self-concept becomes steadily more abstract in the elementary and high school years, coming to include not only actions but also likes and dislikes, beliefs, and more general personality characteristics.
- During adolescence, there may also be a reevaluation of the self, a process Erikson called the identity crisis. In theory, adolescents move from a diffuse sense of future occupational or ideological identity, through a period of reevaluation, to a commitment to a new self-definition. Research findings raise doubts about whether the identity-formation process has such a clear developmental aspect.
- Adolescents of color also construct an ethnic or racial identity. For many, a sense of belonging to two cultures, the dominant society as well as their own ethnic or racial group, appears to be the most adaptive resolution of this process.

Self-Esteem

- Beginning at about age 7 or 8, the child develops a global evaluation of his or her self-worth (self-esteem). Self-esteem is shaped both by the degree of discrepancy between a child's goals and his accomplishments and by the degree of emotional support the child perceives from parents and peers. Self-esteem develops out of a child's experiences with success and failure, the value he ascribes to the activities at which he succeeds or fails, and the feedback he gets from peers and parents about his performance.
- Self-esteem is fairly stable across childhood but somewhat less so in early adolescence. Children with high self-esteem and greater feelings of self-efficacy show lower levels of depression.

The Development of the Concepts of Gender and Sex-Roles

- Children generally acquire gender identity (the ability to correctly identify their own gender and that of others) by about age 2 or 3. They develop gender stability (knowing that people stay the same gender throughout life) by about 4, and they understand gender constancy (that people don't change gender by changing appearance) by about 5 or 6.
- In early elementary school, children create quite rigid rules about what boys and girls ought to do or are allowed to do. Older children are aware that such rules are social conventions and do not treat them as incontrovertible. Sex-typed behavior is evident from about 18 months of age.
- Theorists of several different traditions have attempted to explain observed patterns in sex-role development. The most widely accepted theory is gender schema theory, which proposes that children begin to acquire a rule about what boys do and what girls do as soon as they figure out the difference between boys and girls, and that this schema forms the basis of both stereotyping and sex-typed behavior. Young people also differ in the extent to which they see themselves as having feminine or masculine qualities or traits. Those who describe themselves with qualities from both sets are said to be androgynous. Both girls and boys who describe themselves as androgynous or masculine have somewhat higher self-esteem, at least in U.S. culture.
- Animal studies show that prenatal exposure to testosterone leads to masculine behavior in females, while lack of exposure to this hormone causes male animals to behave in ways that are more typical of females. Research involving children with genetic defects suggests that testosterone may also influence sex-typed behavior in humans.

Key Terms

androgynous (p. 297)
feminine (p. 297)
foreclosure (p. 282)
gender concept (p. 289)
gender constancy (p. 291)
gender identity (p. 291)
gender schema theory (p. 296)

gender stability (p. 291)
identity achievement (p. 282)
identity diffusion (p. 282)
identity versus role confusion (p. 281)
masculine (p. 297)
moratorium (p. 282)
objective self (p. 275)

self-concept (p. 275)
self-esteem (p. 287)
sex role (p. 289)
sex-typed behavior (p. 291)
subjective self (p. 275)
undifferentiated (p. 297)

Self-Concept in Middle Childhood and Adolescence

You can replicate the classic study of Montemayor and Eisen simply by asking children and teenagers from 10 to 18 years of age to answer the question "Who am I?" (Remember to get parents' permission before involving children in any research project.) In each participant's response, count the number of references to physical characteristics and the number to beliefs or ideology. Plot your results on a graph like the one in Figure 10.2 on page 281. If your results differ from those of Montemayor and Eisen, try to determine what may have influenced your results. It may help to think about how the children you questioned might be different from those in the original study or how children's ideas about the self may have been influenced by historical and cultural changes in the three decades since Montemayor and Eisen's data were collected.

Male and Female Stereotypes

You can use the adjectives Williams and Best (1990) used in their research, shown in the table, to examine children's stereotypes. First, find two pictures, one of a man and one of a woman, to use in questioning children. Choose a few traits from each list, and make up a very short behavioral description. For example, you might say, "One of these people *worries* a lot about being safe and is always careful to buckle seat belts in cars and lock the doors. Which one do you think it is?" or "One of these people is very *stubborn* and never gives in to people who try to change his or her mind. Which one do you think it is?" Present the task to a 5-year-old boy and girl and to 8-year-olds of both sexes, as Williams and Best did, as well as to a few adults. Make notes of any age and sex differences in responses.

Male-Associated		Female-Associated	
Active	Loud	Affected	Modest
Adventurous	Obnoxious	Affectionate	Nervous
Aggressive	Opinionated	Appreciative	Patient
Arrogant	Opportunistic	Cautious	Pleasant
Autocratic	Pleasure-seeking	Changeable	Prudish
Bossy	Precise	Charming	Self-pitying
Capable	Progressive	Complaining	Sensitive
Coarse	Quick	Complicated	Sentimental
Conceited	Rational	Confused	Sexy
Confident	Realistic	Curious	Shy
Courageous	Reckless	Dependent	Softhearted
Cruel	Resourceful	Dreamy	Sophisticated
Cynical	Rigid	Emotional	Submissive
Determined	Robust	Excitable	Suggestible
Disorderly	Serious	Fault-finding	Talkative
Enterprising	Sharp-witted	Fearful	Timid
Greedy	Show-off	Fickle	Touchy
Hardheaded	Steady	Foolish	Unambitious
Humorous	Stern	Forgiving	Unintelligent
Indifferent	Stingy	Frivolous	Unstable
Individualistic	Stolid	Fussy	Warm
Initiative	Tough	Gentle	Weak
Interests wide	Unfriendly	Imaginative	Worrying
Inventive	Unscrupulous	Kind	Understanding
Lazy	Witty	Mild	Superstitious

Source: Williams, J., & Best, J. (1994). Cross-cultural views of women and men. In W. Lonner & R. Malpass (Eds). *Psychology and culture* (pp. 191–201). Boston: Allyn & Bacon.

The Development of Social Relationships

11

Many parents endure long commutes to work in order to provide their children with the advantages they believe to be associated with living in a suburban neighborhood.

Low crime rates are among these advantages, and good schools are another. Suburban schools typically turn out students who get high scores on standardized tests, and they offer children many opportunities to participate in extra-curricular activities.

Kingwood, Texas, is one such neighborhood. Located about thirty minutes northeast of Houston, Kingwood is a "master-planned" community through which lush greenbelts and championship golf courses meander. Homes range from upper-middle-class, tract homes to custom-built mansions. As you might expect, there is little crime and almost no gang activity, and Kingwood's schools are among the most highly rated in the state. Consequently, back in 1999, residents were shocked when police revealed the identities of a group of armed robbers who had held up several local stores over a two-month period. The robbers were all current or former students of Kingwood High School, and, surprisingly, they were all girls.

The girls, whose ages ranged from 16 to 18, had named their gang the "Queens of Armed Robbery." Seventeen-year-old Lisa Warzeka typified the group of four girls. Lisa had been an accomplished athlete and successful student at Kingwood High until she began to associate with a couple of girls who used drugs. She changed her appearance to emulate that of her new friends, and her behavior toward her parents became disrespectful. She dropped out of her school activities and eventually quit school altogether. After struggling with Lisa's newfound identity for months, her parents finally made her leave their home in the hope that a "tough-love" approach would turn her around. Lisa moved in with one of her friends, and shortly thereafter the group embarked on their crime spree. Often high on cocaine during their crimes, the girls regarded them as both a source of entertainment and a source of money for drugs and other necessities of the "party-hearty" lifestyle they had adopted.

The partying came to an end when the girls, whose images were plainly visible on several surveillance tapes in the establishments they had robbed, were arrested. One of them received a lenient sentence in exchange for her testimony against the others. One girl decided to fight the charges, but was eventually found guilty and sent to prison anyway. The remaining two, including Lisa, pled guilty in the hope that a remorseful attitude would influence a jury to give them a light sentence. They were wrong; both girls were sentenced to seven years in prison.

While in jail awaiting sentencing, Lisa realized the gravity of what she had become involved in. In search of a haven from the threatening peer environment of the jail, she once again made her bonds with her parents the primary social relationship in her life. In prison, Lisa finished high school and earned an associate's degree. When her application for parole was turned down in 2004, her parents and family were the support network she turned to for consolation. Now she looks forward to getting out of prison at the end of her term and attending the University of Texas at Austin, a path she was on before she got caught up in the lifestyle that eventually led her to prison.

Lisa's experience might be taken as an example of Judith Rich Harris's *group socialization theory* (Harris, 1998). In Harris's view, peers influence children's development more strongly than parents. The reason, says Harris, is that peers are the people with whom children will spend their adult lives. Therefore, they look to peers, more than parents, for behavioral guidelines. Though parents may attempt to influence peer associations by doing things like moving to "good" neighborhoods where they assume most families will share their moral values, group socialization theory predicts that peers will construct their own behavioral standards and provide members with reinforcement for adopting them. Further, this approach would predict that the peers with whom Lisa associates when she gets out of prison will strongly influence the degree to which she accomplishes her goal of graduating from college.

While many developmentalists have criticized group socialization theory for its strong emphasis on peer influences (e.g., Borkowski, Ramey, & Bristol-Power, 2002), most would agree that, at least sometimes, peer influences become more important in children's lives than the guidance of their parents. Still, even Harris notes that an *influence* is quite a different thing from a *relationship*. Parents clearly can't mold children into replicas of themselves, but what they can do is provide them with what Mary Ainsworth called a *secure base*. A secure base is a social safety net to which children can reliably return when their endeavors outside the security of the family environment go awry. Moreover, the secure base gives them encouragement, support, and approval when things go well for them outside the family environment. Look again at Lisa's example. When she was one of the "Queens of Armed Robbery," family relationships meant so little to her that she abandoned them without a thought. But when her world fell apart, those relationships were still there for her to turn to. No doubt they will also be the ones that will help her make the transition from convict to college student when she is released from prison.

Cases like Lisa's can help us understand why most developmentalists believe that it isn't useful to think of parental and peer influences in an *either-or* framework. Instead, both kinds of relationships are important, and the two interact with each other. Many point out that a useful approach to thinking about the issues of parental versus peer influences can be found in a 1989 article by William Hartup, one of the most astute investigators of social development. In the article, Hartup suggests that children need experience in two rather different kinds of relationships: vertical and horizontal. A vertical relationship involves an attachment to someone who has greater social power or knowledge, such as a parent, a teacher, or even an older sibling. A horizontal relationship, in contrast, is reciprocal and egalitarian. The individuals involved, such as same-age peers, have equal social power, and their behavior toward one another comes from the same repertoire. In this chapter, you will learn about both types of relationships.

 # Relationships with Parents

The parent-child relationship has been at the center of much theorizing and research in developmental psychology. To understand the major research findings, you need a basic knowledge of the theoretical foundation on which most research studies have been based.

In this "vertical" social relationship, the son is attached to his dad, but (in Ainsworth's terms) the father's relationship to his son is an affectional bond rather than an attachment.

CRITICAL THINKING ?

Think about your own relationships. In Bowlby's and Ainsworth's terms, which are attachments and which are affectional bonds?

affectional bond A "relatively long-enduring tie in which the partner is important as a unique individual and is interchangeable with none other" (Ainsworth, 1989, p. 711).

attachment A subtype of affectional bond in which the presence of the partner adds a special sense of security, a "safe base," for the individual.

attachment behaviors The collection of (probably) instinctive behaviors of one person toward another that bring about or maintain proximity and caregiving, such as the smile of the young infant; behaviors that reflect an attachment.

ATTACHMENT THEORY: CONCEPTS AND TERMINOLOGY

The strongest theoretical influence in studies of infant-parent relationships is attachment theory, particularly the work of John Bowlby and Mary Ainsworth (Ainsworth, 1972, 1982, 1989; Ainsworth, Blehar, Waters, & Wall, 1978; Bowlby, 1969, 1973, 1980, 1988a, 1988b). You'll recall from Chapter 9 that Bowlby's thinking had roots in psychoanalytic thought, particularly in the emphasis on the significance of the earliest relationship between mother and child. To this theoretical base, he added important evolutionary and ethological concepts. In his view, "the propensity to make strong emotional bonds to particular individuals [is] a basic component of human nature, already present in germinal form in the neonate" (Bowlby, 1988a, p. 3). Such a relationship has survival value because it ensures that the infant will receive nurturance. The relationship is built and maintained by an interlocking repertoire of instinctive behaviors that create and sustain proximity between parent and child.

In Bowlby's and Ainsworth's writings, the key concepts are the affectional bond, attachment, and attachment behaviors. Ainsworth defines an **affectional bond** as "a relatively long-enduring tie in which the partner is important as a unique individual and is interchangeable with none other. In an affectional bond, there is a desire to maintain closeness to the partner" (1989, p. 711). An **attachment** is a subvariety of affectional bond in which a person's sense of security is bound up in the relationship. When you are attached, you feel (or hope to feel) a special sense of security and comfort in the presence of the other, and you can use the other as a safe base from which to explore the rest of the world.

In these terms, the child's relationship with the parent is an attachment, but the parent's relationship with the child is usually not, since the parent presumably does not feel a greater sense of security in the presence of the infant or use the infant as a safe base. A relationship with one's adult partner or with a very close friend, however, is an attachment in the sense Ainsworth and Bowlby meant the term. Of course, adults aren't as dependent on their partners or friends as children are on their parents. Still, there is a certain kind of security that an adult draws from being in such a relationship; knowing that one can rely on the acceptance and support of a romantic partner or a close friend no matter what happens in many ways parallels the safe base function attachment relationships serve for children.

Because affectional bonds and attachments are internal states, developmentalists cannot observe them directly. Instead, they deduce their existence by observing **attachment behaviors**, which are all those behaviors that allow a child or an adult to achieve and retain physical proximity to someone else to whom he is attached. These could include smiling, making eye contact, calling out to the other person across a room, touching, clinging, or crying.

It is important to make clear that there is no one-to-one correspondence between the number of different attachment behaviors a child (or adult) shows on any one occasion and the strength of the underlying attachment. Attachment behaviors are elicited primarily when the individual has need of care or support or comfort. An infant is needy a good deal of the time; an older child would be likely to show attachment behaviors only when he was frightened, tired, or otherwise under stress. It is the pattern of these behaviors, not the frequency, that reveals something about the strength or quality of the attachment or the affectional bond. To understand the early relationship between the parent and the child, developmentalists look at both sides of the equation—at the development of the parent's bond to the child and at the child's attachment to the parent.

THE PARENT'S BOND TO THE CHILD

If you read any popular magazines, you have probably come across articles proclaiming that mothers (or fathers) must have immediate contact with their newborn infant if they are to become properly bonded with the baby. As you'll see, the formation of an attachment relationship to a child is far too complex to be completely dependent on a single, early experience.

The Development of Interactive Skill   What is essential in the formation of an early bond is the opportunity for the parent and infant to develop a mutual, interlocking pattern of attachment behaviors, a smooth "dance" of interaction. The baby signals her needs by crying or smiling; she looks at her parents when they look at her. The parents, in their turn, enter into this interactive dance with their own repertoire of caregiving behaviors. They pick the baby up when she cries, wait for and respond to her signals of hunger or some other need, and so on. Some researchers and theorists have described this as the development of *synchrony* (Isabella, Belsky, & von Eye, 1989).

One of the most intriguing things about this process is that all humans seem to know how to do this particular dance—and do it in very similar ways. In the presence of a young infant, most adults will automatically display a distinctive pattern of interactive behaviors, including a smile, raised eyebrows, and very wide-open eyes. Adults also use their voices in special ways with babies, as you'll remember from the discussion of motherese in Chapter 8. Parents all over the world use the characteristic high-pitched and lilting pattern of motherese; they also use similar intonation patterns. For example, in a study of mother-infant interactions, Hanus and Mechthild Papousek (1991) found that Chinese, German, and American mothers all tended to use a rising voice inflection when they wanted the baby to "take a turn" or contribute to the interaction and a falling intonation when they wanted to soothe the baby.

Yet even though people show these behaviors with many infants, they do not form a bond with every baby they coo at in a restaurant or a grocery store. For an adult, the critical ingredient for the formation of a bond seems to be the opportunity to develop real synchrony—to practice the dance until the partners follow one another's lead smoothly and pleasurably. This takes time and many rehearsals, and some parents (and infants) become more skillful at it than others. In general, the smoother and more predictable the process becomes, the more satisfying it seems to be to the parents and the stronger their bond to the infant becomes.

Father-Child Bonds   Most of the research you have read about so far has involved studies of mothers. Still, many of the same principles seem to hold for fathers as well (Lewis & Lamb, 2003). In particular, fathers seem to direct the same repertoire of attachment behaviors toward their infants as do mothers. In the early weeks of a baby's life, dad touches, talks to, and cuddles the baby in the same ways mom does; both mothers and fathers show the same physiological responses when they interact with their new infant, including increased heart rate and blood pressure (Corter & Fleming, 1995).

After the earliest weeks of life, however, signs of some specialization of parental behaviors with infants become evident. Studies in the United States show that fathers spend more time playing with a baby, using more physical roughhousing. Mothers spend more time in routine caregiving, and they talk to and smile at the baby more (Parke, 1995; Walker, Messinger, Fogel, & Karns, 1992). This does not mean that fathers have a weaker affectional bond with the infant; it does mean that the behaviors they show toward the infant are typically somewhat different from those mothers show. Nevertheless, by 6 months of age, infants are just as likely to show signs of attachment to their fathers as to their mothers (Feldman, 2003). These signs include laughing and wriggling with delight in short, intense bursts while interacting with their fathers. By

Ryan's dad, like most fathers, is far more likely to play with him by tossing him around than is his mom.

contrast, the signs of attachment to mothers are more likely to include slow, gradual smiles. It isn't a matter of liking one parent more than the other. Babies demonstrate through these signs that the specific features of synchronous interaction are different for mothers and fathers.

However, we should not leap to the conclusion that this sex difference is somehow built-in; instead, it appears to rest on cultural patterns. Researchers in England and in India have found higher levels of physical play by fathers than by mothers, but other researchers in Sweden, Israel, Italy, China, and Malaysia have not (Parke & Buriel, 1998). Findings like this nicely illustrate the usefulness of cross-cultural research for identifying patterns of behavior that are influenced by varying cultural expectations or training.

THE CHILD'S ATTACHMENT TO THE PARENT

Like the parent's bond to the baby, the baby's attachment emerges gradually. Bowlby (1969) suggested three phases in the development of the infant's attachment; these are presented schematically in Figure 11.1. Once formed, the attachment relationship changes somewhat as the child gets older.

Phase 1: Nonfocused Orienting and Signaling   Bowlby believed that a baby begins life with a set of innate behavior patterns that orient him toward others and signal his needs. Mary Ainsworth described these as "proximity-promoting" behaviors: They bring people closer. In the newborn's repertoire, these behaviors include crying, making eye contact, clinging, cuddling, and responding to caregiving efforts by being soothed.

At this stage, there is little evidence that the baby is attached to the parents. Nonetheless, the roots of attachment are established. The baby is building up expectancies and schemas about interaction patterns with the parents, as well as developing the ability to discriminate mom and dad from others in many contexts.

Phase 2: Focus on One or More Figures   By 3 months of age, the baby begins to aim her attachment behaviors somewhat more narrowly. She may smile more at the people who regularly take care of her and may not smile readily at a stranger. The infant does not yet have a complete attachment, though. The child still favors a number

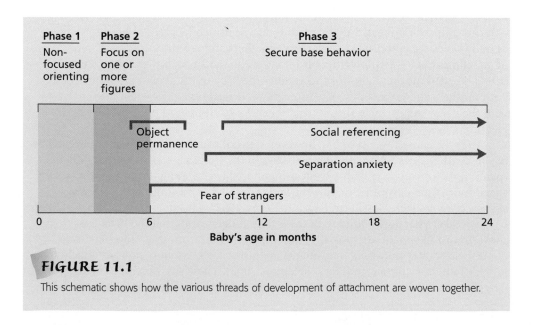

FIGURE 11.1

This schematic shows how the various threads of development of attachment are woven together.

of people with her "proximity-promoting" behaviors, and no one person has yet become the "safe base." Children in this phase show no special anxiety at being separated from their parents and no fear of strangers.

Phase 3: Secure Base Behavior

Only at about 6 months of age, according to Bowlby, does the baby form a genuine attachment—about the same time that he develops some preliminary understanding that objects and people continue to exist when they are out of sight (object permanence). For the first time, the infant uses the "most important" person as a safe base from which to explore the world around him—one of the key signs that an attachment exists. Because the 6- to 7-month-old begins to be able to move about the world more freely by creeping and crawling, he can move toward the caregiver as well as entice the caregiver to come to him. Attachment behaviors therefore shift from mostly "come here" (proximity-promoting) signals to what Ainsworth calls "proximity-seeking" behaviors, which might be thought of as "go there" behaviors.

A few months ago, this baby probably would have let himself be held by just about anyone without a fuss; now all of a sudden he's afraid of strangers. Parents are often puzzled by this behavior, but it is absolutely normal.

Once the child has developed a clear attachment, several related behaviors also appear. One of these is social referencing, which you read about in Chapter 5. The 10-month-old uses his ability to discriminate among various facial expressions to guide his safe-base behavior. He begins to check out mom's or dad's facial expression before deciding whether to venture forth into some novel situation. At about the same age or a little earlier, babies also typically show both fear of strangers and separation anxiety.

Fear of Strangers and Separation Anxiety

Fear of strangers and separation anxiety are two forms of distress that are rare before 5 or 6 months; they appear sometime between 6 and 9 months, rise in frequency until about 12 to 16 months, and then decline after about 24 months. The research findings are not altogether consistent, but it looks as though fear of strangers normally appears first, at about the same time as babies show fearful reactions in other situations. Anxiety at separation starts a bit later but continues to be visible for a longer period, a pattern diagrammed in Figure 11.1.

Such increases in stranger fear and separation anxiety have been observed in children from a number of different cultures and in both home-reared and day-care-reared children in the United States, which suggests that some basic age-related developmental timetables underlie this pattern (Kagan & Herschkowitz, 2005; Kagan, Kearsley, & Zelazo, 1978). Virtually all children show at least mild forms of these two types of distress, although the intensity of the reaction varies widely. Some babies protest briefly; others are virtually inconsolable. Some of this variation undoubtedly reflects basic temperamental differences in behavioral inhibition (Kagan et al., 1994). Heightened fearfulness may also be a response to some upheaval or stress in the child's life, such as a recent move or a change in the daily schedule. Whatever the origin of such variations in fearfulness, the pattern does eventually diminish in most toddlers, typically by the middle of the second year.

Attachments to Mothers and Fathers

From the age of 7 or 8 months, when strong attachments are first seen, infants prefer either the father or the mother to a stranger. And when both the father and the mother are available, an infant will smile at or approach either or both, except when she is frightened or under stress. When that happens, especially between the ages of 8 and 24 months, the child typically turns to the mother rather than the father (Lamb, 1981).

As you might expect, the strength of the child's attachment to the father at this early age seems to be related to the amount of time dad has spent with the child. In one early study, for example, Gail Ross found she could predict a baby's attachment to the father by knowing how many diapers the dad changed in a typical week. The more

Because school-aged children roam farther from home, spending more and more time with peers, it is tempting to assume that they are less strongly attached to their parents. But this assumption is wrong. Children this age still depend on their parents to be a safe base.

diapers, the stronger the attachment (Ross, Kagan, Zelazo, & Kotelchuk, 1975). But greatly increased time with the father does not seem to be the only element, since Michael Lamb and his Swedish colleagues (1983) found that infants whose fathers were their major caregivers for at least a month in the first year of the child's life were nonetheless more strongly attached to their mothers than to their fathers. For the father to be consistently preferred over the mother would probably require essentially full-time paternal care. As this option becomes more common, it will be possible to study such father-child pairs to see whether babies develop a preference for the father.

Cultures with Shared Infant Caretaking   You may be wondering whether attachment patterns vary when an infant has more than one primary caretaker. Edward Tronick and his colleagues (1992) have studied a pygmy group called the Efe, who forage in the forests of Zaire. They live in small groups of perhaps twenty individuals in camps, each consisting of several extended families. Infants in these communities are cared for communally in the early months and years of life. They are carried and held by all the adult women, and they interact regularly with many different adults. They may even be nursed by women other than their mothers, although they normally sleep with their mothers.

Tronick and his colleagues report two things of particular interest about early attachment in this group. First, Efe infants seem to use virtually any adult or older child in their world as a safe base, which suggests that they may have no single central attachment. Second, beginning at about 6 months of age, the Efe infant nonetheless seems to insist on being with his mother more and to prefer her over other women, although other women continue to help care for the child. Thus, even in an extremely communal rearing arrangement, some sign of a central attachment is evident, although it may be less dominant.

Attachments in Early Childhood   By age 2 or 3, although the child's attachment to the mother and father remains powerful, most attachment behaviors have become less continuously visible. Children of this age are cognitively advanced enough to understand mom if she explains why she is going away and says that she will be back, so their anxiety at separation wanes. They can even use a photograph of their mother as a "safe base" for exploration in a strange situation (Passman & Longeway, 1982), which reflects another cognitive advance. By age 3 or 4, a child can also use shared plans offered by parents ("I'll be home after your nap time") to lessen her potential anxiety at separation (Crittenden, 1992). Attachment behaviors have naturally not completely disappeared. Two-year-olds still want to sit on mom's or dad's lap; they are still likely to seek some closeness or proximity when mom returns from some absence. But in nonfrightening or nonstressful situations, toddlers and preschoolers are able to move farther and farther from their safe base without apparent distress.

Bowlby referred to this new form of attachment as a **goal-corrected partnership**. The infant's goal, to put it most simply, is always to have the attachment figure within sight or touch. The preschooler's goal is also to be "in contact" with the parent, but "contact" no longer requires constant physical presence. The preschooler not only understands that his mother will continue to exist when she isn't there; he now also understands that the relationship continues to exist even when the partners are apart. This enables the toddler or preschooler to modify ("correct") her goal of contact with her attachment figure by engaging in collaborative planning: agreeing on when and how the two will be together, for example, or what the child will do if he gets scared or anxious, or who the replacement security person will be.

goal-corrected partnership Term used by Bowlby to describe the form of the child-parent attachment in the preschool years, in which the two partners, through improved communication, negotiate the form and frequency of contact between them.

Attachments in Middle Childhood   In elementary school, overt attachment behaviors such as clinging and crying are even less visible, so it is easy to lose sight of the fact that children this age are still strongly attached to their parents. The elementary school child may take primary responsibility for maintaining contact with the parent (Kerns, 1996), but she wants to know that mom and dad are there when she needs them. Such a need is most likely to arise when the child faces some stressful situation, perhaps the first day of school, an illness or upheaval in the family, or the death of a pet. Because fewer experiences are new and potentially stressful to the 7- or 8-year-old than to the preschooler, there is much less obvious safe-base behavior and less open affection expressed by the child to the parent (Maccoby, 1984). These changes do not, however, signify that the child's attachment to the parent has weakened. In fact, extended separations from parents can be extremely stressful for school-aged children (Smith, Lalonde, & Johnson, 2004).

Although teens have more conflicts with parents than do younger children, they continue to maintain strong attachments to them.

PARENT-CHILD RELATIONSHIPS IN ADOLESCENCE

In adolescence, the form of attachment behaviors shifts somewhat, because teenagers have two apparently contradictory tasks in their relationships with their parents: to establish autonomy from the parents and to maintain their sense of relatedness (attachment) with their parents. The push for autonomy shows itself in increasing conflict between parent and adolescent; the maintenance of connection is seen in the continued strong attachment of child to parent.

Increases in Conflict   The rise in conflict with parents as children enter adolescence has been repeatedly documented (e.g., Flannery, Montemayor, & Eberly, 1994; Laursen, 1995; Steinberg, 1988). In the great majority of families, there is an increase in mild bickering or conflicts over everyday issues such as chores or personal rights—whether the adolescent should be allowed to wear a bizarre hair style or certain clothing or whether and when the teen should be required to do family chores. Teenagers and their parents also interrupt one another more often and become more impatient with one another. They may also argue about the age at which privileges such as dating should be granted (Cunningham, Swanson, Spencer, & Dupree, 2003).

This increase in discord is widely found, but it is important not to assume that it signifies a major disruption of the quality of the parent-child relationship. Laurence Steinberg (1990), one of the key researchers in this area, estimates that only 5–10% of families in the United States experience a substantial or pervasive deterioration in the quality of parent-child relationships in the years of early adolescence. Those families at highest risk for persistently heightened conflict are those in which the parents have a history of low levels of warmth and supportiveness toward their child in earlier years and continue this pattern during adolescence (Rueter & Conger, 1995; Silverberg & Gondoli, 1996). When parents express warmth and supportiveness and are open to hearing the teenager's opinions and disagreements, the period of heightened conflict seems to be relatively brief.

If the rise in conflict doesn't signal that the relationship is falling apart, what does it mean? A variety of theorists have suggested that the temporary discord, far from being a negative event, may instead be a developmentally healthy and necessary part of the adolescent's identity formation. In order to become his own person, the teenager needs to push away from the parents, disagree with them, try out his own limits—a process of **individuation** not unlike that seen in the toddler who begins to say "no" to parents during that famous period called the terrible twos (Grotevant & Cooper, 1985).

individuation The process of psychological, social, and physical separation from parents that begins in adolescence.

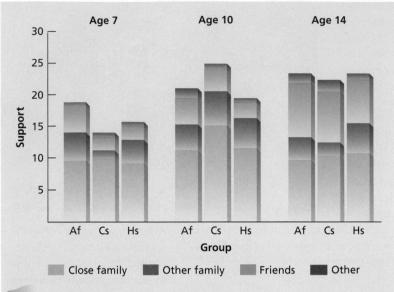

FIGURE 11.2

African American (Af), Caucasian American (Cs), and Hispanic American (Hs) children and teens were asked about the amount and type of support they received from various members of their "social convoy." Note that for teens, friends become more significant sources of support, but parents do not become substantially *less* important.

(*Source*: Levitt, M., Guacci-Franco, N., and Levitt, J., 1993. "Convoys of Social Support in Childhood and Early Adolescence: Structure and Function," *Developmental Psychology*, 29, p. 815. Copyright © 1993 by the American Psychological Association. Reprinted with permission of the American Psychological Association and M. Levitt.)

Before going on...

- Explain the difference between affectional bonds and attachments, and describe attachment behaviors.
- What factors influence the parent's attachment to the child?
- How does the child's attachment to the parent change across infancy, early childhood, and middle childhood?
- What are the characteristics of parent-child relationships in adolescence?

The pattern of causes for parent-teen conflict is obviously complex. Hormonal changes may be causally linked to increases in assertiveness, perhaps especially among boys. Parents' reactions to pubertal changes may also be highly important parts of the mix. Visible pubertal changes, including menarche, alter parents' expectations of the teenager and increase their concern about guiding and controlling the adolescent to help her avoid the pitfalls of too great a level of independence.

Attachment to Parents   Paradoxically, in the midst of this distancing and temporarily heightened family conflict, teenagers' underlying emotional attachment to their parents remains strong. Results from a study by Mary Levitt and her colleagues (1993) illustrate the point. Levitt interviewed African American, Hispanic American, and Caucasian American children aged 7, 10, and 14. All the children were shown a drawing with a set of three concentric circles. They were asked to place in the innermost circle the names of those "people who are the most close and important to you—people you love the most and who love you the most." In the next circle outward, children were asked to place the names of "people who are not quite as close but who are still important—people you really love or like, but not quite as much as the people in the first circle." The last circle contained names of somewhat more distant members of this personal "convoy." For each person listed, the interviewer then asked about the kind of support that person provided.

Levitt found that for all three racial or ethnic groups, at all three ages, parents and other close family were by far the most likely to be placed in the inner circle. Even 14-year-olds rarely placed friends in this position. So the parents remain central. At the same time, it is clear from Levitt's results that peers become increasingly important sources of support, as you can see in Figure 11.2. This figure shows the total amount of support the children and adolescents described from each source. Friends clearly provided more support for the 14-year-olds than they did for the younger children, a pattern that is clear for all three groups.

Despite this evidence of greater support from or intimacy with peers, the research evidence suggests that, in general, a teenager's sense of well-being or happiness is more strongly correlated with the quality of his attachment to his parents than to the quality of his attachments to his peers (Greenberg, Siegel, & Leitch, 1983; Raja, McGee, & Stanton, 1992). In fact, good relationships with parents and peers seem to go hand in hand during the teen years. Teenagers who are close to their parents are also more likely to enjoy positive relationships with their peers than are adolescents who are not close to their parents (Allen, Porter, McFarland, Marsh, & McElhaney, 2005; Turnage, 2004; Weimer, Kerns, & Oldenburg, 2004; Zimmermann, 2004). Furthermore, the stronger the sense of connectedness (attachment) a teenager has with his parents, the less likely he is to engage in any of the risky or delinquent behaviors you learned about in Chapter 4 (Brook, Whiteman, Finch, & Cohen, 2000; Resnick et al., 1997). Thus, even while the teenager is becoming more autonomous, the parents continue to provide a highly important psychological safe base.

Variations in the Quality of Attachments

G
o to a day-care center and watch the way the babies or toddlers greet their parents at the end of the day. Some are calmly pleased to see mom or dad; others may run to the parent, crying and clinging; still others may show little interest. These children may all have formed an attachment to their parents, but the quality of those attachments differs markedly. In Bowlby's terminology, these children have different internal working models of their relationships with parents and key others.

INTERNAL WORKING MODELS OF ATTACHMENT

An **internal working model** of attachment relationships includes such elements as the child's confidence (or lack of it) that the attachment figure will be available or reliable, the child's expectation of rebuff or affection, and the child's sense of assurance that the attachment figure is really a safe base for exploration. The internal model begins to be formed late in the child's first year of life and becomes increasingly elaborated and better established over the first 4 or 5 years. By age 5, most children have clear internal models of the mother (or other caregiver), a self-model, and a model of relationships.

Once formed, such models shape and explain experiences and affect memory and attention. Children notice and remember experiences that fit their model and miss or forget experiences that don't match it. More importantly, the model affects the child's behavior: The child tends to recreate, in each new relationship, the pattern with which he is familiar. Alan Sroufe gives an example that may make this point clearer:

> What is rejection to one child is benign to another. What is warmth to a sec ond child is confusing or ambiguous to another. For example, a child approaches another and asks to play. Turned down, the child goes off and sulks in a corner. A second child receiving the same negative reaction skips on to another partner and successfully engages him in play. Their experiences of rejection are vastly different. Each receives confirmation of quite different inner working models. (1988, p. 23)

In a sense, these internal models are not unlike the social scripts that the preschooler develops in other areas (Bretherton, 1993). They contain expectations for sequences of behavior, rules for behavior with various individuals, and interpretations of others' actions; they help shape what the child pays attention to and what she remembers (Kirsh & Cassidy, 1997).

SECURE AND INSECURE ATTACHMENTS

All attachment theorists share the assumption that the first attachment relationship is the most influential ingredient in the creation of the child's working model. Variations in this first attachment relationship are almost universally described using Mary Ainsworth's category system (Ainsworth et al., 1978). She distinguished between *secure attachment* and two types of *insecure attachment*, which she assessed using a procedure called the Strange Situation.

The **Strange Situation** consists of a series of episodes in a laboratory setting, typically used when the child is between 12 and 18 months of age. The child first spends time with the mother and then with the mother and a stranger; then the child is left alone with the stranger, then completely alone for a few minutes, then reunited with the mother, then left alone again, and finally reunited first with the stranger and then with

internal working model As applied to social relationships, a cognitive construction of the workings of relationships, such as expectations of support or affection, trustworthiness, and so on. The earliest relationships may form the template for such a cognitive construction.

Strange Situation A series of episodes used by Mary Ainsworth and others in studies of attachment. The child is observed with the mother, with a stranger, alone, when reunited with the stranger, and when reunited with the mother.

the mother. Ainsworth suggested that children's reactions to these situations indicated one of three types of attachment: **secure attachment**, shown by a child who uses the parent as a safe base and is readily consoled after separation; and two types of **insecure attachment**, shown by a child who either shows little preference for mother over a stranger (the *insecure/detached* or *insecure/avoidant* child) or is wary of strangers and upset at separation but is not reassured by the mother's return (the *insecure/resistant* or *insecure/ambivalent* child). Mary Main has suggested a fourth type of attachment, which she calls *insecure/disorganized/disoriented* (Main & Solomon, 1990).

Some of the characteristics of the different types of attachment are listed in Table 11.1. As you read the descriptions, note that whether the child cries when he is separated from his mother is not a helpful indicator of the security of his attachment. It is the entire pattern of the child's responses to the Strange Situation that is critical, not any one response.

Origins of Secure and Insecure Attachments

Studies of parent-child interactions suggest that one crucial ingredient for a secure attachment is *emotional availability* on the part of the caregiver (Biringen, 2000). An emotionally available caregiver is one who is able and willing to form an emotional attachment to the infant. For example, economically or emotionally distressed parents may be so distracted by their own problems that they can't invest emotion in the parent-infant relationship. Such parents may meet the baby's physical needs—feeding, changing diapers, and so on—but be unable to respond emotionally.

A number of studies (including some cross-cultural research) further suggest that both acceptance of the infant by the parents and some aspect of sensitivity to the child—a quality that has been measured and given various labels, including *synchrony, mutuality,* and *contingent responsiveness*—are also necessary for the formation of an attachment relationship (De Wolff & van IJzendoorn, 1997; Isabella, 1993; Pederson et al., 1990; Posada et al., 2002; Thompson, 1998). This key quality is more than merely love and affection. To be rated as sensitive, or high in contingent responsiveness, the parents must be attuned to the child's signals and cues and respond appropriately. They smile when the baby smiles, talk to the baby when he vocalizes, pick him up when he cries, and so on (Ainsworth & Marvin, 1995; Sroufe, 1996).

Developmentalists' certainty that this type of responsiveness is a key ingredient in the formation of secure attachment has been strengthened by research in the Netherlands by Dymphna van den Boom (1994), who has demonstrated the link experimen-

secure attachment An internal working model of relationships in which the child uses the parent as a safe base and is readily consoled after separation, when fearful, or when otherwise stressed.

insecure attachment An internal working model of relationships in which the child does not as readily use the parent as a safe base and is not readily consoled by the parent if upset. Includes three subtypes of attachment: avoidant, ambivalent, and disorganized/disoriented.

TABLE 11.1 Categories of Secure and Insecure Attachment in Ainsworth's Strange Situation	
Category	**Behavior**
Secure attachment	Child readily separates from mother and easily becomes absorbed in exploration; when threatened or frightened, child actively seeks contact and is readily consoled; child does not avoid or resist contact if mother initiates it. When reunited with mother after absence, child greets her positively or is easily soothed if upset. Clearly prefers mother to stranger.
Insecure attachment (detached/avoidant)	Child avoids contact with mother, especially at reunion after an absence. Does not resist mother's efforts to make contact, but does not seek much contact. Shows no preference for mother over stranger.
Insecure attachment (resistant/ambivalent)	Child shows little exploration and is wary of stranger. Greatly upset when separated from mother, but not reassured by mother's return or her efforts at comforting. Child both seeks and avoids contact at different times. May show anger toward mother at reunion, and resists both comfort from and contact with stranger.
Insecure attachment (disorganized/disoriented)	Dazed behavior, confusion, or apprehension. Child may show contradictory behavior patterns simultaneously, such as moving toward mother while keeping gaze averted.

Sources: Ainsworth et al., 1978; Carlson and Sroufe, 1995; Main and Solomon, 1990.

tally. She identified 100 lower-class Dutch mothers whose infants had all been rated as high in irritability shortly after birth. Half the mothers were assigned randomly to participate in a set of three relatively brief training sessions aimed at helping them improve their responsiveness to their infants. The other mothers received no such help. When the babies were 12 months old, van den Boom observed the mothers interacting with their infants at home as well as in the standard laboratory Strange Situation. The effects were quite clear: The trained mothers had indeed become more responsive to their babies, and their babies were more likely to be securely attached. In a follow-up study, van den Boom (1995) found that these differences persisted until at least age 18 months.

A low level of responsiveness on the part of caregivers thus appears to be an ingredient in any type of insecure attachment. Each of the several subvarieties of insecure attachment also has additional distinct antecedents. For example, a disorganized/disoriented pattern of attachment seems especially likely when the child has been abused or has parents who had some trauma in their own childhoods, such as either abuse or the early death of a parent (Cassidy & Berlin, 1994; Main & Hesse, 1990). An ambivalent pattern is more common when the mother is inconsistently or unreliably available to the child. Mothers may show such unavailability or periodic neglect for a variety of reasons, but a common one is depression (Teti, Gelfand, Messinger, & Isabella, 1995). When the mother rejects the infant or regularly (rather than intermittently) withdraws from contact with the infant, the infant is more likely to show an avoidant pattern of attachment.

Attachment Quality across Cultures   Studies in a variety of countries have pointed to the possibility that secure attachments may be influenced by culture as well. The most thorough analyses have come from a Dutch psychologist, Marinus van IJzendoorn, who has examined the results of 32 separate studies in 8 different countries. Table 11.2 shows the percentage of babies classified in each category for each country. We need to be cautious about overgeneralizing the information in this table, because in most cases there are only one or two studies from a given country, normally with quite small samples. The single study from China, for example, included only 36 babies. Still, the findings are thought-provoking.

The most striking thing about the data in Table 11.2 is their consistency. In each of the eight countries, a secure attachment is the most common pattern, found in more than half of all babies studied; in five of the eight countries, an avoidant pattern is the more common of the two forms of insecure attachment. Only in Israel and Japan is this pattern significantly reversed. How can such differences be explained?

TABLE 11.2	Secure and Insecure Attachments in Different Cultures			
		Percentage of Children Showing Each Type of Attachment		
Country	**Number of Studies**	**Secure**	**Avoidant**	**Ambivalent**
West Germany	3	56.6	35.3	8.1
Great Britain	1	75.0	22.2	2.8
Netherlands	4	67.3	26.3	6.4
Sweden	1	74.5	21.6	3.9
Israel	2	64.4	6.8	28.8
Japan	2	67.7	5.2	25.0
China	1	50.0	25.0	25.0
United States	18	64.8	21.1	14.1
Overall average		65%	21%	14%

Source: Based on Table 1 of van IJzendoorn and Kroonenberg, 1988, pp. 150–151.

Japanese babies spend more time with their mothers than do infants in Western cultures. As a result, they may exhibit more distress during the Strange Situation and be inappropriately classified as ambivalently attached.

One possibility is that the Strange Situation is simply not an appropriate measure of attachment security in all cultures. For example, because Japanese babies are rarely separated from their mothers in the first year of life, being left totally alone in the midst of the Strange Situation may be far more stressful for them, which might result in more intense, inconsolable crying and hence a classification of ambivalent attachment. The counterargument is that comparisons of toddlers' reactions in the Strange Situation suggest few cultural differences in such behaviors as proximity-seeking or avoidance of the mother, all of which lead to more confidence that the Strange Situation is tapping similar processes among children in many cultures (Sagi, van IJzendoorn, & Koren-Karie, 1991).

It is also possible that the meaning of a "secure" or "avoidant" pattern is different in different cultures, even if the percentages of each category are similar. German researchers, for example, have suggested that, in their culture, an insecure-avoidant classification may reflect not indifference by the mother but rather explicit training toward greater independence in the baby (Grossmann, Grossmann, Spangler, Seuss, & Unzner, 1985).

On the other hand, research in Israel (Sagi, 1990) shows that the attachment classification derived from the Strange Situation predicts the baby's later social skills in much the same way as it does for samples in the United States, which suggests that the classification system is valid in both cultures. The most plausible hypothesis is that the same factors in mother-infant interaction contribute to secure and insecure attachments in all cultures and that these patterns reflect similar internal models. But it will take more research like the Israeli work, in which the long-term outcomes of the various categories are studied, before developmentalists can be sure if this is correct.

STABILITY AND LONG-TERM CONSEQUENCES OF ATTACHMENT QUALITY

Do variations in the quality of a child's early attachment persist over time? This question is a particularly important one for those researchers and therapists who are concerned that the effects of early abuse or neglect or other sources of insecure attachment might be permanent.

Stability of Attachment Classification
Both consistency and inconsistency are evident in attachment relationships over time, depending on the circumstances (Thompson, 1998; van IJzendoorn, 1997). When the child's family environment or life circumstances are reasonably consistent, the security or insecurity of attachment usually remains constant as well, even over many years (Weinfield & Egeland, 2004). For example, in one small study, Claire Hamilton (1995) found that 16 of 18 adolescents who had been rated as insecurely attached at 12 months of age were still rated as insecurely attached at age 17, while 7 of the 11 teens who had been classed as securely attached as infants were still rated as securely attached at 17. Similar high levels of stability have been observed in a sample of children in middle-class families studied by Everett Waters and his colleagues (1995) from infancy to age 18, as well as in a shorter-term study in Germany (Wartner, Grossman, Fremmer-Bombik, & Suess, 1994), in which 82% of a group of youngsters from stable, middle-class families were rated in the same category of attachment at age 6 as they had been at age 1.

When the child's circumstances change in some major way, however—when she starts going to day care or nursery school, when grandma comes to live with the family, or when her parents divorce or move—the security of the child's attachment may change as well, either from secure to insecure or the reverse. For example, in Waters's long-term study (Waters, Treboux, Crowell, Merrick, & Albersheim, 1995), the participants whose attachment classification changed between infancy and young adulthood had nearly all experienced some major upheaval, such as the death of a parent, physical or sexual abuse, or a serious illness.

This elementary school child appears to be securely attached to her parent. Research on the stability of attachment classifications suggests that the secure quality of the relationship was established when the girl was an infant.

The very fact that a child's security can change from one time to another does not refute the notion of attachment as an internal working model. Bowlby suggested that for the first two or three years of life, the particular pattern of attachment shown by a child is in some sense a property of each specific relationship. For example, studies of toddlers' attachments to mothers and fathers show that about 30% of the time, the child is securely attached to one parent and insecurely attached to the other, with both possible combinations equally represented (Fox, Kimmerly, & Schafer, 1991). It is the quality of the particular relationship that determines the child's security with that specific adult. If that relationship changes markedly, the security of the baby's attachment to that individual may change, too. However, Bowlby argued that by age 4 or 5, the internal working model becomes more general, more a property of the child, more generalized across relationships, and thus more resistant to change. At that point, the child tends to impose her working model on new relationships, including relationships with teachers and peers. Thus, a child may "recover" from an initially insecure attachment or lose a secure one. Consistency over time is more typical, however, both because children's relationships tend to be reasonably stable for the first few years and because once the internal model is clearly formed, it tends to perpetuate itself.

Long-Term Consequences of Secure and Insecure Attachment   Ainsworth's classification system has proved to be extremely helpful in predicting a remarkably wide range of other behaviors in children, both toddlers and older children. Dozens of studies (e.g., Carlson, Sampson, & Sroufe, 2003; Carlson & Sroufe, 1995; Leve & Fagot, 1995) show that, compared to children rated as insecurely attached, children rated as securely attached to their mothers in infancy are later more sociable, more positive in their behavior toward friends and siblings, less clinging and dependent on teachers, less aggressive and disruptive, more empathetic, and more emotionally mature in their approach to school and other settings outside the home.

At adolescence, those who were rated as securely attached in infancy or who are classed as secure on the basis of recent interviews have more intimate friendships, are more likely to be rated as leaders, and have higher self-esteem (Black & McCartney, 1995; Lieberman, Doyle, & Markiewicz, 1995; Ostoja, McCrone, Lehn, Reed, & Sroufe, 1995). Those with insecure attachments—particularly those with avoidant attachments—not only have less positive and supportive friendships in adolescence but are also more likely to become sexually active early and to practice riskier sex (Carlson, Sroufe, & Egeland, 2004; O'Beirne & Moore, 1995).

One particularly clear demonstration of some of these links comes from a longitudinal study by Alan Sroufe and his colleagues (1993; Urban, Carlson, Egeland, & Sroufe, 1991; Weinfield, Ogawa, & Sroufe, 1997). These researchers assessed the security of attachment of a group of several hundred infants and then followed the children through childhood and adolescence, testing and observing them at regular intervals. Some of their observations were of participants who had been invited to attend a specially designed summer camp during early adolescence. The counselors rated each child on a range of characteristics, and observers noted how often children spent time together or with the counselors. Naturally, neither the counselors nor the observers knew what the children's initial attachment classification had been. Those children with histories of secure attachment in infancy were rated as higher in self-confidence and social competence. They complied more readily with requests from counselors, expressed more positive emotions, and had a greater sense of their ability to accomplish things. Secure children created more friendships, especially with other securely attached youngsters, and engaged in more complex activities when playing in groups. In contrast, the majority of the children with histories of insecure attachment showed some kind of deviant behavior pattern, such as isolation from peers, bizarre behavior, passivity, hyperactivity, or aggressiveness. Only a few of the originally securely attached children showed any of these patterns.

TEMPERAMENT AND ATTACHMENT

The general timing of the development of attachment behaviors is the same in virtually all children. However, the emotional intensity of the relationship varies considerably from child to child. For example, infants differ widely in how much fear they show toward strangers or toward novel situations. Some of this difference may reflect basic temperamental variations (Kagan, 1994). Heightened fearfulness may also be a response to some upheaval or stress in the child's life, such as a recent move or a parent's job change.

Individual differences in infant temperament may also be related to security of attachment (Zeanah & Fox, 2004). Generally speaking, easy infants, as defined by the Thomas and Chess system (which you read about in Chapter 9), are more likely to be securely attached than babies in the other two categories (Goldsmith & Alansky, 1987; Seifer, Schiller, Sameroff, Resnick, & Riordan, 1996; Vaughn et al., 1992). The relationship makes sense if you think about the traits of infants in the difficult and slow-to-warm-up groups. Difficult infants actively resist comfort; consequently, a parent may be discouraged from establishing a nurturing relationship with a difficult infant. Likewise, slow-to-warm-up babies are less responsive to parental behaviors directed toward them, and the parents of these infants may reduce the frequency of behaviors directed to their unresponsive babies. The result is that the kind of give-and-take relationships most easy infants experience with their parents may never develop for babies who are difficult or slow-to-warm-up (Kagan, 1989).

It's important to remember, however, that a correlation is just a correlation and certainly does not suggest that all easy infants develop secure attachment or that all babies of the other two temperamental types are insecurely attached. In fact, the majority of infants in all three temperament categories are securely attached (van IJzendoorn et al., 1992). In addition, if infant temperament dictated attachment quality, it would be highly unlikely to see infants who are securely attached to one parent but insecurely attached to the other. In reality, this is a very common research finding (e.g., Goossens & van IJzendoorn, 1990).

For these reasons, developmentalists propose that it is not temperament, per se, that influences attachment. Rather, attachment is influenced by the **goodness-of-fit** between the infant's temperament and his or her environment (Thomas & Chess, 1977). For example, if the parents of an irritable baby boy are good at tolerating his irritability and persist in establishing a synchronous relationship with him, then his irritability doesn't lead to the development of an insecure attachment.

DOES QUALITY OF ATTACHMENT MATTER IN ADULTHOOD?

Longitudinal studies show that the effects of attachment status persist into adulthood (Tideman, Nilsson, Smith, & Stjernqvist, 2002). Adults who were securely attached as infants perceive their relationships with their mothers differently than do adults who were insecurely attached. Attachment security in childhood may even find its way into romantic relationships in adulthood. Some studies show that men and women who were securely attached to their parents are more sensitive to their partners' needs (Mikulincer & Shaver, 2005).

Adults' internal models of attachment affect the way they behave with their own children as well. To assess the degree to which they do so, psychologist Mary Main and her colleagues developed a standardized attachment status interview for use with adults (Main & Hesse, 1990; Main, Kaplan, & Cassidy, 1985). They found that an adult's internal working model of attachment can be classified as one of three types:

- *Secure/autonomous/balanced.* These individuals value attachment relations and see their early experiences as influential, but they are objective in describing both good

goodness-of-fit The degree to which an infant's environment and his or her temperament work together.

and bad qualities. They speak coherently about their early experiences and have thoughts about what motivated their parents' behavior.

■ *Dismissing or detached*. These adults minimize the importance or the effects of early family experience. They may idealize their parents, perhaps even denying the existence of any negative childhood experiences. They emphasize their own personal strengths.

■ *Preoccupied or enmeshed*. These adults often talk about inconsistent or role-reversed parenting. They are still engrossed with their relationship with their parents, still actively struggling to please them or very angry at them. They are confused and ambivalent, but still engaged.

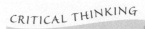

CRITICAL THINKING

How would you rate your own attachment to your parents? Do you think it has any impact on your relationships with other adults?

When adults' models of attachment are related to the security of attachment displayed by their children, the expected pattern emerges strongly: Adults with secure models of attachment to their own parents are much more likely to have infants or toddlers with secure attachments. Those adults with dismissing models are more likely to have infants with avoidant attachments; those with preoccupied attachments are more likely to have infants with ambivalent attachments. Across 20 studies, the typical finding is that three-quarters of the mother-infant pairs share the same attachment category (van IJzendoorn, 1995, 1997). Diane Benoit has even found marked consistency across three generations: grandmothers, young mothers, and infants (Benoit & Parker, 1994).

The cross-generational similarity appears to be a result of each mother's own behavior toward her child, which varies as a function of her own internal working model of attachment (Steele, Hodges, Kaniuk, Hillman, & Henderson, 2003). Mothers who are themselves securely attached are more responsive and sensitive in their behavior toward their infants or young children (van IJzendoorn, 1995). For example, Judith Crowell and Shirley Feldman (1988) observed mothers with their preschoolers in a free-play setting. In the middle of the play period, each mother left her child alone for several minutes and then returned. Mothers who were themselves classed as secure in their attachment model were more likely to prepare the child ahead of time for the impending separation, had less difficulty themselves with the separation, and were most physically responsive to the child during reunion. Preoccupied mothers were themselves more anxious about separating from the child and prepared the child less. Dismissing mothers also prepared the child very little, but they left without difficulty and remained physically distant from their children after returning to the playroom.

Crowell and Feldman also noted that mothers with dismissing or preoccupied internal working models interpreted the child's behavior very differently than did the secure moms: One dismissing mother observed her crying child through the observation window and said, "See, she isn't upset about being left." At reunion, she said to the child, "Why are you crying? I didn't leave" (1991, p. 604). Thus, the mother's own internal model not only affects her actual behavior but also affects the meaning she ascribes to the child's behavior, both of which will affect the child's developing model of attachment.

Before going on . . .

■ Define *internal working model*, and explain how this concept applies to attachment.
■ What are secure and insecure attachments, and how do they develop?
■ Describe the stability and long-term consequences of variations in attachment quality.
■ How does infant temperament influence the attachment process?
■ How do adults' internal working models of attachment influence their parenting behavior?

Relationships with Peers

Because most theories of social and personality development have strongly emphasized the centrality of parent-child interactions, most psychologists thought of relationships with peers as much less important, until recently. That view is now changing as it becomes clear that peer relationships play a unique and significant role in a child's development. We now know that children's relationships with parents and peers are interactive (Chen, He, Chang, & Liu, 2005). That is, good parenting is most effective when children associate with peers who exhibit social competence. Conversely, antisocial peers can undermine the potentially positive effects of good parenting. Thus, developmentalists no longer think of parental and peer relationships as independent

By age 3, most children actually play together with one another in coordinated ways, rather than merely playing side by side.

sets of influences. Of course, children have relationships with parents before they develop them with peers. In this section, we'll discuss how peer relationships change over the years of childhood and adolescence.

PEER RELATIONSHIPS IN INFANCY AND THE PRESCHOOL YEARS

Children first begin to show some positive interest in other infants as early as 6 months of age. If you place two babies of that age on the floor facing each other, they will touch each other, pull each other's hair, and reach for each other's clothing. In 10-month-olds, these behaviors are even more evident. By 14 to 18 months of age, two or more children can play together with toys—occasionally cooperating, but more often simply playing side by side with different toys, a pattern Mildred Parten (1932) first described as **parallel play**. Toddlers of this age express interest in one another, gazing at or making noises at each other. Only at around 18 months of age, however, do toddlers show evidence of coordinated play, such as when one toddler chases another or imitates the other's action with some toy. By 3 or 4, children appear to prefer to play with peers rather than alone, and their play with one another is much more cooperative and coordinated, including various forms of group pretend play.

The first signs of playmate preferences or friendships also emerge in the toddler and preschool years (Hay, Payne, & Chadwick, 2004). A few children show signs of specific playmate preferences as early as age 18 months; by age 3 or 4, more than half of children have at least one mutual friendship. Furthermore, the majority of these friendships last for at least 6 months, many of them for far longer (Dunn, 1993; Howes, 1996).

To be sure, these early "friendships" are not nearly as deep or intimate as those between pairs of older children or adolescents. Toddler friends ignore each other's bids for interaction as often as not. Still, these pairs show unmistakable signs that their relationship is more than merely a passing fancy. They display more mutual liking, more reciprocity, more extended interactions, more positive and less negative behavior, more forgiveness, and more supportiveness in a novel situation than is true of nonfriend pairs at this same age. When they quarrel, they are more likely than nonfriends to try to patch it up (Dunn, 1993; Hartup, Laursen, Stewart, & Eastenson, 1988; Newcomb & Bagwell, 1995).

There is every reason to believe that early play with such a friend is a highly important arena for children to practice a host of social skills (Sebanc, 2003). As John Gottman says, in order to play collaboratively, friends "must coordinate their efforts with all the virtuosity of an accomplished jazz quartet" (1986, p. 3). Often, they must subdue their own desires in the interests of joint play, which requires some awareness of the other's feelings and wishes as well as an ability to modulate one's own emotions. You already know that these cognitive and control skills emerge during the preschool years; what the research on friendships reveals is that play with peers, especially play with friends, may be a crucial ingredient in that development.

One of the really intriguing facts about such early friendships is that they are more likely between same-sex pairs, even among children as young as 2 or 3. John Gottman (1986) reports that perhaps 65% of friendships between preschool children in the United States are with same-sex peers. Social interactions with children other than the chosen friend(s) are also more likely to be with children of the same sex, beginning as early as age 2½ or 3 (Maccoby, 1988, 1990; Maccoby & Jacklin, 1987)—a pattern you already saw in Figure 10.5.

PEER RELATIONSHIPS AT SCHOOL AGE

Peers become even more important among school-aged children. Indeed, for children aged 7 through 10, playing with pals (along with watching TV) takes up virtually all

parallel play Form of play seen in toddlers, in which children play next to, but not with, one another.

their time when they are not in school, eating, or sleeping (Timmer, Eccles, & O'Brien, 1985). As is true among preschoolers, shared play interests form the major basis of peer relationships among school-aged children. Furthermore, children in this age range define play groups in terms of common activities rather than in terms of common attitudes or values. You can see this pattern in Figure 11.3, which shows the results of a study by Susan O'Brien & Karen Bierman (1988). They asked children in 5th, 8th, and 11th grades to tell them about the different groups of kids that hung around together at their school and then to say how they could tell that a particular bunch was a "group." For the 5th graders, the single best criterion of a "group" was that the children did things together. For 8th graders, shared attitudes and common appearance became much more important. By 11th grade, shared attitudes were the most important, and shared

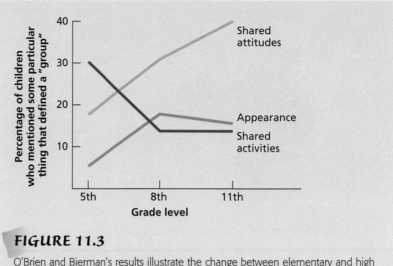

FIGURE 11.3

O'Brien and Bierman's results illustrate the change between elementary and high school in children's ideas about what defines a "group" of peers. (*Source*: O'Brien & Bierman, 1988, Table 1, p. 1363.)

activities the least important. You'll learn more about children's understanding of social relationships and processes in Chapter 12, but note here that this "concreteness" in the elementary school child's view of peers is entirely consistent with what you have already read about children's self-concepts at this age, as well as with Piaget's ideas about concrete operational thinking.

Friendships   Gender segregation is quite pronounced in friendships among school-aged children. In one large study of third and fourth graders, researchers found that only 14% had a cross-sex friendship; for only 3% of these children was the cross-sex relationship the child's primary or most central friendship (Kovacs, Parker, & Hoffman, 1996). School-aged children spend more time with their friends than do preschoolers, and they gradually develop a larger collection of **reciprocal friendships**—pairs in which each child names the other as a friend or as a "best friend." Thomas Berndt, in several studies (e.g., Berndt & Hoyle, 1985), has found that most first graders have only one such reciprocal friendship. This number gradually rises through elementary school, so that by eighth grade, the average child has two or three reciprocal friendships. If researchers simply ask children to name their friends— ignoring the question of whether the friendship is reciprocated—the numbers are still higher. Second graders name about four friends each, and seventh graders name about seven (Reisman & Shorr, 1978). Cross-cultural studies show that best-friend relationships and the belief that having a best friend is important are universal features of school-aged children's social development (Schraf & Hertz-Lazarowitz, 2003).

Children in this age range also behave differently with friends than they do with strangers, just as preschoolers do. They are more open and more supportive with chums, smiling and looking at each other, laughing and touching each other more than nonfriends; they talk more with friends and cooperate with and help each other more. Pairs of friends are also more successful than are nonfriend pairs at solving problems or performing some task together (Newcomb & Bagwell, 1995). Yet school-aged children are also more critical of friends and have more conflicts with them than they do with strangers (Hartup, 1996). At the same time, when such conflicts with friends occur, children are more concerned about resolving them than they are disagreements with nonfriends. Thus, friendships constitute an arena in which children can learn how to manage conflicts (Newcomb & Bagwell, 1995).

Sex Differences in Friendship Quality   The qualities of the friendships girls and boys create differ in intriguing ways. Waldrop and Halverson (1975) refer to boys'

reciprocal friendship A friendship in which each partner identifies the other as a friend; also, a quality of friendship in school-aged children, when friendship is for the first time perceived as being based on reciprocal trust.

Some children prefer solitary activities and are not distressed about their lack of inclusion in peer groups.

relationships as *extensive* and to girls' relationships as *intensive*. Boys' friendship groups are larger and more accepting of newcomers than are girls'. Boy friends play more outdoors and roam over a larger area in their play. Girl friends are more likely to play in pairs or in smaller groups, and they spend more playtime indoors or near home or school (Benenson, 1994; Gottman, 1986).

Sex differences in actual interactions are also evident—a fact that won't surprise you, given what you have already read about the reasons for gender segregation in this age group. Boys' groups and boys' friendships appear to be focused more on competition and dominance than are girls' friendships (Maccoby, 1995). In fact, among school-aged boys, there are higher levels of competition between pairs of friends than between pairs of strangers, the opposite of what can be observed among girls. Friendships between girls also include more agreement, more compliance, and more self-disclosure than those between boys. For example, Campbell Leaper (1991) finds that "controlling" speech—a category that includes rejecting comments, ordering, manipulating or challenging, defying or refuting, or resisting the other's attempt to control—is twice as common among pairs of male friends as among pairs of female friends at ages 7 and 8. Among the 4- and 5-year-olds in this study, there were no sex differences in controlling speech.

None of these observed differences should obscure the fact that the interactions of male and female friends have a great many characteristics in common. For example, collaborative and cooperative exchanges are the most common forms of communication in both boys' and girls' friendships in these years. Nor should we necessarily conclude that boys' friendships are less important to them than are girls'. Nevertheless, it seems clear that there are differences in form and style that may well have enduring implications for the patterns of friendship over the life span.

SOCIAL STATUS

One important aspect of individual differences in peer relationships is the degree to which peers like an individual child. Typically, this variable is called **social status**. Psychologists know a great deal about children in the three traditional status categories—popular, neglected, and rejected. **Popular children** are those who are most often described as well-liked and who are selected as playmates by peers. **Neglected children** are seldom described by peers as either liked or disliked, and **rejected children** are those who are actively disliked and avoided by their peers.

Popular and Neglected Children
Some of the characteristics that differentiate popular children from others are things outside a child's control. In particular, attractive children and physically larger children are more likely to be popular. However, being very different from one's peers may also cause a child to be neglected or rejected. For example, shy children usually have few friends (Fordham & Stevenson-Hinde, 1999). Similarly, highly creative children are often rejected, as are those who have difficulty controlling their emotions (Aranha, 1997; Maszk, Eisenberg, & Guthrie, 1999).

However, children's social behavior seems to be more important than looks or temperament. Most studies show that popular children behave in positive, supporting, nonpunitive, and nonaggressive ways toward most other children. They explain things, take their playmates' wishes into consideration, take turns in conversation, and are able to regulate the expression of their strong emotions. In addition, popular children are usually good at accurately assessing others' feelings (Underwood, 1997). Most are also good at looking at situations from others' perspectives (Fitzgerald & White, 2003).

social status A term used by psychologists to refer to how well an individual child is liked by his or her peers.

popular children Children who are described as well-liked by a majority of peers.

neglected children Children who are seldom described by peers as either liked or disliked.

rejected children Unpopular children who are explicitly avoided and not chosen as playmates or friends.

However, the degree to which popularity represents good adjustment depends on the peer context in which it occurs. Teenagers popular with peers who approve of and value inappropriate behavior—skipping school, for instance—are likely to exhibit such behavior (Allen, Porter, McFarland, Marsh, & McElhaney, 2005). In such cases, popularity may work against the achievement of positive developmental outcomes.

Neglected children share many characteristics of peers who are popular. They often do quite well in school, but they are more prone to depression and loneliness than are popular children (Cillessen, van IJzendoorn, van Lieshout, & Hartup, 1992; Rubin, Hymel, Mills, Rose-Krasnor, 1991; Wentzel & Asher, 1995). This is especially true for girls, who seem to value popularity more than boys do (Oldenburg & Kerns, 1997). Peer neglect may be associated with depression because recent brain-imaging studies show that peer neglect stimulates the same areas of the brain as physical pain (Eisenberger, 2003). In addition, some neglected children have unrealistic expectations about adults' ability to "fix" their situation (Galanaki, 2004). They may think, "Why doesn't the teacher *make* them be my friends?" Such thoughts may lead to feelings of hopelessness.

Nevertheless, many neglected children aren't the least bit concerned about their lack of popularity. Many such children are shy and prefer solitary activities; thus, their neglected status may simply be a function of their own personalities. However, a child's neglected status can change, suggesting that it is a function of both the social context and an individual child's personality. In fact, neglected children often move to the popular category when they become part of a new peer group.

Rejected Children   There are two types of rejected children. *Withdrawn/rejected* children realize that they are disliked by peers (Harrist, Zaia, Bates, Dodge, & Pettit, 1997). After repeated attempts to gain peer acceptance, these children eventually give up and become socially withdrawn. As a result, they often experience feelings of loneliness.

Aggressive/rejected children are often disruptive and uncooperative but usually believe that their peers like them (Zakriski & Coie, 1996). Many appear to be unable to control the expression of strong feelings (Eisenberg, Fabes, et al., 1995; Pettit, Clawson, Dodge, & Bates, 1996). They interrupt their play partners more often and fail to take turns in a systematic way.

Causes and Consequences of Peer Rejection   Much of the information on aggressive/rejected children is consistent with Gerald Patterson's work, whose model is described in Chapter 1 and in Chapter 9. Patterson is persuaded that a child's excess aggressiveness can be traced originally to ineffective parental control. But once the child's aggressiveness is well established, the child displays this same behavior with peers, is rejected by those peers, and is then driven more and more toward the only set of peers who will accept him, usually other aggressive or delinquent youngsters. These aggressive kids are not friendless, but their friends are almost always other kids with similar antisocial patterns. These friendships tend to be fairly transitory and focused on mutual coercion (Dishion, Andrews, & Crosby, 1995).

The seriousness of this set of connected problems is amply demonstrated in a growing body of research showing that rejection by one's peers in elementary school—especially when the rejection is because of excessive aggressiveness—is one of the very few aspects of childhood functioning that consistently predicts behavior problems or emotional disturbances later in childhood, in adolescence, and in adulthood (e.g., Bagwell, Newcomb, & Bukowski, 1998; Dishion, 1990; Ladd & Troop-Gordon, 2003; Serbin, Moskowitz, Schwartzman, & Ledingham, 1991; Stattin & Magnusson, 1996). For example, Melissa DeRosier and her colleagues (1994) followed one group of over 600 children over a 4-year period in the early elementary grades. She found that those children who were most chronically rejected by their peers later showed higher rates of several types of problems, including more absences from school, more depression or sadness, and more behavior problems.

Similarly, John Coie and his colleagues (1995) followed a group of over 1,000 children from the third to the tenth grade. Among the boys, those who were both aggres-

CRITICAL THINKING

Can you remember what your own social status was when you were a child? How do you think your status affected your life in later years?

A pattern of persistent aggression, and the peer rejection that so often accompanies it, is linked to a variety of long-term problems for children.

sive and rejected in third grade were far more likely to show delinquency or other behavior problems in high school than were any other group of boys. Among girls, aggressiveness (but not peer rejection) was linked to later behavior problems.

Such a link between early unpopularity and later behavior problems might be explained in any of several ways. Early problems with peers might be merely the most visible reflection of a general maladjustment that later manifests itself as delinquency or emotional disturbance. Alternatively, developmentalists might hypothesize that a failure to develop friendships itself causes problems that later become more general. Or, the basic difficulty could lie in a seriously warped internal working model of relationships that leads to peer rejection in elementary school and to delinquency. Or, all of the above might be true.

Happily, not all rejected children remain rejected; not all develop serious behavior problems or delinquency. And not all aggressive children are rejected. Research gives a few hints about what may differentiate these several subgroups. For example, some aggressive children also show fairly high levels of altruistic or prosocial behavior, and this mixture of qualities carries a much more positive prognosis than does aggression unleavened by helpfulness (Coie & Cillessen, 1993; Newcomb et al., 1993). Distinctions like these may help developmentalists not only to refine their predictions but to design better intervention programs for rejected/aggressive children.

PEER RELATIONSHIPS IN ADOLESCENCE

Many of the friendship patterns just discussed change at adolescence. Mixed-sex groups begin to appear, conformity to peer group values and behaviors increases, and parents' influence on the child wanes, even though the child's attachment to the parents remains strong. In the United States, teenagers spend more than half their waking hours with other teenagers and less than 5% of their time with either parent. Adolescent friendships are also increasingly intimate, in the sense that the friends share more of their inner feelings and secrets and are more knowledgeable about each other's feelings. Loyalty and faithfulness become centrally valued characteristics of friendship. These adolescent friendships are also more likely to endure for a year or longer (Bowker, 2004). In one longitudinal study, Robert and Beverly Cairns (1994) found that only about 20% of friendships among fourth graders lasted as long as a year, whereas about 40% of friendships formed by these same youngsters when they were tenth graders were long-lasting.

Functions of Adolescent Peer Groups   Just as individual relationships change, the function of the peer group changes in adolescence. In elementary school, peer groups primarily serve as a setting for mutual play (and for all the learning about relationships and the natural world that is part of such play). For teenagers, the peer group has another function. The teenager is struggling to make a slow transition from the protected life of the family to the independent life of adulthood; the peer group becomes the vehicle for that transition.

One sign of this shift is that teenagers begin to confide primarily in their peers, rather than in their parents. You've seen one illustration of this change in Figure 11.2. An equally striking set of findings comes from research by Duane Buhrmester (1996). Figure 11.4 shows the combined findings from several studies in which children, teenagers, or adults were asked to rate the level of intimate disclosure they experienced with parents, friends, and a romantic partner. You can see three clear stages. Before adolescence, children report higher levels of self-disclosure with their parents. At adolescence, this changes in a major way: Self-disclosure with parents declines dramatically, while self-disclosure with friends becomes dominant. Then in adulthood, a second shift occurs as a romantic partner takes the role of primary confidant.

Another aspect of this change in the centrality of peer relationships is a strong clannishness and intense conformity to the group. Such conformity, which Erikson saw as an entirely normal aspect of adolescence, seems to peak at about age 13 or 14 (at about the same time that developmentalists observe a drop in self-esteem); conformity then wanes as the teenager begins to arrive at a sense of identity that is more independent of the peer group.

However, although it is very clear that peers do indeed put pressure on each other to conform to peer group behavior standards, it is also true that peer group pressures are less potent and less negative than popular cultural stereotypes might suggest (Berndt, 1992). Adolescents, like adults, choose their friends, and they are likely to choose to associate with a group that shares their values, attitudes, and behaviors. If the discrepancy between their own ideas and those of their friends becomes too great, teens are more likely to move toward a more compatible group of friends than to be persuaded to shift toward the first group's values or behaviors. Furthermore, teenagers report that explicit peer pressure is most likely to be pressure toward positive activities, such as school involvement, and away from misconduct. Thus, while Erikson appears to be quite correct in saying that peers are a major force in shaping a child's identity development in adolescence, peer influence is neither monolithic nor uniformly negative (Berndt & Keefe, 1995; Brown, Dolcini, & Leventhal, 1995).

One important exception to this rather rosy view of the impact of peer pressure occurs among teens who spend time with peers who lean toward aggressive, delinquent, or disruptive behavior. Such peer subgroups often do provide explicit pressure toward misconduct or lawbreaking, to which some teens are susceptible. Whether an adolescent will be drawn to such a group in the first place, and whether he will be pushed toward more deviant behavior once he begins to "hang out" with such a group, appears to depend a good deal on his individual qualities—such as whether he has good social skills or has already shown some disruptive behavior before adolescence. For example, Frank Vitaro and his colleagues (1997) found that among a group of 868 boys they studied from age 11 to 13, those who had been moderately disruptive at age 11 were more likely to be delinquent at age 13 if they had had aggressive or disruptive friends at ages 11 and 12 than if their friends had been less aggressive or disruptive. Thus, those boys who were leaning toward bad behavior were drawn further in that direction by their friends. However, the boys in this study who were already showing highly disruptive behavior at age 11 most often continued with disruptive behavior at age 13, regardless of the type of friends they hung out with. These teenagers were already set on a course of negative behavior; their friendships with drug users or tough boys did not exacerbate that pattern, nor did nondeviant friends steer them away from delinquent behavior. Findings like these suggest that negative peer group influences primarily affect a particular group of marginal teens, perhaps especially those whose parents are ineffective in monitoring and discipline, or perhaps those who have insecure attachments to their parents (e.g., Dishion, French, & Patterson, 1995; Resnick et al., 1997).

Changes in Peer Group Structure in Adolescence

The structure of the peer group also changes over the years of adolescence. The classic, widely quoted early study is Dexter Dunphy's observation of the forma-

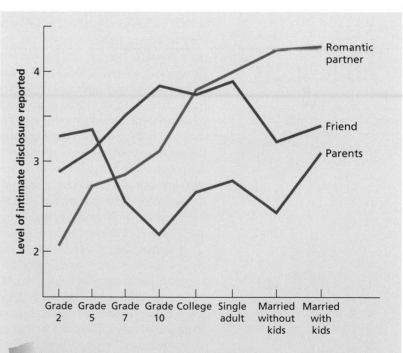

FIGURE 11.4

Before adolescence, parents are most often a child's closest confidants; in adolescence, it is peers in whom the young person confides.

(*Source*: From "Need Fulfillment, Interpersonal Competence, and the Developmental Context of Early Adolescent Friendship" by D. Buhrmester, *The company they keep: Friendship in childhood and adolescence*, W. M. Bukowski, A. F. Newcomb, and W. W. Hartup (eds.), p. 168, Fig. 8.2. © 1996 Cambridge University Press. By permission of Cambridge University Press.)

tion, dissolution, and interaction of teenage groups in a high school in Sydney, Australia, between 1958 and 1960 (Dunphy, 1963). Dunphy identified two important subvarieties of groups. The first type, which he called a **clique**, is made up of four to six young people who appear to be strongly attached to one another. Cliques have strong cohesiveness and high levels of intimate sharing. In the early years of adolescence, cliques are almost entirely same-sex groups—a residual of the preadolescent pattern. Gradually, however, cliques combine into larger sets Dunphy called **crowds**, which include both males and females. Finally, the crowd breaks down again into heterosexual cliques and then into loose associations of couples. In Dunphy's study, children associated with their peers in crowds between approximately ages 13 and 15—the very years when researchers have observed the greatest conformity to peer pressure.

Bradford Brown and other researchers have changed Dunphy's labels somewhat (Brown, 1990; Brown, Mory, & Kinney, 1994). Brown uses the word *crowd* to refer to the "reputation-based" group with which a young person is identified, either by choice or by peer designation. In most U.S. schools, there are any number of crowds—"jocks," "brains," "nerds," "dweebs," "punks," "druggies," "toughs," "normals," "populars," "preppies," or "loners." Studies in junior and senior high schools in the United States make it clear that teenagers can readily identify each of the major crowds in their school, and they offer quite stereotypic—even caricatured—descriptions of them (e.g., "The partiers goof off a lot more than the jocks do, but they don't come to school stoned like the burnouts do"). Each of these descriptions serves as what Brown calls an "identity prototype" (Brown et al., 1994, p. 133): Labeling others and labeling oneself as belonging to one or more of these groups help to create or reinforce the adolescent's own identity. Such labeling also helps the adolescent identify potential friends or foes. Thus, being identified as a member of one crowd or another channels each adolescent toward particular activities and particular relationships.

Within any given school, the various crowds are organized into a fairly clear, widely understood pecking order—that is, more status is attributed to some groups than to others. In U.S. schools, the groups labeled "jocks," "populars," or "normals" (or the equivalent) are typically at the top, with "brains" somewhere in the middle, and "druggies," "loners," and "nerds" at the bottom (Brown et al., 1994). Through the years of junior high and high school, the social system of crowds becomes increasingly differentiated, with more and more distinct groups. For example, in one Midwestern school system, David Kinney (1993) found that junior high students labeled only two major crowds: one small but high-status group (called "trendies" in this school) and the great mass of lower-status students, called "dweebs." A few years later, the same students named five distinct crowds, three with comparatively high social status and two with low status ("grits" and "punkers"). By late high school, these same students identified seven or eight crowds, but the crowds seemed to have become less significant in the students' social organization; mutual friendships and dating pairs had become more central (Urberg, Degirmencioglu, Tolson, & Halliday-Scher, 1995).

Furthermore, researchers have recently discovered that these informal self-groupings carry some significance for future behavior (Barber, Eccles, & Stone, 2001). For example, teens who belong to a "brains" crowd are more likely to graduate from college, and those who belong to a "criminals" group are more likely to engage in anti-social behavior after leaving high school. Thus, the high school crowd with which a given individual adolescent chooses to associate may be indicative of the sense of personal identity he or she will build on in adulthood.

Within (and sometimes across) these crowds, adolescents create smaller friendship groups Brown calls *cliques* (with a definition that is very similar to Dunphy's meaning for the same term). Brown, like Dunphy, notes that in early adolescence, cliques are almost entirely same-sex; by late adolescence, they have become mixed in gender, often composed of groups of dating couples.

Whatever specific clique or crowd a teenager may identify with, theorists agree that the peer group performs the highly important function of helping the teenager shift

CRITICAL THINKING

Think back to your high school years. Can you draw a diagram or a map to show the organization of crowds and cliques? Were those crowds and cliques more important or less important in the last years of high school than they had been earlier?

clique A group of four to six friends with strong affectional bonds and high levels of group solidarity and loyalty; the term is used by researchers to describe a self-chosen group of friends.

crowd A larger and looser group of friends than a clique, normally made up of several cliques that have joined together; a reputation-based group, common in adolescent subculture, with widely agreed-upon characteristics.

from friendships to "partner" social relationships. The 13- or 14-year-old can begin to try out her new relationship skills in the wider group of the clique or crowd. Only after the adolescent develops some confidence do the beginnings of dating and of more committed pair relationships become evident.

Romantic Relationships   Of all the changes in social relationships in adolescence, perhaps the most profound is the shift from the total dominance of same-sex friendships to heterosexual relationships (Richards, Crowe, Larson, & Swarr, 1998). By age 15 or 16, most teens in the United States have begun dating. The change happens gradually but proceeds at a somewhat more rapid pace in girls.

At the beginning of adolescence, teens are still fairly rigid about their preferences for same-sex friends (Bukowski, Sippola, & Hoza, 1999). Over the next year or two, they become more open to opposite-sex friendships (Harton & Latane, 1997; Kuttler, LaGreca, & Prinstein, 1999). The skills they gain in relating to opposite-sex peers in such friendships and in mixed-gender groups enable them to participate in romantic relationships (Feiring, 1999). Thus, while post-pubertal sexual desires are often assumed to be the basis of emergent romantic relationships, it appears that social factors are just as important. In fact, research suggests that social competence across a variety of relationships— with parents, peers, and friends—predicts the ease with which teens move from exclusive same-sex relationships to opposite-sex friendships and romantic relationships (Theriault, 1998).

At a certain age, children move from one kind of clique to another.

Besides their social importance, these new relationships are clearly part of the preparation for assuming a full adult sexual identity. Physical sexuality is part of that role, but so are the skills of personal intimacy with the opposite sex, including flirting, communicating, and reading the form of social cues used by the other gender. In Western societies, adolescents learn these skills first in larger crowds or cliques and then in dating pairs (Zani, 1993).

By age 12 or 13, most adolescents have a prototypical understanding of what it means to be "in love." Interestingly, even though the actual progression toward romantic relationships happens faster for girls, boys report having had the experience of falling in love for the first time at an earlier age. Moreover, by the end of adolescence, the average boy believes he has been in love several more times than the average girl (Montgomery & Sorell, 1998).

The sense of being in love is an important factor in adolescent dating patterns (Montgomery & Sorell, 1998). In other words, teenagers prefer to date those with whom they believe they are in love, and they view falling out of love as a reason for ending a dating relationship. In addition, for girls but not for boys, romantic relationships are seen as a context in which self-disclosure can take place. Put another way, girls seem to want more psychological intimacy from these early relationships than their partners do (Feiring, 1999).

Early dating and early sexual activity are more common among the poor of every ethnic group and among those who experience relatively early puberty. Religious teachings and individual attitudes about the appropriate age for dating and sexual behavior also make a difference, as does family structure. Girls from divorced or remarried families, for example, report earlier dating and higher levels of sexual experience than do girls from intact families, and those with a strong religious identity report later dating and lower levels of sexual experience (Bingham, Miller, & Adams, 1990; Miller &

Moore, 1990). But for every group, adolescence is a time of experimentation with romantic relationships.

SIBLING RELATIONSHIPS

Playmates and friends play a highly significant role in children's development, but so too can brothers and sisters. Sibling relationships are another important type of "horizontal" relationship. The Biblical story of Cain and Abel might lead us to believe that rivalry or jealousy is the key ingredient of sibling relationships. Certainly the birth of a new brother or sister radically changes the life of the older sibling. The parents have less time for the older child, who may feel neglected and angry; such feelings may lead both to more confrontations between the older child and the parents and to feelings of rivalry with the new baby (Furman, 1995).

Yet rivalry is not the only quality of early sibling relationships; observations of preschoolers interacting with their siblings point toward other ingredients as well. Toddlers and preschoolers help their brothers and sisters, imitate them, and share their toys. Judy Dunn, in a detailed longitudinal study of a group of 40 families in England, observed that the older child often imitated a baby brother or sister; by the time the younger child was a year old, however, he or she began imitating the older sibling, and from then on most of the imitation consisted of the younger child copying the older one (Dunn & Kendrick, 1982).

Young brothers and sisters also hit each other, snatch toys, and threaten and insult each other. The older child in a pair of preschoolers is likely to be the leader and is therefore likely to show more of both aggressive and helpful behaviors (Abramovitch, Pepler, & Corter, 1982). For both members of the pair, however, the dominant feature seems to be ambivalence. Both supportive and negative behaviors are evident in about equal proportions. In Abramovitch's research, such ambivalence occurred whether the pair were close in age or further apart and whether the older child was a boy or a girl. Naturally there are variations on this theme; some pairs show mostly antagonistic or rivalrous behaviors, and some show mostly helpful and supportive behaviors. Most sibling pairs show both types of behaviors.

How do those themes play out in middle childhood? As a general rule, sibling relationships seem to be less central in the lives of school-aged children than are relationships with either friends or parents (Buhrmester, 1992). Children of elementary school age are less likely to turn to a sibling for affection than to parents, and they are less likely to turn to a brother or sister for companionship or intimacy than they are to a friend.

Although this general rule seems to hold, sibling relationships also vary enormously. On the basis of direct studies of young children as well as retrospective reports by young adults about their sibling relationships when they were of school age, researchers have identified several patterns or styles of sibling relationships: (1) a *caregiver relationship*, in which one sibling serves as a kind of quasi-parent for the other, a pattern that seems to be more common between an older sister and younger brother than for any other combination of siblings; (2) a *buddy relationship*, in which both members of the pair try to be like one another and take pleasure in being together; (3) a *critical* or *conflictual relationship*, which includes attempts by one sibling to dominate the other, teasing, and quarreling; (4) a *rival relationship*, which contains many of the same elements as a critical relationship but is also low in any form of friendliness or support; and (5) a *casual* or *uninvolved relationship*, in which the siblings have relatively little to do with one another (Murphy, 1993; Stewart, Beilfuss, & Verbrugge, 1995). Rivalrous or critical relationships seem to be more common between siblings who are close together in age (4 or fewer years apart) and in families in which the parents are less satisfied with their marriage (Buhrmester & Furman, 1990; McGuire, McHale, & Updegraff, 1996). Buddy relationships appear to be somewhat more common in pairs of sisters (Buhrmester & Furman, 1990), while rivalry seems to be highest in boy-boy pairs (Stewart et al., 1995).

These patterns appear to vary somewhat when children care for themselves after school while their parents are working. The caregiver relationship predominates, with the older sibling typically given the caregiver role. Longitudinal research suggests that older siblings in such situations can help younger brothers and sisters acquire self-reliance skills (Brody, Kim, Murry, & Brown, 2003). Research also indicates that parents' ability to cope with work-related stress is enhanced by having an older child who is capable of caring for a younger sibling.

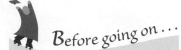

Before going on...
- What are the characteristics of infants' and preschoolers' peer interactions?
- How do peer relationships change during the school years?
- What are the characteristics and consequences of variations in social status?
- What is the significance of peer groups in adolescence?
- Describe the various types of sibling relationships.

Behavior with Peers

The broad sketch of peer relationships from toddlerhood through adolescence that you have just read makes clear the various roles that peers play in children's development over these years. It also points out how central such relationships are. What it does not convey are all the changes in the actual content and quality of children's peer interactions. To fill in some of the gaps, we will consider two specific categories of behavior representing two ends of a continuum: prosocial behavior and aggression.

PROSOCIAL BEHAVIOR

Prosocial behavior is defined by psychologists as "intentional, voluntary behavior intended to benefit another" (Eisenberg, 1992, p. 3). In everyday language, prosocial behavior is essentially what we mean by *altruism*, and it changes with age, just as other aspects of peer behavior change.

Prosocial behaviors first become evident in children of about 2 or 3—at about the same time they begin to show real interest in play with other children. They will offer to help another child who is hurt, offer a toy, or try to comfort another person (Eisenberg & Fabes, 1998; Zahn-Waxler & Radke-Yarrow, 1982; Zahn-Waxler, Radke-Yarrow, Wagner, & Chapman, 1992). As pointed out in Chapter 6, children this young are only beginning to understand that others feel differently than they do, but they obviously understand enough about the emotions of others to respond in supportive and sympathetic ways when they see other children or adults hurt or sad.

After these early years, researchers have noted a number of trends. Older children are more likely to share objects or money with others (such as donating marbles in the game described in Chapter 9). Older children and adolescents are also more likely than preschoolers to provide physical and verbal assistance to someone in need (Eisenberg, 1992). However, not all prosocial behaviors show this pattern of increase with age. Comforting another child, for example, appears to be more common among children in preschool and early elementary grades than among older children (Eisenberg, 1988, 1990).

Developmentalists also know that children vary a lot in the amount of altruistic behavior they show, and that young children who show relatively more empathy and altruism are also those who regulate their own emotions well. They show positive emotions readily and negative emotions less often (Eisenberg et al., 1996). They are also more popular with peers (Mayeux & Cillissen, 2003). These variations in children's levels of empathy or altruism seem to be related to specific kinds of child rearing (see *The Real World*).

prosocial behavior Voluntary behavior intended to benefit another, such as giving away or sharing possessions, money, or time, with no obvious self-gain; altruism.

The Real World

Rearing Helpful and Altruistic Children

Eight-year-old Marisol, perched on a kitchen stool that allowed her to reach the counter, slowly poured cake mix from the box into a large mixing bowl, taking care not to spill any. Her father, Rick, stood by her side ready to assist if his daughter needed help. "Good job," he said as the last of the mix fell into the bowl. "Now we add the eggs." With that, Rick painstakingly showed Marisol how to break an egg. Her first attempt ended with a bit too much shell finding its way into the bowl, so Rick showed her how to remove it. Rick thought to himself that the cake would be finished a lot sooner if he did it himself, without Marisol. But Rick was committed to helping his daughter learn the skills needed to be a contributing member of the Ruiz household.

Teaching children to be helpful can be time-consuming. Helping them learn to be altruistic—that is, to want to help others even when there is no reward involved—can be even more difficult. However, research on the development of prosocial behavior can provide insights into the process (Eisenberg, 1992; Eisenberg & Fabes, 1998; Eisenberg & Murphy, 1995; Grusec, Goodnow, & Cohen, 1996):

- *Capitalize on the child's capacity for empathy.* If your child injures someone, point out the consequences of that injury for the other person: "When you hit Susan, it hurts her" or "See, you made Jimmy cry." This strategy seems to be especially effective when parents use it regularly, when they express their feelings strongly, and when they don't combine it with physical punishment.
- *Create a loving and warm family climate.* When parents express affection and warmth regularly toward their children, the children are more likely to be generous and altruistic.
- *Provide rules or guidelines about helpful behavior.* Clear rules about what to do as well as what not to do are important: "It's always good to be helpful to other people" or "We should share what we have with people who don't have so much." More direct instructions also foster prosocial behavior: "I'd like you to help Keisha with her puzzle" or "Please share your candy with John."
- *Provide prosocial attributions.* Attribute your child's helpful or altruistic action to the child's own internal character: "You're such a helpful child!" or "You certainly do a lot of nice things for other people." This strategy begins to be effective with children at about age 7 or 8, when they are beginning to develop global notions of self-esteem.
- *Have children do helpful things.* Assign them regular household tasks such as helping to cook or clean, taking care of pets, or watching younger siblings. It doesn't seem to matter exactly what the tasks are; what matters is that the child has a regular role in everyday household routines. Having a role to play seems to encourage the development of concern for others as well as a sense of responsibility.
- *Model thoughtful and generous behavior.* Stating the rules will do little good if parents' own behavior does not match what they say! Children (and adults) are simply much more likely to do generous or thoughtful things if they see other people—especially other people in authority, such as parents—being generous and thoughtful.

Having children do helpful things, as these third-graders are doing by sorting recyclable material, is one way to increase altruistic behavior in kids.

Questions for Reflection

1. How might teachers and parents model generosity?
2. Why do you think that a loving and warm family climate promotes altruistic behavior?

AGGRESSION

If you have watched children in pairs or groups, you know that all is not sweetness and light in the land of the young. Children do support and share with their friends, and they do show affectionate and helpful behaviors toward one another, but they also tease, fight, yell, criticize, and argue over objects and territory. Researchers who have studied this more negative side of children's interactions have looked mostly at **aggression**, which can be defined as behavior apparently intended to injure some other person or object.

TABLE 11.3	Percentage of Boys and Girls Aged 4 to 11 Rated by Their Teachers as Displaying Aggressive Behavior	
Behavior	**Boys**	**Girls**
Mean to others	21.8	9.6
Physically attacks people	18.1	4.4
Gets in many fights	30.9	9.8
Destroys own things	10.7	2.1
Destroys others' things	10.6	4.4
Threatens to hurt people	13.1	4.0

Source: Offord et al., 1991, from Table 2.3, p. 39.

Instrumental and Hostile Aggression   Every child shows at least some aggression, but the form and frequency of aggression change over the years of childhood. When 2- or 3-year-old children are upset or frustrated, they are more likely to throw things or to hit each other. Typically, children of this age behave aggressively in order to achieve a goal, such as getting a toy from another child. This kind of aggression is known as **instrumental aggression**. Once the goal is achieved, the aggression stops.

As their verbal skills improve, children shift away from overt physical aggression toward greater use of verbal aggression, such as taunting or name-calling. The purpose of aggression changes as well. Among older preschoolers, **hostile aggression**, the goal of which is to hurt another's feelings rather than to do physical harm, becomes more common. In the elementary school and adolescent years, physical aggression becomes still less common, and children learn the cultural rules about when it is acceptable to display anger or aggression and how much one can acceptably display. In most cultures, this means that anger is increasingly disguised and aggression is increasingly controlled with increasing age (Underwood, Coie, & Herbsman, 1992).

Sex Differences in Aggression   One interesting exception to the general pattern of declining physical aggression with age is that in all-boy pairs or groups, at least in the United States, physical aggression seems to remain both relatively high and constant over the years of childhood. Indeed, at every age, boys show more physical aggression and more assertiveness than do girls, both within friendship pairs and in general (Coie & Dodge, 1998). Table 11.3 gives some highly representative data from a very large, careful survey in Canada (Offord, Boyle, & Racine, 1991) in which both parents and teachers completed checklists describing each child's behavior. Table 11.3 lists only the information provided by teachers, but parent ratings yielded parallel findings. It is clear that boys were described as far more aggressive on nearly any measure of physical aggressiveness.

The social consequences of aggressive behavior vary with gender as well. For girls, aggression seems to lead consistently to peer rejection. Among boys, however, aggression may result in either popularity or rejection (Rodkin, Farmer, Pearl, & Van Acker, 2000; Xie, Cairns, & Cairns, 1999). In fact, aggressiveness seems to be a fairly common characteristic of popular African American boys. In addition, irrespective of their general popularity, the close friends of aggressive boys tend to be aggressive as well. Furthermore, aggressiveness seems to precede these relationships. In other words, boys who are aggressive seek out other boys like themselves as friends, and being friends doesn't seem to make either member of an aggressive friendship pair more aggressive (Poulin & Boivin, 2000). Research also suggests that children have more positive attitudes toward aggressive peers whose aggressive acts are seen as mostly retaliatory in nature and toward those who engage in prosocial as well as aggressive behaviors (Coie &

aggression Behavior that is aimed at harming or injuring another person or object.

instrumental aggression Aggressive behavior intended to achieve a goal, such as obtaining a toy from another child.

hostile aggression Aggressive verbal behavior intended to hurt another's feelings.

Bullies and Victims

At first glance, aggressive interactions among children might appear to be fairly simple: One child hurts another child. However, research shows that, across the middle childhood years, aggressive interactions become increasingly complex (Hay, Payne, & Chadwick, 2004). As children get older, they tend to take on consistent roles across aggressive interactions—perpetrator, victim, assistant to the perpetrator, reinforcing onlooker, nonparticipant onlooker, defender of the victim, and so on (Andreou & Metallidou, 2004). Children's personality traits to some degree determine the roles they assume. For example, shy children usually occupy the nonparticipant onlooker role, while children who are emotionally unstable are more likely to serve as assistants to the perpetrator or as reinforcing onlookers (Tani, Greenman, Schneider, & Fregoso, 2003). The occupant of each of these roles plays a part in maintaining a particular aggressive incident and in determining whether another aggressive interaction involving the same perpetrator and victim will occur in the future.

Until fairly recently, both research on and interventions aimed at reducing aggression focused on the habitual perpetrators, or bullies. However, most developmentalists now believe that changing the behavior of children who occupy other roles in aggressive interactions, especially those who are habitual victims of aggression, may be just as important as intervening with aggressive children themselves (Green, 2001). Dan Olweus (1995) has done the most significant work on bullies and victims. His studies in Sweden indicate that as many as 9% of elementary school children are regularly victims, while 7% could be called bullies—percentages confirmed in studies in other countries (e.g., Perry, Kusel, & Perry, 1988).

Victims have certain characteristics in common, including anxiety, passivity, sensitivity, low self-esteem or self-confidence, lack of humor, and comparative lack of friends (Egan & Perry, 1998; Hodges, Malone, & Perry, 1997; Olweus, 1995). Cross-cultural studies show that these characteristics are found among habitual victims across a wide variety of cultural settings (Eslea et al., 2004). Among boys, victims are also often physically smaller or weaker than their peers. Whether boys or girls, victims seldom assert themselves with their peers, making neither suggestions for play activities nor prosocial actions. Instead, they submit to whatever suggestions others make. Other children do not like this behavior

and thus do not like the victims (Crick & Grotpeter, 1996; Schwartz, Dodge, & Coie, 1993). The consequences of such victimization can include loneliness, school avoidance, low self-esteem, and significant depression at later ages (Kochenderfer & Ladd, 1996; Olweus, 1995).

Still, not all children faced with a passive and unresponsive playmate turn into bullies. Bullies are distinctive because they are typically aggressive in a variety of situations, not just in relationships with selected victims. Bullies also tend to be more aggressive toward adults than do nonbullies, cannot empathize with their victims' pain or unhappiness, feel little or no guilt or shame about their actions, and are often impulsive (Menesini et al., 2003). Olweus's studies do not support the common assumption that bullies are basically insecure children who have developed a tough exterior to cover up their insecurity. In fact, the opposite appears to be true. Bullies most often have low levels of anxiety and insecurity. Olweus proposes that four factors lie behind the development of bullying behavior:

- Indifference toward the child and lack of warmth from the parents in the early years
- Failure by parents to set clear and adequate limits on aggressive behavior
- The parents' use of physical punishment
- A difficult, impulsive temperament in the child

If you look back at Figure 1.2 on page 11 and compare the above list to the factors Gerald Patterson has identified as contributors to the development of delinquent behavior in adolescents, you'll see a great many similarities. Clearly, however, bullying is a complex phenomenon that must be understood as resulting from characteristics of bullies themselves, the family environments in which they are being raised, and the social settings in which bullying incidents occur (Ahmed & Braithwaite, 2004; Rigby, 2005).

Questions for Critical Analysis

1. How might a child's temperament influence parents to exhibit the kinds of parental behaviors Olweus has found to be associated with bullying?
2. Based on the research discussed above, what characteristics should be included in a checklist designed to help teachers and parents identify children who are at high risk of becoming perpetual victims?

Cillessen, 1993; Newcomb, Bukowski, & Pattee, 1993; Poulin & Boivin, 1999). Social approval may not increase boys' aggressiveness, but it does seem to help maintain it, because interventions to reduce aggressive behavior typically have little effect on aggressive boys who are popular (Phillips, Schwean, & Saklofske, 1997). Moreover, the behavior of aggressive boys is often linked to the availability of socially weak and passive peers to serve as victims (see the *Research Report*).

Relational Aggression   The findings of studies examining sex differences in aggression have been so clear and so consistent that most psychologists have concluded that boys are simply "more aggressive" in every possible way. But that conclusion may turn out to be wrong, or at least misleading. Instead, it appears that girls express aggressiveness in a different way, using what has been labeled relational aggression instead of either physical aggression or nasty words (Crick, Casas, & Mosher, 1997; Crick & Grotpeter, 1995; Rys & Bear, 1997; Tomada & Schneider, 1997). Physical aggression hurts others through physical damage or threat of such damage; **relational aggression** is aimed at damaging another person's self-esteem or peer relationships, such as by cruel gossiping, by making facial expressions of disdain, or by ostracizing or threatening to ostracize the other ("I won't invite you to my birthday party if you do that"). Another important difference between hostile and relational aggression is that acts of hostile aggression are more likely to draw adult attention, especially when they involve hitting or other actions that can cause physical harm. Consequently, they may occur less frequently than acts of relational aggression. By contrast, children can engage in relational aggression in ways that escape the notice of adults—such as passing notes containing derogatory statements about peers or subtly moving away from a child who is the target of aggression during recess. As a result, some children may become habitual victims of relational aggression.

Girls are much more likely to use relational aggression than are boys, especially toward other girls, a difference that begins as early as the preschool years and becomes very marked by the fourth or fifth grade. For example, in one study of nearly 500 children in the third through sixth grades, Nicki Crick found that 17.4% of the girls but only 2% of the boys were high in relational aggression—almost precisely the reverse of the rates of physical aggression (Crick & Grotpeter, 1995).

What might be the origins of such sex differences in the form of aggression used? One obvious possibility is that hormone differences play a part. For one thing, higher rates of physical aggression in males have been observed in every human society and in all species of primates. There is some evidence of a link between rates of physical aggression and testosterone levels in males (e.g., Susman et al., 1987), particularly in adolescence and later. Thus, differing rates of physical aggression appear to have at least some biological basis. However, peer reinforcement may also play a role. Researchers have found that children as young as 3 years of age believe that girls are more likely to display relational aggression and boys are more likely to show physical aggression (Giles & Heyman, 2005). Thus, just as children encourage their peers to engage in other types of stereotypical behavior, they may provide rewards for boys and girls who display gender-appropriate aggressive behaviors. Likewise, they may actively sanction peers of both sexes for engaging in gender-inappropriate forms of aggression.

TRAIT AGGRESSION

Earlier in this chapter, you learned that aggressive behavior tends to decrease with age. However, there are a few children, most of them boys, for whom a high level of aggressive behavior in early childhood is predictive of a lifelong pattern of antisocial behavior, a finding that has been supported by cross-cultural research (Derzon, 2001; Hart, Olsen, Robinson, & Mandleco, 1997; Henry, Caspi, Moffitt, & Silva, 1996; Kosterman, Graham, Hawkins, Catalano, & Herrenkohl, 2001; Newman, Caspi, Moffitt, & Silva,

CRITICAL THINKING

Can you think of ways that adults exhibit relational aggression? Do sex differences in types of aggression appear to persist into the adult years? In other words, do men exhibit relational aggression as frequently or less frequently than women?

relational aggression Aggression aimed at damaging another person's self-esteem or peer relationships, such as by using ostracism or threats of ostracism, cruel gossiping, or facial expressions of disdain.

1997). Researchers have searched for causes of this kind of aggression, which psychologists often refer to as *trait aggression*, to distinguish it from developmentally normal forms of aggression.

Some psychologists have looked for a genetic basis for trait aggression and have produced some supportive data (Hudziak et al., 2003; Plomin, 1990; Rowe, 2003; van Beijsterveldt, Bartels, Hudziak, & Boomsma, 2003). Others suggest that trait aggression is associated with being raised in an aggressive environment, such as an abusive family (Dodge, 1993). Family factors other than abuse, such as lack of affection and the use of coercive discipline techniques, also appear to be related to trait aggression, especially in boys (Chang, Schwartz, Dodge, & McBride-Chang, 2003; McFayden-Ketchum, Bates, Dodge, & Pettit, 1996).

Still other developmentalists have discovered evidence that aggressive children may shape their environments in order to gain continuing reinforcement for their behavior. For example, as early as 4 years of age, aggressive boys tend to prefer other aggressive boys as playmates and to form stable peer groups with them. These groups develop their own patterns of interaction and reward each other with social approval for aggressive acts (Farver, 1996). This pattern of association among aggressive boys continues through middle childhood and adolescence.

Finally, a large body of research suggests that highly aggressive children lag behind their peers in understanding others' intentions (Crick & Dodge, 1994). Research demonstrating that teaching aggressive children how to think about others' intentions reduces aggressive behavior also supports this conclusion (Crick & Dodge, 1996; Webster-Stratton & Reid, 2003). Specifically, this research suggests that aggressive school-aged children seem to reason more like 2- to 3-year-olds about intentions. For example, they are likely to perceive a playground incident (such as one child accidentally tripping another during a soccer game) as an intentional act that requires retaliation. Training helps aggressive school-aged children acquire an understanding of others' intentions that most children learn between the ages of 3 and 5. Thus, trait aggression may originate in some kind of deviation from the typical developmental path during the early childhood period.

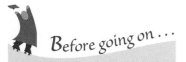

Before going on . . .

■ What are the various elements of prosocial behavior, and how do children acquire them?
■ Define three different forms of aggression, and describe sex differences in their exhibition.
■ What is trait aggression, and how does it differ from developmentally normal forms of aggression?

Summary

Relationships with Parents

● Bowlby and Ainsworth distinguished between an affectional bond (an enduring tie to a partner viewed as unique) and an attachment, which involves feelings of security and having a safe base. An attachment is deduced from the existence of attachment behaviors.

● For parents to form a strong bond to their infant, what is most crucial is not immediate contact at birth but the development and repetition of mutually reinforcing and interlocking attachment behaviors.

● Bowlby proposed that the child's attachment to the caregiver develops through a series of steps, beginning with rather indiscriminate aiming of attachment behaviors toward anyone within reach, through a focus on one or more figures, and finally secure base behavior, beginning at about 6 months of age, which signals the presence of a clear attachment. Attachment behaviors become less visible during the preschool years, except when the child is stressed. By age 4 or 5, the child understands the constancy of the attachment relationship.

● The child's basic attachment to the parents remains strong in adolescence, despite an increase in parent-child conflict, the greater independence of the teenager, and the increased role of the peer group.

Variations in the Quality of Attachments

● Children differ in the security of their first attachments and thus in the internal working models they develop.

● The secure infant uses the parent as a safe base for exploration and can be readily consoled by the parent.

● The security of an initial attachment is reasonably stable and is fostered by sensitivity and contingent responsiveness by the parent. Securely attached children appear to be more socially skillful, more curious and persistent in approaching new tasks, and more mature.

● An infant's temperament may also affect attachment. Infants who have difficult temperaments are more likely to form insecure attachments.

- An adult's internal working model of attachment, based on the security of his or her own attachment to parents in childhood, influences parenting behavior.

Relationships with Peers

- Children's relationships with peers become increasingly significant for their social development after the age of about 2. In elementary school, peer interactions are focused mostly on common activities; in adolescence, peer groups also become a vehicle for the transition from dependence to independence.
- By age 4 or 5, most children have formed individual friendships and show preferential positive behavior toward their friends. Friendships become more common and more stable in the elementary school years, and more intimate in adolescence.
- Popularity among peers, in elementary school or later, is most consistently based on the amount of positive and supportive social behavior shown by a child toward peers. Socially rejected children are often characterized by high levels of aggression or bullying and low levels of agreement and helpfulness. Aggressive/rejected children are likely to show behavior problems in adolescence and a variety of disturbances in adulthood.

- Reputation-based groups, or crowds, are an important part of adolescent social relationships, particularly in the early high school years. Smaller groups of friends, or cliques, are also significant and gradually shift from being same-sex groups to mixed-sex groups to dating pairs. On average in Western cultures, dating begins at about age 15, but there is wide variability.
- Sibling relationships are often thought of as rivalrous, but there are many variations.

Behavior with Peers

- Prosocial behavior, such as helpfulness or generosity, is apparent as early as age 2 or 3 and generally increases throughout childhood.
- Physical aggression peaks at age 3 or 4 and is gradually replaced by more verbal aggression among older children. Boys show more physical aggressiveness at every age; girls show more relational aggression.
- Some children develop a pattern of aggressive behavior, known as trait aggression, that continues to cause problems for them throughout childhood and adolescence.

Key Terms

affectional bond (p. 304)
aggression (p. 329)
attachment (p. 304)
attachment behaviors (p. 304)
clique (p. 324)
crowd (p. 324)
goal-corrected partnership (p. 308)
goodness-of-fit (p. 316)

hostile aggression (p. 329)
individuation (p. 309)
insecure attachment (p. 312)
instrumental aggression (p. 329)
internal working model (p. 311)
neglected children (p. 320)
parallel play (p. 318)
popular children (p. 320)

prosocial behavior (p. 327)
reciprocal friendship (p. 319)
rejected children (p. 320)
relational aggression (p. 331)
secure attachment (p. 312)
social status (p. 320)
Strange Situation (p. 311)

Safe Base Behavior

A playground where toddlers and preschoolers are playing while their parents watch would be an ideal place to carry out a naturalistic observation of safe base behavior. Before you observe any children and parents, be sure to introduce yourself to the parents and explain that you are doing an assignment for your child development class. For a set period of time—say, 15 minutes—observe an individual child and note how many times he or she looks at, speaks to, or moves toward the parent. Repeat the procedure for several other children. Categorize the children as younger or older and compare the number of safe base behaviors for each age group. You should find that the younger children are, the more frequently they make contact with the parent (their safe base).

Development of the Social Convoy

You may find it interesting to replicate Mary Levitt's study of attachment in children and adolescents, described on page 310. First, draw three concentric circles on a sheet of paper and make a few copies. Second, after getting their parents' permission, ask children ranging in age from 7 to 14 to write the names of the people who are most important to them in the innermost circle. Then, tell them to write in the next circle the names of people they like but not in the same way as they do the people in the center circle. Finally, ask your study participants to write in the outermost circle the names of people they spend time with but don't feel particularly close to. In the next phase of the study, ask children how each person whose name they wrote on the paper helps them. Your data should include the relationship categories of all the people children named in each circle. Compare the categories that appear in children's inner circles to those that appear in the inner circles of teenagers. Note any age differences in the presence of parents and peers in the various circles. Your data should also include age-related comparisons of the kind of support each participant gets from the various individuals named. Finally, compare your results to those of Levitt, which are shown in Figure 11.2 on page 310.

Thinking about Relationships: Social-Cognitive and Moral Development

One rarely turns on the television or picks up a newspaper nowadays without encountering some kind of discussion of moral decline.

Increases in the frequency of heinous crimes, together with examples of rude behavior in everyday life, are cited in support of the proposition that society, at least in the West, is less civil than in days gone by. The answer to this problem, some say, is to incorporate *character education* into our schools. Critics, however, point out that ours is a pluralistic, multicultural society. Thus, emphasizing one group's notion of good character over another's might be offensive to some. Advocates of character education counter that there is a common set of values to which all human beings subscribe and that these values should form the core of a formal character education curriculum.

There is some evidence to support the position taken by those who advocate universal character education. Consider, for example, the case of the Kew Primary School in Invercargill, New Zealand (Heenan, 2005). Administrators and teachers at the school were frustrated by the limited success they achieved using behavioral methods such as reinforcement and punishment in their attempts to control troublesome student behaviors such as bullying. They sought an alternative that would help each student construct an internal sense of right and wrong, in the hope that this sense, which they called *character*, would lessen the need for behavioral control measures. A parent survey was one part of the process they used to develop a character education curriculum, because they wanted to be sure that the program included standards and values to which all of their students' families subscribed.

The results of the survey were astonishing, especially given the diverse nature of the school's population. Officials found that 95% of parents approved of their efforts to incorporate character education into the school's academic curriculum. Moreover, values such as truthfulness, honesty, and willingness to accept responsibility for one's actions were endorsed by 100% of parents. Endorsement of values such as respect for others' rights and property, politeness, courtesy, and kindness approached unanimity as well.

Such findings have led a number of educators to develop character education curricula that can be used by any school, regardless of the cultural make-up of its student body. One curriculum has been authored by developmental psychologist Thomas Lickona of the State University of New York at Cortland. For more than 20 years, Lickona has been writing books designed to help parents and teachers apply the findings of developmental research to the task of educating for character. Over the same period, he has participated in numerous studies of the effects of character education on school climate and on individual behavior.

Most recently, Lickona has advocated an approach to character education based on the assumption that ten essential virtues comprise character (Lickona, 2004). The ten virtues are wisdom, justice, fortitude, self-control, love, a positive attitude, hard work, integrity, gratitude, and humility. Lickona claims that, although maturational and developmental processes play important roles in the development of character, for the most part it must be deliberately and systematically transmitted to children by caring adults. His research has shown that when character education is implemented in a school, the frequency of undesirable behaviors declines. And as an added bonus, academic achievement tends to go up.

As a developmental scientist, Lickona argues that character education, like any other kind of instruction, must be based on a sound understanding of child develop-

ment. A developmentally appropriate approach to character education, whether it occurs in one's family home or in a school with hundreds of pupils, begins with an understanding that how individuals think about relationships, a process called *social
cognition*, is at the heart of character. Thus, we begin this chapter with a discussion of
how thinking about social relationships changes over the years of childhood and adolescence and end with an examination of moral development, the process of learning
to distinguish between right and wrong in accordance with cultural values.

The Development of Social Cognition

The topic of **social cognition** should not be entirely new to you. You have read
about many facets of social cognition in previous chapters. The infant's emerging
ability to recognize individuals and to use facial expressions and other body language
for social referencing is one kind of social cognition, as is the growing understanding of
others' emotions and the development of a theory of mind in the preschool years. One
could also argue that an internal working model of attachment is a kind of social cognition, as is the child's self-scheme. However, there are a few other important components of social cognition. Before we consider them, it's important that you understand
a few basic principles.

SOME GENERAL PRINCIPLES AND ISSUES

One way to think about social cognition is simply to conceive of it as the application of
general cognitive processes or skills to a different topic—in this case, people or relationships. In Chapter 6, you learned about how children's thinking changes from infancy through adolescence. At any given age, a child might simply apply her current
ways of thinking to her relationships and to people as well as to objects. In this view,
the child's understanding of self and others, of social relationships, reflects or is based
on her overall level of cognitive development, such as her level of perspective-taking
skills (Rubin, Coplan, Chen, Baskirk, & Wojslawowica, 2005; Selman, 1980).

This approach has a powerful intuitive appeal. After all, as John Flavell points out
(1985), it is the same head doing the thinking whether a child works on a conservation
problem or tries to understand people. Furthermore, as you will see very clearly as we
go through the evidence, many of the same principles that seem to apply to general
cognitive development hold for social cognitive development as well; that is, children's
social cognition develops in certain directions:

- *From outer to inner characteristics.* Younger children pay attention to the surface of
  things, to what things look like; older children look for principles, for causes.
- *From observation to inference.* Young children initially base their conclusions only
  on what they can see or feel; as they grow, they make inferences about what ought
  to be or what might be.
- *From definite to qualified.* Young children's "rules" are very definite and fixed (such
  as sex-role rules); by adolescence, rules begin to be qualified.
- *From observer's view to general view.* Children become less egocentric with time—
  less tied to their own individual views, more able to construct a model of some experience or some process that is true for everyone.

All of these dimensions of change describe children's emerging social cognition,
just as they describe the development of thinking about objects. But thinking about
people or relationships also has some special features that makes it different from
thinking about physical objects.

> **social cognition** Thinking about
> and understanding the emotions
> of and interactions and relation-
> ships among people.

CRITICAL THINKING ?

Think for a minute about how you can tell when someone else is concealing some feeling. What clues do you use? How sure can you be of your interpretation?

One obvious difference is that people, unlike rocks or glasses of water, behave intentionally. In particular, people often attempt to conceal information about themselves; thus, the ability to "read" other people's cues is a key social-cognitive skill. Further, unlike relationships with objects, relationships with people are mutual and reciprocal. Dolls, sets of blocks, or bicycles don't talk back, get angry, or respond in unexpected ways, but people do all these things. In learning about relationships, children must learn enough about other people's motives and feelings to predict such responses.

Children also have to learn special rules about particular forms of social interactions—such as rules about politeness, about when you can and cannot speak, and about power or dominance hierarchies—all of which are forms of social scripts (Schank & Abelson, 1977). The existence of such scripts allows children to develop strong expectations about how people will behave, in what order, in which settings. Furthermore, these scripts probably change with age, not just because children's cognitive skills change, but also simply because the rules (scripts) themselves change from one social setting to another. One obvious example is the set of changes that occurs when children start school. The script associated with the role of "student" is quite different from the one connected with the role of "little kid." Classrooms are more tightly organized, expectations for obedience are higher, and there are more drills and routines to be learned than was probably true at home or even in day care or nursery school. The school script changes when the young adolescent moves into junior high school and then again when she enters high school.

These illustrations make it clear that the development of sophisticated social cognition is more than a simple process of applying basic cognitive processes and strategies to the arena of social interaction. The child must also come to understand the ways in which social relationships are different from interactions with the physical world, and she must learn special rules and strategies. Let's begin with the child's growing ability to describe other people.

DESCRIBING OTHER PEOPLE

Research suggests that there is a shift from observation (what children see) to inference (how they interpret what they see) in children's descriptions of others, as well as a clear change in focus from outer to internal characteristics. There seem to be at least three steps. Up to perhaps ages 6 to 8, children's descriptions of others are focused almost exclusively on external features. Children in this age range describe others' hair color, their relative size, their gender, where they live, and what they like to do. Race is another characteristic that frequently crops up in such descriptions (see *The Real World*). This description by a 7-year-old boy, taken from a classic study in England by Livesley and Bromley, is typical:

> He is very tall. He has dark brown hair, he goes to our school. I don't think he has any brothers or sisters. He is in our class. Today he has a dark orange [sweater] and gray trousers and brown shoes. (1973, p. 213)

When young children do use internal or evaluative terms to describe people, they are likely to use quite global terms, such as *nice* or *mean* and *good* or *bad*. Further, young children do not seem to see these qualities as lasting or general traits of the individual, applicable in all situations or over time (Rholes & Ruble, 1984). In other words, the young child has not yet developed a concept that might be thought of as "conservation of personality."

Then, beginning at about age 7 or 8, at just about the time children seem to develop a global sense of self-esteem, a rather dramatic shift occurs in their descriptions of others. They begin to focus more on the inner traits or qualities of another person and to assume that those traits will be apparent in many situations (Gnepp & Chilamkurti, 1988). Children this age still describe others' physical features, but such descriptions seem to be

The Real World

Learning and Unlearning Racial Prejudice

Mara was excited about her new job teaching first grade in a public school that had a multi-ethnic student population. She became concerned on her first day, however, when she overheard many of the 6-year-olds in her class making remarks about one another's race. Even more alarming to her was her young pupils' tendency to sort themselves according to race and to express dismay when a child of a different race sat by them or tried to join their games. Mara wanted to know how she could help her students learn to be more tolerant.

The classroom is often the only setting in which children of different races come together. Consequently, these classrooms are likely to be important to the development of racial attitudes. Teachers, then, need to be aware of how such attitudes are formed.

Research suggests that racial schemas are well established by age 5 (Pezdek, Blandon-Gitlin, & Moore, 2003). Once these schemas are formed, children use them to make judgments about others. These early judgments probably reflect young children's egocentric thinking. Essentially, children view those like themselves as desirable companions and those who are unlike them—in gender, race, and other categorical variables—as undesirable (Doyle & Aboud, 1995). There is some evidence that these judgments increase in strength as children move through the elementary school years (Nesdale, Durkin, Maass, & Griffiths, 2005). These findings suggest that the characteristics of Piaget's concrete operational stage, the goal of which is to construct a mental model of the outside world, may contribute to school-aged children's tendency to attribute an inappropriate amount of importance to external traits such as race.

Of course, cognitive development doesn't happen in a social vacuum, and by age 5, most white children in English-speaking countries have acquired an understanding of their culture's racial stereotypes and prejudices (Bigler & Liben, 1993). Likewise, African American, Hispanic American, and Native American children become sensitive very early in life to the fact that people of their race are viewed negatively by many whites. Some studies suggest that this early awareness of racial stereotypes negatively influences minority children's self-esteem (Jambunathan & Burts, 2003). Moreover, minority children report a significant number of race-based events to their parents (Bernhard, Lefebvre, Kilbride, Chud, & Lange, 1998).

Psychologists speculate that the combination of immature cognitive development, acquisition of cultural stereotypes, and teachers' insensitivity to racial incidents may foster prejudicial attitudes. The key to preventing racial awareness from developing into racial prejudice, they say, is for preschool teachers to discuss race openly and to make conscious efforts to help children acquire non-prejudiced attitudes (Cushner, McClelland, & Safford, 1992). For example, they can make young children aware of historical realities such as slavery, race segregation, and minority groups' efforts to achieve equal rights. Teachers can also assign children of different races to do projects together. In addition, they can make children aware of each other's strengths as individuals, since both children and adults seem to perceive individual differences only within their own racial group (Ostrom, Carpenter, Sedikides, & Li, 1993).

Ideally, all children should learn to evaluate their own and others' behavior according to individual criteria rather than group membership, and minority children need to be especially encouraged to view their race positively. Preschool teachers are in a position to provide young children with a significant push toward these important goals.

Questions for Reflection

1. How might Mara implement some of the strategies suggested here for reducing prejudice in her classroom?
2. In your view, what is the role of entertainment media in the development of racial prejudice?

---

intended more as examples or elaborations of more general points about internal qualities. You can see the change when you compare the 7-year-old's description above with this (widely quoted) description by a child who is nearly 10:

> He smells very much and is very nasty. He has no sense of humour and is very dull. He is always fighting and he is cruel. He does silly things and is very stupid. He has brown hair and cruel eyes. He is sulky and 11 years old and has lots of sisters. I think he is the most horrible boy in the class. He has a croaky voice and always chews his pencil and picks his teeth and I think he is disgusting. (Livesley & Bromley, 1973, p. 217)

A preschool child would no doubt label this boy's emotion as "sad." A teenager would understand that the emotion might be much more complicated, such as sadness mixed with anger at himself or some other form of ambivalence.

This description still includes many external, physical features, but it goes beyond such concrete surface qualities to the level of personality traits, such as a lack of humor or cruelty.

In adolescence, young people's descriptions begin to include more comparisons of one trait with another or one person with another, more recognition of inconsistencies and exceptions, more shadings of gray (Shantz, 1983), as in this description by a 15-year-old:

> Andy is very modest. He is even shyer than I am when near strangers and yet is very talkative with people he knows and likes. He always seems good tempered and I have never seen him in a bad temper. He tends to degrade other people's achievements, and yet never praises his own. He does not seem to voice his opinions to anyone. He easily gets nervous. (Livesley & Bromley, 1973, p. 221)

Some findings from two early studies by Carl Barenboim illustrate these changes (1977, 1981). He asked children ranging in age from 6 to 16 to describe three people. Any descriptions that involved comparing a child's behaviors or physical features with another child, or with a norm, he called *behavioral comparisons* (such as "Billy runs a lot faster than Jason" or "She draws the best in our whole class"). Statements that involved some internal personality construct he called *psychological constructs* (such as "Sarah is so kind" or "He's a real stubborn idiot!"); any that included qualifiers, explanations, exceptions, or mentions of changes in character he called *organizing relationships* (e.g., "He's only shy around people he doesn't know" or "Usually she's nice to me, but sometimes she can be quite mean"). Figure 12.1 shows the combined findings from the two studies. You can see that behavioral comparisons were most common at around age 8 or 9, psychological constructs increased with age, and organizing relationships did not appear at all until age 10 and were still increasing at age 16.

You may have noticed the strong resemblance between this series of changes and the development of children's self-descriptions outlined in Chapter 10 (Figure 10.2). This parallel illustrates Flavell's basic point, that it is the same head doing the thinking about self and about others.

READING OTHERS' FEELINGS

Both cognitive skill and social information are obviously involved in understanding others' emotions. You need to be able to identify various body signals, including facial expressions; you need to understand various kinds of emotions and know that it is possible for people to feel several emotions at the same time; you need to understand the social context; and you need to have a theory of mind that helps you link the context with the other person's likely feelings. For example, you need the basic understanding that another person will be happy or sad depending on how well he does at something important to him.

Research on children's understanding of others' emotions suggests that they acquire these various forms of knowledge gradually over the years from about age 1 to adolescence (Pons, Harris, & de Rosnay, 2004; Thompson & Goodvin, 2005). You already know from Chapter 5 that by 10 to 12 months of age, babies can tell the difference between positive and negative facial and vocal expressions—at that age, they already show social referencing behavior. By age 3 or 4, the child's emotion-recognition repertoire has expanded considerably, and she has some preliminary understanding of the links between other people's emotions and their situations, such as that someone would be sad if she failed. And by age 10, the child understands and can read some emotional blends, even expressions of ambivalence.

Individual Differences in Emotion Knowledge   Not all children (or all adults) are equally skilled in their ability to read other people's emotions, a point em-

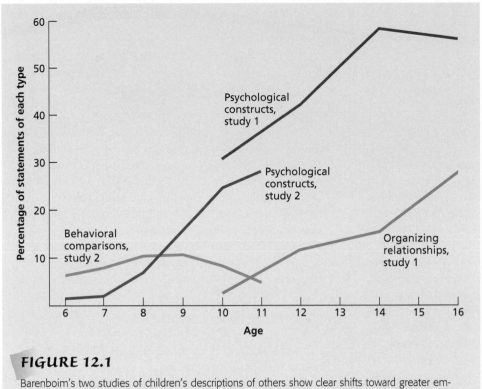

FIGURE 12.1

Barenboim's two studies of children's descriptions of others show clear shifts toward greater emphasis on psychological constructs. Study 1 involved children aged 10 to 16; study 2 involved children 6 to 11.

(*Source*: Barenboim, C., from Fig. 1, p. 134, "The development of person perception in childhood and adolescence" from "Behavioral comparisons to psychological constructs to psychological comparisons," *Child Development*, 52 (1981), 129–144. By permission of the Society for Research in Child Development.)

phasized in Daniel Goleman's popular book *Emotional Intelligence* (1995b). These individual differences turn out to be quite significant for a child's overall social development and social competence. For example, preschoolers who know and use more emotion-related words (*angry, sad*, and so on) are more popular with peers (Fabes, Eisenberg, Hanish, & Spinrad, 2001).

Carol Izard and her colleagues (1997) have shown such a linkage longitudinally. In a group of economically disadvantaged children, Izard found that those who had better and more accurate emotion knowledge in preschool later showed greater social competence and fewer behavior problems in first grade. Such a linkage suggests the possibility that an intervention program designed to improve children's basic emotional competence—their ability both to read others and to control their own emotional expressions—might have wide-ranging benefits. One such intervention, the PATHS program, is described in the *Research Report*.

The Development of Empathy   To explore the development of children's ability to read the emotions and cues of others, psychologists have also studied the development of empathy. **Empathy** involves two aspects: apprehending another person's emotional state or condition and then matching that emotional state oneself. An empathizing person experiences the same feeling he imagines the other person to feel, or a highly similar feeling. Sympathy involves the same process of apprehending another's emotional state, but it is accompanied not by a matching emotion but by a general feeling of sorrow or concern for the other person (Eisenberg & Fabes, 1998; Eisenberg, Fabes, Schaller, & Miller, 1989). Generally speaking, empathy seems to be the earlier response developmentally; among older children and adults, sympathy often seems to grow out of an initial empathetic response.

empathy As defined by Hoffman, "a vicarious affective response that does not necessarily match another's affective state but is more appropriate to the other's situation than to one's own" (1982, p. 285).

An Intervention to Increase Children's Emotional Competence

Surveys showing that 20% of all violent crimes in the United States are committed by individuals under age 18 have increased public awareness of the growing problem of youth violence (National Center for Injury Prevention and Control [NCIPC], 2000). Perhaps not surprisingly, research reveals that most violent youths have poor social-reasoning skills and a poor understanding of others' emotions (Gleason, Jensen-Campbell, & Richardson, 2004). Although programs aimed at improving these skills in teenagers have met with limited success (Armstrong, 2003), research indicates that addressing such deficits in younger children may help to prevent violence in the teen years (DeRosier & Marcus, 2005).

One violence prevention initiative geared toward younger children uses the PATHS (Promoting Alternative THinking Strategies) program, a set of 60 lessons designed to teach elementary school children about emotions and how to read them (Greenberg, 1997; Greenberg, Kusche, Cook, & Quamma, 1995). Children are also taught to label and manage their own feelings.

Researchers used the PATHS curriculum with a group of 900 excessively aggressive early elementary school children in 395 different classrooms in four U.S. cities in a project known as the Fast Track Project (Coie, 1997b; Conduct Problems Prevention Research Group, 2002; Dodge, 1997; McMahon, 1997). The children were divided into experimental and control groups. In special class sessions, children in the experimental group learned how to recognize others' emotions. They also learned strategies for controlling their own feelings, managing aggressive impulses, and resolving conflicts with peers.

The teachers of children in the experimental group were trained to use a series of signals to help children maintain control. For example, a red card or a picture of a red traffic light was used to indicate unacceptable behavior. A yellow card meant something like "Calm down; you're about to lose control." Parenting classes and support groups helped parents learn effective ways of teaching children acceptable behavior, rather than just punishing unacceptable behavior.

After several years of implementation, the program produced the following effects among children in the experimental group:

- Better recognition of emotions
- More competence in social relationships
- Lower ratings of aggressiveness by peers
- Lowered risk of being placed in special education classes
- Less use of physical punishment by parents

This project provides support for the linkage between emotion knowledge and social competence. It also gives psychologists, teachers, and parents some degree of optimism about the prospects for changing the developmental trajectories of aggressive children.

Questions for Critical Analysis

1. Was the Fast Track Project a true experiment? Why or why not?
2. Suppose you were a researcher who wanted to replicate the results of the Fast Track Project. Which of its several components would you choose to manipulate if you had only enough resources to study one of the independent variables? Explain why.

The most thorough analysis of the development of empathy and sympathy has been offered by Martin Hoffman (1982, 1988, 2000), who describes four broad steps, summarized in Table 12.1. The first stage, *global empathy*, which seems to be a kind of automatic empathetic distress response, is visible in quite young infants. Hoffman describes one example:

> An 11-month-old girl, on seeing a child fall and cry, looked as if she was about to cry herself, and then put her thumb in her mouth and buried her head in her mother's lap, which is what she would do if she herself were hurt. (1988, pp. 509–510)

This initial response changes as early as 12 or 18 months, as soon as the child has a clear understanding of the difference between self and others. The toddler still shows a matching emotion but understands that the distress is the other person's and not her

TABLE 12.1	Stages in the Development of Empathy Proposed by Hoffman
Stage	**Description**
Stage 1: Global empathy	Observed during the first year. If the infant is around someone expressing a strong emotion, he may match that emotion—for example, by beginning to cry when he hears another infant crying.
Stage 2: Egocentric empathy	Beginning at about 12 to 18 months of age, when children have developed a fairly clear sense of their separate selves, they respond to another's distress with some distress of their own, but they may attempt to "cure" the other person's problem by offering what they themselves would find most comforting. They may, for example, show sadness when they see another child hurt, and go get their own mother to help.
Stage 3: Empathy for another's feelings	Beginning as young as age 2 or 3 and continuing through elementary school, children note others' feelings, partially match those feelings, and respond to the other's distress in nonegocentric ways. Over these years, children become able to distinguish a wider (and more subtle) range of emotions.
Stage 4: Empathy for another's life condition	In late childhood or adolescence, some children develop a more generalized notion of others' feelings and respond not just to the immediate situation but to the other individual's general situation or plight. Thus, a young person at this level may become more distressed by another person's sadness if she knows that the sadness is chronic or that the person's general situation is particularly tragic than if she sees it as a more momentary problem.

Sources: Hoffman, 1982, 1988, 2000.

own. Nonetheless, her solution to the other's distress is still likely to be egocentric, such as offering the distressed person a teddy bear (Eisenberg & Fabes, 1998).

Children's empathetic and sympathetic responses become more and more subtle over the preschool and elementary school years, as they become better readers of others' emotions. By middle childhood, many children can even empathize with several different emotions at once, as when they see another child make a mistake and fall down during a game. The observing child may see and empathize with both the hurt and the sense of shame or embarrassment, and she may be aware that the child may prefer not to be helped. In adolescence, a still more abstract level emerges, when the child moves beyond the immediate situation and empathizes (or sympathizes) with another person's general plight.

Notice that both developmental progressions—reading others' emotions and empathizing with them—reflect several of the general principles listed earlier in this chapter and parallel the changes Piaget described. In particular, there is a shift from observation to inference: With increasing age, the child's empathetic response is guided less by just the immediate, observed emotions seen in others, such as facial expressions or body language, and more by the child's inferences or deductions about the other person's feelings. This is not a swift change. For example, research in England by Paul Harris and his associates (1981) showed that not until adolescence do young people become fully aware that other people may hide their emotions or act differently from the way they feel "inside."

As you might expect, not all children show equal amounts of such empathetic responses. Some biological disposition toward empathy appears to be part of the story, as evidenced by the greater similarity in levels of empathy among identical twins than among fraternal twins (Zahn-Waxler, Robinson, & Emde, 1992). On the environmental

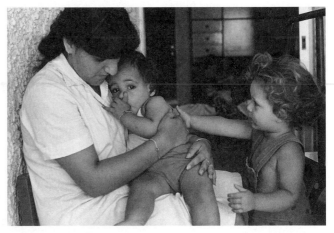

Children as young as 2 or 3 show this kind of empathetic response to other people's distress or delight.

During the preschool years, friendships are based on shared activities. As children get older, reciprocal trust becomes more important than activities.

side, many of the same factors that contribute to greater altruistic behavior (described in *The Real World* in Chapter 11) also appear to contribute to more empathetic responses in young children. For example, greater maternal warmth is linked to increased empathy among toddlers (e.g., Strayer & Roberts, 1989). Like altruistic or kind behavior, empathy is also fostered by parental explanations about the consequences of the child's actions for others and by parental discussions of emotions (e.g., Miller, Eisenberg, Fabes, Shell, & Gular, 1989). Finally, developmentalists have some preliminary evidence that temperamental variables are linked to empathy. Specifically, children who are high in effortful control, the capacity to regulate emotion in order to accomplish goals, are also high in empathy (Valiente et al., 2004). Whatever its source, empathy appears to be critical to controlling aggressive impulses, as children who are high in empathy tend to be low in aggressiveness (Strayer & Roberts, 2004).

DESCRIBING FRIENDSHIPS

Preschool children seem to understand friendships mostly in terms of common activities. If you ask a young child how people make friends, the answer is usually that they "play together" or spend time physically near each other (Damon, 1977, 1983; Hartup & Stevens, 1997; Selman, 1980). Children this age think of friendship as something that involves sharing toys or giving things to one another.

Gradually, this view of friendship begins to shift away from an emphasis on activities (Dunn, Cutting, & Fisher, 2002). Robert Selman's research and extensive studies by Thomas Berndt (1983, 1986) show that the key ingredient of friendships for elementary school children seems to be reciprocal trust: Friends are seen as special people with desired qualities other than mere proximity, as people who are generous with one another, who help and trust one another. Children this age also understand that friendship has a temporal dimension: Friends are people with whom one has a history of connection and interaction, rather than people one has just met or played with once, as Figure 12.2 suggests. Likewise, over the elementary school years, children develop an understanding of gradations in friendships. That is, they understand the difference between "best friends" and other kinds of friends (Schraf & Hertz-Lazarowitz, 2003). Important, too, is the finding that improvements in children's understanding of peer

My definition of a good friend is someone who you can trust, They will never turn their back on you, They will always be there for you. when you are feeling down in the dumps, They'll try to cheer you up, They will never forget about you. They'll always sit next to you at lunch,

FIGURE 12.2

This essay on friendship written by a 10-year-old illustrates the way older school-aged children think about friends.
(*Source*: Author.)

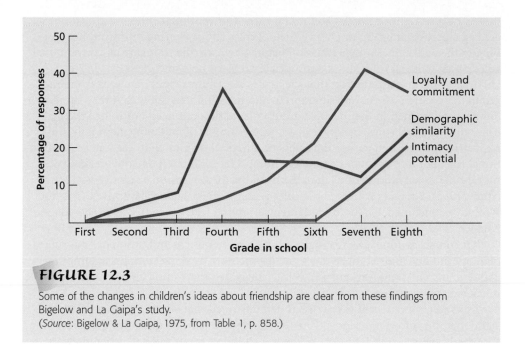

FIGURE 12.3

Some of the changes in children's ideas about friendship are clear from these findings from Bigelow and La Gaipa's study.
(*Source*: Bigelow & La Gaipa, 1975, from Table 1, p. 858.)

relationships are linked to the quantity and quality of children's friendships (Rose & Asher, 2004).

By about age 11 or 12, children begin to talk about intimacy as an important ingredient in friendship; by middle adolescence, they expect a friend to be a confidant and to be supportive and trustworthy (Hartup & Stevens, 1997). Understanding of friendship also becomes more qualified, more shaded. Research suggests that in late adolescence, young people understand that even very close friendships cannot fill every need and that friendships are not static: They change, grow, or dissolve as each member of the pair changes (Damon, 1977). A really good friendship, then, is one that adapts to these changes. Young people of this age say things about friendship like this: "Trust is the ability to let go as well as to hang on" (Selman, 1980, p. 141).

Some research findings from an early cross-sectional study by Brian Bigelow and John La Gaipa (1975) illustrate this pattern of change. These researchers asked several hundred children in Canada to write an essay about how their expectations of friends differed from their expectations of other acquaintances. The answers were scored along many dimensions, three of which are shown in Figure 12.3. You can see that references to demographic similarity (e.g., "We live in the same neighborhood") were highest among fourth graders, whereas comments about loyalty and commitment were highest among seventh graders. References to intimacy potential (e.g., "I can tell her things about myself I can't tell anyone else") did not appear at all until seventh grade but then increased in eighth grade.

From what you have read so far, you can see that the patterns of developmental change in children's understanding of themselves, of others, and of relationships are strikingly similar, shifting in all the ways listed at the beginning of the chapter: from outer to inner characteristics, from observation to inference, from definite to qualified, and from an egocentric to a general view.

UNDERSTANDING RULES AND INTENTIONS

A somewhat different facet of the child's emerging social cognition is her understanding of different categories for social rules. Beginning some time in the elementary school years, children understand the important distinction between what Elliot Turiel

(1983) calls conventional rules and moral rules. **Conventional rules** are arbitrary, created by a particular group or culture. School rules about wearing uniforms, not running in the hall, and asking permission before you leave the room are all conventional rules, as are cultural rules about appropriate dress for boys and girls. By age 7 or 8, children begin to grasp the fact that such rules are arbitrary and may vary from one group to another or from one situation to another. Children know that they should follow such rules when in the specified group or situation but need not follow them at other times. **Moral rules**, in contrast, are seen as universal and obligatory, reflecting basic principles that guarantee the rights of others. Not running in the hall is a conventional rule; not hitting other people is a moral rule. Children judge the breaking of moral rules as far more serious than the breaking of conventional rules (Nucci & Nucci, 1982). Breaking conventional rules is seen as impolite or disruptive but is not typically condemned. Children's judgments of moral transgressions, however, are harsher.

Of course, as adults, we distinguish between intentional and unintentional rule violations, but do children make this same distinction? Working from his assumptions about young children's egocentrism, Piaget suggested that young children are incapable of such discriminations.

However, more recent research has demonstrated that young children do understand intentions to some degree (Zhang & Yu, 2002). For one thing, it's quite common for preschoolers to say "It was an accident . . . I didn't mean to do it" when they are punished. Such protests suggest that children understand that intentional wrongdoing is punished more severely than unintentional transgressions of the rules.

Several studies suggest that children can make judgments about actors' intentions both when presented with abstract problems and when motivated by a personal desire to avoid punishment (Feinfield, Lee, Flavell, Green, & Flavell, 1999). In one classic study, 3-year-olds listened to stories about children playing ball (Nelson, 1980). Pictures were used to convey information about intentions (see Figure 12.4). The children were more likely to label a child who intended to harm a playmate as "bad" or "naughty" than to judge negatively a child who accidentally hit another child in the head with the ball. However, children's judgments were also influenced by outcomes. In other words, they were more likely to say a child who wanted to hurt his playmate was "good" if he failed to hit the child with the ball. These results suggest that children know more about intentions than Piaget thought, but they are still limited in their ability to base judgments entirely on intentions.

Before going on . . .

■ List the general principles of social-cognitive development proposed by Flavell.
■ In what ways do children's descriptions of other people change across childhood and adolescence?
■ Describe individual differences in emotional understanding, and explain how empathy develops.
■ How do descriptions of friendship differ among preschoolers, school-aged children, and adolescents?
■ When do children begin to distinguish between conventional and moral rules, and when do they understand the difference between intentional and unintentional acts?

conventional rules As defined by Turiel, arbitrary, socially defined rules specific to a particular culture, subculture, group, or setting, such as "Don't run in the halls" or "Smoking allowed only in designated areas."

moral rules As defined by Turiel, universal and obligatory rules reflecting basic principles that guarantee the rights of others.

moral development The process of learning to distinguish between right and wrong in accordance with cultural values.

Moral Development

One of parents' and teachers' greatest concerns is helping children learn to be good people, to do the "right" thing according to the standards and values of their culture. **Moral development** is very complex. It has been explained in terms of psychoanalytic, learning, and cognitive-developmental theories. The cognitive-developmental theories, especially that of Lawrence Kohlberg, have been the most influential for the past several decades.

DIMENSIONS OF MORAL DEVELOPMENT

The psychoanalytic, learning, and cognitive-developmental theories each focus on a different aspect of moral development.

Moral Emotions Psychoanalytic theory emphasizes emotions in explaining moral development. According to Freud, the child learns moral rules by identifying with the

FIGURE 12.4

Pictures like these have been used to assess young children's understanding of an actor's intentions.

same-sex parent during the phallic stage. The rules a child learns from her same-sex parent form her *superego*, or her internal moral judge. The superego has two parts: a conscience and an ego ideal. The **conscience** is a list of things that "good boys" and "good girls" don't do, such as telling lies. The **ego ideal** is a list of things that "good boys" and "good girls" do, such as obeying parents. When a child disobeys her conscience, she feels guilt. When she fails to live up to the standards set by the ego ideal, she feels shame. Freud believed children learn to obey the rules of their consciences and ego ideals to avoid these uncomfortable feelings.

To better understand Freud's idea about how the superego works, think about a hungry 7-year-old at the grocery store. He can figure out how to take a candy bar without anyone noticing. However, his superego classifies this behavior as stealing, and thinking about stealing a candy bar makes him feel guilty. This creates a conflict for him. If he steals the candy, he'll feel guilty. If he doesn't, he'll be hungry. If he has a healthy personality, Freud believed, he will obey his superego even though doing so will mean remaining hungry.

Erikson's views on moral development were similar to Freud's. However, Erikson believed that children learn moral rules from both parents. Erikson's theory also claimed that pride is just as important for moral development as guilt and shame. For example, if the boy decides not to take the candy, he will not only avoid feeling guilty but will also feel pride in his ability to resist temptation.

Recently, there has been a resurgence of interest in moral emotions among developmentalists (Eisenberg, 2000). Research has shown, as Freud and Erikson predicted, that feelings of guilt, shame, and pride develop before age 6 (Aksan & Kochanska, 2005; Fung, 1999; Kochanska, Casey, & Fukumoto, 1995; Kochanska, Gross, Lin, & Nichols, 2002). Moreover, as both theorists predicted, the quality of parent-child relationships contributes to the development of moral emotions. For instance, children who have been abused display less understanding than do nonabused children of situations that produce guilt and pride in most people (Koenig, Cicchetti, & Rogosch, 2004).

conscience The list of "don'ts" in the superego; violation of any of these leads to feelings of guilt.

ego ideal The list of "dos" in the superego; violation of any of these leads to feelings of shame.

Researchers infer that children are experiencing shame when they try to hide an act they know to be wrong. In fact, most school-aged children define shame as the emotion people experience when others find out they have done something wrong (Levorato & Donati, 1999). However, it is not until the later school years, at age 10 or so, that children connect shame exclusively to moral wrongs (Olthof, Ferguson, Bloemers, & Deij, 2004). Adolescents' understanding of shame, predictably, is more complex. They tell researchers that people experience shame when they fail to live up to their own standards of behavior as well as when their wrongdoing is exposed to others.

Some research suggests that connections between moral emotions and moral behavior are weaker than Freud believed, because they depend on cognitive development (Hoffman, 1988). Younger children connect moral feelings with adult observation. They seem to think they should feel guilty or ashamed only if a parent or teacher sees them commit a violation of a moral rule. Thus, a 7-year-old candy thief is unlikely to feel guilty unless he gets caught in the act. Later, after age 9 or 10, when children better understand moral feelings, they are more likely to make behavioral choices based on how guilty, ashamed, or proud they think they will feel. For example, when the boy who wants the candy is older, he will be more likely to choose not to take the candy because he knows resisting temptation will make him feel proud of himself.

By contrast, researcher Grazyna Kochanska has found that the guilt-behavior connection is linked to temperament in young children. Children who have a fearful temperament exhibit more signs of guilt, such as body tension, when they believe they have done something wrong (Kochanska et al., 2002). Another contributing factor may be parenting style. Kochanska's research indicates that children of mothers who rely heavily on power-assertive discipline techniques such as yelling and spanking display less guilt.

Moral Behavior   Another way of looking at moral development is through the lens of learning theorist B. F. Skinner's operant conditioning model, which proposes that consequences teach children to obey moral rules. According to Skinner, adults reward children for morally acceptable behavior with praise. At the same time, they punish children for morally unacceptable behavior. As a result, acceptable behavior increases and unacceptable behavior decreases as children get older.

Consequences certainly do influence children's behavior. However, punishment may actually interfere with moral development. For example, if a child's parent spanks him in the grocery store parking lot for having a stolen a candy bar, the parent hopes that the spanking will teach him that stealing is wrong. But the child may learn only that he can't steal when he's with the parent. Similarly, when punishment is severe or embarrassing, children may be distracted from making the connection between their behavior and the punishment. A child who has stolen candy may be so angry at his parent for embarrassing him with a public spanking that he concentrates all his attention on his anger. As a result, he fails to realize that his choice to steal caused the spanking (Hoffman, 1988).

An approach that combines punishment with reasoned explanations may be more effective. On discovering that a 7-year-old had stolen a candy bar, a parent using this approach would respond by telling the child privately that it is wrong to take things that don't belong to you even if you are very hungry. Next, the parent would require the child to right the wrong by admitting his crime, apologizing to the cashier or manager, and paying for the candy. Finally, the 7-year-old would probably have to repay his parents in some way if they gave him the money to pay for the stolen candy. Such a process allows the child to learn both that it is wrong to steal and that, when he breaks a moral rule, he must do something to set things right (Zahn-Waxler, Radke-Yarrow, & King, 1979).

As you may recall from Chapter 1, social-learning theorist Albert Bandura claims that children learn more from observing others than from either rewards or punishments. His theory states that, when a child sees someone rewarded for a behavior, he believes that he will also be rewarded if he behaves in the same way. Similarly, when he sees a model punished, he assumes that he will also experience punishment if he imitates the model's behavior (Bandura, 1977, 1989). For example, a story about a child who was praised by a parent for resisting the temptation to steal may teach the child who hears or reads it that resisting temptation is praiseworthy. Conversely, when a child is exposed to a story about a boy or girl who steals and doesn't get caught, he may learn that it's possible to steal without getting caught.

As Bandura's theory predicts, children learn a lot about moral behavior, both acceptable and unacceptable, from models' behavior. Models can even influence children to change their moral behavior. For example, if a 7-year-old sees another child steal candy after he decides not to, he may change his mind.

Moral Reasoning *Moral reasoning* is the process of making judgments about the rightness or wrongness of specific acts. As you learned earlier in this chapter, children learn to discriminate between intentional and unintentional acts in early childhood. However, using this understanding to make moral judgments is another matter. Piaget claimed that the ability to use reasoning about intentions to make judgments about the moral dimensions of behavior appears to emerge along with concrete operational thinking.

Piaget studied moral development by observing children playing games. As he watched them play, Piaget noticed that younger children seemed to have less understanding of the games' rules. Following up on these observations, Piaget questioned children of different ages about rules. Their answers led him to propose a two-stage theory of moral development (Piaget, 1932).

Children in Piaget's **moral realism stage**, which he found to be typical of children younger than 8, believe that the rules of games can't be changed because they come from authorities, such as parents, government officials, or religious figures. For example, one 6-year-old told Piaget that the game of marbles was invented on Noah's ark. He went on to explain that the rules can't be changed because the "big ones," meaning adults and older children, wouldn't like it (Piaget, 1965, p. 60).

Moral realists also believe that all rule violations result in punishment. For example, Piaget told children a story about a child who fell into a stream when he tried to use a rotten piece of wood as a bridge. Children younger than 8 told him that the child was being punished for something "naughty" he had done in the past.

After age 8, Piaget proposed, children move into the **moral relativism stage**, in which they learn that people can agree to change rules if they want to. They realize that the important thing about a game is that all the players follow the same rules, regardless of what those are. For example, 8- to 12-year-olds know that a group of children playing baseball can decide to give each batter four strikes rather than three. They understand that their agreement doesn't change the game of baseball and that it doesn't apply to other people who play the game. Children in this stage also get better at following the rules of games.

Eight- to twelve-year-olds also know that rule violations don't result in punishment unless you get caught. As a result, they view events like falling into a stream because of using a rotten piece of wood as a bridge as accidents. They understand that accidents are not caused by "naughty" behavior. Children older than 8 also understand the relationship between punishment and intentions. For example, looking back at the situation of a 7-year-old taking a candy bar from a store, Piaget's research suggests that children over 8 would distinguish between a child who unintentionally left without paying for the candy and another who deliberately took it. Older children would likely say that both children should return or pay for the candy, but only the one who intentionally stole it should be punished.

Research supports Piaget's claim that children over 8 give more weight to intentions than to consequences when making moral judgments (Zelazo, Helwig, & Lau, 1996). Although their thinking is more mature than that of preschoolers, school-aged children's moral reasoning is still highly egocentric. For example, every parent has heard the exclamation "It's not fair!" when a child fails to receive the same treat or priv-

moral realism stage The first of Piaget's stages of moral development, in which children believe that rules are inflexible.

moral relativism stage The second of Piaget's stages of moral development, in which children understand that many rules can be changed through social agreement.

The majority of teenagers use stage 3 moral reasoning: What is good is what family or peers define as good and right. Do you think that the level of moral reasoning a teenager shows has any connection to his or her conformity to peers?

ilege as a sibling. However, it is rare, if not completely unknown, for a child to protest the fairness of his receiving something that was not also given to a sibling. Thus, school-aged children still have a long way to go before they are capable of mature moral reasoning. To understand this developmental process, we must turn to the work of Lawrence Kohlberg (1927–1987).

KOHLBERG'S STAGES OF MORAL DEVELOPMENT

Piaget (1932) was the first to offer a description of the development of moral reasoning, but Kohlberg's work has had the most powerful impact on developmentalists' thinking (Colby, Kohlberg, Gibbs, & Lieberman, 1983; Dawson, 2002; Kohlberg, 1964, 1976, 1980, 1981). Building on and revising Piaget's ideas, Kohlberg pioneered the practice of assessing moral reasoning by presenting children with a series of hypothetical dilemmas in story form, each of which highlighted a specific moral issue, such as the value of human life. One of the most famous is the dilemma of Heinz:

> In Europe, a woman was near death from a special kind of cancer. There was one drug that the doctors thought might save her. It was a form of radium that a druggist in the same town had recently discovered. The drug was expensive to make, but the druggist was charging ten times what the drug cost him to make. He paid $200 for the radium and charged $2000 for a small dose of the drug. The sick woman's husband, Heinz, went to everyone he knew to borrow the money, but he could only get together about $1000, which is half of what it cost. He told the druggist that his wife was dying, and asked him to sell it cheaper or let him pay later. But the druggist said, "No, I discovered the drug and I'm going to make money from it." So Heinz got desperate and broke into the man's store to steal the drug for his wife. (Kohlberg & Elfenbein, 1975, p. 621)

After hearing this story, the child or young person is asked a series of questions, such as whether Heinz should have stolen the drug. What if Heinz didn't love his wife? Would that change anything? What if the person dying was a stranger? Should Heinz steal the drug anyway?

On the basis of answers to dilemmas like this one, Kohlberg concluded that there were three main levels of moral reasoning, each with two stages, as summarized briefly in Table 12.2.

Levels and Stages   At Level I, **preconventional morality**, the child's judgments of right and wrong are based on sources of authority who are close by and physically superior to her—usually the parents. Just as the elementary school child's descriptions of others are largely external, her standards for judging rightness or wrongness are also external rather than internal. In particular, it is the outcome or consequences of actions that determine the rightness or wrongness of those actions.

In stage 1 of this level—*the punishment and obedience orientation*—the child relies on the physical consequences of some action to decide whether it is right or wrong. If she is punished, the behavior was wrong; if she is not punished, it was right. She is obedient to adults because they are bigger and stronger.

In stage 2—*individualism, instrumental purpose, and exchange*—the child begins to do things that are rewarded and to avoid things that are punished. (For this reason, the stage is sometimes referred to as *naive hedonism*.) If something feels good or brings pleasant results, it is good. Some beginning of concern for other people is apparent during this stage, but only if that concern can be expressed as something that benefits

preconventional morality The first level of moral development proposed by Kohlberg, in which moral judgments are dominated by consideration of what will be punished and what feels good.

TABLE 12.2	Kohlberg's Stages of Moral Development
Stage	**Description**
LEVEL I: Preconventional Morality	
Stage 1: Punishment and obedience orientation	The child decides what is wrong on the basis of what is punished. Obedience is valued for its own sake, but the child obeys because adults are physically more powerful.
Stage 2: Individualism, instrumental purpose, and exchange	The child follows rules when it is in her immediate interest. What is good is what brings pleasant results.
LEVEL II: Conventional Morality	
Stage 3: Mutual interpersonal expectations, relationships, and interpersonal conformity	Moral actions are those that live up to the expectations of the family or other significant group. "Being good" becomes important for its own sake.
Stage 4: Social system and conscience	Moral actions are those so defined by larger social groups or the society as a whole. One should fulfill duties one has agreed to and uphold laws, except in extreme cases.
LEVEL III: Principled or Postconventional Morality	
Stage 5: Social contract orientation (or utility and individual rights)	Acting so as to achieve the "greatest good for the greatest number." The teenager or adult is aware that most values are relative and laws are changeable, although rules should be upheld in order to preserve the social order. Still, there are some basic nonrelative values, such as the importance of each person's life and liberty.
Stage 6: Universal ethical principles	The adult develops and follows self-chosen ethical principles in determining what is right. These ethical principles are part of an articulated, integrated, carefully thought-out, and consistently followed system of values and principles.

Sources: Kohlberg, 1976; Lickona, 1978.

the child herself as well. So she can enter into agreements such as "If you help me, I'll help you." The following responses to variations of the Heinz dilemma, drawn from studies of children and teenagers in a number of different cultures, illustrate stage 2:

> He should steal the food for his wife because if she dies he'll have to pay for the funeral, and that costs a lot. (Taiwan)

> He should steal the drug because "he should protect the life of his wife so he doesn't have to stay alone in life." (Puerto Rico)

> *Researcher:* Suppose it wasn't his wife who was starving but his best friend. Should he steal the food for his friend?

> *Child:* Yes, because one day when he is hungry his friend would help. (Turkey) (Snarey, 1985, p. 221)

At Level II, **conventional morality**, the young person shifts from judgments based on external consequences and personal gain to judgments based on rules or norms of a group to which he or she belongs, whether that group is the family, the peer group, a church, or the nation. What the chosen reference group defines as right or good is right or good in the child's view, and the child internalizes these norms to a considerable extent.

Stage 3 (the first stage of Level II) is the stage of *mutual interpersonal expectations, relationships, and interpersonal conformity* (sometimes also called the *good boy/nice girl stage*). Children at this stage believe that good behavior is what pleases other people. They value trust, loyalty, respect, gratitude, and maintenance of mutual relationships. Andy, a boy Kohlberg interviewed who was at stage 3, said:

conventional morality The second level of moral development proposed by Kohlberg, in which a person's judgments are dominated by considerations of group values and laws.

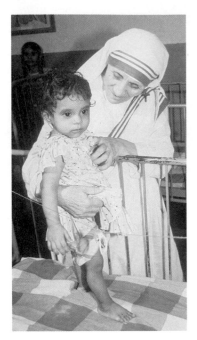

Kohlberg thought that there were at least a few people, such as Mother Teresa, whose moral reasoning was based on universal ethical principles.

I try to do things for my parents, they've always done things for you. I try to do everything my mother says, I try to please her. Like she wants me to be a doctor and I want to, too, and she's helping me get up there. (Kohlberg, 1964, p. 401)

Another mark of stage 3 is that the child begins to make judgments based on intentions as well as on outward behavior. If someone "means well" or "didn't mean to do it," the wrongdoing is seen as less serious than if the person did it "on purpose."

In stage 4, the second stage of conventional morality, the child turns to larger social groups for her norms. Kohlberg labeled this the stage of *social system and conscience*. Children reasoning at this stage focus on doing their duty, respecting authority, following rules and laws. The emphasis is less on what is pleasing to particular people (as in stage 3) and more on adhering to a complex set of regulations. The regulations themselves are not questioned.

The transition to Level III, **principled morality** (also called **postconventional morality**), is marked by several changes, the most important of which is a shift in the source of authority. At Level I, children see authority as totally outside themselves; at Level II, the judgments or rules of external authority are internalized, but they are not questioned or analyzed; at Level III, a new kind of personal authority emerges and allows a person to make individual judgments and choices based on self-chosen principles.

In stage 5 at this level—called the *social contract orientation* by Kohlberg—people show evidence of the beginning of such self-chosen principles. Rules, laws, and regulations are still seen as important because they ensure fairness, and they are seen as logically necessary for society to function. However, people operating at this level also recognize that rules, laws, and regulations sometimes need to be ignored or changed. The system of government in the United States is based on moral reasoning of this kind, since it provides means for changing laws and for allowing personal protests against a given law, such as the civil rights protests of the 1960s and the Vietnam War protests of the 1960s and 1970s.

Stage 6, the second stage in Level III, is simply a further extension of this same pattern, with the individual searching for the highest level of moral principles possible and then trying to live in a way that is consistent with them. Kohlberg referred to this stage as the *universal ethical principles orientation*. People who reason in this way assume personal responsibility for their own actions on the basis of fundamental and universal principles, such as justice and basic respect for persons (Kohlberg, 1978; Kohlberg, Boyd, & Levine, 1990). In their case studies of modern adults who reason and act at this level, Ann Colby and William Damon (1992) note that another quality such people share is "open receptivity"—a willingness to examine their ideas and convictions, even while they act firmly and generously in support of their ideals. Such people are not common. Two famous examples are Mahatma Gandhi and Mother Teresa, both of whom devoted their lives to humanitarian causes.

It is very important to understand that what defines the stage or level of a person's moral development is not the specific moral choices the person makes but the form of reasoning used to justify the choices. For example, either choice—that Heinz should steal the drug or that he should not—can be justified with logic at any given stage. You have already read some examples of stage 2 justifications for Heinz's stealing the drug; the following is a stage 5 justification of the same choice, drawn from a study in India:

What if Heinz was stealing to save the life of his pet animal instead of his wife? If Heinz saves an animal's life his action will be commendable. The right use of the drug is to administer it to the needy. There is some difference, of course—human life is more evolved and hence of greater importance in the scheme of nature—but an animal's life is not altogether bereft of importance. . . . (Snarey, 1985, p. 223, drawn originally from Vasudev, 1983, p. 7)

If you compare this answer to those presented earlier, you can clearly see the difference in the form of reasoning used, even though the action being justified is precisely the same.

principled (postconventional) morality The third level of moral development proposed by Kohlberg, in which considerations of justice, individual rights, and social contracts dominate moral judgment.

Kohlberg argued that this sequence of moral development is both universal and hierarchically organized, just as Piaget thought his proposed stages of cognitive development were universal and hierarchical. That is, each stage follows and grows from the preceding one and has some internal consistency. Individuals should not move backward, or "down" the sequence, but only upward through the stages, if they move at all. Kohlberg did not suggest that all individuals eventually progress through all six stages or even that the stages are always associated with specific ages, but he insisted that their order is invariant and universal.

Age and Moral Reasoning

Kohlberg's own findings, confirmed by many other researchers (e.g., Walker, de Vries, & Trevethan, 1987), show that preconventional moral reasoning (stages 1 and 2) is dominant in elementary school, with stage 2 reasoning still evident among many early adolescents. Conventional reasoning (stages 3 and 4) emerges in middle adolescence and remains the most common form of moral reasoning in adulthood. Postconventional reasoning (stages 5 and 6) is relatively rare, even in adults. For example, in one study of men in their forties and fifties, only 13% were rated as using stage 5 moral reasoning (Gibson, 1990).

Two research examples illustrate these overall age trends. The first, illustrated in Figure 12.5, comes from Kohlberg's own longitudinal study of 58 boys, first interviewed when they were 10, and followed for more than 20 years (Colby et al., 1983). Table 12.3 shows cross-sectional data from a study by Lawrence Walker and his colleagues (1987). They studied 10 boys and 10 girls at each of four ages, interviewing the parents of each child as well. Note that Walker scored each response on a 9-point scale rather than using just the five main stages. This system, which has become quite common, allows for the fact that many people's reasoning falls between two specific stages.

The results of these two studies, although not identical, point to remarkably similar conclusions about the order of emergence of the various stages and about the approximate ages at which they predominate. In both studies, stage 2 reasoning dominates at ages 9 to 10, and stage 3 reasoning is most common at about ages 15 to 16.

Sequence of Stages

The evidence also seems fairly strong that Kohlberg's stages occur in the sequence he proposed. For example, in three long-term longitudinal studies of teenagers and young adults, one in the United States (Colby et al., 1983), one in

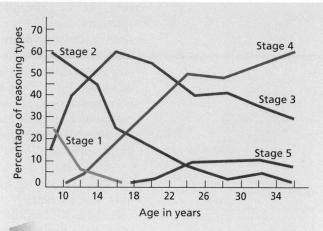

FIGURE 12.5

These findings are from Colby and Kohlberg's long-term longitudinal study of a group of boys who were asked about Kohlberg's moral dilemmas every few years from age 10 through early adulthood. Note that postconventional, or principled, reasoning was quite uncommon, even in adulthood.

(*Source:* Colby et al., from Fig. 1, p. 46, "Longitudinal study of moral judgment," *Monographs of the Society for Research in Child Development*, 48 (1–2, Serial No. 200) (1983). By permission of the Society for Research in Child Development.)

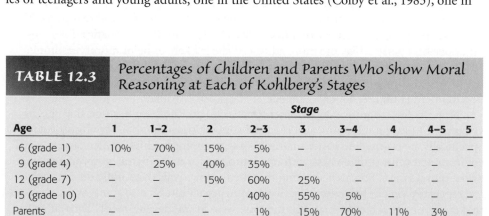

TABLE 12.3	Percentages of Children and Parents Who Show Moral Reasoning at Each of Kohlberg's Stages							
	Stage							
Age	1	1–2	2	2–3	3	3–4	4	4–5	5
6 (grade 1)	10%	70%	15%	5%	–	–	–	–	–
9 (grade 4)	–	25%	40%	35%	–	–	–	–	–
12 (grade 7)	–	–	15%	60%	25%	–	–	–	–
15 (grade 10)	–	–	–	40%	55%	5%	–	–	–
Parents	–	–	–	1%	15%	70%	11%	3%	–

Source: Walker et al., from Table 1, p. 849, "Moral stages and moral orientations in real-life and hypothetical dilemmas," *Child Development*, 60 (1987), 157–160. By permission of the Society for Research in Child Development.

Israel (Snarey, Reimer, & Kohlberg, 1985), and one in Turkey (Nisan & Kohlberg, 1982), the changes in participants' reasoning nearly always occurred in the hypothesized order. Participants did not skip stages, and only about 5–7% of them showed any indication of regression (movement down the sequence of stages rather than up). Similarly, when Walker (1989) retested the participants in his study 2 years later, he found that only 6% had moved down (most only half a stage), while 22% had moved up, and none had skipped a stage. Such a rate of regression is about what researchers would expect to find, given the fact that the measurements of stage reasoning are not perfect. On the whole, the available evidence suggests that moral judgment changes over time in the sequence Kohlberg described (Rest, 1983).

Moral Reasoning Stages across Cultures   Variations of Kohlberg's dilemmas have been presented to children or adults in at least 27 different countries or subcultures, both Western and non-Western, industrialized and nonindustrialized (Snarey, 1985). John Snarey, who has reviewed and analyzed these many studies, notes several things in support of Kohlberg's claim that the stages are universal: (1) Studies of children consistently find an increase in stage of reasoning with age; (2) the few longitudinal studies report "strikingly similar findings" (1985, p. 215), with participants progressing through the stage sequence with few reversals; and (3) cultures differ in the highest level of reasoning observed. In urban societies (both Western and non-Western), stage 5 is typically the highest stage observed, while in those cultures Snarey calls "folk societies," stage 4 is typically the highest. Collectively, this evidence provides quite strong support for the universality of Kohlberg's stage sequence.

CAUSES AND CONSEQUENCES OF MORAL DEVELOPMENT

The most obvious reason for the correlations between Kohlberg's stages and chronological age and for a consistent sequence of stages is that moral reasoning is strongly tied to cognitive development. Further, although the stages have often been criticized for failing to predict moral behavior, research does suggest that there is a link between moral reasoning and moral behavior.

Moral Reasoning and Cognitive Development   It appears that children must have a firm grasp of concrete operational thinking before they can develop or use conventional moral reasoning. Likewise, formal operational thinking appears to be necessary for advancement to the postconventional level. To be more specific, Kohlberg and many other theorists suggest that the decline of egocentrism that occurs as an individual moves through Piaget's concrete and formal operations stages is the cognitive-developmental variable that matters most in the development of moral reasoning. The idea is that the greater a child's or adolescent's ability to look at a situation from another person's perspective, the more advanced she is likely to be in moral reasoning. Psychologists use the term **role-taking** to refer to this ability (Selman, 1980). Research has provided strong support for the hypothesized links between role-taking and moral development (Kuhn, Kohlberg, Languer, & Haan, 1977; Walker, 1980).

Nevertheless, cognitive development isn't enough. Kohlberg thought that the development of moral reasoning also required support from the social environment. Specifically, he claimed, to foster mature moral reasoning, a child's or teenager's social environment must provide him with opportunities for meaningful, reciprocal dialogue about moral issues. Research showing that media portrayals of morally deviant behavior, especially violent behavior, negatively influence children's moral reasoning suggests that environmental factors may also interfere with moral development (Krcmar & Vieira, 2005). Thus, Kohlberg agreed with advocates of character education, as de-

role-taking The ability to look at a situation from another person's perspective.

scribed at the beginning of the chapter, that moral development must be deliberately and systematically encouraged by parents and teachers.

Longitudinal research relating parenting styles and family climate to levels of moral reasoning suggest that Kohlberg was right (Pratt, Arnold, & Pratt, 1999). Parents' ability to identify, understand, and respond to children's and adolescents' less mature forms of moral reasoning seems to be particularly important to the development of moral reasoning. It is important because individuals of all ages have difficulty understanding and remembering moral arguments that are more advanced than their own level (Narvaez, 1998). Thus, a parent who can express her own moral views in terms of a child's level of understanding is more likely to be able to influence that child's moral development.

Moral Reasoning and Moral Behavior Level of moral reasoning appears to be positively correlated with prosocial behavior and negatively related to antisocial behavior (Schonert-Reichl, 1999). In other words, higher levels of prosocial behavior are found among children and teens who are at higher levels of moral reasoning (compared to their peers). Alternatively, the highest levels of antisocial behavior are found among adolescents at the lowest levels of moral reasoning. Moreover, attitudes toward the acceptability of violence also vary with levels of moral reasoning. Individuals at lower levels have more tolerant attitudes toward violence (Sotelo & Sangrador, 1997).

Another connection between moral reasoning and behavior proposed by Kohlberg is that the higher the level of moral reasoning a young person shows, the stronger the link to behavior. Thus, young people reasoning at stage 4 or stage 5 should be more likely to follow their own rules or reasoning than should children reasoning at lower levels.

For example, Kohlberg and Candee (1984) studied students involved in the early "free speech" movement at Berkeley in the late 1960s (a precursor to the Vietnam War protests). They interviewed and tested the moral judgment levels of a group that had participated at a sit-in in the university administration building and of a group randomly chosen from the campus population. Among students who thought it was morally right to sit in, nearly three-quarters of those reasoning at stage 4 or 5 actually did sit in, compared to only about one-quarter of those reasoning at stage 3. Thus, the higher the stage of moral reasoning, the more consistent the behavior was with the reasoning.

In other research, Kohlberg and others simply asked participants whether there is a link between one's stage of moral reasoning and the probability of making some moral choice, such as not cheating. In one early study, Kohlberg (1975) found that only 15% of college students reasoning at stage 5 of the principled level cheated when they were given an opportunity, while 55% of those at the conventional level and 70% of those at the preconventional level cheated.

A similar result comes from studies in which the moral reasoning of highly aggressive or delinquent youngsters is compared to that of nondelinquent peers. The repeated finding is that delinquents (male or female) have lower levels of moral reasoning than do nondelinquents, even when the two groups are carefully matched for levels of education, social class, and IQ (Cheung, Chan, Lee, Liu, & Leung, 2001; Ma, 2003; Smetana, 1990). In one study of this type, Virginia Gregg and her colleagues (1994) found that only 20% of a group of incarcerated male and female delinquents were reasoning at stage 3 or higher, while 59% of a carefully matched comparison group of nondelinquents were reasoning at this level. Like younger children who act out more in school, delinquents are most likely to use highly self-oriented reasoning, at Kohlberg's stage 2 (Richards, Bear, Stewart, & Norman, 1992).

Delinquents appear to be behind their peers in moral reasoning because of deficits in role-taking skills. For example, researchers have found that teenagers who can look at actions they are contemplating from their parents' perspective are less likely to engage in delinquent behavior than adolescents who cannot do so (Wyatt & Carlo, 2002).

Most delinquent teens also seem to be unable to look at their crimes from their victims' perspectives or to assess hypothetical crimes from the victims' perspectives. Thus, programs aimed at helping delinquents develop more mature levels of moral reasoning usually focus on heightening their awareness of the victim's point of view. However, few such programs have been successful (Armstrong, 2003; Moody, 1997; Putnins, 1997).

Finally, despite the abundance of evidence for a link between moral reasoning and behavior, no one has found the correspondence to be perfect. After all, in Kohlberg's studies, 15% of the stage 5 moral reasoners did cheat, and a quarter of stage 4 and stage 5 reasoners who thought it morally right to participate in a sit-in did not do so. As Kohlberg says, "One can reason in terms of principles and not live up to those principles" (1975, p. 672).

ALTERNATIVE VIEWS

Most of the moral dilemmas Kohlberg posed for participants in his studies deal with wrongdoing—with stealing, for example, or disobeying laws. Few of the dilemmas reveal anything about the kind of reasoning children use in justifying prosocial behavior. You learned in Chapter 11 that altruistic behavior is evident in children as young as 2 and 3, but how do children explain and justify such behavior?

Eisenberg's Model of Prosocial Reasoning

Nancy Eisenberg and her colleagues evaluated children's empathy and prosocial behavior by gaining their responses to dilemmas involving self-interest. One story for younger children, for example, involves a child walking to a friend's birthday party. On the way, he comes upon another child who has fallen and hurt himself. If the party-bound child stops to help, he will probably miss the cake and ice cream. What should he do? In response to dilemmas like this, preschool children most often use what Eisenberg calls **hedonistic reasoning**, in which the child is concerned with self-oriented consequences rather than moral considerations. Preschoolers asked about what they would do if they came upon an injured child on their way to a birthday party say things like "I'd help because he'd help me the next time" or "I wouldn't help because I'd miss the party." This approach gradually shifts to one Eisenberg calls **needs-oriented reasoning**, in which the child expresses concern rather directly for the other person's need, even if the other's need conflicts with the child's own wishes or desires. Children operating on this basis say things like "He'd feel better if I helped." These children do not express their choices in terms of general principles or indicate any reflectiveness about generalized values; they simply respond to the other's needs.

Still later, typically in adolescence, children say they will do good things because it is expected of them, a pattern highly similar to Kohlberg's stage 3. Finally, in late adolescence, some young people give evidence that they have developed clear, internalized values that guide their prosocial behavior: "I'd feel a responsibility to help because of my values" or "If everyone helped, society would be a lot better."

Some sample data from Eisenberg's longitudinal study of a small group of U.S. children illustrate the shift from hedonistic to needs-oriented reasoning; see Figure 12.6. By early adolescence, hedonistic reasoning has virtually disappeared and needs-oriented reasoning has become the dominant form. Eisenberg reports that similar patterns have been found among children in West Germany, Poland, and Italy, but that kibbutz-reared Israeli elementary school children show little needs-oriented reasoning (Eisenberg, 1986). Instead, this particular group of Israeli children is more likely to reason on the basis of internalized values and norms and the humanness of recipients, a pattern consistent with the strong emphasis on egalitarianism and communal values in the kibbutzim. These findings suggest that culture may perhaps play a larger role in

hedonistic reasoning A form of prosocial moral reasoning described by Eisenberg in which the child is concerned with consequences to self rather than moral considerations, roughly equivalent to Kohlberg's stage 2.

needs-oriented reasoning A form of prosocial moral reasoning proposed by Eisenberg in which the child expresses concern directly for the other person's need, even if the other's need conflicts with the child's own wishes or desires.

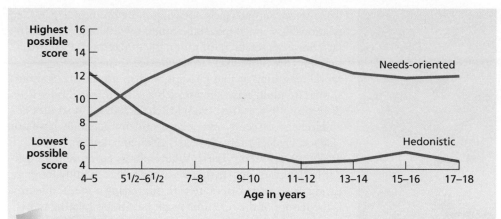

FIGURE 12.6

Every 2 years Eisenberg asked the same group of children what a person should do when confronted with each of a series of dilemmas about doing good, such as helping someone who is hurt. She then analyzed their form of reasoning, using a measure for which the minimum score was 4 and the maximum was 16.

(*Source*: Eisenberg et al., "Pro-social development in late adolescence," *Child Development*, 66, 1995, pp. 1179–1197.)

children's moral reasoning than in their reasoning about justice, although that is still a highly tentative conclusion.

There are obviously strong parallels between the sequences of changes in prosocial reasoning Eisenberg has described and Kohlberg's levels and stages of moral reasoning. Children seem to move from a self-centered orientation ("What feels good to me is right") to a stance in which social approval guides reasoning about both justice and moral behavior ("What is right is what other people define as right; I should do good things because others will approve of me if I do"). Much later, some young people seem to develop internalized, individualized norms to guide both kinds of reasoning. Despite these obvious parallels, though, researchers have typically found only moderate correlations between children's reasoning about prosocial dilemmas such as Eisenberg's and their reasoning about Kohlberg's justice or fairness dilemmas. The sequences of steps may be similar, but as was true of so much of the cognitive development you read about in Chapter 6, children's reasoning in one area doesn't necessarily generalize to a related area.

Eisenberg's research, as well as the work of others in the same field, helps to broaden Kohlberg's original conception, without changing the fundamental arguments. In contrast, Carol Gilligan has questioned some of the basic tenets of Kohlberg's model.

Gilligan's Ethic of Caring   Carol Gilligan (1982; Gilligan & Wiggins, 1987) is fundamentally dissatisfied with Kohlberg's focus on justice and fairness as the defining elements of moral reasoning. Gilligan argues that there are at least two distinct "moral orientations": justice and caring. Each has its own central injunction: not to treat others unfairly (justice), and not to turn away from someone in need (caring). Boys and girls learn both of these injunctions, but Gilligan has hypothesized that girls are more likely to operate from an orientation of caring or connection, while boys are more likely to operate from an orientation of justice or fairness. Because of these differences, she argues, they tend to perceive moral dilemmas quite differently.

Given the emerging evidence on sex differences in styles of interaction and in friendship patterns, which you read about in Chapter 11, Gilligan's hypothesis makes

CRITICAL THINKING **9**

Suppose Gilligan is right, and adult women typically reason based on an ethic of caring while men reason based on an ethic of justice. What do you think the implications of such a difference would be for male-female relationships, for men and women as political leaders, or for other social phenomena?

Gilligan argues that these young women are much more likely to use an "ethic of caring" than an "ethic of justice" as a basis for their moral judgments, while the reverse is true among boys and men. Such a difference may exist among adults, but research on children and adolescents shows no such pattern.

Before going on . . .

■ How do psychoanalytic, learning, and cognitive-developmental theories differ in their explanations of moral development?

■ Describe Kohlberg's preconventional, conventional, and principled (postconventional) levels of moral reasoning and the stages within each.

■ What are the causes and consequences of changes in moral reasoning?

■ Explain Eisenberg's and Gilligan's perspectives on moral reasoning.

some sense. Perhaps girls, focusing more on intimacy in their relationships, judge moral dilemmas by different criteria. In fact, however, research on moral dilemmas has not shown that boys are more likely to use justice as the basis for their moral reasoning or that girls more often use caring. Several studies of adults have shown such a pattern (e.g., Lollis, Ross, & Leroux, 1996; Lyons, 1983; Mitchell, 2002), but studies of children, adolescents, and college students generally have not (Jadack, Hyde, Moore, & Keller, 1995; Smetana, Killen, & Turiel, 1991; Walker, 1991). What matters far more than gender in determining whether a given child or adult will use a caring or a justice orientation in addressing a moral dilemma is the nature of the dilemma itself. Dilemmas relating to interpersonal relationships, for example, are more likely to be addressed using a caring orientation, whereas dilemmas explicitly involving issues of fairness are more likely to be addressed with a justice orientation. It may be that adult women are more likely than men to interpret moral dilemmas as personal, but both men and women use both caring and justice arguments in resolving moral dilemmas (Turiel, 1998).

For example, Lawrence Walker scored children's answers to moral dilemmas using both Kohlberg's fairness scheme and Gilligan's criteria for a caring orientation. He found no sex difference either for hypothetical dilemmas like the Heinz dilemma or for real-life dilemmas suggested by the children themselves (Walker et al., 1987). Only among adults did Walker find a difference in the direction that Gilligan hypothesized.

Gilligan's arguments have often been quoted in the popular press as if they were already proven, when in fact the empirical base is really quite weak. Gilligan herself has done no systematic studies of children's (or adults') caring orientation. Yet despite these weaknesses, most developmentalists are not ready to discard all of her underlying points, primarily because the questions she is asking seem to fit so well with the newer research on sex differences in relationship styles. The fact that researchers typically find no differences between boys and girls in their tendencies to use caring versus justice orientations does not mean that there are no differences in the assumptions males and females bring to relationships or to moral judgments. This seems to be clearly an area in which a great deal more research is needed.

Summary

The Development of Social Cognition

● Many of the general principles that describe overall cognitive development also describe developmental changes in social cognition, including a shift in focus from outer to inner characteristics, from observation to inference, from definite to qualified judgment, and from a particular to a general view. Social and moral reasoning differ from other aspects of cognition, however, in that a child must learn that unlike objects, people behave with intention, mask feelings, and operate by special socially defined scripts or rules.

● Children's descriptions of other people shift from a focus on external features to a focus on personality traits and to

more qualified, comparative descriptions during adolescence; this progression parallels the shifts in children's self-descriptions.

● Children learn to interpret many basic emotional expressions fairly early, but they can correctly read more complex emotions and emotional blends only later. The ability to read others' emotions and intentions is an important element in a child's general social competence; those who are less skilled, who have less "emotion knowledge," are more likely to be rejected by their peers. Empathy—the ability to match or approximate the emotion of another—is seen in young infants, but it becomes less egocentric and more subtle through the preschool and elementary school years.

- Children's thinking about their relationships, especially friendships, also changes developmentally, moving from definitions of friends as people who share physical space or activities, to definitions emphasizing trust, and finally, during adolescence, to definitions emphasizing intimacy.
- By elementary school, children begin to understand the distinction between conventional rules and moral rules. They also distinguish between intentional and unintentional acts.

Moral Development

- Psychoanalytic theories of moral development emphasize emotions, whereas learning theories focus on reinforcement and modeling. Cognitive-developmental theorists study moral reasoning and assert that moral development is strongly related to general cognitive development.
- Kohlberg described six distinct stages in children's (and adults') reasoning about moral issues. These six stages are divided into three levels. The child moves from preconventional morality (dominated by punishment and "what feels good"), to conventional morality (dominated by group norms or laws), to postconventional or principled morality (dominated by social contracts and basic ethical principles).
- Both cognitive-developmental and environmental variables, such as the opportunity to discuss moral issues, contribute to advancement through Kohlberg's stages. A child's or adult's stage predicts prosocial and antisocial behavior and attitudes to some degree.
- Alternative models of moral reasoning include Eisenberg's stages of prosocial reasoning (reasoning about why to do something good) and Gilligan's proposed caring orientation. Gilligan's hypothesis that girls are more likely than boys to use caring, rather than justice, as a basis for moral judgments has not been supported by research with children, adolescents, and college students.

Key Terms

conscience (p. 347)
conventional morality (p. 351)
conventional rules (p. 346)
ego ideal (p. 347)
empathy (p. 341)
hedonistic reasoning (p. 356)

moral development (p. 346)
moral realism stage (p. 349)
moral relativism stage (p. 349)
moral rules (p. 346)
needs-oriented reasoning (p. 356)
preconventional morality (p. 350)

principled (postconventional) morality (p. 352)
role-taking (p. 354)
social cognition (p. 337)

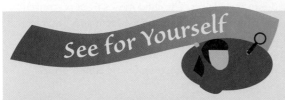

Children's Descriptions of Others

You can replicate Carl Barenboim's classic research by asking children of different ages to describe three specific people. You might begin by asking children to name the three peers they like best. Next, ask them to describe these children. Try to interview children across the same age range as those who participated in Barenboim's studies (6–16 years). Using the examples on page 340 in the text as a guide, count the number of physical/behavioral, psychological, and organizing relationship remarks made by the children you interview. Sum the remarks across the ages of the children you interview, and use the sums to create a graph like the one in Figure 12.1 on page 341.

Piaget's Stages of Moral Reasoning

You can find out more about Piaget's moral realism and moral relativism stages by using the kinds of simple stories employed by Piaget in his research (Piaget, 1965). Present the following stories to a child between 5 and 7 years old and to one between 10 and 12. Ask each child to repeat the stories back to you. Correct any misunderstandings. Then, ask the child the questions.

One day a little girl came inside her house after playing. She had seen a very large dog in a neighbor's yard. She told her mother that she had seen "a dog as big as an elephant."

Another girl came home from school one day. When her mother asked her about her school day, the girl said that she had gotten an "A" on a spelling test, but she had really gotten a "D."

> Moral Judgment Questions
>
> *Did both girls say something that wasn't true?*
> *Did both lie?*
> *Which one told the biggest lie?*
> *Why is her lie bigger than the other girl's?*
> *Should both of them be punished for lying?*
> *If both should be punished, which one should receive the greatest punishment?*

In Piaget's research, younger children (moral realists) said that the child who exaggerated about the size of the dog had told the biggest lie (because there has never been a dog as big as an elephant) and should receive the greater punishment. Older children (moral relativists) distinguished, in a moral sense, between exaggeration and intentional deception. Thus, they judged only the girl who lied about her grade to be deserving of punishment.

The Ecology of Development: The Child within the Family System

I f you have read William Golding's novel The Lord of the Flies or have seen one of the film versions, you know that the former teacher put forward a rather pessimistic view of human nature.

In the story, a group of boys ranging in age from 6 or so to early adolescence are stranded on an island with no adult supervision. The hero, Ralph, attempts to establish a civilized community for the boys, based on the rules of the English society from which they have come. Exploiting the tendency of the younger boys toward fearfulness and superstition, his nemesis, Jack, sets up a "culture" in which he enjoys absolute power. Although there have been many interpretations of Golding's work, one message seems clear: Children need adults to become civilized, or, to put it differently, to channel their natural impulses into behaviors that will enhance both their own development and the collective good of humankind.

While most developmentalists would probably find Golding's characterization of unsupervised children and adolescents a bit too pessimistic, they would probably, nonetheless, agree with the basic premise that children require relationships with adults in order to develop optimally. But will just any adult do, or is there a need for a special adult-child relationship to serve as a context in which culture is transmitted from one generation to the next? In other words, do children really need families?

In search of answers to this question, developmental scientists have turned to systems theory (Lamb & Lewis, 2005). Systems theorists emphasize that any system—biological, economic, or psychological—has several key properties. First and foremost, a system has "wholeness and order," which is another way of saying that the whole is greater than the sum of its parts. The whole consists of the parts and their relationship to one another. Often an analogy is made between a system and a melody. A melody is far more than a set of individual notes: it is the relationship of notes to one another that creates the melody.

A second feature of any system is that it is adaptive in precisely the same way as Piaget theorized the child's cognitive system is. When any part of a system changes or some new element is added, the system "assimilates" if it can but "accommodates" if it must. So systems resist change as much as they can by absorbing new data or new parts into the existing structure; if that doesn't work—as it often doesn't—only then will the system change. For example, when a family's second child is born, the parents may try to keep to their old routines as much as possible; the presence of this new individual in the family system will, however, inevitably force accommodations. That will be particularly true if the new baby is temperamentally very different from the first child.

You can see that these two features of systems—wholeness and adaptivity—cause any change in any one part of a system to affect every other part. Furthermore, systems have feedback loops. For example, a husband who is suffering from depression is likely to be more negative toward his wife than he used to be. This negativity will put a strain on their relationship. The worsening of the relationship, coupled with the man's depression, will cause these parents to treat their children differently—perhaps they will be less attentive in general, but more critical and strict when they do pay attention. The children will react with changes of their own, perhaps becoming defiant. The parents then become more strict and demanding, and a cycle is set in motion.

Viewed from the perspective of systems theory, the boys in Golding's tale adapted to a new context, that of living without adults in a primitive environment, by creating a system of relationships that differed greatly from the social system they had left behind in England. It was not simply the lack of adult supervision that led to the emergence of their rather cruel society. Instead, the perceived necessity of protecting themselves from dangers that they lacked the cognitive development to understand was the driving force behind their behavior and a central theme of the society they constructed. Motivated by fear, the younger boys turned to the most aggressive of the older boys, Jack, for leadership, because they believed him to be the one who was most capable of protecting them. Likewise, they rejected Ralph because he represented a system—rules premised upon adult affection and authority—that had worked well in England but was of little relevance to their new situation. Thus, though nobody would argue that living in a society such as the one depicted in Golding's novel would be beneficial to children's development, it is nonetheless true that the boys' behavior was adaptive in nature, rather than simply morally "bad" behavior that flourished because there were no adults to punish it.

Although virtually all psychologists now accept the general validity of the systems approach, figuring out how to conceptualize and study the various parts of such systems has been no small task (Sameroff & Mackenzie, 2003). To give you some feeling for the complexity of this task, we turn to Urie Bronfenbrenner's (1917–2005) approach to the *bioecology of development*.

Bronfenbrenner's Bioecological Approach

Of all the various systems theories, none has been more influential than that of developmental psychologist Urie Bronfenbrenner (1979, 1989, 2001). For Bronfenbrenner, the family is the filter through which the larger society influences child development. As such, the family can help the larger culture achieve the goal of socializing new members, but it can also serve as a buffer against harmful elements in the culture-at-large. Thus, according to Bronfenbrenner, although other institutions can substitute for it to some degree, the family is "the most efficient means of making human beings human" (Bronfenbrenner, quoted in EBC, 1991).

Of course there are many developmental theories, such as Freud's psychoanalytic theory, that emphasize the importance of the child's family. What distinguishes Bronfenbrenner's bioecological approach from other developmental theories is his attempt to explain how all of the various environmental influences on children's development are related to one another. Moreover, Bronfenbrenner also provides an explanation for how all of these interrelated influences mesh with the child's own biological make-up. For this reason, his theory is now known as the *bioecological approach*.

Just how does Bronfenbrenner achieve such a comprehensive account of the role played by environmental factors in individual development? The fundamental premise of his theory is that the bioecological system in which the child develops can be thought of as a series of layers, or concentric circles. The innermost circle, made up of elements Bronfenbrenner calls *microsystems*, includes all those settings in which the child has direct personal experience, such as the family, a day-care center or a school, and a job setting (for a teenager).

The next layer, which Bronfenbrenner calls *exosystems*, includes a whole range of system elements that the child does not experience directly but that influence the child

CRITICAL THINKING 9

Draw a set of concentric circles like those in Figure 13.1 and describe the ecological system of your life at about age 5. What were the microsystems, exosystems, and macrosystem that affected your life?

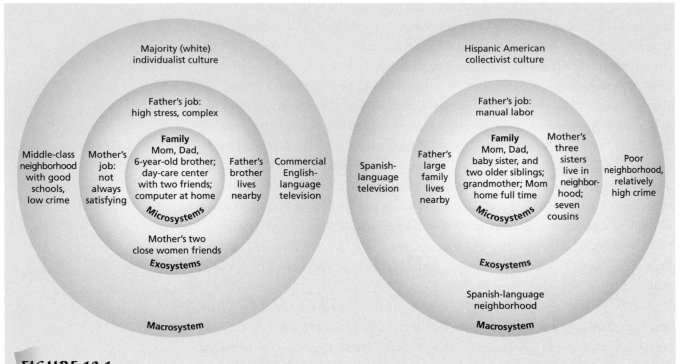

FIGURE 13.1

Two hypothetical children, growing up in widely different ecological settings, illustrate the layers in Bronfenbrenner's model. To understand how the environment affects a child, developmentalists would need to study every aspect of this complex system simultaneously—a tall order.

because they affect one of the microsystems, particularly the family. The parents' work and workplace is one such element, as is the parents' network of friends.

Finally, Bronfenbrenner describes a *macrosystem* that includes the larger cultural or subcultural setting in which both the microsystems and the exosystems are embedded. The poverty or wealth of the family, the neighborhood in which the family lives, the ethnic identity of the family, and the larger culture in which the entire system exists are all parts of this macrosystem.

Figure 13.1 presents these three layers schematically for two hypothetical 4-year-old American children—one from the majority white culture living in an intact middle-class family with two employed parents, the other a Hispanic American child living with both parents and a grandmother in a working-class, largely Spanish-speaking neighborhood, whose mother stays at home full-time. If you try to imagine yourself living within each of these systems, you can get a feeling for the many complex ways in which they differ and how all their pieces interact with one another. Bronfenbrenner's point is that until developmentalists really understand the ways in which all the elements in such complex systems interact to affect the child, they will not understand development.

It is probably obvious that trying to understand child development in this way is immensely difficult. It is hard to keep all the elements of a system in mind at once, let alone to try to study all the relevant parts simultaneously. Perhaps frustrated by that difficulty, or perhaps because of the long tradition of examining family and cultural effects in more linear ways, psychologists have continued to design research that explores only small pieces of the total ecological system. Thus, much of what is known about family and cultural influences on children is piecemeal rather than systemic. Nonetheless, let's plunge in, using Bronfrenbrenner's model as a general framework.

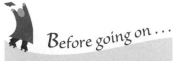

Before going on . . .

■ Explain the various systems proposed by Bronfenbrenner to explain the influence of the child's environment on development.

Dimensions of Family Interaction

Researchers who have focused most directly on patterns of parent-child interaction have identified several major dimensions on which families differ and which seem to be significant for the child. These include the emotional tone of the family, the responsiveness of the parent to the child, the manner in which control is exercised, and the quality and amount of communication.

THE EMOTIONAL TONE OF THE FAMILY

The first key family dimension that has an effect on the child is the relative **warmth versus hostility** of the home. "Warmth" has been difficult to define and measure, but it seems intuitively obvious that it is highly important for the child, and research has supported this intuition. A warm parent cares about the child, expresses affection, frequently or regularly puts the child's needs first, shows enthusiasm for the child's activities, and responds sensitively and empathetically to the child's feelings (Maccoby, 1980). On the other end of this continuum are parents who overtly reject their children—saying in words or by their behavior that they do not love or want them.

Such differences have profound effects. Psychologists have found that children in warm and loving families are more securely attached in the first 2 years of life; have higher self-esteem; are more empathetic, more altruistic, and more responsive to others' hurts or distress; and have higher IQ scores in preschool and elementary school and do better in school (Domitrovich & Bierman, 2001; Maccoby, 1980; Pettit, Bates, & Dodge, 1997; Simons, Robertson, & Downs, 1989). They are also less likely to show high levels of aggression or delinquent behavior in later childhood or in adolescence (Goldstein, Davis-Kean, & Eccles, 2005; Maughan, Pickles, & Quinton, 1995). In addition, teens who were reared in low-warmth families are more likely to have suicidal thoughts and other mental health problems (Lai & McBride-Chang, 2001; Xia & Qian, 2001).

High levels of affection can even buffer a child against the negative effects of otherwise disadvantageous environments. Several studies of children and teens growing up in poor, dangerous neighborhoods show that the single ingredient that most clearly distinguishes the lives of those who do not become delinquent from those who do is a high level of maternal love (Glueck & Glueck, 1972; McCord, 1982). Similarly, in a longitudinal study, Gregory Pettit and his colleagues (Pettit, Bates, & Dodge, 1997) found that children who were growing up in poverty but whose parents provided more "supportive parenting" (including warmth) were less likely to develop aggressive or delinquent behavior than equally poor children in less emotionally supportive families.

At the other end of the continuum from parental warmth, parental hostility is linked to declining school performance and higher risk of delinquency (Melby & Conger, 1996). When such hostility is expressed as physical abuse or neglect, the consequences for the child may be even more severe.

Fostering a secure attachment of the child to the parent appears to be one of the key consequences of emotional warmth. You already know from Chapter 11 that securely attached children are more skillful with their peers, more exploratory, more sure of themselves. Warmth also makes children generally more responsive to guidance, so the parents' affection and warmth increase the potency of the things they say to their children as well as the efficiency of their discipline (MacDonald, 1992).

It is probably obvious that loving a child is a critical ingredient in the child's optimum development—but sometimes it doesn't hurt to restate the obvious.

warmth versus hostility The key dimension of emotional tone used to describe family interactions.

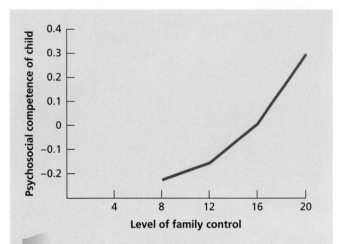

FIGURE 13.2

Junior high school students who report higher levels of parental control and supervision also describe themselves as having higher self-esteem and self-efficacy.
(*Source*: Kurdek, L., and Fine, M., from Fig. 1, p. 1143, "Family acceptance and family control as predictors of adjustments in young adolescents," *Child Development*, 65 (1994), 1137–1146. By permission of the Society for Research in Child Development.)

A second key element of family interaction patterns is **responsiveness** by the parent to the child, a concept you've encountered in earlier chapters. Responsive parents are those who pick up on the child's signals appropriately and then react in sensitive ways to the child's needs (Ainsworth & Marvin, 1995; Sroufe, 1996). Children of parents who do more of this learn language somewhat more rapidly, show higher IQ scores and more rapid cognitive development, and are more likely to be securely attached, more compliant with adult requests, and more socially competent (e.g., Bornstein, 1989; Kochanska, 1997; van den Boom, 1994). Further evidence for the importance of responsiveness comes from research showing that training new parents to be more responsive reduces the odds that an infant will develop an insecure or disorganized attachment (Juffer, Bakermans-Kranenburg, & van IJzendoorn, 2005).

METHODS OF CONTROL

It is the nature of children to do things their parents do not want them to do, ask for things they cannot have, or refuse to obey their parents' requests or demands. Parents are inevitably faced with the task of controlling the child's behavior and training the child to follow basic rules, a process popularly known as *discipline*. Parental control of children's behavior, a third aspect of family interaction, relies on several elements.

One element of control is the consistency of rules—making it clear to the child what the rules are, what the consequences are of disobeying (or obeying) them, and then enforcing them consistently. Some parents are very clear and consistent; others waver or are fuzzy about what they expect or will tolerate. Studies of families show that parents who are clear and consistent have children who are much less likely to be defiant or noncompliant—a pattern you'll remember from Gerald Patterson's research (see Chapter 1). The same pattern, incidentally, can be observed in day-care centers and preschools: Children whose teachers are lax and inconsistent in their response to misbehavior are more likely to misbehave (Arnold, McWilliams, & Arnold, 1998). Consistency of rules does not produce little robots. Children from families with consistent rules are more competent and sure of themselves and less likely to become delinquent or show significant behavior problems than are children from families with less consistent rules.

One piece of research that illustrates this pattern nicely is Lawrence Kurdek and Mark Fine's study of 850 junior high school students (Kurdek & Fine, 1994). They measured the level of control in the family by asking the young adolescents to rate the accuracy of each of the following three statements:

> Someone in my family makes sure that my homework is done.
> Generally, someone in my family knows where I am and what I'm doing.
> Someone in my family keeps a close eye on me.

Kurdek and Fine also had information about each child's self-esteem and sense of self-efficacy, which they combined into a measure of "psychological competence." You can see the relationship between these two pieces of information in Figure 13.2: Greater family control was clearly associated with greater psychological competence.

Such a link between good parental control and positive outcomes for the child has been found among African American as well as Caucasian American youth. For example, Craig Mason and his colleagues (1996; Walker-Barnes & Mason, 2004) have found that among working-class black families, those in which the parents maintained the most consistent monitoring and control over their adolescents had teenagers who were

responsiveness An aspect of parent-child interaction; a responsive parent is sensitive to the child's cues and reacts appropriately, following the child's lead.

least likely to show problem behavior. Interestingly and importantly, the link between parental control and lower rates of problem behavior in Mason's study was especially clear in cases in which the child had many peers who were engaging in problem behavior. Thus, the parents, by applying consistent rules and monitoring the child's activities, could at least partially counteract the negative effects of their children's "hanging out" with misbehaving peers.

This dad seems to be willing to listen carefully to his son, even though the boy is angry and may be accusatory.

A related element of parental control is the level of expectations the parents have for the child's behavior. Is the child expected to show relatively mature behavior, or do the parents feel it is important not to expect too much too soon? Studies of such variations show that, within limits, higher expectations seem to be associated with better outcomes. Children whose parents make high demands on them—expecting them to help around the house or to show relatively mature behavior for their age—have higher self-esteem, show more generosity and altruism toward others, and have lower levels of aggression. Obviously, high expectations can be carried too far. It is unrealistic and counterproductive to expect a 2-year-old to set the table for dinner or to tie his own shoes. But when parents expect a child to be as independent and helpful as possible for his age, they seem to foster a sense of competence in the child that carries over into other situations.

Finally, to understand the process of control, you must understand the role of punishment. Punishment is one form of discipline, one method of training and controlling. It is most often aimed at getting a child to stop doing something prohibited, such as writing on the wall, hitting his brother, or staying out past a curfew, but it may also be used to try to push a child to do something that he is resisting, such as cleaning his room. Punishments almost invariably involve some negative consequence for the child, ranging from withholding privileges or treats, assigning extra chores, sending a child to his room, or "grounding" the child to more severe forms of verbal scolding and even spanking. The most controversial of these is spanking. Because of the importance of the question, the pros and cons of physical punishment are explored in the *Research Report*, but there are two points about punishment strategies in general that you should understand.

First, as Gerald Patterson says, "Punishment 'works.' If you use it properly it will produce rapid changes in the behavior of other people" (1975, p. 19). The operative word here, though, is *properly*. The most effective punishments—those that produce long-term changes in a child's behavior without unwanted or negative side effects—are those used early in some sequence of misbehavior, with the lowest level of emotion possible and the mildest level of punishment possible. Taking a desired toy away when the child first hits a sibling with it or consistently removing small privileges when a child misbehaves will produce the desired results, especially if the parent is also warm, clear about the rules, and consistent. It is far less effective to wait until the sibling's screams have reached a piercing level or until the fourth time a teenager has gone off without telling you where she's going and then weigh in with yelling, critical comments, and strong punishment.

Second, to a considerable degree, parents "get back what they put in" with respect to punishment. As you learned in Chapter 9, children learn by observation as well as by doing, so they learn the adults' ways of coping with stress and their forms of punishment. Yelling at children to get them to stop doing something, for example, may bring a brief change in their behavior (which reinforces the parent for yelling, by the way), but it also increases the chances that the children will yell back on other occasions.

COMMUNICATION PATTERNS

A fourth important dimension of the family system is the quality of the communication between parent and child. Two things about such communication seem to make a

CRITICAL THINKING 9

Think about your own upbringing. What types of control strategies did your parents use? What kinds of punishment did they use? How might you want to change these patterns in bringing up your own children?

To Spank or Not to Spank?

Every culture provides guidelines for how parents ought to discipline children (Giles-Sims & Lockhart, 2005). For example, in Sweden, there is a law against physical punishment of children (Palmérus & Scarr, 1995). In the United States, no such law exists, and 9 out of 10 parents of preschoolers say that they spank their children at least occasionally, most often in response to some aggressive act (Holden, Coleman, & Schmidt, 1995). Among middle-class parents, a quarter say they spank their child with their hand at least weekly; 35% use an object such as a hairbrush to hit their child at least occasionally; and 12% say they hit their child hard enough on occasion to cause considerable pain (Graziano, Hamblen, & Plante, 1996). Spanking teenagers is less common than is spanking preschoolers or elementary school children, but about half of parents of teenagers say they use spanking at least occasionally (Straus, 1991a; Straus & Donnelly, 1993). Researchers have found that parents' decision to spank a child in response to his or her performance of an unacceptable behavior is based on their belief in the efficacy of physical punishment, perceptions of the child's intent, and the degree to which the behavior made them angry (Ateah & Durrant, 2005). With regard to beliefs, parents who spank think of physical punishment as an effective form of discipline. However, many developmentalists disagree, including those in the American Academy of Pediatrics, who addressed the issue in an article on "Guidance for Effective

Discipline" (1998). Here are some of the arguments against using this form of discipline.

In the short term, spanking a child usually does get the child to stop a behavior, and it seems to temporarily reduce the chance that the child will repeat the behavior (Gershoff, 2002). But, even in the short term there are some negative side effects. The child may stop misbehaving, but after a spanking he is likely to be crying, which may be almost as distressing as the original misbehavior. Another short-term side effect is that the parent is being negatively reinforced for spanking whenever the child stops misbehaving. Thus, the parent is being "trained" to use spanking the next time, and a cycle is being built up.

In the longer term, the effects of spanking are clearly negative. The child observes the parent using physical force as a method of solving problems or getting people to do what she wants. By repeatedly pairing her presence with the unpleasant or painful event of spanking, the parent is undermining her own positive value for the child. Over time, this means that she is less able to use any kind of reinforcement effectively. Eventually, even your praise or affection will be less powerful in influencing the child's behavior. That is a very high price to pay.

Spanking also frequently carries a strong underlying emotional message—anger, rejection, irritation, dislike of the child. Even very young children read such emotional

difference for the child: the amount and richness of language used with the child (which you already read about in Chapter 8), and the amount of conversation and suggestions from the child that the parent encourages. Listening is as important as talking.

Listening means something more than merely saying "uh-huh" periodically when the child talks. It also means conveying to the child the sense that what he has to say is worth listening to, that he has ideas, that his ideas are important and should be considered in family decisions.

Developmentalists have conducted much less research on the quality of communication within families than on some of the other dimensions, so they are a long way from understanding all the ramifications of communication style. However, in general, children from families with open communication are seen as more emotionally or socially mature (Baumrind, 1971; Bell & Bell, 1982). Some studies also show that children in such families attain higher levels of academic achievement (Scott, 2004). Moreover, individuals who grow up in families characterized by open communication have good social skills in adulthood (Koesten, 2004).

Open communication may also be important for the functioning of the family as a unit. For example, in a study of a national sample of families with adolescents, Howard Barnes and David Olson (1985) measured communication by asking the parents and teenagers to agree or disagree with statements such as "It is easy for me to express all my true feelings to my messages quite clearly (Rohner, Kean, & Cournoyer, 1991). Spanking thus helps to create a family climate of rejection instead of warmth, with all the attendant negative consequences.

Finally, research evidence suggests that children who are spanked—like children who are abused—at later ages are less popular with their peers and show higher levels of aggression, lower self-esteem, more emotional instability, higher rates of depression and distress, and higher levels of delinquency and later criminality (Fine, Trentacosta, Izard, Mostow, & Campbell, 2004; Laub & Sampson, 1995; Rohner et al., 1991; Strassberg, Dodge, Pettit, & Bates, 1994; Turner & Finkelhor, 1996). As adults, children who have been spanked regularly are more likely to be depressed than are those who were never or rarely spanked (Straus, 1995), and they also have higher risks of various other types of adult problems, including unemployment, divorce or violence within a relationship, and criminality (Maughan et al., 1995). All these negative effects are especially clear if the physical punishment is harsh and erratic, but the risks for these poor outcomes are increased even with fairly mild levels of physical punishment.

Developmentalists who oppose spanking do not mean to suggest that parents should never punish a child. They are saying that physical punishment, such as spanking, is not a good way to go about it. Yelling at the child is not a good alternative strategy, either. Strong verbal aggression by a parent toward a child is also linked to many poor outcomes in the child, including increased risk of delinquency and adult violence (Straus, 1991b).

At the same time, an important caveat is in order. Virtually all the research that shows a link between physical punishment and poor outcomes has been done with Caucasian American children. There are a handful of studies suggesting that the same effects may not occur in African American families. For example, Kirby Deater-Deckard and his colleagues (1996) found that white children whose parents used higher levels of physical punishment were more likely to be aggressive in school; the same link did not occur for black children in the same study, unless the physical discipline was severe. One possible explanation is that spanking and other forms of physical punishment may have negative effects primarily when they are combined with low levels of emotional warmth (Deater-Deckard & Dodge, 1997). If physical discipline is more likely to be combined with emotional coldness in Caucasian American families than it is in African American families, this would help to account for the difference between these racial groups. Another possibility is that parents who are urban, black, and poor, in particular, use physical punishment as a means of maintaining tighter monitoring and control in a highly dangerous environment, and the benefits of improved monitoring may outweigh the adverse effects of physical punishment. Whatever the reason, results like this remind us once again that we must be very careful about generalizing from one group to another. For now, it is reasonable to conclude that for Caucasian American children, spanking seems to have consistently negative consequences and that harsh or erratic physical punishment has negative effects on children in every group studied.

Questions for Critical Analysis

1. Why would it be unethical to use the experimental method to study the effects of spanking?
2. What kinds of variables (e.g., parents' personality traits) might explain the correlation between spanking and poor developmental outcomes?

(mother/father/child)." As you can see in Figure 13.3, the investigators found that compared to those reporting poorer communication, parents and children who reported good, open communication also described their families as more adaptable in the face of stress or change and said that they were more satisfied with their families.

Before going on...

- How do emotional warmth and its opposite—hostility—influence parent-child relationships?
- What are the potential negative effects of physical punishment?
- How do family communication patterns affect family interactions and children's development?

 # Patterns of Child Rearing

Each of the dimensions of parental behavior discussed in the previous section has a demonstrable effect on the child, but if psychologists want to use a systems theory approach, it is not enough to look at each dimension independently. They also have to think about how the dimensions interact to create styles or patterns of child rearing.

PARENTING STYLES

The most influential proposal about styles of child rearing has come from Diana Baumrind (1973), who has looked at combinations of the various dimensions of

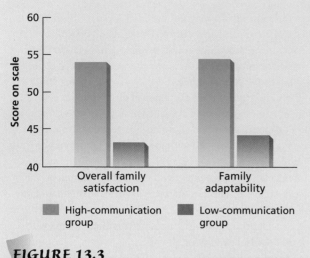

FIGURE 13.3

Good family communication was associated with both satisfaction and adaptability in this study of over 400 adolescents and their parents.
(*Source*: Barnes & Olson, 1985, Table 3, page 445.)

parenting: (1) warmth, or nurturance; (2) level of expectations, which she calls "maturity demands"; (3) the clarity and consistency of rules, referred to as control; and (4) communication between parent and child. Baumrind saw three specific combinations of these characteristics:

- The **permissive style** is high in nurturance but low in maturity demands, control, and communication.
- The **authoritarian style** is high in control and maturity demands but low in nurturance and communication.
- The **authoritative style** is high in all four.

Eleanor Maccoby and John Martin (1983) extended Baumrind's category system, proposing a model that has been widely influential. They emphasized two dimensions, as you can see in Figure 13.4: the degree of control or demand and the level of acceptance/responsiveness. The intersection of these two dimensions creates four parenting types, three of which correspond fairly closely to Baumrind's authoritarian, authoritative, and permissive types. Maccoby and Martin's fourth type, the uninvolved **neglecting style**, was not identified by Baumrind in her early work, although more recent research shows clearly that this is a parenting style that deserves more study.

The Authoritarian Type   Authoritarian parents, as Kristan Glasgow and her colleagues describe them, are highly demanding of their children but at the same time quite unresponsive: "These parents attempt to mold and control the behavior and attitudes of their children according to a set of standards. They tend to emphasize obedience, respect for authority, and order. [They] also discourage verbal give-and-take with their children, expecting rules to be followed without further explanation" (Glasgow, Dornbush, Troyer, Steinberg, & Ritter, 1997, p. 508). Children growing up in such families do less well in school, are typically less skilled with peers, and have lower self-esteem than children from other types of families (Baumrind, 1991; Maccoby & Martin, 1983). Some of these children appear subdued; others may show high levels of aggressiveness or other indications of being out of control (Caputo, 2004). Which of these two outcomes occurs may depend in part on how skillfully the parents use various disciplinary techniques. Patterson finds that the "out-of-control" child is most likely to come from a family in which the parents are authoritarian by inclination but lack the skills to enforce the limits or rules they set.

The Permissive Type   Children growing up with indulgent or permissive parents, who are tolerant and warm but exercise little authority, also show some negative outcomes. They do slightly less well in school in adolescence, and they are likely to be aggressive—particularly if the parents are specifically permissive toward aggressiveness—and to be somewhat immature in their behavior with peers and in school. They are less likely to take responsibility and are less independent (Maccoby & Martin, 1983).

The Authoritative Type   The most consistently positive outcomes have been associated with the authoritative parenting pattern, in which the parents are high in both control and warmth, setting clear limits, expecting and reinforcing socially mature behavior, and at the same time responding to the child's individual needs. Note that parents who use this style of parenting do not let the child rule the roost. Authoritative parents are quite willing to discipline the child appropriately if the child misbehaves. They are less likely to use physical punishment than are authoritarian parents, preferring instead to use time out or other mild punishments, but it is important to understand that such parents

permissive style One of the three parenting styles described by Baumrind, characterized by high levels of nurturance and low levels of control, maturity demands, and communication.

authoritarian style One of the three parental styles described by Baumrind, characterized by high levels of control and maturity demands and low levels of nurturance and communication.

authoritative style One of the three parental styles described by Baumrind, characterized by high levels of control, nurturance, maturity demands, and communication.

neglecting style A fourth parenting style suggested by Maccoby and Martin, involving low levels of both acceptance and control.

are not wishy-washy. Children reared in such families typically show higher self-esteem. They are more independent but at the same time are more likely to comply with parental requests, and they may show more altruistic behavior as well. They are self-confident and achievement-oriented in school and get better grades in elementary school, high school, and college (e.g., Crockenberg & Litman, 1990; Dornbusch, Ritter, Liederman, Roberts, & Fraleigh, 1987; Jackson, Pratt, Hunsberger, & Pancer, 2005; Steinberg, Elmen, & Mounts, 1989; Weiss & Schwarz, 1996).

The Neglecting Type   The most consistently negative outcomes are associated with the fourth parenting pattern, the neglecting or uninvolved type. You may remember from the discussion of secure and insecure attachments in Chapter 11 that one of the characteristics often found in the families of children rated as insecurely attached is the "psychological unavailability" of the mother. The mother may be depressed or may be overwhelmed by problems in her life, or she simply may not have made any deep emotional connection with the child. Whatever the reason, such children continue to show disturbances in their relationships with peers and with adults for many years. At adolescence, for example, youngsters from neglecting families are more impulsive and antisocial and much less achievement-oriented in school (Block, 1971; Caputo, 2004; Lamborn, Mounts, Steinberg, & Dornbusch, 1991; Pulkkinen, 1982). Lack of parental monitoring appears to be critical: Children and teens whose neglecting parents show poor monitoring are far more likely to become delinquent and to engage in sexual activity in early adolescence (Patterson, Read, & Dishion, 1992; Pittman & Chase-Lansdale, 2001; Walker-Barnes & Mason, 2004).

FIGURE 13.4

Maccoby and Martin expanded on Baumrind's categories of parenting style in this two-dimensional typology. (*Source*: Maccoby, E. and Martin, J., adapted from Fig. 2, p. 39, "Socialization in the context of the family: Parent-child interaction," *Handbook of Child Psychology: Socialization, Personality, and Social Development*, Vol. 4, 1983, pp. 1–102. © 1983 by Wiley. By permission.)

CRITICAL THINKING ?

How would you classify your own parents' style? How do you think their parenting style affected your development?

A RESEARCH EXAMPLE: THE WORK OF STEINBERG AND DORNBUSCH

The best single piece of research demonstrating the effects of the several parenting styles is a study of nearly 11,000 high school students in California and Wisconsin that was conducted by Laurence Steinberg and Sanford Dornbusch and their colleagues. Of this sample, 6,902 were followed over a 2-year period, providing valuable longitudinal information (Dornbusch et al., 1987; Glasgow et al., 1997; Lamborn et al., 1991; Steinberg et al., 1989; Steinberg, Mounts, Lamborn, & Dornbusch, 1991; Steinberg, Lamborn, Dornbusch, & Darling, 1992; Steinberg, Lamborn, Darling, Mounts, & Dornbusch, 1994; Steinberg, Darling, Fletcher, Brown, & Dornbusch, 1995). The researchers measured parenting styles by asking the teenagers to respond to questions about their relationship with their parents and their family life, including questions about both parental acceptance/responsiveness and parental control or demand—the dimensions that define Maccoby and Martin's category system. For example, the teenagers were asked to indicate the extent to which each of the following statements was true for them:

> I can count on my parents to help me out if I have some kind of problem.
> When [my father] wants me to do something, he explains why.
> My parents know exactly where I am most afternoons after school.

On the basis of participants' answers to such questions, Steinberg and Dornbusch were able to classify most of their families in the Maccoby and Martin category system and could then look at the relationship between these family styles and a variety of behaviors in the teenagers. They found that teenagers from authoritative families showed the most optimal pattern on every measure they used. These teenagers had higher self-reliance, higher social competence, better grades, fewer indications of psychological distress, and lower levels of school misconduct, drug use, and delinquency. Teenagers from authoritarian families had the lowest scores on the several measures of social competence and self-reliance; those from neglecting families had the least optimal scores on measures of problem behaviors and school achievement (Steinberg et al., 1994). Figure 13.5 illustrates two of these results: variations in grade point average and self-reported delinquent acts (including carrying a weapon, stealing, and getting into trouble with the police).

In an analysis of the data for the nearly 7,000 students on whom they had 2 years of information, Steinberg and Dornbusch found that students who described their parents as most authoritative at the beginning of the study showed more improvement in academic competence and self-reliance and the smallest increases in psychological symptoms and delinquent behavior over the 2 years, suggesting that the family style has a causal and continuing effect. These results have been replicated by many other researchers across a variety of cultures (e.g., Álvarez, Martín, Vergeles, & Martín, 2003).

These results are impressive, but the family system is in fact more complex than the simple comparison of the four parenting types may make it sound. For example, authoritative parents not only create a good family climate and thereby support and motivate their child optimally; they also behave differently toward the child's school. They are much more likely to be involved with the school, attending school functions or talking to teachers, and this involvement seems to play a crucial role. When an otherwise authoritative parent is not also involved with the school, the outcomes for the student are not so clearly positive. Similarly, a teenager whose parent is highly involved with the school but is not authoritative shows less optimal outcomes. It is the combination of authoritativeness and school involvement that is associated with the best results (Steinberg, Lamborn, et al., 1992).

In another indication of the complexity of these relationships, Steinberg and Dornbusch have found that the young people in their study whose friends had more authoritative parents showed more optimal outcomes, regardless of the style of interaction in their own families. Even authoritatively reared teenagers had better grades and lower delinquency when they spent time with friends whose families were also authoritative than when they chose pals from families with other styles (Fletcher, Darling, Steinberg, & Dornbusch, 1995).

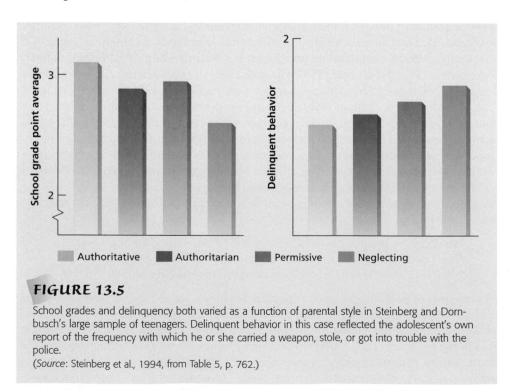

FIGURE 13.5

School grades and delinquency both varied as a function of parental style in Steinberg and Dornbusch's large sample of teenagers. Delinquent behavior in this case reflected the adolescent's own report of the frequency with which he or she carried a weapon, stole, or got into trouble with the police.

(*Source*: Steinberg et al., 1994, from Table 5, p. 762.)

RACIAL AND ETHNIC DIFFERENCES IN PARENTING STYLES

An additional complexity appears in analyses of relationships between parenting styles and developmental outcomes within each of several racial and ethnic groups. Steinberg and Dornbusch's sample was large enough to allow them to do this for subgroups of African American, Hispanic American, and Asian American youth and their families, as well as for Caucasian Americans (Steinberg et al., 1991). The results suggest both common processes and unique cultural variations.

Table 13.1 shows the percentage of families from each of the four racial or ethnic groups involved in this study that could be classed as authoritative, broken down further by social class and by the intactness of the family. The authoritative pattern was most common among Caucasian Americans and least common among Asian Americans, but in each group, authoritative parenting was more common among the middle class and (with one exception) more common among intact families than in single-parent or stepparent families.

The more important question is whether the same predictive relationships between family style and child outcomes apply to all the groups. For some outcomes, the answer is "yes." In all four groups, for example, teenagers from authoritative families showed more self-reliance and less delinquency than did those from nonauthoritative families.

On the other hand, school performance was not linked to authoritative parenting in the same ways in all four groups. In this study, good grades were linked to such a parenting style for Caucasian Americans and for Hispanic Americans, but only very weakly for Asian Americans—a group of students who do extremely well in school even though their parents are among the least authoritative. However, other researchers have found that the pattern of outcomes associated with authoritative and authoritarian parenting among other groups does hold true for Asian families (Chen, Dong, & Zhou, 1997). Among African American families, research results have been inconsistent with regard to linkages between parenting styles and academic achievement (Lamborn, Dornbusch, & Steinberg, 1996; Norwood, 1997).

How can developmentalists explain these differences? One possibility is that the four styles of parenting simply don't capture the most crucial features of family interaction that affect academic performance. Steinberg and Dornbusch have pursued this possibility by examining a wide variety of other aspects of family and cultural systems (Steinberg, Dornbusch, & Brown, 1992). They conclude that an additional key element is the belief students and parents hold about the importance of education for later success in life. All four racial and ethnic groups studied share a belief that doing well in

TABLE 13.1	Racial and Ethnic Differences in Authoritative Parenting

	Percentage of Authoritative Families			
	Working Class		Middle Class	
Ethnic Group	**Intact[a]**	**Not Intact**	**Intact**	**Not Intact**
White	17.2	11.5	25.0	17.6
Black	13.4	12.2	14.0	16.0
Hispanic	10.7	9.8	15.8	12.9
Asian	7.5	6.1	15.6	10.8

[a]*Intact* means the child is still living with both biological parents; *not intact* means a family with a single parent, a stepparent, or configuration other than both natural parents.

Source: Steinberg, L., Mounts, N. S., Lamborn, S. D., and Dornbusch, S. D., from Table 1, p. 25, "Authoritative Parenting and Adolescent Adjustment Roles across Varied Ecological Niches," in *Journal of Research on Adolescence*, 1, 1991. © 1991 by Lawrence Erlbaum Associates, Inc. By permission of the publisher and L. Steinberg.

Asian parents very often score high on measures of authoritarian parental style. But their high level of strictness and control is embedded in a particular set of cultural values, and it thus has a different meaning for the child and a different effect on the child's behavior than such a style might have in a non-Asian family. This is yet another illustration of the fact that psychologists must be careful in generalizing theories and results across cultures.

school will lead to better chances later, but the groups disagree on the consequences of doing poorly in school. Asian American students, more than any other group, believe that a good job is unlikely to follow a bad education, whereas Hispanic Americans and African Americans are more optimistic (or more cavalier) about the risks associated with poor school performance. Perhaps as a result of their greater fear of academic failure, Asian American students spend much more time on homework than do other groups.

Furthermore, Asian American (and Caucasian American students) get very good peer support for academic achievement, whereas African American teens get little. This factor undermines the beneficial effects of any authoritative parenting in this subgroup. Indeed, interviews with the African American students involved in the Steinberg and Dornbusch study suggest that academically oriented African American youths have difficulty finding a peer group that will support their academic goals. As Steinberg puts it, "The sad truth is that many students, and many black students in particular, are forced to choose between doing well in school and having friends" (1996, p. 161).

Another possibility is that the four styles suggested by Maccoby and Martin are themselves ethnocentric and simply do not (perhaps cannot) capture the elements that make individual cultural patterns unique (Parke & Buriel, 1998). For example, Ruth Chao (1994) notes that Chinese American parents, who require obedience, usually score high on traditional measures of authoritarian parenting. But in Asian cultures, strictness and a demand for obedience are perceived as aspects of concern and caring, not as reflections of lack of warmth. For the Chinese, says Chao, the key concept in parenting is training, which means teaching or educating, and training carries with it not only the element of control but also high involvement and closeness to the child. Chinese parents control their children not in order to dominate them—a motivation implicit in the authoritarian style as Baumrind described it—but rather to ensure that harmonious relations within the family and the culture will be maintained. According to Chao, the traditional measures of the authoritarian style simply fail to capture these values and thus badly misrepresent the quality of parent-child interactions within Chinese families.

ADDING UP WHAT IS KNOWN ABOUT PARENTING STYLE

The accumulating evidence makes it clear that the concept of parenting style has been and will continue to be highly useful descriptively and predictively. For one thing, it focuses attention on the family system rather than merely on individual behaviors. However, developmentalists may not yet have zeroed in on the best ways to describe family styles. The four types Baumrind and Maccoby and Martin suggest are probably only a first approximation. Many Caucasian American families cannot be accurately described by this system at all, and—as you've already seen—the model may not capture the important qualities of family interaction in other ethnic or cultural groups.

The model also does not explain why authoritative parenting is linked to greater competence in children (Lamb & Lewis, 2005). Are particular elements of the system especially critical, or is it the full configuration that matters? Addressing this question, Nancy Darling and Laurence Steinberg (1993) propose a major distinction between parental *styles* and parental *behavior*. They suggest that psychologists think of parenting style as a kind of basic climate in the family, as a set of attitudes and values rather than as a set of specific parenting practices or behaviors. Specific parenting behaviors or practices, in contrast, are responses to particular situations or goals, such as getting a child to stop hitting his sister or making sure a child does her homework. Parenting style and parenting behaviors are obviously linked in various ways, because some specific parental practices are more common in some styles than in others, but Darling and Steinberg argue that style and behaviors should be looked at separately. They propose that parenting behaviors affect the child directly, increasing or decreasing the likelihood of specific behaviors on the child's part. Parenting style, in contrast, has a more indirect effect. In particular, Darling and Steinberg argue, parenting style "alters the parents' capacity to socialize their children by changing the effectiveness of their parenting practices" (p. 493).

Thus, an authoritative parenting style is effective because it creates a climate in which the child is more open to the parents' influences and makes the specific parenting practices more potent. One result reported earlier provides support for this idea: Parental involvement with the child's school is more strongly associated with good academic outcomes in authoritative than in authoritarian families. Both types of parents may attend school functions regularly, talk to their children's teachers, and supervise homework. That is, their parenting behavior is the same. But the effects are different. Authoritative parents, by creating a climate that encourages discussion or by offering explanations rather than giving orders, are more effective in their attempts to influence their child's school involvement and success.

Darling and Steinberg's proposal may yet prove to be a heuristic framework, but even this more complex type of analysis of the family system will not be sufficient in the long run. Remember that a great many variables beyond parental style are involved in family dynamics. Each child brings her own temperament and other qualities to the mixture; parents bring their own personalities and habits; the relationship between siblings may have a powerful effect, as the structure of the family itself clearly does. Let's look at each of these added elements in the family system.

Before going on · · ·

- Define the four parenting styles proposed by Maccoby and Martin.
- What have developmental psychologists learned from the research of Steinberg and Dornbusch?
- How do parenting styles and their effects differ across racial and ethnic groups?
- List the general conclusions that can be drawn from developmentalists' knowledge of child-rearing patterns.

Other Aspects of Family Dynamics

One of the most important things to understand about parent-child interactions is that the connections between individuals are not *static*: That is, there are no one-way influences. Instead, relationships are *dynamic* in nature, meaning that influences in the family system flow both ways. Children influence their parents as well as the other way around.

THE CHILD'S CHARACTERISTICS

You have already read about one important influence on family dynamics that originates in the child—the child's temperament. Children with "difficult" temperaments seem to elicit more punishment (especially if the family is under some kind of stress) and may also adversely affect parents' moods (Burt, McGue, Krueger, & Iacono, 2005). More generally, such children may have much more difficulty adapting to any change in the family system, such as a divorce. There are several other influences of this kind.

Birth Order   Children's relationships with their parents may also be affected by their place in the family sequence (referred to as **birth order**, or ordinal position). Early research on birth order suggested that it had, at most, very small effects. Parents generally have higher expectations for maturity in their first-born child and may well be more responsive to or more child-centered with that child. First-borns are also punished more, in part because parents are simply less skilled in using noncoercive forms of control with their first child. Perhaps responding to the higher expectations, oldest

birth order A child's position in the sequence of children within a family, such as first-born, later-born, or only child.

children (first-borns or only children) are somewhat more likely to be achievement-oriented. Compared to later-borns, they achieve cognitive developmental milestones at somewhat earlier ages (Kowalski, Wyver, Masselos, & De Lacey, 2004). As adolescents and adults, first-borns have slightly higher IQ scores, are more likely to go on to college, and are more likely to achieve some degree of eminence (Sutton-Smith, 1982). Various explanations of these slight differences have been offered, but most psychologists concluded from the early research that birth order was not a very helpful way of looking at family interaction patterns.

An intriguing book by historian Frank Sulloway, *Born to Rebel* (1996), however, re-opened the debate. After a detailed analysis of the lives of over 7,000 historical figures, he found that first-borns nearly always support the status quo, while later-borns are the rebels, likely to support new ideas or new political movements. Sulloway's central proposal is that each child must find some niche within the family configuration, some effective way to "curry parental favor." In this battle for successful niches, first-borns have a decided advantage. They are bigger and stronger and can defend the position of "biggest" or "most responsible." First-borns, as a group, have more self-confidence and tend to identify with authority and power. This combination allows them to achieve within the existing social system and commits them to the status quo very early on.

Later-borns, in contrast, are automatically underdogs within the family. Sulloway argues that they are more open to experience, because such an openness helps them to find an unoccupied niche. Their openness also makes them more empathetic, imaginative, and independent-minded than first-borns. Most explorers, heretics, and revolutionaries, according to Sulloway's research, were later-borns.

Sulloway's hypothesis is flexible enough to explain exceptions to these patterns. The key argument is that all children try to find some niche within the family. If the first-born, perhaps because of a genetically patterned difficult temperament, becomes the family rebel, then the second child can capture the niche of the family achiever or traditionalist. Birth order, then, is not destiny. However, if Sulloway is right—and it remains for psychologists to test his theory in various ways—then birth order may give important clues about why children in the same family are often so different.

Child Age

The child's age also makes a difference in family dynamics—a point that may seem obvious but is well worth emphasizing. As the child develops, the parents face very different demands. As any parent can tell you, caring for an infant is quite a different task from caring for a 2-year-old or a 12-year-old. The areas in which control is needed change over time; the degree of push for independence changes; the child's intellectual and language abilities change. Parents quite naturally adapt to these changes, altering their own patterns—perhaps even their style—as the child grows older. At the same time, parents show some consistency in their behavior toward children of the same age. That is, parents behave toward the second child when he is 2 similarly to the way they did toward the first child when she was 2, even though they are now treating the older child as a 4-year-old (Boer, Godhart, & Treffers, 1992). Such a clearly rational set of changes in the parents' behavior as their children grow older has the effect of changing the family system over time.

When children enter school, parents have higher expectations, and the goal of parenting often becomes training the child to regulate his or her own behavior (Lamb & Lewis, 2005). Researchers have learned that there are several parenting variables that contribute to the development of this kind of self-regulation. First, the parents' own ability to self-regulate is important, perhaps because they are providing the child with models of good or poor self-regulation (Prinstein & La Greca, 1999). Also, the degree of self-regulation a parent expects influences the child's self-regulatory behavior. Higher expectations, together with parental monitoring to make certain that expectations are met, are associated with greater self-regulatory competence (Rodrigo, Janssens, & Ceballos, 1999).

Gender

It is clear that parents treat boys and girls differently, beginning in infancy. Some of these differences depend on both the parent's and the baby's sex. For example, parents sing more expressively to same-sex than to opposite-sex infants (Trehub, Hill, & Kamenetsky, 1997). Likewise, mothers of infants maintain more physical and visual contact with daughters than with sons (Lindahl & Haimann, 1977). Differences such as these may contribute in some way to the formation of same-sex alliances between parents and children that may be important later in childhood.

Other kinds of variations in parents' interactions with boys and girls are demonstrated by both mothers and fathers. For example, temperamental differences between boys and girls are much smaller than the differences *perceived* by parents and other adults. In one classic study, researchers found that adults viewing a videotape of an infant interpreted the baby's behavior differently depending on the gender label provided by the researchers. Participants who were told that the baby was a girl interpreted a particular behavior as expressing "fear." Amazingly, those who believed the infant to be male labeled the same behavior "anger" (Condry & Condry, 1976). More recent research employing this technique suggests that the current cohort of adults is somewhat less likely to stereotype infant behavior in this way, although, like their counterparts in the 1970s, they attend to and comment on motor activity more when they believe a target infant is a boy (Pomerleau, Malcuit, Turgeon, & Cossette, 1997). Thus, temperamental stereotyping may affect the quality of the parent-child relationship.

For example, a parent of a calm, quiet girl may view her activity level as a sign of "girlness" and respond to her behavior with acceptance and approval. At the same time, parents of a very active boy may tolerate his activity level, or even encourage it, because they regard it as evidence of the boy's masculinity. But what about parents of active girls and quiet boys? A parent whose female infant is very active may work hard to teach her to be less active because of concerns about the sex-appropriateness of her activity level. Likewise, parents of quiet boys may push them to be more active. In the process, such parents may develop a rejecting, disapproving attitude toward their children that generalizes to all aspects of the parent-child relationships.

Research on another dimension of temperament, emotionality, provides another example. Most studies have found that girls use gestures and language to express emotions more often than boys do, even in infancy (Kuebli, Butler, & Fivush, 1995). Similarly, they are more responsive to others' facial expressions (McClure, 2000). These differences often lead to the perception that girls are more emotionally sensitive. However, in studies of actual behavior, boys are just as affectionate and empathetic as girls during infancy (Melson, Peet, & Sparks, 1991; Zahn-Waxler, Radke-Yarrow, Wagner, & Chapman, 1992).

Nevertheless, a parent's perception of a child's emotional sensitivity affects how the parent responds to the child. Not surprisingly, then, parents initiate conversations about emotions and emotion-provoking events more often with girls than with boys (Kuebli et al., 1995). Therefore, which comes first, girls' greater emotional expressivity or parents' greater willingness to discuss emotions with them? Likewise, are boys less expressive because parents don't frame conversations with them in ways that encourage emotional expression?

Some studies suggest that there are sex differences in parents' expectations with respect to school-aged children's self-regulatory behavior. For example, mothers make different kinds of demands on boys and girls. They appear to provide both with the same types of guidance, but they are more likely to give boys more autonomy over their own behavior than they give girls. Nevertheless, they are also more likely to hold girls to a higher standard of accountability for failure (Pomerantz & Ruble, 1998). Developmentalists speculate that this difference may lead to stronger standards of behavior for girls later in development.

However, the opposite may be true with regard to children who have behavioral difficulties, such as those associated with attention deficit hyperactivity disorder (ADHD). Parents are more likely to attribute such problems to causes outside the child's control when the child is a girl (Maniadaki, Sonuga-Barke, & Kakouros, 2005). By contrast, parents of boys with ADHD are likely to view their sons' behavior as intentional. As a result, the strictness of rules and the harshness of disciplinary techniques is more likely to be increased in response to a son's ADHD symptoms than to a daughter's. Researchers speculate that this pattern, rather than producing higher behavioral standards among boys than among girls, may set up a pattern of hostile and manipulative interactions between parents and sons. Thus, again, we see that parent-child relationships are bidirectional in nature. That is, the effects of any pattern of parent behavior depend to some degree on the characteristics of children. Likewise, children's characteristics influence how parents respond to them.

DIFFERENTIAL TREATMENT OF SIBLINGS

Most children have siblings, and, as you learned in Chapter 11, relationships with them make unique contributions to children's development. But another facet of the sibling relationship involves differential treatment of brothers and sisters by parents. Until recently, most psychologists assumed that if one child experiences an authoritative style, then such a style must characterize the family; all other children in the same household will experience the same style, and the children will therefore end up with similar skills, similar personalities, similar strengths and weaknesses. But both pieces of this assumption now look wrong. Children growing up in the same family end up quite different, and the family system, perhaps even the family style, can be quite different for each child.

Some of the best evidence comes from several studies by Judy Dunn in both England and the United States (Deater-Deckard, Dunn, & Lussier, 2002; Dunn & McGuire, 1994). She has found that parents may express warmth and pride toward one child and scorn toward another, may be lenient toward one and strict with another. Here's an example from one of Dunn's observations, of 30-month-old Andy and his 14-month-old sister, Susie:

> Andy was a rather timid and sensitive child, cautious, unconfident, and compliant. . . . Susie was a striking contrast—assertive, determined, and a handful for her mother, who was nevertheless delighted by her boisterous daughter. In [one] observation of Andy and his sister, Susie persistently attempted to grab a forbidden object on a high kitchen counter, despite her mother's repeated prohibitions. Finally, she succeeded, and Andy overheard his mother make a warm, affectionate comment on Susie's action: "Susie, you are a determined little devil!" Andy, sadly, commented to his mother, "I'm not a determined little devil!" His mother replied, laughing, "No! What are you? A poor old boy!" (Dunn, 1992, p. 6)

Not only are such episodes common in family interactions, but children are highly sensitive to such variations in treatment. Notice that Andy monitored his mother's interaction with Susie and then compared himself to his sister. Children this age are already aware of the emotional quality of exchanges between themselves and their parents as well as between their siblings and their parents. Dunn finds that those who receive less affection and warmth from their mothers are likely to be more depressed, worried, or anxious than are their siblings. And the more differently parents treat siblings, the more rivalry and hostility brothers and sisters are likely to show toward one another (Brody, Stoneman, McCoy, & Forehand, 1992).

Of course, parents treat children differently for many reasons, including their ages. Susie and Andy's mother may have been just as accepting of naughty behavior from Andy when he was a toddler. But Andy does not remember that; what he sees is the contrast between how he is treated and how Susie is treated now. Thus, even when parents are consistent in the way they respond to each child at a given age, they are not behaving consistently toward all the children at any given moment, and the children notice this and create internal models about the meaning of those differences in treatment.

Parents also respond to temperamental differences in their children, to gender differences, and to variations in the children's skills or talents, creating a unique pattern of interaction for each child. If Sulloway's theory is correct, then a child's effort to find

CRITICAL THINKING ?

Are you and your siblings alike in a lot of ways, or do you have quite different traits, skills, and attitudes? Can you trace any of those differences to variations in the way you were treated as children?

her own niche within the family will also affect the way parents (and siblings) respond to her. It is becoming increasingly clear that such differences in treatment are an important ingredient in the child's emerging internal model of self and contribute greatly to variations in behavior among children growing up in the same families (Feinberg & Hetherington, 2001).

THE PARENTS' CHARACTERISTICS

The parents bring their own life histories, their own personalities, and their relationship with each other into the family dynamics as well. Not surprisingly, for example, parents who are high in the trait of neuroticism tend to view their children's behavior more negatively than parents who are more optimistic (Kurdek, 2003). Similarly, significant depression in either parent has a profound effect on the entire family system. You already know from Chapter 11 that an insecure attachment is more likely when the mother is depressed. Depressed parents also perceive their children as more difficult and problematic and are more critical of them, even when objective observers cannot identify any difference in the behavior of such children and the children of nondepressed mothers (Richters & Pellegrini, 1989; Webster-Stratton & Hammond, 1988). Thus, a parent's depression changes not only her behavior but her perception of the child's behavior, both of which alter the family system.

The parent's own internal working model of attachment also seems to have a very strong effect on the family system and thus on the child. You'll also recall from Chapter 11 that those adults who are themselves securely attached are much more likely to have a child who is also securely attached.

Perhaps most broadly, the quality of the parents' own relationship with each other spills over into their relationship with their children. Couples with satisfying marital relationships are more warm and supportive toward their children; those whose marriage is full of discord also have more negative relationships with their children (Erel & Burman, 1995; Parke & Buriel, 1998). Their children show heightened risks of anxiety, depression, and delinquent behavior (Harold & Conger, 1997). In general, fathers' relationships with their children seem to be more strongly affected by the quality of their marital relationship than do mothers' relationships, but the spillover occurs for both parents.

Before going on · · ·

■ How does a child's birth order, age, and gender affect parent-child interactions?
■ In what ways do parents treat siblings differently?
■ What influence do parents' characteristics have on parent-child relationships?

Family Structure, Divorce, and Parental Employment

So far, we haven't considered how the structure of a child's family influences interaction patterns and individual development. To fully understand how families influence development, we need to consider whether **family structure** (the configuration of individuals in a particular child's household) matters and how changes in family structure, such as divorce, contribute.

FAMILY STRUCTURE

Most of you probably know that the proportion of two-parent families in the United States has declined over the past 30 years. In 1970, almost 95% of children lived in such families, but by the end of the 20th century, only about 70% of children were living in two-parent homes (U.S. Bureau of the Census, 2003). Moreover, the proportion of

family structure The configuration of individuals in a child's household.

When they think of "the family," many people still think of a configuration with a father and mother and several children. Although it is still true that most children in the United States live with two biological parents, it is now the exception rather than the rule for a child to spend his or her entire childhood and adolescence in such a family system.

single-parent families in the United States far exceeds that of other industrialized societies. For example, in Korea, Japan, and other Asian nations, only 4–8% of children live with a single parent (Martin, 1995).

Diversity in Two-Parent Families   Two-parent families, though the most common living arrangement for children in the United States, are hardly all alike. Not all two-parent families are happy and harmonious. Researchers have found that, among other variables, hostility in parents' marital relationship is associated with a higher incidence of behavior problems in children (Katz & Woodin, 2002). Conversely, the greater the parents' satisfaction with their marriage, the better able their children are to regulate feelings of sibling rivalry (Volling, McElwain, & Miller, 2002). Such findings underscore the concept of the family as a system in which each relationship affects all others in some way.

The make-up of two-parent families is diverse as well. Only about half of all children in the United States live with both their biological parents (Hernandez, 1997). Between 20% and 30% of two-parent families were created when a divorced or never-married single parent married another single parent or nonparent (Ganong & Coleman, 1994). Thus, even among children in two-parent households, there are many who have experienced single-parenting at one time or another while growing up.

It's also important to keep in mind that any set of statistics on family structure is like a snapshot that fails to capture the number of changes in family structure many children experience across their early years. For example, in some two-parent households, the "parents" are actually the child's grandparents. In most cases, custodial grandparents are caring for the children of a daughter who has some kind of significant problem such as criminal behavior or substance abuse (Jendrek, 1993). These children are likely to have experienced a variety of living arrangements before coming to live with their grandparents. Likewise, many married parents were previously single parents who had relationships with one or more live-in partners.

Single-parent households are diverse as well. In contrast to stereotypes, some single parents are very financially secure. In fact, the proportion of births to single mothers is increasing most rapidly among middle-class professional women who have made an active decision to become single parents (Ingrassia, 1993). Other single parents, especially unmarried teenagers, are likely to live with their own parents (Jorgenson, 1993). Consequently, it's inaccurate to think of single-parent households as any more predictable or homogeneous than two-parent households.

Family Structure and Ethnicity   Looking at family structure across ethnic groups further illustrates family diversity in the United States. You can get some feeling for the degree of variation from Figure 13.6. The figure graphs estimates of the percentages of three family types among white, African American, Asian American, Native American, and Hispanic American children in the United States.

You can see that single-parent families are far more common among African Americans and Native Americans than among other groups. A difference in the proportion of births to unmarried women is one contributing factor. As Figure 13.7 shows, births to single women have increased rather dramatically across all racial and ethnic groups in the United States in the past few decades. However, the rates of such births are much higher among African American and Native American women than in other groups. (By the way, in all groups, more than three-quarters of single women giving birth are over the age of 20. Thus, teenage pregnancy contributes very little to the statistics on single motherhood.)

A second factor is that, although many African American and Native American single mothers eventually marry, adults in these groups—whether parents or not—are

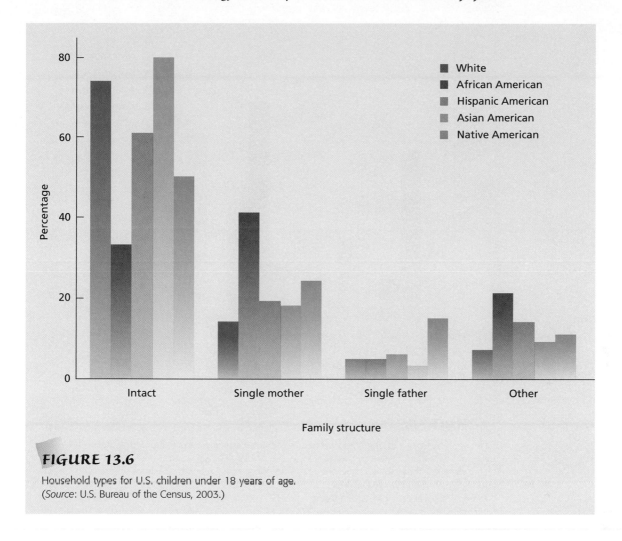

FIGURE 13.6

Household types for U.S. children under 18 years of age.
(*Source*: U.S. Bureau of the Census, 2003.)

less likely to marry. Approximately 37% of African American adults and 27% of Native American adults have never been married. Among whites, only 18% remain single throughout their lives (U.S. Bureau of the Census, 1998).

Of course, statistics can't explain why African American and Native American families are more likely than those of other groups to be headed by single parents. Sociologists speculate that, in the case of African Americans, lack of economic opportunities for men renders them less able to take on family responsibilities (Cherlin, 1992). Others add that grandparents and other relatives in both groups traditionally help support single mothers. For instance, among Native Americans, a traditional cultural value sociologists call *kin orientation* views parenting as the responsibility of a child's entire family, including grandparents and aunts and uncles. As a result, Native American single parents, especially those who live in predominantly Native American communities, receive more material and emotional support than do single parents in other groups and may feel less pressure to marry (Ambert, 2001).

Family Structure Effects The broadest statement psychologists can make about the effects of family structure is that the optimal situation for children, at least in the United States, appears to include two natural parents (Scott, 2004). Never-married mothers, divorced mothers or fathers who have not remarried, and stepparents are frequently linked to less positive outcomes. Variables associated with single-parenthood, such as poverty, may help explain its negative effects on development. Still, the differences between children who never experience single parenting and those who do are too large to be completely explained by other variables. This means that at least part of

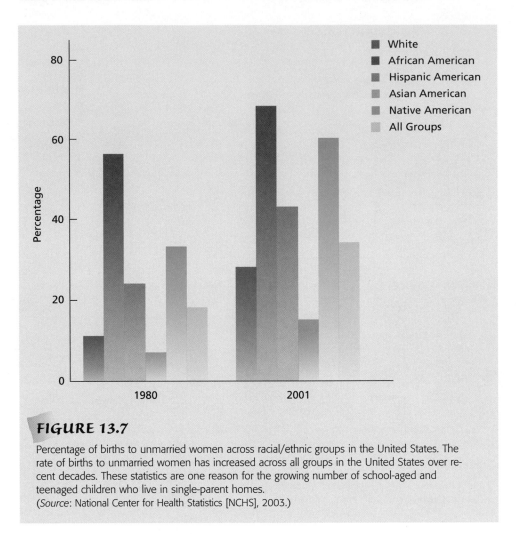

FIGURE 13.7

Percentage of births to unmarried women across racial/ethnic groups in the United States. The rate of births to unmarried women has increased across all groups in the United States over recent decades. These statistics are one reason for the growing number of school-aged and teenaged children who live in single-parent homes.
(*Source*: National Center for Health Statistics [NCHS], 2003.)

the difference is connected to the family structure itself. Thus, it's important to know just what the differences are.

Children growing up in single-parent families are about twice as likely to drop out of high school, twice as likely to have a child before age 20, and less likely to have a steady job in their late teens or early 20s (McLanahan & Sandefur, 1994). Children of adolescent mothers are particularly at risk. Differences between children of teenagers and those whose mothers are older are evident in early childhood. Some studies suggest that preschoolers whose mothers are single teenagers display less advanced cognitive and social development than their peers (Furstenberg, Brooks-Gunn, & Chase-Lansdale, 1989). Other research indicates that, when the children of teen mothers become teens themselves, they are more likely to exhibit behaviors such as truancy, fighting with peers, and early sexual activity than peers whose mothers are older (Levine, Pollack, & Comfort, 2001).

Other Types of Family Structures   In contrast to research comparing two-parent and single-parent families, relatively few studies have looked at the effects of other kinds of family structures. For example, developmentalists know that relationships with grandparents can benefit children, but research on custodial grandparents (grandparents who have full responsibility for raising their grandchildren) tends to focus on the effects of the parenting experience on aging adults. Consequently, researchers know that custodial grandparents' responses to children's problems are quite similar to those of parents (Daly & Glenwick, 2000). However, the stresses of parenting combined with the physical effects of aging are likely to cause older adults to feel more anxious and depressed than younger adults in similar situations (Burton, 1992; Jendrek, 1993). Thus, developmentalists know something about how parenting affects older adults but very little about how being raised by grandparents affects children.

In contrast, concerns about children's sex-role identity and sexual orientation have dominated research on gay and lesbian parenting (Bailey, Brobow, Wolfe, & Mikach, 1995). Studies have generally shown that children raised by gay and lesbian parents develop sex-role identities in the same way as children of heterosexual parents. They are also just as likely to be heterosexual (Golombok & Tasker, 1996).

To help answer general questions about cognitive and social development among the children of gay and lesbian parents, researchers have conducted comprehensive reviews of the small number of studies that have been done. Such reviews have typically found that the majority of studies suggest that children raised by gay and lesbian parents do not differ from those raised by heterosexuals (Fitzgerald, 1999; Lambert, 2005; Patterson, 1997). However, most such studies have involved a very small number of families and children (Schumm, 2004). Moreover, in almost all cases, the children involved have been conceived and reared in heterosexual relationships prior to being parented by a same-sex couple. Thus, the findings of these studies can't be attributed conclusively to the effects of being raised by a gay or lesbian parent.

One study, though, involved 80 school-aged children who had been conceived by artificial insemination (Chan, Raboy, & Patterson, 1998). Researchers compared these children across four types of family structures: lesbian couples, single lesbian mothers, heterosexual couples, and single heterosexual mothers. The study found no differences in either cognitive or social development among the children. However, it did find that the same variables—parenting stress, parental conflict, parental affection—predicted developmental outcomes in all four groups. These findings, much like those contrasting two-parent and single-parent families, suggest that children's development depends more on how parents interact with them than on family configuration.

DIVORCE

There can be little doubt that divorce is traumatic for children. However, this statement must be followed by a note of caution. Some of the negative effects of divorce are due to factors that were present *before* the divorce, such as difficult temperament in the child or excessive marital conflict between the parents (Cherlin, Chase-Lansdale, & McRae, 1998). It's also important to keep in mind that divorce is not a unitary variable; children are probably affected by a multitude of divorce-related factors: parental conflict, poverty, disruptions of daily routine, and so on (Bailey & Zvonkovic, 2003; Hetherington, Bridges, & Insabella, 1998). For this reason, children whose parents separate or stay in conflict-ridden marriages, even if they do not actually divorce, may experience many of the same effects (Ingoldsby, Shaw, Owens, & Winslow 1999).

In the first few years after a divorce, children typically show declines in school performance and show more aggressive, defiant, negative, or depressed behavior (Bonde, Obel, Nedergard, & Thomsen, 2004; Furstenberg & Cherlin, 1991; Hetherington & Clingempeel, 1992; Morrison & Cherlin, 1995; Pagani, Boulerice, Tremblay, & Vitaro, 1997). By adolescence, the children of divorced parents are more likely than peers to become sexually active at an early age, to experiment with drugs and alcohol, and to engage in criminal behavior (Price & Kunz, 2003; Wallerstein & Lewis, 1998). Children living with a parent and a stepparent also have higher rates of delinquency, behavior problems in school, and lower grades than do those living with both natural parents, as indicated in Figure 13.8 (Lee, Burkham, Zimiles, & Ladewski, 1994; Pagani et al., 1997; Hetherington et al., 1999).

The negative effects of divorce seem to persist for many years. For example, children whose parents divorce have a higher risk of mental health problems in adulthood (Chase-Lansdale, Cherlin, & Kiernan, 1995; Cherlin et al., 1998; Wallerstein & Lewis, 1998). Many young adults whose parents are divorced lack the financial re-

Many single parents manage to overcome substantial obstacles and give their children the support and supervision they need.

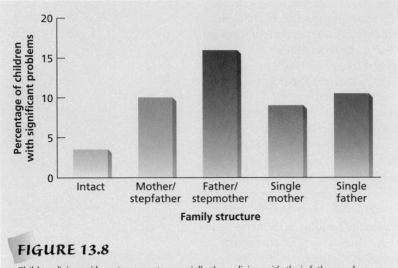

FIGURE 13.8

Children living with a stepparent, especially those living with their father and a stepmother, are more likely than those in intact families to show behavior problems of one type or another.

(*Source*: Lee et al., 1994, from Table 1, p. 417.)

sources and emotional support needed to succeed in college, and a majority report that they struggle with fears of intimacy in relationships (Wallerstein & Lewis, 1998). Not surprisingly, adults whose parents were divorced are themselves more likely to divorce.

As a general rule, these negative effects are more pronounced for boys than for girls. However, some researchers have found that the effects are delayed in girls, making it more difficult to associate the effects with the divorce. Consequently, longitudinal studies often find that girls show equal or even greater negative effects (Amato, 1993; Hetherington, 1991a, 1991b). Age differences in the severity of the reaction have been found in some studies but not others. For example, one longitudinal study found that the effects of parental divorce were most severe in a group of 12-year-olds who experienced the divorce in early childhood rather than during the school years (Pagani et al., 1997).

Race or ethnicity, incidentally, does not appear to be a causal factor. Yes, a larger percentage of African American children grow up in single-parent families. But the same negative outcomes occur in Caucasian American single-parent families, and the same positive outcomes are found in two-parent minority families. For example, the school dropout rate for Caucasian American children from single-parent families is higher than that for Hispanic American or African American children reared in two-parent families (McLanahan & Sandefur, 1994).

UNDERSTANDING THE EFFECTS OF FAMILY STRUCTURE AND DIVORCE

How are developmentalists to understand all these various findings? First, single parenthood or divorce reduces the financial and emotional resources available to support the child. With only one parent, the household typically has only one income and only one adult to respond to the child's emotional needs. Data from the United States indicate that a woman's income drops an average of 40–50% after a divorce (Bradbury & Katz, 2002; Smock, 1993). Remarriage does indeed add a second adult to the family system, which alleviates these problems to some degree, but it adds others (Hetherington et al., 1999).

Second, any family transition involves upheaval. Both adults and children adapt slowly and with difficulty to the subtraction or addition of new adults to the family system (Hetherington & Stanley-Hagan, 1995). The period of maximum disruption appears to last several years, during which the parents often find it difficult to maintain consistent monitoring and control over their children.

Perhaps most importantly, single parenthood, divorce, and stepparenthood all increase the likelihood that the family climate or style will shift away from authoritative parenting. This is evident in the first few years after a divorce, when the custodial parent (usually the mother) is distracted or depressed and less able to manage warm control; it is evident in families with a stepparent as well, where rates of authoritative parenting are lower than in intact families.

Remember, an authoritarian or neglecting parenting style is linked to poor outcomes whether the parenting style is triggered by a divorce, a stressful remarriage, the father's loss of a job, or any other stress (Goldberg, 1990). Ultimately, it is this process within the family, rather than any particular type of disruption, that is significant for the child (see

CRITICAL THINKING ?

Given what you have just read, how would you answer someone who asked you whether it is worse for an unhappy couple to get divorced or to stay together even though they fight all the time?

When Divorce Is Unavoidable

Adriana and Martin have decided to end their marriage, but they are concerned about how their divorce might affect their two children. Like most parents, they know that divorce can be traumatic for children, and they want to do their best to minimize such effects. They have gone to a family therapist to find out how best to achieve this goal. After determining that the couple was sure that their differences could not be reconciled and that there was no alternative to divorce, the therapist advised them that they would not be able to eliminate all of the short-term disruptive effects of such an event on their children. However, the therapist did suggest some specific things that Adriana and Martin could do to soften or reduce the effects:

● *Try to keep the number of separate changes the child has to cope with to a minimum.* If at all possible, keep the children in the same school or day-care setting and the same house or apartment.
● *If the children are teenagers, consider having each child live with the parent of the same gender.* The data are not totally consistent, but it looks as if this may be a less stressful arrangement (Lee et al., 1994).
● *The custodial parent should help children stay in touch with the noncustodial parent.* Likewise, the noncustodial parent should maintain as much contact as possible with children, calling and seeing them regularly, attending school functions, and so on.
● *Keep the conflict to a minimum.* Most of all, try not to fight in front of the children. Open conflict has negative

effects on children whether the parents are divorced or not (Amato, 1993; Coiro, 1995; Isabella, 1995). Thus, divorce is not the sole culprit—divorce combined with open conflict between the adults has worse effects.
● *Parents should not use the children as go-betweens or talk disparagingly about their ex-spouses to them.* Children who feel caught in the middle between the two parents are more likely to show various kinds of negative symptoms, such as depression or behavior problems (Buchanan, Maccoby, & Dornbusch, 1991).
● *Divorced parents need to maintain their own network of support and use that network liberally.* They should stay in touch with friends, seek out others in the same situation, or join a support group.

In the midst of the emotional upheaval that accompanies divorce, these are not easy prescriptions to follow. However, if divorcing parents are able to do so, their children will probably suffer less.

Questions for Reflection

1. What specific strategies can Adriana and Martin employ to achieve the goal of reducing conflict?
2. If you were in this situation, where would you turn for emotional and moral support? Why?

The Real World). After all, three-quarters of children reared in single-parent families or families with a stepparent manage to finish high school, and roughly half of those high school graduates go on to at least some college (McLanahan & Sandefur, 1994).

PARENTS' JOBS

The existing research on the effects of parents' work on children contains an odd quirk. Nearly all the research on mothers' employment compares mothers who work with those who do not, while nearly all the work on the impact of fathers' employment focuses on fathers who have lost their jobs. Little research has studied mothers who lose their jobs or compared stay-at-home fathers with employed fathers. Given the cultural history of most Western industrialized societies, this pattern of research makes sense, although it certainly leaves some significant gaps in developmentalists' knowledge. Fortunately, a new body of work is beginning to emerge that asks a very different kind of question: What is the impact of the quality of the parents' work experience on family life?

Mothers' Employment   How is life different for children whose mothers work outside the home, compared to those whose mothers stay home? Do these two groups of children differ in any systematic way? These questions are obviously not entirely separable from all the issues about child care you'll be reading about in Chapter 14, since it is

In the United States, many two-parent homes are formed when a single parent marries another single parent or a nonparent.

In the United States today, nearly two-thirds of women with children under age 6 and three-quarters of women with school-aged or adolescent children work at least part-time (NICHD Early Child Care Research Network, 2003). In general, the effects seem to be neutral or beneficial for the children.

precisely because the mother is working that most children are in alternative care. But the question is also relevant for families with school-aged children, where the impact of the mother's work is not as confounded with the effects of alternative child care.

Most of the research on the impact of mothers' employment points to a neutral or slightly positive effect for most children (Parke & Buriel, 1998; Scott, 2004). Girls whose mothers work are more independent and admire their mothers more than do girls whose mothers do not work. And both boys and girls whose mothers work have more egalitarian sex-role concepts. The effects of the mother's employment on children's academic performance are less clear. Many studies show no gender differences (e.g., Gottfried, Bathurst, & Gottfried, 1994).

Curiously, some studies suggest that maternal employment in the first year of life has negative effects on white children but positive effects on African American children. In one longitudinal study, researchers examined cognitive and social development in 3- to 4-year-olds of both races whose mothers had been employed between the children's birth and first birthday (Brooks-Gunn, Han, & Waldfogel, 2002; Han, Waldfogel, & Brooks-Gunn, 2001). They found that the white children exhibited negative effects in both domains. Further, when the children were tested again at ages 7 to 8, white children continued to display less advanced development than peers whose mothers had not been employed during the first year after birth. In contrast, African American children whose mothers had been employed during the first year of their lives did not differ from peers whose mothers had not been employed.

One large study (Muller, 1995), involving a nationally representative sample of 24,599 eighth graders, suggested that these effects may continue into early adolescence. Participants in this study showed a very small negative effect from the mother's employment on their math grades and test scores. However, this difference appeared to result from the fact that mothers who work are less involved with the child's school and are less likely to supervise the child's schoolwork during after-school hours, rather than from a long-lasting deficit brought about by maternal employment in the early years. Thus, working mothers who find ways to provide such supervision and who remain involved with their children's schools have kids who do as well as children whose mothers are homemakers.

These findings point to the fact that it is not the mother's job per se that produces the various effects that are linked to maternal employment. Rather, the mother's employment causes changes in daily routines and in interaction patterns, simply because she is not at home for as many hours. Fathers in two-earner families spend somewhat more time in child care and household tasks than do fathers with homemaker wives, although it is still true that working mothers do about twice as much of this labor as do fathers (Blair & Johnson, 1992; Parke & Buriel, 1998). This change in the division of labor may then have an effect on the quality of the father's interactions with the children, as well as altering the role model each parent provides for the child. Finally, of course, when the mother works, she has less time available for one-on-one interaction with the children, including supervision of their homework. Perhaps, then, it isn't surprising that research shows that the effects of maternal employment on infant development depend on how working mothers allocate their time (Huston & Aronson, 2005). Those who compensate for the time they spend at work by reducing the amount of time they devote to other activities that do not involve their children increase the chances that their employment status will have either positive or neutral effects on their babies' development.

Fathers' Employment or Unemployment   Research evidence reveals what you might guess intuitively, that when a man loses his job, it puts enormous strain on his marriage; marital conflict rises, and both parents show more symptoms of depression. The resulting effects on family dynamics look much like those seen in divorcing families or in families facing other sorts of stresses. Both parents become less consistent in their behavior toward their children, less affectionate, and less effective at monitoring them (Conger, Patterson, & Ge, 1995). The children respond to this deterioration in their parents' behavior as they do during a divorce, by exhibiting a variety of symptoms, some-

CRITICAL THINKING ?

Think of your own family's network of support when you were growing up. How did the availability (or lack) of social support help (or hinder) your parents?

times including depression, aggression, or delinquency. Often their school performance declines (Conger, Ge, Elder, Lorenz, & Simons, 1994; Conger et al., 1992; Flanagan & Eccles, 1993). The likelihood of maltreatment, including both neglect and abuse, increases somewhat during periods of paternal unemployment as well (Berger, 2004). Fortunately, these negative effects usually disappear when the father again finds work. But the sequence illustrates nicely how an event outside the family can affect the child through its impact on the parents' behavior toward each other and toward the child.

SOCIAL SUPPORT FOR PARENTS

A second aspect of parents' lives that affects the family system is the quality of their network of relationships and their satisfaction with the social support they receive from that network. The general point is fairly self-evident: Parents who have access to adequate emotional and physical support—from each other or from friends and family—are able to respond to their children more warmly, more consistently, and with better control (Crnic, Greenberg, Ragozin, Robinson, & Basham, 1983; Parke & Buriel, 1998; Taylor, Casten, & Flickinger, 1993). Children whose parents have access to more assistance from friends complete more years of school than do children whose parents have less support of this type (Hofferth, Boisjoly, & Duncan, 1995). The effect of social support on parents is particularly evident when they are experiencing stress of some kind, such as job loss, chronic poverty, teenage childbirth, a temperamentally difficult or handicapped infant, divorce, or even just fatigue.

You may recall that Chapter 9 mentioned a study by Susan Crockenberg (1981) that illustrates the point nicely. She found that temperamentally irritable infants had an increased likelihood of ending up with an insecure attachment to their mothers only when the mother lacked adequate social support. When the mother felt that she had enough support, similarly irritable children were later securely attached. There are many other examples of this "buffering effect" of social support:

- New mothers who lack social and emotional support are more likely to suffer from postpartum depression than are those with adequate support (Cutrona & Troutman, 1986).
- Divorced parents who have help and emotional support from friends or family members are much more able to maintain a stable and affectionate environment for their children than are those who grapple with divorce in isolation (Hetherington, 1989).
- Among African American single mothers, those who have enough aid and emotional support from kin show a more authoritative style of parenting than do single mothers lacking such aid (Taylor et al., 1993).

As a general rule, social support seems to allow parents to mobilize the best parenting skills they have in their repertoire. Of course, not all "help" from family or friends feels like support. (You have probably received unwanted advice from your parents, in-laws, or friends.) The key is not the objective amount of contact or advice received, but rather the parent's satisfaction with the level and quality of the support he or she is experiencing. The moral seems to be that at times of greatest difficulty or stress, you need the emotional and physical support of others the most. Yet if you wait until that difficult moment to look around and see who is there to help, you may not find what you need. Social networks must be developed and nurtured over time. But they certainly seem to pay dividends for parents, and thus for children.

Parents' working conditions represent one of the most important ways in which institutions outside the home influence families and, as a result, influence the development of individual children. Therefore, when workers succeed in improving the conditions under which they work, their efforts may produce long-term benefits for the entire society as well as immediate benefits for themselves and their families.

Before going on . . .

- How is family structure related to children's development?
- How does divorce affect children's behavior in early childhood and in later years?
- What are some possible reasons for the relationship between family structure and children's development?
- How do parents' employment patterns affect children?

Summary

Bronfenbrenner's Bioecological Approach

● Bronfenbrenner conceives of the child's bioecological system as composed of three layers: microsystems, such as the family or the school, in which the child is directly involved; exosystems, such as the parent's jobs, which affect the child indirectly by influencing some aspect of a microsystem; and the macrosystem, including the ethnic subculture and the broader society or culture within which the family exists.

Dimensions of Family Interaction

● Children in families that provide high levels of warmth and affection have more secure attachments and better peer relationships than children in families that are more cold or rejecting.

● Parents who have clear rules and standards and enforce those rules and expectations consistently have children with the greatest self-esteem and the greatest competence across a broad range of situations.

● Children whose parents talk to them frequently, in complex sentences, and who are listened to in turn not only develop language more rapidly but also have more positive and less conflicted relationships with their parents.

Patterns of Child Rearing

● Four styles of parenting suggested by several theorists are authoritarian, authoritative, permissive, and neglecting. The authoritative style appears to be the most generally effective for producing confident, competent, independent, and affectionate children. The most negative outcomes are found with the neglecting style.

● Research by Steinberg and Dornbusch suggests that parenting styles are related to a variety of developmental outcomes, including academic achievement, social functioning, mental health, and delinquency.

● Research has also revealed racial and ethnic differences in the ways in which parenting style affects children. In particular, Asian American children generally do very well in school despite low rates of authoritative parenting, which

may indicate that the categorization of family styles is culture-specific.

● Parenting style classifications are useful for research, but they don't explain how or why parenting behaviors affect children's development.

Other Aspects of Family Dynamics

● The family system is also affected by the child's characteristics, such as temperament, age, gender, and position in the birth order.

● The family system is, in essence, different for each child, which helps explain why siblings growing up in the same family often turn out very differently.

● Parental characteristics that affect the family system include a parent's (especially a mother's) depression, the parent's own internal working model of attachment, and the quality of the parents' marital relationship.

Family Structure, Divorce, and Parental Employment

● The structure of the family has an impact on family functioning, which in turn affects children's behavior. Children reared in single-parent families are at higher risk for a variety of negative outcomes, including dropping out of school, teen parenthood, and delinquency. Having a stepparent is also associated with heightened risks of poorer outcomes for children.

● For most children, divorce results in a decline in standard of living and a decrease in authoritative parenting.

● Any change in family structure, such as a divorce, is likely to produce short-term disruption (often including an increase in authoritarian or neglecting parenting) before the system adapts to a new form.

● A mother's employment affects the family system by changing the mother's self-image, increasing her economic power, and altering the distribution of labor. Loss of job by a father disrupts the family system, increasing authoritarian parenting and reducing marital satisfaction. The character of a parent's job also has an effect on family interactions.

Key Terms

Autobiographical Memories of Divorce

It is likely that a significant proportion of your classmates have experienced a parental divorce. Recruit a few of them to participate in a study of young adults' memories regarding parental divorce. Ask volunteers to tell you how old they were when their parents divorced. Then ask them each to write a brief summary of how the divorce affected them immediately and in the long term. Categorize the summaries by age to determine whether volunteers' experiences vary according to the age at which they confronted parental divorce.

Beyond the Family: The Impact of the Broader Culture

Do you know what momentous event happened on November 10, 1969?

Here's a hint. It seemed relatively insignificant at the time, but it influenced the lives of millions of children and continues to do so today. In fact, there's a good chance that it influenced your own daily routine when you were a preschooler.

November 10, 1969, was the date on which *Sesame Street* made its debut (Palmer, 2003). Although the program is shown in more than 100 nations today, none of those who participated in its creation had any idea that it would become a worldwide phenomenon. Their goal was simply to find an effective way to increase the number of children who were ready for school by the time they reached kindergarten age.

In 1966, developmental psychologist Lloyd Morrisett was supervising educational research at the Carnegie Corporation. After directing numerous experimental studies, Morrisett was certain that low-income preschoolers' school readiness skills could be dramatically improved by providing them with the kinds of academic curricula found in the preschool programs that middle-income parents sent their children to. However, he recognized that, even with millions of dollars in funding, the interventions he had found to be so successful would never reach more than a few thousand children.

As fate would have it, Morrisett found himself at a dinner party in New York City engaged in small talk with Joan Ganz Cooney, a producer for the local public television station. When Morrisett shared his desire to reach millions of children with an effective preschool curriculum, he and Cooney came up with the idea of creating a children's television program based on the interventions he had tested in his studies. They predicted that the combination of Morrisett's expertise in developmental psychology and Cooney's practical knowledge of television programming would result in a unique program that would keep children engaged and entertained while it educated them.

The crowning touch to the plan was Cooney's decision to hire Jim Henson, whose muppets were already familiar to prime-time television viewers, to create a group of characters specifically for the program. Each character was to have a unique personality, and the show's writers were directed to use the characters to teach social skills. Brilliant, too, was Cooney's decision to enlist preschoolers to name the program. While Cooney was working on the creative aspects of the show, Morrisett was busy raising money to fund it and enlisting endorsements from other psychologists.

When the program hit the airwaves, it was an instant success. Incredibly, by the end of its first year, fully half of the 12 million children in the United States were watching *Sesame Street* every day. Still, critics pointed out that the popularity of the show gave no indication as to whether it was achieving its educational goals. In response, psychologists began to study the program's effects on its young viewers. To date, many such studies have been done, and there is little doubt that *Sesame Street* has a positive impact on children's development in both the cognitive and the *social-emotional domains (e.g., Wright et al., 2001). Moreover, the creators of Sesame Street demonstrated that psychological research can serve as a solid foundation on which to build entertainment media for children that are both effective and commercially successful.*

Of course, television is only one force in children's environment. You learned about the importance of families in Chapter 13. In this chapter, we turn our attention to influences beyond the family, including television, that contribute to children's development.

 # Nonparental Care

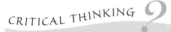

CRITICAL THINKING

If you experienced nonparental care of one sort or another as a child, how do you think your experiences affected your later development?

In 1970, only 18% of married women with children under age 6 were in the U.S. labor force; by 1999, 61% of mothers in this group were employed (NICHD Early Child Care Research Network, 2003). More than half of women with children under age 1—including more than half of women living with a husband—now work outside the home at least part-time, a rate that appears to be higher in the United States than in any other country in the world (Cherlin, 1992; U.S. Bureau of the Census, 1996). It is now typical for infants as well as school-aged children to spend a significant amount of time being cared for by someone other than a parent. One study, based on a carefully selected sample of over 1,300 families from all over the United States, indicated that by age 1, 80% of infants had experienced some regular nonparental child care; the majority entered such care before they were 6 months old (NICHD Early Child Care Research Network, 1997b). Although similar changes have occurred in other countries to a lesser degree, raising the same kinds of fundamental questions, this section is almost exclusively concerned with child care in the United States.

DIFFICULTIES IN STUDYING NONPARENTAL CARE

It might seem that the effect on development of nonparental care could easily be determined by comparing children who receive nonparental care to those who are cared for entirely by their parents. However, both "nonparental care" and "parental care" are among those variables that are actually complex interactions among numerous variables rather than single factors whose effects can be studied independently. Thus, interpretation of research on nonparental care has to take into account a variety of issues.

First, an enormous variety of different care arrangements are all lumped together in the general category of "nonparental care." Children who are cared for by grandparents in their own homes as well as those who are enrolled in day-care centers both receive nonparental care. In addition, these care arrangements begin at different ages for different children and last for varying lengths of time. Some children have the same nonparental caregiver over many years; others shift often from one care setting to another. Moreover, nonparental care varies widely in quality.

Furthermore, distinguishing among the various types of care arrangements still does not begin to convey the enormous variety of solutions parents arrive at in seeking alternative care for their children (Clarke-Stewart, Gruber, & Fitzgerald, 1994). For example, in one national survey, between a quarter and a third of employed mothers reported that their children were in some type of combined care, such as family day care some of the time and care by a relative part of the time (Folk & Yi, 1994).

Families who place their children in nonparental care are also different in a whole host of ways from those who care for their children primarily at home. How can researchers be sure that effects attributed to nonparental care are not the result of these other family differences instead? Mothers also differ in their attitudes toward the care arrangements they have made. Some mothers with children in nonparental care would rather be at home taking care of their children; others are happy to be working. The reverse is also true: Some mothers who are at home full time would rather be working, and some are delighted to be at home.

Most of the research developmentalists have to draw on does not take these complexities into account. Researchers have frequently compared children "in day care" with those "reared at home" and assumed that any differences between the two groups were attributable to the day-care experience. Recent studies are often better, but developmentalists are still a long way from having clear or good answers to even the most basic questions about the impact of day care on children's development. Nonetheless, because the question is so critical, you should be aware of what is known, as well as what is not yet known.

The number of infants in the United States who experience center-based care is increasing.

WHO IS TAKING CARE OF THE CHILDREN?

When most people think of "child care" or "day care," they think of a day-care center. However, in the United States, only a third of children younger than 5 who are in nonparental care are enrolled in such facilities (U.S. House of Representatives, 2004). The most common nonparental care arrangement, involving 45% of these young children, is one in which children are cared for by someone in a home other than their own, an arrangement called *family day care*. The remaining 21% are cared for by a relative or another adult in their own homes. A particularly interesting observation can be made by delving a bit deeper into these statistics. Among children who are not enrolled in child-care centers, a grandparent is the most common caregiver. In fact, almost as many children are cared for by a grandparent, either in the child's own home or in the grandparent's home, as are enrolled in centers.

Not only are there a wide variety of child-care arrangements across families, but it is common for children to experience more than one type of arrangement. For example, a child may attend a center-based program 2 days a week and be cared for by a relative on the other days. One-third of 1-year-olds in the large national sample studied by the National Institute of Child Health and Development (NICHD Early Child Care Research Network, 1997b) had experienced at least three different nonparental care arrangements; more than half had been placed in two different situations.

Child care arrangements also vary by race and ethnicity (U.S. Bureau of the Census, 2001). Hispanic American children are half as likely to be enrolled in day-care centers as African American and Caucasian American children. Among children who are not enrolled in center care, African American and Hispanic American youngsters are more likely to be cared for by relatives than by nonrelatives; the opposite is true of Caucasian American children.

EFFECTS OF NONPARENTAL CARE ON COGNITIVE DEVELOPMENT

In a large study by the NICHD Early Child Care Research Network (1997a), researchers found a small but significant positive effect of high-quality care on children's overall cognitive and language skills. Other research suggests that this positive effect is even larger among infants and children from poor families, who show significant and lasting gains in IQ scores and later school performance after attending highly enriched child care throughout infancy and early childhood—research you'll recall from Chapter 7 (Campbell & Ramey, 1994; Loeb, Fuller, Kagan, & Carrol, 2004; Ramey, 1993; Ramey & Campbell, 1987).

Even middle-class children sometimes show cognitive benefits when they are in good care (e.g., Peisner-Feinberg, 1995). For example, Alison Clarke-Stewart found that regardless of the economic situation of the child's parents, the more cognitively enriched the child's daytime experience was, the higher the child's later cognitive performance (Clarke-Stewart et al., 1994). Children who were read to, talked to, and explicitly taught showed greater cognitive gains than did children who spent their days in less stimulating environments—and this was true whether the children were cared for entirely at home or in some other care setting. Several longitudinal studies in Sweden confirm such a positive effect of high-quality child care (Andersson, 1992; Broberg, Wessels, Lamb, & Hwang, 1997).

A few studies suggest a less rosy picture, perhaps particularly for middle-class children. For example, one large study of over a thousand 3- and 4-year-olds (Baydar & Brooks-Gunn, 1991) found that Caucasian American children—but not African American children—who began some kind of alternative care in the first year of life had the lowest vocabulary scores later in preschool, whether they were from advantaged or poverty-level families. No negative effects were found for those who entered day care after age 1. In a similar large study of 5- and 6-year-olds (Caughy, DiPietro, & Strobino, 1994), researchers found that children from poor families who began day care before age 1 had higher reading or math scores at the start of school, while those from middle-class families who entered day care in infancy had poorer scores.

How can these conflicting findings be reconciled? One fairly straightforward possibility is that the critical factor is the discrepancy between the level of stimulation the child would receive at home and the quality of the child care. Perhaps when a given child's particular day-care setting provides more enrichment than the child would have received at home, day care has some beneficial cognitive effects; when the day care is less stimulating than full-time home care would be for that child, day care may have negative cognitive effects. Most (but not all) of the results you've read about are consistent with this hypothesis, but as yet there are not enough good large studies to be confident that this is the right way to conceptualize the effects.

EFFECTS OF NONPARENTAL CARE ON PERSONALITY

When researchers look at the impact of nonparental child care on children's personality, they find yet another somewhat confusing story. A number of investigators have found that children in day care are more sociable and more popular and have better peer-play skills than do those reared primarily at home. Bengt-Erik Andersson found this in his longitudinal study in Sweden (1989, 1992), as have researchers in the United States (Scarr & Eisenberg, 1993). However, this is by no means the universal finding. Many other researchers find nonparental care linked to heightened aggression with peers and lower compliance with teachers and parents, both during the preschool years and at later ages (Goldstein, Arnold, Rosenberg, Stowe, and Ortiz, 2001; Kim, 1997).

For example, in one very well-designed large study, John Bates and his colleagues (1994) found that kindergarten children who had spent the most time in child care—in infancy, as toddlers, or during the preschool years—were more aggressive and less popular with their peers at school age than were children who had been reared entirely at home or who had spent fewer years in child care. Bates did not find that those who had entered day care early in infancy were worse off; the critical variable was the total length of time in nonparental care, not the timing of that care. These negative effects were fairly small. A child's level of aggressiveness in elementary school is influenced by a wide variety of things, including temperament and the effectiveness of the parents' disciplinary techniques. Yet the fact that nonparental care is implicated in this equation certainly raises a cautionary flag.

Confusing, isn't it? By some measures, day-care children seem to be more socially competent than home-reared children; by other measures, they seem less so. One possible way to resolve this discrepancy is once again to look at the relative quality of care at home or in day care. Consistent with this argument is a finding by Tiffany Field (1991) that the beneficial effects of day-care experience on the child's social competence hold only for good-quality care. Similarly, Alison Clarke-Stewart, in a study comparing various types of nonparental care with home care (Clarke-Stewart et al., 1994), found that what is critical for the child's level of aggression is whether the child spends the daytime hours in an organized, well-structured situation or a messy, unstimulating one—and that it does not matter if the unstructured and messy setting is at home or in day care. If this argument holds, then it is not child care per se that is at issue, but the child's actual day-to-day experiences. Yet even if this turns out to be the best explanation of the observed negative effects, it is hardly cause for cheering. The children in Bates's study, for example, were in ordinary, everyday types of day-care situations. If such run-of-the-mill care is of sufficiently poor quality that it has even small negative effects on children's later behavior, parents and developmentalists ought to be concerned.

EFFECTS OF NONPARENTAL CARE ON ATTACHMENT

Another vital question is whether an infant or toddler can develop a secure attachment to her mother and father if she is repeatedly separated from them. Researchers know that the majority of infants develop secure attachments to their fathers, even though fathers typically go away every day to work, so it is clear that regular separations do not preclude secure attachment. Still, the early research created enough concern that psychologist Jay Belsky, in a series of papers and in testimony before a congressional committee, sounded an alarm (Belsky, 1985, 1992; Belsky & Rovine, 1988). Combining data from several studies, he concluded that there was a slightly heightened risk of insecure attachment among infants who entered day care before their first birthday, compared with those cared for at home throughout the first year. Subsequent analyses supported Belsky's conclusion (Lamb, Sternberg, & Prodromidis, 1992).

Psychologists disagreed strongly and vocally, in person and in print, about the meaning of these findings (e.g., Clarke-Stewart, 1990; Roggman, Langlois, Hubbs-Tait, & Rieser-Danner, 1994; Sroufe, 1990). Some concluded that they implied that day care itself increased the chances of an insecure attachment. Others pointed out that most of the existing research included so many confounding variables that it was impossible to draw any clear conclusion. For example, perhaps the problem was not day care itself, but rather poor-quality day care. The self-selection problem was also troubling. Mothers who work are different in other ways from mothers who do not. More are single mothers, and more prefer to work or find child care onerous. In addition, mothers who prefer center-based care over other arrangements tend to be more insecurely attached to their own parents (Koren-Karie, 2001).

In a wonderful example of the way dispute and disagreement can often lead to very good science, 25 researchers at 14 universities—including all the main protagonists in the dispute that Belsky generated—got together in 1991 to design and carry out a very large study that would address all these questions (NICHD Early Child Care Research Network, 1997c). They enrolled over 1,300 infants and their families in the study, including African American and Hispanic American families, mothers with little education as well as those with college or graduate degrees, and both single mothers and two-parent families.

The basic design of the study is summarized in Table 14.1. As you can see, the researchers first visited each home when the baby was 1 month old. During that visit they obtained information about the family's organization and income and about the mother's temperament, her level of depression, and her attitude toward working. They also asked her to rate the baby's temperament, using a standard questionnaire.

TABLE 14.1	Design of the National Institute of Child Health and Development (NICHD) Study of Early Child Care
Age of Infant at Each Contact	**Measures Used at That Age**
1 month	● Mother's personality ● Mother's level of depression ● Mother's attitude toward employment ● Mother's rating of the infant's temperament ● Household composition and family income
6 months	● Mother's rating of the infant's temperament ● Mother's level of depression ● Observation of quality of home caregiving environment ● Observation of mother and infant during play ● Rating of quality of any nonparental care setting
15 months	● Mother's level of depression ● Observation of mother and child during play ● Observation of quality of home caregiving environment ● Rating of quality of any nonparental care setting ● Child's security of attachment in the Strange Situation

Source: NICHD Early Child Care Research Network, 1997c.

When the babies were 6 months old, the researchers returned to each home, asking the mother again about her level of depression and her view of her child's temperament. During this visit, they also observed the mother's interactions with her infant during a play session and evaluated the quality of the overall caregiving environment in the home, using another standard instrument. In these observations, the researchers were looking particularly at the level of the mother's sensitivity and responsiveness to the infant—a quality known to be linked to security of attachment.

Researchers made one more home visit when the children were 15 months old, repeating their evaluation of the home environment and their direct observation of the mother and child during play. Each pair was also brought to a laboratory where mother and child were put through the series of episodes of the Strange Situation. For those children who were in nonparental care at 6 months and 15 months, the researchers also visited the care setting and rated its quality.

Given the complexity of the study, the results are surprisingly clear: Day care, in itself, was unrelated to the security of the child's attachment. Only among infants whose mothers were relatively insensitive to their needs at home did day care or nonparental care have some negative effects. For these children, low-quality care was linked to less secure attachment. Only the infants who experienced the combination of two poor conditions—an insensitive mother and poor care—had a higher risk of being insecurely attached. Infants with insensitive mothers whose nonparental care was of good quality were just as likely as any other child to be securely attached.

Even this comprehensive research raises a few small cautionary flags, however. The NICHD study researchers also found that the mothers of children in nonparental care showed a very slight (but statistically significant) increase in a tendency to behave less sensitively toward their children, compared to mothers who reared their children entirely at home. Note that this effect was not sufficient to affect the likelihood that the child would be securely attached to the mother. Children in day care were just as likely as those reared entirely at home to be securely attached to their mothers. Still, the research revealed a small potential negative effect.

Researchers continue to monitor the development of the children who participated in the NICHD study. One study looked at aggressiveness during the late elementary school years (NICHD Early Child Care Research Network, 2004). Several different developmental patterns emerged, including the finding that aggressiveness was highly stable in some children. However, there was no correlation between aggressiveness in the late elementary years and participation in nonparental care during the preschool years.

INTERPRETING RESEARCH ON NONPARENTAL CARE

What is it about nonparental care that predisposes infants to become aggressive, disobedient kindergartners? Studies of infants' responses to nonparental care may hold a clue. Researchers have found that levels of the stress hormone *cortisol* increase from morning to afternoon in infants who are enrolled in center-based care (Watamura, Donzella, Alwin, & Gunnar, 2003). By contrast, cortisol levels decrease over the course of the day in home-reared infants. Interestingly, cortisol levels of home-reared and center-care infants are identical on weekends and holidays. Thus, some developmentalists argue that the higher levels of cortisol experienced by center-care infants affect their rapidly developing brains in ways that lead to problem behaviors. However, there is no direct evidence yet to support this hypothesis.

Some developmentalists argue that nonparental care arrangements probably vary in the degree to which they induce stress in infants and young children. In other words, they say, quality of care may be just as important as quantity of care (Maccoby & Lewis, 2003). For example, some researchers have found that, when infants are cared for in high-quality centers, the amount of time they spend in such care is unrelated to social behavior (Love et al., 2003). Thus, developmentalists urge parents, especially those who must leave their infants in center-based care for extended periods of time, to make every effort to ensure that the arrangement they choose has the characteristics discussed in *The Real World*.

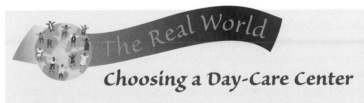

Choosing a Day-Care Center

Rey is a single father who needs to find someone to care for his 14-month-old son while he is at work. Up until now, Rey's mother has been caring for the boy, but she has decided to return to work herself. Rey has heard about studies showing that high-quality care can enhance children's development, but he isn't exactly sure what is meant by the term "high-quality." Here are a few pointers Rey could use to find a high-quality child-care center (Clarke-Stewart, 1992; Howes, Phillips, & Whitebook, 1992; Scarr & Eisenberg, 1993).

- *A low teacher/child ratio.* For children younger than 2, the ratio should be no higher than 1:4; for 2- to 3-year-olds, ratios between 1:4 and 1:10 appear to be acceptable.
- *A small group size.* The smaller the number of children cared for together—whether in one room in a day-care center or in a home—the better for the child. For infants, a maximum of 6 to 8 per group appears best; for 1- to 2-year-olds, between 6 and 12 per group; for older children, groups as large as 15 or 20 appear to be acceptable.
- *A clean, colorful space, adapted to child play.* It is not essential to have lots of expensive toys, but the center must

offer a variety of activities that children find engaging, organized in a way that encourages play.
- *A daily plan.* The daily curriculum should include some structure, some specific teaching, and some supervised activities. However, too much regimentation is not ideal.
- *Sensitive caregivers.* The adults in the day-care setting should be positive, involved, and responsive to the children, not merely custodial.
- *Knowledgeable caregivers.* Training in child development and infant curriculum development helps caregivers provide a day-care setting that meets criteria for good quality.

Questions for Reflection

1. What do you think Rey should do to ease his son's transition from his grandmother's care to a day-care center?
2. One of the criteria is "sensitive caregivers." What kinds of caregiver behaviors might be indicative of this criterion?

Another point to keep in mind is that individual and gender differences have been found to interact with nonparental care. For example, infants who are behaviorally inhibited, in Jerome Kagan's terms, may be more sensitive to the stresses associated with center-based care (Watamura et al., 2003). Moreover, boys in nonparental care are more likely than girls in similar care settings to be insecurely attached to their caregivers (Crockenberg, 2003). For these reasons, more research that takes both temperament and gender into account is needed before we can say for certain that nonparental care has uniformly negative effects on children's social development (Crockenberg, 2003).

Finally, it is important to understand that, on average, the differences between children in nonparental care and their home-reared peers, both positive and negative, are very small (NCIHD Early Child Care Research Network, 2003). Moreover, studies that have attempted to examine all of the complex variables associated with parental and nonparental care, such as parents' level of education, have shown that family variables are more important than the type of day-care arrangements a family chooses (NCIHD Early Child Care Research Network, 2003). Developmental psychologist Sandra Scarr, a leading day-care researcher, has suggested that the kind of day care parents choose is an extension of their own characteristics and parenting styles (Scarr, 1997). For example, poorly educated parents may choose day-care arrangements that do not emphasize infant learning. Similarly, parents whose focus is on intellectual development may not place a high priority on the emotional aspects of a particular day-care arrangement. Thus, Scarr claims, day-care effects are likely to be parenting effects in disguise.

BEFORE- AND AFTER-SCHOOL CARE

Once children reach school age, the issues surrounding nonparental care change to some degree, for both parents and researchers. Many families require care arrangements only for brief periods of time before and after school. Parents of most younger school children provide such arrangements, but as children get older, many families allow children to supervise themselves. In the United States, more than 7 million children are at home by themselves after school for an hour or more each weekday (Crockett, 2003). They are often referred to as *self-care children*. Self-care arrangements differ so much from child to child that it is impossible to say whether, as a group, self-care children differ from others. For example, some self-care children are home alone but are closely monitored by neighbors or relatives, while others are completely without supervision of any kind (Brandon, 1999). Consequently, the global category "self-care children" isn't very useful in research. To compare self-care children to others and to make predictions, investigators have to focus on variables that may affect self-care—such as the crime rate of the neighborhood in which self-care occurs. Thus, developmentalists have learned that the effects of self-care on a child's development depend on behavioral history, age, gender (with girls less negatively affected), the kind of neighborhood the child lives in, and how well parents monitor the child during self-care periods (Casper & Smith, 2002; NICHD Early Child Care Research Network, 2004; Posner & Vandell, 1994; Steinberg, 1986).

Research consistently demonstrates that self-care children are more poorly adjusted in terms of both peer relationships and school performance. They tend to be less socially skilled and to have a greater number of behavior problems. However, some of these differences between self-care children and others arise from the effect of self-care on children who already have social and behavioral difficulties before self-care begins. Investigators have found that children who have such problems in the preschool years, before they experience any self-care, are the most negatively affected by the self-care experience (Pettit, Laird, Bates, & Dodge, 1997).

With respect to age, most developmentalists agree that children under the age of 9 or 10 should not care for themselves. In fact, most cities and/or states have laws specifying the age at which a child may be legally left at home alone for long periods of time. In some areas, this age is in the mid-teens. Thus, parents considering self-care should check with local child protective services to find out the specific regulations in their area.

From a developmental perspective, children younger than 9 do not have the cognitive abilities necessary to evaluate risks and deal with emergencies. Children who start self-care in the early elementary years are vulnerable to older self-care children in their neighborhoods who may hurt or even sexually abuse them and are more likely to have adjustment difficulties in school (Pettit et al., 1997). High-quality after-school programs can help these younger children attain a higher level of achievement (Peterson, Ewigman, & Kivlahan, 1993; Zigler & Finn-Stevenson, 1993).

Children older than 9 may be cognitively able to manage self-care, but they, too, benefit from participation in well-supervised after-school programs. Even part-time participation in supervised activities after school seems to make a difference in the adjustment of self-care children (Pettit et al., 1997). Good programs provide children with opportunities to play, do homework, and get help from adults (Posner & Vandell, 1994).

Self-care has the most negative effects for children in low-income neighborhoods with high crime rates (Marshall et al., 1997). Self-care children in such areas may use after-school time to "hang out" with socially deviant peers who are involved in criminal activity or who have negative attitudes about school. Predictably, then, the positive effects of organized after-school programs on academic achievement are greater for children in low-income neighborhoods (Mason & Chuang, 2001; Posner & Vandell, 1994).

When everything is taken into consideration, the most important factor in self-care seems to be parental monitoring. Many parents, particularly single mothers, enlist the help of neighbors and relatives to keep an eye on their self-care children (Brandon & Hofferth, 2003). Most require children to call them at work when they get home from school to talk about their school day and get instructions about homework and chores. For example, a working mother might tell a fifth-grader, "By the time I get home at 5:00, you should be finished with your math and spelling. Don't work on your history project until I get home and can help you with it. As soon as you finish your math and spelling, start the dishwasher." Research suggests that children whose periods of self-care are monitored in this way are less likely to experience the potential negative effects of self-care (Galambos & Maggs, 1991).

Before going on . . .

- Why is it difficult to study the effects of nonparental care?
- What kinds of nonparental care arrangements are most common in the United States?
- How does nonparental care affect cognitive development?
- How does nonparental care affect personality?
- How does nonparental care affect attachment relationships?
- What variables should be taken into account in interpretations of research on nonparental care?
- How does self-care affect school-aged children's development?

The Impact of Schools

School is another vitally important microsystem experienced by virtually all children in the great majority of cultures. School normally begins between ages 5 and 7, and in industrialized countries, it typically continues through age 16 or older. During these 10 or more years, the child learns an enormous number of facts and develops new and much more complex forms of thinking. What role does the schooling itself play in this set of cognitive changes and in other changes in the social domain?

SCHOOLING AND COGNITIVE DEVELOPMENT

Cross-cultural studies—in Hong Kong and in Mexico, Peru, Colombia, Liberia, Zambia, Nigeria, Uganda, and many other countries—support the conclusion that school experiences are indeed causally linked to the emergence of some advanced cognitive skills. The links are both indirect and direct. One example of an indirect effect is that mothers in non-Western cultures who have attended Western-style schools engage in more teacher-like behavior with their children than their peers who have little or no formal education (Chavajay & Rogoff, 2002). Such a shift in a mother's role and behavior is likely to affect a child's cognitive development. A direct effect of schooling is that children who attend school acquire complex concepts and information-processing strategies that their non-schooled peers do not develop. Schooled children are also better at generalizing a concept or principle they have learned to some new setting than those who do not attend school.

A good example comes from Harold Stevenson's study of the Quechua Indian children of Peru (Stevenson & Chen, 1989; Stevenson, Chen, Lee, & Fuligni, 1991). Stevenson and his associates tested 6- to 8-year-old children, some who had been in school for about 6 months and some who had not yet started school or who were living in an area where no school was available. Stevenson found that in both rural and urban areas, schooled children performed better on virtually all tasks, including a measure of seriation (putting things in serial order, such as by size or length) and a measure of concept formation. These differences remained even if the parents' level of education, the nutritional status of the child, and the amount of educational enrichment offered at home were taken into account.

Schooling also affects the rate at which children move through Piaget's concrete operations stage (Mishra, 1997). You might think that rate of cognitive development doesn't matter, so long as everyone ends up in the same place. However, longitudinal studies show that the rate of progression through concrete operations predicts how well children will reason in adolescence and adulthood (Bradmetz, 1999). Thus, the cognitive-developmental advantage a child gains by attending school is one that probably lasts a lifetime.

Unschooled children are also less proficient at generalizing a learned concept or principle to some new setting. A good illustration comes from studies of South American street vendors, most of whom are of elementary-school age. These children can carry out monetary calculations with lightning speed and impressive accuracy, yet they have trouble translating their mental calculations into written mathematical problems (Schliemann, Carraher, & Ceci, 1997). It seems that the "language" of mathematics children learn in school helps them acquire number knowledge in a far more abstract way than children whose calculation skills develop exclusively in a practical context.

A different way of approaching the question is to compare children whose birthdays fall just before the arbitrary school district cutoff date for entrance into kindergarten or first grade to those whose birthdays fall after the cutoff date. If a particular school district sets September 15 as the cutoff, for example, then a child born on September 10 is eligible for first grade 5 days after he turned 6, whereas a child born on September 20 is not eligible for another year, even though he is only 10 days younger. A year later, these two children are still essentially the same age, but one has had a year of school and the other has not, so investigators can look at the effect of schooling with age held constant (e.g., Morrison, Smith, & Dow-Ehrensberger, 1995; Stelzl, Merz, Ehlers, & Remer, 1995).

Studies comparing early versus late school starters in the United States show that schooling itself, rather than merely age, has a direct effect on some kinds of cognitive skills, such as the ability to use good memory strategies. In one such study, Fred Morrison and his colleagues (1995) found that a big improvement in the use of memory strategies occurred in first grade; children of the same age who spent the year in kindergarten because they just missed the cutoff did not show the same gain in memory skill—although these children would of course acquire such skill in the following year, when they were in first grade.

CRITICAL THINKING

Suppose your child's birthday was right after your local school district's cutoff date for starting school. In light of the evidence about the effects of schooling, would you try to get your child into school early?

FITTING IN AND ADAPTING TO SCHOOL

When parents come to parent-teacher conferences, attend school events, and get involved in supervising homework, children are more strongly motivated, feel more competent, and adapt better to school. They learn to read more readily, get better grades through elementary school, and stay in school for more years (Brody, Stoneman, & Flor, 1995; Grolnick & Slowiaczek, 1994; Reynolds & Bezruczko, 1993). As

Laurence Steinberg puts it, "All other things being equal, children whose parents are involved in school do better than their peers" (1996, pp. 124–125). This effect of parent involvement has been found among groups of poor children as well as among the middle class (e.g., Luster & McAdoo, 1996; Reynolds & Bezruczko, 1993), which confirms that the effect is not just a social class difference in disguise. That is, among poverty-level children, those whose parents are most involved with their school and schooling have a better chance of doing well in school than do equally poor children whose parents have little or no connection to the school.

A range of research reveals that children's school performance improves when their parents participate in school activities such as parent-teacher conferences.

Parental involvement is important not just for the child, but for the parent and for the school. Schools that invite and encourage parents to participate help to create a stronger sense of community, linking parents with one another and with the teachers. Stronger communities, in turn— whether they are in poverty-stricken inner cities or middle-class suburbs—provide better supervision and monitoring of the children in their midst, which benefits the children. Parents who get involved with their children's school also learn ways to help their children; they may even be motivated to continue their own education (Haynes et al., 1996).

A child's early success in school is also affected by whether his own personality or temperament matches the qualities valued and rewarded within the school setting. For example, Karl Alexander and his colleagues (1993) found that children who are enthusiastic, interested in new things, cheerful, and easygoing do better in the early years of school than those who are more withdrawn, moody, or high-strung.

Research also indicates that how a child starts out in the first few years of school has a highly significant effect on the rest of her school experience and success. Children who come to school with good skills quickly acquire new academic skills and knowledge and thereby adapt to later school demands more easily. Children who enter school with poor skills, or with less optimal temperamental qualities, learn less in the early years and are likely to move along a slower achievement trajectory throughout their school years. Such a slow trajectory is not set in stone. Parental involvement can improve the chances of a less advantaged child, as can a particularly skillful kindergarten or first-grade teacher (Pianta, Steinberg, & Rollins, 1995). The key point is that the child does not enter school as a blank slate; she brings her history and her personal qualities with her.

SCHOOL TRANSITIONS

There are many places in the world, including some in North America, where children attend a lower school for 8 years before moving on to a high school. Such an arrangement is known as an 8-4 system. Because students typically show achievement declines after entering high school, educators have developed two models that include a transitional school—a junior high, middle school, or intermediate school—between elementary and high school. The junior high model typically includes 6 years of elementary school followed by 3 years of junior high and 3 years of high school. The middle school model comprises 5 elementary grades, 3 middle school grades, and 4 years of high school.

However, neither the junior high nor the middle school model seems to have solved the transition problem. Students show losses in both achievement and self-esteem across both transition points in the 6-3-3 and 5-3-4 systems. Further, students in both systems show greater losses during the transition to high school than those in 8-4 systems (Alspaugh, 1998; Anderman, 1998). Consequently, educators and developmentalists are searching for explanations and practical remedies.

One potential explanation for transition-related achievement declines is that students' academic goals change once they enter middle school. Researchers classify such goals into two very broad categories: task goals and ability goals. **Task goals** are based on personal standards and a desire to become more competent at something. For example, a runner who wants to improve her time in the 100-meter dash has a task goal. An **ability goal** is one that defines success in competitive terms. A person pursuing an ability goal wants to be better than another person at something. For example, a runner who wants to be the fastest person on his team has an ability goal. Longitudinal research shows that most fifth graders have task goals, but by the time children have been in sixth grade a few months, most have shifted to ability goals (Anderman & Anderman, 1999; Anderman & Midgley, 1997).

A student's goal approach influences her behavior in important ways. Task goals are associated with a greater sense of personal control and positive attitudes about school (Anderman, 1999). A student who takes a task-goal approach to her schoolwork tends to set increasingly higher standards for her performance and attributes success and failure to her own efforts. For example, a task-goal–oriented student is likely to say she received an A in a class because she worked hard or because she wanted to improve her performance.

In contrast, students with ability goals adopt relative standards—that is, they view performance on a given academic task as good so long as it is better than someone else's. Consequently, such students are more strongly influenced by the group with which they identify than by internal standards that define good and bad academic performance. Ability-goal–oriented students are also more likely than others to attribute success and failure to forces outside themselves. For example, such a student might say he got an A in a class because it was easy or because the teacher liked him. Moreover, such students are likely to have a negative view of school (Anderman, 1999).

Because middle schools emphasize ability grouping more than elementary schools, it is likely that many middle-school students change their beliefs about their own abilities during these years (Anderman, Maehr, & Midgley, 1999; Roeser & Eccles, 1998). Thus, high-achieving elementary students who maintain their levels of achievement across the sixth-grade transition gain confidence in their abilities (Pajares & Graham, 1999). In contrast, high achievers, average achievers, and low achievers who fail to meet expectations in middle school undergo a change in self-concept that likely leads to a decline in self-esteem. Once an ability-goal–oriented student adopts the belief that his academic ability is less than adequate, he is likely to stop putting effort into his schoolwork. In addition, such students are likely to use ineffective cognitive strategies when attempting to learn academic material (Young, 1997). Consequently, achievement suffers along with self-esteem.

Educators have devised a number of strategies to address this shift in goal structure. One such approach is based on research demonstrating that the availability of supportive adults outside a child's family makes the transition easier (Galassi, Gulledge, & Cox, 1997; Wenz-Gross, Siperstein, Untch, & Widaman, 1997). For example, some schools pair students with an adult mentor, either a teacher or a volunteer from the community, either for a transitional period or throughout the middle-school years. In one such program, a homeroom teacher monitors several students' daily assignment sheets, homework, grades, and even school supplies. The homeroom teacher also maintains communication with each child's parents regarding these issues. So, if a student in this program isn't doing his math homework or doesn't have any pencils, it is the homeroom teacher's responsibility to tell his parents about the problem. The parents are then responsible for follow-up.

Research suggests that programs of this level of intensity are highly successful in improving middle-schoolers' grades (Callahan, Rademacher, Hildreth, & Hildreth, 1998). Their success probably lies in the fact that the homeroom teacher functions very much like an elementary school teacher—and despite cultural expectations to the contrary, a sixth grader is developmentally a child, whether he is in elementary school or middle school. It isn't surprising that a strategy that makes a middle school more like an elementary school—a school designed for children, not adolescents—is successful.

task goal A goal orientation associated with a desire for self-improvement.

ability goal A goal orientation associated with a desire to be superior to others.

In fact, some observers think that middle schools have failed to meet their goal of easing the transition to secondary schooling because they have simply duplicated high school organization and imposed it on students who are not developmentally ready for it, rather than providing them with a real transition.

One approach aimed at making middle schools truly transitional involves organizing students and teachers into teams. For example, in some schools, sixth, seventh, and eighth grades are physically located in different wings of the school building. In such schools, each grade is like a school-within-a-school. Teachers in each grade-level team work together to balance the demands of different subject-area classes, assess problems of individual students, and devise parent involvement strategies. Preliminary research suggests that the team approach helps to minimize the negative effects of the middle-school transition. As a result, it has become the recommended approach of the National Middle School Association in the United States (Loonsbury, 1992).

Regardless of the type of school they attended prior to high school—middle school, junior high, or grade school—for many teens, a general pattern of success or failure that continues into the adult years is set early in high school. For example, a teen who fails one or more courses in the first year of high school is far less likely than his or her peers to graduate (Roderick & Camburn, 1999). It appears that minority students have a particularly difficult time recovering from early failure.

However, some psychologists emphasize the positive aspects of transition to high school, claiming that participation in activities that are usually offered only in high school allows students opportunities to develop psychological attributes that can't be acquired elsewhere. To demonstrate the point, researchers asked high school students to use pagers to signal them whenever they were experiencing high levels of intrinsic motivation along with intense mental effort (Larson, 2000). The results showed that students experienced both states in elective classes and during extracurricular activities far more often than in required academic classes (Larson, 2000). In other words, a student engaged in an art project or sports practice is more likely to experience this particular combination of states than one who is in a history class. Consequently, educators may be able to ease the transition to high school for many students by offering a wide variety of elective and extracurricular activities and encouraging students to participate.

ENGAGEMENT IN AND DISENGAGEMENT FROM SECONDARY SCHOOL

Some secondary school students benefit little from extracurricular and elective activities because they choose not to be involved in them. For some, the demands of part-time jobs limit the time they have to participate, causing some developmentalists to question the value of these work experiences (see the *Research Report*). Such concerns arise out of research showing that secondary school students fall into two distinct groups. Some students are highly "engaged" in the schooling process, to use Laurence Steinberg's term. They not only enjoy school but are involved in all aspects of it, participating in extracurricular and elective activities, doing their homework, and so on. Others are "disengaged" from schooling, particularly from the academic part of the process. Steinberg argues that a child's level of engagement or disengagement is critical for the child and her future.

Disengaged Students Steinberg (1996) paints quite a gloomy picture of the typical level of engagement of U.S. high school students, based on interviews with and observations of over 20,000 teenagers and their families. A high proportion don't take school or their studies seriously; outside of class, they don't often participate in activities that reinforce what they are learning in school (such as doing their homework); the peer culture denigrates academic success and scorns those students who try to do well

The Effects of Teenaged Employment

In the United States, surveys of teenagers suggest that deciding on a career is one of the central themes of adolescent identity development (Mortimer, Zimmer-Gembeck, Holmes, & Shanahan, 2002). Moreover, many teens believe that engaging in part-time work during high school will help them with this aspect of identity achievement. Parents, too, often encourage their adolescent children to obtain part-time employment on the grounds that it "builds character" and teaches young people about "real life."

Are American teens and parents right about such beneficial effects of work? One frequently cited classic study suggests that the long-term effects of teenaged employment may be quite the opposite. Longitudinal research involving more than 70,000 individuals who graduated from high school in the late 1980s, carried out by Jerald Bachman and John Schulenberg (1993), revealed that the more hours participants worked during high school, the more likely they were to use drugs (alcohol, cigarettes, marijuana, cocaine), to display aggression toward peers, to argue with parents, to get inadequate sleep, and to be dissatisfied with life. More recent studies by Bachman, Schulenberg, and their colleagues have shown a similar pattern among teenagers who were in high school during the late 1990s (Bachman, Safron, Sy, & Schulenberg, 2003). Moreover, as adults, individuals who worked while in high school are less likely than peers who did not work to go to college. Bachman and Schulenberg suggest that

teenaged employment reflects—or perhaps causes—development of a sense of identity that includes disengagement from education. As a result, working may actually decrease teens' chances for successful careers during adulthood, precisely the opposite of what many adolescents and parents believe.

A quite different answer to the question of the impact of teenaged employment comes from studies by Jeylan Mortimer and her colleagues. Their research takes into consideration the kind of work teenagers do, as well as how many hours they spend on the job (Mortimer & Finch, 1996; Mortimer, Finch, Dennehy, Lee, & Beebe, 1995; Mortimer & Harley, 2002). Mortimer's findings indicate that unskilled work that affords little opportunity for independence and little chance to learn long-term job skills is much more likely to be associated with poor outcomes than is complex, skilled work. They also suggest that adolescents who have skill-based work experiences develop increased feelings of competence. In addition, those students who see themselves as gaining useful skills through their work also seem to develop confidence in their ability to achieve economic success in adulthood (Grabowski, Call, & Mortimer, 2001). Thus, Mortimer's findings suggest that part-time employment that involves complex work and affords teens an opportunity to acquire valuable job skills can enhance identity development.

It is not clear how we should add up the results of these several studies. At the very least, this mixture of results should make parents think twice before encouraging teenagers to work. However, parents need to consider the quality of work a teen will do before assuming that a job will negatively affect his or her development.

Questions for Critical Analysis

1. Teenaged employment may be correlated with developmental outcomes because teens who work differ from those who do not in ways that are also related to such outcomes. What variables do you think might distinguish teens who choose to work from their peers who don't?
2. Are there developmental outcomes not addressed by the research described in this discussion that you think might be positively affected by teenaged employment?

in school. Some of the specifics that support these conclusions are summarized in Table 14.2.

Furthermore, a great many U.S. parents are just as disengaged from their children's schooling as their teenagers are. In Steinberg's large study, more than half the high school students said they could bring home grades of C or worse without their parents getting upset; a third said their parents didn't know what they were studying at school; only about a fifth of the parents in this study consistently attended school programs. To use the terminology presented in Chapter 13, parents of disengaged students are most likely to be classed as permissive or authoritarian; parents of engaged students are most likely to be rated as authoritative (Steinberg, 1996).

Parents are not the whole story. Peer group norms and values play an equally important role. Asian American students, for example, are far more likely than African American or Hispanic American students to have friends who value good grades and effort in school; African American and Hispanic American peer groups are much more likely to devalue academic effort or achievement. In these two groups, parental involvement with school or emphasis on the importance of school is undermined by peer norms. To work hard, to try to achieve, is thought of as "acting white" and is thus denigrated.

This problem is not unique to African American or Hispanic American students. Caucasian American teens in the United States today also generally believe that high school students should not seem to be working hard—they should get by, but not show off in the process. To put it another way, the widespread peer norm or goal is the appearance of uninvolvement. Not surprisingly, many teenagers go beyond appearance and become genuinely uninvolved with their schooling, with long-term negative consequences for adult life.

Those Who Drop Out At the extreme end of the continuum of uninvolvement are teenagers who drop out before completing high school. The good news is that the dropout rate has declined significantly over the past several decades. Nevertheless, surveys show that about 10% of 16- to 24-year-olds in the United States left school prior to graduating and do not intend to return (National Center for Education Statistics [NCES], 2005a). If this cohort is like others before it, about 12% will eventually obtain a general equivalency diploma (GED) (Federal Interagency Forum on Child and Family Statistics [FIFCFS], 2000).

Hispanic Americans have the highest dropout rate, at roughly 24% (NCES, 2005a). By comparison, the rate is 12% among African Americans and 6% among Caucasians. Overall, social class is a better predictor of school completion than is race or ethnicity, though. Kids growing up in poor families—especially poor families with a single par-

This high school girl has quite firmly developed beliefs about her abilities and potentials, based on her past school successes and failures. These beliefs contribute significantly to her level of engagement in schooling and will affect important life choices, such as whether to go to college or whether to drop out of school altogether.

TABLE 14.2	Steinberg's Evidence for Widespread Disengagement from Schooling among U.S. Teenagers

- Over one-third of students said they get through the school day mostly by "goofing off with their friends."
- Two-thirds of students said they had cheated on a school test in the past year; nine out of ten said they had copied homework from someone else.
- The average U.S. high school student spends only about 4 hours a week on homework, compared with students in other industrialized countries, who spend 4 hours a *day*.
- Half the students said they did not do the homework they were assigned.
- Two-thirds of U.S. high school students hold paying jobs; half work 15 or more hours a week.
- Only about 20% of students said their friends think it is important to get good grades in school.
- Nearly 20% of students said they do not try as hard as they can in school because they are afraid of what their friends might think.

Source: Steinberg, L., *Beyond the Classroom*, New York: Simon & Schuster, 1996.

Based on the U.S. average, about a tenth of these ninth graders will drop out before finishing high school.

ent—are considerably more likely to drop out of high school than are those from more economically advantaged or intact families. The relationship between social class and dropping out is at least partly explained by the quality of the schools in poor neighborhoods (Cappella & Weinstein, 2001).

Longitudinal studies have found three strong predictors of dropping out: a history of academic failure, a pattern of aggressive behavior, and a tendency to engage in risky behaviors (Cairns & Cairns, 1994; Farmer et al., 2003; Garnier, Stein, & Jacobs, 1997; Jimerson, 1999). With respect to risky behaviors, decisions about sexual intercourse seem to be especially critical. For girls, giving birth and getting married are strongly linked to dropping out.

Another risky behavior, adolescent drug use, is also a strong predictor of dropping out (Garnier et al., 1997). In fact, alcohol and drug use are better predictors of a high school student's grades than are his grades in elementary or middle school. Consequently, decisions about such behaviors seem to be one factor that can cause a teen to deviate from a previously positive developmental pathway.

Peer influence may also be a factor in dropping out. Teens who quit school are likely to have friends who have dropped out or who are contemplating leaving school (Ellenbogen & Chamberland, 1997). Similarly, family variables are linked to dropping out. For example, children whose families move a lot when they are in elementary or middle school are at increased risk for dropping out of high school (Worrell, 1997).

One group of researchers has explored the possibility that by taking into consideration several relevant factors they can devise a general profile of high school students who are potential dropouts. Their research has led to identification of a "type" of high school student who is likely to drop out—one who is quiet, disengaged, low-achieving, and poorly adjusted (Janosz, LeBlanc, Boulerice, & Tremblay, 2000). Many such students show a pattern of chronic class-cutting just prior to dropping out (Fallis & Opotow, 2003).

Whatever its cause, dropping out of high school is associated with a number of long-term consequences. For instance, unemployment is higher among adults who dropped out of high school than among those who graduated, and dropouts who do manage to find jobs earn lower wages than peers who graduate (Crystal, Shae, & Krishnaswami, 1992). In 1998, for example, the average annual income for adults aged 35–44 who had not completed high school was $27,094, compared with $34,786 for those with a high school education and $70,871 for those with a college degree (U.S. Bureau of the Census, 2001). Clearly, those who drop out start on a very different and far less advantageous economic trajectory. For this reason, educators have developed programs aimed at helping dropouts return to school.

The effects of dropping out appear to extend beyond the cognitive domain: Adults who dropped out of high school are also more likely to experience depression (Hagan, 1997). Furthermore, research suggests that staying in school may be an important protective factor for boys who have poor self-regulation skills. When boys who are poor self-regulators stay in school, they appear to be less likely than boys with similar behavior problems who drop out to become involved in criminal activity in early adulthood (Henry et al., 1999).

Engaged Students: Those Who Achieve The other side of the coin are those engaged students who do well in school. Engaged students spend more time on homework, cut class less often, pay more attention in class, and don't cheat. They also tend to spend their time with other students who are engaged or who at least do not ridicule them for making some effort in school, and they are likely to have authoritative parents who expect them to get good grades and who are involved with them and with the school (Brooks-Gunn, Guo, & Furstenberg, 1993; Steinberg, 1996).

You might argue that all the relationships just described exist simply because brighter kids have an easier time with schoolwork, and there is some truth to that. In fact, the best single predictor of a student's academic performance in high school is his or her IQ score. Bright students also have the advantage of many years of successful schooling. Such academic success fosters a greater sense of self-efficacy in these intellectually more able students, in turn increasing their sense of involvement with schooling. Yet Steinberg is also right that the sense of involvement has many other ingredients, which jointly have a strong impact on a teenager's effort and success in school.

While engaged students like these are likely to have the advantage of higher IQ, they are also interested in school and expend effort to do well.

Effort and success, in turn, predict more years of subsequent education, a link that exists among children reared in poverty as well as among the middle class (Barrett & Depinet, 1991). Those extra years of education then have a powerful effect on the career path a young person enters in early adulthood, influencing lifetime income and job success (Featherman, 1980; Rosenbaum, 1984). These are not trivial effects, which is why Steinberg's conclusions about the typical level of school engagement among U.S. high school students are so disturbing.

HOMESCHOOLING

A growing number of parents in the United States are educating their children at home. In 1965, there were only about 2,500 homeschooled children in the United States; by the end of the 20th century, there were more than 1 million homeschooled children (NCES, 2005b). In recent years, homeschooling has grown at a particularly rapid pace among minority families, especially African Americans (Jonsson, 2003). In 1997, there were only about 20,000 homeschooled African American children in the United States. In 2002, the number had grown to approximately 120,000. Homeschooling movements in other nations have experienced similar growth rates. In Canada, for example, homeschool associations estimate that more than 80,000 students are now being educated at home (Basham, 2001). By contrast, in the late 1970s, there were only a few thousand such students. In New Zealand, the number of families involved in homeschooling more than doubled between 1993 and 2003 (New Zealand Ministry of Education, 2003). And in the United Kingdom, homeschooling is now being referred to as the "quiet revolution."

Why would parents want to take on the daunting task of teaching their children at home? Surveys show that the most frequent reason for homeschooling is parents' belief that they can do a better job of educating their children than public or private schools can (Basham, 2001). In addition, many homeschool parents want to be sure that their own religious and moral values are included in their children's education. Many also want to protect their children from negative peer influences or school-based crime.

Special circumstances contribute to the decision to homeschool as well. For instance, some parents who must travel frequently for business reasons choose homeschooling because it allows their families to travel with them. Others want to include activities such as gardening in their children's formal education, and homeschooling allows them the time to do so. Homeschooling also works well for children who are involved in time-consuming pursuits such as elite-level athletic training.

About 8% of homeschool parents have children with disabilities and prefer teaching them at home to having them receive special-education services from local schools (Basham, 2001). The one-on-one teaching these children get at home often helps them achieve more than their disabled peers in public schools are able to (Duvall, Delquadri, & Ward, 2004; Ensign, 1998). In addition, children with disabilities who are homeschooled don't have to deal with teasing from peers.

Research on homeschooling is sparse. Advocates point to a small number of studies showing that homeschooled children are socially competent and emotionally well adjusted and score above average on standardized achievement tests (Ray, 1999). College entrance exam scores of homeschooled students are particularly impressive, ranging from an average score at the 59th percentile for students who were educated at home for one year to an average at the 92nd percentile for those who spent all of their school years in home education (Ray, 1999). However, opponents of homeschooling, a group that includes most professional educators, claim that comparisons of homeschooling and public education are misleading. They point out that researchers have studied only homeschooled children whose families volunteered to participate in research studies. In contrast, most public school achievement test data are based on representative samples or on populations of entire schools.

When comparing homeschooled children to those who attend school, it is also important to know that parents who choose homeschooling differ in significant ways from other families (American Demographics, 2001). One such difference is that 80% of homeschool families have two parents in the home, while among public school families the two-parent-household rate is about 66%. Homeschool parents also tend to have more education; about half possess college degrees, compared to only a third of public school parents. As a result, homeschooling households tend to have higher incomes than those of children who attend public school (Basham, 2001).

Professional educators also argue that homeschooled children miss out on the kinds of socialization opportunities that school attendance provides (Jonsson, 2003). However, advocates of homeschooling counter that homeschooled children have the opportunity to become closer to their parents than children who attend conventional schools. Moreover, homeschoolers typically band together to create music, art, athletic, and social programs for their children. Consequently, most homeschooled children have as many opportunities for socializing with peers as children who attend school.

Before going on . . .

- In what ways does schooling affect cognitive development?
- What factors influence a child's adjustment to school?
- How do children's achievement goals change during the transition to secondary school?
- What have researchers learned about disengaged and engaged students?
- Why do some parents choose to homeschool their children?

The Impact of Entertainment Media

Entertainment media—television, movies, radio, CDs, video games, and the like—are a pervasive part of most children's environments. Of all of these, children and teens devote the most time to television and to video games. In Chapter 4, you learned that the sedentary nature of these activities contributes to the development of obesity in many children. In this section, we will more closely examine the effects of these two forms of entertainment on cognitive and social development.

EFFECTS OF TELEVISION ON LEARNING

Television programs specifically designed to be educational or to teach children positive values do indeed have demonstrable positive effects. This is particularly clear among preschoolers, for whom most such programming is designed. For example, children who regularly watch *Sesame Street* develop larger vocabularies and better school readiness skills than children who do not watch it or who watch it less often, an effect found for children for whom Spanish or English is the dominant language (Huston & Wright, 1998; Rice, Huston, Truglio, & Wright, 1990). And these effects appear to continue well into the high school years (Collins et al., 1997). Programs that emphasize such prosocial behaviors as sharing, kindness, and helpfulness, such as *Mister Rogers'*

Neighborhood, *Sesame Street*, and even *Lassie*, also have some positive impact. Children who regularly view such programs show more kind and helpful behavior than do children who don't view them (Huston & Wright, 1998). Likewise, programs designed to teach racial tolerance to school-aged children have consistently shown positive effects on older children's attitudes and behavior (Persson & Musher-Eizenman, 2003; Shochat, 2003).

However, looking at the total amount of TV viewing rather than at only educational programming reveals a small negative correlation between heavy TV viewing and school grades or achievement test scores. That is, children who are heavy viewers, particularly those who spend more than 30 hours a week watching television, do slightly less well in school (Huston & Wright, 1998). Of course, it is quite possible that children who are already doing poorly in school choose to watch more television, so it may be incorrect to conclude that TV watching is interfering with school performance.

Longitudinal studies give some help in untangling the causal links. Daniel Anderson and his colleagues (Anderson, Huston, Schmitt, Linebarger, & Wright, 2001) found that girls who were heavy TV viewers in preschool got slightly lower school grades overall, especially in science and English, even when researchers controlled statistically for each child's early skill in those areas. For boys in this sample, early heavy viewing had no such persisting effects. Other research, however, suggests that heavy TV viewing may have negative (causal) effects on the development of reading skills for both boys and girls (Ritchie, Price, & Roberts, 1987).

In the United States, children of this age watch an average of 3 to 4 hours of television every day.

TELEVISION AND AGGRESSION

By far the largest body of research has focused on the potential impact of TV viewing on children's aggressiveness (Villani, 2001). The level of violence on U.S. television is remarkably high and has remained high over the past two decades, despite many congressional investigations and cries of alarm. In prime-time programs, there are an average of 5 violent acts per hour; on Saturday morning cartoons, there are 20 to 25 acts of violence per hour (Gerbner, Morgan, & Signorielli, 1994; Murray, 1997). The violence portrayed on these various programs is typically shown as socially acceptable or as a successful way of solving problems; it is frequently rewarded, in that people who are violent often get what they want (Sege, 1998). Further, televised images of actual warfare have become more common in recent years.

Does viewing such a barrage of violence cause higher rates of aggression or violence in children? Unequivocal findings would require an experimental design—a strategy that must be ruled out, for obvious ethical reasons. The most common type of study, the purely correlational design, involves comparing levels of aggression among children who vary in the amount of television they watch in their everyday lives. The almost universal finding is that those who watch more television are more aggressive than their peers who watch less (Huston & Wright, 1998). As is true with all correlational studies, such a result leaves researchers with a problem of interpretation. In particular, children who already behave aggressively appear to choose to watch more television and more violent programs. And families who watch a great deal of television may also be more likely to use patterns of discipline that foster aggressiveness in children.

One partial solution to the interpretation dilemma is to study children longitudinally. In this way, researchers can see whether the amount of violent television a child watches at one age can predict later aggressiveness, taking into account the level of aggression the child already showed at the beginning of the study. There have been several good studies of this type, which show a small but significant effect of TV violence on subsequent aggression. The most famous study in this category is Leonard Eron's 22-year study of aggressiveness from age 8 to age 30 (Eron, 1987).

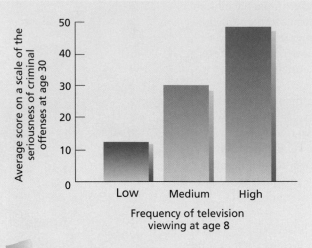

FIGURE 14.1

These data from Leonard Eron's 22-year longitudinal study show the relationships between the amount of television a group of boys watched when they were 8 and the average severity of criminal offenses they had committed by age 30. (*Source*: From Eron, L. D., "The development of aggressive behavior from the perspective of a developing behaviorism," *American Psychologist*, 42 (1987), p. 40. © 1987 by the American Psychological Association. By permission of the author.)

Eron found that the best predictor of a young man's aggressiveness at age 19 was the violence of the TV programs he watched when he was 8. When Eron interviewed the men again when they were 30, he found that those who had watched more television at age 8 were much more likely to have a record of serious criminal behavior in adulthood, a set of results shown in Figure 14.1. The pattern is the same for women, by the way, but the level of criminal offenses is far lower, just as the level of aggression is lower among girls in childhood.

The results shown in the figure, of course, are still a form of correlation. They don't prove that the TV viewing contributed in any causal way to the later criminality, because those children who chose to watch a lot of violent television at age 8 may already have been the most violent children. Indeed, Eron found just such a pattern: Eight-year-old boys who watched a lot of violent television were already more aggressive with their peers, indicating that aggressive boys select more violent TV programs. However, the longitudinal design allowed Eron to discover some additional patterns. In particular, he found that among the already aggressive 8-year-olds, those who watched the most television were more delinquent or aggressive as teenagers and as adults than those who watched less television (Eron, 1987; Huesmann, Lagerspetz, & Eron, 1984). Shorter-term longitudinal studies in Poland, Finland, Israel, and Australia show similar links between TV viewing and later increased aggression among children (Eron, Huesmann, & Zelli, 1991).

A more recent longitudinal study by Frazier, covering children from age 5 to age 12, adds a further note: The impact of higher levels of violent TV viewing at age 5 was substantially stronger among those children whose families also used harsh physical discipline (Frazier, Bates, Dodge, & Pettit, 1997). The combination of physical discipline (spanking) and high levels of violent television was linked to higher levels of later aggression than was either factor by itself.

These findings, along with Eron's, suggest that children are differentially susceptible to the impact of violent television. Not only do aggressive children prefer violent TV programs, but children who are living in families in which aggressive forms of discipline are used are also more susceptible. What seems clear from this research, however, is that the violent television they see causes these children to be more aggressive.

The best evidence of such a causal connection comes from several dozen genuinely experimental studies in which one group of children is exposed to a few episodes of moderately violent television while others watch neutral programs. Collectively, these studies show a significant short-term increase in observable physical aggression among those who watch the violent programs (Huston & Wright, 1998; Paik & Comstock, 1994; Wood, Wong, & Chachere, 1991). In one study of this type, Chris Boyatzis and his colleagues (1995) found that children of elementary school age who were randomly assigned to watch episodes of a then popular (and highly violent) children's program, *The Mighty Morphin Power Rangers*, showed seven times as many aggressive acts during subsequent free play with peers as did comparable children who had not just viewed the violent program. Virtually all psychologists, after reviewing the combined evidence, would agree with Eron's testimony before a Senate committee:

> There can no longer be any doubt that heavy exposure to televised violence is one of the causes of aggressive behavior, crime and violence in society. The ev-

idence comes from both the laboratory and real-life studies. Television violence affects youngsters of all ages, of both genders, at all socioeconomic levels and all levels of intelligence. The effect is not limited to children who are already disposed to being aggressive and is not restricted to this country. (Eron, 1992, p. S8539)

Other evidence suggests that repeated viewing of TV violence leads to emotional desensitization toward violence, to a belief that aggression is a good way to solve problems, and to a reduction in prosocial behavior (Donnerstein, Slaby, & Eron, 1994; Funk, Baldacci, Pasold, & Baumgardner, 2004; Van Mierlo & Van den Bulck, 2004). Violent television is clearly not the only, or even the major, cause of aggressiveness among children or adults. It is nonetheless a significant influence, both individually and at a broader cultural level.

CRITICAL THINKING ❓

As a parent, how could you maximize the benefits and limit the negative effects of TV viewing? Would you be willing to give up having a television altogether if you thought that was necessary for your child's optimal development?

PARENTS' REGULATION OF TELEVISION VIEWING

For parents, the clear message from all the research on television is that it is an educational medium. Children learn from what they watch—vocabulary words, helpful behaviors, attitudes, gender roles, and aggressive behaviors. Huston and Wright point out that "television can be an ally, not an enemy, for parents. Parents can use television programs for their children's benefit just as they use books and toys" (1994, p. 80). However, using television in this way requires considerable vigilance and planning.

Researcher Michelle St. Peters found that she could classify families into one of four types on the basis of the degree of parental regulation or encouragement of TV viewing (St. Peters, Fitch, Huston, Wright, & Eakins, 1991): *Laissez faire* parents had few regulations but did not specifically encourage viewing. *Restrictive* parents had many regulations and provided little encouragement. *Promotive* parents had few regulations and actively encouraged TV viewing. *Selective* parents had many regulations but encouraged some specific types of viewing.

In a 2-year longitudinal study of 5-year-olds and their parents, St. Peters found that children in restrictive families watched the least television (11.9 hours a week). When they watched, they were most likely to view entertainment or educational programs aimed specifically at children (such as *Sesame Street, Mister Rogers' Neighborhood*, or Disney shows). The heaviest viewers were children in promotive families, who watched an average of 21.1 hours a week. They watched not only children's programs but also adult comedy, drama, game shows, and action-adventure shows. Both children in laissez-faire families (16.7 hours) and those in selective families (19.2 hours) watched an intermediate number of hours each week.

The key point is that families create the conditions for children's viewing and thus for what children learn from television. Not only do parents establish a degree of regulation, but they may also watch with the child and interpret what the child sees. A family that wishes to do so can take advantage of the beneficial things television has to offer and can minimize exposure to programs with aggressive, violent, or sexist content.

THE EFFECTS OF VIDEO GAMES

Among preschoolers and school-aged children, television is the most popular form of electronic entertainment. However, as children approach the transition to secondary school at age 11 or 12, the time they spend playing video games approaches and

Some studies suggest that children in the United States now spend more time playing video games than they do watching television.

then exceeds the hours they devote to television ("Children spend more time . . . ," 2004). A recent survey of 1,000 fifth-, eighth-, and eleventh-graders found that, by eighth grade, boys were spending an astonishing 23 hours per week playing video games. Girls spent less time doing so (about 16 hours a week), and time spent video gaming declined somewhat by eleventh grade. These findings help explain why spending on video games has almost surpassed the amount of money families devote to movies (Gentile, 2005). Consequently, developmentalists have begun to study how these games affect children's and teens' cognitive and social development.

Anthropologists propose that video games are one of the many tools industrialized societies use to teach children the technological and intellectual skills they need as adults (Greenfield, 1994). Several studies suggest that playing video games fosters good spatial perception skills (Greenfield, Brannon, & Lohr, 1994). Spatial perception is related to math achievement, a highly valued set of skills in the industrial world. Video games may also help children practice the kind of self-reliance that is so highly valued in Western societies. Researchers have found that both boys and girls who are learning how to play a new game prefer to figure the game out on their own, perhaps by consulting an instruction manual, rather than ask others for help (Blumberg & Sokol, 2004). Thus, the anthropological explanation for the proliferation of video-game playing in technological societies seems to make sense.

Despite these positive effects of video games, research examining their impact on social and emotional development suggests that parents should be cautious about the kinds of games they allow children to play. The linked themes of aggression and power predominate among video games; more than 75% of them involve violence. Further, video-game players, 70–80% of whom are male, overwhelmingly prefer violent games to any other type (Funk & Buchman, 1999).

Researchers have found that playing violent video games leads to immediate increases in aggressive behavior and is associated with long-term increases in such behavior among children who have always been more aggressive than others their age (Anderson & Dill, 2000). In addition, children who play violent video games for 90 minutes or more per day experience higher levels of anxiety and are less able to tolerate frustration than peers (Mediascope, 1999). Indeed, even short-term exposure to violent video games in laboratory settings appears to increase research participants' general level of emotional hostility (Anderson & Dill, 2000). Apparently, increases in emotional hostility and decreases in the capacity to empathize with others, which are engendered by violent video games, are the motivating forces behind the increases in aggressive behavior that often result from playing such games for extended periods of time (Funk, Buchman, Jenks, & Bechtoldt, 2003; Gentile, Lynch, Linder, & Walsh, 2004).

Violent video games also appear to be part of an overall pattern linking preferences for violent stimuli to aggressive behavior. The more violent television programs children watch, the more violent video games they prefer, and the more aggressively they behave toward peers (Mediascope, 1999). This finding holds for both boys and girls; most girls aren't interested in violent games, but those who are tend to be more physically aggressive than average. Consequently, parents who notice that aggressive and violent themes characterize most of their children's leisure-time interests as well as their interactions with peers should worry about their children playing video games (Funk, Buchman, Myers, & Jenks, 2000).

Finally, parents may not be aware of the fact that many video games contain advertising (Gentile, 2005). Such advertising takes the form of "product placement." For example, a character may be shown drinking a particular brand of soda. Thus, encouraging children to buy specific products is another way in which video gaming may influence their development. Parents who are concerned about children's exposure to ads that promote products that they believe to be detrimental to their children's physical or mental health should screen the games they buy for children to determine whether they include objectionable advertisements.

Before going on . . .

■ How does TV viewing affect school achievement?
■ In what way are TV viewing and aggressive behavior related?
■ What does research suggest about the effects of parents' regulations on children's TV viewing?
■ How do video games affect children's cognitive and social development?

Macrosystem Effects: The Impact of the Larger Culture

Finally, we consider explicitly the question of contexts and cultures. Each family, and thus each child, is embedded in a series of overlapping contexts, each of which affects the way the family itself interacts as well as all other parts of the system.

ECONOMIC VARIATIONS: SOCIAL CLASS AND POVERTY

Every society is made up of social layers, usually called **social classes**, each of which has a different degree of access to power, goods, or status. In Western societies, the social class of a given family is most often defined in terms of the income and education of the adults in that family. In the United States, four social classes are usually identified: the upper class, the middle class, the working class, and the lower class (or poverty-level families). Members of each social layer tend to share certain values or styles of interaction, with the largest differences found between families living in poverty and those in higher social classes. For children, it is clear that the disadvantages of poverty are enormous (Mistry, Biesanz, Taylor, Burchinal, & Cox, 2004).

About 16% of children in the United States live below the poverty line—defined as an income of $12,400 or less per year for a family of three (Proctor & Dalaker, 2003). This percentage has dropped somewhat in the past few years. Still, proportionately more children live in poverty in the United States than in any other industrialized country in the world. By way of specific contrast, the percentage of children living in poverty is about 9% in Canada and 2% in Sweden (McLoyd, 1998).

In addition, poverty is not equally distributed across ethnic or racial groups in the United States. Nor is it equally distributed across family structure. African American, Native American, and Hispanic American children, as well as children of single parents, are far more likely to live in poverty than are children in other groups (Evans, 2004; Proctor & Dalaker, 2003). Approximately 60% of African American and Hispanic American children and 40% of Caucasian American children reared by single mothers in the United States live in poverty (Zill & Nord, 1994). Many of these mothers have jobs, but the jobs pay too little to lift the family out of poverty (Lichter & Eggebeen, 1994).

Perhaps more important for the child is the overall family history of poverty. Analyzing economic data this way points to even greater disadvantages for minority children. Greg Duncan notes that 40% of African American children, but only 6% of Caucasian American children, grow up in families that are poor for all of the child's first 5 or 6 years (Duncan, Brooks-Gunn, & Klebanov, 1994). Half of Caucasian American children grow up in families that are never poor and never live in a poor neighborhood; this is true for only 5% of African Americans. Thus, even those African American families that do not fall below the poverty line at any one moment are likely to have fallen below it at some time or to spend some time living in a poor neighborhood.

social class A group with a certain position within a given society, based on income, occupation, and/or education. In the United States, there are four broad social classes: upper class, middle class, working class, and lower class (also called poverty level).

It's not hard to see why some refer to scenes of urban poverty like this as "war zones."

The Effects of Poverty on Families   Among many other things, poverty reduces options for parents. They may not be able to afford prenatal care, so their children are more likely to be born with some sort of disability. When the mother works, she is likely to have fewer choices of affordable child care. Poor children spend more time in poor-quality day care and shift more from one care arrangement to another. Poor families also live in smaller and less adequate housing, often in decaying neighborhoods with high rates of violence, and many of them move frequently, so their children change schools often. The parents are less likely to feel they have adequate social support, and the children often lack a stable group of playmates (Dodge, Pettit, & Bates, 1994). Overall, poor environments are more chaotic, and people living in poverty are more highly stressed with fewer psychological and social resources (Brooks-Gunn, 1995; McLoyd & Wilson, 1991).

Mothers and fathers living in poverty also interact with their children differently than parents in working-class or middle-class families in the United States. Poverty-level parents talk and read to their children less, provide fewer age-appropriate toys, spend less time with them in intellectually stimulating activities, explain things less often and less fully, are less warm, and are stricter and more physical in their discipline (Dodge et al., 1994; Evans, 2004; Sampson & Laub, 1994). In the terms introduced in Chapter 13, in poor families, the parents are more likely to be either neglecting or authoritarian and are less likely to be authoritative.

Some of this pattern of parental behavior is clearly a response to the extraordinary stresses and special demands of the poverty environment—a point buttressed by the repeated observation that those parents living in poverty who nonetheless feel they have enough social support are much less likely to be harshly punitive or unsupportive toward their children (Hashima & Amato, 1994; Taylor & Roberts, 1995). To some extent, the stricter discipline and emphasis on obedience observed among poor parents may be thought of as a logical response to the realities of life in a very poor neighborhood.

Some of the differences in childrearing patterns between poor and nonpoor parents may also result from straightforward modeling of the way these individuals themselves were reared; some inadequate practices may be a product of ignorance of children's needs. Poor parents with relatively more education, for example, typically talk to their children more, are more responsive, and provide more intellectual stimulation than do equally poor parents with lower levels of education (Kelley, Sanchez-Hucles, & Walker, 1993). Whatever the cause, children reared in poverty experience both different physical conditions and quite different interactions with their parents.

The Effects of Poverty on Children   Not surprisingly, children raised in poverty turn out differently. Children from poverty environments have higher rates of illness and disabilities, as you saw in Chapter 4. Typically, they also have lower IQ scores and move through the sequences of cognitive development more slowly—effects that have been found in studies in which researchers controlled for many possible confounding factors, such as the mother's IQ and the family structure (McLoyd, 1998). Children living in poverty are half as likely as their more well-off peers to know the alphabet and to be able to count before they enter school (U.S. Bureau of the Census, 2001). They are twice as likely as nonpoor children to repeat a grade and are less likely to go on to college (Brooks-Gunn, 1995; Huston, 1994; Zill, Moore, Smith, Steif, & Coiro, 1995). Children from low-income homes also exhibit more behavior problems than their better-off peers (Qi & Kaiser, 2003). As adults, children from low-income families are more likely to be poor, thus continuing the cycle through another generation. All these effects are greater for those children who live in poverty in infancy and early childhood and for those who have lived in poverty continuously than for children who have experienced some mixture of poverty and greater affluence (Bolger, 1997; Duncan et al., 1994; Shanahan, Sayer, Davey, & Brooks, 1997; Smith, Brooks-Gunn, & Klebanov, 1997).

Figure 14.2 shows one of these effects, drawn from research by Greg Duncan and his colleagues (1994). Duncan collected information on family income for a large sample of families over the years from the child's birth to age 5. He looked at the child's IQ score at age 5 as a function of whether the family had been poor in every one of those 5 years or in only some years. The figure compares the IQ scores of each of these groups to the benchmark IQ of children who never lived in poverty. It's clear that constant poverty has a greater negative effect than occasional poverty, and both are worse than not being poor. In this analysis, Duncan controlled for the mother's education and the structure of the household (single mother versus two parents, for example), so the differences observed seem to be real effects of poverty.

The Special Case of Inner-City Poverty

All of the effects of poverty are probably much worse for children growing up in poverty-ravaged urban areas, and most such children are African Americans, Hispanic Americans, or other minorities (Brooks-Gunn, Duncan, & Aber, 1997). They are exposed to street gangs and street violence, to drug pushers, to overcrowded homes, and to higher risks of abuse. Entire communities have become like war zones. Predictably, children who are victimized or who witness violent crimes are more likely to suffer from emotional problems than are peers who are spared these experiences (Purugganan, Stein, Johnson Silver, & Benenson, 2003).

Surveys in a number of large cities indicate that nearly half of inner-city elementary and high school students have witnessed at least one violent crime in the past year (Osofsky, 1995); nearly all have heard gunfire, seen someone being beaten up, or observed a drug deal (White, Bruce, Farrell, & Kliewer, 1997); as many as 30% have seen a homicide by the time they are 15 (Garbarino & Kostelny, 1997). In a 1993 national survey by the Centers for Disease Control, 22.1% of high school students reported that they had carried a weapon (gun, knife, or club) some time in the previous 30 days; 7.9% had carried a gun (Kann et al., 1995). Psychologist James Garbarino, who has written extensively about urban poverty, points out that "these figures are much more like the experience of children in the war zones . . . in other countries . . . than they are of what we should expect for our own children, living in 'peace' " (Garbarino & Kostelny, 1997, p. 33).

A growing body of evidence shows that the effect of living in a concentrated pocket of poverty is to intensify all of the ill effects of family poverty (Klebanov, Brooks-Gunn, Hofferth, & Duncan, 1995; Kupersmidt, Griesler, DeRosier, Patterson, & Davis, 1995). Individual family characteristics are still the most important determinants of the child's development, but when the whole neighborhood is poor, especially when the residents of the neighborhood are in constant flux, the negative effects for children are intensified (Brooks-Gunn et al., 1997). In such situations, parents have fewer nonfamily resources to rely on, and children have more violent and fewer supportive adult models; rates of child abuse rise, as do rates of aggression and delinquency by the children (Coulton, Korbin, Su, & Chow, 1995; McLoyd, 1997). When the whole neighborhood also lacks what sociologist William Wilson calls "connectedness and stability"—when the adults do not collaborate to monitor the children and do not provide practical or emotional support to one another—the effects are still worse (Sampson, 1997; Wilson, 1995).

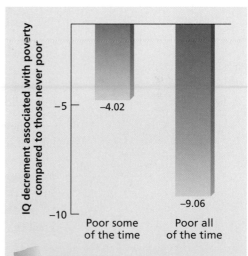

FIGURE 14.2

In this analysis, the zero line represents the average IQ score of a group of 5-year-old children in Duncan's study who had never lived in poverty. Average IQ scores of children who had lived in poverty some of the time or all of the time are compared to that benchmark. You can see that children who spent all of their first 5 years living in poverty had considerably lower average IQs than those who lived in poverty only part of the time, and both groups were significantly lower than the benchmark group.
(*Source*: Duncan et al., 1994, from Table 3, p. 306.)

Many children living in such neighborhoods show all the symptoms of posttraumatic stress disorder (Garbarino, 2002; Garbarino, Dubrow, Kostelny, & Pardo, 1992; Jenkins & Bell, 1997), including sleep disturbances, irritability, inability to concentrate, angry outbursts, and hypervigilance. Many experience flashbacks or intrusive memories of traumatic events. And because they are likely to have missed out on many of the forms of intellectual stimulation and consistent family support that would allow them to succeed in school, they have high rates of behavior problems and academic failure. Fewer than half of urban poor children graduate from high school (Garbarino, Kostelny, & Dubrow, 1991). The reasons for such school failure are complex, but there is little doubt that the chronic stress experienced by these children is one highly significant component.

The Roles of Stress and Protective Factors   Arnold Sameroff and his colleagues (1987) have argued that the effects of various different kinds of stress accumulate. A child may be able to handle one or two, but as the stresses and risks pile up, the probability that the child will thrive intellectually, emotionally, or socially declines steadily. For a child growing up in poverty, perhaps especially urban poverty, the chances of experiencing multiple separate types of stress are very high indeed.

At the same time, studies of resilient and vulnerable children suggest that certain characteristics or circumstances may help to protect some children from the detrimental effects of repeated stresses and upheavals (Cederblad, Pruksachatkunakorn, Boripunkul, Intraprasert, & Hook, 2003; Easterbrooks, Davidson, & Chazan, 1993; Furstenberg & Hughes, 1995; Garmezy & Masten, 1991; Masten, Best, & Garmezy, 1990; Masten & Coatsworth, 1998; Runyan et al., 1998; Townsend & Belgrave, 2003; Winfield, 1995). Table 14.3 lists the key qualities of resilient children suggested by Ann Masten and Douglas Coatsworth in a review (1998). Note that the qualities listed in Table 14.3 are the same qualities that are linked to competence in children who are not growing up in poverty or in other risky environments. As Masten and Coatsworth put it:

> Resilient children do not appear to possess mysterious or unique qualities; rather, they have retained or secured important resources representing basic protective systems in human development. . . . Competence develops in the midst of adversity when, despite the situation at hand, fundamental systems that generally foster competence in development are operating to protect the child or counteract the threats to development. (1998, p. 212)

The results of Emmy Werner's long-term longitudinal study on the Hawaiian island of Kauai demonstrate that these factors operate in real lives (Werner & Smith,

TABLE 14.3	Characteristics of Resilient Children and Adolescents
Source	**Characteristic**
Individual	Good intellectual functioning
	Appealing, sociable, easygoing disposition
	Self-efficacy, self-confidence, high self-esteem
	Talents
	Faith
Family	Close relationship to caring parent figure
	Authoritative parenting: warmth, structure, high expectations
	Socioeconomic advantages
	Connections to extended supportive family networks
Extrafamilial Context	Bonds to prosocial adults outside the family
	Connections to prosocial organizations
	Attending effective schools

Source: From "The development of competence in favorable and unfavorable environments" by Ann S. Masten, *American Psychologist*, 53, p. 212. (1998). Copyright © 1998 by the American Psychological Association. Reprinted within the guidelines of the American Psychological Association and by permission of the author.

1992). The families of the resilient children and adults in her sample were clearly more authoritative, more cohesive, and more loving than were the equally poor families whose children had worse outcomes. Similarly, studies of boys reared in high-crime inner-city neighborhoods show that high intelligence and at least a minimum level of family cohesion are key ingredients affecting a boy's chance of attaining a successful adult life pattern (Long & Vaillant, 1984; McCord, 1982; Sampson & Laub, 1994). Boys reared in poverty-level families plagued by alcoholism, or who had parents with strong antisocial tendencies or low IQs, were simply much less likely to develop the competence needed to bootstrap themselves out of their difficult circumstances. Thus, the outcome depends on some joint effect of the number of stresses the child must cope with and the range of competencies or advantages the child brings to the situation. Poverty does not guarantee bad outcomes, but it stacks the deck against most children.

RACE AND ETHNICITY

These Irish Americans marching in a St. Patrick's Day parade fit the definition of an ethnic group, but they are not a race.

In the United States, because poverty is so much more common among some ethnic groups than others, social class and racial or ethnic group membership are strongly linked. Because of this overlap, it is sometimes tempting to focus attention solely on poverty or social class as the most powerful factor, ignoring the additional impact of race or ethnicity. However, if researchers are to gain an understanding of children's development, they need to understand the separate effects of race or ethnicity. For example, what difference does it make to a child to grow up in a family whose cultural roots emphasize collectivism rather than individualism? You have learned something about these questions throughout the book, but here we will take one final look at what is known about racial and ethnic effects, using the several major groups in the United States as illustration.

We should begin with a definition of **ethnicity**. According to Parke and Buriel, "Ethnicity refers to an individual's membership in a group sharing a common ancestral heritage based on nationality, language, and culture" (1998, p. 496); the group is an **ethnic group**. Ethnicity may include a biological or racial component, but that is not an essential part of the definition. Thus, race and ethnicity are not the same. Ethnicity refers primarily to social and cultural characteristics, whereas race normally designates a group with specific physical characteristics. Thus, African Americans and Asian Americans may be viewed as both ethnic and racial categories, whereas Hispanic Americans, Polish Americans, or Italian Americans would be regarded only as ethnic groups.

African Americans African Americans, the largest minority group in the United States at about 13% of the total population (U.S. Bureau of the Census, 2001), have a culture that has been shaped by their African heritage, their experience of slavery, and a continuing experience of discrimination and segregation. The central values of this culture include the following (Hill, Soriano, Chen, & LaFromboise, 1994):

- Collectivism or communalism, as opposed to individualism; identity is collective as well as personal.
- Person-centered rather than object-centered values; relationships with people are more important than material possessions.
- Mutuality and reciprocity; a belief that "what goes around, comes around," that each person's actions will eventually have repercussions for that individual.
- A strong religious or spiritual orientation, involving acknowledgment of a higher power.
- An emphasis on the importance of children for family continuity.
- Harmony and a sense of connection with nature, including a belief in the "oneness of being" of all humanity.
- Role flexibility.

ethnicity An individual's membership in an ethnic group.

ethnic group "A subgroup whose members are perceived by themselves and others to have a common origin and culture, and shared activities in which the common origin or culture is an essential ingredient" (Porter & Washington, 1993, p. 140).

These values, especially the emphasis on collectivism or communalism and the importance of children, have contributed to a pattern of family structure that is quite different from that of the majority Caucasian American culture. Caucasian Americans think of "the family" as a father, a mother, and several children. Within the African American culture, "family" has a much broader definition, including many variations of extended family structures—a pattern that likely has its roots in West African culture (Sudarkasa, 1993). Martin and Martin, in their book *The Black Extended Family*, defined the African American family as a multigenerational, interdependent kinship system that is welded together by a sense of obligation to relatives; is organized around a dominant figure; extends across geographic boundaries to connect family units to an extended family network; and has a built-in mutual aid system for the welfare of its members and the maintenance of the family as a whole (1978, p. 1). Thus, the key is not just that three or more generations often live in the same household but that contact with nonresident kin is frequent and integral to the functioning of the family unit. When asked, African Americans overwhelmingly report a strong sense of family solidarity (Hatchett & Jackson, 1993; Wilson, 1986, 1989).

Within this subculture, marriage does not play the dominant role in family formation that it does among Caucasian Americans: Fewer African American adults marry; those who do are less likely to be satisfied with their marriages, and divorce is more common (Broman, 1993). One result is that a much larger percentage of African American children are born to or reared by unmarried mothers. However, because of the cultural emphasis on the importance of children and on communalism, these single mothers occupy a different niche within the African American culture than do single mothers in the majority culture. The latter group are more likely to receive financial help from their parents but to live independently; an African American single mother is more likely to live in an extended family with her own mother or grandmother (Wilson, 1986).

These extended family structures allow individuals to pool their economic resources; they also provide important social and emotional support to the members of the household. The presence of the children's grandmother seems to provide especially helpful support for the young single mother; African American children from such three-generation families do better in school and show fewer behavior problems than do African American children reared by single mothers in households without a grandmother. There is also some evidence that the presence of the grandmother increases the chance that an infant will develop a secure rather than an insecure attachment (Egeland & Sroufe, 1981). Thus, the extended family not only has a cultural history but also seems to be a successful adaptive strategy for many African American families.

Religion also appears to play a special, positive role within the African American culture. The church is a place for participation and belonging, an institution in which those who take on specific roles achieve prestige and status, as well as an institution that can provide help in times of physical or emotional need (Dupree, Watson, & Schneider, 2005). For African American children, participation in church activities seems to be a plus as well; a few studies suggest that those who are more active in a church are more likely to be successful in other arenas, such as in school or on the job (Lee, 1985).

The culture of African American families is also profoundly shaped by the persistence of prejudice. African American adolescents who are most aware of such prejudice are most likely to see school achievement as irrelevant (Taylor, Casten, Flickinger, Roberts, & Fulmore, 1994). Even the process of grieving for lost loved ones appears to be complicated by this consciousness of historical racial prejudice. Researchers have found that African Americans' memories of relatives who have passed away are often framed in terms of how racial prejudice interfered with the individual's pursuit of life goals (Rosenblatt & Wallace, 2005). When these memories are shared with children, it is likely that they increase children's awareness of the notion that African Americans often encounter obstacles in life that members of other groups do not. On a positive note, though, these stories may also enhance children's feelings of pride in their family histories and sense of ethnic identity.

Because so many African American families and children live in poverty or near-poverty, it is very difficult to sort out which patterns are due to economic conditions and which are due to distinctive African American cultural processes. These factors obviously interact and are further embedded within the larger culture, in which prejudice and discrimination against African Americans are still a part of everyday life.

This Hispanic American family has obviously assimilated some of the larger American culture: They are celebrating Thanksgiving. At the same time, they have doubtless retained many features of their own culture, including the centrality of family loyalty.

Hispanic Americans Some of the statements made above about African Americans are also true of Hispanic Americans, for whom poverty is also endemic. The term *Hispanic* was chosen by the Department of Commerce to denote any person with family roots in Spanish-speaking countries or from Central or South America. The term *Latino*, which many of these people prefer, is the Spanish word for the same group. Hispanic people represent the fastest-growing minority group in the United States. In 1980, only 6% of the population was Hispanic. By 2000, the proportion had grown to 12% (U.S. Bureau of the Census, 2001).

A number of subgroups, differing somewhat in values and cultural traditions, comprise the Hispanic population in the United States. Just over 60% are Mexican, 12% are Puerto Rican, and 4% are Cuban in origin (U.S. Bureau of the Census, 2001). The rest are from other Central and South American countries. Within this diverse group, Puerto Ricans have the highest poverty rates; their divorce rates are comparable to those among African Americans. Both Mexican Americans and Cuban Americans have divorce rates closer to the rate among white Americans.

These subgroups, however, share a number of cultural values, all of which are aspects of a basic collectivist world view (Hill et al., 1994; Parke & Buriel, 1998):

- Preference for group participation or group work rather than individual effort (*allocentrism*).
- Strong commitment to and adherence to family; placing the family before the individual; self-identity is embedded in the family (*familia*).
- Avoidance of personal conflict; keeping the peace at all costs (*simpatía*).
- Respect for and deference to authority, such as parents, elders, teachers, or government officials (*respeto*).
- High value placed on personal relationships, which are seen as more important than reputation or material gain; feelings and needs of others are paramount; competition is discouraged (*personalismo*).

In addition, of course, there is also the common thread of the Spanish language. The great majority of Hispanic Americans today either speak only Spanish or are bilingual. Because of recent rapid immigration, more than half of Hispanic American school-aged children have only limited English proficiency; a shift toward English as the dominant language generally occurs among second- or third-generation Hispanic Americans, but many if not most continue to speak Spanish in the home (Chapa & Valencia, 1993; Grenier, 1985). Many Hispanic American communities also have Spanish-language newspapers and radio and TV stations; in many neighborhoods, Spanish is the dominant tongue.

The significance of family life within Hispanic American culture is hard to exaggerate. The nuclear family is the core of this kin system, although contact with extended family members and with "fictive kin" is frequent. *Fictive kin*, also common in extended African American family systems, might include a child's godparents or other friends who develop a long-term connection with the family and with each child (Keefe & Padilla, 1987).

This pattern seems to be stronger in first-generation immigrants, who rely almost exclusively on family members for emotional support and problem solving. The children of immigrants seem to have more extensive nonkin networks, and many shift somewhat toward an individualist set of values—with accompanying increases in intrafamily stress (Delgado-Gaitan, 1994; Parke & Buriel, 1998). In both newly immigrant and second-generation families, however, the extended family clearly plays a more central role in the daily life of Hispanic Americans than it does in the majority culture.

This emphasis on the central role of the family is reflected in the values taught to children so that they will become *bien educado*. Literally translated, *bien educado* means "well educated"; the phrase does not primarily connote formal education, however, but rather the ability to function well in any social setting without disrespect or rudeness. Thus, *bien educado* includes politeness, respect, loyalty, and attachment to the extended family and cooperation with others. Hispanic American mothers emphasize the importance of a child's showing proper demeanor in public; a Caucasian American mother, in contrast, is likely to be pleased or even proud when her child behaves in some independent and even slightly naughty way (Harwood, 1992).

These values are taught in the home through all the mechanisms you have read about throughout this book: modeling, direct reinforcement, and style of family interaction. A number of studies suggest that the more fully Hispanic American parents identify with their ethnic heritage, the more likely it is that the child will show these valued qualities, such as concern for others (Knight, Cota, & Bernal, 1993). Moreover, when children of Hispanic immigrants achieve a bicultural identity that includes a strong identification with their parents' culture, along with a sense of belonging in the dominant culture of the United States, they attain higher levels of both social adjustment and academic achievement (Coatsworth, Maldonado-Molina, Pantin, & Szapocznik, 2005).

Asian Americans   Asian American culture, too, places great stress on obedience to family, on respect for elders, and on family honor. Asian American families also resemble Hispanic American families in some respects: They often include three generations in the same household; they are generally hierarchically organized, with the father as the obvious head; and there is a strong emphasis on the interdependence of family members. Despite these surface similarities to other ethnic groups, the mixture of values in Asian American families includes several that are distinct (American Psychological Association, 1993; Park, 2005; Parke & Buriel, 1998):

- Pacifism, self-discipline, and self-control—all values linked to Confucianism, and thus common among Asian groups with a strong Confucian heritage (Chinese, Korean, and Vietnamese particularly, with lesser influence among Japanese).
- An emphasis on hierarchy and respect in social systems and personal relationships (parents are superior to children, men to women), also based on Confucianism.
- Strong family links; young people are expected to obey elders; family solidarity and harmonious relationships are highly valued; family needs come before individual needs.
- A strong belief that each person controls his or her own destiny.
- A powerful work ethic and belief in the importance of achievement.

The Asian American family model includes a striking combination of indulgence, physical contact, comfort, and care on the one hand and high expectations for both obedience and achievement on the other. Children are taught that empathy for others is highly important and yet respecting the privacy of others is also critical (Lebra, 1994). Overall, children are highly valued, although the family's collective needs normally take precedence over the child's individual needs (Rothbaum, Pott, & Morelli, 1995).

Asian Americans also believe in individual effort as one of the primary roads to success (Harrison et al., 1990; Stevenson, 1988). In Caucasian American culture, ability

CRITICAL THINKING

Think about your own beliefs for a moment. Do you think effort or ability is the most significant element in an individual's success? Has this view affected your own choices or behavior at any point in your life?

rather than hard work is seen as the key to success. This difference is not trivial. If you believe in ability as the key ingredient, then there is not much point in pressing for greater effort, and you will accept mediocre performance from your child. An Asian American parent, in contrast, believing in the centrality of effort, takes a very different attitude toward both success and failure by a child: The parent takes success more or less for granted but responds to failure by insisting on more effort. Because of these different belief systems, Asian American parents spend more time tutoring their children and have higher standards for their children's achievement. They are also less likely to be satisfied with their children's schools, believing that schools, too, can always do better. Yet despite what (to Caucasian American eyes) seems like strong pressure to achieve, Asian and Asian American students do not report high feelings of stress or anxiety, whereas high-achieving Caucasian American adolescents do report frequent feelings of stress (Crystal et al., 1994).

Given all these differences, it isn't surprising that Asian American children as a group achieve at higher levels in schools than any other U.S. ethnic group, just as Asian children from Japan, China, Taiwan, and Korea regularly outperform U.S. children and teenagers on standardized tests of math and science. A greater proportion of Asian Americans complete high school and college than any other group in the United States.

Asian American families are also more stable and more upwardly mobile than other ethnic families and are quite unlikely to involve single parents. Collectively, all these factors mean that Asian Americans are least likely to live in poverty of any of the U.S. minority groups.

Nine-year-old Brian gets help with his homework from his dad—a common event in Asian American households, in which parents typically emphasize the importance of hard work in reaching academic goals.

Ethnicity in Perspective What conclusions can be drawn about the role of ethnicity (or, more broadly, culture) in children's development from these three brief (and necessarily simplistic) sketches? Sadly, not many. First and foremost, of course, you have been reading almost entirely about subgroups within U.S. culture, which tells little about other cultural systems. And even within these limits, most research involves comparisons of each ethnic group with children or families in the majority culture. Until recently, most of this research assumed that the dominant culture was right or "normal" and that all other variations were inferior or "deviations" from the standard. That assumption has faded, but developmentalists have very little concurrent information about these groups and even less data about whether the same processes operate in each subgroup. What they are left with is a kind of snapshot of each group, with no way to tell which characteristics are the most crucial, which attitudes or values the most significant.

For example, if developmentalists look for reasons for good or poor school performance in different subcultures, what conclusions can they draw? Bilingualism cannot be the sole factor, because both Asian Americans and Hispanic Americans are typically bilingual; child-rearing style cannot be the sole factor, because Asian American parents are likely to be authoritarian (by current research definitions), yet their children do well in school. Doubtless it is the pattern of values and parental behavior that is crucial, and not any single variable. Cultures and subcultures are incredibly complex systems; their effects come from the combinations of factors, not merely from the adding up of a set of separate variables. In addition, of course, it's essential to try to understand how each subculture, each set of values, combines or conflicts with the values of the majority culture. For a child growing up with one foot in one culture and one in another culture, these are highly important issues.

THE CULTURE AS A WHOLE

A culture as a whole is also a system, made up of values, assumptions, and beliefs, a political and an economic system, patterns of personal relationships, and so forth. Each piece of that system affects all the other parts; changing one part changes the whole.

The wide cultural consequences of the rapid increase in the number of women in the labor force in the United States and other industrialized countries is a very good example. It has led, among many other things, to a fast-growing demand for nonparental care (with consequent changes in children's lives), to changes in male-female relationships, to new political alignments, and to shifts in patterns of interactions within families, which in turn affect children in still other ways.

Throughout this book, you have learned about sequences of children's development that seem to occur regardless of cultural context. At the same time, examples of cultural differences are also evident. At the most visible and measurable level are cultural variations in children's specific beliefs, the social scripts they learn, and the pattern of family and kin relationships they experience.

An interesting example comes from the work of Giyoo Hatano and his colleagues (1993; Inagaki & Hatano, 2004), who compared beliefs about the nature of plants and animals among Japanese, Israeli, and American kindergarten, second-grade, and fourth-grade children. Piaget noted, and others have confirmed, that young children typically view the world through the lens of *animism*, which leads them to attribute not only life but also feelings and self-awareness to inanimate objects, to plants, and to animals. Later, they differentiate among these several facets of life and understand that plants are alive but have no self-awareness. Hatano's study confirms the broad features of this shift: Younger children in all three cultures had much stronger beliefs in animism. But Hatano also found differences in the developmental pattern, depending on the specific cultural beliefs about life.

Japanese culture includes the belief that plants are much like humans; in the Buddhist system, even a blade of grass is thought to have a mind. In contrast, in Israeli language and culture, plants are put into a quite different category from animals and humans. When children in Japan and Israel were asked whether a tree or a tulip was alive, 91% of the Japanese but only 60% of the Israeli fourth graders said that it was. One-fifth of Japanese fourth graders attributed sensory properties to plants, saying that a tree or a tulip could feel chilly or could feel pain if it was hit with a stick. Overall, because of their stronger distinction between plants and animals, Israeli children were much slower than either Japanese or American children to come to the understanding that people, animals, and plants are all alive. This study thus illustrates both an underlying developmental pattern that seems to be shared across cultures and the cultural variations laid over that basic pattern.

It is not hard to generate similar examples. For instance, cultures may vary in the proportion of securely and insecurely attached children because of variations in their typical child rearing styles or beliefs, even though the process by which a child becomes securely or insecurely attached is much the same from one culture to another. In a similar way, adolescents in all cultures need to change their identity to at least some extent in order to move into the adult world, but cultures that provide initiation rituals at puberty may make the process much simpler and less confusing.

Certainly, developmentalists need to know a great deal more about how cultural variations affect development. But as you learned in Chapter 1, they also have to ask a more subtle set of questions. In particular, they need to know whether the relationship between environmental events or a child's characteristics and some outcome for the child is the same in every culture. Is authoritative child rearing optimal in all cultures, or is some other style better for preparing children for adult life in some settings? Are aggressive children unpopular in every culture, or are there some settings in which aggression is highly valued? Indeed, is unpopularity in childhood a major risk factor for adult dysfunction in every culture? As yet there are no answers, although researchers are beginning to ask the questions.

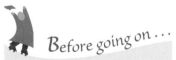

Before going on . . .

- What are the effects of poverty on families and children?
- How do the values of African Americans, Hispanic Americans, and Asian Americans differ?
- In what way does the culture as a whole affect children's development?

Summary

Nonparental Care

- Nonparental care is difficult to study because it involves so many variables. In addition, care arrangements interact with family variables such as income and parents' educational level. Often, it is impossible to separate the effects of nonparental care from the effects of these variables.
- The majority of children in the United States spend a part of their infancy or preschool years in some form of nonparental care.
- Day care often has positive effects on the cognitive development of less advantaged children, but it may have negative effects on advantaged children if there is a large discrepancy between the home environment and the level of stimulation in day care.
- How day care affects a child's personality depends on the quality of the care. An organized, structured situation is preferable.
- A major study showed that day care has no overall negative effect on the security of children's attachment to their parents.
- Infants' physiological responses to the stresses associated with nonparental care may underlie its association with developmental outcomes. The quality of nonparental care a child receives may be as important as the quantity of nonparental care. Individual differences and gender may interact with the quality of a care arrangement, the quantity of outside-the-home care a child receives, or both. Average differences between children who receive nonparental care and those who are cared for entirely in their own home are small.
- Self-care is associated with several negative effects. Girls, children who live in safe neighborhoods, and children whose parents closely monitor their activities after school are the least likely to be negatively affected by self-care.

The Impact of Schools

- Experience with school appears to be causally linked to some aspects of cognitive development, such as the ability to generalize strategies from one situation to another.
- A child's adaptation to school is affected by his readiness to learn to read as well as by his parents' involvement in the school and in his educational attainment.
- Children demonstrate achievement losses at every school transition. They are likely to change their achievement goals and to modify their self-concepts when they move from elementary to secondary school.
- School experience also shapes a child's sense of self-efficacy. By adolescence, children have a clearly developed idea of their comparative skills and abilities. These beliefs are a significant element in decisions about whether to finish high school or drop out.
- Some parents choose to homeschool their children. Generally, homeschooled children exhibit few differences from

their schooled peers, but research has been sparse and includes only those homeschooled children whose families have volunteered to participate.

The Impact of Entertainment Media

- Children who watch specifically educational TV programming can gain skills or positive attitudes. But heavy TV viewing may also contribute to somewhat lower grades and poorer reading skills, although this effect is small and is not found consistently.
- Experts agree that watching violence on television increases the level of aggression shown by a child. This effect appears to be especially strong among children who are already aggressive and among those whose parents use harsh physical punishment.
- Parents vary tremendously in the degree to which they regulate children's television viewing. Variations in parental styles regarding television are linked to the kinds of programs children watch as well as to the amount of time they spend watching.
- Video games may enhance children's spatial cognitive skills; however, those that are violent may also contribute to aggressive behavior. Some video games include subtle forms of advertising.

Macrosystem Effects: The Impact of the Larger Culture

- Children growing up in poverty, perhaps especially urban poverty, are markedly disadvantaged in many ways, including having lower access to medical care and greater exposure to multiple stresses. They do more poorly in school and drop out of school at far higher rates. Some protective factors, including a secure attachment, higher IQ, authoritative parenting, and effective schools, can help to counterbalance poverty effects for some children.
- African American subculture includes a strong emphasis on extended family households and contact and on religion. Hispanic Americans, too, place great emphasis on family ties; their emphasis on family honor and solidarity is heightened by the use of a shared language. In their collectivist cultural system, kin contact is frequent and central to daily life. Asian Americans emphasize respect and loyalty to family as well, but they stress the central importance of effort (rather than inherent ability) as the path to achievement.
- Developmentalists have very little understanding of how cultural variations influence development. Some patterns of development and some basic developmental processes (such as moral development and attachment) appear to be independent of culture. Other processes and patterns are affected by cultural variation.

Key Terms

ability goals (p. 402)   ethnicity (p. 417)   task goals (p. 402)
ethnic group (p. 417)   social class (p. 413)

See for Yourself

Day-Care Arrangements

In the section on nonparental care you learned that many children are placed in multiple care settings. You can find out how frequently such arrangements occur in your own area by surveying parents at a local child-care center. First, explain your project to the center director and get his or her permission to interview parents as they pick up their children each evening. Next, spend a few late afternoons at the center conducting your interviews. Ask parents how many days a week their children attend the center and whether they are also in other kinds of nonparental care. Also ask how many different kinds of care each child has experienced since birth. Keep records of both the number and the types of care arrangements each child is currently experiencing and has been exposed to in the past. Compare your results to the child-care statistics on page 393.

TV Violence

George Gerbner's research on TV violence was completed several years ago. Do you think television has become more or less violent? You can find out by watching a few hours of television and making note of incidents that fit Gerbner's definition of "violence." He defined a violent act as an "overt expression of physical force against others or self, or the compelling of action against one's will on pain of being hurt or killed." To get a good sample, watch a minimum of 4 hours of TV programming. (This doesn't mean watching for 4 hours straight.) Divide the time among educational programs, cartoons, and early evening comedies or dramas that are intended for adults but are popular with children as well. Make notes of the consequences experienced by characters following their acts of violence, and count the number of incidents. When you have arrived at a total number of incidents, calculate the average per hour and compare your findings to Gerbner's. Also, calculate an average for the different types of programs you watched. What does your research tell you about the amount of violence on television? What do your notes about consequences suggest about the media message concerning violence?

Atypical Development

15

C H A P T E R

When Derrick was born, his parents thought he was the most beautiful baby in the world. His grandparents showered him with affection.

Though they were exhausted from getting up for the newborn's feedings in the wee hours of the morning, his parents treasured every moment they spent caring for him.

Prior to Derrick's birth, his parents had purchased a baby book in which to record the important events of his life. One page was titled "Moving On and Moving Up" and included a list of developmental milestones, with a space by each for recording the date on which the milestone was reached. The first item on the list was "rolling over." Derrick's mother had also purchased a book that described the normal sequence of infant development so she would know what kind of skills her son would be acquiring over the first couple of years of his life. The book said that he should begin to try to roll over between 1 and 2 months of age. Consequently, Derrick's mother was not surprised when he reached the age of 1 month and had made no attempt to roll over. She was still unconcerned at the 2-month mark. By 3 months, though, she was beginning to worry. Her concerns were compounded by Derrick's failure to show any of the other milestones described in the book.

Derrick's parents expressed their concerns to their pediatrician, who reassured them that the boy would probably catch up. Privately, though, the doctor worried about the infant's lack of muscle tone and decided to order a few tests. But the tests showed no abnormalities, so the doctor once again told Derrick's parents not to worry. Moreover, when he talked to Derrick's mother, he felt reassured when she told him that the boy was beginning to show some signs of trying to turn over.

Whatever hope Derrick's parents had that he would catch up to his peers had faded significantly by the time he reached his first birthday. Although he had finally been able to turn himself over, his motor development appeared to have stopped at that point. The pediatrician noted that Derrick still had several reflexes that normal infants lose within the first few months of life. Clearly, something was amiss.

Between Derrick's first and second birthdays, his parents spent much of their time in doctors' offices and hospitals. Derrick underwent what seemed to be an endless array of tests, all of which showed nothing that could be pinpointed as the source of his developmental delays. Frustrated, his parents began to consider the possibility that they might never know why Derrick failed to develop like other infants. At the same time, they began to think about the prospect of spending the rest of their lives caring for a person who would never become an independent adult.

Derrick's parents felt that they were making progress when a psychologist provided them with a name for his condition: *profound mental retardation*. But the name had implications that triggered a stressful series of emotional ups and downs. First came grief, a grief so intense that Derrick's mother sometimes thought it would have been easier for them if he had died. She found herself fantasizing about all the things that she had expected her son to do, and often wept in response to passing thoughts about events in a normal child's life, such as the first day of school or the first wobbly bicycle ride. Grief was soon followed by anger. "Why Derrick?" the parents thought. "Why isn't there something that can be done for him?" Next came guilt. "If only I had followed the doctor's dietary recommendations more carefully," Derrick's mother mused. And another thread was woven through all of these feelings—anxiety about their own and Derrick's future. How would they be able to care for Derrick as he got bigger and heavier but remained completely immobile? How would they be able to pay for all the special care he would need? Would he be able to go to school?

Should they consider an institution? If they had another child, would he or she be re-tarded as well? Who would care for Derrick if they died? Hundreds of questions like these flooded their minds during the day and disturbed their sleep at night.

Ultimately, Derrick's parents accepted the fact that they would never have satis-factory answers to all of these questions—that they had no choice but to take each day as it came and try to make the best of it. For some reason, they decided, Derrick had been given to them and allowed to live in this state. Therefore, they would do the best they could to make his life as comfortable as possible. They would find the best educational program they could for him and encourage him to make whatever ad-vances were reasonable to expect.

Derrick's parents' story is similar to those of thousands of parents the world over as they discover that they have a child who is following a developmental pathway dif-ferent from that of most children. These pathways are the topic of this chapter. Fortu-nately, most of them involve deviations and impairments that are far less severe than those associated with profound mental retardation. However, each presents parents with a unique set of challenges. Many parents of children who exhibit atypical devel-opment, no matter how mild their children's disabilities may seem to others, go through the kind of emotional turmoil that Derrick's parents did. The fact that many (even most) of them manage to adapt effectively to the presence of an atypical child is testimony to the devotion and immense effort expended.

Understanding Atypical Development

Perhaps the best starting point for our discussion is to develop a working definition of *atypical development*. There are many behaviors that might be called *atypical* if we went by the literal definition of the term—that is, *not typical*. Most children do things that others would view as odd, but in most cases these behaviors fall within the normal range of variation. By contrast, **atypical development** involves behaviors that are not only unusual, but also part of an enduring pattern that interferes with a child's development in significant ways.

Many of the theories you have read about in earlier chapters have been invoked to explain atypical development. Predictably, psychoanalytic theories emphasize repressed emotions and traumatic experiences, learning theories focus on the environment, and cognitive approaches suggest that faulty thinking underlies deviation from typical de-velopmental pathways. However, in recent years, psychologists have changed the way they think about atypical development. Instead of searching for a single grand theory that can explain everything, they focus on factors that seem to predispose children to problems as well as on variables that appear to protect them.

atypical development An endur-ing pattern of behavior that is un-usual, compared to the behavior of others of the child's age, and that interferes with the child's de-velopment in some significant way.

developmental psychopathology A relatively new approach to the study of deviance that emphasizes that normal and abnormal devel-opment have common roots and that pathology can arise from many different pathways.

DEVELOPMENTAL PSYCHOPATHOLOGY

Developmentalists' knowledge about the dynamics of deviant development in general, and psychopathology in particular, has been enormously enhanced by an approach called **developmental psychopathology**, pioneered by such researchers as Norman Garmezy, Michael Rutter, Dante Cicchetti, Alan Sroufe, and others (e.g., Cicchetti & Cohen, 1995; Davies & Cicchetti, 2004; Rutter & Garmezy, 1983; Rutter & Sroufe, 2000;

Sroufe, 1997). This approach has strongly influenced how both researchers and practitioners think about children's and teenagers' psychological problems (Munir & Beardslee, 2001). It emphasizes several key points.

First, according to developmental psychopathologists, normal and abnormal development both emerge from the same basic processes and are thus interrelated. The task of a developmental psychopathologist is to uncover those basic processes, to learn how they work "correctly" in the case of normal development, and to identify *developmental deviations* and their causes (Sroufe, 1989). Alan Sroufe's studies of the consequences of secure or insecure attachment, which you read about in Chapter 11, are good examples of research based on such assumptions.

Second, the new approach is developmental. Theorists in this subfield are interested in the *pathways* leading to both deviant and normal development, from earliest infancy through childhood and into adult life. A child may follow a continuously maladaptive or adaptive pathway, or he might show initially positive adaptations that later turn maladaptive, or the reverse. The job of psychologists, according to this view, is to try to trace these various pathways: What are the sequences of experiences that lead to increased risk of depression in adolescence? What pathways lead to delinquency or other antisocial behavior or to peer rejection? What factors may inhibit or exacerbate an early deviation or turn an initially normal developmental trajectory into a deviant pattern?

Note that one of the important implications of this model is that the same maladaptive behavior may be reached by many different pathways. Psychologists should not assume that all depressed teenagers or all delinquent teens have the same history, the same roots of their behavior. And it follows that the same treatments will not be effective for all children with similar diagnoses. Another implication of the model is that change is possible at virtually any point. At the same time, it is also true that later changes are at least somewhat constrained by earlier adaptations. As Sroufe puts it, "the longer a maladaptive pathway has been followed . . . the less likely it is that the person will reclaim positive adaptation" (1997, p. 254).

VULNERABILITY AND RESILIENCE

Whether a child or teenager will show a behavior problem in response to stress such as moving to a new home will depend in part on whether he faces other stresses or life changes at the same time—such as perhaps his parents' divorce.

Developmental psychopathologists are especially interested in the concepts of *resilience* and *vulnerability*, two ideas you have encountered in previous chapters. One of the unexpected findings of many recent studies of children thought to be "at risk" for particular kinds of problems, such as children reared by depressed parents, children of divorcing parents, or abused children, has been that some children seem to be unexpectedly resilient in the face of what appear to be disturbing circumstances. The opposite has also been noticed repeatedly: Some children seem to be unexpectedly vulnerable despite what appear to be supportive life circumstances. Developmental psychopathologists such as Rutter and Garmezy have not only taken the lead in studying resilient children but have insisted that these "exceptions" to the general rules offer crucial information about the basic processes of both normal and abnormal development.

This question of vulnerability or resilience has been a persistent theme among developmental psychopathologists (see the *Research Report*). Research findings suggest that the same kinds of protective factors that help poor children rise above their negative circumstances (listed in Chapter 14) also mitigate the effect of other kinds of stresses. Children who are securely attached (whether to a parent or to someone else), who have good cognitive skills, and who have sufficient social skills to make connections with peers are better able to weather the stresses they encounter.

For example, in her classic studies of resilience among school-aged children, Ann Masten (1989) has found that among children who have experienced an extended period of high levels of life stresses, those with higher IQ are much less likely to respond by becoming disruptive. Masten speculates that such children, who have a history of

Why Are Boys More Vulnerable?

One of the most fascinating facts about atypical development is that virtually all disorders are more common in boys than in girls, as you can see in the table. The major exception is depression. How can differences like these be explained?

One possibility is that having an extra X chromosome gives a girl protection from some types of inherited disorder or anomaly. Girls are obviously less likely to inherit any recessive disease that is carried on an X chromosome, because the dominant gene on the other X chromosome is the one that will be expressed. Hormonal differences may be important as well. Since it is possible to construct a persuasive argument for the role of male hormones in aggressive behavior (as you learned in Chapter 11), it is not a very great leap to the hypothesis that the higher incidence of conduct disorders among boys may also be related in some way to hormone variations. And some research suggests that prenatal hormones that cross the placental barrier may predispose boys to disruptive and aggressive behavior.

Experiences after birth may also contribute to the differing rates of deviance. One hypothesis is that adults are simply more tolerant of disruptive or difficult behavior in boys than in girls. By this argument, boys and girls initially respond similarly to stressful situations, but young boys learn that various forms of acting out, tantrums, or defiance are either tolerated or not punished severely. Young girls learn to inhibit these responses—perhaps even to internalize them—because adults respond quite differently to girls. Research provides some fragments of support for such a hypothesis. For example, at least with regard to ADHD, research suggests that the same family variables that predispose boys to the disorder are also present in the families of girls who have the disorder (Faraone et al., 2001).

There is also evidence that the types of disorders from which boys are likely to suffer are more visible than those of girls because they more strongly affect school performance and behavior (Ezpeleta, Keeler, Alaatin, Costello, & Angold, 2001). In other words, at least some of the sex difference may be something of an artifact: Boys' disorders are more likely to get diagnosed and treated because of the environment in which they occur—that is, school. Conversely, girls' disorders tend to be exhibited outside school (in the home, for example), so they may be less likely to be identified.

Whatever the explanation—and none of the existing explanations seems very satisfactory—it is nonetheless extremely interesting that girls do seem to be less vulnerable to virtually any type of atypical development.

Type of Problem	Approximate Ratio of Males to Females
Psychopathologies	
Conduct disorders, including delinquency	5:1
Anxiety and depression in preadolescence	1:1
Anxiety and depression in adolescence	1:2
Attention deficit hyperactivity disorder	3:1–5:1
Estimated number of all children with all diagnoses seen in psychiatric clinics	2:1
Pervasive developmental disorders	**4:1**
Intellectual disabilities	
Mental retardation	3:2
Learning disabilities	3:1
Physical problems	
Blindness or significant visual problems	1:1
Hearing impairment	5:4

Sources: Achenbach, 1982; National Institute of Mental Health [NIMH], 2001; Nolen-Hoeksema and Girgus, 1994; Rutter, 1989; Rutter and Garmezy, 1983; Todd, Swarzenski, Rossi, and Visconti, 1995; Zoccolillo, 1993.

Questions for Critical Analysis

1. One reason suggested for gender differences in atypical development is that parents respond to boys in ways that cause them to believe that disruptive behavior is acceptable. List some possible variables in parents' responses to boys and girls, such as the kinds of verbal reactions to misbehavior, that might be studied in order to test this hypothesis.

2. It was argued that boys' disorders are more "visible" than girls' because they are more likely to occur at school. This statement suggests that teachers and parents have different standards for children's behavior. What kind of study might be done to examine this possibility?

successful problem solving, have a stronger sense of self-efficacy, which may help to make them more resistant to frustration.

On the other side of the coin are the vulnerable children, who are far more likely to show some kind of significant psychopathology in the face of stress. Some kinds of vulnerabilities are inborn, such as physical abnormalities, or are the result of prenatal trauma or preterm birth, prenatal malnutrition, or exposure to disease in utero. A tendency toward a "difficult" temperament, which also seems to be inborn, is another significant vulnerability, not only because, by definition, such children have greater difficulty adapting to new experiences, but also because they are harder to raise; their parents may be less able to establish regular discipline patterns. Research demonstrating that certain patterns of behavior exhibited by preschoolers (e.g., extreme shyness or aggression) strongly predict an individual child's likelihood of being diagnosed with a psychological disorder in later childhood supports the hypothesis that psychopathology arises mostly as a result of inborn vulnerabilities within the child (Biederman et al., 2001; Kochman et al., 2005; Mesman & Koot, 2001; Putnam & Stifter, 2005).

Other vulnerabilities emerge during infancy or early childhood. An insecure early attachment and the internal working model that accompanies it seem to make a child more vulnerable to stress at later ages. And any combination of circumstances that results in a high rate of aggressive or disruptive behavior with peers makes a child more vulnerable to a variety of stresses in the elementary and high school years (Masten, 1989).

Stresses that involve losses of or severe strain within key relationships seem to be especially important in the development of psychopathology. Family violence, for example, is a greater risk factor for psychopathology in children than living in a violent neighborhood (Muller, Goebel-Fabbri, Diamond, & Dinklage, 2000). Emotional rejection of the child by parents is also a factor, as are parental conflict, separation, and divorce (Barnow, Lucht, & Freyberger, 2001; Jenkins, Simpson, Dunn, Rasbash, & O'Connor, 2005; Sourander et al., 2001). On the other hand, having a well-functioning family increases the chances that a child who has a disorder will benefit from treatment (Crawford & Manassis, 2001).

Kenneth Rubin and his colleagues (1991) have proposed a model that combines many of these elements to explain the origins of internalizing disorders. They argue that one important pathway begins with an infant who shows high levels of behavioral inhibition (a temperamental pattern you'll recall from Chapter 9). Among infants with such a tendency, those who become securely attached to their parents appear to do fine. In contrast, those who become insecurely attached tend to move along a path that includes anxiety and fearfulness in the preschool years, then anxiety and perhaps victimization by bullies in the early school years; victimization results in more anxiety and withdrawal from peers, which eventually lead to a failure to develop helpful social skills. By adolescence, these children are at high risk for depression.

Overall, it seems very helpful to think of each child as possessing some inborn vulnerabilities as well as some protective factors, such as a secure attachment or an authoritative family, and some resources, such as higher IQ, an array of friends, or good peer interaction skills. The child's resilience in the face of stress or at normal developmental passages, such as the beginning of school or of adolescence, will depend on the relative weight of these three elements at that time—and on how many separate stresses the child must face simultaneously. No matter how basically resilient he may be, any child is more likely to show at least a short-term behavior problem when multiple stresses pile up at the same time.

TYPES AND FREQUENCY OF PROBLEMS

Most experts in childhood psychopathologies (e.g., Achenbach, 1995) agree that there are three main categories of psychological disorders in children and adolescents. The first two are **attention problems** (most particularly, attention deficit hyperactivity disorder), which impair the ability to concentrate, and **externalizing problems** (also described as *disturbances of conduct*), including both delinquency and excessive

CRITICAL THINKING ?

How would you describe your own vulnerabilities, protective factors, and resources?

attention problems A category of psychopathologies that impair one's ability to concentrate, including attention deficit hyperactivity disorder, attention deficit disorder, and hyperkinetic disorder.

externalizing problems A category of psychopathologies that includes any deviant behavior primarily directed toward others, such as conduct disorders.

aggressiveness or defiance, in which the deviant behavior is directed outward. The third category, **internalizing problems** (also called *emotional disturbances*), includes such problems as depression, anxiety, or eating disorders, in which the deviant behavior is largely directed internally, against the individual herself. You will be reading more about each of these categories later in the chapter.

There are several other types of atypical development that fall outside these three basic categories. For example, individuals at both extremes of the IQ scale are atypical when compared to others of their age. Likewise, children who have average intelligence but who are several years behind their peers in school achievement are considered to be atypical. Children with severe social impairments constitute yet another group of children whose development is atypical. You will also learn about these groups of children.

How common do you think such problems are among children? It is relatively difficult to give a definitive answer to this question. For one thing, the frequency of each type of problem varies across cultures. In one study, John Weisz and his colleagues (1993) compared the incidence of externalizing and internalizing problems among teenagers in a rural group in Kenya (the Embu) and a rural group in Thailand with the rates among rural black and white youth in the United States. Both the Thai and Embu cultures place great emphasis on obedience and politeness, a pattern of cultural values that is thought to be linked to higher rates of "overcontrolled," or internalizing, problems, such as shyness, fearfulness, and depression. In contrast, U.S. culture, with its greater emphasis on individual freedom, appears to foster higher rates of "undercontrolled," or externalizing, problems, such as fighting, showing off, and hyperactivity. As predicted, Weisz found that the Embu teens had the highest rates of internalizing problems and the lowest rates of externalizing problems, whereas white American teens had the highest rates of undercontrol, followed by African American teens; the Thai group showed low rates of both types of problems.

Most children in the United States show some kind of "problem behaviors" at one time or another (Klass & Costello, 2003). For example, parents report that 10–20% of 7-year-olds still wet their beds at least occasionally; 30% have nightmares, 20% bite their fingernails, 10% suck their thumbs, and 10% swear to such an extent that it is considered a problem. Approximately another 30% have temper tantrums (Achenbach & Edelbrock, 1981). Problems like these, especially if they last only a few months, should more properly be considered part of "normal" development (see *The Real World*). Usually, psychologists only label a child's development atypical or deviant if a problem persists for 6 months or longer or if the problem is at the extreme end of the continuum for that behavior. If only such extreme or persisting problems are counted as atypical, the incidence is much lower—although nonetheless higher than most of you may have guessed. Table 15.1 gives some estimates of the incidence of various deviant patterns. Some of these numbers are based on extensive data and are widely accepted, such as the 3.5% rate of mental retardation. Others are still in some dispute, such as the rate of depression in adolescence; in such cases, the table includes a possible range.

Psychologists might also want to combine all these individual rates in some way, to gain some idea of the total percentage of children with one kind of problem or another. Unfortunately this is not a simple matter of addition, since the categories overlap a good deal. For example, many children with serious learning disabilities also show an attention deficit disorder or conduct disorder. Still, even allowing for some overlap, the totals are astonishing: Between 14% and 20% of children and teenagers show at least some form of significant psychopathology (Costello & Angold, 1995; National Institute of Mental Health [NIMH] 2001; Simonoff et al., 1997). If cognitive disorders are added in, the total is at least 20%. That is, at least one in five children (and maybe as many as one in four) will show at least one form of significantly deviant or abnormal behavior at some time in their early years. Rates are similar in many European countries (Lauritsen, Pedersen, & Mortensen, 2004; Wals et al., 2001). The majority of these children will require some type of special help in school, in a child guidance clinic, or in an equivalent setting. When you think of these figures in terms of the demands on the school system and on other social agencies, the prospect is staggering.

internalizing problems A category of psychopathologies that includes anxiety and depression and other conditions in which deviant behavior is directed inwardly, against the self.

TABLE 15.1	Estimated Incidence of Various Types of Developmental Problems in the United States and Other Developed Countries

Type of Problem	Percentage of Children Aged 0–18 with That Problem
Psychopathologies	
Externalizing problems	
1. Conduct disorders	5–7
2. Delinquency (police arrest)	3
Internalizing problems	
1. Significant anxiety and fear	2.5
2. Serious or severe depression	
Elementary school children	1–2
Adolescents	5–7
Attention problems/hyperactivity	3–7
Intellectual Disabilities	
IQ below 70 (mentally retarded)	3.5
Speech and language problems, including delayed language, articulation problems, and stuttering	3.5
Serious learning disability	4
Pervasive Developmental Disorders	**1**

Sources: Barkley, 1997; Brandenburg, Friedman, and Silver, 1990; Broman, Nichols, Shaughnessy, and Kennedy, 1987; Buitelaar and van Engeland, 1996; Cantwell, 1990; Chalfant, 1989; Costello and Angold, 1995; Kopp and Kaler, 1989; Lauritsen, Pedersen, and Mortensen, 2004; Marschark, 1993; Merikangas and Angst, 1995; NIMH, 2001; Nolen-Hoeksema, 1994; Rutter, 1989; Rutter and Garmezy, 1983; Simonoff et al., 1997; Tuna, 1989.

Before going on ...

- What is developmental psychopathology, and how has it changed the way psychologists approach questions about atypical development?
- What are some of the factors that predispose children to atypical development?
- How prevalent is atypical development?

Attention Problems and Externalizing Problems

You will recall that attention problems include disorders in which children's ability to concentrate seems to be impaired. Externalizing problems are disorders that involve outwardly directed inappropriate behaviors, such as aggression.

ATTENTION DEFICIT HYPERACTIVITY DISORDER

A glance at the diagnostic criteria for **attention deficit hyperactivity disorder (ADHD)**, listed in Table 15.2, reveals that the hallmarks of this disorder are physical restlessness and problems with attention—precisely what the name implies. Russell Barkley (1997), one of the major researchers and theorists on ADHD, suggests that the underlying problem is a deficit in the child's ability to inhibit behavior—to keep himself from starting some prohibited or unhelpful behavior or from reacting to some compelling stimulus or to stop behaving in some fashion once he has started. In busy, complex environments with many stimuli (such as a classroom), ADHD children are unable to inhibit their reactions to all the sounds and sights around them, so they appear restless and cannot focus sustained attention on a single activity.

attention deficit hyperactivity disorder (ADHD) A disorder in which a child shows both significant problems in focusing attention and physical hyperactivity.

The Real World

Knowing When to Seek Professional Help

Lucinda is a 4-year-old girl who is currently engaged in an ongoing battle with her parents. The proper arrangement of spaghetti is the central dispute in this battle. Lucinda is convinced that spaghetti and spaghetti sauce should touch each other only in a person's mouth. Consequently, she insists on having her spaghetti served in two separate bowls, one for the pasta and another for the sauce. Furthermore, she requires a spoon for the sauce and a fork for the pasta. She becomes hysterical at even the slightest suggestion that she try having her spaghetti in its more conventional form. Her parents have begun to worry that she might have some kind of serious mental disorder and wonder whether they should consult a child psychologist. Their response is typical of today's parents, many of whom are well informed about child development (Klass & Costello, 2003). But many kinds of difficult behavior can be well within the bounds of normal individual differences. So, it's understandable that parents might fear they are overreacting if they conclude that their child may have a serious problem.

Parents often worry that their children may have some kind of serious mental disorder. However, most problematic behaviors, such as this child's temper tantrum, fall within the range of normal behavior.

Checklists developed by experts in developmental psychopathology can be helpful in distinguishing behavior that is difficult to manage from behavior that may indicate a disorder for which professional care is appropriate. One such checklist has been published by the National Mental Health Association (available at http://www.nmha.org). Here are a few of the warning signs for children and teenagers:

- Changes in grades or behavior reports from teachers
- Changes in patterns of sleeping or eating
- Frequent stomachaches or other minor physical symptoms
- Obsessive concern with weight loss
- A sad facial expression that persists over a period of weeks
- Outbursts of rage that lead to destruction of property or aggression toward others
- Activity far in excess of that exhibited by children of the same age
- Frequent unyielding defiance of parental or teacher authority

Of course, every child or teenager who exhibits such behavior doesn't have a serious psychological disorder. Still, when a child's pattern of difficult behavior matches one or more of these signs, parents should probably adopt the "better safe than sorry" approach and consult a mental health professional.

Questions for Reflection

1. According to the checklist, is Lucinda's spaghetti-eating behavior likely to be a sign of a psychological disorder? Why or why not?
2. What strategies might Lucinda's parents use to get her to try eating spaghetti the way most people do?

Defining the Problem Whether this constellation of problems constitutes a single syndrome or several distinct subvarieties is still a matter of active debate. You'll note that the criteria in Table 15.2 are divided into two sets, those dealing with attention problems and those dealing with hyperactivity, suggesting the existence of two subtypes of attention problem. European psychologists recognize only the hyperactivity subtype, which they label **hyperkinetic syndrome** (Taylor, 1995). Psychologists in the United States agree that there are two subtypes, but they argue that the most common pattern is for both attention deficit and hyperactivity to occur together. When a child shows an attention problem but not hyperactivity, U.S. practitioners normally label the problem **attention deficit disorder (ADD)**.

Because of these variations in definition, it is hard to get a good estimate of just how frequent such problems may be. The best guess, based on studies from around the world, is that between 3.0% and 7.0% of children can be diagnosed with some form of ADHD (NIMH, 2001): Perhaps 1.5% of children show hyperactivity alone, and ADD

hyperkinetic syndrome Term used by European psychologists for attention deficit hyperactivity disorder.

attention deficit disorder (ADD) Term sometimes used interchangeably with ADHD, but more properly used to describe the subset of children who show attention problems without hyperactivity.

TABLE 15.2	Diagnostic Criteria for Attention Deficit Hyperactivity Disorder

- The child must show either significant *inattention* or significant *hyperactivity-impulsivity* (or both).
- Inattention is indicated by any six or more of the following:
  1. Often fails to give close attention to details or makes careless mistakes in schoolwork or other activities.
  2. Often has difficulty sustaining attention in tasks or play.
  3. Often does not seem to listen when spoken to directly.
  4. Often does not follow through on instructions and fails to finish chores, homework, or duties.
  5. Often has difficulty organizing tasks and activities.
  6. Often avoids, dislikes, or is reluctant to engage in tasks that require sustained mental effort.
  7. Often loses things necessary for tasks or activities (e.g., toys, pencils, books, tools).
  8. Is often easily distracted by extraneous stimuli.
  9. Is often forgetful in daily activities.
- Hyperactivity-impulsivity is indicated by the presence of six of the following, persisting over a period of at least six months:
  1. Often fidgets with hands or feet or squirms in seat.
  2. Often leaves seat in classroom or in other situations in which remaining seated is expected.
  3. Often runs about or climbs excessively or reports feeling of restlessness.
  4. Often has difficulty playing quietly.
  5. Is often "on the go" or often acts as if "driven by a motor."
  6. Often talks excessively.
  7. Often blurts out answers before questions are completed.
  8. Often has difficulty waiting for a turn.
  9. Often interrupts or intrudes on others.
- The onset of the problem must be before age 7.
- At least some of the symptoms must be present in two or more settings, such as home and school or school and play with peers.
- The behavior must interfere with developmentally appropriate social, academic, or occupational functioning.

Source: Reprinted with permission from the *Diagnostic and Statistical Manual of Mental Disorders*, 4th edition, Text Revision (Copyright © 2000). American Psychiatric Association.

Children with ADHD are more physically active than peers. Many, like this girl, are also exceptionally adventurous.

alone occurs in perhaps 1.0% (Barkley, 1997; Buitelaar & van Engeland, 1996). The remainder of affected children show both hyperactivity and attention difficulties. All of these patterns are three to five times more common in boys than in girls (Heptinstall & Taylor, 1996)—yet another example of the greater vulnerability of boys.

A further diagnostic problem arises from the fact that a great many children are inattentive or overactive at least some of the time. Both teachers and parents can be tempted to label a boisterous or obstreperous child as having ADD or ADHD. There is no doubt that a good deal of mislabeling of this kind does occur, especially in the United States, where ADD and ADHD are far more common diagnoses than the equivalent diagnosis is in Europe. Further, experimental studies have shown that, on many attention tasks, children diagnosed with ADHD do not differ from nondiagnosed children at all (Lawrence et al., 2004). Where ADHD children do seem to differ markedly from other children is in their overall activity level. However, elevated activity level alone is insufficient to diagnose a child with the disorder. What children must exhibit to be diagnosed with ADHD is high activity along with the characteristics shared by ADHD and ADD. Specifically, children with both types of attention problems differ from peers with regard to their capacity to sustain attention when engaged in boring, repetitive tasks. They also seem to be less able than other children of the same age to control impulses.

By definition, ADHD is an early-developing disorder. The majority of hyperactive children already show some problems focusing attention and inhibiting activity as preschoolers; many have problems making friends or playing effectively with peers because they are not tuned in to their playmates' cues, even at this early age. They are intrusive and insensitive toward peers, showing a variety of annoying behaviors (Hinshaw & Melnick, 1995; Sandberg, Day, & Gotz, 1996). Further, many children with ADHD develop learning disabilities and other disorders (Brook & Boaz, 2005; Decker, McIntosh, Kelly, Nicholls, & Dean, 2001). ADHD persists into adolescence in half to three-quarters of cases and into adulthood in one-third to half of cases (Barkley, 1997).

The severity of the long-term problem seems to be strongly influenced by whether or not the child also develops aggressive behavior. It is the combination of hyperactivity and aggressiveness that is especially likely to lead to significant problems with peer rejection in childhood and to persisting problems, such as substance abuse, in adulthood (Barkley, Fischer, Edelbrock, & Smallish, 1990; Kuperman et al., 2001). One facet of this effect is evident in the results of Terrie Moffitt's longitudinal study (1990), which included 434 boys in New Zealand. When the boys were 13, they were classed in one of four groups based on the presence or absence of two factors: hyperactivity and delinquency. Then, for each group, Moffitt looked back at scores at earlier ages on measures of antisocial behavior, intelligence, and family adversity. You can see the results for antisocial behavior in Figure 15.1. It is clear that the boys who showed both hyperactivity and delinquency as adolescents had been the most antisocial at every earlier age. Hyperactivity that was not accompanied by antisocial behavior at early ages was not linked to delinquency at 13.

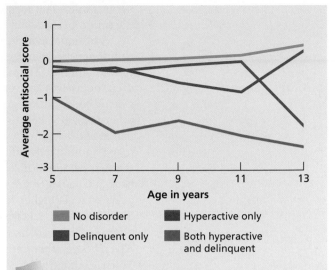

FIGURE 15.1

The boys in Moffitt's study had been studied every 2 years, beginning when they were 5. When they were 13, they were assigned to one of four hyperactivity/delinquency categories, and then Moffitt looked back on the data that had accumulated for each boy. You can see that those who were *both* hyperactive and delinquent at 13 had shown markedly higher rates of antisocial behavior from the time they were 5, whereas those who were only hyperactive at 13 had been much less socially deviant at earlier ages.

(*Source*: Moffitt, T. E., adapted from Fig. 1, p. 899, "Juvenile delinquency and attention deficit disorder: Boys' developmental trajectories from age 3 to age 15," *Child Development*, 61 (1990) pp. 893–910. By permission of the Society for Research in Child Development.)

Origins of the Problem Where might ADD or ADHD come from? Because the behavioral pattern begins so early and has such a strong physical component, most clinicians have assumed that these problems have some kind of biological origin. Early research failed to confirm a biological hypothesis, but more recent evidence makes clear that ADD and ADHD are neuropsychiatric disorders (Goldman, Genel, Bezman, & Slanetz, 1998; Kagan & Herschkowitz, 2005). Three converging lines of evidence support that conclusion.

First, physicians and psychologists have known for some time that a biological treatment is very often effective in reducing or eliminating the deviant behavior. As many as 80% of children diagnosed with ADHD in the United States (but many fewer in Europe) are treated with a stimulant medication called methylphenidate (the most commonly used brand-name drug is Ritalin). The drug works by stimulating the part of the brain that maintains attention. About 70–90% of children treated with this drug show improvement, including decreases in demanding, disruptive, and noncompliant behaviors; lessened aggressiveness and noncompliance; more attentiveness in the classroom; and improved performance on many academic tasks (Gillberg et al., 1997; Goldman et al., 1998; Schachar, Tannock, & Cunningham, 1996). Further, placebo-controlled studies show that it is the real medication that has this effect on the children's behaviors (Pelham et al., 2002; Ridderinkhof, Scheres, Oosterlaan, & Sergeant, 2005). This evidence is consistent with a biological explanation for ADHD. More specifically, it suggests that the problem may lie in one of the brain's neurotransmitters, because stimulant medications of the type used with ADHD children act by altering the action of monoamine, one of the key neurotransmitters (Kado & Takagi, 1996).

Additional evidence for an underlying biological cause comes from research in behavior genetics, which suggests that a pattern of hyperactivity is inherited, at least in certain families (Thapar, 2003). About one-quarter of the parents of hyperactive children themselves have a history of hyperactivity. Studies of twins also suggest there is a genetic contribution. Among identical twins, if one is diagnosed as hyperactive, the other is highly likely to have the same diagnosis; among fraternal twins, this concordance rate is much lower (Kado & Takagi, 1996). Evidence suggesting that inheritance may also indirectly influence the development of ADHD comes from research showing that temperament is related to ADHD. Children who are low in *effortful control* (look back at Chapter 9) are more likely to be diagnosed with the disorder than are their peers who get higher ratings on scales that measure this aspect of temperament (Chang & Burns, 2005). Likewise, longitudinal research has shown that infants who are very outgoing are more likely to be diagnosed with externalizing disorders, including ADHD, when they enter preschool than are infants who are less outgoing (Putnam & Stifter, 2005).

Finally, brain-imaging diagnostic methods have begun to reveal subtle differences in brain structure and brain function between hyperactive and nonhyperactive individuals (Kagan & Herschkowitz, 2005). For example, studies using magnetic resonance imaging (MRI) suggest that in the majority of ADHD children, the right hemisphere of the brain is larger than the left hemisphere, while the majority of non-ADHD children show the reverse (Hynd et al., 1993). Other researchers using positron emission tomography (PET) have found slight differences in brain metabolism (e.g., Zametkin et al., 1990).

With all the evidence supporting the biological basis of ADHD, it might be tempting to conclude that having this disorder dooms a child to underachievement and a difficult social life. However, as the discussion of vulnerability and resilience at the beginning of the chapter suggests, it is more useful to think of ADHD as a single source of vulnerability that may be offset by many protective factors. High IQ is one such protective factor, as is a high degree of intrinsic motivation (Chang & Burns, 2005). Many children with ADHD who are bright and who enjoy intellectual challenges find ways to compensate for their attention difficulties. If they perform poorly in school in spite of these compensatory strategies, they may find extracurricular activities in which they can excel. Further, the heritability of ADHD may actually work to a child's advantage. A parent who struggled with the disorder himself or herself may be able to empathize with the child who has ADHD and offer suggestions as to how to manage it.

Thus, once again, the key to either long-term problems or recovery from difficulties lies in the interaction between the child's inborn or early-developed qualities and the capacity of the family and the environment to support the child's optimum behavior. When parents of ADHD children manage to maintain an authoritative style, their children become less aggressive and more socially competent (Hinshaw, Zupan, Simmel, Nigg, & Melnick, 1997).

CONDUCT DISORDER

The broadest category of externalizing problems is what might be referred to in everyday speech as "antisocial behavior." The American Psychiatric Association's *Diagnostic and Statistical Manual of Mental Disorders* (or DSM) defines **conduct disorder** as a pattern of behavior that includes high levels of aggression, argumentativeness, bullying, disobedience, irritability, and threatening and loud behavior.

conduct disorder Diagnostic term for a pattern of deviant behavior including high levels of aggressive, antisocial, or delinquent acts.

Two Types of Conduct Disorder
Psychologists have known for some time that there are a number of subvarieties of conduct disorder (e.g., Achenbach, 1993). In Sroufe's terms, there are several distinct pathways to conduct disorder, differentiated primarily by the age at which the deviant behavior first begins. For some, aggression

and other antisocial behavior begins in early childhood and persists through adolescence and into adulthood. Children and adolescents who fall in this group also tend to show more serious or severe aggression or delinquent acts than those whose deviant behavior begins later. Stephen Hinshaw and his colleagues (1993) label this subvariety **childhood-onset conduct disorders**; Terrie Moffitt (1993) refers to individuals who show this behavior pattern as *life-course-persistent offenders*. The second subvariety of conduct disorders, labeled **adolescent-onset conduct disorders** by Hinshaw, includes those who begin aggressive or delinquent behavior only in adolescence. Moffitt refers to such individuals as *adolescence-limited delinquents*. Their deviance is typically milder, more transitory, more a function of hanging out with bad companions than a deeply ingrained behavior problem.

In 2002, about 7% of children and teenagers were arrested in the United States.

The developmental pathway for childhood-onset conduct disorders is one you are familiar with by now from what you have read about Patterson's research on aggressive children. These are very often children who begin life with a range of vulnerabilities, including difficult temperament, lower intelligence, or both (e.g., Kochman et al., 2005; Lyons-Ruth, Easterbrooks, & Cibelli, 1997; Newman, Caspi, Moffitt, & Silva, 1997; Prior, Smart, Sanson, & Oberklaid, 1997). In infancy, they are likely to have formed insecure/disorganized or insecure/avoidant attachments (Lynam, 1996; Lyons-Ruth et al., 1997; D. Shaw et al., 1996; van IJzendoorn, 1997). In the preschool years, these children very often throw tantrums and defy parents. They are very difficult children to handle. If the parents are not up to the task of controlling the child, the child's behavior worsens and becomes overt aggression toward others, who then reject the child.

During the school years, these children are less likely than peers to be able to empathize with others' feelings, a social-cognitive deficit that leads to peer rejection (Rey, 2001). Such peer rejection aggravates the problem, pushing the seriously aggressive child in the direction of other children with similar problems, who become the child's only supportive peer group (Shaw, Kennan, & Vondra, 1994). By adolescence, these youngsters are firmly established in delinquent or antisocial behavior, and their friends are drawn almost exclusively from among other delinquent teens (Tremblay, Mâsse, Vitaro, & Dobkin, 1995). They are also highly likely to display a cluster of other problem behaviors, including drug and alcohol use, truancy or dropping out of school, and early and risky sexual behavior, including having multiple sexual partners (Dishion et al., 1995; Kuperman et al., 2001; Wiesner, Kim, & Capaldi, 2005).

CRITICAL THINKING

What kind of implications for social policy (if any) do you see in the fact that childhood-onset conduct disorders are most likely to persist and ultimately to involve adult criminality or violence?

There is also some indication that the early-onset disorder has a much stronger genetic component than the later-onset disorder (Achenbach, 1993; Deater-Deckard & Plomin, 1997; Oosterlaan, Geurts, Knol, & Sergeant, 2005). Thus, the preschooler who already shows defiant and oppositional behavior as well as aggressiveness may have strong inborn propensities for such behavior. But if Patterson is correct, then whether that propensity develops into a full-fledged, persisting conduct disorder will depend on the interactions between the inborn tendency and other aspects of the child's life, including the parents' ability to handle the child's early defiance as well as the general environment in which the child lives, such as inner city versus small town (Gottesman & Goldsmith, 1994; Loeber, Tremblay, Gagnon, & Charlebois, 1989). Parenting style matters as well; research suggests that children who develop conduct disorder have parents who are more permissive than do their peers (Rey, 2001).

Delinquency **Delinquency** is a narrower category of externalizing problems than conduct disorder; it refers only to intentional lawbreaking. Clearly, many children who break laws also show other forms of conduct disorder, so the two categories overlap a great deal. Still, the overlap is not total, so it is useful to look at delinquency separately.

Some willful misbehavior, such as lying or stealing, is fairly common in children as young as 4 or 5, but it is in adolescence that there is a significant increase in the number of youngsters who display such delinquent behaviors, as well as a rise in the seriousness and consistency of the behaviors.

childhood-onset conduct disorder Conduct disorder beginning in childhood; the pattern is linked to rejection by peers and to conduct problems that persist into adolescence and adulthood.

adolescent-onset conduct disorder A conduct disorder that begins only in adolescence; it is typically less severe and persistent than childhood-onset conduct disorder.

delinquency A subcategory of conduct disorder involving explicit lawbreaking.

It is extremely difficult to estimate how many teenagers engage in delinquent behavior. One way to approach the problem is to look at the number of arrests—although arrest rates are arguably only the tip of the iceberg. About 7% of all children under age 18 were arrested in 2002 in the United States (Snyder, Puzzanchera, & Kang, 2005). From age 15 to 17, the arrest rate is closer to 10%—a higher rate than for any other age group across the entire lifespan. Many of these arrests are for relatively minor infractions, but about a third are for serious crimes, including murder, burglary, rape, and arson.

When adolescents themselves describe their own lawbreaking, they report even higher rates. Four-fifths of U.S. youngsters between ages 11 and 17 say that they have been delinquent at some time or another. One-third admit to truancy and disorderly conduct, and one-fifth say that they have committed criminal acts, most often physical assaults or thefts (Dryfoos, 1990). Terrie Moffitt (1993) reports similar figures from his sample of all the children born in a single New Zealand town over a 1-year period (1972–1973), whom Moffitt followed for over 20 years. In this group, 93% of the males acknowledged some form of delinquent activity by age 18.

Serious or persistent delinquency is also more common among teens with lower IQ scores (Lynam, Moffitt, & Stouthamer-Loeber, 1993). This link between IQ score and delinquency cannot be explained away by arguing that the less bright delinquents are more likely to be caught; nor is it simply an artifact of social class or ethnic differences in both delinquency and IQ, because white middle-class delinquents also have lower IQs than their nondelinquent peers. In fact, low IQ scores appear to be a genuine risk factor for delinquency, particularly for children with early-onset types of conduct disorder, for those who show more serious or violent forms of offenses, and for those who experience some school failure (Hämäläinen & Pulkkinen, 1996). The argument offered by Donald Lynam and others (1993) is that school failure reduces a young person's engagement with school and the values it represents. School failure also increases the child's or adolescent's frustration, which raises the likelihood of aggression of some kind. Thus, for many less intelligent young people, the social constraint on delinquent behavior offered by education is simply weaker.

In addition to IQ, variations in self-esteem are related to delinquent behavior. However, there is considerable debate as to whether low or high self-esteem predisposes an adolescent to engage in delinquent behavior. On one side, Brent Donnellan and his colleagues argue that children who develop low self-esteem in elementary school, perhaps brought on by school failure or peer rejection, are more prone to delinquency in later years (Donnellan, Trzesniewski, Robins, Moffitt, & Caspi, 2005). By contrast, Roy Baumeister and others have claimed that the development of an inappropriately high level of self-esteem during childhood, given an individual's real accomplishments, is associated with delinquency (Baumeister, Bushman, & Campbell, 2000; Baumeister, Campbell, Krueger, & Vohs, 2003; Baumeister, Smart, & Boden, 1996). Put differently, Baumeister hypothesizes that *narcissism*, the view that one is the center of the world, is more likely to be at the center of a delinquent teen's sense of self-worth than is low self-esteem. To date, both sides have produced evidence in support of their views. As a result, Donnellan has argued that researchers should probably think of the kind of low self-esteem he measures as being qualitatively distinct from the narcissism that has been studied by Baumeister's group (Donnellan et al., 2005). He says that it is possible for a delinquent teen both to be narcissistic and to have low self-esteem when he judges himself against the criteria he knows to be part of a cultural definition of "good" people. What seems clear is that teens who display delinquent behavior have views of themselves that distinguish them from adolescents who do not engage in such behaviors.

It is important to emphasize, however, that unlike the broader category of conduct disorders, which are quite stable from childhood to adulthood, the milder forms of delinquency do not invariably or even commonly persist into adulthood. Many teens commit only occasional delinquent acts and show no further problem in adulthood. For them, mild delinquent behavior is merely a phase. It is those who show a syndrome of delinquent acts plus high-risk behavior and come from families with low warmth and ineffective control who are quite likely to engage in criminal acts as adults.

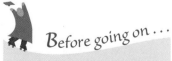
Before going on . . .

- What diagnostic labels are given to children who have attention problems in the United States and in Europe?
- What is conduct disorder, and how does it differ from delinquency?

Internalizing Problems

A s you learned earlier, internalizing problems are so named because they involve deviations from the typical developmental pathway that are directed internally, against the self. Such problems include disturbances of self-concept, as in eating disorders, and disturbances of emotions, as in depression.

EATING DISORDERS

Eating disorders are among the most significant mental health problems of adolescence. Many psychologists argue that these disorders are in fact only the extreme end of a continuum of problems relating to dieting and obsession about body shape and size that appear to be epidemic among white teenaged (and increasingly preteen) girls in the United States and in Britain and some other European countries (e.g., Smolak, Levine, & Streigel-Moore, 1996).

Girls who suffer from anorexia nervosa often have a distorted body image. They see themselves as too fat even when they are severely emaciated.

Bulimia   Bulimia (sometimes called *bulimia nervosa*) involves three elements: (1) a preoccupation with eating and an irresistible craving for food, leading to episodes of binge eating; (2) an intense fear of fatness; and (3) some method of purging to counteract the effects of the binge eating so as to avoid weight gain. Typical purging methods are self-induced vomiting, excessive use of laxatives, or excessive exercise (Garfinkel, 1995). Alternating periods of normal eating and binge eating are common among individuals in all weight groups.

   Only when binge eating occurs as often as twice a week and is combined with repeated episodes of some kind of purging is the syndrome properly called bulimia. Bulimics are ordinarily not exceptionally thin, but they are obsessed with their weight, feel intense shame about their abnormal behavior, and often experience significant depression. The physical consequences of bulimia can include marked tooth decay (from repeated vomiting), stomach irritation, dehydration, lowered body temperature, disturbances of body chemistry, loss of hair, and, in extreme cases, cardiovascular problems (Mitchell, 1995; Muscari, 1996).

   Most experts conclude that the incidence of bulimia has increased in recent decades in many Western countries, although firm data on rates of bulimia have been hard to establish. It has been estimated that from 1% to 3% of adolescent girls and young adult women show the full syndrome of bulimia; as many as 20% of girls in Western industrialized countries show at least some bulimic behaviors, such as occasional purging (Attie & Brooks-Gunn, 1995; Brooks-Gunn & Attie, 1996; Graber, Brooks-Gunn, Paikoff, & Warren, 1994; NIMH, 2001). Many more are sufficiently concerned about their weight to diet regularly or constantly. None of these behaviors is found in countries where food is scarce. Adolescents most at risk for bulimia are those who live in cultures where slenderness is strongly emphasized, particularly those who wish to pursue a career that demands thinness, such as dance, gymnastics, modeling, or acting (Brownell & Fairburn, 1995).

Anorexia Nervosa   Anorexia nervosa is less common than bulimia but potentially more deadly. It is characterized by extreme dieting, intense fear of gaining weight, and obsessive exercise. The weight loss eventually produces a variety of physical symptoms associated with starvation: sleep disturbance, cessation of menstruation, insensitivity to pain, loss of hair, low blood pressure, a variety of cardiovascular problems, and reduced body temperature. Perhaps as many as 10% of anorexics literally starve themselves to death; others die because of some type of cardiovascular dysfunction (Litt, 1996).

bulimia Eating disorder characterized by alternating periods of binging and purging.

anorexia nervosa Eating disorder characterized by self-starvation.

As is true of bulimia, anorexia is far more common among girls and women than among boys or men. In Western countries, 1% to 4% of young women have anorexia (NIMH, 2001). Among European and Caucasian American girls, especially those from professional families, the rate may be as high as 1 in 100 (Brooks-Gunn & Attie, 1996; Litt, 1996). And as is true of bulimia, the rate is considerably higher among subgroups who are under pressure to maintain extreme thinness, such as ballet dancers and high-performance athletes in sports in which thinness is highly valued, such as gymnastics (Stoutjesdyk & Jevne, 1993).

Causes of Eating Disorders   Of the two eating disorders, bulimia is considerably easier to treat; anorexics frequently have relapses, even after extensive treatment. Newer treatment programs, however, offer some promise. In particular, treatment of both types of eating disorders increasingly involves antidepressant drugs, because depression very frequently precedes or accompanies the eating problem (Riggs, 1997). Among bulimics, antidepressant medication appears to be effective in about a third of cases.

Explaining either disorder has proved to be exceptionally difficult. Both bulimia and anorexia typically begin with persistent dieting, reinforcing the idea that eating disorders represent the extreme end of a continuum that includes other forms of concern about weight (Cooper, 1995; Polivy & Herman, 1995). Such a link between dieting and eating disorders is further strengthened by evidence that in countries such as Taiwan, Singapore, and China, where dieting has become a recent fad, eating disorders, which were almost never seen in the past, are becoming more common (Goleman, 1995a; Lai, Tang, & Tse, 2005). Yet a great many young women (and some young men) diet regularly, even obsessively, but never develop an actual eating disorder. Indeed, surveys suggest that only 14% of adolescent girls are actually overweight, but 36% believe that they are too fat (Centers for Disease Control, 2000b). So, what moves a dieter from "normal" dieting into bulimia or anorexia?

Some theorists have proposed biological causes for eating disorders, such as some kind of brain dysfunction in the case of bulimics, who often show abnormal brain waves. Others argue for a psychoanalytic explanation, perhaps a fear of growing up. Childhood sexual abuse also appears to predispose girls to develop eating disorders (Perkins & Luster, 1997; Wonderlich et al., 2001). Family variables, such as the quality of a girl's parents' marriage, may also be important factors (Wade, Bulik, & Kendler, 2001).

The most promising explanation of eating disorders, however, may lie in the discrepancy between the young person's internal image of a desirable body and her perception of her own body (McGee, Hewitt, Sherry, Parkin, & Flett, 2005). This explanation is supported by cross-cultural research demonstrating that adolescents in Western societies, who have the highest rates of eating disorders, are more likely to have negative body images than adolescents in non-Western societies (Akiba, 1998). Moreover, some developmentalists suggest that Western culture's emphasis on thinness as a requirement for attractiveness in a woman contributes to the prevalence of eating disorders.

However, it is likely that family and individual variables mediate cultural influences on teenagers. For example, one study suggested that mothers' beliefs about the desirability of thinness and their daughters' attractiveness may be just as important in the development of eating disorders as the daughters' own views (Hill & Franklin, 1998). The opposite may be true as well. That is, girls whose families place little emphasis on physical appearance may be protected against the tendency to internalize cultural ideals of thinness and physical perfection (Tester & Gleaves, 2005). In addition, images of extremely thin models seem to affect only girls who are already dissatisfied with their bodies (Stice, Spangler, & Agras, 1999).

It is also important to note that a general tendency toward mental illness may also be a factor in eating disorders. One longitudinal study of young women who had been anorexic in adolescence, 94% of whom had recovered from their eating disorders, found that they were far more likely than the general population to suffer from a variety of mental disorders (Nilsson, Gillberg, Gillberg, & Rastam, 1999). Estimates of the proportion of young women who suffer from eating disorders and who also meet the criteria for some other type of psychiatric disorder range as high as 74% (Milos, Spindler, & Schnyder, 2004). An unusually high proportion of them, nearly 25%, have been diagnosed with *obsessive-compulsive disorder*, a disorder that involves an excessive need for control (American Psychiatric Association, 2000a; Milos, Spindler, Ruggiero, Klaghofer, & Schnyder, 2002). These findings suggest that, for many teens, eating disorders may be a manifestation of some larger problem.

DEPRESSION

Children who show internalizing forms of psychopathology exhibit a different set of antecedents and a different pathway to developmental problems than children with conduct disorders. The particular form of deviance that has been most often addressed within the framework of developmental psychopathology is **depression**, persistent feelings of sadness accompanied by impairment in daily functions, such as interacting with family and doing school work.

Both depressed mood and significant clinical depressions rise in frequency in adolescence.

Defining the Problem   For many years, psychiatrists took the position that children or adolescents did not experience significant depression. This turned out to be quite wrong. Researchers have found abundant evidence that depression is actually quite common in adolescence and occurs at least occasionally among younger children. Perhaps 10% of preadolescent children and 30–40% of adolescents experience significant short-term depressed mood or misery (Compas, Hinden, & Gerhardt, 1995; Harrington, Rutter, & Fombonne, 1996; Petersen et al., 1993). When a depressed mood lasts 6 months or longer and is accompanied by other symptoms, such as disturbances of sleeping and eating and difficulty concentrating, it is usually referred to as **clinical depression** or **major depressive disorder**.

Estimates of the frequency of clinical depression among children and adolescents vary somewhat; the best studies suggest that at any given time, about 1.0% of preadolescents and between 1.6% and 8.0% of adolescents are suffering from such an enduring depression (Cicchetti & Toth, 1998). Perhaps twice as many youngsters will experience serious depression at some time in their adolescent years (Compas, Ey, & Grant, 1993; Merikangas & Angst, 1995). These are not trivial states of unhappiness. Not only do they last, on average, for 7 to 9 months, but they are also highly likely to recur: As many as 90% of those who suffer a major depressive episode experience a recurrence within 2 years (Cicchetti & Toth, 1998). Further, depression has serious consequences. For one thing, depression can interfere with learning by slowing down the speed at which the brain processes information (Calhoun & Dickerson Mayes, 2005). Depressed teens are more likely than their nondepressed peers to use drugs (Rey, Sawyer, Raphael, Patton, & Lynskey, 2002). And a significant portion of depressed teens also say that they think about suicide (Fennig et al., 2005). In one longitudinal study of youths growing up in a working-class neighborhood in the United States, one-fifth of those who had had a period of serious depression by age 18 had also attempted suicide (Reinherz et al., 1993).

Interestingly, during the preadolescent years, boys and girls are about equally likely to be unhappy or depressed; however, beginning somewhere between ages 13 and 15, girls are twice as likely to report high or chronic levels of depression. This sex difference persists throughout adulthood and has been found in a number of industrialized countries and among African Americans, Hispanic Americans, and Caucasian Americans (Culbertson, 1997; Hankin et al., 1998; Nolen-Hoeksema & Girgus, 1994; Roberts & Sobhan, 1992).

Causes of Depression   Where does such depression come from, and why do girls experience more of it? The search for the developmental pathways leading to later depression begins with the clear finding that children growing up with depressed parents

depression A combination of sad mood and difficulty carrying out daily functions.

clinical depression (major depressive disorder) A combination of sad mood, sleeping and eating disturbances, and difficulty concentrating that lasts 6 months or longer.

are much more likely than are those growing up with nondepressed parents to develop depression themselves (Merikangas & Angst, 1995). Of course, this finding could indicate a genetic factor, a possibility supported by at least a few studies of twins and adopted children (Petersen et al., 1993). Or, this link between parental and child depression could be explained in terms of the changes in the parent-child interaction that are caused by the parent's depression.

In Chapter 11, you learned that depressed mothers are much more likely than nondepressed mothers to have children who are insecurely attached. In particular, the depressed mother is often so nonresponsive to her child that her behavior seems to foster in the child a kind of helpless resignation. Such a sense of helplessness has been found to be strongly related to depression in both adults and adolescents (Dodge, 1990).

Of course, not all children of depressed parents are themselves depressed. About 60% show no abnormality at all. Whether a child moves along a pathway toward depression seems to be largely a function of the number of other stresses that are present in the family, such as serious illness, family arguments, work stress, loss of income, job loss, or marital separation.

The significant role of stress in the emergence of depression is clear among children whose parent or parents are not depressed. Any combination of stresses—such as the parents' divorce, the death of a parent or another loved person, a parent's loss of job, a move, and/or a change of schools—increases the likelihood of depression in the child (Chang, 2001; Compas et al., 1993). Indeed, the role of such individual life stresses may help to explain the sex differences in depression among adolescents. Anne Petersen has proposed that girls are more likely to experience simultaneous stressful experiences in adolescence, such as pubertal changes combined with a shift in schools (Petersen, Sarigiani, & Kennedy, 1991). In her own longitudinal study, Petersen found that depression was not more common among girls than among boys when both groups had encountered equal levels of life stress or comparable simultaneous stressful experiences.

Susan Nolen-Hoeksema (1994; Nolen-Hoeksema & Girgus, 1994) agrees with Petersen that one of the keys is that teenaged girls face more stresses than do teenaged boys. She also argues that girls respond to their down moods quite differently than boys do. Girls (and women) are more likely to dwell on their sadness or distress ("What does it mean that I feel this way?" "I just don't feel like doing anything"). This coping strategy actually accentuates the depression, producing longer-lasting depressive episodes. Boys (and men), on the other hand, are more likely to use distraction—exercising, playing a game, or working—to deal with their down moods, a coping strategy that tends to reduce depression.

You'll remember from Chapter 10 that low self-esteem, when combined with the traits of external locus of control and neuroticism, greatly increases a teenager's chances of becoming depressed. Susan Harter's studies reveal that young people who feel that they do not measure up to their own standards are much more likely to show symptoms of clinical depression (e.g., Harter & Whitesell, 1996). In fact, high self-esteem and a strong sense of identity seem to protect teens from the potential effects of life stresses (Chang, 2001).

The fact that depression increases markedly in adolescence makes good sense from this point of view. Developmentalists know that adolescents are much more likely than younger children to define themselves and others in comparative terms—to judge themselves against some standard or to see themselves as "less than" or "more than" some other person. Also, in adolescence, physical appearance becomes highly important, and a great many teenagers are convinced that they do not live up to culturally defined appearance standards. Self-esteem thus drops in early adolescence, and depression rises.

Research has taken developmentalists a fair distance in their efforts to understand both the rise in depression in adolescence and the marked gender difference in rates of depression. Yet teenagers still vary widely in their responses to what appear to be the same levels of stress. Not every teenager who faces multiple stresses or fails to live up to some standard is inclined to dwell on her depression rather than use distraction to

CRITICAL THINKING ?

Can you think of any other possible explanations for the higher rates of depression among teenaged girls than among teenaged boys? What sort of study would you have to do to test your hypothesis?

cope; not every teen who is temperamentally shy ends up being clinically depressed. These are all risk factors, but even with these risk factors, some adolescents are more vulnerable than others.

ADOLESCENT SUICIDE

In some teens, sadly, the suicidal thoughts that often accompany depression lead to action. Research with suicidal adults indicates that a preoccupation with planning suicide often begins in adolescence (Glowinski et al., 2001). Surveys suggest that 20% of high school students in the United States have thought seriously about taking their own lives, and approximately 1 in 13 has actually attempted suicide (National Council for Injury Prevention and Control [NCIPC], 2000). A very small proportion of teens, about 12 out of every 100,000, succeed in killing themselves (Blau, 1996). However, public health experts point out that many teen deaths, such as those that result from single-car crashes, may be counted as accidental but are actually suicide (NCIPC, 2000).

Even though depression is more common among girls than boys, the likelihood of succeeding in committing suicide is almost five times as high among adolescent boys as among girls. In contrast, suicide *attempts* are estimated to be three times more common in girls than in boys (Garland & Zigler, 1993; NIMH, 2001). Girls, more often than boys, use less successful methods, such as self-poisoning.

The suicide rate is also nearly twice as high among whites as among nonwhites, except for Native American youth, who attempt and commit suicide at higher rates than any other group (NCIPC, 2000). The rate among Native American teen males is 26.3 per 100,000 per year, compared with about 20 per 100,000 among Caucasian American teen males. Similarly, Hispanic American teen males are more likely to attempt suicide than whites, although the rate of completed suicide among them is lower (NCIPC, 2000). In addition, teen suicide rates are fairly stable in all groups except African American males, among whom the rate more than doubled (from 3.6 to 8.1 per 100,000) during the 1990s (NCIPC, 2000).

It is obviously very difficult to uncover the contributing factors in completed suicides, because the individuals are no longer available to be interviewed. Nonetheless, it does seem clear that some kind of significant psychopathology is virtually a universal ingredient, including but not restricted to depression. Behavior problems such as aggression are also common in the histories of completed suicides, as is a family history of psychiatric disorder or suicide, or a pattern of drug or alcohol abuse (Fennig et al., 2005; Garland & Zigler, 1993; Glowinski et al., 2001). In addition, psychologists suggest at least three other important elements (Shaffer, Garland, Gould, Fisher, & Trautman, 1988; Swedo et al., 1991):

- *Some triggering stressful event*. Studies of suicides suggest that the triggering event is often a disciplinary crisis with the parents or some rejection or humiliation, such as breaking up with a girlfriend or boyfriend or failure in a valued activity.
- *An altered mental state*. Such a state might be an attitude of hopelessness, reduced inhibitions from alcohol consumption, or rage.
- *An opportunity*. For example, a loaded gun available in the house or a bottle of sleeping pills in the parents' medicine cabinet creates an opportunity for a teen to carry out suicidal plans.

Suicide prevention efforts have focused on education, such as providing training to teachers or to teenagers on how to identify students who are at risk for suicide, in the hope that vulnerable individuals might be helped before they make an attempt. For example, self-mutilating behavior such as carving the skin with sharp objects is correlated with extreme feelings of loneliness and hopelessness, two emotions that often lead to suicide (Guertin, Lloyd-Richardson, Spirito, Donaldson, & Boergers, 2001). Thus, teachers who observe such behavior or its effects should refer students to school counselors.

Other professionals who work with teenagers should also take an active role in suicide prevention. For example, checklists have been developed to help physicians and nurses screen adolescents for potential suicide risk when they visit clinics for routine health care (Gould et al., 2005). Further, because teens who have been arrested attempt and complete suicide at higher rates than their peers, many experts on youth suicide recommend that adolescents be formally screened for suicide risk by a mental health professional within 24 hours of an arrest (Gallagher & Dobrin, 2005).

Special training in coping skills has also been offered to students, so that they might be able to find a nonlethal solution to their problems. Unfortunately, most such programs appear to be ineffective in changing student attitudes or knowledge (Shaffer, Garland, Vieland, Underwood, & Busner, 1991). These discouraging results are not likely to improve until psychologists know a great deal more about the developmental pathways that lead to this particular form of psychopathology.

Antidepressants are often prescribed for depressed teens, especially those who are considered to be at high risk for suicide (de Angelis, 2004). Most studies have shown that these medications can be just as effective in treating depression in adolescents as in adults (Findling, Feeny, Stansbrey, Delporto-Bedoya, & Demeter, 2004). However, in the United States, these drugs have yet to be approved by the Food and Drug Administration for treatment of depression in teenagers (de Angelis, 2004). Further, a large-scale British study found that antidepressants may actually increase the risk of suicide in some teens. These findings prompted the FDA to issue a warning against the routine use of these drugs with adolescents (U.S. Food and Drug Administration, 2004).

Before going on …

- What is the difference between bulimia and anorexia, and what do psychologists think about the causes of these eating disorders?
- How is clinical depression defined, and what factors predispose teens to this disorder?
- Describe the various approaches to preventing teen suicide.

Atypical Intellectual and Social Development

I f you look again at Table 15.1, you'll see that the various forms of atypical intellectual development occur as frequently as psychopathologies among children. Roughly 1 in 10 children shows at least some form of intellectual abnormality, including learning disabilities, speech problems, and mental retardation.

MENTAL RETARDATION

mental retardation An intellectual disability defined most often as an IQ below 70 combined with poor adaptive behavior.

Mental retardation (also referred to by many educators today as *intellectual disability* or more generally as *developmental disability*) is normally diagnosed when a child has "consistently subaverage intellectual functioning" (usually defined as an IQ score below 70 or 75) and significant problems in adaptive behavior, such as an inability to dress or feed himself or a problem getting along with others or adjusting to the demands of a regular school classroom (MacMillan & Reschly, 1997). Thus, a low IQ score is a necessary but not sufficient condition for an individual to be classed as retarded. As Thomas Achenbach says, "Children doing well in school are unlikely to be considered retarded no matter what their IQ scores" (1982, p. 214).

Low IQ scores are customarily divided into several ranges, and different labels are attached to children in each range, as you can see in Table 15.3. The lower the IQ range, the fewer children there are. More than 80% of all children with IQs below 70 are considered mildly retarded; only about 2% of low-IQ youngsters (perhaps 3,500 children in the United States) are profoundly retarded (Broman, Nichols, Shaughnessy, & Kennedy, 1987).

Cognitive Functioning of Retarded Children

Some researchers interested in information processing have tried to understand normal intellectual processing by looking at the ways in which retarded children's thinking or approach to problems differ from that of normal-IQ children (Bray, Fletcher, & Turner, 1997; Calhoun & Dickerson Mayes, 2005; Campione, Brown, & Ferrara, 1982; DeLoache & Brown, 1987). This research leads to several major conclusions about retarded children:

| TABLE 15.3 | Categories of Mental Retardation |

Approximate IQ Score Range	Common Label
68–83	Borderline retarded
52–67	Mildly retarded
36–51	Moderately retarded
19–35	Severely retarded
Below 19	Profoundly retarded

- They think and react more slowly than normal-IQ children.
- They think concretely and have difficulty with abstract reasoning.
- They require much more complete and repeated instruction in order to learn new information or a new strategy. (Normal-IQ children may discover a strategy for themselves or be able to proceed with only incomplete instruction.)
- They do not generalize or transfer something they have learned in one situation to a new problem or task. They thus appear to lack those "executive" functions that enable older normal-IQ children and adults to compare a new problem to familiar ones or to scan through a repertoire of strategies until they find one that will work.
- Intellectual deficits often interfere with the development of social skills, such as the ability to recognize and respond to facial expressions (Moore, 2001).

On simple, concrete tasks, retarded children learn in ways and at rates that are similar to younger children with normal IQs. The more significant deficit is in higher-order processing. These children can learn, but they do so more slowly and require far more exhaustive and task-specific instruction.

It's important to note, too, that many of the things you have learned about child development apply to children with mental retardation. Children with intellectual disabilities go through the same Piagetian stages, although at a slower rate, and their motivational characteristics are very much like those of normal children (Blair, Greenberg, & Crnic, 2001). For example, on tasks that normal children are highly intrinsically motivated to learn, such as learning how to play a new video game, children with mental retardation are just as likely to display high levels of intrinsic motivation. And for tasks for which normal children often require extrinsic motivation, such as doing homework, children with intellectual disabilities are also likely to require parent- or teacher-provided incentives.

Causes of Retardation

Mentally retarded children can be divided into two distinct subgroups, depending on the cause of the retardation. The smaller subset, making up about 15–25% of the total, includes children whose retardation is caused by some evident physical damage. Included in this group are those with a genetic anomaly, such as Down syndrome, that probably causes parts of the brain associated with learning to function poorly (Pennington, Moon, Edgin, Stedron, & Nadel, 2003). Damage resulting in retardation can also be caused by a disease, a teratogen such as prenatal alcohol, or severe prenatal malnutrition; it can occur during the birth itself, such as from prolonged anoxia. A small subset of children become retarded as a result of an injury suffered after birth, often in an auto accident or a fall. Certainly, not all children who are injured in accidents or affected by teratogens are retarded. But some children who are mentally retarded have been disabled by some purely physical injury, disease, or anomaly.

The majority of retarded children show no obvious signs of brain damage or other physical disorder. In these cases, the cause of the retardation is some combination of genetic and environmental conditions. Typically, these children come from families in which the parents have low IQ or mental illness or the home life is highly disorganized or emotionally or cognitively deprived. To be sure, in these cases, too, the child's intellectual disability might have been exacerbated by the effects of teratogens or other hazards, such as prenatal alcohol or elevated levels of prenatal or postnatal lead, but it is not thought to be attributable solely to such physical causes.

Large-scale studies have shown quite conclusively that the several causes of retardation are not distributed evenly across the range of low IQ scores. The lower the IQ, the more likely it is that the cause is physical rather than environmental (Broman et al., 1987). One implication of this conclusion is that interventions such as the enriched day care and preschool Ramey devised (see Figure 7.4) are more likely to be effective in countering the effects of family culture in causing milder retardation. This is not to say that educators should ignore environmental enrichment or specific early training for children whose retardation has a physical cause. Greater breadth of experience will enrich their lives and may help to bring their level of functioning closer to the top end of their "reaction range," allowing them to function much more independently (Spiker, 1990). But even massive early interventions are not going to make most brain-damaged or genetically anomalous children intellectually normal.

LEARNING DISABILITIES

Some children with normal IQs and essentially good adaptive functioning nonetheless have difficulty learning to read, write, or do arithmetic. The typical label for this problem is **learning disability (LD)**. Psychologists' definition of this problem includes the presumption that the difficulty arises from some kind of central nervous system dysfunction or damage, in much the same way that many definitions of ADHD assume some kind of biological underpinning. In fact, some children with attention deficit disorder are also diagnosed as learning disabled, so these two sets of problems overlap (Brook & Boaz, 2005). This overlap is far from complete, however, as most children diagnosed as learning disabled do not suffer from ADHD.

Diagnosing Learning Disabilities   Diagnosing a learning disability is extremely tricky, and such a diagnosis is always a residual one—that is, a diagnosis arrived at only by eliminating other possible explanations of a problem. "Learning disabled" is the label normally applied to a child of average or above average intelligence, with normal vision and hearing, who has significant difficulty absorbing, processing, remembering, or expressing some type of information, such as written words or numbers. Children diagnosed as learning disabled do not show persistent or obvious emotional disturbance, and their difficulties cannot be attributed to any clear cultural or educational deprivation. Thus, the working definition focuses on what learning disability is not, rather than what it is. Furthermore, the specific form of a learning disability may vary widely, with some children displaying difficulties in reading only, some having trouble with reading and spelling (such as the boy whose writing sample is shown in Figure 15.2), and others having more difficulty with arithmetic.

Because of such fuzziness in the definition, there is a good deal of dispute about just how many children really have a learning disability. Practically speaking, however, the label of learning disabled is used very broadly within school systems (at least in the United States) to describe children who have unexpected or otherwise unexplainable difficulty with schoolwork, particularly reading. About 5% of all children in the United States are currently labeled in this way (Farnham-Diggory, 1992; U.S. Bureau of the Census, 2001).

Causes of Learning Disabilities   Given such problems with the definition, it's not surprising that the search for causes of learning disabilities has been fraught with difficulties. As Farnham-Diggory says, "We are trying to find out what's wrong with children whom we won't be able to accurately identify until after we know what's wrong with them" (1986, p. 153).

The most central problem has been with the fundamental assumption that learning disabilities have a neurological basis. The difficulty is that children so labeled (like hyperactive children) rarely show signs of major brain damage on standard neurological tests—perhaps because many of the children are mislabeled or perhaps because the brain dysfunction is too subtle to detect with standard tests.

learning disability (LD) A term broadly used to describe an unexpected or unexplained problem in learning to read, spell, or calculate and more precisely used to refer to a neurological dysfunction that causes such effects.

One day me and my brith wit out hunting

The sarking BiT we cume not Fied The sarking is use we doun in a Thoocotei biT we cume not Fied ane is

FIGURE 15.2

This is part of a story written by 13-year-old Luke, who has a significant and persistent learning disability. The little numbers next to some of the words are Luke's word counts. They show that despite his severe writing handicap, his counting abilities are intact.

(*Source*: From *Learning Disabilities: A Psychological Perspective* by Sylvia Farnham-Diggory, p. 61, Copyright © 1978 by Sylvia Farnham-Diggory. By permission of the author.)

Happily, brain-imaging techniques now may make it possible to uncover subtle, but very real and significant, neurological differences between children labeled dyslexic or learning disabled and those who are good readers. A study by Sally Shaywitz and her colleagues (1998) used functional magnetic resonance imaging (fMRI) to identify the parts of the brain that become active when an individual is performing various reading-related tasks. When skillful adult readers in the study were working on these tasks, Shaywitz found that a series of brain regions were activated in turn, beginning with sections of the frontal lobe and then moving backward in the brain. Among the dyslexic adults who participated in this study, however, only the frontal lobe was fully activated, suggesting that their brains functioned quite differently on these tasks. This difference in brain activation patterns was especially vivid when the participants were working on tasks that required them to identify individual sounds, such as in a rhyming task—a finding that makes very good sense in light of all the research you read about in Chapter 8 that links good reading to phonological awareness.

In subsequent research, Shaywitz and his colleagues have found similar patterns of neurological activity in the brains of children with reading disabilities (Pugh et al., 2001; Shaywitz et al., 2002). Such studies suggest that the brains of both children and adults with true dyslexia may not be "wired" in a way that allows them to efficiently analyze sounds into their phonological components. These findings may explain why interventions that provide explicit information about sound-symbol connections (which are typically not emphasized in conventional reading curricula), along with ample opportunities to practice newly acquired skills, have been found to be highly effective in helping people with dyslexia become more fluent readers (Ehri, Nunes, Stahl, & Willows, 2002).

School can be a discouraging and frustrating place for a child with a learning disability.

GIFTEDNESS

Some children lie at the other end of the intellectual continuum and are considered gifted. Finding good programs for such children is a continuing dilemma. A child named Michael, described by Halbert Robinson, is an extreme example of a gifted child:

When Michael was 2 years and 3 months old, the family visited our laboratory. At that time, they described a youngster who had begun speaking at age 5 months and by 6 months had exhibited a vocabulary of more than 50 words.

Elizabeth Lovance of Hartland, Wisconsin (on the right) skipped several grades and graduated from high school at age 14. She said of her experience of being accelerated through school: "I would have had a mental breakdown if I had remained where I was."

He started to read English when he was 13 months old. In our laboratory he spoke five languages and could read in three of them. He understood addition, subtraction, multiplication, division, and square root, and he was fascinated by a broad range of scientific constructs. He loved to make puns, frequently bilingual ones. (1981, p. 63)

Michael's IQ score on the Stanford-Binet was in excess of 180 at age 2; 2 years later, when Michael was 4½, he performed as well as a 12-year-old on the test and was listed as having an IQ score beyond 220.

Definitions and Labels

We can certainly all agree that Michael should be labeled as gifted, but defining the term precisely is difficult (Cramond, 2004). A number of authors (e.g., Gardner, 1983) have argued that people with exceptional specific talents, such as musical, artistic, mathematical, or spatial abilities, should be classed as gifted, along with those with very high IQ scores. This broadening of the definition of giftedness has been widely accepted among theorists, who agree that there are many kinds of exceptional ability, each of which may reflect unusual speed or efficiency with one or another type of cognitive function.

Within school systems, however, giftedness is still typically defined entirely by IQ test scores, such as all scores above 130 or 140. Robinson suggested that it may be useful to divide the group of high-IQ children into two sets, the "garden-variety gifted," who have high IQ scores (perhaps 130 to 150) but no extraordinary ability in any one area, and the "highly gifted" (like Michael) with extremely high IQ scores and/or remarkable skill in one or more areas—a group Ellen Winner (1997) calls the profoundly gifted. These two groups may have quite different experiences at home and in school.

Cognitive and Social Functioning

Gifted children show speedy and efficient processing on simple tasks and flexible use of strategies on more complex tasks. They learn quickly and transfer that learning broadly, and they have remarkably good problem-solving skills—they often leap directly to a solution that requires less gifted individuals many intermediate steps to figure out (Sternberg & Davidson, 1985; Winner, 1997). Further, they seem to have unusually good metacognitive skills: They know what they know and what they don't know, and they spend more time than average-IQ children in planning how to go about solving some problem (Dark & Benbow, 1993). Winner also notes that profoundly gifted children also have a "rage to master," a powerful drive to immerse themselves in learning in some area.

Whether such advanced intellectual abilities transfer to social situations is not so well established. Many parents are concerned about placing their gifted child in a higher grade in school because of fears that the child will not be able to cope socially; others have assumed that rapid development in one area should be linked to rapid development in all areas.

One famous and remarkable early study of gifted children, by Lewis Terman, pointed to the latter conclusion. In the 1920s, Terman selected 1,500 children with high IQ scores from the California school system. These children—now adults in their 80s—have been followed regularly throughout their lives (e.g., Holahan, 1988; Terman, 1925; Terman & Oden, 1959). Terman found that the gifted children he studied were better off than their less gifted classmates in many ways other than school performance. They were healthier, they had wider-ranging interests, and they were more successful in later life. Both the boys and the girls in this study went on to complete many more years of education than was typical in their era, and most had successful careers as adults.

Most research suggests that gifted children have about the same risk of social or emotional problems as normal-IQ children, which means that most are well adjusted and socially adept (Gottfried, Gottfried, Bathurst, & Guerin, 1994; Vida, 2005). Optimism about the social robustness of gifted children may have to be tempered somewhat, however, in the case of the profoundly gifted subgroup, such as those with IQs above 180. These children are so different from their peers that they are likely to be seen as strange or disturbing. They are often socially solitary and introverted as well as fiercely independent and nonconforming; they have difficulties finding peers who can play at their level and are often quite unpopular with classmates (Kennedy, 1995). Profoundly gifted children are about twice as likely as their less gifted peers to show some kind of significant social or emotional problem (Winner, 1997). Also on the negative side of the ledger is the fact that many gifted children are so bored by school that they become disengaged and even drop out, often because their school district does not allow acceleration in grade or has no special programs for the gifted. Given the fact that skipping grades does not seem to be linked to social maladjustment (and is linked to better achievement among the gifted), it seems to make very good sense to encourage accelerated schooling, if only to help ward off extreme boredom in the gifted child.

<aside>
CRITICAL THINKING ?

Are you persuaded by the arguments that gifted children should be encouraged to skip grades? If you were a parent of a gifted child, what kind of data would you want to have to help make a decision on this question?
</aside>

PERVASIVE DEVELOPMENTAL DISORDERS

Many of the atypical patterns of development we have discussed so far may indirectly cause difficulties in children's social relationships. Children with mental retardation, for example, may have problems keeping up with the play interests of children their age. For instance, they may develop the capacity for pretend play at a later age than other children. Thus, a child with mental retardation may be able to build social relationships by playing with other children, but in most cases the children he plays with will be younger than he is.

By contrast, the defining feature of the group of disorders known as **pervasive developmental disorders (PDDs),** or autism spectrum disorders, is the inability to form social relationships. In PDDs, the lack of social skills is itself the disorder rather than an indirect consequence of another atypical developmental pattern. The social difficulties of individuals with PDDs usually derive from their poor communication skills and inability to understand the reciprocal, or give-and-take, aspects of social relationships. Many of these children also exhibit odd, repetitive behaviors, such as hand-flapping. Some develop attachments to objects and become extremely anxious—or even enraged—when separated from them. Others engage in self-injurious behaviors such as head-banging. In the United States, just under 1% of all children have some kind of PDD (Kagan & Herschkowitz, 2005; NIMH, 2001). The rates are similar in European countries (Lauritsen et al., 2005). The two most frequently diagnosed PDDs are *autistic disorder* and *Asperger's disorder*.

The distinguishing symptoms that are exhibited by children with **autistic disorder** include limited or nonexistent language skills, an inability to engage in reciprocal social relationships, and a severely limited range of interests (American Psychiatric Association, 2000b). Most are also mentally retarded, easily distracted, slow to respond to external stimuli, and highly impulsive (Calhoun & Dickerson Mayes, 2005). Some children are helped with symptoms of distractibility and impulsivity by the kinds of stimulant medications that are often prescribed for children with ADHD (Posey, Puntney, Sasher, Kem, & McDougle, 2004).

Many parents of children with autism report having noticed their children's peculiarities during the first few months of life. What strikes these parents is their infants' apparent lack of interest in people. However, in most cases, the disorder is not definitively diagnosed until children's failure to develop normal language skills makes it apparent that they are on an atypical developmental path. This usually occurs between the first and second birthday.

Children with autism who are capable of some degree of normal verbal communication and whose cognitive impairments are minimal are often called *high-functioning*. However, these children's communicative abilities are quite poor because

<aside>
pervasive developmental disorders (PDDs) A group of disorders in which children exhibit severe disturbances in social relationships.

autistic disorder A disorder in which children have much more limited language skills than others of the same age, an inability to engage in reciprocal social relationships, and a severely limited range of interests.
</aside>

Many children with autism display impulsive, bizarre behaviors such as the writhing behavior in which this boy appears to be engaged. They are often unresponsive to the outside world while exhibiting these behaviors, and some injure themselves during these episodes.

Asperger's disorder A disorder in which children possess the other characteristics of autistic disorder but have intact language and cognitive skills.

of their limited ability to engage in social cognition. For example, most never fully develop a theory of mind (Peterson, Wellman, & Liu, 2005). As a result, they typically fail to understand how their statements are perceived by listeners and are incapable of engaging in normal conversations. In addition, the pitch and intonation of their speech is often abnormal. Some utter repetitive phrases, often in robot-like fashion, that are inappropriate for the situation in which they occur.

Asperger's disorder is often thought of as a mild form of autistic disorder. The diagnostic criteria for it are highly similar to those for autistic disorder (American Psychiatric Association, 2000b). However, children with Asperger's disorder have age-appropriate language and cognitive skills and often obtain high scores on IQ tests. Despite their normal language skills, children with Asperger's disorder are incapable of engaging in normal social relationships because, like children with autism who are high-functioning, they usually do not develop the capacity to understand others' thoughts, feelings, and motivations (a theory of mind).

Because of their normal language and cognitive skills, most children with Asperger's disorder don't stand out from their peers until their second or third birthday, when other children begin to engage in cooperative play. However, normal children of this age vary widely, so children with Asperger's disorder are often assumed to be "late bloomers" or "going through a phase." Some are misdiagnosed with ADHD (Pozzi, 2003). Upon entering school, though, many begin to exhibit the odd behaviors that most people associate with pervasive developmental disorders. For example, they may become intensely focused on memorizing things that have little meaning to them, such as airline flight schedules. They may also engage in obsessive behaviors, such as counting and recounting the number of squares on a checkered tablecloth. By school age, their inability to form friendships like those of other children their age is usually quite apparent.

Like ADHD, pervasive developmental disorders were once thought to be the result of poor parenting. However, it is now well established that all of these disorders are of neurological origin (Kagan & Herschkowitz, 2005). However, there is no single brain anomaly or dysfunction that is associated with PDDs. Even for the individual disorders within this category, researchers have not found a single definitive neurological marker. In a few cases, specific genetic defects are known to lead to atypical neurological development and, in turn, cause children to develop pervasive developmental disorders. For instance, *fragile-X syndrome*, as you may recall from Chapter 2, can cause autistic disorder. For the most part, however, the cause of PDDs remains a mystery (Kagan & Herschkowitz, 2005).

Whatever the neurological mechanisms involved in PDDs, twin studies suggest that these disorders are hereditary. When one identical twin is diagnosed with a PDD, there is a 70% to 90% chance that the other twin will be diagnosed as well (Zoghbi, 2003). A wide variety of factors interact with genetic predispositions to trigger the appearance of these disorders (Rutter, 2005). When mothers are depressed, for example, infants have an increased risk of developing the symptoms of a PDD (Pozzi, 2003). However, media reports suggesting that immunizations may cause PDDs have proven to be unfounded (Rutter, 2005a).

Among some children with pervasive developmental disorders, symptoms actually get worse as the children get older (Sigman & McGovern, 2005). Sadly, the minimal language and social skills they appear to acquire through intensive educational programs in the early years of life sometimes deteriorate markedly before they reach adulthood. Many adults with these disorders live in sheltered environments and are employed in jobs that require minimal competencies.

The language skills of a child with a PDD are the best indicator of his or her prognosis in adulthood (American Psychiatric Association, 2000b). Consequently, children with Asperger's disorder have the best hope of attaining independence in adulthood. Thanks to their language and cognitive skills, many are capable of high levels of academic achievement. Indeed, expert reviews of the medical records of one of the most eminent German writers of the twentieth century, Robert Walser, suggest that he probably suffered from Asperger's disorder (Fitzgerald, 2004). His social relationships, however, like those of almost all individuals with this disorder, continued to be impaired throughout his life.

Schooling for Atypical Children

Before going on . . .

■ What are the characteristics of children who have mental retardation?
■ Why has it been so difficult to arrive at a definition of learning disability?
■ What are the characteristics of gifted children?
■ What behaviors are exhibited by children with pervasive developmental disorders?

Atypical children require teachers and schools to make special adaptations. In 1975, largely as a result of pressure from parents of atypical or disabled children, Congress passed Public Law (PL) 94-142, called the Education for All Handicapped Children Act. It specifies that every child in the United States must be given access to an appropriate education in the least restrictive environment possible. PL 94-142 does not say that every disabled child must be educated full-time in a regular classroom. The law allows schools to offer a continuum of services, including separate schools or special classrooms, although it also indicates that a child should be placed in a regular classroom as a first choice and removed from that setting only if her disability is such that she cannot be satisfactorily educated there. Table 15.4 lists the categories of disabilities covered by the law as well as the percentage of school children with disabilities in each category.

PL 94-142 and the supplementary laws that followed it (including the Education of the Handicapped Act of 1986 and the Individuals with Disabilities Education Act of 1990, renewed in 2004) rest most centrally on the philosophical view that children with disabilities have a right to participate in normal school environments (e.g., Stainback & Stainback, 1985). Proponents have further argued that such **inclusive education** aids the disabled child by integrating him into the nondisabled world, thus facilitating the development of important social skills as well as providing more appropriate academic challenges than are often found in separate classrooms or special programs for the disabled (Siegel, 1996). Advocates of inclusion are convinced that mildly retarded children and those with learning disabilities will show greater academic achievement if they are in regular classrooms.

Schools and school districts differ widely in the specific model of inclusion they use, although virtually all models involve a team of educators, including the classroom teacher, one or more special education teachers, classroom aides, and sometimes volunteers. Some schools follow a plan called a *pull-out program*, in which the disabled student is placed in a regular classroom only part of each day, with the remainder of the time spent working with a special education teacher in a special class or resource room. More common are full-inclusion systems in which the child spends the entire school day in a regular class but receives help from volunteers, aides, or special education teachers who come to the classroom to work with the child there. In some districts, a group of disabled children may be assigned to a single regular classroom; in others, no more than one such child is normally assigned to any one class (Baker & Zigmond, 1995).

There is little argument about the desirability of the overall goal: to provide every child with the best education possible, one that challenges the child and gives her the best possible chance to learn the basic intellectual and social skills needed to function in society. Thus, you may be surprised by the finding that teachers who have the most positive attitudes toward inclusion also have the highest burnout rates (Talmor, Reiter,

inclusive education General term for education programs that assign physically, mentally, or emotionally disabled children to regular classrooms and that provide any special services required by the child in that classroom.

TABLE 15.4	Disabilities for Which Children in the United States Received Special Education Services	
Disability Category	**Percentage of Special Education Students in the Category**	**Description of Disability**
Learning Disability	51	Achievement 2 or more years behind expectations based on intelligence tests
		Example: A fourth grader with an average IQ who is reading at a first-grade level
Communication Disorder in Speech or Language	20	A disorder of speech or language that affects a child's education; can be a problem with speech or an impairment in the comprehension or use of any aspect of language
		Example: A first grader who makes errors in pronunciation like those of a 4-year-old and can't connect sounds and symbols
Mental Retardation	11	IQ significantly below average intelligence, together with impairments in adaptive functions
		Example: A school-aged child with an IQ lower than 70 who is not fully toilet-trained and who needs special instruction in both academic and self-care skills
Serious Emotional Disturbance	8	An emotional or behavior disorder that interferes with a child's education
		Example: A child whose severe temper tantrums cause him to be removed from the classroom every day
Other Health Impairments	4	A health problem that interferes with a child's education
		Example: A child with severe asthma who misses several weeks of school each year
Multiple Disabilities	2	Need for special instruction and ongoing support in two or more areas to benefit from education
		Example: A child with cerebral palsy who is also deaf, who thus requires both physical and instructional adaptations
Hearing Impairment	1.3	A hearing problem that interferes with a child's education
		Example: A child who needs a sign-language interpreter in the classroom
Orthopedic Impairment	1.2	An orthopedic handicap that requires special adaptations
		Example: A child in a wheelchair who needs a special physical education class
Visual Impairment	0.5	Impaired visual acuity or a limited field of vision that interferes with education
		Example: A blind child who needs training in the use of Braille to read and write

Sources: Kirk, Gallagher, and Anastasiow, 1993; U.S. Bureau of the Census, 2001.

& Feigin, 2005). Researchers speculate that teachers with idealistic views of inclusion probably work very hard to help students with disabilities succeed. When their efforts meet with limited success, they may suffer from feelings of failure and incompetence and may feel emotionally drained. In some schools, teachers are provided with co-teachers who carry some of the extra burdens involved in teaching a class that includes both typically developing children and children with disabilities. This practice appears to protect some teachers against burnout (Magiera & Zigmond, 2005). Moreover, students with disabilities receive much more direct instruction when both a regular teacher and a co-teacher are available.

Those of you who plan to be teachers should take note of such findings. In addition, be aware that, whatever your views on inclusion, it is a practice that has been mandated by law. Therefore, it is here to stay (Putnam, Spiegel, & Bruininks, 1995). For teachers, the crucial question is a practical one: What works best? That is, among the many varieties of inclusion programs, can features that are consistently associated with better results or poorer results be identified?

This question is extremely hard to answer. For all kinds of perfectly understandable reasons, developmentalists have little of the kind of research needed to answer it. Inclusion programs vary widely in design and serve children with diverse problems. The teachers who implement them range from highly skilled and inventive to overwhelmed and unskilled. If a particular program pattern appears to work in one school, it is often difficult to tell whether it is successful because of the particular teachers involved, because of the specific characteristics of the children being served, or because the program itself is especially well designed.

David, the Down syndrome boy on the left, is in an inclusive elementary school classroom, participating as fully as possible in all activities and assignments.

Given all this, it is not surprising that clear answers to many of the questions about inclusion are still lacking. Still, educators and psychologists have struggled to summarize the information they do have, and most would agree with the following conclusions:

- Children with physical disabilities but no learning problem—such as blind children or some children with spina bifida—make better academic gains in full-inclusion programs (Buysse & Bailey, 1993; MacMillan, Keough, & Jones, 1986; Odom & Kaiser, 1997).

- For children with learning disabilities, however, full-inclusion programs may be less academically supportive than pull-out programs or resource rooms. According to Vaughn and Schumm, "The evidence that does exist for students with learning disabilities suggests that they do not fare well academically in the general education classroom, where undifferentiated, large-group instruction is the norm" (1995, p. 264). Success for learning disabled children in a regular classroom depends heavily on the ability of the teacher to implement an individualized program. Co-teaching arrangements appear to be particularly helpful to children with learning disabilities (Magiera & Zigmond, 2005).

- Although inclusion may provide some social benefits, there are also social risks. Some research shows gains in self-esteem and social skills for disabled children in inclusion programs (e.g., Banerji & Dailey, 1995; Cole, 1991). Yet virtually all groups of disabled children, including the learning disabled, mildly retarded, and physically disabled, are more likely to experience rejection from their peers in regular classes than are nondisabled children (e.g., Sale & Carey, 1995). Learning disabled students, in particular, are often notably unpopular with their peers in regular classes (Roberts & Mather, 1995).

- Effective inclusion programs require, at a minimum, that teachers be given extensive additional training and substantial support from specialists, aides, or volunteers (Roberts & Mather, 1995)—conditions that are very often not met because of budgetary or other reasons. The majority of teachers feel that they are not prepared to teach students with disabilities; many who have such children in their classrooms believe that they do not receive adequate support (Schumm & Vaughn, 1995).

The above list of conclusions should convince you that there is no "magic bullet," no single solution for educators, for parents, or for disabled children. If you are planning to become a teacher, you will need to learn as much as possible about the needs of children with various kinds of disabilities as well as about successful strategies for teaching them; if you are a parent of a disabled child, you will need to inform yourself about all the educational alternatives so that you can become your child's consistent advocate within the school system.

CRITICAL THINKING ?

If you were a parent of a child with mental retardation or learning disabilities, would you want the child to be placed in a regular classroom or a special program? Why?

Before going on · · ·

- What have researchers learned about the effectiveness of inclusive education for children with various kinds of disabilities?

Summary

Understanding Atypical Development

- Studies of psychopathology are more often being cast in a developmental framework, with emphasis on the complex pathways that lead to deviance or normality. Such an approach also emphasizes the importance of the child's own resilience or vulnerability to stresses.
- Family stress or stress that a child experiences directly, especially if there are multiple simultaneous stresses, exacerbates any existing or underlying tendency toward pathology. Children with inborn vulnerabilities (such as difficult temperament or physical problems), few protective factors, and few resources are more likely to respond to stressful circumstances with pathology.
- Psychopathologies are most often divided into three broad groups: disorders of attention, including attention deficit hyperactivity disorder (ADHD); externalizing problems, including conduct disorders; and internalizing problems, including eating disorders and depression. Approximately 20% of all children in the United States will need some form of special assistance for a significant emotional, cognitive, or physical problem at some time in childhood or adolescence.

Attention Problems and Externalizing Problems

- Attention deficit hyperactivity disorder (ADHD), the most common type of disorder of attention, includes both problems in focusing attention and excessive restlessness and activity. Long-term problems are greatest when ADHD is combined with a conduct disorder. ADHD appears to have an initial biological cause, but deviant behavioral patterns are aggravated or improved by subsequent experiences.
- Conduct disorders include patterns of both excess aggressiveness and delinquency. Childhood-onset conduct disorders appear to have a genetic component and are exacerbated by poor family interactions and subsequent poor peer relations. Delinquent acts (lawbreaking) increase in adolescence and are found not only among children with early-onset conduct disorders but also among some teens who show a brief period of delinquency but no long-term negative consequences.

Internalizing Problems

- Eating disorders, including bulimia and anorexia nervosa, probably result from a disordered body image. These disorders are most common in adolescent girls.
- Depression is another type of internalizing problem, relatively uncommon in childhood but common in adoles-

cence. Depressed youngsters are more likely to have a family history of parental depression, to have low self-esteem, or to have a history of being ignored by peers. Depression in adolescence is about twice as common among girls as among boys. No consensus has yet been reached on the explanation for this sex difference.
- Depression sometimes leads to suicidal thoughts. About one-fifth of high school students in the United States report having considered suicide.

Atypical Intellectual and Social Development

- Children with mental retardation, normally defined as having an IQ below 70 combined with significant problems of adaptation, show slower development and more immature or less efficient information-processing strategies. Two types of retarded children can be identified: those whose retardation has a clear physical cause, who are overrepresented among the severely retarded; and those without physical abnormalities, whose retardation is a result of genetic causes, such as low-IQ parents and/or deprived environments, and who are overrepresented among the mildly retarded.
- About 5% of school children in the United States are labeled as learning disabled. There is still considerable dispute about how to identify a genuine learning disability, and many children may be misclassified as learning disabled. Recent research supports the hypothesis that learning disabilities have their roots in atypical brain function, although this conclusion remains tentative.
- Gifted is a term applied to children with very high IQ or to those with unusual creativity or exceptional specific talents. Their information processing is unusually flexible and generalized. Gifted children appear to be socially well-adjusted, except for a small group who are unusually gifted and have a higher risk of psychopathology.
- Children with pervasive developmental disorders (PDDs), also known as autism spectrum disorders, have impaired social relationships. Those who have autistic disorder have limited language skills and are often mentally retarded. Asperger's disorder is a milder form of autistic disorder in which children have normal language and cognitive skills.

Schooling for Atypical Children

- Inclusive education, in which children with disabilities are primarily educated in regular classrooms alongside nondisabled children, is mandated by law in the United States. Programs vary widely; some are effective, others are not.

Key Terms

adolescent-onset conduct disorder (p. 437)
anorexia nervosa (p. 439)
Asperger's disorder (p. 450)
attention deficit disorder (ADD) (p. 433)
attention deficit hyperactivity disorder
  (ADHD) (p. 432)
attention problems (p. 430)
atypical development (p. 427)
autistic disorder (p. 449)

bulimia (p. 439)
childhood-onset conduct disorder (p. 437)
clinical depression (major depressive
  disorder) (p. 441)
conduct disorder (p. 436)
delinquency (p. 437)
depression (p. 441)
developmental psychopathology (p. 427)
externalizing problems (p. 430)

hyperkinetic syndrome (p. 433)
inclusive education (p. 451)
internalizing problems (p. 431)
learning disability (LD) (p. 446)
mental retardation (p. 444)
pervasive developmental disorders (PDDs)
  (p. 449)

See for Yourself

Peer Comparison

When a child is referred to a psychologist because her parents and teacher think she may have ADHD, the psychologist often assesses the child's behavior in the context in which it occurs, in addition to administering standardized tests to the child. To get a feeling for how informative peer comparisons can be, ask an elementary school teacher to allow you to observe his or her class. Your observations should be carried out at times when the children are supposed to be working independently, and you will need a watch or clock with a second hand. Observe a randomly selected sample of five children for a fixed period of time—say, 10 minutes each—and count the number of minutes each child spends working during the period. Be sure to watch only one child at a time. Convert your observations to percentages and average them. Next, follow the same procedure for every other child in the class. Prepare a chart showing how much each child's percentage of on-task behavior deviated from the average percentage of your randomly selected sample. If you were a school psychologist who was gathering data for the purpose of diagnosing a child with ADHD, you would carry out several such observations for the target child. Ideally, you would do your observations over several days across a variety of school subjects (e.g., reading, math). If the child had ADHD, the observations would show a consistent pattern of below-average percentages of on-task behavior.

Inclusion and Burnout

Were you surprised by the finding that teachers with the most positive attitudes toward inclusion also have the highest rates of job burnout? You might find it interesting to interview teachers in your community to see whether these findings hold up. You need to interview a fair number of teachers, 10 or more, to get a feeling for any relationship that may exist. Once you've recruited the teachers, ask them these questions: (1) How do you feel about the inclusion of students with disabilities in the regular classroom? (2) If you have had a student with a disability placed in your classroom, was it a positive experience? (3) Do you feel that your job is satisfying? (4) Do you think you will still be in the teaching profession 10 years from now? Count the number of positive words used in each teacher's answers to the first two questions; this is your measure of positive attitudes toward inclusion. Next, count the number of negative words in each teacher's answers to questions three and four as your measure of burnout. Make a line graph, plotting the number of positive words in each teacher's answers to the first two questions on the vertical axis and the number of negative words in that teacher's answers to the last two on the horizontal axis. If the two are related, the plot points on your graph should form a sloped line. If your findings match those of the study cited in the text, the line will slope in an upward direction from left to right, reflecting a positive correlation between positive attitudes toward inclusion and teacher burnout. In other words, the higher the positive attitudes, the higher the burnout.

Epilogue: Putting It All Together: The Developing Child

At this point, it is likely that you know a good deal about the sequence of development of language and about sequential changes in cognitive functioning and in attachment,

but you may not have a clear idea of how these different developmental sequences connect to one another. If your professor asked you to describe other developmental advances a child is making at the same time as she is first using two-word sentences, you might have a difficult time answering. This epilogue will help to "put the child back together" by looking at how aspects of development fit together chronologically.

Transitions, Consolidations, and Systems

The process of development can be thought of as being made up of a series of alternating periods of rapid growth (accompanied by disruption, or disequilibrium) and periods of comparative calm, or consolidation. Change is obviously going on all the time, from conception to death, but the evidence suggests that there are particular times when the changes pile up or when one highly significant change occurs. The change might be a major physiological development such as puberty, a highly significant cognitive change such as the beginning of symbol usage at about 18 months, or some other major shift.

Such a significant change has two related effects. First, in systems theory terms, any change inevitably affects the entire system. Thus, a rapid increase in skill in one area, such as language, demands adaptation in all parts of the developing system. Because a child learns to talk, her social interactions change, her thinking changes, and no doubt even her nervous system changes as new synapses are created and redundant or underused ones are pruned. Similarly, a child's early attachment may affect her cognitive development by altering the way she approaches new situations, and the hormonal changes of puberty often affect parent-child relations.

Second, when the system changes in such a major way, the child sometimes seems to come "unglued" for a while. The old patterns of relationships, of thinking, of talking, don't work very well anymore, and it takes a while to work out new patterns. Erikson frequently used the word *dilemma* to refer to such a period of semiupheaval. Klaus Riegel (1975) once suggested the term *developmental leaps*, which conveys nicely the sense of energy that often accompanies these pivotal periods. This epilogue will use the less vivid term *transition* to describe a time of change or upheaval and the term *consolidation* to describe an in-between time when change is more gradual. Together, these concepts may help you understand what is happening during each of the major age periods.

From Birth to 18 Months

Figure E.1 shows the various changes during the first 18 months of life. The rows of the figure correspond roughly to the chapters of this book; what you need to do now is read up and down the columns rather than just across the rows.

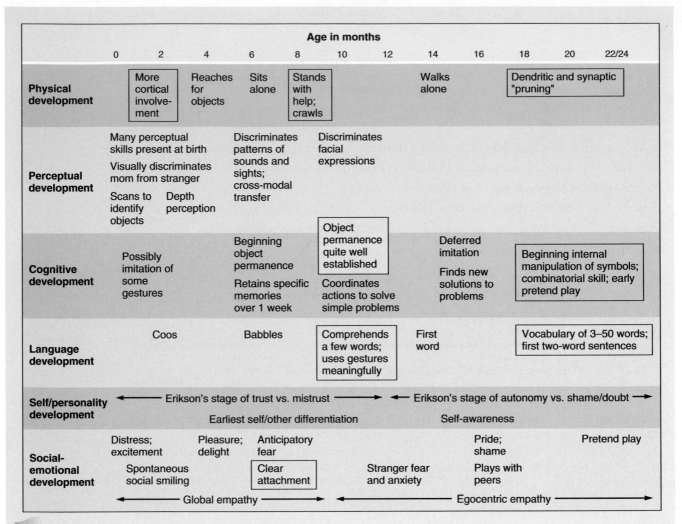

FIGURE E.1

This summary chart shows some of the simultaneous developments during infancy. The several developmental changes that seem to be pivotal—transitional changes—are outlined in boxes.

The overriding impression one gets of the newborn infant—despite her remarkable skills and capacities—is that she is very much on "automatic pilot." There seem to be built-in rules, or schemes, that govern the way an infant looks, listens, explores the world, and relates to others.

One of the really remarkable things about these rules, as you learned in Chapters 3 and 5, is how well designed they are to lead both the child and the caregivers into the "dance" of interaction and attachment. Think of an infant being breast-fed. The baby has the needed rooting, sucking, and swallowing reflexes to take in the milk; when the baby is nursing, the mother's face is at the optimum distance from the baby's eyes for the infant to focus on it; the mother's facial features, particularly her eyes and mouth, are just the sort of visual stimuli that the baby is most likely to look at; the baby is particularly sensitive to the range of sounds of the human voice, especially the upper register, so the infant can easily hear the higher-pitched, lilting voice virtually all mothers use; and during breast-feeding the release of a hormone called cortisol in the mother has the effect of relaxing her and making her more alert to the baby's signals. Both the adult and the infant are thus "primed" to interact with one another.

Sometime around 6 to 8 weeks, there seems to be a change, when these automatic, reflexive responses give way to behavior that appears to be more volitional. The child now looks at objects differently, apparently trying to identify what an object is rather than merely where it is; at this age, she also begins to reliably discriminate one face from another, she smiles more, she sleeps through the night, and she generally becomes a more responsive creature.

Because of these changes in the baby (and also because most mothers by this time have recovered physically from childbirth and most mothers and fathers have begun to adjust to the immense change in their routines), big changes in mother-infant interaction patterns become evident at this time. The need for routine care-taking continues, of course, but as the child stays awake for longer periods and smiles and makes eye contact more, exchanges between parent and child become more playful and smoother.

Once this transition has occurred, there seems to be a brief period of consolidation lasting perhaps 5 or 6 months. Of course, change continues during this consolidation period. Neurological change, in particular, is rapid, with the motor and perceptual areas of the cortex continuing to develop. The child's perceptual skills also show major changes in these months, with depth perception becoming stronger and clear cross-modal transfer and identification of patterns of sounds and sights emerging.

Eight-month-old Laura has a whole set of new skills and understandings: she can crawl, she has a firm attachment to both parents, she can perhaps understand a few words, and she has a beginning understanding of object permanence. All these more or less simultaneous changes profoundly alter the system that is the child.

Despite all these changes, however, there is a kind of equilibrium in this period—an equilibrium that is altered by a series of changes that occur between about 7 and 9 months: (1) The infant forms a strong central attachment, followed a few months later by the development of separation anxiety and fear of strangers; (2) the infant begins to move around independently (albeit very slowly and haltingly at first); (3) communication between infant and parents changes substantially, as the baby begins to use meaningful gestures and to comprehend individual words; (4) the infant begins to understand object permanence, that objects and people can continue to exist even when they are out of sight. At the very least, these changes profoundly alter the parent-child interactive system, requiring the establishment of a new equilibrium (a new consolidation). The infant continues to build gradually on this set of new skills— learning a few spoken words, learning to walk, consolidating the basic attachment— until 18 or 20 months of age, at which point the child's language and cognitive development appear to take another major leap forward.

CENTRAL PROCESSES

What causes all of these changes? Any short list of such causes will inevitably be a gross oversimplification, but four key processes seem to be at work.

Physical Maturation   First and most obviously, the biological clock is ticking very loudly indeed during the early months. Only at adolescence and again in old age is such an obvious maturational pattern at work. In infancy, it is the prepatterned growth of neural dendrites and synapses that appears to be the key. The shift in behavior at 2 months, for example, seems to be governed by just such built-in changes, as synapses in the cortex develop sufficiently to control behavior more fully.

Important as this built-in program is, it nonetheless depends on the presence of a specific factor environment (Greenough, Black, & Wallace, 1987). The brain may be "programmed" to create certain synapses, but the process has to be triggered by exposure to particular kinds of experience. Because virtually all infants encounter such a minimum environment, perceptual, motor, and cognitive developments are virtually identical from one baby to the next. But that does not mean that the environment is unimportant.

The Child's Explorations   A second key process is the child's own exploration of the world around her. She is born ready to explore, to learn from her experience, but she still has to learn the specific connections between seeing and hearing, to tell the differences between mom's face and someone else's, to pay attention to the sounds emphasized in the language she is hearing, to discover that her actions have consequences, and so on.

Clearly, physiological maturation and the child's own explorations are intimately linked in a kind of perpetual feedback loop. The rapid changes in the nervous system, bones, and muscles permit more and more exploration, which in turn affects the child's perceptual and cognitive skills, and these in turn affect the architecture of the brain. For example, researchers have a good deal of evidence that the ability to crawl—a skill that rests on a host of maturationally based physical changes—profoundly affects a baby's understanding of the world. Before the baby can move independently, he seems to locate objects only in relation to his own body; after he can crawl, he begins to locate objects with reference to fixed landmarks. This shift, in turn, probably contributes to the infant's growing understanding of himself as an object in space.

Attachment   A third key process is obviously the relationship between infant and caregiver. It seems likely that Bowlby was right about the built-in readiness of all infants to create an attachment, but the quality of the specific experience the child encounters seems to have a more formative effect on attachment formation than is true for other aspects of development. A wide range of environments are "good enough" to support physical, perceptual, and cognitive growth in these early months. For the establishment of a secure central attachment, however, the acceptable range seems to be narrower.

Still, attachment does not develop along an independent track. Its emergence is linked both to maturational change and to the child's own exploration. For example, the child's understanding of object permanence may be a necessary precondition for the development of a basic attachment. As John Flavell puts it, "How ever could a child persistently yearn and search for a specific other person if the child were still cognitively incapable of mentally representing that person in the person's absence?" (1985, p. 135).

This hypothesis might be turned on its head with the argument that the process of establishing a clear attachment may cause, or at least affect, the child's cognitive development. For example, securely attached youngsters appear to persist longer in their play and to develop object permanence more rapidly (Bates, Bretherton, Beeghly-Smith, & McNew, 1982). Such a connection might exist because the securely attached child is simply more comfortable exploring the world around him from the safe base of his attachment figure. He thus has a richer and more varied set of experiences, which may stimulate more rapid cognitive (and neurological) development.

Internal Working Models   Attachment might also be thought of as a subcategory of a broader process—the creation of internal working models. Seymour Epstein (1991) proposes that what the baby is doing is nothing less than beginning to create a *theory of reality*. In Epstein's view, such a theory includes at least four elements:

- A belief about the degree to which the world is a place of pleasure or pain
- A belief about the extent to which the world is predictable, controllable, and just versus chaotic, uncontrollable, and capricious
- A belief about whether people are desirable or threatening to relate to
- A belief about the worthiness or unworthiness of the self

The roots of this theory of reality, so Epstein and others argue (Bretherton, 1991), lie in the experiences of infancy, particularly experiences with other people. Indeed, Epstein suggests that beliefs created in infancy are likely to be the most basic and therefore the most durable and resistant to change at later ages. Not all psychologists agree with Epstein about the broadness of the infant's theory of reality. However, virtually all agree that the baby begins to create at least two significant internal models, one of the self and one of relationships with others (attachment). Of the two, the attachment model seems to be the most fully developed at 18 or 24 months; the model of the self undergoes many elaborations in the years that follow. You'll recall from Chapter 10 that it is only at about age 6 or 7 that the child seems to have a sense of her global worth (Harter, 1987, 1990).

INFLUENCES ON THE BASIC PROCESSES

The process of creating these two internal models is universal. Nonetheless, infants can be deflected from the common trajectory by several kinds of influences.

Organic Damage　The most obvious potential deflector of development is some kind of damage to the physical organism, from genetic anomalies, inherited disease, or teratogenic effects in utero. Yet even when damage does occur, nature and nurture interact: Recall from Chapter 2 that the long-term consequences of such damage may be more or less severe, depending on the richness and supportiveness of the environment the baby grows up in.

Family Environment　The specific family environment in which the child is reared also affects the developmental trajectory. On one end of the continuum are beneficial effects from an optimal environment that includes a variety of objects for the baby to explore, at least some opportunity to explore freely, and loving, responsive, and sensitive adults who talk to the infant often and respond to his cues (Bradley et al., 1989). Among other things, such enriched environments may contribute to the development and retention of a more elaborate and complex network of neural connections. On the other end of the continuum are some environments that fall outside of the "good enough" range and thus fail to support the child's most basic development. A family that subjected an infant to severe neglect or abuse would fall into this category, as might one in which a parent suffered deep or lasting depression or one characterized by persisting upheaval or stress. In between these extremes are many variations in enrichment, in responsiveness, and in loving support, all of which seem to have at least some impact on the child's pattern of attachment, his motivation, the content of his self-concept, his willingness to explore, and his specific knowledge. The consequences of such differences become evident later in life, when the child faces the challenging tasks of school and the demands of relating to other children.

Influences on the Family　As you've already read many times before, the child is embedded in the family, and the family is part of a larger economic, social, and cultural system, all of which can have both direct and indirect effects on the child. The most obvious example is the impact of poverty or wealth: The parents' overall economic circumstances may have a very wide-ranging impact on a child's life experience. Poor families are less able to provide a safe and secure environment. Their infants are more likely to be exposed to environmental toxins such as lead; less likely to have regular health care, including immunizations; and more likely to have nutritionally inadequate diets. If they must place their infant in day care, poor parents may be unable to afford good quality care, and they are more likely to have to shift the baby from one care arrangement to another. Collectively, these are large differences. The effects do not become evident immediately; babies being reared in poverty-level families do not look much different from babies being reared in more affluent circumstances. By age 2, 3, or 4, though, the differences begin to be obvious.

The Preschool Years

The main theme of the preschool period, as summarized in Figure E.2, is that the child is making a slow but immensely important shift from dependent baby to independent child. The toddler and then the preschooler can move around easily, can communicate more and more clearly, has a growing sense of himself as a separate person with specific qualities, and has the beginning of cognitive and social skills that allow him to interact more fully and successfully with playmates. In these years, the child's thinking is decentering, to use Piaget's term: He shifts away from using himself as the only frame of reference and becomes less tied to physical appearances.

In the beginning, these newfound skills and this new independence are not accompanied by much impulse control. Two-year-olds are pretty good at doing; they are terrible at *not* doing. If frustrated, they hit things, and wail, scream, or shout (isn't language wonderful?). A large part of the conflict parents experience with children of this age arises because the parent must limit the child, not only for the child's own survival but also to help teach the child impulse control (Escalona, 1981).

	Age in years				
	2	**3**	**4**	**5**	**6**
Physical development	Runs easily; climbs stairs one step at a time	Rides tricycle; uses scissors; draws	Climbs stairs one foot per step; kicks and throws large ball	Hops and skips; plays some ball games with more skill	Jumps rope; skips
Cognitive development	Uses symbols; two- and three-step play sequences	Flavell's Level 1 perspective taking	Level 2 perspective taking; understands false belief	Representational theory of mind clearly present; conservation of number and quantity	Some meta-cognition and meta-memory; no spontaneous use of rehearsal in memory tasks
Language development	Two-word sentences	Three- and four-word sentences with grammatical markers	Continued improvement of inflections, past tense, plurals, passive sentences, and tag questions		
Self/personality development	Self-definition based on comparisons of size, age, gender			Categorical self based on physical properties or skills	
	Gender identity		Gender stability	Gender consistency	
	← Erikson's stage of autonomy → vs. shame/doubt	← Erikson's stage of initiative vs. guilt →			
Social development	Attachments to parents shown less frequently, mostly under stress				
	Cooperative play; multistep turn-taking sequences in play with peers	Empathy for another's feelings			
		Some altruism; same-sex peer choice	Beginning signs of individual friendships	Sociodramatic play	Roles in play

FIGURE E.2

A brief summary of parallel developments during the preschool years.

The preschool years also stand out as the period in which the seeds of the child's (and perhaps the adult's) social skills and personality are sown. The attachment process that began in infancy continues to be formative, because it helps to shape the child's internal working model of social relationships. However, in the years from age 2 to 6, this early model is revised, consolidated, and established more firmly. The resultant interactive patterns tend to persist into elementary school and beyond. The 3-, 4-, or 5-year-old who develops the ability to share, to read others' cues well, to respond positively to others, and to control aggression and impulsiveness is likely to be a socially successful, popular 8-year-old. In contrast, the noncompliant, hostile preschooler is far more likely to become an unpopular, aggressive schoolchild (Caspi, 2000).

CENTRAL PROCESSES

Many forces are at play in creating the changes of the preschool years, beginning with two immense cognitive advances in this period: the toddler's new ability to use symbols, and the rapid development, between ages 3 and 5, of a more sophisticated theory of mind.

Pride and independence!

Symbol Use   The development of symbol use is reflected in many different aspects of the child's life. It is evident in the rapid surge of language development, in the child's approach to cognitive tasks, and in play, when the child pretends and has objects stand for something else. The ability to use language more skillfully, in turn, affects social behavior in highly significant ways. For example, the child increasingly uses verbal rather than physical aggression and negotiates with parents instead of having tantrums or using defiant behavior.

Theory of Mind   The emergence of the child's more sophisticated theory of mind has equally broad effects, especially in the social arena, where her newfound abilities to read and understand others' behaviors form the foundation for new levels of interactions with peers and parents. It is probably not accidental that friendships between individual children are first visible at about the time that they also show the sharp drop in egocentrism that occurs with the emergence of the theory of mind.

The seminal role of cognitive changes is also evident in the growing importance of several basic schemes. Not only does the 2- or 3-year-old have an increasingly generalized internal model of attachment; she also develops a self-scheme and a gender scheme, each of which forms part of the foundation of both social behavior and personality.

Social Contacts   Important as these cognitive changes are, they are clearly not the only factors that contribute to developmental changes in the preschool years. Equally important are the child's contacts with adults and peers. When young children play together, they expand each other's experience with objects and suggest new ways of pretending to one another, thus fostering still further cognitive growth. When two children disagree about how to explain something or insist on their own different views, each child gains awareness that there are other ways of thinking or playing, thus creating opportunities to learn about others' mental processes. Just as Vygotsky suggested, social interactions are the arena in which much cognitive growth occurs. For example, in one study, Charles Lewis found that children who have many siblings or who interact regularly with a variety of adult relatives show more rapid understanding of other people's thinking and acting than do children with fewer social partners (Lewis, Freeman, & Maridaki-Kassotaki, 1995). Similarly, Jenkins and Astington (1996) found that children from larger families show more rapid development of a representational theory of mind. Research also shows that children with secure attachments show a more rapid shift to understanding false belief and other aspects of a representational theory of mind than do children with insecure attachments (Charman, Redfern, & Fonagy, 1995;

Steele, Holder, & Fonagy, 1995)—a result that points to the importance of the quality of social interactions as well as their quantity for the child's cognitive development.

Play with other children also forms the foundation of the child's emerging gender scheme. Noticing whether other people are boys or girls and what toys boys and girls play with is the first step in the long chain of sex-role learning.

Naturally enough, it is also social interactions, especially those with parents, that modify or reinforce the child's pattern of social behaviors. The parents' style of discipline becomes critical here. Gerald Patterson's work shows clearly that parents who lack the skills to control the toddler's impulsivity and demands for independence are likely to end up strengthening noncompliant and disruptive behavior (Patterson, Capaldi, & Bank, 1991).

INFLUENCES ON THE BASIC PROCESSES

As is true in infancy, a number of variables influence the basic processes of early childhood development.

Family Dynamics   The family's ability to support the child's development in the preschool years is affected not only by the skills and knowledge the parents bring to the process but also by the amount of stress they are experiencing from outside forces and the quality of support they have in their own lives. In particular, mothers who are experiencing high levels of stress are more likely to be punitive and negative toward their children, with resulting increases in the children's defiant and noncompliant behavior. Maternal negativity, in turn, is implicated in the persistence of noncompliant behavior into elementary school. This link is clear, for example, in Susan Campbell's longitudinal study of a group of noncompliant children (Campbell & Ewing, 1990; Campbell, Pierce, March, & Ewing, 1991). Campbell finds that among a group of 3-year-olds who were labeled "hard to manage," those who had improved by age 6 had mothers who had been less negative.

Stress is obviously not the only factor in the mother's level of negativity toward the child. Depressed mothers are also more likely to show negativity (Thompson & Goodvin, 2005), as are mothers from working-class or poverty-level families, who may well have experienced negativity and harsh discipline in their own childhoods. Even so, stress and lack of personal social support are both part of the equation. Thus, preschoolers, like children of every age, are affected by broader social forces outside the family as well as by the family interaction itself.

 # The Elementary School Years

Figure E.3 summarizes the changes and continuities of middle childhood. There are obviously many gradual changes: increasing physical skill, less reliance on appearance, more attention to underlying qualities and attributes, and a greater role of peers. The one interval during these years in which there seems to be a more rapid change is right at the beginning of middle childhood, at the point of transition from being a preschooler to being a schoolchild.

THE TRANSITION BETWEEN 5 AND 7

Some kind of transition into middle childhood has been noted in a great many cultures. There seems to be widespread recognition that a 6-year-old is somehow qualitatively different from a 5-year-old: more responsible, more able to understand complex

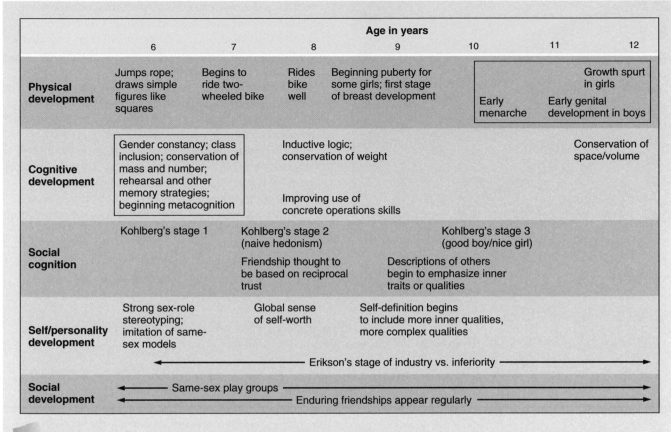

FIGURE E.3

A brief summary of parallel changes during the elementary school years.

ideas. Among the Kipsigis of Kenya, for example, the age of 6 is said to be the first point at which the child has *ng'omnotet*, translated as "intelligence" (Harkness & Super, 1985). The fact that schooling begins at this age seems to reflect an implicit or explicit recognition of this fundamental shift.

Psychologists who have studied development across this transition have pointed to a series of changes children undergo:

- Cognitively, there is a shift to what Piaget calls *concrete operational thinking*. The child now understands conservation problems, seriation, and class inclusion. More generally, the child seems to pay less attention to surface properties of objects and more to underlying continuities and patterns, to be captured less by appearance and to focus on the underlying reality. This can be seen not only in children's understanding of physical objects but also in their understanding of others, of relationships, and of themselves.
- Studies of information processing reveal a parallel rapid increase in the child's use of executive strategies.
- In terms of self-concept, a global judgment of self-worth first emerges at about age 7 or 8.
- In peer relationships, gender segregation becomes virtually complete by age 6 or 7, especially in individual friendships.

The confluence of these changes is impressive and seems to provide some support for the existence of the kind of stage Piaget hypothesized. There appears to be some kind of change in the basic structure of the child's thinking that is reflected in all aspects of the child's functioning. Still, impressive as these changes are, it is not so clear that what

Going to school is a hugely formative experience for children.

is occurring is a rapid, pervasive, structural change to a whole new way of thinking and relating. Children don't make this shift all at once in every area of their cognitive or social functioning. For example, while the shift from a concrete to a more abstract self-concept may become noticeable at age 6 or 7, it occurs quite gradually and is still going on at ages 11 and 12. Similarly, a child may grasp conservation of quantity at age 5 or 6 but typically does not understand conservation of weight until several years later.

Furthermore, expertise, or lack of it, strongly affects the pattern of a child's cognitive progress. Thus, while most psychologists agree that a set of important changes normally emerge together at about this age, most also agree that they do not represent a rapid or abrupt reorganization of the child's basic mode of operating.

CENTRAL PROCESSES

There seem to be three sets of developmental processes at work in the elementary school years: cognitive, social, and physical.

Cognitive Influences   Of the developmental shifts seen during middle childhood, the cognitive changes seem to many psychologists the most central, comprising a necessary but not sufficient condition for the alterations in relationships and in the self-scheme that also occur during this period. A good illustration is the emergence of a global sense of self-worth, which seems to require not only a tendency to look beyond or behind surface characteristics but also the use of inductive logic. The child appears to arrive at a global sense of self-worth by some summative, inductive process.

Similarly, the quality of the child's relationships with peers and parents seems to rest, in part, on a basic cognitive understanding of reciprocity and perspective taking. The child now understands that others read him as much as he reads them. Children of 7 or 8 will say of their friends that they "trust each other," something you would be very unlikely to hear from a 5-year-old.

Peer Group Influences   A bias toward seeing cognitive changes as central dominated theories and research on middle childhood for many decades, largely as a result of the powerful influence of Piaget's theory. This imbalance has begun to be redressed in recent years as the importance of the peer group and the child's social experience has become better understood. There are two reasons for this change in thinking. First, developmentalists have reawakened to the (obvious) fact that a great deal of the experience on which the child's cognitive progress is based occurs in social interactions. Second, they have realized that social relationships present the child with a unique set of demands, both cognitive and interactive, and have unique consequences for the child's social and emotional functioning. It is in the elementary school years, for example, that patterns of peer rejection or acceptance are consolidated, with reverberations through adolescence and into adult life.

Physical Influences   It is not completely clear just what role physical change plays in the various developmental changes of the elementary school years. Clearly, there are physical changes going on. Girls, in particular, begin the early steps toward puberty during elementary school. What developmentalists don't yet know is whether the rate of physical development in these years is connected in any way to the rate of the child's progress through the sequence of cognitive or social understandings. One thing is true: Bigger, more coordinated, early-developing children are likely to have slightly faster cognitive development and to be somewhat more popular with peers. Obviously, this is an area in which developmentalists need far more knowledge.

INFLUENCES ON THE BASIC PROCESSES: THE ROLE OF CULTURE

Most of what you have read about middle childhood (and about other periods as well) is based on research on children growing up in Western cultures. Investigators must ask, therefore, whether the patterns they see are specific to particular cultures or whether they reflect underlying developmental processes common to all children everywhere.

With respect to middle childhood, there are some obvious differences in the experiences of children in Western cultures compared to those growing up in villages in Africa, in Polynesia, or in other parts of the world where families live by subsistence agriculture and schooling is not a dominant force in children's lives (Weisner, 1984). In many such cultures, children of 6 or 7 are thought of as "intelligent" and responsible and are expected to play almost adultlike roles. They are highly likely to be given the task of caring for younger siblings and to begin their apprenticeships in the skills they will need as adults, such as agricultural or animal husbandry skills, learning by working alongside the adults. In some West African and Polynesian cultures, it is also common for children of this age to be sent out to foster care with relatives or to apprentice with a skilled worker.

Such children obviously have a very different set of social tasks to learn in the middle childhood years than do children growing up in industrialized countries. They do not need to learn how to relate to or make friends with same-age strangers in a new environment (school). Instead, from an early age, they need to learn their place in an existing network of roles and relationships. For the Western child, the roles are less prescribed; the choices for adult life are far more varied.

Yet the differences in the lives of children in industrialized and nonindustrialized cultures should not obscure the very real similarities. In all cultures, middle childhood is the period in which children develop individual friendships, segregate their play groups by gender, develop the cognitive underpinnings of reciprocity, learn the beginnings of what Piaget called *concrete operations*, and acquire some of the basic skills that will be required for adult life. These are not trivial similarities. They speak to the power of the common process of development, even in the midst of obvious variations in experience.

 ## Adolescence

Figure E.4 summarizes the various threads of development during adolescence. A number of experts on this developmental period argue that it makes sense to divide the years between 12 and 20 into two subperiods, one beginning at 11 or 12, the other perhaps at 16 or 17. Some label these periods "adolescence" and "youth" (Keniston, 1970); others call them "early" and "late" adolescence (Brooks-Gunn, 1988). However they are labeled, there are distinct differences.

EARLY AND LATE ADOLESCENCE

Early adolescence, almost by definition, is a time of transition, of significant change in virtually every aspect of the child's functioning. Late adolescence is more a time of con-

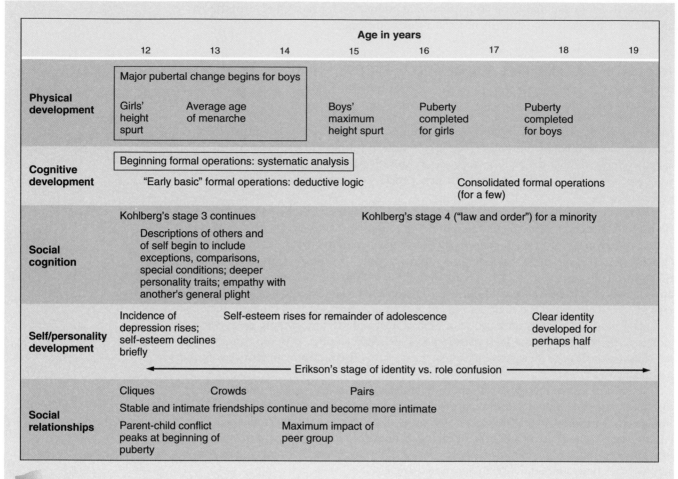

FIGURE E.4

A brief summary of parallel developments during adolescence.

solidation, when the young person establishes a cohesive new identity, with clearer goals and role commitments. Norma Haan (1981), borrowing Piaget's concepts, suggests that early adolescence is a time dominated by assimilation, whereas late adolescence is primarily a time of accommodation.

The 12- or 13-year-old is assimilating an enormous number of new physical, social, and intellectual experiences. While all this absorption is going on, but before the experiences have been digested, the young person is in a more or less continuous state of disequilibrium. Old patterns, old schemes no longer work very well, but new ones have not been established. It is during this early period that the peer group is so centrally important. Ultimately, the 16- or 17- or 18-year-old begins to make the needed accommodations, pulls the threads together, and establishes a new identity, new patterns of social relationships, new goals and roles.

Early Adolescence   In some ways, the early years of adolescence have a lot in common with the toddler years. Two-year-olds are famous for their negativism and for their constant push for more independence. At the same time, they are struggling to learn a vast array of new skills. Teenagers show many of these same qualities, albeit at much more abstract levels. Many of them go through a period of negativism, particularly with parents, right at the beginning of the pubertal changes. And many of the conflicts with parents center on issues of independence—adolescents want to come and go when they please, listen to the music they prefer (at maximum volume), and wear the clothing and hair styles that are currently "in."

As is true of the negativism of 2-year-olds, it is easy to overstate the depth or breadth of the conflict between young teenagers and their parents. For the great majority of teenagers, there is no major turmoil—simply a temporary increase in the frequency of disagreements or disputes. The depiction of adolescence as full of storm and stress is as much an exaggeration as the stereotype of the "terrible twos." What is true is that both ages are characterized by a new push for independence, which is inevitably accompanied by more confrontations with parents over limits. While this push for independence is going on, young adolescents are also facing a new set of demands: new social skills, new and more complex school tasks, a need to form an adult identity. The sharp increase in the rate of depression (especially among girls) and the drop in self-esteem seen at the beginning of adolescence seem to be linked to this surplus of demands and changes. A number of investigators have found that those adolescents who must deal with the greatest number of simultaneous changes at the beginning of puberty—changing to junior high school, moving to a new town or new house, per-

Independence of a new and different kind.

haps a parental separation or divorce—also show the greatest loss in self-esteem, the largest rise in problem behavior, and the biggest drop in grade point average (e.g., Simmons, Burgeson, & Reef, 1988). Young adolescents who can cope with these changes one at a time (for example, youngsters who are able to remain in the same school through eighth or ninth grade before shifting to high school) show fewer symptoms of stress.

Facing major stressful demands, the 2-year-old uses mom (or some other central attachment figure) as a safe base for exploring the world, returning for reassurance when she is fearful. Young adolescents seem to do the same with the family, using it as a safe base from which to explore the rest of the world, including the world of peer relationships. Parents of young adolescents must try to find a balance between providing the needed security, often in the form of clear rules and limits, and still allowing independence—just as parents of 2-year-olds must walk a fine line between allowing exploration and ensuring safety. Among teenagers, as among toddlers, the most confident and successful are those whose families manage this balancing act well.

Drawing a parallel between early adolescents and toddlers also makes sense in that both age groups face the task of establishing a separate identity. The toddler must separate herself from the symbiotic relationship with mom or another central caregiver. The child must figure out not only that she is separate but also that she has abilities and qualities. Physical maturation also allows her new levels of independent exploration. The young adolescent must separate himself from his family and from his identity as a child and begin to form a new identity as an adult.

Late Adolescence

To carry the analogy we've been using further, late adolescence is more like the later preschool years. Major changes have been weathered, and a new balance has been achieved. The physical upheavals of puberty are mostly complete, the family system has changed to allow the teenager more independence and freedom, and the beginnings of a new identity have been created. This period is not without its strains, however. Most young people do not achieve a clear identity until college age, if then, so the identity process continues. And the task of forming emotionally intimate partnerships (whether sexual or not) is a key task of late adolescence. Nonetheless, Haan seems to be correct that this later period is more one of accommodation than assimilation. It is definitely accompanied by rising levels of self-esteem and declining levels of family confrontation or conflict.

By late adolescence, the form of peer interaction has shifted from mixed-sex cliques to loose associations of pairs.

CENTRAL PROCESSES AND THEIR CONNECTIONS

It seems clear that changes in one or another of the facets of development may be central to the constellation of transformations seen at a given age. In infancy, underlying physiological change and the creation of a first central attachment appear to have such key causal roles; in the preschool years, cognitive changes seem especially dominant; among school-aged children, both cognitive and social changes appear to be formative. In adolescence, every domain shows significant change. At this point, developmentalists simply do not have the research data to clarify the basic causal connections among the transformations in these various areas. Nevertheless, they have some information about linkages.

The Role of Puberty   One obvious factor to emphasize in discussions of adolescence is puberty itself. Puberty not only defines the beginning of early adolescence; it clearly affects all other facets of the young person's development, either directly or indirectly. There are several direct effects. Most clearly, the surges of pubertal hormones stimulate sexual interest while triggering body changes that make adult sexuality and fertility possible. These changes seem inescapably and causally linked to the gradual shift (for the great majority of teens) from same-sex peer groupings to heterosexual crowds and finally to heterosexual pair relationships.

Hormone changes may also be directly implicated in the increases in confrontation or conflict between parents and children and in various kinds of aggressive or delinquent behavior. Lawrence Steinberg's research (1988) suggests such a direct link; he found pubertal stage and not age to be the critical variable in predicting the level of adolescents' conflict with their parents. Other investigators have found that in girls, the rise in estradiol at the beginning of puberty is associated with increases in verbal aggression and a loss of impulse control, while in boys, increases in testosterone are correlated with increases in irritability and impatience (Paikoff & Brooks-Gunn, 1990). However, many studies find no such connections (e.g., Coe, Hayashi, & Levine, 1988), so most theorists conclude that the links between pubertal hormones and changes in adolescent social behavior are considerably more complicated than they had first imagined.

One factor that complicates the analysis is that the physical changes of puberty have highly significant indirect effects as well as direct consequences. When a child's body grows and becomes more like that of an adult, the parents begin to treat the child differently, and the child begins to see himself as a soon-to-be-adult. Both of these changes may be linked to the brief rise in parent-adolescent confrontation and may help to trigger some of the searching self-examinations that are part of this period of life.

Physiological changes might conceivably also play some role in the shift to formal operations. There is some indication, for example, that synaptic and dendritic pruning continues through early adolescence, so a final reorganization of the brain may be occurring in these years. At the same time, any link between formal operational thinking and pubertal change cannot be inevitable, because all adolescents experience puberty, but not all make the transition to formal operations. The best guess at the moment is that neurological or hormonal changes at adolescence may be necessary for further cognitive gains, but they cannot be sufficient conditions for such developments.

The Role of Cognitive Changes   An equally attractive possibility to many theorists is the proposition that it is the cognitive changes that are pivotal in adolescent development. The cognitive shift from concrete to formal operations obviously does not *cause* pubertal changes, but cognitive development may make possible many of the other changes seen in adolescence, including changes in self-concept, the process of identity formation, increases in level of moral reasoning, and changes in peer relationships.

There is ample evidence, for example, that the greater abstractness in the adolescent's self-concept and in her descriptions of others is intimately connected to the broader changes in cognitive functioning (Harter, 1990). You will also remember from Chapter 12 that the shift in the child's thinking from concrete operations to at least beginning formal operations seems to be a necessary precondition for the emergence of more advanced forms of social cognition and moral judgment. Finally, some ability to use formal operations may also be necessary but not sufficient for the formation of a clear identity. One of the characteristics of formal operational thinking is the ability to imagine possibilities that you have never experienced and to manipulate ideas in your head. These new skills may help to foster the questioning of old values and old patterns that is a central part of identity formation. For example, several studies show that among high school and college students, those in Marcia's status of identity achievement or moratorium are much more likely also to be using formal operations reasoning than are those in the status of diffusion or foreclosure. In Rowe and Marcia's study (1980), the only individuals who showed full identity achievement were those who were also using full formal operations. But the converse was not true. That is, there were a number of participants in the study who used formal operations but had not yet established a clear identity. Thus, formal operational thinking may enable the young person to rethink many aspects of her life, but it does not guarantee that she will do so.

Overall, both the physical changes of puberty and the potential cognitive changes of formal operations appear to be central to the phenomena of adolescence, but the connections between them, and their impact on social behavior, remain unclear.

INFLUENCES ON THE BASIC PROCESSES

There is not enough space in this epilogue (or perhaps in this entire book) to detail all the factors that influence the teenager's experience of adolescence. You have already read about many of these factors, including the timing of the child's pubertal development, the degree of personal or familial stress, and such cultural variations as the use of initiation rites. But one more general point is worth repeating: Adolescence, like every other developmental period, does not begin as a clean slate. The individual youngster's own temperamental qualities, behavioral habits, and internal models of interaction, established in earlier years of childhood, obviously have a profound effect on the experience of adolescence. Examples are easy to find:

- Teens who are high in neuroticism and introversion, who have low self-esteem, and who tend to blame external agents for their problems are at higher risk for mental health problems than are peers who have a more optimistic outlook on life (Beautrais, Joyce, & Mulder, 1999).
- Alan Sroufe's longitudinal study (1989), described in Chapter 11, showed that those who had been rated as having a secure attachment in infancy were more self-confident and more socially competent with peers at the beginning of adolescence.
- Delinquency and heightened aggressiveness in adolescence are most often preceded by earlier behavior problems and by inadequate family control as early as the child's toddler years (Dishion, French, & Patterson, 1995). Even those who show such antisocial behavior for the first time as teenagers enter adolescence with different qualities, including poorer-quality friendships (Berndt & Keefe, 1995).
- Depression in the teenage years is more likely among those who enter adolescence with low self-esteem (Harter, 1987).

Avshalom Caspi and Terrie Moffitt (1991) make the more general point that any major life crisis or transition, including adolescence, has the effect of accentuating earlier personality or behavioral patterns rather than creating new ones. This is not unlike the observation that the child's attachment to the parent is revealed only when the child is under stress. As one example of the more general process, Caspi and Moffitt point out that girls who experience very early puberty have higher rates of psychological problems, on average, than do those who experience puberty at a more normal or average age. However, closer analysis reveals that it is only the early-maturing girls who already had social problems before puberty began whose pubertal experience and adolescence is more negative. Very early puberty does not induce psychological problems in girls who were psychologically healthier to begin with.

Caspi and Moffitt's observation appears to be important for understanding the various transitions of adult life as well as those of adolescence. Not only do we "carry ourselves with us" as we move through the roles and demands of adult life, but existing patterns may be most highly visible when we are under stress. This does not mean that we never change or learn new and more effective ways of responding—obviously many of us do. Still, it is important not to lose sight of the fact that by adolescence, and certainly by adulthood, people's internal working models and repertoires of coping behaviors are already established, creating a bias in the system. Another way of putting it is that while change is possible, continuity is the default option.

A Return to Some Basic Questions

With this brief overview in mind, let's now go back to some of the questions raised in Chapter 1 and see if the answers can be made any clearer.

WHAT ARE THE MAJOR INFLUENCES ON DEVELOPMENT?

Throughout this book, you have read about the arguments for and against both nature and nurture, or nativism and empiricism, as basic explanations of developmental patterns. In every instance, you learned that the real answer lies in the interaction between the two. To make the point more clearly, we might go back to Aslin's five models of environmental and internal influences on development, illustrated in Figure 1.1. You'll recall that Aslin proposed one purely physical model (which he calls maturation), according to which some particular development occurs regardless of environmental input, and one purely environmental pattern (which he calls induction) according to which some development is entirely a function of experience. These two "pure" alternatives make logical sense, but in actuality, probably neither occurs at all. All of development is a product of various forms of interaction between internal and external influences.

Even in the case of development that appears to be the most clearly biologically determined or influenced, such as physical development or early perceptual development, normal development can occur only if the child is growing in an environment that falls within an adequate or sufficient range. The fact that the vast majority of environments fall within that range in no way reduces the crucial importance of the environment. As John Flavell puts it, "Environmental elements do not become any less essential to a particular form of development just because they are virtually certain to be available for its use" (1985, p. 284). Similarly, even those aspects of development that seem most obviously to be products of the environment, such as the quality of the child's first attachment, rest on a physiological foundation and on instinctive patterns of attachment behaviors. The fact that all normal children possess that foundation and those instincts makes them no less essential for development.

Rutter's Five Principles of the Interaction of Nature and Nurture   It is not enough merely to say that all development is a product of interaction between nature and nurture. Developmentalists want to be able to specify much more clearly just how that interaction operates. Michael Rutter and his colleagues (1997) have proposed a set of five general principles governing the interplay between nature and nurture; these go beyond Aslin's models and provide a helpful summary analysis:

- *"Individuals differ in their reactivity to the environment"* (p. 338). Some babies, children, and adults are highly reactive, highly sensitive to stress or strangeness; others react with much less volatility. Variations in such reactivity may rest on basic inborn temperamental differences, or they may be the product of cumulative experience. A child exposed to high levels of stress over many months or years, for example, may become more reactive—just as adults who have experienced higher levels of stress are more likely to catch a cold when exposed to a virus (Cohen, Tyrrell, & Smith, 1991).

- *"There is a two-way interplay between individuals and their environments"* (p. 338). It is important not to think of the influences of the environment as a one-way street. Influences go back and forth. One example illustrates Rutter's point: Mothers who experience higher levels of stress are more likely to become depressed; then, once they become depressed, the women are likely to experience still higher rates of stressful life events. Thus, influence occurs in both directions: Stress leads to more depression, and depression leads to more stress (Pianta & Egeland, 1994b). Another example: Children whose inborn skills or disabilities make it difficult for them to learn to read will naturally read less. Reading less, in turn, means that they will have fewer of the experiences that help build reading skill. These back-and-forth influences tend to move the child (or the adult) farther and farther along the original trajectory.

- *"The interplay between persons and their environments needs to be considered within an ecological framework"* (p. 339). Although research nearly always treats environmental events (for example, divorce) as if they were the same for everyone, they are not. The event itself will differ as a function of culture, poverty, family structure, and a whole host of other variables.

- *"People process their experiences rather than just serve as passive recipients of environmental forces"* (p. 339). This point has been made throughout the book, but it is good to repeat it. Children are actively trying to understand their experience. They create theories or models to explain that experience. Internal models of attachment, of the self, of gender, of relationships, are all examples of this principle, but the principle is even more general. As Chapter 1 noted, it is the meaning each child attaches to an experience that governs the effect, not the experience itself. Thus, the "same" experience can have widely differing effects, depending on how the child (or adult) processes or interprets it.

- *"People act on their environment so as to shape and select their experiences"* (p. 339). Experiences are not distributed randomly and independently of how the child or adult behaves. We each choose behaviors and niches within the family or within other social groups.

The fact that virtually all babies have some chance to reach for and examine objects does not mean that such experience is unimportant in the child's emerging perceptual or motor skills. Most (if not all) so-called maturational sequences require particular kinds of environmental inputs if they are to occur at all.

A Continuum of Environmental Influences

Another point, not included in Rutter's list, is that the form and extent of the interaction between nature and nurture may well vary as a function of the aspect of development in question. It may help to think of different facets of development along a continuum, with those most fully internally programmed on one end and those most externally influenced on the other.

Physical development defines one end of this continuum, since it is very strongly shaped by internal forces. Given the minimum necessary environment, physical maturational timetables are extremely powerful and consistent, particularly during infancy and adolescence. Next along the continuum is probably language (although some experts might argue with this conclusion, given the possible dependence of language development on prior cognitive developments). Language seems to emerge with only minimal environmental support—though again, the environment must fall within some acceptable range. At the very least, the child must hear language spoken (or see it signed). Still, specific features of the environment seem to matter a bit more in the case of language development than is true for physical development. For example, parents who respond appropriately to their children's vocalizations seem to be able to speed up the process, an example of what Aslin calls *facilitation*.

Cognitive development falls somewhere in the middle of the continuum. Clearly, powerful internal forces are at work here. As John Flavell expressed it, "There is an impetus to childhood cognitive growth that is not ultimately explainable by this environmental push or that experiential shove" (1985, p. 283). Developmentalists don't yet know whether the impressive regularity of the sequences of cognitive development arises from built-in processes such as assimilation and accommodation or from physiological changes such as synapse formation and pruning, or from some combination of causes. However, developmentalists do know that specific qualities of the environment affect both cognitive power and structure. Children with varied and age-appropriate toys, who receive encouragement for exploration and achievement, whose parents are responsive to their overtures—who experience, in Aslin's terms, not just facilitation but attunement—show faster cognitive development and higher IQ scores.

Social and emotional development lie at the other end of the continuum, where the impact of the environment seems to be the greatest, although even here genetic factors are obviously at work. Some aspects of temperament seem clearly to be built-in, or genetic, and attachment behaviors may be instinctive; both of these inborn factors certainly shape the child's earliest encounters with others. In this developmental area, however, the balance of nature and nurture seems to lean more toward nurture. In particular, the security of the child's attachment and the quality of the child's relationships with others outside of the family seem to be powerfully affected by the specific quality of the interactions within the family.

DOES TIMING MATTER?

It's also important to remember that the impact of any experience can vary depending on when it occurs during development. This issue has been explored in a variety of ways throughout the book.

Early Experience as Critical
The most pervasive version of the timing question has asked whether the early years of life are a critical or sensitive period for the establishment of many of the trajectories of the child's later development. To borrow Ann Clarke's analogy (Clarke & Clarke, 1976): In the construction of a house, does the shape of the foundation determine the final structure partially or completely, or can later structures be built on the original foundation? Are any flaws or weaknesses in the original foundation permanent, or can they be corrected later, after the house is completed?

There are arguments on both sides. Some psychologists, such as Sandra Scarr, point to the fact that virtually all children successfully complete the sensorimotor period, and even mild and moderately retarded children achieve some form of Piaget's concrete operations. The term that has been widely used to describe such developmental patterns is *canalization*, a notion borrowed from embryologist C. H. Waddington (1957). He suggested that development can be thought of metaphorically as a marble rolling down gully on a hillside, as in Figure E.5. When a gully is narrow and deep, development is said to be highly canalized. The marble will roll down that gully with little deviation. Other aspects of development, in contrast, might be better depicted with much flatter or wider gullies, with many side branches, where the marble will be more likely to deviate from a given path. Scarr and others argue that in the early years

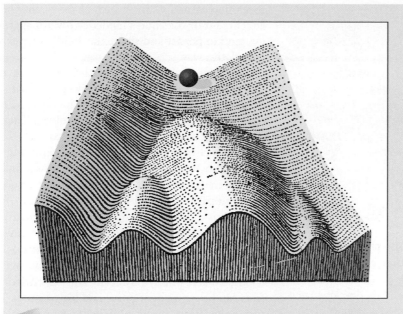

FIGURE E.5

Waddington's visual depiction of the concept of canalization. A narrow and deep gully depicts strong canalization. If infancy is highly canalized, it means that almost any environment will support or sustain that development.
(*Source*: "A catastrophic theory of evolution" by C. H. Waddington in the *Annals of the New York Academy of Science*, 231, pp. 32–42 (1974). By permission.)

of life, development is highly canalized, with strong "self-righting" tendencies. Even if deflected, the baby's pattern of development rapidly returns to the bottom of the gully and proceeds along the normal track. Such self-righting is illustrated, for example, by the large percentage of low-birth-weight or other initially vulnerable babies who nonetheless catch up to their normal-birth peers in physical and cognitive development by age 2 or 3.

Michael Lewis, in his book *Altering Fate* (1997), makes an even more sweeping argument against the primacy of early experience:

> I wish to argue against the idea that development is a sequence of small progressions that are gradual but accumulative, that it has clear directionality, that it is causal—earlier events are connected to later ones—and that prediction therefore is possible. Instead, I would like to argue for the idea that development is based on the pragmatic needs of the present, that the contextual flow of our lives determines our development through adaptation to the current. (pp. 15–16)

Lewis makes the point that chance encounters, upheavals, joys, and stresses change each of us; in a sense, he is saying that we remake ourselves moment to moment and that it is simply a mistake to think of development as if it were a cumulative process, with the earliest steps determining the trajectory of all that follows. Some developmentalists believe that Lewis has taken this argument too far, but he has certainly raised some important and provocative issues.

On the other side of the argument are a whole group of psychologists—much of whose thinking is rooted in psychoanalytic theory—who see infancy and early childhood as especially formative (e.g., Sroufe, 1983). They note that some prenatal influences are permanent; some effects of early cognitive impoverishment, malnutrition, or abuse may also be long-lasting. There is also a good deal of evidence that early

If infancy is a critical period for some aspects of personality development, then these preschoolers' characters are already well formed. Whether or not this is true remains one of the most crucial theoretical and practical issues in developmental psychology.

psychological adaptations, such as the quality of the earliest attachment or the child's tendency toward aggressive behavior, tend to persist and shape the child's later experiences in a cumulative way.

It seems likely that both of these perspectives are valid: The early years of life are a sensitive period for some kinds of development and at the same time highly canalized. How can such an apparent paradox be resolved? There are at least two possible ways. First, canalization could be seen not just as a product of powerful built-in programming but as the result of such programming being expressed in a sufficiently supportive environment. Viewed this way, a good deal of the apparent paradox disappears (Turkheimer & Gottesman, 1991). It is only when a child's particular environment falls outside the range of sufficiently supportive environments that there is a so-called environmental effect. So, for a child reared in an extremely impoverished orphanage setting or a child who is regularly physically abused, environmental effects can be strongly negative and long-lasting. The earlier such a deviation from a sufficiently supportive environment occurs, the more pervasive the effects seem to be. In this way of looking at critical periods versus canalization, a normally supported infancy may be less pivotal in the pattern of the child's development than minor deviations during toddlerhood or the preschool years. But if the deviations in infancy are extreme enough to deflect the infant from the normal developmental path—as in the case of severe abuse or malnutrition—the effect is larger than for deviations at any other age.

Robert Cairns (1991) offers a second resolution to the paradox when he points out that in any given period, some facets of development may be highly canalized and other facets may be strongly responsive to environmental variation. In infancy, for example, physical, perceptual, and perhaps linguistic development may be strongly canalized, but the development of internal working models of attachment is clearly affected by the child's specific family experiences. Indeed, all internal working models— whether of attachment, of gender identity and self-concept, or of peer relations—are likely to be more powerfully affected by early than by later experiences, simply because the model, once formed, affects and filters all later experience.

A particularly nice example of this kind of early effect comes from one of Alan Sroufe's studies of the long-term consequences of attachment security. Sroufe and his colleagues (Sroufe, Egeland, & Kreutzer, 1990) compared two groups of elementary school children. One group had formed secure attachments in infancy but for various reasons had not functioned well in the preschool years. The second group had shown poor adaptation at both ages. When these two groups of children were assessed at elementary school age, Sroufe found that those who had had a good early start "rebounded" better. They had better emotional health and social skills than did those who had had poor adaptation in infancy, even though both groups had functioned poorly as preschoolers. The infancy experience is not totally formative; the child's current circumstances also have a major impact. But, at least with respect to attachment security, early experience leaves a lingering trace.

Psychological Tasks at Different Ages   Another way to think about timing is to identify specific psychological tasks to be dealt with at different ages. Erikson's theory, for example, emphasizes a series of psychological dilemmas. Any experience that affects the way a child resolves a particular task will be formative at that time; at an earlier or later time, the same experience might have much less effect. Alan Sroufe and Michael Rutter (1984) have offered a broader list of age-related tasks, presented in Table E.1. In this way of looking at things, the child is seen as focusing on different as-

TABLE E.1	Issues or Tasks in Each of Several Age Periods

Age in Years	Issues or Tasks
0–1	Biological regulation; harmonious interactions with parents and/or caregivers; formation of an effective attachment relationship
1–2 1/2	Exploration, experimentation, and mastery of the world of objects (caregiver as secure base); individuation and autonomy; responding to external control of impulses
3–5	Flexible self-control; self-reliance; initiative; gender identification and gender concept; establishing effective peer contacts (empathy)
6–12	Social understanding (equity, fairness); gender constancy; same sex friendships; sense of "industry" (competence); school adjustment
13+	Formal operations (flexible perspective taking, "what-if" thinking); loyal friendships (same sex); beginning heterosexual relationships; emancipation; identity

Source: Table 1, p. 22, "The domain of developmental psychopathology" by L. A. Sroufe and M. Rutter, *Child Development*, 55 (1984), 17–29. By permission of the Society for Research in Child Development.

pects of the environment at different times. Thus, during the period from age 1 to 2 1/2, when the child is focused on mastery of the world of objects, the quality and range of inanimate experiences to which the child has access may be of special importance.

Overall, most developmentalists today do not think that any specific age is "critical" for all aspects of development; most do think, though, that for any aspect of development, some ages are more critical than others, and that patterns that affect later experience are set during those times. As Alan Sroufe says, "Development is hierarchical; it is not a blackboard to be erased and written upon again. Even when children change rather markedly, the shadows of the earlier adaptation remain" (1983, pp. 73–74).

WHAT IS THE NATURE OF DEVELOPMENTAL CHANGE?

On balance, it seems likely that developmental change is more qualitative than quantitative. Certainly, over the years of development, the child acquires more vocabulary words, more information-processing strategies. But these tools and skills are used in different ways by older children than they are by younger ones. Further, it seems clear that these qualitative changes occur in sequences. Such sequences are apparent in physical development, in cognitive development, and in social and moral development.

Stages Whether it is meaningful to speak of stages of development, however, is still an open question. Some hierarchically organized stages have certainly been identified, the most obvious example being Kohlberg's stages of moral reasoning. And researchers can certainly find examples of apparently stagelike changes across several developmental areas—for example, at about 18 to 24 months, the child seems to discover the ability to combine symbols, a change that is evident in two-word sentences, in thinking, and in multistep play with other children. There also appears to be a quite stagelike shift between ages 3 and 4, of which the theory of mind is the centerpiece. Nevertheless, each new skill or understanding seems to be acquired in a fairly narrow area first and is generalized more fully only later. In fact, one of the things that differentiates the gifted or higher-IQ child from the lower-IQ or retarded child is how quickly and broadly the child generalizes some new concept or strategy to new instances.

Despite this nonstagelike quality of most developmental change, it is nonetheless true that the patterns of relationships, of thinking, and of problem solving of two children of widely different ages (say, a 5-year-old and an 11-year-old) differ in almost every respect. So there is certainly orderliness in the sequences, and there are some links between them, but there probably are not major stages as Piaget proposed them.

Continuities   In the midst of all this change, all these sequences, all the new ways of relating and thinking, there is also continuity. Each child carries forward some core of individuality. The notion of temperament certainly implies such a core, as does the concept of an internal working model. Alan Sroufe once again offers an elegant way of thinking about this central core. Continuity in development, he says, "takes the form of coherence across transformations" (1983, p. 51). Thus, the specific behavior exhibited by a child may change—the clinging toddler may not become a clinging 9-year-old—but the underlying attachment model or the temperament that led to the clinging will still be at least partially present, manifesting itself in new ways. In particular, it has become increasingly clear that maladaptations often persist over time, as seen in the consistency of high levels of aggression or tantrum behavior and in the persistence of some of the maladaptive social interactions that flow from insecure attachments. The task of developmental psychologists is to understand both coherence (consistency) and the underlying patterns of transformation (development).

WHAT IS THE SIGNIFICANCE OF INDIVIDUAL DIFFERENCES?

The issue of individual continuities emphasizes the fact that development is individual as well as collective. By definition, and as the core of its basic approach, developmental psychology concerns itself with the typical rather than with deviations from what is expected. Still, you have read about individual differences in virtually every chapter, so you know that both inborn differences and emergent or environmentally produced variations are present for children in every aspect of development. It seems instructive to tie together many of the threads woven throughout this epilogue by returning to the dimension of individual difference you have read about several times—vulnerability versus resilience.

It may be useful to define these concepts somewhat differently than we did in earlier chapters, in terms of the range of environments that will be sufficiently supportive for optimal development. By this definition, a vulnerable infant is one with a narrow range of potentially supportive environments. For such a child, only the most stimulating, the most responsive, the most adaptive environment will do. When the child's environment falls outside that range, the probability of a poor outcome is greatly increased. A resilient child, in contrast, is one for whom any of a very wide range of environments will support optimal development. A resilient child may thus be more strongly canalized, and a vulnerable child less so.

Some kinds of vulnerabilities are inborn, caused by genetic abnormalities, prenatal trauma or stress, preterm birth, or malnutrition. Any child suffering from these problems will thrive only in a highly supportive environment. You've encountered this pattern again and again through the chapters of this book:

- Low-birth-weight infants typically have normal IQs if they are reared in middle-class homes, but they have a high risk of retardation if they are reared in nonstimulating poverty-level homes (Bradley et al., 1994).
- Prenatally malnourished infants or those who suffered other complications in utero or during delivery develop more or less normally if they attend highly stimulating special preschools, but they have significantly lower IQs if reared at home by mothers with limited education (Breitmayer & Ramey, 1986; Zeskind & Ramey, 1981).
- Children born with cytomegalovirus are much more likely to have learning problems in school if they are reared in poverty-level environments than if they are reared in middle-class families (Hanshaw et al., 1976).

These examples are fairly straightforward. But "vulnerability" in this sense does not remain constant throughout life. A more general proposition, which you might think of as a working hypothesis, is that each time a given child's environment falls outside the range of acceptable supportiveness (that is, each time a mismatch occurs between the child's needs and what is available), the child becomes more vulnerable; on the other hand, every time the child's needs are met, the child becomes more resilient. For example, a temperamentally difficult child whose family environment is nonetheless sufficient to foster a secure attachment will become more resilient, more able to handle the next set of tasks; a temperamentally easy child who for some reason developed an insecure attachment would become more vulnerable to later stress or environmental insufficiency.

Furthermore, the qualities of the environment that are critical for a child's optimal development no doubt change as the child passes from one age to another. Responsive and warm interactions with parents seem particularly important in the period from perhaps 6 months to 18 months; richness of cognitive stimulation seems particularly critical between perhaps 1 year and 4 years; opportunity for practicing social skills with peers may be especially crucial at a later age. Thus, as the tasks change with age, the optimal environment changes also. Among other things, this means that the same family may be very good with a child of one age and not so good with a child of another age.

Most generally, the vulnerability/resilience model leads to the conclusion that even the most "vulnerable" child can show improvement if her environment improves markedly. Because some congenitally vulnerable children do not encounter sufficiently supportive environments, their vulnerability continues to increase. For this reason, early problems often persist. At the same time, improvement is possible, even likely. Most children manage to survive and thrive, despite stresses and vulnerabilities. As Emmy Werner puts it, "We could not help being deeply impressed by the resilience of most children and youth and their capacity for positive change and personal growth" (1986, p. 5).

This photo has been used at the end of every edition of this text because it speaks so eloquently of the joy and discovery that are so much a part of development.

A FINAL POINT: THE JOY OF DEVELOPMENT

To end both this epilogue and the book on an optimistic note, remember that in the midst of all the "crises" and "transitions" and "vulnerabilities," development has a special joyous quality. When a child masters a new skill, she is not just pleased—she is delighted and will repeat that new skill at length, quite obviously getting vast satisfaction from it. A 5-year-old who learns to draw stars may draw them on everything in sight, including paper, walls, clothes, and napkins, simply because it is so much fun to draw stars. A 10-year-old who learns to do cartwheels will delightedly display this new talent to anyone who will watch and will practice endlessly.

The same joyous quality can be part of the family's development as well. Confronting and moving successfully through any of the periodic and inevitable upheavals in family life can be immensely pleasing. Watching your child progress, liking your child, and enjoying being together are all deeply satisfying parts of rearing children. When parents cry at their son's or daughter's high school graduation or wedding, it is not merely sentiment. It is an expression of that sense of love, pride, and wonderment that they and their children have come so far.

Glossary

ability goal A goal orientation associated with a desire to be superior to others.

accommodation That part of the adaptation process proposed by Piaget by which a person modifies existing schemes as a result of new experiences or creates new schemes when old ones no longer handle the data.

achievement test Test designed to assess a child's learning of specific material taught in school, such as spelling or arithmetic computation; in the United States, achievement tests are typically given to all children in designated grades.

adaptive reflexes Reflexes that are essential to the infant's survival but that disappear in the first year of life.

adolescent-onset conduct disorder A conduct disorder that begins only in adolescence; it is typically less severe and persistent than childhood-onset conduct disorder.

affectional bond A "relatively long-enduring tie in which the partner is important as a unique individual and is interchangeable with none other" (Ainsworth, 1989, p. 711).

aggression Behavior that is aimed at harming or injuring another person or object.

agreeableness One of the Big Five personality traits; a person who scores high on this trait is characterized by trust, generosity, kindness, and sympathy.

amnion The sac, or bag, filled with liquid in which the embryo/fetus floats during prenatal life.

analytical intelligence One of three types of intelligence in Sternberg's triarchic theory of intelligence; the type of intelligence typically measured on IQ tests, including the ability to plan, remember facts, and organize information.

androgynous One of four sex-role types suggested by the work of Bem and others; a type characterized by high levels of both masculine and feminine qualities.

anorexia nervosa Eating disorder characterized by self-starvation.

anoxia A shortage of oxygen. This is one of the potential risks at birth, and it can result in brain damage if it is prolonged.

Asperger's disorder A disorder in which children possess the other characteristics of autistic disorder but have intact language and cognitive skills.

assimilation That part of the adaptation process proposed by Piaget that involves absorbing new experiences or information into existing schemes. Experience is not taken in "as is," however, but is modified (or interpreted) somewhat so as to fit the preexisting schemes.

association areas Parts of the brain where sensory, motor, and intellectual functions are linked.

attachment A subtype of affectional bond in which the presence of the partner adds a special sense of security, a "safe base," for the individual.

attachment behaviors The collection of (probably) instinctive behaviors of one person toward another that bring about or maintain proximity and caregiving, such as the smile of the young infant; behaviors that reflect an attachment.

attention deficit disorder (ADD) Term sometimes used interchangeably with ADHD, but more properly used to describe the subset of children who show attention problems without hyperactivity.

attention deficit hyperactivity disorder (ADHD) A disorder in which a child shows both significant problems in focusing attention and physical hyperactivity.

attention problems A category of psychopathologies that impair one's ability to concentrate, including attention deficit hyperactivity disorder, attention deficit disorder, and hyperkinetic disorder.

atypical development An enduring pattern of behavior that is unusual, compared to the behavior of others of the child's age, and that interferes with the child's development in some significant way.

auditory acuity How well one can hear.

authoritarian style One of the three parental styles described by Baumrind, characterized by high levels of control and maturity demands and low levels of nurturance and communication.

authoritative style One of the three parental styles described by Baumrind, characterized by high levels of control, nurturance, maturity demands, and communication.

autistic disorder A disorder in which children have much more limited language skills than others of the same age, along with an inability to engage in reciprocal social relationships, and a severely limited range of interests.

automaticity The ability to recall information from long-term memory without effort.

axon The long-tubular extension of a neuron; the terminal fibers of the axon serve as transmitters in the synaptic connection with the dendrites of other neurons.

babbling The repetitive vocalizing of consonant-vowel combinations by an infant, typically beginning at about 6 months of age.

Babinski reflex A reflex found in very young infants that causes them to splay out their toes in response to a stroke on the bottom of the foot.

Bayley Scales of Infant Development The best-known and most widely used test of infant "intelligence."

behavior genetics The study of the genetic contributions to behavior or traits such as intelligence or personality.

behaviorism The theoretical view that defines development in terms of behavior changes caused by environmental influences.

Big Five The five primary dimensions of adult personality identified by researchers: extraversion, agreeableness, conscientiousness, neuroticism, and openness/intellect.

bilingual education As practiced in the United States, a school program for students who are not proficient in English in which instruction in basic subject matter is given in the children's native language during the first 2 or 3 years of schooling, with a gradual transition to full English instruction over several years.

birth order A child's position in the sequence of children within a family, such as first-born, later-born, or only child.

blastocyst Name for the mass of cells from roughly 4 to 10 days after fertilization.

bone age A measure of physical maturation based on x-ray examination of bones, typically the wrist and hand bones. Two children of the same chronological age may have different bone age because their rates of physical maturation differ.

bulimia Eating disorder characterized by alternating periods of binging and purging.

case studies In-depth studies of individuals.

cephalocaudal One of two basic patterns of physical development in infancy (the other is proximodistal), in which development proceeds from the head downward.

cesarean section (c-section) Delivery of the child through an incision in the mother's abdomen.

childhood-onset conduct disorder Conduct disorder beginning in childhood; the pattern is linked to rejection by peers and to conduct problems that persist into adolescence and adulthood.

chorion The outer layer of cells of the blastocyst during prenatal development, from which both the placenta and the umbilical cord are formed.

chromosomes The structures, arrayed in 23 pairs, within each cell in the body that contain genetic information. Each chromosome is made up of many segments, called genes.

class inclusion The principle that subordinate classes of objects are included in superordinate classes.

classical conditioning One of three major types of learning. An automatic, or unconditioned, response such as an emotion or a reflex comes to be triggered by a new cue, called the conditional stimulus, after having been paired several times with that stimulus.

clinical depression (major depressive disorder) A combination of sad mood, sleeping and eating disturbances, and difficulty concentrating that lasts 6 months or longer.

clique A group of four to six friends with strong affectional bonds and high levels of group solidarity and loyalty; the term is used by researchers to describe a self-chosen group of friends.

cognitive-developmental theories Developmental theories that emphasize children's actions on the environment and suggest that age-related changes in reasoning precede and explain changes in other domains.

colic A pattern of persistent and often inconsolable crying, totaling more than 3 hours a day, found in some infants in the first 3 to 4 months of life.

color constancy The ability to see the color of an object as remaining the same despite changes in illumination or shadow.

competence A person's basic, underlying level of skill, displayed under ideal circumstances. It is not possible to measure competence directly.

concrete operations stage Piaget's term for the stage of development between ages 6 and 12, during which children become able to think logically.

conduct disorder Diagnostic term for a pattern of deviant behavior including high levels of aggressive, antisocial, or delinquent acts.

conscience The list of "don'ts" in the superego; violation of any of these leads to feelings of guilt.

conscientiousness One of the Big Five personality traits; a person who scores high on this trait is characterized by efficiency, organization, planfulness, and reliability.

conservation The understanding that the quantity or amount of a substance remains the same even when there are external changes in its shape or arrangement. Typically, children do not have this understanding until after age 5.

constraint As used in discussions of language development, an assumption that is presumed to be built-in or learned early (a "default option") by

which a child figures out what words refer to. Examples include the principle of contrast and the whole object constraint.

control group A group of participants in an experiment who receive either no special treatment or some neutral treatment.

conventional morality The second level of moral development proposed by Kohlberg, in which a person's judgments are dominated by considerations of group values and laws.

conventional rules As defined by Turiel, arbitrary, socially defined rules specific to a particular culture, subculture, group, or setting, such as "Don't run in the halls" or "Smoking allowed only in designated areas."

cooing Making repetitive vowel sounds, particularly the *uuu* sound; the behavior develops early in the prelinguistic period, when babies are between about 1 and 4 months of age.

corpus callosum The structure that connects the right and left hemispheres of the cerebral cortex.

correlation A statistic used to describe the strength of a relationship between two variables. It can range from -1.00 to $+1.00$. The closer it is to $+1.00$ or -1.00, the stronger the relationship being described.

cortex The convoluted gray portion of the brain, which governs most complex thought, language, and memory.

creative intelligence One of three types of intelligence described by Sternberg in his triarchic theory of intelligence; includes insightfulness and the ability to see new relationships among events or experiences.

critical period Any time period during development when an organism is especially responsive to and learns from a specific type of stimulation. The same stimulation at other points in development has little or no effect.

cross-cultural research Any study that involves comparisons of different cultures or contexts.

cross-modal transfer The ability to transfer information gained through one sense to another sense at a later time (for example, identifying visually something you had previously explored only tactually).

cross-sectional design A form of research study in which samples of participants from several different age groups are studied at the same time.

crowd A larger and looser group of friends than a clique, normally made up of several cliques that have joined together; a reputation-based group, common in adolescent subculture, with widely agreed-upon characteristics.

cumulative deficit Any difference between groups in IQ or achievement test scores that becomes larger over time.

deductive logic Reasoning from the general to the particular, from a rule to an expected instance or from a theory to a hypothesis, characteristic of formal operational thinking.

delinquency A subcategory of conduct disorder involving explicit law-breaking.

dendrites The branchlike part of a neuron that forms one half of a synaptic connection to other nerves. Dendrites develop rapidly in the final 2 prenatal months and the first year after birth.

deoxyribonucleic acid (DNA) The chemical of which chromosomes are composed.

dependent variable The variable in an experiment that is expected to show the impact of manipulations of the independent variable; also called the *outcome variable*.

depression A combination of sad mood and difficulty carrying out daily functions.

developmental psychopathology A relatively new approach to the study of deviance that emphasizes that normal and abnormal development have common roots and that pathology can arise from many different pathways.

developmental science The study of age-related changes in behavior, thinking, emotions, and social relationships.

difficult child An infant who is irritable and irregular in behavior.

dilation A key process in the first stage of childbirth, during which the cervix widens sufficiently to allow the infant's head to pass into the birth canal. Full dilation is 10 centimeters.

dominant/recessive pattern of inheritance The pattern of genetic transmission in which a single dominant gene influences a person's phenotype, but an individual must have two recessive genes to express a recessive trait.

Down syndrome (trisomy 21) A genetic anomaly in which every cell contains three copies of chromosome 21 rather than two. Children born with this genetic pattern are usually mentally retarded and have characteristic physical features.

easy child An infant who adapts easily to change and who exhibits regular patterns of eating, sleeping, and alertness.

eclecticism The use of multiple theoretical perspectives to explain and study human development.

effacement The flattening of the cervix, which, along with dilation, is a key process of the first stage of childbirth.

ego In Freudian theory, the portion of the personality that organizes, plans, and keeps the person in touch with reality. Language and thought are both ego functions.

egocentrism A cognitive state in which the individual (typically a child) sees the world only from his own perspective, without awareness that there are other perspectives.

ego ideal The list of "dos" in the superego; violation of any of these leads to feelings of shame.

embryo The name given to the developing organism during the period of prenatal development between about 2 weeks and 8 weeks after conception, beginning with implantation of the blastocyst in the uterine wall.

embryonic stage The second stage of prenatal development, from week 2 through week 8, when the embryo's organs form.

empathy As defined by Hoffman, "a vicarious affective response that does not necessarily match another's affective state but is more appropriate to the other's situation than to one's own" (1984, p. 285).

empiricism The view that perceptual abilities are learned.

endocrine glands Glands (including the adrenals, the thyroid, the pituitary, the testes, and the ovaries) that secrete hormones governing overall physical growth and sexual maturing.

English-as-a-second-language (ESL) An alternative to bilingual education; children who are not proficient in English attend academic classes taught entirely in English but then spend several hours in a separate class to receive English-language instruction.

equilibration The third part of the adaptation process proposed by Piaget, involving a periodic restructuring of schemes to create a balance between assimilation and accommodation.

ethnic group "A subgroup whose members are perceived by themselves and others to have a common origin and culture, and shared activities in which the common origin or culture is an essential ingredient" (Porter & Washington, 1993, p. 140).

ethnicity An individual's membership in an ethnic group.

experiment A research method for testing a causal hypothesis, in which participants are assigned randomly to experimental and control groups and the experimental group is then provided with a particular experience that is expected to alter behavior in some fashion.

experimental group A group of participants in an experiment who receive a particular treatment intended to produce some specific effect.

expressive language Sounds, signs, or symbols used to communicate meaning.

externalizing problems A category of psychopathologies that includes any deviant behavior primarily directed toward others, such as conduct disorders.

extraversion One of the Big Five personality traits; a person who scores high on this trait is characterized by assertiveness, energy, enthusiasm, and outgoingness.

extremely low birth weight (ELBW) Term for any baby born with a weight below 1,000 grams (2.2 pounds).

fallopian tube The tube between the ovary and the uterus down which the ovum travels to the uterus and in which conception usually occurs.

false belief principle The understanding that another person might have a false belief and the ability to determine what information might cause the false belief. A child's understanding of the false belief principle is one key sign of the emergence of a representational theory of mind.

family structure The configuration of individuals in a child's household.

fast-mapping The ability to categorically link new words to real-world referents.

feminine One of four sex-role types suggested by the work of Bem and others; a type characterized by high scores on femininity measures and low scores on masculinity measures.

fetal alcohol syndrome (FAS) A pattern of abnormalities, including mental retardation and minor physical anomalies, often found in children born to alcoholic mothers.

fetal stage The third stage of prenatal development, from week 8 to birth, when growth and organ refinement take place.

fetus The name given to the developing organism from about 8 weeks after conception until birth.

fontanel One of several "soft spots" in the skull that are present at birth but disappear when the bones of the skull grow together.

foreclosure One of four identity statuses proposed by Marcia, involving an ideological or occupational commitment without a previous reevaluation.

formal operations stage Piaget's name for the fourth and final major stage of cognitive development, occurring during adolescence, when the child becomes able to manipulate and organize ideas or hypothetical situations as well as objects.

fraternal (dizygotic) twins Children carried in the same pregnancy but who develop from two separately fertilized ova. They are no more alike genetically than other pairs of siblings.

full scale IQ The WISC-IV score that takes into account verbal and non-verbal scale scores.

gametes Sperm and ova. These cells, unlike all other cells of the body, contain only 23 chromosomes rather than 23 pairs.

gender concept The full understanding that gender is constant and permanent, unchanged by appearance.

gender constancy The final stage in development of gender concept, in which the child understands that gender doesn't change even though there may be external changes (in clothing or hair length, for example).

gender identity The first stage in the development of gender concept, in which a child labels self and others correctly as male or female.

gender schema theory A theory of the development of gender concept and sex-role behavior that proposes that, between about 18 months and age 2 or 3, a child creates a fundamental schema by which to categorize people, objects, activities, and qualities by gender.

gender stability The second stage in the development of gender concept, in which the child understands that a person's gender stays the same throughout life.

gene A uniquely coded segment of DNA in a chromosome that affects one or more specific body processes or developments.

genotype The pattern of characteristics and developmental sequences mapped in the genes of any specific individual, which will be modified by individual experience into the phenotype.

germinal stage The first stage of prenatal development, beginning at conception and ending at implantation of the zygote in the uterus (approximately the first 2 weeks).

glial cells One of two major classes of cells making up the nervous system; glial cells provide firmness and structure, the "glue" to hold the system together.

goal-corrected partnership Term used by Bowlby to describe the form of the child-parent attachment in the preschool years, in which the two partners, through improved communication, negotiate the form and frequency of contact between them.

gonadotrophic hormones Two hormones secreted by the pituitary gland at the beginning of puberty that stimulate the development of glands in the testes and ovaries, which then begin to secrete testosterone or estrogen.

goodness-of-fit The degree to which an infant's environment and his or her temperament work together.

habituation An automatic decrease in the intensity of a response to a repeated stimulus, enabling a child or adult to ignore the familiar and focus attention on the novel.

handedness A strong preference for using primarily one hand or the other; it develops between 3 and 5 years of age.

hedonistic reasoning A form of prosocial moral reasoning described by Eisenberg in which the child is concerned with consequences to self rather than moral considerations, roughly equivalent to Kohlberg's stage 2.

heterozygous Term describing the genetic pattern when the two genes in the pair at any given genetic locus carry different instructions, such as a gene for blue eyes from one parent and a gene for brown eyes from the other parent.

hippocampus A brain structure that is involved in the transfer of information to long-term memory.

holophrase A combination of a gesture and a single word that conveys more meaning than just the word alone; often seen and heard in children between 12 and 18 months old.

homozygous Term describing the genetic pattern when the two genes in the pair at any given genetic locus both carry the same instructions.

horizontal decalage Piaget's term for school-aged children's inconsistent performance on concrete operations tasks.

hostile aggression Aggressive verbal behavior intended to hurt another's feelings.

hyperkinetic syndrome Term used by European psychologists for attention deficit hyperactivity disorder.

hypothetico-deductive reasoning Piaget's term for the form of reasoning that is part of formal operational thought and involves not just deductive logic but also the ability to consider hypotheses and hypothetical possibilities.

id In Freudian theory, the inborn, primitive portion of the personality, the storehouse of libido, the basic energy that continually pushes for immediate gratification.

identical (monozygotic) twins Children carried in the same pregnancy who develop from the same fertilized ovum. They are genetic clones of each other.

identification The process of taking into oneself (incorporating) the qualities and ideas of another person, which Freud thought was the result of the

Oedipus conflict between ages 3 and 5. The child attempts to become like the parent of the same sex.

identity achievement One of four identity statuses proposed by Marcia, involving the successful resolution of an identity "crisis" and resulting in a new commitment.

identity diffusion One of four identity statuses proposed by Marcia, involving neither a current reevaluation of identity nor a firm personal commitment.

identity versus role confusion As hypothesized by Erikson, the psychosocial stage in which a teenager must develop a sense of personal identity or else enter adulthood with a sense of confusion about his or her place in the world.

inclusive education General term for education programs that assign physically, mentally, or emotionally disabled children to regular classrooms and that provide any special services required by the child in that classroom.

independent variable A condition or event that an experimenter varies in some systematic way in order to observe the impact of that variation on participants' behavior.

individuation The process of psychological, social, and physical separation from parents that begins in adolescence.

inductive logic Reasoning from the particular to the general, from experience to broad rules, characteristic of concrete operational thinking.

information-processing theories A set of theories based on the idea that humans process information in ways that are similar to those used in computers.

insecure attachment An internal working model of relationships in which the child does not as readily use the parent as a safe base and is not readily consoled by the parent if upset. Includes three subtypes of attachment: avoidant, ambivalent, and disorganized/disoriented.

instrumental aggression Aggressive behavior intended to achieve a goal, such as obtaining a toy from another child.

intelligence A set of abilities defined in various ways by different psychologists but generally agreed to include the ability to reason abstractly, the ability to profit from experience, and the ability to adapt to varying environmental contexts.

intelligence quotient (IQ) Originally defined in terms of a child's mental age and chronological age, IQ is now computed by comparing a child's performance with that of other children of the same chronological age.

internalizing problems A category of psychopathologies that includes anxiety and depression and other conditions in which deviant behavior is directed inwardly, against the self.

internal models of experience A theoretical concept emphasizing that each child creates a set of core ideas or assumptions about the world, the self, and relationships with others through which all subsequent experience is filtered.

internal working model As applied to social relationships, a cognitive construction of the workings of relationships, such as expectations of support or affection, trustworthiness, and so on. The earliest relationships may form the template for such a cognitive construction.

intersensory integration The combining of information from two or more senses to form a unified perceptual whole (such as combining the sight of mouth movements with the sound of particular words).

invented spelling A strategy young children with good phonological awareness skills use when they write.

lateralization The process through which brain functions are divided between the two hemispheres of the cerebral cortex.

learning disability (LD) A term broadly used to describe an unexpected or unexplained problem in learning to read, spell, or calculate and more precisely used to refer to a neurological dysfunction that causes such effects.

learning theories Psychological theories that explain development in terms of accumulated learning experiences.

libido The term used by Freud to describe the basic, unconscious, instinctual sexual energy in each individual.

longitudinal design A form of research study in which the same participants are observed or assessed repeatedly over a period of months or years.

low birth weight (LBW) Term for any baby born with a weight below 2,500 grams (5.5 pounds), including both those born too early (preterm) and those who are small for date.

masculine One of four sex-role types suggested by the work of Bem and others; a type characterized by high scores on masculinity measures and low scores on femininity measures.

maturation Sequential patterns of change that are governed by instructions contained in the genetic code and shared by all members of a species.

mean length of utterance (MLU) The average number of meaningful units in a sentence. Each basic word is one meaningful unit, as is each inflection.

medulla A portion of the brain that lies immediately above the spinal cord; it is largely developed at birth.

menarche Onset of menstruation.

mental age Term used by Binet and Simon and Terman in the early calculation of IQ scores to refer to the age level of IQ test items a child could successfully answer. Used in combination with the child's chronological age to calculate an IQ score.

mental retardation An intellectual disability defined most often as an IQ below 70 combined with poor adaptive behavior.

metacognition General and rather loosely used term describing knowledge of one's own thinking processes: knowing what one knows, and how one learns.

metamemory Knowledge about one's own memory processes.

midbrain A section of the brain lying above the medulla and below the cortex that regulates attention, sleeping, waking, and other automatic functions; it is largely developed at birth.

moral development The process of learning to distinguish between right and wrong in accordance with cultural values.

moral realism stage The first of Piaget's stages of moral development, in which children believe that rules are inflexible.

moral relativism stage The second of Piaget's stages of moral development, in which children understand that many rules can be changed through social agreement.

moral rules As defined by Turiel, universal and obligatory rules reflecting basic principles that guarantee the rights of others.

moratorium One of four identity statuses proposed by Marcia, involving an ongoing reexamination of identity but no new commitment.

Moro reflex The reflex that causes infants to extend their legs, arms, and fingers, arch the back, and draw back the head when startled (for example, by a loud sound or a sensation of being dropped).

motherese (infant-directed speech) The simplified, higher-pitched speech that adults use with infants and young children.

motor development Growth and change in ability to perform both gross motor skills (such as walking or throwing) and fine motor skills (such as drawing or writing).

multifactorial pattern of inheritance The pattern of genetic transmission in which both genes and environment influence the phenotype.

multiple intelligences Eight types of intelligence (linguistic, logical/mathematical, spatial, bodily kinesthetic, musical, interpersonal, intrapersonal, and naturalistic) proposed by Howard Gardner.

myelination The process by which an insulating layer of a substance called myelin is added to neurons.

nativism The view that perceptual abilities are inborn.

naturalistic observation A research method in which participants are observed in their normal environments.

needs-oriented reasoning A form of prosocial moral reasoning proposed by Eisenberg in which the child expresses concern directly for the other person's need, even if the other's need conflicts with the child's own wishes or desires.

negative reinforcement The process of strengthening a behavior by the removal or cessation of an unpleasant stimulus.

neglected children Children who are seldom described by peers as either liked or disliked.

neglecting style A fourth parenting style suggested by Maccoby and Martin, involving low levels of both acceptance and control.

neo-Piagetian theory A theory of cognitive development that assumes that Piaget's basic ideas are correct but that uses concepts from information-processing theory to explain children's movement from one stage to the next.

neurons The cells in the nervous system that are responsible for transmission and reception of nerve impulses.

neuroticism One of the Big Five personality traits; a person who scores high on this trait is characterized by anxiety, self-pity, tenseness, and emotional instability.

neurotransmitters Chemicals that accomplish the transmission of signals from one neuron to another at synapses.

norms Average ages at which developmental events happen.

obesity Most often defined as a body weight 20% or more above the normal weight for height, or a Body Mass Index at the 85th percentile or above.

object constancy The general phrase describing the ability to see objects as remaining the same despite changes in sensory information about them.

objective self The component of the self-concept that involves awareness of the self as an object with properties.

object permanence The understanding that objects continue to exist even when they cannot be directly perceived.

Oedipus conflict The pattern of events that Freud believed occur between ages 3 and 5, when the child experiences a sexual desire for the parent of the opposite sex; the resulting fear of possible reprisal from the parent of the same sex is resolved when the child identifies with that parent.

openness/intellect One of the Big Five personality traits; a person who scores high on this trait is characterized by curiosity, imagination, insight, originality, and wide interests.

operant conditioning The type of learning in which the probability of a person's performing some behavior is increased or decreased because of the consequences it produces.

operation Term used by Piaget for a complex, internal, abstract scheme, first seen at about age 6.

operational efficiency A neo-Piagetian term for the number of schemes an individual can place into working memory at one time.

ossification The process of hardening by which soft tissue becomes bone.

overextension The inappropriate use of a word to designate an entire category of objects, such as when a child uses the word *kitty* to refer to all animate objects.

ovum The cell released monthly from a woman's ovaries, which, if fertilized, forms the basis for the developing organism.

parallel play Form of play seen in toddlers, in which children play next to, but not with, one another.

perceptual constancies A collection of mental rules that allow humans to perceive shape, size, and color as constant even when perceptual conditions (such as amount of light, angle of view, and the like) change.

perceptual reasoning index Tests on the WISC-IV, such as block design and picture completion, that tap nonverbal visual-processing abilities.

performance The behavior shown by a person under real-life rather than ideal circumstances. Even when researchers are interested in competence, all they can ever measure is performance.

permissive style One of the three parenting styles described by Baumrind, characterized by high levels of nurturance and low levels of control, maturity demands, and communication.

personality The collection of relatively enduring patterns of reacting to and interacting with others and the environment that distinguishes each child or adult.

pervasive developmental disorders (PDDs) A group of disorders in which children exhibit severe disturbances in social relationships.

phenotype The expression of a particular set of genetic information in a specific environment; the observable result of the joint operation of genetic and environmental influences.

phonological awareness Understanding of the rules governing the sounds of a language as well as knowledge of the connection between sounds and the way they are represented in written language.

phonology The sound patterns of a particular language and the rules for combining them.

pituitary gland Gland that provides the trigger for release of hormones from other glands.

placenta An organ that develops between the fetus and the wall of the uterus during gestation.

polygenic pattern of inheritance Any pattern of genetic transmission in which multiple genes contribute to the outcome, such as is presumed to occur for complex traits such as intelligence or temperament.

popular children Children who are described as well-liked by a majority of peers.

positive reinforcement The process of strengthening a behavior by the presentation of some pleasurable or positive stimulus.

practical intelligence One of three types of intelligence in Sternberg's triarchic theory of intelligence; often called "street smarts," this type of intelligence includes skill in applying information to the real world or solving practical problems.

pragmatics The rules for the use of language in communicative interaction, such as the rules for taking turns and the style of speech that is appropriate for different listeners.

preconventional morality The first level of moral development proposed by Kohlberg, in which moral judgments are dominated by consideration of what will be punished and what feels good.

prelinguistic phase The period before a child speaks his or her first words.

preoperational stage Piaget's term for the second major stage of cognitive development, from about 18 months to about age 6, marked by the ability to use symbols.

preterm infant An infant born before 38 weeks gestational age.

primary circular reactions Piaget's phrase to describe a baby's simple repetitive actions in substage 2 of the sensorimotor stage, organized around the baby's own body; the baby repeats some action in order to have some desired outcome occur again, such as putting his thumb in his mouth to repeat the good feeling of sucking.

primitive reflexes Collection of reflexes seen in young infants that gradually disappear during the first year of life, including the Moro and Babinski reflexes.

principled (postconventional) morality The third level of moral development proposed by Kohlberg, in which considerations of justice, individual rights, and social contracts dominate moral judgment.

principle of contrast The assumption that every word has a different meaning, which leads a child to assume that two or more different words refer to different objects.

processing speed index Timed tests on the WISC-IV, such as symbol search, that measure how rapidly an examinee processes information.

production deficiency A pattern whereby an individual can use some mental strategy if reminded to do so but fails to use the strategy spontaneously.

prosocial behavior Voluntary behavior intended to benefit another, such as giving away or sharing possessions, money, or time, with no obvious self-gain; altruism.

proximodistal One of two basic patterns of physical development in infancy (the other is cephalocaudal), in which development proceeds from the center outward, that is, from the trunk to the limbs.

psychoanalytic theories Developmental theories based on the assumption that age-related change results from maturationally determined conflicts between internal drives and society's demands.

psychosexual stages The stages of personality development suggested by Freud, consisting of the oral, anal, phallic, latency, and genital stages.

psychosocial stages The stages of personality development suggested by Erikson, involving tasks centered on trust, autonomy, initiative, industry, identity, intimacy, generativity, and ego integrity.

puberty The series of hormonal and physical changes at adolescence that bring about sexual maturity.

punishment The removal of a desirable stimulus or the administration of an unpleasant consequence after some undesired behavior in order to stop the behavior.

reaction range Term used by some psychologists for the range of possible outcomes (phenotypes) for some variable, given basic genetic patterning (the genotype). In the case of IQ scores, the reaction range is estimated at 20 to 25 points.

receptive language Comprehension of spoken language.

reciprocal friendship A friendship in which each partner identifies the other as a friend; also, a quality of friendship in school-aged children, when friendship is for the first time perceived as being based on reciprocal trust.

reflexes Automatic body reactions to specific stimulation, such as the knee jerk or the Moro reflex. Adults have many reflexes, but the newborn also has some primitive reflexes that disappear as the cortex develops.

rejected children Unpopular children who are explicitly avoided and not chosen as playmates or friends.

relational aggression Aggression aimed at damaging another person's self-esteem or peer relationships, such as by using ostracism or threats of ostracism, cruel gossiping, or facial expressions of disdain.

relative right-left orientation The ability to identify right and left from multiple perspectives.

respiratory distress syndrome A problem frequently found in infants born more than 6 weeks before term, in which the infant's lungs lack a chemical (surfactant) needed to keep air sacs inflated.

responsiveness An aspect of parent-child interaction; a responsive parent is sensitive to the child's cues and reacts appropriately, following the child's lead.

reticular formation The part of the brain that regulates attention.

reversibility One of the most critical of the operations Piaget identified as part of the concrete operations period: the understanding that actions and mental operations can be reversed.

role-taking The ability to look at a situation from another person's perspective.

rooting reflex The reflex that causes an infant to automatically turn toward a touch on the cheek, open the mouth, and make sucking movements.

scaffolding The term used by Bruner to describe the process by which a teacher (or parent, older child, or other person in the role of teacher) structures a learning encounter with a child, so as to lead the child from step to step—a process consistent with Vygotsky's theory of cognitive development.

schematic learning The development of expectancies concerning what actions lead to what results or what events tend to go together.

scheme Piaget's word for the basic actions of knowing, including both physical actions (sensorimotor schemes, such as looking or reaching) and mental actions (such as classifying, comparing, and reversing). An experience is assimilated into a scheme, and the scheme is created or modified through accommodation.

secondary circular reactions Repetitive actions in substage 3 of the sensorimotor period, oriented around external objects; the infant repeats some action in order to have some outside event recur, such as hitting a mobile repeatedly so that it moves.

secular trend A pattern of change in some characteristic over several cohorts, such as systematic changes in the average timing of menarche or in average height or weight.

secure attachment An internal working model of relationships in which the child uses the parent as a safe base and is readily consoled after separation, when fearful, or when otherwise stressed.

selective attention The ability to focus cognitive activity on the important elements of a problem or situation.

self-concept One's knowledge of and thoughts about the set of qualities attributed to the self.

self-efficacy Bandura's term for an individual's belief in his or her ability to accomplish tasks.

self-esteem A global evaluation of one's own worth; an aspect of self-concept.

semantics A particular language's system of meaning and the rules for conveying meaning.

sensation-seeking A strong desire to experience the emotional and physical arousal associated with risky behaviors such as fast driving and unprotected sex.

sensitive period A period during which particular experiences can best contribute to proper development. It is similar to a critical period, but the effects of deprivation during a sensitive period are not as severe as during a critical period.

sensorimotor stage Piaget's term for the first major stage of cognitive development, from birth to about 18 months, when the child uses sensory and motor skills to act on the environment.

sequential design A form of research study that combines cross-sectional and longitudinal designs in some way.

sex role The set of behaviors, attitudes, rights, duties, and obligations that are seen as appropriate for being male or female in any given culture.

sex-typed behavior Behavior that matches a culturally defined sex role.

sexually transmitted diseases (STDs) Category of disease spread by sexual contact, including chlamydia, genital warts, syphilis, gonorrhea, and HIV; also called venereal diseases.

shape constancy The ability to see an object's shape as remaining the same despite changes in the shape of the retinal image; a basic perceptual constancy.

short-term storage space (STSS) A neo-Piagetian term for working memory capacity.

size constancy The ability to see an object's size as remaining the same despite changes in size of the retinal image; a key element in size constancy is the ability to judge depth.

slow-to-warm-up child An infant who may seem unresponsive but who simply takes more time to respond than other infants do.

small-for-date infant An infant who weighs less than is normal for the number of weeks of gestation completed.

social class A group with a certain position within a given society, based on income, occupation, and/or education. In the United States, there are four broad social classes: upper class, middle class, working class, and lower class (also called poverty level).

social cognition Thinking about and understanding the emotions of and interactions and relationships among people.

social referencing Using another person's emotional reaction to some situation as a basis for deciding one's own reaction. A baby does this when she checks her parent's facial expression or body language before responding positively or negatively to something new.

social status A term used by psychologists to refer to how well an individual child is liked by his or her peers.

spatial cognition The ability to infer rules from and make predictions about the movement of objects in space.

spatial perception The ability to identify and act on relationships of objects in space; in most people, this skill is lateralized to the right cerebral hemisphere.

sperm The cells produced in a man's testes that may fertilize an ovum following intercourse.

Stanford-Binet The best-known U.S. intelligence test. It was written by Lewis Terman and his associates at Stanford University and based on the first tests by Binet and Simon.

states of consciousness The periodic shifts in alertness, sleepiness, crankiness, and so on that characterize an infant's behavior.

Strange Situation A series of episodes used by Mary Ainsworth and others in studies of attachment. The child is observed with the mother, with a stranger, alone, when reunited with the stranger, and when reunited with the mother.

structured immersion An alternative to traditional bilingual education used in classrooms in which all children speak the same non-English native language. All basic instruction is in English, paced so that the children can comprehend, with the teacher translating only when absolutely necessary.

subjective self The component of the self-concept that involves awareness of the "I," the self that is separate from others.

submersion An approach to education of non–English-speaking students in which they are assigned to a classroom where instruction is given in English and are given no supplemental language assistance; also known as the "sink or swim" approach.

sudden infant death syndrome (SIDS) The unexpected death of an infant who otherwise appears healthy; also called crib death. The cause of SIDS is unknown.

superego In Freudian theory, the "conscience" part of personality, which contains parental and societal values and attitudes incorporated during childhood.

synapse The point of communication between two neurons, where nerve impulses are passed from one neuron to another by means of chemicals called neurotransmitters.

synaptogenesis The process of synapse formation.

syntax The rules for forming sentences in a particular language.

task goal A goal orientation associated with a desire for self-improvement.

telegraphic speech Term used by Roger Brown to describe the earliest sentences created by most children, which sound a bit like telegrams because they include key nouns and verbs but generally omit all other words and grammatical inflections.

temperament Inborn predispositions that form the foundations of personality.

teratogens Substances such as viruses and drugs or events that can cause birth defects.

tertiary circular reactions The deliberate experimentation with variations of previous actions, characteristic of substage 5 of the sensorimotor period, according to Piaget.

theory of mind Ideas that collectively explain other people's ideas, beliefs, desires, and behavior.

tracking Following a moving object with the eyes.

triarchic theory of intelligence A theory advanced by Robert Sternberg, proposing the existence of three types of intelligence: analytical, creative, and practical.

umbilical cord The cord connecting the embryo/fetus to the placenta, containing two arteries and one vein.

underextension The use of words to apply only to specific objects, such as a child's use of the word *cup* to refer only to one particular cup.

undifferentiated One of four sex-role types suggested by the work of Bem and others; a type characterized by low scores on both masculinity and femininity measures.

uterus The female organ in which the embryo/fetus develops (popularly referred to as the *womb*).

utilization deficiency Using some specific mental strategy without deriving benefit from it.

verbal comprehension index Tests on the WISC-IV that tap verbal skills such as knowledge of vocabulary and general information.

very low birth weight (VLBW) Term for any baby born with a weight below 1,500 grams (3.3 pounds).

visual acuity How well one can see.

warmth versus hostility The key dimension of emotional tone used to describe family interactions.

WISC-IV The most recent revision of the Wechsler Intelligence Scales for Children, a well-known IQ test developed in the United States that includes both verbal and performance (nonverbal) subtests.

working memory index Tests on the WISC-IV, such as digit span, that measure working memory efficiency.

WPPSI-III The third revision of the Wechsler Preschool and Primary Scale of Intelligence.

zone of proximal development In Vygotsky's theory, the range of tasks that are slightly too difficult for a child to do alone but that can be accomplished successfully with guidance from an adult or more experienced child.

zygote The single cell formed from separate sperm and egg cells at conception.

References

Abdelrahman, A., Rodriguez, G., Ryan, J., French, J., & Weinbaum, D. (1998). The epidemiology of substance use among middle school students: The impact of school, familial, community and individual risk factors. *Journal of Child & Adolescent Substance Abuse, 8,* 55–75.

Aboud, F. E., & Doyle, A. B. (1995). The development of in-group pride in black Canadians. *Journal of Cross-Cultural Psychology, 26,* 243–254.

Abramovitch, R., Pepler, D., & Corter, C. (1982). Patterns of sibling interaction among preschool-age children. In M. E. Lamb & B. Sutton-Smith (Eds.), *Sibling relationships: Their nature and significance across the life-span* (pp. 61–86). Hillsdale, NJ: Erlbaum.

Abrams, B. (1994). Weight gain and energy intake during pregnancy. *Clinical Obstetrics and Gynecology, 37,* 515–527.

Abrams, E. J., Matheson, P. B., Thomas, P. A., Thea, D. M., Krasinski, K., Lambert, G., Shaffer, N., Bamji, M., Hutson, D., Grimm, K., Kaul, A., Bateman, D., Rogers, M., & New York City Perinatal HIV Transmission Collaborative Study Group. (1995). Neonatal predictors of infection status and early death among 332 infants at risk of HIV-1 infection monitored prospectively from birth. *Pediatrics, 96,* 451–458.

Accardo, P., Tomazic, T., Fete, T., Heaney, M., Lindsay, R., & William, B. (1997). Maternally reported fetal activity levels and developmental diagnoses. *Clinical Pediatrics, 36,* 279–283.

Achenbach, T. M. (1982). *Developmental psychopathology* (2nd ed.). New York: Wiley.

Achenbach, T. M. (1993). Taxonomy and comorbidity of conduct problems: Evidence from empirically based approaches. *Development and Psychopathology, 5,* 51–64.

Achenbach, T. M. (1995). Developmental issues in assessment, taxonomy, and diagnosis of child and adolescent psychopathology. In D. Cicchetti & D. J. Cohen (Eds.), *Developmental psychopathology: Vol. 1. Theory and methods* (pp. 57–80). New York: Wiley.

Achenbach, T. M., & Edelbrock, C. S. (1981). Behavioral problems and competencies reported by parents of normal and disturbed children aged 4 through 16. *Monographs of the Society for Research in Child Development, 46*(1, Serial No. 188).

Adab, N., Jacoby, A., Smith, D., & Chadwick, D. (2001). Additional educational needs in children born to mothers with epilepsy. *Journal of Neurology, Neurosurgery & Psychiatry, 70,* 15–21.

Adachi, M., Trehub, S., & Abe, J. (2004). Perceiving emotion in children's songs across age and culture. *Japanese Psychological Research, 46,* 322–336.

Adams, M., & Henry, M. (1997). Myths and realities about words and literacy. *School Psychology Review, 26,* 425–436.

Adams, M. J. (1990). *Beginning to read: Thinking and learning about print.* Cambridge, MA: MIT Press.

Adams, M. J., Trieman, R., & Pressley, M. (1998). Reading, writing, and literacy. In W. Damon (Ed.), *Handbook of child psychology: Vol 4. Child psychology in practice* (5th ed., pp. 275–355). New York: Wiley.

Adelman, W., & Ellen, J. (2002). Adolescence. In A. Rudolph, R. Kamei, & K. Overby (Eds.), *Rudolph's fundamentals of pediatrics* (3rd ed., pp. 70–109) New York: McGraw-Hill.

Adesman, A. R. (1996). Fragile X syndrome. In A. J. Capute & P. J. Accardo (Eds.), *Developmental disabilities in infancy and childhood: Vol. 2. The spectrum of developmental disabilities* (2nd ed., pp. 255–269). Baltimore: Brookes.

Adolph, K., & Berger, S. (2005). Physical and motor development. In M. Bornstein & M. Lamb (Eds.), *Developmental science: An advanced textbook* (5th ed., pp. 223–283). Hillsdale, NJ: Erlbaum.

Agnew, J., Dorn, C., & Eden, G. (2004). Effect of intensive training on auditory processing and reading skills. *Brain & Language, 88,* 21–25.

Ahadi, S. A., & Rothbart, M. K. (1994). Temperament, development, and the Big Five. In C. F. Halverson, Jr., G. A. Kohnstamm, & R. P. Martin (Eds.), *The developing structure of temperament and personality from infancy to adulthood* (pp. 189–207). Hillsdale, NJ: Erlbaum.

Ahlsten, G., Cnattingius, S., & Lindmark, G. (1993). Cessation of smoking during pregnancy improves foetal growth and reduces infant morbidity in the neonatal period: A population-based prospective study. *Acta Paediatrica, 82,* 177–182.

Ahmed, E., & Braithwaite, V. (2004). Bullying and victimization: Cause for concern for both families and schools. *Social Psychology of Education, 7,* 35–54.

Aiken, L. (1997). *Psychological testing and assessment* (9th ed.). Boston: Allyn & Bacon.

Ainsworth, M. D. S. (1972). Attachment and dependency: A comparison. In J. L. Gewirtz (Ed.), *Attachment and dependency* (pp. 97–138). Washington, DC: Winston.

Ainsworth, M. D. S. (1982). Attachment: Retrospect and prospect. In C. M. Parkes & J. Stevenson-Hinde (Eds.), *The place of attachment in human behavior* (pp. 3–30). New York: Basic Books.

Ainsworth, M. D. S. (1989). Attachments beyond infancy. *American Psychologist, 44,* 709–716.

Ainsworth, M. D. S., Blehar, M., Waters, E., & Wall, S. (1978). *Patterns of attachment.* Hillsdale, NJ: Erlbaum.

Ainsworth, M. D. S., & Marvin, R. S. (1995). On the shaping of attachment theory and research: An interview with Mary D. S. Ainsworth (Fall 1994). *Monographs of the Society for Research in Child Development, 60*(244, Nos. 2–3), 3–21.

Akhtar, N., Carpenter, M., & Tomasello, M. (1996). The role of discourse novelty in early word learning. *Child Development, 67,* 635–645.

Akiba, D. (1998). Cultural variations in body esteem: How young adults in Iran and the United States view their own appearances. *The Journal of Social Psychology, 138,* 539–540.

Aksan, N., & Kochanska, G. (2005). Conscience in childhood: Old questions, new answers. *Developmental Psychology, 41,* 506–516.

Aksu-Koc, A. A., & Slobin, D. I. (1985). The acquisition of Turkish. In D. I. Slobin (Ed.), *The crosslinguistic study of language acquisition: Vol. 1. The data* (pp. 839–878). Hillsdale, NJ: Erlbaum.

Alan Guttmacher Institute. (2004). *U.S. teenage pregnancy statistics with comparative statistics for women aged 20–24.* Retrieved May 6, 2005, from http://www.guttmacher.org/pubs/teen_stats.html

Alexander, K. L., Entwisle, D. R., & Dauber, S. L. (1993). First-grade classroom behavior: Its short- and long-term consequences for school performance. *Child Development, 64,* 801–814.

Alho, O., Laära, E., & Oja, H. (1996). How should relative risk estimates for acute otitis media in children aged less than 2 years be perceived? *Journal of Clinical Epidemiology, 49,* 9–14.

Allen, C., & Kisilevsky, B. (1999). Fetal behavior in diabetic and nondiabetic pregnant women: An exploratory study. *Developmental Psychobiology, 35,* 69–80.

Allen, J., Porter, M., McFarland, F., Marsh, P., & McElhaney, K. (2005). The two faces of adolescents' success with peers: Adolescent popularity, social adaptation, and deviant behavior. *Child Development, 76,* 747–760.

Allen, K., & Rainie, L. (2002). *Parents online.* Retrieved March 16, 2004, from http://www.pewinternet.org

Allen, M. (2004). Minority language school systems: A profile of students, schools and communities. *Education Quarterly Review, 9,* 9–29.

Alsaker, F. D. (1995). Timing of puberty and reactions to pubertal change. In M. Rutter (Ed.), *Psychosocial disturbances in young people: Challenges for prevention* (pp. 37–82). Cambridge, England: Cambridge University Press.

Alsaker, F. D., & Olweus, D. (1992). Stability of global self-evaluations in early adolescence: A cohort longitudinal study. *Journal of Research on Adolescence, 2,* 123–145.

Alspaugh, J. (1998). Achievement loss associated with the transition to middle school and high school. *Journal of Educational Research, 92,* 20–25.

Alt, M., Plante, E., & Creusere, M. (2004). Semantic features in fast-mapping: Performance of preschoolers with specific language impairment versus preschoolers with normal language. *Journal of Speech, Language, & Hearing Research, 47*, 407–420.

Álvarez, J., Martín, A. F., Vergeles, M., & Martín, A. H. (2003). Substance use in adolescence: Importance of parental warmth and supervision. *Psicothema, 15*, 161–166.

Amato, P. R. (1993). Children's adjustment to divorce: Theories, hypotheses, and empirical support. *Journal of Marriage and the Family, 55*, 23–38.

Amato, S. (1998). Human genetics and dysmorphy. In R. Behrman & R. Kliegman (Eds.), *Nelson essentials of pediatrics* (3rd ed., pp. 129–146). Philadelphia: Saunders.

Ambert, A. (2001). *Families in the new millennium.* Boston, MA: Allyn & Bacon.

Ambuel, B. (1995). Adolescents, unintended pregnancy, and abortion: The struggle for a compassionate social policy. *Current Directions in Psychological Science, 4*, 1–5.

American Academy of Pediatrics Committee on Infectious Diseases (2000). Recommended childhood immunization schedule. *Pediatrics, 97*, 143–146.

American Academy of Pediatrics Committee on Psychosocial Aspects of Child and Family Health. (1998). Guidance for effective discipline. *Pediatrics, 101*, 723–728.

American College of Obstetrics and Gynecology (ACOG). (2001, December 12). *ACOG addresses latest controversies in obstetrics.* Retrieved April 1, 2004, from http://www.acog.org

American College of Obstetrics and Gynecology (ACOG). (2002, November 29). *Rubella vaccination recommendation changes for pregnant women.* Retrieved April 2, 2004, from http://www.acog.org

American College of Obstetrics and Gynecology (ACOG). (2004). *Ethics in obstetrics and gynecology.* Washington, DC: Author.

American Demographics. (2001). It's all homework. Retrieved June 23, 2004, from http://articles.findarticles.com/p/articles/mi_m4021/is_2001_Nov_1/ai_79501196

American Psychiatric Association. (2000a). *Practice guidelines for eating disorders.* Retrieved June 9, 2005, from http://www.psych.org

American Psychiatric Association. (2000b). *The diagnostic and statistical manual of mental disorders* (4th ed., Text Revision). Washington, DC: Author

American Psychological Association. (1993). *Violence and youth: Psychology's response: Vol. 1. Summary report of the American Psychological Association Commission on Violence and Youth.* Washington, DC: American Psychological Association.

Anderman, E. (1998). The middle school experience: Effects on the math and science achievement of adolescents with LD. *Journal of Learning Disabilities, 31*, 128–138.

Anderman, E., Maehr, M., & Midgley, C. (1999). Declining motivation after the transition to middle school: Schools can make a difference. *Journal of Research & Development in Education, 32*, 131–147.

Anderman, E., & Midgley, C. (1997). Changes in achievement goal orientations, perceived academic competence, and grades across the transition to middle-level schools. *Contemporary Educational Psychology, 22*, 269–298.

Anderman, L. (1999). Classroom goal orientation, school belonging and social goals as predictors of students' positive and negative affect following the transition to middle school. *Journal of Research & Development in Education, 32*, 89–103.

Anderman, L., & Anderman, E. (1999). Social predictors of changes in students' achievement goal orientations. *Contemporary Educational Psychology, 24*, 21–37.

Anderson, C., & Dill, K. (2000). Video games and aggressive thoughts, feelings, and behavior in the laboratory and in life. *Journal of Personality & Social Psychology, 78*, 772–790.

Anderson, D., Huston, A., Schmitt, K., Linebarger, D., & Wright, J. (2001). Early childhood television viewing and adolescent behavior: The recontact study. *Monographs of the Society for Research in Child Development, 66*, vii–147.

Anderson, R. (1998). Examining language loss in bilingual children. *Electronic Multicultural Journal of Communication Disorders, 1*.

Andersson, B. (1989). Effects of public day-care: A longitudinal study. *Child Development, 60*, 857–886.

Andersson, B. (1992). Effects of day-care on cognitive and socioemotional competence of thirteen-year-old Swedish schoolchildren. *Child Development, 63*, 20–36.

Andreou, E., & Metallidou, P. (2004). The relationship of academic and social cognition to behaviour in bullying situations among Greek primary school children. *Educational Psychology, 24*, 27–41.

Andreucci, C. (2003). Comment l'idée d'instabilité du volume vient aux enfants. *Enfance, 55*, 139–158.

Anglin, J. M. (1993). Vocabulary development: A morphological analysis. *Monographs of the Society for Research in Child Development, 58*(Serial No. 238).

Anglin, J. M. (1995, April). *Word learning and the growth of potentially knowable vocabulary.* Paper presented at the biennial meetings of the Society for Research in Child Development, Indianapolis.

Anisfeld, M. (1991). Neonatal imitation. *Developmental Review, 11*, 60–97.

Anisfeld, M., Turkewitz, G., Rose, S., Rosenberg, F., Sheiber, F., Couturier-Fagan, D., Ger, J., & Sommer, I. (2001). No compelling evidence that newborns imitate oral gestures. *Infancy, 2*, 111–122.

Annett, M. (2003). Do the French and the English differ for hand skill asymmetry? Handedness subgroups in the sample of Doyen and Carlier (2002) and in English schools and universities. *Laterality: Asymmetries of Body, Brain, & Cognition, 8*, 233–245.

Anshel, M. H. (1990). *Sport psychology: From theory to practice.* Scottsdale, AZ: Gorsuch Scarisbrick.

Anthony, J., & Lonigan, C. (2004). The nature of phonological awareness: Converging evidence from four studies of preschool and early grade school children. *Journal of Educational Psychology, 96*, 43–55.

Apgar, V. A. (1953). A proposal for a new method of evaluation of the newborn infant. *Current Research in Anesthesia and Analgesia, 32*, 260–267.

Aranha, M. (1997). Creativity in students and its relation to intelligence and peer perception. *Revista Interamericana de Psicologia, 31*, 309–313.

Armstrong, T. (2003). Effect of moral reconation therapy on the recidivism of youthful offenders: A randomized experiment. *Criminal Justice & Behavior, 30*, 668–687.

Arn, P., Chen, H., Tuck-Muller, C. M., Mankinen, C., Wachtel, G., Li, S., Shen, C.-C., & Wachtel, S. S. (1994). SRVX, a sex reversing locus in Xp21.2 → p22.11. *Human Genetics, 93*, 389–393.

Arnold, D. H., McWilliams, L., & Arnold, E. H. (1998). Teacher discipline and child misbehavior in day care: Untangling causality with correlational data. *Developmental Psychology, 34*, 276–287.

Arseneault, R., Tremblay, R., Boulerice, B., & Saucier, J. (2002). Obstetrical complications and violent delinquency: Testing two developmental pathways. *Child Development, 73*, 496–508.

Aslin, R., Saffran, J., & Newport, E. (1998). Computation of conditional probability statistics by 8-month-old infants. *Psychological Science, 9*, 321–324.

Aslin, R. N. (1981). Experiential influences and sensitive periods in perceptual development: A unified model. In R. N. Aslin, J. R. Alberts, & M. R. Petersen (Eds.), *Development of perception. Psychobiological perspectives: Vol. 2. The visual system* (pp. 45–93). New York: Academic Press.

Aslin, R. N. (1987). Motor aspects of visual development in infancy. In P. Salapatek & L. Cohen (Eds.), *Handbook of infant perception: Vol. 1. From sensation to perception* (pp. 43–113). Orlando, FL: Academic Press.

Assibey-Mensah, G. (1997). Role models and youth development: Evidence and lessons from the perceptions of African-American male youth. *Western Journal of Black Studies, 21*, 242–252.

Associated Press. (2005, February 8). "World's smallest baby goes home." Retrieved July 5, 2005, from http://www.cbsnews.com/stories/2005/02/08/health/main672488.shtml

Astington, J., & Jenkins, J. (1999). A longitudinal study of the relation between language and theory-of-mind development. *Developmental Psychology, 35*, 1311–1320.

Astington, J. W., & Jenkins, J. M. (1995, April). *Language and theory of mind: A theoretical review and a longitudinal study.* Paper presented at the biennial meetings of the Society for Research in Child Development, Indianapolis.

Ateah, C., & Durrant, J. (2005). Maternal use of physical punishment in response to child misbehavior: Implications for child abuse prevention. *Child Abuse & Neglect, 29*, 169–185.

Attie, I., & Brooks-Gunn, J. (1995). The development of eating regulation across the life span. In D. Cicchetti & D. J. Cohen (Eds.), *Developmental psychopathology: Vol. 2. Risk, disorder, and adaptation* (pp. 332–368). New York: Wiley.

Australian Clearinghouse for Youth Studies. (2005). *Australian youth facts and stats.* Retrieved July 9, 2005, from http://www.youthfacts.com.au/index.php?option=displaypage&Itemid=209&op=page

Avis, J., & Harris, P. L. (1991). Belief-desire reasoning among Baka children: Evidence for a universal conception of mind. *Child Development, 62*, 460–467.

Aylward, G. (2002). Cognitive and neuropsychological outcomes: More than IQ scores. *Mental Retardation & Developmental Disabilities Research Reviews, 8*, 234–240.

Bachman, J., Safron, D., Sy, S., & Schulenberg, J. (2003). Wishing to work: New perspectives on how adolescents' part-time work intensity is linked to educational disengagement, substance use, and other problem behaviours. *International Journal of Behavioral Development, 27*, 301–315.

Bachman, J. G., & Schulenberg, J. (1993). How part-time work intensity relates to drug use, problem behavior, time use, and satisfaction among high school seniors: Are these consequences or merely correlates? *Developmental Psychology, 29*, 220–235.

Baghurst, P. A., McMichael, A. J., Tong, S., Wigg, N. R., Vimpani, G. V., & Robertson, E. F. (1995). Exposure to environmental lead and visual-motor integration at age 7 years: The Port Pirie cohort study. *Epidemiology, 6*, 104–109.

Baghurst, P. A., McMichael, A. J., Wigg, N. R., Vimpani, G. V., Robertson, E. F., Roberts, R. J., & Tong, S. (1992). Environmental exposure to lead and children's intelligence at the age of seven years. *New England Journal of Medicine, 327*, 1279–1284.

Bagwell, C. L., Newcomb, A. F., & Bukowski, W. M. (1998). Preadolescent friendship and peer rejection as predictors of adult adjustment. *Child Development, 69*, 140–153.

Bahrick, L., & Lickliter, R. (2000). Intersensory redundancy guides attentional selectivity and perceptual learning in infancy. *Developmental Psychology, 36*, 190–201.

Bailey, J., Brobow, D., Wolfe, M., & Mikach, S. (1995). Sexual orientation of adult sons of gay fathers. *Developmental Psychology, 31*, 124–129.

Bailey, J., Pillard, R., Dawood, K., Miller, M., Farrer, L., Trivedi, S., & Murphy, R. (1999). A family history study of male sexual orientation using three independent samples. *Behavior Genetics, 29*, 79–86.

Bailey, J., & Zucker, K. (1995). Childhood sex-typed behavior and sexual orientation: A conceptual analysis and quantitative review. *Developmental Psychology, 31*, 43–55.

Bailey, J. M., & Pillard, R. C. (1991). A genetic study of male sexual orientation. *Archives of General Psychiatry, 48*, 1089–1096.

Bailey, J. M., Pillard, R. C., Neale, M. C., & Agyei, Y. (1993). Heritable factors influence sexual orientation in women. *Archives of General Psychiatry, 50*, 217–223.

Bailey, S., & Zvonkovic, A. (2003). Parenting after divorce: Nonresidential parents' perceptions of social and institutional support. *Journal of Divorce & Remarriage, 39*, 59–80.

Baillargeon, R. (1994). How do infants learn about the physical world? *Current Directions in Psychological Science, 3*, 133–140.

Baker, J. M., & Zigmond, N. (1995). The meaning and practice of inclusion for students with learning disabilities: Themes and implications from the five cases. *The Journal of Special Education, 29*, 163–180.

Baker, S., Victor, J., Chambers, A., & Halverson, C. (2004). Adolescent personality: A five-factor model construct validation. *Assessment, 11*, 303–315.

Baker-Ward, L. (1995, April). *Children's reports of a minor medical emergency procedure.* Paper presented at the biennial meetings of the Society for Research in Child Development, Indianapolis.

Baker-Ward, L., Gordon, B. N., Ornstein, P. A., Larus, D. M., & Clubb, P. A. (1993). Young children's long-term retention of a pediatric examination. *Child Development, 64*, 1519–1533.

Bakketeig, L. S., Cnattingius, S., & Knudsen, L. B. (1993). Socioeconomic differences in fetal and infant mortality in Scandinavia. *Journal of Public Health Policy, 14*(Spring), 82–90.

Balaban, M. T. (1995). Affective influences on startle in five-month-old infants: Reactions to facial expressions of emotion. *Child Development, 66*, 28–36.

Ball, E. (1997). Phonological awareness: Implications for whole language and emergent literacy programs. *Topics in Language Disorders, 17*, 14–26.

Bamford, F. N., Bannister, R. P., Benjamin, C. M., Hillier, V. F., Ward, B. S., & Moore, W. M. O. (1990). Sleep in the first year of life. *Developmental Medicine and Child Neurology, 32*, 718–724.

Bandura, A. (1973). *Aggression: A social learning analysis.* Englewood Cliffs, NJ: Prentice Hall.

Bandura, A. (1977). *Social learning theory.* Englewood Cliffs, NJ: Prentice Hall.

Bandura, A. (1982). Self-efficacy mechanism in human agency. *American Psychologist, 37*, 122–147.

Bandura, A. (1986). *Social foundations of thought and action: A social cognitive theory.* Englewood Cliffs, NJ: Prentice Hall.

Bandura, A. (1989). Social cognitive theory. *Annals of Child Development, 6*, 1–60.

Bandura, A. (1997). *Self-efficacy. The exercise of control.* New York: Freeman.

Bandura, A. (2004). Swimming against the mainstream: The early years from chilly tributary to transformative mainstream. *Behaviour Research & Therapy, 42*, 613–630.

Bandura, A., & Bussey, K. (2004). On broadening the cognitive, motivational, and sociostructural scope of theorizing about gender development and functioning: Comment on Martin, Ruble, and Szkrybalo (2002). *Psychological Bulletin, 130*, 691–701.

Bandura, A., Caprara, G., Barbaranelli, C., Gerbino, M., & Pastorelli, C. (2003). Role of affective self-regulatory efficacy in diverse spheres of psychosocial functioning. *Child Development, 74*, 769–782.

Banerji, M., & Dailey, R. A. (1995). A study of the effects of an inclusion model on students with specific learning disabilities. *Journal of Learning Disabilities, 28*, 511–522.

Bangerter, A., & Heath, C. (2004). The Mozart effect: Tracking the evolution of a scientific legend. *British Journal of Social Psychology, 43*, 605–623.

Barber, B., Eccles, J., & Stone, M. (2001). Whatever happened to the jock, the brain, and the princess? Young adult pathways linked to adolescent activity involvement and social identity. *Journal of Adolescent Research, 16*, 429–455.

Bardoni, B., Zanaria, E., Guioli, S., Floridia, G., Worley, K. C., Tonini, G., Ferrante, E., Chiumello, G., McCabe, E. R. B., Fraccaro, M., Zuffardi, O., & Camerino, G. (1994). A dosage sensitive locus at chromosome Xp21 is involved in male to female sex reversal. *Nature Genetics, 7*, 497–501.

Barenboim, C. (1977). Developmental changes in the interpersonal cognitive system from middle childhood to adolescence. *Child Development, 48*, 1467–1474.

Barenboim, C. (1981). The development of person perception in childhood and adolescence: From behavioral comparisons to psychological constructs to psychological comparisons. *Child Development, 52*, 129–144.

Barkley, R. A. (1997). Behavioral inhibition, sustained attention, and executive functions: Constructing a unifying theory of ADHD. *Psychological Bulletin, 121*, 65–94.

Barkley, R. A., Fischer, M., Edelbrock, C. S., & Smallish, L. (1990). The adolescent outcome of hyperactive children diagnosed by research criteria: I. An 8-year prospective follow-up study. *Journal of the American Academy of Child and Adolescent Psychiatry, 29*, 546–557.

Barnard, K. E., Hammond, M. A., Booth, C. L., Bee, H. L., Mitchell, S. K., & Spieker, S. J. (1989). Measurement and meaning of parent-child interaction. In J. J. Morrison, C. Lord, & D. P. Keating (Eds.), *Applied developmental psychology* (Vol. 3, pp. 40–81). San Diego, CA: Academic Press.

Barnes, H. L., & Olson, D. H. (1985). Parent-adolescent communication and the circumplex model. *Child Development, 56*, 438–447.

Barness, L. A., & Curran, J. S. (1996). Nutrition. In R. E. Behrman, R. M. Kliegman, & A. M. Arvin (Eds.), *Nelson textbook of pediatrics* (15th ed., pp. 141–184). Philadelphia: Saunders.

Barnett, D., Manley, J., & Cicchetti, D. (1993). Defining child maltreatment: The interface between policy and research. In D. Cicchetti & S. Toth (Eds.), *Child abuse, child development, and social policy* (pp. 7–73). Norwood, NJ: Ablex.

Barnett, W. S. (1993). Benefit-cost analysis of preschool education: Findings from a 25-year follow-up. *American Journal of Orthopsychiatry, 63*, 500–508.

Barnow, S., Lucht, M., & Freyberger, H. (2001). Influence of punishment, emotional rejection, child abuse, and broken home on aggression in adolescence: An examination of aggressive adolescents in Germany. *Psychopathology, 34*, 167–173.

Barr, R., Hopkins, B., & Green, J. (2000). *Crying as a sign, a symptom, and a signal.* New York: Cambridge University Press.

Barrett, G. V., & Depinet, R. L. (1991). A reconsideration of testing for competence rather than for intelligence. *American Psychologist, 46*, 1012–1024.

Bartels, M., Rietveld, M., Van Baal, G., & Boomsma, D. (2002). Genetic and environmental influences on the development of intelligence. *Behavior Genetics, 32*, 237–249.

Barth, R. (2001). Research outcomes of prenatal substance exposure and the need to review policies and procedures regarding child abuse reporting. *Child Welfare, 80*, 275–296.

Bartsch, K. (1993). Adolescents' theoretical thinking. In R. M. Lerner (Ed.), *Early adolescence. Perspectives on research, policy, and intervention* (pp. 143–157). Hillsdale, NJ: Erlbaum.

Basham, P. (2001). Home schooling: From the extreme to the mainstream. *Public Policy Sources/The Fraser Institute, 51.* Retrieved June 23, 2004, from http://www.fraserinstitute.ca/admin/books/files/homeschool.pdf

Bass, C., & Coleman, H. (1997). Enhancing the cultural identity of early adolescent male African Americans. *Professional School Counseling, 1,* 48–51.

Bates, E. (1993). Commentary: Comprehension and production in early language development. *Monographs of the Society for Research in Child Development, 58*(3–4, Serial No. 233), 222–242.

Bates, E., Bretherton, I., Beeghly-Smith, M., & McNew, S. (1982). Social bases of language development: A reassessment. In H. W. Reese & L. P. Lipsitt (Eds.), *Advances in child development and behavior* (Vol. 16, pp. 8–68). New York: Academic Press.

Bates, E., Marchman, V., Thal, D., Fenson, L., Dale, P., Reznick, J. S., Reilly, J., & Hartung, J. (1994). Developmental and stylistic variation in the composition of early vocabulary. *Journal of Child Language, 21,* 85–123.

Bates, E., O'Connell, B., & Shore, C. (1987). Language and communication in infancy. In J. D. Osofsky (Ed.), *Handbook of infant development* (2nd ed., pp. 149–203). New York: Wiley.

Bates, J. E. (1989). Applications of temperament concepts. In G. A. Kohnstamm, J. E. Bates, & M. K. Rothbart (Eds.), *Temperament in childhood* (pp. 321–356). Chichester, England: Wiley.

Baumeister, R., Bushman, B., & Campbell, W. (2000). Self-esteem, narcissism, and aggression: Does violence result from low self-esteem or from threatened egotism? *Current Directions in Psychological Science, 9,* 26–29.

Baumeister, R., Campbell, J., Krueger, J., & Vohs, K. (2003). Does high self-esteem cause better performance, interpersonal success, happiness, or healthier lifestyles? *Psychological Science in the Public Interest, 4*(1), 1–44.

Baumeister, R., Smart, L., & Boden, J. (1996). Relation of threatened egotism to violence and aggression: The dark side of high self-esteem. *Psychological Review, 103,* 5–33.

Bauminger, N., & Kasari, C. (1999). Brief report: Theory of mind in high-functioning children with autism. *Journal of Autism & Developmental Disorders, 29,* 81–86.

Baumrind, D. (1971). Current patterns of parental authority. *Developmental Psychology Monograph, 4*(1, Part 2).

Baumrind, D. (1973). The development of instrumental competence through socialization. In A. D. Pick (Ed.), *Minnesota symposium on child psychology* (Vol. 7, pp. 3–46). Minneapolis: University of Minnesota Press.

Baumrind, D. (1991). The influence of parenting style on adolescent competence and substance use. *Journal of Early Adolescence, 11,* 56–95.

Baydar, N., & Brooks-Gunn, J. (1991). Effects of maternal employment and child-care arrangements on preschoolers' cognitive and behavioral outcomes: Evidence from the children of the National Longitudinal Survey of Youth. *Developmental Psychology, 27,* 932–945.

Baydar, N., & Brooks-Gunn, J., & Furstenberg, F. F. (1993). Early warning signs of functional illiteracy: Predictors in childhood and adolescence. *Child Development, 64,* 815–829.

Bayley, N. (1969). *Bayley Scales of Infant Development.* New York: Psychological Corporation.

Bayley, N. (1993). *Bayley Scales of Infant Development: Birth to two years.* San Antonio, TX: Psychological Corporation.

Beaudry, M., Dufour, R., & Marcoux, S. (1995). Relation between infant feeding and infections during the first six months of life. *Journal of Pediatrics, 126,* 191–197.

Beautrais, A., Joyce, P., & Mulder, R. (1999). Personality traits and cognitive styles as risk factors for serious suicide attempts among young people. *Suicide & Life-Threatening Behavior, 29,* 37–47.

Bee, H. L., Barnard, K. E., Eyres, S. J., Gray, C. A., Hammond, M. A., Spietz, A. L., Snyder, C., & Clark, B. (1982). Prediction of IQ and language skill from perinatal status, child performance, family characteristics, and mother-infant interaction. *Child Development, 53,* 1135–1156.

Behrend, D., Scofield, J., & Kleinknecht, E. (2001). Beyond fast mapping: Young children's extensions of novel words and novel facts. *Developmental Psychology, 37,* 690–705.

Beilstein, C., & Wilson, J. (2000). Landmarks in route learning by girls and boys. *Perceptual & Motor Skills, 91,* 877–882.

Bell, J., & Bromnick, R. (2003). The social reality of the imaginary audience: A ground theory approach. *Adolescence, 38,* 205–219.

Bell, L. G., & Bell, D. C. (1982). Family climate and the role of the female adolescent: Determinants of adolescent functioning. *Family Relations, 31,* 519–527.

Belsky, J. (1985). Prepared statement on the effects of day care. In *Improving child care services: What can be done?* Select Committee on Children, Youth, and Families, House of Representatives, 98th Cong., 2d Sess., Washington, DC: U.S. Government Printing Office.

Belsky, J. (1992). Consequences of child care for children's development: A deconstructionist view. In A. Booth (Ed.), *Child care in the 1990s. Trends and consequences* (pp. 83–94). Hillsdale, NJ: Erlbaum.

Belsky, J. (2001). Developmental risks (still) associated with early child care. *Journal of Child Psychology & Psychiatry & Allied Disciplines, 42,* 845–859.

Belsky, J. (2002). Quantity counts: Amount of child care and children's socioemotional development. *Journal of Developmental and Behavioral Pediatrics, 23,* 167–170.

Belsky, J., Friedman, S., & Hsieh, K. (2001). Testing a core emotion-regulation prediction: Does early attentional persistence moderate the effect of infant negative emotionality on later development? *Child Development, 72,* 123–133.

Belsky, J., Hsieh, K., & Crnic, K. (1996). Infant positive and negative emotionality: One dimension or two? *Developmental Psychology, 32,* 289–298.

Belsky, J., Lang, M. E., & Rovine, M. (1985). Stability and change in marriage across the transition to parenthood: A second study. *Journal of Marriage and the Family, 47,* 855–865.

Belsky, J., & Rovine, M. (1988). Nonmaternal care in the first year of life and the security of infant-parent attachment. *Child Development, 59,* 157–167.

Bem, S. L. (1974). The measurement of psychological androgyny. *Journal of Consulting and Clinical Psychology, 42,* 155–162.

Bem, S. L. (1981). Gender schema theory: A cognitive account of sex-typing. *Psychological Review, 88,* 354–364.

Bem, S. L. (1989). Genital knowledge and gender constancy in preschool children. *Child Development, 60,* 649–662.

Benbow, C. P. (1988). Sex differences in mathematical reasoning ability in intellectually talented preadolescents: Their nature, effects, and possible causes. *Behavioral & Brain Sciences, 11,* 169–232.

Bender, S. L., Word, C. O., DiClemente, R. J., Crittenden, M. R., Persaud, N. A., & Ponton, L. E. (1995). The developmental implications of prenatal and/or postnatal crack cocaine exposure in preschool children: A preliminary report. *Journal of Developmental and Behavioral Pediatrics, 16,* 418–424.

Benenson, J. F. (1994). Ages four to six years: Changes in the structures of play networks of girls and boys. *Merrill-Palmer Quarterly, 40,* 478–487.

Benoit, D., & Parker, K. C. H. (1994). Stability and transmission of attachment across three generations. *Child Development, 65,* 1444–1456.

Berch, D. B., & Bender, B. G. (1987, December). Margins of sexuality. *Psychology Today, 21,* 54–57.

Berger, L. (2004). Income, family structure, and child maltreatment risk. *Children and Youth Services Review, 26,* 725–748.

Bergeson, T., & Trehub, S. (1999). Mothers' singing to infants and preschool children. *Infant Behavior and Development, 22,* 53–64.

Berkowitz, G. S., Skovron, M. L., Lapinski, R. H., & Berkowitz, R. L. (1990). Delayed childbearing and the outcome of pregnancy. *New England Journal of Medicine, 322,* 659–664.

Bernardo, A., & Calleja, M. (2005). The effects of stating problems in bilingual students' first and second languages on solving mathematical word problems. *Journal of Genetic Psychology, 166,* 117–128.

Berndt, T. J. (1983). Social cognition, social behavior, and children's friendships. In E. T. Higgins, D. N. Ruble, & W. W. Hartup (Eds.), *Social cognition and social development: A sociocultural perspective* (pp. 158–192). Cambridge, England: Cambridge University Press.

Berndt, T. J. (1986). Children's comments about their friendships. In M. Perlmutter (Ed.), *Minnesota symposia on child psychology* (Vol. 18, pp. 189–212). Hillsdale, NJ: Erlbaum.

Berndt, T. J. (1992). Friendship and friends' influence in adolescence. *Current Directions in Psychological Science, 1,* 156–159.

Berndt, T. J., & Hoyle, S. G. (1985). Stability and change in childhood and adolescent friendships. *Developmental Psychology, 21,* 1007–1015.

Berndt, T. J., & Keefe, K. (1995). Friends' influence on adolescents' adjustment to school. *Child Development, 66,* 1312–1329.

Berney, B. (1996). Epidemiology of childhood lead poisoning. In S. M. Pueschel, J. G. Linakis, & A. C. Anderson (Eds.), *Lead poisoning in childhood* (pp. 15–35). Baltimore: Brookes.

Bernhard, J., Lefebvre, M., Kilbride, K., Chud, G., & Lange, R. (1998). Troubled relationships in early childhood education: Parent-teacher interactions in ethnoculturally diverse child care settings. *Early Education & Development, 9*, 5–28.

Berninger, V., Abbott, R., Zook, D., Ogier, S., et al. (1999). Early intervention for reading disabilities: Teaching the alphabet principle in a connectionist framework. *Journal of Learning Disabilities, 32*, 491–503.

Berninger, V., & Richards, T. (2002). *Brain literacy for educators and psychologists*. San Diego, CA: Academic Press.

Berry, D., Sheehan, R., Heschel, R., Knafl, K., Melkus, G., & Grey, M. (2004). Family-based interventions for childhood obesity: A review. *Journal of Family Nursing, 10*, 429–449.

Bertenthal, B. I., & Campos, J. J. (1987). New directions in the study of early experience. *Child Development, 58*, 560–567.

Berthier, N., DeBlois, S., Poirier, C., Novak, M., & Clifton, R. (2000). Where's the ball? Two- and three-year-olds reason about unseen events. *Developmental Psychology, 36*, 394–401.

Bethus, I., Lemaire, V., Lhomme, M., & Goodall, G. (2005). Does prenatal stress affect latent inhibition? It depends on the gender. *Behavioural Brain Research, 158*, 331–338.

Bettes, B. A. (1988). Maternal depression and motherese: Temporal and intonational features. *Child Development, 59*, 1089–1096.

Bhatt, R. S., & Rovee-Collier, C. (1996). Infants' forgetting of correlated attributes and object recognition. *Child Development, 67*, 172–187.

Bialystok, E. (1997). Effects of bilingualism and biliteracy on children's emerging concepts of print. *Developmental Psychology, 33*.

Bialystok, E., & Majumder, S. (1998). The relationship between bilingualism and the development of cognitive processes in problem solving. *Applied Psycholinguistics, 19*, 69–85.

Bialystok, E., Majumder, S., & Martin, M. (2003). Developing phonological awareness: Is there a bilingual advantage? *Applied Linguistics, 24*, 27–44.

Bialystok, E., Shenfield, T., & Codd, J. (2000). Languages, scripts, and the environment: Factors in developing concepts of print. *Developmental Psychology, 36*, 66–76.

Biederman, J., Hirshfeld-Becker, D., Rosenbaum, J., Herot, C., Friedman, D., Snidman, N., Kagan, J., & Faraone, S. (2001). Further evidence of association between behavioral inhibition and social anxiety in children. *American Journal of Psychiatry, 158*, 1673–1679.

Bigelow, B. J., & La Gaipa, J. J. (1975). Children's written descriptions of friendships: A multidimensional analysis. *Developmental Psychology, 11*, 857–858.

Bigler, R., & Liben, S. (1993). The role of attitudes and interventions in gender-schematic processing. *Child Development, 61*, 1440–1452.

Bigler, R. S. (1995). The role of classification skill in moderating environmental influences on children's gender stereotyping: A study of the functional use of gender in the classroom. *Child Development, 66*, 1072–1087.

Billy, J. O. G., Brewster, K. L., & Grady, W. R. (1994). Contextual effects on the sexual behavior of adolescent women. *Journal of Marriage and the Family, 56*, 387–404.

Binet, A., & Simon, T. (1905). Méthodes nouvelles pour le diagnostic du niveau intellectuel des anormaux [New methods for diagnosing intellectual level in the abnormal]. *Année Psychologie, 11*, 191–244.

Bingham, C. R., Miller, B. C., & Adams, G. R. (1990). Correlates of age at first sexual intercourse in a national sample of young women. *Journal of Adolescent Research, 5*, 18–33.

Birch, D. (1998). The adolescent parent: A fifteen year longitudinal study of school-age mothers and their children. *International Journal of Adolescent Medicine & Health, 10*, 141–153.

Biringen, A. (2000). Emotional availability: Conceptualization and research findings. *American Journal of Orthopsychiatry, 70*, 104–114.

Birney, D., Citron-Pousty, J., Lutz, D., & Sternberg, R. (2005). The development of cognitive and intellectual abilities. In M. Bornstein & M. Lamb (Eds.), *Developmental science: An advanced textbook* (5th ed., pp. 327–358). Hillsdale, NJ: Erlbaum.

Biswas, M. K., & Craigo, S. D. (1994). The course and conduct of normal labor and delivery. In A. H. DeCherney & M. L. Pernoll (Eds.), *Current obstetric and gynecologic diagnosis & treatment* (pp. 202–227). Norwalk, CT: Appleton & Lange.

Bivens, J. A., & Berk, L. E. (1990). A longitudinal study of the development of elementary school children's private speech. *Merrill-Palmer Quarterly, 36*, 443–463.

Bjorklund, D. F., & Coyle, T. R. (1995, April). *Utilization deficiencies, multiple strategy use, and memory development*. Paper presented at the biennial meetings of the Society for Research in Child Development, Indianapolis.

Bjorklund, D. F., Miller, P. H., Coyle, T. R., & Slawinski, J. L. (1997). Instructing children to use memory strategies: Evidence of utilization deficiencies in memory training studies. *Developmental Review, 17*, 411–441.

Bjorklund, D. F., & Muir, J. E. (1988). Remembering on their own: Children's development of free recall memory. In R. Vasta (Ed.), *Annals of child development* (Vol. 5, pp. 79–124). Greenwich, CT: JAI Press.

Black, K. A., & McCartney, K. (1995, April). *Associations between adolescent attachment to parents and peer interactions*. Paper presented at the biennial meetings of the Society for Research in Child Development, Indianapolis.

Blair, C., Greenberg, M., & Crnic, K. (2001). Age-related increases in motivation among children with mental retardation and MA- and CA-matched controls. *American Journal on Mental Retardation, 106*, 511–524.

Blair, S. L., & Johnson, M. P. (1992). Wives' perceptions of the fairness of the division of household labor: The intersection of housework and ideology. *Journal of Marriage and the Family, 54*, 570–581.

Blake, I. K. (1994). Language development and socialization in young African-American children. In P. M. Greenfield & R. R. Cocking (Eds.), *Cross-cultural roots of minority child development* (pp. 167–195). Hillsdale, NJ: Erlbaum.

Blake, S., Ledsky, R., Lehman, T., Goodenow, C., Sawyer, R., & Hack, T. (2001). Preventing sexual risk behaviors among gay, lesbian, and bisexual adolescents. *American Journal of Public Health, 91*, 940–946.

Blass, E. M., Ganchrow, J. R., & Steiner, J. E. (1984). Classical conditioning in newborn humans 2–48 hours of age. *Infant Behavior and Development, 7*, 223–235.

Blau, G. (1996). Adolescent depression and suicide. In G. Blau & T. Gullotta (Eds.), *Adolescent dysfunctional behavior: Causes, interventions, and prevention* (pp. 187–205). Newbury Park, CA: Sage.

Blickstine, I., Jones, C., & Keith, L. (2003). Zygotic-splitting rates after single-embryo transfers in in vitro fertilization. *New England Journal of Medicine, 348*, 2366–2367.

Block, J. (1971). *Lives through time*. Berkeley, CA: Bancroft.

Block, J., & Robins, R. W. (1993). A longitudinal study of consistency and change in self-esteem from early adolescence to early adulthood. *Child Development, 64*, 909–923.

Bloom, L. (1973). *One word at a time*. The Hague: Mouton.

Bloom, L. (1991). *Language development from two to three*. Cambridge, England: Cambridge University Press.

Bloom, L. (1993). *The transition from infancy to language: Acquiring the power of expression*. Cambridge, England: Cambridge University Press.

Bloom, L. (1997, April). *The child's action drives the interaction*. Paper presented at the biennial meetings of the Society for Research in Child Development, Washington, DC.

Bloom, L. (1998). Language acquisition in its developmental context. In W. Damon (Ed.), *Handbook of child psychology: Vol. 2. Cognition, perception, and language* (5th ed., pp. 309–370). New York: Wiley.

Blumberg, F., & Sokol, L. (2004). Boys' and girls' use of cognitive strategies when learning to play video games. *Journal of General Psychology, 131*, 151–158.

Boer, F., Godhart, A. W., & Treffers, P. D. A. (1992). Siblings and their parents. In F. Boer & J. Dunn (Eds.), *Children's sibling relationships: Developmental and clinical issues* (pp. 41–54). Hillsdale, NJ: Erlbaum.

Bogenschneider, K., Wu, M., Raffaelli, M., & Tsay, J. (1998). "Other teens drink, but not my kid": Does parental awareness of adolescent alcohol use protect adolescents from risky consequences? *Journal of Marriage and the Family, 60*, 356–373.

Bohman, M., & Sigvardsson, S. (1990). Outcome in adoption: Lessons from longitudinal studies. In D. M. Brodzinsky (Ed.), *The psychology of adoption* (pp. 93–106). New York: Oxford University Press.

Boldizar, J. P. (1991). Assessing sex typing and androgyny in children: The Children's Sex Role Inventory. *Developmental Psychology, 27*, 505–515.

Bolger, K. (1997, April). *Children's adjustment as a function of timing of family economic hardship*. Paper presented at the biennial meetings of the Society for Research in Child Development, Washington, DC.

Bond, L., Braskamp, D., & Roeber, E. (1996). *The status report of the assessment programs in the United States*. Oakbrook, IL: North Central Regional Educational Laboratory. ERIC Document No. ED 401 333.

Bond, M. H., Nakazato, H., & Shiraishi, D. (1975). Universality and distinctiveness in dimensions of Japanese person perception. *Journal of Cross-Cultural Psychology, 6*, 346–357.

Bonde, E., Obel, C., Nedergard, N., & Thomsen, P. (2004). Social risk factors as predictors for parental report of deviant behaviour in 3-year-old children. *Nordic Journal of Psychiatry, 58*, 17–23.

Bong, M. (1998). Tests of the internal/external frames of reference model with subject-specific academic self-efficacy and frame-specific academic self-concepts. *Journal of Educational Psychology, 90,* 102–110.

Borkenau, P., & Ostendorf, F. (1990). Comparing exploratory and confirmatory factor analysis: A study on the five-factor model of personality. *Personality and Individual Differences, 11,* 515–524.

Borkowski, J., Ramey, S., & Bristol-Power, M. (2002). *Parenting and the child's world.* Hillsdale, NJ: Erlbaum.

Bornstein, M., Arterberry, M., & Nash, C. (2005). Perceptual development. In M. Bornstein & M. Lamb (Eds.), *Developmental science: An advanced textbook* (5th ed., pp. 283–326). Hillsdale, NJ: Erlbaum.

Bornstein, M., DiPietro, J., Hahn, C., Painter, K., Haynes, O., & Costigan, K. (2002). Prenatal cardiac function and postnatal cognitive development: An exploratory study. *Infancy, 3,* 475–494.

Bornstein, M. H. (1995). Parenting infants. In M. H. Bornstein (Ed.), *Handbook of parenting: Vol 1. Children and parenting* (pp. 3–39). Mahwah, NJ: Erlbaum.

Bornstein, M. H. (Ed.). (1989). Maternal responsiveness: Characteristics and consequences. *New Directions for Child Development, 43.*

Bornstein, M. H., Tamis-LeMonda, C. S., Tal, J., Ludemann, P., Toda, S., Rahn, C. W., Pecheux, M., Azuma, H., & Vardi, D. (1992). Maternal responsiveness to infants in three societies: The United States, France, and Japan. *Child Development, 63,* 808–821.

Bosch, L., & Sebastian-Galles, N. (1997). Native-language recognition abilities in 4-month-old infants from monolingual and bilingual environments. *Cognition, 65,* 33–69.

Bosworth, R., & Birch, E. (2005). Motion detection in normal infants and young patients with infantile esotropia. *Vision Research, 45,* 1557–1567.

Bouchard, T. J., Jr., & McGue, M. (1981). Familial studies of intelligence: A review. *Science, 212,* 1055–1059.

Bowen, J., Gibson, F., & Hand, P. (2002). Educational outcome at 8 years for children who were born extremely prematurely: A controlled study. *Journal of Pediatrics & Child Health, 38,* 438–444.

Bower, T. G. R. (1966). The visual world of infants. *Scientific American, 215,* 80–92.

Bowerman, M. (1985). Beyond communicative adequacy: From piecemeal knowledge to an integrated system in the child's acquisition of language. In K. E. Nelson (Ed.), *Children's language* (Vol. 5, pp. 369–398). Hillsdale, NJ: Erlbaum.

Bowker, A. (2004). Predicting friendship stability during early adolescence. *Journal of Early Adolescence, 24,* 85–112.

Bowlby, J. (1969). *Attachment and loss: Vol. 1. Attachment.* New York: Basic Books.

Bowlby, J. (1973). *Attachment and loss: Vol. 2. Separation, anxiety, and anger.* New York: Basic Books.

Bowlby, J. (1980). *Attachment and loss: Vol. 3. Loss, sadness, and depression.* New York: Basic Books.

Bowlby, J. (1988a). Developmental psychiatry comes of age. *American Journal of Psychiatry, 145,* 1–10.

Bowlby, J. (1988b). *A secure base.* New York: Basic Books.

Bowler, D., Briskman, J., & Grice, S. (1999). Experimenter effects on children's understanding of false drawings and false beliefs. *Journal of Genetic Psychology, 160,* 443–460.

Boyatzis, C. J., Matillo, G., Nesbitt, K., & Cathey, G. (1995, April). *Effects of "The Mighty Morphin Power Rangers" on children's aggression and prosocial behavior.* Paper presented at the biennial meetings of the Society for Research in Child Development, Indianapolis.

Bradbury, K., & Katz, J. (2002). Women's labor market involvement and family income mobility when marriages end. *New England Economic Review, Q4,* 41–74.

Bradley, R. H., Caldwell, B. M., Rock, S. L., Barnard, K. E., Gray, C., Hammond, M. A., Mitchell, S., Siegel, L., Ramey, C. D., Gottfried, A. W., & Johnson, D. L. (1989). Home environment and cognitive development in the first 3 years of life: A collaborative study involving six sites and three ethnic groups in North America. *Developmental Psychology, 25,* 217–235.

Bradley, R. H., Whiteside, L., Mundfrom, D. J., Casey, P. H., Kelleher, K. J., & Pope, S. K. (1994). Early indications of resilience and their relation to experiences in the home environments of low birthweight, premature children living in poverty. *Child Development, 65,* 346–360.

Bradmetz, J. (1999). Precursors of formal thought: A longitudinal study. *British Journal of Developmental Psychology, 17,* 61–81.

Brand, A., & Brinich, P. (1999). Behavior problems and mental health contacts in adopted, foster, and nonadopted children. *Journal of Child Psychology & Psychiatry & Allied Disciplines, 40,* 1221–1229.

Brandenburg, N. A., Friedman, R. M., & Silver, S. E. (1990). The epidemiology of childhood psychiatric disorders: Prevalence findings from recent studies. *Journal of the American Academy of Child and Adolescent Psychiatry, 29,* 76–83.

Brandon, P. (1999). Determinants of self-care arrangements among school-age children. *Children & Youth Services Review, 21,* 497–520.

Brandon, P., & Hofferth, S. (2003). Determinants of out-of-school childcare arrangements among children in single-mother and two-parent families. *Social Science Research, 32,* 129–147.

Bray, N. W., Fletcher, K. L., & Turner, L. A. (1997). Cognitive competencies and strategy use in individuals with mental retardation. In W. E. MacLean, Jr. (Ed.), *Ellis' handbook of mental deficiency: Psychological theory and research* (3rd ed., pp. 197–217). Mahwah, NJ: Erlbaum.

Brazelton, T. D. (1984). *Neonatal Behavioral Assessment Scale.* Philadelphia: Lippincott.

Breitmayer, B. J., & Ramey, C. T. (1986). Biological nonoptimality and quality of postnatal environment as codeterminants of intellectual development. *Child Development, 57,* 1151–1165.

Breland, H. M. (1974). Birth order, family configuration, and verbal achievement. *Child Development, 45,* 1011–1019.

Brennan, F., & Ireson, J. (1997). Training phonological awareness: A study to evaluate the effects of a program of metalinguistic games in kindergarten. *Reading & Writing, 9,* 241–263.

Bretherton, I. (1991). Pouring new wine into old bottles: The social self as internal working model. In M. R. Gunnar & L. A. Sroufe (Eds.), *The Minnesota symposia on child development* (Vol. 23, pp. 1–42). Hillsdale, NJ: Erlbaum.

Bretherton, I. (1993). From dialogue to internal working models: The co-construction of self in relationships. In C. A. Nelson (Ed.), *The Minnesota symposia on child psychology* (Vol. 26, pp. 237–264). Hillsdale, NJ: Erlbaum.

Briones, T., Klintsova, A., & Greenough, W. (2004). Stability of synaptic plasticity in the adult rat visual cortex induced by complex environment exposure. *Brain Research, 1018,* 130–135.

British Columbia Ministry of Education. (2001). *English as a second language.* Retrieved October 6, 2001, from http://www.bced.gov.bc.ca/esl/policy/introduction.htm

Broberg, A. G., Wessels, H., Lamb, M. E., & Hwang, C. P. (1997). Effects of day care on the development of cognitive abilities in 8-year-olds: A longitudinal study. *Developmental Psychology, 33,* 62–69.

Brockington, I. (1996). *Motherhood and mental health.* Oxford, England: Oxford University Press.

Brody, G., Kim, S., Murry, V., & Brown, A. (2003). Longitudinal direct and indirect pathways linking older sibling competence to the development of younger sibling competence. *Developmental Psychology, 39,* 618–628.

Brody, G. H., Stoneman, Z., & Flor, D. (1995). Linking family processes and academic competence among rural African American youths. *Journal of Marriage and the Family, 47,* 567–579.

Brody, G. H., Stoneman, Z., McCoy, J. K., & Forehand, R. (1992). Contemporaneous and longitudinal associations of sibling conflict with family relationship assessments and family discussions about sibling problems. *Child Development, 63,* 391–400.

Brody, N. (1992). *Intelligence* (2nd ed.). San Diego, CA: Academic Press.

Brody, N. (1997). Intelligence, schooling, and society. *American Psychologist, 52,* 1046–1050.

Broman, C. L. (1993). Race differences in marital well-being. *Journal of Marriage and the Family, 55,* 724–732.

Broman, S. H., Nichols, P. L., & Kennedy, W. A. (1975). *Preschool IQ: Prenatal and early developmental correlates.* Hillsdale, NJ: Erlbaum.

Broman, S. H., Nichols, P. L., Shaughnessy, P., & Kennedy, W. (1987). *Retardation in young children.* Hillsdale, NJ: Erlbaum.

Bronfenbrenner, U. (1979). *The ecology of human development.* Cambridge, MA: Harvard University Press.

Bronfenbrenner, U. (1989). Ecological systems theory. *Annals of Child Development, 6,* 187–249.

Bronfenbrenner, U. (2001). The bioecological theory of human development. In N. Smelser & P. Baltes (Eds.), *International encyclopedia of the social and behavioral sciences* (pp. 6963–6970). New York: Elsevier.

Bronson, G. W. (1991). Infants' differences in rate of visual encoding. *Child Development, 62,* 44–45.

Bronson, G. W. (1994). Infants' transitions toward adult-like scanning. *Child Development, 65,* 1253–1261.

Brook, J., Whiteman, M., Finch, S., & Cohen, P. (2000). Longitudinally foretelling drug use in the late twenties: Adolescent personality and social-environmental antecedents. *Journal of Genetic Psychology, 161,* 37–51.

Brook, U., & Boaz, M. (2005). Attention deficit and hyperactivity disorder/learning disabilities (ADHD/LD): Parental characterization and perception. *Patient Education & Counseling, 57,* 96–100.

Brooks-Gunn, J. (1987). Pubertal processes and girls' psychological adaptation. In R. M. Lerner & T. T. Foch (Eds.), *Biological-psychosocial interactions in early adolescence* (pp. 123–154). Hillsdale, NJ: Erlbaum.

Brooks-Gunn, J. (1988). Commentary: Developmental issues in the transition to early adolescence. In M. R. Gunnar & W. A. Collins (Eds.), *Minnesota symposia on child psychology* (Vol. 21, pp. 189–208). Hillsdale, NJ: Erlbaum.

Brooks-Gunn, J. (1995). Children in families in communities: Risk and intervention in the Bronfenbrenner tradition. In P. Moen, G. H. Elder Jr., & K. Lüscher (Eds.), *Examining lives in context: Perspectives on the ecology of human development* (pp. 467–519). Washington, DC: American Psychological Association.

Brooks-Gunn, J., & Attie, I. (1996). Developmental psychopathology in the context of adolescence. In M. F. Lenzenweger & J. J. Haugaard (Eds.), *Frontiers of developmental psychopathology* (pp. 148–189). New York: Oxford University Press.

Brooks-Gunn, J., & Duncan G. J. (1997). The effects of poverty on children. *The Future of Children, 7*(2), 55–71.

Brooks-Gunn, J., Duncan, G. J., & Aber, J. L. (Eds.). (1997). *Neighborhood poverty: Vol 1. Context and consequences for children.* New York: Russell Sage Foundation.

Brooks-Gunn, J., Guo, G., & Furstenberg, F. F., Jr. (1993). Who drops out of and who continues beyond high school? A 20-year follow-up of black urban youth. *Journal of Research on Adolescence, 3,* 271–294.

Brooks-Gunn, J., Han, W., & Waldfogel, J. (2002). Maternal employment and child cognitive outcomes in the first three years of life: The NICHD study of early child care. *Child Development, 73,* 1052–1072.

Brooks-Gunn, J., & Matthews, W. S. (1979). *He and she: How children develop their sex-role identity.* Englewood Cliffs, NJ: Prentice Hall.

Brooks-Gunn, J., & Warren, M. P. (1985). The effects of delayed menarche in different contexts: Dance and nondance students. *Journal of Youth and Adolescence, 13,* 285–300.

Brosnan, M. (1998). Spatial ability in children's play with Lego blocks. *Perceptual & Motor Skills, 87,* 19–28.

Brost, B. C., Goldenberg, R. L., Mercer, B. M., Iams, J. D., Meis, P. J., Moawad, A. H., Newman, R. B., Miodovnik, M., Caritis, S. N., Thurnau, G. R., Bottoms, S. F., Das, A., & McNellis, D. (1997). The preterm prediction study: Association of cesarean delivery with increases in maternal weight and body mass index. *American Journal of Obstetrics and Gynecology, 177,* 333–341.

Broverman, I. K., Broverman, D., Clarkson, F. E., Rosenkrantz, P. S., & Vogel, S. R. (1970). Sex-role stereotypes and clinical judgments of mental health. *Journal of Consulting and Clinical Psychology, 34,* 1–7.

Brown, A. (2000–2001). Prenatal infection and adult schizophrenia: A review and synthesis. *International Journal of Mental Health, 29,* 22–37.

Brown, A., & Day, J. (1983). Macrorules for summarizing text: The development of expertise. *Journal of Verbal Learning and Verbal Behavior, 22,* 1–14.

Brown, B. B. (1990). Peer groups and peer cultures. In S. S. Feldman & G. R. Elliott (Eds.), *At the threshold: The developing adolescent* (pp. 171–196). Cambridge, MA: Harvard University Press.

Brown, B. B., Dolcini, M. M., & Leventhal, A. (1995, April). *The emergence of peer crowds: Friend or foe to adolescent health?* Paper presented at the biennial meetings of the Society for Research in Child Development, Indianapolis.

Brown, B. B., Mory, M. S., & Kinney, D. (1994). Casting adolescent crowds in a relational perspective: Caricature, channel, and context. In R. Montemayor, G. R. Adams, & T. P. Gullotta (Eds.), *Personal relationships during adolescence* (pp. 123–167). Thousand Oaks, CA: Sage.

Brown, L., Karrison, T., & Cibils, L. A. (1994). Mode of delivery and perinatal results in breech presentation. *American Journal of Obstetrics and Gynecology, 171,* 28–34.

Brown, R. (1973). *A first language: The early stages.* Cambridge, MA: Harvard University Press.

Brown, R., & Bellugi, U. (1964). Three processes in the acquisition of syntax. *Harvard Educational Review, 334,* 133–151.

Brown, R., & Hanlon, C. (1970). Derivational complexity and order of acquisition. In J. R. Hayes (Ed.), *Cognition and the development of language* (pp. 155–207). New York: Wiley.

Brown, W., Kesler, S., Eliez, S., Warsofsky, I., Haberecht, M., Patwardhan, A., Ross, J., Neely, E., Zeng, S., Yankowitz, J., & Reiss, A. (2002). Brain development in Turner syndrome: A magnetic resonance imaging study. *Psychiatry Research: Neuroimaging, 116,* 187–196.

Brownell, C. A. (1990). Peer social skills in toddlers: Competencies and constraints illustrated by same-age and mixed-age interaction. *Child Development, 61,* 836–848.

Brownell, K. D., & Fairburn, C. G. (Eds.). (1995). *Eating disorders and obesity: A comprehensive handbook.* New York: Guilford Press.

Bruck, M., & Ceci, S. J. (1997). The suggestibility of young children. *Current Directions in Psychological Science, 6,* 75–79.

Bruck, M., Ceci, S. J., & Hembrooke, H. (1998). Reliability and credibility of young children's reports: From research to policy and practice. *American Psychologist, 53,* 136–151.

Bruer, J. (1999). *The myth of the first three years.* New York: Free Press.

Bryant, P., MacLean, M., & Bradley, L. (1990). Rhyme, language, and children's reading. *Applied Psycholinguistics, 11,* 237–252.

Bryant, P. E., MacLean, M., Bradley, L. L., & Crossland, J. (1990). Rhyme and alliteration, phoneme detection, and learning to read. *Developmental Psychology, 26,* 429–438.

Buchanan, C. M., Maccoby, E. E., & Dornbusch, S. M. (1991). Caught between parents: Adolescents' experience in divorced homes. *Child Development, 62,* 1008–1029.

Bugental, D., & Happaney, K. (2004). Predicting infant maltreatment in low-income families: The interactive effects of maternal attributions and child status at birth. *Developmental Psychology, 40,* 234–243.

Buhrmester, D. (1992). The developmental courses of sibling and peer relationships. In F. Boer & J. Dunn (Eds.), *Children's sibling relationships: Developmental and clinical issues.* Hillsdale, NJ: Erlbaum.

Buhrmester, D. (1996). Need fulfillment, interpersonal competence, and the developmental contexts of early adolescent friendship. In W. M. Bukowski, A. F. Newcomb, & W. W. Hartup (Eds.), *The company they keep: Friendship in childhood and adolescence* (pp. 158–185). Cambridge, England: Cambridge University Press.

Buhrmester, D., & Furman, W. (1990). Perceptions of sibling relationships during middle childhood and adolescence. *Child Development, 61,* 1387–1398.

Buitelaar, J. K., & van Engeland, H. (1996). Epidemiological approaches. In S. Sandberg (Ed.), *Hyperactivity disorders of childhood* (pp. 26–68). Cambridge, England: Cambridge University Press.

Bukowski, W., Sippola, L., & Hoza, B. (1999). Same and other: Interdependency between participation in same- and other-sex friendships. *Journal of Youth & Adolescence, 28,* 439–459.

Burchinal, M., Lee, M., & Ramey, C. (1989). Type of day-care and preschool intellectual development in disadvantaged children. *Child Development, 60,* 128–137.

Burchinal, M. R., Campbell, F. A., Bryant, D. M., Wasik, B. H., & Ramey, C. T. (1997). Early intervention and mediating processes in cognitive performance of children of low-income African American families. *Child Development, 68,* 935–954.

Burgess, S. (1997). The role of shared reading in the development of phonological awareness: A longitudinal study of middle to upper class children. *Early Child Development & Care, 127–128,* 191–199.

Burgess, S. (2005). The preschool home literacy environment provided by teenage mothers. *Early Child Development & Care, 175,* 249–258.

Burn, S., O'Neil, A., & Nederend, S. (1996). Childhood tomboyishness and adult androgyny. *Sex Roles, 34,* 419–428.

Burnett, J. W., Anderson, W. P., & Heppner, P. P. (1995). Gender roles and self-esteem: A consideration of environmental factors. *Journal of Counseling and Development, 73,* 323–326.

Burt, S., McGue, M., Krueger, R., & Iacono, W. (2005). How are parent-child conflict and childhood externalizing symptoms related over time? Results from a genetically informative cross-lagged study. *Journal of Child Psychology and Psychiatry, 46,* 263–274.

Burton, L. (1992). Black grandparents rearing children of drug-addicted parents: Stressors, outcomes, and the social service needs. *Gerontologist, 31,* 744–751.

Bus, A., & van IJzendoorn, M. (1999). Phonological awareness and early reading: A meta-analysis of experimental training studies. *Journal of Educational Psychology, 91,* 403–414.

Buss, A. H. (1989). Temperaments as personality traits. In G. A. Kohnstamm, J. E. Bates, & M. K. Rothbart (Eds.), *Temperament in childhood* (pp. 39–58). Chichester, England: Wiley.

Buss, A. H., & Plomin, R. (1984). *Temperament: Early developing personality traits*. Hillsdale, NJ: Erlbaum.

Buss, A. H., & Plomin, R. (1986). The EAS approach to temperament. In R. Plomin & J. Dunn (Eds.), *The study of temperament: Changes, continuities and challenges* (pp. 67–80). Hillsdale, NJ: Erlbaum.

Bussey, K., & Bandura, A. (2004). Social cognitive theory of gender development and functioning. In E. Eagly, A. Beall, & R. Sternberg (Eds.), *The psychology of gender* (2nd ed., pp. 92–119). New York: Guilford.

Bussing, R., Zima, B., Gary, F., & Garvan, C. (2002). Use of complementary and alternative medicine for symptoms of attention-deficit hyperactivity disorder. *Psychiatric Services, 53,* 1096–1102.

Butterfield, S., Lehnhard, R., Lee, J., & Coladarci, T. (2004). Growth rates in running speed and vertical jumping by boys and girls ages 11–13. *Perceptual & Motor Skills, 99,* 225–234.

Butterworth, C. E., Jr., & Bendich, A. (1996). Folic acid and the prevention of birth defects. *Annual Review of Nutrition, 16,* 73–97.

Buysse, V., & Bailey, D. B., Jr. (1993). Behavioral and developmental outcomes in young children with disabilities in integrated and segregated settings: A review of comparative studies. *The Journal of Special Education, 26,* 434–461.

Buzi, R., Roberts, R., Ross, M., Addy, R., & Markham, C. (2003). The impact of a history of sexual abuse on high-risk sexual behaviors among females attending alternative school. *Adolescence, 38,* 595–605.

Cairns, R. B. (1991). Multiple metaphors for a singular idea. *Developmental Psychology, 27,* 23–26.

Cairns, R. B., & Cairns, B. D. (1994). *Lifelines and risks: Pathways of youth in our time*. Cambridge, England: Cambridge University Press.

Calhoun, S., & Dickerson Mayes, S. (2005). Processing speed in children with clinical disorders. *Psychology in the Schools, 42,* 333–343.

Callaghan, T., Rochat, P., Lillard, A., Claux, M., Odden, H., Itakura, S., Tapanya, S., & Singh, S. (2005). Synchrony in the onset of mental-state reasoning: Evidence from five cultures. *Psychological Science, 16,* 378–384.

Callahan, K., Rademacher, J., Hildreth, B., & Hildreth, B. (1998). The effect of parent participation in strategies to improve the homework performance of students who are at risk. *Remedial & Special Education, 19,* 131–141.

Camaioni, L., & Longobardi, E. (1995). Nature and stability of individual differences in early lexical development of Italian-speaking children. *First Language, 15,* 203–218.

Cameron, L. (1998). *The music of light: The extraordinary story of Hikari and Kenzaburo Oe*. New York: Free Press.

Campbell, F., Pungello, E., Miler-Johnson, S., Burchinal, M., & Ramey, C. (2001). The development of cognitive and academic abilities: Growth curves from an early childhood educational experiment. *Developmental Psychology, 37,* 231–242.

Campbell, F. A., & Ramey, C. T. (1994). Effects of early intervention on intellectual and academic achievement: A follow-up study of children from low-income families. *Child Development, 65,* 684–698.

Campbell, R. L., & Bickhard, M. H. (1992). Types of constraints on development: An interactivist approach. *Developmental Review, 12,* 311–338.

Campbell, S. B., & Ewing, L. J. (1990). Follow-up of hard-to-manage preschoolers: Adjustment at age 9 and predictors of continuing symptoms. *Journal of Child Psychology and Psychiatry, 31,* 871–889.

Campbell, S. B., Pierce, E. W., March, C. L., & Ewing, L. J. (1991). Noncompliant behavior, overactivity, and family stress as predictors of negative maternal control with preschool children. *Development and Psychopathology, 3,* 175–190.

Campione, J. C., & Brown, A. L. (1984). Learning ability and transfer propensity as sources of individual differences in intelligence. In P. H. Brooks, C. McCauley, & R. Sperber (Eds.), *Learning and cognition in the mentally retarded*. Hillsdale, NJ: Erlbaum.

Campione, J. C., Brown, A. L., & Ferrara, R. A. (1982). Mental retardation and intelligence. In J. R. Sternberg (Ed.), *Handbook of human intelligence* (pp. 392–492). Cambridge, England: Cambridge University Press.

Campione, J. C., Brown, A. L., Ferrara, R. A., Jones, R. S., & Steinberg, E. (1985). Breakdowns in flexible use of information: Intelligence-related differences in transfer following equivalent learning performance. *Intelligence, 9,* 297–315.

Cantwell, D. P. (1990). Depression across the early life span. In M. Lewis & S. M. Miller (Eds.), *Handbook of developmental psychopathology* (pp. 293–310). New York: Plenum Press.

Capirci, O., Iverson, J., Montanari, S., & Volterra, V. (2002). Gestural, signed and spoken modalities in early language development: The role of linguistic input. *Bilingualism: Language & Cognition, 5,* 25–37.

Cappella, E., & Weinstein, R. (2001). Turning around reading achievement: Predictors of high school students' academic resilience. *Journal of Educational Psychology, 93,* 758–771.

Capron, C., & Duyme, M. (1989). Assessment of effects of socio-economic status on IQ in a full cross-fostering study. *Nature, 340,* 552–554.

Capute, A. J., Palmer, F. B., Shapiro, B. K., Wachtel, R. C., Ross, A., & Accardo, P. J. (1984). Primitive reflex profile: A quantification of primitive reflexes in infancy. *Developmental Medicine and Child Neurology, 26,* 375–383.

Caputo, R. (2004). Parent religiosity, family processes, and adolescent outcomes. *Families in Society, 85,* 495–510.

Carey, S., & Bartlett, E. (1978). Acquiring a single new word. *Papers & Reports on Child Language Development, 15,* 17–29.

Carlson, E., Sampson, M., & Sroufe, A. (2003). Implications of attachment theory and research for developmental-behavioral pediatrics. *Journal of Developmental and Behavioral Pediatrics, 24,* 364–379.

Carlson, E., Sroufe, A., & Egeland, B. (2004). The construction of experience: A longitudinal study of representation and behavior. *Child Development, 75,* 66–83.

Carlson, E. A., & Sroufe, L. A. (1995). Contribution of attachment theory to developmental psychopathology. In D. Cicchetti & D. J. Cohen (Eds.), *Developmental psychopathology: Vol. 1. Theory and methods* (pp. 581–617). New York: Wiley.

Carmichael, S. L., & Abrams, B. (1997). A critical review of the relationship between gestational weight gain and preterm delivery. *Obstetrics and Gynecology, 89,* 865–873.

Carnoy, M., Loeb, S., & Smith, T. (2001). *Do higher state test scores in Texas make for better high school outcomes?* Philadelphia: Consortium for Policy Research in Education/University of Pennsylvania, #RR0047. Retrieved November 11, 2004, from http://www.cpre.org/publications /rr47.pdf

Caron, A. J., & Caron, R. F. (1981). Processing of relational information as an index of infant risks. In S. Friedman & M. Sigman (Eds.), *Preterm birth and psychological development* (pp. 219–240). New York: Academic Press.

Caron, A. J., Caron R. F., Roberts, J., & Brooks, R. (1997). Infant sensitivity to deviations in dynamic facial-vocal displays: The role of eye regard. *Developmental Psychology, 33,* 802–813.

Carson, D., Klee, T., & Perry, C. (1998). Comparisons of children with delayed and normal language at 24 months of age on measures of behavioral difficulties, social and cognitive development. *Infant Mental Health, 19,* 59–75.

Carter, A., Garrity-Rokous, F., Chazan-Cohen, R., Little, C., & Briggs-Gowan, M. (2001). Maternal depression and comorbidity: Predicting early parenting, attachment security, and toddler social-emotional problems and competencies. *Journal of the American Academy of Child and Adolescent Psychiatry, 40,* 18–26.

Carver, P., Egan, S., & Perry, D. (2004). Children who question their heterosexuality. *Developmental Psychology, 40,* 43–53.

Carver, R. P. (1990). Intelligence and reading ability in grades 2–12. *Intelligence, 14,* 449–455.

Casasola, M., & Cohen, L. (2000). Infants' association of linguistic labels with causal actions. *Developmental Psychology, 36,* 155–168.

Case, R. (1985). *Intellectual development: Birth to adulthood*. New York: Academic Press.

Case, R. (1991). Stages in the development of the young child's first sense of self. *Developmental Review, 11,* 210–230.

Case, R. (1992). *The mind's staircase: Exploring thought and knowledge*. Hillsdale, NJ: Erlbaum.

Caselli, C., Casadio, P., & Bates, E. (1997). *A cross-linguistic study of the transition from first words to grammar* (Technical Report No. CND-9701). Center for Research in Language, University of California, San Diego.

Casey, B., McIntire, D., & Leveno, K. (2001). The continuing value of the Apgar score for the assessment of newborn infants. *New England Journal of Medicine, 344,* 467–471.

Casey, M. B. (1986). Individual differences in selective attention among prereaders: A key to mirror-image confusions. *Developmental Psychology, 22,* 58–66.

Cashon, C., & Cohen, L. (2000). Eight-month-old infants' perceptions of possible and impossible events. *Infancy, 1,* 429–446.

Caslyn, C., Gonzales, P., & Frase, M. (1999). *Highlights from the third international Mathematics and Science Study*. Washington, DC: National Center for Educational Statistics.

Casper, L., & Smith, K. (2002). Dispelling the myths: Self-care, class, and race. *Journal of Family Issues, 23,* 716–727.

Caspi, A. (1998). Personality development across the life course. In W.

Damon (Ed.), *Handbook of child psychology: Vol. 3. Social, emotional, and personality development* (5th ed., pp. 311–388). New York: Wiley.

Caspi, A. (2000). The child is father of the man: Personality continuities from childhood to adulthood. *Journal of Personality & Social Psychology, 78,* 158–172.

Caspi, A., Harkness, A. R., Moffitt, T. E., & Silva, P. A. (1996). Intellectual performance: Continuity and change. In P. A. Silva & W. R. Stanton (Eds.), *From child to adult: The Dunedin Multidisciplinary Health and Development Study* (pp. 59–74). Aukland: Oxford University Press.

Caspi, A., Harrington, H., Milne, B., Amell, J., Theordore, R., & Moffitt, T. (2003). Children's behavioral styles at age 3 are linked to their adult personality traits at age 26. *Journal of Personality, 71,* 495–513.

Caspi, A., Lynam, D., Moffitt, T. E., & Silva, P. A. (1993). Unraveling girls' delinquency: Biological, dispositional, and contextual contributions to adolescent misbehavior. *Developmental Psychology, 29,* 19–30.

Caspi, A., & Moffitt, T. E. (1991). Individual differences are accentuated during periods of social change: The sample case of girls at puberty. *Journal of Personality and Social Psychology, 61,* 157–168.

Caspi, A., Roberts, B., & Shiner, R. (2005). Personality development: Stability and change. *Annual Review of Psychology, 56,* 453–484.

Cassidy, J., & Berlin, L. J. (1994). The insecure/ambivalent pattern of attachment: Theory and research. *Child Development, 65,* 971–991.

Castellino, D., Lerner, J., Lerner, R., & von Eye, A. (1998). Maternal employment and education: Predictors of young adolescent career trajectories. *Applied Developmental Science, 2,* 114–126.

Castle, J., Groothues, C., Bredenkamp, D., Beckett, C., et al. (1999). Effects of qualities of early institutional care on cognitive attainment. *American Journal of Orthopsychiatry, 69,* 424–437.

Cato, J., & Canetto, S. (2003). Attitudes and beliefs about suicidal behavior when coming out is the precipitant of the suicidal behavior. *Sex Roles, 49,* 497–505.

Caughy, M. O., DiPietro, J. A., & Strobino, D. M. (1994). Day-care participation as a protective factor in the cognitive development of low-income children. *Child Development, 65,* 457–471.

Cavill, S., & Bryden. P. (2003). Development of handedness: Comparison of questionnaire and performance-based measures of preference. *Brain & Cognition, 53,* 149–151.

Ceci, S. J., & Bruck, M. (1993). Suggestibility of the child witness: A historical review and synthesis. *Psychological Bulletin, 113,* 403–439.

Ceci, S. J., & Bruck, M. (1995). *Jeopardy in the courtroom: A scientific analysis of children's testimony.* Washington, DC: American Psychological Association.

Ceci, S. J., & Bruck, M. (1998). Children's testimony: Applied and basic issues. In W. Damon (Ed.), *Handbook of child psychology: Vol. 4. Child psychology in practice* (5th ed., pp. 713–774). New York: Wiley.

Cederblad, M., Hook, B., Irhammar, M., & Mercke, A. (1999). Mental health in international adoptees as teenagers and young adults: An epidemiological study. *Journal of Child Psychology & Psychiatry & Allied Disciplines, 40,* 1239–1248.

Cederblad, M., Pruksachatkunakorn, P., Boripunkul, T., Intraprasert, S., & Hook, B. (2003). Sense of coherence in a Thai sample. *Transcultural Psychiatry, 40,* 585–600.

Centers for Disease Control and Prevention (CDC). (2004a). Sexually transmitted disease surveillance 2001,supplement, chlamydia prevalence monitoring project. Retrieved May 4, 2005, from http://www.cdc.gov/std /Chlamydia2003/

Centers for Disease Control and Prevention (CDC). (2004b). Surveillance summaries. *Morbidity & Mortality Weekly Report, 53,* 2–29.

Centers for Disease Control National Immunization Program. (1999, April 2). Achievements in public health, 1900–1999: Impact of vaccines universally recommended for children. *Morbidity & Mortality Weekly Report, 48(12),* 243–248.

Centers for Disease Control National Immunization Program. (2000, January 21). 2000,childhood immunization schedule. *Morbidity & Mortality Weekly Report, 49,* 35–38.

Centers for Disease Control. (1992). Pregnancy risks determined from birth certificate data—United States, 1989. *Morbidity & Mortality Weekly Report, 41(30),* 556–563.

Centers for Disease Control. (1995a). Chorionic villus sampling and amniocentesis: Recommendations for prenatal counseling. *Morbidity & Mortality Weekly Report, 44(RR-9),* 1–12.

Centers for Disease Control. (1995b). U.S. Public Health Service recommendations for human immunodeficiency virus counseling and voluntary testing for pregnant women. *Mortality & Morbidity Weekly Report, 44(RR-7),* 1–15.

Centers for Disease Control. (1996). Population-based prevalence of perinatal exposure to cocaine: Georgia, 1994. *Morbidity & Mortality Weekly Report, 45,* 887.

Centers for Disease Control. (2000). Youth risk behavior surveillance—United States, 1999. *Morbidity & Mortality Weekly Report, 49,* 1–96.

Chabris, C. F. (1999). Prelude or requiem for the 'Mozart effect'? *Nature, 400,* 826–827.

Chalfant, J. C. (1989). Learning disabilities: Policy issues and promising approaches. *American Psychologist, 44,* 392–398.

Chan, R., Raboy, B., & Patterson, C. (1998). Psychosocial adjustment among children conceived via donor insemination by lesbian and heterosexual mothers. *Child Development, 69,* 443–457.

Chang, E. (2001). Life stress and depressed mood among adolescents: Examining a cognitive-affective mediation model. *Journal of Social & Clinical Psychology, 20,* 416–429.

Chang, F., & Burns, B. (2005). Attention in preschoolers: Associations with effortful control and motivation. *Child Development, 76,* 247–263.

Chang, L., & Murray, A. (1995, April). *Math performance of 5- and 6-year-olds in Taiwan and the U.S.: Maternal beliefs, expectations, and tutorial assistance.* Paper presented at the biennial meetings of the Society for Research in Child Development, Indianapolis.

Chang, L., Schwartz, D., Dodge, K., & McBride-Chang, C. (2003). Harsh parenting in relation to child emotion regulation and aggression. *Journal of Family Psychology, 17,* 598–606.

Chao, R. K. (1994). Beyond parental control and authoritarian parenting style: Understanding Chinese parenting through the cultural notion of training. *Child Development, 65,* 1111–1119.

Chapa, J., & Valencia, R. R. (1993). Latino population growth, demographic characteristics, and educational stagnation: An examination of recent trends. *Hispanic Journal of Behavioral Sciences, 15,* 165–187.

Charity, A., Scarborough, H., & Griffin, D. (2004). Familiarity with school English in African American children and its relation to early reading achievement. *Child Development, 75,* 1340–1356.

Charman, T., Redfern, S., & Fonagy, P. (1995, April). *Individual differences in theory of mind acquisition: The role of attachment security.* Paper presented at the biennial meetings of the Society for Research in Child Development, Indianapolis.

Charman, T., Ruffman, T., & Clements, W. (2002). Is there a gender difference in false belief development? *Social Development, 11,* 1–10.

Chase-Lansdale, P., Cherlin, A., & Kiernan, K. (1995). The long-term effects of parental divorce on the mental health of young adults: A developmental perspective. *Child Development, 66,* 1614–1634.

Chavajay, P., & Rogoff, B. (2002). Schooling and traditional collaborative social organization of problem solving by Mayan mothers and children. *Developmental Psychology, 38,* 55–66.

Chen, E. (2004). Why socioeconomic status affects the health of children: A psychosocial perspective. *Current Directions in Psychological Science, 13,* 112–115.

Chen, X., He, Y., Chang, L., & Liu, H. (2005). The peer group as a context: Moderating effects on relations between maternal parenting and social and school adjustment in Chinese children. *Child Development, 76,* 417–434.

Chen, Z. (1999). Ethnic similarities and differences in the association of emotional autonomy and adolescent outcomes: Comparing Euro-American and Asian-American adolescents. *Psychological Reports, 84,* 501–516.

Chen, Z., Dong, Q., & Zhou, H. (1997). Authoritative and authoritarian parenting practices and social and school performance in Chinese children. *International Journal of Behavioral Development, 21,* 855–873.

Cherlin, A. (1992). *Marriage, divorce, remarriage.* Cambridge, MA: Harvard University Press.

Cherlin, A., Chase-Lansdale, P., & McRae, C. (1998). Effects of parental divorce on mental health throughout the life course. *American Sociological Review, 63,* 239–249.

Cherlin, A. J. (1992). Infant care and full-time employment. In A. Booth (Ed.), *Child care in the 1990s: Trends and consequences* (pp. 209–214). Hillsdale, NJ: Erlbaum.

Cherry, V., Belgrave, F., Jones, W., Kennon, D., Gray, F., & Phillips, F. (1998). NTU: An Africentric approach to substance abuse prevention among African American youth. *Journal of Primary Prevention, 18,* 319–339.

Chess, S., & Thomas, A. (1984). *Origins and evolution of behavior disorders: Infancy to early adult life.* New York: Brunner/Mazel.

Cheung, C., Chan, W., Lee, T., Liu, S., & Leung, K. (2001). Structure of moral consciousness and moral intentions among youth in Hong Kong *International Journal of Adolescence & Youth, 9,* 83–116.

Chi, M. T. (1978). Knowledge structure and memory development. In R. S. Siegler (Ed.), *Children's thinking: What develops?* (pp. 73–96). Hillsdale, NJ: Erlbaum.

Chiappe, P., & Siegel, L. (1999). Phonological awareness and reading acquisition in English- and Punjabi-speaking Canadian children. *Journal of Educational Psychology, 91*, 20–28.

"Children spend more time playing video games than watching TV, MSU survey shows." (2004, April 4). Retrieved July 23, 2005, from http://www.newsroom.msu.edu/site/indexer/1943/content.htm

Chincotta, D., & Underwood, G. (1997). Estimates, language of schooling and bilingual digit span. *European Journal of Cognitive Psychology, 9*, 325–348.

Chisholm, J. S. (1989). Biology, culture, and the development of temperament: A Navaho example. In J. K. Nugent, B. M. Lester, & T. B. Brazelton (Eds.), *The cultural context of infancy: Vol. 1. Biology, culture, and infant development*. Norwood, NJ: Ablex.

Choi, S. (2000). Caregiver input in English and Korean: Use of nouns and verbs in book-reading and toy-play contexts. *Journal of Child Language, 27*, 69–96.

Chomsky, N. (1965). *Aspects of a theory of syntax*. Cambridge, MA: MIT Press.

Chomsky, N. (1975). *Reflections on language*. New York: Pantheon Books.

Chomsky, N. (1986). *Knowledge of language: Its nature, origin, and use*. New York: Praeger.

Chomsky, N. (1988). *Language and problems of knowledge*. Cambridge, MA: MIT Press.

Chopak, J., Vicary, J., & Crockett, L. (1998). Predicting alcohol and tobacco use in a sample of rural adolescents. *American Journal of Health Behavior, 22*, 334–341.

Christakis, D., Zimmerman, F., Giuseppe, D., & McCarty, C. (2004). Early television exposure and subsequent attentional problems in children. *Pediatrics, 113*, 708–713.

Christensen, C. (1997). Onset, rhymes, and phonemes in learning to read. *Scientific Studies of Reading, 1*, 341–358.

Chudley, A., Conry, J., Cook, J., Loock, C., Rosales, T., & LeBlanc, N. (2005). Fetal alcohol spectrum disorder: Canadian guidelines for diagnosis. *Canadian Medical Association Journal, 172*, S1–S21.

Ciancio, D., Sadovsky, A., Malabonga, V., Trueblood, L., et al. (1999). Teaching classification and seriation to preschoolers. *Child Study Journal, 29*, 193–205.

Cicchetti, D., & Cohen, D. J. (1995). Perspectives on developmental psychopathology. In D. Cicchetti & D. J. Cohen (Eds.), *Developmental psychopathology. Vol 1: Theory and methods* (pp. 3–20). New York: Wiley.

Cicchetti, D., Rogosch, F., Maughan, A., Toth, S., & Bruce, J. (2003). False belief understanding in maltreated children. *Development & Psychopathology, 15*, 1067–1091.

Cicchetti, D., & Toth, S. L. (1998). The development of depression in children and adolescents. *American Psychologist, 53*, 221–241.

Cillessen, A. H. N., van IJzendoorn, H. W., van Lieshout, C. F. M., & Hartup, W. W. (1992). Heterogeneity among peer-rejected boys: Subtypes and stabilities. *Child Development, 63*, 893–905.

Clark, E. V. (1975). Knowledge, context, and strategy in the acquisition of meaning. In D. P. Date (Ed.), *Georgetown University round table on language and linguistics*. Washington, DC: Georgetown University Press.

Clark, E. V. (1983). Meanings and concepts. In J. H. Flavell & E. M. Markman (Eds.), *Handbook of child psychology: Cognitive development* (Vol. 3, pp. 787–840). New York: Wiley.

Clark, E. V. (1990). On the pragmatics of contrast. *Journal of Child Language, 41*, 417–431.

Clarke, A. M., & Clarke, A. D. B. (1976). *Early experience: Myth and evidence*. New York: Free Press.

Clarke-Stewart, A. (1990). "The 'effects' of infant day care reconsidered" reconsidered: Risks for parents, children, and researchers. In N. Fox & G. G. Fein (Eds.), *Infant day care: The current debate* (pp. 61–86). Norwood, NJ: Ablex.

Clarke-Stewart, A. (1992). Consequences of child care for children's development. In A. Booth (Ed.), *Child care in the 1990s: Trends and consequences* (pp. 63–82). Hillsdale, NJ: Erlbaum.

Clarke-Stewart, K. A., Gruber, C. P., & Fitzgerald, L. M. (1994). *Children at home and in day care*. Hillsdale, NJ: Erlbaum.

Clayton, V. (2004, September 8). *What's to blame for the rise in ADHD?* Retrieved November 22, 2004, from http://www.msnbc.msn.com/id/5933775/

Cnattingius, S., Berendes, H. W., & Forman, M. R. (1993). Do delayed childbearers face increased risks of adverse pregnancy outcomes after the first birth? *Obstetrics and Gynecology, 81*, 512–516.

Coatsworth, J., Maldonado-Molina, M., Pantin, H., & Szapocznik, J. (2005). A person-centered and ecological investigation of acculturation strategies in Hispanic immigrant youth. *Journal of Community Psychology, 33*, 157–174.

Cobb, K. (2000, September 3). Breaking in drivers: Texas could join states restricting teens in effort to lower rate of fatal accidents. *Houston Chronicle*, A1, A20.

Cocodia, E., Kim, J., Shin, H., Kim, J., Ee, J., Wee, M., & Howard, R. (2003). Evidence that rising population intelligence is impacting formal education. *Personality & Individual Differences, 35*, 797–810.

Coe, C., Hayashi, K. T., & Levine, S. (1988). Hormones and behavior at puberty: Activation or concatenation? In M. R. Gunnar & W. A. Collins (Eds.), *Development during the transition to adolescence: Minnesota symposia on child psychology* (Vol. 21, pp. 17–42). Hillsdale, NJ: Erlbaum.

Cohen, D., Pichard, N., Tordjman, S., Baumann, C., Burglen, L., Excoffier, E., Lazar, G., Mazet, P., Pinquier, C., Verloes, A., & Heron, D. (2005). Specific genetic disorders and autism: Clinical contribution towards their identification. *Journal of Autism & Developmental Disorders, 35*, 103–116.

Cohen, S., Tyrrell, D., & Smith, A. (1991). Psychological stress and susceptibility to the common cold. *New England Journal of Medicine, 325*, 606–612.

Coie, J. D. (1997a, April). *Initial outcome evaluation of the prevention trial*. Paper presented at the biennial meetings of the Society for Research in Child Development, Washington, DC.

Coie, J. D. (1997b, August). *Testing developmental theory of antisocial behavior with outcomes from the Fast Track Prevention Project*. Paper presented at the annual meeting of the American Psychological Association, Chicago.

Coie, J. D., & Cillessen, A. H. N. (1993). Peer rejection: Origins and effects on children's development. *Current Directions in Psychological Science, 2*, 89–92.

Coie, J. D., & Dodge, K. A. (1998). Aggression and antisocial behavior. In W. Damon (Ed.), *Handbook of child psychology: Vol. 3. Social, emotional, and personality development* (5th ed., pp. 779–862). New York: Wiley.

Coie, J. D., Terry, R., Lenox, K., Lochman, J., & Hyman, C. (1995). Childhood peer rejection and aggression as predictors of stable patterns of adolescent disorder. *Development and Psychopathology, 7*, 697–713.

Coiro, M. J. (1995, April). *Child behavior problems as a function of marital conflict and parenting*. Paper presented at the biennial meetings of the Society for Research in Child Development, Indianapolis.

Colby, A., & Damon, W. (1992). *Some do care: Contemporary lives of moral commitment*. New York: Free Press.

Colby, A., Kohlberg, L., Gibbs, J., & Lieberman, M. (1983). A longitudinal study of moral judgment. *Monographs of the Society for Research in Child Development, 48*(1–2, Serial No. 200).

Cole, D. A. (1991). Social integration and severe disabilities: A longitudinal analysis of child outcomes. *The Journal of Special Education, 25*, 340–351.

Cole, M. (2005). Culture in development. In M. Bornstein & M. Lamb (Eds.), *Developmental science: An advanced textbook* (5th ed., pp. 45–102). Hillsdale, NJ: Erlbaum.

Cole, P., Martin, S., & Dennis, T. (2004). Emotion regulation as a scientific construct: Methodological challenges and directions for child development research. *Child Development, 75*, 317–333.

Collaer, M. L., & Hines, M. (1995). Human behavioral sex differences: A role for gonadal hormones during early development? *Psychological Bulletin, 118*, 55–107.

Collet, J. P., Burtin, P., Gillet, J., Bossard, N., Ducruet, T., & Durr, F. (1994). Risk of infectious diseases in children attending different types of daycare setting. Epicreche Research Group. *Respiration, 61*, 16–19.

Collins, P. A., Wright, J. C., Anderson, D. R., Huston, A. C., Schmitt, K. L., McElroy, E. S., & Linebarger, D. L. (1997, April). *Effects of early childhood media use on academic achievement*. Paper presented at the biennial meetings of the Society for Research in Child Development, Washington, DC.

Colombo, J. (1993). *Infant cognition: Predicting later intellectual functioning*. Newbury Park, CA: Sage.

Colton, M., Buss, K., Mangelsdorf, S., Brooks, C., Sorenson, D., Stansbury, K., Harris, M., & Gunnar, M. (1992). Relations between toddler coping strategies, temperament, attachment and adrenocortical stress responses. Poster presented at the Eighth International Conference on Infant Studies, Miami, FL.

Compas, B. E., Ey, S., & Grant, K. E. (1993). Taxonomy, assessment, and diagnosis of depression during adolescence. *Psychological Bulletin, 114*, 323–344.

Compas, B. E., Hinden, B. R., & Gerhardt, C. A. (1995). Adolescent development: Pathways and processes of risk and resilience. *Annual Review of Psychology, 46*, 265–293.

Condry, J., & Condry, S. (1976). Sex differences: A study in the eye of the beholder. *Child Development, 47*, 812–819.

Conduct Problems Prevention Research Group. (2002). The implementation of the Fast Track Program: An example of a large-scale prevention science efficacy trial. *Journal of Abnormal Child Psychology, 30*, 1–17.

Conger, R. D., Conger, K. J., Elder, G. H., Jr., Lorenz, F. O., Simons, R. L., & Whitbeck, L. B. (1992). A family process model of economic hardship and adjustment of early adolescent boys. *Child Development, 63*, 526–541.

Conger, R. D., Ge, X., Elder, G. H., Jr., Lorenz, F. O., & Simons, R. L. (1994). Economic stress, coercive family process, and developmental problems of adolescence. *Child Development, 65*, 541–561.

Conger, R. D., Patterson, G. R., & Ge, X. (1995). It takes two to replicate: A mediational model for the impact of parents' stress on adolescent adjustment. *Child Development, 66*, 80–97.

Connolly, K., & Dalgleish, M. (1989). The emergence of a tool-using skill in infancy. *Developmental Psychology, 25*, 894–912.

Connor, P., Sampson, P., Bookstein, F., Barr, H., & Streissguth, A. (2001). Direct and indirect effects of prenatal alcohol damage on executive function. *Developmental Neuropsychology, 18*, 331–354.

"Convicted Day-Care Rapist Released." (2004, April 30). TheBostonChannel.com. Retrieved May 16, 2005, from http://www.thebostonchannel.com/print/3255987/detail.html

Cooper, P. J. (1995). Eating disorders and their relationship to mood and anxiety disorders. In K. D. Brownell & C. G. Fairburn (Eds.), *Eating disorders and obesity: A comprehensive handbook* (pp. 159–164). New York: Guilford Press.

Cooper, R. P., & Aslin, R. N. (1994). Developmental differences in infant attention to the spectral properties of infant-directed speech. *Child Development, 65*, 1663–1677.

Cornelius, M., Goldschmidt, L., Day, N., & Larkby, C. (2002). Alcohol, tobacco and marijuana use among pregnant teenagers: 6-year follow-up of offspring growth effects. *Neurotoxicology & Teratology, 24*, 703–710.

Corter, C. M., & Fleming, A. S. (1995). Psychobiology of maternal behavior in human beings. In M. H. Bornstein (Ed.), *Handbook of parenting: Vol. 2. Biology and ecology of parenting* (pp. 87–116). Mahwah, NJ: Erlbaum.

Costa, P. T., Jr., & McCrae, R. R. (1984). Personality as a lifelong determinant of wellbeing. In C. Z. Malatesta & C. E. Izard (Eds.), *Emotion in adult development* (pp. 141–158). Beverly Hills, CA: Sage.

Costa, P. T., Jr., & McCrae, R. R. (1994). Set like plaster? Evidence for the stability of adult personality. In T. F. Hetherton & J. L. Weinberger (Eds.), *Can personality change?* (pp. 21–40). Washington, DC: American Psychological Association.

Costello, E. J., & Angold, A. (1995). Developmental epidemiology. In D. Cicchetti & D. J. Cohen (Eds.), *Developmental psychopathology: Vol. 1. Theory and methods* (pp. 23–56). New York: Wiley.

Coté, J. E. (1996). Identity: A multidimensional analysis. In J. G. Adams, R. Montemayor, & T. P. Gullotta (Eds.), *Psychosocial development during adolescence: Progress in developmental contextualism* (pp. 131–180). Thousand Oaks, CA: Sage.

Coulton, C. J., Korbin, J. E., Su, M., & Chow, J. (1995). Community level factors and child maltreatment rates. *Child Development, 66*, 1262–1276.

Council of the Great City Schools. (1997). Standard English Proficiency Program: A program in the Oakland Unified School District to facilitate standard English proficiency and self-esteem. In *What Works in Urban Education: Achievement* [Online brochure]. Retrieved January 15, 2001, from http://www.cgcs.org/promise/whatworks/achievement/part27.html

Council on Basic Education. (1998). *Quality Counts* [Online report]. Retrieved October 21, 1998, http://www.c-b-e.org

Coury, D. (2002). Developmental and behavioral pediatrics. In A. Rudolph, R. Kamei, & K. Overby (Eds.), *Rudolph's fundamentals of pediatrics* (3rd ed., pp. 110–124). New York: McGraw-Hill.

Cowan, N., Nugent, L. D., Elliott, E., Ponomarev, I., & Saults, J. (1999). The role of attention in the development of short-term memory: Age differences in the verbal span of apprehension. *Child Development, 70*, 1082–1097.

Cox, T. (1983). Cumulative deficit in culturally disadvantaged children. *British Journal of Educational Psychology, 53*, 317–326.

Cramer, P. (2000). Defense mechanisms in psychology today. *American Psychologist, 55*, 637–646.

Cramond, B. (2004). Can we, should we, need we agree on a definition of giftedness? *Roeper Review, 27*, 15–16.

Crawford, A., & Manassis, K. (2001). Familial predictors of treatment outcome in childhood anxiety disorders. *Journal of the American Academy of Child and Adolescent Psychiatry, 40*, 1182–1189.

Crawford, J. (1991). *Bilingual education: History, politics, theory, and practice* (2nd ed.). Los Angeles: Bilingual Education Services.

Crick, N., & Dodge, K. (1994). A review and reformulation of social information processing mechanisms in children's social adjustment. *Psychological Bulletin, 115*, 74–101.

Crick, N., & Dodge, K. (1996). Social information-processing mechanisms in reactive and proactive aggression. *Child Development, 67*, 993–1002.

Crick, N. R., Casas, J. F., & Mosher, M. (1997). Relational and overt aggression in preschool. *Developmental Psychology, 33*, 579–588.

Crick, N. R., & Grotpeter, J. K. (1995). Relational aggression, gender, and social-psychological adjustment. *Child Development, 66*, 710–722.

Crick, N. R., & Grotpeter, J. K. (1996). Children's treatment by peers: Victims of relational and overt aggression. *Development and Psychopathology, 8*, 367–380.

Crittenden, P. M. (1992). Quality of attachment in the preschool years. *Development and Psychopathology, 4*, 209–241.

Crnic, K. A., Greenberg, M. T., Ragozin, A. S., Robinson, N. M., & Basham, R. B. (1983). Effects of stress and social support on mothers and premature and full-term infants. *Child Development, 43*, 209–217.

Crockenberg, S. (2003). Rescuing the baby from the bath water: How gender and temperament (may) influence how child care affects child development. *Child Development, 74*, 1034–1038.

Crockenberg, S., & Leerkes, E. (2004). Infant and maternal behaviors regulate infant reactivity to novelty at 6 months. *Developmental Psychology, 40*, 1123–1132.

Crockenberg, S. B. (1981). Infant irritability, mother responsiveness, and social support influences on the security of infant-mother attachment. *Child Development, 52*, 857–865.

Crockenberg, S. B. (1987). Predictors and correlates of anger toward and punitive control of toddlers by adolescent mothers. *Child Development, 48*, 964–975.

Crockenberg, S. B., & Litman, C. (1990). Autonomy as competence in 2-year-olds: Maternal correlates of child defiance, compliance, and self-assertion. *Development Psychology, 26*, 961–971.

Crockett, D. (2003). Critical issues children face in the 2000s. *School Psychology Quarterly, 18*, 446–453.

Crone, E., & van der Molen, M. (2004). Developmental changes in real life decision making: Performance on a gambling task previously shown to depend on the ventromedial prefrontal cortex. *Developmental Neuropsychology, 25*, 251–279.

Crook, C. (1987). Taste and olfaction. In P. Salapatek & L. Cohen (Eds.), *Handbook of infant perception, Vol. 1: From sensation to perception* (pp. 237–264). Orlando, FL: Academic Press.

Crossman, A., Scullin, M., & Melnyk, L. (2004). Individual and developmental differences in suggestibility. *Applied Cognitive Psychology, 18*, 941–945.

Crowell, J. A., & Feldman, S. S. (1988). Mothers' internal models of relationships and children's behavioral and developmental status. A study of mother-child interaction. *Child Development, 50*, 1273–1285.

Crowell, J. A., & Feldman, S. S. (1991). Mothers' working models of attachment relationships and mother and child behavior during separation and reunion. *Developmental Psychology, 27*, 597–605.

Crystal, D. S., Chen, C., Fuligni, A. J., Stevenson, H. W., Hsu, C., Ko, H., Kitamura, S., & Kimura, S. (1994). Psychological maladjustment and academic achievement: A cross-cultural study of Japanese, Chinese, and American high school students. *Child Development, 65*, 738–753.

Crystal, D. S., Watanabe, H., & Chen, R. (2000). Reactions to morphological deviance: A comparison of Japanese and American children and adolescents. *Social Development, 9*, 40–61.

Crystal, S., Shae, D., & Krishnaswami, S. (1992). Educational attainment, occupational history, and stratification: Determinants of later-life economic outcomes. *Journals of Gerontology: Social Sciences, 47*, S213–S221.

Culbertson, F. M. (1997). Depression and gender: An international review. *American Psychologist, 52*, 25–31.

Cummings, E. M., & Davies, P. T. (1994). Maternal depression and child development. *Journal of Child Psychology and Psychiatry, 35*, 73–112.

Cunningham, M. (2001). The influence of parental attitudes and behaviors on children's attitudes toward gender and household labor in early adulthood. *Journal of Marriage and the Family, 63*, 111–122.

Cunningham, M., Swanson, D., Spencer, M., & Dupree, D. (2003). The association of physical maturation with family hassles among African

American adolescent males. *Cultural Diversity and Ethnic Minority Psychology, 9,* 276–288.

Currie, J., & Thomas, D. (1997). Can Head Start lead to long term gains in cognition after all? *SRCD Newsletter, 40*(2), 3–5.

Curry, C. (2002). An approach to clinical genetics. In A. Rudolph, R. Kamei, & K. Overby (Eds.), *Rudolph's fundamentals of pediatrics* (3rd ed., pp. 184–220). New York: McGraw-Hill.

Cushner, K., McClelland, A., & Safford, P. (1992). *Human diversity in education.* New York: McGraw-Hill.

Custodero, L., Britto, P., & Brooks-Gunn, J. (2003). Musical lives: A collective portrait of American parents and their young children. *Journal of Applied Developmental Psychology, 24,* 553–572.

Custodero, L., & Johnson-Green, E. (2003). Passing the cultural torch: Musical experience and musical parenting of infants. *Journal of Research in Music Education, 51,* 102–114.

Cutrona, C. E., & Troutman, B. R. (1986). Social support, infant temperament, and parenting self-efficacy: A mediational model of post-partum depression. *Child Development, 57,* 1507–1518.

Cuvo, A. (1974). Incentive level influence on overt rehearsal and free recall as a function of age. *Journal of Experimental Child Psychology, 18,* 167–181.

Daley, T., Whaley, S., Sigman, M., Espinosa, M., & Neumann, C. (2003). IQ on the rise: The Flynn effect in rural Kenyan children. *Psychological Science, 14,* 215–219.

Daly, K. A. (1997). Definition and epidemiology of otitis media. In J. E. Roberts, I. F. Wallace, & F. W. Henderson (Eds.), *Otitis media in young children: Medical, developmental, and educational considerations* (pp. 3–42). Baltimore: Brookes.

Daly, S., & Glenwick, D. (2000). Personal adjustment and perceptions of grandchild behavior in custodial grandmothers. *Journal of Clinical Child Psychology, 29,* 108–118.

Daly, S., Mills, J. L., Molloy, A. M., Conley, M., Lee, Y. J., Kirke, P. N., Weir, D. G., & Scott, J. M. (1997). Minimum effective dose of folic acid for food fortification to prevent neural-tube defects. *The Lancet, 350,* 1666–1669.

Dammeijer, P., Schlundt, B., Chenault, M., Manni, J., & Anteunis, I. (2002). Effects of early auditory deprivation and stimulation on auditory brainstem responses in the rat. *Acta Oto-Laryngologica, 122,* 703–708.

Damon, W. (1977). *The social world of the child.* San Francisco: Jossey-Bass.

Damon, W. (1983). The nature of social-cognitive change in the developing child. In W. F. Overton (Ed.), *The relationship between social and cognitive development* (pp. 103–142). Hillsdale, NJ: Erlbaum.

Danby, S., & Baker, C. (1998). How to be masculine in the block area. *Childhood: A Global Journal of Child Research, 5,* 151–175.

Dark, V. J., & Benbow, C. P. (1993). Cognitive differences among the gifted: A review and new data. In D. K. Detterman (Ed.), *Current topics in human intelligence: Vol. 3. Individual differences and cognition* (pp. 85–120). Norwood, NJ: Ablex.

Darling, N., & Steinberg, L. (1993). Parenting style as context: An integrative model. *Psychological Bulletin, 113,* 487–496.

Darlington, R. B. (1991). The long-term effects of model preschool programs. In L. Okagaki & R. J. Sternberg (Eds.), *Directors of development* (pp. 203–215). Hillsdale, NJ: Erlbaum.

Davies, G. M. (1993). Children's memory for other people: An integrative review. In C. A. Nelson (Ed.), *The Minnesota symposia on child psychology* (Vol. 26, pp. 123–157). Hillsdale, NJ: Erlbaum.

Davies, P., & Cicchetti, D. (2004). Toward an integration of family systems and developmental psychopathology approaches. *Development and Psychopathology, 16,* 477–481.

Davies, P., & Rose, J. (1999). Assessment of cognitive development in adolescents by means of neuropsychological tasks. *Developmental Neuropsychology, 15,* 227–248.

Dawson, D. A. (1991). Family structure and children's health and well-being: Data from the 1988 National Health Interview Survey on Child Health. *Journal of Marriage and the Family, 53,* 573–584.

Dawson, G., Panagiotides, H., Klinger, L. G., & Spieker, S. (1997). Infants of depressed and nondepressed mothers exhibit differences in frontal brain electrical activity during the expression of negative emotions. *Developmental Psychology, 33,* 650–656.

Dawson, T. (2002). New tools, new insights: Kohlberg's moral judgement stages revisited. *International Journal of Behavioral Development, 26,* 154–166.

de Angelis, T. (2004). Should we be giving psychotropics to children? *APA Monitor on Psychology, 35,* 42.

Deary, I., Thorpe, G., Wilson, V., Starr, J., & Whalley, L. (2003). Population sex differences in IQ at age 11: The Scottish mental survey 1932. *Intelligence, 31,* 533–542.

Deary, I., Whiteman, M., Starr, J., Whalley, L., & Fox, H. (2004). The impact of childhood intelligence on later life: Following up the Scottish mental surveys of 1932 and 1947. *Journal of Personality & Social Psychology, 86,* 139–147.

Deater-Deckard, K., & Dodge, K. A. (1997). Externalizing behavior problems and discipline revisited: Nonlinear effects and variation by culture, context, and gender. *Psychological Inquiry, 8,* 161–175.

Deater-Deckard, K., & Plomin, R. (1997, April). *An adoption study of the etiology of teacher reports of externalizing problems in middle childhood.* Paper presented at the biennial meetings of the Society for Research in Child Development, Washington, DC.

Deater-Deckard, K., Dodge, K. A., Bates, J. E., & Pettit, G. S. (1996). Physical discipline among African American and European American mothers: Links to children's externalizing behaviors. *Developmental Psychology, 32,* 1065–1072.

Deater-Deckard, K., Dunn, J., & Lussier, G. (2002). Sibling relationships and social-emotional adjustment in different family contexts. *Social Development, 11,* 571–590.

DeCasper, A. J., & Spence, M. J. (1986). Prenatal maternal speech influences newborns' perception of speech sounds. *Infant Behavior and Development, 9,* 133–150.

DeCasper, A. J., Lecaneut, J., Busnel, M., Granier-DeFerre, C., & Maugeais, R. (1994). Fetal reactions to recurrent maternal speech. *Infant Behavior and Development, 17,* 159–164.

Deci, E., Koestner, R., & Ryan, R. (1999). A meta-analytic review of experiments examining the effects of extrinsic rewards on intrinsic motivation. *Psychological Bulletin, 125,* 627–668.

Decker, S., McIntosh, D., Kelly, A., Nicholls, S., & Dean, R. (2001). Comorbidity among individuals classified with attention disorders. *International Journal of Neuroscience, 110,* 43–54.

de Haan, M., Luciana, M., Maslone, S. M., Matheny, L. S., & Richards, M. L. M. (1994). Development, plasticity, and risk: Commentary on Huttenlocher, Pollit and Gorman, and Gottesman and Goldsmith. In C. A. Nelson (Ed.), *The Minnesota symposia on child psychology* (Vol. 27, pp. 161–178). Hillsdale, NJ: Erlbaum.

de la Chica, R., Ribas, I., Giraldo, J., Egozcue, J., & Fuster, C. (2005). Chromosomal instability in amniocytes from fetuses of mothers who smoke. *JAMA: Journal of the American Medical Association, 293,* 1212–1222.

de Lacoste, M., Horvath, D., & Woodward, J. (1991). Possible sex differences in the developing human fetal brain. *Journal of Clinical and Experimental Neuropsychology, 13,* 831.

del Barrio, V., Moreno-Rosset, C., Lopez-Martinez, R., & Olmedo, M. (1997). Anxiety, depression and personality structure. *Personality & Individual Differences, 23,* 327–335.

Delaney-Black, V., Covington, C., Templin, T., Kershaw, T., Nordstrom-Klee, B., Ager, J., Clark, N., Surendran, A., Martier, S., & Sokol, R. (2000). Expressive language development of children exposed to cocaine prenatally: Literature review and report of a prospective cohort study. *Journal of Communication Disorders, 33,* 463–481.

Delgado-Gaitan, C. (1994). Socializing young children in Mexican-American families: An intergenerational perspective. In P. M. Greenfield & R. R. Cocking (Eds.), *Crosscultural roots of minority child development* (pp. 55–86). Hillsdale, NJ: Erlbaum.

Dellatolas, G., de Agostini, M., Curt, F., Kremin, H., Letierce, A., Maccario, J., & Lellouch, J. (2003). Manual skill, hand skill asymmetry, and cognitive performance in young children. *Laterality: Asymmetries of Body, Brain, & Cognition, 8,* 317–338.

DeLoache, J. (1989). Young children's understanding of the correspondence between a scale model and a larger space. *Cognitive Development, 4,* 121–139.

DeLoache, J., Simcock, G., & Marzolf, D. (2004). Transfer by very young children in the symbolic retrieval task. *Child Development, 75,* 1708–1718.

DeLoache, J. S. (1989). The development of representation in young children. In H. W. Reese (Ed.), *Advances in child development and behavior* (Vol. 22, pp. 2–37). San Diego, CA: Academic Press.

DeLoache, J. S. (1995). Early understanding and use of symbols: The model model. *Current Directions in Psychological Science, 4,* 109–113.

DeLoache, J. S., & Brown, A. L. (1987). Differences in the memory-based searching of delayed and normally developing young children. *Intelligence, 11,* 277–289.

Delpit, L. (1990). Language diversity and learning. In S. Hynds & D. Rubin (Eds.), *Perspectives on talk and learning* (pp. 247–266). Urbana, IL: National Council on Teacher Education.

DeMars, C. (2000). Test stakes and item format interactions. *Applied Measurement in Education, 13,* 55–77.

Dempster, F. (1981). Memory span: Sources of individual and developmental differences. *Psychological Bulletin, 89,* 63–100.

Denham, S., Blair, K., DeMulder, E., Levitas, J., Sawyer, K., Auerbach-Major, S., & Queenan, P. (2003). Preschool emotional competence: Pathway to social competence. *Child Development, 74,* 238–256.

Dennis, W. (1960). Causes of retardation among institutional children: Iran. *Journal of Genetic Psychology, 96,* 47–59.

Den Ouden, L., Rijken, M., Brand, R., Verloove-Vanhorick, S. P., & Ruys, J. H. (1991). Is it correct to correct? Developmental milestones in 555 "normal" preterm infants compared with term infants. *Journal of Pediatrics, 118,* 399–404.

DeRosier, M., & Marcus, S. (2005). Building friendships and combating bullying: Effectiveness of S.S.GRIN at one-year follow-up. *Journal of Clinical Child & Adolescent Psychology, 34,* 140–150.

DeRosier, M. E., Kupersmidt, J. B., & Patterson, C. J. (1994). Children's academic and behavioral adjustment as a function of the chronicity and proximity of peer rejection. *Child Development, 65,* 1799–1831.

Derryberry, D., & Rothbart, M. K. (1998). Reactive and effortful processes in the organization of temperament. *Development and Psychopathology, 9,* 633–652.

Derzon, J. (2001). Antisocial behavior and the prediction of violence: A meta-analysis. *Psychology in the Schools, 38,* 93–106.

de Villiers, P. A., & de Villiers, J. G. (1992). Language development. In M. H. Bornstein & M. E. Lamb (Eds.), *Developmental psychology: An advanced textbook* (3rd ed., pp. 337–418). Hillsdale, NJ: Erlbaum.

De Wolff, M. S., & van IJzendoorn, M. H. (1997). Sensitivity and attachment: A meta-analysis on parental antecedents of infant attachment. *Child Development, 68,* 571–591.

Dick, D., Rose, R., Viken, R., & Kaprio, J. (2000). Pubertal timing and substance use: Associations between and within families across late adolescence. *Developmental Psychology, 36,* 180–189.

Dickens, W., & Flynn, J. (2001). Heritability estimates versus large environmental effects: The IQ paradox resolved. *Psychological Review, 108,* 346–369.

Diehl, L., Vicary, J., & Deike, R. (1997). Longitudinal trajectories of self-esteem from early to middle adolescence and related psychosocial variables among rural adolescents. *Journal of Research on Adolescence, 7,* 393–411.

Diener, M., & Kim, D. (2004). Maternal and child predictors of preschool children's social competence. *Journal of Applied Developmental Psychology, 25,* 3–24.

Dieter, J., Field, T., Hernandez-Reif, M., Emory, E., & Redzepi, M. (2003). Stable preterm infants gain more weight and sleep less after five days of massage therapy. *Journal of Pediatric Psychology, 28,* 403–411.

Dieterich, S., Hebert, H., Landry, S., Swank, P., & Smith, K. (2004). Maternal and child characteristics that influence the growth of daily living skills from infancy to school age in preterm and term children. *Early Education & Development, 15,* 283–303.

Dietrich, K. N., Berger, O. G., Succop, P. A., Hammond, P. B., & Bornschein, R. L. (1993). The developmental consequences of low to moderate prenatal and postnatal lead exposure: Intellectual attainment in the Cincinnati Lead Study cohort following school entry. *Neurotoxicology and Teratology, 15,* 37–44.

Dietz, W. (2001). Breastfeeding may help prevent childhood overweight. *Journal of the American Medical Association, 285,* 2506–2507.

Digman, J. M. (1990). Personality structure: Emergence of the five-factor model. *Annual Review of Psychology, 41,* 417–440.

Diller, L. (2001). *Defusing the explosive child: The debate between drugs and discipline for raising extremely difficult children.* Retrieved May 30, 2005, from http://cyc-net.org/today2001/today010730.html

Dillingham, R., & Guerrant, R. (2004). Childhood stunting: Measuring and stemming the staggering costs of inadequate water and sanitation. *Lancet, 363,* 94–95.

DiPietro, J. (2004). The role of prenatal maternal stress in child development. *Current Directions in Psychological Science, 13,* 71–74.

DiPietro, J., Bornstein, M., Costigan, K., Pressman, E., Hahn, C., Painter, K., Smith, B., & Yi, L. (2002). What does fetal movement predict about behavior during the first two years of life? *Psychobiology, 40,* 358–371.

DiPietro, J., Costigan, K., & Gurewitsch, E. (2003). Fetal response to induced maternal stress. *Early Human Development, 74,* 125–138.

DiPietro, J., Hilton, S., Hawkins, M., Costigan, K., & Pressman, E. (2002). Maternal stress and affect influence fetal neurobehavioral development. *Developmental Psychology, 38,* 659–668.

DiPietro, J., Hodgson, D., Costigan, K., Hilton, S., & Johnson, T. (1996). Fetal neurobehavioral development. *Child Development, 67,* 2553–2567.

DiPietro, J., Hodgson, D., Costigan, K., & Johnson, T. (1996). Fetal antecedents of infant temperament. *Child Development, 67,* 2568–2583.

Dishion, T. J. (1990). The family ecology of boys' peer relations in middle childhood. *Child Development, 61,* 874–892.

Dishion, T. J., Andrews, D. W., & Crosby, L. (1995). Antisocial boys and their friends in early adolescence: Relationship characteristics, quality, and interactional process. *Child Development, 66,* 139–151.

Dishion, T. J., French, D. C., & Patterson, G. R. (1995). The development and ecology of antisocial behavior. In D. Cicchetti & D. J. Cohen (Eds.), *Developmental psychopathology: Vol. 2. Risk, disorder, and adaptation* (pp. 421–471). New York: Wiley.

Dishion, T. J., Patterson, G. R., Stoolmiller, M., & Skinner, M. L. (1991). Family, school, and behavioral antecedents to early adolescent involvement with antisocial peers. *Developmental Psychology, 27,* 172–180.

Dockett, S., & Smith, I. (1995, April). *Children's theories of mind and their involvement in complex shared pretense.* Paper presented at the biennial meetings of the Society for Research in Child Development, Indianapolis.

Dodge, K. (1993). Social-cognitive mechanisms in the development of conduct disorder and depression. *Annual Review of Psychology, 44,* 559–584.

Dodge, K. A. (1990). Developmental psychopathology in children of depressed mothers. *Developmental Psychology, 26,* 3–6.

Dodge, K. A. (1997, April). *Testing developmental theory through prevention trials.* Paper presented at the biennial meetings of the Society for Research in Child Development, Washington, DC.

Dodge, K. A., Pettit, G. S., & Bates, J. E. (1994). Socialization mediators of the relation between socioeconomic status and child conduct problems. *Child Development, 65,* 649–665.

Domitrovich, C., & Bierman, K. (2001). Parenting practices and child social adjustment: Multiple pathways of influence. *Merrill-Palmer Quarterly, 47,* 235–263.

Donnellan, M., Trzesniewski, K., Robins, R., Moffitt, T., & Caspi, A. (2005). Low self-esteem is related to aggression, antisocial behavior, and delinquency. *Psychological Science, 16,* 328–335.

Donnerstein, E., Slaby, R. G., & Eron, L. D. (1994). The mass media and youth aggression. In L. D. Eron, J. H. Gentry, & P. Schlegel (Eds.), *Reason to hope: A psychosocial perspective on violence and youth* (pp. 219–250). Washington, DC: American Psychological Association.

Donohew, R., Hoyle, R., Clayton, R., Skinner, W., Colon, S., & Rice, R. (1999). Sensation seeking and drug use by adolescents and their friends: Models for marijuana and alcohol. *Journal of Studies on Alcohol, 60,* 622–631.

Dornbusch, S. M., Ritter, P. L., Liederman, P. H., Roberts, D. F., & Fraleigh, M. J. (1987). The relation of parenting style to adolescent school performance. *Child Development, 58,* 1244–1257.

Doyle, A. B., & Aboud, F. E. (1995). A longitudinal study of white children's racial prejudice as a social-cognitive development. *Merrill-Palmer Quarterly, 41,* 209–228.

Drum, P. (1985). Retention of text information by grade, ability and study. *Discourse Processes, 8,* 21–52.

Dryfoos, J. (1990). *Adolescents at risk: Prevalence and prevention.* New York: Oxford University Press.

DuBois, D. L., Felner, R. D., Brand, S., Phillips, R. S. C., & Lease, A. M. (1996). Early adolescent self-esteem: A developmental-ecological framework and assessment strategy. *Journal of Research on Adolescence, 6,* 543–579.

Duke, P. M., Carlsmith, J. M., Jennings, D., Martin, J. A., Dornbusch, S. M., Gross, R. T., & Siegel-Gorelick, B. (1982). Educational correlates of early and late sexual maturation in adolescence. *Journal of Pediatrics, 100,* 633–637.

Duncan, G. (1993, April). *Economic deprivation and childhood development.* Paper presented at the biennial meetings of the Society for Research in Child Development, New Orleans.

Duncan, G. J., Brooks-Gunn, J., & Klebanov, P. K. (1994). Economic deprivation and early childhood development. *Child Development, 65,* 296–318.

Duncan, R. M. (1995). Piaget and Vygotsky revisited: Dialogue or assimilation? *Developmental Review, 15,* 458–472.

Dunham, P. J., Dunham, F., & Curwin, A. (1993). Joint-attentional states and lexical acquisition at 18 months. *Developmental Psychology, 29,* 827–831.

Dunn, J. (1992). Siblings and development. *Current Directions in Psychological Science, 1,* 6–9.

Dunn, J. (1993). *Young children's close relationships.* Newbury Park, CA: Sage.

Dunn, J. (1994). Experience and understanding of emotions, relationships, and membership in a particular culture. In P. Ekman & R. J. Davidson (Eds.), *The nature of emotion: Fundamental questions* (pp. 352–355). New York: Oxford University Press.

Dunn, J., Cutting, A., & Fisher, N. (2002). Old friends, new friends: Predictors of children's perspective on their friends at school. *Child Development, 73*, 621–635.

Dunn, J., & Kendrick, C. (1982). Siblings and their mothers: Developing relationships within the family. In M. E. Lamb & B. Sutton-Smith (Eds.), *Sibling relationships: Their nature and significance across the lifespan* (pp. 39–60). Hillsdale, NJ: Erlbaum.

Dunn, J., & McGuire, S. (1994). Young children's nonshared experiences: A summary of studies in Cambridge and Colorado. In E. M. Hetherington, D. Reiss, & R. Plomin (Eds.), *Separate social worlds of siblings: The impact of nonshared environment on development* (pp. 111–128). Hillsdale, NJ: Erlbaum.

Dunphy, D. C. (1963). The social structure of urban adolescent peer groups. *Sociometry, 26*, 230–246.

Dupree, L., Watson, M., & Schneider, M. (2005). Preferences for mental health care: A comparison of older African Americans and older Caucasians. *Journal of Applied Gerontology, 24*, 196–210.

Durston, S., Pol, H., Casey, B., Giedd, J., Buitelaar, J., & van Engeland, H. (2001). Anatomical MRI of the developing human brain: What have we learned? *Journal of the American Academy of Child and Adolescent Psychiatry, 40*, 1012–1020.

Duvall, S., Delquadri, J., & Ward, D. (2004). A preliminary investigation of the effectiveness of homeschool instructional environments for students with attention-deficit/hyperactivity disorder. *School Psychology Review, 33*, 140–158.

Eagly, A. H. (1995). The science and politics of comparing women and men. *American Psychologist, 50*, 145–158.

Easterbrooks, M. A., Davidson, C. E., & Chazan, R. (1993). Psychosocial risk, attachment, and behavior problems among school-aged children. *Development and Psychopathology, 5*, 389–402.

EBC (1991). *Childhood: In the land of giants.* [Television series]. New York: Public Broadcasting System.

Egan, S., & Perry, D. (2001). Gender identity: A multidimensional analysis with implications for psychosocial adjustment. *Developmental Psychology, 37*, 451–463.

Egan, S. K., & Perry, D. G. (1998). Does low self-regard invite victimization? *Developmental Psychology, 34*, 299–309.

Egeland, B., & Sroufe, L. A. (1981). Attachment and early maltreatment. *Child Development, 52*, 44–52.

Ehri, L., Nunes, S., Stahl, S., & Willows, D. (2001). Systematic phonics instruction helps students learn to read: Evidence from the National Reading panel's meta-analysis. *Review of Educational Research, 71*, 393–447.

Eisenberg, N. (1986). *Altruistic emotion, cognition, and behavior.* Hillsdale, NJ: Erlbaum.

Eisenberg, N. (1988). The development of prosocial and aggressive behavior. In M. H. Bornstein & M. E. Lamb (Eds.), *Developmental psychology: An advanced textbook* (2nd ed., pp. 461–496). Hillsdale, NJ: Erlbaum.

Eisenberg, N. (1990). Prosocial development in early and mid-adolescence. In R. Montemayor, G. R. Adams, & T. P. Gullotta (Eds.), *From childhood to adolescence: A transitional period?* (pp. 240–268). Newbury Park, CA: Sage.

Eisenberg, N. (1992). *The caring child.* Cambridge, MA: Harvard University Press.

Eisenberg, N. (2000). Emotion, regulation, and moral development. *Annual Review of Psychology, 51*, 665–697.

Eisenberg, N. (2001). The core and correlates of affective social competence. *Social Development, 10*, 120–124.

Eisenberg, N., Fabes, R., Murphy, B., Shepard, S., Guthrie, I., Mazsk, P., Paulin, R., & Jones, S. (1999). Prediction of elementary school children's socially appropriate and problem behavior from anger reactions at age 4–6 years. *Journal of Applied Developmental Psychology, 20*, 119–142.

Eisenberg, N., & Fabes, R. A. (1998). Prosocial behavior. In W. Damon (Ed.), *Handbook of child psychology: Vol 3. Social, emotional, and personality development* (5th ed., pp. 701–778). New York: Wiley.

Eisenberg, N., Fabes, R. A., Murphy, B., Karbon, M., Smith, M., & Maszk, P. (1996). The relations of children's dispositional empathy-related responding to their emotionality, regulation, and social functioning. *Developmental Psychology, 32*, 195–209.

Eisenberg, N., Fabes, R. A., Murphy, B., Maszk, P., Smith, M., & Karbon, M. (1995). The role of emotionality and regulation in children's social functioning: A longitudinal study. *Child Development, 66*, 1360–1384.

Eisenberg, N., Fabes, R. A., Schaller, M., & Miller, P. A. (1989). Sympathy and personal distress: Development, gender differences, and interrelations of indexes. *New Directions for Child Development, 44*, 107–126.

Eisenberg, N., Gershoff, E., Fabes, R., Shepard, S., Cumberland, A., Losoya, S., Guthrie, I., & Murphy, B. (2001). Mother's emotional expressivity and children's behavior problems and social competence: Mediation through children's regulation. *Developmental Psychology, 37*, 475–490.

Eisenberg, N., Liew, J., & Pidada, S. (2001). The relations of parental emotional expressivity with quality of Indonesian children's social functioning. *Emotion, 1*, 116–136.

Eisenberg, N., & Murphy, B. (1995). Parenting and children's moral development. In M. H. Bornstein (Ed.), *Handbook of parenting: Vol. 4. Applied and practical parenting* (pp. 227–257). Mahwah, NJ: Erlbaum.

Eisenberg, N., Sadovsky, A., Spinrad, T., Fabes, R., Losoya, S., Valiente, C., Reiser, M., Cumberland, A., & Shepard, S. (2005). The relations of problem behavior status to children's negative emotionality, effortful control, and impulsivity: Concurrent relations and prediction of change. *Developmental Psychology, 41*, 193–211.

Eisenberger, N. (2003). Does rejection hurt? An fMRI study of social exclusion. *Science, 302*, 290–292.

Eisenberger, R., Pierce, W., & Cameron, J. (1999). Effects of reward on intrinsic motivation—negative, neutral, and positive: Comment on Deci, Koestner, and Ryan. *Psychological Bulletin, 125*, 677–691.

Ekman, P. (1972). Universals and cultural differences in facial expressions of emotion. In J. Cole (Ed.), *Nebraska symposium on motivation, 1971* (pp. 207–282). Lincoln: University of Nebraska Press.

Ekman, P. (1973). Cross-cultural studies of facial expression. In P. Ekman (Ed.), *Darwin and facial expression* (pp. 169–222). New York: Academic Press.

Ekman, P. (1989). The argument and evidence about universals in facial expressions of emotion. In H. Wagner & A. Manstead (Eds.), *Handbook of social psychophysiology* (pp. 143–164). Chichester, England: Wiley.

Elkind, D. (1967). Egocentrism in adolescence. *Child Development, 38*, 1025–1034.

Ellenbogen, S., & Chamberland, C. (1997). The peer relations of dropouts: A comparative study of at-risk and not at-risk youths. *Journal of Adolescence, 20*, 355–367.

Ellickson, P., Martino, S., & Collins, R. (2004). Marijuana use from adolescence to young adulthood: Multiple developmental trajectories and their associated outcomes. *Health Psychology, 23*, 299–307.

Elliot, A., & Hall, N. (1997). The impact of self-regulatory teaching strategies on "at-risk" preschoolers' mathematical learning in a computer-mediated environment. *Journal of Computing in Childhood Education, 8*, 187–198.

Ellsworth, C. P., Muir, D. W., & Hains, S. M. J. (1993). Social competence and person-object differentiation: An analysis of the still-face effect. *Developmental Psychology, 29*, 63–73.

Emery, R. E., & Laumann-Billings, L. (1998). An overview of the nature, causes, and consequences of abusive family relationships: Toward differentiating maltreatment and violence. *American Psychologist, 53*, 121–135.

Englund, M., Luckner, A., Whaley, G., & Egeland, B. (2004). Children's achievement in early elementary school: Longitudinal effects of parental involvement, expectations, and quality of assistance. *Journal of Educational Psychology, 96*, 723–730.

Ensign, J. (1998). *Defying the stereotypes of special education: Homeschool students.* Paper presented at the annual meeting of the American Education Research Association, San Diego, CA.

Entwisle, D. R., & Alexander, K. L. (1990). Beginning school math competence: Minority and majority comparisons. *Child Development, 61*, 454–471.

Epstein, S. (1991). Cognitive-experiential self theory: Implications for developmental psychology. In M. R. Gunnar & L. A. Sroufe (Eds.), *The Minnesota symposia on child development* (Vol. 23, pp. 79–123). Hillsdale, NJ: Erlbaum.

Erel, O., & Burman, B. (1995). Interrelatedness of marital relations and parent-child relations: A meta-analytic review. *Psychological Bulletin, 118*, 108–312.

Ericsson, K. A., & Crutcher, R. J. (1990). The nature of exceptional performance. In P. B. Baltes, D. L., Featherman, & R. M. Lerner (Eds.), *Life-span development and behavior* (Vol. 10, pp. 188–218). Hillsdale, NJ: Erlbaum.

Ernst, M., Moolchan, E., & Robinson, M. (2001). Behavioral and neural consequences of prenatal exposure to nicotine. *Journal of the American Academy of Child and Adolescent Psychiatry, 40*, 639–641.

Eron, L. D. (1987). The development of aggressive behavior from the perspective of a developing behaviorism. *American Psychologist, 42*, 435–442.

Eron, L. D. (1992). Testimony before the Senate Committee on Governmental Affairs. *Congressional Record, 88*(June 18), S8538–S8539.

Eron, L. D., Huesmann, L. R., & Zelli, A. (1991). The role of parental variables in the learning of aggression. In D. J. Pepler & K. H. Rubin (Eds.),

The development and treatment of childhood aggression (pp. 169–188). Hillsdale, NJ: Erlbaum.

Escalona, K. S. (1981). The reciprocal role of social and emotional developmental advances and cognitive development during the second and third years of life. In E. K. Shapiro & E. Weber (Eds.), *Cognitive and affective growth: Developmental interaction* (pp. 87–108). Hillsdale, NJ: Erlbaum.

Escorihuela, R. M., Tobena, A., & Fernández-Teruel, A. (1994). Environmental enrichment reverses the detrimental action of early inconsistent stimulation and increases the beneficial effects of postnatal handling on shuttlebox learning in adult rats. *Behavioural Brain Research, 61,* 169–173.

Eslea, M., Menesini, E., Morita, Y., O'Moore, M., Mora-Merchan, J., Pereira, B., & Smith, P. (2004). Friendship and loneliness among bullies and victims: Data from seven countries. *Aggressive Behavior, 30,* 71–83.

Espy, K., Stalets, M., McDiarmid, M., Senn, T., Cwik, M., & Hamby, A. (2002). Executive functions in preschool children born preterm: Application of cognitive neuroscience paradigms. *Child Neuropsychology, 8,* 83–92.

Evans, G. (2004). The environment of childhood poverty. *American Psychologist, 59,* 77–92.

Ex, C. & Janssens, J. (1998). Maternal influences on daughters' gender role attitudes. *Sex Roles, 38,* 171–186.

Ezpeleta, L., Keeler, G., Alaatin, E., Costello, E., & Angold, A. (2001). Epidemiology of psychiatric disability in childhood and adolescence. *Journal of Child Psychology & Psychiatry & Allied Disciplines, 42,* 901–914.

Fabes, R., Eisenberg, N., Hanish, L., & Spinrad, T. (2001). Preschoolers' spontaneous emotion vocabulary: Relations to likability. *Early Education & Development, 12,* 11–27.

Fagan, J. F., III, & Singer, L. T. (1983). Infant recognition memory as a measure of intelligence. In L. P. Lipsitt (Ed.), *Advances in infancy research* (Vol. 2, pp. 31–78). Norwood, NJ: Ablex.

Fagard, J., & Jacquet, A. (1989). Onset of bimanual coordination and symmetry versus asymmetry of movement. *Infant Behavior and Development, 12,* 229–235.

Fagot, B. I. (1995). Parenting boys and girls. In M. H. Bornstein (Ed.), *Handbook of parenting: Vol. 1. Children and parenting* (pp. 163–183). Mahwah, NJ: Erlbaum.

Fagot, B. I., & Hagan, R. (1991). Observations of parent reactions to sex-stereotyped behaviors: Age and sex effects. *Child Development, 62,* 617–628.

Fagot, B. I., & Leinbach, M. D. (1989). The young child's gender schema: Environmental input, internal organization. *Child Development, 60,* 663–672.

Fagot, B. I., & Leinbach, M. D. (1993). Gender-role development in young children: From discrimination to labeling. *Developmental Review, 13,* 205–224.

Fagot, B. I., Leinbach, M. D., & O'Boyle, C. (1992). Gender labeling, gender stereotyping, and parenting behaviors. *Developmental Psychology, 28,* 225–230.

Fair Test. (2004). *No Child Left Behind after two years: A track record of failure.* Retrieved May 26, 2005, from http://www.fairtest.org/Nclb%20flaw%20fact%20sheet%201-7-04.html

Fallis, R., & Opotow, S. (2003). Are students failing school or are schools failing students? Class cutting in high school. *Journal of Social Issues, 59,* 103–119.

Fantuzzo, J., Sekino, Y., & Cohen, H. (2004). An examination of the contributions of interactive peer play to salient classroom competencies for urban Head Start children. *Psychology in the Schools, 41,* 323–336.

Fantz, R. L. (1956). A method for studying early visual development. *Perceptual & Motor Skills, 6,* 13–15.

Faraone, S., Biederman, J., Mick, E., Doyle, A., Wilens, T., Spencer, T., Frazier, E., & Mullen, K. (2001). A family study of psychiatric comorbidity in girls and boys with attention-deficit/hyperactivity disorder. *Biological Psychiatry, 50,* 586–592.

Farmer, T., Estell, D., Leung, M., Trott, H., Bishop, J., & Cairns, B. (2003). Individual characteristics, early adolescent peer affiliations, and school dropout: An examination of aggressive and popular group types. *Journal of School Psychology, 41,* 217–232.

Farnham-Diggory, S. (1978). On the logic and pitfalls of logograph research. *Journal of Experimental Child Psychology, 25,* 366–370.

Farnham-Diggory, S. (1986). Time, now, for a little serious complexity. In S. J. Ceci (Ed.), *Handbook of cognitive, social, and neuropsychological aspects of learning disability* (Vol. 1). Hillsdale, NJ: Erlbaum.

Farnham-Diggory, S. (1992). *The learning-disabled child.* Cambridge, MA: Harvard University Press.

Farrar, M. J. (1992). Negative evidence and grammatical morpheme acquisition. *Developmental Psychology, 28,* 90–98.

Farver, J. (1996). Aggressive behavior in preschoolers' social networks: Do birds of a feather flock together? *Early Childhood Research Quarterly, 11,* 333–350.

Farver, J., Bhadha, B., & Narang, S. (2002). Acculturation and psychological functioning in Asian Indian adolescents. *Social Development, 11,* 11–29.

Fearon, I., Hains, S., Muir, D., & Kisilevsky, B. (2002). Development of tactile responses in human preterm and full-term infants from 30 to 40 weeks postconceptional age. *Infancy, 3,* 31–51.

Featherman, D. L. (1980). Schooling and occupational careers: Constancy and change in worldly success. In O. G. Brim Jr. & J. Kagan (Eds.), *Constancy and change in human development* (pp. 675–738). Cambridge, MA: Harvard University Press.

Federal Interagency Forum on Child and Family Statistics (FIFCFS). (2000). *America's children: Key national indicators of well-being 2000.* Washington, DC: Author.

Fein, J., Durbin, D., & Selbst, S. (2002). Injuries and emergencies. In A. Rudolph, R. Kamei, & K. Overby (Eds.), *Rudolph's fundamentals of pediatrics* (3rd ed., pp. 390–436). New York: McGraw-Hill.

Feinberg, M., & Hetherington, E. (2001). Differential parenting as a within-family variable. *Journal of Family Psychology, 15,* 22–37.

Feinfield, K., Lee, P., Flavell, E., Green, F., & Flavell, J. (1999). Young children's understanding of intention. *Cognitive Development, 14,* 463–486.

Feiring, C. (1999). Other-sex friendship networks and the development of romantic relationships in adolescence. *Journal of Youth & Adolescence, 28,* 495–512.

Feldman, D. (2004). Piaget's stages: The unfinished symphony of cognitive development. *New Ideas in Psychology, 22,* 175–131.

Feldman, R. (2003). Paternal socio-psychological factors and infant attachment: The mediating role of synchrony in father-infant interactions. *Infant Behavior and Development, 25,* 221–236.

Feldman, R., & Eidelman, A. (2003). Skin-to-skin contact (Kangaroo Care) accelerates autonomic and neurobehavioural maturation in preterm infants. *Developmental Medicine & Child Neurology, 45,* 274–281.

Feldman, S. S. (1987). Predicting strain in mothers and fathers of 6-month-old infants. A short-term longitudinal study. In P. W. Berman & F. A. Pedersen (Eds.), *Men's transitions to parenthood* (pp. 13–36). Hillsdale, NJ: Erlbaum.

Fennig, S., Geva, K., Zalzman, G., Weitzman, A., Fennig, S., & Apter, A. (2005). Effect of gender on suicide attempters versus nonattempters in an adolescent inpatient unit. *Comprehensive Psychiatry, 46,* 90–97.

Fenson, L., Dale, P. S., Reznick, J. S., Bates, E., Thal, D. J., & Pethick, S. J. (1994). Variability in early communicative development. *Monographs of the Society for Research in Child Development, 59*(5, Serial No. 242).

Ferber, R., & Boyer, R. (1985). *Solve your child's sleep problems.* New York: Simon & Schuster.

Fernald, A. (1993). Approval and disapproval: Infant responsiveness to vocal affect in familiar and unfamiliar languages. *Child Development, 64,* 657–674.

Fernald, A., & Kuhl, P. (1987). Acoustic determinants of infant preference for motherese speech. *Infant Behavior and Development, 10,* 279–293.

Fernald, A., & Morikawa, H. (1993). Common themes and cultural variations in Japanese and American mothers' speech to infants. *Child Development, 64,* 637–656.

Fernald, A., Taeschner, T., Dunn, J., Papousek, M., Boysson-Bardies, B., & Fukui, I. (1989). A cross-language study of prosodic modifications in mothers' and fathers' speech to preverbal infants. *Journal of Child Language, 16,* 477–501.

Fewell, R., & Deutscher, B. (2003). Contributions of early language and maternal facilitation variables to later language and reading abilities. *Journal of Early Intervention, 26,* 132–145.

Field, T., Diego, M., Hernandez-Reif, M., Vera, Y., Gil, K., Schanberg, S., Kuhn, C., & Gonzalez-Garcia, A. (2004). Prenatal predictors of maternal and newborn EEG. *Infant Behavior and Development, 27,* 533–536.

Field, T. M. (1977). Effects of early separation, interactive deficits, and experimental manipulations on infant-mother face-to-face interaction. *Child Development, 48,* 763–771.

Field, T. M. (1991). Quality infant day-care and grade school behavior and performance. *Child Development, 62,* 863–870.

Field, T. M. (1995). Psychologically depressed parents. In M. H. Bornstein (Ed.), *Handbook of parenting: Vol. 4. Applied and practical parenting* (pp. 85–99). Mahwah, NJ: Erlbaum.

Field, T. M., Healy, B., Goldstein, S., & Guthertz, M. (1990). Behavior-state matching and synchrony in mother-infant interactions of non-depressed versus depressed dyads. *Developmental Psychology, 26,* 7–14.

Field, T. M., Woodson, R., Greenberg, R., & Cohen, D. (1982). Discrimination and imitation of facial expressions by neonates. *Science, 218,* 179–181.

Fifer, W. P., & Moon, C. M. (1994). The role of mother's voice in the organization of brain function in the newborn. *Acta Paediatrica, 397*(Suppl.), 86–93.

Fillmore, C. (1997). *A linguist looks at the Ebonics debate.* Washington, DC: Center for Applied Linguistics.

Findling, R., Feeny, N., Stansbrey, R., Delporto-Bedoya, D., & Demeter, C. (2004). Special articles: Treatment of mood disorders in children and adolescents: Somatic treatment for depressive illnesses in children and adolescents. *Psychiatric Clinics of North America, 27,* 113–137.

Fine, L., Trentacosta, C., Izard, C., Mostow, A., & Campbell, J. (2004). Anger perception, caregivers' use of physical discipline, and aggression in children at risk. *Social Development, 13,* 213–228.

Fischer, K., & Rose, S. (1994). Dynamic development of coordination of components in brain and behavior: A framework for theory and research. In K. Fischer & G. Dawson (Eds.), *Human behavior and the developing brain* (pp. 3–66). New York: Guilford.

Fitzgerald, B. (1999). Children of lesbian and gay parents: A review of the literature. *Marriage & Family Review, 29,* 57–75.

Fitzgerald, D., & White, K. (2003). Linking children's social worlds: Perspective-taking in parent-child and peer contexts. *Social Behavior & Personality, 31,* 509–522.

Fitzgerald, M. (2004). The case of Robert Walser (1878–1956). *Irish Journal of Psychological Medicine, 21,* 138–142.

Flanagan, C. A., & Eccles, J. S. (1993). Changes in parents' work status and adolescents' adjustments at school. *Child Development, 64,* 246–257.

Flannery, D. J., Montemayor, R., & Eberly, M. B. (1994). The influence of parent negative emotional expression on adolescents' perceptions of their relationships with their parents. *Personal Relationships, 1,* 259–274.

Flavell, J. (1999). Cognitive development: Children's knowledge about the mind. *Annual Review of Psychology, 50,* 21–45.

Flavell, J. (2000). Development of children's knowledge about the mental world. *International Journal of Behavioral Development, 24,* 14–23.

Flavell, J. (2004). Theory-of-mind development: Retrospect and prospect. *Merrill-Palmer Quarterly, 50,* 274–290.

Flavell, J., & Green, F. (1999). Development of intuitions about the controllability of different mental states. *Cognitive Development, 14,* 133–146.

Flavell, J., Green, F., & Flavell, E. (1998). The mind has a mind of its own: Developing knowledge about mental uncontrollability. *Cognitive Development, 13,* 127–138.

Flavell, J., Green, F., & Flavell, E. (2000). Development of children's awareness of their own thoughts. *Journal of Cognition and Development, 1,* 97–112.

Flavell, J., Green, F., Flavell, E., & Lin, N. (1999). Development of children's knowledge about unconsciousness. *Child Development, 70,* 396–412.

Flavell, J. H. (1985). *Cognitive development* (2nd ed.). Englewood Cliffs, NJ: Prentice Hall.

Flavell, J. H. (1986). The development of children's knowledge about the appearance-reality distinction. *American Psychologist, 41,* 418–425.

Flavell, J. H. (1993). Young children's understanding of thinking and consciousness. *Current Directions in Psychological Science, 2,* 40–43.

Flavell, J. H., Green, F. L., & Flavell, E. R. (1989). Young children's ability to differentiate appearance-reality and level 2 perspectives in the tactile modality. *Child Development, 60,* 201–213.

Flavell, J. H., Green, F. L., & Flavell, E. R. (1990). Developmental changes in young children's knowledge about the mind. *Cognitive Development, 5,* 1–27.

Flavell, J. H., Green, F. L., & Flavell, E. R. (1995). Young children's knowledge about thinking. *Monographs of the Society for Research in Child Development, 60*(1, Serial No. 243).

Flavell, J. H., Green, F. L., Wahl, K. E., & Flavell, E. R. (1987). The effects of question clarification and memory aids on young children's performance on appearance-reality tasks. *Cognitive Development, 2,* 127–144.

Flavell, J. H., Miller, P. H., & Miller, S. A. (1993). *Cognitive development* (3rd ed.). Englewood Cliffs, NJ: Prentice Hall.

Flavell, J. H., Zhang, X., Zou, H., Dong, Q., & Qi, S. (1983). A comparison of the appearance-reality distinction in the People's Republic of China and the United States. *Cognitive Psychology, 15,* 459–466.

Fletcher, A. C., Darling, N. E., Steinberg, L., & Dornbusch, S. M. (1995). The company they keep: Relation of adolescents' adjustment and behavior to their friends' perceptions of authoritative parenting in the social network. *Developmental Psychology, 31,* 300–310.

Flynn, J. (1999). Searching for justice: The discovery of IQ gains over time. *American Psychologist, 54,* 5–20.

Flynn, J. R. (1994). IQ gains over time. In *The Encyclopedia of Human Intelligence* (pp. 617–623). New York: Macmillan.

Folk, K. F., & Yi, Y. (1994). Piecing together child care with multiple arrangements: Crazy quilt or preferred pattern for employed parents of preschool children? *Journal of Marriage and the Family, 56,* 669–680.

Folven, R., & Bonvillian, J. (1991). The transition from nonreferential to referential language in children acquiring American Sign Language. *Developmental Psychology, 27,* 806–816.

Fordham, K., & Stevenson-Hinde, J. (1999). Shyness, friendship quality, and adjustment during middle childhood. *Journal of Child Psychology & Psychiatry & Allied Disciplines, 40,* 757–768.

Foulder-Hughes, L., & Cooke, R. (2003a). Do mainstream schoolchildren who were born preterm have motor problems? *British Journal of Occupational Therapy, 66,* 9–16.

Foulder-Hughes, L., & Cooke, R. (2003b). Motor, cognitive, and behavioural disorders in children born very preterm. *Developmental Medicine & Child Neurology, 45,* 97–103.

Fox, N., Henderson, H., Rubin, K., Calkins, S., & Schmidt, L. (2001). Continuity and discontinuity of behavioral inhibition and exuberance: Psychophysiological and behavioral influences across the first four years of life. *Child Development, 72,* 1–21.

Fox, N. A., Kimmerly, N. L., & Schafer, W. D. (1991). Attachment to mother/attachment to father: A meta-analysis. *Child Development, 62,* 210–225.

Francis, P. L., Self, P. A., & Horowitz, F. D. (1987). The behavioral assessment of the neonate: An overview. In J. D. Osofsky (Ed.), *Handbook of infant development* (2nd ed., pp. 723–779). New York: Wiley-Interscience.

Franco, N., & Levitt, M. (1998). The social ecology of middle childhood: Family support, friendship quality, and self-esteem. *Family Relations: Interdisciplinary Journal of Applied Family Studies, 47,* 315–321.

Fraser, A. M., Brockert, J. E., & Ward, R. H. (1995). Association of young maternal age with adverse reproductive outcomes. *New England Journal of Medicine, 332,* 1113–1117.

Frazier, S., Bates, J. E., Dodge, K. A., & Pettit, G. S. (1997, April). *The effects of television violence and early harsh discipline on children's social cognitions and peer-directed aggression.* Paper presented at the biennial meetings of the Society for Research in Child Development, Washington, DC.

Fredricks, J., & Eccles, J. (2002). Children's competence and value beliefs from childhood through adolescence: Growth trajectories in two male sex-typed domains. *Developmental Psychology, 38,* 519–533.

Fredricks, J., & Eccles, J. (2005). Family socialization, gender, and sport motivation and involvement. *Journal of Sport & Exercise Psychology, 27,* 3–31.

Freedman, D. G. (1979). Ethnic differences in babies. *Human Nature, 2,* 36–43.

Fretts, R. C., Schmittdiel, J., McLean, F. H., Usher, R. H., & Goldman, M. B. (1995). Increased maternal age and the risk of fetal death. *New England Journal of Medicine, 333,* 953–957.

Freud, S. (1905). *The basic writings of Sigmund Freud* (A. A. Brill, Trans.). New York: Random House.

Freud, S. (1920). *A general introduction to psychoanalysis* (J. Riviere, Trans.). New York: Washington Square Press.

Frey, K. S., & Ruble, D. N. (1992). Gender constancy and the "cost" of sex-typed behavior: A test of the conflict hypothesis. *Developmental Psychology, 28,* 714–721.

Fried, P., & Smith, A. (2001). A literature review of the consequences of prenatal marihuana exposure: An emerging theme of a deficiency in aspects of executive function. *Neurotoxicology & Teratology, 23,* 1–11.

Fry, A. F., & Hale, S. (1996). Processing speed, working memory, and fluid intelligence. *Psychological Science, 7,* 237–241.

Fuchs, L., Fuchs, D., Karns, K., Hamlett, C., Dutka, S., & Katsaroff, M. (2000). The importance of providing background information on the structure and scoring of performance assessments. *Applied Measurement in Education, 13,* 134.

Fuligni, A., Yip, T., & Tseng, V. (2002). The impact of family obligation on the daily activities and psychological well-being of Chinese American adolescents. *Child Development, 73,* 302–314.

Fung, H. (1999). Becoming a moral child: The socialization of shame among young Chinese children. *Ethos, 27,* 180–209.

Funk, J., Baldacci, H., Pasold, T., & Baumgardner, J. (2004). Violence exposure in real-life, video games, television, movies, and the Internet: Is there desensitization? *Journal of Adolescence, 27,* 23–39.

Funk, J., & Buchman, D. (1999). Playing violent video and computer games and adolescent self-concept. *Journal of Communication, 46,* 19–32.

Funk, J., Buchman, D., Jenks, J., & Bechtoldt, H. (2003). Playing violent video games, desensitization, and moral evaluation in children. *Journal of Applied Developmental Psychology, 24,* 413–436.

Funk, J., Buchman, D., Myers, B., & Jenks, J. (2000, August). *Asking the right questions in research on violent electronic games.* Paper presented at the annual meeting of the American Psychological Association, Washington, DC.

Furman, E. (1995). Memories of a "qualified student." *Journal of Child Psychotherapy, 21,* 309–312.

Furman, L., Wilson-Costello, D., Friedman, H., Taylor, H., Minich, N., & Hack, M. (2004). The effect of neonatal maternal milk feeding on the neurodevelopmental outcome of very low birth weight infants. *Journal of Developmental and Behavioral Pediatrics, 25,* 247–253.

Furnham, A. (2000). Parents' estimates of their own and their children's multiple intelligences. *British Journal of Developmental Psychology, 18,* 583–594.

Furnham, A., Petrides, K., Tsaousis, I., Pappas, K., & Garrod, D. (2005). A cross-cultural investigation into the relationships between personality traits and work values. *Journal of Psychology: Interdisciplinary & Applied, 139,* 5–32.

Furrow, D. (1984). Social and private speech at two years. *Child Development, 55,* 355–362.

Furrow, D., & Nelson, K. (1984). Environmental correlates of individual differences in language acquisition. *Journal of Child Language, 11,* 523–534.

Furstenberg, F., Brooks-Gunn, J., & Chase-Lansdale, L. (1989). Teenaged pregnancy and childbearing. *American Psychologist, 44,* 313–320.

Furstenberg, F. F., Jr., & Cherlin, A. J. (1991). *Divided families: What happens to children when parents part.* Cambridge, MA: Harvard University Press.

Furstenberg, F. F., Jr., & Hughes, M. E. (1995). Social capital and successful development among at-risk youth. *Journal of Marriage and the Family, 57,* 580–592.

Galambos, D. L., & Maggs, J. (1991). Out-of-school care of young adolescents and self-reported behavior. *Developmental Psychology, 27,* 644–655.

Galanaki, E. (2004). Teachers and loneliness: The children's perspective. *School Psychology International, 25,* 92–105.

Galassi, J., Gulledge, S., & Cox, N. (1997). Middle school advisories: Retrospect and prospect. *Review of Educational Research, 67,* 301–338.

Gale, C., O'Callaghan, F., Godfrey, K., Law, C., & Martyn, C. (2004). Critical periods of brain growth and cognitive function in children. *Brain, 127,* 321–329.

Gallagher, C., & Dobrin, A. (2005). The association between suicide screening practices and attempts requiring emergency care in juvenile justice facilities. *Journal of the American Academy of Child and Adolescent Psychiatry, 44,* 485–493.

Gallahue, D. L., & Ozmun, J. C. (1995). *Understanding motor development* (3rd ed.). Madison, WI: Brown & Benchmark.

Galliher, R., Rostosky, S., & Hughes, H. (2004). School belonging, self-esteem, and depressive symptoms in adolescents: An examination of sex, sexual attraction status, and urbanicity. *Journal of Youth & Adolescence, 33,* 235–245.

Ganchrow, J. R., Steiner, J. E., & Daher, M. (1983). Neonatal facial expressions in response to different qualities and intensities of gustatory stimuli. *Infant Behavior and Development, 6,* 189–200.

Ganong, L., & Coleman, M. (1994). *Remarried family relationships,* Thousand Oaks, CA: Sage.

Garbarino, J. (2002). Foreward: Pathways from childhood traumas to adolescent violence and delinquency. *Journal of Aggression, Maltreatment, & Trauma, 6,* xxv–xxxi.

Garbarino, J., Dubrow, N., Kostelny, K., & Pardo, C. (1992). *Children in danger: Coping with the consequences of community violence.* San Francisco: Jossey-Bass.

Garbarino, J., & Kostelny, K. (1997). What children can tell us about living in a war zone. In J. D. Osofsky (Ed.), *Children in a violent society* (pp. 32–41). New York: Guilford Press.

Garbarino, J., Kostelny, K., & Dubrow, N. (1991). *No place to be a child: Growing up in a war zone.* Lexington, MA: Lexington Books.

Gardner, H. (1983). *Frames of mind: The theory of multiple intelligence.* New York: Basic Books.

Gardner, R., Friedman, B., & Jackson, N. (1999). Body size estimations, body dissatisfaction, and ideal size preferences in children six through thirteen. *Journal of Youth & Adolescence, 28,* 603–618.

Garfinkel, P. E. (1995). Classification and diagnosis of eating disorders. In K. D. Brownell & C. G. Fairburn (Eds.), *Eating disorders and obesity: A comprehensive handbook* (pp. 125–134). New York: Guilford Press.

Garland, A. F., & Zigler, E. (1993). Adolescent suicide prevention: Current research and social policy implications. *American Psychologist, 48,* 169–182.

Garmezy, N. (1993). Vulnerability and resilience. In D. C. Funder, R. D. Parke, C. Tomlinson-Keasey, & K. Widaman (Eds.), *Studying lives through time: Personality and development* (pp. 377–398). Washington, DC: American Psychological Association.

Garmezy, N., & Masten, A. S. (1991). The protective role of competence indicators in children at risk. In E. M. Cummings, A. L. Green, & K. H. Karraker (Eds.), *Life-span developmental psychology: Perspectives on stress and coping* (pp. 151–174). Hillsdale, NJ: Erlbaum.

Garmezy, N., & Rutter, M. (Eds.). (1983). *Stress, coping, and development in children.* New York: McGraw-Hill.

Garnier, H., Stein, J., & Jacobs, J. (1997). The process of dropping out of high school: A 19-year perspective. *American Educational Research Journal, 34,* 395–419.

Gathercole, S., Pickering, S., Ambridge, B., & Wearing, H. (2004). The structure of working memory from 4 to 15 years of age. *Developmental Psychology, 40,* 177–190.

Gauvain, M., Fagot, B., Leve, C., & Kavanagh, K. (2002). Instruction by mothers and fathers during problem solving with their young children. *Journal of Family Psychology, 16,* 81–90.

Gavazzi, A., Alford, K. A., & McKenry, P. (1996). Culturally specific programs for foster care youth: The sample case of an African American rites of passage program. *Family Relations: Journal of Applied Family & Child Studies, 45,* 166–174.

Gavazzi, S., & Law, J. (1997). Creating definitions of successful adulthood for families with adolescents: A therapeutic intervention from the Growing Up FAST" program. *Journal of Family Psychotherapy, 8,* 21–38.

Ge, X., Brody, G., Conger, R., Simons, R., et al. (2002). Contextual amplification of pubertal transition effects on deviant peer affiliation and externalizing behavior among African American children. *Developmental Psychology, 38,* 42–54.

Ge, X., & Conger, R. (1999). Adjustment problems and emerging personalty characteristics from early to late adolescence. *American Journal of Community Psychology, 27,* 429–459.

Ge, X., Conger, R., & Elder, G. (2001). The relation between puberty and psychological distress in adolescent boys. *Journal of Research in Adolescence, 11,* 49–70.

Geary, D., Lin, F., Chen, G., Saults, S., et al. (1999). Contributions of computational fluency to cross-national differences in arithmetical reasoning abilities. *Journal of Educational Psychology, 91,* 716–719.

Geary, D. C. (1996). International differences in mathematical achievement: Their nature, causes, and consequences. *Current Directions in Psychological Science, 5,* 133–137.

Geary, D. C., Bow-Thomas, C. C., Liu, F., & Siegler, R. S. (1996). Development of arithmetical competencies in Chinese and American children: Influences of age, language, and schooling. *Child Development, 65,* 2022–2044.

Gee, C., & Rhodes, J. (1999). Postpartum transitions in adolescent mothers' romantic and maternal relationships. *Merrill-Palmer Quarterly, 45,* 512–532.

Gee, C., & Rhodes, J. (2003). Adolescent mothers' relationship with their children's biological fathers: Social support, social strain and relationship continuity. *Journal of Family Psychology, 17,* 370–383.

Geissbuehler, V., & Eberhard, J. (2002). Fear of childbirth during pregnancy: A study of more than 8000 pregnant women. *Journal of Psychosomatic Obstetrics & Gynecology, 23,* 229–235.

Gelman, R. (1972). Logical capacity of very young children: Number invariance rules. *Child Development, 43,* 75–90.

Gentile, D., Lynch, P., Linder, J., & Walsh, D. (2004). The effects of violent video game habits on adolescent hostility, aggressive behaviors, and school performance. *Journal of Adolescence, 27,* 5–22.

Gentile, G. (2005). *Products placed liberally in video games.* Retrieved July 23, 2005, from http://www.spinwatch.org/modules.php?name=News&file=article&sid=1011

Gentner, D. (1982). Why nouns are learned before verbs: Linguistic relativity versus natural partitioning. In S. A. Kuczaj, II (Ed.), *Language development: Vol. 2, Language, thought, and culture* (pp. 301–334). Hillsdale, NJ: Erlbaum.

Georgieff, M. K. (1994). Nutritional deficiencies as developmental risk factors: Commentary on Pollitt and Gorman. In C. A. Nelson (Ed.), *The Minnesota symposia on child development* (Vol. 27, pp. 145–159). Hillsdale, NJ: Erlbaum.

Gerbner, G., Morgan, M., & Signorielli, N. (1994). *Television violence profile no. 16: The turning point—from research to action.* Unpublished manuscript, Annenberg School of Communications, University of Pennsylvania.

Gerhardstein, P., Adler, S., & Rovee-Collier, C. (2000). A dissociation in infants' memory for stimulus size: Evidence for the early development of multiple memory systems. *Developmental Psychobiology, 36*, 123–135.

Gershkoff-Stowe, L., Thal, D. J., Smith, L. B., & Namy, L. L. (1997). Categorization and its developmental relation to early language. *Child Development, 68*, 843–859.

Gershoff, E. (2002). Corporal punishment by parents and associated child behaviors and experiences: A meta-analytic and theoretical review. *Psychological Bulletin, 128*, 539–579.

Gesell, A. (1925). *The mental growth of the preschool child.* New York: Macmillan.

Gibson, D. R. (1990). Relation of socioeconomic status to logical and sociomoral judgment of middle-aged men. *Psychology and Aging, 5*, 510–513.

Gibson, E. (2002). *Perceiving the affordances: A portrait of two psychologists.* Hillsdale, NJ: Erlbaum.

Gibson, E. J., & Walk, R. D. (1960). The "visual cliff." *Scientific American, 202*, 80–92.

Giedd, J., Blumenthal, J., Jeffries, N., Castellanos, F., Lui, H., & Paus, T. (1999). Brain development during childhood and adolescence: A longitudinal MRI study. *Nature Neuroscience, 2*, 861–863.

Gilbertson, M., & Bramlett, R. (1998). Phonological awareness screening to identify at-risk readers: Implications for practitioners. *Language, Speech, & Hearing Services in Schools, 29*, 109–116.

Giles, J., & Heyman, G. (2005). Young children's beliefs about the relationship between gender and aggressive behavior. *Child Development, 76*, 207–121.

Giles-Sims, J., & Lockhart, C. (2005). Culturally shaped patterns of disciplining children. *Journal of Family Issues, 26*, 196–218.

Gillberg, C., Melander, H., von Knorring, A., Janols, L., Thernlund, G., Hägglöf, B., Eidevall-Wallin, L., Gustafsson, P., & Kopp, S. (1997). Long-term stimulant treatment of children with attention-deficit hyperactivity disorder symptoms: A randomized, double-blind, placebo-controlled trial. *Archives of General Psychiatry, 54*, 857–864.

Gilligan, C. (1982). *In a different voice: Psychological theory and women's development.* Cambridge, MA: Harvard University Press.

Gilligan, C., & Wiggins, G. (1987). The origins of morality in early childhood relationships. In J. Kagan & S. Lamb (Eds.), *The emergence of morality in young children* (pp. 277–307). Chicago: University of Chicago Press.

Gladue, B. A. (1994). The biopsychology of sexual orientation. *Current Directions in Psychological Science, 3*, 150–154.

Glaser, D. (2000). Child abuse and neglect and the brain a review. *Journal of Child Psychology & Psychiatry & Allied Disciplines, 41*, 97–116.

Glasgow, K. L., Dornbusch, S. M., Troyer, L., Steinberg, L., & Ritter, P. L. (1997). Parenting styles, adolescents' attributions, and educational outcomes in nine heterogeneous high schools. *Child Development, 68*, 507–529.

Gleason, K., Jensen-Campbell, L., & Richardson, D. (2004). Agreeableness as a predictor of aggression in adolescence. *Aggressive Behavior, 30*, 43–61.

Gleitman, L. R., & Gleitman, H. (1992). A picture is worth a thousand words, but that's the problem: The role of syntax in vocabulary acquisition. *Current Directions in Psychological Science, 1*, 31–35.

Gleitman, L. R., & Wanner, E. (1988). Current issues in language learning. In M. H. Bornstein & M. E. Lamb (Eds.), *Developmental psychology: An advanced textbook* (2nd ed., pp. 297–358). Hillsdale, NJ: Erlbaum.

Glenn, N. D. (1990). Quantitative research on marital quality in the 1980s: A critical review. *Journal of Marriage and the Family, 52*, 818–831.

Glowinski, A., Bucholz, K., Nelson, E., Fu, Q., Madden, P., Reich, W., & Heath, A. (2001). Suicide attempts in an adolescent female twin sample. *Journal of the American Academy of Child and Adolescent Psychiatry, 40*, 1300–1307.

Glueck, S., & Glueck, E. (1972). *Identification of pre-delinquents: Validation studies and some suggested uses of Glueck table.* New York: Intercontinental Medical Book Corp.

Gnepp, J., & Chilamkurti, C. (1988). Children's use of personality attributions to predict other people's emotional and behavioral reactions. *Child Development, 50*, 743–754.

Goldberg, S. (1972). Infant care and growth in urban Zambia. *Human Development, 15*, 77–89.

Goldberg, W. A. (1990). Marital quality, parental personality, and spousal agreement about perceptions and expectations for children. *Merrill-Palmer Quarterly, 36*, 531–556.

Golden, M., & Birns, B. (1983). Social class and infant intelligence. In M. Lewis (Ed.), *Origins of intelligence: Infancy and early childhood* (2nd ed., pp. 347–398). New York: Plenum Press.

Goldenberg, C. (1996). Latin American immigration and U.S. schools. *Social Policy Report, Society for Research in Child Development, 10*(1), 1–29.

Goldfield, B. A. (1993). Noun bias in maternal speech to one-year-olds. *Journal of Child Language, 20*, 85–99.

Goldfield, B. A., & Reznick, J. S. (1990). Early lexical acquisition: Rate, content, and the vocabulary spurt. *Journal of Child Language, 17*, 171–183.

Golding J., Emmett, P. M., & Rogers, I. S. (1997a). Gastroenteritis, diarrhoea and breast feeding. *Early Human Development, 49*(Suppl.), S83–S103.

Golding, J., Emmett, P. M., & Rogers, I. S. (1997b). Does breast feeding protect against non-gastric infections? *Early Human Development, 49*(Suppl.), S105–S120.

Goldman, L. S., Genel, M., Bezman, R. J., & Slanetz, P. J. (1998). Diagnosis and treatment of attention-deficit/hyperactivity disorder in children and adolescents. *Journal of the American Medical Association, 279*, 1100–1107.

Goldsmith, H., & Alansky, J. (1987). Maternal and infant temperamental predictors of attachment: A meta-analytic review. *Journal of Consulting and Clinical Psychology, 55*, 805–806.

Goldsmith, H. H., Buss, K. A., & Lemery, K. S. (1997). Toddler and childhood temperament: Expanded content, stronger genetic evidence, new evidence for the importance of environment. *Developmental Psychology, 33*, 891–905.

Goldsmith, H. H., Gottesman, I. I., & Lemery, K. S. (1997). Epigenetic approaches to developmental psychopathology. *Development and Psychopathology, 9*, 365–387.

Goldstein, N., Arnold, D., Rosenberg, J., Stowe, R., & Ortiz, C. (2001). Contagion of aggression in day care classrooms as a function of peer and teacher responses. *Journal of Educational Psychology, 93*, 708–719.

Goldstein, S., Davis-Kean, P., & Eccles, J. (2005). Parents, peers, and problem behavior: A longitudinal investigation of the impact of relationship perceptions and characteristics on the development of adolescent problem behavior. *Developmental Psychology, 41*, 401–413.

Goleman, D. (1995a, October 4). Eating disorder rates surprise the experts. *The New York Times*, p. B7.

Goleman, D. (1995b). *Emotional intelligence.* New York: Bantam Books.

Golinkoff, R. M., Mervis, C. B., & Hirsh-Pasek, K. (1994). Early object labels: The case for lexical principles. *Journal of Child Language, 21*, 125–155.

Gollan, T., & Silverberg, N. (2001). Tip-of-the-tongue states in Hebrew-English bilinguals. *Bilingualism: Language & Cognition, 4*, 63–83.

Golombok, S., & Fivush, R. (1994). *Gender development.* Cambridge, England: Cambridge University Press.

Golombok, S., & Tasker, F. (1996). Do parents influence the sexual orientation of their children? Findings from a longitudinal study of lesbian families. *Developmental Psychology, 32*, 3–11.

Gomez, R., Bounds, J., Homberg, K., Fullarton, C., & Gomez, A. (1999). Effects of neuroticism and avoidant coping style on maladjustment during early adolescence. *Personality & Individual Differences, 26*, 305–319.

Gomez, R., Gomez, A., & Cooper, A. (2002). Neuroticism and extraversion as predictors of negative and positive emotional information processing: Comparing Eysenck's, Gray's and Newman's theories. *European Journal of Personality, 16*, 333–350.

Gomez, R., Homberg, K., Bounds, J., Fullarton, C., & Gomez, A. (1999). Neuroticism and extraversion as predictors of coping styles during early adolescence. *Personality & Individual Differences, 27*, 3–17.

Gonzalez, J., & Valle, I. (2000). Word identification and reading disorders in the Spanish language. *Journal of Learning Disabilities, 33*, 44–60.

Goodsitt, J. V., Morse, P. A., Ver Hoeve, J. N., & Cowan, N. (1984). Infant speech recognition in multisyllabic contexts. *Child Development, 55*, 903–910.

Goossens, L., Beyers, W., Emmen, M., & van Aken, M. (2002). The imaginary audience and personal fable: Factor analyses and concurrent validity of the "New Look" measures. *Journal of Research on Adolescence, 12*, 193–215.

Goossens, R., & van IJzendoorn, M. (1990). Quality of infants' attachments to professional caregivers: Relation to infant-parent attachment and daycare characteristics. *Child Development, 61*, 832–837.

Gopnik, A., & Astington, J. W. (1988). Children's understanding of representational change and its relation to the understanding of false belief and the appearance-reality distinction. *Child Development, 59*, 26–37.

Gopnik, A., & Meltzoff, A. (1987). The development of categorization in the second year and its relation to other cognitive and linguistic developments. *Child Development, 58*, 1523–1531.

Gopnik, A., & Meltzoff, A. N. (1992). Categorization and naming: Basic-level sorting in eighteen-month-olds and its relation to language. *Child Development, 63*, 1091–1103.

Gordon, N. (1995). Apoptosis (programmed cell death) and other reasons for elimination of neurons and axons. *Brain & Development, 17*, 73–77.

Gorter, A. C., Sanchez, G., Pauw, J., Perez, R. M., Sandiford, P., & Smith, G. O. (1995). Childhood diarrhea in rural Nicaragua: Beliefs and traditional health practices. *Boletin de la Oficina Sanitaria Panamericana, 119*, 337–390.

Gottesman, I. I., & Goldsmith, H. H. (1994). Developmental psychopathology of antisocial behavior: Inserting genes into its ontogenesis and epigenesis. In C. A. Nelson (Ed.), *The Minnesota symposia on child psychology* (Vol. 27, pp. 69–104). Hillsdale, NJ: Erlbaum.

Gottfried, A. E., Bathurst, K., & Gottfried, A. W. (1994). Role of maternal and dual-earner employment status in children's development: A longitudinal study from infancy through early adolescence. In A. E. Gottfried & A. W. Gottfried (Eds.), *Redefining families: Implications for children's development* (pp. 55–97). New York: Plenum Press.

Gottfried, A. W., Gottfried, A. E., Bathurst, K., & Guerin, D. W. (1994). *Gifted IQ: Early developmental aspects.* New York: Plenum Press.

Gottlieb, G. (1976a). Conceptions of prenatal development: Behavioral embryology. *Psychological Review, 83*, 215–234.

Gottlieb, G. (1976b). The roles of experience in the development of behavior and the nervous system. In G. Gottlieb (Ed.), *Neural and behavioral specificity*. New York: Academic Press.

Gottman, J. M. (1986). The world of coordinated play: Same- and cross-sex friendship in young children. In J. M. Gottman & J. G. Parker (Eds.), *Conversations of friends: Speculations on affective development* (pp. 139–191). Cambridge, England: Cambridge University Press.

Gould, M., Marrocco, F., Kleinman, M., Thomas, J., Mostkoff, K., Cote, J., & Davies, M. (2005). Evaluating iatrogenic risk of youth suicide screening programs: A randomized controlled trial. *Journal of the American Medical Association, 293*, 1635–1643.

Graber, J. A., Brooks-Gunn, J., Paikoff, R. L., & Warren, M. P. (1994). Prediction of eating problems: An 8-year study of adolescent girls. *Developmental Psychology, 30*, 823–834.

Grabowski, L., Call, K., & Mortimer, J. (2001). Global and economic self-efficacy in the educational attainment process. *Social Psychology Quarterly, 64*, 164–197.

Graham, S., & Harris, K. (1997). It can be taught, but it does not develop naturally: Myths and realities in writing instruction. *School Psychology Review, 26*, 414–424.

Gravel, J. S., & Nozza, R. J. (1997). Hearing loss among children with otitis media with effusion. In J. E. Roberts, I. F. Wallace, & F. W. Henderson (Eds.), *Otitis media in young children: Medical, developmental, and educational considerations* (pp. 63–92). Baltimore: Brookes.

Graziano, A. M., Hamblen, J. L., & Plante, W. A. (1996). Subabusive violence in child rearing in middle-class American families. *Pediatrics, 98*, 845–848.

Green, E., Deschamps, J., & Páez, D. (2005). Variation of individualism and collectivism within and between 20 countries: A typological analysis. *Journal of Cross-Cultural Psychology, 36*, 321–339.

Green, S. (2001). Systemic vs. individualistic approaches to bullying. *Journal of the American Medical Association, 286*, 787.

Green, S., Pring, L., & Swettenham, J. (2004). An investigation of first-order false belief understanding of children with congenital profound visual impairment. *British Journal of Developmental Psychology, 22*, 1–17.

Greenberg, M. T. (1997, April). *Improving peer relations and reducing aggressive behavior: The classroom level effects of the PATHS curriculum.* Paper presented at the biennial meetings of the Society for Research in Child Development, Washington, DC.

Greenberg, M. T., Kusche, C. A., Cook, E. T., & Quamma, J. P. (1995). Promoting emotional competence in school-aged children: The effects of the PATHS curriculum. *Development and Psychopathology, 7*, 117–136.

Greenberg, M. T., Siegel, J. M., & Leitch, C. J. (1983). The nature and importance of attachment relationships to parents and peers during adolescence. *Journal of Youth & Adolescence, 12*, 373–386.

Greenberger, E., & Steinberg, L. (1986). *When teenagers work: The psychological and social costs of adolescent employment.* New York: Basic Books.

Greene, R. (1998). *Explosive child: A new approach for understanding and parenting easily frustrated, "chronically inflexible" children.* New York: Harper Collins.

Greenfield, P. (1994). Video games as cultural artifacts. *Journal of Applied Developmental Psychology, 15*, 3–12.

Greenfield, P. (1995). Profile: On teaching. Culture, ethnicity, race, and development: Implications for teaching theory and research. *SRCD Newsletter* (Winter), 3–4, 12.

Greenfield, P., Brannon, C., & Lohr, D. (1994). Two-dimensional representation of movement through three-dimensional space: The role of video game expertise. *Journal of Applied Developmental Psychology, 15*, 87–104.

Greenough, W. T. (1991). Experience as a component of normal development: Evolutionary considerations. *Developmental Psychology, 27*, 11–27.

Greenough, W. T., Black, J. E., & Wallace, C. S. (1987). Experience and brain development. *Child Development, 58*, 539–559.

Gregg, V., Gibbs, J. C., & Basinger, K. S. (1994). Patterns of developmental delay in moral judgment by male and female delinquents. *Merrill-Palmer Quarterly, 40*, 538–553.

Grenier, G. (1985). Shifts to English as usual language by Americans of Spanish mother tongue. In R. O. De La Garza, F. D. Bean, C. M. Bonjean, R. Romo, & R. Alvarez (Eds.), *The Mexican American experience: An interdisciplinary anthology* (pp. 347–358). Austin: University of Texas Press.

Griffith, D. R., Azuma, S. D., & Chasnoff, I. J. (1994). Three-year outcome of children exposed prenatally to drugs. *Journal of the American Academy of Child and Adolescent Psychiatry, 33*, 20–27.

Grigorenko, E. (2003). Intraindividual fluctuations in intellectual functioning: Selected links between nutrition and the mind. In R. Sternberg, J. Lautrey, & T. Lubart (Eds.), *Models of intelligence: International perspectives* (pp. 91–116). Washington, DC: American Psychological Association.

Grimes, D. A. (1996). Stress, work, and pregnancy complications. *Epidemiology, 7*, 337–338.

Grolnick, W. S., & Slowiaczek, M. L. (1994). Parents' involvement in children's schooling: A multidimensional conceptualization and motivational model. *Child Development, 65*, 237–252.

Groome, L., Mooney, D., Holland, S., Smith, L., Atterbury, J., & Dykman, R. (1999). Behavioral state affects heart rate response to low-intensity sound in human fetuses. *Early Human Development, 54*, 39–54.

Grossmann, K., Grossmann, K. E., Spangler, G., Suess, G., & Unzner, L. (1985). Maternal sensitivity and newborns' orientation responses as related to quality of attachment in northern Germany. *Monographs of the Society of Research in Child Development, 50* (1–2, Serial No. 209), 233–256.

Grotevant, H. D., & Cooper, C. R. (1985). Patterns of interaction in family relationships and the development of identity exploration in adolescence. *Child Development, 56*, 415–428.

Grusec, J. E. (1992). Social learning theory and developmental psychology: The legacies of Robert Sears and Albert Bandura. *Developmental Psychology, 28*, 776–786.

Grusec, J. E., Goodnow, J. J., & Cohen, L. (1996). Household work and the development of concern for others. *Developmental Psychology, 32*, 999–1007.

Grusec, J. E., Saas-Kortsaak, P., & Simutis, Z. M. (1978). The role of example and moral exhortation in the training of altruism. *Child Development, 49*, 920–923.

Guerin, D. W., & Gottfried, A. W. (1994a). Temperamental consequences of infant difficultness. *Infant Behavior and Development, 17*, 413–421.

Guerin, D. W., & Gottfried, A. W. (1994b). Developmental stability and change in parent reports of temperament: A ten-year longitudinal investigation from infancy through preadolescence. *Merrill-Palmer Quarterly, 40*, 334–355.

Guerin, T., Lloyd-Richardson, E., Spirito, A., Donaldson, D., & Boergers, J. (2001). Self-mutilative behavior in adolescents who attempt suicide by overdose. *Journal of the American Academy of Child and Adolescent Psychiatry, 40*, 1062–1069.

Gunnar, M., Sebanc, A., Tout, K., Donzella, B., & Van Dulmen, M. (2003). Peer rejection, temperament, and cortisol activity in preschoolers. *Developmental Psychobiology, 43*, 346–358.

Gunnar, M. R. (1994). Psychoendocrine studies of temperament and stress in early childhood: Expanding current models. In J. E. Bates & T. D. Wachs (Eds.), *Temperament: Individual differences at the interface of biology and behavior* (pp. 175–198). Washington, DC: American Psychological Association.

Guralnick, M. J., & Paul-Brown, D. (1984). Communicative adjustments during behavior-request episodes among children at different developmental levels. *Child Development, 55*, 911–919.

Gurnáková, J., & Kusá, D. (2004). Gender self-concept in personal theories of reality. *Studia Psychologica, 46*, 49–61.

Guttentag, R. E., Ornstein, P. A., & Siemens, L. (1987). Children's spontaneous rehearsal: Transitions in strategy acquisition. *Cognitive Development, 2*, 307–326.

Guttman, A., & Dick, P. (2004). Infant hospitalization and maternal depression, poverty and single parenthood: A population-based study. *Child: Care, Health & Development, 30*, 67–75.

Guyer, B., MacDorman, M. F., Anderson, R. N., & Strobino, D. M. (1997). Annual summary of vital statistics—1996. *Pediatrics, 100*, 905–918.

Gzesh, S. M. & Surber, C. F. (1985). Visual perspective-taking skills in children. *Child Development, 56*, 1204–1213.

Haan, N. (1981). Adolescents and young adults as producers of their own development. In R. M. Lerner & N. A. Busch-Rossnagel (Eds.), *Individuals as producers of their own development* (pp. 155–182). New York: Academic Press.

Hack, M., Taylor, C. B. H., Klein, N., Eiben, R., Schatschneider, C., & Mercuri-Minich, N. (1994). School-age outcomes in children with birth weights under 750 g. *New England Journal of Medicine, 331*, 753–759.

Hagan, J. (1997). Defiance and despair: Subcultural and structural linkages between delinquency and despair in the life course. *Social Forces, 76*, 119–134.

Hagekull, B., & Bohlin, G. (1998). Preschool temperament and environmental factors related to the five-factor model of personality in middle childhood. *Merrill-Palmer Quarterly, 44*, 194–215.

Hagerman, R. J. (1996). Growth and development. In W. W. Hay, Jr., J. R. Groothuis, A. R. Hayward, & M. J. Levin (Eds.), *Current pediatric diagnosis and treatment* (12th ed., pp. 65–84). Norwalk, CT: Appleton & Lange.

Haith, M. M. (1980). *Rules that babies look by.* Hillsdale, NJ: Erlbaum.

Hakansson, G., Salameh, E., & Nettelbladt, U. (2003). Measuring language development in bilingual children: Swedish-Arabic children with and without language impairment. *Linguistics, 41*, 255–288.

Hale, S., Fry, A. F., & Jessie, K. A. (1993). Effects of practice on speed of information processing in children and adults: Age sensitivity and age invariance. *Developmental Psychology, 29*, 880–892.

Halford, G. S., Maybery, M. T., O'Hare, A. W., & Grant, P. (1994). The development of memory and processing capacity. *Child Development, 65*, 1338–1356.

Hall, G. (2003, September). Primary elective C-section up 20% from 1999 to 2001. *OB/GYN News.* Retrieved April 1, 2004, from http://www.imng.com

Halpern, C. T., Udry, J. R., Campbell, B., & Suchindran, C. (1993). Testosterone and pubertal development as predictors of sexual activity: A panel analysis of adolescent males. *Psychosomatic Medicine, 55*, 436–447.

Halpern, D. (1986). *Sex differences in cognitive abilities.* Hillsdale, NJ: Erlbaum.

Halpern, D., & Tan, U. (2001). Stereotypes and steroids: Using a psychobiosocial model to understand cognitive sex differences. *Brain & Cognition, 45, 392–414.*

Halverson, C., Havill, V., Deal, J., Baker, S., Victor, J., Pavlopoulous, V., Besevegis, E., & Wen, L. (2003). Personality structure as derived from parental ratings of free descriptions of children: The inventory of child individual differences. *Journal of Personality, 71*, 995–1026.

Hämäläinen, M., & Pulkkinen, L. (1996). Problem behavior as a precursor of male criminality. *Development and Psychopathology, 8*, 443–455.

Hamilton, C. E. (1995, April). *Continuity and discontinuity of attachment from infancy through adolescence.* Paper presented at the biennial meetings of the Society for Research in Child Development, Indianapolis.

Hamm, J. (2000). Do birds of a feather flock together? The variable bases for African American, Asian American, and European American adolescents' selection of similar friends. *Developmental Psychology, 36*, 209–219.

Hamvas, A., Wise, P. H., Yang, R. K., Wampler, N. S., Noguchi, A., Maurer, M. M., Walentik, C. A., Schramm, W. F., & Cole, F. S. (1996). The influence of the wider use of surfactant therapy on neonatal mortality among blacks and whites. *New England Journal of Medicine, 334*, 1635–1640.

Han, W., Waldfogel, J., & Brooks-Gunn, J. (2001). The effects of early maternal employment on later cognitive and behavioral outcomes. *Journal of Marriage and the Family, 63*, 336–354.

Hankin, B. L., Abramson, L. Y., Moffitt, T. E., Silva, P. A., McGee, R., & Angell, K. E. (1998). Development of depression from preadolescence to young adulthood: Emerging gender differences in a 10-year longitudinal study. *Journal of Abnormal Psychology, 107*, 128–140.

Hanlon, H., Thatcher, R., & Cline, M. (1999). Gender differences in the development of EEG coherence in normal children. *Developmental Neuropsychology, 17*, 199–223.

Hanna, E., & Meltzoff, A. N. (1993). Peer imitation by toddlers in laboratory, home, and day-care contexts: Implications for social learning and memory. *Developmental Psychology, 29*, 701–710.

Hannon, E., & Trehub, S. (2005). Metrical categories in infancy and adulthood. *Psychological Science, 16*, 48–55.

Hansen, J., & Bowey, J. A. (1994). Phonological analysis skills, verbal working memory, and reading ability in second-grade children. *Child Development, 65*, 938–950.

Hansen, M., Kurinczuk, J., Bower, C., & Webb, S. (2002). The risk of major birth defects after intracytoplasmic sperm injection and in vitro fertilization. *New England Journal of Medicine, 346*, 725–730.

Hanshaw, J. B., Scheiner, A. P., Moxley, A. W., Gaeav, L., Abel, V., & Scheiner, B. (1976). School failure and deafness after "silent" congenital cytomegalovirus infection. *New England Journal of Medicine, 295*, 468–470.

Hardy, C., & Van Leeuwen, S. (2004). Interviewing young children: Effects of probe structures and focus of rapport-building talk on the qualities of young children's eyewitness statements. *Canadian Journal of Behavioral Science, 36*, 155–165.

Harkness, S. (1998). Time for families. *Anthropology Newsletter, 39*, 1, 4.

Harkness, S., & Super, C. M. (1985). The cultural context of gender segregation in children's peer groups. *Child Development, 56*, 219–224.

Harkness, S., & Super, C. M. (1995). Culture and parenting. In M. H. Bornstein (Ed.), *Handbook of parenting: Vol. 2. Biology and ecology of parenting* (pp. 211–234). Mahwah, NJ: Erlbaum.

Harold, G. T., & Conger, R. D. (1997). Marital conflict and adolescent distress: The role of adolescent awareness. *Child Development, 68*, 333–350.

Harrington, R., Rutter, M., & Fombonne, E. (1996). Developmental pathways in depression: Multiple meanings, antecedents, and endpoints. *Development and Psychopathology, 8*, 601–616.

Harris, J. (1998). *The nurture assumption: Why kids turn out the way they do: Parents matter less than you think and peers matter more.* New York: Free Press.

Harris, M. (1992). *Language experience and early language development: From input to uptake.* Hove, England: Erlbaum.

Harris, P. L. (1989). *Children and emotion: The development of psychological understanding.* Oxford: Basil Blackwell.

Harris, P. L., Olthof, T., & Terwogt, M. M. (1981). Children's knowledge of emotion. *Journal of Child Psychology and Psychiatry, 22*, 247–261.

Harrison, A. O., Wilson, M. N., Pine, C. J., Chan, S. Q., & Buriel, R. (1990). Family ecologies of ethnic minority children. *Child Development, 61*, 347–362.

Harrist, A., Zaia, A., Bates, J., Dodge, K., & Pettit, G. (1997). Subtypes of social withdrawal in early childhood: Sociometric status and social-cognitive differences across four years. *Child Development, 68*, 278–294.

Hart, B., & Risley, T. R. (1995). *Meaningful differences in the everyday experience of young American children.* Baltimore, MD: Brookes.

Hart, C., Olsen, S., Robinson, C., & Mandleco, B. (1997). The development of social and communicative competence in childhood: Review and a model of personal, familial, and extrafamilial processes. *Communication Yearbook, 20, 305–373.*

Hart, S., Boylan, L., Border, B., Carroll, S., McGunegle, D., & Lampe, R. (2004). Breast milk levels of cortisol and Secretory Immunoglobulin A (SIgA) differ with maternal mood and infant neuro-behavioral functioning. *Infant Behavior and Development, 27*, 101–106.

Hart, S., Jones, N., Field, T., & Lundy, B. (1999). One-year-old infants of intrusive and withdrawn depressed mothers. *Child Psychiatry and Human Development, 30*, 111–120.

Harter, S. (1987). The determinants and mediational role of global self-worth in children. In N. Eisenberg (Ed.), *Contemporary topics in developmental psychology* (pp. 219–242). New York: Wiley-Interscience.

Harter, S. (1990). Processes underlying adolescent self-concept formation. In R. Montemayor, G. R. Adams, & T. P. Gullotta (Eds.), *From childhood to adolescence: A transitional period?* (pp. 205–239). Newbury Park, CA: Sage.

Harter, S. (1998). The development of self-representations. In W. Damon (Ed.), *Handbook of child psychology: Vol. 3. Social, emotional, and personality development* (5th ed., pp. 553–617). New York: Wiley.

Harter, S. (1999). *Developmental approaches to self processes.* New York: Guilford.

Harter, S., & Monsour, A. (1992). Developmental analysis of conflict caused by opposing attributes in the adolescent self-portrait. *Developmental Psychology, 28*, 251–260.

Harter, S., & Pike, R. (1984). The Pictorial Perceived Competence Scale for Young Children. *Child Development, 55*, 1969–1982.

Harter, S., & Whitesell, N. (2003). Beyond the debate: Why some adolescents report stable self-worth over time and situation, whereas others report changes in self-worth. *Journal of Personality, 71*, 1027–1058.

Harter, S., & Whitesell, N. R. (1996). Multiple pathways to self-reported depression and psychological adjustment among adolescents. *Development and Psychopathology, 8*, 761–777.

Harton, H., & Latane, B. (1997). Social influence and adolescent lifestyle attitudes. *Journal of Research on Adolescence, 7*, 197–220.

Hartshorn, K., & Rovee-Collier, C. (1997). Infant learning and long-term memory at 6 months: A confirming analysis. *Developmental Psychobiology, 30*, 71–85.

Hartup, W. (1989). Social relationships and their developmental significance. *American Psychologist, 44*, 120–126.

Hartup, W. W. (1996). The company they keep: Friendships and their developmental significance. *Child Development, 67,* 1–13.

Hartup, W. W., Laursen, B., Stewart, M. I., & Eastenson, A. (1988). Conflict and the friendship relations of young children. *Child Development, 59,* 1590–1600.

Hartup, W. W., & Stevens, N. (1997). Friendships and adaptation in the life course. *Psychological Bulletin, 121,* 355–370.

Hartup, W. W., & van Lieshout, C. F. M. (1995). Personality development in social context. *Annual Review of Psychology, 46,* 655–687.

Harvey, A., & Coleman, A. (1997). An Afrocentric program for African American males in the juvenile justice system. *Child Welfare, 76,* 197–211.

Harvey, A., & Hill, R. (2004). Afrocentric youth and family rites of passage program: Promoting resilience among at-risk African American youths. *Social Work, 49,* 65–74.

Harvey, A., & Rauch, J. (1997). A comprehensive Afrocentric rites of passage program for black male adolescents. *Health & Social Work, 22,* 30–37.

Harwood, R. L. (1992). The influence of culturally derived values on Anglo and Puerto Rican mothers' perceptions of attachment behavior. *Child Development, 63,* 822–839.

Hashima, P. Y., & Amato, P. R. (1994). Poverty, social support, and parental behavior. *Child Development, 65,* 394–403.

Haskins, R. (1989). Beyond metaphor: The efficacy of early childhood education. *American Psychologist, 44,* 274–282.

Hatano, G., Siegler, R. S., Richards, D. D., Inagaki, K., Stavy, R., & Wax, N. (1993). The development of biological knowledge: A multi-national study. *Cognitive Development, 8,* 47–62.

Hatchett, S. J., & Jackson, J. S. (1993). African American extended kin systems: An assessment. In H. P. McAdoo (Ed.), *Family ethnicity: Strength in diversity* (pp. 90–108). Newbury Park, CA: Sage.

Haviland, J. M., & Lelwica, M. (1987). The induced affect response: 10-week-old infants' responses to three emotional expressions. *Developmental Psychology, 23,* 97–104.

Havill, V. L., Allen, K., Halverson, C. F., Jr., & Kohnstamm, G. A. (1994). Parents' use of Big Five categories in their natural language descriptions of children. In C. F. Halverson, Jr., G. A. Kohnstamm, & R. P. Martin (Eds.), *The developing structure of temperament and personality from infancy to adulthood* (pp. 371–386). Hillsdale, NJ: Erlbaum.

Hay, D., Payne, A., & Chadwick, A. (2004). Peer relations in childhood. *Journal of Child Psychology and Psychiatry, 45,* 84–108.

Hayne, H., & Rovee-Collier, C. (1995). The organization of reactivated memory in infancy. *Child Development, 66,* 893–906.

Haynes, N. M., Ben-Avie, M., Squires, D. A., Howley, J. P., Negron, E. N., & Corbin, J. N. (1996). It takes a whole village: The SDP school. In J. P. Corner, N. M. Haynes, E. T. Joyner, & M. Ben-Avie (Eds.), *Rallying the whole village: The Comer process for reforming education* (pp. 42–71). New York: Teachers College Press.

Hedegaard, M., Henriksen, T. B., Secher, N. J., Hatch, M. C., & Sabroe, S. (1996). Do stressful life events affect duration of gestation and risk of preterm delivery? *Epidemiology, 7,* 339–345.

Heenan, J. (2005). *Character education transforms school.* Retrieved July 19, 2005, from http://www.cornerstonevalues.org/kew2.htm

Heidelise, A., Duffy, F., McAnulty, G., Rivkin, M., Vajapeyam, S., Mulkern, R., Warfield, S., Huppi, P., Butler, S., Conneman, N., Fischer, C., & Eichenwald, E. (2004). Early experience alters brain function and structure. *Pediatrics, 113,* 846–857.

Henneborn, W. J., & Cogan, R. (1975). The effect of husband participation on reported pain and the probability of medication during labour and birth. *Journal of Psychosomatic Research, 19,* 215–222.

Henriksen, T. B., Hedegaard, M., Secher, N. J., & Wilcox, A. J. (1995). Standing at work and preterm delivery. *British Journal of Obstetrics and Gynecology, 102,* 198–206.

Henry, B., Caspi, A., Moffitt, T., Harrington, H., et al. (1999). Staying in school protects boys with poor self-regulation in childhood from later crime: A longitudinal study. *International Journal of Behavioral Development, 23,* 1049–1073.

Henry, B., Caspi, A., Moffitt, T., & Silva, P. (1996). Temperamental and familial predictors of violent and nonviolent criminal convictions: Age 3 to age 18. *Developmental Psychology, 32,* 614–623.

Heptinstall, E., & Taylor, E. (1996). Sex differences and their significance. In S. Sandberg (Ed.), *Hyperactivity disorders of childhood* (pp. 329–439). Cambridge, England: Cambridge University Press.

Hepworth, S., Rovet, J., & Taylor, M. (2001). Neurophysiological correlates of verbal and nonverbal short-term memory in children: Repetition of words and faces. *Psychophysiology, 38,* 594–600.

Herbert, J., Eckerman, C., Goldstein, R., & Stanton, M. (2004). Contrasts in infant classical eyeblink conditioning as a function of premature birth. *Infancy, 5,* 367–383.

Hernandez, D. (1997). Child development and the social demography of childhood. *Child Development, 68,* 149–169.

Herrenkohl, E., Herrenkohl, R., Egolf, B., & Russo, M. (1998). The relationship between early maltreatment and teenage parenthood. *Journal of Adolescence, 21,* 291–303.

Herrera, N., Zajonc, R., Wieczorkowska, G., & Cichomski, B. (2003). Beliefs about birth rank and their reflection in reality. *Journal of Personality & Social Psychology, 85,* 142–150.

Hess, E. H. (1972). "Imprinting" in a natural laboratory. *Scientific American, 227,* 24–31.

Hetherington, E. (1991a). Presidential address: Families, lies, and videotapes. *Journal of Research on Adolescence, 1,* 323–348.

Hetherington, E. (1991b). The role of individual differences and family relationships in children's coping with divorce and remarriage. In P. A. Cowen & M. Hetherington (Eds.), *Family transitions* (pp. 165–194). Hillsdale, NJ: Erlbaum.

Hetherington, E., Bridges, M., & Insabella, G. (1998). What matters? What does not? Five perspectives on the association between marital transitions and children's adjustment. *American Psychologist, 53,* 167–184.

Hetherington, E., Henderson, S., Reiss, D., Anderson, E., et al. (1999). Adolescent siblings in stepfamilies: Family functioning and adolescent adjustment. *Monographs of the Society for Research in Child Development, 64,* 222.

Hetherington, E. M. (1989). Coping with family transitions: Winners, losers, and survivors. *Child Development, 60,* 1–14.

Hetherington, E. M., & Clingempeel, W. G. (1992). Coping with marital transitions: A family systems perspective. *Monographs of the Society for Research in Child Development, 57*(2–3, Serial No. 227).

Hetherington, E. M., & Stanley-Hagan, M. M. (1995). Parenting in divorced and remarried families. In M. H. Bornstein (Ed.), *Handbook of parenting: Vol. 3. Status and social conditions of parenting* (pp. 233–254). Mahwah, NJ: Erlbaum.

Hewitt, L., Hammer, C., Yount, K., & Tomblin, B. (2005). Language sampling for kindergarten children with and without SLI: Mean length of utterance, IPSYN, and NDW. *Journal of Communication Disorders, 38,* 197–213.

Heyman, G., (2001). Children's interpretation of ambiguous behavior: Evidence for a "boys are bad" bias. *Social Development, 10,* 230–247.

Hickey, C. A., Cliver, S. P., McNeal, S. F., Hoffman, H. J., & Goldenberg, R. L. (1996). Prenatal weight gain patterns and birth weight among nonobese black and white women. *Obstetrics and Gynecology, 88,* 490–496.

Hill, A., & Franklin, J. (1998). Mothers, daughters, and dieting: Investigating the transmission of weight control. *British Journal of Clinical Psychology, 37,* 3–13.

Hill, H. M., Soriano, F. I., Chen, S. A., & LaFromboise, T. D. (1994). Sociocultural factors in the etiology and prevention of violence among ethnic minority youth. In L. D. Eron, J. H. Gentry, & P. Schlegel (Eds.), *Reason to hope: A psychosocial perspective on violence and youth* (pp. 59–97). Washington, DC: American Psychological Association.

Hinshaw, S. P., Lahey, B. B., & Hart, E. L. (1993). Issues of taxonomy and comorbidity in the development of conduct disorder. *Development and Psychopathology, 5,* 31–49.

Hinshaw, S. P., & Melnick, S. M. (1995). Peer relationships in boys with attention-deficit hyperactivity disorder with and without comorbid aggression. *Development and Psychopathology, 7,* 627–647.

Hinshaw, S. P., Zupan, B. A., Simmel, C., Nigg, J. T., & Melnick, S. (1997). Peer status in boys with and without attention-deficit hyperactivity disorder: Predictions from overt and covert antisocial behavior, social isolation, and authoritative parenting beliefs. *Child Development, 68,* 880–896.

Hirsh-Pasek, K., Trieman, R., & Schneiderman, M. (1984). Brown and Hanlon revisited: Mothers' sensitivity to ungrammatical forms. *Journal of Child Language, 11,* 81–88.

Ho, C., & Bryant, P. (1997). Learning to read Chinese beyond the logographic phase. *Reading Research Quarterly, 32,* 276–289.

Hodge, K. P., & Tod, D. A. (1993). Ethics of childhood sport. *Sports Medicine, 15,* 291–298.

Hodges, E. V. E., Malone, M. J., & Perry, D. G. (1997). Individual risk and social risk as interacting determinants of victimization in the peer group. *Developmental Psychology, 33,* 1032–1039.

Hoeksma, J., Oosterlaan, J., & Schipper, E. (2004). Emotion regulation and the dynamics of feelings: A conceptual and methodological framework. *Child Development, 75,* 354–360.

Hofferth, S. L., Boisjoly, J., & Duncan, G. (1995, April). *Does children's school attainment benefit from parental access to social capital?* Paper presented at the biennial meetings of the Society for Research in Child Development, Indianapolis.

Hoffman, H. J., & Hillman, L. S. (1992). Epidemiology of the sudden infant death syndrome: Maternal, neonatal, and postneonatal risk factors. *Clinics in Perinatology, 19*(4), 717–737.

Hoffman, M. (2000). *Empathy and moral development: Implications for caring and justice.* Cambridge, England: Cambridge University Press.

Hoffman, M. L. (1982). Development of prosocial motivation: Empathy and guilt. In N. Eisenberg (Ed.), *The development of prosocial behavior* (pp. 281–314). New York: Academic Press.

Hoffman, M. L. (1988). Moral development. In M. H. Bornstein & M. E. Lamb (Eds.), *Developmental psychology: An advanced textbook* (2nd ed., pp. 497–548). Hillsdale, NJ: Erlbaum.

Holahan, C. K. (1988). Relation of life goals at age 70 to activity participation and health and psychological well-being among Terman's gifted men and women. *Psychology and Aging, 3,* 286–291.

Holden, G. W., Coleman, S. M., & Schmidt, K. L. (1995). Why 3-year-old children get spanked: Parent and child determinants as reported by college-educated mothers. *Merrill-Palmer Quarterly, 41,* 431–452.

Holobow, N., Genesee, F., & Lambert, W. (1991). The effectiveness of a foreign language immersion program for children from different ethnic and social class backgrounds: Report 2. *Applied Psycholinguistics, 12,* 179–198.

Holowka, S., Brosseau-Lapré, F., & Petitto, L. (2002). Semantic and conceptual knowledge underlying bilingual babies' first signs and words. *Language Learning, 52,* 205–262.

Honzik, M. P. (1986). The role of the family in the development of mental abilities: A 50-year study. In N. Datan, A. L. Greene, & H. W. Reese (Eds.), *Life-span developmental psychology: Intergenerational relations* (pp. 185–210). Hillsdale, NJ: Erlbaum.

Horowitz, F. D. (1987). *Exploring developmental theories: Toward a structural/behavioral model of development.* Hillsdale, NJ: Erlbaum.

Horowitz, F. D. (1990). Developmental models of individual differences. In J. Colombo & J. Fagen (Eds.), *Individual differences in infancy: Reliability, stability, prediction* (pp. 3–18). Hillsdale, NJ: Erlbaum.

Houck, G., & Lecuyer-Marcus, E. (2004). Maternal limit setting during toddlerhood, delay of gratification, and behavior problems at age five. *Infant Mental Health Journal, 25,* 28–46.

Hovell, M., Blumberg, E., Sipan, C., Hofstetter, C., Burkham, S., Atkins, C., & Felice, M. (1998). Skills training for pregnancy and AIDS prevention in Anglo and Latino youth. *Journal of Adolescent Health, 23,* 139–149.

Hovell, M., Sipan, C., Blumberg, E., Atkins, C., Hofstetter, C. R., & Kreitner, S. (1994). Family influences on Latino and Anglo adolescents' sexual behavior. *Journal of Marriage and the Family, 56,* 973–986.

Howes, C. (1996). The earliest friendships. In W. M. Bukowski, A. F. Newcomb, & W. W. Hartup (Eds.), *The company they keep: Friendship in childhood and adolescence* (pp. 66–86). Cambridge, England: Cambridge University Press.

Howes, C., Phillips, D. A., & Whitebook, M. (1992). Thresholds of quality: Implications for the social development of children in center-based child care. *Child Development, 63,* 449–460.

Hoyert, D., Kung, H., & Smith, B. (2005). Deaths: Preliminary data for 2003. *National Vital Statistics Reports, 53:*15, 1–48.

Hoyert, D. L. (1996). Fetal mortality by maternal education and prenatal care, 1990. *Vital and Health Statistics, Series 20*(No. 30), 1–7.

Huang, H., & Hanley, J. (1997). A longitudinal study of phonological awareness, visual skills, and Chinese reading acquisition among first-graders in Taiwan. *International Journal of Behavioral Development, 20,* 249–268.

Hubel, D. H., & Weisel, T. N. (1963). Receptive fields of cells in striate cortex of very young, visually inexperienced kittens. *Journal of Neurophysiology, 26,* 994–1002.

Hudziak, J., van Beijsterveldt, C., Bartels, M., Rietveld, M., Rettew, D., Derks, E., & Boomsma, D. (2003). Individual differences in aggression: Genetic analyses by age, gender, and informant in 3-, 7-, and 10-year-old Dutch twins. *Behavior Genetics, 33,* 575–589.

Huesmann, L. R., Lagerspetz, K., & Eron, L. D. (1984). Intervening variables in the television violence-aggression relation: Evidence from two countries. *Developmental Psychology, 20,* 746–775.

Huey, S. J., Jr., & Weisz, J. R. (1997). Ego control, ego resiliency, and the five-factor model as predictors of behavioral and emotional problems in clinic-referred children and adolescents. *Journal of Abnormal Psychology, 106,* 404–415.

Huffman, L. C., Bryan, Y. E., Pedersen, F. A., Lester, B. M., Newman, J. D., & del Carmen, R. (1994). Infant cry acoustics and maternal ratings of temperament. *Infant Behavior and Development, 17,* 45–53.

Hughes, C., Jaffee, S., Happé, F., Taylor, A., Caspi, A., & Moffitt, T. (2005).

Origins of individual differences in theory of mind: From nature to nurture? *Child Development, 76,* 356–370.

Hulbert, A. (2003). *Raising America: Experts, parents, and a century of advice about children.* New York: Alfred A. Knopf.

Hunfeld, J., Tempels, A., Passchier, J., Hazebroek, F., et al. (1999). Parental burden and grief one year after the birth of a child with a congenital anomaly. *Journal of Pediatric Psychology, 24,* 515–520.

Huntington, L., Hans, S. L., & Zeskind, P. S. (1990). The relations among cry characteristics, demographic variables, and developmental test scores in infants prenatally exposed to methadone. *Infant Behavior and Development, 13,* 533–538.

Hurt, H., Malmus, D., Betancourt, L., Brodsky, N., & Giannetta, J. (2001). A prospective comparison of developmental outcomes of children with in utero cocaine exposure and controls using the Battelle Developmental Inventory. *Journal of Developmental and Behavioral Pediatrics, 22,* 27–34.

Hurwitz, E., Gunn, W. J., Pinsky, P. F., & Schonberger, L. B. (1991). Risk of respiratory illness associated with day-care attendance: A nationwide study. *Pediatrics, 87,* 62–69.

Huston, A., & Aronson, S. (2005). Mothers' time with infant and time in employment as predictors of mother-child relationships and children's early development. *Child Development, 76,* 467–482.

Huston, A. C. (1994). Children in poverty: Designing research to affect policy. *Social Policy Report, Society for Research in Child Development, 8*(2), 1–12.

Huston, A. C., & Wright, J. C. (1994). Educating children with television: The forms of the medium. In D. Zillmann, J. Bryant, & A. C. Huston (Eds.), *Media, children, and the family: Social scientific, psychodynamic, and clinical perspectives* (pp. 73–84). Hillsdale, NJ: Erlbaum.

Huston, A. C., & Wright, J. C. (1998). Mass media and children's development. In W. Damon (Ed.), *Handbook of child psychology: Vol. 4. Child psychology in practice* (5th ed., pp. 999–1058). New York: Wiley.

Hutt, S. J., Lenard, H. G., & Prechtl, H. E. R. (1969). Psychophysiological studies in newborn infants. In L. P. Lipsitt & H. W. Reese (Eds.), *Advances in child development and behavior* (Vol. 4, pp. 128–173). New York: Academic Press.

Huttenlocher, J. (1995, April). *Children's language in relation to input.* Paper presented at the biennial meetings of the Society for Research in Child Development, Indianapolis.

Huttenlocher, P. R. (1994). Synaptogenesis, synapse elimination, and neural plasticity in human cerebral cortex. In C. A. Nelson (Ed.), *The Minnesota symposia on child psychology* (Vol. 27, pp. 35–54). Hillsdale, NJ: Erlbaum.

Hynd, G. W., Hern, K. L., Novey, E. S., Eliopolus, D., Marshall, R., Gonzalez, J. J., & Voeller, K. K. (1993). Attention deficit-hyperactivity disorder and asymmetry of the caudate nucleus. *Journal of Child Neurology, 8,* 339–347.

Inagaki, K., & Hatano, G. (2004). Vitalistic causality in young children's naive biology. *Trends in Cognitive Sciences, 8,* 356–362.

Ingoldsby, E., Shaw, D., Owens, E., & Winslow, E. (1999). A longitudinal study of interparental conflict, emotional and behavioral reactivity, and preschoolers' adjustment problems among low-income families. *Journal of Abnormal Child Psychology, 27,* 343–356.

Ingram, D. (1981). Early patterns of grammatical development. In R. E. Stark (Ed.), *Language behavior in infancy and early childhood* (pp. 327–358). New York: Elsevier/North-Holland.

Ingrassia, M. (1993, August 2). Daughters of Murphy Brown. *Newsweek,* 58–59.

Inhelder, B., & Piaget, J. (1958). *The growth of logical thinking from childhood to adolescence.* New York: Basic Books.

Interactive Digital Software Association. (1998). *Deep impact: How does the interactive entertainment industry affect the U.S. economy?* Retrieved from http://www.idsa.com

Isabella, G. M. (1995, April). *Varying levels of exposure to marital conflict: Prediction of adolescent adjustment across intact families and stepfamilies.* Paper presented at the biennial meetings of the Society for Research in Child Development, Indianapolis.

Isabella, R. A. (1993). Origins of attachment: Maternal interactive behavior across the first year. *Child Development, 64,* 605–621.

Isabella, R. A., Belsky, J., & von Eye, A. (1989). Origins of infant-mother attachment: An examination of interactional synchrony during the infant's first year. *Developmental Psychology, 25,* 12–21.

Issiaka, S., Cartoux, M., Zerbo, O., Tiendrebeogo, S., Meda, N., Dabis, F., & Van de Perre, P. (2001). Living with HIV: Women's experience in Burkina Faso, West Africa. *AIDS Care, 13,* 123–128.

Itier, R., & Taylor, M. (2004). Face inversion and contrast-reversal effects across development: In contrast to the expertise theory. *Developmental Science, 7,* 246–260.

Izard, C., & Abe, J. (2004). Developmental changes in facial expressions of emotions in the strange situation during the second year of life. *Emotion, 4,* 251–265.

Izard, C. E., Fantauzzo, C. A., Castle, J. M., Haynes, O. M., Rayias, M. F., & Putnam, P. H. (1995). The ontogeny and significance of infants' facial expressions in the first 9 months of life. *Developmental Psychology, 31,* 997–1013.

Izard, C. E., & Harris, P. (1995). Emotional development and developmental psychopathology. In D. Cicchetti & D. J. Cohen (Eds.), *Developmental psychopathology: Vol. 1. Theory and methods* (pp. 467–503). New York: Wiley.

Izard, C. E., & Malatesta, C. Z. (1987). Perspectives on emotional development I: Differential emotions theory of early emotional development. In J. D. Osofsky (Ed.), *Handbook of infant development* (2nd ed., pp. 494–554). New York: Wiley-Interscience.

Izard, C. E., Schultz, D., & Ackerman, B. P. (1997, April). *Emotion knowledge, social competence, and behavior problems in disadvantaged children.* Paper presented at the biennial meetings of the Society for Research in Child Development, Washington, DC.

Jackson, D., & Tein, J. (1998). Adolescents' conceptualization of adult roles: Relationships with age, gender, work goal, and maternal employment. *Sex Roles, 38,* 987–1008.

Jackson, E., Campos, J. J., & Fischer, K. W. (1978). The question of decalage between object permanence and person permanence. *Developmental Psychology, 14,* 1–10.

Jackson, L., & Bracken, B. (1998). Relationship between students' social status and global and domain-specific self-concepts. *Journal of School Psychology, 36,* 233–246.

Jackson, L., Pratt, M., Hunsberger, B., & Pancer, S. (2005). Optimism as a mediator of the relation between perceived parental authoritativeness and adjustment among adolescents: Finding the sunny side of the street. *Social Development, 14,* 273–304.

Jacobs, J., Lanza, S., Osgood, D., Eccles, J., & Wigfield, A. (2002). Changes in children's self-competence and values: Gender and domain differences across grades one through twelve. *Child Development, 73,* 509–527.

Jadack, R. A., Hyde, J. S., Moore, C. F., & Keller, M. L. (1995). Moral reasoning about sexually transmitted diseases. *Child Development, 66,* 167–177.

Jahnke, H. C., & Blanchard-Fields, F. (1993). A test of two models of adolescent egocentrism. *Journal of Youth & Adolescence, 22,* 313–326.

Jain, T., Harlow, B., & Hornstein, M. (2002). Insurance coverage and outcomes of in vitro fertilization. *New England Journal of Medicine, 347,* 661–666.

Jain, T., Missmer, S., & Hornstein, M. (2004). Trends in embryo-transfer practice and in outcomes of the use of assisted reproductive technology in the United States. *New England Journal of Medicine, 350,* 1639–1645.

Jambunathan, S., & Burts, D. (2003). Comparison of perception of self-competence among five ethnic groups of preschoolers in the US. *Early Childhood Education, 173,* 651–660.

James, W. (1890). *Principles of psychology.* Chicago: Encyclopaedia Britannica.

James, W. (1892). *Psychology: The briefer course.* New York: Holt.

Janosz, M., LeBlanc, M., Boulerice, B., & Tremblay, R. (2000). Predicting different types of school dropouts: A typological approach with two longitudinal samples. *Journal of Educational Psychology, 92,* 171–190.

Janssen, P. A., Holt, V. L., & Myers, S. J. (1994). Licensed midwife-attended, out-of-hospital births in Washington State: Are they safe? *Birth, 21,* 141–148.

Janssen, T., & Carton, J. (1999). The effects of locus of control and task difficulty on procrastination. *Journal of Genetic Psychology, 160,* 436–442.

Jendrek, M. (1993). Grandparents who parent their grandchildren: Effects on lifestyle. *Journal of Marriage and the Family, 55,* 609–621.

Jenkins, E. J., & Bell, C. C. (1997). Exposure and response to community violence among children and adolescents. In J. D. Osofsky (Ed.), *Children in a violent society* (pp. 9–31). New York: Guilford Press.

Jenkins, J., & Astington, J. (2000). Theory of mind and social behavior: Causal models tested in a longitudinal study. *Merrill-Palmer Quarterly, 46,* 203–220.

Jenkins, J., Simpson, A., Dunn, J., Rasbash, J., & O'Connor, T. (2005). Mutual influence of marital conflict and children's behavior problems: Shared and nonshared family risks. *Child Development, 76,* 24–39.

Jenkins, J. M., & Astington, J. W. (1996). Cognitive factors and family structure associated with theory of mind development in young children. *Developmental Psychology, 32,* 70–78.

Jensen, A. R. (1980). *Bias in mental testing.* New York: Free Press.

Jessor, R. (1992). Risk behavior in adolescence: A psychosocial framework for understanding and action. *Developmental Review, 12,* 374–390.

Jimerson, S. (1999). On the failure of failure: Examining the association between early grade retention and educational and employment outcomes during late adolescence. *Journal of School Psychology, 37,* 243–272.

John, O. P., Caspi, A., Robins, R. W., Moffitt, T. E., & Stouthamer-Loeber, M. (1994). The "little five": Exploring the nomological network of the five-factor model of personality in adolescent boys. *Child Development, 65,* 160–178.

Johnson, J. W. C., & Yancey, M. K. (1996). A critique of the new recommendations for weight gain in pregnancy. *American Journal of Obstetrics and Gynecology, 174,* 254–258.

Johnson, K., & Daviss, B. (2005). Outcomes of planned home births with certified professional midwives: Large prospective study in North America. *British Medical Journal, 330,* 1416.

Johnson, M. (2005). Developmental neuroscience, psychophysiology, and genetics. In M. Bornstein & M. Lamb (Eds.), *Developmental science: An advanced textbook* (5th ed., pp. 187–222). Hillsdale, NJ: Erlbaum.

Johnston, J., Durieux-Smith, A., & Bloom, K. (2005). Teaching gestural signs to infants to advance child development: A review of the evidence. *First Language, 25,* 235–251.

Jones, M. C. (1924). A laboratory study of fear: The case of Peter. *Pedagogical Seminary, 31,* 308–315.

Jones, S., & Zigler, E. (2002). The Mozart effect: Not learning from history. *Journal of Applied Developmental Psychology, 23,* 355–372.

Jonsson, P. (2003). The new face of homeschooling. *Christian Science Monitor Online.* Retrieved June 23, 2004,from http://www.csmonitor.com /2003/0429/p01s01-ussc.html

Jordan, N. C., Huttenlocher, J., & Levine, S. C. (1992). Differential calculation abilities in young children from middle- and low-income families. *Developmental Psychology, 28,* 644–653.

Jorgenson, S. (1993). Adolescent pregnancy and parenting. In T. Gullotta, G. Adams, & R. Montemayor (Eds.), *Adolescent sexuality* (pp. 103–140). Thousand Oaks, CA: Sage.

Joseph, K., Young, D., Dodds, L., O'Connell, C., Allen, V., Chandra, S., & Allen, A. (2003). Changes in maternal characteristics and obstetric practice and recent increases in primary cesarean delivery. *Obstetrics and Gynecology, 102,* 791–800.

Joseph, R. (2000). Fetal brain behavior and cognitive development. *Developmental Review, 20,* 81–98.

Josephs, R., Newman, M., Brown, R., & Beer, J. (2003). Status, testosterone, and human intellectual performance. *Psychological Science, 14,* 158–163.

Joshi, M. S., & MacLean, M. (1994). Indian and English children's understanding of the distinction between real and apparent emotion. *Child Development, 65,* 1372–1384.

Juffer, E., & Rosenboom, L. (1997). Infant mother attachment of internationally adopted children in the Netherlands. *International Journal of Behavioral Development, 20,* 93–107.

Juffer, F., Bakermans-Kranenburg, M., & van IJzendoorn, M. (2005). The importance of parenting in the development of disorganized attachment: Evidence from a preventive intervention study in adoptive families. *Journal of Child Psychology and Psychiatry, 46,* 263–274.

Jusczyk, P., & Hohne, E. (1997). Infants' memory for spoken words. *Science, 277,* n.p.

Justice, L., Invernizzi, M., Geller, K., Sullivan, A., & Welsch, J. (2005). Descriptive-developmental performance of at-risk preschoolers on early literacy tasks. *Reading Psychology, 26,* 1–25.

Kado, S., & Takagi, R. (1996). Biological aspects. In S. Sandberg (Ed.), *Hyperactivity disorders of childhood* (pp. 246–279). Cambridge, England: Cambridge University Press.

Kagan, J. (1971). *Change and continuity in infancy.* New York: Wiley.

Kagan, J. (1989). *Unstable ideas: Temperament, cognition, and self.* Cambridge, MA: Harvard University Press.

Kagan, J. (1994). *Galen's prophecy.* New York: Basic Books.

Kagan, J. (1997). Temperament and the reactions to unfamiliarity. *Child Development, 68,* 139–143.

Kagan, J., Arcus, D., Snidman, N., Feng, W. Y., Hendler, J., & Greene, S. (1994). Reactivity in infants: A cross-national comparison. *Developmental Psychology, 30,* 342–345.

Kagan, J., & Herschowitz, N. (2005). *A young mind in a growing brain.* Hillsdale, NJ: Erlbaum.

Kagan, J., Kearsley, R., & Zelazo, P. (1978). *Infancy: Its place in human development.* Cambridge, MA: Harvard University Press.

Kagan, J., Reznick, J. S., & Snidman, N. (1990). The temperamental qualities of inhibition and lack of inhibition. In M. Lewis & S. M. Miller (Eds.), *Handbook of developmental psychopathology* (pp. 219–226). New York: Plenum Press.

Kagan, J., Snidman, N., & Arcus, D. (1993). On the temperamental categories of inhibited and uninhibited children. In K. H. Rubin & J. B. Asendorpf (Eds.), *Social withdrawal, inhibition, and shyness in childhood* (pp. 19–28). Hillsdale, NJ: Erlbaum.

Kahana-Kalman, R., & Walker-Andrews, A. (2001). The role of person familiarity in young infants' perception of emotional expressions. *Child Development, 72,* 352–369.

Kail, R. (1990). *The development of memory in children* (3rd ed.). New York: Freeman.

Kail, R. (1991). Processing time declines exponentially during childhood and adolescence. *Developmental Psychology, 27,* 259–266.

Kail, R. (1997). Processing time, imagery, and spatial memory. *Journal of Experimental Child Psychology, 64,* 67–78.

Kail, R. (2004). Cognitive development includes global and domain-specific processes. *Merrill-Palmer Quarterly, 50,* 445–455.

Kail, R., & Hall, L. (1999). Sources of developmental change in children's word-problem performance. *Journal of Educational Psychology, 91,* 660–668.

Kail, R., & Hall, L. K. (1994). Processing speed, naming speed, and reading. *Developmental Psychology, 30,* 949–954.

Kaltiala-Heino, R., Rimpela, M., Rissanen, A., & Rantanen, P. (2001). Early puberty and early sexual activity are associated with bulimic-type eating pathology in middle adolescence. *Journal of Adolescent Health, 28,* 346–352.

Kamps, D., Tankersley, M., & Ellis, C. (2000). Social skills interventions for young at-risk students: A 2-year follow-up study. *Behavioral Disorders, 25,* 310–324.

Kandel, D., & Wu, P. (1995). The contributions of mothers and fathers to the intergenerational transmission of cigarette smoking in adolescence. *Journal of Research on Adolescence, 5,* 225–252.

Kann, L., Warren, C. W., Harris, W. A., Collins, J. L., Douglas, K. A., Collins, M. E., Williams, B. I., Ross, J. G., & Kolbe, L. J. (1995). Youth risk behavior surveillance—United States, 1993. *Morbidity & Mortality Weekly Reports, 44*(SS 1), 1–55.

Kaplan, P., Bachorowski, J., Smoski, M., & Zinser, M. (2001). Role of clinical diagnosis and medication use in effects of maternal depression on infant directed speech. *Infancy, 2,* 537–548.

Karadi, K., Szabo, I., Szepesi, T., Kallai, J., & Kovacs, B. (1999). Sex differences on the hand mental rotation task for 9-year-old children and young adults. *Perceptual & Motor Skills, 89,* 969–972.

Kashima, Y., Kashima, E., Chiu, C., Farsides, T., Gelfand, M., Hong, Y., Kim, U., Strack, F., Werth, L., Yuki, M., & Yzerbyt, V. (2005). Culture, essentialism, and agency: Are individuals universally believed to be more real entities than groups? *European Journal of Social Psychology, 35,* 147–169.

Katz, L., & Woodin, E. (2002). Hostility, hostile detachment, and conflict engagement in marriages: Effects on child and family functioning. *Child Development, 73,* 636–652.

Katz, P. A., & Ksansnak, K. R. (1994). Developmental aspects of gender role flexibility and traditionality in middle childhood and adolescence. *Developmental Psychology, 30,* 272–282.

Kaufman, M. (1997). The teratogenic effects of alcohol following exposure during pregnancy, and its influence on the chromosome constitution of the pre-evaluator egg. *Alcohol & Alcoholism, 32,* 113–128.

Kavšek, M. (2002). The perception of static subjective contours in infancy. *Child Development, 73,* 331–344.

Kaye, K. (1982). *The mental and social life of babies: How parents create persons.* Chicago: University of Chicago Press.

Keating, D. P. (1980). Thinking processes in adolescence. In J. Adelson (Ed.), *Handbook of adolescent psychology* (pp. 211–246). New York: Wiley.

Keating, D. P., List, J. A., & Merriman, W. E. (1985). Cognitive processing and cognitive ability: Multivariate validity investigation. *Intelligence, 9,* 149–170.

Keech, R. (2002). Ophthalmology. In A. Rudolph, R. Kamei, & K. Overby (Eds.), *Rudolph's fundamentals of pediatrics* (3rd ed., pp. 847–862). New York: McGraw-Hill.

Keefe, S. E., & Padilla, A. M. (1987). *Chicano ethnicity.* Albuquerque: University of New Mexico Press.

Keen, R. (2003). Representation of objects and events: Why do infants look so smart and toddlers look so dumb? *Current Directions in Psychological Science, 12,* 79–83.

Keeney, T. J., Cannizzo, S. R., & Flavell, J. H. (1967). Spontaneous and induced verbal rehearsal in a recall task. *Child Development, 38,* 935–966.

Kelley, M. L., Sanchez-Hucles, J., & Walker, R. R. (1993). Correlates of disciplinary practices in working- to middle-class African-American mothers. *Merrill-Palmer Quarterly, 39,* 252–264.

Kemper, K. J. (1996). *The wholistic pediatrician.* New York: HarperCollins.

Kendall-Tackett, K. A., Williams, L. M., & Finkelhor, D. (1993). Impact of sexual abuse on children: A review and synthesis of recent empirical studies. *Psychological Bulletin, 113,* 164–180.

Keniston, K. (1970). Youth: A "new" stage in life. *American Scholar, 8* (Autumn), 631–654.

Kennedy, D. M. (1995). Glimpses of a highly gifted child in a heterogeneous classroom. *Roeper Review, 17,* 164–168.

Kerns, K. A. (1996). Individual differences in friendship quality: Links to child-mother attachment. In W. M. Bukowski, A. F. Newcomb, & W. W. Hartup (Eds.), *The company they keep: Friendship in childhood and adolescence* (pp. 137–157). Cambridge, England: Cambridge University Press.

Khlat, M., Sermet, C., & Le Pape, A. (2000). Women's health in relation with their family and work roles: France in the early 1990s. *Social Science & Medicine, 50,* 1807–1825.

Kidger, J. (2004). 'You realise it could happen to you': The benefits to pupils of young mothers delivering school sex education. *Sex Education, 4,* 185–197.

Kilgore, P. E., Holman, R. C., Clarke, M. J., & Glass, R. I. (1995). Trends of diarrheal disease-associated mortality in US children, 1968 through 1991. *Journal of the American Medical Association, 274,* 1143–1148.

Killen, M., Pisacane, K., Lee-Kim, J., & Ardila-Rey, A. (2001). Fairness or stereotypes? Young children's priorities when evaluating group exclusion and inclusion. *Developmental Psychology, 37,* 587–596.

Kilpatrick, S. J., & Laros, R. K. (1989). Characteristics of normal labor. *Obstetrics and Gynecology, 74,* 85–87.

Kim, H., Baydar, N., & Greek, A. (2003). Testing conditions influence the race gap in cognition and achievement estimated by household survey data. *Journal of Applied Developmental Psychology, 23,* 567–582.

Kim, S. (1997). Relationships between young children's day care experience and their attachment relationships with parents and socioemotional behavior problems. *Korean Journal of Child Studies, 18,* 5–18.

Kinney, D. A. (1993). From "nerds" to normals: Adolescent identity recovery within a changing social system. *Sociology of Education, 66,* 21–40.

Kirk, K., Bailey, J., & Martin, N. (2000). Etiology of male sexual orientation in an Australian twin sample. *Psychology, Evolution, & Gender, 2,* 301–311.

Kirk, S., Gallagher, J., & Anastasiow, N. (1993). *Educating exceptional children* (7th ed.). Boston: Houghton Mifflin.

Kirkcaldy, B., Siefen, G., Surall, D., & Bischoff, R. (2004). Predictors of drug and alcohol abuse among children and adolescents. *Personality & Individual Differences, 36,* 247–265.

Kirsh, S., & Cassidy, J. (1997). Preschoolers' attention to and memory for attachment-relevant information. *Child Development, 68,* 1143–1153.

Klaczynski, P., Fauth, J., & Swanger, A. (1998). Adolescent identity: Rational vs. experiential processing, formal operations, and critical thinking beliefs. *Journal of Youth & Adolescence, 27,* 185–207.

Klahr, D. (1992). Information-processing approaches to cognitive development. In M. H. Bernstein & M. E. Lamb (Eds.), *Developmental psychology: An advanced textbook* (3rd ed., pp. 273–335). Hillsdale, NJ: Erlbaum.

Klass, P., & Costello, E. (2003). *Quirky kids: Understanding and helping your child who doesn't fit in—when to worry and when not to worry.* New York: Ballantine Books.

Klebanov, P. K., Brooks-Gunn, J., Hofferth, S., & Duncan, G. J. (1995, April). *Neighborhood resources, social support and maternal competence.* Paper presented at the biennial meetings of the Society for Research in Child Development, Indianapolis.

Klein, A. & Swartz, S. (1996). *Reading Recovery in California: Program overview.* San Francisco: San Francisco Unified School District.

Klein, J. O. (1994). Otitis media. *Clinical Infectious Diseases, 19,* 823–833.

Kliegman, R. (1998). Fetal and neonatal medicine. In R. Behrman & R. Kliegman (Eds.), *Nelson essentials of pediatrics* (3rd ed., pp. 167–225). Philadelphia: Saunders.

Knight, G. P., Cota, M. K., Bernal, M. E. (1993). The socialization of cooperative, competitive, and individualistic preferences among Mexican American children: The mediating role of ethnic identity. *Hispanic Journal of Behavioral Sciences, 15,* 291–309.

Kochanska, G. (1997). Mutually responsive orientation between mothers and their young children: Implications for early socialization. *Child Development, 68,* 94–112.

Kochanska, G., Casey, R., & Fukumoto, A. (1995). Toddlers' sensitivity to standard violations. *Child Development, 66,* 643–656.

Kochanska, G., Gross, J., Lin, M., & Nichols, K. (2002). Guilt in young children: Development, determinants, and relations with a broader system of standards. *Child Development, 73,* 461–482.

Kochanska, G., Murray, K., & Coy, K. C. (1997). Inhibitory control as a contributor to conscience in childhood: From toddler to early school age. *Child Development, 68,* 263–277.

Kochenderfer, B. J., & Ladd, G. W. (1996). Peer victimization: Cause or consequence of school maladjustment. *Child Development, 67*, 1305–1317.

Kochman, F., Hantouche, E., Ferrari, P., Lancrenon, S., Bayart, D., & Akiskal, H. (2005). Cyclothymia temperament as a prospective predictor of bipolarity and suicidality in children and adolescents with major depressive disorder. *Journal of Affective Disorders, 85*, 181–189.

Kodituwakku, P., May, P. A., Clericuzio, C., & Weers, D. (2001). Emotion-related learning in individuals prenatally exposed to alcohol: An investigation of the relation between set shifting, extinction of responses, and behavior. *Neuropsychologia, 39*, 699–708.

Koenig, A., Cicchetti, D., & Rogosch, F. (2004). Moral development: The association between maltreatment and young children's prosocial behaviors and moral transgressions. *Social Development, 13*, 97–106.

Koeppe, R. (1996). Language differentiation in bilingual children: The development of grammatical and pragmatic competence. *Linguistics, 34*, 927–954.

Koesten, J. (2004). Family communication patterns, sex of subject, and communication competence. *Communication Monographs, 71*, 226–244.

Kohlberg, L. (1964). Development of moral character and moral ideology. In M. L. Hoffman & L. W. Hoffman (Eds.), *Review of child development research* (Vol. 1, pp. 283–332). New York: Russell Sage Foundation.

Kohlberg, L. (1966). A cognitive-developmental analysis of children's sex-role concept and attitudes. In E. E. Maccoby (Ed.), *The development of sex differences* (pp. 82–172). Stanford, CA: Stanford University Press.

Kohlberg, L. (1975). The cognitive-developmental approach to moral education. *Phi Delta Kappan*, 670–677.

Kohlberg, L. (1976). Moral stages and moralization: The cognitive-developmental approach. In T. Lickona (Ed.), *Moral development and behavior: Theory, research, and social issues* (pp. 31–53). New York: Holt.

Kohlberg, L. (1978). Revisions in the theory and practice of moral development. *New Directions for Child Development, 2*, 83–88.

Kohlberg, L. (1980). *The meaning and measurement of moral development.* Worcester, MA: Clark University Press.

Kohlberg, L. (1981). *Essays on moral development: Vol. 1. The philosophy of moral development.* New York: Harper & Row.

Kohlberg, L., Boyd, D. R., & Levine, C. (1990). The return of stage 6: Its principle and moral point of view. In T. E. Wren (Ed.), *The moral domain: Essays in the ongoing discussion between philosophy and the social sciences.* Cambridge: MIT Press.

Kohlberg, L., Candee, D. (1984). The relationship of moral judgment to moral action. In W. M. Kurtines & J. L. Gewirtz (Eds.), *Morality, moral behavior, and moral development* (pp. 52–73). New York: Wiley.

Kohlberg, L., & Elfenbein, D. (1975). The development of moral judgments concerning capital punishment. *American Journal of Orthopsychiatry, 54*, 614–640.

Kohlberg, L., & Ullian, D. Z. (1974). Stages in the development of psychosexual concepts and attitudes. In R. C. Friedman, R. M. Richart, & R. L. Vande Wiele (Eds.), *Sex differences in behavior* (pp. 209–222). New York: Wiley.

Kohnstamm, G. A., Halverson, C. F., Jr., Havill, V. L., & Mervielde, I. (1994). Parents' free descriptions of child characteristics: A crosscultural search for the roots of the Big Five. In S. Harkness & C. M. Super (Eds.), *Parents' cultural belief system: Cultural origins and developmental consequences.* New York: Guilford Press.

Kopp, C. B., & Kaler, S. R. (1989). Risk in infancy: Origins and implications. *American Psychologist, 44*, 224–230.

Koren-Karie, N. (2001). Mothers' attachment representations and choice of infant care: Center care vs. home. *Infant & Child Development, 10*, 117–127.

Korkman, M., Liikanen, A., & Fellman, V. (1996). Neuropsychological consequences of very low birth weight and asphyxia at term: Follow-up until school-age. *Journal of Clinical and Experimental Neuropsychology, 18*, 220–233.

Korner, A. F., Hutchinson, C. A., Koperski, J. A., Kraemer, H. C., & Schneider, P. A. (1981). Stability of individual differences of neonatal motor and crying patterns. *Child Development, 52*, 83–90.

Koskinen, P., Blum, I., Bisson, S., Phillips, S., et al. (2000). Book access, shared reading, and audio models: The effects of supporting the literacy learning of linguistically diverse students in school and at home. *Journal of Educational Psychology, 92*, 23–36.

Kost, K. (1997). The effects of support on the economic well-being of young fathers. *Families in Society, 78*, 370–382.

Kostanski, M., & Gullone, E. (1999). Dieting and body image in the child's world: Conceptualization and behavior. *Journal of Genetic Psychology, 160*, 488–499.

Kosterman, R., Graham, J., Hawkins, J., Catalano, R., & Herrenkohl, T. (2001). Childhood risk factors for persistence of violence in the transition to adulthood: A social development perspective. *Violence & Victims, 16*, 355–369.

Kovacs, D. M., Parker, J. G., & Hoffman, L. W. (1996). Behavioral, affective, and social correlates of involvement in cross-sex friendship in elementary school. *Child Development, 67*, 2269–2286.

Kowalski, H., Wyver, S., Masselos, G., & De Lacey, P. (2004). Toddlers' emerging symbolic play: A first-born advantage? *Early Child Development & Care, 174*, 389–400.

Krakovsky, M. (2005, February 2). Dubious Mozart effect remains music to many Americans' ears. *Stanford Report.* Retrieved May 3, 2005, from http://new-service.stanford.edu/news/2005/february2/mozart-0202

Krcmar, M., & Vieira, E. (2005). Imitating life, imitating television: The effects of family and television models on children's moral reasoning. *Communication Research, 32*, 267–294.

Kronlund, A., & Whittlesea, B. (2005). Seeing double: Levels of processing can cause false memory. *Canadian Journal of Experimental Psychology, 59*, 11–16.

Kuczaj, S. A., II (1977). The acquisition of regular and irregular past tense forms. *Journal of Verbal Learning and Verbal Behavior, 49*, 319–326.

Kuczaj, S. A., II (1978). Children's judgments of grammatical and ungrammatical irregular past tense verbs. *Child Development, 49*, 319–326.

Kuebli, J., Butler, S., & Fivush, R. (1995). Mother-child talk about past emotions: Relationships of maternal language and child gender over time. *Cognition and Emotion, 9*, 265–283.

Kuhl, P. K. (1993). Developmental speech perception: Implications for models of language impairment. *Annals of the New York Academy of Sciences, 682*(July 14), 248–263.

Kuhl, P. L., & Meltzoff, A. N. (1984). The intermodal representation of speech in infants. *Infant Behavior and Development, 7*, 361–381.

Kuhn, D. (1992). Cognitive development. In M. H. Bornstein & M. E. Lamb (Eds.), *Developmental psychology: An advanced textbook* (3rd ed., pp. 211–272). Hillsdale, NJ: Erlbaum.

Kuhn, D., Garcia-Mila, M., Zohar, A., Andersen, C. (1995). Strategies of knowledge acquisition. *Monographs of the Society for Research in Child Development, 60*(Serial No. 245).

Kuhn, D., Kohlberg, L., Languer, J., & Haan, N. (1977). The development of formal operations in logical and moral judgment. *Genetic Psychology Monographs, 95*, 97–188.

Kuperman, S., Schlosser, S., Kramer, J., Bucholz, K., Hesselbrock, V., Reich, T., & Reich, W. (2001). Developmental sequence from disruptive behavior diagnosis to adolescent alcohol dependence. *American Journal of Psychiatry, 158*, 2022–2026.

Kupersmidt, J. B., Griesler, P., DeRosier, M. E., Patterson, C. J., & Davis, P. W. (1995). Childhood aggression and peer relations in the context of family and neighborhood factors. *Child Development, 66*, 360–375.

Kurcinka, M. (1992). *Raising your spirited child: A guide for parents whose child is more intense, sensitive, perceptive, persistent, energetic.* New York: Harper Collins.

Kurdek, L. (2003). Correlates of parents' perceptions of behavioral problems in their young children. *Journal of Applied Developmental Psychology, 24*, 457–473.

Kurdek, L. A., & Fine, M. A. (1994). Family acceptance and family control as predictors of adjustment in young adolescents: Linear, curvilinear, or interactive effects? *Child Development, 65*, 1137–1146.

Kuttler, A., LaGreca, A., & Prinstein, M. (1999). Friendship qualities and social-emotional functioning of adolescents with close, cross-sex friendships. *Journal of Research on Adolescence, 9*, 339–366.

Ladd, G., & Troop-Gordon, W. (2003). The role of chronic peer difficulties in the development of children's psychological adjustment problems. *Child Development, 74*, 1344–1367.

La Freniere, P., Strayer, F. F., Gauthier, R. (1984). The emergence of same-sex affiliative preferences among preschool peers: A developmental/ethological perspective. *Child Development, 55*, 1958–1965.

Lafuente, M., Grifol, R., Segarra, J., Soriano, J., Gorba, M., & Montesinos, A. (1997). Effects of the Firstart method of prenatal stimulation on psychomotor development: The first six months. *Pre- & Peri-Natal Psychology Journal, 11*, 151–162.

Lai, B., Tang, C., & Tse, W. (2005). Prevalence and psychosocial correlates of disordered eating among Chinese pregnant women in Hong Kong. *Eating Disorders: The Journal of Treatment & Prevention, 13*, 171–186.

Lai, K., & McBride-Chang, C. (2001). Suicidal ideation, parenting style, and family climate among Hong Kong adolescents. *International Journal of Psychology, 36*, 81–87.

Laing, S. (2003). Assessment of phonology in preschool African American vernacular English speakers using an alternate response mode. *American Journal of Speech-Language Pathology, 12,* 273–281.

Lamb, M., & Lewis, C. (2005). The role of parent-child relationships in child development. In M. Bornstein & M. Lamb (Eds.), *Developmental science: An advanced textbook* (5th ed., pp. 429–468). Hillsdale, NJ: Erlbaum.

Lamb, M. E. (1981). The development of father-infant relationships. In M. E. Lamb (Ed.), *The role of the father in child development* (2nd ed., pp. 459–488). New York: Wiley.

Lamb, M. E., Frodi, M., Hwang, C., Frodi, A. M. (1983). Effects of paternal involvement on infant preferences for mothers and fathers. *Child Development, 54,* 450–458.

Lamb, M. E., Sternberg, K. J., & Prodromidis, M. (1992). Nonmaternal care and the security of infant-mother attachment: A reanalysis of the data. *Infant Behavior and Development, 15,* 71–83.

Lambert, S. (2005). Gay and lesbian families: What we know and where to go from here. *Family Journal: Counseling & Therapy, 13,* 43–51.

Lamborn, S. D., Dornbusch, S. M., & Steinberg, L. (1996). Ethnicity and community context as moderators of the relations between family decision making and adolescent adjustment. *Child Development, 67,* 283–301.

Lamborn, S. D., Mounts, N. S., Steinberg, L., & Dornbusch, S. M. (1991). Patterns of competence and adjustment among adolescents from authoritative, authoritarian, indulgent, and neglectful families. *Child Development, 62,* 1049–1065.

Lamke, L. K. (1982). Adjustment and sex-role orientation. *Journal of Youth & Adolescence, 11,* 247–259.

Landry, S., Smith, K., Miller-Loncar, C., & Swank, P. (1997). Predicting cognitive-linguistic and social growth curves from early maternal behaviors in children at varying degrees of biologic risk. *Developmental Psychology, 33,* 1040–1053.

Landry, S., Smith, K., Swank, P., Assel, M., & Vellet, S. (2001). Does early responsive parenting have a special importance for children's development or is consistency across early childhood necessary? *Developmental Psychology, 37,* 387–403.

Landry, S. H., Garner, P. W., Swank, P. R., & Baldwin, C. D. (1996). Effects of maternal scaffolding during joint toy play with preterm and full-term infants. *Merrill-Palmer Quarterly, 42,* 177–199.

Laney, D. (2002). The gastrointestinal tract & liver. In A. Rudolph, R. Kamei, & K. Overby (Eds.), *Rudolph's fundamentals of pediatrics* (3rd ed., pp. 466–512).

Langlois, J. H., Ritter, J. M., Roggman, L. A., & Vaughn, L. S. (1991). Facial diversity and infant preferences for attractive faces. *Developmental Psychology, 27,* 79–84.

Langlois, J. H., Roggman, L. A., Casey, R. J., Ritter, J. M., Rieser-Danner, L. A., & Jenkins, V. Y. (1987). Infant preferences for attractive faces: Rudiments of a stereotype? *Developmental Psychology, 23,* 363–369.

Langlois, J. H., Roggman, L. A., & Rieser-Danner, L. A. (1990). Infants' differential social responses to attractive and unattractive faces. *Developmental Psychology, 26,* 153–159.

La Paro, K., Justice, L., Skibbe, L., & Pianta, R. (2004). Relations among maternal, child, and demographic factors and the persistence of preschool language impairment. *American Journal of Speech-Language Pathology, 13,* 291–303.

Lapsley, D. K. (1993). Toward an integrated theory of adolescent ego development: The "new look" at adolescent egocentrism. *American Journal of Orthopsychiatry, 63,* 562–571.

Lapsley, D. K., & Murphy, M. N. (1985). Another look at the theoretical assumptions of adolescent egocentrism. *Developmental Review, 5,* 201–217.

Larson, R. (2000). Toward a psychology of positive youth development. *American Psychologist, 55,* 170–183.

Lau, A., Uba, A., & Lehman, D. (2002). Infectious diseases. In A. Rudolph, R. Kamei, & K. Overby (Eds.), *Rudolph's fundamentals of pediatrics* (3rd ed., pp. 289–389).

Laub, J. H., & Sampson, R. J. (1995). The long-term effect of punitive discipline. In J. McCord (Ed.), *Coercion and punishment in long-term perspectives* (pp. 247–258). Cambridge, England: Cambridge University Press.

Laumann, E. O., Gagnon, J. H., Michael, R. T., & Michaels, S. (1994). *The social organization of sexuality: Sexual practices in the United States.* Chicago: University of Chicago Press.

Lauritsen, M., Pedersen, C., & Mortensen, P. (2004). The incidence and prevalence of pervasive developmental disorders: A Danish population-based study. *Psychological Medicine, 34,* 1339–1346.

Laursen, B. (1995). Conflict and social interaction in adolescent relationships. *Journal of Research on Adolescence, 5,* 55–70.

Lawrence, A. (2003). Factors associated with satisfaction or regret following male-to-female sex reassignment surgery. *Archives of Sexual Behavior, 32,* 299–315.

Lawrence, V., Houghton, S., Douglas, G., Durkin, K., Whiting, K., & Tannock, R. (2004). Children with ADHD: Neuropsychological testing and real-world activities. *Journal of Attention Disorders, 7,* 137–149.

Layton, L., Deeny, K., Tall, G., & Upton, G. (1996). Researching and promoting phonological awareness in the nursery class. *Journal of Research in Reading, 19,* 1–13.

Leaper, C. (1991). Influence and involvement in children's discourse: Age, gender, and partner effects. *Child Development, 62,* 797–811.

Learmonth, A., Lamberth, R., & Rovee-Collier, C. (2004). Generalization of deferred imitation during the first year of life. *Journal of Experimental Child Psychology, 88,* 297–318.

Lebra, T. S. (1994). Mother and child in Japanese socialization: A Japan-U.S. comparison. In P. M. Greenfield & R. R. Cocking (Eds.), *Cross-cultural roots of minority child development* (pp. 259–274). Hillsdale, NJ: Erlbaum.

Lee, C. C. (1985). Successful rural black adolescents: A psychological profile. *Adolescence, 20,* 129–142.

Lee, D., & Quintana, S. (2005). Benefits of cultural exposure and development of Korean perspective-taking ability for transracially adopted Korean children. *Cultural Diversity & Ethnic Minority Psychology, 11,* 130–143.

Lee, M., Law, C., & Tam, K. (1999). Parenthood and life satisfaction: A comparison of single and dual-parent families in Hong Kong. *International Social Work, 42,* 139–162.

Lee, V. E., Burkham, D. T., Zimiles, H., & Ladewski, B. (1994). Family structure and its effect on behavioral and emotional problems in young adolescents. *Journal of Research on Adolescence, 4,* 405–437.

Leff, M., Moolchan, E., Cookus, B., Spurgeon, L., Evans, L., London, E., Kimes, A., Schroeder, J., & Ernst, M. (2003). Predictors of smoking initiation among at risk youth: A controlled study. *Journal of Child & Adolescent Substance Abuse, 13,* 59–76.

Legerstee, M., Pomerleau, A., Malcuit, G., & Feider, H. (1987). The development of infants' responses to people and a doll: Implications for research in communication. *Infant Behavior and Development, 10,* 81–95.

Leichtman, M. D., & Ceci, S. J. (1995). The effects of stereotypes and suggestions on preschoolers' reports. *Developmental Psychology, 31,* 568–578.

Lengua, L., & Kovacs, E. (2005). Bidirectional associations between temperament and parenting and the prediction of adjustment problems in middle childhood. *Journal of Applied Developmental Psychology, 26,* 21–38.

Lerner, R., Theokas, C., & Bobek, C. (2005). Concepts and theories of human development: Historical and contemporary dimensions. In M. Bornstein & M. Lamb (Eds.), *Developmental science: An advanced textbook* (5th ed., pp. 3–44). Hillsdale, NJ: Erlbaum.

Lesaux, N., & Siegel, L. (2003). The development of reading in children who speak English as a second language. *Developmental Psychology, 39,* 1005–1019.

Lester, B. M. (1987). Prediction of developmental outcome from acoustic cry analysis in term and preterm infants. *Pediatrics, 80,* 529–534.

Lester, B. M., Boukydis, C. F. Z., Garcia-Coll, C. T., Hole, W., & Peucker, M. (1992). Infantile colic: Acoustic cry characteristics, maternal perception of cry, and temperament. *Infant Behavior and Development, 15,* 15–26.

Lester, B. M., & Dreher, M. (1989). Effects of marijuana use during pregnancy on newborn cry. *Child Development, 60,* 765–771.

Lester, B. M., Freier, K., LaGasse, L. (1995). Prenatal cocaine exposure and child outcome: What do we really know? In M. Lewis & M. Bendersky (Eds.), *Mothers, babies, and cocaine: The role of toxins in development* (pp. 19–39). Hillsdale, NJ: Erlbaum.

Leve, L. D., & Fagot, B. I. (1995, April). *The influence of attachment style and parenting behavior on children's prosocial behavior with peers.* Paper presented at the biennial meetings of the Society for Research in Child Development, Indianapolis.

Levine, D. (2002). MR imaging of fetal central nervous system abnormalities. *Brain & Cognition, 50,* 432–448.

Levine, J., Pollack, H., & Comfort, M. (2001). Academic and behavioral outcomes among the children of young mothers. *Journal of Marriage and the Family, 63,* 355–369.

Levine, S., Huttenlocher, J., Taylor A., & Langrock, A. (1999). Early sex differences in spatial skill. *Developmental Psychology, 35,* 940–949.

Levitt, M. J., Guacci-Franco, N., & Levitt, J. L. (1993). Convoys of social support in childhood and early adolescence: Structure and function. *Developmental Psychology, 29,* 811–818.

Levorato, M., & Donati, V. (1999). Conceptual and lexical knowledge of shame in Italian children and adolescents. *International Journal of Behavioral Development, 23,* 873–898.

Levy, G. D., & Fivush, R. (1993). Scripts and gender: A new approach for examining gender-role development. *Developmental Review, 13,* 126–146.

Levy-Shiff, R., Lerman, M., Har-Even, D., & Hod, M. (2002). Maternal adjustment and infant outcome in medically defined high-risk pregnancy. *Developmental Psychology, 38,* 93–103.

Levy-Shiff, R., Vakil, E., Dimitrovsky, L., Abramovitz, M., Shahar, N., Har-Even, D., Gross, S., Lerman, M., Levy, L., Sirota, L., & Fish, B. (1998). Medical, cognitive, emotional, and behavioral outcomes in school-age children conceived by in-vitro fertilization. *Journal of Clinical Child Psychology, 27,* 320–329.

Lewis, C., & Lamb, M. E. (2003). Fathers' influences on children's development: The evidence from two-parent families. *European Journal of Psychology of Education, 18,* 211–228.

Lewis, C. C. (1981). How adolescents approach decisions: Changes over grades seven to twelve and policy implications. *Child Development, 52,* 538–544.

Lewis, C. N., Freeman, N. H., & Maridaki-Kassotaki, K. (1995, April). *The social basis of theory of mind: Influences of siblings and, more importantly, interactions with adult kin.* Paper presented at the biennial meetings off the Society for Research in Child Development, Indianapolis.

Lewis, M. (1997). *Altering fate.* New York: Guilford Press.

Lewis, M., Allesandri, S. M., & Sullivan, M. W. (1992). Differences in shame and pride as a function of children's gender and task difficulty. *Child Development, 63,* 630–638.

Lewis, M., & Brooks, J. (1978). Self-knowledge and emotional development. In M. Lewis & L. A. Rosenblum (Eds.), *The development of affect* (pp. 205–226). New York: Plenum Press.

Lewis, M., & Ramsay, D. (2004). Development of self-recognition, personal pronoun use, and pretend play during the 2nd year. *Child Development, 75,* 1821–1831.

Lewis, M., & Sullivan, M. W. (1985). Infant intelligence and its assessment. In B. B. Wolman (Ed.), *Handbook of intelligence* (pp. 505–599). New York: Wiley-Interscience.

Lewis, M., Sullivan, M. W., Stanger, C., & Weiss, M. (1989). Self development and self-conscious emotions. *Child Development, 60,* 146–156.

Lewis, M. D. (1993). Early socioemotional predictors of cognitive competence at 4 years. *Developmental Psychology, 29,* 1036–1045.

Lewkowicz, D. J. (1994). Limitations on infants' response to rate-based auditory-visual relations. *Developmental Psychology, 30,* 880–892.

Li, S., Lindenberger, U., Hommel, B., Aschersleben, G., Prinz, W., & Baltes, P. (2004). Transformations in the couplings among intellectual abilities and constituent cognitive processes across the life span. *Psychological Science, 15,* 155–163.

Liben L., Bigler, R., & Krogh, H. (2001). Pink and blue collar jobs: Children's judgments of job status and job aspirations in relation to sex of worker. *Journal of Experimental Child Psychology, 79,* 346–363.

Lichter, D., & Eggebeen, D. (1994). The effect of parental employment on child poverty. *Journal of Marriage and the Family, 56,* 633–645.

Lickliter, R., Bahrick, L., & Honeycutt, H. (2002). Intersensory redundancy facilitates prenatal perceptual learning in bobwhite quail *(colinus virginianus)* embryos. *Developmental Psychology, 38,* 15–23.

Lickona, T. (1978). Moral development and moral education. In J. M. Gallagher & J. J. A. Easley (Eds.), *Knowledge and development* (Vol. 2, pp. 21–74). New York: Plenum.

Lickona, T. (2004). *Character matters: How to help our children develop good judgment, integrity, and other essential virtues.* New York: Simon & Schuster.

Lidz, C., & Macrine, S. (2001). An alternative approach to the identification of gifted culturally and linguistically diverse learners: The contribution of dynamic assessment. *School Psychology International, 22,* 74–96.

Lieberman, M., Doyle, A., & Markiewicz, D. (1995, April). *Attachment to mother and father: Links to peer relations in children.* Paper presented at the biennial meetings of the Society for Research in Child Development, Indianapolis.

Liew, J., Eisenberg, N., & Reiser, M. (2004). Preschoolers' effortful control and negative emotionality, immediate reactions to disappointment, and quality of social functioning. *Journal of Experimental Child Psychology, 89,* 298–313.

Lillard, A. S., & Flavell, J. H. (1992). Young children's understanding of different mental states. *Developmental Psychology, 28,* 626–634.

Lin, C., Hsiao, C., & Chen, W. (1999). Development of sustained attention assessed using the Continuous Performance Test among children 6–15 years of age. *Journal of Abnormal Child Psychology, 27,* 403–412.

Lindahl, L., & Haimann, M. (1997). Social proximity in early mother-infant

interactions: Implications for gender differences? *Early Development & Parenting, 6,* 83–88.

Linnet, K., Dalsgaard, S., Obel, C., Wisborg, K., Henriksen, T., Rodriquez, A., Kotimaa, A., Moilanen, I., Thomsen, P., Olsen, J., & Jarvelin, M. (2003). Maternal lifestyle factors in pregnancy risk of attention deficit hyperactivity disorder and associated behaviors: Review of the current evidence. *American Journal of Psychiatry, 160,* 1028–1040.

Lippa, R. (2005). *Gender, nature, and nurture* (2nd ed.). Hillsdale, NJ: Erlbaum.

Litt, I. F. (1996). Special health problems during adolescence. In R. E. Behrman, R. M. Kliegman, & A. M. Arvin (Eds.), *Nelson textbook of pediatrics* (15th ed., pp. 541–565). Philadelphia: Saunders.

Litt, J., Taylor, H., Klein, N., & Hack, M. (2005). Learning disabilities in children with very low birthweight: Prevalence, neuropsychological correlates, and educational interventions. *Journal of Learning Disabilities, 38,* 130–141.

Liu, J., Raine, A., Venables, P., & Mednick, S. (2004). Malnutrition at age 3 years and externalizing behavior problems at ages 8, 11, and 17 years. *American Journal of Psychiatry, 161,* 2005–2013.

Livesley, W. J., & Bromley, D. B. (1973). *Person perception in childhood and adolescence.* London: Wiley.

Loeb, S., Fuller, B., Kagan, S., & Carrol, B. (2004). Child care in poor communities: Early learning effects of type, quality, and stability. *Child Development, 75,* 47–65.

Loeber, R., Tremblay, R. E., Gagnon, C., Charlebois, P. (1989). Continuity and desistance in disruptive boys' early fighting at school. *Development and Psychopathology, 1,* 39–50.

Loehlin, J. C., Horn, J. M., & Willerman, L. (1994). Differential inheritance of mental abilities in the Texas Adoption Project. *Intelligence, 19,* 324–336.

Loftus, E. (1993). The reality of repressed memories. *American Psychologist, 48,* 518–537.

Lollis, S., Ross, H., Leroux, L. (1996). An observational study of parents' socialization of moral orientation during sibling conflicts. *Merrill-Palmer Quarterly, 42,* 475–494.

Long, J. V. F., & Vaillant, G. E. (1984). Natural history of male psychological health: Escape from the underclass. *American Journal of Psychiatry, 141,* 341–346.

López-Alarcón, M., Villapando, S., & Fajardo, A. (1997). Breast-feeding lowers the frequency and duration of acute respiratory infection and diarrhea in infants under six months of age. *Journal of Nutrition, 127,* 436–443.

Loonsbury, J. (1992). Interdisciplinary instruction: A mandate for the nineties. In J. Loonsbury (Ed.), *Connecting the curriculum through interdisciplinary instruction.* Columbus, OH: National Middle School Association.

Louhiala, P. J., Jaakkola, N., Ruotsalainen, R., Jaakkola, J. J. K. (1995). Form of day care and respiratory infections among Finnish children. *American Journal of Public Health, 85,* 1109–1112.

Love, J., Harrison, L., Sagi-Schwartz, A., van IJzendoorn, M., Ross, C., Ungerer, J., Raikes, H., Brady-Smith, C., Boller, K., Brooks-Gunn, J., Constantine, J., Kisker, E., Paulsell, D., & Chazan-Cohen, R. (2003). Child care quality matters: How conclusions may vary with context. *Child Development, 74,* 1021–1033.

Lüdtke, O., Trautwein, N., & Köller, O. (2004). A validation of the NEO-FFI in a sample of young adults: Effects of the response format, factorial validity, and relations with indicators of academic achievement. *Diagnostica, 50,* 134–144.

Lundy, J. (2002). Age and language skills of deaf children in relation to theory of mind development. *Journal of Deaf Studies & Deaf Education, 7,* 41–56.

Luster, T., Lekskul, K., & Oh, S. (2004). Predictors of academic motivation in first grade among children born to low-income adolescent mothers. *Early Childhood Research Quarterly, 19,* 337–353.

Luster, T., & McAdoo, H. P. (1995). Factors related to self-esteem among African American youths: A secondary analysis of the High/Scope Perry Preschool data. *Journal of Research on Adolescence, 5,* 451–467.

Luster, T., & McAdoo, H. (1996). Family and child influences on educational attainment: A secondary analysis of the High/Scope Perry Preschool data. *Developmental Psychology, 32,* 26–39.

Luthar, S. S., & Zigler, E. (1992). Intelligence and social competence among high-risk adolescents. *Development and Psychopathology, 4,* 287–299.

Lynam, D. R. (1996). Early identification of chronic offenders: Who is the fledgling psychopath? *Psychological Bulletin, 120,* 209–234.

Lynam, D. R., Moffitt, T. E., & Stouthamer-Loeber, M. (1993). Explaining the relation between IQ and delinquency: Class, race, test motivation, school failure, or self-control? *Journal of Abnormal Psychology, 102*, 187–196.

Lynn, R. (1991). Intelligence in China. *Social Behavior and Personality, 19*, 1–4.

Lynn, R., & Song, M. (1992). General intelligence, visuospatial and verbal abilities in Korean children. *Journal of the Indian Academy of Applied Psychology, 18*, 1–3.

Lyon, T. D., & Flavell, J. H. (1994). Young children's understanding of "remember" and "forget." *Child Development, 65*, 1357–1371.

Lyons, N. P. (1983). Two perspectives: On self, relationships, and morality. *Harvard Educational Review, 53*, 125–145.

Lyons-Ruth, K., Easterbrooks, M. A., Cibelli, C. D. (1997). Infant attachment strategies, infant mental lag, and maternal depressive symptoms: Predictors of internalizing and externalizing problems at age 7. *Developmental Psychology, 33*, 681–692.

Lytle, L., Bakken, L., & Romig, C. (1997). Adolescent female identity development. *Sex Roles, 37*, 175–185.

Lytton, H., & Romney, D. M. (1991). Parents' differential socialization of boys and girls: A meta-analysis. *Psychological Bulletin, 109*, 267–296.

Ma, H. (2003). The relation of moral orientation and moral judgment to prosocial and antisocial behaviour of Chinese adolescents. *International Journal of Psychology, 38*, 101–111.

Maccoby, E., & Lewis, C. (2003). Less day care or different day care? *Child Development, 74*, 1069–1075.

Maccoby, E. E. (1980). *Social development: Psychological growth and the parent-child relationship.* New York: Harcourt Brace Jovanovich.

Maccoby, E. E. (1984). Middle childhood in the context of the family. In W. A. Collins (Ed.), *Development during middle childhood: The years from six to twelve* (pp. 184–239). Washington, DC: National Academy Press.

Maccoby, E. E. (1988). Gender as a social category. *Developmental Psychology, 24*, 755–765.

Maccoby, E. E. (1990). Gender and relationships: A developmental account. *American Psychologist, 45*, 513–520.

Maccoby, E. E. (1995). The two sexes and their social systems. In P. Moen, G. H. Elder, Jr., & K. Luscher (Eds.), *Examining lives in context: Perspectives on the ecology of human development* (pp. 347–364). Washington, DC: American Psychological Association.

Maccoby, E. E., & Jacklin, C. N. (1987). Gender segregation in childhood. In H. W. Reese (Ed.), *Advances in child development and behavior* (Vol. 20, pp. 239–288). Orlando, FL: Academic Press.

Maccoby, E. E., & Martin, J. A. (1983). Socialization in the context of the family: Parent-child interaction. In E. M. Hetherington (Ed.), *Handbook of child psychology: Socialization, personality, and social development* (Vol. 4, pp. 1–102). New York: Wiley.

MacDonald, K. (1992). Warmth as a developmental construct: An evolutionary analysis. *Child Development, 63*, 753–773.

MacDorman, M., & Atkinson, J. (1999). Infant mortality statistics from the 1997 period linked birth/infant death data set. *National Vital Statistics Reports, 47*(23). Hyattsville, MD: National Center for Health Statistics.

MacFarlane, A. (1977). *The psychology of child birth.* Cambridge, MA: Harvard University Press.

MacLean, M., Bryant, P., & Bradley, L. (1987). Rhymes, nursery rhymes, and reading in early childhood. *Merrill-Palmer Quarterly, 33*, 255–281.

MacMillian, D. L., Keogh, B. K., Jones, R. L. (1986). Special educational research on mildly handicapped learners. In M. C. Wittrock (Ed.), *Handbook of research on teaching* (3rd ed., pp. 686–724). New York: Macmillan.

MacMillan, D. L., & Reschly, D. J. (1997). Issues of definition and classification. In W. E. MacLean, Jr. (Ed.), *Ellis' handbook of mental deficiency: Psychological theory and research* (pp. 47–74). Mahwah, NJ: Erlbaum.

MacWhinney, B. (2005). Language development. In M. Bornstein & M. Lamb (Eds.), *Developmental science: An advanced textbook* (5th ed., pp. 359–390). Hillsdale, NJ: Erlbaum.

Madan-Swain, A., Brown, R., Foster, M., Verga, R., et al. (2000). Identity in adolescent survivors of childhood cancer. *Journal of Pediatric Psychology, 25*, 105–115.

Maffeis, C., Schutz, Y., Piccoli, R., Gonfianttini, E., Pinelli, L. (1993). Prevalence of obesity in children in north-east Italy. *International Journal of Obesity, 14*, 287–294.

Magiera, K., & Zigmond, N. (2005). Co-teaching in middle school classrooms under routine conditions: Does the instructional experience differ for students with disabilities in co-taught and solo-taught classes? *Learning Disabilities Research & Practice, 20*, 79–85.

Main, M., & Heese, E. (1990). Parents' unresolved traumatic experiences are related to infant disorganized attachment status: Is frightened and/or frightening parental behavior the linking mechanism? In M. T. Greenberg, D. Cicchetti, E. M. Cummings (Eds.), *Attachment in the preschool years: Theory, research, and intervention* (pp. 151–182). Chicago: University of Chicago Press.

Main, M., Kaplan, N., & Cassidy, J. (1985). Security in infancy, childhood, and adulthood: A move to the level of representation. *Monographs of the Society for Research in Child Development, 50*(Serial No. 209), 66–104.

Main, M., & Solomon, J. (1990). Procedures for identifying infants as disorganized/disoriented during the Ainsworth Strange Situation. In M. T. Greenberg, D. Cicchetti, E. M. Cummings (Eds.), *Attachment in the preschool years: Theory, research, and intervention* (pp. 121–160). Chicago: University of Chicago Press.

Mainemer, H., Gilman, L., & Ames, E. (1998). Parenting stress in families adopting children from Romanian orphanages. *Journal of Family Issues, 19*, 164–180.

Maitel, S., Dromi, E., Sagi, A., & Bornstein, M. (2000). The Hebrew Communicative Development Inventory: Language-specific properties and cross-linguistic generalizations. *Journal of Child Language, 27*, 43–67.

Malamitsi-Puchner, A., Protonotariou, E., Boutsikou, T., Makrakis, E., Sarandakou, A., & Creatsas, G. (2005). The influence of the mode of delivery on circulating cytokine concentrations in the perinatal period. *Early Human Development, 81*, 387–392.

Malina, R. M. (1990). Physical growth and performance during the transitional years (9–16). In R. Montemayor, G. R. Adams, & T. P. Gullotta (Eds.), *From childhood to adolescence: A transitional period?* (pp. 41–62). Newbury Park, CA: Sage.

Malina, R. M. (1994). Physical growth and biological maturation of young athletes. In J. O. Holloszy (Ed.), *Exercise and sports sciences reviews* (Vol. 22, pp. 389–433). Baltimore: Williams & Wilkins.

Malinosky-Rummell, R., & Hansen, D. J. (1993). Long-term consequences of childhood physical abuse. *Psychological Bulletin, 114*, 68–79.

Maniadaki, K., Sonuga-Barke, E., & Kakouros, E. (2005). Parents' causal attributions about attention deficit/hyperactivity disorder: The effect of child and parent sex. *Child: Care, Health & Development, 31*, 331–340.

Maratsos, M. (1983). Some current issues in the study of the acquisition of grammar. In J. H. Flavell & E. M. Markman (Eds.), *Handbook of child psychology: Cognitive development* (pp. 707–786). New York: Wiley.

Maratsos, M. (1998). The acquisition of grammar. In W. Damon (Ed.), *Handbook of child psychology, Vol. 2: Cognition, perception, and language* (5th ed., pp. 421–466). New York: Wiley.

Maratsos, M. (2000). More overregularizations after all: New data and discussion on Marcus, Pinker, Ullman, Hollander, Rosen, & Xu. *Journal of Child Language, 27*, 183–212.

March of Dimes. (2004). *Environmental risks and pregnancy.* Retrieved September 21, 2004, from http://www.marchofdimes.com/professionals/681_9146.asp

Marcia, J. (2002). Identity and psychosocial development in adulthood. *Identity, 2*, 7–28.

Marcia, J. E. (1966). Development and validation of ego identity status. *Journal of Personality & Social Psychology, 3*, 551–558.

Marcia, J. E. (1980). Identity in adolescence. In J. Adelson (Ed.), *Handbook of adolescent psychology* (pp. 159–187). New York: Wiley.

Marcia, J. E. (1993). The status of the statuses: Research review. In J. E. Marcia, A. S. Waterman, D. R. Matteson, S. L. Archer, & J. L. Orlofsky (Eds.), *Ego identity: A handbook for psychosocial research* (pp. 22–41). New York: Springer-Verlag.

Marcovitch, S., Goldberg, S., Gold, A., & Washington, J. (1997). Determinants of behavioural problems in Romanian children adopted in Ontario. *International Journal of Behavioral Development, 20*, 17–31.

Marcus, G. F., Pinker, S., Ullman, M., Hollander, M., Rosen, T. J., & Fei, X. (1992). Overregularization in language acquisition. *Monographs of the Society for Research in Child Development, 57*(4, Serial No. 228).

Marean, G. C., Werner, L. A., & Kuhl, P. K. (1992). Vowel categorization by very young infants. *Developmental Psychology, 2*, 396–405.

Margolin, G., & Gordis, E. (2000). The effects of family and community violence on children. *Annual Review of Psychology, 51*, 445–479.

Marschark, M. (1993). *Psychological development of deaf children.* New York: Oxford University Press.

Marsh, H., Hau, K., & Kong, C. (2000). Late immersion and language of instruction in Hong Kong high schools. Achievement growth in language and nonlanguage subjects. *Harvard Educational Review, 70*, 302–346.

Marsh, H., & Yeung, A. (1997). Coursework selection: Relations to academic self-concept and achievement. *American Educational Research Journal, 34*, 691–720.

Marshall, N. L., Coll, C. G., Marx, F., McCartney, K., Keefe, N., Ruh, J. (1997). After-school time and children's behavioral adjustment. *Merrill-Palmer Quarterly, 43,* 497–514.

Martin, C., & Ruble, D. (2004). Children's search for gender cues: Cognitive perspectives on gender development. *Current Directions in Psychological Science, 13,* 67–70.

Martin, C. L. (1991). The role of cognition in understanding gender effects. In H. W. Reese (Ed.), *Advances in child development and behavior* (Vol. 23, pp. 113–150). San Diego, CA: Academic Press.

Martin, C. L. (1993). New directions for investigating children's gender knowledge. *Developmental Review, 13,* 184–204.

Martin, C. L., & Halverson, C. F. (1983). Gender constancy: A methodological and theoretical analysis. *Sex Roles, 9,* 775–790.

Martin, C. L., & Halverson, C. F., Jr. (1981). A schematic processing model of sex typing and stereotyping in children. *Child Development, 52,* 1119–1134.

Martin, C. L., & Little, J. K. (1990). The relation of gender understanding to children's sex-typed preferences and gender stereotypes. *Child Development, 66,* 1427–1439.

Martin, E. P., & Martin, J. M. (1978). The black extended family. Chicago: University of Chicago Press.

Martin, E. W. (1995). Case studies on inclusion: Worst fears realized. *The Journal of Special Education, 29,* 192–199.

Martin, J., & D'Augelli, A. (2003). How lonely are gay and lesbian youth? *Psychological Reports, 93,* 486.

Martin, J., & Nguyen, D. (2004). Anthropometric analysis of homosexuals and heterosexuals: Implications for early hormone exposure. *Hormones & Behavior, 45,* 31–39.

Martin, R., Noyes, J., Wisenbaker, J., & Huttunen, M. (1999). Prediction of early childhood negative emotionality and inhibition from maternal distress during pregnancy. *Merrill-Palmer Quarterly, 45,* 370–391.

Martin, R. P., Wisenbaker, J., & Huttunen, M. (1994). Review of factor analytic studies of temperament measures based on the Thomas-Chess structural model: Implications for the Big Five. In C. F. Halverson, Jr., G. A. Kohnstamm, & R. P. Martin (Eds.), *The developing structure of temperament and personality from infancy to adulthood* (pp. 157–172). Hillsdale, NJ: Erlbaum.

Martorano, S. C. (1977). A developmental analysis of performance on Piaget's formal operations tasks. *Developmental Psychology, 13,* 666–672.

Masataka, N. (1999). Preference for infant-directed singing in 2-day-old hearing infants of deaf parents. *Developmental Psychology, 35,* 1001–1005.

Mascolo, M. F., & Fischer, K. W. (1995). Developmental transformations in appraisals for pride, shame, and guilt. In J. P. Tangney & K. W. Fischer (Eds.), *Self-conscious emotions: The psychology of shame, guilt, embarrassment, and pride* (pp. 64–113). New York: Guilford Press.

Mason, C. A., Cauce, A. M., Gonzales, N., & Hiraga, Y. (1996). Neither too sweet nor too sour: Problem peers, maternal control, and problem behavior in African American adolescents. *Child Development, 67,* 2115–2130.

Mason, M., & Chuang, S. (2001). Culturally-based after-school arts programming for low-income urban children: Adaptive and preventive effects. *Journal of Primary Prevention, 22,* 45–54.

Massad, C. M. (1981). Sex role identity and adjustment during adolescence. *Child Development, 52,* 1290–1298.

Masten, A. S. (1989). Resilience in development: Implications of the study of successful adaptation for developmental psychopathology. In D. Cicchetti (Ed.), *The emergence of a discipline: Rochester symposium on developmental psychopathology* (Vol. 1, pp. 261–294. Hillsdale, NJ: Erlbaum.

Masten, A. S., Best, K. M., & Garmezy, N. (1990). Resilience and development: Contributions from the study of children who overcome adversity. *Development and Psychopathology, 2,* 425–444.

Masten, A. S., & Coatsworth, J. D. (1995). Competence, resilience, and psychopathology. In D. Cicchetti & D. J. Cohen (Eds.), *Developmental psychopathology: Vol. 2. Risk, disorder, and adaptation* (pp. 715–752). New York: Wiley-Interscience.

Masten, A. S., & Coatsworth, J. D. (1998). The development of competence in favorable and unfavorable environments: Lessons from research on successful children. *American Psychologist, 53,* 205–220.

Masur, E. F. (1995). Infants' early verbal imitation and their later lexical development. *Merrill-Palmer Quarterly, 41,* 286–306.

Maszk, P., Eisenberg, N., & Guthrie, I. (1999). Relations of children's social status to their emotionality and regulation: A short-term longitudinal study. *Merrill-Palmer Quarterly, 454,* 468–492.

Matarazzo, J. D. (1992). Biological and physiological correlates of intelligence. *Intelligence, 16,* 257–258.

Mather, P. L., & Black, K. N. (1984). Heredity and environmental influences on preschool twins' language skills. *Developmental Psychology, 20,* 303–308.

Matthews, T. (2005). Racial/ethnic disparities in infant mortality—United States, 1995–2002. *Morbidity & Mortality Weekly Report, 54,* 553–556.

Maughan, B., Pickles, A., & Quinton, D. (1995). Parental hostility, childhood behavior, and adult social functioning. In J. McCord (Ed.), *Coercion and punishment in long-term perspectives* (pp. 34–58). Cambridge, England: Cambridge University Press.

Mayes, L., Cicchetti, D., Acharyya, S., & Zhang, H. (2003). Developmental trajectories of cocaine-and-other-drug-exposed and non-cocaine-exposed children. *Journal of Developmental and Behavioral Pediatrics, 24,* 323–335.

Mayeux, L., & Cillessen, A. (2003). Development of social problem solving in early childhood: Stability, change, and associations with social competence. *Journal of Genetic Psychology, 164,* 153–173.

Mayringer, H., & Wimmer, H. (2000). Pseudoname learning by German-speaking children with dyslexia: Evidence for a phonological learning deficit. *Journal of Experimental Child Psychology, 75,* 116–133.

McAllister, D., Kaplan, B., Edworthy, S., Martin, L., et al. (1997). The influence of systemic lupus erythematosus on fetal development: Cognitive, behavioral, and health trends. *Journal of the International Neurological Society, 3,* 370–376.

McAndrew, F. T., King, J. C., & Honoroff, L. R. (2002). A sociobiological analysis of namesaking patterns in 322 American families. *Journal of Applied Social Psychology, 32,* 851–864.

McBride-Chang, C. (1998). The development of invented spelling. *Early Education & Development, 9,* 147–160.

McBride-Chang, C., & Ho, C. (2000). Developmental issues in Chinese children's character acquisition. *Journal of Educational Psychology, 92,* 50–55.

McBride-Chang, C., Shu, H., Zhou, C., & Wagner, R. (2004). Morphological awareness uniquely predicts young children's Chinese character recognition. *Journal of Educational Psychology, 96,* 743–751.

McCall, R. B. (1993). Developmental functions for general mental performance. In D. K. Detterman (Ed.), *Current topics in human intelligence: Vol. 3. Individual differences and cognition* (pp. 3–30). Norwood, NJ: Ablex.

McClure, E. (2000). A meta-analytic review of sex differences in facial expression processing and their development in infants, children, and adolescents. *Psychological Bulletin, 126,* 242–453.

McCord, J. (1982). A longitudinal view of the relationship between parental absence and crime. In J. Gunn & D. P. Farrington (Eds.), *Abnormal offenders, delinquency, and the criminal justice system* (pp. 113–128). London: Wiley.

McCrae, R., Costa, P., Ostendorf, F., & Angleitner, A. (2000). Nature over nurture: Temperament, personality, and life span development. *Journal of Personality & Social Psychology, 78,* 173–186.

McCrae, R., & Terracciano, A. (2005). Universal features of personality traits from the observer's perspective: Data from 50 cultures. *Journal of Personality & Social Psychology, 88,* 547–561.

McCrae, R. R., & Costa, P. T., Jr. (1994). The stability of personality: Observations and evaluations. *Current Directions in Psychological Science, 3,* 173–175.

McCrae, R. R., & John, O. P. (1992). An introduction to the five-factor model and its applications. *Journal of Personality, 50,* 175–215.

McCune, L. (1995). A normative study of representational play at the transition to language. *Developmental Psychology, 31,* 198–206.

McElree, B., Jia, G., & Litvak, A. (2000). The time course of conceptual processing in three bilingual populations. *Journal of Memory & Language, 42,* 229–254.

McFalls, J. A., Jr. (1990). The risks of reproductive impairment in the later years of childbearing. *Annual Review of Sociology, 16,* 491–519.

McFayden-Ketchum, S., Bates, J., Dodge, K., & Pettit, G. (1996). Patterns of change in early childhood aggressive-disruptive behavior: Gender differences in predictions from early coercive and affectionate mother-child interactions. *Child Development, 67,* 2417–2433.

McGee, B., Hewitt, P., Sherry, S., Parkin, M., & Flett, G. (2005). Perfectionistic self-presentation, body image, and eating disorder symptoms. *Body Image, 2,* 29–40.

McGrath, M., & Sullivan, M. (2002). Birth weight, neonatal morbidities, and school age outcomes in full-term and preterm infants. *Issues in Comprehensive Pediatric Nursing, 25,* 231–254.

McGue, M. (1994). Why developmental psychology should find room for behavior genetics. In C. A. Nelson (Ed.), *The Minnesota symposia on child development* (Vol. 27, pp. 105–119). Hillsdale, NJ: Erlbaum.

McGuire, S., McHale, S. M., & Updegraff, K. (1996). Children's perceptions of the sibling relationship in middle childhood: Connections within and between family relationships. *Personal Relationships, 3,* 229–239.

McKelvie, P., & Low, J. (2002). Listening to Mozart does not improve children's spatial ability: Final curtains for the Mozart effect. *British Journal of Developmental Psychology, 20,* 241–258.

McKown, C., & Weinstein, R. (2003). The development and consequences of stereotype consciousness in middle childhood. *Child Development, 74,* 498–515.

McLanahan, S. S., & Sandefur, G. (1994). *Growing up with a single parent: What hurts, what helps.* Cambridge, MA: Harvard University Press.

McLoyd, V. (1997, April). *Reducing stressors, increasing supports in the lives of ethnic minority children in America: Research and policy issues.* Paper presented at the biennial meetings of the Society for Research in Child Development, Washington, DC.

McLoyd, V., & Wilson, L. (1991). The strain of living poor: Parenting, social support, and child mental health. In A. C. Huston (Ed.), *Children in poverty: Child development and public policy* (pp. 105–135). Cambridge, England: Cambridge University Press.

McLoyd, V. C. (1998). Socioeconomic disadvantage and child development. *American Psychologist, 53,* 185–204.

McMahon, R. J. (1997, April). *Prevention of antisocial behavior: Initial findings from the Fast Track Project.* Symposium presented at the biennial meetings of the Society for Research in Child Development, Washington, DC.

McManis, M., Kagan, J., Snidman, N., & Woodward, S. (2002). EEG asymmetry, power, and temperament in children. *Developmental Psychobiology, 41,* 169–177.

McRorie, M., & Cooper, C. (2004). Psychomotor movement and IQ. *Personality & Individual Differences, 37,* 523–531.

Measor, L. (2004). Young people's views of sex education: Gender, information and knowledge. *Sex Education, 4,* 153–166.

Mediascope Press. (1999). *The social effects of electronic interactive games: An annotated bibliography.* Studio City, CA: Mediascope Inc.

Medvedova, L. (1998). Personality dimensions—"little five"—and their relationships with coping strategies in early adolescence. *Studia Psychologica, 40,* 261–265.

Melby, J. N., & Conger, R. D. (1996). Parental behaviors and adolescent academic performance: A longitudinal analysis. *Journal of Research on Adolescence, 6,* 113–137.

Melinder, A., Goodman, G., Eilertsen, D., & Magnussen, S. (2004). Beliefs about child witnesses: A survey of professionals. *Psychology, Crime, & Law, 10,* 347–365.

Melot, A., & Houde, O. (1998). Categorization and theories of mind: The case of the appearance/reality distinction. *Cahiers de Psychologie Cognitive/Current Psychology of Cognition, 17,* 71–93.

Melson, G., Peet, S., & Sparks, C. (1991). Children's attachments to their pets: Links to socioemotional development. *Children's Environmental Quarterly, 8,* 55–65.

Meltzoff, A. N. (1988). Infant imitation and memory: Nine-month-olds in immediate and deferred tasks. *Child Development, 59,* 217–225.

Meltzoff, A. N. (1995). Understanding the intentions of others: Re-enactment of intended acts by 18-month-old children. *Developmental Psychology, 31,* 838–850.

Meltzoff, A. N., & Moore, M. K. (1977). Imitation of facial and manual gestures by human neonates. *Science, 198,* 75–78.

Menesini, E., Sanchez, V., Fonzi, A., Ortega, R., Costabile, A., & Lo Feudo, G. (2003). Moral emotions and bullying: A cross-national comparison of differences between bullies, victims and outsiders. *Aggressive Behavior, 29,* 515–530.

Merikangas, K. R., & Angst, J. (1995). The challenge of depressive disorders in adolescence. In M. Rutter (Ed.), *Psychosocial disturbances in young people: Challenges for prevention* (pp. 131–165). Cambridge, England: Cambridge University Press.

Merrick, J., & Morad, M. (2002). Adolescent pregnancy in Israel. *International Journal of Adolescent Medicine, 14,* 161–164.

Merriman, W. E. (1991). The mutual exclusivity bias in children's word learning: A reply to Woodward and Markman. *Developmental Review, 11,* 164–191.

Merriman, W. E., & Bowman, L. L. (1989). The mutual exclusivity bias in children's word learning. *Monographs of the Society for Research in Child Development, 54*(Serial No. 220).

Mervis, C. B., & Bertrand, J. (1994). Acquisition of the novel name-nameless category (N3C) principle. *Child Development, 65,* 1646–1662.

Meschyan, G., & Hernandez, A. (2002). Is native-language decoding skill related to second-language learning? *Journal of Educational Psychology, 94,* 14–22.

Mesman, J., & Koot, H. (2001). Early preschool predictors of preadolescent internalizing and externalizing DSM-IV diagnoses. *Journal of the American Academy of Child and Adolescent Psychiatry, 40,* 1029–1036.

Meyer-Bahlburg, H. F. L., Ehrhardt, A. A., Rosen, L. R., Gruen, R. S., Veridiano, N. P., Vann, F. H., & Neuwalder, H. F. (1995). Prenatal estrogens and the development of homosexual orientation. *Developmental Psychology, 31,* 12–21.

Mikulincer, M., & Shaver, P. (2005). Attachment security, compassion, and altruism. *Current Directions in Psychological Science, 14,* 34–38.

Miller, B., Benson, B., & Galbraith, K. (2001). Family relationships and adolescent pregnancy risk: A research synthesis. *Developmental Review, 21,* 1–38.

Miller, B., Norton, M., Curtis, T., Hill, E., Schvaneveldt, P., & Young, M. (1998). The timing of sexual intercourse among adolescents: Family, peer, and other antecedents: Erratum. *Youth & Society, 29,* 390.

Miller, B. C., & Moore, K. A. (1990). Adolescent sexual behavior, pregnancy, and parenting: Research through the 1980s. *Journal of Marriage and the Family, 52,* 1025–1044.

Miller, P. (2002). *Theories of development* (4th ed.). New York: Worth.

Miller, P., Eisenberg, N., Fabes, R., Shell, R., & Gular, S. (1989). Mothers' emotional arousal as a moderator in the socialization of children's empathy. *New Directions for Child Development, 44,* 65–83.

Mills, D., Coffey-Corina, S., & Neville, H. (1994). Variability in cerebral organization during primary language acquisition. In G. Dawson & K. Fischer (Eds.), *Human behavior and the developing brain.* New York: Guilford.

Milos, G., Spindler, A., Ruggiero, G., Klaghofer, R., & Schnyder, U. (2002). Comorbidity of obsessive-compulsive disorders and duration of eating disorders. *International Journal of Eating Disorders, 31,* 284–289.

Milos, G., Spindler, A., & Schnyder, U. (2004). Psychiatric comorbidity and Eating Disorder Inventory (EDI) profiles in eating disorder patients. *Canadian Journal of Psychiatry, 49,* 179–184.

Minty, B. (1999). Outcomes in long-term foster family care. *Journal of Child Psychology and Psychiatry & Allied Disciplines, 40,* 991–999.

Mischel, W. (1966). A social learning view of sex differences in behavior. In E. E. Maccoby (Ed.), *The development of sex differences* (pp. 56–81). Stanford, CA: Stanford University Press.

Mischel, W. (1970). Sex typing and socialization. In P. H. Mussen (Ed.), *Carmichael's manual of child psychology* (Vol. 2, pp. 3–72). New York: Wiley.

Mishra, R. (1997). Cognition and cognitive development. In J. Berry, P. Dasen, & T. Saraswathi (Eds.), *Handbook of cross-cultural psychology: Vol. 2. Basic processes and human development.* Boston: Allyn & Bacon.

Misra, G. (1983). Deprivation and development: A review of Indian studies. *Indian Educational Review, 18,* 12–32.

Mistry, R., Biesanz, J., Taylor, L., Burchinal, M., & Cox, M. (2004). Family income and its relation to preschool children's adjustment for families in the NICHD Study of Early Child Care. *Developmental Psychology, 40,* 727–745.

Mitchell, A. (2002). Infertility treatment: More risks and challenges. *New England Journal of Medicine, 346,* 769–770.

Mitchell, C., O'Nell, T., Beals, J., Dick, R., Keane, E., & Manson, S. (1996). Dimensionality of alcohol use among American Indian adolescents: Latent structure, construct validity, and implications for developmental research. *Journal of Research on Adolescence, 6,* 151–180.

Mitchell, E. A., Tuohy, P. G., Brunt, J. M., Thompson, J. M. D., Clements, M. S., Stewart, A. W., Ford, R. P. K., & Taylor, B. J. (1997). Risk factors for sudden infant death syndrome following the presentation campaign in New Zealand: A prospective study. *Pediatrics, 100,* 835–840.

Mitchell, J. E. (1995). Medical complications of bulimia nervosa. In K. D. Brownell & C. G. Fairburn (Eds.), *Eating disorders and obesity: A comprehensive handbook* (pp. 271–275). New York: Guilford Press.

Mitchell, K. (2002). Women's morality: A test of Carol Gilligan's theory. *Journal of Social Distress & the Homeless, 11,* 81–110.

Mitchell, P. R., & Kent, R. D. (1990). Phonetic variation in multisyllable babbling. *Journal of Child Language, 17,* 247–265.

Mofenson, L. (2002). U.S. Public Health Service Task Force recommendations for use of antiretroviral drugs in pregnant HIV-1 infected women for maternal health and interventions to reduce perinatal HIV-1 transmission in the United States. *Morbidity & Mortality Weekly Report, 51,* 1–38.

Moffitt, T. E. (1990). Juvenile delinquency and attention deficit disorder: Boys' developmental trajectories from age 3 to age 15. *Child Development, 61,* 893–910.

Moffitt, T. E. (1993). Adolescence-limited and life-course-persistent antisocial behavior: A developmental taxonomy. *Psychology Review, 100,* 674–701.

Moffitt, T. E., & Harrington, H. L. (1996). Delinquency: The natural history of antisocial behavior. In P. A. Silva & W. R. Stanton (Eds), *From child to adult: The Dunedin multidisciplinary health and development study* (pp. 163–185). Aukland: Oxford University Press.

Mohanty, A., & Perregaux, C. (1997). Language acquisition and bilingualism. In J. Berry, P. Dasen, & T. Saraswathi (Eds.) *Handbook of cross-cultural psychology: Vol. 2. Basic processes and human development.* Boston: Allyn & Bacon.

Mohsin, M., Wong, F., Bauman, A., & Bai, J. (2003). Maternal and neonatal factors influencing premature birth and low birth weight in Australia. *Journal of Biosocial Science, 35,* 161–174.

Molfese, V. J., DiLalla, L. F., & Bunce, D. (1997). Prediction of the intelligence test scores of 3- to 8-year-old children by home environment, socioeconomic status, and biomedical risks. *Merrill-Palmer Quarterly, 43,* 219–234.

Money, J. (1975). Ablatio penis: Normal male infant sex-reassignment as a girl. *Archives of Sexual Behavior, 4,* 65–71.

Montemayor, R., & Eisen, M. (1977). The development of self-conceptions from childhood to adolescence. *Developmental Psychology, 13,* 314–319.

Montgomery, M., & Sorell, G. (1998). Love and dating experience in early and middle adolescence: Grade and gender comparisons. *Journal of Adolescence, 21,* 677–689.

Moody, E. (1997). Lessons from pair counseling with incarcerated juvenile delinquents. *Journal of Addictions & Offender Counseling, 18,* 10–25.

Moon, C., & Fifer, W. P. (1990). Syllables as signals for 2-day-old infants. *Infant Behavior and Development, 13,* 377–390.

Mooney, L., Knox, D., & Schacht, C. (2000). *Social problems.* Belmont, CA: Wadsworth.

Moore, C., Barresi, J., & Thompson, C. (1998). The cognitive basis of future-oriented prosocial behavior. *Social Development, 7,* 198–218.

Moore, D. (2001). Reassessing emotion recognition performance in people with mental retardation: A review. *American Journal on Mental Retardation, 106,* 481–502.

Moore, E. G. J. (1986). Family socialization and the IQ test performance of traditionally and transracially adopted black children. *Developmental Psychology, 22,* 317–326.

Moore, K. L., & Persaud, T. V. N. (1993). *The developing human: Clinically oriented embryology* (5th ed.). Philadelphia: Saunders.

Moore, R., Vadeyar, S., Fulford, J., Tyler, D., Gribben, C., Baker, P., James, D., & Gowland, P. (2001). Antenatal determination of fetal brain activity in response to an acoustic stimulus using functional magnetic resonance imaging. *Human Brain Mapping, 12,* 94–99.

Morelli, G. A., Rogoff, B., Oppenheim, D., & Goldsmith, D. (1992). Cultural variation in infants' sleeping arrangements: Questions of independence. *Developmental Psychology, 28,* 604–613.

Moretti, M., & Wiebe, V. (1999). Self-discrepancy in adolescence: Own and parental standpoints on the self. *Merrill-Palmer Quarterly, 45,* 624–649.

Morgan, J. L. (1994). Converging measures of speech segmentation in preverbal infants. *Infant Behavior and Development, 17,* 389–403.

Morgan, J. L., Bonamo, K. M., & Travis, L. L. (1995). Negative evidence on negative evidence. *Developmental Psychology, 31,* 180–197.

Morrison, D. R., & Cherlin, A. J. (1995). The divorce process and young children's well-being: A prospective analysis. *Journal of Marriage and the Family, 57,* 800–812.

Morrison, F. J., Smith, L., & Dow-Ehrensberger, M. (1995). Education and cognitive development: A natural experiment. *Developmental Psychology, 31,* 789–799.

Morrissette, P. (1999). Post-traumatic stress disorder in child sexual abuse: Diagnostic and treatment considerations. *Child & Youth Care Forum, 28,* 205–219.

Morrongiello, B. A. (1988). Infants' localization of sounds along the horizontal axis: Estimates of minimum audible angle. *Developmental Psychology, 24,* 8–13.

Morrongiello, B. A., Fenwick, K. D., & Chance, G. (1990). Sound localization acuity in very young infants: An observer-based testing procedure. *Developmental Psychology, 26,* 75–84.

Morse, P. A., & Cowan, N. (1982). Infant auditory and speech perception. In T. M. Field, A. Houston, H. C. Quay, L. Troll, & G. E. Finley (Eds.), *Review of human development* (pp. 32–61). New York: Wiley.

Mortensen, E., Andresen, J., Kruuse, E., Sanders, S., & Reinisch, J. (2003). IQ stability: The relation between child and young adult intelligence test scores in low-birthweight samples. *Scandinavian Journal of Psychology, 44,* 395–398.

Mortimer, J., & Harley, C. (2002). The quality of work and youth mental health. *Work & Occupations, 29,* 166–197.

Mortimer, J., Zimmer-Gembeck, M., Holmes, M., & Shanahan, M. (2002). The process of occupational decision making: Patterns during the transition to adulthood. *Journal of Vocational Behavior, 61,* 439–465.

Mortimer, J. T., & Finch, M. D. (1996). Work, family, and adolescent development. In J. T. Mortimer & M. D. Finch (Eds.), *Adolescents, work, and family: An intergenerational developmental analysis* (pp. 1–24). Thousand Oaks, CA: Sage.

Mortimer, J. T., Finch, M. D., Dennehy, K., Lee, C., & Beebe, T. (1995, April). *Work experience in adolescence.* Paper presented at the biennial meetings of the Society for Research in Child Development, Indianapolis.

Moses, L., Baldwin, D., Rosicky, J., & Tidball, G. (2001). Evidence for referential understanding in the emotions domain at twelve and eighteen months. *Child Development, 72,* 718–735.

Moshman, D. (2005). *Rationality, morality, and identity.* Hillsdale, NJ: Erlbaum.

Mott, J., Crowe, P., Richardson, J., & Flay, B. (1999). After-school supervision and adolescent cigarette smoking: Contributions of the setting and intensity of after-school self-care. *Journal of Behavioral Medicine, 22,* 35–58.

Mueller, U., Overton, W., & Reene, K. (2001). Development of conditional reasoning: A longitudinal study. *Journal of Cognition & Development, 2,* 27–49.

Muhuri, P. K., Anker, M., & Bryce, J. (1996). Treatment patterns for childhood diarrhoea: Evidence from demographic and health surveys. *Bulletin of the World Health Organization, 74,* 135–146.

Muir-Broaddus, J. E. (1997, April). *The effects of social influence and psychological reactance on children's responses to repeated questions.* Paper presented at the biennial meetings of the Society for Research in Child Development, Washington, DC.

Muller, C. (1995). Maternal employment, parent involvement, and mathematics achievement among adolescents. *Journal of Marriage and the Family, 57,* 85–100.

Muller, R., Goebel-Fabbri, A., Diamond, T., & Dinklage, D. (2000). Social support and the relationship between family and community violence exposure and psychopathology among high risk adolescents. *Child Abuse & Neglect, 24,* 449–464.

Munir, K., & Beardslee, W. (2001). A developmental and psychobiological framework for understanding the role of culture in child and adolescent psychiatry. *Child & Adolescent Psychiatric Clinics of North America, 10,* 667–677.

Munro, G., & Adams, G. R. (1977). Ego-identity formation in college students and working youth. *Developmental Psychology, 13,* 523–524.

Munroe, R. H., Shimmin, H. S., & Munroe, R. L. (1984). Gender understanding and sex role preference in four cultures. *Developmental Psychology, 20,* 673–682.

Muraskas, J., & Hasson, A. (2004). A girl with a birth weight of 280 g, now 14 years old. *New England Journal of Medicine, 324,* 1598–1599.

Murphy, S. O. (1993, April). *The family context and the transition to siblinghood: Strategies parents use to influence sibling-infant relationships.* Paper presented at the biennial meetings of the Society for Research in Child Development, New Orleans.

Murray, A. D., & Hornbaker, A. V. (1997). Maternal directive and facilitative interaction styles: Associations with language and cognitive development of low risk and high risk toddlers. *Development and Psychopathology, 9,* 507–516.

Murray, B. (1998, June). Dipping math scores heat up debate over math teaching. *APA Monitor, 29,* 34–35.

Murray, J. P. (1997). Media violence and youth. In J. D. Osofsky (Ed.), *Children in a violent society* (pp. 72–96). New York: Guilford Press.

Murray, L., Sinclair, D., Cooper, P., Ducournau, P., et al. (1999). The socio-emotional development of 5-year-old children of postnatally depressed mothers. *Journal of Child Psychology & Psychiatry & Allied Disciplines, 40,* 1259–1271.

Muscari, M. E. (1996). Primary care of adolescents with bulimia nervosa. *Journal of Pediatric Health Care, 10,* 17–25.

Must, O., Must, A., & Raudik, V. (2003). The secular rise in IQs: In Estonia, the Flynn effect is not a Jensen effect. *Intelligence, 31,* 461–471.

Nachmias, M. (1993, April). *Maternal personality relations with toddler's attachment classification, use of coping strategies, and adrenocortical stress response.* Paper presented at the biennial meetings of the Society for Research in Child Development, New Orleans.

Nagy, E., & Molnar, P. (2004). Homo imitans or homo provocans? Human imprinting model of neonatal imitation. *Infant Behavior and Development, 27,* 54–63.

Nagy, W., Berninger, V., Abbott, R., Vaughan, K., & Vermeulen, K. (2004). Relationship of morphology and other language skills to literacy skills in at-risk second-grade readers and at-risk fourth-grade writers. *Journal of Educational Psychology, 96*, 730–742.

Nakata, T., & Trehub, S. (2004). Infants' responsiveness to maternal speech and singing. *Infant Behavior and Development, 27*, 455–464.

Narvaez, D. (1998). The influence of moral schemas on the reconstruction of moral narratives in eighth graders and college students. *Journal of Educational Psychology, 47*, 218–228.

National Abortion and Reproductive Rights Action League (NARAL). (1997). Limitations on the rights of pregnant women [NARAL Factsheet]. Retrieved March 5, 2001, from http://www.naral.org/publications /facts

National Center for Chronic Disease Prevention and Health Promotion (NCCDPHP). (2000). Obesity epidemic increases dramatically in the United States [Online press release]. Retrieved August 23, 2000, from http://www.cdc.gov

National Center for Education Statistics (NCES). (1997). *Condition of Education/1997.* Washington, DC: U.S. Department of Education.

National Center for Education Statistics (NCES). (1999). *Guide to the National Assessment of Educational Progress* [Online version]. Retrieved February 15, 2001, from http://www.nces.ed.gov/nationsreportcard/guide

National Center for Education Statistics (NCES). (2000). *Trends in international mathematics and science study: TIMSS results.* Retrieved May 26, 2005, from http://nces.ed.gov/tims/results.asp

National Center for Education Statistics (NCES). (2003a). *Overview of public elementary and secondary schools and districts: School year 2001–2002.* Retrieved July 9, 2005, from http://nces.ed.gov/pubs2003/overview03 /table_10.asp

National Center for Education Statistics (NCES). (2003b). *Characteristics of the 100 largest public elementary and secondary school districts in the United States: 2001–2002.* Retrieved July 9, 2005, from http://nces.ed.gov/pubs 2003/100_largest/table_20_1.asp

National Center for Education Statistics (NCES). (2003c). *Highlights from the TIMSS 1999 video study of eighth-grade mathematics teaching* (NCES Publication No. 2003011). Washington, DC: Author.

National Center for Education Statistics (NCES). (2005a). The condition of education 2005, in brief. Retrieved July 23, 2005, from http://nces.ed.gov /pubs2005/2005095.pdf

National Center for Education Statistics (NCES). (2005b). The condition of education 2000–2005. Retrieved July 23, 2005, from http://nces.ed.gov /programs/coe/

National Center for Health Statistics (NCHS). (1996a). Guidelines for school health programs to promote lifelong healthy eating. *Morbidity & Mortality Weekly Report, 45*, 1–33.

National Center for Health Statistics (NCHS). (1996b). Leading causes of death by age, sex, race, and Hispanic origin: United States, 1992. *Vital and Health Statistics, Series 20*(29, June).

National Center for Health Statistics (NCHS). (1999, September 14). Trends in twin and triplet births: 1980–1997. *National Vital Statistics Reports, 47*(24).

National Center for Health Statistics (NCHS). (2001). Prevalence of overweight among children and adolescents: United States, 1999 [Online report]. Retrieved September 16, 2002, from http://www.cdc.gov/nchs /products/pubs/pubd/hestats/overwgt99.htm

National Center for Health Statistics (NCHS). (2003). *Births: Final data for 2002.* Retrieved June 18, 2004, from http://www.cdc.gov/nchs/pressroom /03facts/teenbirth.htm

National Center for Health Statistics (NCHS). (2005). Obesity trends in the United States, 1999–2002. Retrieved May 5, 2005, from http://www.cdc .gov/nchs/products/pubs/pubd/hestats/over.html

National Council for Injury Prevention and Control (NCIPC). (2000). *Fact Book for the Year 2000.* Washington, DC: Author.

National Institute of Mental Health (NIMH). (2001). *The numbers count: Mental disorders in America.* NIH Publication No. 01-4584. Retrieved June 10, 2005, from http://www.nimh.nih.gov

National Literacy Trust. (2003). *Mother tongues: What languages are spoken in the UK?* Retrieved July 9, 2005, from http://www.literacytrust.org.uk /Research/lostop3.html

Needleman, H. L., Riess, J. A., Tobin, M. J., Biesecker, G. E., & Greenhouse, J. B. (1996). Bone lead levels and delinquent behavior. *Journal of the American Medical Association, 275*, 363–369.

Needlman, R., Frank, D. A., Augustyn, M., & Zuckerman, B. S. (1995). Neurophysiological effects of prenatal cocaine exposure: Comparison of human and animal investigations. In M. Lewis & M. Bendersky (Eds.), *Mothers, babies, and cocaine: The role of toxins in development* (pp. 229–250). Hillsdale, NJ: Erlbaum.

Needlman, R. D. (1996). Growth and development. In R. E. Behrman, R. M. Kliegman, & A. M. Arvin (Eds.), *Nelson textbook of pediatrics* (15th ed., pp. 30–72). Philadelphia: Saunders.

Neill, M. (2000). Too much harmful testing? *Educational Measurement: Issues & Practice, 16*, 57–58.

Neisser, U., Boodoo, G., Bouchard, T. J., Jr., Boykin, A. W., Brody, N., Ceci, S. J., Halpern, D. F., Loehlin, J. C., Perloff, R., Sternberg, R. J., & Urbina, S. (1996). Intelligence: Knowns and unknowns. *American Psychologist, 51*, 77–101.

Nelson, C. A. (1987). The recognition of facial expression in the first two years of life: Mechanisms of development. *Child Development, 58*, 889–909.

Nelson, C. A. (1994). Neural bases of infant temperament. In J. E. Bates & T. D. Wachs (Eds.), *Temperament: Individual differences at the interface of biology and behavior* (pp. 47–82). Washington, DC: American Psychological Association.

Nelson, J., Benner, G., & Gonzalez, J. (2005). An investigation of the effects of a prereading intervention on the early literacy skills of children at risk of emotional disturbance and reading problems. *Journal of Emotional & Behavioral Disorders, 13*, 3–12.

Nelson, K. (1977). Facilitating children's syntax acquisition. *Developmental Psychology, 13*, 101–107.

Nelson, K. (1985). *Making sense: The acquisition of shared meaning.* New York: Academic Press.

Nelson, K. (1988). Constraints on word learning. *Cognitive Development, 3*, 221–246.

Nelson, S. (1980). Factors influencing young children's use of motives and outcomes as moral criteria. *Child Development, 51*, 823–829.

Nesdale, D., Durkin, K., Maass, A., & Griffiths, J. (2005). Threat, group identification, and children's ethnic prejudice. *Social Development, 14*, 189–205.

Nettelbeck, T. & Wilson, C. (2004). The Flynn effect: Smarter not faster. *Intelligence, 32*, 85–93.

New Zealand Ministry of Education. (2003). Homeschooling in 2003. Retrieved June 23, 2004, from http://www.minedu.govt.nz/index.cfm ?layout=document&documentid=6893&indexid=6852&indexparentid =5611

Newcomb, A. F., & Bagwell, C. L. (1995). Children's friendship relations: A meta-analytic review. *Psychological Bulletin, 117*, 306–347.

Newcomb, A. F., Bukowski, W. M., & Pattee, L. (1993). Children's peer relations: A meta-analytic review of popular, rejected, neglected, controversial, and average sociometric status. *Psychological Bulletin, 113*, 99–128.

Newcombe, N. S., & Baenninger, M. (1989). Biological change and cognitive ability in adolescence. In G. R. Adams, R. Montemayor, & T. P. Gullotta (Eds.), *Biology of adolescent behavior and development* (pp. 168–194). Newbury Park, CA: Sage.

Newman, D., Caspi, A., Moffitt, T., & Silva, P. (1997). Antecedents of adult interpersonal functioning: Effects of individual differences in age 3 temperament. *Developmental Psychology, 33*, 206–217.

Newman, R. (2005). The cocktail party effect in infants revisited: Listening to one's name in noise. *Developmental Psychology, 41*, 352–362.

NICHD Early Child Care Research Network. (1997a, April). *Mother-child interaction and cognitive outcomes associated with early child care: Results of the NICHD study.* Paper presented at the biennial meetings of the Society for Research in Child Development, Washington, DC.

NICHD Early Child Care Research Network. (1997b). Child care in the first year of life. *Merrill-Palmer Quarterly, 43*, 340–360.

NICHD Early Child Care Research Network. (1997c). The effects of infant child care on infant-mother attachment security: Results of the NICHD study of early child care. *Child Development, 68*, 860–879.

NICHD Early Child Care Research Network. (1999). Chronicity of maternal depressive symptoms, maternal sensitivity, and child functioning at 36 months. *Developmental Psychology, 35*, 1297–1310.

NICHD Early Child Care Research Network. (2003). Does amount of time spent in child care predict socioemotional adjustment during the transition to kindergarten? *Child Development, 74*, 976–1005.

NICHD Early Child Care Research Network. (2004). Are child developmental outcomes related to before- and after-school care arrangements? Results from the NICHD Study of Early Child Care. *Child Development, 75*, 280–295.

Nicholls, C. (2005). Death by a thousand cuts: Indigenous language bilingual education programmes in the northern territory of Australia, 1972–1998. *International Journal of Bilingual Education & Bilingualism, 8*, 160–177.

Nicholson, J. (1998). Inborn errors of metabolism. In R. Behrman & R. Kliegman (Eds.), *Nelson essentials of pediatrics* (3rd ed., pp. 147–166). Philadelphia: Saunders.

Nilsson, E., Gillberg, C., Gillberg, I., & Rastam, M. (1999). Ten-year follow-up of adolescent-onset anorexia nervosa: Personality disorders. *Journal of the American Academy of Child and Adolescent Psychiatry, 38*, 1389–1395.

Nisan, M., & Kohlberg, L. (1982). Universality and variation in moral judgment: A longitudinal and cross-sectional study in Turkey. *Child Development, 53*, 865–876.

Nolen-Hoeksema, S. (1994). An interactive model for the emergence of gender differences in depression in adolescence. *Journal of Research on Adolescence, 4*, 519–534.

Nolen-Hoeksema, S., & Girgus, J. S. (1994). The emergence of gender differences in depression during adolescence. *Psychological Bulletin, 115*, 424–443.

Norboru, T. (1997). A developmental study of wordplay in preschool children: The Japanese game of "Shiritori." *Japanese Journal of Developmental Psychology, 8*, 42–52.

Nordentoft, M., Lou, H. C., Hansen, D., Nim, J., Pryds, O., Rubin, P., & Hemmingsen, R. (1996). Intrauterine growth retardation and premature delivery: The influence of maternal smoking and psychosocial factors. *American Journal of Public Health, 86*, 347–354.

Norwood, M. K. (1997, April). *Academic achievement in African-American adolescents as a function of family structure and child-rearing practices.* Paper presented at the biennial meetings of the Society for Research in Child Development, Washington, DC.

Nowakowski, R. S. (1987). Basic concepts of CNS development. *Child Development, 58*, 568–595.

Nucci, L. P., & Nucci, M. S. (1982). Children's social interactions in the context of moral and conventional transgressions. *Child Development, 53*, 403–412.

Nugent, J. K., Lester, B. M., Greene, S. M., Wieczorek-Deering, D., & O'Mahony, P. (1996). The effects of maternal alcohol consumption and cigarette smoking during pregnancy on acoustic cry analysis. *Child Development, 67*, 1806–1815.

Nutter, J. (1997). Middle school students' attitudes and use of anabolic steroids. *Journal of Strength Conditioning Research, 11*, 35–39.

Oates, J. (1998). Risk factors for infant attrition and low engagement in experiments and free play. *Infant Behavior and Development, 21*, 555–569.

O'Beirne, H., & Moore, C. (1995, April). *Attachment and sexual behavior in adolescence.* Paper presented at the biennial meetings of the Society for Research in Child Development, Indianapolis.

O'Brien, M. (1992). Gender identity and sex roles. In V. B. Van Hasselt & M. Hersen (Eds.), *Handbook of social development: A lifespan perspective* (pp. 325–345). New York: Plenum Press.

O'Brien, S. F., & Bierman, K. L. (1988). Conceptions and perceived influence of peer groups: Interviews with preadolescents and adolescents. *Child Development, 59*, 1360–1365.

O'Connor, B. P. (1995). Identity development and perceived parental behavior as sources of adolescent egocentrism. *Journal of Youth & Adolescence, 24*, 205–227.

O'Connor, T., Bredenkamp, D., & Rutter, M. (1999). Attachment disturbances and disorders in children exposed to early severe deprivation. *Infant Mental Health Journal, 20*, 10–29.

Odom, S. L., & Kaiser, A. P. (1997). Prevention and early intervention during early childhood: Theoretical and empirical bases for practice. In W. E. MacLean, Jr. (Ed.), *Ellis' handbook of mental deficiency: Psychological theory and research* (pp. 137–172). Mahwah, NJ: Erlbaum.

Offer, D., Kaiz, M., Howard, K., & Bennett, E. (1998). Emotional variables in adolescence and their stability and contribution to the mental health of adult men: Implications for early intervention strategies. *Journal of Youth & Adolescence, 27*, 675–690.

Offord, D. R., Boyle, M. H., & Racine, Y. A. (1991). The epidemiology of antisocial behavior in childhood and adolescence. In D. J. Pepler & K. H. Rubin (Eds.), *The development and treatment of childhood aggression* (pp. 31–54). Hillsdale, NJ: Erlbaum.

Ogbu, J. (2004). Collective identity and the burden of "acting white" in black history, community, and education. *Urban Review, 36*, 1–35.

Ogbu, J. U. (1994). From cultural differences to differences in cultural frame of reference. In P. M. Greenfield & R. R. Cocking (Eds.), *Cross-cultural roots of minority child development* (pp. 365–391). Hillsdale, NJ: Erlbaum.

Ohgi, S., Takahashi, T., Nugent, J., Arisawa, K., & Akiyama, T. (2003). Neonatal behavioral characteristics and later behavioral problems. *Clinical Pediatrics, 42*, 679–686.

Oldenburg, C., & Kerns, K. (1997). Associations between peer relationships and depressive symptoms: Testing moderator effects of gender and age. *Journal of Early Adolescence, 17*, 319–337.

O'Leary, S., Smith Slep, A., & Reid, M. (1999). A longitudinal study of mothers' overreactive discipline and toddlers' externalizing behavior. *Journal of Abnormal Child Psychology, 27*, 331–341.

Olivan, G. (2003). Catch-up growth assessment in long-term physically neglected and emotionally abused preschool age male children. *Child Abuse & Neglect, 27*, 103–108.

Oller, D., Cobo-Lewis, A., & Eilers, R. (1998). Phonological translation in bilingual and monolingual children. *Applied Psycholinguistics, 19*, 259–278.

Oller, D., Eilers, R., Urbano, R., & Cobo-Lewis, A. (1997). Development of precursors to speech in infants exposed to two languages. *Journal of Child Language, 24*, 407–425.

Oller, D. K. (1981). Infant vocalizations: Exploration and reflectivity. In R. E. Stark (Ed.), *Language behavior in infancy and early childhood* (pp. 85–104). New York: Elsevier North-Holland.

Olshan, A. F., Baird, P. A., & Teschke, K. (1989). Paternal occupational exposures and the risk of Down syndrome. *American Journal of Human Genetics, 44*, 646–651.

Olson, H. C., Sampson, P. D., Barr, H., Streissguth, A. P., & Bookstein, F. L. (1992). Prenatal exposure to alcohol and school problems in late childhood: A longitudinal prospective study. *Development and Psychopathology, 4*, 341–359.

Olson, S. L., Bates, J. E., & Kaskie, B. (1992). Caregiver-infant interaction antecedents of children's school-age cognitive ability. *Merrill-Palmer Quarterly, 38*, 309–330.

Olthof, T., Ferguson, T., Bloemers, E., & Deij, M. (2004). Morality- and identity-related antecedents of children's guilt and shame attributions in events involving physical illness. *Cognition & Emotion, 18*, 383–404.

Olweus, D. (1995). Bullying or peer abuse at school: Facts and intervention. *Current Directions in Psychological Science, 4*, 196–200.

O'Neill, D. K., Astington, J. W., & Flavell, J. H. (1992). Young children's understanding of the role that sensory experiences play in knowledge acquisition. *Child Development, 63*, 474–490.

Oosterlaan, J., Geurts, H., Knol, D., & Sergeant, J. (2005). Low basal salivary cortisol is associated with teacher-reported symptoms of conduct disorder. *Psychiatry Research, 134*, 1–10.

O'Shea, T. M., Klinepeter, K. L., Goldstein, D. J., Jackson, B. W., & Dillard, R. G. (1997). Survival and developmental disability in infants with birth weights of 501 to 800 grams, born between 1979 and 1994. *Pediatrics, 100*, 982–986.

Osofsky, J. D. (1995). The effects of exposure to violence on young children. *American Psychologist, 50*, 782–788.

Osofsky, J. D., Hann, D. M., & Peebles, C. (1993). Adolescent parenthood: Risks and opportunities for mothers and infants. In C. H. Zeanah, Jr. (Ed.), *Handbook of infant mental health* (pp. 106–119). New York: Guilford.

Ostoja, E., McCrone, E., Lehn, L., Reed, T., & Sroufe, L. A. (1995, April). *Representations of close relationships in adolescence: Longitudinal antecedents from infancy through childhood.* Paper presented at the biennial meetings of the Society for Research in Child Development, Indianapolis.

Ostrom, T., Carpenter, S., Sedikides, C., & Li, F. (1993). Differential processing of in-group and out-group information. *Journal of Personality & Social Psychology, 64*, 21–34.

Ott, W. J. (1995). Small for gestational age fetus and neonatal outcome: Reevaluation of the relationship. *American Journal of Perinatology, 12*, 396–400.

Overby, K. (2002). Pediatric health supervision. In A. Rudolph, R. Kamei, & K. Overby (Eds.), *Rudolph's fundamentals of pediatrics* (3rd ed., pp. 1–69). New York: McGraw-Hill.

Overton, W. F., & Reese, H. W. (1973). Models of development: Methodological implications. In J. R. Nesselroade & H. W. Reese (Eds.), *Lifespan developmental psychology: Methodological issues* (pp. 65–86). New York: Academic Press.

Overton, W. F., Ward, S. L., Noveck, I. A., Black, J., & O'Brien, D. P. (1987). Form and content in the development of deductive reasoning. *Developmental Psychology, 23*, 22–30.

Owens, J., Spirito, A., McGuinn, M., & Nobile, C. (2000). Sleep habits and sleep disturbance in elementary school-aged children. *Journal of Developmental & Behavioral Pediatrics, 21*, 27–36.

Oyserman, D., Harrison, K., & Bybee, D. (2001). Can racial identity be promotive of academic efficacy? *International Journal of Behavioral Development, 25*, 379–385.

Paarlberg, K., Vingerhoets, A. J., Passchier, J., Dekker, G., & van Geign, H. (1995). Psychosocial factors and pregnancy outcome review with emphasis on methodological issues. *Journal of Psychosomatic Research, 39*, 563–595.

Pagani, L., Boulerice, B., Tremblay, R., & Vitaro, F. (1997). Behavioural development in children of divorce and remarriage. *Journal of Child Psychology & Psychiatry & Allied Disciplines, 38*, 769–781.

Page, D. C., Mosher, R., Simpson, E. M., Fisher, E. M. C., Mardon, G., Pollack, J., McGillivray, B., de la Chapelle, A., & Brown, L. G. (1987). The sex-determining region of the human Y chromosome encodes a finger protein. *Cell, 51*, 1091–1104.

Paik, H., & Comstock, G. (1994). The effects of television violence on antisocial behavior: A meta-analysis. *Communication Research, 21*, 516–546.

Paikoff, R. L., & Brooks-Gunn, J. (1990). Physiological processes: What role do they play during the transition to adolescence? In R. Montemayor, G. R. Adams, & T. P. Gullotta (Eds.), *From childhood to adolescence: A transitional period?* (pp. 63–81). Newbury Park, CA: Sage.

Painter, M., & Bergman, I. (1998). Neurology. In R. Behrman & R. Kliegman (Eds.), *Nelson essentials of pediatrics* (3rd ed., pp. 694–745). Philadelphia: Saunders.

Pajares, F., & Graham, L. (1999). Self-efficacy, motivation constructs, and mathematics performance of entering middle school students. *Contemporary Educational Psychology, 24*, 124–139.

Pajulo, M., Savonlahti, E., Sourander, A., Helenius, H., & Piha, J. (2001). Antenatal depression, substance dependency and social support. *Journal of Affective Disorders, 65*, 9–17.

Palkovitz, R. (1985). Fathers' birth attendance, early contact, and extended contact with their newborns: A critical review. *Child Development, 56*, 392–406.

Palmer, A. (2003). The street that changed everything. *APA Monitor on Psychology, 34*, 90.

Palmérus, K., & Scarr, S. (1995, April). *How parents discipline young children: Cultural comparisons and individual differences.* Paper presented at the biennial meetings of the Society for Research in Child Development, Indianapolis.

Papousek, H., & Papousek, M. (1991). Innate and cultural guidance of infants' integrative competencies: China, the United States, and Germany. In M. H. Bornstein (Ed.), *Cultural approaches to parenting* (pp. 23–44). Hillsdale, NJ: Erlbaum.

Paradise, J. L., Rockette, H. E., Colborn, D. K., Bernard, B. S., Smith, C. G., Kurs-Lasky, M., & Janosky, J. E. (1997). Otitis media in 2253 Pittsburgh-area infants: Prevalence and risk factors during the first two years of life. *Pediatrics, 99*, 318–333.

Parault, S., & Schwanenflugel, P. (2000). The development of conceptual categories of attention during the elementary school years. *Journal of Experimental Child Psychology, 75*, 245–262.

Park, N. (2005). Life satisfaction among Korean children and youth: A developmental perspective. *School Psychology International, 26*, 209–223.

Parke, R. (2004). The Society for Research in Child Development at 70: Progress and promise. *Child Development, 75*, 1–24.

Parke, R. D. (1995). Fathers and families. In M. H. Bornstein (Ed.), *Handbook of parenting: Vol. 3. Status and social conditions of parenting* (pp. 27–63). Mahwah, NJ: Erlbaum.

Parke, R. D., & Buriel, R. (1998). Socialization in the family: Ethnic and ecological perspectives. In W. Damon (Ed.), *Handbook of child psychology: Vol 3. Social, emotional, and personality development* (5th ed., pp. 463–552). New York: Wiley.

Parmelee, A. H., Jr., Wenner, W. H., & Schulz, H. R. (1964). Infant sleep patterns from birth to 16 weeks of age. *Journal of Pediatrics, 65*, 576–582.

Parten, M. B. (1932). Social participation among preschool children. *Journal of Abnormal and Social Psychology, 27*, 243–269.

Pascalis, O., de Schonen, S., Morton, J., Derulle, C., & Fabre-Grenet, M. (1995). Mother's face recognition by neonates: A replication and extension. *Infant Behavior and Development, 18*, 79–85.

Passman, R. H., & Longeway, K. P. (1982). The role of vision in maternal attachment: Giving 2-year-olds a photograph of their mother during separation. *Developmental Psychology, 18*, 530–533.

Patterson, C. (1997). Children of lesbian and gay parents. *Advances in Clinical Child Psychology, 19*, 235–282.

Patterson, G. R. (1975). *Families: Applications of social learning to family life.* Champaign, IL: Research Press.

Patterson, G. R. (1996). Some characteristics of a developmental theory for early-onset delinquency. In M. F. Lenzenweger & J. J. Haugaard (Eds.), *Frontiers of developmental psychopathology* (pp. 81–124). New York: Oxford University Press.

Patterson, G. R., Capaldi, D., & Bank, L. (1991). An early starter model for predicting delinquency. In D. J. Pepler & K. H. Rubin (Eds.), *The development and treatment of childhood aggression* (pp. 139–168). Hillsdale, NJ: Erlbaum.

Patterson, G. R., DeBarsyshe, B. D., & Ramsey, E. (1989). A developmental perspective on antisocial behavior. *American Psychologist, 44*, 329–335.

Patterson, G. R., Reid, J. B., & Dishion, T. J. (1992). *Antisocial boys.* Eugene, OR: Castalia Press.

Patterson, J. (1998). Expressive vocabulary of bilingual toddlers: Preliminary findings. *Electronic Multicultural Journal of Communication Disorders, 1.* Retrieved April 11, 2001, from http://www.asha.ucf.edu/patterson.html

Pederson, D. R., Moran, G., Sitko, C., Campbell, K., Ghesquire, K., & Acton, H. (1990). Maternal sensitivity and the security of infant-mother attachment: A Q-sort study. *Child Development, 61*, 1974–1983.

Pedlow, R., Sanson, A., Prior, M., & Oberklaid, F. (1993). Stability of maternally reported temperament from infancy to 8 years. *Developmental Psychology, 29*, 998–1007.

Pegg, J. E., Werker, J. F., & McLeod, P. J. (1992). Preference for infant-directed over adult-directed speech: Evidence from 7-week-old infants. *Infant Behavior and Development, 15*, 325–345.

Peipert, J. F., & Bracken, M. B. (1993). Maternal age: An independent risk factor for cesarean delivery. *Obstetrics and Gynecology, 81*, 200–205.

Peisner-Feinberg, E. S. (1995, April). *Developmental outcomes and the relationship to quality of child care experiences.* Paper presented at the biennial meetings of the Society for Research in Child Development, Indianapolis.

Peisner-Feinberg, E. S., & Burchinal, M. R. (1997). Relations between preschool children's child-care experiences and concurrent development: The Cost, Quality, and Outcomes Study. *Merrill-Palmer Quarterly, 43*, 451–477.

Pelham, W., Hoza, B., Pillow, D., Gnagy, E., Kipp, H., Greiner, A., Waschbusch, D., Trane, S., Greenhouse, J., Wolfson, L., & Fitzpatrick, E. (2002). Effects of methylphenidate and expectancy on children with ADHD: Behavior, academic performance, and attributions in a summer treatment program and regular classroom settings. *Journal of Consulting and Clinical Psychology, 70*, 320–335.

Pennington, B., Moon, J., Edgin, J., Stedron, J., & Nadel, L. (2003). The neuropsychology of Down syndrome: Evidence of hippocampal dysfunction. *Child Development, 74*, 75–93.

Peoples, C. E., Fagan, J. F., III, & Drotar, D. (1995). The influence of race on 3-year-old children's performance on the Stanford-Binet: Fourth edition. *Intelligence, 21*, 69–82.

Pereverzeva, M., Hui-Lin Chien, S., Palmer, J., & Teller, D. (2002). Infant photometry: Are mean adult isoluminance values a sufficient approximation to individual infant values? *Vision Research, 42*, 1639–1649.

Perkins, D. F., & Luster, T. (1997, April). *The relationship between sexual abuse and a bulimic behavior: Findings from community-wide surveys of female adolescents.* Paper presented at the biennial meetings of the Society for Research in Child Development, Washington, DC.

Perlman, M., Claris, O., Hao, Y., Pandid, P., Whyte, H., Chipman, M., & Liu, P. (1995). Secular changes in the outcomes to eighteen to twenty-four months of age of extremely low birth weight infants, with adjustment for changes in risk factors and severity of illness. *Journal of Pediatrics, 126*, 75–87.

Perry, D., Kusel, S. K., & Perry, L. C. (1988). Victims of peer aggression. *Developmental Psychology, 24*, 807–814.

Perry, T., Ohde, R., & Ashmead, D. (2001). The acoustic bases for gender identification from children's voices. *Journal of the Acoustical Society of America, 109*, 2988–2998.

Persson, A., & Musher-Eizenman, D. (2003). The impact of a prejudice-prevention television program on young children's ideas about race. *Early Childhood Research Quarterly, 18*, 530–546.

Petersen, A. C. (1987). The nature of biological-psychosocial interactions: The sample case of early adolescence. In R. M. Lerner & T. T. Foch (Eds.), *Biological-psychosocial interactions in early adolescence* (pp. 35–62). Hillsdale, NJ: Erlbaum.

Petersen, A. C., Compas, B. E., Brooks-Gunn, J., Stemmler, M., Ey, S., & Grant, K. E. (1993). Depression in adolescence. *American Psychologist, 48*, 155–168.

Petersen, A. C., Sarigiani, P. A., & Kennedy, R. E. (1991). Adolescent depression: Why more girls? *Journal of Youth & Adolescence, 20*, 247–272.

Petersen, A. C., & Taylor, B. (1980). The biological approach to adolescence. In J. Adelson (Ed.), *Handbook of adolescent psychology* (pp. 117–158). New York: Wiley.

Peterson, C., & Bell, M. (1996). Children's memory for traumatic injury. *Child Development, 67,* 3045–3070.

Peterson, C., & Siegal, M. (1999). Representing inner worlds: Theory of mind in autistic, deaf, and normal hearing children. *Psychological Science, 10,* 126–129.

Peterson, C., Wellman, H., & Liu, D. (2005). Steps in theory-of-mind development for children with deafness or autism. *Child Development, 76,* 502–517.

Peterson, C. C., & Siegal, M. (1995). Deafness, conversation and theory of mind. *Journal of Child Psychology and Psychiatry, 36,* 459–474.

Peterson, J., Pihl, R., Higgins, D., Seguin, J., & Tremblay, R. (2003). Neuropsychological performance, IQ, personality, and grades in a longitudinal grade-school male sample. *Individual Differences Research, 1,* 159–172.

Peterson, L., Ewigman, B., & Kivlahan, C. (1993). Judgments regarding appropriate child supervision to prevent injury: The role of environmental risk and child age. *Child Development, 64,* 934–950.

Petitto, L., Katerelos, M., Levy, B., Gauna, K., Tetreault, K., & Ferraro, V. (2001). Bilingual signed and spoken language from birth: Implications for the mechanisms underlying early bilingual language acquisition. *Journal of Child Language, 28,* 453–496.

Petitto, L. A. (1988). "Language" in the prelinguistic child. In F. S. Kessell (Ed.), *The development of language and language researchers: Essays in honor of Roger Brown* (pp. 187–222). Hillsdale, NJ: Erlbaum.

Pettit, G. S., Bates, J. E., & Dodge, K. A. (1997). Supportive parenting, ecological context, and children's adjustment: A seven-year longitudinal study. *Child Development, 68,* 908–923.

Pettit, G. S., Clawson, M. A., Dodge, K. A., & Bates, J. E. (1996). Stability and change in peer-rejected status: The role of child behavior, parenting, and family ecology. *Merrill-Palmer Quarterly, 42,* 295–318.

Pettit, G. S., Laird, R. D., Bates, J. E., & Dodge, K. A. (1997). Patterns of after-school care in middle childhood: Risk factors and developmental outcomes. *Merrill-Palmer Quarterly, 43,* 515–538.

Pezdek, K., Blandon-Gitlin, I., & Moore, C. (2003). Children's face recognition memory: More evidence for the cross-race effect. *Journal of Applied Psychology, 88,* 760–763.

Phillips, D., Schwean, V., & Saklofske, D. (1997). Treatment effect of a school-based cognitive-behavioral program for aggressive children. *Canadian Journal of School Psychology, 13,* 60–67.

Phinney, J., Horenczyk, G., Liebkind, K., & Vedder, P. (2001). Ethnic identity, immigration, and well-being: An interactional perspective. *Journal of Social Issues, 57,* 493–510.

Phinney, J., Kim-Jo, T., Osorio, S., & Vilhjalmsdottir, P. (2005). Autonomy and relatedness in adolescent-parent disagreements: Ethnic and developmental factors. *Journal of Adolescent Research, 20,* 8–39.

Phinney, J. S. (1990). Ethnic identity in adolescents and adults: Review of research. *Psychological Bulletin, 108,* 499–514.

Phinney, J. S., & Devich-Navarro, M. (1997). Variations in bicultural identification among African American and Mexican American adolescents. *Journal of Research on Adolescence, 7,* 3–32.

Phinney, J. S., Ferguson, D. L., & Tate, J. D. (1997). Intergroup attitudes among ethnic minority adolescents: A causal model. *Child Development, 68,* 955–969.

Phinney, J. S., & Rosenthal, D. A. (1992). Ethnic identity in adolescence: Process, context, and outcome. In G. R. Adams, T. P. Gullotta, & R. Montemayor (Eds.), *Adolescent identity formation* (pp. 145–172). Newbury Park, CA: Sage.

Piaget, J. (1932). *The moral judgment of the child.* New York: Macmillan.

Piaget, J. (1952). *The origins of intelligence in children.* New York: International Universities Press.

Piaget, J. (1954). *The construction of reality in the child.* New York: Basic Books. (Originally published 1937)

Piaget, J. (1962). *Play, dreams, and imitation in childhood.* New York: W. W. Norton.

Piaget, J. (1965). *The moral judgment of the child,* New York: Free Press.

Piaget, J. (1970). Piaget's theory. In P. H. Mussen (Ed.), *Carmichael's manual of child psychology* (3rd ed., Vol. 1, pp. 703–732). New York: Wiley.

Piaget, J. (1977). *The development of thought: Equilibration of cognitive structures.* New York: Viking Press.

Piaget, J., & Inhelder, B. (1969). *The psychology of the child.* New York: Basic Books.

Pianta, R. C., & Egeland, B. (1994a). Predictors of instability in children's mental test performance at 24, 48, and 96 months. *Intelligence, 18,* 145–163.

Pianta, R. C., & Egeland, B. (1994b). Relation between depressive symptoms and stressful life events in a sample of disadvantaged mothers. *Journal of Consulting and Clinical Psychology, 62,* 1229–1234.

Pianta, R. C., Steinberg, M. S., & Rollins, K. B. (1995). Teacher-child relationships and deflections in children's classroom adjustment. *Development and Psychopathology, 7,* 295–312.

Pickens, J. (1994). Perception of auditory-visual distance relations by 5-month-old infants. *Developmental Psychology, 30,* 537–544.

Pickens, J., & Field, T. (1993). Facial expressivity in infants of depressed mothers. *Developmental Psychology, 29,* 986–988.

Pickering, L. K., Granoff, D. M., Erickson, J. R., Masor, M. L., Cordle, C. T., Schaller, J. P., Winship, T. R., Paule, C. L., & Hilty, M. D. (1998). Modulation of the immune system by human milk and infant formula containing nucleotides. *Pediatrics, 101,* 242–249.

Pilgrim, C., Luo, Q., Urberg, K., & Fang, X. (1999). Influence of peers, parents, and individual characteristics on adolescent drug use in two cultures. *Merrill-Palmer Quarterly, 45,* 85–107.

Pillard, R. C., & Bailey, J. M. (1995). A biologic perspective on sexual orientation. *The Psychiatric Clinics of North America, 18*(1), 71–84.

Pillow, B. (1999). Children's understanding of inferential knowledge. *Journal of Genetic Psychology, 160,* 419–428.

Pilowsky, T., Yirmiya, N., Arbelle, S., & Mozes, T. (2000). Theory of mind abilities of children with schizophrenia, children with autism, and normally developing children. *Schizophrenia Research, 42,* 145–155.

Pinker, S. (1994). *The language instinct: How the mind creates language.* New York: Morrow.

Pisecco, S., Wristers, K., Swank, P., Silva, P., & Baker, D. (2001). The effect of academic self-concept on ADHD and antisocial behaviors in early adolescence. *Journal of Learning Disabilities, 34,* 459–461.

Pittman, L., & Chase-Lansdale, P. (2001). African American adolescent girls in impoverished communities: Parenting style and adolescent outcomes. *Journal of Research on Adolescence, 11,* 199–224.

Plomin, R. (1990). *Nature and nurture: An introduction to behavior genetics,* Pacific Grove, CA: Brooks/Cole.

Plomin, R. (1995). Genetics and children's experiences in the family. *Journal of Child Psychology and Psychiatry, 36,* 33–68.

Plomin, R. (2001). Genetics and behavior. *Psychologist, 14,* 134–139.

Plomin, R. (2004). Genetics and developmental psychology. *Merrill-Palmer Quarterly, 50,* 341–352.

Plomin, R., & DeFries, J. C. (1985). *Origins of individual differences in infancy: The Colorado Adoption Project.* Orlando, FL: Academic Press.

Plomin, R., Loehlin, J. C., & DeFries, J. C. (1985). Genetic and environmental components of "environmental" influences. *Developmental Psychology, 21,* 391–402.

Plomin, R., Reiss, D., Hetherington, E. M., & Howe, G. W. (1994). Nature and nurture: Genetic contributions to measures of the family environment. *Developmental Psychology, 30,* 32–43.

Plomin, R., & Rende, R. (1991). Human behavioral genetics. *Annual Review of Psychology, 42,* 161–190.

Polivy, J., & Herman, C. P. (1995). Dieting and its relation to eating disorders. In K. D. Brownell & C. G. Fairburn (Eds.), *Eating disorders and obesity: A comprehensive handbook* (pp. 83–86). New York: Guilford Press.

Polka, L., & Werker, J. F. (1994). Developmental changes in perception of nonnative vowel contrasts. *Journal of Experimental Psychology: Human Perception and Performance, 20,* 421–435.

Pollitt, E., & Gorman, K. S. (1994). Nutritional deficiencies as developmental risk factors. In C. A. Nelson (Ed.), *The Minnesota symposia on child development* (Vol. 27, pp. 121–144). Hillsdale, NJ: Erlbaum.

Pomerantz, E., & Ruble, D. (1998). The role of maternal control in the development of sex differences in child self-evaluative factors. *Child Development, 69,* 458–478.

Pomerleau, A., Malcuit, G., Turgeon, L., & Cossette, L. (1997). Effects of labelled gender on vocal communication of young women with 4-month-old infants. *International Journal of Psychology, 32,* 65–72.

Pomerleau, A., Scuccimarri, C., & Malcuit, G. (2003). Mother-infant behavioral interactions in teenage and adult mothers during the first six months postpartum: Relations with infant development. *Infant Mental Health Journal, 24,* 495–509.

Pons, F., Harris, P., & de Rosnay, M. (2004). Emotion comprehension between 3 and 11 years: Developmental periods and hierarchical organization. *Journal of Developmental Psychology, 1,* 127–152.

Ponsonby, A., Dwyer, T., Gibbons, L. E., Cochrane, J. A., & Wang, Y. (1993). Factors potentiating the risk of sudden infant death syndrome associated with the prone position. *New England Journal of Medicine, 329,* 377–382.

Population Resource Center. (2004). *Latina teen pregnancy: Problems and prevention*. Retrieved May 6, 2005, from http://ww.prcds.org/summaries/latinapreg04/latinapreg04/html

Porter, J., & Washington, R. (1993). Minority identity and self-esteem. *Annual Review of Sociology, 19*, 139–161.

Posada, G., Jacobs, A., Richmond, M., Carbonell, O., Alzate, G., Bustamante, M., & Quiceno, J. (2002). Maternal caregiving and infant security in two cultures. *Developmental Psychology, 38*, 67–78.

Posey, D., Puntney, J., Sasher, T., Kem, D., & McDougle, C. (2004). Guanfacine treatment of hyperactivity and inattention in pervasive developmental disorders: A retrospective analysis of 80 cases. *Journal of Child & Adolescent Psychopharmacology, 14*, 233–241.

Posner, J., & Vandell, D. (1994). Low-income children's after-school care: Are there beneficial effects of after-school programs? *Child Development, 65*, 440–456.

Posthuma, D., de Geus, E., & Boomsma, D. (2003). Genetic contributions to anatomical, behavioral, and neurophysiological indices of cognition. In R. Plomin, J. DeFries, I. Craig, & P. McGuffin (Eds.), *Behavioral genetics in the postgenomic era* (pp. 141–161). Washington, DC: American Psychological Association.

Poulin, F., & Boivin, M. (1999). Proactive and reactive aggression and boys' friendship quality in mainstream classrooms. *Journal of Emotional & Behavioral Disorders, 7*, 168–177.

Poulin, F., & Boivin, M. (2000). The role of proactive and reactive aggression in the formation and development of boys' friendships. *Developmental Psychology, 36*, 233–240.

Poulin-Dubois, D., Serbin, L. A., Kenyon, B., & Derbyshire, A. (1994). Infants' intermodal knowledge about gender. *Developmental Psychology, 30*, 436–442.

Poulson, C. L., Nunes, L. R. D., & Warren, S. F. (1989). Imitation in infancy: A critical review. In H. W. Reese (Ed.), *Advances in child development and behavior* (Vol. 22, pp. 272–298). San Diego, CA: Academic Press.

Power, T. (2000). *Play and exploration in children and animals*. Hillsdale, NJ: Erlbaum.

Powlishta, K. K., Serbin, L. A., Doyle, A., & White, D. R. (1994). Gender, ethnic, and body type biases: The generality of prejudice in childhood. *Developmental Psychology, 30*, 526–536.

Pozzi, M. (2003). A three-year-old boy with ADHD and Asperger's syndrome treated with parent-child psychotherapy. *Journal of the British Association of Psychotherapists, 41*, 16–31.

Prat-Sala, M., Shillcock, R., & Sorace, A. (2000). Animacy effects on the production of object-dislocated description by Catalan-speaking children. *Journal of Child Language, 27*, 97–117.

Pratt, M., Arnold, M., & Pratt, A. (1999). Predicting adolescent moral reasoning from family climate: A longitudinal study. *Journal of Early Adolescence, 19*, 148–175.

Prechtl, H., & Beintema, D. (1964). *The neurological examination of the full-term newborn infant: Clinics in developmental medicine*. London: Heinemann.

Prentice, A. (1994). Extended breast-feeding and growth in rural China. *Nutrition Reviews, 52*, 144–146.

Prentice, D., & Miller, D. (2002). The emergence of homegrown stereotypes. *American Psychologist, 57*, 352–359.

Pressley, M., & Dennis-Rounds, J. (1980). Transfer of a mnemonic keyword strategy at two age levels. *Journal of Educational Psychology, 72*, 575–582.

Pressley, M., & Wharton-McDonald, R. (1997). Skilled comprehension and its development through instruction. *School Psychology Review, 26*, 448–466.

Pressman, E., DiPietro, J., Costigan, K., Shupe, A., & Johnson, T. (1998). Fetal neurobehavioral development: Associations with socioeconomic class and fetal sex. *Developmental Psychobiology, 33*, 79–91.

Price, C., & Kunz, J. (2003). Rethinking the paradigm of juvenile delinquency as related to divorce. *Journal of Divorce & Remarriage, 39*, 109–133.

Prinstein, M., & La Greca, A. (1999). Links between mothers' and children's social competence and associations with maternal adjustment. *Journal of Clinical Child Psychology, 28*, 197–210.

Prior, M., Smart, D., Sanson, A., & Oberklaid, F. (1997, April). *Longitudinal trajectories in aggressive behaviour: Infancy to adolescence*. Paper presented at the biennial meetings of the Society for Research in Child Development, Washington, DC.

Proctor, B., & Dalaker, J. (2003). *Poverty in the United States: 2002*. Retrieved July 1, 2004, from http://www.census.gov/hhes/www/poverty02.html

Public Health Policy Advisory Board. (2001). *Health and the American child: A focus on mortality among children*. Washington, D.C.: Author.

Pugh, K., Mencl, W., Jenner, A., Lee, J., Katz, L., Frost, S., Shaywitz, S., &

Shaywitz, B. (2001). Neuroimaging studies of reading development and reading disability. *Learning Disabilities Research & Practice, 16*, 240–249.

Pujol, J., Deus, J., Losilla, J., & Capdevila, A. (1999). Cerebral lateralization of language in normal left-handed people: Studies by function MRI. *Neurology, 52*, 1038–1043.

Pulkkinen, L. (1982). Self-control and continuity from childhood to late adolescence. In P. Baltes & O. G. Brim, Jr. (Eds.), *Life span development and behavior* (Vol. 4, pp. 64–107). New York: Academic Press.

Purugganan, O., Stein, R., Johnson Silver, E., & Benenson, B. (2003). Exposure to violence and psychosocial adjustment among urban school-aged children. *Journal of Developmental and Behavioral Pediatrics, 24*, 424–430.

Putnam, J. W., Spiegel, A. N., & Bruininks, R. H. (1995). Future directions in education and inclusion of students with disabilities: A Delphi investigation. *Exceptional Children, 61*, 553–576.

Putnam, S., & Stifter, C. (2005). Behavioral approach-inhibition in toddlers: Prediction from infancy, positive and negative affective components, and relations with behavior problems. *Child Development, 76*, 212–226.

Putnins, A. (1997). Victim awareness programs for delinquent youths: Effects on moral reasoning maturity. *Adolescence, 32*, 709–714.

Pye, C. (1986). Quiche Mayan speech to children. *Journal of Child Language, 13*, 85–100.

Pynoos, R. S., Steinberg, A. M., & Wraith, R. (1995). A developmental model of childhood traumatic stress. In D. Cicchetti & D. J. Cohen (Eds.), *Developmental psychopathology: Vol. 2. Risk, disorder, and adaptation*. New York: Wiley.

Qi, C., & Kaiser, A. (2003). Behavior problems of preschool children from low-income families: Review of the literature. *Early Childhood Special Education, 23*, 188–216.

Rabinowitz, D. (2003). *No crueler tyrannies: Accusation, false witness, and other terrors of our time*. New York: Wall Street Journal Books.

Raffaelli, M., & Ontai, L. (2004). Gender socialization in Latino/a families: Results from two retrospective studies. *Sex Roles, 50*, 287–299.

Ragnarsdottir, H., Simonsen, H., & Plunkett, K. (1999). The acquisition of past tense morphology in Icelandic and Norwegian children: An experimental study. *Journal of Child Language, 26*, 577–618.

Raja, S. N., McGee, R., & Stanton, W. R. (1992). Perceived attachments to parents and peers and psychological well-being in adolescence. *Journal of Youth & Adolescence, 21*, 471–485.

Ramey, C., & Ramey, S. (2004). Early learning and school readiness: Can early intervention make a difference? *Merrill-Palmer Quarterly, 50*, 471–491.

Ramey, C. T. (1993). A rejoinder to Spitz's critique of the Abecedarian experiment. *Intelligence, 17*, 25–30.

Ramey, C. T., & Campbell, F. A. (1987). The Carolina Abecedarian Project. An educational experiment concerning human malleability. In J. J. Gallagher & C. T. Ramey (Eds.), *The malleability of children* (pp. 127–140). Baltimore: Brookes.

Ramey, C. T., & Ramey, S. L. (1998). Early intervention and early experience. *American Psychologist, 53*, 109–120.

Rattaz, C., Goubet, N., & Bullinger, A. (2005). The calming effect of a familiar odor on full-term newborns. *Journal of Developmental and Behavioral Pediatrics, 26*, 86–92.

Räty, H., Vänskä, J., Kasanen, K., & Kärkkäinen, R. (2002). Parents' explanations of their child's performance in mathematics and reading: A replication and extension of Yee and Eccles. *Sex Roles, 46*, 121–128.

Rauscher, F. H., Shaw, G. L., & Ky, K. N. (1993). Music and spatial task performance. *Nature, 365*, 611.

Ray, B. (1999). *Home schooling on the threshold: A survey of research at the dawn of the new millenium*. Washington, DC: Home Education Research Institute.

Rebollo, M., Molina, M., & Mu—oz, I. (2004). Problemas de conducta, evaluados con el CBCL, en adolescentes adoptados espa—oles. *Analisis y Modificacion de Conducta, 30*, 663–691.

Rees, J. M., Lederman, S. A., & Kiely, J. L. (1996). Birth weight associated with lowest neonatal mortality: Infants of adolescent and adult mothers. *Pediatrics, 98*, 1161–1166.

Reilly, J., Jackson, D., Montgomery, C., Kelly, L., Slater, C., Grant, S., & Paton, J. (2004). Total energy expenditure and physical activity in young Scottish children: Mixed longitudinal study. *Lancet, 363*, 211–212.

Reiner, W., & Gearhardt, J. (2004). Discordant sexual identity in some genetic males with cloacal exstrophy assigned to female sex at birth. *New England Journal of Medicine, 350*, 333–341.

Reinherz, H. Z., Giaconia, R. M., Pakiz, B., Silverman, A. B., Frost, A. K., & Lefkowitz, E. S. (1993). Psychosocial risks for major depression in late adolescence: A longitudinal community study. *Journal of the American Academy of Child and Adolescent Psychiatry, 32,* 1155–1163.

Reis, S., & Park, S. (2001). Gender differences in high-achieving students in math and science. *Journal for the Education of the Gifted, 25,* 52–73.

Reisman, J. E. (1987). Touch, motion, and proprioception. In P. Salapatek & L. Cohen (Eds.), *Handbook of infant perception, Vol 1: From sensation to perception* (pp. 265–304). Orlando, FL: Academic Press.

Reisman, J. M., & Shorr, S. I. (1978). Friendship claims and expectations among children and adults. *Child Development, 49,* 913–916.

Reiss, D. (1998). Mechanisms linking genetic and social influences in adolescent development: Beginning a collaborative search. *Current Directions in Psychological Science, 6,* 100–105.

Remafedi, G., French, S., Story, M., Resnick, M., & Blum, R. (1998). The relationship between suicide risk and sexual orientation: Results of a population-based study. *American Journal of Public Health, 88,* 57–60.

Remafedi, G., Resnick, M., Blum, R., & Harris, L. (1998). Demography of sexual orientation in adolescents. *Pediatrics, 89,* 714–721.

Renouf, A. G., & Harter, S. (1990). Low self-worth and anger as components of the depressive experience in young adolescents. *Development and Psychopathology, 2,* 293–310.

Resnick, M. D., Bearman, P. S., Blum, R. W., Bauman, K. E., Harris, K. M., Jones, J., Tabor, J., Beuhring, T., Sieving, R. E., Shew, M., Ireland, M., Bearinger, L. H., & Udry, J. R. (1997). Protecting adolescents from harm: Findings from the National Longitudinal Study on Adolescent Health. *Journal of the American Medical Association, 278,* 823–832.

Rest, J. R. (1983). Morality. In J. H. Flavell & E. M. Markman (Eds.), *Handbook of child psychology: Cognitive development* (Vol. 3, pp. 556–629). New York: Wiley.

Retz, W., Retz-Junginger, P., Hengesch, G., Schneider, M., Thome, J., Pajonk, F., Salahi-Disfan, A., Rees, O., Wender, P., & Rösler, M. (2004). Psychometric and psychopathological characterization of young male prison inmates with and without attention deficit/hyperactivity disorder. *European Archives of Psychiatry & Clinical Neuroscience, 254,* 201–208.

Rey, C. (2001). Empathy in children and adolescents with disocial conduct disorder, and the degree of rejection, affective marginalization and permissiveness tolerated by their fathers and mothers. *Avances en Psicologia Clinica Latinoamericana, 19,* 25–36.

Rey, J., Sawyer, M., Raphael, B., Patton, G., & Lynskey, M. (2002). Mental health of teenagers who use cannabis: Results of an Australian survey. *British Journal of Psychiatry, 180,* 216–221.

Reynolds, A. J. (1994). Effects of a preschool plus follow-on intervention for children at risk. *Developmental Psychology, 30,* 787–804.

Reynolds, A. J., & Bezruczko, N. (1993). School adjustment of children at risk through fourth grade. *Merrill-Palmer Quarterly, 39,* 457–480.

Rholes, W. S., & Ruble, D. N. (1984). Children's understanding of dispositional characteristics of others. *Child Development, 55,* 550–560.

Ricci, C. M., Beal, C. R., & Dekle, D. J. (1995, April). *The effect of parent versus unfamiliar interviewers on young witnesses' memory and identification accuracy.* Paper presented at the biennial meetings of the Society for Research in Child Development, Indianapolis.

Rice, M. L., Huston, A. C., Truglio, R., & Wright, J. (1990). Words from "Sesame Street": Learning vocabulary while viewing. *Developmental Psychology, 26,* 421–428.

Richards, H. C., Bear, G. G., Stewart, A. L., & Norman, A. D. (1992). Moral reasoning and classroom conduct: Evidence of a curvilinear relationship. *Merrill-Palmer Quarterly, 38,* 176–190.

Richards, M., Hardy, R., Kuh, D., & Wadsworth, M. (2001). Birth weight and cognitive function in the British 1946 birth cohort: Longitudinal population-based study. *BMJ: British Medical Journal, 322,* 199–203.

Richards, M. H., Crowe, P. A., Larson, R., & Swarr, A. (1998). Developmental patterns and gender differences in the experience of peer companionship during adolescence. *Child Development, 69,* 154–163.

Richardson, G. A., & Day, N. L. (1994). Detrimental effects of prenatal cocaine exposure: Illusion or reality? *Journal of the American Academy of Child and Adolescent Psychiatry, 33,* 28–34.

Richters, J., & Pellegrini, D. (1989). Depressed mothers' judgments about their children: An examination of the depression-distortion hypothesis. *Child Development, 60,* 1068–1075.

Rickards, A., Kelly, E., Doyle, L., & Callanan, C. (2001). Cognition, academic progress, behavior and self-concept at 14 years of very low birth weight children. *Journal of Developmental and Behavioral Pediatrics, 22*(1), 11–18.

Ridderinkhof, K., Scheres, A., Oosterlaan, J., & Sergeant, J. (2005). Delta plots in the study of individual differences: New tools reveal response in-hibition deficits in AD/HD that are eliminated by methylphenidate treatment. *Journal of Abnormal Psychology, 114,* 197–215.

Riegel, K. F. (1975). Adult life crises: A dialectic interpretation of development. In N. Datan & L. H. Ginsberg (Eds.), *Lifespan developmental psychology: Normative life crises* (pp. 99–128). New York: Academic Press.

Rierdan, J., & Koff, E. (1993). Developmental variables in relation to depressive symptoms in adolescent girls. *Development and Psychopathology, 5,* 485–496.

Rigby, K. (2005). Why do some children bully at school? The contributions of negative attitudes towards victims and the perceived expectations of friends, parents and teachers. *School Psychology International, 26,* 147–161.

Riggs, L. L. (1997, April). *Depressive affect and eating problems in adolescent females: An assessment of direction and influence using longitudinal data.* Paper presented at the biennial meetings of the Society for Research in Child Development, Washington, D.C.

Righetti, P. (1996). The emotional experience of the fetus: A preliminary report. *Pre- & Peri-Natal Psychology Journal, 11,* 55–65.

Rinderman, H., & Neubauer, A. (2004). Processing speed, intelligence, creativity, and school performance: Testing of causal hypotheses using structural equation models. *Intelligence, 32,* 573–589.

Ripple, C., & Zigler, E. (2003). Research, policy, and the federal role in prevention initiatives for children. *American Psychologist, 58,* 482–490.

Ritchie, D., Price, V., & Roberts, D. (1987). Television, reading, and reading achievement: A reappraisal. *Communication Research, 14,* 292–315.

Roberts, J., & Bell, M. (2000). Sex differences on a mental rotation task: Variations in electroencephalogram hemispheric activation between children and college students. *Developmental Neuropsychology, 17,* 199–223.

Roberts, J. E., & Wallace, I. F. (1997). Language and otitis media. In J. E. Roberts, I. F. Wallace, & F. W. Henderson (Eds.), *Otitis media in young children: Medical, developmental, and educational considerations* (pp. 133–162). Baltimore: Brookes.

Roberts, R., & Mather, N. (1995). The return of students with learning disabilities to regular classrooms: A sellout? *Learning Disabilities Research & Practice, 10,* 46–58.

Roberts, R. E., & Sobhan, M. (1992). Symptoms of depression in adolescence: A comparison of Anglo, African, and Hispanic Americans. *Journal of Youth & Adolescence, 21,* 639–651.

Robins, L. N., & McEvoy, L. (1990). Conduct problems as predictors of substance abuse. In L. N. Robins & M. Rutter (Eds.), *Straight and devious pathways from childhood to adulthood* (pp. 182–204). Cambridge, England: Cambridge University Press.

Robinson, H. B. (1981). The uncommonly bright child. In M. Lewis & L. A. Rosenblum (Eds.), *The uncommon child* (pp. 57–82). New York: Plenum Press.

Robinson, N., Lanzi, R., Weinberg, R., Ramey, S., & Ramey, C. (2002). Family factors associated with high academic competence in former Head Start children at third grade. *Gifted Child Quarterly, 46,* 278–290.

Robinson, N. M., & Janos, P. M. (1986). Psychological adjustment in a college-level program of marked academic acceleration. *Journal of Youth & Adolescence, 15,* 51–60.

Rochat, P., & Striano, T. (2002). Who's in the mirror? Self-other discrimination in specular images by four- and nine-month-old infants. *Child Development, 73,* 35–46.

Roche, A. F. (1979). Secular trends in human growth, maturation, and development. *Monographs of the Society for Research in Child Development, 44*(3–4, Serial No. 179).

Rock, A., Trainor, L., & Addison, T. (1999). Distinctive messages in infant-directed lullabies and play songs. *Developmental Psychology, 35,* 527–534.

Roderick, M., & Camburn, E. (1999). Risk and recovery from course failure in the early years of high school. *American Educational Research Journal, 36,* 303–343.

Rodkin, P., Farmer, T., Pearl, R., & Van Acker, R. (2000). Heterogeneity of popular boys: Antisocial and prosocial configurations. *Developmental Psychology, 36,* 14–24.

Rodrigo, M., González, A., de Vega, M., Muñetón-Ayala, M., & Rodríguez, G. (2004). From gestural to verbal deixis: A longitudinal study with Spanish infants and toddlers. *First Language, 24,* 71–90.

Rodrigo, M., Janssens, J., & Ceballos, E. (1999). Do children's perceptions and attributions mediate the effects of mothers' child rearing actions? *Journal of Family Psychology, 13,* 508–522.

Roebers, C., & Schneider, W. (2001). Individual differences in children's eyewitness recall: The influence of intelligence and shyness. *Applied Developmental Science, 5,* 9–20.

Roeser, R., & Eccles J. (1998). Adolescents' perceptions of middle school: Relation to longitudinal changes in academic and psychological adjustment. *Journal of Research on Adolescence, 8,* 123–158.

Rogers, J. L., Rowe, D. C., & May, K. (1994). DF analysis of NLSY IQ/achievement data: Non-shared environmental influences. *Intelligence, 19,* 157–177.

Rogers, P. T., Roizen, N. J., & Capone, G. T. (1996). Down syndrome. In A. J. Capute & P. J. Accardo (Eds.), *Developmental disabilities in infancy and childhood: Vol 2. The spectrum of developmental disabilities* (2nd ed., pp. 221–243). Baltimore: Brookes.

Roggman, L. A., Langlois, J. H., Hubbs-Tait, L., & Rieser-Danner, L. A. (1994). Infant daycare, attachment, and the "file drawer problem." *Child Development, 65,* 1429–1443.

Rogosch, F. A., Cicchetti, D., & Aber, J. L. (1995). The role of child maltreatment in early deviations in cognitive and affective processing abilities and later peer relationship problems. *Development and Psychopathology, 7,* 591–609.

Rogosch, F. A., Cicchetti, D., Shields, A., & Toth, S. L. (1995). Parenting dysfunction in child maltreatment. In M. H. Bornstein (Ed.), *Handbook of parenting: Vol. 4. Applied and practical parenting* (pp. 127–159). Mahwah, NJ: Erlbaum.

Rohner, R. P., Kean, K. J., & Cournoyer, D. E. (1991). Effects of corporal punishment, perceived caretaker warmth, and cultural beliefs on the psychological adjustment of children in St. Kitts, West Indies. *Journal of Marriage and the Family, 53,* 681–693.

Rolls, E. (2000). Memory systems in the brain. *Annual Review of Psychology, 51,* 599–630.

Rooks, J. P., Weatherby, N. L., Ernst, E. K. M., Stapleton, S., Rosen, D., & Rosenfield, A. (1989). Outcomes of care in birth centers: The National Birth Center Study. *New England Journal of Medicine, 321,* 1804–1811.

Rose, A., & Asher, S. (2004). Children's strategies and goals in response to help-giving and help-seeking tasks within a friendship. *Child Development, 75,* 749–763.

Rose, A. J., & Montemayor, R. (1994). The relationship between gender role orientation and perceived self-competence in male and female adolescents. *Sex Roles, 31,* 579–595.

Rose, R. J. (1995). Genes and human behavior. *Annual Review of Psychology, 56,* 625–654.

Rose, S., Feldman, J., & Jankowski, J. (2004). Infant visual recognition memory. *Developmental Review, 24,* 74–100.

Rose, S. A., & Feldman, J. F. (1995). Prediction of IQ and specific cognitive abilities at 11 years from infancy measures. *Developmental Psychology, 31,* 685–696.

Rose, S. A., & Feldman, J. F. (1997). Memory and speed: Their role in the relation of infant information processing to later IQ. *Child Development, 68,* 630–641.

Rose, S. A., & Ruff, H. A. (1987). Cross-modal abilities in human infants. In J. D. Osofsky (Ed.), *Handbook of infant development* (2nd ed., pp. 318–362). New York: Wiley-Interscience.

Rosenbaum, J. E. (1984). *Career mobility in a corporate hierarchy.* New York: Academic Press.

Rosenberg, M. (1986). Self-concept from middle childhood through adolescence. In J. Suls & A. G. Greenwald (Eds.), *Psychological perspectives on the self* (Vol. 3, pp. 107–136). Hillsdale, NJ: Erlbaum.

Rosenblatt, P., & Wallace, B. (2005). Narratives of grieving African Americans about racism in the lives of deceased family members. *Death Studies, 29,* 217–235.

Rosenthal, R. (1994). Interpersonal expectancy effects: A 30-year perspective. *Current Directions in Psychological Science, 3,* 176–179.

Rosenthal, S., & Gitelman, S. (2002). Endocrinology. In A. Rudolph, R. Kamei, & K. Overby (Eds.), *Rudolph's fundamentals of pediatrics* (3rd ed., pp. 747–795). New York: McGraw-Hill.

Rosenthal, S., Lewis, L., Succop, P., & Burklow, K. (1997). Adolescent girls' perceived prevalence of sexually transmitted diseases and condom use. *Journal of Developmental and Behavioral Pediatrics, 18,* 158–161.

Ross, G., Kagan, J., Zelazo, P., & Kotelchuk, M. (1975). Separation protest in infants in home and laboratory. *Developmental Psychology, 11,* 256–257.

Rossell, C., & Baker, K. (1996). The educational effectiveness of bilingual education. *Research in the Teaching of English, 30,* 1–68.

Rostosky, S., Owens, G., Zimmerman, R., & Riggle, E. (2003). Associations among sexual attraction status, school belonging, and alcohol and marijuana use in rural high school students. *Journal of Adolescence, 26,* 741–751.

Rothbart, M. (2004). Temperament and the pursuit of an integrated developmental psychology. *Merrill-Palmer Quarterly, 50,* 492–505.

Rothbart, M., Ahadi, S., & Evans, D. (2000). Temperament and personality: Origins and outcomes. *Journal of Personality & Social Psychology, 78,* 83–116.

Rothbart, M., Ahadi, S., Hersey, K., & Fisher, P. (2001). Investigations of temperament at three to seven years: The Children's Behavior Questionnaire. *Child Development, 72,* 1394–1408.

Rothbart, M. K., & Bates, J. E. (1998). Temperament. In W. Damon (Ed.), *Handbook of child psychology: Vol 3. Social, emotional, and personality development* (5th ed., pp. 105–176). New York: Wiley.

Rothbaum, F., Pott, M., & Morelli, G. (1995, April). *Ties that bind: Cultural differences in the development of family closeness.* Paper presented at the biennial meetings of the Society for Research in Child Development, Indianapolis.

Rothman, K. J., Moore, L. L., Singer, M. R., Nguyen, U. D. T., Mannino, S., & Milunsky, A. (1995). Teratogenicity of high Vitamin A intake. *New England Journal of Medicine, 333,* 1369–1373.

Rotter, J. (1990). Internal versus external control of reinforcement: A case history of a variable. *American Psychologist, 45,* 489–493.

Rovee-Collier, C. (1986). The rise and fall of infant classical conditioning research: Its promise for the study of early development. In L. P. Lipsitt & C. Rovee-Collier (Eds.), *Advances in infancy research* (Vol. 4, pp. 139–162). Norwood, NJ: Ablex.

Rovee-Collier, C. (1993). The capacity for long-term memory in infancy. *Current Directions in Psychological Science, 2,* 130–135.

Rovet, J., & Netley, C. (1983). The triple X chromosome syndrome in childhood: Recent empirical findings. *Child Development, 54,* 831–845.

Rowe, D. (2003). Assessing genotype-environment interactions and correlations in the postgenomic era. In R. Plomin, J. DeFries, I. Craig, & P. McGuffin (Eds.), *Behavioral genetics in the postgenomic era* (pp. 71–86). Washington, DC: American Psychological Association.

Rowe, I., & Marcia, J. E. (1980). Ego identity status, formal operations, and moral development. *Journal of Youth & Adolescence, 9,* 87–99.

Roy, E., Bryden, P., & Cavill, S. (2003). Hand differences in pegboard performance through development. *Brain & Cognition, 53,* 315–317.

Roy, P., Rutter, M., & Pickles, A. (2000). Institutional care: Risk from family background or patterns of rearing. *Journal of Child Psychology & Psychiatry & Allied Disciplines, 41,* 139–149.

Rubin, K., Burgess, K., Dwyer, K., & Hastings, P. (2003). Predicting preschoolers' externalizing behaviors from toddler temperament, conflict, and maternal negativity. *Developmental Psychology, 39,* 164–176.

Rubin, K., Burgess, K., & Hastings, P. (2002). Stability and social-behavioral consequences of toddlers' inhibited temperament and parenting behaviors. *Child Development, 73,* 483–495.

Rubin, K., Cheah, C., & Fox, N. (2001). Emotion regulation, parenting, and display of social reticence in preschoolers. *Early Education & Development, 12,* 97–115.

Rubin, K., & Coplan, R. (2004). Paying attention to and not neglecting social withdrawal and social isolation. *Merrill-Palmer Quarterly, 50,* 506–534.

Rubin, K., Coplan, R., Chen, X., Baskirk, A., & Wojslawowica, J. (2005). Peer relationships in childhood. In M. Bornstein & M. Lamb (Eds.), *Developmental science: An advanced textbook* (5th ed., pp. 469–512). Hillsdale, NJ: Erlbaum.

Rubin, K. H., Hastings, P. D., Stewart, S. L., Henderson, H. A., & Chen, X. (1997). The consistency and concomitants of inhibition: Some of the children, all of the time. *Child Development, 68,* 467–483.

Rubin, K. H., Hymel, S., Mills, R. S. L., & Rose-Krasnor, L. (1991). Conceptualizing different developmental pathways to and from social isolation in childhood. In D. Cicchetti & S. L. Toth (Eds.), *Internalizing and externalizing expressions of dysfunction: Rochester symposium on developmental psychopathology* (Vol. 2, pp. 91–122). Hillsdale, NJ: Erlbaum.

Ruble, D. N. (1987). The acquisition of self-knowledge: A self-socialization perspective. In N. Eisenberg (Ed.), *Contemporary topics in developmental psychology* (pp. 243–270). New York: Wiley-Interscience.

Ruble, D. N., & Martin, C. L. (1998). Gender development. In W. Damon (Ed.), *Handbook of child psychology: Vol 3. Social, emotional, and personality development* (5th ed., pp. 933–1016). New York: Wiley.

Rueter, M. A., & Conger, R. D. (1995). Antecedents of parent-adolescent disagreements. *Journal of Marriage and the Family, 57,* 435–448.

Runyan, D. K., Hunter, W. M., Socolar, R. R. S., Amaya-Jackson, L., English, D., Landsverk, J., Dubowitz, H., Browne, D. H., Bandiwala, S. I., & Mathew, R. M. (1998). Children who prosper in unfavorable environments: The relationship to social capital. *Pediatrics, 101,* 12–18.

Rushton, J., & Jensen, A. (2005). Thirty years of research on race differences in cognitive ability. *Psychology, Public Policy, & Law, 11,* 235–294.

Russell, J. A. (1989). Culture, scripts, and children's understanding of emotion. In C. Saarni & P. L. Harris (Eds.), *Children's understanding of emotion* (pp. 293–318). Cambridge, England: Cambridge University Press.

Rutter, D. R., & Durkin, K. (1987). Turn-taking in mother-infant interaction: An examination of vocalizations and gaze. *Developmental Psychology, 23,* 54–61.

Rutter, M. (1978). Early sources of security and competence. In J. S. Bruner & A. Garton (Eds.), *Human growth and development* (pp. 33–61). London: Oxford University Press.

Rutter, M. (1987). Continuities and discontinuities from infancy. In J. D. Osofsky (Ed.), *Handbook of infant development* (2nd ed., pp. 1256–1296). New York: Wiley-Interscience.

Rutter, M. (1989). Isle of Wight revisited: Twenty-five years of child psychiatric epidemiology. *Journal of the American Academy of Child and Adolescent Psychiatry, 28,* 633–653.

Rutter, M. (2002). Nature, nurture, and development: From evangelism through science toward policy and practice. *Child Development, 73,* 1–21.

Rutter, M. (2005a). Aetiology of autism: Findings and questions. *Journal of Intellectual Disability Research, 49,* 231–238.

Rutter, M. (2005b). Environmentally mediated risks for psychopathology: Research strategies and findings. *Journal of the American Academy of Child and Adolescent Psychiatry, 44,* 3–18.

Rutter, M., Dunn, J., Plomin, R., Simonoff, E., Pickles, A., Maughan, B., Ormel, J., Meyer, J., & Eaves, L. (1997). Integrating nature and nurture: Implications of person-environment correlations and interactions for developmental psychopathology. *Development and Psychopathology, 9,* 335–364.

Rutter, M., & Garmezy, N. (1983). Developmental psychopathology. In E. M. Hetherington (Ed.), *Handbook of child psychology: Vol 4. Socialization, personality, and social development* (pp. 775–912). New York: Wiley.

Rutter, M., & Sroufe, A. (2000). Developmental psychopathology: Concepts and challenges. *Development and Psychopathology, 12,* 265–296.

Rybakowski, J. (2001). Moclobemide in pregnancy. *Pharmacopsychiatry, 34,* 82–83.

Rys, G. S., & Bear, G. G. (1997). Relational aggression and peer relations: Gender and developmental issues. *Merrill-Palmer Quarterly, 43,* 87–106.

Saccuzzo, D. P., Johnson, N. E., & Guertin, T. L. (1994). Information processing in gifted versus nongifted African American, Latino, Filipino, and white children: Speeded versus nonspeeded paradigms. *Intelligence, 19,* 219–243.

Sackett, P., Hardison, C., & Cullen, M. (2004a). On interpreting stereotype threat as accounting for African American–White differences on cognitive tests. *American Psychologist, 59,* 7–13.

Sackett, P., Hardison, C., & Cullen, M. (2004b). On the value of correcting mischaracterizations of stereotype threat research. *American Psychologist, 59,* 38–49.

Sackett, P., Hardison, C., & Cullen, M. (2005). On interpreting research on stereotype threat and test performance. *American Psychologist, 60,* 271–272.

Sadeh, A., Gruber, R., & Raviv, A. (2002). Sleep, neurobehavioral functioning, and behavior problems in school-age children. *Child Development, 73,* 405–417.

Saewyc, E., Bearinger, L., Heinz, P., Blum, R., & Resnick, M. (1998). Gender differences in health and risk behaviors among bisexual and homosexual adolescents. *Journal of Adolescent Health, 23,* 181–188.

Safren, S., & Heimberg, R. (1999). Depression, hopelessness, suicidality, and related factors in sexual minority and heterosexual adolescents. *Journal of Consulting and Clinical Psychology, 67,* 859–866.

Sagi, A. (1990). Attachment theory and research from a cross-cultural perspective. *Human Development, 33,* 10–22.

Sagi, A., van IJzendoorn, M. H., & Koren-Karie, N. (1991). Primary appraisal of the Strange Situation: A cross-cultural analysis of preseparation episodes. *Developmental Psychology, 27,* 587–596.

Sai, F. (2005). The role of the mother's voice in developing mother's face preference: Evidence for intermodal perception at birth. *Infant & Child Development, 14,* 29–50.

Saigal, S., Szatmari, P., Rosenbaum, P., Campbell, D., & King, S. (1991). Cognitive abilities and school performance of extremely low birth weight children and matched term control children at age 8 years: A regional study. *Journal of Pediatrics, 118,* 751–760.

Sale, P., & Carey, D. M. (1995). The sociometric status of students with disabilities in a full-inclusion school. *Exceptional Children, 62,* 6–19.

Sameroff, A., & Mackenzie, M. (2003). Research strategies for capturing transactional models of development: The limits of the possible. *Development and Psychopathology, 15,* 613–640.

Sameroff, A. J., Seifer, R., Barocas, R., Zax, M., & Greenspan, S. (1987). Intelligence quotient scores of 4-year-old children: Social-environmental risk factors. *Pediatrics, 79,* 343–350.

Sampson, R. J. (1997, April). *Child and adolescent development in community context: New findings from a multilevel study of 80 Chicago neighborhoods.* Paper presented at the biennial meetings of the Society for Research in Child Development, Washington, DC.

Sampson, R. J., & Laub, J. H. (1994). Urban poverty and the family context of delinquency: A new look at structure and process in a classic study. *Child Development, 65,* 523–540.

Samuels, S., & Flor, R. (1997). The importance of automaticity for developing expertise in reading. *Reading & Writing Quarterly: Overcoming Learning Difficulties, 13,* 107–121.

Samuelson, L. K., & Smith, L. B. (1998). Memory and attention make smart word learning: An alternative account of Akhtar, Carpenter, and Tomasello. *Child Development, 69,* 94–104.

Sandberg, S., Day, R., & Gotz, E. T. (1996). Clinical aspects. In S. Sandberg (Ed.), *Hyperactivity disorders of childhood* (pp. 69–106). Cambridge, England: Cambridge University Press.

Sandelowski, M. (1994). Separate, but less unequal: Fetal ultrasonography and the transformation of expectant mother/fatherhood. *Gender & Society, 8,* 230–245.

Sandman, C., Wadhwa, P., Hetrick, W., Porto, M., & Peeke, H. (1997). Human fetal heart rate dishabituation between thirty and thirty-two weeks. *Child Development, 68,* 1031–1040.

Sandven, K., & Resnick, M. (1990). Informal adoption among Black adolescent mothers. *American Journal of Orthopsychiatry, 60,* 210–224.

Sani, F., & Bennett, M. (2001). Contextual variability in young children's gender ingroup stereotypes. *Social Development, 10,* 221–229.

Sato, S., Shimonska, Y., Nakazato, K., & Kawaai, C. (1997). A life-span developmental study of age identity: Cohort and gender differences. *Japanese Journal of Developmental Psychology, 8,* 88–97.

Saudino, K., Wertz, A., Gagne, J., & Chawla, S. (2004). Night and day: Are siblings as different in temperament as parents say they are? *Journal of Personality & Social Psychology, 87,* 698–706.

Saudino, K. J. (1998). Moving beyond the heritability question: New directions in behavioral genetic studies of personality. *Current Directions in Psychological Science, 6,* 86–90.

Saudino, K. J., & Plomin, R. (1997). Cognitive and temperamental mediators of genetic contributions to the home environment during infancy. *Merrill-Palmer Quarterly, 43,* 1–23.

Savage, J., Brodsky, N., Malmud, E., Giannetta, J., & Hurt, H. (2005). Attentional functioning and impulse control in cocaine-exposed and control children at age ten years. *Journal of Developmental and Behavioral Pediatrics, 26,* 42–47.

Savage, M., & Holcomb, D. (1999). Adolescent female athletes' sexual risk-taking behaviors. *Journal of Youth & Adolescence, 28,* 583–594.

Savage-Rumbaugh, E. S., Murphy, J., Sevcik, R. A., Brakke, K. E., Williams, S. L., & Rumbaugh, D. M. (1993). Language comprehension in ape and child. *Monographs of the Society for Research in Child Development, 58*(3–4, Serial No. 223).

Savin-Williams, R., & Ream, G. (2003). Suicide attempts among sexual-minority male youth. *Journal of Clinical Child & Adolescent Psychology, 32,* 509–522.

Scarr, S. (1997). Why child care has little impact on most children's development. *Current Directions in Psychological Science, 6,* 143–147.

Scarr, S., & Eisenberg, M. (1993). Child care research: Issues, perspectives, and results. *Annual Review of Psychology, 44,* 613–644.

Scarr, S., & McCartney, K. (1983). How people make their own environments: A theory of genotype/environment effects. *Child Development, 54,* 424–435.

Scarr, S., Weinberg, R. A., & Waldman, I. D. (1993). IQ correlations in transracial adoptive families. *Intelligence, 17,* 541–555.

Scerif, G., Karmiloff-Smith, A., Campos, R., Elsabbagh, M., Driver, J., & Cornish, K. (2005). To look or not to look? Typical and atypical development of oculomotor control. *Journal of Cognitive Neuroscience, 17,* 591–604.

Schaal, B., Marlier, L., & Soussignan, R. (1998). Olfactory function in the human fetus: Evidence from selective neonatal responsiveness to the odor of amniotic fluid. *Behavioral Neuroscience, 112,* 1438–1449.

Schachar, R., Tannock, R., & Cunningham, C. (1996). Treatment. In S. Sandberg (Ed.), *Hyperactivity disorders of childhood* (pp. 433–476). Cambridge, England: Cambridge University Press.

Schaffer, H. R. (1996). *Social development.* Oxford, England: Blackwell.

Schank, R. C., & Abelson, R. (1977). *Scripts, plans, goals, and understanding.* Hillsdale, NJ: Erlbaum.

Schatschneider, C., Fletcher, J., Francis, D., Carlson, C., & Foorman, B. (2004). Kindergarten prediction of reading skills: A longitudinal comparative analysis. *Journal of Educational Psychology, 96*, 265–282.

Schatschneider, C., Francis, D., Foorman, B., Fletcher, J., & Mehta, P. (1999). The dimensionality of phonological awareness: An application of item response theory. *Journal of Educational Psychology, 91*, 439–449.

Schieve, L., Meikle, S., Ferre, C., Peterson, H., Jeng, G., & Wilcox, L. (2002). Low and very low birth weight in infants conceived with the use of assisted reproductive technology. *New England Journal of Medicine, 346*, 731–737.

Schieve, L., Peterson, H., Meikle, S., Jeng, G., Danel, I., Burnett, N., & Wilcox, L. (1999). Birth rates and multiple-birth risk using in vitro fertilization. *Journal of the American Medical Association, 282*, 1832–1838.

Schlagmüller, M., & Schneider, W. (2002). The development of organizational strategies in children: Evidence from a microgenetic longitudinal study. *Journal of Experimental Child Psychology, 81*, 298–319.

Schliemann, A., Carraher, D., & Ceci, S. (1997). Everyday cognition. In J. Berry, P. Dasen, & T. Saraswathi (Eds.), *Handbook of cross-cultural psychology. Vol. 2: Basic processes and human development.* Boston: Allyn & Bacon.

Schlyter, S. (1996). Bilingual children's stories: French passe compose/imparfait and their correspondences in Swedish. *Linguistics, 34*, 1059–1085.

Schmidt, L., Trainor, L., & Santesso, D. (2003). Development of frontal electroencephalogram (EEG) and heart rate (ECG) responses to affective musical stimuli during the first 12 months of post-natal life. *Brain & Cognition, 52*, 27–32.

Schmidt, P. (2000, January 21). Colleges prepare for the fallout from state testing policies. *Chronicle of Higher Education, 46*, A26–A28.

Schmitz, S., Fulker, D., Plomin, R., Zahn-Waxler, C., Emde, R., & DeFries, J. (1999). Temperament and problem behavior during early childhood. *International Journal of Behavioral Development, 23*, 333–355.

Schneider, B., Hieshima, J. A., Lee, S., & Plank, S. (1994). East-Asian academic success in the United States: Family, school, and community explanations. In P. M. Greenfield & R. R. Cocking (Eds.), *Cross-cultural roots of minority child development* (pp. 323–350). Hillsdale, NJ: Erlbaum.

Schneider, M. L. (1992). The effect of mild stress during pregnancy on birthweight and neuromotor maturation in rhesus monkey infants *(Macaca mulatta). Infant Behavior and Development, 15*, 389–403.

Schneider, W., & Bjorklund, D. F. (1992). Expertise, aptitude, and strategic remembering. *Child Development, 63*, 461–473.

Schneider, W., & Bjorklund, D. F. (1998). Memory. In W. Damon (Ed.), *Handbook of child psychology: Vol. 2. Cognition, perception, and language* (5th ed., pp. 467–521). New York: Wiley.

Schneider, W., Gruber, H., Gold, A., & Opwis, K. (1993). Chess expertise and memory for chess positions in children and adults. *Journal of Experimental Child Psychology, 56*, 328–349.

Schneider, W., Reimers, P., Roth, E., & Visé, M. (1995, April). *Short- and long-term effects of training phonological awareness in kindergarten: Evidence from two German studies.* Paper presented at the biennial meetings of the Society for Research in Child Development, Indianapolis.

Schoendorf, K., Hogue, C., Kleinman, J., & Rowley, D. (1992). Mortality among infants of black as compared with white college-educated parents. *New England Journal of Medicine, 326*, 1522–1526.

Schonert-Reichl, K. (1999). Relations of peer acceptance, friendship adjustment, and social behavior to moral reasoning during early adolescence. *Journal of Early Adolescence, 19*, 249–279.

Schothorst, P., & van Engeland, H. (1996). Long-term behavioral sequelae of prematurity. *Journal of the American Academy of Child and Adolescent Psychiatry, 35*, 175–183.

Schott, J., & Rossor, M. (2003). The grasp and other primitive reflexes. *Journal of Neurology, Neurosurgery & Psychiatry, 74*, 558–560.

Schraf, M., & Hertz-Lazarowitz, R. (2003). Social networks in the school context: Effects of culture and gender. *Journal of Social & Personal Relationships, 20*, 843–858.

Schumm, J. S., & Vaughn, S. (1995). Getting ready for inclusion: Is the stage set? *Learning Disabilities Research and Practice, 10*, 169–179.

Schumm, W. (2004). What was really learned from Tasker and Golombok's (1995) study of lesbian and single parent mothers? *Psychological Reports, 94*, 422–424.

Schvaneveldt, P., Miller, B., Berry, E., & Lee, T. (2001). Academic goals, achievement, and age at first sexual intercourse: Longitudinal, bidirectional influences. *Adolescence, 36*, 767–787.

Schwartz, C., Wright, C., Shin, L., Kagan, J., & Rauch, S. (2003). Inhibited and uninhibited infants "grown up": Adult amygdalar response to novelty. *Science, 300*, 1952–1953.

Schwartz, C. E., Snidman, N., & Kagan, J. (1996). Early childhood temperament as a determinant of externalizing behavior in adolescence. *Development and Psychopathology, 8*, 527–537.

Schwartz, D., Dodge, K. A., & Coie, J. D. (1993). The emergence of chronic peer victimization in boys' play groups. *Child Development, 64*, 1755–1772.

Schwartz, J. (1994). Low-level lead exposure and children's IQ: A meta-analysis and search for a threshold. *Environmental Research, 65*, 42–55.

Schwartz, R. M., Anastasia, M. L., Scanlon, J. W., & Kellogg, R. J. (1994). Effect of surfactant on morbidity, mortality, and resource use in newborn infants weighing 500 to 1500 g. *New England Journal of Medicine, 330*, 1476–1480.

Schwebel, D., Rosen, C., & Singer, J. (1999). Preschoolers' pretend play and theory of mind: The role of jointly constructed pretence. *British Journal of Developmental Psychology, 17*, 333–348.

Schweinle, A., & Wilcox, T. (2004). Intermodal perception and physical reasoning in young infants. *Infant Behavior and Development, 27*, 246–265.

Scollon, R. (1976). *Conversations with a one-year-old.* Honolulu: University of Hawaii Press.

Scott, J. (1998). Hematology. In R. Behrman & R. Kliegman (Eds.), *Nelson essentials of pediatrics* (3rd ed., pp. 545–582). Philadelphia: Saunders.

Scott, J. (2004). Family, gender, and educational attainment in Britain: A longitudinal study. *Journal of Comparative Family Studies, 35*, 565–589.

Sears, R. R., Maccoby, E. E., & Levin, H. (1977). *Patterns of child rearing.* Stanford, CA: Stanford University Press. (Originally published 1957 by Row, Peterson)

Sebanc, A. (2003). The friendship features of preschool children: Links with prosocial behavior and aggression. *Social Development, 12*, 249–268.

Sege, R. D. (1998). Life imitating art: Adolescents and television violence. In T. P. Gullotta, G. R. Adams, & R. Montemayor (Eds.), *Delinquent violent youth: Theory and interventions.* Thousand Oaks, CA: Sage.

Segers, E., & Verhoeven, L. (2004). Computer-supported phonological awareness intervention for kindergarten children with specific language impairment. *Language, Speech, & Hearing Services in Schools, 35*, 229–239.

Seibt, B., & Förster, J. (2004). Stereotype threat and performance: How self-stereotypes influence processing by inducing regulatory foci. *Journal of Personality & Social Psychology, 87*, 38–56.

Seidman, E., Allen, L., Aber, J. L., Mitchell, C., & Feinman, J. (1994). The impact of school transitions in early adolescence on the self-system and perceived social context of poor urban youth. *Child Development, 65*, 507–522.

Seifer, R., Schiller, M., Sameroff, A., Resnick, S., & Riordan, K. (1996). Attachment, maternal sensitivity, and infant temperament during the first year of life. *Developmental Psychology, 32*, 12–25.

Seligman, S. (2005). Dynamic systems theories as a metaframework for psychoanalysis. *Psychoanalytic Dialogues, 15*, 285–319.

Selman, R. L. (1980). *The growth of interpersonal understanding.* New York: Academic Press.

Serbin, L., Moskowitz, D. S., Schwartzman, A. E., & Ledingham, J. E. (1991). Aggressive, withdrawn, and aggressive/withdrawn children in adolescence: Into the next generation. In D. J. Pepler & K. H. Rubin (Eds.), *The development and treatment of childhood aggression* (pp. 55–70). Hillsdale, NJ: Erlbaum.

Serbin, L. A., Powlishta, K. K., & Gulko, J. (1993). The development of sex typing in middle childhood. *Monographs of the Society for Research in Child Development, 58*(2, Serial No. 232).

Serpell, R., & Hatano, G. (1997). Education, schooling, and literacy. In J. Berry, P. Dasen, & T. Saraswathi (Eds.), *Handbook of cross-cultural psychology. Vol. 2: Basic processes and human development.* Boston: Allyn & Bacon.

Shaffer, D., Garland, A., Gould, M., Fisher, P., & Trautman, P. (1988). Preventing teenage suicide: A critical review. *Journal of the American Academy of Child and Adolescent Psychiatry, 27*, 675–687.

Shaffer, D., Garland, A., Vieland, V., Underwood, M., & Busner, C. (1991). The impact of curriculum-based suicide prevention programs for teenagers. *Journal of the American Academy of Child and Adolescent Psychiatry, 30*, 588–596.

Shakib, S. (2003). Female basketball participation. *American Behavioral Scientist, 46*, 1405–1422.

Shanahan, M., Sayer, A., Davey, A., & Brooks, J. (1997, April). *Pathways of poverty and children's trajectories of psychosocial adjustment.* Paper presented at the biennial meetings of the Society for Research in Child Development, Washington, DC.

Shantz, C. U. (1983). Social cognition. In J. H. Flavell & E. M. Markman

(Eds.), *Handbook of child psychology: Vol. 3. Cognitive development* (pp. 495–555). New York: Wiley.

Sharma, V., & Sharma, A. (1997). Adolescent boys in Gujrat, India: Their sexual behavior and their knowledge of acquired immunodeficiency syndrome and other sexually transmitted diseases. *Journal of Developmental and Behavioral Pediatrics, 18,* 399–404.

Sharpe, P. (2002). Preparing for primary school in Singapore: Aspects of adjustment to the more formal demands of the primary one mathematics syllabus. *Early Child Development & Care, 172,* 329–335.

Shaw, D. S., Kennan, K., & Vondra, J. I. (1994). Developmental precursors of externalizing behavior: Ages 1 to 3. *Developmental Psychology, 30,* 355–364.

Shaw, D. S., Owens, E. B., Vondra, J. I., Keenan, K., & Winslow, E. B. (1996). Early risk factors and pathways in the development of early disruptive behavior problems. *Development and Psychopathology, 8,* 679–700.

Shaywitz, B., Shaywitz, S., Pugh, K., Mencl, W., Fulbright, R., Skudlarksi, P., Constable, R., Marchione, K., Fletcher, J., Lyon, G., & Gore, J. (2002). Disruption of posterior brain systems for reading in children with developmental dyslexia. *Journal of Biological Psychiatry, 52,* 101–110.

Shaywitz, S. E., Shaywitz, B. A., Pugh, K. R., Fulbright, R. K., Constable, R. T., Mencl, W. E., Shankweiler, D. P., Liberman, A. M., Skudlarski, P., Fletcher, J. M., Katz, L., Marachione, K. E., Lacadie, C., Gatenby, C., & Gore, J. C. (1998). Functional disruption in the organization of the brain for reading in dyslexia. *Proceedings of the National Academy of Sciences, USA, 95,* 2636–2641.

Shiner, R. (2000). Linking childhood personality with adaptation: Evidence for continuity and change across time into late adolescence. *Journal of Personality & Social Psychology, 78,* 310–325.

Shirley, L., & Campbell, A. (2000). Same-sex preference in infancy. *Psychology, Evolution & Gender, 2,* 3–18.

Shochat, L. (2003). *Our Neighborhood*: Using entertaining children's television to promote interethnic understanding in Macedonia. *Conflict Resolution Quarterly, 21,* 79–93.

Shore, C. (1986). Combinatorial play, conceptual development, and early multiword speech. *Developmental Psychology, 22,* 184–190.

Shore, C. M. (1995). *Individual differences in language development.* Thousand Oaks, CA: Sage.

Shore, R. (1997). *Rethinking the brain: New insights into early development.* New York: Families and Work Institute.

Shu, H., Anderson, R., & Wu, N. (2000). Phonetic awareness: Knowledge of orthography-phonology relationships in the character acquisition of Chinese children. *Journal of Educational Psychology, 92,* 56–62.

Sicotte, C., & Sternberger, R. (1999). Do children with PDDNOS have a theory of mind? *Journal of Autism & Developmental Disorders, 29,* 225–233.

Siegel, B. (1996). Is the emperor wearing clothes? Social policy and the empirical support for full inclusion of children with disabilities in the preschool and early elementary grades. *Social Policy Report, Society for Research in Child Development, 10*(2–3), 2–17.

Siegler, R. (1996). *Emerging minds: The process of change in children's thinking.* New York: Oxford University Press.

Siegler, R., & Chen, Z. (2002). Development of rules and strategies: Balancing the old and the new. *Journal of Experimental Child Psychology, 81,* 446–457.

Siegler, R., & Svetina, M. (2002). A microgenetic/cross-sectional study of matrix completion: Comparing short-term and long-term change. *Child Development, 73,* 793–809.

Siegler, R. S., & Ellis, S. (1996). Piaget on childhood. *Psychological Science, 7,* 211–215.

Sigman, M., & McGovern, C. (2005). Improvement in cognitive and language skills from preschool to adolescence in autism. *Journal of Autism & Developmental Disorders, 35,* 15–23.

Sigman, M., Neumann, C., Carter, E., Cattle, D. J., D'Souza, S., & Bwibo, N. (1988). Home interactions and the development of Embu toddlers in Kenya. *Child Development, 59,* 1251–1261.

Signorella, M. L., Bigler, R. L., & Liben, L. S. (1993). Developmental differences in children's gender schemata about others: A meta-analytic review. *Developmental Review, 13,* 147–183.

Silbereisen, R. K., & Kracke, B. (1993). Variations in maturational timing and adjustment in adolescence. In S. Jackson & H. Rodrigues-Tomé (Eds.), *Adolescence and its social worlds* (pp. 67–94). Hove, England: Erlbaum.

Silverberg, S. B., & Gondoli, D. M. (1996). Autonomy in adolescence: A contextualized perspective. In G. R. Adams, R. Montemayor, & T. P. Gullotta (Eds.), *Psychosocial development during adolescence: Progress in developmental contextualism* (pp. 12–61). Thousand Oaks, CA: Sage.

Simmons, R. G., Burgeson, R., & Reef, M. J. (1988). Cumulative change at entry to adolescence. In M. R. Gunnar & W. A. Collins (Eds.), *The Minnesota symposia on child psychology* (Vol. 21, pp. 123–150). Hillsdale, NJ: Erlbaum.

Simonoff, E., Pickles, A., Meyer, J. M., Silberg, J. L., Maes, H. H., Loeber, R., Rutter, M., Hewitt, J. K., & Eaves, L. J. (1997). The Virginia twin study of adolescent behavioral development. *Archives of General Psychiatry, 54,* 801–808.

Simons, R. L., Robertson, J. F., & Downs, W. R. (1989). The nature of the association between parental rejection and delinquent behavior. *Journal of Youth & Adolescence, 18,* 297–309.

Simpkins, S., Davis-Kean, P., & Eccles, J. (2005). Parents' socializing behavior and children's participation in math, science, and computer out-of-school activities. *Applied Development Science, 9,* 14–30.

Singer, L., Arendt, R., & Minnes, S. (1993). Neurodevelopmental effects of cocaine. *Clinics in Perinatology, 20,* 245–262.

Singh, G. K., & Yu, S. M. (1996). US childhood mortality, 1950 through 1993: Trends and socioeconomic differentials. *American Journal of Public Health, 86,* 505–512.

Singh, S., & Darroch, J. (2000). Adolescent pregnancy and childbearing: Levels and trends in industrialized countries. *Family Planning Perspectives, 32,* 14–23.

Skinner, B. F. (1957). *Verbal behavior.* New York: Prentice Hall.

Slaby, R. G., & Frey, K. S. (1975). Development of gender constancy and selective attention to same-sex models. *Child Development, 46,* 849–856.

Slater, A. (1995). Individual differences in infancy and later IQ. *Journal of Child Psychology and Psychiatry, 36,* 69–112.

Slaughter-Defoe, D., & Rubin, H. (2001). A longitudinal case study of Head Start eligible children: Implications for urban education. *Educational Psychologist, 36,* 31–44.

Sligh, A., & Conners, F. (2003). Relation of dialect to phonological processing: African American Vernacular English vs. Standard American English. *Contemporary Educational Psychology, 28,* 205–228.

Slobin, D. I. (1985a). Introduction: Why study acquisition crosslinguistically? In D. I. Slobin (Ed.), *The crosslinguistic study of language acquisition, Vol. 1: The data* (pp. 3–24). Hillsdale, NJ: Erlbaum.

Slobin, D. I. (1985b). Crosslinguistic evidence for the language-making capacity. In D. I. Slobin (Ed.), *The crosslinguistic study of language acquisition, Vol. 2: Theoretical issues* (pp. 1157–1256). Hillsdale, NJ: Erlbaum.

Small, S. A., & Luster, T. (1994). Adolescent sexual activity: An ecological risk-factor approach. *Journal of Marriage and the Family, 56,* 181–192.

Smetana, J. G. (1990). Morality and conduct disorders. In M. Lewis & S. M. Miller (Eds.), *Handbook of developmental psychopathology* (pp. 157–180). New York: Plenum Press.

Smetana, J. G., Killen, M., & Turiel, E. (1991). Children's reasoning about interpersonal and moral conflicts. *Child Development, 62,* 629–644.

Smith, A., Lalonde, R., & Johnson, S. (2004). Serial migration and its implications for the parent-child relationship: A retrospective analysis of the experiences of the children of Caribbean immigrants. *Cultural Diversity & Ethnic Minority Psychology, 10,* 107–122.

Smith, J. R., Brooks-Gunn, J., & Klebanov, P. K. (1997). Consequences of living in poverty for young children's cognitive and verbal ability and early school achievement. In G. J. Duncan & J. Brooks-Gunn (Eds.), *Consequences of growing up poor* (pp. 132–179). New York: Russell Sage Foundation.

Smith, R. E., & Smoll, F. L. (1997). Coaching the coaches: Youth sports as a scientific and applied behavioral setting. *Current Directions in Psychological Science, 6,* 16–21.

Smith, S., Howard, J., & Monroe, A. (1998). An analysis of child behavior problems in adoptions in difficulty. *Journal of Social Service Research, 24,* 61–84.

Smith, S., Howard, J., & Monroe, A. (2000). Issues underlying behavior problems in at-risk adopted children. *Children and Youth Services Review, 22,* 539–562.

Smock, P. J. (1993). The economic costs of marital disruption for young women over the past two decades. *Demography, 30,* 353–371.

Smolak, L., Levine, M. P., & Streigel-Moore, R. (Eds.). (1996). *The developmental psychopathology of eating disorders.* Mahwah, NJ: Erlbaum.

Smoll, F. L., & Schutz, R. W. (1990). Quantifying gender differences in physical performance: A developmental perspective. *Developmental Psychology, 26,* 360–369.

Snarey, J. R. (1985). Cross-cultural universality of social-moral development: A critical review of Kohlbergian research. *Psychological Bulletin, 97,* 202–232.

Snarey, J. R., Reimer, J., & Kohlberg, L. (1985). Development of social-moral reasoning among kibbutz adolescents: A longitudinal cross-sectional study. *Developmental Psychology, 21,* 3–17.

Snow, C. E. (1997, April). *Cross-domain connections and social class differences: Two challenges to nonenvironmentalist views of language development.* Paper presented at the biennial meetings of the Society for Research in Child Development, Washington, DC.

Snyder, H., Puzzanchera, C., & Kang, W. (2005). *Easy access to FBI arrest statistics 1994–2002.* Retrieved June 10, 2005, from http://ojjdp.ncjrs.org/ojstabb/ezaucr/

Snyder, J., Edwards, P., McGraw, K., Kilgore, K., & Holton, A. (1994). Escalation and reinforcement in mother-child conflict: Social processes associated with the development of physical aggression. *Development and Psychopathology, 6,* 305–321.

Society for Assisted Reproductive Technology. (2004). *Guidelines on number of embryos transferred: Committee report.* Retrieved August 18, 2004, from http://www.sart.org

Soken, N. H., & Pick, A. D. (1992). Intermodal perception of happy and angry expressive behaviors by seven-month-old infants. *Child Development, 63,* 787–795.

Sola, A., Rogido, M., & Partridge, J. (2002). The perinatal period. In A. Rudolph, R. Kamei, & K. Overby (Eds.), *Rudolph's fundamentals of pediatrics* (3rd ed., pp. 125–183). New York: McGraw-Hill.

Somers, C., & Surmann, A. (2004). Adolescents' preferences for source of sex education. *Child Study Journal, 34,* 47–59.

Sonnenschein, S. (1986). Development of referential communication skills: How familiarity with a listener affects a speaker's production of redundant messages. *Developmental Psychology, 22,* 549–552.

Sophian, C. (1995). Representation and reasoning in early numerical development: Counting, conservation, and comparisons between sets. *Child Development, 66,* 559–577.

Sotelo, M., & Sangrador, J. (1997). Psychological aspects of political tolerance among adolescents. *Psychological Reports, 81,* 1279–1288.

Sourander, A., Helstelae, L., Ristkari, T., Ikaeheimo, K., Helenius, H., & Piha, J. (2001). Child and adolescent mental health service use in Finland. *Social Psychiatry & Psychiatric Epidemiology, 36,* 294–298.

Sowell, E., Peterson, B., Thompson, P., Welcome, S., Henkenius, A., & Toga, A. (2003). Mapping cortical change across the human life span. *Nature Neuroscience, 6,* 309–315.

Spector, S. A. (1996). Cytomegalovirus infections. In A. M. Rudolph, J. I. E. Hoffman, & C. D. Rudolph (Eds.), *Rudolph's pediatrics* (pp. 629–633). Stanford, CT: Appleton & Lange.

Spelke, E. S. (1979). Exploring audible and visible events in infancy. In A. D. Pick (Ed.), *Perception and its development: A tribute to Eleanor J. Gibson* (pp. 221–236). Hillsdale, NJ: Erlbaum.

Spelke, E. S. (1982). Perceptual knowledge of objects in infancy. In J. Mehler, E. C. T. Walker, & M. Garrett (Eds.), *Perspectives on mental representation* (pp. 409–430). Hillsdale, NJ: Erlbaum.

Spelke, E. S. (1985). Perception of unity, persistence, and identity: Thoughts on infants' conceptions of objects. In J. Mehler & R. Fox (Eds.), *Neonate cognition* (pp. 89–113). Hillsdale, NJ: Erlbaum.

Spelke, E. S. (1991) Physical knowledge in infancy: Reflections on Piaget's theory. In S. Carey & R. Gelman (Eds.), *The epigenesis of mind: Essays on biology and cognition* (pp. 133–169). Hillsdale, NJ: Erlbaum.

Spelke, E. S., von Hofsten, C., & Kestenbaum, R. (1989). Object perception in infancy: Interaction of spatial and kinetic information for object boundaries. *Developmental Psychology, 25,* 185–196.

Spence, J. T., & Helmreich, R. L. (1978). *Masculinity and femininity.* Austin: University of Texas Press.

Spieker, S. J., Bensley, L., McMahon, R. J., Fung, H., & Ossiander, E. (1996). Sexual abuse as a factor in child maltreatment by adolescent mothers of preschool aged children. *Development and Psychopathology, 8,* 497–509.

Spiker, D. (1990). Early intervention from a developmental perspective. In D. Cicchetti & M. Beeghly (Eds.), *Children with Down syndrome: A developmental perspective* (pp. 424–448). Cambridge, England: Cambridge University Press.

Spreen, O., Risser, A., & Edgell, D. (1995). *Developmental neuropsychology.* New York: Oxford University Press.

Sroufe, A., Egeland, B., & Kreutzer, T. (1990). The fate of early experience following developmental change: Longitudinal approaches to individual adaptation in childhood. *Child Development, 61,* 1363–1373.

Sroufe, L., Bennett, C., England, M., Urban, J., & Shulman, S. (1993). The significance of gender boundaries in preadolescence: Contemporary correlates and antecedents of boundary violations and maintenance. *Child Development, 64,* 455–466.

Sroufe, L. A. (1983). Infant-caregiver attachment and patterns of adaptation

in preschool: The roots of maladaption and competence. In M. Perlmutter (Ed.), *The Minnesota symposia on child psychology* (Vol. 16, pp. 41–84). Hillsdale, NJ: Erlbaum.

Sroufe, L. A. (1988). The role of infant-caregiver attachment in development. In J. Belsky & T. Nezworski (Eds.), *Clinical implications of attachment* (pp. 18–40). Hillsdale, NJ: Erlbaum.

Sroufe, L. A. (1989). Pathways to adaptation and maladaptation: Psychopathology as developmental deviation. In D. Cicchetti (Ed.), *The emergence of a discipline: Rochester symposium on developmental psychopathology* (pp. 13–40). Hillsdale, NJ: Erlbaum.

Sroufe, L. A. (1990). A developmental perspective on day care. In N. Fox & G. G. Fein (Eds.), *Infant day care: The current debate* (pp. 51–60). Norwood, NJ: Ablex.

Sroufe, L. A. (1996). *Emotional development: The organization of emotional life in the early years.* Cambridge, England: Cambridge University Press.

Sroufe, L. A. (1997). Psychopathology as an outcome of development. *Development and Psychopathology, 9,* 251–268.

Sroufe, L. A., Carlson, E., & Schulman, S. (1993). Individuals in relationships: Development from infancy through adolescence. In D. C. Funder, R. D. Parke, C. Tomlinson-Keasey, & K. Widaman (Eds.), *Studying lives through time: Personality and development* (pp. 315–342). Washington, DC: American Psychological Association.

Sroufe, L. A., & Rutter, M. (1984). The domain of developmental psychopathology. *Child Development, 55,* 17–29.

Stainback, S., & Stainback, W. (1985). The merger of special and regular education: Can it be done? A response to Lieberman and Mesinger. *Exceptional Children, 51,* 517–521.

Starfield, B. (1991). Childhood morbidity: Comparisons, clusters, and trends. *Pediatrics, 88,* 519–526.

Statistics Canada. (2000). *Canada at a glance* (2nd ed.). Retrieved November 19, 2001, from http://www.statcan.ca/english/freepub/12-581-XIE/12-581-XIE.pdf

Stattin, H., & Klackenberg-Larsson, I. (1993). Early language and intelligence development and their relationship to future criminal behavior. *Journal of Abnormal Psychology, 102,* 369–378.

Stattin, H., & Magnusson, D. (1996). Antisocial development: A holistic approach. *Development and Psychopathology, 8,* 617–646.

Steele, C., & Aronson, J. (1995). Stereotype threat and the intellectual test performance of African Americans. *Journal of Personality & Social Psychology, 69,* 797–811.

Steele, C., & Aronson, J. (2004). Stereotype threat does not live by Steele and Aronson (1995) alone. *American Psychologist, 59,* 47–48.

Steele, H., Holder, J., & Fonagy, P. (1995, April). *Quality of attachment to mother at one year predicts belief-desire reasoning at five years.* Paper presented at the biennial meetings of the Society for Research in Child Development, Indianapolis.

Steele, J., & Mayes, S. (1995). Handedness and directional asymmetry in the long bones of the human upper limb. *International Journal of Osteoarchaeology, 5,* 39–49.

Steele, K. M., Bass, K. E., & Crook, M. D. (1999). The mystery of the Mozart effect: Failure to replicate. *Psychological Science, 10,* 366–369.

Steele, M., Hodges, J., Kaniuk, J., Hillman, S., & Henderson, K. (2003). Attachment representations and adoption: Associations between maternal states of mind and emotion narratives in previously maltreated children. *Journal of Child Psychotherapy, 29,* 187–205.

Stein, K., Roeser, R., & Markus, H. (1998). Self-schemas and possible selves as predictors and outcomes of risky behaviors in adolescents. *Nursing Research, 47,* 96–106.

Stein, Z., Susser, M., Saenger, G., & Morolla, F. (1975). *Famine and human development: The Dutch hunger winter of 1944–1945.* New York: Oxford University Press.

Steinberg, E., Tanofsky-Kraff, M., Cohen, M., Elberg, J., Freedman, R., Semega-Janneh, M., Yanovski, S., & Yanovski, J. (2004). Comparison of the child and parent forms of the Questionnaire on Eating and Weight Patterns in the assessment of children's eating-disordered behaviors. *International Journal of Eating Disorders, 36,* 183–194.

Steinberg, L. (1986). Latchkey children and susceptibility to peer pressure: An ecological analysis. *Developmental Psychology, 22,* 433–439.

Steinberg, L. (1988). Reciprocal relation between parent-child distance and pubertal maturation. *Developmental Psychology, 24,* 122–128.

Steinberg, L. (1990). Autonomy, conflict and harmony in the parent-adolescent relationship. In S. S. Feldman & G. R. Elliott (Eds.), *At the threshold: The developing adolescent* (pp. 255–276). Cambridge, MA: Harvard University Press.

Steinberg, L. (1996). *Beyond the classroom: Why school reform has failed and what parents need to do*. New York: Simon & Schuster.

Steinberg, L., Darling, N. E., Fletcher, A. C., Brown, B. B., & Dornbusch, S. M. (1995). Authoritative parenting and adolescent adjustment: An ecological journey. In P. Moen, G. H. Elder, Jr., & K. Lüscher (Eds.), *Examining lives in context: Perspectives on the ecology of human development* (pp. 423–466). Washington, DC: American Psychological Association.

Steinberg, L., & Dornbusch, S. M. (1991). Negative correlates of part-time employment during adolescence: Replication and elaboration. *Developmental Psychology, 27*, 304–313.

Steinberg, L., Dornbusch, S. M., & Brown, B. B. (1992). Ethnic differences in adolescent achievement: An ecological perspective. *American Psychologist, 47*, 723–729.

Steinberg, L., Elmen, J. D., & Mounts, N. S. (1989). Authoritative parenting, psychosocial maturity, and academic success among adolescents. *Child Development, 60*, 1424–1436.

Steinberg, L., Lamborn, S. D., Darling, N., Mounts, N. S., & Dornbusch, S. M. (1994). Over-time changes in adjustment and competence among adolescents from authoritative, authoritarian, indulgent, and neglectful families. *Child Development, 65*, 754–770.

Steinberg, L., Lamborn, S. D., Dornbusch, S. M., & Darling, N. (1992). Impact of parenting practices on adolescent achievement: Authoritative parenting, school involvement, and encouragement to succeed. *Child Development, 63*, 1266–1281.

Steinberg, L., Mounts, N. S., Lamborn, S. D., & Dornbusch, S. D. (1991). Authoritative parenting and adolescent adjustment across varied ecological niches. *Journal of Research on Adolescence, 1*, 19–36.

Steiner, J. E. (1979). Human facial expressions in response to taste and smell stimulation. In H. W. Reese & L. P. Lipsitt (Eds.), *Advances in child development and behavior* (Vol. 13, pp. 257–296). New York: Academic Press.

Stelzl, I., Merz, F., Ehlers, T., & Remer, H. (1995). The effect of schooling on the development of fluid and crystallized intelligence: A quasi-experimental study. *Intelligence, 21*, 279–296.

Sternberg, R. (2001). What is the common thread of creativity? Its dialectical relation to intelligence and wisdom. *American Psychologist, 56*, 360–362.

Sternberg, R. (2003). Construct validity of the theory of successful intelligence. In R. Sternberg, J. Lautrey, & T. Lubart (Eds.), *Models of intelligence: International perspectives* (pp. 55–80). Washington, DC: American Psychological Association.

Sternberg, R., Castejon, J., Prieto, M., Hautamaeki, J., & Grigorenko, E. (2001). Confirmatory factor analysis of the Sternberg Triarchic Abilities Test in three international samples: An empirical test of the triarchic theory of intelligence. *European Journal of Psychological Assessment, 17*, 1–16.

Sternberg, R., Grigorenko, E., & Bundy, D. (2001). The predictive value of IQ. *Merrill-Palmer Quarterly, 47*, 1–41.

Sternberg, R. J. (1985). *Beyond IQ: A triarchic theory of human intelligence*. New York: Cambridge University Press.

Sternberg, R. J., & Davidson, J. E. (1985). Cognitive development in the gifted and talented. In F. D. Horowitz & M. O'Brien (Eds.), *The gifted and talented: Developmental perspectives* (pp. 37–74). Washington, DC: American Psychological Association.

Sternberg, R. J., & Wagner, R. K. (1993). The g-ocentric view of intelligence and job performance is wrong. *Current Directions in Psychological Science, 2*, 1–5.

Sternberg, R. J., Wagner, R. K., Williams, W. M., & Horvath, J. A. (1995). Testing common sense. *American Psychologist, 50*, 912–927.

Stevenson, H. W. (1988). Culture and schooling: Influences on cognitive development. In E. M. Hetherington, R. M. Lerner, & M. Perlmutter (Eds.), *Child development in life span perspective* (pp. 241–258). Hillsdale, NJ: Erlbaum.

Stevenson, H. W., & Chen, C. (1989). Schooling and achievement: A study of Peruvian children. *International Journal of Educational Research, 13*, 883–894.

Stevenson, H. W., Chen, C., Lee, S., & Fuligni, A. J. (1991). Schooling, culture, and cognitive development. In L. Okagaki & R. J. Sternberg (Eds.), *Directors of development* (pp. 243–268). Hillsdale, NJ: Erlbaum.

Stevenson, H. W., & Lee, S. (1990). Contexts of achievement: A study of American, Chinese, and Japanese children. *Monographs of the Society for Research in Child Development, 55*(1–2, Serial No. 221).

Stevenson, H. W., Lee, S., Chen, C., Lummis, M., Stigler, J., Fan, L., & Ge, F. (1990). Mathematics achievement of children in China and the United States. *Child Development, 61*, 1053–1066.

Stewart, R. B., Beilfuss, M. L., & Verbrugge, K. M. (1995, April). *That was then, this is now: An empirical typology of adult sibling relationships*. Paper presented at the biennial meetings of the Society for Research in Child Development, Indianapolis.

Stice, E., Spangler, D., & Agras, W. (1999, August). *Effects of long-term exposure to fashion magazines on adolescent girls: Effects of media-portrayed thin-ideal images*. Paper presented at the annual meeting of the American Psychological Association, Boston, MA.

Stigler, J. W., Lee, S., & Stevenson, H. W. (1987). Mathematics classrooms in Japan, Taiwan, and the United States. *Child Development, 58*, 1272–1285.

Stigler, J. W., & Stevenson, H. W. (1991, Spring). How Asian teachers polish each lesson to perfection. *American Educator 12–20*, 43–47.

Stipek, D. (1992). The child at school. In M. H. Bornstein & M. E. Lamb (Eds.), *Developmental psychology: An advanced textbook* (3rd ed., pp. 579–625). Hillsdale, NJ: Erlbaum.

St. James-Roberts, I., Bowyer, J., Varghese, S., & Sawdon, J. (1994). Infant crying patterns in Manila and London. *Child: Care, Health and Development, 20*, 323–337.

Stolarova, M., Whitney, H., Webb, S., deRegnier, R., Georgieff, M., & Nelson, C. (2003). Electrophysiological brain responses of six-month-old low risk premature infants. *Infancy, 4*, 437–450.

Storter, M. D. (1990). *Intelligence and giftedness*. San Francisco: Jossey-Bass.

Stoutjesdyk, D., & Jevne, R. (1993). Eating disorders among high performance athletes. *Journal of Youth & Adolescence, 22*, 271–282.

St. Peters, M., Fitch, M., Huston, A. C., Wright, J. C., & Eakins, D. J. (1991). Television and families: What do young children watch with their parents? *Child Development, 62*, 1409–1423.

Strassberg, Z., Dodge, K. A., Pettit, G. S., & Bates, J. E. (1994). Spanking in the home and children's subsequent aggression toward kindergarten peers. *Development and Psychopathology, 6*, 445–461.

Stratton, K. R., Howe, C. J., & Battaglia, F. C. (Eds.). (1996). *Fetal alcohol syndrome: Diagnosis, epidemiology, prevention and treatment*. Washington, DC: National Academy Press.

Straus, M. A. (1991a). Discipline and deviance: Physical punishment of children and violence and other crime in adulthood. *Social Problems, 38*, 133–152.

Straus, M. A. (1991b). New theory and old canards about family violence research. *Social Problems, 38*, 180–194.

Straus, M. A. (1995). Corporal punishment of children and adult depression and suicidal ideation. In J. McCord (Ed.), *Coercion and punishment in long-term perspectives* (pp. 59–77). Cambridge, England: Cambridge University Press.

Straus, M. A., & Donnelly, D. A. (1993). Corporal punishment of adolescents by American parents. *Youth & Society, 24*, 419–442.

Strayer, J., & Roberts, W. (1989). Children's empathy and role-taking: Child and parental factors and relations to prosocial behavior. *Journal of Applied Developmental Psychology, 10*, 227–239.

Strayer, J., & Roberts, W. (2004). Empathy and observed anger and aggression in five-year-olds. *Social Development, 13*, 1–13.

Streissguth, A., Bookstein, F., Barr, H., Sampson, P., O'Malley, K., & Young, J. (2004). Risk factors for adverse life outcomes in fetal alcohol syndrome and fetal alcohol effects. *Journal of Developmental and Behavioral Pediatrics, 25*, 228–238.

Streissguth, A. P., Barr, H. M., & Sampson, P. D. (1990). Moderate prenatal alcohol exposure: Effects on child IQ and learning problems at age $7\frac{1}{2}$ years. *Alcoholism: Clinical and Experimental Research, 14*, 662–669.

Streissguth, A. P., Barr, H. M., Sampson, P. D., Darby, B. L., & Martin, D. C. (1989). IQ at age 4 in relation to maternal alcohol use and smoking during pregnancy. *Developmental Psychology, 25*, 3–11.

Streissguth, A. P., Bookstein, F. L., Sampson, P. D., & Barr, H. M. (1995). Attention: Prenatal alcohol and continuities of vigilance and attentional problems from 4 through 14 years. *Development and Psychopathology, 7*, 419–446.

Streissguth A. P., Landesman-Dwyer, S., Martin, J. C., & Smith, D. W. (1980). Teratogenic effects of alcohol in humans and laboratory animals. *Science, 209*, 353–361.

Streissguth, A. P., Martin, D. C., Barr, H. M., Sandman, B. M., Kirchner, G. L., & Darby, B. L. (1984). Intrauterine alcohol and nicotine exposure: Attention and reaction time in 4-year-old children. *Developmental Psychology, 20*, 533–541.

Streissguth, A. P., Martin, D. C., Martin, J. C., & Barr, H. M. (1981). The Seattle longitudinal prospective study on alcohol and pregnancy. *Neurobehavioral Toxicology and Teratology, 3*, 223–233.

Stroganova, T., Posikera, I., Pushina, N., & Orekhova, E. (2003). Lateralization of motor functions in early human ontogeny. *Human Physiology, 29*, 48–58.

Stunkard, A. J., Harris, J. R., Pedersen, N. L., & McClearn, G. E. (1990). The body-mass index of twins who have been reared apart. *New England Journal of Medicine, 322*, 1483–1487.

Sudarkasa, N. (1993). Female-headed African American households: Some neglected dimensions. In H. P. McAdoo (Ed.), *Family ethnicity* (pp. 81–89). Newbury Park, CA: Sage.

Sue, S., & Okazaki, S. (1990). Asian-American educational achievements: A phenomenon in search of an explanation. *American Psychologist, 45*, 913–920.

Sulkes, S. (1998). Developmental and behavioral pediatrics. In R. Behrman & R. Kliegman (Eds.), *Nelson essentials of pediatrics* (3rd ed.). Philadelphia: Saunders.

Sullivan, K., Zaitchik, D., & Tager-Flusberg, H. (1994). Preschoolers can attribute second-order beliefs. *Developmental Psychology, 30*, 395–402.

Sulloway, F. (1996). *Born to rebel.* New York: Pantheon Books.

Susman, E. J., Inoff-Germain, G., Nottelmann, E. D., Loriaux, D. L., Cutler, G. B., Jr., & Chrousos, G. P. (1987). Hormones, emotional dispositions, and aggressive attributes in young adolescents. *Child Development, 58*, 1114–1134.

Sutton-Smith, B. (1982). Birth order and sibling status effects. In M. E. Lamb & B. Sutton-Smith (Eds.), *Sibling relationships: Their nature and significance across the lifespan* (pp. 153–165). Hillsdale, NJ: Erlbaum.

Suzuki, L., & Aronson, J. (2005). The cultural malleability of intelligence and its impact on the racial/ethnic hierarchy. *Psychology, Public Policy, & Law, 11*, 320–327.

Swain, I. U., Zelazo, P. R., & Clifton, R. K. (1993). Newborn infants' memory for speech sounds retained over 24 hours. *Developmental Psychology, 29*, 312–323.

Swayze, V. W., Johnson, V. P., Hanson, J. W., Piven, J., Sato, Y., Geidd, J. N., Mosnik, D., & Andreasen, N. C. (1997). Magnetic resonance imaging of brain anomalies in fetal alcohol syndrome. *Pediatrics, 99*, 232–240.

Swedo, S. E., Rettew, D. C., Kuppenheimer, M., Lum, D., Dolan, S., & Goldberger, E. (1991). Can adolescent suicide attempters be distinguished from at-risk adolescents? *Pediatrics, 88*, 620–629.

Sweeting, H., & West, P. (2002). Gender differences in weight related concerns in early to late adolescence. *Journal of Family Issues, 23*, 728–747.

Talan, J. (1998, October 28). Possible genetic link found for right-handedness, not for left. *Seattle Times.*

Talmor, R., Reiter, S., & Feigin, N. (2005). Factors relating to regular education teacher burnout in inclusive education. *European Journal of Special Needs Education, 20*, 215–229.

Tamis-LeMonda, C., Shannon, J., Cabrera, N., & Lamb, M. (2004). Fathers and mothers at play with their 2- and 3-year-olds: Contributions to language and cognitive development. *Child Development, 76*, 1806–1820.

Tani, F., Greenman, P., Schneider, B., & Fregoso, M. (2003). Bullying and the Big Five: A study of childhood personality and participant roles in bullying incidents. *School Psychology International, 24*, 131–146.

Tanner, J. M. (1990). *Foetus into man* (revised and enlarged ed.). Cambridge, MA: Harvard University Press.

Tan-Niam, C., Wood, D., & O'Malley, C. (1998). A cross-cultural perspective on children's theories of mind and social interaction. *Early Child Development & Care, 144*, 55–67.

Tanofsky-Kraff, M., Yanovski, S., & Yanovski, J. (2005). Comparison of child interview and parent reports of children's eating disordered behaviors. *Eating Behaviors, 6*, 95–99.

Tardif, T., & Wellman, H. (2000). Acquisition of mental state language in Mandarin- and Cantonese-speaking children. *Developmental Psychology, 36*, 25–43.

Taylor, E. (1995). Dysfunctions of attention. In D. Cicchetti & D. J. Cohen (Eds.), *Developmental psychopathology: Vol. 2. Risk, disorder, and adaptation* (pp. 243–273). New York: Wiley.

Taylor, H., Klein, N., Minich, N., & Hack, M. (2000). Middle-school-aged outcomes in children with very low birthweight. *Child Development, 71*, 1495–1511.

Taylor, J. A., Krieger, J. W., Reay, D. T., Davis, R. L., Harruff, R., & Cheney, L. K. (1996). Prone sleep position and the sudden infant death syndrome in King County, Washington: A case-control study. *Journal of Pediatrics, 128*, 626–630.

Taylor, M. G. (1996). The development of children's beliefs about social and biological aspects of gender differences. *Child Development, 67*, 1555–1571.

Taylor, R. D., Casten, R., & Flickinger, S. M. (1993). Influence of kinship social support on the parenting experiences and psychosocial adjustment of African-American adolescents. *Developmental Psychology, 29*, 382–388.

Taylor, R. D., Casten, R., Flickinger, S. M., Roberts, D., & Fulmore, C. D. (1994). Explaining the school performance of African-American adolescents. *Journal of Research on Adolescence, 4*, 21–44.

Taylor, R. D., & Roberts, D. (1995). Kinship support and maternal and adolescent well-being in economically disadvantaged African-American families. *Child Development, 66*, 1585–1597.

Taylor, W., Ayars, C., Gladney, A., Peters, R., Roy, J., Prokhorov, A., Chamberlain, R., & Gritz, E. (1999). Beliefs about smoking among adolescents: Gender and ethnic differences. *Journal of Child & Adolescent Substance Abuse, 8*, 37–54.

Teachman, J. D., Paasch, K. M., Day, R. D., & Carver, K. P. (1997). Poverty during adolescence and subsequent educational attainment. In G. J. Duncan & J. Brooks-Gunn (Eds.), *Consequences of growing up poor* (pp. 382–418). New York: Russell Sage Foundation.

ter Laak, J., de Goede, M., Alevan, L., Brugman, G., van Leuven, M., & Hussmann, J. (2003). Incarcerated adolescent girls: Personality, social competence and delinquency. *Adolescence, 38*, 251–265.

Terman, L. (1916). *The measurement of intelligence.* Boston: Houghton Mifflin.

Terman, L. (1925). *Genetic studies of genius: Vol. 1. Mental and physical traits of a thousand gifted children.* Stanford: CA: Stanford University Press.

Terman, L., & Merrill, M. A. (1937). *Measuring intelligence: A guide to the administration of the new revised Stanford-Binet tests.* Boston: Houghton Mifflin.

Terman, L., & Oden, M. (1959). *Genetic studies of genius: Vol. 5. The gifted group at mid-life.* Stanford, CA: Stanford University Press.

Tershakovec, A., & Stallings, V. (1998). Pediatric nutrition and nutritional disorders. In R. Behrman & R. Kliegman (Eds.), *Nelson essentials of pediatrics* (3rd ed.). Philadelphia: Saunders.

Tesman, J. R., & Hills, A. (1994). Developmental effects of lead exposure in children. *Social Policy Report, Society for Research in Child Development, 8*(3), 1–16.

Tessier, R., Cristo, M., Velez, S., Giron, M., Line, N., Figueroa de Calume, Z., Ruiz-Palaez, J., & Charpak, N. (2003). Kangaroo Mother Care: A method for protecting high-risk low-birth-weight and premature infants against developmental delay. *Infant Behavior and Development, 26*, 384–397.

Tester, M., & Gleaves, D. (2005). Self-deceptive enhancement and family environment: Possible protective factors against internalization of the thin ideal. *Eating Disorders: The Journal of Treatment & Prevention, 13*, 187–199.

Teti, D. M., Gelfand, D. M., Messinger, D. S., & Isabella, R. (1995). Maternal depression and the quality of early attachment: An examination of infants, preschoolers, and their mothers. *Developmental Psychology, 31*, 364–376.

Thal, D., Tobias, S., & Morrison, D. (1991). Language and gesture in late talkers: A 1-year follow-up. *Journal of Speech & Hearing Research, 34*, 604–612.

Thapar, A. (2003). Attention deficit hyperactivity disorder: New genetic findings, new directions. In R. Plomin, J. DeFries, I. Craig, & P. McGuffin (Eds.), *Behavioral genetics in the postgenomic era* (pp. 445–462). Washington, DC: American Psychological Association.

Tharenou, P. (1999). Is there a link between family structures and women's and men's managerial career advancement? *Journal of Organizational Behavior, 20*, 837–863.

Thelen, E. (1983). Learning to walk is still an "old" problem: A reply to Zelazo. *Journal of Motor Behavior, 15*, 139–161.

Thelen, E. (1995). Motor development: A new synthesis. *American Psychologist, 50*, 79–95.

Thelen, E., & Adolph, K. E. (1992). Arnold L. Gesell: The paradox of nature and nurture. *Developmental Psychology, 28*, 368–380.

Theriault, J. (1998). Assessing intimacy with the best friend and the sexual partner during adolescence: The PAIR-M inventory. *Journal of Psychology, 132*, 493–506.

Thomas, A., Bulevich, J., & Loftus, E. (2003). Exploring the role of repetition and sensory elaboration in the imagination inflation effect. *Memory & Cognition, 31*, 630–640.

Thomas, A., & Chess, S. (1977). *Temperament and development.* New York: Brunner/Mazel.

Thomas, M. (2000). *Comparing theories of child development* (5th ed.). Pacific Grove, CA: Brooks/Cole.

Thomas, M., & Karmiloff-Smith, A. (2003). Connectionist models of development, developmental disorders, and individual differences. In R. Sternberg, J. Lautrey, & T. Lubart (Eds.), *Models of intelligence: International perspectives* (pp. 133–150). Washington, DC: American Psychological Association.

Thomas, R. M. (1990). Motor development. In R. M. Thomas (Ed.), *The encyclopedia of human development and education: Theory, research, and studies* (pp. 326–330). Oxford: Pergamon Press.

Thompson, P., Giedd, J., Woods, R., MacDonald, D., Evans, A., & Toga, A. (2000). Growth patterns in the developing brain detected by using continuum mechanical tensor maps. *Nature, 404,* 190–193.

Thompson, R., & Goodvin, R. (2005). The individual child: Temperament, emotion, self, and personality. In M. Bornstein & M. Lamb (Eds.), *Developmental science: An advanced textbook* (5th ed., pp. 391–428). Hillsdale, NJ: Erlbaum.

Thompson, R., McKerchar, P., & Dancho, K. (2004). The effects of delayed physical prompts and reinforcement on infant sign language acquisition. *Applied Behavior Analysis, 37,* 379–383.

Thompson, R. A. (1998). Early sociopersonality development. In W. Damon (Ed.), *Handbook of child psychology: Vol. 3. Social, emotional, and personality development* (5th ed., pp. 25–104). New York: Wiley.

Thompson, S. K. (1975). Gender labels and early sex role development. *Child Development, 46,* 339–347.

Thorn, A., & Gathercole, S. (1999). Language-specific knowledge and short-term memory in bilingual and non-bilingual children. *Quarterly Journal of Experimental Psychology: Human Experimental Psychology, 52A,* 303–324.

Tideman, E., Nilsson, A., Smith, G., & Stjernqvist, K. (2002). Longitudinal follow-up of children born preterm: The mother-child relationship in a 19-year perspective. *Journal of Reproductive & Infant Psychology, 20,* 43–56.

Tiedemann, J. (2000). Parents' gender stereotypes and teachers' beliefs as predictors of children's concept of their mathematical ability in elementary school. *Journal of Educational Psychology, 92,* 144–151.

Timmer, S. G., Eccles, J., & O'Brien, K. (1985). How children use time. In F. T. Juster & F. P. Stafford (Eds.), *Time, goods, and well-being* (pp. 353–369). Ann Arbor: Institute for Social Research, University of Michigan.

Todd, R. D., Swarzenski, B., Rossi, P. G., & Visconti, P. (1995). Structural and functional development of the human brain. In D. Cicchetti & D. J. Cohen (Eds.), *Developmental psychopathology: Vol. 1. Theory and methods* (pp. 161–194). New York: Wiley.

Tomada, G., & Schneider, B. H. (1997). Relational aggression, gender, and peer acceptance: Invariance across culture, stability over time, and concordance among informants. *Developmental Psychology, 33,* 601–609.

Tomasello, M., & Mannle, S. (1985). Pragmatics of sibling speech to one-year-olds. *Child Development, 56,* 911–917.

Tomlinson-Keasey, C., Eisert, D. C., Kahle, L. R., Hardy-Brown, K., & Keasey, B. (1979). The structure of concrete operational thought. *Child Development, 50,* 1153–1163.

Toomela, A. (1999). Drawing development: Stages in the representation of a cube and a cylinder. *Child Development, 70,* 1141–1150.

Torgesen, J., Wagner, R., Rashotte, C., Rose, E., et al. (1999). Preventing reading failure in young children with phonological processing disabilities: Group and individual responses to instruction. *Journal of Educational Psychology, 91,* 594–603.

Toronto District School Board (2001). *Facts and figures about the TDSB.* Retrieved October 6, 2001, from http://www.tdsb.on.ca/communications/TDSBFacts.html

Torrey, E. (1992). *Freudian fraud: The malignant effect of Freud's theory on American thought and culture.* New York: HarperCollins.

Tortora, G., & Derrickson, B. (2005). *Principles of anatomy and physiology* (11th ed.). New York: Wiley.

Tortora, G., & Grabowski, S. (1993). *Principles of anatomy and physiology.* New York: HarperCollins.

Townsend, G., & Belgrave, F. (2003). The influence of cultural and racial identification on the psychosocial adjustment of inner-city African American children in school. *American Journal of Community Psychology, 32,* 217–228.

Trainor, L., Anonymous, & Tsang, C. (2004). Long-term memory for music: Infants remember tempo and timbre. *Developmental Science, 7,* 289–296.

Trainor, L., Clark, E., Huntley, A., & Adams, B. (1997). The acoustic basis of preferences for infant-directed singing. *Infant Behavior and Development, 20,* 383–396.

Trainor, L., Tsang, C., & Cheung, V. (2002). Preference for sensory consonance in 2- and 4-month-old infants. *Music Perception, 20,* 187–194.

Trautner, H., Gervai, J., & Nemeth, R. (2003). Appearance-reality distinction and development of gender constancy understanding in children. *International Journal of Behavioral Development, 27,* 275–283.

Trehub, S. (2003). The developmental origins of musicality. *Nature Neuroscience, 6,* 669–673.

Trehub, S., Hill, D., & Kamenetsky, S. (1997). Parents' sung performances for infants. *Canadian Journal of Experimental Psychology, 51,* 385–396.

Trehub, S. E., Bull, D., & Thorpe, L. A. (1984). Infants' perception of melodies: The role of melodic contour. *Child Development, 55,* 821–830.

Trehub, S. E., & Rabinovitch, M. S. (1972). Auditory-linguistic sensitivity in early infancy. *Developmental Psychology, 6,* 74–77.

Trehub, S. E., Thorpe, L. A., & Morrongiello, B. A. (1985). Infants' perception of melodies: Changes in a single tone. *Infant Behavior and Development, 8,* 213–223.

Treiman, R. (2004). Spelling and dialect: Comparisons between speakers of African American vernacular English and White speakers. *Psychonomic Bulletin & Review, 11,* 338–342.

Tremblay, R. E., Kurtz, L., Mêsse, L. C., Vitaro, F., & Pihl, R. O. (1995). A bimodal preventive intervention for disruptive kindergarten boys: Its impact through mid-adolescence. *Journal of Consulting and Clinical Psychology, 63,* 560–568.

Tremblay, R. E., Mêsse, L. C., Vitaro, F., & Dobkin, P. L. (1995). The impact of friends' deviant behavior on early onset of delinquency: Longitudinal data from 6 to 13 years of age. *Development and Psychopathology, 7,* 649–667.

Tronick, E. Z., Morelli, G. A., & Ivey, P. K. (1992). The Efe forager infant and toddler's pattern of social relationships: Multiple and simultaneous. *Developmental Psychology, 28,* 568–577.

Tuna, J. M. (1989). Mental health services for children: The state of the art. *American Psychologist, 44,* 188–199.

Turecki, S. (1985). *The difficult child.* New York: Bantam.

Turiel, E. (1983). *The development of social knowledge: Morality and convention.* New York: Cambridge University Press.

Turiel, E. (1998). The development of morality. In W. Damon (Ed.), *Handbook of child psychology: Vol. 3. Social, emotional, and personality development* (5th ed., pp. 863–932). New York: Wiley.

Turkheimer, E., & Gottesman, I. I. (1991). Individual differences and the canalization of human behavior. *Developmental Psychology, 27,* 18–22.

Turkheimer, E., Haley, A., Waldron, M., D'Onofrio, B., & Gottesman, I. (2003). Socioeconomic status modifies heritability of IQ in young children. *Psychological Science, 14,* 623–628.

Turnage, B. (2004). African American mother-daughter relationships mediating daughter's self-esteem. *Child & Adolescent Social Work Journal, 21,* 155–173.

Turner, H. A., & Finkelhor, D. (1996). Corporal punishment as a stressor among youth. *Journal of Marriage and the Family, 58,* 155–166.

U.S. Bureau of the Census. (1995). *Statistical abstract of the United States: 1995.* Washington, DC: U.S. Government Printing Office.

U.S. Bureau of the Census. (1996). *Statistical abstract of the United States: 1996* (116th ed.). Washington, DC: U.S. Government Printing Office.

U.S. Bureau of the Census. (1997). *Statistical abstract of the United States: 1997* (117th ed.). Washington, DC: U.S. Government Printing Office.

U.S. Bureau of the Census. (1998). *Statistical abstract of the United States: 1998* (118th ed.). Washington, DC: U.S. Government Printing Office.

U.S. Bureau of the Census. (2001). *Statistical abstract of the United States: 2000.* Washington, DC: U.S. Government Printing Office.

U.S. Bureau of the Census. (2003). *2002, American Community Survey.* Retrieved June 18, 2004, from http://www.census.gov/acs/www/index.html

U.S. Department of Education. (2004). *No child left behind: Introduction.* Retrieved May 26, 2005, from http://www.ed.gov/print/nclb/overview/intro/index.html

U.S. Department of Energy (2001). The Human Genome Program [Online report]. Retrieved July 6, 2001, from http://www.ornl.gov/TechResources/Human_Genome/home.html

U.S. Food and Drug Administration. (2004, October 15). Suicidality in children and adolescents being treated with antidepressant medication. Retrieved May 12, 2005, from http://www.fda.gov/cder/drug/antidepressants/SSRIPHA200410.htm

U.S. House of Representatives. (2004). Green book: Background material and data on programs within the jurisdiction of the Committee on Ways and Means. Retrieved July 23, 2005, from http://waysandmeans.house.gov/media/pdf/greenbook2003/Section9.pdf

Udry, J. R., & Campbell, B. C. (1994). Getting started on sexual behavior. In A. S. Rossi (Ed.), *Sexuality across the life course* (pp. 187–208). Chicago: University of Chicago Press.

Ukeje, I., Bendersky, M., & Lewis, M. (2001). Mother-infant interaction at 12 months in prenatally cocaine-exposed children. *American Journal of Drug & Alcohol Abuse, 27,* 203–224.

Umberson, D., & Gove, W. R. (1989). Parenthood and psychological well-being. Theory, measurement, and stage in the family life course. *Journal of Family Issues, 10,* 440–462.

Umetsu, D. (1998). Immunology and allergy. In R. Behrman & R. Kliegman (Eds.), *Nelson essentials of pediatrics* (3rd ed.). Philadelphia: Saunders.

Underwood, M. (1997). Peer social status and children's understanding of the expression and control of positive and negative emotions. *Merrill-Palmer Quarterly, 43*, 610–634.

Underwood, M. K., Coie, J. D., & Herbsman, C. R. (1992). Display rules for anger and aggression in school-age children. *Child Development, 63*, 366–380.

Underwood, M. K., Kupersmidt, J. B., & Coie, J. D. (1996). Childhood peer sociometric status and aggression as predictors of adolescent childbearing. *Journal of Research on Adolescence, 6*, 201–224.

Ungerer, J. A., & Sigman, M. (1984). The relation of play and sensorimotor behavior to language in the second year. *Child Development, 55*, 1448–1455.

Uno, D., Florsheim, P., & Uchino, B. (1998). Psychosocial mechanisms underlying quality of parenting among Mexican-American and white adolescent mothers. *Journal of Youth & Adolescence, 27*, 585–605.

Urban, J., Carlson, E., Egeland, B., & Sroufe, L. A. (1991). Patterns of individual adaptation across childhood. *Development and Psychopathology, 3*, 445–460.

Urberg, K., Degirmencioglu, S., & Pilgrim, C. (1997). Close friend and group influence on adolescent cigarette smoking and alcohol use. *Developmental Psychology, 33*, 834–844.

Urberg, K. A., Degirmencioglu, S. M., Tolson, J. M., & Halliday-Scher, K. (1995). The structure of adolescent peer networks. *Developmental Psychology, 31*, 540–547.

Valiente, C., Eisenberg, N., Fabes, R., Shepard, S., Cumberland, A., & Losoya, S. (2004). Prediction of children's empathy-related responding from their effortful control and parents' expressivity. *Developmental Psychology, 40*, 911–926.

van Balen, F. (1998). Development of IVF children. *Developmental Review, 18*, 30–46.

van Beijsterveldt, C., Bartels, M., Hudziak, J., & Boomsma, D. (2003). Causes of stability of aggression from early childhood to adolescence: A longitudinal genetic analysis in Dutch twins. *Behavior Genetics, 33*, 591–605.

van den Boom, D. C. (1994). The influence of temperament and mothering on attachment and exploration: An experimental manipulation of sensitive responsiveness among lower-class mothers with irritable infants. *Child Development, 65*, 1457–1477.

van den Boom, D. C. (1995). Do first-year intervention effects endure? Follow-up during toddlerhood of a sample of Dutch irritable infants. *Child Development, 66*, 1798–1816.

Van den Broek, P., Lynch, J., Naslund, J., Ievers-Landis, C., & Verduin, K. (2004). The development of comprehension of main ideas in narratives: Evidence from the selection of titles. *Journal of Educational Psychology, 96*, 707–718.

van der Molen, M., & Molenaar, P. (1994). Cognitive psychophysiology: A window to cognitive development and brain maturation. In G. Dawson & K. Fischer (Eds.), *Human behavior and the developing brain*. New York: Guilford.

Vander Wal, J., & Thelen, M. (2000). Eating and body image concerns among obese and average-weight children. *Addictive Behaviors, 25*, 775–778.

van IJzendoorn, M., Juffer, F., & Poelhuis, C. (2005). Adoption and cognitive development: A meta-analytic comparison of adopted and nonadopted children's IQ and school performance. *Psychological Bulletin, 131*, 301–316.

van IJzendoorn, M. H. (1995). Adult attachment representations, parental responsiveness, and infant attachment: A meta-analysis on the predictive validity of the Adult Attachment Interview. *Psychological Bulletin, 117*, 387–403.

van IJzendoorn, M. H. (1997, April). *Attachment, morality, and aggression: Toward a developmental socioemotional model of antisocial behavior.* Paper presented at the biennial meetings of the Society for Research in Child Development, Washington, DC.

van IJzendoorn, M. H., Goldberg, S., Kroonenberg, P. M., & Frenkel, O. J. (1992). The relative effects of maternal and child problems on the quality of attachment: A meta-analysis of attachment in clinical samples. *Child Development, 63*, 840–858.

van IJzendoorn, M. H., & Kroonenberg, P. M. (1988). Cross-cultural patterns of attachment: A meta-analysis of the Strange Situation. *Child Development, 59*, 147–156.

van Lieshout, C. F. M., & Haselager, G. J. T. (1994). The Big Five personality factors in Q-sort descriptions of children and adolescents. In C. F. Halverson, Jr., G. A. Kohnstamm, & R. P. Martin (Eds.), *The developing*

structure of temperament and personality from infancy to adulthood (pp. 293–318). Hillsdale, NJ: Erlbaum.

Van Mierlo, J., & Van den Bulck, J. (2004). Benchmarking the cultivation approach to video game effects: A comparison of the correlates of TV viewing and game play. *Journal of Adolescence, 27*, 97–111.

van Wormer, K., & McKinney, R. (2003). What schools can do to help gay/lesbian/bisexual youth: A harm reduction approach. *Adolescence, 38*, 409–420.

Vartanian, L. (2000). Revisiting the imaginary audience and personal fable constructs of adolescent egocentrism: A conceptual review. *Adolescence, 35*, 639–661.

Vartanian, L. (2001). Adolescents' reactions to hypothetical peer group conversations: Evidence for an imaginary audience? *Adolescence, 36*, 347–380.

Vartanian, L. R. (1997). Separation-individuation, social support, and adolescent egocentrism: An exploratory study. *Journal of Early Adolescence, 17*, 245–270.

Vartanian, L. R., & Powlishta, K. K. (1996). A longitudinal examination of the social-cognitive foundations of adolescent egocentrism. *Journal of Early Adolescence, 16*, 157–178.

Vaughn, B., Stevenson-Hinde, J., Waters, E., Kotsaftis, A., Lefever, G., Shouldice, A., Trudel, M., & Belsky, J. (1992). Attachment security and temperament in infancy and early childhood: Some conceptual clarification. *Developmental Psychology, 28*, 463–473.

Vaughn, S., & Schumm, J. S. (1995). Responsible inclusion for students with learning disabilities. *Journal of Learning Disabilities, 28*, 264–270.

Ventura, S., Mosher, W., Curtin, S., Abma, J., & Henshaw, S. (2000). Trends in pregnancies and pregnancy rates by outcome: Estimates for the United States, 1976–1996. *Vital Health Statistics, 21*, n.p.

Verhulst, F., & Versluis-Den Bieman, H. (1995). Development course of problem behaviors in adolescent adoptees. *Journal of the American Academy of Child and Adolescent Psychiatry, 34*, 151–159.

Vernon, P. A. (Ed.). (1987). *Speed of information-processing and intelligence.* Norwood, NJ: Ablex.

Vernon, P. A. (1993). Intelligence and neural efficiency. In D. K. Detterman (Ed.), *Current topics in human intelligence: Vol. 3. Individual differences and cognition* (pp. 171–187). Norwood, NJ: Ablex.

Vernon, P. A., & Mori, M. (1992). Intelligence, reaction times, and peripheral nerve conduction velocity. *Intelligence, 16*, 273–288.

Vernon-Feagans, L., Manlove, E. E., & Volling, B. L. (1996). Otitis media and the social behavior of day-care-attending children. *Child Development, 67*, 1528–1539.

Victorian Infant Collaborative Study Group. (1991). Eight-year outcome in infants with birth weight of 500–999 grams: Continuing regional study of 1979 and 1980 births. *Journal of Pediatrics, 118*, 761–767.

Vida, J. (2005). Treating the "wise baby." *American Journal of Psychoanalysis, 65*, 3–12.

Vikat, A., Rimpela, A., Kosunen, E., & Rimpela, M. (2002). Sociodemographic differences in the occurrence of teenage pregnancies in Finland in 1987–1998: A follow up study. *Journal of Epidemiology & Community Health, 56*, 659–670.

Villani, S. (2001). Impact of media on children and adolescents: A 1-year review of the research. *Journal of the American Academy of Child and Adolescent Psychiatry, 40*, 392–401.

Vitaro, F., Tremblay, R. E., Kerr, M., Pagani, L., & Bukowski, W. M. (1997). Disruptiveness, friends' characteristics, and delinquency in early adolescence: A test of two competing models of development. *Child Development, 68*, 676–689.

Volling, B., McElwain, N., & Miller, A. (2002). Emotion regulation in context: The jealousy complex between young siblings and its relations with child and family characteristics. *Child Development, 73*, 581–600.

Voyer, D., Voyer, S., & Bryden, M. P. (1995). Magnitude of sex differences in spatial abilities: A meta-analysis and consideration of critical variables. *Psychological Bulletin, 117*, 250–270.

Vuchinich, S., Bank, L., & Patterson, G. R. (1992). Parenting, peers, and the stability of antisocial behavior in preadolescent boys. *Developmental Psychology, 28*, 510–521.

Vuorenkoski, L., Kuure, O., Moilanen, I., & Peninkilampi, V. (2000). Bilingualism, school achievement, and mental wellbeing: A follow-up study of return migrant children. *Journal of Child Psychology & Psychiatry & Allied Disciplines, 41*, 261–266.

Vygotsky, L. S. (1978). *Mind and society: The development of higher mental processes.* Cambridge, MA: Harvard University Press. (Original works published 1930, 1933, and 1935)

Waddington, C. H. (1957). *The strategy of the genes.* London: Allen.

Waddington, C. H. (1974). A catastrophe theory of evolution. *Annals of the New York Academy of Sciences, 231*, 32–41.

Wade, T., Bulik, C., & Kendler, K. (2001). Investigation of quality of the parental relationship as a risk factor for subclinical bulimia nervosa. *International Journal of Eating Disorders, 30*, 389–400.

Wagner, R. K., Torgesen, J. K., Rashotte, C. A., Hecht, S. A., Barker, T. A., Burgess, S. R., Donahue, J., & Garon, T. (1997). Changing relations between phonological processing abilities and word-level reading as children develop from beginning to skilled readers: A 5-year longitudinal study. *Developmental Psychology, 33*, 468–479.

Waldrop, M., & Halverson, C. (1975). Intensive and extensive peer behavior: Longitudinal and cross-sectional analyses. *Child Development, 46*, 19–26.

Walker, H., Messinger, D., Fogel, A., & Karns, J. (1992). Social and communicative development in infancy. In V. B. Van Hasselt & M. Hersen (Eds.), *Handbook of social development: A lifespan perspective* (pp. 157–181). New York: Plenum Press.

Walker, L. (1980). Cognitive and perspective-taking prerequisites for moral development. *Child Development, 51*, 131–139.

Walker, L. J. (1989). A longitudinal study of moral reasoning. *Child Development, 60*, 157–160.

Walker, L. J. (1991). Sex differences in moral reasoning. In W. M. Kurtines & J. L. Gewirtz (Eds.), *Handbook of moral behavior and development: Vol. 2. Research* (pp. 333–364). Hillsdale, NJ: Erlbaum.

Walker, L. J., de Vries, B., & Trevethan, S. D. (1987). Moral stages and moral orientations in real-life and hypothetical dilemmas. *Child Development, 58*, 842–858.

Walker-Andrews, A. S. (1997). Infants' perception of expressive behaviors: Differentiation of multimodal information. *Psychological Bulletin, 121*, 437–456.

Walker-Andrews, A. S., & Lennon, E. (1991). Infants' discrimination of vocal expressions: Contributions of auditory and visual information. *Infant Behavior and Development, 14*, 131–142.

Walker-Barnes, C., & Mason, C. (2004). Delinquency and substance use among gang-involved youth: The moderating role of parenting practices. *American Journal of Community Psychology, 34*, 235–250.

Wallerstein, J., & Lewis, J. (1998). The long-term impact of divorce on children: A first report from a 25-year study. *Family & Concilation Courts Review, 36*, 368–383.

Wals, M., Hillegers, M., Reichart, C., Ormel, J., Nolen, W., & Verhulst, F. (2001). Prevalence of psychopathology in children of a bipolar parent. *Journal of the American Academy of Child and Adolescent Psychiatry, 40*, 1094–1102.

Walters, R. H., & Brown, M. (1963). Studies of reinforcement of aggression: III. Transfer of responses to an interpersonal situation. *Child Development, 34*, 563–571.

Walton, G. E., Bower, N. J. A., & Bower, T. G. R. (1992). Recognition of familiar faces by newborns. *Infant Behavior and Development, 15*, 265–269.

Walton, G. E., & Bower, T. G. R. (1993). Amodal representation of speech in infants. *Infant Behavior and Development, 16*, 233–253.

Wang, C., & Chou, P. (1999). Risk factors for adolescent primigravida in Kaohsium county, Taiwan. *American Journal of Preventive Medicine, 17*, 43–47.

Wang, X., Dow-Edwards, D., Anderson, V., Minkoff, H., & Hurd, Y. (2004). In utero marijuana exposure associated with abnormal amygdala dopamine D-sub-2 gene expression in the human fetus. *Biological Psychiatry, 56*, 909–915.

Ward, S. L., & Overton, W. F. (1990). Semantic familiarity, relevance, and the development of deductive reasoning. *Developmental Psychology, 26*, 488–493.

Warfield-Coppock, N. (1997). The balance and connection of manhood and womanhood training. *Journal of Prevention & Intervention in the Community, 16*, 121–145.

Warren, S., & Simmens, S. (2005). Predicting toddler anxiety/depressive symptoms: Effects of caregiver sensitivity on temperamentally vulnerable children. *Infant Mental Health Journal, 26*, 40–55.

Wartner, U. B., Grossman, K., Fremmer-Bombik, E., & Suess, G. (1994). Attachment patterns at age six in south Germany: Predictability from infancy and implications for preschool behavior. *Child Development, 65*, 1014–1027.

Watamura, S., Donzella, B., Alwin, J., & Gunnar, M. (2003). Morning-to-afternoon increases in cortisol concentrations for infants and toddlers at child care: Age differences and behavioral correlates. *Child Development, 74*, 1006–1020.

Waterman, A. S. (1985). Identity in the context of adolescent psychology. *New Directions for Child Development, 30*, 5–24.

Waterman, A. S. (1988). Identity status theory and Erikson's theory: Communalities and differences. *Developmental Review, 8*, 185–208.

Waterman, A. S. (1992). Identity as an aspect of optimal psychological functioning. In G. R. Adams, T. P. Gullotta, & R. Montemayor (Eds.), *Adolescent identity formation* (pp. 50–72). Newbury Park, CA: Sage.

Waters, E., Merrick, S. K., Albersheim, L. J., & Treboux, D. (1995, April). *Attachment security from infancy to early adulthood: A 20-year longitudinal study.* Paper presented at the biennial meetings of the Society for Research in Child Development, Indianapolis.

Waters, E., Treboux, D., Crowell, J., Merrick, S., & Albersheim, L. (1995, April). *From the Strange Situation to the Adult Attachment Interview: A 20-year longitudinal study of attachment security in infancy and early adulthood.* Paper presented at the biennial meetings of the Society for Research in Child Development, Indianapolis.

Watson, A., Nixon, C., Wilson, A., & Capage, L. (1999). Social interaction skills and theory of mind in young children. *Developmental Psychology, 35*, 386–391.

Watson, J. B. (1913). Psychology as the behaviorist views it. *Psychological Review, 20*, 158–177.

Watson, J. B. (1928). *Psychological care of the infant and child.* New York: Norton.

Watson, J. B. (1930). *Behaviorism.* New York: Norton.

Watson, J. B., & Rayner, R. (1920). Conditioned emotional reactions. *Journal of Experimental Psychology, 3*, 1–14.

Watson, M. W., & Getz, K. (1990a). Developmental shifts in Oedipal behaviors related to family role understanding. *New Directions for Child Development, 48*, 29–48.

Watson, M. W., & Getz, K. (1990b). The relationship between Oedipal behaviors and children's family role concepts. *Merrill-Palmer Quarterly, 36*, 487–506.

Waxman, S. R., & Hall, D. G. (1993). The development of a linkage between count nouns and object categories: Evidence from fifteen- to twenty-one-month-old infants. *Child Development, 64*, 1224–1241.

Waxman, S. R., & Kosowski, T. D. (1990). Nouns mark category relations: Toddlers' and preschoolers' word-learning biases. *Child Development, 61*, 1461–1473.

Weaver, S., Clifford, E., Hay, D., & Robinson, J. (1997). Psychosocial adjustment to unsuccessful IVF and GIFT treatment. *Patient Education & Counseling, 31*, 7–18.

Webb, R., Lubinski, D., & Benbow, C. (2002). Mathematically facile adolescents with math-science aspirations: New perspectives on their educational and vocational development. *Journal of Educational Psychology, 94*, 785–794.

Webster-Stratton, C., & Hammond, M. (1988). Maternal depression and its relationship to life stress, perceptions of child behavior problems, parenting behaviors and child conduct problems. *Journal of Abnormal Child Psychology, 16*, 299–315.

Webster-Stratton, C., & Reid, M. (2003). Treating conduct problems and strengthening social and emotional competence in young children: The dina dinosaur treatment program. *Journal of Emotional & Behavioral Disorders, 11*, 130–143.

Wechsler, D. (1974). *Manual for the Wechsler Intelligence Scale for Children-Revised.* New York: Psychological Corp.

Weimer, B., Kerns, K., & Oldenburg, C. (2004). Adolescents' interactions with a best friend: Associations with attachment style. *Journal of Experimental Psychology, 88*, 102–120.

Weinberg, R. A. (1989). Intelligence and IQ: Landmark issues and great debates. *American Psychologist, 44*, 98–104.

Weindrich, D., Jennen-Steinmetz, C., Laucht, M., & Schmidt, M. (2003). Late sequelae of low birthweight: Mediators of poor school performance at 11 years. *Developmental Medicine and Child Neurology, 45*, 463–469.

Weinfeld, N., & Egeland, B. (2004). Continuity, discontinuity, and coherence in attachment from infancy to late adolescence: Sequelae of organization and disorganization. *Attachment & Human Development, 6*, 73–97.

Weinfield, N. M., Ogawa, J. R., & Sroufe, L. A. (1997). Early attachment as a pathway to adolescent peer competence. *Journal of Research on Adolescence, 7*, 241–265.

Weinstock, L. (1999). Gender differences in the presentation and management of social anxiety disorder. *Journal of Clinical Psychiatry, 60*, 9–13.

Weisner, T. S. (1984). Ecocultural niches of middle childhood: A cross-cultural perspective. In W. A. Collins (Ed.), *Development during middle childhood: The years from six to twelve* (pp. 335–369). Washington, DC: National Academy Press.

Weiss, L. H., & Schwarz, J. C. (1996). The relationship between parenting types and older adolescents' personality, academic achievement, adjustment, and substance use. *Child Development, 67,* 2101–2114.

Weisz, J. R., Sigman, M., Weiss, B., & Mosk, J. (1993). Parent reports of behavioral and emotional problems among children in Kenya, Thailand, and the United States. *Child Development, 64,* 98–109.

Welch-Ross, M. (1997). Mother-child participation in conversation about the past: Relationships to preschoolers' theory of mind. *Developmental Psychology, 33,* 618–629.

Wellman, H. M. (1982). The foundations of knowledge: Concept development in the young child. In S. G. Moore & C. C. Cooper (Eds.), *The young child: Reviews of research* (Vol. 3, pp. 115–134). Washington, DC: National Association for the Education of Young Children.

Wellman, H. M., & Hickling, A. K. (1994). The mind's "I": Children's conception of the mind as an active agent. *Child Development, 65,* 1564–1580.

Wentzel, K. R., & Asher, S. R. (1995). The academic lives of neglected, rejected, popular, and controversial children. *Child Development, 66,* 754–763.

Wenz-Gross, M., Siperstein, G., Untch, A., & Widaman, K. (1997). Stress, social support, and adjustment of adolescents in middle school. *Journal of Early Adolescence, 17,* 129–151.

Werker, J. F., & Desjardins, R. N. (1995). Listening to speech in the first year of life: Experiential influences on phoneme perception. *Current Directions in Psychological Science, 4,* 76–81.

Werker, J. F., Pegg, J. E., & McLeod, P. J. (1994). A cross-language investigation of infant preference for infant-directed communication. *Infant Behavior and Development, 17,* 323–333.

Werker, J. F., & Tees, R. C. (1984). Cross-language speech perception: Evidence for perceptual reorganization during the first year of life. *Infant Behavior and Development, 7,* 49–63.

Werler, M. M., Louik, C., Shapiro, S., & Mitchell, A. A. (1996). Prepregnant weight in relation to risk of neural tube defects. *Journal of the American Medical Association, 275,* 1089–1092.

Werner, E., & Smith, R. (2001). *Journeys from childhood to midlife: Risk, resilience, and recovery.* Ithaca, NY: Cornell University Press.

Werner, E. E. (1986). A longitudinal study of perinatal risk. In D. C. Farran & J. D. McKinney (Eds.), *Risk in intellectual and psychosocial development* (pp. 3–28). Orlando, FL: Academic Press.

Werner, E. E. (1993). Risk, resilience, and recovery: Perspectives from the Kauai Longitudinal Study. *Development and Psychopathology, 5,* 503–515.

Werner, E. E. (1995). Resilience in development. *Current Directions in Psychological Science, 4,* 81–85.

Werner, E. E., & Smith, R. S. (1992). *Overcoming the odds: High risk children from birth to adulthood.* Ithaca, NY: Cornell University Press.

Werner, L. A., & Gillenwater, J. M. (1990). Pure-tone sensitivity of 2- to 5-week-old infants. *Infant Behavior and Development, 13,* 355–375.

West, P., Sweeting, H., & Ecob, R. (1999). Family and friends' influences on the uptake of regular smoking from mid-adolescence to early adulthood. *Addiction, 97,* 1397–1411.

Whitam, F. L., Diamond, M., & Martin, J. (1993). Homosexual orientation in twins: A report on 61 pairs and three triplet sets. *Archives of Sexual Behavior, 22,* 187–206.

White, K. S., Bruce, S. E., Farrell, A. D., & Kliewer, W. L. (1997, April). *Impact of exposure to community violence on anxiety among urban adolescents: Family social support as a protective factor.* Paper presented at the biennial meetings of the Society for Research in Child Development, Washington, DC.

White, M., & Glick, J. (2000). Generation status, social capital, and the routes out of high school. *Sociological Forum, 15,* 671–691.

Whitehurst, G. J. (1995, April). *Levels of reading readiness and predictors of reading success among children from low-income families.* Paper presented at the biennial meetings of the Society for Research in Child Development, Indianapolis.

White-Traut, R., Nelson, M., Silvestri, J., Vasan, U., Littau, S., Meleedy-Rey, P., Gu, G., & Patel, M. (2002). Effect of auditory, tactile, visual, and vestibular intervention on length of stay, alertness, and feeding progression in preterm infants. *Developmental Medicine and Child Neurology, 44,* 91–97.

Whiting, B. B., & Edwards, C. P. (1988). *Children of different worlds: The formation of social behavior.* Cambridge, MA: Harvard University Press.

Wickrama, K., Conger, R., Lorenz, F., & Elder, G. (1998). Parental education and adolescent self-reported physical health. *Journal of Marriage and the Family, 60,* 967–978.

Wickrama, K., Lorenz, F., & Conger, R. (1997). Parental support and adolescent physical health status: A latent growth-curve analysis. *Journal of Health & Social Behavior, 38,* 149–163.

Wiehe, V. (2003). Empathy and narcissism in a sample of child abuse perpetrators and a comparison sample of foster parents. *Child Abuse & Neglect, 27,* 541–555.

Wierson, M., & Forehand, R. (1994). Parent behavioral training for child noncompliance: Rationale, concepts, and effectiveness. *Current Directions in Psychological Science, 3,* 146–150.

Wiesenfeld, A. R., Malatesta, C. Z., & DeLoach, L. L. (1981). Differential parental response to familiar and unfamiliar infant distress signals. *Infant Behavior and Development, 4,* 281–296.

Wiesner, M., Kim, H., & Capaldi, D. (2005). Developmental trajectories of offending: Validation and prediction to young adult alcohol use, drug use, and depressive symptoms. *Development and Psychopathology, 17,* 251–270.

Wigfield, A., Eccles, J. S., MacIver, D., Reuman, D. A., & Midgley, C. (1991). Transitions during early adolescence: Changes in children's domain-specific self-perceptions and general self-esteem across the transition to junior high school. *Developmental Psychology, 27,* 552–565.

Williams, J., & Best, J. (1994). Cross-cultural views of women and men. In W. Lonner & R. Malpass (Eds.), *Psychology and culture* (pp. 191–201). Boston: Allyn & Bacon.

Williams, J., Wake, M., Hesketh, K., Maher, E., & Waters, E. (2005). Health-related quality of life of overweight and obese children. *Journal of the American Medical Association, 293,* 1–5.

Williams, J. E., & Best, D. L. (1990). *Measuring sex stereotypes: A multination study* (rev. ed.). Newbury Park, CA: Sage.

Williams, W. (1998). Are we raising smarter children today? School and home related influences on IQ. In U. Neisser (Ed.), *The rising curve: Long-term gains in IQ and related measures* (pp. 125–154). Washington, DC: American Psychological Association.

Williams, W. M., & Ceci, S. J. (1997). Are Americans becoming more or less alike? Trends in race, class, and ability differences in intelligence. *American Psychologist, 52,* 1226–1235.

Willinger, M., Hoffman, H. J., & Hartford, R. B. (1994). Infant sleep position and risk for sudden infant death syndrome: Report of meeting held January 13 and 14, 1994, National Institutes of Health, Bethesda, MD. *Pediatrics, 93,* 814–819.

Wilson, M. N. (1986). The black extended family: An analytical consideration. *Developmental Psychology, 22,* 246–258.

Wilson, M. N. (1989). Child development in the context of the black extended family. *American Psychologist, 44,* 380–385.

Wilson, W. J. (1995). Jobless ghettos and the social outcome of youngsters. In P. Moen, G. H. Elder, Jr., & K. Lüscher (Eds.), *Examining lives in context: Perspectives on the ecology of human development* (pp. 527–543). Washington, DC: American Psychological Association.

Winfield, L. F. (1995). The knowledge base on resilience in African-American adolescents. In L. J. Crockett & A. C. Crouter (Eds.), *Pathways through adolescence* (pp. 87–118). Mahwah, NJ: Erlbaum.

Winner, E. (1997). Exceptionally high intelligence and schooling. *American Psychologist, 52,* 1070–1081.

Wolfram, W. (1990). *Incorporating dialect study into the language arts class.* Washington, DC: ERIC Clearinghouse on Languages and Linguistics. ERIC digest No. ED 318231.

Wolfram, W., Schilling-Estes, N., & Hazen, K. (1996). *Dialects and the Ocracoke brogue. Eighth grade curriculum.* Raleigh, NC: North Carolina Language and Life Project.

Wonderlich, S., Crosby, R., Mitchell, J., Thompson, K., Redlin, J., Demuth, G., Smith, J., & Haseltine, B. (2001). Eating disturbance and sexual trauma in childhood and adulthood. *International Journal of Eating Disorders, 30,* 401–412.

Wong, C., & Tang, C. (2004). Coming out experiences and psychological distress of Chinese homosexual men in Hong Kong. *Archives of Sexual Behavior, 33,* 149–157.

Wong, D., (1993). *Whaley & Wong's essentials of pediatric nursing.* St. Louis, MO: Mosby-Yearbook, Inc.

Wood, C., & Terrell, C. (1998). Pre-school phonological awareness and subsequent literacy development. *Educational Psychology, 18,* 253–274.

Wood, D. J., Bruner, J. S., & Ross, G. (1976). The role of tutoring in problem solving. *Journal of Child Psychology and Psychiatry, 17,* 89–100.

Wood, W., Wong, F. Y., & Chachere, J. G. (1991). Effects of media violence on viewers' aggression in unconstrained social interaction. *Psychological Bulletin, 109,* 371–383.

Woodward, A. L., & Markman, E. M. (1998). Early word learning. In W. Damon (Ed.), *Handbook of child psychology: Vol. 2. Cognition, perception, and language* (5th ed., pp. 371–420). New York: Wiley.

Woodward, S., McManis, M., Kagan, J., Deldin, P., Snidman, N., Lewis, M., &

Kahn, V. (2001). Infant temperament and the brainstem auditory evoked response in later childhood. *Developmental Psychology, 37*, 533–538.

Worrell, F. (1997). Predicting successful or non-successful at-risk status using demographic risk factors. *High School Journal, 81*, 46–53.

Wright, J., Huston, A., Murphy, K., St. Peters, M., Pinon, M., Scantlin, R., & Kotler, J. (2001). The relations of early television viewing to school readiness and vocabulary of children from low-income families: The early window project. *Child Development, 72*, 1347–1366.

Wright, K., Fineberg, D., Brown, K., & Perkins, A. (2005). Theory of mind may be contagious, but you don't catch it from your twin. *Child Development, 76*, 97–106.

Wright, V., Schieve, L., Reynolds, M., & Jeng, G. (2005). Assisted reproductive technology surveillance—United States, 2002. *Morbidity & Mortality Weekly Report, 54*, 1–24.

Wyatt, J., & Carlo, G. (2002). What will my parents think? Relations among adolescents' expected parental reactions, prosocial moral reasoning and prosocial and antisocial behaviors. *Journal of Adolescent Research, 17*, 646–666.

Xia, G., & Qian, M. (2001). The relationship of parenting style to self-reported mental health among two subcultures of Chinese. *Journal of Adolescence, 24*, 251–260.

Xie, H., Cairns, R., & Cairns, B. (1999). Social networks and configurations in inner-city schools: Aggression, popularity, and implications for students with EBD. *Journal of Emotional & Behavioral Disorders, 7*, 147–155.

Yamada, A., & Singelis, T. (1999). Biculturalism and self-construal. *International Journal of Intercultural Relations, 23*, 697–709.

Yeung, A., Chui, H., & Lau, I. (1999). Hierarchical and multidimensional academic self-concept of commercial students. *Contemporary Educational Psychology, 24*, 376–389.

Yirmiya, N., Eriel, O., Shaked, M., & Solomonica-Levi, D. (1998). Meta-analyses comparing theory of mind abilities of individuals with autism, individuals with mental retardation, and normally developing individuals. *Psychological Bulletin, 124*, 283–307.

Yirmiya, N., & Shulman, C. (1996). Seriation, conservation, and theory of mind abilities in individuals with autism, individuals with mental retardation, and normally developing children. *Child Development, 67*, 2045–2059.

Yirmiya, N., Solomonica-Levi, D., Shulman, C., & Pilowsky, T. (1996). Theory of mind abilities in individuals with autism, Down syndrome, and mental retardation of unknown etiology: The role of age and intelligence. *Journal of Child Psychology & Psychiatry & Allied Disciplines, 37*, 1003–1014.

Yonas, A. (1981). Infants' responses to optical information for collision. In R. Aslin, J. R. Alberts, & M. R. Peterson (Eds.), *Development of perception: Vol. 2. From perception to cognition* (pp. 80–122). Orlando, FL: Academic Press.

Yonas, A., & Owsley, C. (1987). Development of visual space perception. In P. Salapatek & L. Cohen (Eds.), *Handbook of infant perception: Vol. 2. From perception to cognition* (pp. 80–122). Orlando, FL: Academic Press.

Young, A. (1997). I think, therefore I'm motivated: The relations among cognitive strategy use, motivational orientation and classroom perceptions over time. *Learning & Individual Differences, 9*, 249–283.

Young, M., & Bradley, M. (1998). Social withdrawal: Self-efficacy, happiness, and popularity in introverted and extroverted adolescents. *Canadian Journal of School Psychology, 14*, 21–35.

Zahn-Waxler, C., & Radke-Yarrow, M. (1982). The development of altruism: Alternative research strategies. In N. Eisenberg (Ed.), *The development of prosocial behavior* (pp. 109–138). New York: Academic Press.

Zahn-Waxler, C., Radke-Yarrow, M., & King, R. (1979). Child rearing and children's prosocial initiations toward victims of distress. *Child Development, 50*, 319–330.

Zahn-Waxler, C., Radke-Yarrow, M., Wagner, E., & Chapman, M. (1992). Development of concern for others. *Developmental Psychology, 28*, 125–136.

Zahn-Waxler, C., Robinson, J., & Emde, R. N. (1992). The development of empathy in twins. *Developmental Psychology, 28*, 1038–1047.

Zajonc, R. B. (1983). Validating the confluence model. *Psychological Bulletin, 93*, 457–480.

Zajonc, R. B., & Marcus, G. B. (1975). Birth order and intellectual development. *Psychological Review, 82*, 74–88.

Zajonc, R. B., & Mullally, P. R. (1997). Birth order: Reconciling conflicting effects. *American Psychologist, 52*, 685–699.

Zakriski, A., & Coie, J. (1996). A comparison of aggressive-rejected and nonaggressive-rejected children's interpretation of self-directed and other-directed rejection. *Child Development, 67*, 1948–2070.

Zametkin, A. J., Nordahl, T. E., Gross, M., King, A. C., Semple, W. E., Rumsey, J., Hamburger, S., & Cohen, R. M. (1990). Cerebral glucose metabolism in adults with hyperactivity of childhood onset. *New England Journal of Medicine, 323*, 1361–1366.

Zani, B. (1993). Dating and interpersonal relationships in adolescence. In S. Jackson & H. Rodrigues-Tomé (Eds.), *Adolescence and its social worlds* (pp. 95–119). Hove, England: Erlbaum.

Zaslow, M. J., & Hayes, C. D. (1986). Sex differences in children's responses to psychosocial stress: Toward a cross-context analysis. In M. E. Lamb, A. L. Brown, & B. Rogoff (Eds.), *Advances in developmental psychology* (Vol. 4, pp. 285–338). Hillsdale, NJ: Erlbaum.

Zeanah, C., & Fox, N. (2004). Temperament and attachment disorders. *Journal of Clinical Child & Adolescent Psychology, 33*, 32–41.

Zelazo, P., Helwig, C., & Lau, A. (1996). Intention, act, and outcome in behavioral prediction and moral judgment. *Child Development, 67*, 2478–2492.

Zelazo, P. R., Zelazo, N. A., & Kolb, S. (1972). "Walking" in the newborn. *Science, 176*, 314–315.

Zeskind, P. S., & Barr, R. G. (1997). Acoustic characteristics of naturally occurring cries of infants with "colic." *Child Development, 68*, 394–403.

Zeskind, P. S., & Ramey, C. T. (1981). Preventing intellectual and interactional sequelae of fetal malnutrition: A longitudinal, transactional, and synergistic approach to development. *Child Development, 52*, 213–218.

Zhang, R., & Yu, Y. (2002). A study of children's coordinational ability for outcome and intention information. *Psychological Science (China), 25*, 527–530.

Zhou, W., & Olsen, J. (1997). Gestational weight gain as a predictor of birth and placenta weight according to pre-pregnancy body mass index. *Acta Obstetrica Scandinavica, 76*, 300–307.

Zigler, E., & Finn-Stevenson, M. (1993). *Children in a changing world: Developmental and social issues*. Pacific Grove, CA: Brooks/Cole.

Zigler, E. F., & Hodapp, R. M. (1991). Behavioral functioning in individuals with mental retardation. *Annual Review of Psychology, 42*, 29–50.

Zigler, E. F., & Styfco, S. (1996). Head Start and early childhood intervention: The changing course of social science and social policy. In E. F. Zigler, S. L. Kagan, & N. W. Hall (Eds.), *Children, families, and government* (pp. 132–154). Cambridge, England: Cambridge University Press.

Zigler, E. F., & Styfco, S. J. (1993). Using research and theory to justify and inform Head Start expansion. *Social Policy Report, Society for Research in Child Development, 7*(2), 1–21.

Zill, N., & Nord, C. W. (1994). *Running in place: How American families are faring in a changing economy and an individualistic society*. Washington, DC: Child Trends.

Zill, N., Moore, K. A., Smith, E. W., Stief, T., & Coiro, M. J. (1995). The life circumstances and development of children in welfare families: A profile based on national survey data. In P. L. Chase-Lansdale & J. Brooks-Gunn (Eds.), *Escape from poverty: What makes a difference for children?* (pp. 39–59). Cambridge, England: Cambridge University Press.

Zimmerman, M., Copeland, L., Shope, J., & Dielman, T. (1997). A longitudinal study of self-esteem: Implications for adolescent development. *Journal of Youth & Adolescence, 26*, 117–141.

Zimmermann, P. (2004). Attachment representations and characteristics of friendship relations during adolescence. *Journal of Experimental Child Psychology, 88*, 83–101.

Zoccolillo, M. (1993). Gender and the development of conduct disorder. *Development and Psychopathology, 5*, 65–78.

Zoghbi, H. (2003). Postnatal neurodevelopmental disorders. *Science, 302*, 826–830.

Photo Credits

Name Index

and Health Promotion (NCCDPHP), 115, 116, 118
National Center for Education Statistics (NCES), 191, 203, 204, 238, 239, 240, 241, 407
National Center for Health Statistics (NCHS), 40, 58, 68, 71, 115, 118, 382
National Center for Injury Prevention and Control (NCIPC), 114, 342, 443
National Institute of Mental Health (NIMH), 429, 431, 432, 433, 439, 440, 443, 449
National Literary Trust, 239
Neale, M. C., 112
Nederend, S., 296
Nedergard, N., 383
Needleman, H. L., 57
Needlman, R., 55
Needlman, R. D., 45, 77, 101, 103
Neill, M., 191
Neisser, U., 191, 199, 200
Nelson, C. A., 144, 253
Nelson, J., 235
Nelson, K., 219, 223, 230
Nelson, S., 346
Nemeth, R., 291
Nesdale, D., 339
Netley, C., 51
Nettelbladt, U., 239
Nettlebeck, T., 186
Neubauer, A., 206
Neumann, C., 186
Neville, H., 97
Newcomb, A. F., 318, 319, 321, 322, 331
Newcombe, N. S., 205
Newman, D., 331, 437
Newman, M., 205
Newman, R., 137
Newport, E., 136
New Zealand Ministry of Education, 407
Nguyen, D., 113
NICHD Early Child Care Research Network, 145, 386, 392, 393, 395, 396, 398
Nicholls, C., 239
Nicholls, S., 435
Nichols, K., 347
Nichols, P. L., 194, 432, 444
Nicholson, J., 47
Nigg, J. T., 436
Nilsson, A., 316
Nilsson, E., 440
Nisan, M., 354
Nixon, C., 160
Nobile, C., 114
Nolen-Hoeksema, S., 429, 432, 441, 442
Norboru, T., 236
Nord, C. W., 413
Noredentoft, M., 54
Norman, A. D., 355
Novak, M., 141
Nowakowski, R. S., 94
Noyes, J., 60
Nozza, R. J., 87
Nucci, L. P., 346
Nucci, M. S., 346
Nugent, J., 73
Nugent, J. K., 77
Nugent, L. D., 173
Nunes, L. R. D., 156

Nunes, S., 447
Nutter, J., 118

Oates, J., 60
O'Beirne, H., 315
Obel, C., 383
Oberklaid, F., 253
O'Boyle, C., 295
O'Brien, K., 319
O'Brien, M., 294
O'Brien, S. F., 319
O'Callaghan, F., 194
O'Connell, B., 217
O'Conner, B. P., 172
O'Connor, T., 267, 430
Oden, M., 448
Odom, S. L., 453
Oe, H., 183, 184
Oe, K., 182, 183
Offer, D., 290
Offord, D. R., 329
Ogawa, J. R., 315
Ogbu, J. U., 201
Oh, S., 195
O'Hare, A. W., 173
Ohde, R., 291
Ohgi, S., 73
Oja, H., 87
Okazaki, S., 200
Oldenburg, C., 310, 321
O'Leary, S., 145
Olivan, G., 117
Oller, D., 238
Oller, D. K., 217
Olmedo, M., 290
Olsen, J., 58
Olsen, S., 331
Olshan, A. F., 49
Olson, D. H., 368
Olson, H. C., 54
Olson, S. L., 195
Olthof, T., 348
Olweus, D., 288, 330
O'Mahony, P., 77
O'Malley, C., 162, 164
O'Neil, A., 296
O'Neill, D. K., 176
Ontai, L., 294
Oosterlaan, J., 278, 435, 437
Opotow, S., 406
Opwis, K., 179
Orekhova, E., 99
Ornstein, P. A., 174, 178
Ortiz, C., 394
Osgood, D., 287
Osofsky, J. D., 112, 415
Osorio, S., 285
Ossiander, E., 116
Ostendorf, F., 248, 250
Ostoja, E., 315
Ostrom, T., 339
Ott, W. J., 72
Overby, K., 84, 85, 103, 114, 115, 116, 117
Overton, W., 168
Overton, W. F., 171, 269
Owens, E., 383
Owens, E. B., 58
Owens, G., 113

Owens, J., 114
Owsley, C., 134
Oyersman, D., 285
Ozmun, J. C., 103

Paarlberg, K., 60
Paasch, K. M., 192
Padilla, A. M., 419
Páez, D., 12
Pagani, L., 383, 384
Page, D. C., 36
Paik, H., 410
Paikoff, R. L., 439, 470
Painter, M., 48
Pajares, F., 402
Pajulo, M., 54
Palkovitz, R., 66
Palmer, A., 391
Palmer, J., 131
Palmérus, K., 368
Panagiotides, H., 145
Pancer, S., 371
Pantin, H., 420
Papousek, H., 305
Papousek, M., 305
Pappas, K., 248
Paradise, J. L., 86
Parault, S., 176
Pardo, C., 416
Park, S., 206
Parke, R., 22
Parke, R. D., 305, 306, 374, 379, 386, 387, 417, 419, 420
Parker, J. G., 319
Parker, K. C. H., 317
Parkin, M., 440
Parmelee, A. H., Jr., 76
Parten, M. B., 318
Partridge, J., 65, 72, 73, 76
Pascalis, O., 135, 136
Pasold, T., 411
Passchier, J., 60
Passman, R. H., 308
Pastorelli, C., 259
Patel, R., 50
Patel, S., 50
Pattee, L., 331
Patterson, C., 383
Patterson, C. J., 321, 415
Patterson, G. R., 10, 11, 256, 257, 321, 323, 366, 367, 371, 386, 464, 471
Patterson, J., 239, 383
Patton, G., 441
Paul-Brown, D., 159
Pavlov, I., 17
Payne, A., 318, 330
Pearl, R., 329
Pedersen, C., 431, 432
Pedersen, N. L., 117
Pederson, D. R., 312
Pedlow, R., 253
Peebles, C., 112
Peeke, H., 46
Peet, S., 377
Pegg, J. E., 230
Peipert, J. F., 59
Peisner-Feinberg, E. S., 394
Pelham, W., 435

Subject Index